SEVENTH EDITION

Elementary and Middle School Mathematics

Teaching Developmentally

John A. Van de Walle
Late of Virginia Commonwealth University

Karen S. Karp
University of Louisville

Jennifer M. Bay-Williams
University of Louisville

Allyn & Bacon

Boston   New York   San Franc
Mexico City   Montreal   Toronto   London   Ma
Hong Kong   Singapore   Tokyo   Cape T

Acquisitions Editor: Kelly Villella Canton
Senior Development Editor: Shannon Steed
Editorial Assistant: Annalea Manalili
Senior Marketing Manager: Darcy Betts
Editorial Production Service: Omegatype Typography, Inc.
Composition Buyer: Linda Cox
Manufacturing Buyer: Megan Cochran
Electronic Composition: Omegatype Typography, Inc.
Interior Design: Carol Somberg
Cover Administrator: Linda Knowles

For related titles and support materials, visit our online catalog at www.pearsonhighered.com.

Between the time website information is gathered and then published, it is not unusual for some sites to have closed. Also, the transcription of URLs can result in typographical errors. The publisher would appreciate notification where these errors occur so that they may be corrected in subsequent editions.

Library of Congress Cataloging-in-Publication Data

Van de Walle, John A.
    Elementary and middle school mathematics: teaching developmentally. —
7th ed. / John A. Van de Walle, Karen S. Karp, Jennifer M. Bay-Williams.
        p.   cm.
    Includes bibliographical references and index.
    ISBN-13: 978-0-205-57352-3
    ISBN-10: 0-205-57352-5
    1. Mathematics—Study and teaching (Elementary)   2. Mathematics—
Study and teaching (Middle school)   I. Karp, Karen.   II. Bay-Williams, Jennifer M.   III. Title.
    QA135.6.V36 2008
    510.71'2—dc22

                                                        2008040112

Printed in the United States of America

10   9   8   7   6   5   4   WEB   13   12   11   10

Allyn & Bacon
is an imprint of

www.pearsonhighered.com

ISBN-10: 0-205-57352-5
ISBN-13: 978-0-205-57352-3

In Memoriam

"Do you think anyone will ever read it?" our father asked with equal parts hope and terror as the first complete version of the first manuscript of this book ground slowly off the dot matrix printer. Dad envisioned his book as one that teachers would not just read but use as a toolkit and guide in helping students discover math. With that vision in mind, he had spent nearly two years pouring his heart, soul, and everything he knew about teaching mathematics into "the book." In the two decades since that first manuscript rolled off the printer, "the book" became a part of our family—sort of a child in need of constant love and care, even as it grew and matured and made us all enormously proud.

Many in the field of math education referred to our father as a "rock star," a description that utterly baffled him and about which we mercilessly teased him. To us, he was just our dad. If we needed any proof that Dad was in fact a rock star, it came in the stories that poured in when he died—from countless teachers, colleagues, and most importantly from elementary school students about how our father had taught them to actually *do* math. Through this book, millions of children all over the world will be able to use math as a tool that they understand, rather than as a set of meaningless procedures to be memorized and quickly forgotten. Dad could not have imagined a better legacy.

Our deepest wish on our father's behalf is that with the guidance of "the book," teachers will continue to show their students how to discover and to own for themselves the joy of doing math. Nothing would honor our dad more than that.

"Believe in kids!"
—*John A. Van de Walle*

Gretchen Van de Walle

Bridget Van de Walle Phipps

—Gretchen Van de Walle and Bridget Phipps
(daughters of John A. Van de Walle)

Dedication

As many of you may know, John Van de Walle passed away suddenly after the release of the sixth edition. It was during the development of the previous edition that we (Karen and Jennifer) first started writing for this book, working toward becoming coauthors for the seventh edition. Through that experience, we appreciate more fully John's commitment to excellence—thoroughly considering recent research, feedback from others, and quality resources that had emerged. His loss was difficult for all who knew him and we miss him greatly.

We believe that our work on this edition reflects our understanding and strong belief in John's philosophy of teaching and his deep commitment to children and prospective and practicing teachers. John's enthusiasm as an advocate for meaningful mathematics instruction is something we keep in the forefront of our teaching, thinking, and writing. In recognition of his contributions to the field and his lasting legacy in mathematics teacher education, we dedicate this book to John A. Van de Walle.

Karen S. Karp

Jennifer M. Bay-Williams

Over the past 20 years, many of us at Pearson Allyn & Bacon and Longman have had the privilege to work with John Van de Walle, as well as the pleasure to get to know him. Undoubtedly, *Elementary and Middle School Mathematics: Teaching Developmentally* has become the gold standard for elementary mathematics methods courses. John set the bar high for math education. He became an exemplar of what a textbook author should be: dedicated to the field, committed to helping all children make sense of mathematics, focused on helping educators everywhere improve math teaching and learning, diligent in gathering resources and references and keeping up with the latest research and trends, and meticulous in the preparation of every detail of the textbook and supplements. We have all been fortunate for the opportunity to have known the man behind "the book"—the devoted family man and the quintessential teacher educator. He is sorely missed and will not be forgotten.

—Pearson Allyn & Bacon

About the Authors

John A. Van de Walle was a professor emeritus at Virginia Commonwealth University. He was a mathematics education consultant who regularly gave professional development workshops for K–8 teachers in the United States and Canada. He visited and taught in elementary school classrooms and worked with teachers to implement student-centered math lessons. He co-authored the Scott Foresman-Addison Wesley *Mathematics K–6* series and contributed to the new Pearson School mathematics program, *enVisionMATH*. Additionally, he wrote numerous chapters and articles for the National Council of Teachers of Mathematics (NCTM) books and journals and was very active in NCTM. He served as chair of the Educational Materials Committee and program chair for a regional conference. He was a frequent speaker at national and regional meetings, and was a member of the board of directors from 1998–2001.

Karen S. Karp is a professor of mathematics education at the University of Louisville (Kentucky). Prior to entering the field of teacher education she was an elementary school teacher in New York. Karen is a coauthor of *Feisty Females: Inspiring Girls to Think Mathematically*, which is aligned with her research interests on teaching mathematics to diverse populations. With Jennifer, Karen co-edited *Growing Professionally: Readings from NCTM Publications for Grades K–8*. She is a member of the board of directors of the NCTM and a former president of the Association of Mathematics Teacher Educators (AMTE).

Jennifer M. Bay-Williams is an associate professor of mathematics education at the University of Louisville (Kentucky). Jennifer has published many articles on teaching and learning in NCTM journals. She has also coauthored the following books: *Math and Literature: Grades 6–8*, *Math and Nonfiction: Grades 6–8*, and *Navigating Through Connections in Grades 6–8*. Jennifer taught elementary, middle, and high school in Missouri and in Peru, and continues to work in classrooms at all levels with students and with teachers. Jennifer serves as the president of the Association of Mathematics Teacher Educators (AMTE) and chair of the NCTM Emerging Issues Committee.

Brief Contents

Contents

SECTION I

Teaching Mathematics: Foundations and Perspectives

The fundamental core of effective teaching of mathematics combines an understanding of how children learn, how to promote that learning by teaching through problem solving, and how to plan for and assess that learning on a daily basis. Introductory chapters in this section provide perspectives on trends in mathematics education and the process of doing mathematics. These chapters develop the core ideas of learning, teaching, planning, and assessment. Additional perspectives on mathematics for children with diverse backgrounds and the role of technology are also discussed.

CHAPTER 6

Teaching Mathematics Equitably to All Children   93

CHAPTER 7

Using Technology to Teach Mathematics   111

SECTION II

Development of Mathematical Concepts and Procedures

This section serves as the application of the core ideas of Section I. Here you will find chapters on every major content area in the pre-K–8 mathematics curriculum. Numerous problem-based activities to engage students are interwoven with a discussion of the mathematical content and how children develop their understanding of that content. At the outset of each chapter, you will find a listing of "Big Ideas," the mathematical umbrella for the chapter. Also included are ideas for incorporating children's literature, technology, and assessment. These chapters are designed to help you develop pedagogical strategies and to serve as a resource for your teaching now and in the future.

CHAPTER 13

Using Computational Estimation with Whole Numbers 240

CHAPTER 14

Algebraic Thinking: Generalizations, Patterns, and Functions 254

CHAPTER 18

Proportional Reasoning   348

CHAPTER 19

Developing Measurement Concepts   369

CHAPTER 22

Exploring Concepts of Probability   456

CHAPTER 23

Developing Concepts of Exponents, Integers, and Real Numbers   473

Preface

WHAT YOU WILL FIND IN THIS BOOK

If you look at the table of contents, you will see that the chapters are separated into two distinct sections. The first section, consisting of seven chapters, deals with important ideas that cross the boundaries of specific areas of content. The second section, consisting of 16 chapters, offers teaching suggestions for every major mathematics topic in the pre-K–8 curriculum. Chapters in Section I offer perspective on the challenging task of helping children learn mathematics. The evolution of mathematics education and underlying causes for those changes are important components of your professional knowledge as a mathematics teacher. Having a feel for the discipline of mathematics—that is, to know what it means to "do mathematics"—is also a critical component of your profession. The first two chapters address these issues.

Chapters 2 and 3 are core chapters in which you will learn about a constructivist view of learning, how that is applied to learning mathematics, and what it means to teach through problem solving. Chapter 4 will help you translate these ideas of how children best learn mathematics into the lessons you will be teaching. Here you will find practical perspectives on planning effective lessons for all children, on the value of drill and practice, and other issues. A sample lesson plan is found at the end of this chapter. Chapter 5 explores the integration of assessment with instruction to best assist student learning.

In Chapter 6, you will read about the diverse student populations in today's classrooms including students who are English language learners, are gifted, or have special needs. Chapter 7 provides perspectives on the issues related to using technology in the teaching of mathematics. A strong case is made for the use of handheld technology at all grade levels. Guidance is offered for the selection and use of computer software and resources on the Internet.

Each chapter of Section II provides a perspective of the mathematical content, how children best learn that content, and numerous suggestions for problem-based activities to engage children in the development of good mathematics. The problem-based tasks for students are integrated within the text, not added on. Reflecting on the activities as you read can help you think about the mathematics from the perspective of the student. Read them along with the text, not as an aside. As often as possible, take out pencil and paper and try the problems so that you actively engage in *your learning* about *children learning* mathematics.

SOME SPECIAL FEATURES OF THIS TEXT

By flipping through the book, you will notice many section headings, a large number of figures, and various special features. All are designed to make the book more useful as a textbook and as a long-term resource. Here are a few things to look for.

NEW! MyEducationLab ▶

New to this edition, you will find margin notes that connect chapter ideas to the MyEducationLab website (www.myeducationlab.com). Every chapter in Section I connects to new video clips of John Van de Walle presenting his ideas and activities to groups of teachers. For a complete list of the new videos of John Van de Walle, see the inside front cover of your text.

Think of MyEducationLab as an extension of the text. You will find practice test questions, lists of children's literature organized by topic, links to useful websites, classroom videos, and videos of John Van de Walle talking with students and teachers. Each of the Blackline Masters mentioned in the book can be downloaded as a PDF file. You will also find seven Expanded Lesson plans based on activities in the book. MyEducationLab is easy to use! In the textbook, look for the MyEducationLab logo in the margins and follow links to access the multimedia assignments in MyEducationLab that correspond with the chapter content.

myeducationlab
Go to the Activities and Application section of Chapter 3 of MyEducationLab. Click on Videos and watch the video entitled "**John Van de Walle on Teaching Through Problem Solving**" to see him working on a problem with teachers during a training workshop.

Big Ideas

Much of the research and literature espousing a student-centered approach suggests that teachers plan their instruction around "big ideas" rather than isolated skills or concepts. At the beginning of each chapter in Section II, you will find a list of the key mathematical ideas associated with the chapter. Teachers find these lists helpful for quickly getting a picture of the mathematics they are teaching.

Mathematics Content Connections

Following the Big Ideas lists are brief descriptions of other content areas in mathematics that are related to the content of the current chapter. These lists are offered to help you be more aware of the potential interaction of content as you plan lessons, diagnose students' difficulties, and learn more yourself about the mathematics you are teaching.

◄ Activities

The numerous activities found in every chapter of Section II have always been rated by readers as one of the most valuable parts of the book. Some activity ideas are described directly in the text and in the illustrations. Others are presented in the numbered Activity boxes. Every activity is a problem-based task (as described in Chapter 3) and is designed to engage students in doing mathematics. Some activities incorporate calculator use; these particular activities are marked with a calculator icon.

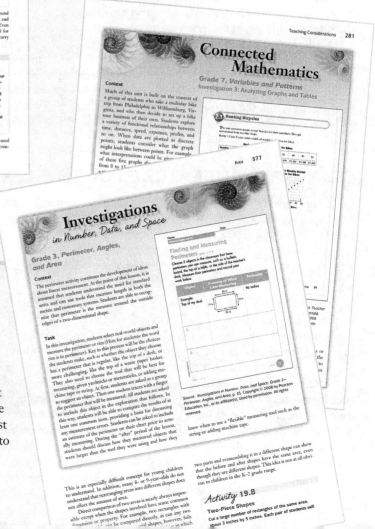

Investigations in Number, Data, and Space and *Connected Mathematics* ►

In Section II, four chapters include features that describe an activity from the standards-based curriculum *Investigations in Number, Data, and Space* (an elementary curriculum) or *Connected Mathematics Project (CMP II)* (a middle school curriculum). These features include a description of an activity in the program as well as the context of the unit in which it is found. The main purpose of this feature is to acquaint you with these materials and to demonstrate how the spirit of the NCTM *Standards* and the constructivist theory espoused in this book have been translated into existing commercial curricula.

Assessment Notes ▶

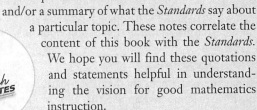

Assessment should be an integral part of instruction. Similarly, it makes sense to think about what to be listening for (assessing) as you read about different areas of content development. Throughout the content chapters, you will see assessment icons indicating a short description of ways to assess the topic in that section. Reading these assessment notes as you read the text can also help you understand how best to help your students.

NCTM Standards ▶

Throughout the book, you will see an icon indicating a reference to NCTM's *Principles and Standards for School Mathematics*. The NCTM Standards notes typically consist of a quotation from the *Standards* and/or a summary of what the *Standards* say about a particular topic. These notes correlate the content of this book with the *Standards*. We hope you will find these quotations and statements helpful in understanding the vision for good mathematics instruction.

Tech Notes ▶

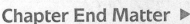

An icon marks each Tech Notes section, which discuss how technology can be used to help with the content just discussed. Descriptions include open-source software, interactive applets, and other Web-based resources. Note that there are suggestions of NCTM e-Examples that connect to full lessons on the NCTM Illuminations website. (Inclusion of any title or website in these notes should not be seen as an endorsement.)

Chapter End Matter ▶

The end of each chapter is reorganized to include two major subsections: Reflections, which includes Writing to Learn and For Discussion and Exploration; and Resources, which includes Literature Connections (found in all Section II chapters), Recommended Readings, Online Resources, and Field Experience Guide Connections.

Writing to Learn

To help you focus on the important pedagogical ideas, a list of focusing questions is found at the end of every chapter under the heading "Writing to Learn." These study questions are designed to help you reflect on the main points of the chapter. Actually writing out the answers to these questions in your own words is one of the best ways for you to develop your understanding of each chapter's main ideas.

For Discussion and Exploration

These questions ask you to explore an issue, reflect on observations in a classroom, compare ideas from this book with those found in curriculum materials, or perhaps take a position on a controversial issue. There are no "right" answers to these questions, but we hope that they will stimulate thought and cause spirited conversations.

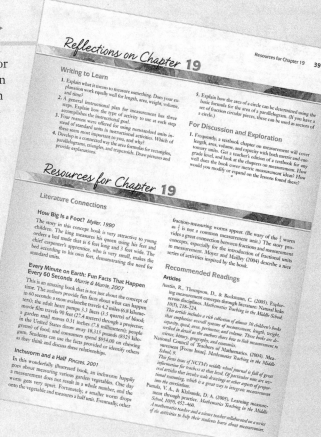

Literature Connections

Section II chapters contain end-of-chapter Literature Connections sections. These have been completely updated and expanded. For each children's literature title suggested, there is a brief description of how the mathematics concepts in the chapter can be connected to the story. These sections will get you started using this exciting vehicle for teaching mathematics.

Recommended Readings

In this section, you will find an annotated list of articles and books to augment the information found in the chapter. These recommendations include NCTM articles and books, and other professional resources designed for the classroom teacher. (In addition to the Recommended Readings, there is a References list at the end of the book for all sources cited within the chapters.)

A more complete listing of books and articles related to each chapter of the book can be found on the MyEducationLab site for this book at www.myeducationlab.com.

Online Resources

Today there are many mathematics-learning resources available free on the Internet. Most are in the form of interactive applets that allow students to explore a specific mathematics concept or skill. At the end of each chapter, you will find an annotated list of some of the best of these resources along with their website addresses. Exploring these Web-based resources will be a learning experience for you as well as your students.

An easy method of accessing these sites is to visit the MyEducationLab site for this book. There, each Web-based resource and applet can be accessed with a simple click of the mouse.

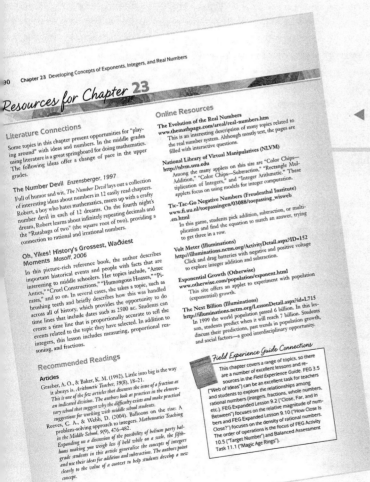

NEW!

◀ **Field Experience Guide Connections**

This new feature showcases resources from the *Field Experience Guide* that directly connect to the content and topics within each chapter. The *Field Experience Guide*, a supplement to *Elementary and Middle School Mathematics*, is for observation, practicum, and student teaching experiences at the elementary and middle school levels. The guidebook contains two parts: Part I provides tasks for preservice teachers to do in the field; Part II provides three types of activities: Expanded Lessons, Mathematics Activities, and Balanced Assessment Tasks. We hope this Field Experience Guide Connections section will help you better integrate information from the text with your work in schools.

NCTM Standards Appendixes

NCTM's *Principles and Standards for School Mathematics* is described in depth in Chapter 1, referred to periodically by the NCTM Standards notes, and reflected in spirit throughout the book. In Appendix A, you will find a copy of the appendix to that document, listing the content standards and goals for each of the following grade bands: pre-K–2, 3–5, and 6–8.

Appendix B contains the seven revised Standards for Teaching Mathematics from *Mathematics Teaching Today* (NCTM, 2007a).

Expanded Lessons ▼

An example of an Expanded Lesson can be found at the end of Chapter 4. In addition, seven similar Expanded Lessons can be found on MyEducationLab at www.myeducationlab.com. An additional 24 Expanded Lessons spanning all content areas can be found in the *Field Experience Guide*. The Expanded Lessons follow the lesson structure described in Chapter 4 and include mathematical goals, notes on preparation, specific student expectations, notes for assessment, and Blackline Masters when needed. They provide a model for converting an activity description into a real lesson plan and indicate the kind of thinking that is required in doing so.

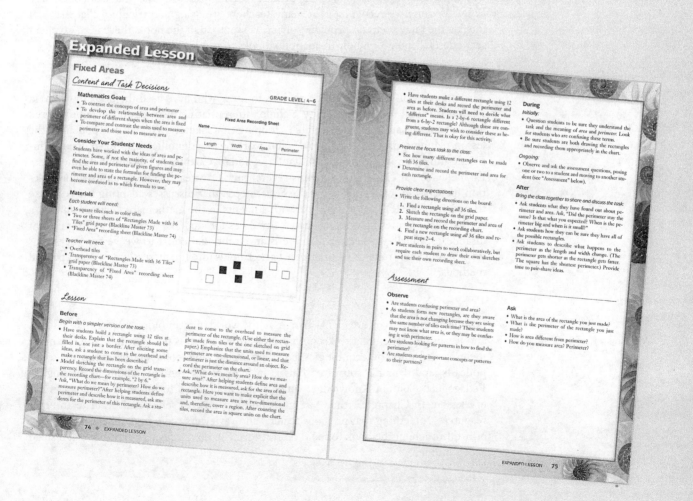

CHANGES IN THIS EDITION

Some changes are more obvious; for others you have to look closely. No chapter was left untouched. All features from the sixth edition remain, although some have been revised and expanded. Recommendations for additional resources are now shorter and more focused, and Literature Connections are found at the end of the content chapters with the other resources. Also, there are new MyEducationLab features, including video of John Van de Walle working with teachers. In addition, each chapter now concludes with a section connecting to the *Field Experience Guide*. Following are highlights of the changes in the seventh edition.

Doing and Understanding Mathematics

You will immediately note that there is one fewer chapter. Chapters 2 and 3 in the sixth edition separated the doing and understanding of mathematics. Now Chapter 2 connects the theories of learning "why do" to the implementation of "doing" mathematics. The theories of constructivism and sociocultural theory are concisely and clearly described, followed by implications for teaching. Many reviewers requested this melding of the two chapters, and the resulting chapter explicitly ties theory to practice.

Problem Solving

Although problem solving is integrated throughout the book, in Section I chapters you will find a new emphasis on teaching problem solving with a focus on the work of George Polya. Because we recognize that many teachers are using a curriculum that may not include the same focus on problem solving as espoused in the book, there is an excellent section in Chapter 3 on how to adapt textbooks to promote problem solving.

Diversity

The emphasis on diversity will be obvious to those who have used the book in the past. Discussions that focus on diversity include differentiating instruction (including tiered lessons) and the advantages of flexible grouping (in Chapter 4), a new component of the lesson planning process (Chapter 4), and working with families who have diverse linguistic and cultural backgrounds (Chapters 4 and 6). Chapter 6, "Teaching Mathematics Equitably to All Children," contains several new features, including an expanded section for working with students with special needs that discusses adapting the response to intervention (RTI) model for use with students in the mathematics classroom, and a revised section offering research-based strategies for students with mild and significant disabilities. Finally, in Section II there is an intentional effort to weave considerations for working with students from diverse backgrounds into the discussions of concepts and methods.

Technology

Not surprisingly, there are many changes in the world of technology since the last edition and it will be challenging to keep up even as this edition is published. There is a more inclusive definition of technologies including digital tools, collaborative authoring tools, podcasts, and dynamic software. This is in light of the thinking about Technological Pedagogical Content Knowledge, which reflects the need to infuse technology in every lesson. In Chapter 7, there are guidelines on how to select and evaluate Internet resources, something that previous readers and reviewers requested. There is a distinct effort throughout the book to focus on software you do not need to buy, but can instead access online.

Algebraic Thinking

One of the most important changes in this edition is the treatment of algebraic thinking in Chapter 14, "Algebraic Thinking: Generalizations, Patterns, and Functions." Although revised in the sixth edition, the chapter is now reorganized around five critical themes of algebraic thinking: generalization from arithmetic and from patterns in all of mathematics, meaningful use of symbols, study of structure in the number system, study of patterns and functions, and the process of mathematical modeling, which integrates the first four. In addition, there is increased attention to developing meaningful contexts for algebraic thinking across grades pre-K–8, including connections to other subject areas.

Statistics and Data Analysis

Since the sixth edition, the American Statistical Association published the *Guidelines for Assessment and Instruction in Statistics Education (GAISE) Report.* This important document outlines a process for doing statistics that provides the foundation for Chapter 21. While data analysis remains an essential focus of this chapter, there are now added sections on posing questions, data collection, and drawing inferences.

Developing as a Professional

There is also a new emphasis on your long-term professional growth, from keeping you abreast of the most current documents in mathematics education to a whole new section in Chapter 1 that invites you to grow and learn as you become a teacher of mathematics. In Chapter 1, you will be introduced to the *Curriculum Focal Points.* You will also be made aware of all new NCTM position statements, thinking on Grade Level Expectations, and the results of major national and international assessments. In addition, there is a specific section in Chapter 1 that emphasizes your responsibility to develop your personal knowledge of mathematics, persistence, positive attitude, readiness for change, and reflective disposition. These are the elements of becoming a lifelong learner.

Other Changes

Here are some other highlights new to the seventh edition:

- Chapter 5, "Building Assessment into Instruction," now includes definitions of formative and summative assessment, rubrics that are clearly focused on the collection of evidence, and a section on diagnostic interviews to support you when working with students who are struggling.

- Chapter 10, "Helping Children Master the Basic Facts," has been reorganized to place more emphasis on the Make 10 strategy, which research indicates is most effective. In addition, a new section on what to do and what not to do provides more guidance to teachers about how to implement the strategies.

- Chapter 15, "Developing Fraction Concepts," now includes a section on the meaning of fractions and gives a list of strategies to remember when teaching fractions.

- Chapter 19, "Developing Measurement Concepts," now includes the topic of money that was previously discussed in the chapter on place value.

- Chapter 22, "Exploring Concepts of Probability," includes many more real and engaging contexts for exploring probability, as well as an increased focus on the important concepts of sample size and variability.

ACKNOWLEDGMENTS

Many talented people have contributed to the success of this book, and we are deeply grateful to all those who have assisted over the years. Without the success of the first edition, there would certainly not have been a second, much less seven editions. The following people worked closely with John and he was sincerely indebted to Warren Crown (Rutgers), John Dossey (Illinois State University), Bob Gilbert (Florida International University), and Steven Willoughby (University of Arizona), who gave time and great care in offering detailed comments on the original manuscript. Few mathematics educators of their stature would take the time and effort that they gave to that endeavor.

In preparing this seventh edition, we have received thoughtful input from the following educators who offered comments on the sixth edition or on the manuscript for the seventh:

Fran Arbaugh, *University of Missouri*
Suzanne Brown, *University of Houston–Clear Lake*
Mary Margaret Capraro, *Texas A&M University*
Frank D'Angelo, *Bloomsburg University*
David Fuys, *Brooklyn College*
Yvelyne Germaine-McCarthy, *University of New Orleans*
Dianne S. Goldsby, *Texas A&M University*
Margo Lynn Mankus, *State University of New York at New Paltz*
Ruben D. Schwieger, *University of Southern Indiana*
David J. Sills, *Molloy College*
Stephen P. Smith, *Northern Michigan University*
Diana Treahy, *College of Charleston*
Elaine Young, *Texas A&M University–Corpus Christi*

Each reviewer challenged us to think through important issues. Many specific suggestions have found their way into this book, and their feedback helped us focus on important ideas. We are indebted to these committed professionals.

We also extend our thanks to the members of the seventh edition advisory council who offered their feedback and advice on multiple aspects of the text and supplements throughout the development process:

Suzanne Brown, *University of Houston–Clear Lake*
Mary Margaret Capraro, *Texas A&M University*
Dionne I. Cross, *Indiana University–Bloomington*
Frank D'Angelo, *Bloomsburg University*
Nedra J. Davis, *Chapman University College*
Virgil G. Fredenberg, *University of Alaska Southeast*
David Fuys, *Brooklyn College*
Dianne S. Goldsby, *Texas A&M University*
Olga Kosheleva, *University of Texas at El Paso*
Elizabeth Kreston, *The University of the Incarnate Word*
Mona C. Majdalani, *University of Wisconsin–Eau Claire*
Dawn Parker, *Texas A&M University*
David J. Sills, *Molloy College*
Stephen P. Smith, *Northern Michigan University*
Brian K. Tate, *East Tennessee State University*
Annette R. True, *East Tennessee State University*
Elaine A. Tuft, *Utah Valley University*
Trena L. Wilkerson, *Baylor University*
Elaine Young, *Texas A&M University–Corpus Christi*

Special thanks goes to Jon Wray of Howard County Public Schools (Maryland), who reviewed every technology reference in the seventh edition and provided general feedback across all chapters. His vast knowledge of emerging technologies helped add a new level of currency to the technology chapter and all end-of-chapter online resources. We are also grateful for the work of Margaret (Peg) Darcy, a master middle school teacher, and E. Todd Brown at the University of Louisville for their thoughtful contributions to the revised *Field Experience Guide*.

We received indispensable support and advice from colleagues at Pearson/Allyn & Bacon. We are fortunate to work with Kelly Villella Canton, our acquisitions editor, who guided us throughout our journey in revising the seventh edition. Her ability to respond to questions as our roles changed during the process and to give us high-quality input on our thinking was invaluable. We extend deep gratitude to Shannon Steed, our development editor, who gently nurtured us while guiding us forward at a steady pace. She was able to encourage us to think critically about our decisions and provide "real time" feedback resulting in a higher-quality product. In addition, we would like to thank Maxine Chuck, who was also a supportive mentor in her role as editor. We also wish to thank Karla Walsh and the rest of the production and editing team at Omegatype Typography, Inc.

We also would each like to thank our families for their many contributions and sacrifices along the way. On behalf of John, we thank his wife of more than 40 years, Sharon. Sharon was John's biggest supporter in this process and remained a sounding board for his many decisions as he wrote the first six editions of this book. We also thank his daughters, Bridget (a fifth-grade teacher in Chesterfield County, Virginia) and Gretchen (an associate professor of psychology at Rutgers University–Newark). They were John's first students and he tested many ideas that are in this book by their sides. We can't forget those who called John "Math Grandpa": his granddaughters, Maggie, Aidan, and Gracie.

From Karen Karp: Thanks to my husband, Bob, who as a mathematics educator himself graciously responded to revision considerations and offered insights and encouragement. In addition, I thank my children, Matthew, Tammy, Joshua, Misty, Matt, Christine, Jeffrey, and Pamela for their support and inspiration. I also thank my grandchildren, Jessica and Zane, who have helped deepen my understanding about how children think.

From Jennifer Bay-Williams: I thank all of my family for their constant support. First and foremost I want to thank my husband, Mitch; his willingness to do whatever needs to be done enables me to take on major projects. I also want to thank my daughter, MacKenna (5 years), and son, Nicolas (2 years), for their love and patience. I offer thanks to my parents, siblings, and nieces and nephews for their support and willingness to talk and do mathematics. Finally, it was two high school English teachers (yes, English!)—Mrs. Carol Froehlke and Mr. Conrad Stawski (Rock Bridge High School)—who made such a difference in helping me become a writer.

Most importantly, we thank all the teachers and students who gave of themselves by assessing what worked and what didn't work in the many iterations of this book. If future teachers learn how to teach mathematics from this book, it is because teachers and children before them shared their best ideas and thinking with the authors.

SUPPLEMENTS

Qualified college adopters can contact their Pearson sales representatives for information on ordering any of the supplements below. The instructor supplements are all available for download from the Pearson Instructor Resource Center at www.pearson highered.com/irc.

Instructor Supplements

Instructor's Manual   Written by the authors, the Instructor's Manual for the seventh edition includes a wealth of resources designed to help instructors teach the course, including chapter notes, activity suggestions, suggested assessment and test questions, and instructor transparency masters.

Computerized Test Bank   The Computerized Test Bank contains hundreds of challenging questions in fill-in-the-blank, multiple-choice, true/false, and essay formats. Instructors can choose from these questions and create their own customized exams.

PowerPoint™ Presentation   Ideal for instructors to use for lecture presentations or student handouts, the PowerPoint presentation provides dozens of ready-to-use graphic and text images tied to the text. Also included are the transparency masters from the Instructor's Manual.

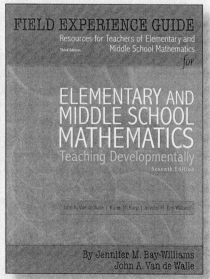

Student Supplements

◄ **Field Experience Guide**   This guidebook for both practicum experiences and student teaching at the elementary and middle school levels has been revised for the seventh edition. The author, Jennifer Bay-Williams, has developed this guide to directly address the NCATE accreditation requirements. It contains numerous field-based assignments. Each includes reproducible forms to record your experiences to turn in to your instructor. The guide includes additional activities for students, full-size versions of all of the Blackline Masters in this text, and 24 additional Expanded Lesson plans that guide teachers from planning to implementing student-centered lessons.

If this *Field Experience Guide* did not come packaged with your book, you may purchase it online at www.mypearsonstore.com.

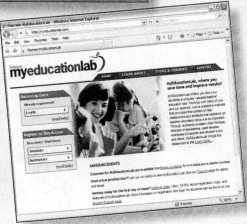

◄ **MyEducationLab**   Think of MyEducationLab as an extension of the text. You will find practice test questions, lists of children's literature organized by topic, links to useful websites, classroom videos, and videos of John Van de Walle talking with students and teachers. Each of the Blackline Masters mentioned in the book can be downloaded as a PDF file. You will also find seven Expanded Lesson plans based on activities in the book.

New to this edition you will find integration of the Scott Foresman-Addison Wesley *enVisionMATH K–6* mathematics program. MyEducationLab features topics from the *enVisionMATH* teacher's edition e-book correlated to the text. This K–6 curriculum includes daily problem-based interactive learning followed by visual learning strategies.

This curriculum is designed to deepen conceptual understanding by making meaningful connections for students and delivering strong, sequential visual/verbal connections through the Visual Learning Bridge in every lesson. Ongoing diagnosis and intervention and daily data-driven differentiation ensure that *enVisionMATH* gives every student the opportunity to succeed. The MyEducationLab website offers 16 topics from grades K–6 to give future teachers an opportunity to explore this mathematics curriculum used in elementary school classrooms throughout the country.

MyEducationLab is easy to use! In the textbook, look for the MyEducationLab logo in the margins and follow links to access the multimedia assignments in MyEducationLab that correspond with the chapter content.

If the access code for MyEducationLab did not come packaged with your book, you may purchase access at www.myeducationlab.com.

Chapter 1

Teaching Mathematics in the Era of the NCTM Standards

In this changing world, those who understand and can do mathematics will have significantly enhanced opportunities and options for shaping their futures. Mathematical competence opens doors to productive futures. A lack of mathematical competence keeps those doors closed. . . . All students should have the opportunity and the support necessary to learn significant mathematics with depth and understanding. There is no conflict between equity and excellence.

NCTM (2000, p. 50)

Someday soon you will find yourself in front of a class of students, or perhaps you are already teaching. What general ideas will guide the way you will teach mathematics? This book will help you become comfortable with the mathematics content of the pre-K–8 curriculum. You will also learn about research-based strategies for helping children come to know mathematics and be confident in their ability to do mathematics. These two things—your knowledge of mathematics and how students learn mathematics—are the most important tools you can acquire to be an effective teacher of mathematics. However, outside influences and research will affect the mathematics teaching in your classroom as well.

For at least two decades, mathematics education has been undergoing slow but steady changes. The impetus for these changes, in both the content of school mathematics and the way mathematics is taught, can be traced to various sources, including knowledge gained from research. One significant factor in this change has been the professional leadership of the National Council of Teachers of Mathematics (NCTM), an organization of teachers and mathematics educators. Another factor is the public or political pressure for change in mathematics education due largely to less-than-stellar U.S. student performance in international studies. In reaction, state standards and the No Child Left Behind Act (NCLB) press for higher levels of achievement, more testing, and increased teacher accountability. The reform agendas of NCTM and those of the political sector often seem to press

teachers in different directions. Although high expectations for students are important, testing alone is not an appropriate approach to improved student learning. According to NCTM, "Learning mathematics is maximized when teachers focus on mathematical thinking and reasoning" (www.nctm.org). The views of NCTM are clearly reflected in the ideas discussed in this book.

As you prepare to help children learn mathematics, it is important to have some perspective on the forces that affect change in the mathematics classroom. This chapter addresses the leadership that NCTM provides for mathematics education and also the major pressures on mathematics education from outside influences.

Ultimately, it is you, the teacher, who will shape mathematics for the children you teach. Your beliefs about what it means to know and do mathematics and about how children come to make sense of mathematics will affect how you approach instruction. These beliefs will undoubtedly be affected, directly or indirectly, by the significant ideas on mathematics education that you will read about in this chapter.

The National Standards-Based Movement

In April 2000, the National Council of Teachers of Mathematics (NCTM) released *Principles and Standards for School Mathematics*, an update of its original standards document released 11 years earlier in 1989. With this most important document, the council continues to guide a revolutionary reform movement in mathematics education, not just in the United States and Canada but also throughout the world.

The momentum for reform in mathematics education began in the early 1980s in response to a "back to basics" movement that emphasized "reading, writing, and arithmetic." As a result, problem solving became an important strand in the mathematics curriculum. The work of Jean

Piaget and other developmental psychologists helped to focus research on how children can best learn mathematics.

This momentum came to a head in 1989, when NCTM published *Curriculum and Evaluation Standards for School Mathematics* and the standards movement or reform era in mathematics education began. It continues today. No other document has ever had such an enormous effect on school mathematics or on any other area of the curriculum. In 1991, NCTM published *Professional Standards for Teaching Mathematics*. The *Professional Standards* and the companion document *Mathematics Teaching Today* articulate a vision of teaching mathematics and build on the notion found in the *Curriculum Standards* that significant mathematics achievement is a vision for all children, not just a few. NCTM completed the package with the *Assessment Standards for School Mathematics* in 1995 (see Chapter 5). The *Assessment Standards* shows clearly the necessity of integrating assessment with instruction and indicates the key role that assessment plays in implementing change.

From 1989 to 2000, these three documents guided the reform movement in mathematics education, directly leading in 2000 to the publication of *Principles and Standards for School Mathematics*, which is an update of all three original standards documents and further articulates the ideals, processes, and content that should be emphasized in pre-K through grade 12 classrooms and programs. In 2006, NCTM released *Curriculum Focal Points*, a little publication with a big message—mathematics at each grade level needs to focus, go into more depth, and show connections. With continued guidance from NCTM and the sustained hard work of teachers and mathematics educators at all levels, mathematics teaching and learning will continue to improve and move the country forward to a curriculum that is more challenging and meaningful to students. In the following sections, we discuss these documents, especially the *Principles and Standards*, as well as other reports, because their message is critical to your work as a mathematics teacher.

Principles and Standards for School Mathematics

Principles and Standards for School Mathematics (2000) is designed to provide guidance and direction for teachers and other leaders in pre-K–12 mathematics education. After almost 10 years, *Principles and Standards* remains the most significant reference for these educators on mathematical knowledge. While it is important that teachers read and reflect on the actual document, the next few pages will provide you with an idea of what you will find there.

The Six Principles

One of the most important features of *Principles and Standards for School Mathematics* is the articulation of six principles fundamental to high-quality mathematics education:

- Equity
- Curriculum
- Teaching
- Learning
- Assessment
- Technology

According to *Principles and Standards*, these principles must be "deeply intertwined with school mathematics programs" (NCTM, 2000, p. 12). The principles make it clear that excellence in mathematics education involves much more than simply listing content objectives.

The Equity Principle

> Excellence in mathematics education requires equity—high expectations and strong support for all students. (NCTM, 2000, p. 12)

The strong message of the Equity Principle is high expectations for all students. All students must have the opportunity and adequate support to learn mathematics "regardless of personal characteristics, backgrounds, or physical challenges" (p. 12). The message of high expectations for all is interwoven throughout the document as a whole.

The Curriculum Principle

> A curriculum is more than a collection of activities: it must be coherent, focused on important mathematics, and well articulated across the grades. (NCTM, 2000, p. 14)

Coherence speaks to the importance of building instruction around "big ideas" both in the curriculum and in daily classroom instruction. Students must be helped to see that mathematics is an integrated whole, not a collection of isolated bits and pieces.

Mathematical ideas are "important" if they help in the development of other ideas, link ideas one to another, or serve to illustrate the discipline of mathematics as a human endeavor.

The Teaching Principle

> Effective mathematics teaching requires understanding what students know and need to learn and then challenging and supporting them to learn it well. (NCTM, 2000, p. 16)

What students learn about mathematics almost entirely depends on the experiences that teachers provide every day in the classroom. To provide high-quality mathematics education, teachers must (1) understand deeply the mathematics they are teaching; (2) understand how children learn mathematics, including a keen awareness of the individual mathematical development of their own students; and (3) select instructional tasks and strategies that will enhance learning.

"Teachers' actions are what encourage students to think, question, solve problems, and discuss their ideas, strategies, and solutions" (p. 18).

The Learning Principle

> Students must learn mathematics with understanding, actively building new knowledge from experience and prior knowledge. (NCTM, 2000, p. 20)

The learning principle is based on two fundamental ideas. First, learning mathematics with understanding is essential. Mathematics today requires not only computational skills but also the ability to think and reason mathematically in order to solve the new problems and learn the new ideas that students will face in the future.

Second, the principle states quite clearly that students *can* learn mathematics with understanding. Learning is enhanced in classrooms where students are required to evaluate their own ideas and those of others, are encouraged to make mathematical conjectures and test them, and are helped to develop their reasoning skills.

The Assessment Principle

> Assessment should support the learning of important mathematics and furnish useful information to both teachers and students. (NCTM, 2000, p. 22)

In the authors' words, "Assessment should not merely be done *to* students; rather, it should also be done *for* students, to guide and enhance their learning" (p. 22). Ongoing assessment highlights for students the most important mathematics concepts. Assessment that includes ongoing observation and student interaction encourages students to articulate and, thus, clarify their ideas. Feedback from daily assessment helps students establish goals and become more independent learners.

Assessment should also be a major factor in making instructional decisions. By continuously gathering information about student growth and understanding, teachers can better make the daily decisions that support student learning. For assessment to be effective, teachers must use a variety of assessment techniques, understand their mathematical goals deeply, and have a good idea of how their students may be thinking about or misunderstanding the mathematics that is being developed.

The Technology Principle

> Technology is essential in teaching and learning mathematics; it influences the mathematics that is taught and enhances students' learning. (NCTM, 2000, p. 24)

Calculators, computers, and other technologies should be seen as essential tools for doing and learning mathematics in the classroom. Technology permits students to focus on mathematical ideas, to reason, and to solve problems in ways that are often impossible without these tools. Technology enhances the learning of mathematics by allowing for increased exploration and enhanced representation of ideas. It extends the range of problems that can be accessed.

The Five Content Standards

Principles and Standards includes four grade bands: pre-K–2, 3–5, 6–8, and 9–12. The new emphasis on preschool recognizes the need to highlight the critical years before children enter kindergarten. Rather than use different sets of mathematical topics for each grade band, the authors agreed on a common set of five content standards throughout the grades (see Appendix A). Section 2 of this book (Chapters 8 through 23) is devoted to elaborating on each of the content standards listed below:

- Number and Operations
- Algebra
- Geometry
- Measurement
- Data Analysis and Probability

Each content standard includes a small set of goals applicable to all grade bands. Then, each grade-band chapter provides specific expectations for what students should know. These grade-band expectations are also concisely listed in the appendix to the *Standards* and in Appendix A of this book.

Pause and Reflect

Pause now and turn to Appendix A. Spend a few minutes with these expectations for the grade band in which you are most interested. How do these expectations compare with the mathematics you experienced when you were in school?

Although the same five content standards apply across all grades, you should not infer that each strand has equal weight or emphasis in every grade band. Number and Operations is the most heavily emphasized strand from pre-K through grade 5 and continues to be important in the middle grades, with a lesser emphasis in grades 9–12. That same emphasis is reflected in this book, with Chapters 8 to 13 and 15 to 18 addressing content found in the Number and Operations standard.

Algebra is clearly intended as a strand for all grades. This was likely not the case when you were in school. Today, most states and provinces include algebra objectives at every grade level. In this book, Chapter 14 addresses this strand.

Note that Geometry and Measurement are separate strands, suggesting the unique importance of each of these two areas to the elementary and middle grades curriculum.

The Five Process Standards

Following the five content standards, *Principles and Standards* lists five process standards:

- Problem Solving
- Reasoning and Proof

- Communication
- Connections
- Representation

The process standards refer to the mathematical process through which students should acquire and use mathematical knowledge. The statement of the five process standards can be found in Table 1.1.

These five processes should not be regarded as separate content or strands in the mathematics curriculum. Rather, they direct the methods or processes of doing all mathematics and, therefore, should be seen as integral components of all mathematics learning and teaching.

To teach in a way that reflects these process standards is one of the best definitions of what it means to teach "according to the *Standards*."

The **Problem Solving** standard clearly views problem solving as the vehicle through which children develop mathematical ideas. Learning and doing mathematics *as you solve problems* is probably the most significant difference in the *Standards* approach versus previous methodologies.

If problem solving is the focus of mathematics, the **Reasoning and Proof** standard emphasizes the logical thinking that helps us decide if and why our answers make sense. Students need to develop the habit of providing a rationale as an integral part of every answer. It is essential for students to learn the value of justifying ideas through logical argument.

The **Communication** standard points to the importance of being able to talk about, write about, describe, and explain mathematical ideas. Learning to communicate in mathematics fosters interaction and exploration of ideas in the classroom as students learn in an active, verbal environment. No better way exists for wrestling with or cementing an idea than attempting to articulate it to others.

The **Connections** standard has two separate thrusts. First, it refers to connections within and among mathematical ideas. For example, fractional parts of a whole are connected to concepts of decimals and percents. Students need opportunities to see how mathematical ideas build on one another in a useful network of connected ideas.

Second, mathematics should be connected to the real world and to other disciplines. Children should see that mathematics plays a significant role in art, science, language arts, and social studies. This suggests that mathematics should frequently be integrated with other discipline areas and that applications of mathematics in the real world should be explored.

The **Representation** standard emphasizes the use of symbols, charts, graphs, manipulatives, and diagrams as powerful methods of expressing mathematical ideas and relationships. Symbolism in mathematics, along with visual aids such as charts and graphs, should be understood by students as ways of communicating mathematical ideas to other people. Moving from one representation to another

Table 1.1

The Five Process Standards from *Principles and Standards for School Mathematics*

Problem Solving Standard Instructional programs from prekindergarten through grade 12 should enable all students to—	• Build new mathematical knowledge through problem solving • Solve problems that arise in mathematics and in other contexts • Apply and adapt a variety of appropriate strategies to solve problems • Monitor and reflect on the process of mathematical problem solving
Reasoning and Proof Standard Instructional programs from prekindergarten through grade 12 should enable all students to—	• Recognize reasoning and proof as fundamental aspects of mathematics • Make and investigate mathematical conjectures • Develop and evaluate mathematical arguments and proofs • Select and use various types of reasoning and methods of proof
Communication Standard Instructional programs from prekindergarten through grade 12 should enable all students to—	• Organize and consolidate their mathematical thinking through communication • Communicate their mathematical thinking coherently and clearly to peers, teachers, and others • Analyze and evaluate the mathematical thinking and strategies of others • Use the language of mathematics to express mathematical ideas precisely
Connections Standard Instructional programs from prekindergarten through grade 12 should enable all students to—	• Recognize and use connections among mathematical ideas • Understand how mathematical ideas interconnect and build on one another to produce a coherent whole • Recognize and apply mathematics in contexts outside of mathematics
Representation Standard Instructional programs from prekindergarten through grade 12 should enable all students to—	• Create and use representations to organize, record, and communicate mathematical ideas • Select, apply, and translate among mathematical representations to solve problems • Use representations to model and interpret physical, social, and mathematical phenomena

is an important way to add depth of understanding to a newly formed idea.

NCTM
Standards Throughout this book, this icon will alert you to specific information in *Principles and Standards* relative to the information you are reading. However, these notes and the brief descriptions you have just read should not be a substitute for reading the *Standards* documents. Members of NCTM have access online to the complete *Principles and Standards* document as well as the three previous standards documents. Nonmembers can sign up for 120 days of free access to the *Principles and Standards* at www.nctm.org. The website also contains a number of free applets (referred to as "e-Examples"), which are interactive tools for learning about mathematical concepts. ◆

Curriculum Focal Points: A Quest for Coherence

The goals established by states are sometimes broad and numerous (discussed more thoroughly later in this chapter in the section "Grade-Level Expectations"), often covering many topics in 1 year without clearly indicating how those topics should be connected. Once again, NCTM responded to the needs expressed by teachers of mathematics, state curriculum leaders, and other educators at a variety of agencies to pinpoint mathematical "targets" for each grade level that specify the big ideas for the most significant concepts and skills. NCTM brought together a variety of experts who researched this topic and wrote *The Curriculum Focal Points for Prekindergarten through Grade 8 Mathematics: A Quest for Coherence* (2006). This document is organized by grade level and NCTM content strands, emphasizing for each grade three essential areas (Focal Points) as the primary focus of that year's instruction. The topics relating to that focus are organized to show the importance of a *coherent* curriculum rather than a curriculum with a list of isolated topics. The expectation is that those focal points along with integrated process skills and connecting experiences would form the fundamental core content of that grade. The *Curriculum Focal Points* are, in fact, a stimulus for conversations among teachers, administrators, families, and other interested stakeholders about the emphasis, depth, and sequence of key ideas for their child, classroom, school, or state. Not surprisingly, over half the states are already aligning their curriculum with the Focal Points. Besides focusing instruction, the document provides guidance to profession-

als about ways to refine and streamline the existing curriculum in light of competing priorities.

The Professional Standards for Teaching Mathematics and Mathematics Teaching Today

Although *Principles and Standards* incorporates principles of teaching and assessment, the emphasis is on curriculum. In contrast, *The Professional Standards for Teaching Mathematics* (1991) (available free online to NCTM members) and its companion document, *Mathematics Teaching Today* (2007) (see Appendix B), focus on teaching. Through detailed classroom stories (vignettes) of real teachers, the documents articulate the careful, reflective work that must go into the teaching of mathematics.

Shifts in the Classroom Environment

The introduction to *Mathematics Teaching Today* lists six major shifts in the environment of the mathematics classroom that are necessary to allow students to develop mathematical understanding:

- Communities that offer an equal opportunity to learn to all students
- A balanced focus on conceptual understanding as well as on procedural fluency
- Active student engagement in problem solving, reasoning, communicating, making connections, and using multiple representations
- Well-equipped learning centers in which technology is used to enhance understanding
- Incorporation of multiple assessments that are aligned with instructional goals and practices
- Mathematics authority that lies within the power of sound reasoning and mathematical integrity (NCTM, 2007, p. 7).

The Teaching Standards

Mathematics Teaching Today contains chapters on (1) teaching and learning; (2) observation, supervision, and improvement of mathematics teaching; (3) education and continued professional growth of teachers; (4) working together to achieve the vision; and (5) questions for the reflective practitioner. In the teaching and learning section there are seven mathematics teaching standards:

1. Knowledge of Mathematics and General Pedagogy
2. Knowledge of Student Mathematical Learning
3. Worthwhile Mathematical Tasks

myeducationlab
Go to the Activities and Application section of Chapter 1 of MyEducationLab. Click on Online Resources and then on the link entitled **"Curriculum Focal Points"** to explore mathematical topics for each grade level.

4. Learning Environment
5. Discourse
6. Reflection on Student Learning
7. Reflection on Teaching Practice

Mathematics Teaching Today (and its predecessor) is an excellent resource to help you envision your role as a teacher in creating a classroom that supports the *Principles and Standards*.

━━ II ━━━━━━━━━━ *Pause and Reflect*

The seven teaching standards are located in Appendix B of this book. Take a moment now to look over this one-page listing. Select one or two of the standards that seem especially significant to you. Put a sticky note on the page to remind you to return to these important ideas from time to time as you work through this book.

Influences and Pressures on Mathematics Teaching

NCTM has provided the major leadership and vision for reform in mathematics education. However, no single factor controls the direction of change. National and international comparisons of student performance continue to make headlines, provoke public opinion, and pressure legislatures to call for tougher standards backed by testing. The pressures of testing policies exerted on schools and ultimately on teachers may have an impact on instruction that is different from the vision of the NCTM *Standards*. In addition to these pressures, there is also the strong influence of the textbook or curriculum materials that are provided to teachers, which may not be aligned with state standards.

National and International Studies

Large studies that tell the American public how the nation's children are doing in mathematics receive a lot of attention. They influence political decisions as well as provide useful data for mathematics education researchers. Why do these studies matter? Because international and national assessments provide strong evidence that mathematics teaching *must* change if our students are to be competitive in the global market and able to understand the complex issues they must confront as responsible citizens.

National Assessment of Educational Progress. Since the late 1960s and at regular intervals (2 and 4 years), the United States gathers national data on how students are doing in mathematics (and other content areas) through the National Assessment of Educational Progress (NAEP). These data provide an important tool for policy makers

and educators to measure the overall improvement of U.S. students over time. Reported in what is called the "Nation's Report Card," NAEP examines both national and state-level trends. NAEP rates students in grades 4, 8, and 12 using four performance levels: Below Basic, Basic, Proficient, and Advanced (with Proficient and Advanced representing substantial grade-level achievement). The criterion-referenced test is designed to reflect current curriculum. In the most recent assessment in 2007, less than half of all U.S. students in grades 4 and 8 performed at the desirable range between Proficient and Advanced (39 percent in each case) (U.S. Department of Education, 2008). Although the No Child Left Behind legislation expects that all students will be at or above the Proficient level by 2014, NAEP data suggest that goal is probably not attainable. Most troubling, approximately 18 percent of fourth-grade students and 29 percent of eighth-grade students were at the Below Basic level. Despite small gains in the NAEP scores over the last 30 years, U.S. students' performance has remained at discouraging levels of competency (full information can be found at http://nationsreportcard.gov/math_2007).

Trends in International Mathematics and Science Study. In 1995 and 1996, 41 nations participated in the Third International Mathematics and Science Study (TIMSS), the largest study of mathematics and science education ever conducted. Data were gathered in grades 4, 8, and 12 from 500,000 students as well as from teachers. The most widely reported results are that U.S. fourth-grade students are above the average of the TIMSS countries, below the international average at the eighth grade, and significantly below average at the twelfth grade (U.S. Department of Education, 1997a).

In 1999 (38 countries), 2003 (46 countries), and 2007 (63 countries), repeat TIMSS studies were conducted. (The acronym TIMSS now standing for Trends in International Mathematics and Science Study.) The most recent version analyzed (2003) finds that although the rank ordering for fourth grades places the United States above the average, 11 countries (or parts of countries) have significantly higher scores (Singapore, Hong Kong, Japan, Chinese Taipei, Flemish Belgium, Netherlands, Latvia, Lithuania, Russian Federation, England, and Hungary). Only 7 percent of U.S. fourth graders would fall in the Advanced International Benchmark. This is in stark contrast with Singapore at 44 percent, Chinese Taipei at 38 percent, and Japan at 24 percent (Mullis, Martin, Gonzales, & Chrostowski, 2004).

A major finding of the original TIMSS curriculum analysis called the U.S. mathematics curriculum "a mile wide and an inch deep" (Schmidt, McKnight, & Raizen, 1996, p. 62), meaning it was found to be unfocused, pursuing many more topics than other countries while yet involving a great deal of repetition. The U.S. curriculum attempted to do everything and, as a consequence, rarely provided depth of study, making reteaching all too common (Schmidt et al., 1996). In response, the purpose of the *Curriculum Focal Points* is to assist states and districts in moving away from this "mile wide, inch deep" curriculum to one that is focused and goes into depth at each grade level.

One of the most interesting components of the 1999 study was the inclusion of a video study conducted in eighth-grade classrooms in the United States, Australia, and five of the highest-achieving countries. The results indicate that teaching is a cultural activity, and the differences for countries were often striking despite many similarities. In all countries problems or tasks were frequently used to begin the lesson. However, as a lesson progressed, the way these problems were handled in the United States was in stark contrast to the high-achieving countries. Analysis revealed that although the world is for all purposes unrecognizable from what it was 100 years ago, the U.S. approach to teaching mathematics during the same time frame was essentially unchanged.

Does the following typical U.S. lesson sound at all familiar? The teacher begins with a review of previous materials or homework and then demonstrates a problem at the board. Students practice similar basic problems at their desks, the teacher checks the seatwork, and then assigns further problems for either the remainder of the class session or homework. In more than 99.5 percent of the U.S. lessons the teacher reverts to showing students how to solve the problems. In not one of the 81 videotaped U.S. lessons was any high-level mathematics content observed; in contrast, 30 to 40 percent of lessons in Germany and Japan contained high-level content. As we stated previously, the teachers knew the research team was coming to videotape; nevertheless, 89 percent of the U.S. lessons consisted exclusively of low-level content. In the Czech Republic, Hong Kong, and Japan, lessons incorporated a variety of methods, but they frequently began with a problem-solving approach and continued in that spirit with an emphasis on conceptual understanding and true problem solving (Hiebert et al., 2003). Teaching in the high-achieving countries more closely resembles the recommendations of the NCTM *Standards* than does the teaching in the United States.

State Standards

The term *standards* was popularized by NCTM in 1989. Today it is used by nearly every state in the nation to refer to a grade-by-grade listing of very specific mathematics objectives. These state standards or objectives vary considerably from state to state. Even the grade level at which basic facts for each of the operations are expected to be mastered varies by as much as three grade levels. Although the NCTM *Standards* document lists goals for each of four grade bands, it is not a national curriculum. The United States and Canada are the only industrialized countries in the world without a national curriculum.

Grade-Level Expectations. In 2001 the legislation commonly known as No Child Left Behind (NCLB) was enacted, requiring highly qualified teachers in every classroom, proficiency from all students by 2014, incremental annual achievement based on assessments of adequate yearly progress (AYP), and development by states of content standards that are rigorous and specific. These grade-level learning expectations (GLEs) help guide textbook selection, inform the topics taught and assessed at different grades, and eventually direct what is taught to prospective teachers at universities. But as you might suspect, GLEs vary from state to state—sometimes dramatically (Reys & Lappan, 2007). For example, just in total numbers alone, at the fourth-grade level Florida has 89 GLEs in mathematics and North Carolina has 26. Textbook publishers try to cover as many states' requirements as possible, particularly populous states, in order to maximize sales of textbooks. However, this burdens teachers who must sort through many topics and corresponding lessons in a given book to eliminate some materials while sometimes needing to supplement the text with other resources to cover missing topics. Researchers also point out that textbooks' "limited overlap" and "large number of unique learning expectations" result in shallow treatment of many topics (Reys, Chval, Dingman, McNaught, Regis, & Togashi, 2007, p. 11). As more states consider such research in combination with the NCTM *Curriculum Focal Points*, we hope that collaboration may yield consensus and a narrowing of emphasis or focus will occur.

Assessments. Associated with every set of state standards is some form of testing program. Publicly reported test scores place pressure on superintendents, then on principals, and ultimately on teachers, who feel enormous pressure to raise test scores at all costs (Schmidt et al., 1996). For a teacher who has little or no experience with the spirit of the *Standards*, it is very difficult to adopt the student-centered approach to mathematics when preoccupied with preparing for high-stakes tests. Unfortunately for children, the resulting drill, review, and practice tests produce mathematics experiences with little or no high-level thinking, problem solving, or reasoning.

Are state standards incompatible with the *Standards*? Good mathematics teaching is about helping children understand concepts and become confident in their abilities to do mathematics and solve problems. There are many wonderful examples of teaching in the spirit of the NCTM standards. Children in these classrooms achieve quite well, even on the most traditional of standardized tests.

Curriculum

In most classrooms, the textbook is the single most influential factor in determining the what, when, and how of actual teaching. What is becoming increasingly complicated is how teachers and school systems attempt to align the textbook or other curriculum materials with the mandated state pre-standards. Though possibly an oversimplification, mathematics curriculum materials that are used in pre-K–8 classrooms can be categorized as either traditional or standards-based—meaning reflecting the spirit of the NCTM *Standards*.

myeducationlab

Go to the Activities and Application section of Chapter 1 of MyEducationLab. Click on Online Resources and then on the link entitled **"Standards-Based Curricula"** for a list of standards-based curricula and their developers, publishers, and Internet contacts.

Traditional Curricula. The term "traditional textbook" is used here to describe books that are developed by major publishing companies based on market research. Though traditional textbooks vary in some ways among one another, there are several characteristics that tend to be true for all of them. First, traditional textbooks reflect publishers' efforts to cover the topics in every state's curriculum documents. Since states vary widely in the topics they include at a particular grade level, this approach of including everything results in a very large textbook with many, many topics. Second, because there are so many topics, most of them are covered in a one-day lesson, which may be inadequate in developing a deep understanding. Third, traditional texts incorporate the implied instructional model of the teacher demonstrating and explaining how to do the mathematics and students then practicing those procedures. Fourth, and perhaps most challenging in terms of the international research previously discussed, is the traditional emphasis on mathematical procedures at the expense of conceptual understanding. For example, in a unit on fractions, a traditional text is likely to focus on showing students how to do the computation rather than focus on when that computation might be needed or how that topic is related to other mathematics strands.

Textbooks greatly influence teaching practice. A teacher using a traditional textbook is more likely to cover many topics, spend one day on each topic, use a teacher-directed instructional approach, and focus on procedures. If a teacher wants to devote more time to a concept, teach it more deeply, or focus on conceptual understanding, for example, he or she may need to adapt and extend the lessons in the textbook.

Standards-Based Curricula. In contrast to traditional textbooks, standards-based textbooks are not based on market research but on research related to how students learn mathematics and how concepts should develop over time. Therefore, they tend to cover fewer topics, spend more time on each concept, and make connections among concepts. Many of the standards-based programs are designed for students to learn through inquiry-oriented approaches—not through teacher explanation. Finally, all of the standards-based programs have a strong emphasis on conceptual understanding (not just procedures) and on solving problems.

At present, there are three elementary and four middle school programs commonly recognized as standards-based curricula. A hallmark of these standards-based or alternative programs is student engagement. Children are challenged to make sense of new mathematical ideas through explorations and projects, often in real contexts. Written and oral communication is strongly encouraged.

Data concerning the effectiveness of standards-based curricula as measured by traditional testing programs continue to be gathered. It is safe to say that students in standards-based programs perform much better on problem-solving measures and at least as well on traditional skills as students in traditional programs (Bell, 1998; Boaler, 1998; Fuson, Carroll, & Drueck, 2000; Hiebert, 2003; Reys, Robinson, Sconiers, & Mark, 1999; Riordin & Noyce, 2001; Stein, Grover, & Henningsen, 1996; Stein & Lane, 1996; Wood & Sellers, 1996, 1997).

Because textbooks are so central in current teaching, use of a standards-based textbook strongly influences what teachers do. Interesting and meaningful tasks are easily accessible, so the teacher is much more likely to have math lessons that link important mathematics concepts to contexts that engage students. The teacher is more likely to spend more time on concepts rather than an exclusive focus on procedures, because the student investigations are conceptually oriented. Writing, speaking, working in groups, and problem solving are more likely to be commonplace components. Comparing any of these activities to procedures associated with a corresponding traditional textbook would be an effective way to understand what reform or standards-based mathematics is all about.

In Chapters 9, 14, 18, and 19 of Section 2 you will find features describing activities from two standards-based programs: *Investigations in Number, Data, and Space* (Grades K–5) or *Connected Mathematics* (Grades 5–8). These features are included to offer you some insight into these nontraditional programs as well as to offer good ideas for instruction.

A Changing World Economy

The Glenn Commission Report, headed by former astronaut and senator John Glenn, states, "60% of all new jobs in the early 21st century will require skills that are possessed by only 20% of the current workforce" (U.S. Department of Education, 2000, p. 11). The report found that schools are not producing "graduates with the kinds of skills our economy needs to remain on the competitive cutting edge" (p. 12). These skills are often the mathematical skills that build the infrastructure of our nation.

In his book *The World Is Flat* (2007), Thomas Friedman discusses the need for people to have skills that are lasting and will survive the ever-changing landscape of available jobs. These are what he calls "the untouchables"—the individuals who will make it through all economic revolutions. He suggests that if people can fit into several of the broad categories he defines then they will not be challenged by a shifting job market. One of these safety-ensuring categories in his analysis is "math lovers." Friedman points out that in a world that is digitized and surrounded by algorithms, the math lover will always have opportunities and options. Now it becomes the job of the teacher to develop this passion in students. As Lynn Arthur Steen, a well-known mathematician and educator, states, "As information becomes ever more quantitative and as society relies increasingly on computers and the data they produce, an innumerate citizen today is as vulnerable as the illiterate peasant of Gutenberg's time" (1997, p. xv).

The changing world influences what should be taught in pre-K–8 mathematics classrooms. As we prepare elementary students for jobs that possibly do not currently exist, we do know that there are few jobs for people where they just do simple computation. We can predict that there will be work that requires interpreting complex data, designing algorithms to make predictions, and using the ability to approach new problems in a variety of ways.

An Invitation to Learn and Grow

The mathematics education described in the NCTM *Standards* may not be the same as the mathematics and the mathematics teaching you experienced in grades K through 8. Along the way, you may have had some excellent teachers who really did reflect the current reform spirit. Examples of good standards-based curriculum have been around since the early 1990s, and you may have benefited from one of them. But for the most part, the goals of the reform movement at the end of its second decade have yet to be realized in the large majority of school districts in North America.

As a practicing or prospective teacher facing the challenge of the *Standards*, this book may require you to confront some of your personal beliefs—about what it means to *do mathematics*, how one goes about *learning mathematics*, how to *teach mathematics through problem solving*, and what it means to *assess mathematics* integrated with instruction.

As part of this personal assessment, you should understand that mathematics is seen as the subject that people love to hate. At parties or even at parent–teacher conferences, other adults will respond to the fact that you are a teacher of mathematics with comments such as "I could never do math," or "I can't even balance my checking account." Instead of just dismissing these disclosures, they are not to be taken lightly. Would people confide that they don't read and hadn't read a book in years? That is not likely. Families' and teachers' attitudes toward mathematics may enhance or detract from children's ability to do math. It is important for you and for students' families to know that math ability is not inherited—anyone can learn mathematics. Moreover,

learning mathematics is an essential life skill. You need to find ways of countering these statements, especially if they are stated in the presence of children, pointing out the importance of the topic and the fact that all people have the capacity to learn it. Only in that way can the long-standing pattern that passes this apprehension from family member to child (or in rare cases teacher to child) be broken. There is much joy to be had in solving mathematical problems, and you need to nurture that passion in children.

Children and adults alike need to think of themselves as mathematicians, in the same way as they think of themselves as readers. As all people interact with our increasingly mathematical and technological world, they need to construct, modify, or integrate new information in many forms. Solving novel problems and approaching circumstances with a mathematical perspective should come as naturally as reading new materials to comprehend facts, insights, or news. Thinking and talking about mathematics instead of focusing on the "one right answer" is a strategy that will serve us well in becoming a society where all citizens are confident that they can do math.

Becoming a Teacher of Mathematics

This book and this course of study are critical to your professional teaching career. The mathematics education course you are taking now will be the foundation for much of the mathematics instruction you do in your classroom for the next decade. The authors of this book take that seriously, as we know you do. Therefore, this section lists and describes the characteristics, habits of thought, skills, and dispositions you will need to succeed as a teacher of mathematics.

Knowledge of Mathematics. You will need to have a profound, flexible, and adaptive knowledge of mathematics content (Ma, 1999). This statement is not intended to scare you if you feel that mathematics is not your strong suit, but it is meant to help you prepare for a serious semester of learning about mathematics and how to teach it. The "school effects" for mathematics are great, meaning that unlike other subject areas, where children have frequent interactions with their family or others outside of school on topics such as reading books, exploring nature, or discussing current events, in the area of mathematics what we do in school is "it" for many children. This adds to the earnestness of your responsibility, because a student's learning for the year in mathematics will likely come only from you. If you are not sure of a fractional concept or other aspect of the mathematics curriculum, now is the time to make changes in your depth of understanding to best prepare for your role as an instructional leader. This book and your professor will help you in that process.

Persistence.

You need the ability to stave off frustration and demonstrate persistence. This is the very skill that your students must have to conduct mathematical investigations. As you move through this book and work the problems yourself, you will learn methods and strategies that help you anticipate the barriers to student learning and identify strategies to get past these stumbling blocks. It is likely that what works for you as a learner will work for your students. As you experience the material in this book, if you ponder, struggle, talk about your thinking, and reflect on how it all fits or doesn't fit, then you enhance your repertoire as a teacher. Remember you need to demonstrate these characteristics so your students can model them.

Positive Attitude.

Arm yourself with a positive attitude toward the subject of mathematics. Research shows that teachers with positive attitudes teach math in more successful ways that result in their students liking math more (Karp, 1991). If in your heart you say, "I never liked math," that will be evident in your instruction. The good news is that research shows that attitudes toward mathematics are relatively easy to change (Tobias, 1995) and that the changes are long-lasting. Through expanding your knowledge of the subject and trying new ways to approach problems, you can learn to enjoy mathematical activities. Not only can you acquire a positive attitude toward mathematics, it is essential that you do.

Readiness for Change.

Demonstrate a readiness for change, even for change so radical that it may cause disequilibrium. You may find that what is familiar will become unfamiliar and, conversely, what is unfamiliar will become familiar. For example, you may have always referred to "reducing fractions" as the process of changing $\frac{2}{4}$ to $\frac{1}{2}$, but is "reducing" what is going on conceptually? Are reduced fractions getting smaller? Such terminology can lead to mistaken connections that children will naturally make ("Did the reduced fraction go on a diet?"). A careful look will point out that "reducing" is not a good term to use when focusing on conceptual knowledge. Even though you have used this familiar expression for years, it is inappropriate, because it does not explain what is really happening. We will discuss innovative and conceptually sound methods for teaching fractions in Chapter 15.

On the other hand what is unfamiliar will become more comfortable. It may feel uncomfortable for you to be asking students, "Did anyone solve it differently?" if you are worried that you won't understand their explanations. Yet bravely using this strategy will lead you to understand the concept better yourself as you ask students to re-explain how they solved a problem so that you can understand their thinking.

Another potentially difficult change is toward a focus on concepts. What happens in a procedure-focused classroom when a student doesn't understand division of fractions? A teacher who only has procedural knowledge is often left with just one approach: repeating, louder and slower. "Just change the division sign to multiplication, flip over the second fraction, and multiply." We know this approach doesn't work well, so let's think about another. Consider $3\frac{1}{2} \div \frac{1}{2} = $ _____. In a conceptual approach, you might relate to a whole number problem such as $25 \div 5 = $ _____. A corresponding story problem might be, "How many orders of 5 pizzas are there in a group of 25 pizzas?" Returning to the fraction problem, ask students to put words around the division problem, such as "You plan to serve each guest $\frac{1}{2}$ a pizza. If you have $3\frac{1}{2}$ pizzas, how many guests can you serve?" Yes, there are seven halves in $3\frac{1}{2}$ and therefore 7 guests you can serve. Are you surprised that you can do this problem mentally?

To respond to students' challenges, uncertainties, and frustrations you need to unlearn and relearn mathematical concepts, developing comprehensive understanding and substantial representations along the way. Supporting your knowledge on solid, well-supported terrain is your best hope of making a lasting difference—so be ready for change. What you already understand will provide you with many "Aha" moments as you read this book and connect new information to the mathematics knowledge currently stored in your memory.

Reflective Disposition.

Make time to be self-conscious and reflective. As Steve Leinwand, the former director of mathematics education in Connecticut, wrote, "If you don't feel inadequate, you're probably not doing the job" (2007, p. 583). No matter if you are a preservice teacher or an experienced teacher, there is more to learn about the content and methodology of teaching mathematics. The ability to examine oneself for areas that need improvement or to reflect on successes and challenges is critical for growth and development. The best teachers are always trying to improve their practice through the latest article, the newest book, the most recent conference, or by signing up for the next series of professional development opportunities. These teachers don't say, "Oh, that's what I am already doing"; instead, they identify and celebrate one small tidbit that adds to their repertoire. The best teachers never finish learning all that they need to know, they never exhaust the number of new connections that they make, and, as a result, they never see teaching as stale or stagnant. An ancient Chinese proverb states, "The best time to plant a tree is twenty years ago; the second best time is today." So, as John Van de Walle said with every new edition, "Enjoy the journey!"

Reflections on Chapter 1

Writing to Learn

At the end of each chapter of this book, you will find a series of questions under this same heading. The questions are designed to help you reflect on the most important ideas of the chapter. Writing (or talking aloud with a peer) is an excellent way to explore new ideas and incorporate them into your own knowledge base. The writing (or discussion) will help make the ideas your own.

1. What are the five content strands (standards) defined by *Principles and Standards*? How are they emphasized differently in different grade bands?
2. What is meant by a *process* as referred to in the *Principles and Standards* process standards? Give a brief description of each of the five process standards.
3. Among the ideas in *Mathematics Teaching Today* are six shifts in the classroom environment. Examine these six shifts, and describe in a few sentences what aspects of each shift seem most significant to you.
4. Describe two results derived from NAEP data. What are the implications?
5. Describe two results derived from TIMSS data. What are the implications?

For Discussion and Exploration

1. In recent years, the outcry for "basics" was again being heard from a variety of sources. The debate between reform and the basics is both important and interesting. For an engaging discussion of the reform movement in light of the "back to basics" outcry, read the three free online articles from the February 1999 edition of the *Phi Delta Kappan* at www.pdkintl.org/kappan/khome/karticle.htm. Where do you stand on the issue of reform versus the basics?
2. Examine a traditional textbook at any grade level of your choice. If possible, use a teacher's edition. Page through any chapter and look for signs of the five process standards. To what extent are children who are being taught from this book likely to be doing and learning mathematics in ways described by those processes? What would you have to do to supplement the general approach of this text?
3. Examine a unit from any one of the standards-based curriculum programs and see how it reflects the NCTM vision of reform, especially the five process standards. How do these curriculum programs differ from traditional textbook programs? Do you need to supplement this text?

Resources for Chapter 1

Recommended Readings

Articles

Hoffman, L., & Brahier, D. (2008). Improving the planning and teaching of mathematics by reflecting on research. *Mathematics Teaching in the Middle School, 13*(7), 412–417.
This article addresses how a teacher's philosophy and beliefs influence his or her mathematics instruction. Using TIMSS and NAEP studies as a foundation, the authors talk about posing higher-level problems, asking thought-provoking questions, facing students' frustration, and using mistakes to enhance understanding of concepts. They pose a set of reflective questions that are good for self-assessment or discussion with peers.

Books

Ferrini-Mundy, J. (2000). The standards movement in mathematics education: Reflections and hopes. In M. J. Burke (Ed.), *Learning mathematics for a new century* (pp. 37–50). Reston, VA: NCTM.
In this chapter, written before Standards was released, the author shares her unique and very well-informed view of this important publication, how it came to be, the impact of the earlier document,

the political climate in which Standards was released, and the intentions that NCTM had for the document. This article will provide an understanding of Standards that is impossible to get from the document itself.

Hiebert, J. (2003). What research says about the NCTM standards. In J. Kilpatrick, W. G. Martin, & D. Schifter (Eds.), *A research companion to Principles and Standards for School Mathematics* (pp. 5–23). Reston, VA: NCTM.
This chapter provides one of the best perspectives on what we have learned since Standards was released. It also offers some perspective on typical U.S. classrooms and offers contrasts between traditional mathematics programs and those called "standards based."

National Research Council. (2001). *Adding it up: Helping children learn mathematics*. J. Kilpatrick, J. Swafford, & B. Findell (Eds.). Mathematics Learning Study Committee, Center for Education, Division of Behavioral and Social Sciences and Education. Washington, DC: National Academy Press.
This book is the effort of a select committee representing mathematics educators, mathematicians, school administrators, and industry. A hallmark of this book is the formulation of five strands of "mathematical proficiency": conceptual understanding, procedural fluency, strategic competence, adaptive reasoning, and

productive disposition. Educators and policy makers will cite this book for many years to come.

Standards-Based Curricula

Elementary Programs

UCSMP Elementary: Everyday Mathematics (K–6)

Investigations of Number, Data, and Space (K–5) (samples included throughout the book)

Math Trailblazers: A Mathematical Journey Using Science and Language Arts (K–5)

Middle School Programs

Connected Mathematics (CMP) (6–8) (samples included throughout the book)

Mathematics in Context (MIC) (5–8)

MathScape (6–8)

Middle Grades Math Thematics (STEM) (6–8)

Middle School Mathematics Through Applications Project (MMAP) (6–8)

Online Resources

Illuminations
www.illuminations.nctm.org

A companion website to NCTM sponsored by NCTM and Marcopolo. Provides lessons, interactive applets, and links to websites for learning and teaching mathematics.

Key Issues in Math
www.mathforum.org/social/index.html

Part of the Math Forum at Drexel University, this page lists numerous questions concerning issues in mathematics education with answers supplied by experts in short articles or excerpts.

NAEP (National Assessment of Educational Progress, "The Nation's Report Card")
http://nces.ed.gov/nationsreportcard/mathematics

Past and current data and reports related to NAEP assessments.

National Council of Teachers of Mathematics
www.nctm.org

Here you can find all about NCTM, its belief statements, and positions on important topics. Also find an overview of

Principles and Standards and free access to interactive applets (see Standards—Electronic), membership and conference information, publications catalog, links to related sites, and much more. Members have access to even more information.

State Mathematics Standards Database
http://mathcurriculumcenter.org/states.php

This site from The Center for the Study of Mathematics Curriculum (CSMC) has the complete set of hotlinks to current state-level K–12 mathematics curriculum standards. In some cases states provide multiple documents, including their standards for assessment or other important information for teachers of mathematics.

TIMSS (Trends in International Mathematics and Science Study)
http://nces.ed.gov/timss

Access articles and data from TIMSS.

Field Experience Guide Connections

The *Field Experience Guide: Resources for Teachers of Elementary and Middle School Mathematics* (FEG) is a workbook designed to respond to both the variety of teacher preparation programs and the NCTE recommendation that students have the opportunity to engage in diverse activities. At the end of each chapter, you will find a brief note that connects chapter content to activities and experiences within the guide. Many of the field experiences focus on aligning practice with the standards. For example, see the observation protocol for shifts in the classroom environment (FEG 1.2), a teacher interview based on the teaching standards (FEG 1.3), and observation protocol for the process standards (FEG 4.1). Developing a reflective disposition is the purpose of FEG 3.7, 4.8, 5.5, and 6.4. These opportunities for reflection focus on your students' learning and your own professional growth.

Chapter 2

Exploring What It Means to Know and Do Mathematics

No matter how lucidly and patiently teachers explain to their students, they cannot understand for their students.

Schifter and Fosnot (1993, p. 9)

What does it mean to know a mathematics topic? Take division of fractions, for example. If you know this topic well, what do you know? As mentioned in Chapter 1, the answer is more broad than knowing a procedure you may have memorized (invert the second fraction and multiply). Knowing division of fractions means that you can not only think of examples that fit division of fractions, you can also use alternative strategies to solve problems, estimate an answer, or draw a diagram to show what happens when a number is divided by a fraction. Unfortunately, too much mathematics instruction is limited to simple algorithms without allowing students to deeply learn about different topics.

This chapter is about the learning theory of teaching developmentally and the knowledge necessary for students to learn mathematics with understanding. You might consider this chapter the what, why, and how of teaching mathematics. The "how" is addressed first—how should mathematics be experienced by a learner? Second, "why" should mathematics look this way? And, finally, "what" does it mean to understand mathematics?

Before you read about learning theory and knowledge in mathematics, however, it is important for you to have a chance to "do mathematics" in a way that nurtures understanding and builds connections. These experiences will serve as exemplars when we turn to the discussion of learning theory and knowledge.

What Does It Mean to Do Mathematics?

Stop for a moment and write a few sentences about what it means to do and know mathematics, based on your own experiences. Then put your paper aside until you have finished this chapter.

The description of doing mathematics presented here may not match your personal experiences. That's okay! However, it is not okay to be closed off to new ideas that may clash with your perceptions or to refuse to acknowledge that teaching mathematics could be dramatically different than your previous experience.

Mathematics is more than completing sets of exercises or mimicking processes the teacher explains. Doing mathematics means generating strategies for solving problems, applying those approaches, seeing if they lead to solutions, and checking to see if your answers make sense. Doing mathematics in classrooms should closely model the act of doing mathematics in the real world.

Mathematics Is the Science of Pattern and Order

This wonderfully simple description of mathematics, found in the thought-provoking publication *Everybody Counts* (Mathematical Sciences Education Board, 1989), challenges the popular view of mathematics as a discipline dominated by computation and rules without reasons. Science is a process of figuring out or making sense. Although you may never have thought of it in quite this way, mathematics is a science of concepts and processes that have a pattern of regularity and logical order. Finding and exploring this regularity or order, and then making sense of it, is what doing mathematics is all about.

Even the youngest schoolchildren can and should be involved in the science of pattern and order.

Have you ever noticed that 6 + 7 is the same as 5 + 8 and 4 + 9? What is the pattern? What are the relationships? When two odd numbers are multiplied, the result is also odd, but if the same numbers are added or subtracted, the result is even.

In middle school, students graph linear functions (i.e., functions that can be represented as $y = mx + b$). Graphing functions can be narrowly explored by following a set of steps or rules, but understanding why certain forms of equations, situations, or models are growing in a linear manner involves a search for patterns. Discovering what types of real-world relationships are represented by linear graphs is more scientific—and infinitely more valuable—than creating a graph from an equation without connection to the world.

Engaging in the science of pattern and order—doing mathematics—takes time and effort. Consider topics that show up on lists of "basic skills," such as knowing basic facts for addition and multiplication and having efficient methods of computing whole numbers, fractions, and decimals. Studying relationships on the multiplication chart or analyzing patterns in place value (discussed in detail in the related content chapters) helps students understand what they are doing, therefore increasing their accuracy and retention. To master these topics as facts and procedures by memorization alone is no more doing mathematics than playing scales on the piano is making music.

⏸ ———————— *Pause and Reflect*

Envision for a moment an elementary or middle school mathematics class where students are doing mathematics as "a study of patterns." What action verbs would students use to describe what they are doing? Make a short list before reading further.

A Classroom Environment for Doing Mathematics

To create a setting where students are doing mathematics means a shift in the tasks given to students and how classrooms are organized for mathematics lessons. Doing mathematics begins with posing worthwhile tasks and then creating a risk-taking environment where students share and defend mathematical ideas.

The Language of Doing Mathematics. Children in traditional mathematics classes often describe mathematics as "work" or "getting answers." They talk about "plussing" and "doing times" (multiplication). In contrast, the following collection of verbs can be found in most of the literature describing the authentic work of doing mathematics, and all are used in *Principles and Standards* (NCTM, 2000):

explore	justify	construct	develop
investigate	represent	verify	describe
conjecture	formulate	explain	use
solve	discover	predict	

These verbs require higher-level thinking and encompass "making sense" and "figuring out." Children engaged in these actions in mathematics classes will be actively thinking about the mathematical ideas that are involved. Contrast these with the verbs that might reflect the traditional mathematics classroom: listen, copy, memorize, drill. These are lower-level thinking activities and do not adequately prepare students for the real act of doing mathematics. Mathematics requires effort and it is important that students, parents, and the community acknowledge and honor the fact that effort is what leads to learning in mathematics (National Mathematics Advisory Panel, 2008). In classrooms pursuing higher-level mathematics activities on a daily basis, the students are getting an empowering message: "You are capable of making sense of this—you are capable of doing mathematics!"

Every idea introduced in the mathematics classroom can and should be understood by every child. There are no exceptions! All children are capable of learning the mathematics we want them to learn. Their learning becomes meaningful when they are taught using the verbs listed here to perform challenging and engaging mathematics.

The Setting for Doing Mathematics. The teacher's role is to create this spirit of inquiry, trust, and expectation. Within that environment, students are invited to do mathematics. You pose problems; students wrestle toward solutions. The focus is on students actively figuring things out by testing ideas, making conjectures, developing reasons, and offering explanations. In *Classroom Discussions*, a teacher resource describing how to implement effective discourse in the classroom, Chapin, O'Conner, and Anderson (2003) write, "When a teacher succeeds in setting up a classroom in which students feel obligated to listen to one another, to make their own contributions clear and comprehensible, and to provide evidence for their claims, that teacher has set in place a powerful context for student learning" (p. 9).

In the classic book *Making Sense* (Hiebert et al., 1997), the authors describe four features of a productive classroom culture for mathematics in which students can learn from each other.

1. *Ideas are the currency of the classroom.* Ideas, expressed by any participant, have the potential to contribute to everyone's learning and consequently warrant respect and response.
2. *Students have autonomy with respect to the methods used to solve problems.* Students must respect the need for everyone to understand their own methods and must recognize that there are often a variety of methods that will lead to a solution.
3. *The classroom culture exhibits an appreciation for mistakes as opportunities to learn.* Mistakes afford opportunities to examine errors in reasoning, and thereby raise everyone's level of analysis. Mistakes are not to be covered up; they are to be used constructively.

4. *The authority for reasonability and correctness lies in the logic and structure of the subject, rather than in the social status of the participants.* The persuasiveness of an explanation or the correctness of a solution depends on the mathematical sense it makes, not on the popularity of the presenter. (pp. 9–10)

In classrooms that embrace this culture for learning, the way students think about mathematics changes. Rather than students asking (or thinking) "What do you want me to do?" problem ownership shifts the situation to "I think I am going to . . ." (Baker & Baker, 1990). In the latter example the student feels empowered to come up with his or her own approach rather than depend on the teacher to offer an approach. This is foundational in creating an environment for doing mathematics. More information on creating a community of learners is found in Chapter 3.

An Invitation to Do Mathematics

If your goal is to create a classroom environment where children are truly doing mathematics, it is important that you have a personal feel for doing mathematics. The purpose of this section is to provide *you* with opportunities to engage in the science of pattern and order—to do some mathematics. If possible, find one or two peers to work with you so that you can experience sharing and exchanging ideas.

Don't read too much at once. Some hints and suggestions follow each task. Do as much as you can until you are stuck—really stuck—and then read a bit more.

Let's Do Some Mathematics!

We will explore four different problems. Each is independent of the others. None requires any sophisticated mathematics, not even algebra. But they do require higher-level thinking and reasoning. Try out your ideas! Devote time and effort—persist—these are the keys for being successful at mathematics. Have fun!

Start and Jump Numbers: Searching for Patterns

You will need to make a list of numbers that begin with a "start number" and increase by a fixed amount we will call the "jump number." First try 3 as the start number and 5 as the jump number. Write the start number at the top of your list, then 8, 13, and so on, "jumping" by 5 each time until your list extends to about 130.

Examine this list of numbers and find as many patterns as you can. Share your ideas with the group, and write down every pattern you agree really is a pattern.

Do not read on until you have listed as many patterns as you can identify.

A Few Ideas. Here are some patterns you might consider:

- Do you see at least one alternating pattern?
- Have you looked at odd and even numbers?
- What can you say about the number in the tens place?
- How did you think about the first two numbers with no tens-place digits?
- Have you tried doing any adding of numbers? Numbers in the list? Digits in the numbers?

If there is an idea in this list you haven't tried, try that now.

Don't forget to think about what happens to your patterns after the numbers go over 100. How are you thinking about 113? One way is as 1 hundred, 1 ten, and 3 ones. But, of course, it could also be "eleventy-three," where the tens digit has gone from 9 to 10 to 11. How do these different perspectives affect your patterns? What would happen after 999?

When you added the digits in the numbers, the sums are 3, 8, 4, 9, 5, 10, 6, 11, 7, 12, 8, ... Did you look at every other number in this string? And what is the sum of the digits for 113? Is it 5 or is it 14? (There is no "right" answer here. But it is interesting to consider different possibilities.)

Next Steps. Sometimes when you have discovered some patterns in mathematics, it is a good idea to make some changes and see how the changes affect the patterns. What changes might you make in this problem?

Try some ideas now before going on.

Your changes may be even more interesting than the following suggestions. But here are some ideas:

- Change the start number but keep the jump number equal to 5. What is the same and what is different?
- Keep the same start number and examine different jump numbers. You will find out that changing jump numbers really "messes things up" a lot compared to changing the start numbers.
- If you have patterns for several different jump numbers, what can you figure out about how a jump number

Figure 2.1 For jumps of 3, this cycle of digits will occur in the ones place. The start number determines where the cycle begins.

affects the patterns? For example, when the jump number was 5, the ones-digit pattern repeated every two numbers—it had a "pattern length" of two. But when the jump number is 3, the length of the ones-digit pattern is ten! Do other jump numbers create different pattern lengths?

- For a jump number of 3, how is the ones-digit pattern related to the circle of numbers in Figure 2.1? Are there other circles of numbers for other jump numbers?
- Using the circle of numbers for 3, find the pattern for jumps of multiples of 3, that is, jumps of 6, 9, or 12.

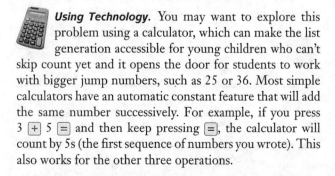

Using Technology. You may want to explore this problem using a calculator, which can make the list generation accessible for young children who can't skip count yet and it opens the door for students to work with bigger jump numbers, such as 25 or 36. Most simple calculators have an automatic constant feature that will add the same number successively. For example, if you press 3 ⊞ 5 ⊟ and then keep pressing ⊟, the calculator will count by 5s (the first sequence of numbers you wrote). This also works for the other three operations.

Two Machines, One Job

Ron's Recycle Shop started when Ron bought a used paper-shredding machine. Business was good, so Ron bought a new shredding machine. The old machine could shred a truckload of paper in 4 hours. The new machine could shred the same truckload in only 2 hours. How long will it take to shred a truckload of paper if Ron runs both shredders at the same time?

 ——————————————

Do not read on until you either get an answer or get stuck. Can you check that you are correct? Are you sure you are stuck?

A Few Ideas. Are you overlooking any assumptions made in the problem? Do the machines run simultaneously? The problem says "at the same time." Do they run just as fast when working together as when they work alone?

 ——————————————

If this gives you an idea, pursue it before reading more.

Have you tried to predict approximately how much time you think it should take the two machines? Just make an estimate in round numbers. For example, will it be closer to 1 hour or closer to 4 hours? What causes you to answer as you have? Can you tell if your "guestimate" makes sense or is at least in the ballpark? Checking a guess in this way sometimes leads to a new insight.

Some people draw pictures to solve problems. Others like to use something they can move or change. For example, you might draw a rectangle or a line segment to stand for the truckload of paper, or you might get some counters (chips, plastic cubes, pennies) and make a collection that stands for the truckload.

 ——————————————

Go back and work on the problem more.

Consider Solutions of Others. Here are solutions of teachers who worked on this problem (adapted from Schifter & Fosnot, 1993, pp. 24–27). Here is Betsy's solution (she teaches sixth grade):

Betsy holds up a bar of plastic cubes. "Let's say these 16 cubes are the truckload of paper. In 1 hour, the new machine shreds 8 cubes and the old machine 4 cubes." Betsy breaks off 8 cubes and then 4 cubes. "That leaves these 4 cubes. If the new machine did 8 cubes' worth in 1 hour, it can do 2 cubes' worth in 15 minutes. The old machine does half as much, or 1 cube." As she says this, she breaks off 3 more cubes. "That is 1 hour and 15 minutes, and we still have 1 cube left." Long pause. "Well, the new machine did 2 cubes in 15 minutes, so it will do this cube in $7\frac{1}{2}$ minutes. Add that onto the 1 hour and 15 minutes. The total time will be 1 hour $22\frac{1}{2}$ minutes." (See Figure 2.2.)

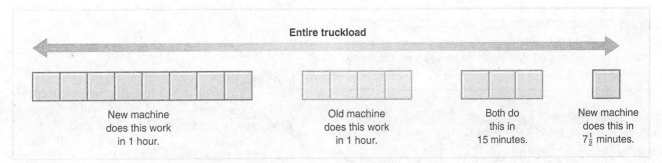

Figure 2.2 Betsy's solution to the paper-shredding problem.

Cora, a fourth-grade teacher, disagrees with Betsy's answer. Here is Cora's proposal:

"This rectangle [see Figure 2.3] stands for the whole truckload. In 1 hour, the new machine will do half of this." The rectangle is divided in half. "In 1 hour, the old machine could do $\frac{1}{4}$ of the paper." The rectangle is divided accordingly. "So in 1 hour, the two machines have done $\frac{3}{4}$ of the truck, and there is $\frac{1}{4}$ left. What is left is one-third as much as what they already did, so it should take the two machines one-third as long to do that part as it took to do the first part. One-third of an hour is 20 minutes. That means it takes 1 hour and 20 minutes to do it all."

Sylvia, a third-grade teacher, reports on her group's strategy:

At first, we solved the problem by averaging. We decided that it would take 3 hours because that's the average. Then Deborah asked how we knew to average. We thought we had a reason, but then Deborah asked how Ron would feel if his two machines together took longer than just the new one that could do the job in only 2 hours. So we can see that 3 hours doesn't make sense. So we still don't know whether it's 1 hour and 20 minutes or 1 hour and $22\frac{1}{2}$ minutes.

As with the teachers in these examples, it is important to decide if your solution is correct through justifying why you did what you did, as this reflects real problem solving (rather than checking with an answer key). After you have justified that you have solved the problem in a correct manner, try to find other ways to reach that solution or try to understand others' approaches to the problem—in considering other ways, you can expand your repertoire of problem-solving strategies.

One Up, One Down

For Grades 1–3. When you add 7 to itself, you get 14. When you make the first number 1 more and the second number 1 less, you get the same answer:

$\uparrow \quad \downarrow$

7 + 7 = 14 has the same answer as 8 + 6 = 14

It works for 5 + 5 too:

$\uparrow \quad \downarrow$

5 + 5 = 10 has the same answer as 6 + 4 = 10

What can you find out about this?

For Grades 4–8. What happens when you change addition to multiplication in this exploration?

$\uparrow \quad \downarrow$

7 × 7 = 49 has an answer that is one more than 8 × 6 = 48

It works for 5 × 5 too:

$\uparrow \quad \downarrow$

5 × 5 = 25 has an answer that is one more than 6 × 4 = 24

What can you find out about this situation?

Can this pattern be extended to other situations?

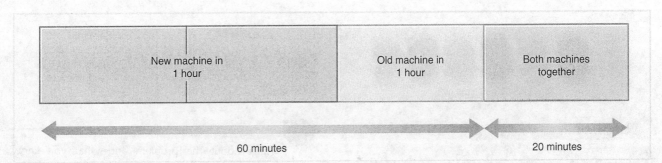

Figure 2.3 Cora's solution to the paper-shredding problem.

STOP
Work on the multiplication pattern. Explore until you have developed some ideas. Write down whatever ideas you discover.

A Few Ideas. Use a physical model or picture. You have probably found some interesting patterns. Can you tell why these patterns work? In the case of addition, it is fairly easy to see that when you take from one number and give to the other, the total stays the same. With multiplication, that is not the case. Why? One way to explore this is to draw rectangles with a length and height of each of the factors (e.g., for the first problem, a 7-by-7-unit rectangle and a 6-by-4-unit rectangle). See how the rectangles compare (Figure 2.4(a)).

You may prefer to think of multiplication as equal sets. For example, using stacks of chips, 7 × 7 is seven stacks with seven chips in each stack (set). The expression 8 × 6 is represented by eight stacks of six (though six stacks of eight is a possible interpretation). See how the stacks for each expression compare (Figure 2.4(b)).

STOP
Work with one or both of these approaches to see if you get any insights.

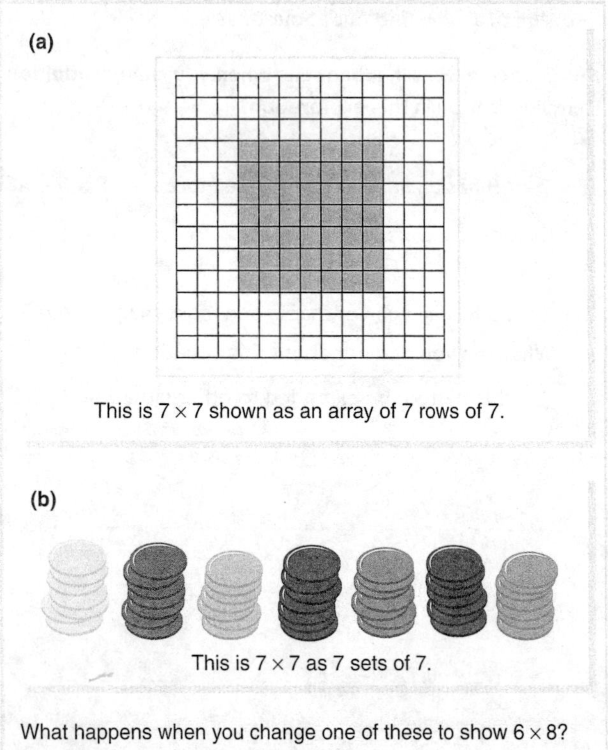

(a)

This is 7 × 7 shown as an array of 7 rows of 7.

(b)

This is 7 × 7 as 7 sets of 7.

What happens when you change one of these to show 6 × 8?

Figure 2.4 Two physical ways to think about multiplication that might help in the exploration.

Additional Patterns to Explore. There is a lot to find out about multiplication patterns. Think of the many "what if"s that are possible. Here are a few. If you have found other ones—great. There are many ways to explore this problem.

- Have you looked at how the first two numbers are related? For example, 7 × 7, 5 × 5, and 9 × 9 are all products with like factors. What if the product was two consecutive numbers (e.g., 8 × 7 or 13 × 12)? What if the factors differ by 2 or by 3?
- Think about adjusting by numbers other than one. What if you adjust up two and down two (e.g., 7 × 7 to 9 × 5)?
- What happens if you use big numbers instead of small ones (e.g., 30 × 30)?
- If both factors increase, is there a pattern?

We hope you have made your own conjectures and explored them or at least added to the "what if" list. Scientists (including mathematicians) explore new ideas that strike them as interesting and promising rather than blindly following procedures.

The Best Chance of Purple

Three students are spinning to "get purple" with two spinners, either by spinning first red and then blue or first blue and then red (see Figure 2.5). They may choose to spin each spinner once or one of the spinners twice. Mary chooses to spin twice on spinner A; John chooses to spin twice on spinner B; and Susan chooses to spin first on spinner A and then on spinner B. Who has the best chance of getting a red and a blue? (Lappan & Even, 1989, p. 17)

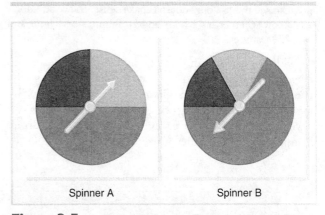

Spinner A   Spinner B

Figure 2.5 You may spin A twice, B twice, or A then B. Which option gives you the best chance of spinning a red and a blue?

STOP
Think about the problem and what you know. Experiment.

A Few Ideas. Sometimes it is tough to get a feel for problems that are abstract or complex. In situations involving chance, find a way to experiment and see what happens. For this problem, you can make spinners using a freehand drawing on paper, a paper clip, and a pencil. Put your pencil point through the loop of the clip and on the center of your spinner. Now you can spin the paper clip "pointer." Try at least 20 pairs of spins for each choice and keep track of what happens.

Consider these issues as you explore:

* For Susan's choice (A then B), would it matter if she spun B first and then A? Why or why not?
* Explain why you think purple is more or less likely in one of the three cases compared to the other two. It sometimes helps to talk through what you have observed to come up with a way to apply some more precise reasoning.

Try these suggestions before reading on.

Strategy 1: Tree Diagrams. On spinner A, the four colors each have the same chance of coming up. You could make a tree diagram for A with four branches, and all the branches would have the same chance (see Figure 2.6). Spinner B has different-sized sections, leading to the following questions:

* What is the relationship between the blue region and each of the others?
* How could you make a tree diagram for B with each branch having the same chance?
* How can you add to the diagram for spinner A so that it represents spinning A twice in succession?
* Which branches on your diagram represent getting purple?
* How could you make tree diagrams for John's and Susan's choices? Why do they make sense?

Test your ideas by actually spinning the spinner or spinners.

Tree diagrams are only one way to approach this. You may have a different way. As long as your way seems to be

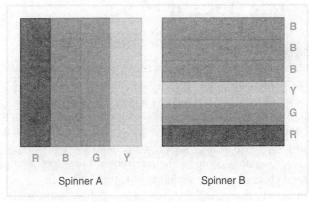

Figure 2.7 A square shows the chance of obtaining each color for the spinners in Figure 2.5.

getting you somewhere, stick with it. There is one more suggestion to follow, but don't read further if you are ready to solve the problem.

Strategy 2: Grids. Suppose that you had a square that represented all the possible outcomes for spinner A and a similar square for spinner B. Although there are many ways to divide a square in four equal parts, if you use lines going all in the same direction, you can make comparisons of all the outcomes of one event (one whole square) with the outcomes of another event (drawn on a different square). When the second event (here the second spin) follows the first event, make the lines on the second square go the opposite way from the lines on the first. Make a tracing of one square in Figure 2.7 and place it on the other. You end up with 24 little sections.

Why are there six subdivisions for the spinner B square? What does each of the 24 little rectangles stand for? What sections would represent purple? In any other method you have been trying, did 24 come into play when you were looking at spinner A followed by B?

Where Are the Answers?

No answers or solutions are given in this text. How do you feel about that? What about the "right" answers? Are your answers correct? What makes the solution to any investigation "correct"?

In the classroom, the ready availability of the answer book or the teacher's providing the solution or verifying that an answer is correct sends a clear message to students about doing mathematics: "Your job is to find the answers that the teacher already has." In the real world of problem solving outside the classroom, there are no teachers with answers and no answer books. Doing mathematics includes using justification as a means of determining if an answer is correct.

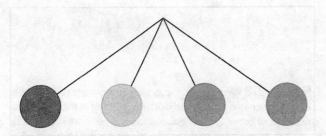

Figure 2.6 A tree diagram for spinner A in Figure 2.5.

What Does It Mean to Learn Mathematics?

Now that you have had the chance to experience doing mathematics, you may have a series of questions: Can students solve such challenging tasks? Why take the time to solve these problems—isn't it better to do a lot of shorter problems? Why should students be doing problems like this, especially if they are reluctant to do so? Collectively, these questions could be summarized as "How does 'doing mathematics' relate to student learning?" The answer lies in current theory and research on how people learn, as discussed in the following sections. The experiences we provide in classrooms should be designed to maximize learning opportunities for students.

Constructivist Theory

Constructivism is rooted in the cognitive school of psychology and in the work of Jean Piaget, who introduced the notion of mental schema and developed a theory of cognitive development in the 1930s (translated to English in the 1950s). At the heart of constructivism is the notion that children (or any learners) are not blank slates but rather creators of their own learning. Integrated networks, or *cognitive schemas*, are both the product of constructing knowledge and the tools with which additional new knowledge can be constructed. As learning occurs, the networks are rearranged, added to, or otherwise modified. Piaget suggested that schemas can be changed in two ways—*assimilation* and *accommodation*. Assimilation occurs when a new concept "fits" with prior knowledge and the new information expands an existing network. Accommodation takes place when the new concept does not "fit" with the existing network, so the brain revamps or replaces the existing schema. Through *reflective thought*, people modify their existing schemas to incorporate new ideas (Fosnot, 1996). Reflective thought means sifting through existing ideas (also called prior knowledge) to find those that seem to be related to the current thought, idea, or task.

Existing schemas are often referred to as prior knowledge. One basic tenet of constructivism is that people construct their own knowledge based on their prior knowledge. All people, all of the time, construct or give meaning to things they perceive or think about. As you read these words, you are giving meaning to them. Whether listening passively to a lecture or actively engaging in synthesizing findings in a project, your brain is applying prior knowledge to make sense of the new information.

Construction of Ideas.   To construct or build something in the physical world requires tools, materials, and effort. How we construct ideas can be viewed in an analogous manner. The tools we use to build understanding are our existing ideas and knowledge. The materials we use to build understanding may be things we see, hear, or touch—elements of our physical surroundings. Sometimes the materials are our own thoughts and ideas. The effort required is active and reflective thought.

In Figure 2.8 blue and red dots are used as symbols for ideas. Consider the picture to be a small section of our cognitive makeup. The blue dots represent existing ideas. The lines joining the ideas represent our logical connections or relationships that have developed between and among ideas. The red dot is an emerging idea, one that is being constructed. Whatever existing ideas (blue dots) are used in the construction will necessarily be connected to the new idea (red dot) because those were the ideas that gave meaning to it. If a potentially relevant idea (blue dot) is not accessed by the learner when learning a new concept (red dot), then that potential connection will not be made.

Constructing knowledge is an active endeavor on the part of the learner (Baroody, 1987; Cobb, 1988; Fosnot, 1996; von Glasersfeld, 1990, 1996). To construct and understand a new idea requires actively thinking about it. "How does this fit with what I already know?" "How can I understand this in the context of my current understanding of this idea?" Knowledge cannot be "poured into" a learner. Put simply, constructing knowledge requires *reflective thought*, actively thinking about or mentally working on an idea.

Learners will vary in the number and nature of connections they make between a new idea and existing ideas.

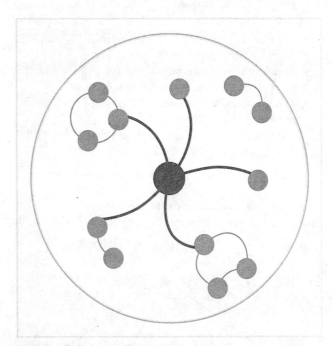

Figure 2.8 We use the ideas we already have (blue dots) to construct a new idea (red dot), developing in the process a network of connections between ideas. The more ideas used and the more connections made, the better we understand.

The construction of an idea is going to be different for each learner, even within the same environment or classroom. Though learning is constructed within the self, the classroom culture contributes to learning while the learner contributes to the culture in the classroom (Yackel & Cobb, 1996). Yackel and Cobb argue that the learner and the culture of the classroom are reflexively related—one influencing the other.

Sociocultural Theory

In the same way that the work of Piaget led to constructivism, the work of Lev Vygotsky, a Russian psychologist, has greatly influenced sociocultural theory. Vygotsky's work also emerged in the 1920s and 1930s, though it was not translated until the late 1970s. There are many concepts that these theories share (for example the learning process as active meaning-seeking on the part of the learner), but sociocultural theory has several unique foundational concepts. One is that mental processes exist between and among people in social learning settings, and that from these social settings the learner moves ideas into his or her own psychological realm (Forman, 2003).

Second, the way in which information is internalized (or learned) depends on whether it was within a learner's zone of proximal development (ZPD), which is the difference between a learner's assisted and unassisted performance on a task (Vygotsky, 1978). Simply put, the ZPD refers to a "range" of knowledge that may be out of reach for a person to learn on his or her own, but is accessible if the learner has support of peers or more knowledgeable others. "[T]he ZPD is not a physical space, but a symbolic space created through the interaction of learners with more knowledgeable others and the culture that precedes them" (Goos, 2004, p. 262). Both Cobb (1994) and Goos (2004) suggest that in a true mathematical community of learners there is something of a common ZPD that emerges across learners as well as the ZPDs of individual learners.

Another major concept in sociocultural theory is *semiotic mediation*, a term used to describe how information moves from the social plane to the individual plane. It is defined as the "mechanism by which individual beliefs, attitudes, and goals are simultaneously affected and affect sociocultural practices and institutions" (Forman & McPhail, 1993, p. 134). Semiotic mediation involves interaction through language but also through diagrams, pictures, and actions. Language and these other objects and actions are considered the "tools" of mediation.

Social interaction is essential for mediation. The nature of the community of learners is affected by not just the culture the teacher creates, but the broader social and historical culture of the members of the classroom (Forman, 2003). In summary, from a sociocultural perspective, learning is dependent on the learners (working within their ZPD), the social interactions in the classroom, and the culture within and beyond the classroom.

Implications for Teaching Mathematics

It is not necessary to choose between a social constructivist theory that favors the views of Vygotsky and a cognitive constructivism built on the theories of Piaget (Cobb, 1994). In fact, when considering classroom practices that maximize opportunities to construct ideas, or to provide tools to promote mediation, they are quite similar. Classroom discussion based on students' own ideas and solutions to problems is absolutely "foundational to children's learning" (Wood & Turner-Vorbeck, 2001, p. 186).

It is important to restate that a learning theory is not a teaching strategy, but the theory *informs* teaching. In this section teaching strategies that reflect constructivist and sociocultural perspectives are briefly discussed. You will see these strategies revisited in Chapters 3 and 4, where a problem-based model for instruction is discussed, and throughout the content chapters, where you learn how to apply these ideas to specific areas of mathematics.

Build New Knowledge from Prior Knowledge.   Consider the following task, posed to a class of fourth graders who are learning division of whole numbers.

> Four children had 3 bags of M&Ms. They decided to open all 3 bags of candy and share the M&Ms fairly. There were 52 M&M candies in each bag. How many M&M candies did each child get? (Campbell & Johnson, 1995, pp. 35–36)

Note: You may want to select a nonfood context, such as decks of cards, or any culturally relevant or interesting item that would come in similar quantities.

STOP

Consider how you might introduce division to fourth graders and what your expectations might be for this problem as a teacher grounding your work in constructivist or sociocultural learning theory.

The student work samples in Figure 2.9 are from a classroom that is grounded in constructivist ideas—that students should develop, or invent, strategies for doing mathematics using their prior knowledge, therefore making connections among mathematics concepts.

Marlena interpreted the task as "How many sets of 4 can be made from 156?" She first used facts that were either easy or available to her: 10 × 4 and 4 × 4. These totals she subtracted from 156 until she got to 100. This seemed to cue her to use 25 fours. She added her sets of 4 and knew the answer was 39 candies for each child. Marlena is using an equal subtraction approach and known multiplication facts. Note the "blue dots" that she is connecting in order to begin learning about the newer concept of division. While this is not the most efficient approach, it demonstrates that

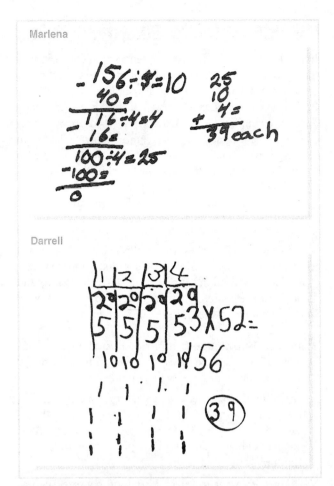

Figure 2.9 Two fourth-grade children invent unique solutions to a computation.

Source: Reprinted with permission from P. F. Campbell and M. L. Johnson, "How Primary Students Think and Learn," in I. M. Carl (Ed.), *Prospects for School Mathematics* (pp. 21–42), copyright © 1995 by the National Council of Teachers of Mathematics, Inc. www.nctm.org.

Marlena understands the concept of division and can move towards more efficient approaches.

Darrell's approach was more directly related to the sharing context of the problem. He formed four columns and distributed amounts to each, accumulating the amounts mentally and orally as he wrote the numbers. Darrell used a counting-up approach, first giving each student 20 M&Ms, seeing they could get more, distributed 5, then 10, then singles until he reached the total. Like Marlena, Darrell used facts and procedures that he knew. The context of sharing provided a "blue dot" for Darrell, as he was able to think about the problem in terms of equal distribution.

Provide Opportunities to Talk about Mathematics. Learning is enhanced when the learner is engaged with others working on the same ideas. A worthwhile goal is to create an environment in which students interact with each other and with you. The rich interaction in such a classroom allows students to engage in reflective thinking and to internalize concepts that may be out of reach without the interaction and input from peers and their teacher. In discussions with peers, students will be adapting and expanding on their existing networks of concepts.

Build In Opportunities for Reflective Thought. Classrooms need to provide structures and supports to help students make sense of mathematics in light of what they know. For a new idea you are teaching to be interconnected in a rich web of interrelated ideas, children must be mentally engaged. They must find the relevant ideas they possess and bring them to bear on the development of the new idea. In terms of the dots in Figure 2.8, we want to activate every blue dot students have that is related to the new red dot we want them to learn.

As you will see in Chapter 3 and throughout this book, a significant key to getting students to be reflective is to engage them in problems where they use their prior knowledge as they search for solutions and create new ideas in the process. The problem-solving approach requires not just answers but also explanations and justifications for solutions.

Encourage Multiple Approaches. Teaching should provide opportunities for students to build connections between what they know and what they are learning. The student whose work is presented in Figure 2.10 may not understand the algorithm she is trying to use. If instead she was asked to use her own approach to find the difference, she might be able to get to a correct solution and build on her understanding of place value and subtraction.

Even learning a basic fact, like 7×8, can have better results if a teacher promotes multiple strategies. Imagine a class where children discuss and share clever ways to figure out the product. One child might think of 5 eights and then 2 more eights. Another may have learned 7×7 and added on 7 more. Still another might take half of the sevens (4×7) and double that. A class discussion sharing these ideas brings to the fore a wide range of useful mathematical "dots" relating addition and multiplication concepts.

In contrast, facts such as 7×8 can be learned by rote (memorized). While that knowledge is still constructed, it is not connected to other knowledge. Rote learning can be thought of as a "weak construction" (Noddings, 1993). Students can recall it if they remember it, but if they forget, they don't have 7×8 connected to other knowledge pieces that would allow them to redetermine the fact.

Treat Errors as Opportunities for Learning. When students make errors, it can mean a misapplication of their prior knowledge in the new situation. Remember that from a constructivist perspective, the mind is sifting through what it knows in order to find useful approaches for the new situation. Knowing that children rarely give random

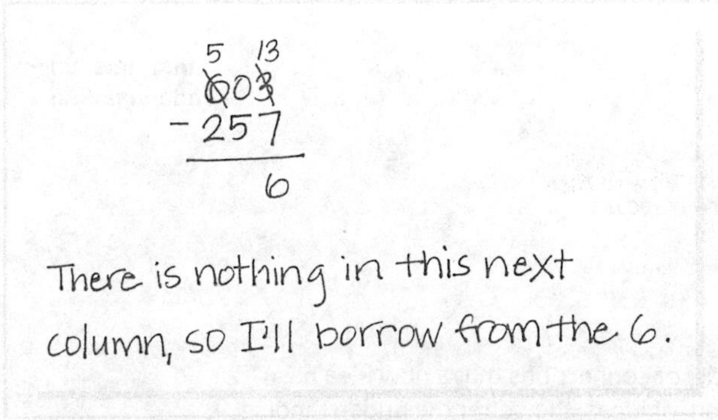

$$\begin{array}{r} \overset{5}{\cancel{6}}\overset{13}{\cancel{0}}\overset{}{3} \\ -\ 2\ 5\ 7 \\ \hline 6 \end{array}$$

There is nothing in this next column, so I'll borrow from the 6.

Figure 2.10 This student's work indicates that she has a misconception about place value and regrouping.

responses (Ginsburg, 1977; Labinowicz, 1985) gives insight into addressing student misconceptions and helping students accommodate new learning. For example, students comparing decimals may incorrectly apply "rules" of whole numbers, such as "the longer the number the bigger" (Martinie, 2007; Resnick, Nesher, Leonard, Magone, Omanson, & Peled, 1989).

Figure 2.10 is an example of a student incorrectly applying what she learned about regrouping. If the teacher tries to help the student by re-explaining the "right" way to do the problem, the student loses the opportunity to reflect on and correct her misconceptions. If the teacher instead asks the student to explain her regrouping process, the student must engage her reflective thought and think about what was regrouped and how to keep the number equivalent.

Scaffold New Content.   The concept of *scaffolding*, which comes out of sociocultural theory, is based on the idea that a task otherwise outside of a student's ZPD can become accessible if it is carefully structured. For concepts completely new to students, the learning requires more structure or assistance, including the use of tools like manipulatives or more assistance from peers. As students become more comfortable with the content, the scaffolds are removed and the student becomes more independent. Scaffolding can provide support for those students who may not have a robust collection of "blue dots."

Honor Diversity.   Finally, and importantly, these theories emphasize that each learner is unique, with a different collection of prior knowledge and cultural experiences. Since new knowledge is built on existing knowledge and experience, effective teaching incorporates and builds on what the students bring to the classroom, honoring those experiences. Thus, lessons begin with eliciting prior experiences, and understandings and contexts for the lessons are selected based on students' knowledge and experiences. Some students will not have the "blue dots" they need—it is your job

to provide experiences where those blue dots are developed and then connected to the concept being learned.

Classroom culture influences the individual learning of your students. As stated previously, you should support a range of approaches and strategies for doing mathematics. Students' ideas should be valued and included in classroom discussion of the mathematics. This shift in practice, away from the teacher telling one way to do the problem, establishes a classroom culture where ideas are valued. This approach values the uniqueness of each individual.

What Does It Mean to Understand Mathematics?

Both constructivist and sociocultural theories emphasize the learner building connections (blue dots to the red dots) among existing and new ideas. So you might be asking, "What is it they should be learning and connecting?" Or "What are those blue dots?" This section focuses on mathematics content required in today's classrooms.

It is possible to say that we know something or we do not. That is, an idea is something that we either have or don't have. Understanding is another matter. For example, most fifth graders know something about fractions. Given the fraction $\frac{6}{8}$, they likely know how to read the fraction and can identify the 6 and 8 as the numerator and denominator, respectively. They know it is equivalent to $\frac{3}{4}$ and that it is more than $\frac{1}{2}$.

Students will have different *understandings*, however, of such concepts as what it means to be equivalent. They may know that $\frac{6}{8}$ can be simplified to $\frac{3}{4}$ but not understand that $\frac{3}{4}$ and $\frac{6}{8}$ represent identical quantities. Some may think that simplifying $\frac{6}{8}$ to $\frac{3}{4}$ makes it a smaller number. Some students will be able to create pictures or models to illustrate equivalent fractions or will have many examples of how $\frac{6}{8}$ is used outside of class. In summary, there is a range of ideas that students often connect to their individualized *understanding* of a fraction—each student brings a different set of blue dots to his or her knowledge of what a fraction is.

Understanding can be defined as a measure of the quality and quantity of connections that an idea has with existing ideas. Understanding is not an all-or-nothing proposition. It depends on the existence of appropriate ideas and on the creation of new connections, varying with each person (Backhouse, Haggarty, Pirie, & Stratton, 1992; Davis, 1986; Hiebert & Carpenter, 1992; Janvier, 1987; Schroeder & Lester, 1989).

One way that we can think about understanding is that it exists along a continuum from a relational understanding—knowing what to do and why—to an instrumental understanding—doing without understanding (see Figure 2.11). The two ends of this continuum were named by Richard Skemp (1978), an educational psychologist who has had a major influence on mathematics education.

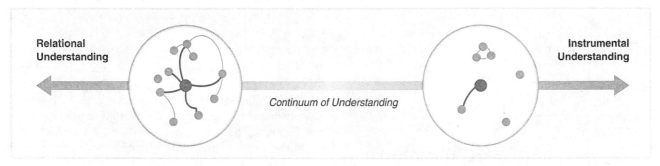

Figure 2.11 Understanding is a measure of the quality and quantity of connections that a new idea has with existing ideas. The greater the number of connections to a network of ideas, the better the understanding.

In the $\frac{6}{8}$ example, the student who can draw diagrams, give examples, find equivalencies, and approximate the size of $\frac{6}{8}$ has an understanding toward the relational end of the continuum, while a student who only knows the names and a procedure for simplifying $\frac{6}{8}$ to $\frac{3}{4}$ has an understanding more on the instrumental end of the continuum.

Mathematics Proficiency

Much work has emerged since Skemp's classic work on relational and instrumental understanding focusing on what mathematics should be learned, all of it based on the need to include more than learning procedures.

Conceptual and Procedural Understanding. Conceptual understanding is knowledge about the relationships or foundational ideas of a topic. Procedural understanding is knowledge of the rules and procedures used in carrying out mathematical processes and also the symbolism used to represent mathematics. Consider the task of multiplying 47 × 21. The conceptual understanding of this problem includes such ideas as that multiplication is repeated addition and that the problem could represent the area of a rectangle with dimensions of 47 inches and 21 inches. The procedural knowledge could include the standard algorithm or invented algorithms (e.g., multiplying 47 by 10, doubling it, then adding one more 47). The ability to employ invented strategies, such as the one described here, requires a conceptual understanding of place value and multiplication.

In fact, it is well established in research on mathematics learning that conceptual understanding is an important component of procedural proficiency (Bransford, Brown, & Cocking, 2000; National Mathematics Advisory Panel, 2008; NCTM, 2000). The *Principles and Standards* Learning Principle states it well:

 "The alliance of factual knowledge, procedural proficiency, and conceptual understanding makes all three components usable in powerful ways" (p. 19). ◆

Recall the two students who used their own invented procedure to solve 156 ÷ 4 (see Figure 2.9). Clearly, there was an active and useful interaction between the procedures the children invented and the concepts they knew about multiplication and were constructing about division.

The common practice of teaching procedures in the absence of conceptual understanding leads to errors and a dislike of mathematics. One way to help your students (and you) think about all the interrelated ideas for a concept is to create a network or web of associations, as demonstrated in Figure 2.12 for the concept of ratio. Note how much is involved in having a relational understanding of ratio. Compare that to the instrumental treatment of ratio in some textbooks that have a single lesson on the topic with prompts such as "If the ratio of girls to boys is 3 to 4, then how many girls are there if there are 24 boys?"

Five Strands of Mathematical Proficiency. While conceptual and procedural understanding of any concept are essential, they are not sufficient. Being mathematically proficient means that people exhibit behaviors and dispositions as they are "doing mathematics." *Adding It Up* (NRC, 2001), an influential report on how students learn mathematics, describes five strands involved in being mathematically proficient: (1) conceptual understanding, (2) procedural fluency, (3) strategic competence, (4) adaptive reasoning, and (5) productive disposition. Figure 2.13 illustrates these interrelated and interwoven strands, providing a definition of each.

Recall the problems that you solved in the "Let's Do Some Mathematics" section. In approaching each problem, if you felt like you could design a strategy to solve it (or try new approaches if one didn't work), then that is evidence of strategic competence. In each of the problems selected, you were asked to explain or justify solutions. If you were able to reason about a pattern and tell how you knew it would work, this is evidence of adaptive reasoning. Finally, if you were committed to making sense of and solving those tasks, knowing that if you kept at it, you would get to a solution, then you have a productive disposition.

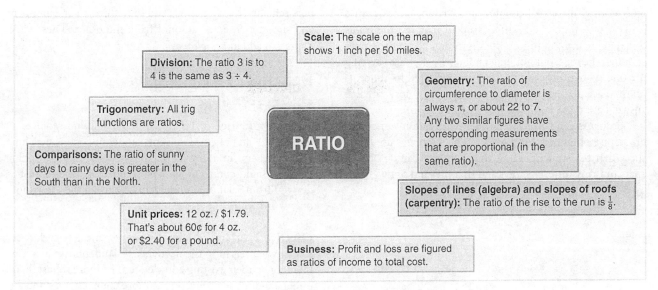

Figure 2.12 Potential web of ideas that could contribute to the understanding of "ratio."

The last three of the five strands develop only when students have experiences that involve these processes. We hope you have noticed that the terms used here are very similar to the ones in the previous learning theory discussion. Reflection, using prior knowledge, social interaction, and solving problems in a variety of ways, among other strategies, are essential to learning and therefore becoming mathematically proficient.

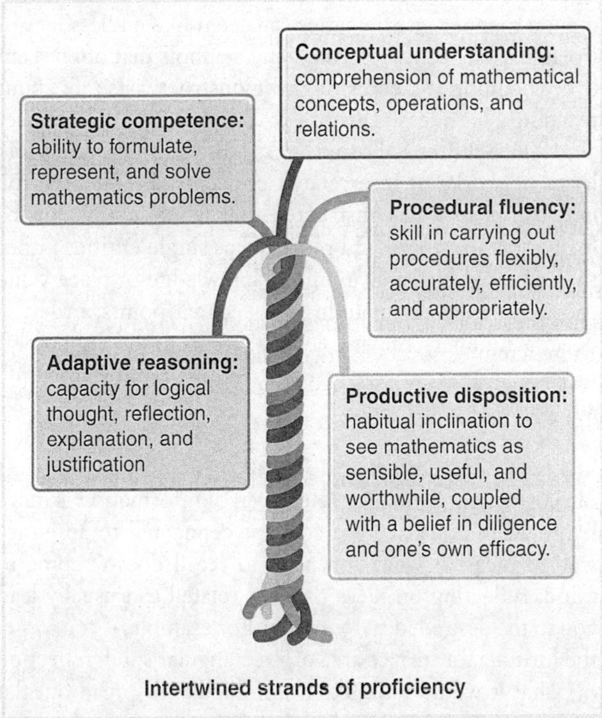

Implications for Teaching Mathematics

If we accept the notion that understanding has both qualitative and quantitative differences from knowing, the question "Does she know it?" must be replaced with "How does she understand it? What ideas does she connect with it?" In the following examples, you will see how different children may well develop different ideas about the same knowledge and, thus, have different understandings.

Early Number Concepts. Consider the concept of "7" as constructed by a child in the first grade. A first grader most likely connects "7" to the counting procedure and the construct of "more than," probably understanding it as less than 10 and more than 2. What else will this child eventually connect to the concept of 7? It is 1 more than 6; it is 2 less than 9; it is the combination of 3 and 4 or 2 and 5; it is odd; it is small compared to 73 and large compared to $\frac{1}{10}$; it is the number of days in a week; it is "lucky"; it is prime; and on and on. The web of potential ideas connected to a number can grow large and involved.

Computation. Computation is much more than memorizing a procedure; analyzing a student's strategy provides a good opportunity to see how understanding can differ from one child to another. For addition and subtraction with two- or three-digit numbers, a flexible and rich understanding of numbers and place value is very helpful. How might different children approach the task of finding the sum of 37 and 28? For children whose understanding of 37 is based only

Figure 2.13 *Adding It Up* describes five strands of mathematical proficiency.
Source: Adding It Up: Helping Children Learn Mathematics, p. 5. Reprinted with permission from the National Academies Press, copyright © 2001, National Academy of Sciences.

Intertwined strands of proficiency

Conceptual understanding: comprehension of mathematical concepts, operations, and relations.

Strategic competence: ability to formulate, represent, and solve mathematics problems.

Procedural fluency: skill in carrying out procedures flexibly, accurately, efficiently, and appropriately.

Adaptive reasoning: capacity for logical thought, reflection, explanation, and justification

Productive disposition: habitual inclination to see mathematics as sensible, useful, and worthwhile, coupled with a belief in diligence and one's own efficacy.

on counting, the use of counters and a count-all procedure is likely (see Figure 2.14(a)). A student may use the traditional algorithm, lining up the digits and adding the ones and then the tens, but not understand why they are carrying the one. When procedures are not connected to concepts (in this case place-value concepts), errors and unreasonable answers are more common (see Figure 2.14(b)).

Students can solve the problem using an invented approach (see Figure 2.14(c) & (d)). The strategies used here show that the students know that numbers can be broken apart in many different ways and that the sum of two numbers remains the same if you add something to one number and subtract an equal amount from the other. These students can add in *flexible* ways.

Benefits of a Relational Understanding

To teach for a rich or relational understanding requires a lot of work and effort. Concepts and connections develop over time, not in a day. Tasks must be selected that help students build connections. The important benefits to be derived from relational understanding make the effort not only worthwhile but also essential.

Effective Learning of New Concepts and Procedures. Recall what learning theory tells us—students are actively building on their existing knowledge. The more robust their understanding of a concept, the more connections students are building, and the more likely it is they can connect new ideas to the existing conceptual webs they have. Fraction knowledge and place-value knowledge come together to make decimal learning easier, and decimal concepts directly enhance an understanding of percentage concepts and procedures. Without these and many other connections, children will need to learn each new piece of information they encounter as a separate, unrelated idea.

Less to Remember. When students learn in an instrumental manner, mathematics can seem like endless lists of isolated skills, concepts, rules, and symbols that often seem overwhelming to keep straight. Constructivists talk about teaching "big ideas" (Brooks & Brooks, 1993; Hiebert et al., 1996; Schifter & Fosnot, 1993). Big ideas are really just large networks of interrelated concepts. Frequently, the network is so well constructed that whole chunks of information are stored and retrieved as single entities rather than isolated bits. For example, knowledge of place value subsumes rules about lining up decimal points, ordering decimal numbers, moving decimal points to the right or left in decimal-percent conversions, rounding and estimating, and a host of other ideas.

Increased Retention and Recall. Memory is a process of retrieving information. Retrieval of information is more likely when you have the concept connected to an entire web of ideas. If what you need to recall doesn't come to mind, reflecting on ideas that are related can usually lead you to the desired idea eventually. For example, if you forget the formula for surface area of a rectangular solid, reflecting on what it would look like if unfolded and spread out flat can help you remember that there are six rectangular faces in three pairs that are each the same size.

Enhanced Problem-Solving Abilities. The solution of novel problems requires transferring ideas learned in one

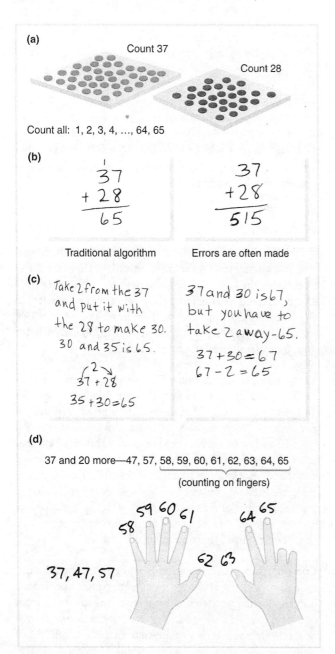

Figure 2.14 A range of computational examples showing different levels of understanding.

context to new situations. When concepts are embedded in a rich network, transferability is significantly enhanced and, thus, so is problem solving (Schoenfeld, 1992). When students understand the relationship between a situation and a context, they are going to know when to use a particular approach to solve a problem. While many students may be able to do this with whole-number computation, once problems increase in difficulty and numbers move to rational numbers or unknowns, students without a relational understanding are not able to apply the skills they learned to solve new problems.

Improved Attitudes and Beliefs.   Relational understanding has an affective as well as a cognitive effect. When ideas are well understood and make sense, the learner tends to develop a positive self-concept about his or her ability to learn and understand mathematics. There is a definite feeling of "I can do this! I understand!" There is no reason to fear or to be in awe of knowledge learned relationally. At the other end of the continuum, instrumental understanding has the potential of producing mathematics anxiety, a real phenomenon that involves fear and avoidance behavior.

Multiple Representations to Support Relational Understanding

The more ways that children are given to think about and test an emerging idea, the better chance they will correctly form and integrate it into a rich web of concepts and therefore develop a relational understanding. Lesh, Post, and Behr (1987) offer five "representations" for concepts (see Figure 2.15). Their research has found that children who have difficulty translating a concept from one representation to another also have difficulty solving problems and understanding computations. Strengthening the ability to move between and among these representations improves student understanding and retention. Discussion of oral language, real-world situations, and written symbols is woven into this chapter, but it is important that you have a good perspective on how manipulatives and models can help or fail to help children construct ideas.

Models and Manipulatives.   A *model for a mathematical concept* refers to any object, picture, or drawing that represents the concept or onto which the relationship for that concept can be imposed. In this sense, any group of 100 objects can be a model of the concept "hundred" because we can impose the 100-to-1 relationship on the group and a single element of the group. *Manipulatives* are physical objects that students and teachers can use to illustrate and discover mathematical concepts, whether made specifically for mathematics, like connecting cubes, or objects that were created for other purposes.

It is incorrect to say that a model "illustrates" a concept. To illustrate implies showing. Technically, all that you

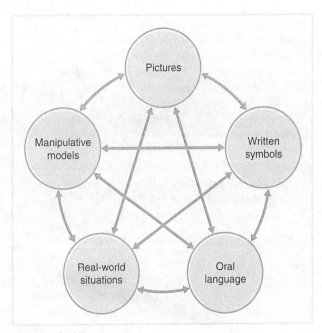

Figure 2.15 Five different representations of mathematical ideas. Translations between and within each can help develop new concepts.

actually see with your eyes is the physical object; only your mind can impose the mathematical relationship on the object (Suh, 2007; Thompson, 1994).

Models can be a testing ground for emerging ideas. It is sometimes difficult for students (of all ages) to think about and test abstract relationships using only words or symbols. For example, to explore the idea of area of a triangle, knowing the area of a parallelogram, requires the use of pictures and/or manipulatives to build the connections. A variety of models should be accessible for students to select and use freely. You will undoubtedly encounter situations in which you use a model that you think clearly illustrates an idea but a student just doesn't get it, whereas a different model is very helpful.

Examples of Models.   Physical materials or manipulatives in mathematics abound—from common objects such as lima beans and string to commercially produced materials such as wooden rods (e.g., Cuisenaire rods) and blocks (e.g., Pattern Blocks). Figure 2.16 shows six models, each representing a different concept, giving only a glimpse into the many ways each manipulative can be used to support the development of mathematics concepts and procedures.

STOP

Consider each of the concepts and the corresponding model in Figure 2.16. Try to separate the physical model from the relationship that you must impose on the model in order to "see" the concept.

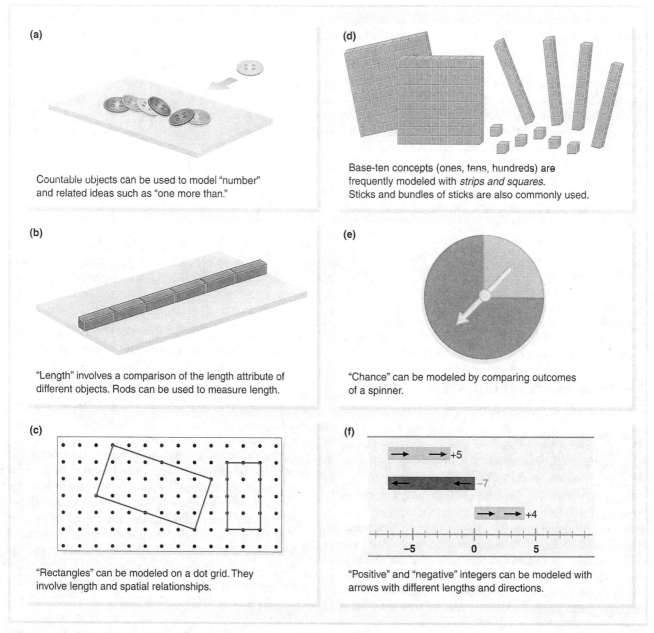

(a) Countable objects can be used to model "number" and related ideas such as "one more than."

(b) "Length" involves a comparison of the length attribute of different objects. Rods can be used to measure length.

(c) "Rectangles" can be modeled on a dot grid. They involve length and spatial relationships.

(d) Base-ten concepts (ones, tens, hundreds) are frequently modeled with *strips and squares*. Sticks and bundles of sticks are also commonly used.

(e) "Chance" can be modeled by comparing outcomes of a spinner.

(f) "Positive" and "negative" integers can be modeled with arrows with different lengths and directions.

Figure 2.16 Examples of models to illustrate mathematics concepts.

The examples in Figure 2.16 are models that can show the following concepts:

a. The concept of "6" is a relationship between sets that can be matched to the words *one*, *two*, *three*, *four*, *five*, or *six*. Changing a set of counters by adding one changes the relationship. The difference between the set of 6 and the set of 7 is the relationship "one more than."

b. The concept of "measure of length" is a comparison of the length attribute of different objects. The length measure of an object is a comparison relationship of the length of the object to the length of the unit.

c. The concept of "rectangle" includes both spatial and length relationships. The opposite sides are of equal length and parallel and the adjacent sides meet at right angles.

d. The concept of "hundred" is not in the larger square but in the relationship of that square to the strip ("ten") and to the little square ("one").

e. "Chance" is a relationship between the frequency of an event's happening compared with all possible outcomes. The spinner can be used to create relative frequencies. These can be predicted by observing relationships of sections of the spinner.

f. The concept of a "negative integer" is based on the relationships of "magnitude" and "is the opposite of." Negative quantities exist only in relation to positive quantities. Arrows on the number line model the opposite of relationship in terms of direction and size or magnitude relationship in terms of length.

Ineffective Use of Models and Manipulatives.
In addition to not making the distinction between the model and the concept, there are other ways that models or manipulatives can be used ineffectively. One of the most widespread misuses occurs when the teacher tells students, "Do as I do." There is a natural temptation to get out the materials and show children exactly how to use them. Children mimic the teacher's directions, and it may even look as if they understand, but they could be just mindlessly following what they see. It is just as possible to get students to move blocks around mindlessly as it is to teach them to "invert and multiply" mindlessly. Neither promotes thinking or aids in the development of concepts (Ball, 1992; Clements & Battista, 1990; Stein & Bovalino, 2001).

A natural result of overly directing the use of models is that children begin to use them as answer-getting devices rather than as tools used to explore a concept. For example, if you have carefully shown and explained to children how to get an answer to a multiplication problem with a set of base-ten blocks, then students may set up the blocks to get the answer but not focus on the patterns or processes that can be seen in modeling the problem with the blocks. A mindless procedure with a good manipulative is still just a mindless procedure.

Conversely, leaving students with insufficient focus or guidance results in nonproductive and unsystematic investigation (Stein & Bovalino, 2001). Students may be engaged in conversations about the model they are using, but if they do not know what the mathematical goal is, the manipulative is not serving as a tool for developing the concept.

Technology-Based Models.
Technology provides another source of models and manipulatives. There are websites, such as the Utah State University National Library of Virtual Manipulatives, that have a range of manipulatives available (e.g., geoboards, base-ten blocks, spinners, number lines). Virtual manipulatives are a good addition to physical models, as some students will prefer the electronic version; moreover, they may have access to these tools outside of the classroom.

It is important to include calculators as a tool. The calculator models a wide variety of numeric relationships by quickly and easily demonstrating the effects of these ideas. For example, you can skip-count by hundredths from 0.01 (press 0.01 [+] .01 [=], [=], [=] . . .) or from another beginning number such as 3 (press [+] 0.01 [=], [=], [=] . . .). How many presses of [=] are required to get from 3 to 4? Many more similar ideas are presented in Chapter 7.

Connecting the Dots

It seems appropriate to close this chapter by connecting some dots, especially because the ideas represented here are the foundation for the approach to each topic in the content chapters. This chapter began with discussing what *doing* mathematics is and challenging you to do some mathematics. Each of these tasks offered opportunities to make connections among mathematics concepts—connecting the blue dots.

myeducationlab

Go to the Activities and Application section of Chapter 2 of MyEducationLab. Click on Videos and watch the video entitled "**John Van de Walle on Connecting the Dots**" to see him talk with teachers about understanding students' thinking.

Second, you read about learning theory—the importance of having opportunities to connect the dots. The best learning opportunities, according to constructivism and sociocultural theories, are those that engage learners in using their own knowledge and experience to solve problems through social interactions and reflection. This is what you were asked to do in the four tasks. Did you learn something new about mathematics? Did you connect an idea that you had not previously connected?

Finally, you read about understanding—that to have the relational knowledge (knowledge where blue dots are well connected) requires conceptual and procedural understanding, as well as other proficiencies. The problems that you solved in the first section included a focus on concepts and procedures while placing you in a position to use strategic competence, adaptive reasoning, and productive disposition.

This chapter focused on connecting the dots between theory and practice—building a case that your teaching must focus on opportunities for students to develop their own networks of blue dots. As you plan and design instruction, you should constantly reflect on how to elicit prior knowledge by designing tasks that reflect the social and cultural backgrounds of students, to challenge students to think critically and creatively, and to include a comprehensive treatment of mathematics.

Reflections on Chapter 2

Writing to Learn

1. How would you describe what it means to "do mathematics"?
2. Explain why we should assume that each child's knowledge and understanding of an idea are unique for that child.
3. What is reflective thought? Why is reflective thinking so important in the development of conceptual ideas in mathematics?
4. What does it mean to say that understanding exists on a continuum from relational to instrumental? Give an example of an idea, and explain how a student's understanding might fall on either end of the continuum.
5. Explain why a model for a mathematical idea is not really an example of the idea. If it is not an example of the concept, what does it mean to say we "see" the concept when we look at the model?

For Discussion and Exploration

1. Read the following problem and respond to the listed items:
   - Solve it, using a strategy of choice.
   - Explain in words how you solved it.
   - Justify that your solution is correct.

   Some people say that to add four consecutive numbers, you add the first and the last numbers and multiply by 2. Is this always true? How do you know? (Stoessiger & Edmunds, 1992)

2. Consider the following task and respond to these three questions.
   - What features of "doing mathematics" does it have?
   - To what extent does it lead students to develop a relational understanding?
   - To what extent does it develop mathematical proficiency? (See Figure 2.13 on page 25.)

   The Sole D'Italia Pizzeria sells small, medium, and large pizzas. The small pie is 9 inches in diameter, the medium pie is 12 inches in diameter, and the large pie is 15 inches in diameter. For a plain cheese small pizza, Sole D'Italia charges $6; for a medium pizza, it charges $9; for a large pizza, it charges $12.

   ◆ **Which measures should be most closely related to the prices charged—circumference, area, radius, or diameter? Why?**
   ◆ **Use your results to write a report on the fairness of Sole D'Italia's pizza prices.**

3. Not every educator believes in the constructivist-oriented approach to teaching mathematics. Some of their reasons include the following: There is not enough time to let kids discover everything. Basic facts and ideas are better taught through quality explanations. Students should not have to "reinvent the wheel." How would you respond to these arguments?

Resources for Chapter 2

Recommended Readings

Articles

Ball, D. L. (1997). From the general to the particular: Knowing our own students as learners of mathematics. *Mathematics Teacher, 90*(9), 732–737.
Deborah Ball, one of the leading advocates for classroom discourse and listening to children, offers a thought-provoking example of third-grade thinking about fractions while raising our awareness of how difficult it is to see into the minds of children.

Berkman, R. M. (2006). One, some, or none: Finding beauty in ambiguity. *Mathematics Teaching in the Middle School, 11*(7), 324–327.
This article offers a great teaching strategy for nurturing relational thinking. Examples of the engaging "one, some, or none" activity are given for geometry, number, and algebra activities.

Buschman, L. (2003). Children who enjoy problem solving. *Teaching Children Mathematics, 9*(9), 539–544.
The focus of this article is the enjoyment that students achieve when they are making sense of mathematics themselves rather than following rules.

Flores, A., & Klein, E. (2005). From students' problem solving strategies to connections with fractions. *Teaching Children Mathematics, 11*(9), 452–457.
This outstanding article focuses on fractions, a topic for which students (and adults) often lack relational understanding, and describes how connections can be made to other concepts.

Hedges, M., Huinker, D., & Steinmeyer, M. (2005). Unpacking division to build teachers' mathematical knowledge. *Teaching Children Mathematics, 11*(9), 478–483.
Like the Flores and Klein article, this article offers a wonderful explanation of the concepts related to division. Student strategies

are examined and from that a collection of related concepts are proposed.

Suh, J. (2007). Tying it all together: Classroom practices that promote mathematical proficiency for all students. *Teaching Children Mathematics, 14*(3), 163–169.

This is an excellent resource for teachers wanting to implement strategies for developing the five strands of mathematics proficiency described in Adding It Up *(NRC, 2001).*

Books

Lampert, M. (2001). *Teaching problems and the problems of teaching.* New Haven, CT: Yale University Press.

Lampert reflects on her personal experiences in teaching fifth grade and shares with us her perspectives on the many issues and complexities of teaching. It is wonderfully written and easily accessed at any point in the book.

Mokros, J., Russell, S. J., & Economopoulos, K. (1995). *Beyond arithmetic: Changing mathematics in the elementary classroom.* Palo Alto, CA: Dale Seymour Publications.

These authors/researchers of the Investigations in Number, Data, and Space *curriculum use numerous examples from the elementary classroom to develop an image of teaching mathematics from a problem-solving perspective. In looking at teaching, curriculum, and assessment, the importance of problem solving as a way of learning mathematics is quite clear.*

Online Resources

A Maths Dictionary for Kids
www.amathsdictionaryforkids.com
An extensive dictionary with each word illustrated by a small interactive explanation.

Classic Problems
www.mathforum.org/dr.math/faq/faq.classic.problems.html
A nice collection of well-known problems ("Train A leaves the station at . . .") along with discussion, solutions, and extensions.

Constructivism
http://carbon.cudenver.edu/~mryder/itc_data/constructivism.html
Based at the University of Colorado, Denver, this site lists definitions and numerous papers on constructivist theories from Dewey to von Glasersfeld and Vygotsky.

Constructivism in the Classroom
http://mathforum.org/mathed/constructivism.html
Provided by the Math Forum, this page contains links to numerous sites concerning constructivism as well as articles written by researchers.

Utah State University National Library of Virtual Manipulatives
http://nlvm.usu.edu/en/nav/vlibrary.html
A robust collection of virtual manipulatives. A great site to bookmark and use. Here are two favorite applets to check out from this site:

Circle 21
http://nlvm.usu.edu/en/nav/frames_asid_188_g_2_t_1.html
A puzzle that involves adding positive and negative integers to sum to twenty-one.

How High?
http://nlvm.usu.edu/en/nav/category_g_3_t_3.html
This is a conservation of volume activity—the student predicts how high the liquid in one container will be when moved to one of a different shape.

Field Experience Guide Connections

An environment for doing mathematics is the focus of Chapter 1 of the *Field Experience Guide*. Activities include observation protocols, teacher and student interviews, teaching, and a project. The act of doing mathematics is also the focus of an observation targeting higher-level thinking (FEG 2.2). In addition, Chapter 4 of the guide includes experiences related to conceptual and procedural knowledge, building on prior knowledge and creating a web of ideas.

Chapter 3

Teaching Through Problem Solving

Allowing the subject to be problematic means allowing students to wonder why things are, to inquire, to search for solutions, and to resolve incongruities. It means that both the curriculum and instruction should begin with problems, dilemmas, and questions for students.

Hiebert et al. (1996, p. 12)

For over two decades since publication of the original NCTM *Standards* document (1989), evidence has continued to mount that problem solving is a powerful and effective vehicle for learning. As *Principles and Standards* (2000) states:

> Solving problems is not only a goal of learning mathematics but also a major means of doing so. . . . Problem solving is an integral part of all mathematics learning, and so it should not be an isolated part of the mathematics program. Problem solving in mathematics should involve all the five content areas described in these Standards. . . . Good problems will integrate multiple topics and will involve significant mathematics. (p. 52)

In a classic publication (Schroeder & Lester, 1989), two researchers in the area of problem solving in mathematics identified three ways that problem solving might be incorporated into mathematics instruction:

1. *Teaching for problem solving.* This approach can be summarized as teaching a skill so that a student can later problem solve, which follows the format of many textbooks designed with skills taught first. Rather than building on prior knowledge, teaching for problem solving often starts with learning the abstract concept and then moving to solving problems as a way to apply the learned skills. For example, students learn the algorithm for adding fractions, and once that is mastered, solve story problems that involve adding fractions.

2. *Teaching about problem solving.* This second approach involves teaching students *how* to problem solve, which can include teaching the process (understand, design a strategy, implement, look back) or strategies for solving a problem. An example of a strategy is "draw a picture," in which students use a picture or diagram to help solve a problem. This is discussed in more detail in the section "Teaching about Problem Solving" later in this chapter.

3. *Teaching through problem solving.* This approach generally means that students learn mathematics *through* real contexts, problems, situations, and models. The contexts and models allow students to build meaning for the concepts so that they can move to abstract concepts. Teaching *through* problem solving might be described as upside down from teaching *for* problem solving—with the problem(s) presented at the beginning of a lesson and skills emerging from working with the problem(s). For example, in exploring the situation of combining $\frac{1}{2}$ and $\frac{1}{3}$ feet of ribbon to figure out how long the ribbon is, students would be led to discover the procedure for adding fractions.

Teaching through problem solving is the topic of this chapter and a theme of this book.

Teaching Through Problem Solving

Most, if not all, important mathematics concepts and procedures can best be taught through problem solving. This statement is a reflection of the *Principles and Standards* quote and represents current thinking of researchers in mathematics education.

myeducationlab

Go to the Activities and Application section of Chapter 3 of MyEducationLab. Click on Videos and watch the video entitled **"John Van de Walle on Teaching Through Problem Solving"** to see him working on a problem with teachers during a training workshop.

Tasks or problems can and should be posed that engage students in thinking about and developing the important mathematics they need to learn. Let's examine why this approach better supports student learning.

Problems and Tasks for Learning Mathematics

A *problem* is defined here as any task or activity for which the students have no prescribed or memorized rules or methods, nor is there a perception by students that there is a specific "correct" solution method (Hiebert et al., 1997).

A *problem* for learning mathematics also has these features:

- *It must begin where the students are.* The design or selection of the task must take into consideration the students' current understanding. They should have the appropriate ideas to engage and solve the problem and yet still find it challenging and interesting.

- *The problematic or engaging aspect of the problem must be due to the mathematics that the students are to learn.* In solving the problem or doing the activity, students should be concerned primarily with making sense of the mathematics involved and thereby developing their understanding of those ideas. Although it is desirable to have contexts for problems that make them interesting, these aspects should not be the focus of the activity. Nor should nonmathematical activity (e.g., cutting and pasting, coloring graphs, etc.) detract from the mathematics involved.

- *It must require justifications and explanations for answers and methods.* Students should understand that the responsibility for determining if answers are correct and why they are correct rests within themselves and not with the teacher. Justification should be an integral part of doing mathematics.

It is important to understand that mathematics is to be taught *through* problem solving. That is, problem-based tasks or activities are the vehicle by which the desired curriculum is developed. The learning is an outcome of the problem-solving process.

A Shift in the Role of Problems

Schroeder and Lester's first way to use problem solving, teaching *for* problem solving (described earlier), is strongly engrained in our culture as the way to teach mathematics. The teacher presents the mathematics; the students practice the skill and then study word or story problems involving that skill. Unfortunately, this approach to mathematics teaching has not been successful in supporting student learning and retention of mathematics concepts.

- The approach assumes that all students have the necessary prior knowledge (the blue dots described in Chapter 2) to understand the teacher's explanations.
- The teacher usually only presents one way to do the problem, which may not be the most accessible approach for all students, while communicating that there is only one way to solve the problem, which is almost never the case.
- A show-and-tell approach places the student as a passive learner, dependent on the teacher to present ideas, rather than as an independent thinker who can develop an approach to solve the problem with the knowledge he or she possesses.
- Problem solving becomes a separate activity from skills and concepts, diminished as part of learning mathematics. Consequently, students do not feel capable of solving the problems they encounter, because they do not see the relationship to the skills and concepts learned earlier.
- Students accustomed to being told how to do mathematics are not likely to attempt a new problem without explicit instructions on *how* to solve it. But—that's what doing mathematics is—figuring out an approach to solve the problem at hand.

Some teachers may think that showing students how to solve a set of problems is the best approach for students, preventing struggling while saving time. However, students are not learning content with deep understanding, often forgetting what they have learned; they need a more effective approach to learning mathematics.

Effective lessons begin where the students are, not where teachers are. That is, teaching should begin with the ideas that children already have, the ideas they will use to create new ones. To engage students requires tasks or activities that are problem-based and require thought. Students learn mathematics as a *result* of solving problems. Mathematical ideas are the *outcomes* of the problem-solving experience rather than elements that must be taught before problem solving (Hiebert et al., 1996, 1997). Furthermore, the process of solving problems is now completely interwoven with the learning; children are *learning* mathematics by *doing* mathematics!

The Value of Teaching Through Problem Solving

Teaching through problem solving requires a paradigm shift, which means that a teacher is changing more than just a few things about her teaching; she is changing her philosophy of how she thinks children learn and how she can best help them learn. At first glance, it may seem that the teacher's role is less demanding because the students are doing the thinking, but the reverse is actually the case. Teachers must select quality tasks that allow students to learn the content by figuring out their own strategies and solutions. Teachers must then develop and ask the high-quality questions that allow students to verify and relate their strategies. This process allows students to understand mathematics on a deeper level. There are good reasons to go to the effort involved in teaching through problem solving.

- *Focuses students' attention on ideas and sense making.* When solving problems, students are necessarily reflecting on the concepts inherent in the problems. Emerging concepts are more likely to be integrated with existing ones, thereby improving understanding. By contrast, no matter how skillfully a teacher provides explanations and directions, students will attend to the directions but rarely to the concepts and connections.

> **myeducationlab**
>
> Go to the Activities and Application section of Chapter 3 of MyEducationLab. Click on Videos and watch the video entitled "**John Van de Walle on the Value of Teaching Through Problem Solving**" to see his conversation with teachers during a training workshop.

- *Develops student confidence that they are capable of doing mathematics and that mathematics makes sense.* Every time teachers pose a problem-based task and expect a solution, they say to students, "I believe you can do this." Every time the class solves a problem and students develop their understanding, confidence and self-worth are enhanced.
- *Provides a context to help students build meaning for the concept.* Providing a context, especially when that context is grounded in an experience familiar to students, supports the development of mathematics concepts. Such an approach provides students access to the mathematics, allowing them to successfully learn the content.
- *Allows an entry point for a wide range of students.* Good problem-based tasks have multiple paths to the solution. Students may solve 42 – 26 by counting out a set of 42 counters and removing 26, by adding onto 26 in various ways to get to 42, by subtracting 20 from 42 and then taking off 6 more, by counting forward (or backward) on a hundreds chart, or by using a standard computational method. Each student gets to make sense of the task using his or her own ideas. Furthermore, students expand on these ideas and grow in their understanding as they hear and reflect on the solution strategies of others. In contrast, the teacher-directed approach ignores diversity, to the detriment of most students.
- *Provides ongoing assessment data useful for making instructional decisions, helping students succeed, and informing parents.* As students discuss ideas, draw pictures or use manipulatives, defend their solutions and evaluate those of others, and write reports or explanations, they provide the teacher with a steady stream of valuable information. These products provide rich evidence of how students are solving problems, what misconceptions they might have, and how they are connecting and applying new concepts. With a better understanding of what students know, a teacher

can plan more effectively and accommodate each student's learning needs.

- *Allows for extensions and elaborations.* Extensions and "what if" questions can motivate advanced learners or quick finishers, resulting in increased learning and enthusiasm for doing mathematics. Such problems can be configured to meet the needs of a range of learners.
- *Engages students so that there are fewer discipline problems.* Many discipline issues in a classroom are the result of students becoming bored, not understanding the teacher directions, or simply finding little relevance in the task. Most students like to be challenged and enjoy being permitted to solve problems in ways that make sense to them, giving them less reason to act out or cause trouble.
- *Develops "mathematical power."* Students solving problems in class will be engaged in all five of the processes of doing mathematics—the process standards described by the *Principles and Standards* document: problem solving, reasoning, communication, connections, and representation.
- *Is a lot of fun!* Teachers who teach through problem solving never return to a teach-by-telling mode. The excitement of students' developing understanding through their own reasoning is worth all the effort.

As this list illustrates, teaching through problem solving has benefits for student learning and for engagement. The next section discusses the types of tasks teachers can use to teach through problem solving.

Examples of Problem-Based Tasks

In Chapter 2, you saw that mathematical ideas could be categorized as conceptual or procedural. Students can learn both types of mathematics through problem-based activities, as shown in the following examples.

Conceptual Mathematics. As described in Chapter 2, concepts are the foundational ideas on which understanding builds. Concepts related to multiplication, for example, include the idea of repeated addition ($4 \times 5 = 5 + 5 + 5 + 5$) and area (a rug that is 4 by 5 has an area of 20 square feet). The following three examples briefly describe how concepts can be presented through problem solving.

Concept: Partitioning
Grades: K–1

Think about the number 6 broken into two different amounts. Draw a picture to show a way that six things can be broken in two parts. Think up a story to go with your picture.

At the kindergarten or first-grade level, the teacher may want students simply to think about different parts of 6 and to connect these ideas into a context. In first or second grade, the teacher may challenge children to find all of the combinations rather than focus on the story or context. There is a nice relationship and pattern to be constructed. In a class discussion following work on the task, students are likely to develop an orderly process for listing all seven of the combinations: As one part grows from 0 to 6, the other part begins at 6 and shrinks by ones to 0.

The second task is focused on the approximate size of a fraction, a concept poorly understood by most students.

Concept: Estimating Fractions Greater Than 1
Grades: 4–6

Place an X on the number line about where $\frac{11}{8}$ would be. Explain why you put your X where you did. Perhaps you will want to draw and label other points on the line to help explain your answer.

0   2

Note that the task includes a suggestion for how to respond but does not specify exactly what must be done. Students are able to use their own level of reasoning and understanding to justify their answers. In the follow-up discussion, the teacher may well expect to see a variety of justifications from which to help the class refine ideas about fractions greater than 1.

Concept: Comparing Ratios and Proportional Reasoning
Grade: 6–8

Jack and Jill were at the bottom of a hill, hoping to fetch a pail of water. Jack walks uphill at 5 steps every 25 seconds, while Jill walks uphill at 3 steps every 10 seconds. Assuming constant walking rate, who will get to the pail of water first?

Students can solve this problem in a variety of ways, including setting up ratios. Students may also use a rate approach, determining the number of steps taken per minute for each person. The discussion about this task, and the others, will focus on the ways that students compared the ratios, which is the essence of proportional reasoning. This task is one of four used to introduce proportional reasoning in an Expanded Lesson that can be found in the *Field Experience Guide*, pp. 113–114.

Algorithms and Processes.   Some teachers falsely assume that procedures must be taught through direct instruction. In reality, students can develop algorithms via a problem-solving approach. The distinction between direct instruction and the problem-solving approach is in who

determines the approach to solving the problem. When students learn computation through problem solving, they figure out how they will solve the problem. This is a major shift from showing students only one algorithm that they are to use. The following two examples demonstrate this approach.

The first example is a grade 1–2 lesson on two-digit addition. The lesson begins with the teacher posing the following questions: *What is the sum of 48 and 25? How did you figure it out?* Even though there is no story or situation to resolve, this is a problem because students must figure out *how* they are going to approach the task. Students work on the problem, using manipulatives, pictures, or other tools. After students have solved the problem in their own way, the teacher gathers the students together to hear one another's strategies and solutions.

In one second-grade classroom, at least seven different solution methods were offered by the students (Russell, 1997). Two children employed two different counting techniques using a hundreds chart (a 10-by-10 chart numbered 1 to 100 from top to bottom). Here are some of the other solutions:

4⃞8⃞ + 2⃞5⃞   (Boxed digits help "hold" them.)
40 + 20 = 60
8 + 2 = 10   ⃞3⃞   (The 3 is left from the 5.)
60 + 10 = 70
70 + 3 = 73

---
40 + 20 = 60
60 + 8 = 68
68 + 5 = 73

---
48 + 20 = 68
68 + 2 ("*from the 5*") = 70
"*Then I still have that 3 from the 5.*"
70 + 3 = 73

---
25 + 25 = 50   ⃞23⃞
50 + 23 = 73
Teacher: Where does the 23 come from?
"*It's sort of from the 48.*"
How did you split up the 48?
"*20 and 20 and I split the 8 into 5 and 3.*"

---
48 − 3 = 45   ⃞3⃞
45 + 25 = 70
70 + 3 = 73

The students in this class show a variety of levels of thinking and many interesting techniques. They had learned from each other the trick of placing numbers in "hold boxes," although not everyone used it. The children who are counting on the hundreds chart are showing that they may not yet have developed adequate place-value tools to understand these more sophisticated methods. Or the class discussion may help them activate those ideas or "dots" they simply had not considered. One question asks whether these invented methods are efficient or adequate. Students need to consider a variety of methods and make this determination.

Imagine for yourself what might happen if fifth-grade students were asked to add 3.72 + 1.6 before learning about lining up decimal points. Many students will do it incorrectly, perhaps aligning the 2 and 6. The decimal may be placed in various places. But students asked to defend their solutions will need to confront the size of the answer and the meaning of the digits in each position. A class of practiced problem solvers will soon develop a solid approach for adding decimals.

Gary Tsuruda is a middle school teacher who wrote a book about his successful problem-based mathematics classroom (Tsuruda, 1994). His classes frequently work in small groups to solve problems. The following example (Figure 3.1) is a lesson on the formula for area of a trapezoid. Rather than state the algorithm and have students plug numbers

into the formula, students use a problem-based approach that fosters understanding of the formula. Notice that the initial questions bring the requisite ideas needed for the task to the students' conscious level. Next they are asked to do some exploration and look for patterns. From these explorations the group must come up with a formula, test it, describe how it was developed, and illustrate its use.

Tsuruda (1994) reports that every group was able to produce a formula. "Not all the formulas looked like the typical textbook formula, but they were all correct, and more important, each formula made sense according to the way the students in that group had constructed the knowledge from the data they themselves had generated" (p. 6).

In all of these examples of problem-based lessons, the students are very much engaged in the processes of doing mathematics—figuring out procedures rather than not accepting them blindly. What is abundantly clear is that the more problem solving students do, the more willing and confident they are to solve problems and the more methods they develop for attacking future problems (Boaler, 1998, 2002; Boaler & Humphreys, 2005; Buschman, 2003a,b; Campbell, 1996; Rowan & Bourne, 1994; Silver, Smith, & Nelson, 1995; Silver & Stein, 1996; Wood, Cobb, Yackel, & Dillon, 1993).

Selecting or Designing Problem-Based Tasks and Lessons

A key element in teaching with problems is the selection of appropriate problems or tasks. A task is effective when it helps students learn the ideas you want them to learn. It must be the mathematics in the task that makes it problematic for the students so that it is the mathematical ideas that are their primary concern. Therefore, the first and most important consideration for selecting any task for your class must be the mathematics. That said, what do you look for in tasks and where do you find them?

Multiple Entry Points

One of the advantages of a problem-based approach is that it can help accommodate the diversity of learners in every classroom. A problem-based approach does not dictate how a child must think about a problem in order to solve it. When a task is posed, students are told, in essence, "Use the ideas *you* own to solve this problem." Because of the range of students' mental tools, concepts, and ideas, many students in a class will have different ideas about the best way to complete a task. Thus, access to the problem by all students demands that there be multiple entry points— different places to "get on the ramp"—to reach solutions.

Trapezoid Area

Problem: *Find an easy way to determine the area of any trapezoid.*

Be sure that you understand the answers to each of these questions:

1. What does "area" mean?
2. What is a trapezoid?
3. How do you find the area of other polygons? Show as many different ways as you can.

Now see if your group can find an easy way to determine the area of any trapezoid.

Hints:

1. Draw several trapezoids on dot paper and find their areas. Look for patterns.
2. Consider how you find the area of other polygons. Are any of the key ideas similar?
3. You might try cutting out trapezoids and piecing them together.
4. If you find a way to determine the area, make sure it is as easy as you can make it and that it works for *any* trapezoid.

Write-up:

1. Explain your answers to the first three questions in detail. Tell how your group reached agreement on the answers.
2. Tell what you did to get your formula for the area of any trapezoid. Did you use any of the hints? How did they help you?
3. Show your formula and give an illustration of how it works.

Figure 3.1 A middle school example in which students construct a formula.

Source: Reprinted with permission from *Putting It Together: Middle School Math in Transition* (p. 7) by G. Tsuruda. Copyright © 1994 by G. Tsuruda. Published by Heinemann, a division of Reed Elsevier, Inc. Portsmouth, NH. All rights reserved.

Once we stop thinking that there is only one way to solve a problem, it is not quite as difficult to develop good "ramp-up problems" or problems with multiple entry points. Although many problems have singular correct answers, there are often numerous ways to get there. Nearly all the problems presented in this chapter have multiple entry points, as in the following two examples.

Concept: Area
Grades: 3–4

Find the area of the cover of your math book. That is, how many square tiles will fit on the cover of the book?

Concept: Division of Fractions
Grades: 5–7

Clara has 2 whole pizzas and $\frac{1}{3}$ of another. All of the pizzas are the same size. If each of her friends will want to eat $\frac{1}{4}$ of a pizza, how many friends will she be able to feed with the $2\frac{1}{3}$ pizzas?

 Pause and Reflect

See if you can think of more than one path to solving these two problems. Try to think of an approach that is near the bottom of the "ramp" (less sophisticated) and another that is closer to the middle or the top of the "ramp." Do this now before reading further.

The area problem can be solved with materials that directly attack the meaning of the problem. The cover of the book can be completely covered with tiles and then counted one at a time. Moving slightly up the ramp to a higher entry point, a child may cover the book with tiles but count only the length of the row and the number of rows, multiplying to get the total. Another child may place tiles only along the edges of the book and multiply. Yet another child, noting that the tiles are 1 inch on each side, may use a ruler to measure the book edges.

For the pizza task a direct approach is also possible. Using plastic circular fraction pieces (or a drawing) to represent $2\frac{1}{3}$ pizzas, $\frac{1}{4}$ pieces can be placed on top until no more will fit. Another child may know that four fourths make a whole; therefore, two of the pizzas will feed eight friends. Children may or may not know how many fourths they can get from the $\frac{1}{3}$ piece and will have to tackle that part accordingly. A guess-and-check approach is possible, starting with perhaps six children, then seven, and so on until the pizza is gone. A few children may have learned a computational method for dividing $2\frac{1}{3}$ by $\frac{1}{4}$.

Having thought about these possible entry points, the teacher will be better prepared to suggest appropriate hints

for any student who is "stuck," depending on what that student brings to the task.

Creating Meaningful and Engaging Contexts

Certainly one of the most powerful features of teaching through problem solving is that the problem that begins the lesson can get students excited about learning mathematics. Compare these two sixth-grade introductory lessons on ratios:

> "Today we are going to explore ratios and see how ratios can be used to compare amounts."

> "In a minute, I am going to read to you a passage from Harry Potter about how big Hagrid is. We are going to use ratios to compare our heights and widths to Hagrid's."

Contexts can also be used to learn about cultures, such as those of students in your classroom. Contexts can also be used to connect to other subjects, as shown in the following sections. Children's literature, culturally relevant applications, and linking to other disciplines (e.g., science) are explored here for their potential to engage students in learning mathematics.

NCTM Standards "By analyzing and adapting a problem, anticipating the mathematical ideas that can be brought out by working on the problem, and anticipating students' questions, teachers can decide if particular problems will help to further their mathematical goals for the class" (NCTM, 2000, p. 53). ◆

Children's Literature. Children's literature is a rich source of problems at all levels, not just primary. Children's stories can be used in numerous ways to create a variety of reflective tasks, and there are many excellent books to help you in this area (Bay-Williams & Martinie, 2004; Bresser, 1995; Burns, 1992; Karp, Brown, Allen, & Allen, 1998; Sheffield, 1995; Theissen, Matthias, & Smith, 1998; Ward, 2006; Welchman-Tischler, 1992; Whitin & Whitin, 2004; Whitin & Wilde, 1992, 1995).

By way of example, a very popular children's picture book, *The Doorbell Rang* (Hutchins, 1986), can be used to explore different concepts at various grade levels. The story is a sequential tale of children sharing 12 cookies. On each page, more children come to the kitchen, and the 12 cookies must be redistributed. This simple yet engaging story can lead to exploring ways to make equal parts of almost any number for children at the K–2 level. It is a springboard for multiplication and division at the 3–4 level. It can also be used to explore fraction concepts at the 4–6 level.

In *Harry Potter and the Sorcerer's Stone* (Rowling, 1998), referred to earlier, the lesson is based on a description of

Hagrid as twice as tall and five times as wide as the average man. Students in grades 2–3 can cut strips of paper (like adding machine paper) that is as tall as they are and as wide as their shoulders are. Then they can figure out how big Hagrid would be if he were twice as tall and five times as wide as they are. In grades 4–5, students can create a table that shows each student's height and width and look for a pattern (it turns out to be about 3 to 1). Then they can figure out Hagrid's height and width and see if they keep the same ratio (it is 5 to 2). In grades 6–8, students can create a scatter plot of their widths and heights and see where Hagrid's data would be plotted on the graph. Measurement, number, and algebra content are all embedded in these examples. Whether students are 6 or 13, literature resonates with them, making them more enthusiastic about solving the related mathematics problems and more likely to learn and to see mathematics as a useful tool for exploring the world.

Several recent teacher resources focus on using nonfiction literature in teaching mathematics (Bay-Williams & Martinie, 2008; Petersen, 2004; Sheffield & Gallagher, 2004). Nonfiction literature can include newspapers, magazines, and the Web—all great sources for problems that have the added benefit of students learning about the world around them.

For example, an article appeared in the *Manchester Evening News*, in England (Leeming, 2007), explaining that the Cool Cash Lottery Scratchcard, created by a company named Camelot, had to be recalled—the integer values were too difficult for many people:

> To qualify for a prize, users had to scratch away a window to reveal a temperature lower than the value displayed on each card. As the game had a winter theme, the temperature was usually below freezing. Camelot received dozens of complaints on the first day from players who could not understand how, for example, –5 is higher than –6. . . . [One person] said: "On one of my cards it said I had to find temperatures lower than –8. The numbers I uncovered were –6 and –7 so I thought I had won, and so did the woman in the shop. But when she scanned the card the machine said I hadn't."

Can you think of a good problem to pose to students? One task could be to ask students to prepare an illustration and explanation that can help grown-ups understand the value of negative numbers.

The end of the chapters in Section 2 include a section titled "Literature Connections" that suggests picture books, poetry, and novels that can be used to explore the mathematics of that chapter. Literature ideas are often found in the articles of NCTM's journals, because it is an exciting approach to creating problem-solving scenarios.

Links to Other Disciplines. Finding relevant contexts for engaging all students is always a challenge in classes of diverse learners. Using contexts familiar for all students can be effective. An excellent source for problems, therefore, is the other subject matter that students are studying. Elementary teachers can pull ideas from the topics being taught in social studies, science, and language arts; likewise, middle school teachers can link to these subjects through their grade-level colleagues. Other familiar contexts such as art, sports, and pop culture can also be valuable.

In kindergarten, students can bring their study of natural systems into mathematics by sorting leaves based on a range of rules, such as color, smooth or jagged edges, feel of the leaf, and shape. Students learn about rules for sorting and possibly Venn diagrams (mathematics) and about observing and analyzing what is common and different in leaves from different trees (science). Sorting and measuring, topics in both mathematics and science, are more concepts to explore with leaves. Older students can learn in science about why different leaves have different shapes, sizes, and textures while in mathematics, students can find the perimeter and area of various types of leaves.

AIMS (Activities in Mathematics and Science), a series of teacher resource books integrating mathematics and science, has fantastic ideas in every book. See www.aimsedu .org for more information. In *Looking at Lines* (AIMS, 2001), a middle school AIMS books, students hang paperclips from a handmade balance to learn about linear equations (mathematics) and force and motion (science).

Social studies is rich with opportunities to do mathematics. Timelines of historic events are excellent opportunities for students to work on the relative sizes of numbers and to make better sense of history. Students can explore the areas and populations of various countries or U.S. states and compare the population densities, while in social studies they can talk about how life differs for regions with 200 people living in a square mile from regions with 5 people per square mile.

 The Equity Principle challenges teachers to believe that every student brings something of value to the tasks that they pose to their classes. The Teaching Principle calls for teachers to select tasks that "can be solved in more than one way, such as using an arithmetic counting approach, drawing a geometric diagram and enumerating possibilities, or using algebraic equations [so that tasks are] accessible to students with varied prior knowledge and experience" (NCTM, 2000, p. 19). ◆

How to Find Quality Tasks and Problem-Based Lessons

Abundant mathematics teaching resources are available in print along with a nearly endless supply of ideas on the Web. Searching for the right task for a particular lesson can be time-consuming or confusing. Knowing what makes a good task and where to start looking can help.

A Task Selection Guide. Throughout this book, in every student textbook, and in every article you read or in-service workshop you attend, you will find suggestions for activities, problems, tasks, or explorations that someone believes are effective in helping children learn some aspect of mathematics. As well-known mathematics educators Lappan and Briars (1995) contend, selecting activities or tasks is the most significant decision teachers make to affect students' learning. Figure 3.2 shows a four-step guide you can use when considering a new activity for your students.

The third step in Figure 3.2 is the most important point in determining if an activity is a good fit for the content you are teaching. What is problematic about the activity? How will the activity improve the chances that the children will be mentally active, reflecting on and constructing the ideas you identified for the lesson?

Practice using this evaluation and selection guide with activities throughout this book. Work toward thinking about tasks or activities from the view of what is likely to happen inside children's minds, not just what they are doing with their hands. Good tasks are minds-on activities, not just hands-on activities.

 — Pause and Reflect

Suppose your goal is for students to learn some of the harder multiplication facts they have not yet mastered (grade 3 or 4). You pose the task on page 50 about finding a helping fact. Think about the questions in step 3 of Figure 3.2. Do you think this will be an effective activity for your students? Why? Can you make it better? How?

Illuminations, a resource website of NCTM, is perhaps the best portal for finding high-quality lessons on the Internet. Besides over 100 activities posted that use engaging applets, there are more than 500 full lesson plans as well as links to many high-quality websites, searchable by content and by grade band. A definite site to bookmark on your computer! (http://illuminations.nctm.org). ◆

Standards-Based Curriculum. If your school is using a standards-based mathematics program, you will find an increased emphasis on learning mathematics through problem solving. This is certainly true with *Investigations in Number, Data, and Space* and *Connected Mathematics Project* (CMP II), which follow a before, during, and after lesson approach as described later in this chapter.

The CMP II lesson in Figure 3.3 is the first lesson on multiplication of fractions. In the problem, a familiar context is used: a pan of brownies. This context helps students use prior knowledge to think about and solve the problem. The lesson begins with posing the problem, "How much of the pan have we sold?" (*before*).

Next, students explore questions A through D using the square pan as a model (*during*). Notice how the questions are (1) grounded in the context of brownies, (2) placed in order of increasing difficulty, and (3) focused on connecting the concept to the procedure. Notice that parts A and B are very conceptual, and by C and D students are being asked to use the patterns they noticed in their problem solving to develop a rule or algorithm for multiplying fractions.

Finally, students are gathered back as a whole group and asked questions that focus on the concept of multiplication of fractions—taking a part of a part (*after*). In the Teacher Guide that accompanies the curriculum, the following questions are suggested for the discussion:

- How did you decide what fraction of a whole pan is being bought?
- Can someone suggest a way to mark the brownie pan so it is easy to see what part of the whole pan is being bought?

Activity Evaluation and Selection Guide

STEP 1: How Is the Activity Done?
Actually do the activity. Try to get "inside" the task or activity to see how it is done and what thinking might go on.
How would *children* do the activity or solve the problem?
- What materials are needed?
- What is written down or recorded?
- What misconceptions may emerge?

STEP 2: What Is the Purpose of the Activity?
What *mathematical ideas* will the activity develop?
- Are the ideas concepts or procedural skills?
- Will there be connections to other related ideas?

STEP 3: Can the Activity Accomplish Your Learning Goals?
What is *problematic* about the activity? Is the problematic aspect related to the mathematics you identified in the purpose?
What *must* children reflect on or think about to complete the activity? (Don't rely on wishful thinking.)
Is it possible to complete the activity without much reflective thought? If so, can it be modified so that students will be required to think about the mathematics?

STEP 4: What Must You Do?
What will you need to do in the *before* portion of your lesson?
- How will you activate students' prior knowledge?
- What will the students be expected to produce?
What might you anticipate seeing and asking in the *during* portion of your lesson?
What will you want to focus on in the *after* portion of your lesson?

Figure 3.2 A process for selecting effective mathematics tasks or activities.

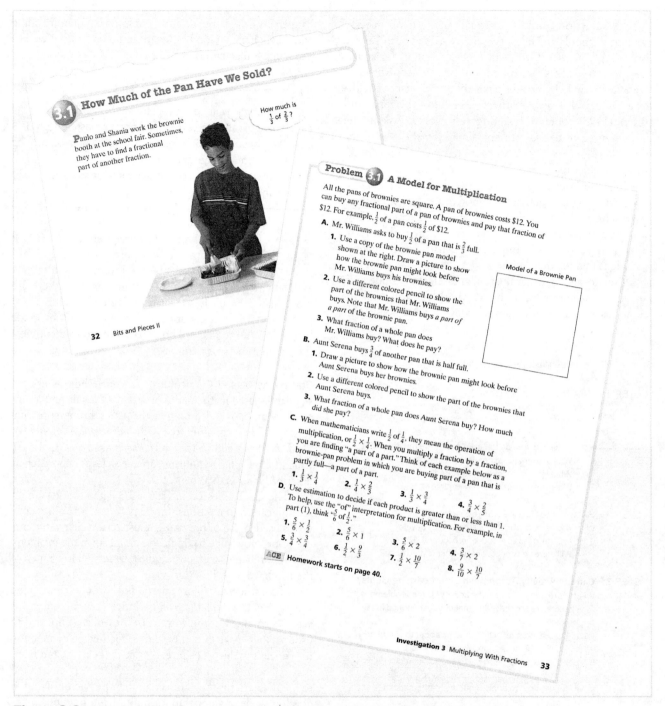

Figure 3.3 First lesson on multiplying fractions in a standards-based mathematics program.
Source: Connected Mathematics: Bits and Pieces II: Student Edition by G. Lappan, J. Fey, W. Fitzgerald, S. Friel, and E. Phillips,
pp. 32–33. Copyright © 2006 by Michigan State University. Used by permission of Pearson Education, Inc. All rights reserved.

• What number sentences [equations] could I write for Question A?

This is just one lesson in a series of lessons to build meaning for multiplication of fractions, all designed in the teaching through problem solving style.

Ⅱ ———————— *Pause and Reflect*

Name three distinct aspects about this approach to multiplication of fractions that differ from the traditional approach. What advantages and challenges do you anticipate in using a teaching through problem solving approach?

Adapting a Non-Problem-Based Lesson. Most teachers find their textbook to be the main guide to their day-to-day curriculum. However, when teachers let the text determine the next lesson, they assume that children learned from each page what was intended. Avoid the "myth of coverage": If we covered it, they must have learned it. Good teachers use their text as a resource and as a basic guide to their curriculum, enhancing what is given to better meet the needs of students.

Many traditional textbooks are designed for teacher-directed classrooms, a contrast to the approach you have been reading about. Adopt a unit perspective. Avoid the idea that every lesson and idea in the unit requires attention. Examine a chapter or unit from beginning to end and identify the two to four big ideas, the essential mathematics in the chapter. (Big ideas are listed at the start of each chapter in Section 2 of this book. These may be helpful as a reference.) With the big ideas of the unit in mind, you now have two choices: (1) adapt the best or most important lessons in the chapter to a problem-based format or (2) create or find tasks in the textbook and other resources that address the major concepts.

Example 1: Addition. Figure 3.4 shows a page from a first-grade textbook. The lesson addresses an important idea: the connection between addition and subtraction. The approach on this page is fine: A picture of two sets of counters is used to suggest an addition and a subtraction equation, thus connecting these concepts. However, the expectation for students is limited to filling in the blanks.

Imagine for a moment how you might help students complete this page. It is easy to slip into a "how-to" mode focused more on the blanks than on the concepts of addition and subtraction. Let's convert this lesson to a problem-based one.

Figure 3.4 A first-grade lesson from a traditional textbook. *Source: Scott Foresman–Addison Wesley Math: Grade 1* (p. 137), by R. I. Charles et al. Copyright © 2004 Pearson Education, Inc., or its affiliate(s). Used by permission. All rights reserved.

❚❚ ——————— *Pause and Reflect*

How can students be challenged to wrestle with this task? How might a different approach allow for multiple entry points? If this problem is redesigned to be more open-ended, how will it affect the challenge and learning in the lesson?

One possibility is to provide a set of perhaps eight counters and have students separate the set into two parts. The students' task is to write addition and subtraction equations that represent how they separated the counters. Students can be asked to draw a picture to show the two parts of the set. In addition, they can be challenged to see how many different ways they can separate the eight counters, recording the possible addition and subtraction number sentences for each.

Another possibility is to create a scenario in which there are two amounts, such as toy cars, on two different shelves. *In the toy store, there were 11 cars, 4 on the top shelf and 7 on the next shelf.* Have the students create two story problems about the 11 cars, one that is an addition story and another that is a related subtraction story.

In both of these modifications, the students will solve only one or two problems rather than the eight provided. But in the *during* and *after* portions of either modified lesson, there will be a much greater opportunity for students to develop the connection between the operations for addition and subtraction.

Example 2: Classifying Triangles. Figure 3.5 is the second page of a geometry lesson from a sixth-grade book. The content involves classification of triangles by relative side lengths and by the sizes of the angles, but notice how much of the lesson is simply providing definitions. Here the question at the top of the page (How can you draw and classify triangles?) is the essence of a good problem-based task. Consider what *you* might do before reading on.

To make this a classification task, students need some triangles in all six categories, with two or three triangles per category. You might prepare a set of triangles, reproduce

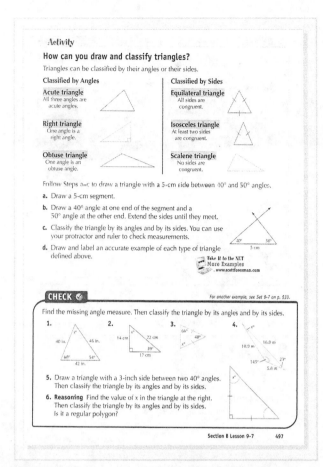

Figure 3.5 A page from a sixth-grade lesson from a traditional textbook.

Source: Scott Foresman–Addison Wesley Math: Grade 6 (p. 497), by R. I. Charles et al. Copyright 2004 Pearson Education, Inc., or its affiliate(s). Used by permission. All rights reserved.

them, and have students cut them out, or geoboards could be used if they are available. (See Activity 20.8 on page 413 and Blackline Master 58 for details.) Given the set of triangles, the task is to find two ways to sort the triangles into three separate piles. You could specify doing this first with a rule about sides and then a rule about angles, or let students develop their own classification schemes. In the *during* portion, you can approach struggling students and provide hints that will help ensure that they create categories. After students have created the categories, you can introduce the appropriate vocabulary.

Teaching about Problem Solving

As discussed in the first section of this chapter, teaching about problem solving means explicitly teaching

students how to solve problems. This is also a part of teaching through problem solving, though sometimes in classrooms there are days when a teacher's goal is to teach students a new problem-solving strategy, such as "Make an organized list." In teaching about problem solving, it is not only important to seek understanding of the process for solving problems; it is also important to teach general strategies useful for solving problems.

Four-Step Problem-Solving Process

George Polya, a famous mathematician, wrote a classic book, *How to Solve It* (1945), that outlined four steps for doing mathematics. These widely adopted steps for problem solving have appeared and continue to appear in many resource books and textbooks. Explicitly teaching these four steps to students can improve their ability to solve problems. The four steps are described very briefly in the following list:

1. *Understanding the problem.* Briefly, this means figuring out what the problem is about, identifying what question or problem is being posed.

2. *Devising a plan.* In this phase you are thinking about how to solve the problem. Will you want to write an equation? Will you want to model the problem with a manipulative? (See the next section, "Problem-Solving Strategies," for more on this one.)

3. *Carrying out the plan.* This is the implementation of your plan.

4. *Looking back.* This phase, arguably the most important as well as most skipped by students, is the moment you determine if your answer from step 3 answers the problem as originally understood in step 1. Does your answer make sense?

As you teach through problem solving, using these steps to help guide your students will foster success. Once you pose a problem to students, your first step is to be sure they understand it, which is the first step of Polya's process (and part of the *before* phase). You may also ask students for ideas on which strategies might work for this problem to get some ideas started for step 2. In the *during* phase of the lesson, students are devising and carrying out a strategy they have selected) (steps 2 and 3). Then they look back to see if their solution makes sense (step 4). The *after* phase of the lesson is a time where students share their strategy (step 2), how they solved it (step 3), and how they know it is correct (step 4). The beauty of Polya's framework is generality; it can and should be applied to many different types of problems, from simple computational exercises to difficult multistep word problems.

Problem-Solving Strategies

Strategies for solving problems are identifiable methods of approaching a task that are completely independent of the specific topic or subject matter. Students select or design a strategy as they devise a plan (step 2). When students discover important or especially useful strategies, they should be identified, highlighted, and discussed. Labeling a strategy provides a useful means for students to talk about their methods and for you to provide hints and suggestions, which can be appropriate in the *before* or *during* phases of your lesson. The following labeled strategies are commonly encountered in K–8 mathematics, though some may not be used at every grade.

- *Draw a picture, act it out, use a model.* The strategy of using models and manipulatives is described in Chapter 2. "Act it out" extends models to a real interpretation of the problem situation.
- *Look for a pattern.* Pattern searching is at the heart of many problem-based tasks, especially in the algebraic reasoning strand. Patterns in number and in operations play a huge role in helping students learn and master basic skills starting at the earliest levels and continuing into the middle and high school years.
- *Guess and check.* This might be called "Try and see what you can find out." A good way to work on a task that has you stumped is to try something. Make an attempt! Reflection even on a failed attempt can lead to a better idea.
- *Make a table or chart.* Charts of data, function tables, tables for operations, and tables involving ratios or measurements are a major form of analysis and communication. The use of a chart is often combined with pattern searching as a means of solving problems or constructing new ideas.
- *Try a simpler form of the problem.* Modify or simplify the quantities in a problem so that the resulting task is easier to understand and analyze. Solving the easier problem can sometimes lead to insights that can then be used to solve the original, more complex problem.
- *Make an organized list.* Systematically accounting for all possible outcomes in a situation can show the number of possibilities there are or verify that all possible outcomes have been included. One subject area where organized lists are essential is probability.
- *Write an equation.* As it implies, in this strategy, the story is converted into numbers or symbols, and the equation is solved.

It is important not to "proceduralize" problem solving. In other words, don't take the problem solving out of problem solving by telling students the strategy they should pick and how to do it. Instead, pose a problem that lends itself to the strategy you would like them to develop (e.g., make an organized list) and allow students to solve the problem any way they like. During the sharing of results, highlight student work that uses a list, or if none uses a list, ask, "Could we have made an organized list to solve the problem more efficiently? What would that look like? Give it a try!"

 The first two goals of the problem-solving standard concern teaching through problem solving. The third and fourth goals refer to students learning about problem solving. It would be beneficial to check these goals for the grade band that interests you most. ◆

Teaching in a Problem-Based Classroom

The ideas expressed throughout this chapter have been gathered both from the research literature on teaching through problem solving and from elementary and middle school teachers who have been working hard at developing a problem-based approach in their classrooms. The following are important distinctions and considerations in planning for such a mathematics classroom.

myeducationlab

Go to the Activities and Application section of Chapter 3 of MyEducationLab. Click on Videos and watch the video entitled **"Math Strategies for Problem Solving"** to see teachers using problem-based teaching methods.

Let Students Do the Talking

The value of classroom discussion of ideas cannot be overemphasized. As students describe and evaluate solutions to tasks, share approaches, and make conjectures, learning will occur in ways that are otherwise unlikely to occur. Students begin to take ownership of ideas and develop a sense of power in making sense of mathematics.

When students are given a task, they should understand that one of their responsibilities is to prepare for a discussion that will occur after they have had an opportunity to work on the problem. One fourth-grade teacher discovered that she was too involved when she realized that the students tended to wait for her questions rather than tell about their solutions. To help her students be more personally responsible, she devised three posters, inscribed as follows:

1. How did you solve the problem?
2. Why did you solve it this way?
3. Why do you think your solution is correct and makes sense?

In the beginning, students referred to the posters as they made presentations to the class, but soon that was not necessary. They continued to refer to the posters as they wrote up the solutions to problems in the *during* portion of lessons. Students began to prompt presenters: "You didn't answer the second question on the poster." One of the best results of these posters was that they helped remove the teacher from the content of the discussions.

Regardless of the exact structure or timeframe for a lesson, an opportunity for discourse should always be included. After students have played a game, worked in a learning center, completed a challenging worksheet, or engaged in a mental math activity with a full class, they can still discuss their activity: *What strategies worked well in the game? What did you find out in the learning center? What are different ways to do this exercise?*

How Much to Tell and Not to Tell

When teaching through problem solving, one of the most perplexing dilemmas is how much to tell. On one hand, telling diminishes student reflection. Students who sense that the teacher has a preferred method or approach are more reluctant to use their own strategies. Nor will students develop self-confidence and problem-solving abilities by watching the teacher do the thinking. On the other hand, to tell too little can sometimes leave students floundering and waste precious class time.

While noting that there will never be a simple solution to this dilemma, researchers offer the following guidance: Teachers should feel free to share relevant information as long as the mathematics in the task remains problematic for the students (Hiebert et al., 1997). That is, "information can and should be shared as long as it does not solve the problem [and] does not take away the need for students to reflect on the situation and develop solution methods they understand" (p. 36). They go on to suggest three types of information that teachers should provide to their students:

- *Mathematical conventions.* The social conventions of symbolism and terminology that are important in mathematics will never be developed through reflective thought. For example, representing "three and five equals eight" as "3 + 5 = 8" is a convention. Definitions and labels are also conventions. It is important to offer these symbols and words only when students need them or will find them useful. As a rule of thumb, symbolism and terminology should be introduced *after* concepts have been developed and then specifically as a means of expressing or labeling ideas.

- *Alternative methods.* You can, with care, suggest to students an alternative method or approach for solving a problem. You may also suggest more efficient recording procedures for student-invented computational methods. For example, suggesting that students draw a vertical line between the tens and ones place as a way of keeping track of the value of the digits can be effective for students with learning disabilities. The value of a procedure should be grounded in both accuracy and efficiency. Engage students

in evaluating procedures by asking whether their procedure always works and if it is efficient and by encouraging students to decide which procedure they might use the next time they encounter a similar problem.

- *Clarification of students' methods.* You should help students clarify or interpret their ideas and perhaps point out related ideas. A student may add 38 and 5 by noting that 38 and 2 more is 40 with 3 more making 43. This strategy can be related to the Make 10 strategy used to add 8 + 5. The selection of 40 as a midpoint in this procedure is an important place-value concept. Such clarifications reinforce the students who have the ideas. Discussion or clarification of students' ideas focuses attention on ideas you want the class to learn. Teacher attention to one method should not be done in such a way as to suggest that it is the preferred approach.

The Importance of Student Writing

There are many reasons to use writing in a mathematics classroom. The most important is that it improves student learning and understanding (Bell & Bell, 1985; Pugalee, 2005; Steele, 2007), although there are other interrelated reasons as well.

- *The act of writing is a reflective process.* As students make an effort to explain their thinking and defend their answers, they will spend more focused time thinking about the ideas involved.

- *A written report is a rehearsal for the discussion period.* It is difficult for students to explain how they solved a problem 15 minutes after they have done so. Students can always refer to a written report when asked to share. Even a kindergarten child can show a picture and talk about it. When every student has written about his or her solution, you need not ask for volunteers to share ideas.

- *A written report is also a written record that remains when the lesson is finished.* The reports can be collected and looked at later. The information can be used for planning, for finding out who needs help or opportunities to extend their knowledge, and for evaluation and parent conferences.

It is important to help students understand what they are trying to accomplish in their written report. When you ask students to explain how they got their answer, they may just repeat each step, rather than explaining why they did what they did. Figures 3.6 and 3.7 illustrate a range of quality in student explanations. Modeling for students how to explain their thinking is essential. Using student work samples, such as those illustrated, can help students understand your expectations for them. To help elicit better explanations, you might consider the following two possible types of directions:

- Give students a template to begin their report: "I (We) think the answer is _____. We think this because _____."

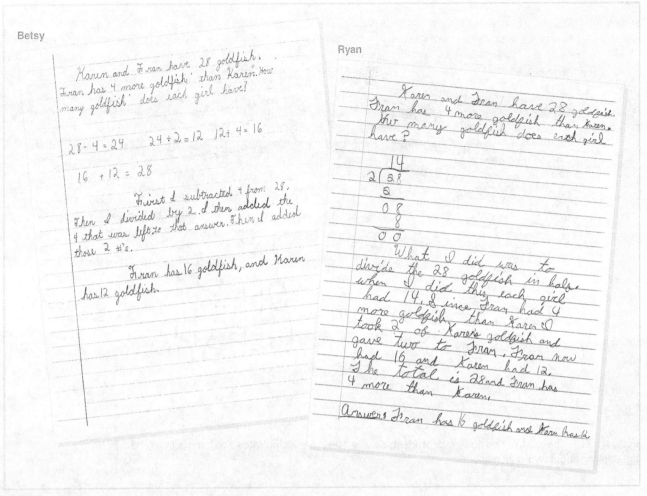

Figure 3.6 Betsy tells each step in her solution but provides no explanation. In contrast, Ryan's work includes reasons for his steps.

- "Use words, pictures, and numbers to explain how you got your answer and why you think your answer makes sense and is correct."

Technology Tools in Writing. Take advantage of the following free programs as part of allowing students to write, edit, and submit work to you electronically:

Text Editing
(real-time, collaborative tools)
- Google Docs & Spreadsheets (http://docs.google.com)
- Synchroedit (www.synchroedit.com)
- OpenEffort (www.openeffort.com/oe)
- Zoho Writer (http://zoho.com)

Wikis
(free, asynchronous, collaborative website creation tools)
- Wikispaces—includes ability to use math equations (www.wikispaces.com)

- Wiki-site—includes ability to use math equations (www.wiki-site.com)
- XWiki—includes ability to use math equations (www.xwiki.com/xwiki/bin/view/Main/WebHome)
- Wikidot—includes ability to use math equations; no ads (www.wikidot.com)

Blogging Tools
- Blogger (www.blogger.com)
- WordPress (http://wordpress.com)

Web-based tools such as these can be used inside and outside of the (physical) mathematics classroom to allow students and teachers to collaboratively draft, read, and edit each other's mathematical ideas. Students who are reluctant to write by hand or in a word document could be motivated by the more interactive technologies, increasing the likelihood that they will produce quality written explanations and illustrations.

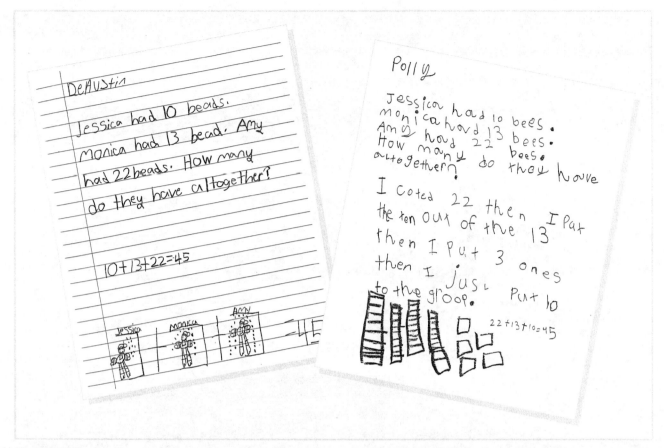

Figure 3.7 The work of two first-grade students solving 10 + 13 + 22 indicates a difference in how children are thinking about two-digit numbers.

Metacognition

Metacognition refers to conscious monitoring (being aware of how and why you are doing something) and regulation (choosing to do something or deciding to make changes) of your own thought process. Good problem solvers monitor their thinking regularly and automatically. They recognize when they are stuck or do not fully understand. They make conscious decisions to switch strategies, rethink the problem, search for related content knowledge that may help, or simply start afresh (Schoenfeld, 1992).

There is evidence that metacognitive behavior can be learned (Campione, Brown, & Connell, 1989; Garofalo, 1987; Lester, 1989; Thomas, 2006). Furthermore, students can learn to monitor and regulate their own problem-solving behaviors and those who do so show improvement in problem solving.

We know that it is important to help students learn to monitor and control their own progress in problem solving. A simple formula that can be employed consists of three questions: *What* are you doing? *Why* are you doing it? *How* does it help you? An elaboration of these three questions is proposed in the THINK framework (Thomas, 2006):

Talk about the problem.
How can it be solved?
Identify a strategy to solve the problem.
Notice how your strategy helped you solve the problem.
Keep thinking about the problem. Does it make sense?
    Is there another way to solve it?

Students who used the THINK framework improved in their problem solving more than those who did not use it (Thomas, 2006). The key to success is being intentional and consciously developing the metacognitive skills to monitor and reflect on the problems being solved.

Fostering metacognition spans all three lesson phases. In the *before* phase, students begin to address *what* strategies they are using and *why*. As they move into the *during* phase, they continue to consider *what*, *why*, and even *how*. You can support metacognition by using prompts that will help students use the THINK framework. You can ask the questions as you interact with individuals or small groups. By joining a group, you can model questions you want the students to ask each other and themselves. In the upper grades, each group can have a designated monitor, whose job is to be the reflective questioner that you have modeled when working with the group.

You can also help students develop self-monitoring habits after their problem-solving activity is over, when a discussion can focus on what was done to solve the problem. In addition to discussing solution strategies, the *after* phase of the lesson should include opportunities to reflect on the metacognitive questions noted above. This can be accomplished through journals (Roberts & Tayeh, 2007) or classroom discussions, prompted by such questions as:

- What did you do that helped you understand the problem?
- Did you find any numbers or information you didn't need? How did you know?
- How did you decide what to do?
- Did you think about your answer after you got it?
- How did you decide if your answer was right?
- Did you try something that didn't work? How did you figure out it was not going to work out?
- Can something you did in this problem help you solve other problems?

As students become more independent in their study of mathematics, they are less likely to need the support of a teacher to solve problems. Their attitudes and dispositions shift related to what they think mathematics is and how competent they feel in doing mathematics.

Disposition

Disposition refers to the attitudes and beliefs that students possess about doing mathematics. Students' beliefs concerning their abilities to do mathematics and to understand the nature of mathematics have a significant effect on how they approach problems and ultimately on how well they succeed.

Students who enjoy solving problems and feel they will be successful at conquering a perplexing problem are much more likely to persevere, make second and third attempts, and even search out new problems. A lack of productive disposition has just the opposite effect.

Attitudinal Goals

- *Gaining confidence and belief in abilities* is important for a student to want to do mathematics and confront unfamiliar tasks.
- *Being willing to take risks and to persevere* improves a student's willingness to attempt unfamiliar problems and to develop perseverance in solving problems without being discouraged by initial setbacks.
- *Enjoying doing mathematics* helps a student sense personal reward in the process of thinking, searching for patterns, and solving problems.

A classroom environment built on high expectations for all students and respect for each student's thoughts will go a long way toward achieving attitudinal goals. Here are some additional ideas to help with these goals for all students.

- *Build in success.* In the beginning of the year, plan problems that you are confident your students can solve. Avoid creating a false success that depends on your showing the way at every step and barrier.
- *Praise efforts and risk taking.* Students need to hear frequently that they are "good thinkers" capable of good, productive thought. When students volunteer ideas, listen carefully and actively to each idea and give credit for the thinking and the risk that children take by venturing to speak out. Be careful to focus praise on the risk or effort and not the products (i.e., answers) of that effort, as noted earlier.
- *Listen to all students.* Avoid ending a discussion with the first correct answer. As you make nonevaluative responses, you will find many children with different approaches to the same problem or different ways to explain the same strategy. By noting their contribution, use of good mathematical language, or novel approach, you build that student's confidence and increase other students' understanding of what you expect of them.

When students have confidence, show perseverance, and enjoy mathematics, it makes sense that they will achieve at a higher level and want to continue learning about mathematics—opening many doors to them in the future. As noted earlier, though, teaching in this manner is a complete reconceptualization of your role as the teacher and of the student's role as the student. In considering such a transformation, questions are likely to arise. Even if you feel these new methods contain really good ideas, you may be wondering how to accomplish some of the recommendations and how to fit new approaches into a lesson. In the following section, a three-phase lesson plan model is explained. An adaptation of the inquiry-based science lesson model, this process will enable you to engage students in learning through problem solving and learning about problem solving.

A Three-Phase Lesson Format

In a non-problem-based lesson, teachers typically spend a small portion of a lesson explaining or reviewing an idea and then go into "production mode," where students wade through a set of exercises. Lessons organized in this explain-then-practice pattern condition students to focus on procedures, often at the expense of understanding what they are doing. Teachers find themselves going from desk to desk reteaching and explaining to individuals. This approach is in significant contrast to a problem-based lesson that tends to be built around a single problem.

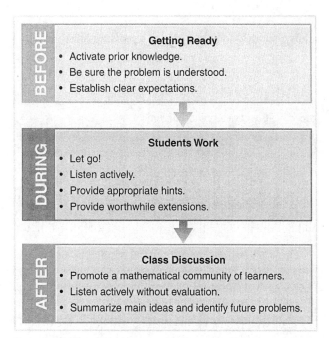

Figure 3.8 Teaching through problem solving lends itself to a three-phase structure for lessons.

It is useful to think of a problem-based lesson as consisting of three parts—before, during, and after (see Figure 3.8). If time is allotted for each segment, one problem may take a full day or even longer. There are times when a task may not merit a full lesson; a mental mathematics activity is a good example. Even here, it is useful to keep the same three components of a lesson in mind. Each part of the lesson has a specific agenda or objective. How you attend to these agendas in each portion of the lesson may vary depending on the class, the problem itself, and the purpose of the lesson.

The *Before* Phase of a Lesson

There are three related agendas for the *before* phase of a lesson:

1. Get students mentally prepared to work on the problem and think about the previous knowledge they have that will be most helpful.
2. Be sure students understand the problem so that they are ready to engage in solving it. You will not need to clarify or explain to individuals later in the lesson.
3. Clarify your expectations to students before they begin working on the problem. This includes both how they will be working (individually or in pairs or small groups) and what product you expect in addition to an answer.

These *before* phase agendas need not be addressed in the order listed. For example, for some lessons you will do a short activity to activate students' prior knowledge for the problem and then present the problem and clarify expectations.

Other lessons may begin with a statement of the problem and may or may not have a readiness activity.

Teacher Actions in the *Before* Phase

What you do in the *before* portion of a lesson will vary with the task. Some tasks you can begin with immediately. For example, if your students are used to solving story problems and know they are expected to use words, pictures, and numbers to explain their solutions in writing, all that may be required is to read through the problem with them and be sure all understand it. The actual presentation of the task or problem may occur at the beginning or at the end of your *before* actions.

1. Activate Prior Knowledge. Activate specific prior knowledge related to today's concept. What form this preparation activity might take will vary with the topic, as shown in the following options and examples.

Begin with a Simple Version of the Task. Suppose that you are interested in developing some ideas about area and perimeter. Begin by presenting the following task (Lappan & Even, 1989).

Concept: Perimeter
Grades: 4–6

Assume that the edge of a square is 1 unit. Add squares to this shape so that it has a perimeter of 18.

Instead of beginning your lesson with this problem, you might consider activating prior knowledge in one of the following ways:

• Draw a 3-by-5 rectangle of squares on the board and ask students what they know about the shape. (It's a rectangle. It has squares. There are 15 squares. There are three rows of five.) If no one mentions the words *area* and *perimeter*, you could write them on the board and ask if those words can be used in talking about this figure.

• Provide students with some square tiles or grid paper and say, "I want everyone to make a shape that has a perimeter of 12 units. After you make your shape, find out what its area is." After a short time, have several students share their shapes.

Each of these "warm-ups" uses the vocabulary needed for the focus task. The second activity suggests the tiles as a possible model students may elect to use and introduces the idea that there are different figures with the same perimeter.

The following problem is designed to help students use addition to solve a subtraction problem.

Concept: Subtraction
Grades: 2–3

Dad says it is 503 miles to the beach. When we stopped for gas, we had gone 267 miles. How much farther do we have to drive?

Before presenting this problem, you can elicit prior knowledge by asking them to supply the missing part of 100 after you give one part. Try numbers like 80 or 30 at first; then try 47 or 62. When you present the actual task, you might ask students if the answer to the problem is more or less than 300 miles.

Brainstorm Solutions. The following problem is designed to address ratios and data analysis.

Concepts: Ratios and Statistics
Grades: 6–7

Enrollment data for the school provide information about the students and their families from one class as compared to the whole school.

	School	Class
Siblings		
None	36	5
One	89	4
Two	134	17
More than two	93	3
Race		
African American	49	11
Asian American	12	0
White	219	15
Travel-to-school method		
Walk	157	10
Bus	182	19
Other	13	0

If someone asked you how typical the class was of the rest of the school, how would you answer? Write an explanation of your answer. Include one or more charts or graphs that you think would support your conclusion.

This problem does not lend itself to posing a simpler problem, but instead solicits students' prior knowledge during their thinking about how to approach the problem.

For example, students might discuss (e.g., think-pair-share) what "typical" means and how they could determine what a typical class is. The teacher can list the ideas on the board for students to consider when they move into the *during* part of the lesson.

Estimate or Use Mental Computation. When the task is aimed at the development of a computational procedure, a useful *before* action is to have students actually do the computation mentally or suggest an estimated answer. This practice will not spoil the problem for the class; in fact, it may raise curiosity as to what the answer might be. This technique is appropriate for the earlier problem concerning how many more miles to go to the beach. The following task is another example in which preliminary estimates or mental computations would activate prior knowledge.

Concept: Multiplication
Grades: 4–5

How many small unit squares will fit in a rectangle that is 54 units long and 36 units wide? Use base-ten blocks to help you with your solution. Note that base-ten blocks come in ones (one cube), tens (a row of ten cubes), and hundreds (a ten-by-ten grid). Make a plan for figuring out the total number of squares without doing too much counting. Explain how your plan would work on a rectangle that is 27 units by 42 units.

Prior to estimation or mental computation for this problem, beginning with several simpler problems can help—for example, rectangles such as 30 by 8 or 40 by 60.

2. Be Sure the Problem Is Understood. Understanding the problem is not optional! You must always be sure that students understand the problem before setting them to work. It is important for you to analyze the problem in order to anticipate student approaches and possible misinterpretations or misconceptions (Wallace, 2007). Time spent at this stage of the problem-solving process is critical to the rest of the lesson. You can ask questions to clarify student understanding of the problem (i.e., knowing what it means rather than how they will solve it). For example, ask, "What do you know?" and "What do you need to know?" Wallace, a mathematics researcher and teacher, notes, "The more I questioned *prior to* giving the problem, the less help the students needed from me *during* problem solving" (p. 510).

Consider a problem-based approach to mastering the multiplication facts, a term used for the basic multiplication tables. The most difficult facts can each be connected or related to an easier fact already learned.

Concept: Multiplication Facts
Grades: 3–4

Use a "helping fact" (a multiplication fact you already know) to help you solve each of these problems: 4 × 6, 6 × 8, 7 × 6, 3 × 8.

For this task, it is essential that students understand the idea of using a helping fact. They have most likely used helping facts in addition. You can build on this prior knowledge by asking, "When you were learning addition facts, how could knowing 6 + 6 help you figure out 6 + 7?" You may also need to help students understand what is meant by a fact they know—one they have mastered and know without counting.

In the case of a word problem, like the one below, it is important to help them understand the meaning of the sentences, without giving away how to solve the problem.

Concept: Multiplication and Division
Grades: 3–5

The local candy store purchased candy in cartons holding 12 boxes per carton. The price paid for one carton was $42.50. Each box contained 8 candy bars that the store planned to sell individually. What was the candy store's cost for each candy bar?

Questions might include: "What did the candy store do? What is in a carton? What is in a box? What is the price of one carton? What does that mean when it says 'each box'?" The last question here is to identify vocabulary that may be misunderstood. It is also useful to be sure students can explain to you what the problem is asking. Asking students to reread a problem does little

good, but asking students to restate the problem in their own words helps them figure out what the problem is asking.

If you have struggling readers or English language learners, additional support may be needed. Explicit attention to vocabulary is critical. Graphic organizers (handouts with places to record needed information) can aid in reading and understanding the text. For more on supporting English language learners, see Table 4.1 in Chapter 4 and Chapter 6.

3. Establish Clear Expectations. There are two components to establishing expectations: how students are to work and what products they are to prepare for the discussion in the third part of the lesson. Each of these is essential; they cannot be skipped.

Whether or not you have students work in groups, it is always a good idea for students to have some opportunity to discuss their ideas with one or more classmates prior to sharing their thoughts in the *after* phase of the lesson. When students work alone, they have no one to look to for an idea or a way to get started if they are stuck. On the other hand, when students work in groups, there is always the possibility of students not contributing or of a dominating student overshadowing the others.

Buschman (2003b), a leader in mathematics education, suggests a *think-write-pair-share* approach, adding that students should first write or illustrate their solutions to the problem before sharing with a partner. With written work to share, the two students have something to talk about. Although appropriate for all students, the think-write-pair-share method is especially helpful for K–1 students who often do not know how to go about discussing a solution or even how to work together.

Teaching through problem solving requires that students focus on not just the solution, but how they reached that solution. Therefore, it is important to model and explain your expectations of what their final product might be. One expectation could be a written explanation of the problem. Writing supports student learning in mathematics (Pugalee, 2005; Steele, 2007) and can be a support to students during discussions, as they can refer to their own written explanation. Students may also or instead choose to prepare an illustration, diagram, or graph with or without a written explanation (see Figure 3.9). In this example, the student was asked to show how many different ways five people could be on the two stories of a house. Discuss with students what they might draw that will show their thinking. Just as it is important to ascertain that students understand the problem itself, it is also important to check that students have a clear understanding of the expectations for the product they will be sharing in the *after* phase of the lesson.

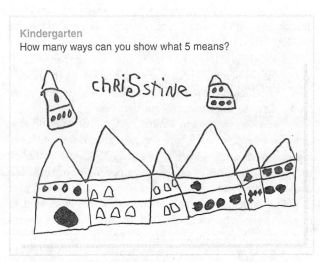

Figure 3.9 A kindergarten student shows her thinking about ways to make 5.

The *During* Phase of a Lesson

In the *during* phase of the lesson students explore the focus task (alone, with partners, or in small groups). There are clear agendas that you will want to attend to:

1. *Let go!* Give students a chance to work without too much guidance. Allow and encourage students to embrace the struggle—it is an important part of doing mathematics.
2. *Listen actively.* Take this time to find out how different students are thinking, what ideas they are using, and how they are approaching the problem. This is a time for observation and assessment—not teaching.
3. *Provide appropriate hints.* Base any hints on students' ideas and ways of thinking. Be careful not to imply that you have the *correct* method of solving the problem.
4. *Provide worthwhile extensions.* Have something prepared for students who finish quickly.

Teacher Actions in the *During* Phase

With the exception of preparing for early finishers, these agendas can challenge teachers who tend to help too much. The teacher is a facilitator, carefully making decisions about when to let go and when to provide a hint. These decisions are based on carefully listening to students and knowing the content goals of the lesson.

1. Let Go! Once students understand what the problem is asking, it is time to LET GO. While it is tempting to "step in front of the struggle" in the *during* phase, you need to hold yourself back. Doing mathematics takes time, and solutions are not always obvious. It is important to communicate to students that spending time on a task, trying different approaches, and consulting each other are impor-

tant to learning and understanding mathematics. When students are stuck, you can ask questions like, "Is this like another problem we have solved?" "Did you try to make a picture?" "What is it about this problem that is difficult?" This approach is effective in helping students because you are supporting their thinking, yet you are not telling them how to solve the problem.

Students will look to you for approval of their results or ideas. Avoid being the source of right and wrong. When asked if a result or method is correct, respond by saying, "How can you decide?" or "Why do you think that might be right?" or "Can you check that somehow?" Asking "How can we tell if that makes sense?" reminds students that answers without understanding are not acceptable.

Letting go also means allowing students to make mistakes. When you observe an error or incorrect thinking, do not correct it at this point. Students must learn from the very beginning that their mistakes can be opportunities for learning (Boaler & Humphreys, 2005). The best discussions occur when students disagree.

When students make mistakes, ask them to explain their process or approach to you. They may catch their own mistake. In addition, in the *after* portion of the lesson, students will have an opportunity to explain, justify, defend, and challenge solutions and strategies. This process provides an opportunity for mistakes and misconceptions to be treated as opportunities for learning.

2. Listen Actively. "Listening actively" means that you are trying to understand a student's approach to a problem. Consequently your questions must probe your students' thinking; the result may be unexpected. This is different from listening for a particular response or for what you know to be *the* answer and trying to elicit that response. This process is referred to as "funneling" students toward a response that approaches what you have in mind.

The *during* phase is one of two opportunities you have (the other is in the *after* phase) to find out what your students know, how they think, and how they are approaching the task you have given them. You might sit down with a group and simply listen for a while, letting the students explain what they are doing as you take occasional notes. If you want further information, try saying, "Tell me what you are doing" or "I see you have started to multiply these numbers. Can you tell me why you are multiplying?" You want to convey a genuine interest in what students are doing and thinking. This is not the time to evaluate or to tell students how to solve the problem.

"It's easy." "Let me help you." These two simple sentences send two disastrous messages to the student who hears them. For the student who asks for help, it is not easy! Students may think, "If it's easy and I can't get it, I must be stupid." The second sentence can also send a negative message. It implies, "You are not capable of doing this on your own. I have to help you."

Listening actively includes asking questions, such as the following:

- What ideas have you tried so far?
- Can you tell more more about . . . ?
- Why did you . . . ?
- How did you solve it?

By asking questions you find out where students are in their understanding of the concepts.

3. Provide Appropriate Hints. If a group or student is searching for a place to begin, a hint may be appropriate. You might suggest that the students try using a particular manipulative, draw a picture, or make a table if one of these ideas seems appropriate. You might also ask questions like those mentioned in the "Let Go!" section.

Concept: Percent Increase and Decrease
Grades: 6–8

In Fern's Furniture Store, Fern has priced all of her furniture at 20 percent over wholesale. In preparation for a sale, she tells her staff to cut all prices by 10 percent. Will Fern be making 10 percent profit, less than 10 percent profit, or more than 10 percent profit? Explain your answer.

For this problem, consider the following hints:

- Try drawing a picture or a diagram of something that shows what 10 percent off means.
- Try drawing a picture or a diagram that shows what 20 percent more means.
- Maybe you could pick a sample initial price and see what happens when you add 20 percent and then reduce 10 percent.
- Let's try a simpler problem. Suppose that you had 8 blocks and got 25 percent more. Then you lost 25 percent of the new collection.

Notice that these suggestions are not directive but, rather, they serve as starters. Even here, the choice of a hint is best made after listening carefully to what the student has been trying or thinking. After offering a hint, walk away. Don't hover or the student is apt to seek further direction.

4. Provide Worthwhile Extensions. Some students will always finish earlier than their classmates. Early finishers can often be challenged in some manner connected to the problem just solved without it seeming like extra work. (See Chapter 6 for discussion of strategies for students who are talented and gifted.) Ongoing extended projects should be used as another part of your mathematics program. Sometimes students finishing early can use this time to work on their mathematics projects.

Many good problems are simple on the surface. It is the extensions that are challenging. The area and perimeter

task in this chapter is a case in point. Many students will quickly come up with one or two solutions. "I see you found one way to do this. Are there any other solutions? Are any of the solutions different or more interesting than others? Which of the shapes with a perimeter of 18 has the largest area and which has the smallest area? Does the perimeter always change when you add another tile?"

Questions that begin "What if . . . ?" or "Would that same idea work for . . . ?" are ways to extend student thinking in a motivating way. For example, "Suppose you tried to find all the shapes possible with a perimeter of 18. What could you find out about the areas?"

The value of students' solving a problem in more than one way cannot be overestimated. It shifts the value system in the classroom from answers to processes and thinking. It is a good way for students to make new and different connections.

As an example, consider the following sixth-grade problem.

Concept: Percent Increase and Decrease
Grades: 6–8

The dress was originally priced at $90. If the sale price is 25 percent off, how much will it cost on sale?

This is an example of a straightforward problem with a single answer. Many students will solve it by multiplying by 0.25 and subtracting the result from $90. The suggestion to find another way may be all that is necessary. Others may require specific directions: "How would you solve it using fractions instead of decimals?" "Draw me a diagram that explains what you did." "How could this be done in just one step?" "Think of a way that you could do this mentally."

Second graders will frequently solve the next problem by counting or using addition.

Concept: Addition and Subtraction
Grades: K–2

Maxine had saved up $9. The next day she received her allowance. Now she has $12. How much allowance did she get?

"How would you do that on a calculator?" and "Can you write two equations that represent this situation?" are ways of encouraging children to connect $9 + ? = 12$ with $12 - 9 = ?$.

The *After* Phase of a Lesson

In the *after* phase of the lesson, your students will work as a community of learners, discussing, justifying, and challenging various solutions to the problem all have just worked on. Here is where much of the learning will occur as students reflect individually and collectively on the ideas they have explored. It is challenging but critical to plan sufficient time for a discussion and make sure the *during* portion does not go on too long. The agendas for the *after* phase are easily stated but difficult to achieve:

1. *Promote a mathematical community of learners.* Includes all learners. Engage the class in productive discussion, helping students work together as a community of learners.

2. *Listen actively without evaluation.* Take this second major opportunity to find out how students are thinking—how they are approaching the problem. Evaluating methods and solutions is the duty of your students.

3. *Summarize main ideas and identify future problems to explore.* You can lay the groundwork for future activities as a natural part of this phase.

Teacher Actions in the *After* Phase

Be certain to plan ample time for this portion of the lesson and then be certain to *save* the time. Twenty minutes or more is not at all unreasonable for a good class discussion and sharing of ideas. It is not necessary for every student to have finished. This is not a time to check answers but for the class to share ideas.

Over time, you will develop your class into a mathematical community of learners where students feel comfortable taking risks and sharing ideas, where students and the teacher respect one another's ideas even when they disagree, where ideas are defended and challenged respectfully, and where logical or mathematical reasoning is valued above all. This atmosphere will not develop easily or quickly. You must teach your students about your expectations for this time and how to interact respectfully with their peers.

1. Promote a Mathematical Community of Learners That Includes All Children.

NCTM in its *Standards* documents is very clear in expressing the belief that all children can learn important mathematics. This view is supported by a number of prominent mathematics educators who have worked extensively with at-risk populations (Campbell, 1996; Gutstein, Lipman, Hernandez, & Reyes, 1997; Silver & Stein, 1996; Trafton & Claus, 1994).

Because the needs and abilities of children are different, conducting a large group discussion that is balanced and that includes all children requires skill and practice. Rowan and Bourne (1994) offer excellent suggestions based on their work in an urban, multiethnic, low-socioeconomic school district. They emphasize that the most important factor is to be clear about the purpose of group discussion—that is, to share and explore the variety of strategies, ideas, and solutions generated by the class and to learn to communicate these ideas in a rich mathematical discourse. Every class has a handful of students who are always ready to respond. Other children learn to be passive or do not participate. So, step one is to be sure the discussion involves all students.

Considerable research into how mathematical communities develop and operate provides us with additional insight for developing effective classroom discourse (e.g., Rasmussen, Yackel, & King, 2003; Stephan & Whitenack, 2003; Wood, Williams, & McNeal, 2006; Yackel & Cobb, 1996). Suggestions from this research include the following:

- Encourage student–student dialogue rather than student–teacher conversations that exclude the class. "Juanita, can you answer Lora's question?" "Devon, can you explain that so that LaToya and José can understand what you are saying?" When students have differing solutions, have students work these ideas out as a class. "George, I noticed that you got a different answer than Tomeka. What do you think about her explanation?"
- Request explanations to accompany *all* answers. Soon the request for an explanation will not signal an incorrect response, as children will initially believe. Correct answers may not represent the conceptual thinking you assumed. Incorrect answers may only be the result of an easily corrected error. By requiring explanations, students learn that reasoning in mathematics is important and useful.
- Call on students for their ideas, often calling first on the children who tend to be shy or lack the ability to express themselves well. When asked to participate early and given sufficient time to formulate their thoughts, these reticent children can more easily participate and thus be valued. Asking "Who wants to explain their solution?" will result in the same three or four eager students raising their hands. Other students tend to accept that these students are generally correct and may be reluctant to offer ideas that are different from the well-known leaders. Use the *during* portion of a lesson to walk around the room and identify interesting solutions that will add to your discussion—including those that are incorrect. All students should be prepared to share as part of their everyday expectations.
- Encourage students to ask questions. "Pete, did you understand how they did that? Do you want to ask Antonio a question?"
- Be certain that your students also understand what you understand. Your knowledge of the topic may cause you to accept a less than clear explanation because you hear what the student means to say. Select important points in a student's explanation and express your own "confusion." "Carlos, I don't quite get why you subtracted 9 here in this step. Can you tell us why you did that?" Demonstrate to students that it is okay to be confused and that asking clarifying questions is appropriate. One teaching goal is for students to ask these questions without your input.

• Occasionally ask those who understand to offer explanations for others. "Thandie, perhaps you can explain this idea in your own words so that some of the rest of us can understand better." Don't assume that a student who says he or she understands really does.

• Move students to more conceptually based explanations when appropriate. For example, if a student says that he knows 4.17 is more than 4.1638, you can ask him (or another student) to explain why this is so. Another technique is to use a "fooler." With pretend confusion, ask, "How can this be? It seems like the longer decimal ought to be a larger number." Similarly, move students away from simply listing steps in their solutions. "I see *what* you did but I think some of us are confused about *why* you did it that way and why you think that will give us the correct solution."

2. Listen Actively Without Evaluation.

By being a facilitator and not an evaluator, students will be more willing to share their ideas during discussions. This is your window into their thinking and therefore an assessment of their learning. Listen carefully to the discussion without too much interference. You can use this information to plan for tomorrow's lesson and in general to decide on the direction you wish to take in your current unit.

Try to take a neutral position with respect to *all* responses. Resist the temptation to judge the correctness of an answer. You can ask questions to help clarify a response—both right and wrong. When you say, "That's correct, Dewain," there is no longer a reason for students to evaluate the response. Had students disagreed with Dewain's response or had a question about it, they will not challenge or question it since you've said it was correct. Consequently, you will not have the chance to hear and learn from them. You can support student thinking without evaluation. "Does someone have a different idea or want to comment on what Dewain just said?"

Use praise cautiously. Praise offered for correct solutions or excitement over interesting ideas suggests that the students did something unusual or unexpected. This can be negative feedback for those who do not get praise. Comments such as "Good job!" and "Super work!" roll off the tongue easily. However, there is evidence to suggest that we should be careful with expressions of praise, especially with respect to student products and solutions (Kohn, 1993; Schwartz, 1996).

In place of praise that is judgmental, Schwartz (1996) suggests comments of interest and extension: "I wonder what would happen if you tried . . ." or "Please tell me how you figured that out." Notice that these phrases express interest and value the student's thinking.

There will be times when a student will get stuck in the middle of an explanation or when a response is simply not forthcoming. Be sensitive about calling on someone else to "help out." You may be communicating that the child is not capable on his or her own. Always allow ample time. You can sometimes suggest taking additional time to get thoughts together and promise to return to the student later—and then be certain to hear what the student figured out.

3. Summarize Main Ideas and Identify Future Problems.

A wide variety of approaches can be used to summarize ideas. A whole class discussion can bring to light main ideas in students' words. There are numerous ways to share verbally, such as a partner exchange, where one partner tells one key idea and the other partner gives an example. Following oral summaries with individual written summaries is important to ensure that you know what each child has learned from the lesson. Exit slips, for example, are handouts with one or two prompts that ask students to explain the main ideas of the lesson (or ask for pictures from younger students). These are handed in as an "exit" from the math lesson. Or ask students to write a newspaper headline to describe the day's activity and a brief column to describe it. There are many different templates and writing starters that could be engaging for your students.

When ideas have been well developed, reinforce appropriate terminology, definitions, or symbols. Vocabulary should come after ideas have been established, not before. If a problem involves creating a procedure such as a method of computing, a strategy for basic facts, or a formula in measurement, record useful methods on the board. These can be labeled with the student's name and an example. These strategies are then available in future lessons for students to try.

Often someone will make a generalization or an observation that he or she strongly believes in but cannot completely justify. Untested ideas can be written up on the board, named after the student with the conjecture—for example, "Andrea's Hypothesis." Explain the meaning of *hypothesis* as an idea that may or may not be true. Testing the hypothesis may become a future problem, or the hypothesis may simply be kept on the board until additional evidence comes up that either supports or disproves it. For example, when comparing fractions, suppose that a group makes this generalization and you write it on the board: *When deciding which fraction is larger, the fraction in which the bottom number is closer to the top number is the larger fraction. Example: $\frac{4}{7}$ is not as big as $\frac{7}{8}$ because 7 is only 1 from 8 but 4 is 3 away from 7.* This is not an unusual conclusion, but it is not correct in all instances. A problem for a subsequent day would be to decide if the hypothesis is always right or to find fractions for which it is not right (counterexamples).

Even when students have not suggested hypotheses, discussions will often turn up interesting questions that can be used for a follow-up investigation to help further develop an emerging concept.

Frequently Asked Questions

The following are questions teachers have asked about implementing a teaching through problem solving approach to instruction.

1. *How can I teach all the basic skills I have to teach?* It is tempting, especially with pressures of state testing programs, to resort to rote drill and practice to teach "basic skills." Some people believe that mastery of the basics is incompatible with a problem-based approach. However, the evidence strongly suggests otherwise. In fact, drill-oriented approaches in U.S. classrooms have consistently produced poor results (Battista, 1999; Kamii & Dominick, 1998; O'Brien, 1999). Short-term gains on low-level skills may possibly result from drill, but even state testing programs require more than low-level skills.

Second, research data indicate that students in programs based on a problem-based approach do as well or better than students in traditional programs on basic skills as measured by standardized tests (Campbell, 1995; Carpenter, Franke, Jacobs, Fennema, & Empson, 1998; Hiebert, 2003; Hiebert & Wearne, 1996; Riordan & Noyce, 2001; Silver & Stein, 1996). Any deficit in skill development is more than outweighed by strength in concepts and problem solving.

Finally, traditional skills such as basic fact mastery and computation can be effectively taught in a problem-solving approach (for example, see Campbell, Rowan, & Suarez, 1998; Huinker, 1998).

2. *Why is it often better for students to "tell" or "explain" than for me?* First, students' explanations are grounded in their own understanding. Second, as students communicate their mathematical ideas in words, they are solidifying their own understanding. Third, there are implications for creating a community of learners. Students will question their peers when an explanation does not make sense to them, whereas explanations from the teacher are usually accepted without scrutiny (and possibly without understanding). Finally, when students are responsible for explaining, the class members develop a sense of pride and confidence that *they* can figure things out and make sense of mathematics. *They* have power and ability.

3. *Is it okay to help students who have difficulty solving a problem?* Of course, you will want to help students who are struggling. However, as Buschman (2003b) suggests, rather than propose how to solve a problem, a better approach is to try to find out *why* the student is having difficulty. If you jump in with help, you may not even be addressing the real reason the student is struggling. It may be as simple as not understanding the problem or as complex as a lack of understanding of a fundamental concept. "Tell me what you are thinking" is a good beginning.

Recall our previous discussion of the negative consequences of these two simple sentences: *It's easy! Let me help you.* Rather, try to build on the student's knowledge. Do not rob students of the feeling of accomplishment and the true growth in understanding that come from solving a problem themselves.

4. *Where can I find the time to cover everything?* Mathematics is much more connected and integrated than a look at the itemized objectives found on many state "standards" lists might suggest. To deal with coverage, the first suggestion is to teach with a goal of developing the "big ideas," the main concepts in a unit or chapter. Most of the skills and ideas on your list of objectives will be addressed as you progress. If you focus separately on each item on the list, then big ideas and connections, the essence of understanding, are unlikely to develop. Second, we spend far too much time reteaching because students don't retain ideas. Time spent up front to help students develop meaningful networks of ideas drastically reduces the need for reteaching and remediation, thus creating time in the long term.

5. *How much time does it take for students to become a community of learners and really begin to share and discuss ideas?* It generally takes more time than we anticipate, and discussions may seem strained or nonproductive at first. Students have to be coached in how to participate in a classroom discussion about a problem and how to work collaboratively in small groups. For the first weeks of school, time must be devoted to explicitly teaching and modeling these skills. Frequent reinforcement of participation and listening is needed initially; then the support becomes less necessary as the community is established. Students in the primary grades will adapt much more quickly than students in the upper grades, as they have not yet developed an expectation that mathematics class is about sitting quietly and following the rules. You might expect it to take as long as 6 weeks before students begin to assume responsibility for making sense of mathematics. Probing and asking good questions and developing a community of learners requires a long-term commitment. Don't give up!

6. *Can I use a combination of student-oriented problem-based teaching with a teacher-directed approach?* Switching instructional approaches is not recommended. By switching methods, students become confused as to what is expected of them. More importantly, students will come to believe that their own ideas do not really matter because the teacher will eventually tell them the "right" way to do it (Mokros, Russell, & Economopoulos, 1995). In order for students to become invested in a problem-based approach they must deeply believe that their ideas are important and that the source of knowledge is themselves—every day.

7. *Is there any place for drill and practice?* Absolutely! The error is to believe that drill is a method of developing or reinforcing concepts. Drill is only appropriate when (a) the desired concepts have been meaningfully developed,

(b) flexible and useful procedures have been developed, *and* (c) speed and accuracy are needed. With drill and practice, the important thing to remember is a little goes a long way. Drilling on basic facts should take no more than 10 minutes in one sitting. Five multiplication problems can be as sufficient in assessing student understanding of the procedure as 25 problems; therefore, not much is gained from the additional 20 problems. Also, when students are making mistakes, more drill and practice is not the solution—identifying and addressing misconceptions is far more effective. For example, some middle school students still do not know their multiplication facts. Drilling on the 144 facts won't help nearly as much as working on strategies for the targeted facts a student is forgetting (e.g., helping facts). (See Chapter 10 for many more strategies for basic facts.)

8. *What do I do when a problem-based lesson bombs?* It will happen, although not as often as you think, that students just do not know what to do with a problem you pose, no matter how many hints and suggestions you offer. Do not give in to the temptation to "tell them." Set it aside for the moment. Ask yourself why it didn't work well. Did the students have the prior knowledge they needed? Was the task too advanced? Often we need to regroup and offer students a simpler related task that gets them prepared for the one that proved too difficult. When you sense that a task is not going anywhere, regroup! Don't spend days just hoping that something wonderful might happen. If you listen to your students, you will get ideas on where to go next.

Reflections on Chapter 3

Writing to Learn

1. Which of the benefits of teaching with problems resonates the most with you? Why?
2. Describe what is meant by tasks or problems that can be used for teaching mathematics. Be sure to include the three important features that are required to make this method effective.
3. Polya's four-step process maps to a *before, during, after* lesson plan model. What questions might you ask students to support their thinking in each of the four steps?
4. Discuss the benefits of using children's literature in teaching mathematics.
5. What are some of the benefits of having students write in mathematics class? When should the writing take place? How can very young students "write"?
6. Describe in your own words what is meant by a "mathematical community of learners."
7. What is the teacher's purpose or agenda in each of the three parts of a lesson—before, during, and after?

8. Describe the kinds of actions a teacher should be doing in each of the three parts of a lesson. (Note that not all of these would be done in every lesson.) Which actions should you use almost all of the time?
9. "It's easy! Let me help you." Not a good idea? What is a better way of helping a student who is having difficulty solving a problem?

For Discussion and Exploration

1. Select an activity from any chapter in Section 2 of this text. How can the activity be used as a problem or task for the purpose of instruction as described in this chapter? If you were using this activity in the classroom, what specifically would you do during the *before* section of the lesson?
2. Find a traditional textbook for any grade level. Look through a chapter and find at least one lesson that you could convert to a problem-based lesson without drastically altering the lesson as it was written.

Resources for Chapter 3

Recommended Readings

Articles

Buschman, L. E. (2005). Isn't that interesting! *Teaching Children Mathematics, 12*(1), 34–40.
Buschman uses the prompt that is the title of this article to get his students to articulate their mathematics processes. In this article he shares several rich tasks and the different ways students approach the problems. The tasks themselves are worthy of a look, and the

discussion of what he learned by asking for elaboration highlights the fact that as teachers, we can jump to incorrect conclusions if we don't listen carefully.
Hartweg, K., & Heisler, M. (2007). No tears here! Third-grade problem solvers. *Teaching Children Mathematics, 13*(7), 362–368.
This article is a great complement to this chapter. The authors elaborate on how they have implemented the before, during, and after lesson phases. They offer suggestions for supporting student

understanding of the problem, questioning, and templates for student writing. The data they gathered on the response of teachers and students are also impressive!

Reinhart, S. C. (2000). Never say anything a kid can say! *Mathematics Teaching in the Middle School, 5*(8), 478–483.

The author is an experienced middle school teacher who questioned his own "masterpiece" lessons after realizing that his students were often confused. The article is the result of the realization that he was doing the talking and explaining, and that was causing the confusion. Reinhart's suggestions for questioning techniques and involving students are superb!

Rigelman, N. R. (2007). Fostering mathematical thinking and problem solving: The teacher's role. *Teaching Children Mathematics, 13*(6), 308–314.

This is a wonderful article for illustrating the subtle (and not so subtle) differences between true problem solving and "proceduralizing" problem solving—in other words, showing students how to solve problems. Because two contrasting vignettes are offered, it gives an excellent opportunity for discussing how the two teachers differ philosophically and in their practices.

Books

Boaler, J., & Humphreys, C. (2005). *Connecting mathematical ideas: Middle school video cases to support teaching and learning.* Portsmouth, NH: Heinemann.

Cathy Humphreys teaches seventh grade. Jo Boaler is a respected researcher who is interested in the impact of different teaching approaches. This book offers cases from Cathy's classroom based on different content areas and issues in teaching. Each case is followed by Jo's commentary and expert perspective. Accompanying the book are two CDs that provide videos of the cases.

Buschman, L. (2003). *Share and compare: A teacher's story about helping children become problem solvers in mathematics.* Reston, VA: NCTM.

Larry Buschman is an experienced elementary teacher who has taught with a problem-based approach for many years. In this book he describes in detail how he makes this work in his classroom. Much of the book is written as if a teacher were interviewing Larry as he answers the kinds of questions you will undoubtedly have as you begin to teach.

Hiebert, J., Carpenter, T. P., Fennema, E., Fuson, K., Wearne, D., Murray, H., Olivier, A., & Human, P. (1997). *Making sense: Teaching and learning mathematics with understanding.* Portsmouth, NH: Heinemann.

The authors of this significant book are each connected to one of four problem-based, long-term research projects. They make one of the best cases currently in print for developing mathematics through problem solving.

Lester, F. K., & Charles, R. I. (Eds.). (2003). *Teaching mathematics through problem solving: Pre-K to 6.* Reston, VA: NCTM.

This is an important and valuable publication from NCTM. The 17 chapters, all written by top authors in the field, provide an in-depth examination of using a problem-based approach to teaching for understanding.

Sakshaug, L. E., Olson, M., & Olson, J. (2002). *Children are mathematical problem solvers.* Reston, VA: NCTM.

This excellent problem-solving collection includes 29 tasks that appeared in Teaching Children Mathematics' *Problem Solvers column. Each task is followed by student solutions, the problem, and a reflection on what these students are telling us.*

Online Resources

Annenberg/CPB
www.learner.org/index.html

A unit of the Annenberg Foundation, Annenberg/CPB offers professional development information and useful information for teachers who want to learn about and teach mathematics.

MathSolutions Lessons from the Classroom
www.mathsolutions.com/index.cfm?page=wp9&crid=56

This is a great collection of lessons for teaching through problem solving.

ENC Online (Eisenhower National Clearinghouse)
www.goenc.com

Click on Digital Dozen, Lessons and Activities, or Web Links. The ENC site is full of useful information for teachers who are planning lessons and activities or searching for professional development resources

Writing and Communication in Mathematics
http://mathforum.org/library/ed_topics/writing_in_math

This Math Forum page lists numerous articles and Web links concerning the value of writing in mathematics at all levels.

Field Experience Guide Connections

Just as problem solving will be found throughout this book, it is found throughout the *Field Experience Guide.* The task selection guide (Figure 3.2 on p. 39) is adapted to a field-based activity in FEG 2.3 and 2.4. FEG 2.5 provides a template for planning a problem-based lesson and FEG 4.7 provides a process for teaching a standards-based lesson. FEG 2.6 focuses on using children's literature as a context for doing meaningful, worthwhile mathematics. Chapter 9 of the guide offers 24 Expanded Lessons, all designed using the *before, during,* and *after* model. Chapter 10 using the guide offers worthwhile tasks that can be developed into problem-based lessons.

Chapter 4

Planning in the Problem-Based Classroom

Natural learning . . . doesn't happen on a time schedule and often requires more time than schools are organized to provide. Problem-solving experiences take time. It's essential that teachers provide the time that's needed for children to work through activities on their own and that teachers not slip into teaching-by-telling for the sake of efficiency.

Burns (1992, p. 30)

The three-phase lesson format described in Chapter 3 provided a basic structure for problem-based lessons, based on the need for students to be engaged in problems followed by time for discussion and reflection. However, to successfully implement this instructional model, it is necessary to consider a range of pragmatic issues.

This chapter begins with a step-by-step guide for planning problem-based lessons. Also explored here are some variations of the three-phase structure, tips for supporting diverse learners, issues related to drill and practice, homework recommendations, and effective use of textbooks. In short, this chapter discusses the "nuts and bolts" of planning a problem-based mathematics lesson.

Planning a Problem-Based Lesson

Regardless of your experience, it is crucial that you give substantial thought to the planning of your lessons. There is no such thing as a "teacher-proof" curriculum—where you can simply teach every lesson as it is planned and in the order it appears. Every class of students is different. Choices of which tasks to use and how they are presented to students must be made daily to best fit the needs of your diverse students and the state and local curriculum objectives you are hired to teach.

Planning Process for Developing a Lesson

Planning lessons is usually couched within the planning of an instructional unit, each lesson building from the prior lesson to accomplish the unit goals and objectives. This book does not address unit development but instead focuses on how to develop a problem-based lesson within a unit. Figure 4.1 provides an outline of the considerations involved in planning a lesson. Content and task decisions (the first column) are often overlooked when lessons are planned without considering the content expectations and the needs of students—yet this is the most important part of the planning process. Once these decisions are made, the lesson is ready to be designed (see purple-shaded steps in Figure 4.1). Here the focus is on designing activities for students that accomplish the goals outlined in Chapter 3 for the three lesson phases (*before*, *during*, and *after*). It is through these three phases that the content goals are accomplished. Once the plan is drafted, it is important to review and finalize the plan, taking into consideration the flow of the lesson, the anticipated challenges, expected responses from students, and the questions or prompts that can best support the learner. Each of the considerations in planning a problem-based lesson is briefly discussed in this section. Within the considerations, an example lesson titled Fixed Area is discussed, as an illustration of how the process is implemented (this lesson plan is also found at the end of the chapter). The *Field Experience Guide* also offers a template that can provide support for completing a lesson plan.

Step 1: Determine the Mathematics and Learning Goals. How do you decide what mathematics your students need to learn?

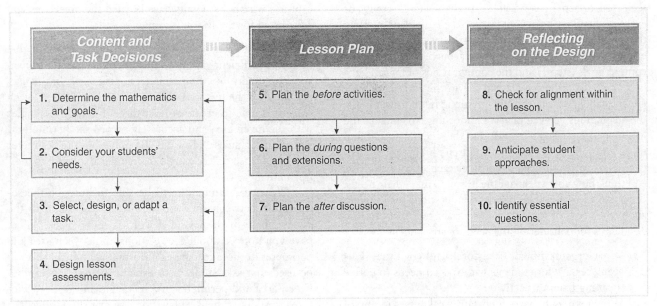

Figure 4.1 Planning steps for a problem-based lesson.

Prior to planning this lesson, either you or a group in your district identified the mathematics goals for the year and you have identified the important mathematics to emphasize in the current unit. (*Field Experience Guide* Task 2.1 offers a template for interviewing a teacher related to selecting goals and objectives.) At the lesson level, it is important to look at both your state standards and your local curriculum guide for your grade level and ask yourself, "What is it that my students should be able to do when this lesson is over?" Keep in mind that a lesson can take several days to accomplish. As you respond to this question, be sure you are focused on the mathematics and not the activity you want to do.

Example: Fixed Areas. In looking at the district expectations for measurement, you see perimeter and area (grade 5). A possible goal for one unit lesson on this topic is for students to explore the relationship between area and perimeter, specifically that one can change while the other stays the same.

This goal leads to the development of *observable* and *measurable* objectives. The objectives are the very things you want to see your students *do* or *say* to demonstrate what they know. There are numerous formats for lesson objectives, but there is consensus that an objective must state clearly what the student will do.

Example: Fixed Areas. Students will be able to draw a sufficient variety of possible rectangles for a given area and determine the perimeters. Students will be able to describe the relationship between area and perimeter. Students will describe a process (their own algorithm) for finding perimeter of a rectangle.

Non-Example: Fixed Areas. Students will understand that the perimeter can change and the area can stay the same.

Note that the "example" objectives are actions you can *see* or *hear*. The "non-example," although a reasonable goal to guide your planning, is not an objective because understanding is not observable or measurable.

Step 2: Consider Your Students' Needs. What do your students already know or understand about the selected mathematics concepts? Are they ready to tackle this bit of mathematics or are there some background ideas that they have not yet developed? Perhaps they already have some knowledge of the content you have been working on, which this lesson is aimed at expanding or refining. Be sure that the mathematics you identified in step 1 includes something new or at least slightly unfamiliar to your students. At the same time, be certain that your objectives are not out of reach.

Consider the individual needs of each student, including learning disabilities, learning styles, and each person's strengths and weaknesses. In addition, language and culture must be a consideration. What might students already know about this topic that can serve as a launching point? What context might be engaging to the range of learners in the classroom? What learning gaps or misconceptions might need to be addressed? What visuals or models might support student understanding? What vocabulary support might be needed?

Example: Fixed Areas. Students are likely to have prior knowledge of the terms *perimeter* and *area*. However, they may also confuse the meaning of the two. They may have a misconception that for a given area, there is only one perimeter, or vice versa.

Step 3: Select, Design, or Adapt a Task. With your goals and students in mind, you are ready to consider what focus task or activity you will use, perhaps a task, activity, or exercises that may be in your textbook. At this planning step, the question to ask yourself is "Does the task you are considering (from the textbook or any other source) accomplish the content goals (step 1) and the content needs of my students (step 2)?" (Experiences 2.3 and 2.4 in the *Field Experience Guide* can help you address this question.) If the answer is yes, the adaptations you can plan are minor ways to enhance the lesson, perhaps using a context that the students would find more engaging or including a children's literature connection. Next, you will need to consider each of your students and think how you will adapt the lesson to meet their needs. Karp and Howell (2004) offer three questions for thinking about the needs of students with special needs that can be a good basis for considering the needs of any student:

1. What organizational, behavioral, and cognitive skills are necessary for students with special needs to derive meaning from this activity?
2. Which students have important weaknesses in any of these skills?
3. How can I provide support in these areas of weakness so that students with special needs can focus on the conceptual task at hand?

If you look at the given lesson tasks and find that they do not fit your content and student needs, then you will need to either make substantial modifications to the lesson or find a substitute.

Good tasks need not be elaborate. Often a simple story problem is all that is necessary as long as the solution involves children in the intended mathematics.

Chapter 3 gave examples of tasks and suggestions for creating or selecting them. This book is full of tasks. The more experience you have with the content in planning step 1 and the longer you have had to build a repertoire of tasks from journals, resource books, conferences, and professional development, the easier this important step in planning will become.

Step 4: Design Lesson Assessments. You might wonder why you are thinking about assessment before you have even introduced the lesson, but thinking about what it is you want students to know and how they are going to show that to you *is* assessment. The sentence you just read may give you a déjà-vu experience related to the section on objectives—and so it should. Your assessments are derived from your objectives. It is important to assess in a variety of ways—see Chapter 5 for extended discussions of assessment strategies. Formative assessment is the type of information gathering that lets you know how students are doing on each of the objectives during the lesson. This information can be used for adjusting the lesson midstream or making changes for the next day. Formative assessment also informs the questions you pose in the discussion of the task for the *after* phase of the lesson. Summative assessment

captures whether students have learned the objectives you have listed for the lesson (or unit).

Example: Fixed Areas. *Objective 1:* Students will be able to draw a sufficient variety of possible rectangles for a given area and determine the perimeters. *Assessment:* In the *during* phase of the lesson, I will use a checklist to see if each student is able to create at least three different rectangles with the given area and accurately record the perimeter. I will ask individuals, "How did you figure out the perimeter of that (point at one rectangle) rectangle? Explain it to me." [formative]

Objective 2: Students will be able to describe the relationship between area and perimeter. *Assessment:* In the *during* phase of the lesson, I will ask individuals, "What have you noticed about the relationship between area and perimeter of these rectangles?" [formative] An exit slip will be used that asks students to explain the relationship between area and perimeter of a rectangle and to draw pictures to support their explanation. An exit slip is a written response turned in at the end of class—as an "exit" to the lesson. [summative]

Objective 3: Students will describe a process (their own algorithm) for finding perimeter of a rectangle. *Assessment:* In the *during* phase of the lesson, I will ask, "How are you finding perimeter? Are you seeing any patterns or shortcuts? Explain it to me." [formative] In the *after* phase, this will be the focus of a discussion. [formative]

Steps 1 through 4 define the heart of your lesson. The next three steps explain how you will carry the plan out in your classroom.

Step 5: Plan the *Before* Phase of the Lesson. As discussed in Chapter 3 in the section titled "Teacher Actions in the *Before* Phase," the beginning of the lesson should elicit students' prior knowledge, provide context, and establish expectations. You need to think about the task you have selected and how you will introduce it. What terminology and background might students need to be ready for the task? Will you read a children's book that connects to the task and builds interest for students? Is there a current or popular event that could be used to introduce the topic? Sometimes you can simply begin with the task and articulation of students' responsibilities. But, in many instances, you will want to prepare students by posing a related task or some related warm-up exercise that builds background and elicits prior knowledge.

Consider how you will present the task. Options include having it written on paper, taken from their texts, shown on the overhead, or written on the board or on chart paper. Be sure to tell students about their responsibilities. For nearly every task, you want students to be able to tell you

- What they did to get the answer
- Why they did it that way
- Why they think the solution is correct or reasonable

Decide how you want students to supply this information. If responding in writing, will students write individually or prepare a group presentation? Will they write in their journals, on paper to be turned in, on a worksheet, on chart paper to present to the class, or on acetate to use on the overhead? Will they prepare a PowerPoint presentation?

Estimate how much time you think students should be given for the task. It is useful to tell students in advance. Some teachers set a timer that all students can see. Plan to be somewhat flexible, but do not give up your time for discussion at the end of the lesson.

Example: Fixed Areas. Building off of fifth graders' interest in *High School Musical*, the lesson context will be building a stage that has an area of 36 square meters. Students will explain what the perimeter and area of the stage floor are, and the teacher will draw and label this on the board. A focus question to raise curiosity is: Does it matter what the length and width are for the stage floor? Would one shape of rectangle be better or worse than another? Let's see what the possibilities are and then pick one that will best serve the actors and dancers.

Step 6: Plan the *During* Phase of the Lesson.

While it may seem that this phase is when the students are working independently, this is a critical time for teaching. The teacher's role is to monitor and assess student progress and to provide hints as necessary. For example, you might make one quick visit to each group to verify that each understands the task and is engaged in solving the problem.

What hints or assists can you plan in advance for students who may be stuck or who may need accommodations? Are there particular groups or individual students you wish to specially observe or assess during this lesson? Make a note to do so. Think of extensions or challenges you can pose to students who are gifted or others who finish early.

After the initial round to see that each group has started, the next rounds are your opportunity to learn what your students know and can do (see planning steps 1 and 4). Students should become accustomed to the fact that in the *during* phase of the lesson you will be asking them to explain what they are thinking and doing. This phase is also a time for you to see which groups or individuals should be sharing their work in the *after* phase of the lesson.

Example: Fixed Areas. After distributing 36 tiles to each pair of students, make one trip around the room to see that students are actually building a rectangle, recording its dimensions on the grid sheet accurately, and labeling each side. After confirming that all students have completed this for the first rectangle, make more trips around asking the assessment questions. The goal is to get each student to explain how he or she found the perimeter of the rectangles and what patterns he or she is noticing, but if you can't get to everyone, target those that you missed in the next lesson.

Step 7: Plan the *After* Phase of the Lesson.

How will you begin your discussion? One option is to simply list all of the different answers from groups or individuals, doing so without comment, and then returning to students or groups to explain their solutions and justify their answers. You may also begin with full explanations from each group or student before you get all the answers. If you accept oral reports, think about how you will record on the board what is being said.

Plan an adequate amount of time for your discussion. Five minutes is almost never sufficient. A rich problem can take 15 to 20 minutes to discuss.

Example: Fixed Areas. First, get all the possibilities of the rectangles with a given area posted, so have an overhead copy of grid paper and ask each group to report one that they found. Quickly sketch and label the dimensions of each one. Second, ask different groups to report on the perimeter and area of each one and go back and add this information. This visual will stay posted for the focus discussion:

- How did you find the perimeters of these rectangles? (Collect different ideas—look for shortcuts and note those responses in words and symbols on the board.)
- What do you notice about the relationship between area and perimeter? (Students should notice that there are a number of possible perimeters for a given area and that the perimeter is less when the shape is more "square.")
- If you were the stage architect for *High School Musical*, which of the rectangles would you pick and why?

After the discussion, distribute the exit slip titled "Advice to the Architect" that asks students to explain the second question above to the architect, using illustrations to support the explanation.

Steps 5, 6, and 7 have resulted in a tentative instructional plan. The next three steps are designed to review this tentative plan in light of some critical considerations, making changes or additions as needed.

Step 8: Check for Alignment Within the Lesson.

A well-prepared lesson that maximizes the opportunity for students to learn must be focused and aligned. There is often a temptation to do a series of "fun" activities that seem to relate to a topic but that are intended for slightly different learning goals. First, look to see that three parts of the plan are clearly aligned, sometimes nearly identical: the objectives, the assessment, and the questions asked in the *during* and *after* phases. If the questions are all focused on only one objective, add questions to address each objective or remove the objective that is not addressed.

Second, the lesson should have a reasonable flow to it, building in sophistication. The *before* activity should be related to the focus task in the *during* phase but will likely be less involved. The *after* phase should take students from looking at the task itself to generalizing ideas about mathematics concepts. If you feel like you are doing one activity, then switching to another, and you don't know how to pull it together in the end, it may be that the lesson is not aligned. Look back to the objectives and make sure all activities support these objectives and build in critical thinking and challenges.

Example: Fixed Areas. The area lesson demonstrates alignment. The objectives were used to write the assessments and the assessment questions were written to match the phases of the lesson. The lesson starts with an example to get students thinking about the use of area and perimeter, builds on this foundation by having them create as many rectangles with an area of 36 as they can, and then engages them in a discussion by focusing on generalized ideas of the relationship between area and perimeter and ways to find perimeter.

Step 9: Anticipate Student Approaches. In reflecting on the task that is chosen, it is important to consider what strategies students might use and how you might respond. What misconceptions might students have? What common barriers might need to be addressed? Which of these do you want to address prior to the activity starting and which ones do you want to see emerge from their work?

Example: Fixed Areas. Students are likely to debate about whether the 6 by 6 square should be one of their rectangles. This will not be addressed up front, as a conversation around whether a square is a rectangle is a worthy class discussion. Second, students may initially consider a 4 by 9 rectangle different from a 9 by 4 rectangle. This will be addressed in the *before* as being considered the same for this activity—so that students don't get bogged down in making too many rectangles. Students may confuse the terms *perimeter* and *area*, so in the *before* phase, we will discuss strategies for remembering which is which and students will be encouraged to use these appropriate terms as they work with their partner.

Step 10: Identify Essential Questions. While this might sound redundant after the previous steps, the quality of your questioning in a lesson is so critically important to the potential learning that it is a fitting last step. Using your objectives as the focus, review the lesson to see that in the *before* phase you are posing questions that focus students' attention and raise curiosity about how to solve the problem. In the *during* and *after* phases, you are using questions from the objectives to focus students' thinking on the salient features of the task and what you want them to learn. Research on questioning indicates that teachers rarely ask higher-level questions—this is your chance to review and be sure that you have included some challenging questions that ask students to extend, analyze, compare, generalize, and synthesize. These questions help students more deeply understand the concepts they are studying.

Example: Fixed Areas. Higher-level questions based on the objectives are posed to students in the *during* and *after* phases. Some additional questions to have ready for the discussion or for early finishers or advanced students include the following:

> What if the perimeter was set at 36 meters? Would there be different possible areas?
> Which one might an architect prefer for a dance stage?
> Is a square a rectangle? Explain using what you know of the characteristics of the shapes.

Applying the Planning Process

The importance of using the planning process cannot be overemphasized. Sometimes teachers are pulled to spend more time on grading papers than preparing a lesson for an upcoming concept. This may result in a poor quality lesson that means less is learned. Then the teacher has even more work in trying to remediate students and respond to misconceptions.

A finished lesson plan often has the following components, though the order may vary:

- State and/or local mathematics standards
- Lesson goals and learning objectives
- Assessment(s)
- Accommodations
- Materials needed
- *Before* phase
- *During* phase
- *After* phase

Because the lessons discussed in the next section were developed for an unknown population of students and state standards vary from state to state, the lesson plan design for the Expanded Lessons does not include accommodations or standards.

Examples of Lessons: Expanded Lessons. Attention to the first two planning steps (the mathematics in your curriculum and the particular needs of your students relative to the mathematics) is critical to a successful lesson. Therefore, to plan a lesson without a real class in mind is somewhat artificial. However, a sample lesson, called an Expanded Lesson, is found at the end of this chapter to illustrate the thinking involved.

The Expanded Lesson on area and perimeter has served as an example for each of the planning steps in a problem-based lesson.

It is designed as a full-class lesson for fourth or fifth grade. In addition to this sample lesson, the MyEducationLab (www.myeducationlab.com) website and *Field Experience Guide* have Expanded Lessons that elaborate on activities from each content chapter in Section 2 of this book.

Look for this icon **myeducationlab** indicating that a lesson related to that activity or concept is found on MyEducationLab. At the end of every chapter, you will find Field Experience Guide Connections that connect lessons and activities from the *Field Experience Guide* to chapter coverage.

Variations of the Three-Phase Lesson

The basic lesson structure we have been discussing assumes that a class will be given a task or problem, allowed to work on it, and end with a discussion. Certainly, not every lesson is developed around a task given to a full class. However, the basic concept of tasks and discussions can be adapted to most problem-based lessons.

Minilessons. Many tasks do not require the full class period. The three-part format can be compressed to as little as 10 minutes. You might plan two or three cycles in a single lesson. For example, consider these tasks:

Grades K–1: Make up two questions that we can answer using the information in our graph.

Grades 2–3: If you have forgotten the answer to the addition fact 9 + 5, how might you figure it out in your head?

Grades 4–5: On your geoboard, make a figure that has line symmetry but not rotational symmetry. Make a second figure that has rotational symmetry but not line symmetry.

Grades 6–7: Without finding the common denominator, find a way to determine which of the fractions in the pair is larger. Explain your strategy.

$\frac{1}{8}$ and $\frac{1}{10}$ $\frac{9}{20}$ and $\frac{13}{25}$ $\frac{3}{4}$ and $\frac{3}{8}$ $\frac{9}{10}$ and $\frac{10}{11}$

These are worthwhile tasks but probably would not require a full class period to do and discuss.

An effective strategy for short tasks is *think-pair-share*. Students are first directed to spend a minute developing their own thoughts and ideas on how to approach the task or even what they think may be a solution. Then they pair with a classmate and discuss each other's strategies. This provides an opportunity to test out ideas and to practice articulating them. The last step is to share the idea with the rest of the class. The pair may actually have two ideas or can be told to come to a single decision. The entire process, including some discussion, may take less than 15 minutes.

Stations. It is often useful for students to work at different tasks at various locations around the room. Stations are a good way to manage materials without the need to distribute and collect them. They also help when it is unreasonable or impossible for all students to have access to the required materials for an activity. Because good computer tasks do exist, especially applets found on the Web, one station can be a computer station allowing all students an opportunity to have a turn on the computer. Stations also allow you to differentiate tasks when your students are at different stages in their conceptual understanding.

You may want students to work at stations in small groups or individually. Therefore, for a given topic you might prepare from four to eight different activities. Not every station has to be different. Materials required for the activity or game, including any special recording sheets, are placed in a container or folder to be quickly positioned at different locations in the classroom.

A good idea for younger children or for games and computer activities is to explain or teach the activity to the full class ahead of time in addition to having the instructions at the station. In this way students should not waste time when they get to the station and you will not have to run around the room explaining what to do. Also, you can involve parents or other volunteers.

A good task for a station activity is one that can be profitably repeated several times. For example, students might play a "game" where one student covers part of a known number of counters and the other student names the amount in the covered part. "Fraction Game" in the NCTM Illuminations Lessons (http://illuminations.nctm.org/ActivityDetail.aspx?ID=18) can be played repeatedly, each time strengthening students' understanding of fractions.

A game or other repeatable activity may not seem to incorporate a problem but it can nonetheless be a problem-based task. The determining factor is whether the activity causes students to be reflective about new or developing mathematical relationships. Remember that it is reflective thought that causes growth and therefore learning. If the activity merely has students repeating a procedure without wrestling with an emerging idea, then it is not a problem-based experience. However, the few examples just mentioned and many others do have children thinking through concepts that they have not yet developed well. In this sense, they fit the definition of problem-based tasks.

The time during which students are working at stations is analogous to the *during* portion of a lesson. What kinds of things could you do for the *after* portion of the lesson? Discussions with students who have been working on a task are just as important for games and stations. These discussions might take place in small groups. For example, you might sit down with students at a station and ask about what they have been doing, what strategies they have discovered, or how they have been going about the activity in general. Try to get at the reasoning behind what they are doing. Another possibility is to wait until all in the class have worked each of the stations. Then you can have a full class discussion about the mathematics concepts embedded in the activities.

Just as with any task, some form of recording or writing should be included with stations whenever possible. Students solving a problem on a computer can write up what they did and explain what they learned. Students playing a game can keep records and then tell about how they played the game and what thinking or strategies they used.

Textbooks as Resources

The textbook remains the most significant factor influencing instruction in the elementary and middle school classroom. With exceptions found in occasional lessons, most traditional textbooks remain very close to a "teach by telling" instructional approach. However, standards-based textbooks are very different from traditional texts. The instructional model in standards-based mathematics texts, such as the two featured throughout this book (*Investigations in Number, Data, and Space* and *Connected Mathematics Project II*), align to the *before*, *during*, and *after* lesson phases described in this chapter and Chapter 3. For more on the characteristics of traditional and standards-based textbooks, see Chapter 1.

If you are using a traditional textbook, one way to make it more standards-based is to increase the emphasis of the NCTM process standards within the lesson (problem solving, reasoning and proof, communication, connections, and representations). As you plan for instruction see where you can add in meaningful contexts (to build connections), include opportunities for open-ended questioning (to build in communication), adapt straightforward questions to more complex higher-level thinking questions (to enable problem solving and reasoning to occur), and consider what models or visuals you might employ (to use more representations). Sometimes the problems that appear in the examples section or at the end of the homework section (the story problems) are a good source for making the lesson more problem-based. See Chapter 3 for more on how to adapt a non-problem-based lesson.

Other approaches to using textbooks as sources of ideas are offered here:

- Teach to the big ideas or concepts, not the pages. The chapter or unit viewpoint will help focus on the big ideas rather than the activity required to complete a page.
- Consider the conceptual portions of lessons as ideas or inspirations for planning more problem-based activities. The students do not actually have to do the activities on that page.
- Let the pace of your lessons through a unit be determined by student performance and understanding rather than the artificial norm of a lesson a day.
- Remember that there is no law saying every page must be done or every exercise completed. Select lessons or activities that suit your state standards, your instructional goals, and your students, rather than designing instruction to match the text. Omit pages and activities you believe to be inappropriate and use only what is needed.

Planning for All Learners

Perhaps one of the most important challenges for teachers today is to reach all of the students in their increasingly diverse classrooms. Every teacher faces this dilemma because every classroom contains a range of student abilities and backgrounds.

Interestingly and perhaps surprisingly to some, the problem-based approach to teaching is the best way to teach mathematics and attend to the range of students. In the problem-based classroom, children are making sense of the mathematics in *their* way, bringing to the problems only the skills and ideas that they own. In contrast, in a traditional highly directed lesson, it is often assumed that all students will understand and use the same approach and the same ideas as determined by the textbook or the teacher. Students not ready to understand the ideas presented must focus their attention on following the teacher rules or directions in an instrumental manner (i.e., without a conceptual understanding). This, of course, leads to endless difficulties and leaves many students behind or in need of serious remediation.

In addition to using a problem-based approach, there are specific improvements you can make to help attend to the diversity of learners in your classroom. Chapter 6 is devoted to offering strategies for the diverse range of students you will have in your classroom. In this chapter, the focus is specifically on the planning steps during the development of a problem-based lesson that are essential if you are to do the best you can do for all learners. Specifically, this section briefly discusses:

- Accommodations and modifications
- Differentiated instruction

- Flexible groups
- Example of accommodating a lesson: English language learners

Make Accommodations and Modifications

There are two paths to making a given task accessible to all students: *accommodation* and *modification*. An *accommodation* is a provision of a different environment or circumstance made with particular students in mind. For example, you might write down instructions instead of just saying them orally. Accommodations do not alter the task. A *modification* refers to a change in the problem or task itself. For example, suppose the task begins with finding the area of a compound shape as shown here.

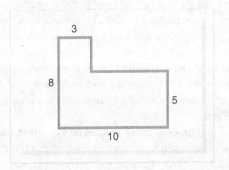

If you decide instead to focus on simple rectangular regions, then that is a modification. However, if you decide to begin with rectangular regions and build to connected compound shapes composed of rectangles, you have *scaffolded* the lesson in a way to ramp up to the original task. Scaffolding a task in this manner is an accommodation. In planning accommodations and modifications the goal is to enable each child to successfully reach your learning objectives, not to change the objectives. This is how equity is achieved in the classroom.

Differentiating Instruction

Differentiating instruction means that a teacher's plan includes strategies to support the range of different academic backgrounds frequently found in classrooms that are academically, culturally, and linguistically heterogeneous (Tomlinson, 1999).

When considering what to differentiate, consider the learning profile of each student, student interest, and student readiness. Second, consider what can be differentiated across three critical elements: content (what do you want each student to be able to do), process (how will you engage them in that learning), and product (what will they have to show for what they have learned when the lesson is over). Third, consider how the physical learning environment

might be adapted. This might include seating arrangement, specific grouping strategies, and access to materials. Some common ways to differentiate include adapting the task to different levels (tiered lessons) and using centers or stations.

Tiered Lessons. In a tiered lesson, the teacher determines the learning goals for all students, but the level of difficulty of the task is adapted up and down to meet the range of learners. Teachers can identify the challenge of each of the defined tiers in a lesson to determine which best meets the learning needs of the students in the classroom (Kingore, 2006; Tomlinson, 1999). The level of difficulty is not just about the *content*, but can be any of the following (Kingore, 2006):

1. *The degree that the teacher provides assistance.* This might include providing examples or partnering students.
2. *How structured the lesson is.* Students with special needs, for example, benefit from highly structured tasks, but gifted students often benefit from a more open-ended structure.
3. *The complexity of the task(s) given.* This can include making a task more concrete or more abstract or including more difficult problems or applications.
4. *The complexity of process.* This includes how quickly paced the lesson is, how many instructions you give at one time, and how many higher-level thinking questions are included as part of the task.

Consider the following task for grades 1–2, focused on concepts of addition:

Original Task

Eduardo had 9 toy cars. Erica came over to play and brought 8 cars. Can you figure out how many cars Eduardo and Erica have together? Explain how you know.

The teacher has distributed cubes to students to model the problem and paper and pencil to illustrate and record how they solved the problem. He asks students to model the problem and be ready to explain their solution.

Adapted Task

Eduardo had some toy cars. Erica came over to play and brought her cars. Can you figure out how many cars Eduardo and Erica have together? Explain how you know.

The teacher asks students what is happening in this problem and what they are going to be doing. Then he distributes Task Cards that tell how many cars Eduardo and Erica have. He has varied how hard the numbers are, giving the students who are struggling numbers less than ten and the more advanced students numbers greater than ten.

Card 1 (easier)

Eduardo has 6 cars and
Erica has 8 cars.

Card 2 (middle)

Eduardo has 13 cars and
Erica has 16 cars.

Card 3 (advanced)

Eduardo has ____ cars and
Erica has ____ cars. Together
they have 25 cars. How many
cars might Eduardo have and
how many might Erica have?

In each case, students must illustrate using words, pictures, models, or numbers on paper how they figured out the solution. Various tools are provided (connecting cubes, sticks, and hundreds chart) for their use.

In this adapted lesson, there are several options for how to organize the use of the Task Cards. First, the teacher can give everyone the cards in order. Second, the teacher can give students only one card, based on their current academic readiness (e.g., easy cards to those that have not

yet mastered addition of single-digit numbers). Third, the teacher can give out cards 1 and 2, based on ability and use card 3 as an extension for those that have successfully completed card 1 or 2. In each of these three cases, the teacher will know at the end of the lesson which students are able to model and explain addition problems and plan the next lesson accordingly.

There are several other ways you can effectively differentiate a task. One way to differentiate a task is to present a situation with related but different questions that can be asked. The situation might be data in a chart or graph, a measurement task, or a geometry task. Here is an example:

Topic: Properties of Parallelograms
Grade: 5–8

Students are given a collection of parallelograms including squares and rectangles as well as nonrectangular parallelograms. The following questions can be posed:

- **Select a shape and draw at least three new shapes that are like it in some way. Tell how your new shapes are both similar to and different from the shape you selected.**
- **Draw diagonals in these shapes and measure them. See what relationships you can discover about the diagonals.**
- **Make a list of all of the properties that you can think of that every parallelogram in this set has.**

In this task there is a challenge to engage nearly every student.

For many problems involving computations, you can insert multiple sets of numbers. In the following problem students are permitted to select the first, second, or third number in each bracket.

Topic: Subtraction
Grades: 2–3

Eduardo had {12, 60, 121} marbles. He gave Erica {5, 15, 46} marbles. How many marbles does Eduardo have now?

Students tend to select the numbers that provide them with the greatest challenge without being too difficult. In the discussions, all children benefit and feel as though they worked on the same task.

❚❚ —————————— *Pause and Reflect*

How might you change the parallelogram task to adjust the level of difficulty, giving consideration to the four levels of difficulty (Kingore, 2006) described earlier?

Flexible Groupings

Allowing students to collaborate on tasks provides support and challenge for students, increasing their chance to communicate about mathematics and build understanding. Collaboration is also an important life skill. "Flexible grouping" means that the size and makeup of small groups vary in a purposeful and strategic manner. In other words, sometimes students are working in partner groups because the nature of the task best suits only two people working together and at other times they are in groups of four because the task has enough tasks or roles to warrant a larger team. Also, groups are selected based on the students' academic abilities, language needs, social dynamics, and behavior. It is often most effective to use mixed-ability (heterogeneous) groups, strategically placing struggling learners with more capable students who are likely to be helpful.

Groups may stay the same for a full unit so that the students become skilled at working with one another. If students are seated with their groups in clusters of four, they can still pair with one person from their group when the task is better suited for only two students.

Regardless of whether groups have two or four members or whether you have grouped by mixed ability or similar ability (homogeneous), the key to successful grouping is *individual accountability*. That means that while the group is working together on a product, each individual must be able to explain the process, the content, and the product. While this concept may sound easy, it is not. Second, and equally challenging, is building a sense of *shared responsibility* within a group. At the start of the year, it is important to do team building activities and to set the standard that all members will participate and that all team members are responsible to make sure all the people in their group understand the process, content, and product.

Good resources for team building activities (though there are many) include *Team Building Activities for Every Group* by Alanna Jones (1999) and *Feeding the Zircon Gorilla and Other Team Building Activities* by Sam Sikes (1995). For a free downloadable collection, Tom Heck has created eight fun activities, all done with shoestrings, in the e-book, *Team Building Games on a Shoestring* (www.teachmeteamwork .com).

To reinforce individual accountability and shared responsibility means a shift in your role as the teacher. When a member of a small group asks you a question, your response is not to answer the question but to inquire to the whole group what they think. Students will soon learn that they must use their teammates as their first resource and seek teacher help only when the whole group needs help. Also, when observing groups, rather than ask Angela what she is doing, you can ask Bernard to explain what Angela is doing. Having all students participate in their oral report to the whole class also builds in individual accountability. Letting students know that you may call on any of their members to explain what they did is a good way to be sure all group members understand what they did. Additionally, having students individually write and record their strategies and solutions is important. The more you use these strategies and others like them, the more effectively will groups function and the more successfully will students learn the concepts.

Avoid ability grouping! Trying to split a class into ability groups is futile; every group will still have diversity. It is demeaning to those students not in the top groups. Students in the lower group will not experience the thinking and language of the top group, and top students will not hear the often unconventional but interesting approaches to tasks in the lower group.

Example of Accommodating a Lesson: ELLs

We have already seen some strategies that promote equity for all students. To be an equitable teacher, you must keep your eye on the mathematical goals for your lessons and at the same time attend to the specific learning needs of each child. Attention to the needs of the English language learner must be considered at each step of the ten-step planning guide detailed in Table 4.1.

In the NCTM Equity Principle, the two phrases "high expectations" and "strong support" are one idea, not two. In the following example, the teacher uses several techniques that provide support for her English language learners while keeping expectations high.

Ms. Steimer is working on a third-grade lesson that involves the concepts of estimating length (in inches) and measuring to the nearest half inch. The task asks students to use estimation to find three objects that are about 6 inches long, three objects that are about 1 foot long, and three objects that are about 2 feet long. Once identified, students are to measure the nine objects to the nearest half inch and compare the measurements with their estimates. Ms. Steimer has a child from Korea who knows only a little English, and she has a child from Mexico who speaks English well but is new to U.S. schools. These two students are not familiar with feet or inches, so they will likely struggle in trying to estimate or measure in inches.

Ms. Steimer takes time to address the language and the increments on the ruler to the entire class. Because the word foot has two meanings, Ms. Steimer decides to address that explicitly before launching into the lesson. She begins by asking students what a "foot" is. She allows time for them to discuss the word with a partner and then share their answers with the class. She explains that today they are going to be using the measuring unit of a foot (while holding up the ruler). She asks students what other units can be used to measure. In particular, she asks her English language learners to share what units they use in their countries of

Table 4.1

An At-a-Glance Look at General Planning Steps and Additional Considerations for ELLs		
Steps	**General Description**	**Additional Considerations for English Language Learners**
1. Determine the mathematics and goals	• Identify the mathematical concepts that align with state and district standards. • Formulate learning objectives.	• Establish language objectives (e.g., include reading, writing, speaking, and listening) in the lesson plan. • Post content and language objectives, using kid-friendly words.
2. Consider your students' needs	• Relate concepts to previously learned concepts and experiences.	• Consider students' social/cultural backgrounds and previously learned content and vocabulary.
3. Select, design, or adapt a task	• Select a task that will enable students to explore the concept(s) selected in step 1.	• Include a context that is meaningful to the students' cultures and backgrounds. • Analyze the task for language pitfalls. Identify words that need to be discussed and eliminate terms that are not necessary to understanding the task. • Watch for homonyms, homophones, and words that have special meanings in math (e.g., mean, similar, product).
4. Design lesson assessments	• Determine the types of assessments that will be used for each objective. • Use a variety of assessments.	• Build in questions to diagnose understanding. Use translators if needed. • If a student is not succeeding, seek alternative strategies to diagnose if the problem is with language, content, or both.
5. Plan the *before* activities	• Determine how you will introduce the task. • Consider warm-ups that orient student thinking.	• Build background! Link task to prior learning and to familiar contexts. • Review key vocabulary needed for the task. List key vocabulary in a prominent location. • Provide visuals and real objects related to the selected task. • Present the task in written and oral format. • Check for understanding (e.g., ask students to pair-share).
6. Plan the *during* questions and extensions	• Think about hints or assists you might give as students work. • Consider extensions or challenges.	• Group students for both academic and language support. • Encourage students to draw pictures, make diagrams, and/or use manipulatives/models. • Maximize language. Ask students to explain and defend. • Consider using a graphic organizer. Ideas include: sentence starters (e.g., "I solved the problem by . . ."), recording tables, and concept maps. • Maximize language use in nonthreatening ways (e.g., think-pair-share).
7. Plan the *after* discussion	• How will students report their findings? • Determine how you will format the discussion of the task.	• Encourage students to use visuals in reports. • Give advance notice that students will be speaking, so they can plan. • Encourage students to choose the language they wish to use, using a translator if possible. • Provide appropriate "wait time."
8. Check for alignment within the lesson	• Check that all aspects of the lesson target the objectives.	• Review lesson phases to see if key vocabulary is supported throughout the lesson. • Review lesson phases to see that visuals and other supports are in place.
9. Anticipate student approaches	• Reflect on how students will respond to the task and what misconceptions may occur. • Determine how to address these issues.	• Consider approaches that might be used in other countries and encourage students to share different approaches. • Encourage pictures to replace words, as appropriate for age and language proficiency.
10. Identify essential questions	• Using your objectives as a guide, what questions will you ask in each lesson phase?	• If possible, translate essential questions. • Word questions in straightforward, simple sentence structures.

origin, *having metric rulers to show the class. She asks students to study the ruler and compare the centimeter to the inch by posing these questions: "Can you estimate about how many centimeters are in an inch? In 6 inches? In a foot?"*

Moving to the lesson objectives, Ms. Steimer asks students to compare how the halfway points are marked for the inches and the centimeters. Then she asks students without using rulers to tear a piece of paper that they think is about one-half of a foot long. Students then measure their paper strips to see how close their strips are to 6 inches. Now she has them ready to begin estimating and measuring.

Pause and Reflect

Review Ms. Steimer's lesson. What specific strategies to support English language learners can you identify?

Discussion of the word *foot* using the think-pair-share technique recognized the potential language confusion and allowed students the chance to talk about it before becoming confused by the task. The efforts to use visuals and concrete models (the ruler and the torn paper strip) and to build on students' prior experience (use of the metric system in Korea and Mexico) provided support so that the ELLs could succeed in this task. Most importantly, Ms. Steimer did not diminish the challenge of the task with these strategies. If she had altered the task, for example, not expecting the ELLs to estimate since they didn't know the inch very well, she would have lowered her expectations. Conversely, if she had simply posed the problem without taking time to have students study the ruler or to provide visuals, she may have kept her expectations high but failed to provide the support that would enable her students to succeed. Finally, by making a connection for all students to the metric system, she showed respect for the students' cultures and broadened the horizons of other students to measurement in other countries.

Pause and Reflect

Examine the Expanded Lesson at the end of the chapter. Look for evidence within the lesson that there is already support for the ELL. What additional opportunities can you find in the lesson to provide support for the ELL?

Additional information for working with students who are English learners in mathematics can be found in Chapter 6.

Drill or Practice?

Drill and practice, if not a hallmark of American instructional methods in mathematics, is present to at least some degree in nearly every classroom. Most lessons in traditional textbooks end with a section consisting of exercises, usually of a similar nature and always completely in line with the ideas that were just taught in the lesson. This repetitive procedural work is supposed to cement the ideas just learned. In addition to this common textbook approach, drill-and-practice workbooks and computer drill programs abound.

A question worth asking is "What has all of this drill gotten us?" It has been an ever-present component of mathematics classes for decades and yet the adult population is replete with those who almost proudly proclaim "I was never any good at mathematics" and who understand little more about the subject than basic arithmetic. This section offers a different perspective.

New Definitions of Drill and Practice

The phrase "drill and practice" slips off the tongue so rapidly that the two words *drill* and *practice* appear to be synonyms—and, for the most part, they have been. In the interest of developing a new or different perspective on drill and practice, consider definitions that differentiate between these terms as different types of activities rather than link them together.

Practice refers to different problem-based tasks or experiences, spread over numerous class periods, each addressing the same basic ideas.

Drill refers to repetitive, *non*-problem-based exercises designed to improve skills or procedures already acquired.

Pause and Reflect

How are these two definitions different? Which is more in keeping with the view of drill and practice (as a singular term) with which you are familiar? How do each of these align with what we know about how people learn (see Chapter 2)?

Using these definitions as a point of departure, it is now useful to examine what benefits we can get from each and when each is appropriate.

What Drill Provides

Drill can provide students with the following:

- An increased facility with a procedure but *only* with a procedure already learned
- A review of facts or procedures so they are not forgotten

Limitations of drill include:

- A focus on a singular method and an exclusion of flexible alternatives
- A false appearance of understanding
- A rule-oriented or procedural view of what mathematics is about

The popular belief is that somehow students learn through drill. In reality, drill can only help students get faster at what they already know. Students who count on their fingers to answer basic fact questions only get very good at counting on their fingers. Drill is not a reflective activity. The nature of drill asks students to do what they already know how to do, even if they just learned it. The focus of drill is on procedural skill.

For most school-level mathematics, including computation, there are numerous ways of getting answers. For example, how many different mental methods can you think of to add 48 + 35? To find 25 percent of $84 you can divide by 4 rather than multiply by 0.25. What approach would you use to find 17 percent of $84? Similar examples of the value of flexible thinking are easily found. Drill has a tendency to narrow one's thinking to one approach rather than promote flexibility.

When students successfully complete a page of routine exercises, teachers (and even students) often believe that this is an indication that they've "got it." In fact, what they most often have is a very temporary ability to reproduce a procedure recently shown to them. The short-term memory required of a student to complete the exercises at the end of the traditional lesson is no indication of understanding. Superficially learned procedures are easily and quickly forgotten and confused. As noted in Chapter 6, one of the obstacles for students with special needs is memorization. An approach to instruction where students are to memorize and drill on a fact or procedure is not in the best interests of these students, as well as the many other students who are not good memorizers but are good thinkers.

When drill is such a prevalent component of the mathematics classroom, it is no wonder that so many students and adults dislike mathematics. Real mathematics is about sense making and reasoning—it is a science of pattern and order. Students cannot possibly obtain this view of the discipline when constantly being asked to repeat procedural skills over and over.

What is most important to understand is this: Drill will *not* help with conceptual understanding. Drill will *not* provide any new skills or strategies. Drill focuses only on retaining what is already known.

What Practice Provides

In essence, practice is what this book is about—providing students with ample and varied opportunities to reflect on or create new ideas through problem-based tasks. The following list of outcomes of practice should not be surprising:

- An increased opportunity to develop conceptual ideas and more elaborate and useful connections
- An opportunity to develop alternative and flexible strategies

- A greater chance for all students to understand, particularly students with special needs
- A clear message that mathematics is about figuring things out and that it makes sense

Each of the preceding benefits has been explored in this or previous chapters and should require no further discussion. However, it is important to point out that practice can and does develop skills. The fear that without extensive drill students will not master "basic skills" is not supported by recent research on standards-based curriculum or practices (see Chapter 1). These programs include lots of practice as defined here and include appropriate amounts of drill. Students in these programs perform about as well as students in traditional programs on computational skills and much better on nearly every other measure.

When Is Drill Appropriate?

Yes, there is a place for drill in mathematics but it need not be as frequent or lengthy as is often the case. Consider these two proposed criteria for determining whether the drill is appropriate:

- An efficient strategy for the skill to be drilled is already in place.
- Automaticity with the skill or strategy is a desired outcome, which means that the skill can be performed efficiently and effectively.

Is it possible to have a skill and still need to perfect it or to drill it? Clearly this happens outside of mathematics all the time, with sports and music as good examples. We learn how to dribble a soccer ball or play the chords shown on a sheet of music. At the outset of instruction, we are given the necessary bits of information to perform these skills. Initially, the skills are weak and unperfected. They must be repeated in order to hone them to a state of efficiency. However, if the skill is not there to begin with, no amount of drill will create it.

When drill is appropriate—for example, practicing basic facts—a little bit goes a long way. Practicing a set of 10 facts, for example, is more effective than a page of 50 facts that have to be done within a set timeframe. (See Chapter 10 for elaboration on effective teaching of the basic facts.) Also, drill, because it is review, is best if limited to 5 to 10 minutes. Devoting extensive time to repeating a procedure is not effective and can negatively impact students' perceptions, motivation, and understanding.

Finally, students often quit thinking when they have to solve problem after problem the same way. Consider the problem 301 – 298. Students who find themselves solving large sets of these will perform the algorithm for subtraction here, borrowing from the 3 across the zero, which oftentimes results in an error. They don't stop to see that these numbers are only three apart and that the difference is therefore 3. And, in fact, they don't need to follow an algorithm.

‖ ——————— *Pause and Reflect*

Stop and make a mental list of the things in pre-K–8 mathematics with which you think students should have automaticity.

Probably your list includes how to count, read, and write numbers. It should include mastery of basic facts (e.g., 3 + 9 or 8 × 6). If you are like most people, you may have computation with whole numbers and even with fractions and decimals on your list. Certainly we want students to be fluent in computation, but not limited to a single method or one that does not make sense to them. There are more items that are candidates for the list of desired automaticity but generally these will be small bits of mathematics, not big ideas. In fact, the list of things for which automaticity is required is actually quite short and the time devoted to these topics should reflect this.

Students Who Don't Get It

As discussed earlier, the diversity in classrooms is a challenge for all teachers. For those students who don't pick up new ideas as quickly as most in the class, there is an overwhelming temptation to give in and "just drill 'em." Before committing to this solution, ask yourself these two questions: *Will drill build understanding? What is this telling the child?* The child who has difficulties has certainly been drilled in the past. It is naive to believe that the drill you provide will be more beneficial than the drills this child has undoubtedly endured in the past. Although drill may provide some very short-term success, an honest reflection and much research suggest that drill will have little effect in the long run. What these children learn from more drill is simple: "I'm no good at math. I don't like math. Math is rules."

The earlier section of this chapter, "Planning for All Learners," suggests strongly that a conceptual approach is the best way to help students who struggle. Drill is simply not the answer.

Homework

Data from the Third International Mathematics and Science Study (TIMSS) suggest that U.S. fourth graders are assigned about as much homework as students in most other countries (U.S. Department of Education, 1997c). U.S. eighth graders are assigned more homework and spend more time in class talking about homework than do Japanese students, who significantly outperform the U.S. students (U.S. Department of Education, 1996). The real value of homework is unclear. Many parents expect to see homework and most teachers do assign homework.

But what should homework be in a problem-based curriculum? How do you effectively support students and their families to be successful with homework? The distinction between drill and practice as described in the previous section provides a useful lens for looking at homework.

Practice as Homework

Homework is a perfectly appropriate way to engage students in problem-based activities—in practice. A problem-based task similar to those described in Chapter 3 can be assigned for homework provided that the difficulty of the task is within reach of most of the students. The difference is that, when at home, students will be working alone rather than with a partner or group.

The process of giving homework can mimic the three-phase lesson model. Complete a brief version of the *before* phase of a lesson to be sure the task is understood before students go home. At home students complete the *during* phase. When they return with the work completed, apply the sharing techniques of the *after* phase of the lesson. They can even practice the *after* phase with their family if this is encouraged through parent/guardian communications. Some form of written work must be required so that students are held responsible for the task and are prepared for the class discussion.

Homework of this nature communicates to families the problem-based or sense-making nature of your classroom and can help them see the value in this approach. Families want to see homework but some will not have any experience with the type of instruction you have been reading about. Providing guidance and support to families can make a big difference in their understanding of the approach and their ability to help their student(s).

Drill as Homework

Do not assign drill as a substitute for practice or before the requisite concepts have been developed. When assigning drill for homework, here are some things to think about:

- Keep it short. Lengthy drill is not productive.
- Provide an answer key. At grade 3 and above, students are capable of checking their own work. Students can be required to repeat the missed exercises and/or write a sentence indicating where they had difficulty and what they do not understand. If you respond to these notes with assistance, students will begin to understand that homework drills are a way for them to receive help.
- Never grade homework based on correctness. Instead, grade only that it was or was not completed. Rather than penalize wrong answers, use wrong answers as an opportunity to assist students and promote growth. This suggestion also applies equally well to practice homework.

- Do not waste valuable classroom time going over drill homework. Especially if the last two suggestions are followed, simply observing that it is complete is all that is required.

Provide Homework Support

Families also benefit from strategies for doing homework problems. Providing guiding questions for parents or guardians, for example, can help them help their child and understand your emphasis on a problem-based approach to instruction. Figure 4.2 provides some guiding questions that can be included in the students' notebooks and shared with parents or guardians.

Check to see what online resources your textbook provides. Sometimes textbooks websites have online resources for homework and for parents or guardians, including flash-based tutorials, video resources, resources

These guiding questions are designed for helping your child think through their math homework problems:

- What do you need to figure out? What is the problem about?
- What words are confusing? What words are familiar?
- Did you solve problems like this one in class today?
- What have you tried so far?
- Can you make a drawing to help you think about the problem?
- Does your answer make sense?
- Is there more than one answer?

Figure 4.2 Questions for families for helping with homework.

for parents or guardians, connections to careers and real applications, multilingual glossaries, audio podcasts, and more.

Reflections on Chapter 4

Writing to Learn

1. Not every lesson will be built around a single task. What are other ways to structure problem-based activities in the class?
2. How can a game be considered a problem-based task?
3. How do you do the *after* portion of a lesson when students are working at stations?
4. Why is a problem-based approach a good way to reach all students in a diverse classroom?
5. Discuss what is meant by (a) differentiated tasks and (b) tiered lessons.
6. What teacher actions are needed for groups to function effectively?
7. What is the difference between making an accommodation for students and making a modification in a lesson? Explain why this distinction is important.
8. This chapter suggests a distinction between drill and practice. Explain the difference and what each can provide.
9. What is the major difference between the instructional method described in this book and the predominant approach found in most traditional textbooks? Describe briefly

what is meant by the "two-page lesson format" that is often adhered to in traditional textbooks. What is a serious drawback of this form?

For Discussion and Exploration

1. Examine a textbook for any grade level. Look at a topic for a whole chapter and determine the two or three main objectives or big ideas covered in the chapter. Restrict yourself to no more than three. Now look at the individual lessons. Are the lessons aimed at the big ideas you have identified? Will the lessons effectively develop the big ideas for this chapter? Are the lessons problem-based? If not, how can they be adapted to be problem-based?
2. When planning a lesson for a class that includes English language learners, there are many points you might consider at each stage of the planning process. Take the Expanded Lesson from this book or one from the *Field Experience Guide* and describe the adaptations you would incorporate for students with special needs and English language learners (ELLs). Use the key ideas for English language learners described in Table 4.1.

Resources for Chapter 4

Recommended Readings

Articles

Holden, B. (2008). Preparing for problem solving. *Teaching Children Mathematics, 14*(5), 290–295.

This excellent "how to" article shares how a first-grade teacher working in an urban high-poverty setting incorporated differentiated instruction. Holden describes how she prepared her classroom and her students to be successful through six specific steps. For new and experienced teachers, this provides great insights into how to structure a successful problem-based classroom.

Reeves, C. A., & Reeves, R. (2003). Encouraging students to think about how they think! *Mathematics Teaching in the Middle School, 8*(7), 374–377.

When students (and also adults) get into a habit of mind—or, in this case, a pattern for solving a problem—they often continue to use this pattern even when easier methods are available. The authors explore this idea with simple tasks you can try. The point is that too much drill with little variability may have negative effects.

Williams, L. (2008). Tiering and scaffolding: Two strategies for providing access to important mathematics. *Teaching Children Mathematics, 14*(6), 324–330.

Using a second-grade fraction lesson and a third-grade geometry lesson as examples, Williams shares how they were tiered and then how scaffolds, or supports, were built into the lesson. The focus on individual learners and equity makes this a very worthwhile article.

Books

Burns, M., & Silbey, R. (2000). *So you have to teach math? Sound advice for K–6 teachers.* Sausalito, CA: Math Solutions Publications.

This is a must read for new teachers and also for veteran teachers who are switching grades. Burns and Silbey offer practical advice on leading class discussions, using manipulatives, incorporating writing into your classroom, creating useful homework, working with families, and more. Each topical chapter is organized by questions teachers typically ask. Filled with practical tips, this will be a resource to come back to often.

Litton, N. (1998). *Getting your math message out to parents: A K–6 resource.* Sausalito, CA: Math Solutions Publications.

Well-meaning parents and other family members who remember mathematics as memorization and worksheets often challenge a constructivist, student-oriented approach to teaching. Litton is a classroom teacher who has practical suggestions for communicating with family members. The book includes chapters on parent conferences, newsletters, homework, and family math night.

Online Resources

Illuminations
www.illuminations.nctm.org

This is a favorite of many math teachers. Click on "Lessons" and you can then select grade band and content to search for lessons—all of them excellent!

The Math Forum: Internet Mathematics Library
http://mathforum.org/library

Here you will find links to all sorts of information that will be useful in both planning and assessment in a problem-based classroom.

Ask Dr. Math
http://mathforum.org/dr.math

Ask Dr. Math is a great homework resource for families, students, and teachers. Dr. Math has answers to all the classic math questions students have, like why a negative times a negative is a positive.

Field Experience Guide Connections

Chapter 2 of the *Field Experience Guide* offers a range of experiences related to planning. In Chapter 4 of the guide, several activities focus on different types of instruction. For example, FEG 4.3 focuses on cooperative groups and FEG 4.6 focuses on small-group instruction. Chapter 8 of the guide provides experiences focused on the needs of individual learners. For example, FEG 8.5 focuses on sheltering instruction for an English language learner. Chapter 9 in the guide offers 24 Expanded Lessons, all designed in the *before, during,* and *after* model. Chapter 10 offers worthwhile mathematics activities that can be developed into problem-based lessons, like the one at the end of this chapter.

Expanded Lesson

Fixed Areas

Content and Task Decisions

Mathematics Goals

- To contrast the concepts of area and perimeter
- To develop the relationship between area and perimeter of different shapes when the area is fixed
- To compare and contrast the units used to measure perimeter and those used to measure area

Consider Your Students' Needs

Students have worked with the ideas of area and perimeter. Some, if not the majority, of students can find the area and perimeter of given figures and may even be able to state the formulas for finding the perimeter and area of a rectangle. However, they may become confused as to which formula to use.

Materials

Each student will need:

- 36 square tiles such as color tiles
- Two or three sheets of centimeter grid paper
- "Rectangles Made with 36 Tiles" recording sheet (Blackline Master 73)
- "Fixed Area" recording sheet (Blackline Master 74)

Teacher will need:

- Overhead tiles
- Transparency of "Rectangles Made with 36 Tiles" recording sheet (Blackline Master 73)
- Transparency of "Fixed Area" recording sheet (Blackline Master 74)

Fixed Area Recording Sheet

Name _____

Length	Width	Area	Perimeter

Lesson

Before

Begin with a simpler version of the task:

- Have students build a rectangle using 12 tiles at their desks. Explain that the rectangle should be filled in, not just a border. After eliciting some ideas, ask a student to come to the overhead and make a rectangle that has been described.
- Model sketching the rectangle on the grid transparency. Record the dimensions of the rectangle in the recording chart—for example, "2 by 6."
- Ask, "What do we mean by perimeter? How do we measure perimeter?" After helping students define perimeter and describe how it is measured, ask students for the perimeter of this rectangle. Ask a stu-

dent to come to the overhead to measure the perimeter of the rectangle. (Use either the rectangle made from tiles or the one sketched on grid paper.) Emphasize that the units used to measure perimeter are one-dimensional, or linear, and that perimeter is just the distance around an object. Record the perimeter on the chart.

- Ask, "What do we mean by area? How do we measure area?" After helping students define area and describe how it is measured, ask for the area of this rectangle. Here you want to make explicit that the units used to measure area are two-dimensional and, therefore, cover a region. After counting the tiles, record the area in square units on the chart.

- Have students make a different rectangle using 12 tiles at their desks and record the perimeter and area as before. Students will need to decide what "different" means. Is a 2-by-6 rectangle different from a 6-by-2 rectangle? Although these are congruent, students may wish to consider these as being different. That is okay for this activity.

Present the focus task to the class:

- See how many different rectangles can be made with 36 tiles.
- Determine and record the perimeter and area for each rectangle.

Provide clear expectations:

- Write the following directions on the board:
  1. Find a rectangle using *all* 36 tiles.
  2. Sketch the rectangle on the grid paper.
  3. Measure and record the perimeter and area of the rectangle on the recording chart.
  4. Find a new rectangle using *all* 36 tiles and repeat steps 2–4.
- Place students in pairs to work collaboratively, but require each student to draw their own sketches and use their own recording sheet.

During

Initially:

- Question students to be sure they understand the task and the meaning of *area* and *perimeter*. Look for students who are confusing these terms.
- Be sure students are both drawing the rectangles and recording them appropriately in the chart.

Ongoing:

- Observe and ask the assessment questions, posing one or two to a student and moving to another student (see "Assessment" below).

After

Bring the class together to share and discuss the task:

- Ask students what they have found out about perimeter and area. Ask, "Did the perimeter stay the same? Is that what you expected? When is the perimeter big and when is it small?"
- Ask students how they can be sure they have all of the possible rectangles.
- Ask students to describe what happens to the perimeter as the length and width change. (The perimeter gets shorter as the rectangle gets fatter. The square has the shortest perimeter.) Provide time to pair-share ideas.

Assessment

Observe

- Are students confusing perimeter and area?
- As students form new rectangles, are they aware that the area is not changing because they are using the same number of tiles each time? These students may not know what area is, or they may be confusing it with perimeter.
- Are students looking for patterns in how to find the perimeter?
- Are students stating important concepts or patterns to their partners?

Ask

- What is the area of the rectangle you just made?
- What is the perimeter of the rectangle you just made?
- How is area different from perimeter?
- How do you measure area? Perimeter?

Chapter 5

Building Assessment into Instruction

Assessment should be the servant of teaching and learning. Without information about their students' skills, understanding, and individual approaches to mathematics, teachers have nothing to guide their work.

Mokros, Russell, and Economopoulos (1995, p. 84)

What ideas about assessment come to mind from your personal experiences? Tests? Pop quizzes? Grades? Studying? Anxiety? Getting the correct answers? All of these are typical memories. Now suppose that you are told that assessment in the classroom should be designed to help students learn and to help teachers teach. How can assessment do those things?

Integrating Assessment into Instruction

The Assessment Principle in *Principles and Standards* stresses two main ideas: (1) Assessment should enhance students' learning, and (2) assessment is a valuable tool for making instructional decisions. Assessments can be formative or summative. Formative assessment is a planned process of regularly checking students' understanding during your instructional activities (Popham, 2008; Wiliam, 2008). When implemented well, formative assessment can dramatically increase the speed of student learning (Nyquist, 2003; Wiliam, 2007) by providing feedback that promotes learning and using the results and evidence collected to improve instruction—either for the whole class or individual students. Quick feedback gives students useful information to adjust their current learning approaches and take ownership of their own education. The data you collect will inform your decision making for the next steps in the learning progression.

In the following pages we will discuss several formative approaches that include performance-based tasks, journals, observations of students solving problems, and student diagnostic interviews. Summative assessments are cumulative evaluations that might generate a single score such as an end-of-unit test or the standardized test that is used in your state or school district. If summative assessment could be described as a digital snapshot, formative assessment is like streaming video. One is a picture of what a student knows that is captured in a single moment of time and the other is a moving picture that demonstrates active student thinking and reasoning.

> **myeducationlab**
> Go to the Building Teaching Skills and Dispositions section of Chapter 5 of MyEducationLab. Click on Videos and watch the video entitled "**Authentic Assessment**" to see classroom examples that demonstrate how students communicate their understanding is as important as how they solve the problem.

What Is Assessment?

The term *assessment* is defined in the NCTM *Assessment Standards* as "the process of gathering evidence about a student's knowledge of, ability to use, and disposition toward mathematics and of making inferences from that evidence for a variety of purposes" (NCTM, 1995, p. 3). It is important to note that "gathering evidence" is not the same as giving a test or quiz. Assessment can and should happen every day as an integral part of instruction. If you restrict your view of assessment to tests and quizzes, you will miss seeing how assessment can inform instruction and help students grow.

The *Assessment Standards*

Traditional testing has focused on what students *do not know* (how many wrong answers). In the 1989 *Curriculum Standards* the authors called for a shift toward assessing

Table 5.1

The NCTM Assessment Standards	
The Mathematics Standard	• Use NCTM and state or local standards to establish what mathematics students should know and be able to do and base assessments on those essential concepts and processes • Develop assessments that encourage the application of mathematics to real and sometimes novel situations • Focus on significant and correct mathematics
The Learning Standard	• Incorporate assessment as an integral part of instruction and not an interruption or a singular event at the end of a unit of study • Inform students about what content is important and what is valued by emphasizing those ideas in your instruction and matching your assessments to the models and methods used • Listen thoughtfully to your students so that further instruction will not be based on guesswork but instead on evidence of students' misunderstandings or needs
The Equity Standard	• Respect the unique qualities, experiences, and expertise of all students • Maintain high expectations for students while recognizing their individual needs • Incorporate multiple approaches to assessing students, including the provision of accommodations and modifications for students with special needs
The Openness Standard	• Establish with students the expectations for their performance and how they can demonstrate what they know • Avoid just looking at answers and give attention to the examination of the thinking processes students used • Provide students with examples of responses that meet expectations and those that don't meet expectations
The Inferences Standard	• Reflect seriously and honestly on what students are revealing about what they know • Use multiple assessments (e.g., observations, interviews, tasks, tests) to draw conclusions about students' performance • Avoid bias by establishing a rubric that describes the evidence needed and the value of each component used for scoring
The Coherence Standard	• Match your assessment techniques with both the objectives of your instruction and the methods of your instruction • Ensure that assessments are a reflection of the content you want students to learn • Develop a system of assessment that allows you to use the results to inform your instruction in a feedback loop

what students *do know* (what ideas they bring to a task, how they reason, what processes they use). This shift to finding out more about students is also a theme of the *Assessment Standards for School Mathematics* published by NCTM in 1995. The *Assessment Standards* contains six standards for assessment that are deserving of some reflection (see Table 5.1).

Why Do We Assess?

Even a cursory glance at the six assessment standards suggests a complete integration of assessment and instruction. The *Assessment Standards* outlines four specific purposes of assessment as depicted in Figure 5.1. With each purpose, an arrow points to a corresponding result on the outside ring.

Monitoring Student Progress.   Assessment should provide both teacher and students with ongoing feedback concerning progress toward lesson objectives and long-term goals. Assessment during instruction should inform each individual student and the teacher about problem-solving ability and growth toward understanding of mathematical concepts, not just mastery of procedural skills.

Making Instructional Decisions.   Teachers planning tasks to develop student understanding must have information about how students are thinking and what ideas they are

using and developing. Daily problem solving and discussion provide a much richer and more useful array of data than can ever be gathered from a chapter test. This gathering of

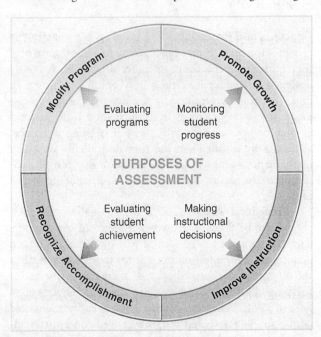

Figure 5.1 Four purposes of assessment and their results (in the outer ring).
Source: Adapted with permission from *Assessment Standards for School Mathematics*, p. 25, copyright 1995 by the National Council of Teachers of Mathematics, Inc. www.nctm.org.

evidence comes at a time when you can actually formulate plans to help students develop ideas rather than remediate after the fact.

Evaluating Student Achievement. *Evaluation* is "the process of determining the worth of, or assigning a value to, something on the basis of careful examination and judgment" (NCTM, 1995, p. 3). Evaluation involves a teacher's collecting of evidence to make an informed judgment. It may include test data but should take into account a wide variety of sources and types of information gathered during the course of instruction. Most important, evaluation should reflect performance criteria about what students know and understand; it should not be used to compare one student with another.

Evaluating Programs. Assessment data should be used as one component in answering the question "How well did this program or unit of study work to achieve my goals?" For the classroom teacher, this includes selection of tasks, sequence of activities, kinds of questions developed, and use of models.

What Should Be Assessed?

The broader view of assessment promoted here and by NCTM requires that appropriate assessment reflect the full range of mathematics: concepts and procedures, mathematical processes, and even students' disposition to mathematics.

Concepts and Procedures. A good assessment strategy provides the opportunity for students to demonstrate how they understand the concepts under discussion. A poorly designed test generally targets only one way to know an idea—the way determined by the designer of the assessment. If you collect formative information from students as they complete an activity, while it is being discussed, as results are justified—in short, while students are doing mathematics—you will gain information that provides insight into the nature of the students' understanding of that idea.

Procedural knowledge, including skill proficiency, should also be assessed. However, if a student can compute with fractions yet has no idea of why he needs a common denominator for addition but not for multiplication, then the rules that have been "mastered" are poorly connected to meaning. This would indicate only the most tenuous presence of a skill. Whereas a routine skill can easily be checked with a simple fact-based test, the desired conceptual connections require different assessments.

Mathematical Processes. Guidelines for defining the specifics of mathematical power can be found in the five process standards of *Principles and Standards*. Now it is not reasonable to try to assess all of these processes, and certainly not every day. For each grade band, *Principles and Standards* describes what the process standards might look like at that level. Use these descriptions to craft statements about doing mathematics that your students can understand. Here are a few examples, but you should write your own or use those provided by your school system or state guidelines.

Problem Solving

- Works to fully understand problems before beginning
- Uses drawings, graphs, and physical models to help think about and solve problems
- Knows a variety of strategies
- Uses appropriate strategies for solving problems
- Assesses the reasonableness of answers

Reasoning

- Justifies solution methods and results
- Makes conjectures based on reasoning
- Observes and uses patterns in mathematics

Communication

- Explains ideas in writing using words, pictures, and numbers
- Communicates ideas clearly in class discussions

These statements should be discussed with your students to help them understand these components and to let students know that these are processes you value. Periodically, use the statements to evaluate students' mathematical processes based on their individual work, group work, and participation in class discussions. If you use portfolios consisting of work developed and collected over time, assessment that focuses on process should be considered. Processes must also be assessed as part of your grading or evaluation scheme, or students will not take them seriously.

Productive Disposition. Collecting data on students' confidence and beliefs in their own mathematical abilities as well as their likes and dislikes about mathematics is also an important assessment. This information is most easily obtained with self-reported checklists, interviews, and journal writing. Information on perseverance and willingness to attempt problems is available to you every day when you use a problem-solving approach.

Performance-Based Assessments

Recall from Chapter 3 that a problem is any task or activity for which students have no prescribed or memorized rules or solution method. The same definition should be used for assessment tasks. Perhaps you have heard about *performance assessment tasks* or *alternative assessments*. These terms refer to tasks that are connected to actual problem-solving activities used in instruction. A good problem-based task designed to promote learning is often the best type of task for assessment.

Good tasks should permit every student in the class, regardless of mathematical prowess, to demonstrate knowledge, skills, or understanding. Students who are struggling should be encouraged to use ideas they possess to work on a problem even if these are not the same skills or strategies used by others in the room.

Often assessments' tasks include real-world or authentic contexts for problems. Although contextual situations are often important, how a student completes a task and justifies the solution should inform us about his or her understanding of the mathematics. That agenda should not be overshadowed because of difficulties that may arise from context, especially for students who are English language learners.

The justifications for answers, even when given orally, will almost certainly provide more information than the answers alone. Perhaps no better method exists for getting at student understanding.

Examples of Performance-Based Tasks

Each of the following tasks provides ample opportunity for students to learn. At the same time, each will provide data for the teacher to use in assessment. Notice that these are not elaborate tasks and yet when followed by a discussion, each could engage students for most of a period. What mathematical ideas are required to successfully respond to each of these tasks? Will the task help you understand how well students understand these ideas?

Shares (Grades K–3)

Leila has 6 gumdrops, Darlene has 2, and Melissa has 4. They want to share them equally. How will they do it? Draw a picture to help explain your answer.

At second or third grade, the numbers in the Shares task should probably be larger. What additional concepts would be involved if the task was about sharing cookies and the total number of cookies was 14?

Subtraction (Grades 1–2)

If you did not know the answer to 12 – 7, what are some ways you could find the answer?

How Much? (Grades 1–2)

Gustavo has saved $15 to buy a game that he wants. The game costs $23. How much money does Gustavo still need? Explain how you got your answer.

These two problems are similar in that they involve subtraction and allow the teacher to see what strategies a student might use. In the second problem, the context increases the chances that students will use an "add-on" approach (15 and how much more to make 23?). Contrast the benefits of using these tasks with simply giving the corresponding computations.

The Whole Set (Grades 3–5)

Mary counted 15 cupcakes left from the whole batch that her mother made for the picnic. "We've already eaten two-fifths," she noted. How many cupcakes did her mother bake?

This problem could easily have been posed without any context. What is the value of using a real-world context in tasks such as these?

In the following task, students are asked to judge the performances of other students. Analysis of student performance is a good way to create tasks.

Decimals (Grades 4–6)

Alan tried to make a decimal number as close to 50 as he could using the digits 1, 4, 5, and 9. He arranged them in this order: 51.49. Jerry thinks he can arrange the same digits to get a number that is even closer to 50. Do you agree or disagree? Explain.

Mental Math (Grades 4–8)

Explain two different ways to multiply 4 × 276 in your head. Which way is easier to use? Would you use a different way to multiply 5 × 98? Explain why you would use the same method or a different method.

Mental computation tasks should be done frequently at all grade levels beginning around grade 2. Other students can pick up the methods that students share in class. The explanations also offer evidence about students' understanding of concepts and strategy use. This observational information can be recorded over time with a variety of simple methods.

Two Triangles (Grades 4–8)

Tell everything you can about these two triangles.

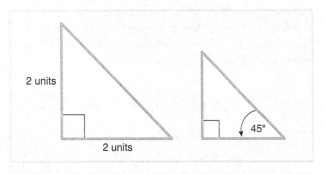

This task is a good example of an open-ended assessment. Consider how much more valuable this task is than asking for the angle measure in the triangle on the left.

Algebra: Graphing (Grades 7–8)

Does the graph of $y = x^2$ ever intersect the graph of $y = x^2 + 2$? What are some ways that you could test your idea?

Even with a graphing calculator, proving that these two graphs will not intersect requires reasoning and an understanding of how graphs are related to equations and tables.

Thoughts about Assessment Tasks

In some instances, the real value of the task or what can be learned about students' understanding will come only in the discussion that follows. For others, the information will be in the written report. In many of Marilyn Burns's books, you will see the phrase "We think the answer is . . . We think this because . . . ." Students must develop the habit of sharing, writing, and listening to justifications. If explanations are not regularly practiced in your classroom, it may be unrealistic to expect students to offer good explanations in assessments.

Many activities have no written component and no "answer" or result. For example, students may be playing a game in which dice or dominoes are being used. A teacher who sits in on the game will see great differences in how children use numbers. Some will count every dot on the card or domino. Others will use a counting-on strategy. (A student using a counting-on strategy to find the total on a domino, for example, will see four dots on one side and count on from four to tally the total number.) Some will recognize certain patterns without counting. Others may

be unsure if 13 beats 11. This evidence differentiates students relative to their understanding of number concepts. Data gathered from listening to a pair of children work on a simple activity or an extended project provide significantly greater insight into students' thinking than almost any written test we could devise. Data from student conversations and observations of student behavior can be recorded and used for the same purposes as written data, including evaluation and grading. Especially in the case of grading, it is important to keep dated written anecdotal notes that can be referred to later. (See the section "Anecdotal Notes" later in this chapter.)

You can move from instruction to assessment and make performance-based tasks into evaluation tools aligned with your goals. The process of moving from teaching tasks to assessment tasks involves the addition of a rubric. The next section will explain how you can create and use both generic rubrics that describe general qualities of performance and topic-specific rubrics that include criteria based on your particular lesson objectives.

Rubrics and Performance Indicators

Problem-based tasks may tell us a great deal about what students know, but how do we handle this information? Often there is only one problem for students to work on in a given period. There is no way to simply count the percent correct and put a mark in the grade book. It may be helpful to make a distinction between *scoring* and *grading*. "*Scoring* is comparing students' work to criteria or rubrics that describe what we expect the work to be. *Grading* is the result of accumulating scores and other information about a student's work for the purpose of summarizing and communicating to others" (Stenmark & Bush, 2001, p. 118). The scores can be used (or perhaps not used) along with other information to create a grade. One valuable tool for scoring is a rubric.

A *rubric* is a framework that can be designed or adapted by the teacher for a particular group of students or a particular mathematical task (Kulm, 1994). A rubric consists of a scale of three to six points that is used as a rating of performance on a single task rather than a count of how many items in a series of exercises are correct or incorrect. The rating or score is applied by examining total performance.

Simple Rubrics

The following simple four-point rubric was developed by the New Standards Project.

4	Excellent: Full Accomplishment
3	Proficient: Substantial Accomplishment
2	Marginal: Partial Accomplishment
1	Unsatisfactory: Little Accomplishment

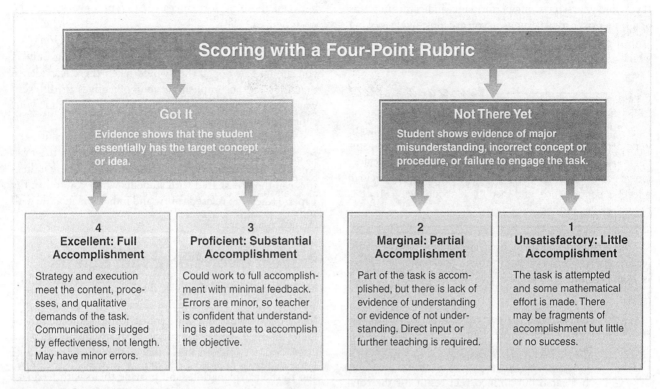

Figure 5.2 With a four-point rubric, performances are first sorted into two categories. Each performance is then considered again and assigned to a point on the scale.

This simple rubric allows a teacher to score performances by first sorting into two categories, as illustrated in Figure 5.2. The broad categories of the first sort are relatively easy to discern. The scale then allows you to separate each category into two additional levels as shown. A rating of 0 is given for no response or effort or for responses that are completely off task.

The advantage of the four-point scale is the relatively easy initial sort into "Got It" or "Not There Yet." Others prefer a three-point rubric such as the following example:

3   Above and beyond—uses exemplary methods, shows creativity, goes beyond the requirements of the problem

2   On target—completes the task with only minor errors, uses successful approaches

1   Not there yet—makes significant errors or omissions, uses unsuccessful approaches

These relatively simple scales are *generic rubrics*. They label general categories of performance but do not define the specific criteria for a particular task. For any given task or process, it is usually helpful to create specific performance indicators for each level.

Performance Indicators

Performance indicators are task-specific statements that describe what performance looks like at each level of the rubric and in so doing establish criteria for acceptable performance.

A rubric and its performance indicators should focus you and your students on the objectives and away from the self-limiting question "How many can you miss and still get an A?" Like athletes who continually strive for better performances rather than "good enough," students should always see the possibility to excel. When you take into account the total performance (processes, answers, justifications, extension, and so on), it is always possible to "go above and beyond."

When you create your task-specific rubric, what performance at different levels of your rubric will or should look like may be difficult to predict. Much depends on your experience with children at that grade level, your past experiences with students working on the same task, and your insights about the task itself. One important part of helping you set performance levels is students' common misconceptions or the expected thinking or approaches to the same or similar problems.

If possible, it is good to write out indicators of "proficient" or "on target" performances before you use the task in class. This is an excellent self-check to be sure that the task is likely to accomplish the purpose you selected it for in the first place. Think about how children are likely to approach the activity.

Remember that topic-specific rubrics are applied to a single task, although the task may have multiple components.

If you find yourself writing performance indicators in terms of number of correct responses, you are most likely looking at drill exercises and not the performance-based tasks for which a rubric is appropriate.

⏸ ———————————— *Pause and Reflect*

Consider the fraction problem titled "The Whole Set" on page 79. Assume you are teaching fourth grade and wish to write performance indicators that you can share with your students using a four-point rubric (Figure 5.2). What indicators would you use for level-3 and level-4 performances? Start with a level-3 performance, and then think about level 4. Try this before reading further.

Determining performance indicators is always a subjective process based on your professional judgment. Here is one possible set of indicators for "The Whole Set" task:

3   Determines the correct answer or uses an approach that would yield a correct answer if not for minor errors. Reasons are either missing or incorrect. Giving a correct result for the number eaten but an incorrect result for the total baked would also be a level-3 performance.

4   Determines the total number baked and uses words, pictures, and numbers to explain and justify the result and how it was obtained. Demonstrates a knowledge of fractional parts and the relation to the whole.

Indicators such as these should be shared ahead of time with students. Sharing indicators before working on a task clearly conveys what is valued and expected. If you review the indicators with students when you return papers, try including the correct answers and some examples of successful responses. This will help students understand how they may have done better. Often it is useful to show work from classmates (anonymously) or from a prior class. Students need to see models of what a level-4 performance looks like.

What about level-1 and level-2 performances? Here are suggestions for the same task:

2   Uses some aspect of fractions appropriately (e.g., divides the 15 into 5 groups instead of 3) but fails to illustrate an understanding of how to determine the whole. The meanings of numerator and denominator are incorrect or confused.

1   Shows some effort but little or no understanding of a fractional part relative to the whole.

Frequently it is not necessary to share indicators for level-1 and level-2 performances unless students or parents request further explanation. However, you often will be aided in your work if you articulate the differences between these performances so students' growth can be documented.

Unexpected methods and solutions happen. Don't box students into demonstrating their understanding only as you thought or hoped they would when there is evidence that they are accomplishing your objectives in different ways. Such occurrences can help you revise or refine your rubric for future use.

When you have finished your sorting process, use the results to write additional rubric indicators for the task. Keep the descriptions as general as possible. These indicators can then be shared with students when you return the papers. Keep the revised rubric and indicators in a file with the task for future use.

Student Involvement with Rubrics

In the beginning of the year, discuss your generic rubric (such as Figure 5.2) with the class. Post it prominently. Many teachers use the same rubric for all subjects; others prefer to use a specialized rubric for mathematics. In your discussion, let students know that as they do activities and solve problems in class, you will look at their work and listen to their explanations and provide them with feedback in terms of the rubric, rather than as a letter grade or a percentage.

When students start to understand what the rubric really means, begin to discuss performance on tasks in terms of the generic rubric. You might have students self-assess their own work using the generic rubric and explain their reasons for the rating. Older students can do this in written form, and you can respond in writing. For all students, you can have class discussions about a task that has been done and what might constitute proficient and excellent performance.

Observation Tools

All teachers learn useful bits of information about their students every day. When the three-part lesson format suggested in Chapter 3 is used, the flow of evidence about student performance increases dramatically, especially in the *during* and *after* portions of lessons. If you have a systematic plan for gathering this information while observing and listening to students, at least two very valuable results occur. First, information that may have gone unnoticed is suddenly visible and important. Second, observation data gathered systematically can be added to other data and used in planning lessons, providing feedback to students, conducting parent conferences, and determining grades.

Depending on what information you may be trying to gather, a single observation of a whole class may require several days to 2 weeks before all students have been observed. Shorter periods of observation will focus on a particular cluster of concepts or skills or particular students. Over longer periods, you can note growth in mathematical processes, such as problem solving, representation, reasoning, or communication. To use observation effectively as a means of gathering assessment data from performance tasks, you should take seriously the following maxim: *Do not attempt to record data on every student in a single class period.*

Observation methods vary with the purposes for which they are used. Further, formats and methods of gathering observation data are going to be influenced by your individual teaching style and habits.

Anecdotal Notes

One system for recording observations is to write short notes either during or immediately after a lesson in a brief narrative style. One possibility is to have a card for each student. Some teachers keep the cards on a clipboard with each taped at the top edge (see Figure 5.3). Another option

is to focus your observations on about five students a day. On another day, different students are selected. The students selected may be members of one or two cooperative groups. An alternative to cards is the use of large peel-off file labels, possibly preprinted with student names. The label notes are then moved to a more permanent notebook page for each student.

Observation Rubric

Another possibility is to use your three- or four-point generic rubric on a reusable form as in Figure 5.4. Include space for content-specific indicators and another column to jot down names of students. A quick note or comment may be added to a name. This method is especially useful for planning purposes.

Checklists for Individual Students

To cut down on writing and to help focus your attention, a checklist with several specific processes or content areas of interest can be devised and duplicated for each student (see

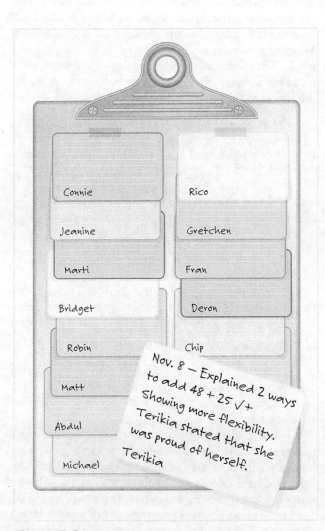

Figure 5.3 Preprinted cards for observation notes can be taped to a clipboard or folder for quick access.

Observation Rubric		
Making Whole Given Fraction Part (3/17)		
Above and Beyond Clear understanding. Communicates concept in multiple representations. Shows evidence of using idea without prompting.	Sally	
	Latania	
Fraction whole made from parts in rods and in sets. Explains easily.	Greg	Zal
On Target Understands or is developing well. Uses designated models.	Lavant (rod)	Tanisha (rod)
	Julie (rod)	Lee (set)
Can make whole in either rod or set format (note). Hesitant. Needs prompt to identify unit fraction.	George (set)	J.B. (rod)
	Maria (set)	John H. (rod)
Not There Yet Some confusion or misunderstands. Only models idea with help.	John S.	Mary
Needs help to do activity. No confidence.		

Figure 5.4 Record names in a rubric during an activity or for a single topic over several days.

Figure 5.5). Some teachers have found methods of printing these on sticky labels or cards using a computer printer. Once a template is created, it is easy to edit the items in the checklist file without retyping all the student names. Regardless of the checklist format, a place for comments should be included.

Checklists for Full Classes

Another format involves listing all students in a class on a single page or not more than three pages (see Figure 5.6). Across the top of the page are specific abilities or deficiencies to look for. Pluses and minuses, checks, or codes corresponding to your general rubric can be entered in the grid. A space left for comments is useful. A full-class checklist is more likely to be used for long-term objectives. Topics that might be appropriate for this format include problem-

solving processes, communication skills, and such subject areas as basic facts or estimation. Dating entries or noting specific activities observed is also helpful.

Writing and Journals

We have been emphasizing that instruction and assessment should be integrated. No place is this more evident than in students' writing. Writing is both a learning and an assessment opportunity. Though some students initially have difficulty writing in mathematics, persistence pays off and students come to see writing as a natural part of the mathematics class.

The Value of Writing

When students write, they express their own ideas and use their own words and language. It is personal. In contrast, oral communication in the classroom is very public. Ideas "pop out" of students' mouths without editing or revision. Meaning is negotiated or elaborated on by the class as a whole. The individual reflective quality of writing as compared to classroom discourse is an important factor in considering the value of writing in mathematics.

> The process of writing requires gathering, organizing, and clarifying thoughts. It demands finding out what you know and don't know. It calls for thinking clearly. Similarly, doing mathematics depends on gathering, organizing, and clarifying thoughts, finding out what you know and don't know, and thinking clearly. Although the final representation of a mathematical pursuit looks very different from the final product of a writing effort, the mental journey is, at its base, the same—making sense of an idea and presenting it effectively. (Burns, 1995b, p. 3)

As an assessment tool writing provides a unique window to students' perceptions and the way a student is thinking about an idea. Even a kindergartener can express ideas in drawings or other markings on paper and begin to explain what he or she is thinking. Finally, student writing is an excellent form of communication with parents during conferences. Writing shows evidence of students' thinking to their parents, telling them much more than any grade or test score.

When students write about their solutions to a task prior to the class discussion the writing can serve as a rehearsal for the conversation about the work. Students who otherwise have difficulty thinking on their feet now have a script to support their contributions. This avoids having the few highly verbal students providing all of the input for the discussion. Call on these more reluctant talkers first so that their ideas are heard and valued.

NAME: *Sharon V.*

FRACTIONS	NOT THERE YET	ON TARGET	ABOVE AND BEYOND	COMMENTS
Understands numerator/denominator		✓		
Area models		✓		*Used pattern blocks to show 2/3 and 3/6*
Set models	✓			
Uses fractions in real contexts	✓			
Estimates fraction quantities		✓		*Showing greater reasonableness*
PROBLEM SOLVING				
Understands problem before beginning work		✓		*Stated problem in own words*
Is willing to take risks	✓			*Reluctant to use abstract models*
Justifies results				

Figure 5.5 A focused computer-generated checklist and rubric can be printed for each student.

Topic: Mental Computation Adding 2-digit numbers **Names**	Not There Yet *Can't do mentally*	On Target *Has at least one strategy*	Above and Beyond *Uses different methods with different numbers*	Comments
Lalie		✓ *3-18-09* *3-21-09*		
Pete	✓ *3-20-09*	✓ *3-24-09*		*Difficulty with problems requiring regrouping*
Sid			✓ + *3-20-09*	*Flexible approaches used*
Lakeshia		✓		*Counts by tens, then adds ones*
George		✓		
Pam	✓			*Beginning to add the group of tens first*
Maria		✓ *3-24-09*		*Using a posted hundreds chart*

Figure 5.6 A full-class observation checklist can be used for longer-term objectives or for several days to cover a short-term objective.

Journals

Journals are a way to make written communication a regular part of doing mathematics. The feedback you provide to students should move their learning forward. Journals are a place for students to write about various aspects of their mathematics experiences:

- Their conceptual understandings and problem solving, including descriptions of ideas, solutions, and justifications of problems, graphs, charts, and observations
- Their questions concerning the current topic, an idea that they may need help with, or an area they don't quite understand
- Their attitudes toward mathematics, their confidence in their understanding, or their fears of being wrong

Even if you have students write in their journals regularly, be sure that these journals are special places for writing about mathematics thinking. Drill or lengthy projects done over several days, for example, are not best carried out in journals. A performance-based assessment task you plan to use primarily for evaluation purposes should probably not be in a journal. But the work for many of your instructional tasks can and should go in the journal, communicating that the work is important and you do want to see it even if you are not always going to grade it.

Grading journals would communicate that there is a specific "right" response you are seeking. It is essential, however, that you read and respond to journal writing. One form of response for a performance task would be to use the classroom's generic rubric along with a helpful comment. This is another way to distinguish between rubrics and grades and still provide feedback.

Writing Prompts and Ideas

Students should always have a clear, well-defined purpose for writing in their journals. They need to know exactly what to write about and who the audience is (you, a student in a lower grade, an adult, a new student to the school), and they should be given a definite time frame within which to write. Journal writing that is completely open-ended without a stated goal or purpose will not be a good use of time. Here are some suggestions for writing prompts to get you thinking; however, the possibilities are endless.

Concepts and Processes

- "I think the answer is . . . I think this because . . . ." (The journal can be used to solve and explain any problem. Some teachers duplicate the problem and have students tape it into the journal.)
- Write an explanation for a new or younger student of why 4×7 is the same as 7×4 and if this works for 6×49 and 49×6. If so, why?
- Explain to a student in a different grade or class (or who was absent today) what you learned about decimals.
- What mathematics work that we did today was easy? What was hard? What do you still have questions about?
- If you got stuck today in solving a problem, where in the problem did you get stuck? Why do you think you had trouble there?
- After you got the answer to today's problem, what did you do so that you were convinced your answer was correct? How sure are you that you got the correct answer?

- Write a story problem that goes with this equation (this graph, this diagram, this picture).

Productive Dispositions

- "What I like the most (or least) about mathematics is . . . ."
- Write a mathematics autobiography. Tell about your experiences in mathematics outside of school and how you feel about the subject.
- What was the most interesting mathematics idea you learned this week?

Journals for Early Learners

If you are interested in working with pre-K–1 children, the writing prompts presented may have sounded too advanced; it is difficult for prewriters and beginning writers to express ideas like those suggested. There are specific techniques for journals in kindergarten and first grade that have been used successfully.

The Giant Journal.   To begin the development of the writing-in-mathematics process, one kindergarten teacher uses a language experience approach. After an activity, she writes "Giant Journal" and a topic or prompt on a large flipchart. Students respond to the prompt, and she writes their ideas, adding the contributor's name and even drawings when appropriate, as in Figure 5.7.

Drawings and Early Writing.   All students can draw pictures of some sort to describe what they have done. Dots can represent counters or blocks. Shapes and special figures can be cut out from duplicated sheets and pasted onto journal pages.

The "writing" should be a record of something the student has just done and is comfortable with. Figure 5.8 shows problems solved in first and second grade. Do not be concerned about invented spellings to communicate ideas. Have students read their papers to you.

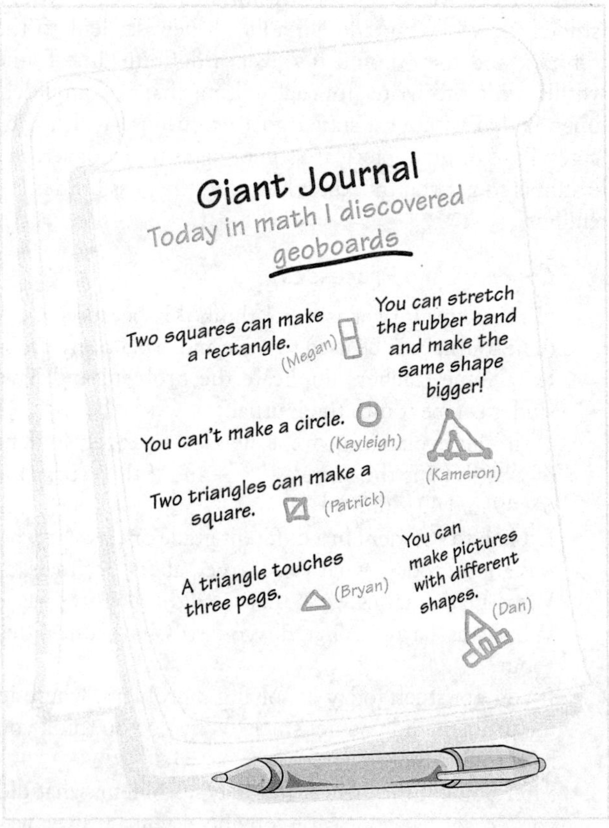

Figure 5.7 A journal in kindergarten may be a class product on a flipchart.

Figure 5.8 Journal entries of children in grades 1 and 2.

Student Self-Assessment

Stenmark (1989) notes that "the capability and willingness to assess their own progress and learning is one of the greatest gifts students can develop. . . . Mathematical power comes with knowing how much we know and what to do to learn more" (p. 26). Student self-assessment should not be your only measure of their learning or disposition, but rather a record of how *they perceive* these things.

As you plan for a self-assessment, consider how you want the assessment to help you as a teacher. Tell your students why you are having them do this activity. Encourage them to be honest and candid.

You can gather self-assessment data in several ways. An open-ended writing prompt such as was suggested for journals is a successful method of getting self-assessment data:

- How well do you think you understand the work we have been doing on fractions during the last few days? If there is something that is causing you difficulty with fractions, please tell me what it is.
- Write one thing you liked and one thing you did not like about class today (or this week).
- As you worked in your group today, what was your contribution?

Another method is to use some form of a questionnaire to which students respond. These can have open-ended questions, response choices (e.g., *seldom, sometimes, often; disagree, don't care, agree*), mind maps, drawings, and so on. Many such instruments appear in the literature, and many textbook publishers provide examples. Whenever you use a form or questionnaire that someone else has devised, be certain that it serves the purpose you intend.

Students may find it difficult to write about attitudes and beliefs. A questionnaire where they can respond "yes," "maybe," or "no" to a series of statements is often a successful approach. Encourage students to add comments under an item if they wish. Here are some items you could use to build such a questionnaire:

- I feel sure of myself when I get an answer to a problem.
- I sometimes just put down anything so I can get finished.
- I like to work on really hard math problems.
- Math class makes me feel nervous.
- If I get stuck, I feel like quitting or going to another problem.
- I am not as good in mathematics as most of the other students in this class.
- Mathematics is my favorite subject.
- I do not like to work at problems that are hard to understand.
- Memorizing rules is the only way I know to learn mathematics.
- I will work a long time at a problem until I think I've solved it.

Another technique is to ask students to write a sentence at the end of any work they do in mathematics class saying how that activity made them feel. Young children can draw a face on each page to tell you about their feelings.

Diagnostic Interviews

Diagnostic interviews are a means of getting in-depth information about an individual student's knowledge and mental strategies about the concept under investigation. These interviews, although often labor intensive, are rich assessments that provide evidence of misunderstandings and explore students' ways of thinking about important concepts. In each case a student is given a problem and asked to verbalize his or her thinking at points in the process. Sometimes students self-correct a mistake but more frequently teachers can unearth a student's misunderstanding or reveal what strategies students have mastered.

The problems you select should match the essential understanding for the topic your students are studying. In every case have paper, pencils, and a variety of materials available, particularly those you have been using during your instruction. It is often useful to have a scoring guide or rubric available to jot down notes about emerging understandings, common methods you expect to see used, or common misunderstandings that may come to light.

Here are suggested problems that can be used for diagnostic interviews.

> **myeducationlab**
>
> Go to the Activities and Application section of Chapter 5 of MyEducationLab. Click on Simulation Exercise and read "**Interviewing**," a vignette that models diagnostic interviewing.

Does the 1 in each of the following problems represent the same amount? (Philipp, Schappelle, Siegfried, Jacobs, & Lamb, 2008)

$$
\begin{array}{r}
2\overset{1}{5}9 \\
+\ 38 \\
\hline
297
\end{array}
\qquad
\begin{array}{r}
\overset{3}{4}\overset{1}{2}9 \\
-\ 34 \\
\hline
395
\end{array}
$$

After students have given their answer you should ask them to explain why in addition (as in the first problem) the 1 is added to the 5, but in subtraction (as in the second problem) 10 is added to the 2. This problem helps you understand whether your students are only working from a procedural knowledge or if they have a conceptual knowledge of the operations of addition and subtraction. Whether the student gives attention to place-value concepts and the quantities involved in regrouping or if they believe the number is the same in each problem will provide valuable information that enhances professional judgment for your subsequent instructional decisions.

The following problem can be used in an interview to assess knowledge of comparing fractions. Figure 5.9 shows student work comparing $\frac{4}{4}$ and $\frac{4}{8}$.

Which is more—$\frac{4}{4}$ or $\frac{4}{8}$? (Ball, 2008)

In this case students should be encouraged to show their thinking about this comparison. Possibly they will select an area model or a number line in their attempt to make their mental processes apparent and justify their answer. Some students may draw diagrams of different-sized rectangles which will reveal their understandings or misunderstandings about the whole as a constant unit for this comparison. For example, in a presentation by Deborah Ball, a noted mathematics educator, one of the children in her class drew an area model of the four-fourths and then used the same sized pieces to draw four-eighths, resulting in a whole that was twice the size of the original (2008). But he then self-corrected when he saw another student who had drawn two rectangles of the same size and divided one into fourths, shading all four, and another into eighths, shading four (or only half) of the pieces. During a diagnostic interview the students will not be able to benefit from the explanations of other students, but these are the discoveries and results that

can inform and improve your instruction. This information will also help you in redirecting or reinforcing students' thinking and strategies.

Tests

Tests will always be a part of assessment and evaluation no matter how adept we become at blending assessment with instruction. However, a test need not be a collection of low-level skill exercises that are simple to grade. Although simple tests of computational skills may have some role in your classroom, the use of such tests should be only one aspect of your assessment. Like all other forms of assessment, tests should match the goals of your instruction. Tests can be designed to find out what concepts students understand and how their ideas are connected. Tests of procedural knowledge should go beyond just knowing how to perform an algorithm and should allow and require the student to demonstrate a conceptual basis for the process. The following examples will illustrate these ideas.

1. Write a multiplication problem that has an answer that falls between the answers to these two problems:

$$\begin{array}{cc} 49 & 45 \\ \times\ 25 & \times\ 30 \end{array}$$

2. a. In this division exercise, what number tells how many tens were shared among the 6 sets?
   b. Instead of writing the remainder as "R 2," Elaine writes "$\frac{1}{3}$." Explain the difference between these two ways of recording the leftover part.

$$\begin{array}{cc} 49\text{R}2 & 49\frac{1}{3} \\ 6\overline{)296} & 6\overline{)296} \end{array}$$

3. On a grid, draw two figures with the same area but different perimeters. List the area and perimeter of each.

4. For each subtraction fact, write an addition fact that helps you think of the answer to the subtraction.

$$\begin{array}{cccc} 12 & 9 & 9 & 14 \\ -3 & +3 & -4 & -7 \\ \hline 9 & 12 & & \end{array}$$

5. Draw pictures of arrows to show why $^-3 + {^-4}$ is the same as $^-3 - {^+4}$.

If a test is well constructed, much more information can be gathered than simply the number of correct or incorrect answers. The following considerations can help maximize the value of your tests:

1. *Permit students to use calculators.* Except for tests of computational skills, calculators allow students to focus on what you really want to test. Permitting calculators also communicates a positive attitude about calculator use to your students.

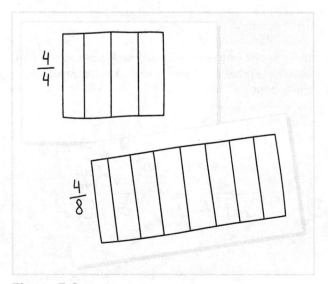

Figure 5.9 Student work comparing fractions.

2. *Use manipulatives and drawings.* Students can use appropriate models to work on test questions when those same models have been used during instruction to develop concepts. (Note the use of grids and drawings in previous examples.) Simple drawings can be used to represent counters, base-ten pieces, fraction pieces, and the like (see Figure 5.10). Be sure to provide examples in class of how to draw the models before you ask students to draw on a test.

3. *Include opportunities for explanations.*

4. *Avoid always using "preanswered" tests.* Tests in which questions have only one correct answer, whether it is a calculation, a multiple-choice, or a fill-in-the-blank question, tend to fragment what children have learned and hide most of what they know. Rather, construct tests that allow students the opportunity to show what they know.

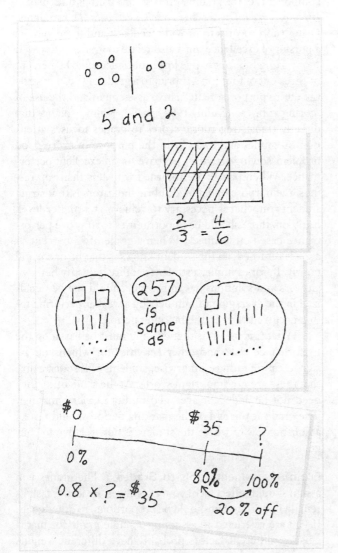

Figure 5.10 Students can use drawings to illustrate concepts on tests.

Improving Performance on High-Stakes Tests

The No Child Left Behind Act mandates that every state test children in mathematics at every grade beginning with grade 3 through grade 8. The method of testing and even the objectives to be tested are left up to individual states. Many districts test their students in mathematics at every grade level.

Whatever the details of the testing program in your particular state, these external tests (originating externally to the classroom) impose significant pressures on school districts, which in turn put pressure on principals, who then place pressure on teachers.

External testing that has consequences for students and teachers is typically referred to as *high-stakes* testing. High stakes make the pressures of testing significant for both students (Will I pass? Will my parents be upset?) and teachers (Will my class meet state proficiency levels? My students' scores have been below passing—I've got to get them up.). The pressures certainly have an effect on instruction.

You will not be able to avoid the pressures of high-stakes testing. The question is "How will you respond?"

Teach Fundamental Concepts and Processes

The best advice for succeeding on high-stakes tests is to teach to the big ideas in the mathematics curriculum that are aligned with your state and local standards. Students who have learned conceptual ideas in a relational manner and who have learned the processes of doing mathematics will perform well on tests, regardless of the format or specific objectives.

Examine lists of state or district skills and objectives and identify the broader conceptual foundations on which they depend. Be certain that you provide students with an opportunity to learn the content in the standards. At the start of each chapter of Section 2 of this book, you will find a short list of Big Ideas followed by a section called Mathematics Content Connections. These will help you identify the broader ideas behind the objectives that you need to teach so you can help students deepen their understanding of connecting ideas and strands. All programs should have a common focus on conceptual development, problem solving, reasoning, and communication of mathematical understanding. In short, a problem-based approach is the best course of action for raising scores.

Test-Taking Strategies

Another common approach to raising test scores is to teach students specific noncontent strategies useful for taking tests. With a healthy dose of caution and keeping in mind the following caveats, this approach may help some students. First, if the students have not developed the concepts, the test strategies will be useless. Second, time teaching test strategies is best spent shortly before a test. Here are a few test-taking strategies that may have some positive effect.

- *Familiarize students with different question formats.* Research the types of formats the standardized test in your state will employ and be sure to use these question formats regularly (not exclusively) in class.
- *Teach test-taking strategies.* Students are often not very efficient test takers, so helping them learn how to take tests can result in benefits. Here are some teachable strategies:
  - Read questions carefully. Practice identifying what questions are asking and what information is needed to get the answer.
  - Estimate the answer before spending time with computation. On multiple-choice tests, estimation and good number sense are often all that are needed to select the correct answer.
  - Eliminate choices. Look at the available options. Some will almost certainly be unreasonable. Does a choice make sense? Can looking at the ones digit eliminate answers?
  - Work backward from an answer.

Remember! Successful test-taking strategies require understanding concepts, skills, and number sense.

Grading

A grade is a statistic used to communicate to others the achievement level that a student has attained in a particular area of study. The accuracy or validity of the grade is dependent on the information used in generating the grade, the professional judgment of the teacher, and the alignment of the assessments with the true goals and objectives of the instruction. Look again at the definition of grading on p. 80. Notice that it says scores are used along with "other information about a student's work" to determine a grade. There is no mention of averaging scores.

Most experienced teachers will tell you that they know a great deal about their students in terms of what the students know, how they perform in different situations, their attitudes and beliefs, and their levels of skill attainment. Successful teachers have always been engaged in ongoing performance assessment, albeit informal and sometimes with no recording. A better approach is to record all important assessment information that reflects an accurate picture of your students' performance.

The practice of grading by statistical number crunching is so firmly ingrained in schooling at all levels that you may find it hard to abandon. One concept that should be clear from the discussions in this chapter is that it is quite useful to gather a wide variety of rich information about students' understanding, problem-solving processes, and attitudes and beliefs. To ignore all of this information in favor of a small set of numbers based on tests, especially tests that may focus on low-level skills, is unfair to students, to parents, and to you as the teacher.

Grading Issues

For effective use of the assessment information gathered from problems, tasks, and other appropriate methods to assign grades, some hard decisions are inevitable. Some are philosophical, some require school or district policies about grades, and all require us to examine what we value and the objectives we communicate to students and parents.

What Gets Graded Gets Valued. Among the many components of the grading process, one truth is undeniable: *What gets graded* by teachers *is what gets valued* by students. Using rubric scores to provide feedback and to encourage a pursuit of excellence must also relate to grades. However, "converting four out of five [on a rubric score] to 80 percent or three out of four [on a rubric] to a grade of C can destroy the entire purpose of alternative assessment and the use of scoring rubrics" (Kulm, 1994, p. 99). Kulm explains that directly translating rubric scores to grades focuses attention on grades and away from the purpose of every good problem-solving activity—to strive for an excellent performance. When papers are returned with less than top ratings, the purpose of detailed rubric indicators is to instruct students on what is necessary to achieve at a higher level. Early on, there should be opportunities to improve performance based on feedback. When a grade of 75 percent or a C– is returned, all the student knows is that he or she did poorly. If, for example, a student's ability to justify her own answers and solutions has improved, should she be penalized in the averaging of numbers by a weaker performance that occurred early in the marking period?

What this means is that grading must be based on the performance tasks and other activities for which you assigned rubric ratings; otherwise, students will soon realize that these are not important scores. At the same time, they need not be added or averaged in any numeric manner. The grade at the end of the marking period should reflect a holistic view of where the student is now relative to your goals.

From Assessment Tools to Grades. The grades you assign should reflect all of your objectives. Procedural skills remain important but should be proportional to other goals. If you are restricted to assigning a single grade for mathematics, different factors probably have different weights or values in making up the grade. Student X may be strong in reasoning and truly love mathematics yet be weak in computational skills. Student Y may be mediocre in problem solving but possess good skills in communicating her mathematical thinking. How much weight should you give to cooperation in groups, to written versus oral reports, to computational skills? There are no simple answers to these questions. However, they should be addressed at the beginning of the grading period and not the night you set out to assign report card grades.

A multidimensional reporting system that relies on multiple assessments is important for improving the validity of a grading system. If you can assign several grades for mathematics and not just one, your report to families is more meaningful. Even if the school's report card does not permit multiple grades, you can devise a supplement indicating several ratings for different objectives. A place for comments is also helpful. This form can be shared with

students periodically during a grading period and can easily accompany a report card.

The process of grading your students using multiple forms of assessments has the potential to enhance your students' achievement. As you develop your own tools to match your instruction and provide valuable evidence of your students' understanding, work with colleagues. In small groups or with a grade-level partner, you can share tasks, look at samples of students' work to try and decipher errors or celebrate a student's novel approach, and engage in discussions about how they have responded to similar student misconceptions. Working as a team to create and implement sound assessments will enrich your ability to select and administer meaningful performance-based questions or tasks and enhance your professional judgment by questioning or confirming your thinking.

Reflections on Chapter 5

Writing to Learn

1. What is the difference between formative and summative assessment? Give examples of each.
2. What is the difference between scoring and grading? What is the purpose of a score if it is not a grade?
3. Describe the essential features of a rubric. What are performance indicators?
4. How can students be involved in understanding and using rubrics to help with their learning?
5. How can you incorporate observational assessments into your daily lessons? What is at least one method of getting observations recorded? Do you have to observe every student?
6. How can children with limited writing skills "write" in mathematics journals?
7. How do diagnostic interviews help to capture student thinking?

For Discussion and Exploration

1. Examine a few end-of-chapter tests in various mathematics textbooks. How well do the tests assess what is important in the chapter? Concepts and understanding? Mathematical processes?
2. Access your state's department of education website and find a few released test items used by your state to determine annual yearly progress (AYP) as required by NCLB. For the released test items, first decide if they are good problem-based assessments that would help you find out about student understanding of the concepts involved. Then, if necessary, try to improve the item so that it becomes a problem-based assessment that would be useful in the classroom.
3. How are teachers in your area responding to the pressures of state testing programs? What are they doing in order to improve students' performance on these tests?

Resources for Chapter 5

Recommended Readings

Articles

Kitchen, R., Cherrington, A., Gates, J., Hitchings, J., Majka, M., Merk, M., & Trubow, G. (2002). Supporting reform through performance assessment. *Mathematics Teaching in the Middle School, 8*(1), 24–30.
Six of the seven authors are middle school teachers working together in the same school. As part of implementing a standards-based curriculum in a school that had recently dropped tracking, these teachers wrote and refined assessments they believed would help promote higher-order thinking. The article includes interesting examples and provides useful and inspiring information that is applicable across the grades.

Leatham, K. R., Lawrence, K., & Mewborn, D. (2005). Getting started with open-ended assessment. *Teaching Children Mathematics, 11*(8), 413–419.
In this article, the definition of an open-ended assessment item includes the potential for a range of responses and a balance between too much and too little information given. Examples are

included. The teacher-author (Lawrence) talks personally about getting started in her third–fourth grade class of "culturally and economically diverse" students and the values that accrued for both her and her class.

Books

Bush, W. S., & Leinwand, S. (Eds.). (2000). *Mathematics assessment: A practical handbook for grades 6–8.* Reston, VA: NCTM.

Glanfield, F., Bush, W. S., & Stenmark, J. K. (Eds.). (2003). *Mathematics assessment: A practical handbook for grades K–2.* Reston, VA: NCTM.

Stenmark, J. K., & Bush, W. S. (Eds.). (2001). *Mathematics assessment: A practical handbook for grades 3–5.* Reston, VA: NCTM.

These three NCTM books are part of a K–12 series on assessment. The handbooks offer practical advice for classroom teachers that is considerably beyond the scope of this chapter. The four chapters in each book essentially cover the kinds of assessment options that are best used, practical guidelines for implementing a quality assessment program in your classroom, and suggestions for dealing with the assessment data once gathered.

Wright, R., Martland, J., & Stafford, A. (2006). *Early numeracy: Assessment for teaching and intervention.* London: Paul Chapman Educational Publishers.

This book includes six diagnostic interviews for assessing young children's knowledge and strategy use related to numbers and the operations of addition and subtraction. Using a series of frameworks the authors help teachers pinpoint students' misconceptions and support appropriate interventions.

Online Resources

NCTM Research Clips and Briefs—Formative Assessment
www.nctm.org/clipsandbriefs.aspx

NCTM provides information on the definition of formative assessment and Five Key Strategies for effective formative assessment, including an example of a task for a diagnostic interview. They also include an excellent set of references for further investigation.

NCTM's Position Statement—High-Stakes Tests (Jan. 2006)
http://nctm.org/about/content.aspx?id=6356

This position statement provides information about NCTM's position on the role of high-stakes testing in making decisions for schools, students, and instruction.

20 Math Rubrics
http://intranet.cps.k12.il.us/Assessments/Ideas_and_Rubrics/Rubric_Bank/MathRubrics.pdf

Although this site is maintained by the Chicago Public Schools' Bureau of Assessment, you will find rubrics from many different states and national projects. Some are generic rubrics for problem solving, communication, and concept knowledge, but many have useful indicators and performance levels that can be adapted for many purposes.

Field Experience Guide Connections

Student learning and assessment is the focus of Chapter 7 of the *Field Experience Guide*, where seven different opportunities are designed to help you learn to assess. Designing and using rubrics, for example, are the focus of FEG 7.4 and 7.5. Also, FEG 1.4 (a student interview on attitudes) and FEG 7.2 (on assessing student understanding) are good assessment tasks to learn about students and about teaching. Chapter 11 of the guide offers three excellent balanced assessment tasks, complete with rubrics and guidance on how to score students.

Chapter 6

Teaching Mathematics Equitably to All Children

It was a wise man who said that there is no greater inequality than the equal treatment of unequals.

Supreme Court Justice Felix Frankfurter in
Dennis v. U.S., 339 US 162 (1950), p. 184.

Educational equity is a key component of helping all students meet the goals of the NCTM standards. The Equity Principle states, "Excellence in mathematics education requires equity—high expectations and strong support for all students" (NCTM, 2000, p. 12). Students need opportunities to advance their knowledge supported by teaching that gives attention to their individual learning goals. In years past (and in some cases still today) some students were not expected to do as well in mathematics as others, including students with special needs, students of color, speakers of languages other than English, females, and those of low socioeconomic status. Although all students should have equal chances to learn grade-level curriculum, this does not mean the instruction for every child should be equal.

Creating Equitable Instruction

Teaching for equity is much more than providing students with an equal opportunity to learn mathematics. It is not enough to require the same mathematics courses, give the same assignments, and use the identical assessment criteria. Instead, teaching for equity attempts to attain equal outcomes for all students by being sensitive to individual differences. Teaching for equity encourages teachers to treat students fairly and impartially by considering a complex array of information collected on every child. Ensuring that children of poverty and students in urban and sometimes rural schools will succeed requires you to

challenge widespread assumptions about children's ability to learn and the power of educational reform. Teachers who make change in their mathematics instruction by adjusting to children's needs and who celebrate classroom diversity are those who truly support student learning. You can have a transformational role when you view teaching in this way. In fact, there cannot be excellent schools without equitable schools.

Principles and Standards states, "All students, regardless of their personal characteristics, backgrounds, or physical challenges must have opportunities to study—and support to learn—mathematics. Equity does not mean that every student should receive identical instruction; instead, it demands that reasonable and appropriate accommodations be made as needed to promote access and attainment for all students" (NCTM, 2000, p. 12). Former NCTM president Shirley Frye said this as simply: "All children can learn but not in the same way and not on the same day."

myeducationlab

Go to the Activities and Application section of Chapter 6 of MyEducationLab. Click on Videos and watch the video entitled "**John Van de Walle on Creating Equitable Instruction**" to see him talk with teachers about teaching for equity.

One way to teach for equity, supported by extensive research, is guaranteeing that students have a highly qualified teacher with a strong knowledge of and experience teaching mathematics. "The most direct route to improving mathematics [and science] achievement for all students is better mathematics [and science] teaching.... Evidence of the positive effect of better teaching is unequivocal; indeed, the most consistent and powerful predictors of student achievement in mathematics [and science] are full teaching certification and a college major in the field being taught" (Glenn, 2000). Unfortunately, urban schools are most likely to have high turnover rates and the greatest number of teachers without certification or without a strong background in mathematics content. If teachers cannot provide deep mathematical understandings they may produce students who are underprepared or worse—inaccurately prepared. Therefore, it is not surprising to see gaps in performance comparing students from districts and schools with "master" teachers to those having teachers with weak backgrounds.

Many *achievement* gaps are actually *instructional* gaps or *expectation* gaps. Elementary and middle school teachers must prepare students by knowing as much mathematics content as possible to set students on a solid foundation. It is not helpful when teachers establish low expectations for students as when they say, "I just cannot put this class into groups to work; they are too unruly" or "My students can't solve word problems—they don't have the reading skills" or "I am not doing as many writing activities during math instruction as I have many English language learners in my class." All of these statements represent a lack of high expectations for all students. Going in with an attitude that some students cannot "do" will ensure that they don't have ample opportunities to prove otherwise.

NCTM views the education of *every* child as its most compelling objective. When thinking about creating and maintaining an equitable classroom environment, NCTM states, "Excellence in mathematics education rests on equity—high expectations, respect, understanding and strong support for all students. Policies, practices, attitudes, and beliefs related to mathematics teaching and learning must be assessed continually to ensure that all students have equal access to the resources with the greatest potential to promote learning. A culture of equity maximizes the learning potential of all students" (2008).

Mathematics for All Children

Most teachers, particularly new teachers, are committed to supporting each child in their classrooms. Therefore, equipping yourself with a large collection of strategies for children is critical. A strategy that works for one child may be completely ineffective with another, even for a child with the same exceptionality.

Pause and Reflect

Stop and think for a minute. Do you personally believe a "culture of equity" is necessary or even possible? Children with learning disabilities, children from impoverished homes, English language learners—can all of these children learn to think mathematically?

Diversity in Today's Classroom

The range of abilities, disabilities, and socioeconomic circumstances in the regular classroom poses significant challenges to teachers. Addressing the needs of *all* children means providing opportunity for any or all of the following:

* Students who are identified as having a specific learning disability
* Students from different cultural backgrounds
* Students who are English language learners
* Students who are mathematically gifted

In this chapter we will examine issues of diversity in the mathematics classroom and approaches that might be successful in helping every child reach mathematical literacy. You may think, "I do not need to read the section on culturally and linguistically diverse (CLD) students because I plan on working in a place that doesn't have any immigrants." Did you know that the number of Hispanics registered in schools rose from 6 percent in 1972 to 20 percent in 2008? During the same period, the number of whites registered in school has decreased from 78 percent of the population to 57 percent (U.S. Department of Education, 2008). You may think, "I can skip the section on mathematically promising students because they will be pulled out for math enrichment." Children who are gifted need to be challenged in daily instruction, not just when they are pulled out for a gifted program.

Recall that issues of equity and English language learners were addressed in Chapter 4 as they relate to planning effective lessons. As you read each section in this chapter, you will discover ways to create more equitable classrooms and you will find the means of helping all students become more mathematically literate.

The goal of equity is to offer all students access to important mathematics. Yet inequities exist, even if unintentionally. For example, if a teacher does not build in opportunities for student-to-student interaction in a lesson, he or she may not be addressing the needs of girls, who are often social learners, or English language learners, who need opportunities to talk, listen, and write in small-group situations. It takes more than just wanting to be fair or equitable; it takes knowing the strategies that accommodate each type of learner and making every effort to incorporate those strategies into your teaching. Although all students should have equal chances to learn grade-level curriculum, equal instruction is not a goal.

Tracking and Flexible Grouping

Tracking students is a significant culprit in creating differential expectations of students. Once students are placed in a lower-level track or in a "slow" class, expectations decline accordingly. Students in low tracks are frequently denied access to challenging material, high-quality instruction, and the best teachers (Burris & Welner, 2005; Futrell & Gomez, 2008; Samara, 2007). The mathematics for the lower tracks or classes is often oriented toward remedial drill with minimal success and little excitement. Low expectations are reinforced because students are not encouraged to think, nor are they engaged in activities and interactions that encourage problem solving and reasoning. This is particularly discouraging because minority and low-socioeconomic-status (low-SES) students are over-represented in lower-level tracks (Samara, 2007; Wyner, Bridgeland, & Dilulio, 2007).

The effect of tracking exaggerates initial differences among students rather than trying to bridge them. The talk about how groups are flexible and students can move to higher levels is in reality just that—talk. Groups usually remain fixed and the overall effect is cumulative. For a student to move to a higher track requires almost superhuman intensity—catching up on previously missed material while staying current on new content presented at a faster pace than the student is accustomed to and also learning the social and academic "rules" of the new classroom.

Nor does tracking particularly benefit higher-achieving students. Gains made by students in the highest groups have been found to be minimal when compared to similar students in heterogeneous classes. At the same time, low-achieving groups are deprived of quality instruction. Support for tracking of students at the K–8 level cannot be found in international comparisons either. This is particularly true in Asian countries. Among major industrialized countries, only the United States and Canada seem to maintain an interest in tracking (NRC, 2001).

In heterogeneous classes, expectations are often turned upside down as children once perceived as less able demonstrate understanding and work meaningfully with concepts to which they would never be exposed in a low-track class. Exposing all students to higher-level thinking and quality mathematics avoids compounding differences from year to year caused by low-track expectations.

Instructional Principles for Diverse Learners

Across the wonderful and myriad diversities of our students, all children essentially learn in the same way (Fuson, 2003). The authors of *Adding It Up* (NRC, 2001) conclude that all children are best served when attention is given to the following three principles:

1. Learning with understanding is based on connecting and organizing knowledge around big conceptual ideas.
2. Learning builds on what students already know.
3. Instruction in school should take advantage of the children's informal knowledge of mathematics.

These principles should come as no surprise. The tenets of constructivism described in Chapter 2 apply to all learners, not just the middle range of a so-called typical classroom.

Having said this, it is worth revisiting two ideas from Chapter 4: accommodation and modification (see pp. 65–69). An accommodation is a response to the needs of the environment or the learner but does not alter the task. A modification changes the task, making it more accessible to the student. When modifications result in an easier or less demanding task, expectations are lowered. Modifications should be made as a way to lead back to the original task, providing scaffolding or support for learners who may need it.

The following section discusses accommodations for the wide range of students likely to sooner or later appear in your classroom.

Providing for Students with Special Needs

One of the basic tenets of special education is the need for individualization of the content taught and the methods used for students with special needs. Many students with disabilities have an individualized education program (IEP) as mandated by the Individuals with Disabilities Education Act (IDEA) that was originally signed in 1975 and amended several times since, most recently in 2004. This law guarantees students access to the mathematics curriculum in the general education classroom, emphasizing the placement of as many students with special needs as possible in general elementary and middle grades classrooms. This legislation implies that educators consider individual learning needs not only in terms of *what* mathematics is taught but also *how* it is taught. "Equity does not mean that every student should receive identical instruction; instead, it demands that reasonable and appropriate accommodations be made as needed to promote access and attainment for all students" (NCTM, 2000, p. 12).

> **myeducationlab**
>
> Go to the Building Teaching Skills and Dispositions section of Chapter 6 of MyEducationLab. Click on Simulation Exercise and complete the simulation **"Providing Instructional Supports,"** which focuses on supporting the individual needs of students.

Response to Intervention

Determining eligibility for special education services for students with learning disabilities is shifting under the 2004 reauthorization of IDEA to include an approach called response to intervention (RTI). In the past students with learning disabilities were identified for special education through a marked discrepancy between their IQ scores and academic performance. But identifying those who need special services through testing alone limits the chance for students to get immediate assistance, a delay that oftentimes can mean learning problems become harder to fix. In addition, using testing alone does not take into consideration the strategies a teacher used to try to assist the student. Approaches such as RTI were designed to address these issues and distinguish between low achievement due to a lack of appropriate mathematic instruction, or "teacher-disabled students" (Ysseldyke, 2002), and low achievement due to a true learning disability.

RTI is a three-tiered student support system that focuses on the results of implementing instructional interventions in a model of prevention. Each tier represents a level of intervention with corresponding monitoring of results and outcomes as shown in Figure 6.1. The foundational and largest portion of the triangle represents Tier 1, which is the primary instruction that should be used with

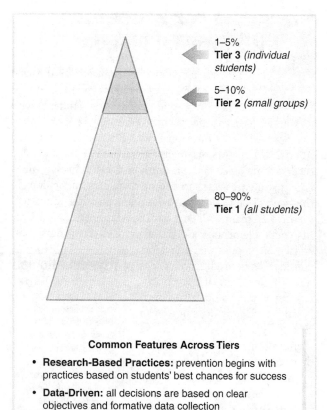

Common Features Across Tiers

- **Research-Based Practices:** prevention begins with practices based on students' best chances for success

- **Data-Driven:** all decisions are based on clear objectives and formative data collection

- **Instructional:** prevention and intervention involve effective instruction, prompts, cues, practice, and environmental arrangements

- **Context Specific:** all strategies and measures selected to fit individual schools, classrooms, or students

Figure 6.1 Response to intervention—using effective prevention strategies for all children.
Source: Scott, Terence, and Lane, Holly. (2001). *Multi-Tiered Interventions in Academic and Social Contexts.* Unpublished manuscript, University of Florida, Gainesville.

all students—in most cases a high-quality mathematics curriculum with high-quality instructional practices (i.e., manipulatives, conceptual emphasis, etc.). These instructional practices address principles of universal design that benefit all typically developing students while addressing students with special needs. At tier 1 a variety of assessments should be used to allow all students to demonstrate the knowledge and skills expected by grade-level state or national standards. Tier 2 represents "prereferral" students who did not reach the level of achievement expected during tier 1 activities but are not yet considered as needing special education services. Students in tier 2 should receive additional targeted instruction using modifications that include more explicit instruction with systematic teaching of critical skills, more intensive and frequent instructional opportunities, and more supportive and precise prompts to students, using more scaffolding (Torgesen, 2002). If further assessment reveals favorable progress, the students are weaned from the extra support. If challenges and struggles still exist, the interventions can be adjusted or the students are referred to the next tier of support. Tier 3 is for students who need more intensive levels of assistance, including a referral for special education evaluation or special education services. This intervention is "reserved for disorders that prove resistant to lower levels of prevention and require more heroic action to preclude serious complications" (Fuchs & Fuchs, 2001). The teacher will likely be required to show that a variety of ordinarily effective instructional interventions were attempted and that the student did not respond adequately to those more intensive strategies and approaches. Rather than waiting for a student to fail to show the dramatic discrepancies mandated by previous laws, RTI builds in a prevention model with structured support allowing students to progress. Strategies for the three tiers are outlined in Table 6.1.

Research into use of the RTI model reveals that although most students remain in tier 1, approximately 15 percent of students fail to demonstrate the full growth expected (Fuchs & Fuchs, 2001). Eventually nearly 40 percent of students targeted to move to tier 2 are returned to tier 1. Only about 13 percent of the original group moved to the second tier are considered for individual services from a special educator at the tier 3 level (Fuchs & Fuchs, 2005, 2007). If using an example of a group of 100 children, this would mean that their research showed that 15 students would move to tier 2. Then after intervention 6 would return to tier 1 and, of the remaining 9 students left in tier 2, approximately 2 students would move to tier 3 for more individualized services.

Students with Mild Disabilities

Students with learning disabilities have very specific difficulties with perceptual or cognitive processing and are identified as needing tier 3 services. These difficulties may affect memory; general strategy use; attention; or the ability

Table 6.1

RTI Interventions for Teaching Mathematics

RTI Level	Interventions
Tier 3	**Highly qualified special education teacher:** • Works one on one with student • Uses tailored instruction on specific areas of weakness • Modifies instructional methods, motivates students, and adapts curricula further • Uses explicit contextualization of skills-based instruction
Tier 2	**Highly qualified regular classroom teacher with possible collaboration from a highly qualified special education teacher:** • Conducts individual diagnostic interviews (see Chapter 5) • Collaborates with special education teacher • Creates lessons that emphasize the big ideas (focal points) or themes • Incorporates explicit systematic strategy instruction (directly summarizes key points, reviews key vocabulary or concepts prior to the lesson) • Models specific behaviors and strategies, such as how to handle measuring materials or geoboards • Uses mnemonics or steps written on cards or posters to help students follow problem-solving steps • Uses peer-assisted learning where one student requires help that another student can provide • Tutors on specific areas of weakness outside of the regular math instruction using volunteers such as grandparents • Supplies families with additional support materials to use at home • Encourages student use of self-regulation and self-instructional strategies such as revising notes, writing summaries, identifying main ideas • Teaches test-taking strategies, allows the students to use a highlighter on the test to emphasize important information • Slices back (Fuchs & Fuchs, 2001) to material from a previous grade to ramp back up

Tier 1	**Highly qualified regular classroom teacher:**
	• Incorporates high-quality curriculum and challenging standards for achievement
	• Commits to teaching the curriculum as defined
	• Uses manipulatives and visual models
	• Monitors progress to identify struggling students
	• Uses flexible student grouping
	• Fosters active involvement
	• Communicates high expectations
	• Uses graphic organizers in the before, during, and after stages of the lesson
	    Before. States purpose, introduces new vocabulary, clarifies concepts from the prior knowledge in a visual organizer, defines tasks of group members if using groups
	    During. Lays out the directions in a chart, poster, or list; provides a set of guiding questions in a chart with blank spaces for responses
	    After. Presents summary and list of important concepts as they relate to one another

to speak or express ideas in writing, perceive auditory, visual, or written information, or integrate abstract ideas. Although each student will have a unique profile of weaknesses and strengths, there are ways to support students in all phases of the planning, teaching, and assessing of the mathematics lesson.

NCTM has gathered a set of research-based effective strategies (NCTM, 2007) for teaching students with difficulties in mathematics (such as students in RTI tier 2), highlighting the use of several key strategies (Baker, Gersten, & Lee, 2002; Gersten, Chard, Jayanthi, & Baker, 2006), including systematic and explicit strategy instruction, student think-alouds, visual and graphic representation of problems, peer-assisted learning activities, and formative assessment data provided to students and teachers. These research-based approaches, proven to show effectiveness, in some cases represent principles quite different from those at the primary and secondary level of prevention found in tiers 1 and 2. Tier 3 intervention and instruction focuses on an individual student, whereas instruction in primary and secondary prevention emphasizes work with the whole class or small groups. The information that follows is for use with the small subset of students for whom the primary prevention strategies (tier 1) are unsuccessful.

Explicit Strategy Instruction. Explicit instruction is often characterized by highly structured, direct, teacher-led instruction on a specific strategy. The teacher does not merely model the strategy and have students practice it, but attempts to illuminate the decision making that may be troublesome for these learners. In this model, teaching routines are used that include a tightly scripted demonstration-prompt-practice sequence. Instruction is highly organized in a step-by-step format and involves direct teacher-led explanations of concepts including the critical connection building and meaning making that will help these learners place the knowledge of mathematics with other concepts they have learned. For example, let's look at a classroom teacher using explicit instruction:

As you enter Mr. Logan's classroom, you see a small group of students seated at a table listening to the teacher's detailed explanation and watching his demonstration of equivalent fraction concepts. Children are using manipulatives, as prescribed by Mr. Logan. He tells the students to take out the red "one-fourth" pieces and asks them to check how many will exactly cover the blue "one-half" piece. Then he asks them to compare the brown "eighths" and the yellow "sixths" to the piece representing one-half. Children are taking turns answering these questions out loud. During the lesson Mr. Logan frequently stops the group, interjects points of clarification, and directly highlights critical components of the task. Vocabulary words, such as numerator *and* denominator, *are written on the chalkboard and the definitions of these terms are reviewed and reinforced throughout the lesson. At the completion of the lesson, students are given several practice examples of the kind of comparisons discussed in the lesson.*

A number of aspects of direct instruction can be seen in Mr. Logan's approach to teaching fraction concepts. He employs a teacher-directed teaching format, prescribes the use of manipulatives, and incorporates a demonstration-prompt-practice sequence in the form of verbal instructions with demonstrations followed by prompting and questioning and then independent practice. Mr. Logan uses primarily teacher-led activities. Children are deriving mathematical knowledge from oral, written, and visual clues presented to them by the teacher.

As students solve problems they are given explicit strategy instruction to guide them in carrying out tasks such as reading and restating the problem, drawing a picture, developing a plan by identifying the type of problem, writing the problem in a mathematical sentence, breaking the problem into smaller pieces, carrying out operations, and checking using a calculator. These self-instructive prompts, or self-questions, structure the entire learning process from beginning to end. Unlike the more inquiry-based instruction in tier 1, the teacher models these steps and explains components using terminology that is easily understood by students with disabilities who did not discover them independently through tier 1 or 2 activities.

Physical models also can be used with explicit strategy instruction. For example, a teacher demonstrating a multiplication array with cubes might say, "Watch me. Now make a rectangle with the cubes that looks just like mine." In contrast, a teacher with a more constructivist approach might say, "Using these cubes, how can you show me a representation for 4 × 5?"

There are a number of possible advantages to the use of explicit strategy instruction for students with disabilities. This approach helps uncover or make overt the covert thinking strategies that support mathematical problem solving. Students with disabilities may otherwise not have access to these strategies, as they may be unable to acquire or apply them without explicit instruction. More explicit approaches are also less dependent on the student's ability to draw concepts from experience or to operate in an efficient and self-directed manner in loosely structured learning activities.

Along with the advantages, several possible challenges have been identified in using explicit strategy instruction for students with disabilities. Some aspects of this approach rely on memory, which can be one of the weakest areas for students with special needs. Taking a known weakness and building a learning strategy around it is often not productive. There is also the concern that highly teacher-controlled approaches such as direct, explicit instruction promote prolonged dependency on teacher assistance. This is of particular concern for students with disabilities, because many of them are described as passive learners. Students learn what they have the opportunity to practice. Students who are never given opportunities to engage in self-directed learning (based on the assumption that this is not an area of strength) will be deprived of the opportunity to develop skills in this area. In fact, the best direct instruction moves to multiple models, examples, and nonexamples and immediate error correction with fading of prompts to help students move to independence. Another possible challenge of explicit approaches is the depth of understanding that can be expected as a result. Experiential-based learning that centers on active problem solving and the construction of knowledge produces deeper understanding of mathematics and enhances student ability to retain, generalize, and apply information, all factors that are vital to long-term success in mathematics while too often problem areas for students with mild disabilities.

Peer-Assisted Learning.   Children with special needs benefit from others' modeling and support, including the modeling by their classmates or peers (Fuchs, Fuchs, Yazdian, & Powell, 2002). In this approach, what happens in the classroom design reflects the basic notion that children learn best when they are placed in the role of an apprentice mastering school tasks. The students are encouraged to think about learning events in ways that approximate the thinking of those who are more skilled experts. Although the peer-assisted learning approach shares some of the characteristics of the explicit strategy instruction model described above, there are a number of important distinctions. One of these is the notion that knowledge is presented on an "as-needed" basis as opposed to a predetermined sequence. Peers share knowledge with others when that knowledge is required. The students can be paired with older children or peers who have more sophisticated understandings of a concept. In other cases, tutors and tutees can change roles during the tasks.

Student Think-Alouds.   "Think-aloud" is an instructional strategy that involves demonstrating the steps to accomplish a task while you verbalize the thinking process and reasoning that accompanies the steps. The student follows this instruction by imitating these steps on a different, but parallel, task. This derives from the model in which "expert" learners share strategies with "novice" learners. Consider a problem in which fourth-grade students are given the task of determining how much paint will be needed to cover the walls of their classroom. Rather than merely demonstrating, for example, how to use a ruler to measure the distance across a wall, the think-aloud strategy would involve talking through the steps and identifying the reasons for each step while measuring the space. As the teacher places a mark on the wall to indicate where the ruler ended in the first measurement, she states, "I used this line to mark off where the ruler ends. How should I use this line as I measure the next section of the floor? I know I have to move the ruler, but should I copy what I did the first time?" All of this dialogue occurs prior to placing the ruler for a second measurement. Often teachers share alternatives about how they could have carried out the task but decided to do something else. When using this strategy, teachers try to model possible approaches while making their invisible thinking processes visible.

Although you will choose strategies as needed, your goal is always working toward high student responsibility for learning. Movement to higher levels of understanding of content can be likened to the need to move to a higher level on a hill. For some, formal stair steps with support along the way is necessary (explicit strategy instruction); for others ramps with encouragement at the top of the hill will work (peer-assisted learning). Other students can find a path up the hill on their own with some guidance (constructivist approach). All people can relate to the need to have different support during different times of their lives or under different circumstances, and it is no different for students with special needs. Yet they must eventually learn to create a path to new learning on their own as that is what will be required in the real world after schooling. Leaving children only knowing how to climb steps with support and having them face hills without stair steps or constant assistance from others will not help students attain their goals. The following suggestions may help you provide lesson modifications and adaptations for particular students with special needs in the three critical instructional stages—before, during, and after (Karp & Howell, 2004).

BEFORE
Structure the Environment

- *Centralize attention.* Move the student close to the board or teacher. Face students when you speak to them.
- *Help families play a part.* If possible, provide an extra mathematics textbook to be taken home.
- *Remove competing stimuli.* Conduct assessments in another space that is quieter or has fewer distractions.
- *Adjust curricular objectives.* Adapt the number of learning goals for particular students so that they focus on the "big ideas" while allowing other students to explore topics in greater depth or complexity.

- *Avoid confusion.* Word directions carefully and specifically and ask the child to repeat them. Give one direction at a time.
- *Smooth the periods between instruction.* Ensure that transitions between activities have clear directions and limited chances to get "off task."
- *Preteach or preview math concepts or vocabulary.* Familiarize students with important terms.

Identify Potential Barriers

- *Find ways to help students remember.* Recognizing that memory is often not a strong suit for students with special needs, develop mnemonics (memory aids) for familiar steps or write directions that can be referred to throughout the lesson. For example, **STAR** is a mnemonic for problem solving: **S**earch the word problem for important information; **T**ranslate the words into models, pictures, or symbols; **A**nswer the problem; **R**eview your solution for reasonableness (Gagnon & Maccini, 2001).
- *Reinforce key vocabulary and symbols.* Create a word and symbol wall to provide visual cues. Highlight math vocabulary and symbols for students with language processing problems.
- *Use friendly numbers.* Instead of using $6.13 use $6.00 to emphasize conceptual understanding rather than mixing computation and conceptual goals at the same time. Remember, this technique is only used when computation and operation skills are *not* the lesson objective.
- *Vary the task size.* Assign students with special needs fewer problems to solve. Some students can become frustrated by the enormity of the task. Find ways to adapt the size of the activity to be challenging but doable.
- *Remember the timeframe.* Give students additional reminders about the time left for exploring the materials, completing tasks, or finishing assessments. This will help students with time management.
- *Modify the level of support.* Allow more support either through your own attention or instruction or the attention of teaching assistants or peers. Consider the support of a variety of learning tools including manipulative materials and technology.
- *Pair and share.* Have students share ideas to help increase students' risk taking and willingness to discuss ideas with the whole class.

DURING
Provide Clarity

- *Ask students to share their thinking.* Use the think-aloud method or think-pair-share (first *think* about the question, then *pair* with a classmate and compare ideas, finally *share* the best thinking with the rest of the class).

- *Link the model to an action and words.* For example, as you fold a strip of paper into fourths, point out the part-whole relationship with gestures as you pose a question about the relationship between $\frac{2}{4}$ and $\frac{1}{2}$.
- *Adjust the visual display.* Design assessments and tasks so that there is not too much on a single page. Sometimes the density of words, illustrations, and numbers can overload students. Find ways to put one problem on a page, increase font size, or just reduce the visual display to a workable amount.
- *Emphasize the relevant points.* Some students with special needs may inappropriately focus on the color of a cube instead of the quantity of cubes.
- *Utilize methods for organizing written work.* Provide tools and templates so students can focus on the mathematics rather than the organization of a table or chart. Also use organizers, picture-based models, and paper with columns or grids
- *Provide examples and nonexamples.* Give examples of triangles as well as shapes that are not triangles. Help students focus on the characteristics that differentiate the examples from those that are not examples.
- *Support connections.* Provide concrete representations, pictorial representations, and numerical representations. Have students connect the linkages through carefully phrased questions.
- *Adapt delivery modes.* Incorporate a variety of materials, images, examples, and models for students who may be more visual learners. Some students may need to have the problem or assessment read to them or generated with voice creation software. Provide written instructions with oral instructions.

AFTER

Consider Alternative Assessments

- *Propose alternative products.* Provide options for the ways that students with special needs respond to the tasks. They may need to provide a verbal response that is written by someone else or tape recorded. They may use voice recognition software or word prediction software that can generate a whole menu of word choices from typing a few letters. For an assessment they might use materials to demonstrate their understanding of a mathematics concept rather than a reply through a written record.
- *Consider feedback charts.* Monitor students' growth and chart progress over time. This is important reinforcement for students and the teacher.

Emphasize Practice and Summary

- *Help students bring ideas together.* Create study guides that summarize the key mathematics concepts and allow for review.
- *Provide extra practice.* Use carefully selected problems (not a large number) and allow use of familiar physical models for a longer period of time.

- *Make practice routines developmental.* Begin practice using only one problem type and then move to practice with multiple types of problems.

Students with Significant Disabilities

Students with significant cognitive disabilities often need extensive modifications and individualized supports to understand the mathematics curriculum. Cognitive problems include severe autism, sensory disorders, multiple disabilities including combinations of limitations affecting movement, or cognitive processing disorders such as mental retardation and cerebral palsy. IDEA (1990, 1997, 2004) mandated access for all students to the general grade-level curriculum. No Child Left Behind has moved from access to now requiring evidence that students learn the content, incorporating expectations that students with moderate to severe disabilities will be working toward grade-appropriate alternate proficiencies on state-designated alternative standards in mathematics. To demonstrate their serious intent, some states are now including students with significant disabilities in their annual formal accountability programs for assessing student progress.

Originally, the functional curriculum for students with severe disabilities was often narrowed to life-related skills such as managing money; telling time; or matching numbers to complete such tasks as entering a telephone number, identifying a house number, using a calculator, or measuring. Now, state initiatives and assessments have broadened the curriculum to address the five NCTM content strands that were specifically delineated by grade level in the *Curriculum Focal Points* (NCTM, 2006). For example, one key approach emphasizes numeracy through real-world representations as a way to prepare all students to be mathematically literate citizens. Using money to study place-value concepts or posing problems in the context of making purchases are approaches with multiple benefits.

At a beginning level, students work on identifying numbers by holding up fingers or pictures. To develop number sense, counting up can be linked to counting off daily tasks to be accomplished, and counting down can mark a period of cleanup after an activity or to complete self-care routines (brushing teeth). Students with moderate or severe disabilities should have opportunities to use measuring tools, compare graphs, explore place-value concepts (often linked to money use), use the number line, and compare quantities. Each time the content should be connected to life skills and possible features of jobs—such as restocking supplies (Hughes & Rusch, 1989). Shopping skills or activities in which food is prepared are both options for mathematical problem-solving situations. At other times, just linking mathematical learning objectives to everyday events is practical. For example, when studying the operation of division, figuring how candy can be equally shared at Halloween or dealing cards to play a game would be appropriate. Students can also undertake a small project such as constructing a box to store different items as a way to explore shapes and measurements.

Do not believe that all facts must be mastered before students with moderate or severe disabilities can move forward in the curriculum; students can learn geometric or measuring concepts without having mastered addition and subtraction facts. Geometry for students with moderate and severe disabilities is more than merely identifying shapes but is in fact critical for orienting themselves in the real world. The practical aspects emerge when such concepts as parallel and perpendicular lines and curves and straight sides become helpful for interpreting maps of the local area. Students' use of public transportation can be supported by using maps related to bus or subway routes as teaching materials. Students who learn to count bus stops and judge time can be helped to successfully navigate their world.

Table 6.2 offers some suggested approaches to different content areas. You will need to blend the curriculum for a particular grade level with the basic skills a student needs in a functional context. If other students are studying the measures of various angles of triangles, the student with moderate disabilities can sort triangles into groups with the same angle as a given triangle. For example in matching right-angled triangles to a model on a mat as part of learning about right angles, the content area remains within grade-level mathematics objectives while being adapted to meet the long-term needs of students with moderate disabilities to grow in concepts, vocabulary, and symbol use.

The following list indicates other ideas for modifying grade-level instruction.

Additional Strategies for Supporting Students with Moderate and Severe Disabilities

- *Systematic instruction.* Use repeated trials, systematic prompting, and corrective feedback to reach a particular outcome.
- *Visual supports.* Visual cues, color coding, and simplified numerical expressions using dots or other pictorial clues can focus learning for some students.
- *Response prompt.* Ask a student, "What is three plus three?" while visually showing 3 + 3. Say "Six" and then state to the student again, "Three plus three is six." Next give a stimulus-response prompt—"What's three plus three?"
- *Task chaining.* Task analyze. Take one step at a time with a prompt for students at each step. Fade the number of prompts based on student performance.
- *Problem solving.* State the problem. For example, pass out paper plates for students at the table with an incorrect number and some plates missing. Ask students, "What is the problem?" The students should state a solution and suggest that more materials are needed. "How many more plates are needed?" When that amount is given, students have solved the problem. Use a visual showing a one-to one correspondence between people and plates to show how to record the situation. Then write and read the corresponding equation.
- *Self-determination skills and independent self-directed learning.* Support opportunities for students to make choices in decision making and goal setting.

Table 6.2

Activities for Students with Moderate and Severe Disabilities	
Content Area	**Activity**
Number and Operations	• Count out a variety of items for general classroom activities. • Create a list of supplies that need to be ordered for the classroom or a particular event. • Calculate the number of calories in a given meal. • Compare the cost of two meals on menus from local restaurants.
Algebra	• Show an allowance or wage on a chart to demonstrate growth over time. Write an equation to show how much they would have in a month or year. • Calculate the slope of a wheelchair ramp or driveway.
Geometry	• Use spatial relationships to identify a short path between two locations on a map. • Tessellate several figures to show how a variety of shapes fit together. Using tangrams to fill a space will also develop these important workplace skills.
Measurement	• Fill different-shaped items with water, sand, or rice to assess volume, ordering the vessels from least to most. • Take body temperature and use an enlarged thermometer to show comparison to outside temperatures. • Calculate the amount of paint needed to cover the walls or ceiling of the classroom, using area. • Estimate the amount of time it would take to travel to a known location using a map.
Data Analysis and Probability	• Survey students on favorite games (either electronic or other) using the top five as choices for the class. Make a graph to represent and compare the results. • Tally the number of students ordering school lunch. • Examine the outside temperatures for the past week and discuss the probability of the temperatures for the next days being within a particular range.

Culturally and Linguistically Diverse Students

The United States has been called both a melting pot and a salad bowl. In reality, it is both. Many students in our classrooms have parents or grandparents of mixed heritage, yet they have been raised in the United States and their first language is English. The United States also has many students who have not been blended into mainstream American culture. They are first- or second-generation children from another culture who may speak another language as their first language. You will better serve the needs of your students who are culturally and linguistically diverse (CLD) by valuing their culture and language and not trying to force them into local culture and language. This section discusses ways to develop a culturally competent set of instructional practices.

Windows and Mirrors

You are not the only one who needs to expand your cultural horizons to enhance mathematics learning; the students do too. In the words of Emily Style, a former diversity coordinator of the Morristown, New Jersey, schools,

> An inclusive curriculum provides students with a balance of windows to frame and acknowledge the diverse experience of others and mirrors to reflect the reality and validity of each student. (1988)

As you work with students' areas of strength you should identify opportunities to stretch their thinking in ways that move unfamiliar experiences to familiar ones. For example, if you are working with children in an urban setting and using an example discussing plots of farm land or gardens, it would be wise to read a story that could improve understanding for the whole class. *City Green* by DyAnne Disalvo-Ryan helps make the unknown known. Students can see how a lot in an urban community can be divided and shared among neighbors. With this approach, all students can experience the background needed for the task. Another part of a supportive context is creating a safe and nurturing environment where students care for one another. Students should feel responsible for each other's success in mathematical tasks and feel supported in their work. Giving students an opportunity to communicate as part of an emphasis on the social and affective domains is critical to creating classrooms where a variety of cultures are celebrated.

Culturally Relevant Mathematics Instruction

You have probably heard it said that "mathematics is a universal language." This common misconception can lead to inequities in the classroom. For example, language needs for students who are CLD tend to be ignored in mathematics instruction (Lee & Jung, 2004). There are three different perspectives on how to support students who are CLD:

1. Limit the use of language and focus primarily on symbols.
2. Implement the NCTM *Principles and Standards*, using language-rich tasks.
3. Integrate a standards-based curriculum with CLD strategies (Bay-Williams & Herrera, 2007).

We will look briefly at each of these three approaches, including their advantages and disadvantages.

The rationale for the limited-language approach is that the student will understand the symbols, which are universal. There are many problems with this viewpoint. First, symbols are not universal. For example, in Mexico textbooks may refer to angle B as $\hat{B}$ or $\widehat{ABC}$ rather than $\angle B$ or $\angle ABC$ as in the United States. An English language learner may not recognize the angle symbol and might confuse it with the "less than" symbol. The numeral 9 as written in Latin American countries can easily be confused with a lowercase g. What is called "billions" in the United States is called "thousand millions" in Mexico (Perkins & Flores, 2002). Second, symbols are abstract. As discussed in Chapter 2, students should begin with concrete materials and problems that provide situations familiar to the student. Third, the use of language, in written and oral forms, is essential to developing a deep understanding of mathematics (Khisty, 1997). Finally, a belief that symbols are easier for students who are CLD often causes a teacher too quickly to use symbolic representations and, therefore, limits a student's conceptual understanding (Garrison & Mora, 1999).

The second approach to teaching students who are CLD is to embrace the recommendations outlined in *Principles and Standards*. A standards-based teacher may use inquiry, student–student interactions (pairs and small groups), discussions, and alternative assessments, all of which can support the learning of a student who is also learning English or who is not familiar with particular aspects of U.S. culture (Echevarria, Vogt, & Short, 2008).

Standards-based teaching supports the English language learner more effectively than traditional teaching because many of the strategies used are especially helpful for students who are CLD. For example, the *Standards* encourages a learning environment whereby students solve a problem using a strategy of their own choosing and later explain how they solved the problem. A student from a different culture may have learned different strategies for that concept or for related skills. In addition, explaining their strategy allows students opportunities to develop their language skills.

However, even in classrooms where teachers incorporate many standards-based practices, an achievement gap may still exist. What is often lacking is an intentional effort to help students develop their language skills, which is what the third approach offers.

Creating effective learning for students who are CLD involves integrating principles of bilingual education with standards-based content instruction (see Table 4.1). That is, lessons must be based on problems and discussions while also attending to the culture and the language of the students. To operate from this perspective requires exploring how to embrace culture while supporting language development. Although discussed separately in the next two sections, they are interrelated and should not be separated in instruction.

Ethnomathematics

The combination of culture, mathematics, and education activities is often referred to as *ethnomathematics*. Many societies have different mathematical traditions and have developed various strands of mathematical thought. Teaching mathematics with respect to culture is one way to honor diversity within the classroom. Students can be personally engaged in mathematics by examining their own culture's impact on the ways they use, practice, and think about mathematics. A study of mathematics within other cultures provides an opportunity for students to "put faces" on mathematical contributions instead of erroneously thinking that mathematics is a result of some mystical phenomenon.

Bishop (1991) defines six categories in which we find mathematics linking culture and linguistic diversity: counting (e.g., learning the numbers systems of other nations), measuring (e.g., using other countries' measuring tools or units), locating (e.g., using maps and geography to locate places), designing and building (e.g., considering the living space in African round and square houses), playing (e.g., "Mancala," "Nine Men's Morris"), and explaining (e.g., describing how family members are related on a family tree or telling stories through African sand painting patterns, or *sona*).

There are many ways to approach mathematics from a cultural perspective (e.g., biographies of mathematicians or historical development of concepts, games, children's literature, and thematic units). Ethnomathematics provides a natural bridge between mathematics and other subjects in the curriculum. Mathematics is the by-product of human ideas, creativity, problem solving, recreation, beliefs, values, and survival. Contributions to the field of mathematics have come from diverse people all over the world, including many women and people of color whose important contributions to mathematics have been overlooked.

English Language Learners (ELLs)

How many students attending U.S. schools are not fluent in English? Nationally, more than 5 million students (10.5 percent) were receiving ELL services in 2005. This is not just a statistic for urban centers; ELL services are needed in every state in the United States and every province in Canada. For example, the states with the largest increase in ELL students from 1995 to 2005 are South Carolina (714%), Kentucky (417%), Indiana (408%), North Carolina (372%), and Tennessee (370%). Hispanics continue to be the largest minority group in the United States, representing 58 percent of all immigrant schoolchildren and more than 75 percent of ELL students (Kohler & Lazarin, 2007).

English language learners enter the mathematics classroom from homes in which English is not the primary language of communication. Although a person might develop conversational English language skills in a few years, it takes as many as 7 years to learn "academic language," which is the language specific to a content area such as mathematics (Cummins, 1994). Academic language is harder to learn because it is not used in a student's everyday world. When learning about mathematics, students might be learning content in English that they have no words for in their native language. For example, in studying the measures of central tendency (*mean, median,* and *mode*), they may not know words for these terms in their first language, increasing the challenge for learning academic language in their second language. In addition, story problems are difficult for ELLs not just due to the language but also to the fact that sentences in story problems are often structured differently than sentences in conversational English.

Teachers of English to Speakers of Other Languages (TESOL) developed standards for effective instruction of English as a second language (ESL) to pre-K–12 students in the United States (TESOL, 1997). TESOL's vision of effective education for students learning English includes developing proficiency in English and the maintenance and promotion of students' native languages. TESOL standards state that students will use English to

1. "interact in the classroom"
2. "obtain, process, construct, and provide subject matter information in spoken and written form"
3. "use appropriate learning strategies to construct and apply academic knowledge" (TESOL, 1997, p. 9)

Notice that students are to use English in their academic content courses. This does not mean "English only," but rather an approach that encourages the use of native language and the development of English. Also note that the emphasis for ELLs is providing these language opportunities: reading, writing, speaking, and listening. When these are incorporated effectively into instruction, both mathematical understanding and language can be learned.

Strategies for Teaching Mathematics to ELLs

Among the many classroom supports for students who are learning English, the strategies discussed in this section are critical to mathematics instruction. They are among the ideas that teachers and researchers most commonly mention as increasing the academic achievement of ELLs in mathematics classrooms (also see Table 4.1 in Chapter 4).

Write and State the Content and Language Objectives.   Every lesson should begin with telling students what they will be learning. You do not give away what they will discover in their exploration, but you state the larger purpose of what they are doing; in other words, provide a road map. If students know the purpose of the lesson, they are better able to make sense of the details in light of the bigger picture. For example, when teaching a lesson about using different strategies for multiplication and division, you would write student-friendly objectives on the board such as the following:

1. Find different ways to multiply and divide numbers. (content)
2. Explain how you completed a multiplication and division problem when you were given the first step. (language and content)
3. Write the way you would pick to solve the division problem. (language)

Build Background.   This is similar to building on prior knowledge, but it takes into consideration native language and culture as well as content. If possible, use a context and any appropriate visuals to help students understand the task you want them to solve. Link the lesson to prior learning: yesterday's lesson, a real-world problem, or something you did earlier in the month. For example, you might have a discussion of what 22×42 could refer to (perhaps it refers to the measurements of a picture hanging on the wall or the amount of money it will cost to buy stamps for each member of a class of 22 students).

Encourage Use of Native Language.   Research shows that students' cognitive development progresses more readily in their native language. In a mathematics classroom, students can communicate in their native language and continue their English language development. For example, a good strategy for students working in small groups is having students who speak Spanish first discuss the problem in Spanish. If a student knows enough English, then the presentation during the *after* phase of the lesson can be assigned as "English preferred." If the student knows little or no English, then he or she can explain in Spanish using a translator.

Use Comprehensible Input.   *Comprehensible input* as used in bilingual education that means that the message you are communicating is understandable to students. It means to simplify sentence structures and limit the use of nonessential or confusing vocabulary; it does not mean to lower expectations for the lesson. It also means to use strategies to help students understand the language they encounter. Sometimes teachers put many unnecessary words and phrases into questions, making them less clear to nonnative speakers. Compare the following sets of teachers' directions:

> Not Modified: You have a labsheet in front of you that I just gave out. For every situation, I want you to determine the total area for the shapes. You will be working with your partners, but each of you needs to record your answers on your own paper and explain how you got your answer. If you get stuck on a problem raise your hand.

> Modified: Please look at your paper. (Holds paper and points to it. Pointing to the first picture.) You will find the area. What does *area* mean? (Allows wait time.) How can you calculate area? (*Calculate* is more like the Spanish word *calcular,* so it is more accessible to Spanish speakers.) Talk to your partners. (Points to mouth and then to a pair of students as she says this.) Write your answers. (Makes a writing motion over paper.)

Notice that three things have been done: sentences shortened, removal of confusing words, and use of gestures and motions that link to the vocabulary. Also notice the "wait time" the teacher gives. It is very important to provide extra time after posing a question or giving instructions to allow ELLs time to translate, make sense of the request, and then participate.

Another way to provide comprehensible input is to use a variety of tools to help students visualize and understand what is verbalized. In the preceding example, the teacher is modeling the instructions. When introducing a lesson, include pictures, real objects, and diagrams. For example, if teaching integers, having a real thermometer, as well as an overhead of a thermometer, will help provide a visual (and a context). You might even add pictures of places covered in snow and position them near the low temperatures and so on. Students should also be expected to include multiple representations in their work. Expect students to draw, write, and explain what they have done. This is helpful to them and to their peers who will be seeing their solutions. Supplemental materials you should consider using include manipulatives, real objects, pictures, visuals, multimedia, demonstrations, and children's books (Echevarria, Vogt, & Short, 2008).

Explicitly Teach Vocabulary.   One popular technique to reinforce vocabulary development is a mathematics word wall. As you encounter vocabulary essential for learning mathematics, students participate in creating and adding to the word wall. When a word is selected, students can create cards that include the word in English, translations to languages represented in your room, pictures, and a student-made description (not a formal definition) in English or in several languages.

In addition to word walls, there are many ways to explicitly teach vocabulary. For example, students can create concept maps, linking concepts and terms as they study the relationships among fractions, decimals, and percents. Students can keep "personal math dictionaries" of terms they need to know, which include the word, illustrations, and examples. As you use a mathematical term that has been previously addressed, stop and make sure that students remember the term. As new terms are introduced, the word itself should be discussed, sharing the root and related words (Rubenstein, 2000). There are many terms that have different meanings in mathematics from everyday activities, such as *product, mean, sum, factor, acute, foot, division, difference, similar, angle.*

Plan Cooperative/Interdependent Groups to Support Language. English language learners need opportunities to speak, write, talk, and listen in nonthreatening situations. The best way to accomplish such goals is through cooperative/interdependent groups. In grouping, you must consider a student's language skills. Placing an ELL with two English-speaking students may result in the ELL being left out entirely. It is better to place a bilingual student in this group or to place students that have the same first language together if possible (Garrison, 1997; Khisty, 1997). Pairs may be more appropriate than groups of three or four. As with all group work, rules or structures should be in place to make sure that each student is able to participate and is accountable for the activity assigned. ELLs will recognize that you have established a haven that is supportive and nurturing when they find that you see their culture and language as a resource to be valued rather than a drawback to be managed.

Create Partnerships with Families. All students achieve more when their families support their learning. Parents or guardians must be made aware of test results and what they can do to make positive changes in their children's performance to help reduce any gaps in understanding. However, it can be difficult to build good relationships when family members have negative memories of their own schooling or their attempts at mathematics. In the way many of you might feel uneasy entering a hospital because you or a loved one may have had a difficult experience there, family members can feel that way about returning to a school setting, especially the mathematics classroom. On occasion teachers and administrators need to go out into the community to share with families the message that working together to have all students learn mathematics is the best way for students to "win." *Win* is an important word here as most communities are eager to rally around strategies for winning. A vital aspect of having a strong, inclusive mathematics program is gathering support and trust from families who see their role as critical to a partnership for helping their child learn.

Significant mathematics learning occurs before children even enter the classroom. This household knowledge of mathematics is a good foundation for building new experiences and can set the stage for higher-level learning as teachers build on these assets. Bringing a child's family into the mathematics equation is a critical part of developing a classroom community and learning about ways to make the curriculum culturally relevant. Families need to share the mathematics their children learn so they can value it, even though it may be different from their own school experiences learning mathematics. Newsletters including tips for families, puzzles, games, and problems can be sent home for family exploration. Invitations for Family Math Night (Stenmark, Thompson, & Cossey, 1986) or suggestions for ways that families can be helpful with homework are all means to a better partnership. Finding ways to draw children away from television and computer games and toward mathematics activities with family members that stimulate the imagination or call on problem-solving skills are essential to building lasting educational partnerships. As teachers learn to respect the contributions of the families' culture to the classroom, the families, in turn, gain respect for the work of the classroom teacher. The following family-oriented math project is descriptive of the kind of meaning you can bring to the mathematics class by honoring family history and culture.

I read a book called the Hundred Penny Box (Mathis, 1986) to my class each day after lunch. This is the touching and poignant story of a boy's great-great-Aunt Dew, an elderly African American woman who has collected in an old cigar box one penny from each of the hundred years she has been alive. Plucking a penny out of the box, she can remember an important event that happened to her that year. Each penny is more than a piece of money; it is a "memory trigger" for her life. Taking a cue from the book, I asked each child to collect one penny from each year they were alive starting from the year of their birth and not missing a year. Students were encouraged to bring in additional pennies their classmates might need. Then the students consulted with family members to create a penny time line of important events in their lives. Using information gathered at home they started with the year they were born listing their birthday and went on to record first steps, accidents, vacations, pets, and births of siblings in those early years. Then I asked students to determine how many years between certain events or to calculate their age when they adopted a pet or learned to ride a bicycle.

Besides connecting to a sense of community and building of links to families, the project established a classroom climate of respect and rapport. Students and families worked together to investigate the child's personal history and decide which events were most important to highlight, many times revealing cultural values. Matching episodes to chronological time on a time line linked well with skills being learned in social studies.

Working Toward Gender Equity

Based on the results of NAEP tests, gender gaps in mathematics achievement remained small but fairly consistent from 1990 to 2007, with males outperforming females in grades 4, 8, and 12. Yet a recent study (Hyde, Lindberg, Linn, Ellis, & Williams, 2008) reveals that in analyzing the standardized test scores from more than 7.2 million U.S. students in grades 2–11, there were no differences in math scores for girls and boys. Hyde stated that "girls who believe the stereotype wind up avoiding harder math classes" but the carefully designed efforts over the past 20 years are showing results. However, after high school, more males than females enter fields of study that include heavy emphases on mathematics and science. The president of the Society of Women Engineers stated, "Why, while girls comprise 55 percent of undergraduate students, do they account for only 20 percent of engineering majors, and boys remain four times more likely to enroll in undergraduate engineering programs?" (Tortolani, 2007). It remains important to be aware of and address gender equity issues in your classroom.

Possible Causes of Gender Inequity

As Becker and Jacobs (2001) point out, most of the research "is moving away from 'sex differences' to 'gender differences' in acknowledgment that gender is socially constructed and the differences are not biologically determined" (p. 2). We can find some of the causes of gender inequity in the classroom.

Belief Systems Related to Gender. The belief that mathematics is a male activity persists in our society and is held by both sexes. Stereotypes that boys are better in math shape girls' self-perceptions and motivations (Nosek, Banaji, & Greenwald, 2002). What may result is a decrease in emerging interest in math. "The relative absence of females in math and science careers fuels the stereotype that girls cannot succeed in math-related areas and thus young girls are, often subtly, steered away from them" (Barnett, 2007).

Teacher Interactions and Gender. Teachers may not consciously seek to stereotype students by gender; however, the gender-based biases of our society often affect teachers' interactions with students (Martin, Sexton, Wagner, & Gerlovich, 1997). According to Janet Hyde, "[b]oth parents and teachers continue to hold the stereotype that boys are better than girls [at math]" (Seattle Times News Services, 2008). Observations of teachers' gender-specific interactions in the classroom indicate that boys get more attention and different kinds of attention than girls do. Boys receive more criticism for wrong answers as well as more praise for correct answers. Boys also tend to be more involved in discipline-related attention and have their work monitored more carefully (Campbell, 1995). Attention is interpreted as value, with a predictable effect on both sexes. Often females in math classes go unobserved and a study found them to be the "quiet achievers" (Clark et al., 2001).

What Can Be Done?

As already noted, the causes of girls' perceptions of themselves vis-à-vis mathematics are partially a function of the educational environment. That is where we should look for solutions.

Awareness. As a teacher, you need to work at ensuring equitable treatment of boys and girls. As you interact with students, try to be sensitive to the following interactions with both gender groups:

- Number and type of questions you ask
- Amount of attention given to disturbances
- Kinds and topics of projects and activities assigned
- Praise given in response to students' participation
- Makeup of small groups
- Contexts of problems
- Characters in children's literature used in mathematics instruction (Karp, Brown, Allen, & Allen, 1998)

Being aware of your gender-specific actions is more difficult than it may sound. To receive feedback, try video-recording a class or two on a periodic basis. Tally the number of questions asked of boys and girls. Also note which students ask questions and what kind of questions are being asked. Where do you stand in the room? At first, you may be surprised at any gender-biased behaviors. Awareness takes effort.

Involve All Students. Find ways to involve all students in your class, not just those who seem eager. Girls may tend to shy away from involvement and are not as quick to seek help. Perhaps the best suggestion for involving students is to follow the tenets of this book—use a problem-based approach to instruction. Mau and Leitze (2001) make the case that when teachers are in a show-and-tell mode, there is significantly more opportunity for the teacher to reinforce boys' more overt behaviors as well as girls' more passive behaviors. In a classroom influenced by constructivist theory, all students are expected to both talk and listen. More mathematical thinking is constructed with less teacher talk and more student conversation about ideas. Authority resides in the students and in their arguments.

—————————— *Pause and Reflect*

Stop for a moment and envision the teaching model you experienced as a student. Can you remember situations in which one gender was favored, encouraged, reprimanded, or assisted by the teacher—even without consciously being aware of any differential treatment? How would these differences possibly disappear in a problem-based, student-discourse-oriented environment?

Reducing Resistance and Building Resilience

There are children who make a decision along the way in their formal education that they won't learn mathematics, so why try? Teachers need to "reach beyond the resistance" and find ways to listen to children and affirm their abilities. Here are a few key strategies for getting there.

Give Children Choices and Capitalize on Their Unique Strengths. Children often need to have power over something with a stake and a say in what is happening. Therefore, focus on making classrooms inviting and familiar as you connect students' voices to the content. Setting up situations where these students feel success with mathematics tasks can bring them closer to stopping the willful avoidance of learning mathematics. Schools, like families and communities, are protective support systems that can foster resilience and persistence in children.

Nurture Traits of Resilience. Benard (1991) suggests there are four traits found in resilient individuals—social competence, problem-solving skills, autonomy, and a sense of purpose and future. We in mathematics education can use these characteristics to help students reach success. Encourage children to be successful despite risk and adversity. Get students to think critically and be flexible in solving novel problems. This skill is key to developing strategies that will serve students in all aspects of their lives. Also continue to nurture high levels of student responsibility and autonomy, intentionally nurturing in students a disposition that they can and will be able to master mathematical concepts.

Demonstrate an Ethic of Caring. It is especially critical in mathematics, which is sometimes seen as a mechanical process, to foster a caring atmosphere. For example, work with students to identify pressures and burdens to thereby help students navigate life stresses and create a refuge in the mathematics classroom, because "when schools focus on what really matters in life, the cognitive ends we now pursue so painfully and artificially will be achieved somewhat more naturally. . . . It is obvious that children will work harder and do things—even things like adding fractions—for people they love and trust" (Noddings, 1988, p. 32).

Make Mathematics Irresistible. Motivation is based on what students expect they can do and what they value (Feather, 1982). The use of games, brainteasers, mysteries that can be solved through mathematics, and counterintuitive problems that leave students asking, "How is that possible?" help generate excitement for the subject. But the main thrust of the motivation emerges from you. Teachers communicate a passion for the content. Be enthusiastic and show that mathematics can make a difference in their lives. Well-known science educator David Hawkins once stated that "some things are best known by falling in love with them" (Hawkins, 1965, p. 3).

Give Students Some Leadership in Their Own Learning. High-achieving students tend to suggest their failures were from lack of effort. They see the failure as a temporary condition that can be resolved with hard work and renewed efforts. On the other hand, children with any history of academic failure can attribute their failures to lack of ability. This internal attribution is more difficult to counteract as they think their innate lack of mathematical ability prevents them from doing well no matter what they do. One strategy is to help students develop personal goals for their learning of mathematics. They might reflect on their performance on a unit assessment and what their goals are for the next unit, or they might personally monitor how they are doing on their basic fact memorization and set weekly goals.

Providing for Students Who Are Mathematically Gifted

Students who are mathematically gifted include those who have high ability or high interest. Some of the students in this group may be gifted with an intuitive knowledge of mathematical concepts, whereas others have a passion for the subject even though they may have to work hard to learn it. The National Association for Gifted Children (NAGC) describes a gifted student as "someone who shows, or has the potential for showing, an exceptional level of performance in one or more areas of expression" (NAGC, 2007). Many gifted students make themselves apparent to parents, guardians, and teachers by grasping and articulating mathematics concepts at an age earlier than expected.

They are often found to easily make connections among topics of study and frequently are unable to explain how they quickly got an answer (Rotigel & Fello, 2005). Generally, as in tier 1 of the response to intervention model used to identify students with special needs, the assumption is that good teaching is often able to respond to the varying needs of diverse learners, including the talented and gifted. Yet for some gifted students who seek additional challenges in their conceptual knowledge and skills, researchers (Lynch, 1992; Renzulli, 1986; VanTassel-Baska, 1998) suggest the curriculum should be adapted to consider level, complexity, breadth, depth, and pace.

Strategies to Avoid

There is a tendency for many beginning teachers to respond to mathematically gifted students with three rather ineffective approaches. The first is to offer high-ability students more of the same work when teachers find them rapidly completing their tasks. This is the least appropriate way to respond to mathematically gifted students and the most likely to result in students' hiding their ability. The approach to provide more of the same problems is described by a quotation from Persis Herold, a math center director in Washington, D.C., "as all scales and no music" (quoted in Tobias, 1995, p. 168). Another way to not capitalize on students' talents is allowing them to have free time if they finish faster than the others. Although students find this rewarding, it does not maximize their intellectual growth. A third approach pairs struggling students with gifted students who serve as mentors for assigned tasks. Routinely assigning gifted students to teach others what they have mastered is an error in judgment, because it puts mathematically talented students in a constant position of tutoring rather than allowing them to create deeper and more complex levels of understanding. Instead of relying on such options, mathematically gifted students need a variety of choices. Sheffield writes that gifted students should be introduced to the "joys and frustrations of thinking deeply about a wide range of original, open-ended, or complex problems that encourage them to respond creatively in ways that are original, fluent, flexible and elegant" (1999, p. 46).

Strategies to Incorporate

There are four basic categories for adapting mathematics content for gifted mathematics students: *acceleration, enrichment, sophistication,* and *novelty* (Gallagher & Gallagher, 1994). In each of these cases students should be asked to apply rather than just acquire information. The emphasis on implementing ideas must overshadow the mental collection of facts and even concepts.

Acceleration. Acceleration recognizes that students may already understand the mathematics content that will be presented. Some teachers use "curriculum compacting" (Renzulli, Smith, & Reis, 1982) to give a short overview of the content and assess students' ability to respond to tasks that would demonstrate their proficiency. Then teachers can either reduce the amount of time these students spend on aspects of the topic or move altogether to other more advanced and complex content. Allowing students to pace their own learning can give them access to curriculum above their grade level while demanding more independence as they are provided with materials and tools that vary from the rest of the class. More frequently students explore similar topics but include higher-level thinking, more complex or abstract ideas, and deeper levels of understanding or content. Research reveals that when gifted students are accelerated through the curriculum they become more likely to explore science, technology, engineering, and mathematics (STEM) (Sadler & Tai, 2007).

Enrichment. Enrichment activities go beyond the topic of study to content that is not specifically a part of the grade-level curriculum but is aligned with the lesson objectives. Most enrichment activities include extensions to the original mathematical tasks. For example, when a second-grade class is using a spinner with three divisions of different colors to explore probability, an extension for enrichment could include asking a group of students to create six different spinners that demonstrate the following cases: red is certain to win; red can't possibly win; blue is likely to win; red, blue, green, yellow, and orange are all equally likely to win; blue or green will probably win; and red, blue, and green have the same chance to win while yellow and orange can't possibly win. Other times the format of enrichment can involve studying the same topic as the rest of the class while differing on the means and outcomes of the work. Examples include group investigations, solving real problems in the community, writing letters to outside audiences, or identifying applications of the mathematics learned.

Sophistication. Another strategy is to increase the sophistication of a topic by raising the level of complexity or pursuing more depth. In mathematics this can mean exploring a larger set of ideas in which a mathematics topic exists. For example, while studying a unit on place value, mathematically gifted students can stretch their knowledge to study other numeration systems such as Roman, Mayan, Egyptian, Babylonian, Chinese, and Zulu. This provides a multicultural view of how our system fits within the number systems of the world. In the algebra strand, when students study sequences or patterns of numbers, mathematically gifted students can learn about Fibonacci sequences and their appearances in the natural world.

Novelty. Novelty, the fourth adaptation, introduces completely different material from the regular curriculum and frequently takes place in after-school clubs, out-of-class projects, or collaborative school experiences. The collaborative experiences include students from a variety of grades and classes volunteering for special mathematics projects, with a classroom teacher, principal, or resource teacher taking the lead. The novelty approach allows gifted students to explore topics that are within their developmental grasp but may be outside of the regular curriculum. For example, students may look at mathematical "tricks" using the binary numbers to guess classmates' birthdays or solve reasoning problems using a logic matrix. The novelty approach may also involve explorations of topics such as topology through the creation of paper "knots" called flexagons or large-scale investigations of the amount of food thrown away at lunchtime. A group might create tetrahedron kites or find mathematics in art. Another aspect of the novelty approach provides different options for students in culminating performances of their understanding, such as demonstrating their knowledge through inventions, experiments, simulations, dramatizations, visual displays, and oral presentations.

An additional concern that must be addressed as you work with your students who are gifted and talented is the consistent media image of students who do well in mathematics as appearing strange looking or acting weird (Sheffield, 1997). Children are bombarded with television and movie characters that represent successful, smart mathematics and science students as socially inept outcasts. Just as students mimic behaviors of popular media figures, they absorb powerful messages about negative consequences of showing their intelligence in public settings as they regularly view these performances. A survey of more than 20,000 students revealed that when given a choice of preferred group membership, they selected "druggies" over "brains" (Steinberg, Brown, & Dornbusch, 1996). The repeated presentation of an anti-intellectual bias in popular media needs to be countered with the consistent message that "smart wins." Influencing media portrayals is challenging, so finding ways to identify "math-smart" role models in the world of television, movies, and literature, as well as the real world, encourages and supports your students who are gifted and talented.

Final Thoughts

The late Asa Hilliard, a professor and expert on diversity, stated, "To restructure we must first look deeply at the goals that we set for our children and the beliefs that we have about them. Once we are on the right track there, then we must turn our attention to the delivery systems, as we have begun to do. Untracking is right. Mainstreaming is right. Decentralization is right. Cooperative learning is right. Technology access for all is right. Multiculturalism is right. But none of these approaches or strategies will mean anything if the fundamental belief does not fit with new structures that are being created" (1991, p. 36). As you move into the schools as a teacher of your own class, your high expectations for all students to succeed will make a lasting difference, as you incorporate the following general strategies that support diversity:

- Identify children's current knowledge base and build instructions with that in mind
- Push all students to high-level thinking
- Maintain high expectations
- Use a multicultural approach
- Recognize, value, explore, and incorporate the home culture
- Use alternative assessments to broaden the variety of indicators of students' performance
- Measure progress over time rather than taking short snapshots of student work
- Promote the importance of effort and resilience

Reflections on Chapter **6**

Writing to Learn

1. How is equity in the classroom different from teaching all students equally?
2. For children with learning disabilities and special learning needs, how should content and instruction each be modified using the response to intervention model?
3. What are some of the specific difficulties English language learners may encounter in the mathematics class?
4. In the context of providing for the mathematically gifted, what is meant by depth?

For Discussion and Exploration

1. Develop your own philosophical statement for "all students" or "every child." Design a visual representation for your statement. Read the Equity Principle in *Principles and Standards* and see if your position is in accord with that principle.
2. What would you do if you found yourself teaching a class with one mathematically gifted child who had no equal in the room? Assume that acceleration to the next grade has been ruled out due to social adjustment factors.

Resources for Chapter 6

Recommended Readings

Articles

Berry, R. Q., III. (2004). The Equity Principle through the voices of African American males. *Mathematics Teaching in the Middle School, 10*(2), 100–103.

Berry provides the reader with a realistic view of adolescent African American males who can and do find their way in mathematics. It is clear that it is the teacher who makes a difference.

Lee, H., & Jung, W. S. (2004). Limited English-proficient (LEP) students and mathematical understanding. *Mathematics Teaching in the Middle School, 9*(5), 269–272.

The article helps teachers design instruction to assist students who know little or no English. Specific examples will help the reader go beyond guiding principles.

National Council of Teachers of Mathematics. (2004). Teaching mathematics to special needs students [Focus Issue]. *Teaching Children Mathematics, 11*(3).

The first article in this focus issue by Karp and Howell tackles the reality that children with special needs truly are different and need special support to meet high standards. Other articles in the journal address assessment issues for special students, strategies for differentiation, and more.

Witzel, B., & Allsopp, D. (2007). Dynamic concrete instruction in an inclusive classroom. *Mathematics Teaching in the Middle School, 13*(4), 244–248.

This article highlights the use of manipulative materials for middle grade students with high incidence disabilities such as attention-deficit hyperactivity disorder (ADHD). They discuss through two classroom vignettes three main strategies: (1) linking prior knowledge to new concepts, (2) emphasizing thinking-aloud modeling, and (3) applying multisensory cueing (p. 244).

Books

Secada, W. G. (Series Ed.). (1999–2002). *Changing the faces of mathematics* (6 volumes). Reston, VA: NCTM.

These six books present perspectives on Asian Americans and Pacific Islanders, Native Americans, Latinos, African Americans, multiculturalism, and gender equity. Each volume explores curriculum, instruction, and assessment issues relevant to the topic for all grade levels.

Online Resources

LDOnline
www.ldonline.org

This site offers identification and assessment tools, teaching strategies, recommended readings, and interesting articles on mathematical disabilities in the "LD in Depth" section.

Teaching Diverse Learners—Culturally Responsive Teaching
www.alliance.brown.edu/tdl/tl-strategies/crt-principles-prt.shtml

This site includes several characteristics of culturally relevant teaching, explaining the importance of each and giving concrete examples of how to implement each characteristic in the classroom.

National Association for Gifted Children (NAGC)
www.nagc.org

NAGC, which has been in existence for over 50 years, is dedicated to serving professionals who work on behalf of gifted children. The site has a "Tools for Educators" section that includes online articles and resources.

Field Experience Guide Connections

Chapter 8 of the *Field Experience Guide* focuses on diversity. Experiences include observing one child's experience (FEG 8.1), interviewing a teacher about strategies they use to meet the needs of all students (FEG 8.2), and reflecting on meeting the needs of all students (FEG 8.6). The assessment tasks in Chapter 7 of the guide also provide great opportunities to focus on the needs of individual learners.

Chapter 7

Using Technology to Teach Mathematics

Technology is an essential tool for learning mathematics in the 21st century, and all schools must ensure that all their students have access to technology. Effective teachers maximize the potential of technology to develop students' understanding, stimulate their interest, and increase their proficiency in mathematics. When technology is used strategically, it can provide access to mathematics for all students.

NCTM Position Statement on the Role
of Technology in the Teaching and
Learning of Mathematics (March 2008)

The term *technology* in the context of school mathematics refers to digital tools, desktop and laptop computers, calculators and other handheld devices, collaborative authoring tools, computer algebra systems, dynamic geometry software, online digital games, podcasts, interactive presentation devices, spreadsheets, as well as the available, often Internet-based resources for use with these devices and tools. Technology is one of the six principles in the *Principles and Standards* documents, an emphasis reinforced by the aforementioned position statement to make clear that NCTM regards technology as an *essential tool* for both learning and teaching mathematics. Thinking of technology as an "extra" added on to the list of things you are trying to accomplish in your classroom is not an effective approach. Instead, technology should be seen as an integral part of your instructional arsenal of tools for learning. It can enlarge the scope of the content students can learn and it can broaden the range of problems that students are able to tackle (Ball & Stacey, 2005; NCTM Position Statement, 2008). However, it cannot be a replacement for the full conceptual understanding of mathematics content.

Pedagogical content knowledge (PCK) is the intersection of mathematics content knowledge with the pedagogical knowledge of teaching and learning (Shulman, 1986), a body of information possessed by teachers that the average person, even one strong in mathematics, would not likely know. PCK represents the specific strategies and approaches that teachers use to deliver mathematical content to students. Technological, pedagogical, and content knowledge (TPACK), as shown in Figure 7.1, describes the infusion of technology to this mix (Mishra & Koehler, 2006; Niess, 2008). We suggest that teachers consider technology as a conscious component of each lesson and each strategy for enhancing student learning. This chapter's emphasis on the importance of technology in instruction is carried over throughout the content chapters, especially in sections highlighted with the technology icon. Its value becomes evident when technological features embedded in a lesson enhance students' opportunities to learn important mathematics, serving as a basic learning tool rather than an add-on or a once-a-week opportunity in a computer lab.

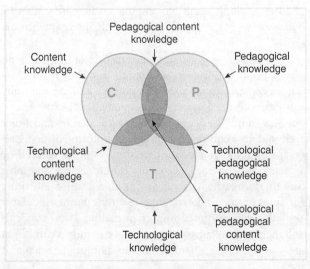

Figure 7.1 TPACK framework.

Calculators in Mathematics Instruction

In its 2005 Position Statement on Computation, Calculators, and Common Sense, NCTM clarified its long-standing view by stating, "Students need an understanding of number and operations, including the use of computational procedures, estimation, mental mathematics, and the appropriate use of the calculator." They go on to say, "Teachers can capitalize on the appropriate use of this technology to expand students' mathematical understanding, not to replace it."

myeducationlab

Go to the Building Teaching Skills and Dispositions section of Chapter 7 of MyEducationLab. Click on Videos and watch the video entitled "**Graphing Calculators**" to see students using graphing calculators.

Even with everyday use of calculators in society and the professional support of calculators in schools, use of calculators is not always central to instruction in a mathematics classroom, especially at the elementary level. Sometimes educators and students' families are concerned that just allowing students to use calculators when solving problems will replace children's learning the basic facts to reach computational proficiency. However, rather than an either-or choice, just as with the use of the Internet, there are conditions when students should use the technology and other times when they must call on their own resources.

Based on efficiency and effectiveness, the student should learn when to use mental mathematics, when to use estimation, when to tackle a problem with paper and pencil, and when to use a calculator. Ignoring the potential benefits of calculators by prohibiting their use entirely can inhibit students' learning. Helping students know when to grab a calculator and when not to use one is precisely the work of the teacher. Sometimes using a calculator during instruction allows students to explore a higher-level topic or identify a complex pattern. Expanding students' abilities to think about challenging mathematics must be balanced with the development of their computational skills.

Help families understand that calculator use will in no way prevent children from learning rigorous mathematics: in fact, calculators used thoughtfully and meaningfully can enhance the learning of mathematics. Furthermore, families should be made aware that calculators and other technologies require students to be problem solvers. Calculators can only calculate according to input entered by humans. In isolation, calculators cannot answer the most meaningful mathematics tasks and they cannot substitute for thinking or understanding. Sending home calculator activities that reinforce important mathematical concepts and including calculator activities on a Family Math Night are ways to educate families about appropriate calculator use.

When to Use a Calculator

If the primary purpose of the instructional activity is to practice computational skills, students should not be using a calculator. On the other hand, students should have full access to calculators when they are exploring patterns, conducting investigations, testing conjectures, and solving problems. Situations involving computations that are beyond students' ability without the aid of a calculator are not necessarily beyond their ability to think about meaningfully.

As students come to fully understand the meanings of the operations, they should be exposed to realistic problems with realistic numbers. For example, young children may want to calculate how many seconds they have been alive. They can think conceptually about how many seconds in a minute, hour, day, and so on. But the actual calculations and those that continue to weeks and years can be done more efficiently on a calculator.

Also include calculators when the goal of the instructional activity is not to compute, but computation is involved in the problem solving. For example, students in the middle grades may be asked to identify the "best buy" when there are different percentages off different merchandise. Whether purchasing a bicycle or getting a deal on ride tickets at the fair, the goal is to define the most economical relationship given a set of choices by calculating the various percentage discounts with a calculator. Calculators are also valuable for generating and analyzing patterns. For example, when finding the decimal equivalent of $\frac{8}{9}, \frac{7}{9}, \frac{5}{9}$, and so on, a neat pattern emerges. Let students explore other "ninths" and make conjectures as to why the pattern occurs. Again, the emphasis is not to determine a computational solution but instead to use the calculator to help find a pattern.

Finally, calculators can be used as accommodations for students with special needs. When used for instruction that is not centered on developing computation skills, calculators can help ensure that all students have appropriate access to the curriculum to the maximum extent possible.

Benefits of Calculator Use

Understanding how calculators contribute to the learning of mathematics includes recognizing that the "use of calculators does not threaten the development of basic skills and that it can enhance conceptual understanding, strategic competence, and disposition toward mathematics" (NRC, 2001, p. 354). This includes four-function, scientific, and graphing calculators. A specific discussion of graphing calculators is found later in this chapter.

Calculators Can Be Used to Develop Concepts and Enhance Problem Solving. The calculator can be much more than a device for calculation. As shown in an analysis of more than 79 research studies, K–12 students (with the exception of grade 4) who used calculators improved their "basic skills with paper-pencil tasks both in computational operations and in problem solving" (Hembree & Dessert, 1986; 1992, p. 96). Other researchers confirm that students with long-term experience using calculators performed better overall than children without such experience on both mental computation and paper-and-pencil problems (Ellington, 2003; Smith, 1997b; Wareham, 2005). There has been a call for more studies on the long-term use of calculators (National Mathematics Advisory Panel, 2008), and additional research is likely to result.

Although some worry that calculator use can impede instruction in number and operations, the reverse is actually the case, as shown in the following examples. (Also see the calculator activities in the following chapters, on number and operations.) In K–1, children who are exploring concepts of quantity can use the calculator as a counting machine. Using the automatic-constant feature (not all calculators perform this in the same way—so check how it works on your calculator) children can count. For example, press the following keys—[0] [+] [1] [=] [=] [=]—to count by ones, pressing the equals key for as long as the count continues. Help children try this feature. The "count by ones" on the calculator can reinforce students' oral counting, identification of patterns, and can even be used by one child to count their classmates as they enter in the morning. Children's literature with repeated phrases, such as the classic *Goodnight Moon* (Brown, 1947), provides an opportunity for students to count. Children can press the equals sign each time the little rabbit says goodnight in his bedtime routine. At the completion of the book they can compare how many "goodnights" were recorded. Follow-up activities include using the same automatic-constant feature on the calculator with different stories or books to skip-count by twos (e.g., pairs of animals or people), fives (e.g., fingers on one hand or people in a car), or tens (e.g., dimes, "ten in a bed," apples in a tree).

Older students can investigate decimal concepts with a calculator, as in the following examples. On the calculator, $796 \div 42 = 18.95348$. Consider the task of using the calculator to determine the whole-number remainder. Another example is to use the calculator to find a number that when multiplied by itself will produce 43. In this situation, a student can press 6.1 [×] [=] to get the square of 6.1. For students who are just beginning to understand decimals, the activity will demonstrate that numbers such as 6.3 and 6.4 are between 6 and 7. Furthermore, 6.55 is between 6.5 and 6.6. For students who already understand decimals, the same activity serves as a meaningful and conceptual introduction to square roots.

Calculators Can Be Used for Drill. Students who want to practice the multiples of 7 can press 7 [×] 3 and delay pressing the [=]. The challenge is to answer the fact to themselves before pressing the [=] key. Subsequent multiples of 7 can be checked by simply pressing the second factor and the [=]. The TI-10 (Texas Instruments) and TI-15 calculators now have built-in problem-solving modes in which students can practice facts, develop lists of related facts, and test equations or inequalities with arithmetic expressions on both sides of the relationship symbol (http://education.ti.com/educationportal/sites/US/productCategory/us_elementary.html).

A class can be split in half with one half required to use a calculator and the other required to do the computations mentally. For 3000 + 1765, the mental group wins every time. It will also win for simple facts and numerous problems that lend themselves to mental computation. Of course, there are many computations, such as 537 × 32, where the calculator team will be faster. Not only does this simple exercise provide practice with mental math, but it also demonstrates to students that it is not always effective to reach for the calculator.

Calculators Can Improve Attitudes and Motivation. Research results reveal that students who frequently use calculators have better attitudes toward the subject of mathematics (Ellington, 2003). There is also evidence that students are more motivated when their anxiety is reduced; therefore, supporting students during problem-solving activities with calculators is important. A student with special needs who is left out of the problem-solving lesson due to weak knowledge of basic facts will not pursue the worthwhile explorations the teacher plans. That does not excuse them from learning their facts. As we try to increase students' confidence that they can solve challenging mathematics problems, we can expand their motivation to be persistent and stay engaged in the process of thinking about numbers. Again, the strategic use of the calculator is guided by the plans of the teacher and the eventual decision making of the students.

Calculators Are Commonly Used in Society. Calculators are used in every facet of life that involves any sort of exact computation by almost everyone. Students should be taught how to use this commonplace tool effectively and also learn to judge when to use it. Many adults have not learned how to use the automatic-constant feature of a calculator and are not practiced in recognizing common errors that are often made on calculators. Effective use of calculators is an important skill that is best learned by using them regularly in meaningful problem-solving activities.

Graphing Calculators

Graphing calculators help students visualize concepts as they make real-world connections with data. When students can actually see expressions, formulas, graphs, and the results of changing a variable on those visual representations, a deeper understanding of concepts can result. Graphing calculators are used with upper-elementary-age students to high school students and beyond, but the most common use is at the secondary level. Since graphing calculators are permitted and in some cases required on such tests as the SAT, ACT, PSAT, or AP exams, it is critical for all students to be familiar with their use.

myeducationlab

Go to the Activities and Application section of Chapter 7 of MyEducationLab. Click on Videos and watch the video entitled "**John Van de Walle on the Benefits of Calculator Use**" to see him talk with Canadian teachers about using calculators.

It is a mistake to think that graphing calculators are only for doing "high-powered" mathematics. The following list demonstrates some features the graphing calculator offers, every one of which is useful within the standard middle school curriculum.

- The display window permits compound expressions such as $3 + 4(5 - 6/7)$ to be shown completely before being evaluated. Furthermore, once evaluated, previous expressions can be recalled and modified. This promotes an understanding of notation and order of operations. The graphing calculator is also a significant tool for exploring patterns and solving problems. Expressions can include exponents, absolute values, and negation signs, with no restrictions on the values used.

- Even without using function definition capability, students can insert values into expressions or formulas without having to enter the entire formula for each new value. The results can be entered into a list or table of values and stored directly on the calculator for further analysis.

- Variables can be used in expressions and then assigned different values to see the effect on expressions. This simple method helps with the idea of a variable as something that varies.

- The distinction between "negative" and "subtract" is clear and very useful. A separate key is used to enter the negative of a quantity. The display shows the negative sign as a superscript. If $^-5$ is stored in the variable B, then the expression $^-2 - {}^-B$ will be evaluated correctly as $^-7$. This feature is a significant aid in the study of integers and variables.

- Points can be plotted on a coordinate screen either by entering coordinates and seeing the result or by moving the cursor to a particular coordinate on the screen.

- Very large and very small numbers are managed without error. The calculator will quickly compute factorials, even for large numbers, as well as permutations and combinations. For example, $23! = 1.033314797 \times 10^{40}$.

- Built-in statistical functions allow students to examine the means, medians, and standard deviations of large sets of realistic data without a computer. Data are entered, ordered, added to, or changed almost as easily as on a spreadsheet.

- Graphs for data analysis are available, including box-and-whisker plots, histograms, and, on some calculators, circle graphs, bar graphs, and pictographs.

- Random number generators allow for the simulation of a variety of probability experiments that would be difficult without such a device.

- Scatter plots for ordered pairs of real data can be entered, plotted, and examined for trends. The calculator will calculate the equations of best-fit linear, quadratic, cubic, or logarithmic functions.

- Functions can be explored in three modes: equation, table, and graph. Because the calculator easily switches from one to the other and because of the trace feature, the connections between these modes become quite clear.

- The graphing calculator is programmable. Programs are very easily written and understood. For example, a program involving the Pythagorean theorem can be used to find the lengths of sides of right triangles.

- Students can share data programs and functions from one calculator to another, connect their calculators to a classroom display screen, save information on a computer, and download software applications that give additional functionality for special uses.

Most of the ideas on this list are explored briefly in appropriate chapters in this book.

A new graphing calculator, the TI-Nspire (www.ti-nspire.com/tools/nspire/index.html) is beginning to make its way into classrooms. This handheld device links up to four representations of the same data on a single screen, including graphs, tables, visual images, and even written representations. For example, a student can explore how changing the width of a rectangle but keeping the perimeter constant impacts the area. Simultaneously on the screen the student can see the visual image of the rectangle that they can manipulate to desired dimensions, a table of matching values, and a graph of the resulting area. Rather than toggling from one representation to another, they can all be considered at one time, which strengthens the ability to see patterns. There are even options for writing notes to record discoveries or findings. Again, however, this device is only as useful as the tasks teachers create for students.

Arguments against graphing calculators are similar to those for other calculators—and are equally unsubstantiated. These amazing tools have the potential of providing students with significant opportunities for exploring real mathematics.

Data-Collection Devices

In addition to the capabilities of the graphing calculator alone, electronic data-collection devices make them even more remarkable. Texas Instruments calls its version the

CBL (for *computer-based laboratory*), which has become the generic acronym for such devices. Casio's current version, the EA-200, is nearly identical in design. These devices accept a variety of data-collection probes, such as temperature or light sensors and motion detectors, that can be used to gather real physical data. The data can be transferred to the graphing calculator, where they are stored in one or more lists. The calculator can then produce scatter plots or prepare other analyses. With appropriate software, the data can also be transferred to a computer.

These instruments help students connect graphs with real-world physical events. They emphasize the relationships between variables and can dispel some of the common misconceptions students have about interpreting graphs (Lapp, 2001). Lapp explains that students confuse the fastest rate of change with the highest point on the graph or they may erroneously think that the shape of the graph is the shape of the motion (like a bicycle going up the hill is faster—increasing speed—than a bicycle going downhill). The fact that the graph can be produced immediately is a powerful feature of the device so that these "miss-steps" in thinking can be tested and discussed.

The most popular probe for mathematics teachers is the motion detector. Texas Instruments has a special motion detector called a Ranger or CBR that connects directly to the calculator without requiring a CBL unit. Experiments with a motion detector include analysis of objects rolling down an incline, bouncing balls, or swinging pendulums. The device actually detects the distance an object is from the sensor. When distance is plotted against time, the graph shows velocity. Students can plot their own motion walking toward or away from the detector or match the motion shown in a graph already produced. The concept of rate when interpreted as the slope of a distance-to-time curve can become quite dramatic.

One of the most exciting aspects of data-collection devices involves the melding of science and mathematics learning. For example, the Concord Consortium's Technology Enhanced Elementary and Middle School Science (TEEMSS II) project blends science and mathematics inquiry for grades 3–8 (http://teemss.concord.org). Through curriculum and software (free after registration), they share investigations in which real-time data in physical science, life science, earth science, technology, and engineering are collected, analyzed, and shared.

Computers in Mathematics Instruction

A number of powerful software tools have been created for use in the mathematics classroom, existing both as stand-alone programs that can be purchased from software publishers and as Internet-based applications accessible through Web browsers such as Microsoft Internet Explorer, Apple's Safari, Mozilla's Firefox, and others.

Java applets are much smaller, more targeted programs than commercial software and have the significant advantage that they can be freely accessed on the Internet. Many can also be downloaded so that an Internet connection is not required for student use. Some of these applets are described briefly throughout this book and at the end of each chapter. The sites listed at the end of this chapter collectively offer well over 100 applets. You are strongly urged to browse and play. Many of these are lots of fun!

A mathematical software tool is somewhat like a physical manipulative; by itself, it does not teach. However, the user of a well-designed tool has an electronic "thinker toy" with which to explore mathematical ideas.

Tools for Developing Numeration

Programs providing screen versions of popular manipulative models for counting, place value, and fractions are available for students to work with freely without the computer posing problems, evaluating results, or telling the students what to do.

At the earliest level there are programs that provide "counters" such as colored tiles, pictures of assorted objects, five/ten frames, and more. Typically, students can drag counters to any place on the screen, change the colors, and put them in groupings. Some programs have options that turn on counters for the screen or subsets of the screen. Nonmathematical programs such as *Kidspiration* (Inspiration Software, 2008) can also be used to "stamp" discrete objects on the screen, explore shapes, word process, and more.

Base-ten blocks (ones, tens, and hundreds models), assorted fraction pieces, and Cuisenaire rods (centimeter rods) are available in some software packages as well as in Web-based applets. These include both pure tool programs and instructional software programs that attempt to teach or tutor. Some fraction models are more flexible than physical models. For example, a circular region might be subdivided into many more fractional parts than is reasonable with physical models. When the models are connected with on-screen counters, it is possible with some programs to have fraction or decimal representations shown so that connections between fractions and decimals can be illustrated. *Odyssey Math* (CompassLearning, 2008) or *Destination Math* (Riverdeep Interactive Learning Limited, 2008) do a nice job of connecting these types of representations for fractions.

Web-based tools or applets exist that are designed so that students may manipulate them without constraint. For example, the Base Ten Block Applet (www.arcytech.org/java/b10blocks/b10blocks.html) allows children to collect as many flats, rods, and units as they wish, gluing together groups of ten, or breaking a flat into ten rods or a rod into ten units.

The obvious question is, Why not simply use the actual physical models? Electronic or virtual manipulatives have some advantages that merit integrating them into your instruction—not just adding them on as extras.

- *Qualitative Differences in Use.* Usually it is at least as easy to manipulate virtual manipulatives as it is to use their physical counterparts. However, control of materials on the screen requires a different, perhaps more deliberate, mental action that is "more in line with the *mental actions* that we want children to carry out" (Clements & Sarama, 2005, p. 53). For example, the base-ten rod representing a ten can be broken into ten single blocks by clicking on it with a hammer icon. With physical blocks, the ten must be traded for the equivalent blocks counted out by the student.
- *Connection to Symbolism.* Most virtual manipulatives for number include dynamic numerals or odometers that change as the representation on the screen changes. This direct and immediate connection to numeral representation is more challenging with physical models.
- *Unlimited Materials with Easy Cleanup.* With virtual manipulatives, students can easily erase the screen and begin a new problem with the click of a mouse. They will never run out of materials. For place value, even the large 1000 cubes are readily available in quantity. And there is no storage or cleanup to worry about.
- *Accommodations for Special Purposes.* For English language learners or visually impaired students, some programs come with speech enhancements so that the students hear the names of the materials or the numbers. Some programs and applets are available in Spanish. For students with physical disabilities, the computer models are often easier to access and use than physical models.

Many software-based programs also offer a word-processing capability connected to the workspace, allowing students to write a sentence or two to explain what they have done or perhaps to create a story problem to go with their work. Printing a picture of the workspace, with or without a written attachment, creates a record of the work for the teacher or parent that is more challenging with physical models. Note, however, that Web-based applets typically do not have print capabilities.

Tools for Developing Geometry

Computer tools for geometric exploration are much closer to pure tools than those just described for numeration. That is, students can use most of these tools without any constraints. They typically offer some significant advantages over physical models, although the computerized tools should never replace physical models in the classroom.

Blocks and Tiles.   Programs that allow students to "stamp" geometric tiles or blocks on the screen are quite common. Typically, there is a palette of blocks, often the same as pattern blocks or tangrams, from which students can choose by clicking the mouse. Often the blocks can be made "magnetic" so that when they are released close to another block, the two will snap together, matching like sides. Blocks can usually be rotated, either freely or in set increments. Figure 7.2 shows a simple yet powerful applet that permits a student to slice any of the three shapes in any place and then manipulate the pieces. This is a good example of something a student can do with a computer that would be difficult or impossible with physical models. You may find the following:

- The ability to enlarge or reduce the size of blocks, usually by set increments
- The ability to "glue" blocks together to make new blocks
- The ability to reflect one or more blocks across a line of symmetry or to rotate them about a point
- The ability to measure area or perimeters
- The ability to select polygons with a variable number of sides
- The possibility of creating three-dimensional shapes and rotating them in space

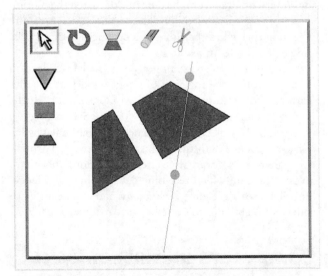

Figure 7.2 The Cutting Shapes Tool applet.
Used with permission from the CD-ROM included with the NCTM pre-K–2 *Navigations* book for geometry by C. R. Findell, L. Davey, C. E. Greens, and L. J. Sheffield. Copyright © 2001 by the National Council of Teachers of Mathematics, Inc. All rights reserved. The presence of the screenshot from *Navigations* does not constitute or imply an endorsement by NCTM.

For students who have poor motor coordination or a physical disability that makes block manipulation difficult, the computer versions of blocks are a real plus. Colorful printouts can be displayed, discussed, and taken home if that option is available.

Drawing Programs.   For younger students, drawing shapes on a grid is much easier and more useful for geometric exploration than free-form drawing. Several programs offer electronic geoboards on which lines can be drawn between points on a grid. When a shape such as a triangle is formed, it can typically be altered just as you would a rubber band on a geoboard. For an example, check NCTM's Illuminations website. The electronic geoboard programs offer a larger grid on which to draw, ease of use, and the ability to save and print. Some include measuring capabilities as well as reflection and rotation of shapes, things that are difficult or impossible to do on a physical geoboard. An example of a good Internet applet for drawing is the Isometric Drawing Tool found at NCTM's website (see Figure 7.3).

Dynamic Geometry Environments.   Dynamic geometry programs allow students to create shapes on the computer screen and then manipulate and measure them by dragging vertices. The most well-known are *The Geometer's Sketchpad* (Key Curriculum Press), *Cabri Geometry II* (Texas Instruments), and the public domain *Wingeom* (http://math.exeter.edu/rparris/wingeom.html). Dynamic geometry programs allow the creation of geometric objects (lines, circles) so that their relationship to another screen object is established. For example, a new line can be drawn through a point and perpendicular to another line. A midpoint can be established on any line segment. Once created, these

relationships are preserved no matter how the objects are moved or altered. Dynamic geometry software can dramatically both change and improve the teaching of geometry in grade 3 and beyond. The ability of students to explore geometric relationships with this software is unmatched with any noncomputer mode. More detailed discussion of these programs can be found in Chapter 20.

Tools for Developing Probability and Data Analysis

These computer tools allow for the entry of data and a wide choice of graphs made from the data. In addition, most will produce typical statistics such as mean, median, and range. Some programs are designed for students in the primary grades. Others are more sophisticated and can be used through the middle grades. For example, TinkerPlots (Key Curriculum Press, 2005), for students in grades 4–8, can generate graphs in a variety of forms for analyzing data and producing statistics. The dynamic nature of the program allows students to drag an outlier to see how the mean, median, and mode change. Using a "stack, order, and separate" framework, the software not only provides a sound approach to thinking about the graphs, but gives more than 40 data sets to use in investigating real-world information. These programs make it possible to change the emphasis in data analysis from "how to construct graphs" to "which graph best tells the story."

Probability Tools.   These programs make it easy to conduct controlled probability experiments and see graphical representations of the results. For example, the National Library of Virtual Manipulatives (see websites section at end of chapter) provides options for coin tossing and spinners with regions that can be customized. The young student using these programs must accept that when the computer "flips a coin" or "spins a spinner," the results are just as random and have the same probabilities as if done with real coins or spinners. The value of these programs is found in the ease with which experiments can be designed and large numbers of trials conducted, which allows more time for analyzing results.

Spreadsheets and Data Graphers.   *Spreadsheets* are programs that can manipulate rows and columns of numeric data. Values taken from one position in the spreadsheet can be used in formulas to determine entries elsewhere in the spreadsheet. When an entry is changed, the spreadsheet updates all values immediately.

Because the spreadsheet is among the most popular pieces of standard tool software outside of schools, it is often available in integrated packages you may already have on your computer. Students as early as third grade can use these programs to organize data, display data graphically in

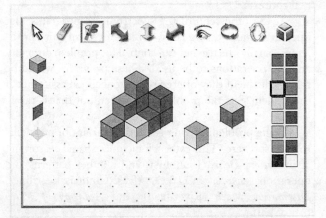

Figure 7.3 The Isometric Drawing Tool applet from NCTM's Illuminations website.

various ways, and do numeric calculations such as finding how changing gas prices impact the family budget. Students only need to know how to use the capabilities of the spreadsheet that they will be using.

The Illuminations website from NCTM offers a couple of very nice spreadsheet Internet applets, *Spreadsheet* and *Spreadsheet and Graphing Tool*. They can be used while connected to the Internet, or they can be downloaded to your computer. In addition, MCES Kidszone (at http://nces .ed.gov/nceskids/index.asp) has both graphing tools and probability simulations for elementary and middle school students.

Tools for Developing Algebraic Thinking

Very young children can use virtual pattern blocks to create patterns for copying, continuing, transforming, and for analysis (see www.arcytech.org/java/patterns). The unending supply of any pattern block does not restrict children by the number of available materials. Copies of their designs can be printed through a screen capture so that other students can be challenged to identify the pattern. Teachers of older students can use virtual pattern blocks either on their interactive whiteboard or accessed from the National Library of Virtual Manipulatives website to create a growing pattern, recording the number of squares needed at each step (or term). Students can explore the sequence of squares to make a conjecture as to how many squares will be needed at the tenth term or the ninth term of the pattern.

For older students, function graphing software permits the user to create the graph of almost any function very quickly. Multiple functions can be plotted on the same axis. It is usually possible to trace along the path of a curve and view the coordinates at any point. The dimensions of the viewing area can be changed easily so that it is just as easy to look at a graph for x and y between –10 and +10 as it is to look at a portion of the graph thousands of units away from the origin. By "zooming in" on the intersection of two graphs, it is possible to find points of intersection without algebraic manipulation. Similarly, the point where a graph crosses the axis can be found to as many decimal places as is desired.

The function graphing features just described are available on all graphing calculators. Computer programs can add speed, color, visual clarity, and a variety of other interesting features to help students analyze functions.

Instructional Software

Instructional software is designed for student interaction in a manner similar to the textbook or a tutor. It is designed to teach. The distinction between tool and instructional software is not always clear since some packages include a tool-only component. In the following discussion, the intent is to provide some perspective on the different kinds of input to your mathematics program that instructional software might offer.

Concept Instruction

A growing number of programs make an effort to offer conceptual instruction. Some, like the *Math Adventures* series of programs (Tom Snyder Productions) and the *Prime Time Math* series (Tom Snyder Productions), rely on real-world contexts to illustrate mathematical ideas. Using problem-solving situations, specific concepts are developed in a guided manner to solve the problem.

What is most often missing is a way to make the mathematics problem-based or to connect the conceptual activity with the symbolic techniques. Furthermore, when students work on a computer, there is little opportunity for discourse, conjecture, or original ideas. Some software even presents concepts in such a fashion as to remove learners from thinking and constructing their own understanding. In some instances, the programs might be best used with the teacher controlling the program on a large display screen with the class. In this way, the teacher can pose questions and entertain discussion that is simply not possible with one student on a computer.

Problem Solving

With the current focus on problem solving, more software publishers purport to teach students to solve problems. But problem solving is not the same as solving problems. The *Thinkport* series demonstrates good examples of problem solving. Here the problems are not typical story problems awaiting a computation but more thoughtful stories set in real contexts.

At the other end of the spectrum are programs that offer little more than a large library of typical story problems. Usually, the teacher can control for problem difficulty and the operations to be used. These programs would be more valuable if they offered some conceptual assistance if the student gets the problems incorrect, but that is rarely the case.

Logic problem solving is another variant of problem-solving software. This category includes spatial reasoning, as in *Factory Deluxe* (Sunburst) and number patterns and operation sense, as in *Odyssey Math* (CompassLearning), *Destination Math* (Riverdeep), and *Academy of Math* (AutoSkill).

Drill and Reinforcement

Drill programs give students practice with skills that are assumed to have been previously taught. In general, a drill program poses questions that are answered directly or by selecting from a multiple-choice list. Many of these programs are set in arcade formats that make them exciting for students who like video games, although the format has nothing to do with the practice involved.

Drill programs evaluate responses immediately. How they respond to the first or second incorrect answer is one important distinguishing feature. At one extreme, the answer is simply recorded as wrong. There may be a second or third chance to correct it. At the other extreme, the program may branch to an explanation of the correct response. Others may provide a useful hint or supply a visual model to help with the task. Some programs also offer record-keeping features for the teacher to keep track of individual student's progress.

One software feature worth mentioning is differentiated drill, such as is found in *FASTT Math* (Tom Snyder Productions, www.tomsnyder.com/fasttmath/overview.html). The *FASTT Math* (Fluency and Automaticity through Systematic Teaching with Technology) program works to help all students develop fluency with math facts. In short sessions that are customized for individual learners, the software automatically differentiates instruction based on each student's previous performance.

Guidelines for Selecting and Using Software

There is so much software for mathematics today. Commercially published software is becoming increasingly expensive which is why we suggest open-source software where possible. Even though most Internet-based applets are free to use, schools must still provide for Internet access and the appropriate hardware. In either case, it is important to make informed decisions when investing limited resources.

Guidelines for Using Software

How software is used in mathematics instruction will vary considerably with the topic, the grade level, and the software itself. The following are offered as considerations that you should keep in mind.

- Software should contribute to the objectives of the lesson or unit. It should not be used as an add-on or substitute for more accessible approaches. Its use should take advantage of what technology can do efficiently and well.
- For individualized or small-group use, plan to provide specific instructions for using the software and also plan to provide time for students to freely explore or practice using the software.

- Combine software activities with off-computer activities (e.g., collect measurement data in the classroom to enter into a spreadsheet).
- Create a management plan for using the software. This could include a schedule for using the software (e.g., during centers, during small-group work) and a way to assess the effectiveness of the software use. Although some software programs include a way to keep track of student performance, you may need to rely on other assessment strategies to determine whether the software is effectively meeting the objectives of the lesson or unit.

How to Select Software

The most important requirement for purchasing effective software is to be well informed about the product and to evaluate its merits in an objective manner.

Gathering Information.   One of the best sources of information concerning new software is the review section of the NCTM journals or other journals that you respect. Many websites offer reviews on both commercially available software and Internet-based applets. The Math Forum at Drexel University at http://mathforum.org is one such site.

One important consideration is whether the software is accessible for all students, including individuals with disabilities. Can the text be enlarged or highlighted as it is read aloud? Are the graphics easily recognizable, containing mouse-overs (where the action is written or spoken as the mouse is moved over the image) and not dependent on color for meaning? Can the software be used with a keyboard instead of a mouse? All these questions are derived from the universal design principles defined at www.design.ncsu.edu/cud/about_ud/udprinciplestext.htm.

TechMatrix at www.techmatrix.org "is a powerful tool for finding educational and assistive technology products for students with special needs" (National Center for Technology Innovation, 2008). Select mathematics under the heading subjects and take a look at how the learning support "matrix" list indicates the presence of a variety of elements in software programs. The matrix you generate will compare whether different software products for mathematics learning contain such elements as differentiation features, text to speech capability, word prediction, eye-tracking cursors, output options in Braille, voice recognition, and other useful information. Clicking on "Research" and then "Math" at the top of the home page displays a list of research-based reports related to the use of technology in the mathematics classroom for students with and without disabilities.

When selecting any computer-based tool or instructional software, it is important to evaluate it appropriately. Try first to get a preview copy or at least a demonstration version. Take advantage of any option that allows users to download software for 30-day approval. Before purchasing, try the software with kids in the grade that will be using it. Remember, it is the content you are interested in, not the game the students will be playing.

Criteria. Think about the following points as you review software before purchasing it or using it in your classroom (also see the rubric in the *Field Experience Guide*):

- What does this do better than can be done without the computer? Don't select or use software just to put your students on the computer. Get past the clever graphics and the games and focus on what students will be learning.
- How are students likely to be engaged with the *content* (not the frills)? Remember that student reflective thought is the most significant factor in effective instruction. Is the mathematics presented so that it is problematic for the student?
- How easy is the program to use? There should not be so much tedium in using the program that attention is diverted from the content or students become frustrated.
- How does the program develop conceptual knowledge that supports understanding of concepts? In drill programs, how are wrong answers handled? Are the models or explanations going to be helpful for student understanding?
- What controls and assessments are provided to the teacher? Are there options that can be turned on and off (e.g., sound, types of feedback or help, levels of difficulty)? Is there a provision for record keeping so that you will know what progress individual students have made?
- Is a manual or online instruction available? What is the quality of the manual or instructions? Minimally, the manual should make it clear how the program is to operate and provide assistance for troubleshooting.
- Is the program equitable in its consideration of gender and culture?
- What is the nature of the licensing agreement? In the case of purchased software, is a site license or network license available? If you purchase a single-user package, it is not legal to install the software on multiple computers. Internet applets require the computer to be connected to the Internet and software such as Java (Sun Microsystems) to view the applets. Do these constraints fit with your school situation?
- Be sure that the program will run on the computers at your school. The software description should indicate the compatible platform(s) (Windows/Macintosh) and the version of the required operating systems.

Resources on the Internet

In addition to access to Internet-based software applications, or applets, the World Wide Web is a wellspring of information and resources for both teachers and students interested in mathematics and teaching mathematics.

Instead of using a standard search engine to find mathematics-related information, it is better to have some places to begin. Several good websites in different categories will usually provide you with more links to other sites than you will have time to search. One source for good websites is this book. At the end of every chapter and on the MyEducationLab website (www.myeducationlab.com) you will find a list of Web-based resources. Although a brief description accompanies each listing, you are encouraged to check these out yourself as websites are frequently modified. The types of resources you can expect to find include professional information, teacher resources, digital tools, and open-source software.

How to Select Internet Resources

The massive amount of information available on the Internet must be sifted through for accuracy and sorted by quality when you plan instruction or when the students in your class gather information or research a mathematics topic. For example, identifying a mathematics lesson plan on the Internet does not ensure that it is of high quality, as anyone can publish any idea they have on the Web. When students complete a WebQuest (http://webquest.org) or an I Search (www2.edc.org/FSC/MIH) about a famous mathematician for example, how can they be sure the information is trustworthy? To use the Web as a teaching toolbox for locating successful mathematics tasks, motivating enrichment activities, or supportive strategies to assist struggling learners, it is better to go to trustworthy, high-quality sites than merely plugging a few key words into available search engines. We suggest that you add the end-of-chapter sites in this book or MyEducationLab to your computer "favorites" and go to them as a first-level source of support and information. If you choose to explore Web pages, Web logs (blogs), or wikis (collaboratively created and updated Web pages) more broadly, take the elements enumerated in Table 7.1 into consideration. These criteria are critical for your use as a discerning educator and can be adapted or simplified for your students as they evaluate material on the Web. The main topics are adapted from a group of considerations suggested by Smith (1997a).

Emerging Technologies

Emerging technologies refers to the ever-changing landscape of technological tools and advances. In our increasingly technological society, we know that we can only do our best in helping students be able to respond to the

Table 7.1

Evaluating Web Resources		
Criteria	**Justification**	**Evidence/Verification**
Authority • Page should identify the authors and their qualifications. • Site should be associated with a reputable educational institution or organization.	• Anyone can publish pages on the Web. You want to be assured that the information is from a reliable source and is of high quality.	• Contact information for the author or organization is easily available. Is there a link to the organization's home page? • Do the authors establish their expertise? • Use www.whois.net domain research service to identify the author of the site. • Is the URL domain .org, .edu, .gov, .net, or .com?
Content • Site should match topic of interest. • The materials should add depth to your information.	• The information should be useful facts rather than opinions. • The text should be actual information from an expert and not paraphrased from another site.	• Is it a list of links from other sites? • Are the statements verified by footnotes and research articles? • Do the authors indicate criteria for including information?
Objectivity • Site should not reflect a biased point of view. • Authors should present facts and not try to sway the reader.	• Websites can try to influence the readers rather than provide independent and evenhanded information sources.	• Are there advertisements or sponsors either on the page or linked to the page? • Does the author discuss multiple theories or points of view?
Accuracy • Information should be free of errors. • Verification of information confirmed by reviewers or fact-checkers.	• Websites can be published without reviewers or accuracy checks.	• Does the page contain obvious errors in grammar, spelling, or mathematics? • Are original sources clearly documented in a list of references? • Can the information be cross-checked through another source? • Are charts, graphs, or statistical information labeled clearly?
Currency • Site should be current and frequently revised.	• Information is changing so rapidly that pages that are not maintained and up-to-date cannot provide the reliable information needed. • Currency is a key advantage of the Web over print sources. If there is no evidence of currency the site loses its potential to add to knowledge in the field.	• Look for dates and updates for the page. • Links should be current and not lead to dead sites. • References should include recent citations. • Photos and videos should be up-to-date (unless related to a historical topic).
Audience • Site should clearly target whether it is for your own use or the potential use of students in your classroom. • Site should detail whether it is a self-created site or has been created by others. • Site should be accessible by all learners, particularly those with special needs.	• In education the audience may be students, families, teachers, or administrators. Presenting information for a well-defined audience is critical.	• Check for suggested grade levels or ages. • Does the site allow for easy use through menus or search features that help children find information? • What is the reading level of the narrative? • Are there options for students with special needs? Do they adhere to the principles of universal design by, for example, considering students with visual impairments by using increased font size, synthesized speech, or a screen reader, or considering students with hearing impairments by including captions for video or audio materials? See http://webxact.watchfire.com to assess a website for accessibility.

newest hardware and software with a curious mind and a sensible approach to learning about the innovation. One area of growing interest is Web 2.0 tools that encourage collaboration, communication, and construction of knowledge, including blogs, wikis, and audio or video presentations frequently referred to as podcasts.

Podcasts. Podcasts refer to audio or video files that automatically download to subscribers over the Internet and are listened to or watched on mobile media players. Students and teachers create these podcasts so they can replay information related to a particular topic or lesson. Teachers produce podcasts to create downloadable digital instruction that supports classroom lessons. Students develop these as culminating projects, such as a report on the Pythagorean theorem or a persuasive argument that results from collecting data of real-world significance.

Wikis. Wikis are Web-based publishing tools built through the combined collective wisdom of multiple contributors. Members of the contributing group add, remove, edit, or otherwise change content. This process of collaborative authorship can encourage students to find new information, assess and evaluate information already in place, and build new knowledge. Although information that is misleading or inaccurate can get posted, that defect helps to develop the ability to scrutinize Web information as a savvy consumer. You can easily see how a topic in social studies such as the civil rights movement or a piece of literature can spark the start of a wiki, but mathematics topics are worthy starting points for wikis, too. Numeration systems, geometric transformations, the interpretation of a set of data, or the mathematics in a photograph, book, or movie represent a variety of options for wikis emerging from mathematics lessons.

Web Logs. Web logs are electronic documents or websites where people discuss events, post comments, or just give their opinions about a variety of topics. Sharing resources or thoughts and having others respond is a powerful tool in getting students to communicate and evaluate ideas. At a basic level your class Web log (blog) can archive homework assignments or other materials of interest to families—even a place to post an outstanding assignment. Web logs can also hold portfolios of students' work that can be shared for conferences or just reflect the pattern of growth in mathematics learning throughout a grading period or year. The site can become a place to store math games, problems of the week, or writing prompts, such as mathematics poetry templates. Remember to develop a policy so that everyone (including family members) understands how the blog should and should not be used.

Digital Gaming. Some experts agree that digital gaming is the direction that online educational websites are headed. Considering that many young students' first encounters with technology are digital games they played on the computer as toddlers, new games out there are familiar and attractive means to support mathematics learning by solving complex problems. Just as in other video games, these mathematics games require resolve, concentration, the use of a variety of strategies, imagination, and creativity. Through interactive virtual worlds, young students can use what they know to learn new concepts. For example, Maryland Public Television's *Thinkport* site is a leader in developing innovative and engaging websites to support instruction in various disciplines (www.thinkport.org/technology/gotgame/default.tp). One of their digital games, "Lure of the Labyrinth" (http://labyrinth.thinkport.org) is an example of a higher-level activity geared toward middle school mathematics students. Linked to NCTM standards, the "Labyrinth" engages students in a storyline designed to develop critical thinking on the topics of proportionality, variables and equations, and number and operations. Gamers learn from experience and are the "experts" in charge of their own failure or success. As the game keeps track of progress, students can get help "just in time" when they need it. If you click on "For Educators" you see a user-friendly explanation of the game as well as background on gaming through key papers on the topic, lesson plans, classroom management strategies, and the mathematics standards connection chart.

Reflections on Chapter 7

Writing to Learn

1. Technology has affected the mathematics curriculum and how it is taught in many ways. Explain at least three, and give examples to support your explanation. Can you think of examples that are not included in this chapter?

2. Describe some of the benefits of using calculators regularly in the mathematics classroom. Which of these seem to you to be the most compelling? What are some of the arguments against using calculators? Answer each of the arguments against calculators as if you were giving a speech at your PTA meeting or arguing for regular use of calculators before your principal.

3. Name at least three features of graphing calculators that truly improve the learning of mathematics in the middle grades?

4. What are some criteria that seem most important to you when selecting software?

5. What kind of information can you expect to find on the Internet that would be useful in teaching mathematics? How can you evaluate the quality of that information?

6. What are some of the emerging technologies? How can you be ready for new technologies in the future?

For Discussion and Exploration

1. Talk with some teachers about their use of calculators in the classroom. How do they make a decision as to when to use them? Read the NCTM Position Statement on Computation, Calculators, and Common Sense? How do the reasons given by the teachers you talked with compare to the NCTM position?
2. Among the software kept at your school, find one example of instructional software for mathematics. Try it and decide how it would be used in your classroom (if at all). Be sure to check the documentation for suggested grade levels.
3. Check out at least three of the websites suggested below or at MyEducationLab. Be sure to follow some of the links to other sites. Create your own "top ten" to bookmark as favorites on your computer.
4. Explore three or four applets from one or more of the sites listed under Applets (see below). Select one and try it with children. Teach a lesson that incorporates the applet as either a teacher tool or student activity.

Resources for Chapter 7

Recommended Readings

Articles

McGehee, J., & Griffith, L. K. (2004). Technology enhances student learning across the curriculum. *Mathematics Teaching in the Middle School, 9*(6), 344–349.

Five examples using technology are explored, including understanding graphs (rate of change), decimals, geometry, measurement, and data analysis. This is a good introduction to the use of technology in any of these domains.

National Council of Teachers of Mathematics. (2002–present). *ON-Math* is an online NCTM journal that can be accessed on the Web by all NCTM members at www.nctm.org/publications/onmath.aspx.

However, anyone can go into the "Articles by Grade" section and see titles of the variety of articles for pre-K–12 teachers. There are actual classroom activities, enhanced lessons, and more general suggestions for technology use delivered with interactive software, virtual manipulatives, video clips, and sound effects.

Thompson, T., & Sproule, S. (2005). Calculators for students with special needs. *Teaching Children Mathematics, 11*(7), 391–395.

An excellent argument is made for the use of calculators for students who have learning problems that affect their mathematical skills. A framework or flowchart that is easily used to make decisions about when to allow calculator use is not only appropriate for special students but also for every child. This short article can help counter any objections raised by calculator critics.

Books

Masalski, W. J., & Elliott, P. C. (Eds.). (2005). *Technology-supported mathematics learning environments: Sixty-seventh yearbook.* Reston, VA: NCTM.

An excellent collection of perspectives on the use of technology across the grades by noted authorities and practicing teachers alike. Topics include strategies for effective use of technology, examination of virtual manipulatives for young students, dynamic geometry software, the spreadsheet, and much more. A CD is included to illustrate many of the ideas found in the book.

Online Resources

Professional Information

National Council of Teachers of Mathematics (NCTM)
www.nctm.org

The NCTM website is a must for every elementary teacher and teacher of mathematics. It includes specific information for teachers, parents, leaders, and researchers. The home page changes almost monthly, providing up-to-date information about conferences, publications, news, and more. The site also provides a mechanism for joining the council, registering for conferences, purchasing publications and products, and linking to the Illuminations site (see separate entry). Members can access their journals online, subscribe to a special electronic journal, and renew memberships. You can choose to receive a monthly e-mail update informing you of recent additions to the website.

Association for Supervision and Curriculum Development (ACSD)
www.ascd.org

ASCD is an international nonprofit educational association that is committed to successful teaching and learning for all.

International Society for Technology in Education (ISTE)
www.iste.org

ISTE is the professional organization for educators interested in infusing technology into instruction. It maintains an exciting set of resources for teachers including website links, professional development, and publications. The next generation of ISTE's National Educational Technology Standards (NETS-S) for students can be found by clicking the NETS section from the home page. The standards address such topics as creativity and innovation; communication and collaboration; research and information fluency; critical thinking, problem solving, and decision making; digital citizenship; and technology operations and concepts.

Teacher Resources

NCTM Illuminations
http://illuminations.nctm.org

This is an incredible site developed by NCTM to provide Internet resources for teaching and learning intended to "illuminate" *Principles and Standards for School Mathematics*. You can find resources from lesson ideas to "math-lets" (applets designed to provide tools for developing understanding in mathematics). Also at this site are multimedia investigations for students and links to video vignettes designed to promote professional reflection.

The Illuminations website continues to be updated with the addition of many new lessons. In addition the Illuminations Game Room Project allows students to explore mathematics topics while playing mathematics games with one another over the Web.

The Math Forum
http://mathforum.org

Along with the NCTM sites, this may be your most important source of information and links to useful sites. The forum has resources (Math Tools) for both teachers and students. There are suggestions for lessons, puzzles, and activities, plus links to other sites with similar information. There are forums where teachers can talk with other teachers. Two pages accept questions about mathematics from students or teachers (Ask Dr. Math) and about teaching mathematics from teachers (Teacher 2 Teacher). Problems are regularly posted, and solutions can be entered via the Internet.

Annenberg/CPB Projects
www.learner.org

This tremendous resource lists free online learning activities, including information about all sorts of interesting uses of mathematics and science in the real world, resources for free and inexpensive materials from Annenberg, and information about funding opportunities.

Center for Implementing Technology in Education (CITEd): Tech Matrix
www.techmatrix.org

CITEd's Tech Matrix is a useful database of technology products that supports instruction in mathematics for students with special needs. Each product evaluation includes a link to the supplier's website.

Applets

National Council of Teachers of Mathematics e-Examples
http://standards.nctm.org/document/eexamples/index.htm

Many of these applets are referenced in and directly support the text of *Principles and Standards for School Mathematics*. They are also available on the CD version of the *Standards*. Most are also available on the Illuminations site.

NCTM Illuminations
http://illuminations.nctm.org

Check both the i-Math Investigations (interactive math lessons, most built around applets) and Interactive Math-lets (a collection of applets). The Math-let applications cover the K–12 spectrum. They are ordered alphabetically, so be sure to check out the full list. This is a good collection of quality tools. The i-Math Investigations include all of the applets from the e-Examples.

The National Library for Virtual Manipulatives and eNLVM
http://nvlm.usu.edu/en/nav/vlibrary.html

This NSF-funded site located at Utah State University contains a huge collection of applets organized by the five content strands of the *Standards* and also by the same four grade bands. The eNVLM section contains online units, customizable student activities, and tools to help teachers develop activities collaboratively.

Arcytech
http://arcytech.org/java

This site includes tool applets for base-ten blocks, pattern blocks, Cuisenaire rods, fraction bars, and integer bars. There is also an extended interactive lesson developing the Pythagorean theorem.

Shodor Interactivate (Shodor Education Foundation)
www.shodor.org/interactivate

The site contains a huge list of applets that continues to grow. In addition, there are lessons and activities. Applets (referred to as "activities") are arranged by content rather than grade level, so be sure to look through the full list. This is a valuable site, especially for teachers in the upper grades and middle school.

Field Experience Guide Connections

Technology is the focus of Chapter 5 of the *Field Experience Guide*. Projects and teaching opportunities in this section focus on the role of technology in supporting student learning. For example, in FEG 5.4 you develop a learning center involving the use of a calculator or computer. Several of the Expanded Lessons in Chapter 9—such as FEG 9.22, "Bar Graphs to Circle Graphs," and FEG 9.19, "Triangle Midsegments"—lend themselves to the use of technology.

Chapter 8

Developing Early Number Concepts and Number Sense

Children come to school with many ideas about number. These ideas should be built upon as we work with children and help them develop new relationships. It is sad to see the large number of students in grades 4, 5, and above who essentially know little more about number than how to count. It takes time and lots of experiences for children to develop a full understanding of number that will grow and develop into more advanced number-related concepts in higher grades.

This chapter looks at the development of number ideas for numbers up to about 20. These foundational ideas can all be extended to larger numbers, operations, basic facts, and computation.

Big Ideas

1. Counting tells how many things are in a set. When counting a set of objects, the last word in the counting sequence names the quantity for that set.

2. Numbers are related to each other through a variety of number relationships. The number 7, for example, is more than 4, two less than 9, composed of 3 and 4 as well as 2 and 5, is three away from 10, and can be quickly recognized in several patterned arrangements of dots. These ideas further extend to an understanding of 17, 57, and 370.

3. Number concepts are intimately tied to the world around us. Application of number relationships to real settings marks the beginning of making sense of the world in a mathematical manner.

Mathematics Content Connections

Early number development is related to other areas in the curriculum in two ways: content that interacts with and enhances the development of number and content that is directly affected by how well early number concepts have been developed. Measurement, data, and the meanings of operations fall in the first category. Basic facts, place value, and computation fall in the second.

- **Operations** (Chapter 9): As children solve story problems for any of the four operations, they count on, count back, make and count groups, and make comparisons. In the process, they form new relationships and methods of working with numbers.

- **Measurement** (Chapter 19): The determination of measures of length, height, size, or weight is an important use of number for the young child. Measurement involves meaningful counting and comparing (number relationships) and connects number to the world in which the child lives.

- **Data** (Chapter 21): Data, like measurement, involve counts and comparisons to both aid in developing number and connecting it to real-world situations.

- **Basic Facts** (Chapter 10): A rich and thorough development of number relationships is a critical foundation for mastering basic facts. Without number relationships, facts must be rotely memorized. With number understanding, facts for addition and subtraction are relatively simple extensions.

- **Place Value and Computation** (Chapters 11 and 12): Many of the ideas that contribute to computational fluency and flexibility with numbers are extensions of how numbers are related to ten and how numbers can be taken apart and recombined in different ways.

Promoting Good Beginnings

In 2002 NCTM and the National Association for the Education of Young Children (NAEYC) collaboratively produced a joint position statement emphasizing that all children need an early start in learning mathematics. This emphasis on readiness aligns with the recent findings of the National Mathematics Advisory Panel (2008). The position statement suggests ten research-based recommendations to help teachers develop high-quality learning activities for children aged 3 to 6:

1. Enhance children's natural interest in mathematics and their disposition to use it to make sense of their physical and social worlds

2. Build on children's experience and knowledge, including their family, linguistic, cultural, and community backgrounds; their individual approaches to learning; and their informal knowledge

3. Base mathematics curriculum and teaching practices on knowledge of young children's cognitive, linguistic, physical, and social-emotional development

4. Use curriculum and teaching practices that strengthen children's problem-solving and reasoning processes as well as representing, communicating, and connecting mathematical ideas

5. Ensure that the curriculum is coherent and compatible with known relationships and sequences of important mathematical ideas

6. Provide for children's deep and sustained interaction with key mathematical ideas

7. Integrate mathematics with other activities and other activities with mathematics

8. Provide ample time, materials, and teacher support for children to engage in play, a context in which they explore and manipulate mathematical ideas with keen interest

9. Introduce mathematical concepts, methods, and language, through a range of appropriate experiences and teaching strategies

10. Support children's learning by thoughtfully and continually assessing all children's mathematical knowledge, skills, and strategies

❚❚ ————— *Pause and Reflect*

Although all of these recommendations are critical, which two do you consider most important for you to work on first as you develop as a teacher?

Number Development in Pre-K and Kindergarten

Families help children count their fingers, toys, people at the table, and other small sets of objects. Questions concerning "who has more?" or "are there enough?" are part of the daily lives of children as young as 2 or 3 years

of age. Considerable evidence indicates that these children have beginning understandings of the concepts of number and counting (Baroody & Wilkins, 1999; Fuson, 1988; Gelman & Gallistel, 1978; Gelman & Meck, 1986; NRC, 2001). We therefore include abundant activities to support a variety of different experiences that young children need to gain a full understanding of the concepts.

The Relationships of More, Less, and Same

The concepts of "more," "less," and "same" are basic relationships contributing to the overall concept of number. Children begin to develop relational ideas before they begin school. Almost any child entering kindergarten can choose the set that is *more* if presented with two sets that are quite obviously different in number. In fact, Baroody (1987) states, "A child unable to use 'more' in this intuitive manner is at considerable educational risk" (p. 29). Classroom activities should help children build on this basic notion and refine it.

Though the concept of less is logically related to the concept of more (selecting the set with more is the same as *not* selecting the set with less), the word *less* proves to be more difficult for children than *more*. A possible explanation is that children have many opportunities to use the word *more* but have limited exposure to the word *less*. To help children with the concept of less, frequently pair it with the word *more* and make a conscious effort to ask "which is less?" questions as well as "which is more?" questions. For example, suppose that your class has correctly selected the set that has more from two that are given. Immediately follow with the question "Which is less?" In this way, the concept can be connected with the better-known idea and the term *less* can become more familiar.

For all three concepts (more, less, and same), children should construct sets using counters as well as make comparisons or choices between two given sets. The following activities should be conducted in a spirit of inquiry accompanied whenever possible with requests for explanations. "Why do you think this set has less?"

Activity 8.1

Make Sets of More/Less/Same

At a workstation or table, provide about eight cards with sets of 4 to 12 objects, a set of small counters or blocks, and some word cards labeled *More, Less,* and *Same.* Next to each card have students make three collections of counters: a set that is more, one that is less, and one that is the same. The appropriate labels are placed on the sets (see Figure 8.1).

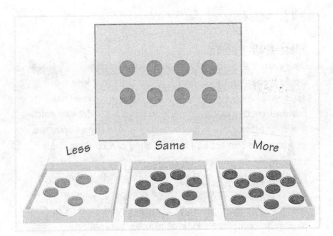

Figure 8.1 Making sets that are more, less, and the same.

In Activity 8.1, students create a set with counters, which gives them the opportunity to reflect on the sets and adjust them as they work. The next activity is done without counters. Although it addresses the same basic ideas, it provides a different problem situation.

Activity 8.2

Find the Same Amount

Give children a collection of cards with sets on them. Dot cards are one possibility (see Blackline Masters 3–8). Have the children pick up any card in the collection and then find another card with the same amount to form a pair. Continue to find other pairs. This activity can be altered to have children find dot cards that are "less" or "more."

Observe children as they do this task. Children whose number ideas are completely tied to counting and nothing more will select cards at random and count each dot. Others will begin by selecting a card that appears to have about the same number of dots. This demonstrates a significantly higher level of understanding. Also observe how the dots are counted. Are the counts made accurately? Is each counted only once? Does the child need to touch the dot when counting? A significant milestone for children occurs when they begin recognizing small patterned sets without counting.

▮▮ ———————— *Pause and Reflect*

You have begun to see some of the early foundational ideas about number. Stop now and make a list of all of the important ideas that you think children should *know about* the number 8 by the time they finish first grade. (The number 8 is used as an example. The list could be about any number from, say, 6 to 12.) Put your thoughts aside and we will revisit these ideas later.

Early Counting

Meaningful counting activities begin in preschool. Generally, children at midyear in kindergarten should have a fair understanding of counting, but children must construct this idea. It cannot be forced. Only the counting sequence is a rote procedure. The *meaning* attached to counting is the key conceptual idea on which all other number concepts are developed.

The Development of Counting Skills. Counting involves at least two separate skills. First, a child must be able to produce the standard list of counting words in order: "One, two, three, four, . . . " Second, a child must be able to connect this sequence in a one-to-one manner with the items in the set being counted. Each item must get one and only one count.

Experience and guidance are the major factors in the development of these counting skills. Many children come to kindergarten able to count sets of ten or beyond. At the same time, children with weak background knowledge may require additional practice to enhance their background experiences. The size and arrangement of the set are also factors related to success in counting. Obviously, longer number strings require more practice to learn. The first 12 counts involve no pattern or repetition, and many children do not easily recognize a pattern in the teens. Children still learning the skills of counting—that is, matching oral number words with objects—should be given sets of blocks or counters that they can move or pictures of sets that are arranged in a pattern for easy counting.

Meaning Attached to Counting. Fosnot and Dolk (2001) make it very clear that an understanding of cardinality and the connection to counting is not a simple matter for 4-year-olds. Children will learn *how* to count (matching counting words with objects) before they understand that the last count word indicates the *amount* of the set or the *cardinality* of the set. Children who have made this connection are said to have the *cardinality principle*, which is a refinement of their early ideas about quantity. Most, but certainly not all, children by age $4\frac{1}{2}$ have made this connection (Fosnot & Dolk, 2001; Fuson & Hall, 1983).

 Young children who can count orally may not have attached meaning to their counts. Show a child a card with five to nine large dots in a row so that they can be easily counted. Ask the child to count the dots. If the count is accurate, ask "How many dots are on the card?" Many children will count again. One indication of understanding the first count will be a response that reflects the first count without recounting. Now have the child get that same number of counters from a collection of counters: "Please get the same number of counters as there are dots on the card." There are several indicators to watch for. Will the child recount to know how many to get? Does the child count the counters or place them one-to-one on the dots? Is the child confident that there is the same number of counters as dots? ◆

Fosnot and Dolk discuss a class of 4-year-olds in which children who knew there were 17 children in the class were unsure how many milk cartons they should get so that each could have one.

To develop their understanding of counting, engage children in almost any game or activity that involves counts and comparisons. The following is a simple suggestion.

Activity 8.3

Fill the Chutes

Create a simple game board with four "chutes." Each consists of a column of about twelve 1-inch squares with a star at the top. Children take turns rolling a die and collecting the indicated number of counters. They then place these counters in one of the chutes. The object is to fill all of the chutes with counters. As an option, require that the chutes be filled exactly. A roll of 5 cannot be used to fill a chute with four empty spaces.

This "game" provides opportunities for you to talk with children about number and assess their thinking. Watch how the children count the dots on the die. Ask, "How do you know you have the right number of counters?" and "How many counters did you put in the chute? How many more do you need to fill the chute?"

Activities 8.1 and 8.2 also provide opportunities for formative assessment. Regular classroom activities, such as counting how many napkins are needed at snack time, are additional opportunities for children to learn about number and for teachers to listen to students' ideas.

Numeral Writing and Recognition

Helping children read and write single-digit numerals is similar to teaching them to read and write letters of the alphabet. Neither has anything to do with number concepts. Traditionally, instruction has involved various forms of repetitious practice. Children trace over pages of numerals, repeatedly write the numbers from 0 to 10, make the numerals from clay, trace them in sand, write them on the chalkboard or in the air, and so on.

The calculator is a good instructional tool for numeral recognition. In addition to helping children with numerals, early activities can help develop familiarity with the calculator so that more complex activities are possible.

Activity 8.4

Find and Press

Every child should have a calculator. Always begin by having the children press the clear key. Then you say a number, and the children press that number on the calculator. If you have an overhead calculator, or interactive whiteboard, you can then show the children the correct key so that they can confirm their responses, or you can write the number on the board for children to check. Begin with single-digit numbers. Later, progress to two or three numbers called in succession. For example, call, "Three, seven, one." Children press the complete string of numbers as called.

Perhaps the most common preschool and kindergarten exercises have children match sets with numerals (see Blackline Master 2). Children are given pictured sets and asked to write or match the number that tells how many. Alternatively, they may be given a number and told to make or draw a set with that many objects. Although many teacher resource books describe learning center activities where children put a numeral with the correct-sized set, such as numbered frogs on lily pads (with dots), it is important to note that these activities involve only the skills of counting sets and numeral recognition or writing. When children are successful with these activities, it is time to move on to more advanced concepts.

Counting On and Counting Back

Although the forward sequence of numbers is relatively familiar to most young children, counting on and counting back are difficult skills for many. Frequent short practice drills are recommended.

Activity 8.5

Up and Back Counting

Counting up to and back from a target number in a rhythmic fashion is an important counting exercise. For example, line up five children and five chairs in front of the class. As the whole class counts from 1 to 5, the children sit down one at a time. When the target number, 5, is reached, it is repeated; the child who sat on 5 now stands, and the count goes back to 1. As the count goes back, the children stand up one at a time, and so on, "1, 2, 3, 4, 5, 5, 4, 3, 2, 1, 1, 2, ..." Preschool, kindergarten, and first-grade children find exercises such as this both fun and challenging. Any movement (clapping, turning around) can be used as the count goes up and back in a rhythmic manner.

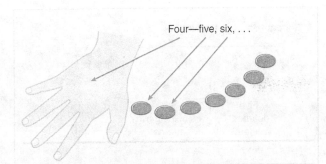

Four—five, six, . . .

Figure 8.2 Counting on: "Hide four. Count, starting from the number of counters hidden."

Figure 8.3 How many in all? How do children count to tell the total? Dump the counters? Count up from 1 without dumping the counters? Count on?

The last activity is designed only to help students become fluent with the number words in both forward and reverse order and to begin counts with numbers other than 1. Although not at all easy for young students, these activities do not address counting on or counting back in a meaningful manner. Fosnot and Dolk (2001) describe the ability to count on as a "landmark" on the path to number sense. The next two activities are designed for that purpose.

Activity 8.6

Counting On with Counters

Give each child a collection of 10 or 12 small counters that the children line up left to right on their desks. Tell them to count four counters and push them under their left hands or place them in a cup (see Figure 8.2). Then say, "Point to your hand. How many are there?" (Four.) "So let's count like this: f-o-u-r (pointing to their hand), five, six, . . . Repeat with other numbers under the hand.

The following activity addresses the same concept in a somewhat more problem-based manner.

Activity 8.7

Real Counting On

This "game" for two children requires a deck of cards with numbers 1 to 7, a die, a paper cup, and some counters. The first player turns over the top number card and places the indicated number of counters in the cup. The card is placed next to the cup as a reminder of how many are there. The second child rolls the die and places that many counters next to the cup. (See Figure 8.3.) Together they decide how many counters in all. A record sheet with columns for "In the Cup," "On the Side," and "In All" is an option. The largest number in the card deck can be adjusted if needed.

Watch how children determine the total amounts in this last activity. Children who are not yet counting on may want to dump the counters from the cup or will count up from one without dumping out the counters. Be sure to permit these strategies. As children continue to play, they will eventually count on as that strategy becomes meaningful and useful.

Early Number Sense

Number sense was a term that became popular in the late 1980s, even though terms such as this have somewhat vague definitions. Howden (1989) described number sense as a "good intuition about numbers and their relationships. It develops gradually as a result of exploring numbers, visualizing them in a variety of contexts, and relating them in ways that are not limited by traditional algorithms" (p. 11). This may still be the best definition.

NCTM Standards In *Principles and Standards*, the term *number sense* is used freely throughout the Number and Operations standard. "As students work with numbers, they gradually develop flexibility in thinking about numbers, which is a hallmark of number sense. . . . Number sense develops as students understand the size of numbers, develop multiple ways of thinking about and representing numbers, use numbers as referents, and develop accurate perceptions about the effects of operations on numbers" (p. 80). ◆

The discussion of number sense begins as we look at the kinds of relationships and connections children should be making about smaller numbers up to about 20. But "good intuition about numbers" does not end with these smaller whole numbers. Children continue to develop number sense as they begin to use numbers in operations, build an understanding of place value, and devise flexible methods of computing and making estimates involving large numbers, fractions, decimals, and percents.

The early number ideas that have been discussed to this point in the chapter are the rudimentary aspects of number. Unfortunately, too many traditional textbooks move directly from these beginning ideas to addition and subtraction, leaving students with a very limited collection of ideas about number to bring to these new topics. The result is often that children continue to count by ones to solve simple story problems and have difficulty mastering basic facts. Early number sense development should demand significantly more attention than it is given in most traditional pre-K–2 programs.

Relationships among Numbers 1 Through 10

Once children have acquired a concept of cardinality and can meaningfully use their counting skills, little more is to be gained from the kinds of counting activities described so far. More relationships must be created for children to develop number sense, a flexible concept of number not completely tied to counting.

Figure 8.4 illustrates the four different types of relationships that children can and should develop with numbers:

- *Patterned sets.* Children can learn to recognize sets of objects in patterned arrangements and tell how many without counting. For most numbers, there are several common patterns. For smaller numbers, patterns can also be made up of two or more easier patterns.
- *One and two more, one and two less.* The two-more-than and two-less-than relationships involve more than just the ability to count on two or count back two. Children should know that 7, for example, is 1 more than 6 and also 2 less than 9.
- *Anchors or "benchmarks" of 5 and 10.* Since 10 plays such a large role in our numeration system and because two fives make up 10, it is very useful to develop relationships for the numbers 1 to 10 to the important anchors of 5 and 10.
- *Part-part-whole relationships.* To conceptualize a number as being made up of two or more parts is the most important relationship that can be developed about numbers. For example, 7 can be thought of as a set of 3 and a set of 4 or a set of 2 and a set of 5.

The principal tool that children will use as they construct these relationships is the one number tool they possess: counting. Initially, then, you will notice a lot of counting, and you may wonder if you are making progress. Have patience! Counting will become less and less necessary as children construct these new relationships and begin to use more powerful ideas.

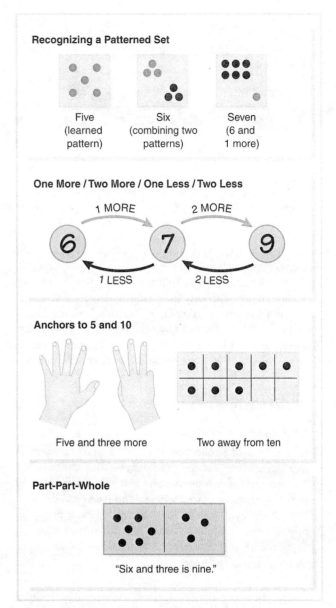

Figure 8.4 Four number relationships for children to develop.

Patterned Set Recognition

Many children learn to recognize the dot arrangements on standard dice due to the many games they have played that use dice. Similar instant recognition (also known as *subitizing*) can be developed for other patterns. The activities suggested here encourage reflective thinking about the patterns so that the relationships will be constructed. Naming amounts without the routine of counting can then aid in "counting on" (from a known patterned set) or learning combinations of numbers (seeing a pattern of two known smaller patterns).

Good materials to use in pattern recognition activities include a set of dot plates. These can be made using small

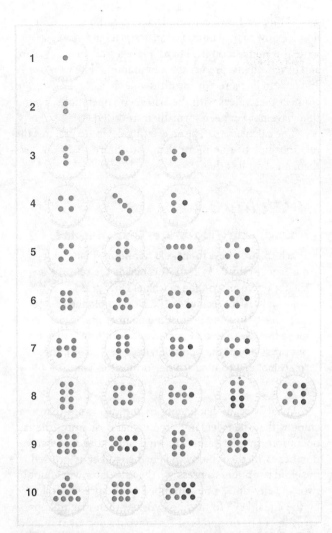

Figure 8.5 A collection of dot patterns for "dot plates."

paper plates and the peel-off dots commonly available in office supply stores. A collection of patterns is shown in Figure 8.5. Note that some patterns are combinations of two smaller patterns or a pattern with one or two additional dots. These should be made in two colors. Keep the patterns compact. If the dots are spread out, the patterns are hard to identify.

Activity 8.8

Learning Patterns

To introduce the patterns, provide each student with about ten counters and a piece of construction paper as a mat. Hold up a dot plate for about 3 seconds. "Make the pattern you saw on the plate using the counters on the mat. How many dots did you see? What did the pattern look like?" Spend some time discussing the configuration of the pattern and how many dots. Do this with a few new patterns each day.

Activity 8.9

Dot Plate Flash

Hold up a dot plate for only 1 to 3 seconds. "How many dots did you see? What did the pattern look like?" Children like to see how quickly they can recognize and say how many dots. Include lots of easy patterns and a few with more dots as you build their confidence. Students can also flash the dot plates to each other as a workstation activity.

The instant recognition activities with the plates are exciting and can be done in 5 minutes at any time of day or between lessons. There is value in using them at any primary grade level and at any time of year.

One and Two More, One and Two Less

When children count, they have no reason to reflect on the way one number is related to another. The goal is only to match number words with objects until they reach the end of the count. To learn that 6 and 8 are related by the twin relationships of "two more than" and "two less than" requires reflection on these ideas within tasks that permit counting. Counting on (or back) one or two counts is a useful tool in constructing these ideas.

Note that the relationship of "two more than" is significantly different than "comes two counts after." This latter relationship is applied to the string of number words, not to the quantities they represent. A comes-two-after relationship can be applied to letters of the alphabet. The letter *H* comes two after the letter *F*. However, there is no numeric or quantitative difference between *F* and *H*. The quantity 8 would still be two more than 6 even if there were no number string to count these quantities. It is the numeric relationship you want to develop.

The following activity is a good place to begin helping children with these relationships. As described, it focuses on the two-more-than relationship although it can be used just as well for any of the four relationships.

Activity 8.10

Make a Two-More-Than Set

Provide students with about six dot cards. Their task is to construct a set of counters that is two more than the set shown on the card. Similarly, spread out eight to ten dot cards, and ask students to find another card for each that is two less than the card shown. (Omit the 1 and 2 cards for two less than, and so on.)

In activities in which children find a set or make a set, they can add a numeral card (a small card with a number written on it) to all of the sets involved. They can also be encouraged to take turns reading a number sentence to their partner. If, for example, a set has been made that is two more than a set of four, the child can read this by saying the number sentence, "Two more than four is six" or "Six is two more than four." The next activity combines the relationships.

Activity 8.11

More or Less

This is an activity for two players or a small group. Use Blackline Master 1 to make a deck of More-or-Less cards as shown in Figure 8.6. Make four or five of each type of card. You will also need a set of cards (Blackline Master 2) with the numbers 3 to 10 (2 each). One child draws a number card and places it face up where all can see. That number of counters are put into a cup. Next, another child draws one of the More-or-Less cards and places it next to the number card. For the More cards, counters are added accordingly to the cup. For the Less cards, counters are removed from the cup. For Zero cards, no change is made. Once the cup has been adjusted, each child predicts how many counters are now in the cup. The counters are dumped out and counted, ending that round of the game and a new number card is drawn.

Figure 8.6 Materials to play "More or Less" (see Blackline Master 1).

"More or Less" can be played with the class. You announce how many counters you are placing in the cup and write this number on the board. Have a student draw a card and have students predict the new amount. The words *more* and *less* can be paired or substituted with *add* and *subtract* to connect these ideas with the arithmetic operations, even if they have not yet been formally introduced.

The calculator can be an exciting device to practice the relationships of one more than, two more than, one less than, and two less than.

Activity 8.12

A Calculator Two-More-Than Machine

Teach children how to make a two-more-than machine. Press 0 [+] 2 [=]. This makes the calculator a two-more-than machine. Now press any number—for example, 5. Children hold their finger over the [=] key and predict the number that is two more than 5. Then they press [=] to confirm. If they do not press any of the operation keys (+, −, ×, ÷), the "machine" will continue to perform in this way.

What is really happening in the two-more-than machine is that the calculator "remembers" or stores the last operation, in this case "+2," and adds that to whatever number is in the window when the [=] key is pressed. If the child continues to press [=], the calculator will count by twos. At any time, a new number can be pressed followed by the equal key. To make a two-less-than machine, press 2 [−] 2 [=]. (The first press of 2 is to avoid a negative number.) In the beginning, students forget and press operation keys, which change what their calculator is doing. Soon, however, they get the hang of using the calculator as a function machine.

The "two-more-than" calculator will give the number two more than any number pressed, including those with two or more digits. The two-more-than relationship should be extended to two-digit numbers as soon as students are exposed to them. One way to do this is to ask for the number that is two more than 7. After getting the correct answer, ask "What is two more than 37?" and similarly for other numbers that end in 7. When you try this for 8 or 9, expect difficulties and unusual responses such as two more than 28 is "twenty-ten." In the first grade, this struggle can prove quite valuable. The "More or Less" activity can also be extended to larger numbers if no actual counters are used.

Anchoring Numbers to 5 and 10

Here again, we want to help children relate a given number to other numbers, specifically 5 and 10. These relationships

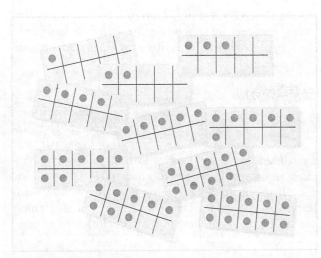

Figure 8.7 Ten-frames.

are especially useful in thinking about various combinations of numbers. For example, in each of the following, consider how the knowledge of 8 as "5 and 3 more" and as "2 away from 10" can play a role: 5 + 3, 8 + 6, 8 − 2, 8 − 3, 8 − 4, 13 − 8. (It may be worth stopping here to consider the role of 5 and 10 in each of these examples.) Later similar relationships can be used in the development of mental computation skills on larger numbers such as 68 + 7.

The most common and perhaps most important model for this relationship is the ten-frame. The ten-frame is simply a 2 × 5 array in which counters or dots are placed to illustrate numbers (see Figure 8.7). Ten-frames can be simply drawn on a full sheet of construction paper (or use Blackline Master 10). Nothing fancy is required, and each child can have one. The ten-frame has been incorporated into a variety of activities in this book and is often found in mathematics textbooks.

For children in kindergarten or early first grade who have not yet explored a ten-frame, it is a good idea to begin with a five-frame. This row of five sections is also drawn on a sheet of construction paper (or use Blackline Master 9). Provide children with about ten counters that will fit in the five-frame sections and conduct the following activity.

Activity 8.13

Five-Frame Tell-About

Explain that only one counter is permitted in each section of the five-frame. No other counters are allowed on the five-frame mat. Have the children show 3 on their five-frame. "What can you tell us about 3 from looking at your mat?" After hearing from several children, try other numbers from 0 to 5. Children may

place their counters on the five-frame in any manner. What they observe will differ a great deal from child to child. For example, with four counters, a child with two on each end may say, "It has a space in the middle" or "It's two and two." Accept all correct answers. Focus attention on how many more counters are needed to make 5 or how far away from 5 a number is. Next try numbers between 5 and 10. The rule of one counter per section still holds. As shown in Figure 8.8, numbers greater than 5 are shown with a full five-frame and additional counters on the mat but not in the frame. In discussion, focus attention on these larger numbers as 5 and some more: "Seven is five and two more."

Notice that the five-frame really focuses on the relationship to 5 as an anchor for numbers but does not anchor numbers to 10. When five-frames have been used for a week or so, introduce ten-frames (see Blackline Master 10). You may want to play a ten-frame version of a "Five-Frame Tell-About" but soon introduce the following rule for showing numbers on the ten-frame: *Always fill the top row first, starting on the left, the same way you read. When the top row is full, counters can be placed in the bottom row, also from the left.* This will produce the "standard" way to show numbers on the ten-frame as in Figure 8.7.

For a while, many children will count every counter on their ten-frame. Some will take all counters off and begin each number from a blank frame. Others will soon learn to adjust numbers by adding on or taking off only what is required, often capitalizing on a row of five without counting. Do not pressure students. With continued practice, all students will grow. How they are using the ten-frame provides you with insights into students' current number concept development.

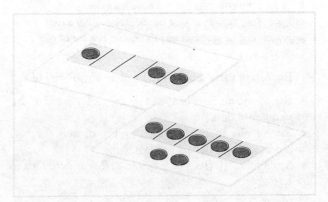

Figure 8.8 A five-frame focuses on the 5 anchor. Counters are placed one to a section, and students tell about how they see their number in the frame.

Activity 8.14

Crazy Mixed-Up Numbers

This activity is adapted from *Mathematics Their Way* (Baratta-Lorton, 1976). All children make their ten-frame show the same number. The teacher then calls out random numbers between 0 and 10. After each number, the children change their ten-frames to show the new number. Children can play this game independently by preparing lists of about 15 "crazy mixed-up numbers." One child plays "teacher," and the rest use the ten-frames. Children like to make up their own number lists.

"Crazy Mixed-Up Numbers" is much more of a problem than it first appears. How do you decide how to change your ten-frame? Some children will wipe off the entire frame and start over with each number. Others will have learned what each number looks like. To add another dimension, have the children tell, *before changing their ten-frames*, how many more counters need to be added ("plus") or removed ("minus"). They then should state plus or minus the correct amount. If, for example, the frames showed 6, and the teacher called out "four," the children would respond, "Minus two!" and then change their ten-frames accordingly. A discussion of how they know what to do is valuable.

Ten-frame flash cards are an important variation of ten-frames. Make cards from tagboard about the size of a small index card, with a ten-frame on each and dots drawn in the frames. A set of 20 cards consists of a 0 card, a 10 card, and two each of the numbers 1 to 9. The cards allow for simple drill activities to reinforce the 5 and 10 anchors as in the following activity.

Activity 8.15

Ten-Frame Flash

Flash ten-frame cards to the class or group and see how fast the children can tell how many dots are shown. This activity is fast-paced, takes only a few minutes, can be done at any time, and is a lot of fun.

Important variations of "Ten-Frame Flash" include

- Saying the number of spaces on the card instead of the number of dots
- Saying one more than the number of dots (or two more, and also one or two less than)
- Saying the "10 fact"—for example, "Six and four make ten"

Ten-frame tasks are surprisingly problematic for students. Students must reflect on the two rows of five, the spaces remaining, and how a particular number is more or less than 5 and how far away from 10. The early discussions of how numbers are seen on the five-frames or ten-frames are examples of brief *after* activities in which students learn from one another.

 How well students can respond to the cards in "Ten-Frame Flash" is a good quick assessment of a child's current number concept level. Include as well the variations of the activity that were listed. Since the distance to 10 is so important, another assessment is to point to a numeral less than ten and ask, "If this many dots were on a ten-frame, how many blank spaces would there be?" Or you can also simply ask, "If I have seven, how many more do I need to make ten?" ◆

Part-Part-Whole Relationships

⏸ ──────── *Pause and Reflect*

Before reading on, get some simple counters or coins. Count out a set of eight counters in front of you as if you were a first- or second-grade child counting them.

Any child who has learned how to count meaningfully can count out eight objects as you just did. What is significant about the experience is what it did *not* cause you to think about. Nothing in counting a set of eight objects will cause a child to focus on the fact that it could be made of two parts. For example, separate the counters you just set out into two piles and reflect on the combination. It might be 2 and 6, 7 and 1, or 4 and 4. Make a change in your two piles of counters and say the new combination to yourself. Focusing on a quantity in terms of its parts has important implications for developing number sense. A noted researcher in children's number concepts, Lauren Resnick (1983), states:

> Probably the major conceptual achievement of the early school years is the interpretation of numbers in terms of part and whole relationships. With the application of a Part-Whole schema to quantity, it becomes possible for children to think about numbers as compositions of other numbers. This enrichment of number understanding permits forms of mathematical problem solving and interpretation that are not available to younger children. (p. 114)

Basic Ingredients of Part-Part-Whole Activities. Most part-part-whole activities focus on a single number for the entire activity. For example, a child or group of children working together might work on the number 7 throughout the activity. Children can either build the designated quantity in two or more parts, or else they start with the full amount and separate it into two or more parts. A group of two or three children may work on one number in one activity for 5 to 20 minutes. Kindergarten children will usually begin these activities working on the number 4 or 5. As concepts develop, children can extend their work to numbers 6 to 12. A wide variety of materials and formats for these activities can help maintain student interest. It is not unusual to find second graders who have not developed firm part-part-whole constructs for numbers in the 7-to-12 range.

When children do these activities, have them say or "read" the parts aloud or write them down on some form of recording sheet (or do both). Reading or writing the combinations serves as a means of encouraging reflective thought focused on the part-whole relationship. Writing can be in the form of drawings, numbers written in blanks (_____ and _____), or addition equations if these have been introduced ($3 + 5 = 8$). There is a clear connection between part-part-whole concepts and addition and subtraction ideas.

Part-Part-Whole Activities. The following activity and its variations may be considered the "basic" part-part-whole activity.

Activity 8.16

Build It in Parts

Provide children with one type of material, such as connecting cubes or squares of colored paper. The task is to see how many different combinations for a particular number they can make using two parts. (If you wish, you can allow for more than two parts.) Each different combination can be displayed on a small mat, such as a quarter-sheet of construction paper. Here are just a few ideas, each of which is illustrated in Figure 8.9.

* Use two-color counters such as lima beans spray painted on one side (also available in plastic).
* Make bars of connecting cubes. Make each bar with two colors. Keep the colors together.
* Make combinations using two dot strips—strips of poster board about 1 inch wide with stick-on dots. (Make lots of strips with from one to four dots and fewer strips with from five to ten dots.)
* Make combinations of two Cuisenaire rods to match a given amount.

As you observe children working on the "Build It in Parts" activity, ask them to "read" a number sentence to go with each of their combinations. Encourage children to read their number sentences to each other. Two or three children working together with the same materials may have quite a large number of combinations including lots of repeats. Remember, the children are focusing on the combinations.

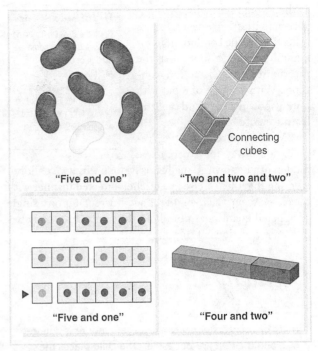

"Five and one"   Connecting cubes   "Two and two and two"

"Five and one"   "Four and two"

Figure 8.9 Assorted materials for building parts of 6.

The following activity is strictly symbolic. However, children should use counters if they feel they need to.

Activity 8.17

Two Out of Three

Make lists of three numbers, two of which total the whole that children are focusing on. Here is an example list for the number 5:

    2–3–4
    5–0–2
    1–3–2
    3–1–4
    2–2–3
    4–3–1

With the list on the board, overhead, or worksheet, children can take turns selecting the two numbers that make the whole. As with all problem-solving activities, children should be challenged to justify their answers.

Missing-Part Activities. A special and important variation of part-part-whole activities is referred to as *missing-part* activities. In a missing-part activity, children know the whole amount and use their already developed knowledge of the parts of that whole to try to tell what the covered or hidden part is. If they do not know or are unsure, they simply uncover the unknown part and say the full combination as they would normally. Missing-part activities provide maximum reflection on the combinations for a number. They also serve as the forerunner to subtraction concepts. With a whole of 8 but with only 3 showing, the child can later learn to write "8 − 3 = 5."

Missing-part activities require some way for a part to be hidden or unknown. Usually this is done with two children working together or else in a teacher-directed manner with the class. Again, the focus of the activity remains on a single designated quantity as the whole. The next three activities illustrate variations of this important idea.

myeducationlab

Go to the Building Teaching Skills and Dispositions section of Chapter 8 of MyEducationLab. Click on Expanded Lessons to download the Expanded Lesson for **"I Wish I Had"** and complete the related activities.

Activity 8.18

Covered Parts

A set of counters equal to the target amount is counted out, and the rest are put aside. One child places the counters under a margarine tub or piece of tagboard. The child then pulls some out into view. (This amount could be none, all, or any amount in between.) For example, if 6 is the whole and 4 are showing, the other child says, "Four and *two* is six." If there is hesitation or if the hidden part is unknown, the hidden part is immediately shown (see Figure 8.10).

Activity 8.19

Missing-Part Cards

For each number 4 to 10, make missing-part cards on strips of 3-by-9-inch tagboard. Each card has a numeral for the whole and two dot sets with one set covered by a flap. For the number 8, you need nine cards with the visible part ranging from zero to eight dots. Students use the cards as in "Covered Parts," saying, "Four and two is six" for a card showing four dots and hiding two (see Figure 8.10).

Activity 8.20

I Wish I Had

Hold out a bar of connecting cubes, a dot strip, a two-column strip, or a dot plate showing 6 or less. Say, "I wish I had six." The children respond with the part that is needed to make 6. Counting on can be used to check. The game can focus on a single whole, or the "I wish I had" number can change each time (see Figure 8.10).

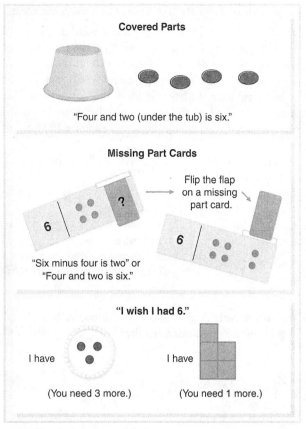

Covered Parts

"Four and two (under the tub) is six."

Missing Part Cards

6 ? Flip the flap on a missing part card.

6

"Six minus four is two" or "Four and two is six."

"I wish I had 6."

I have (You need 3 more.)   I have (You need 1 more.)

Figure 8.10 Missing-part activities.

Tech NOTES
There are lots of ways you can use computer software to create part-part-whole activities. All that is needed is a program that permits students to create sets of objects on the screen. Scott Foresman's *eTools* (Pearson Education, 2004) includes a variety of background screens for counters. This activity is also available free at www.kyrene.org/mathtools. If you use the online version choose "Counters" and under "workspaces" on the bottom left, select the bucket icon. Then select the bathtub and add boat, duck, or goldfish counters. As shown in Figure 8.11, children can stamp these three different types of bathtub toys either in the tub (unseen) or outside the tub. The numeral on the tub shows how many are in the tub or it can be fixed to show a question mark (?) for missing-part thinking. The total is shown at the bottom. By clicking on the lightbulb above the tub, the contents of the tub can be seen (Figure 8.11b). In the hands of a teacher, this program offers a great deal of diversity and challenge for both part-part-whole and missing-part activities. ◆

Ⅱ ——————————— *Pause and Reflect*

Remember the list you made earlier in the chapter about what children should know about the number 8? Get it out now and see if you would add to it or revise it based on what you have read to this point. Do this before reading on.

(a)

(b)

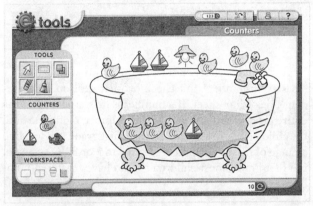

Figure 8.11 The counters tool in Scott Foresman's *eTools* software is useful for exploring part-part-whole and missing-part ideas as well as earlier number concepts and early addition/subtraction ideas.

Source: Scott Foresman Addison-Wesley Math Electronic-Tools CD-ROM Grade K Through 6. Copyright © 2004 Pearson Education, Inc., or its affiliate(s). Used by permission. All rights reserved.

Here is a possible list of the kinds of things that children should know about the number 8 (or any number up to about 12) by the end of the first grade.

- Count to eight (know the number words and their order)
- Count eight objects and know that the last number word tells how many
- Write the numeral 8
- Recognize and read the numeral 8

The preceding list represents the minimal skills of number. In the following list are the relationships students should have that contribute to number sense:

- More and less by 1 and 2: 8 is one more than 7, one less than 9, two more than 6, and two less than 10.
- Spatial patterns for 8 such as

- Anchors to 5 and 10: 8 is 3 more than 5 and 2 away from 10.
- Part-whole relationships: 8 is 5 and 3, 2 and 6, 7 and 1, and so on. This includes knowing the missing part of 8.
- Doubles: double 4 is 8.
- Relationships to the real world: my brother is 8 years old, my reading book is 8 inches wide.

Dot Cards as a Model for Teaching Number Relationships

Many good number development activities involve more than one of the relationships discussed so far. As children learn about ten-frames, patterned sets, and other relationships, the dot cards in Blackline Masters 3–8 provide a wealth of activities (see Figure 8.12). The cards contain dot patterns, patterns that require counting, combinations of two and three simple patterns, and ten-frames with "standard" as well as unusual placements of dots. When children use these cards for any activity that involves number concepts, the cards make them think about numbers in many

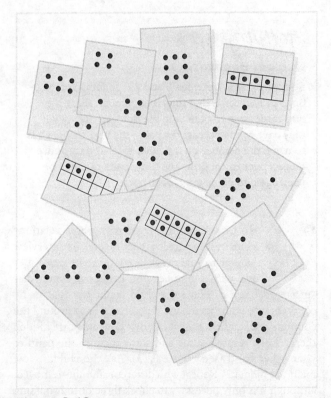

Figure 8.12 Dot cards can be made using Blackline Masters 3–8.

different ways. The dot cards add another dimension to many of the activities already described and can be used effectively in the following activities.

Activity 8.21

Double War

The game of "Double War" (Kamii, 1985) is played like war, but on each play, both players turn up two cards instead of one. The winner is the player with the larger total number. Children playing the game can use many different number relationships to determine the winner without actually finding the total number of dots.

Activity 8.22

Difference War

Deal out the cards to the two players as in regular "War" and prepare a pile of 30 to 40 counters. On each play, the players turn over their cards as usual. The player with the greater number of dots wins as many counters from the pile as the difference between the two cards. The players keep their cards. The game is over when the counter pile runs out. The player with the most counters wins the game.

Activity 8.23

Number Sandwiches

Select a number between 5 and 12, and find combinations of two cards that total that number. Place the two cards back to back with the dot side out. When they have found at least ten pairs, the next challenge is to name the number on the other side. The cards are flipped over to confirm. The same pairs can then be used again to name the hidden part.

To assess the important part-whole relationships, use a missing-part diagnostic interview similar to Activity 8.18 ("Covered Parts"). Begin with a number you believe the child has "mastered," say, 5. Have the child count out that many counters into your open hand. Close your hand around the counters and confirm that she knows how many are hidden there. Then remove some and show them in the palm of your other hand (see Figure 8.13). Ask the child, "How many are hidden?" Repeat with different amounts removed, although it is only necessary to check three or four missing parts for each number. If the child responds quickly and

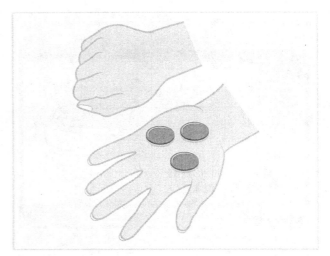

Figure 8.13 A missing-part number assessment. Eight in all. "How many are hidden?"

correctly and is clearly not counting in any way, call that a "mastered number" and check off that skill on your student's recording sheet. If a number is mastered, repeat the entire process with the next higher number. Continue until the child begins to stumble. In early first grade you will find a range of mastered numbers from 4 to 7 or 8. By spring of the first grade, most children should have mastered numbers to 10. ◆

Relationships for Numbers 10 Through 20

Even though kindergarten, first-, and second-grade children experience numbers up to 20 and beyond daily, it should not be assumed that they will automatically extend the set of relationships they developed on smaller numbers to the numbers beyond 10. And yet these numbers play a big part in many simple counting activities, in basic facts, and in much of what we do with mental computation. Relationships with these numbers are just as important as relationships involving the numbers through 10.

Pre-Place-Value Concepts

A set of ten should play a major role in children's early understanding of numbers between 10 and 20. When children see a set of six with a set of ten, they should know without counting that the total is 16. However, the numbers between 10 and 20 are not an appropriate place to discuss place-value concepts. That is, prior to a much more complete development of place-value concepts (see *Curriculum*

Focal Points for grade 2), children should not be expected to explain the 1 in 16 as representing "one ten."

II ———————— *Pause and Reflect*

Say to yourself, "One ten." Now think about that from the perspective of a child just learning to count to 20! What could "one ten" possibly mean when ten tells me how many fingers I have and is the number that comes after nine? How can it be one of something?

Initially, children do not see a numeric pattern in the numbers between 10 and 20. Rather, these number names are simply ten additional words in the number sequence. The concept of a single ten is challenging for a kindergarten or early first-grade child to grasp. Some would say that it is not appropriate for grade 1 at all (Kamii, 1985). The inappropriateness of discussing "one ten and six ones" (what's a one?) does not mean that a set of ten should not figure prominently in the discussion of the teen numbers. The following activity illustrates this idea.

Activity 8.24

Ten and Some More

Use a simple two-part mat and have children count out ten counters onto one side. Next have them put five counters on the other side. Together count all of the counters by ones. Chorus the combination: "Ten and five is fifteen." Turn the mat around: "Five and ten is fifteen." Repeat with other numbers in a random order but without changing the 10 side of the mat.

Activity 8.24 is designed to teach new number names and, thus, requires a certain amount of teacher-directed teaching. Following this activity, explore numbers to 20 in a more open-ended manner. Provide each child with two ten-frames drawn one under the other on a construction paper mat or use Blackline Master 11. In random order, have children show numbers to 20 on their mats. That is, play "Crazy Mixed-Up Numbers" (Activity 8.14) with two ten-frames and numbers to 20. There is no preferred way to do this as long as there are the correct number of counters. What is interesting is to discuss how the counters can be arranged on the mat so that it is easy to see how many are there. Have children share their ideas. Not every child will use a full set of ten, but as this idea becomes more popular, the notion that ten and some more is a teen amount will soon be developed. As you listen to your children, you may want to begin challenging them to find ways to show 26 counters or even more.

Extending More Than and Less Than Relationships

The relationships of one more than, two more than, one less than, and two less than are important for all numbers. However, these ideas are built on or connected to the same concepts for numbers less than 10. The fact that 17 is one less than 18 is connected to the idea that 7 is one less than 8. Children may need help in making this connection.

Activity 8.25

More and Less Extended

On the overhead, or whiteboard, show seven counters and ask what is two more, or one less, and so on. Now add a filled ten-frame to the display (or 10 in any pattern) and repeat the questions. Pair up questions by covering and uncovering the ten-frame as illustrated in Figure 8.14.

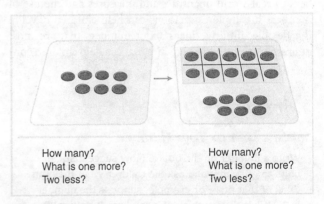

How many?
What is one more?
Two less?

How many?
What is one more?
Two less?

Figure 8.14 Extending relationships to the teens.

Doubles and Near-Doubles

The use of doubles (double 6 is 12) and near-doubles (13 is double 6 and 1 more) is generally considered a strategy for memorizing basic addition facts. There is no reason why children should not begin to develop these relationships long before they are concerned with memorizing basic facts. Doubles and near-doubles are simply special cases of the general part-part-whole construct.

Relate the doubles to special images. Children can draw pictures or make posters that illustrate the doubles for each number. Any images that are strong ideas for your children will be good for them.

Periodically conduct oral exercises in which students double the number you say. Ask children to explain how they knew a particular double. Many will not use the pictures.

Activity 8.26

The Double Maker

Make the calculator into a "double maker" by pressing 2 ☒ ⊟. Now a press of any digit followed by ⊟ will produce the double of that number. Children can work in pairs or individually to try to beat the calculator.

As a related oral task, say a number, and ask students to tell what double it is. "What is fourteen?" (Double 7.) When students can do this well, use any number up to 20. "What is seventeen?" (Double 8 and 1 more.)

Number Sense in Their World

Here we examine ways to broaden the early knowledge of numbers in a different way. Relationships of numbers to real-world quantities and measures and the use of numbers in simple estimations can help children develop the flexible, intuitive ideas about numbers that are most desired. Here are some activities that can help children connect numbers to real situations.

Activity 8.27

Add a Unit to Your Number

Write a number on the board. Now suggest some units to go with it and ask the children what they can think of that fits. For example, suppose the number is 9. "What do you think of when I say 9 *dollars*? 9 *hours*? 9 *cars*? 9 *kids*? 9 *meters*? 9 *o'clock*? 9 *hand spans*? 9 *gallons*?" Spend some time in discussion of each. Let children suggest units as well. Be prepared to explore some of the ideas either immediately or as projects or tasks to share with parents or guardians at home.

Activity 8.28

Is It Reasonable?

Select a number and a unit—for example, 15 feet. Could the teacher be 15 feet tall? Could your living room be 15 feet wide? Can a man jump 15 feet high? Could three children stretch their arms 15 feet? Pick any number, large or small, and a unit with which children are familiar. Then make up a series of these questions.

Once children are familiar with Activity 8.28, have them select the number and the unit or things (10 kids, 20 bananas, . . .), and see what kinds of questions children make up. When a difference of opinion develops, capitalize on the opportunity to explore and experiment. Resist the temptation to supply your adult-level knowledge. Rather, say, "Well, how can we find out if it is or is not reasonable? Who has an idea about what we could do?"

These activities are problem-based in the truest sense. Not only are there no clear answers, but children can easily begin to pose their own questions and explore number in the part of the environment most interesting to them. Children will not have these real-world connections when you begin, and you may be disappointed in their initially limited ideas about number. Howden (1989) writes about a first-grade teacher of children from very impoverished backgrounds who told her, "They all have fingers, the school grounds are strewn with lots of pebbles and leaves, and pinto beans are cheap. So we count, sort, compare, and talk about such objects. We've measured and weighed almost everything in this room and almost everything the children can drag in" (p. 6). This teacher's children had produced a wonderfully rich and long list of responses to the question "What comes to your mind when I say twenty-four?" In another school in a professional community where test scores are high, the same question brought almost no response from a class of third graders. It can be a very rewarding effort to help children connect their number ideas to the real world.

Estimation and Measurement

One of the best ways for children to think of real quantities is to associate numbers with measures of things. In the early grades, measures of length, weight, and time are good places to begin. Just measuring and recording results will not be very effective unless there is a reason for children to be interested in or think about the result. To help children think or reflect on what number might tell how long the desk is or how heavy the book is, it would be good if they could first write down or tell you an estimate. To produce an estimate is, however, a very difficult task for young children. They do not easily grasp the concept of "estimate" or "about." For example, suppose that you have cut out of poster board a set of very large footprints, say, about 18 inches long. All are exactly the same size. You would like to ask the class, "About how many footprints will it take to measure across the rug in our reading corner?" The key word here is *about*, and it is one that you will need to spend a lot of time helping children understand. To this end, the request of an estimate can be made in ways that help with the concept of "about" yet not require students to give a specific number.

The following estimation questions can be used with most early estimation activities:

- *More or less than*_____? Will it be more or less than 10 footprints? Will the apple weigh more or less than 20 wooden blocks? Are there more or less than 15 connecting cubes in this long bar?
- *Closer to* _____ or to _____? Will it be closer to 5 footprints or closer to 20 footprints? Will the apple weigh closer to 10 blocks or closer to 30 blocks? Does this bar have closer to 10 cubes or closer to 50 cubes?
- *About* _____. Use one of these numbers: 5, 10, 15, 20, 25, 30, 35, 40, . . . About how many footprints? About how many blocks will the apple weigh? About how many cubes are in this bar?

Asking for estimates using these formats helps children learn what you mean by "about." Every child can make an estimate without having to pull a number out of the air. However, rewarding students for the closest estimate in a competitive fashion will often result in their learning to seek precision and not actually estimate. Instead, it is best to discuss all answers that fall into a reasonable range.

To help with numbers and measures, estimate several things in succession using the same unit. For example, suppose that you are estimating and measuring "around things" using a string. To measure, the string is wrapped around the object and then measured in some unit such as craft sticks. After measuring the distance around Demetria's head, estimate the distance around the wastebasket or around the globe or around George's wrist. Each successive measure helps children with the new estimates.

Data Collection and Analysis

Graphing activities are another good way to connect children's worlds with number. Chapter 21 discusses ways to make graphs with children in grades pre-K–2. Graphs can be quickly made of almost any data that can be gathered from the students, such as: favorite ice cream, color, sports team, pet; number of sisters and brothers; transportation to school; types of shoes; number of pets; and so on. Graphs can be connected to content in other areas. A unit on water might lead to a graph of items that float or sink.

Once a simple bar graph is made, it is very important to take time to ask as many number questions as is appropriate for the graph. In the early stages of number development (grades pre-K–1), the use of graphs for number relationships and for connecting numbers to real quantities in the children's environment is a more important reason for building graphs than the graphs themselves. The graphs focus attention on counts of realistic things. Equally important, bar graphs clearly exhibit comparisons between and among numbers that are rarely made when only one number or quantity is considered at a time. See Figure 8.15 for an example of a graph and questions that can be asked. At first, children may have trouble with the questions involving differences, but repeated exposure to these ideas in a bar graph format will improve their understanding. These comparison concepts add considerably to children's understanding of number.

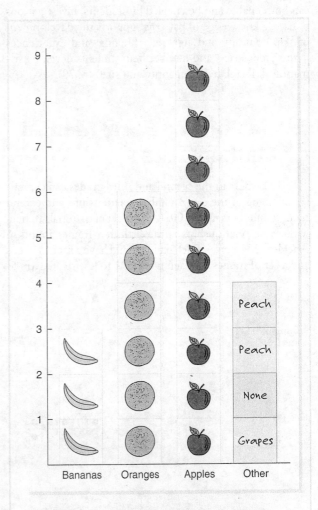

Class graph showing fruit brought for snack. Paper cutouts for bananas, oranges, apples, and cards for "others."

- Which snack (or refer to what the graph represents) is most, least?
- Which are more (less) than 7 (or some other number)?
- Which is one less (more) than this snack (or use fruit name)?
- How much more is _____ than _____ ? (Follow this question immediately by reversing the order and asking how much less.)
- How much less is _____ than _____ ? (Reverse this question after receiving an answer.)
- How much difference is there between _____ and _____ ?
- Which two bars together are the same as _____ ?

Figure 8.15 Relationships and number sense in a bar graph.

NCTM Standards The *Standards* clearly recognizes the value of integrating number development with other areas of the curriculum. "Students' work with numbers should be connected to their work with other mathematics topics. For example, computational fluency . . . can both enable and be enabled by students' investigations of data; a knowledge of patterns supports the development of skip counting and algebraic thinking; and experiences with shape, space, and number help students develop estimation skills related to quantity and size" (p. 79). ◆

Extensions to Early Mental Mathematics

Teachers in the second and third grades can capitalize on some of the early number relationships and extend them to numbers up to 100. A useful set of materials to help with these relationships is the little ten-frames found in Blackline Master 16. Each child should have a set of 10 tens and a set of frames for each number 1 to 9 with an extra 5.

The following three ideas can be demonstrated using the little ten-frames in Figure 8.16. First are the relationships of one more than and one less than. If you understand that one more than 6 is 7, then in a similar manner, one more ten than 60 is 70. The second idea is really a look ahead to fact strategies. If a child has learned to think about adding on to 8 or 9 by first adding up to 10 and then adding the rest, the extension to similar two-digit numbers is quite simple; see Figure 8.16(b). Finally, the most powerful idea for small numbers is thinking of them in parts. It is a very useful idea to take apart larger numbers to begin to develop some flexibility in the same way. Children can begin by thinking of ways to take apart a multiple of 10 such as 80. Once they do it with tens, the challenge can be to think of ways to take apart 80 when one part has a 5 in it, such as 25 or 35.

More will be said about early mental computation in Chapter 12. The point to be made here is that early number relationships have a greater impact on what children know than may be apparent at first. Even teachers in the upper grades may consider the benefits of using ten-frames and part-part-whole activities.

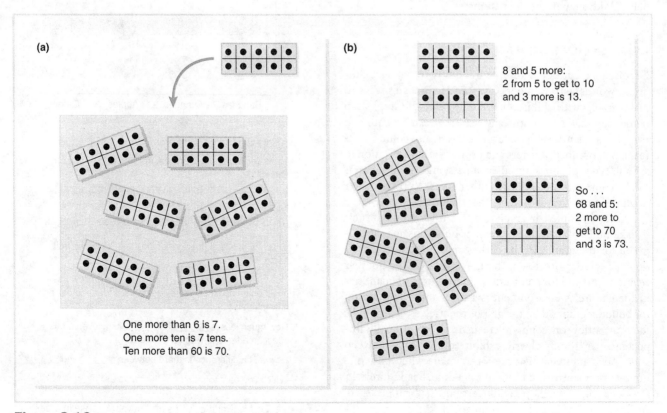

Figure 8.16 Extending early number relationships to mental computation activities.

Reflections on Chapter 8

Writing to Learn

1. What must a child be able to do in order to count a set accurately?
2. Describe an activity that is a "set-to-numeral match" activity. What ideas must a child have to do these activities meaningfully and correctly?
3. How can "Real Counting On" (Activity 8.7) be used as an assessment to determine if children understand counting on or are still in a transitional stage?
4. What are the four types of relationships that have been described for numbers from 1 to 10? Explain briefly what each of these means and suggest at least one activity for each.
5. How can a teacher assess the number relationships of part-whole?
6. How can a calculator be used to develop early counting ideas connected with number? How can a calculator be used to help a child practice number relationships such as part-part-whole or one less than?
7. For numbers between 10 and 20, describe how to develop each of these ideas:
   a. The idea of the teens as a set of ten and some more
   b. Extension of the one-more/one-less concept to the teens

8. What are three ways that children can be helped to connect numbers to real-world ideas?

For Discussion and Exploration

1. Examine the *Curriculum Focal Points* document (available online at www.nctm.org). Look at the CFPs suggested for children in grades pre-K–2 under the concept of "number" and compare them with the ideas presented in this chapter. What ideas are stressed? What ideas are not included in the CFPs? How can you use both resources to plan your number concept development program?
2. You've noticed that a student you are working with is counting items with an accurate sequence of the numbers in our system, but is not attaching one number to each item. Therefore, their final count is inconsistent and inaccurate. What would you plan to help this student develop a better grasp of one-to-one correspondence?

Resources for Chapter 8

Literature Connections

Children's literature abounds with wonderful counting books. Be sure to go beyond simply reading a counting book or a number-related book and looking at the pictures. Find a way to extend the book into the children's world. Create problems related to the story. Have children identify the mathematics in the story. Extend the numbers and see what happens. Talk about how old the book is by looking at the copyright. Here are a few ideas for making literature connections to number concepts and number sense.

Anno's Counting House, *Anno, 1982*

This book shows ten children in various parts of a house. As the pages are turned, the house front covers the children, and a few are visible through cutout windows. A second house is on the opposite page. As you move through the book, the children move one at a time to the second house, creating the potential for a 10–0, 9–1, 8–2, . . . , 0–10 pattern of pairs. But as each page partially shows the children through the window, there is an opportunity to discuss how many in the missing part. Have children use counters to model the story as you "read" it the second or third time.

What if the children moved in pairs instead of one at a time? What if there were three houses? What if there were more children?

The Very Hungry Caterpillar, *Carle, 1969*

This is a predictable-progression counting book about a caterpillar who eats first one thing, then two, and so on. Children can create their own eating stories and illustrate them. What if more than one type of thing were eaten at each stop? What combinations for each number are there? Are seven little things more or less than three very large things?

Two Ways to Count to Ten, *Dee, 1988*

This Liberian folktale is about King Leopard's search for the best animal to marry his daughter. The task devised involves throwing a spear and counting to 10 before the spear lands. Many animals try and fail. Counting by ones proves too lengthy. Finally, the antelope succeeds by counting "2, 4, 6, 8, 10."

The story is a perfect lead-in to skip counting. Can you count to 10 by threes? How else can you count to 10? How many ways can you count to 48? What numbers can you reach if you count by fives? A hundreds board or counters are useful in helping with these problems. Be sure to have children write about what they discover in their investigations.

Another fun book to use is *The King's Commissioners* (Friedman, 1994), a hilarious tale that also opens up opportunities to count by different groupings or skip counting.

Recommended Readings

Articles

Fuson, K. C., Grandau, L., & Sugiyama, P. A. (2001). Achievable numerical understandings for all young children. *Teaching Children Mathematics, 7*(9), 522–526.
Researchers who have long worked with the number development of young children provide the reader with a concise overview of number development from ages 3 to 7. This practical reporting of their research is quite useful.

Griffin, S. (2003). Laying the foundation for computational fluency in early childhood. *Teaching Children Mathematics, 9*(6), 306–309.
This short article lays out clearly five stages of number development based on a simple addition story problem task. This is followed by activities to develop number at each stage. A useful article, especially for diagnosis and remediation of early number development.

Losq, C. (2005). Number concepts and special needs students: The power of ten-frame tiles. *Teaching Children Mathematics, 11*(6), 310–315.
This is a very useful article to engage struggling learners in the use of a countable and visually unique model—the ten-frame tile. Losq positions the ten-frames described in this chapter in a vertical position to enhance subitizing or instant recognition and provide useful tools for formative assessment.

Books

Fosnot, C. T., & Dolk, M. (2001). *Young mathematicians at work: Constructing number sense, addition, and subtraction.* Portsmouth, NH: Heinemann.
One of three books in a series by these authors, they describe clearly the development of number concepts. Dolk represents the view of the Freudenthal Institute in the Netherlands and Fosnot is a respected mathematician and theoretician in the United States. This book demonstrates a sensitivity for children and a detailed perspective on children's number development.

Richardson, K. (2003). *Assessing math concepts: The hiding assessment.* Bellingham, WA: Mathematical Perspectives.
One of a series of nine assessment books covering number topics from counting through two-digit numbers. The assessments are designed for diagnostic interviews. Extensive explanations and levels with examples are provided. Richardson is a leading expert on early number development and assessment.

Online Resources

Count Us In
www.abc.net.au/countusin/default.htm
A site full of downloadable activities and games for early number development.

Let's Count to 5 (Grades K–2)
http://illuminations.nctm.org/LessonDetail.aspx?id=U57
This site contains seven lessons with links to resources and downloads for student recording sheets. Children can make sets of zero through five objects and connect number words or numerals to the sets. Familiar songs, rhymes, and a variety of activities that appeal to visual, auditory, and kinesthetic learners are included. In a similar fashion see the following site for higher numbers.

Let's Count to 10 (Grades K–2)
http://illuminations.nctm.org/LessonDetail.aspx?id=U147

Let's Count to 20 (Grades K–2)
http://illuminations.nctm.org/LessonDetail.aspx?id=U153
These lessons emphasize the process standards of Communication and Reasoning.

Toy Shop Numbers (Grades K–2)
http://illuminations.nctm.org/LessonDetail.aspx?id=L216
Using the setting of a toy shop, these activities focus on finding numbers in the real world.

Representing Data—Baby Weight (Grades K–8)
http://illuminations.nctm.org/LessonDetail.aspx?ID=L170
In this grades 1–2 lesson, students work with data to complete an organized chart by doubling or halving numbers and compare data using bar graphs.

Math Tools: Math 1, Number Sense
http://mathforum.org/mathtools/cell/m1,3.2,ALL,ALL
On this one page of the Math Tools website you will find activities and lessons appropriate for first-grade number sense. Explore other options on the site as well.

Ten Frame (NCTM illuminations Tools)
http://illuminations.nctm.org/activitydetail.aspx?id=75
A nice manipulative version of the ten-frame. Four games that help students develop counting and addition skills are included in this activity.

Early Childhood Mathematics: Promoting Good Beginnings
www.naeyc.org/about/positions/pdf/psmath.pdf
The full position statement of the National Association for the Education of Young Children (NAEYC) and the National Council for Teachers of Mathematics (NCTM) is found at this location.

Field Experience Guide Connections

FEG Expanded Lessons 9.3, 9.12, 9.15, and 9.20 are focused on early number concepts and number concepts applied to measurement and data. FEG Activity 10.1 ("The Find!") and FEG Activity 10.2 ("Odd or Even?") are also engaging activities for young children.

Chapter 9

Developing Meanings
for the Operations

This chapter is about helping children connect different meanings, interpretations, and relationships to the four operations of addition, subtraction, multiplication, and division so that they can effectively use these operations in real-world settings.

The main thrust of this chapter is helping children develop what might be termed *operation sense*, a highly integrated understanding of the four operations and the many different but related meanings these operations take on in real contexts.

As you read this chapter, pay special attention to the impact on number development, basic fact mastery, and computation. As children develop their understanding of operations, they can and should simultaneously be developing additional ideas about number and ways to think about basic fact combinations. Story problems for operations meaning are also a method of developing computational skills.

Big Ideas

1. Addition and subtraction are connected. Addition names the whole in terms of the parts, and subtraction names a missing part.

2. Multiplication involves counting groups of like size and determining how many are in all (multiplicative thinking).

3. Multiplication and division are related. Division names a missing factor in terms of the known factor and the product.

4. Models can be used to solve contextual problems for all operations and to figure out what operation is involved in a problem regardless of the size of the numbers. Models also can be used to give meaning to number sentences.

Mathematics
Content Connections

The ideas in this chapter are most directly linked to concepts of numeration and the development of invented computation strategies.

- **Number Development** (Chapter 8): As children learn to think about number in terms of parts and missing parts, they should be relating these ideas to addition and subtraction. Multiplication and division require students to think about numbers as units: In 3×6 each of the three sixes is counted as a unit.

- **Basic Facts** (Chapter 10): A good understanding of the operations can firmly connect addition and subtraction so that subtraction facts are a natural consequence of having learned addition. A firm connection between multiplication and division provides a similar benefit.

- **Whole-Number Place Value and Computation** (Chapters 11 and 12): Students work with and develop ideas about the base-ten number system as they solve story problems involving larger numbers. It is reasonable to have children invent strategies for computing with two-digit numbers as they build their understanding of the operations.

- **Algebraic Thinking** (Chapter 14): Representing contextual situations in equations is at the heart of algebraic thinking. This is exactly what students are doing as they learn to write equations to go with their solutions to story problems.

- **Fraction and Decimal Computation** (Chapters 16 and 17): These topics for the upper elementary and middle grades depend on a firm understanding of the operations.

Addition and Subtraction Problem Structures

We begin this chapter with a look at four categories of problem structure for additive situations (which include both addition and subtraction) and later explore four problem structures for multiplicative situations (which include both multiplication and division). Although these categories are not knowledge that students are expected to master, teachers are expected to learn these categories as part of pedagogical content knowledge (PCK) (Shulman, 1986), which is the deep understanding that teachers need to effectively organize and support students' mathematics learning. Teachers who are not aware of the variety of situations and structures may randomly offer problems to students without the proper sequencing to support students' full grasp of the meaning of the operations, thus not preparing students for the variety of real-world contexts they will encounter. By knowing the logical structure of these problems you will be able to help students interpret a variety of mathematical situations. Again, students will not need to identify a problem with a "join" or "separate" classification by name, but as a teacher you will need to present a variety of problem types as well as recognize which structures cause the greatest challenges for students.

Researchers have separated addition and subtraction problems into categories based on the kinds of relationships involved. These include *join* problems, *separate* problems, *part-part-whole* problems, and *compare* problems (Carpenter, Carey, & Kouba, 1990; Carpenter, Fennema, Franke, Levi, & Empson, 1999; Gutstein & Romberg, 1995). The basic structure for each of these four types of problems is illustrated in Figure 9.1. Each structure involves a number "family" such as 3, 5, 8. A different problem type results depending on which of the three quantities in the situation is unknown.

Examples of the Four Problem Structures

The number family 4, 8, 12 is used in each of the story problems that follow and can be connected to the structure in Figure 9.1. These drawings are not intended for students but to help you as a teacher. Also note that the problems are described in terms of their structure and interpretation and not as addition or subtraction problems. Contrary to what you may have thought, a joining action does not always mean addition, nor does separate or remove always mean subtraction.

Join Problems. For the action of joining, there are three quantities involved: an initial or starting amount, a change amount (the part being added or joined), and the resulting amount (the total amount after the change takes place). In Figure 9.1(a) this is illustrated by the change being "added to" the initial amount. Any one of these three quantities can be unknown in a problem as shown here.

Join: Result Unknown

Sandra had 8 pennies. George gave her 4 more. How many pennies does Sandra have altogether?

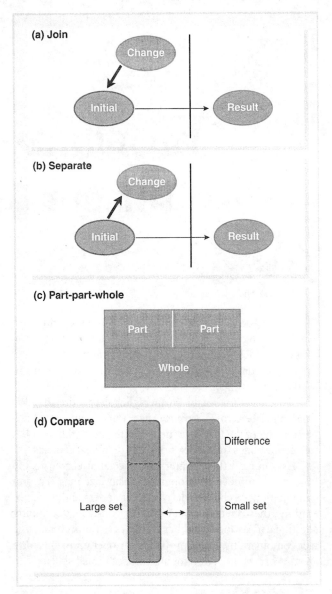

Figure 9.1 Four basic structures for addition and subtraction story problem types. Each structure has three numbers. Any one of the three numbers can be the unknown in a story problem.

Join: Change Unknown

Sandra had 8 pennies. George gave her some more. Now Sandra has 12 pennies. How many did George give her?

Join: Initial Unknown

Sandra had some pennies. George gave her 4 more. Now Sandra has 12 pennies. How many pennies did Sandra have to begin with?

Separate Problems. Notice that in the "separate" problems, the initial amount is the whole or the largest amount, whereas in the "join" problems, the result is the whole. In "separate" problems the change is that an amount is being removed from the initial value. Again, refer to Figure 9.1(b) as you consider these problems.

Separate: Result Unknown

Sandra had 12 pennies. She gave 4 pennies to George. How many pennies does Sandra have now?

Separate: Change Unknown

Sandra had 12 pennies. She gave some to George. Now she has 8 pennies. How many did she give to George?

Separate: Initial Unknown

Sandra had some pennies. She gave 4 to George. Now Sandra has 8 pennies left. How many pennies did Sandra have to begin with?

Part-Part-Whole Problems. Part-part-whole problems involve two parts that are combined into one whole as in Figure 9.1(c). The combining may be a physical action, or it may be a mental combination where the parts are not physically combined.

There is no meaningful distinction between the two parts in a part-part-whole situation, so there is no need to have a different problem for each part as the unknown. For each possibility (whole unknown and part unknown), two problems are given here. The first is a mental combination where there is no action. The second problem involves a physical action.

Part-Part-Whole: Whole Unknown

George has 4 pennies and 8 nickels. How many coins does he have?

George has 4 pennies and Sandra has 8 pennies. They put their pennies into a piggy bank. How many pennies did they put into the bank?

Part-Part-Whole: Part Unknown

George has 12 coins. Eight of his coins are pennies, and the rest are nickels. How many nickels does George have?

George and Sandra put 12 pennies into the piggy bank. George put in 4 pennies. How many pennies did Sandra put in?

Compare Problems. Compare problems involve the comparison of two quantities. The third amount does not actually exist but is the difference between the two amounts. Figure 9.1(d) illustrates the comparison problem type. There are three ways to present compare problems, corresponding to which quantity is unknown (smaller, larger, or difference). For each of these, two examples are given: one problem where the difference is stated in terms of more and another in terms of less.

Compare: Difference Unknown

George has 12 pennies and Sandra has 8 pennies. How many more pennies does George have than Sandra?

George has 12 pennies. Sandra has 8 pennies. How many fewer pennies does Sandra have than George?

Compare: Larger Unknown

George has 4 more pennies than Sandra. Sandra has 8 pennies. How many pennies does George have?

Sandra has 4 fewer pennies than George. Sandra has 8 pennies. How many pennies does George have?

Compare: Smaller Unknown

George has 4 more pennies than Sandra. George has 12 pennies. How many pennies does Sandra have?

Sandra has 4 fewer pennies than George. George has 12 pennies. How many pennies does Sandra have?

❚❚ ———————— *Pause and Reflect*

Go back through all of these examples and match the numbers in the problems with the components of the structures in Figure 9.1. For each problem, do two additional things. First, use a set of counters or coins to model (solve) the problem as you think children in the primary grades might do. Second, for each problem, write either an addition or subtraction equation that you think best represents the problem as you did it with counters.

In most curricula, the overwhelming emphasis is on the easier join and separate problems with the result unknown. These become the de facto definitions of addition and subtraction: Addition is "put together" and subtraction is "take away." The fact is, these are *not* the definitions of addition and subtraction.

When students develop these limited put-together and take-away definitions for addition and subtraction, they often have difficulty later when addition or subtraction is called for but the structure is other than put together or take away. It is important that children be exposed to all forms within these four problem structures.

Problem Difficulty. The various types of problems are not at all equal in difficulty for children. The join or separate problems in which the initial part is unknown are among the most difficult, probably because children modeling the problems directly do not know how many counters to put down to begin with. Problems in which the change amounts are unknown are also difficult.

Many children will solve compare problems as part-part-whole problems without making separate sets of counters for the two amounts. The whole is used as the large amount, one part for the small amount and the second part for the difference. Which method did *you* use? There is absolutely no reason this should be discouraged as long as children are clear about what they are doing.

As students begin to translate the variety of story problems in the previous pages into equations to solve, they may be challenged in creating a matching equation that emphasizes the corresponding operation. This is particularly important as students move into explorations that develop algebraic thinking. The structure of the equations also may cause difficulty for English language learners who may not initially have the flexibility in creating equivalent equations due to reading comprehension issues with the situation described in the story. Therefore, we need to look at how knowing about computational and semantic forms of equations will help you help your students.

Computational and Semantic Forms of Equations. If you wrote an equation for each of the problems as just suggested, you may have some equations where the unknown quantity is not isolated on one side of the equal sign. For example, a likely equation for the join problem with initial part unknown is $\square + 4 = 12$. This is referred to as the *semantic* equation for the problem since the numbers are listed in the order that follows the meaning of the problem. Figure 9.2 shows the semantic equations for the six join and separate problems on the previous pages. Note that the two result-unknown problems place the unknown alone on one side of the equal sign. An equation that isolates the unknown in this way is referred to as the *computational* form of the equation. When the semantic form is not also the computational form, an equivalent equation can be written. For example, the equation $\square + 4 = 12$ can be written equivalently as $12 - 4 = \square$. The computational form is the one you would need to use if you were to solve these equations with a calculator. Students need to see that there are several ways to represent a situation in an equation. As numbers increase in size and children are not solving equations with counters, they must eventually learn to see the equivalence between different forms of the equations.

Quantity Unknown	Join Problems	Separate Problems
Result	8 + 4 = [ ]	12 − 4 = [ ]
Change	8 + [ ] = 12	12 − [ ] = 8
Initial	[ ] + 4 = 12	[ ] − 4 = 8

Figure 9.2 The semantic equation for each of the six join and separate problems on pages 146–147. Notice that for results-unknown problems the semantic form is also the computational form. The computational form for the other four problems is an equivalent equation that isolates the unknown quantity.

Teaching Addition and Subtraction

So far you have seen a variety of types of story problems for addition and subtraction and you probably have used some counters to help you understand how these problems can be solved by children. Combining the use of contextual problems and models (counters, drawings, number lines) is important in helping students construct a rich understanding of these two operations. Let's examine how each approach can be used in the classroom. As you move through this section, note that addition and subtraction are taught at the same time.

myeducationlab

Go to the Activities and Application section of Chapter 9 of MyEducationLab. Click on Videos and watch the video entitled "**Strategies for Learning About Operations**" to see two classroom teachers use a variety of strategies to develop students' understanding of the operations.

Contextual Problems

There is more to think about than simply giving students problems to solve. In contrast with the rather sterile story problems in the previous section, consider the following problem.

Yesterday we were measuring how tall we were. You remember that we used the connecting cubes to make a big train that was as long as we were when we were lying down. Dion and Rosa were wondering how many cubes long they would be if they lay down head to foot. Dion had measured Rosa and she was 84 cubes long. Rosa measured Dion and she was 102 cubes long. Let's see if we can figure out how long they will be end to end, and then we can check by actually measuring them.

Fosnot and Dolk (2001) point out that in story problems, children tend to focus on getting the answer. "Context problems, on the other hand, are connected as closely as possible to children's lives, rather than to 'school mathematics.' They are designed to anticipate and to develop children's mathematical modeling of the real world" (p. 24). Contextual problems might derive from recent experiences in the classroom, a field trip, a discussion you have been having in art, science, or social studies, or from children's literature.

Lessons Built on Context or Story Problems.

The tendency in the United States is to have students solve a lot of problems in a single class period. The focus of these lessons seems to be on how to get answers. In Japan, however, a complete lesson will often revolve around one or two problems and the related discussion (Reys & Reys, 1995).

What might a good lesson for second graders that is built around word problems look like? The answer comes more naturally if you think about students not just solving the problems but also using words, pictures, and numbers to explain how they went about solving the problem and why they think they are correct. Children should be allowed to use whatever physical materials they feel they need to help them, or they can simply draw pictures. Whatever they put on their paper should explain what they did well enough to allow someone else to understand their thinking (allow at least a half page of space for a problem).

The second-grade curriculum of *Investigations in Number, Data, and Space* places a significant emphasis on connecting addition and subtraction concepts. In the excerpt shown on page 150, you can see an activity involving word problems for subtraction. Take special note of the emphasis on students' visualizing the situation mentally and putting the problem in their own words.

Choosing Numbers for Problems.

Even pre-K and kindergarten children should be expected to solve story problems. Their methods of solution will typically involve using counters or actual experiments in a very direct modeling of the problems. This is what makes the join and separate problems with the initial parts unknown so difficult. For these problems, children initially use a trial-and-error approach (Carpenter, Fennema, Franke, Levi, & Empson, 1999).

Although the structure of the problems will cause the difficulty to vary, the numbers in the problems should be in accord with the number development of the children. Pre-K and kindergarten children can use numbers as large as they can grasp conceptually, which is usually to about 10 or 12.

Second-grade children are also learning about two-digit numbers and are beginning to understand how our base-ten system works. Rather than waiting until students have learned about place value and have developed techniques for computing numbers, word problems are a problem-based opportunity to learn about number and computation at the same time. For example, a problem involving the combination of 30 and 42 has the potential to help students focus on sets of ten. As they begin to think of 42 as 40 and 2, it is not at all unreasonable to think that they will add 30 and 40 and then add 2 more. As you learn more about invented strategies for computation in Chapter 12, you will develop a better understanding of how to select numbers for the problems you use in your lessons to aid in computational development.

 The *Standards* authors make clear the value of connecting addition and subtraction. "Teachers should ensure that students repeatedly encounter situations in which the same numbers appear in different contexts. For example, the numbers 3, 4, and 7 may appear in problem-solving situations that could be represented by $4 + 3$, $3 + 4$, or $7 - 3$, or $7 - 4$. . . . Recognizing the inverse relationship between addition and subtraction can allow students to be flexible in using strategies to solve problems" (p. 83). ◆

Introducing Symbolism.

Very young children do not need to understand the symbols +, −, and = to learn about addition and subtraction concepts. However, these symbolic conventions are important. When you feel your students are ready to use these symbols, introduce them in the discussion portion of a lesson where students have solved story problems. Say, "You had the whole number of 12 in your problem and the number 8 was one of the parts of 12. You found out that the part you did not know was 4. Here is a way we can write that: $12 - 8 = 4$." The minus sign should be read as "minus" or "subtract" but not as "take away." The plus sign is easier since it is typically a substitute for "and."

Some care should be taken with the equal sign. The equal sign means "is the same as." However, most children come to think of it as a symbol that tells you that the "answer is coming up." It is interpreted in much the same way as the ⊟ on a calculator. That is, it is the key you press to get the answer. An equation such as $4 + 8 = 3 + 9$ has no "answer" and is still true because both sides stand for the same quantity. A good idea is to often use the phrase "is the same as" in place of or in conjunction with "equals" as you read equations with students.

Another approach is to think of the equal sign as a balance; whatever is on one side of the equation "balances" or equals what is on the other side. This will support algebraic thinking in future grades if developed early (Knuth, Stephens, McNeil, & Alibali, 2006). (See Chapter 14 for a more detailed look at teaching the equal sign as "is the same as" rather than "give me the answer.")

Investigations
in Number, Data, and Space

Grade 2, *Counting, Coins, and Combinations*

Context

The Counting, Coins, and Combinations unit is the first of nine curriculum units for the second grade. It is one of four units in which the work on addition, subtraction, and the number system is undertaken. Children begin with the facts and move to two-digit problems using student-invented strategies. The focus on whole-number operations includes understanding the structure of the problem, developing strategies to solve story problems, and using words, pictures, and numbers to communicate solutions. Over the series of units, the full variety of problem structures presented previously in this chapter will be developed. There is an emphasis on a variety of problem types to assist the students in thinking about different situations and perspectives rather than focusing on one action or visualization.

Task Description

Counting, Coins, and Combinations has students explore addition and subtraction problems together within story situations and then visualizing and modeling the actions described. The discussions that follow these activities embody a definite effort to use the story problems to connect the concepts of addition and subtraction. The subtraction task shown on this page is one of several presented individually on a chart or in another prominent location. Each of the story problems is set up to represent a range of the structures discussed in this chapter. This subtraction task, for example, demonstrates a separate problem with the result unknown. To begin their work, students are told that they will be hearing a story, to visualize the situation in their minds, and be ready to put the problem in their own words.

Since subtraction situations are often more challenging to follow, students are asked if the answer will be more or less than 16. They should be able to share why they think so. Then students are to use whatever methods and materials they wish to solve the problem but are required to show their work so that "someone else should be able to look at your work and understand what you did to solve it" (p. 41).

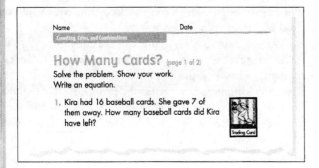

In a full-class session following this activity, students are given an opportunity to share their strategies with the teacher who helps deepen their understanding by posing questions. In addition the teacher can ask another student to model the solution suggested by a classmate—such as using the cubes or hundreds chart as shown in the students' work samples. Other students can also be asked to try the strategy. Poll students to see who also used a similar approach to give them ownership while you get a sense of the students' development. Before leaving the problem you can discuss strategies not already presented.

It is important to also link to the symbolic representation through writing the equation for the problem. Talk about how this can be linked to an addition story using the same numbers.

Take time to look at the two student work samples shown. What do you notice in their recording of their thinking? Can you follow their strategy use? Is one approach more prone to errors? Does one display a more sophisticated level of understanding?

Watching how children solve story problems will give you a lot of information about children's understanding of number as well as the more obvious information about problem solving and their understanding of addition and subtraction. The CGI project (Carpenter et al., 1999) has found that children progress in their problem-solving strategies from kindergarten to grade 2. These strategies are a reflection of students' understanding of number and of their emerging mastery of basic fact strategies. For example, early on, students will use counters and count each addend and then recount the entire set for a join-result-unknown problem. With more practice, they will count on from the first set. This strategy will be modified to count on from the larger set; that is, for 4 + 7 the child will begin with 7 and count on, even though 4 is the initial amount in the problem. Eventually, students will begin to use facts retrieved from memory and rely on counters or other models only when necessary. Watching how students solve problems provides evidence to help you decide what numbers to use in problems and how to make decisions about what questions to ask students that will focus attention on more efficient strategies. ◆

Model-Based Problems

Many children will use counters or number lines (models) to solve story problems. The model is a thinking tool to help them both understand what is happening in the problem and a means of keeping track of the numbers and solving the problem. Problems can also be posed using models when there is no context involved.

Addition. When the parts of a set are known, addition is used to name the whole in terms of the parts. This simple definition of addition serves both action situations (join and separate) and static or no-action situations.

Each of the part-part-whole models shown in Figure 9.3 is a model for 5 + 3 = 8. Some of these are the result of a definite put-together or joining action, and some are not. Notice that in every example, both of the parts are distinct, even after the parts are joined. If counters are used, the two parts should be kept in separate piles or in separate sections of a mat or should be two distinct colors. For children to see a relationship between the two parts and the whole, the image of the 5 and 3 must be kept as two separate sets. This helps children reflect on the action after it has taken place. "These red chips are the ones I started with. Then I added these three blue ones, and now I have eight altogether."

A number line presents some real conceptual difficulties for first and second graders. Its use as a model at that level is generally not recommended. A number line measures distances from zero the same way a ruler does. In the early grades, children focus on the hash marks or numerals

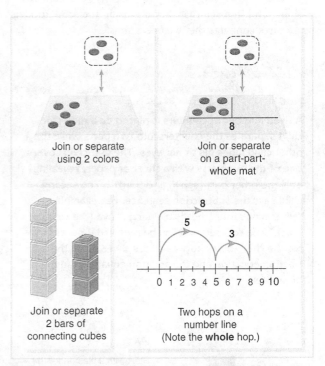

Figure 9.3 Part-part-whole models for 5 + 3 = 8 and 8 − 3 = 5.

on a number line instead of the spaces. However, if arrows (hops) are drawn for each number in an exercise, the length concept is more clearly illustrated. To model the part-part-whole concept of 5 + 3, start by drawing an arrow from 0 to 5, indicating, "This much is five." Do not point to the hash mark for 5, saying "This is five."

Activity 9.1

Up and Down the Line

Create a large number line on the floor of your classroom or hang one on the chalkboard tray. Use an eraser for hopping on the chalkboard tray number line or a student to walk the number line on the floor. Talk about the movement required for each of a variety of different equations. This emphasizes the spaces on the number line and is a wonderful mental image for thinking about the meaning of addition and subtraction.

Subtraction. In a part-part-whole model, when the whole and one of the parts are known, subtraction names the other part. This definition is consistent with the overused language of "take away." If you start with a whole set of 8 and remove a set of 3, the two sets that you know are the sets of 8 and 3. The expression 8 − 3, read "eight minus three," names the five remaining. Therefore, eight minus three is five. Notice that the models in Figure 9.3 are models for subtraction as well as addition (except for the action).

Helping children see that they are using the same models or pictures connects the two operations.

Activity 9.2

Missing-Part Subtraction

A fixed number of counters is placed on a mat. One child separates the counters into two parts while the other child hides his or her eyes. The first child covers one of the two parts with a sheet of paper, revealing only the other part (see Figure 9.4(b)). The second child says the subtraction sentence. For example, "Nine minus four [the visible part] is five [the covered part]." The covered part can be revealed if necessary for the child to say how many are there. Both the subtraction equation and the addition equation can then be written.

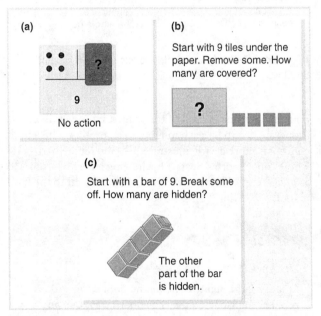

Figure 9.4 Models for 9 – 4 as a missing-part problem.

Subtraction as Think-Addition. Note that in Activity 9.2, the situation ends with two parts clearly distinct, even when there is a remove action. The removed part remains in the activity or on the mat as a model for an addition equation to be written after writing the subtraction equation. A discussion of how these two equations can be written for the same model situation is an important opportunity to connect addition and subtraction. This modeling and discussion of addition and subtraction connections is significantly better than the traditional activity of "fact families" in which children are given a family of numbers such as 3, 5, and 8 and are asked to write two addition equations and two

subtraction equations. This often becomes a rote process of dropping the numbers into slots.

Thinking about subtraction as "think-addition" rather than "take-away" is extremely significant for mastering subtraction facts. Because the counters for the remaining or unknown part are left hidden under the cover, when children do these activities, they are encouraged to think about the hidden part: "What goes with the part I see to make the whole?" For example, if the total or whole number of counters is 9, and 6 are removed from under the cover, the child is likely to think in terms of "6 and what makes 9?" or "What goes with 6 to make 9?" The mental activity is "think-addition" instead of "count what's left." Later, when working on subtraction facts, a subtraction fact such as $9 - 6 = \square$ should trigger the same thought pattern: "6 and what makes 9?"

Comparison Models. Comparison situations involve two distinct sets or quantities and the difference between them. Several ways of modeling the difference relationship are shown in Figure 9.5. The same model can be used whether the difference or one of the two quantities is unknown.

Note that it is not immediately clear how you would associate either the addition or subtraction operations with a comparison situation. From an adult vantage point, you can see that if you match part of the larger amount with the smaller amount, the large set is now a part-part-whole model that can help you solve the problem. In fact, many

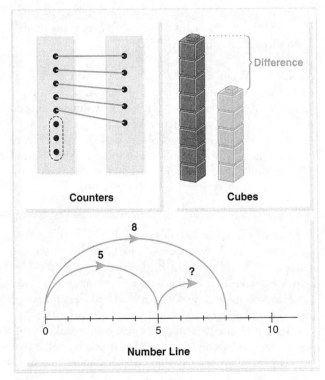

Figure 9.5 Models for the difference between 8 and 5.

children do model compare problems in just this manner. But that is a very difficult idea to show children if they do not construct the idea themselves.

Have children make two amounts, perhaps with two bars of connecting cubes. Discuss the difference between the two bars to generate the third number. For example, if the children make a bar of 10 and a bar of 6, ask, "How many more do we need to match the 10 bar?" The difference is 4. "What equations can we make with these three numbers?" Have children make up story problems that involve the two amounts of 10 and 6. Discuss which equations go with the problems that are created.

Properties of Addition and Subtraction

The Commutative Property for Addition. The commutative property for addition says that it makes no difference in which order two numbers are added. Although the commutative property may seem obvious to us (simply reverse the two piles of counters on the part-part-whole mat), it may not be as obvious to children. Because this property is quite useful in problem solving, mastering basic facts, and mental mathematics, there is value in spending some time helping children construct the relationship. Students do not need to be able to name the property as much as they need to understand the concept and apply it.

Schifter (2001) describes a class of early second-grade students who discovered the "turn-around" property while examining sums to ten. Later, the teacher wondered if they really understood this idea and asked the children if they thought it would always work. Many in the class were unsure if it worked all of the time and were especially unsure about it working with large numbers. The point is that children may see and accept the commutative property for sums they've experienced but not be able to explain or even believe that this simple yet important property works for all addition combinations.

To help children focus on the commutative property, pair problems that have the same addends but in different orders. The context for each problem should be different. For example:

Tania is on page 32 in her book. Tomorrow she hopes to read 15 more pages. What page will she be on if she reads that many pages?

The milk tray in the cafeteria was down to only 15 cartons. Before lunch, the delivery person brought in some more milk. She filled up the tray with 32 more cartons. How many cartons does the milk tray hold?

Ask if anyone notices how these problems are alike. If done as a pair, some (not all) students will see that having solved one they have essentially solved the other.

The Associative Property for Addition. The associative property for addition states that when adding three or more numbers, it does not matter whether the first pair are added first or if you start with any other pair of addends. There is much flexibility in addition, and students can change the order in which they group numbers to work with combinations they know. Notice the following examples involve mentally grouping numbers to add in an order different from just reading the expressions from left to right.

Activity 9.3

More Than Two Addends

Give students six sums to find involving three or four addends. Prepare these on one page divided into six sections so that there is space to write beneath each sum. Within each, include at least one pair with a sum of ten or perhaps a double: 4 + 7 + 6, 5 + 9 + 9, or 3 + 4 + 3 + 7. Students should show how they added the numbers. Allow students to find the sums without any other directions.

Figure 9.6 illustrates how students might show their thinking. As they share their solutions, almost certainly there will be students who added using a different order but got the same result. From this discussion you can help them conclude that you can add numbers in any order. You are also using the associative property but it is the commutative property that is more important. This is also an excellent number sense activity because many students will find combinations of ten in these sums or will use doubles. Learning to adjust strategies to fit the numbers is the beginning of the road to computational fluency.

The Zero Property. Story problems involving zero and or using zeros in the three-addend sums are also a good method of helping students understand zero as an identity element in addition or subtraction (*Curriculum Focal Points*

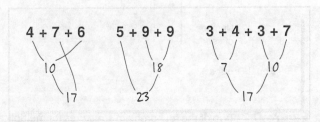

Figure 9.6 Students show how they added.

[CFP], Grade 1). Occasionally students feel that 6 + 0 must be more than 6 because "adding makes numbers bigger" or that 12 − 0 must be 11 because "subtracting makes numbers smaller." Instead of making arbitrary-sounding rules about adding and subtracting zero, build opportunities for discussing zero into the problem-solving routine.

At present, few curricular programs offer addition and subtraction word problems with the variety of problem types we have just explored. However, there are two other ways that you can take advantage of your classroom computers using almost any basic tool software you happen to have. First, you can provide problems yourself using your word processing software or any program that allows shapes to be easily drawn and words to be typed. Open a new file and write a word problem in an appropriate space. Students open the file and use the drawing capabilities to record their solution. You can also have children write story problems on the computer for pictures you create. ◆

Multiplication and Division Problem Structures

Like addition and subtraction, there are problem structures that will help you as the teacher in formulating and assigning multiplication and division tasks. As with the additive problem structures, these are for you, not for your students.

Most researchers identify four different classes of multiplicative structures (Greer, 1992). (The term *multiplicative* is used here to describe all types of problems that involve multiplication and division.) Of these, the two described in Figure 9.7, *equal groups* (*repeated addition*, *rates*) and *multiplicative comparison*, are by far the most prevalent in the elementary school. Problems matching these structures can be modeled with sets of counters, number lines, or arrays. They represent a large percentage of the multiplicative problems in the real world.

Examples of the Four Problem Structures

In multiplicative problems one number or *factor* counts how many sets, groups, or parts of equal size are involved. The other factor tells the size of each set or part. The third number in each of these two structures is the *whole* or *product* and is the total of all of the parts. The parts and wholes terminology is useful in making the connection to addition.

Equal-Group Problems.   When the number and size of groups are known, the problem is a multiplication situation. When either the number of sets or the size of sets is unknown, then the problem is a division situation. But note that these division situations are not alike. Problems in

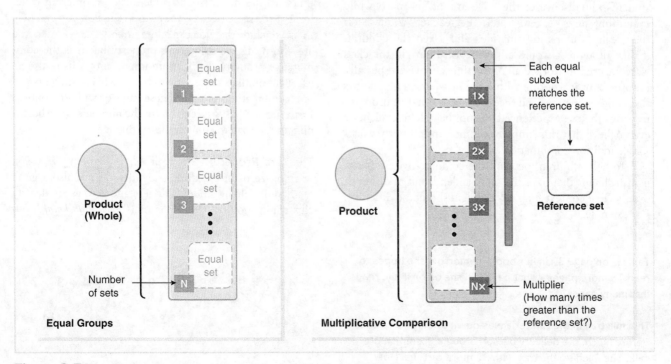

Equal Groups

Multiplicative Comparison

Figure 9.7 Two of the four problem structures for multiplication and division story problems. Each structure has three numbers. Any one of the three numbers can be the unknown in a story problem.

which the size of the sets is unknown are called *fair-sharing* or *partition* problems. The whole is shared or distributed among a known number of sets to determine the size of each. If the number of sets is unknown but the size of the equal sets is known, the problems are called *measurement* or sometimes *repeated-subtraction* problems. The whole is "measured off" in sets of the given size. These terms are used with the examples to follow. Keep in mind the structure in Figure 9.7 to see which numbers are given and which are unknown.

There is also a subtle difference between equal group problems (also called *repeated-addition* problems, such as "If three children have four apples each, how many apples are there?") and those that might be termed *rate* problems ("If there are four apples per child, how many apples would three children have?"). For each category, two examples of rate problems are provided.

Equal Groups: Whole Unknown (Multiplication)

Mark has 4 bags of apples. There are 6 apples in each bag. How many apples does Mark have altogether? (*repeated addition*)

If apples cost 7 cents each, how much did Jill have to pay for 5 apples? (*rate*)

Peter walked for 3 hours at 4 miles per hour. How far did he walk? (*rate*)

Equal Groups: Size of Groups Unknown (Partition Division)

Mark has 24 apples. He wants to share them equally among his 4 friends. How many apples will each friend receive? (*fair sharing*)

Jill paid 35 cents for 5 apples. What was the cost of 1 apple? (*rate*)

Peter walked 12 miles in 3 hours. How many miles per hour (how fast) did he walk? (*rate*)

Equal Groups: Number of Groups Unknown (Measurement Division)

Mark has 24 apples. He put them into bags containing 6 apples each. How many bags did Mark use? (*repeated subtraction*)

Jill bought apples at 7 cents apiece. The total cost of her apples was 35 cents. How many apples did Jill buy? (*rate*)

Peter walked 12 miles at a rate of 4 miles per hour. How many hours did it take Peter to walk the 12 miles? (*rate*)

Comparison Problems. In multiplicative comparison problems, there are really two different sets, as there were with comparison situations for addition and subtraction. One set consists of multiple copies of the other. Two examples of each possibility are provided here. In the former, the comparison is an amount or quantity difference. In multiplicative situations, the comparison is based on one set being a particular multiple of the other.

Comparison: Product Unknown (Multiplication)

Jill picked 6 apples. Mark picked 4 times as many apples as Jill. How many apples did Mark pick?

This month Mark saved 5 times as much money as last month. Last month he saved $7. How much money did Mark save this month?

Comparison: Set Size Unknown (Partition Division)

Mark picked 24 apples. He picked 4 times as many apples as Jill. How many apples did Jill pick?

This month Mark saved 5 times as much money as he did last month. If he saved $35 this month, how much did he save last month?

Comparison: Multiplier Unknown (Measurement Division)

Mark picked 24 apples, and Jill picked only 6. How many times as many apples did Mark pick as Jill did?

This month Mark saved $35. Last month he saved $7. How many times as much money did he save this month as last?

⏸ ——————————— *Pause and Reflect*

What you just read is a lot to take in without reflection. Stop now and get a collection of counters—at least 35. Use the counters to solve each of the problems. Look first at the equal-group problems and do the "Mark" problems or the first problem in each set. Match the numbers with the structure model in Figure 9.7. How are these problems alike and how are they different, especially the two types of division problems? Repeat the exercise with the "Jill" problems and then the "Peter" problems. Can you see how the problems in each problem structure are alike and how the problems across structures such as the problems about "Mark" are related?

When you are comfortable with the equal-group problems, repeat the same process with the multiplicative comparison problems. Again, start with the first problem in all three sets and then the second problem in all three sets. Reflect on the same questions posed earlier.

There is evidence that kindergarten and first-grade children are quite successful at solving multiplication and division problems, even division involving remainders (Carpenter, Ansell, Franke, Fennema, & Weisbeck, 1993; Carpenter et al., 1999). Mulligan and Mitchelmore (1997), based on their own research and that of others, make a strong argument that students should be exposed to all four operations from the first year of school and that multiplication and division should be much more closely linked in the curriculum.

Although the following two multiplicative structures are slightly more complex and therefore not a good introductory point, it is important that you recognize them as two other categories of multiplicative situations.

Combinations or *Cartesian products* and *area* and other *product-of-measures* problems (e.g., length times width equals area) are less frequently mentioned within the multiplication and division sections of most curricula but are used with older elementary and middle grade students.

Combinations Problems. Combinations problems involve counting the number of possible pairings that can be made between two sets. The product consists of pairs of things, one member of each pair taken from each of the two given sets.

Combinations: Product Unknown

Sam bought 4 pairs of pants and 3 jackets, and they all can be worn together. How many different outfits consisting of a pair of pants and a jacket does Sam have?

An experiment involves tossing a coin and rolling a die. How many different possible results or outcomes can this experiment have?

In these two examples, the product is unknown and the size of the two sets is given. It is possible—rarely—to have related division problems for the combinations concept.

Figure 9.8 shows two common methods of modeling combination problems: an array and a tree diagram. Counting how many combinations of two or more things or events are possible is important in determining probabilities. For example, to determine the probability of a head and either a 1 or a 6, one needs to know that there are 12 possible outcomes for the head and die experiment. The combinations concept is most often found in the probability strand.

Area and Other Product-of-Measures Problems. What distinguishes product-of-measures problems from the others is that the product is literally a different type of unit from the other two factors. In a rectangle, the product of two lengths (length × width) is an area, usually square

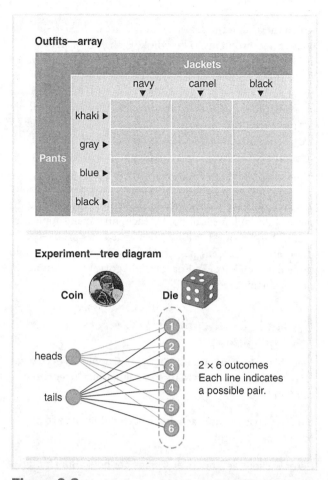

Figure 9.8 Models for combinations situations.

units. Figure 9.9 illustrates how different the square units are from each of the two factors of length: 4 feet times 7 feet is not 28 feet but 28 square feet. The factors are each one-dimensional entities, but the product consists of *two-dimensional* units.

Two other fairly common examples in this category are number of workers × hours worked = worker-hours and kilowatts × hours = kilowatt-hours.

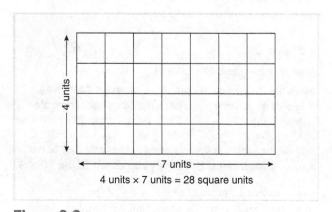

Figure 9.9 Length times length equals area.

Teaching Multiplication and Division

Multiplication and division are taught separately in most textbooks, with multiplication preceding division. It is important, however, to combine multiplication and division soon after multiplication has been introduced in order to help students see how they are related. In most curricula, these topics are first presented in grade 2 (CFP) and then become a main focus of the third grade with continued development in the fourth and fifth grades.

A major conceptual hurdle in working with multiplicative structures is understanding groups of items as single entities while also understanding that a group contains a given number of objects (Blote, Lieffering, & Ouewhand, 2006; Clark & Kamii, 1996). Children can solve the problem *How many apples in 4 baskets of 8 apples each?* by counting out four sets of eight counters and then counting all. To think multiplicatively about this problem as four *sets of eight* requires children to conceptualize each group of eight as a single item to be counted. Experiences with making and counting groups, especially in contextual situations, are extremely useful. (See the discussion of the book *Each Orange Had 8 Slices* at the end of this chapter.)

> **myeducationlab**
>
> Go to the Building Teaching Skills and Dispositions section of Chapter 9 of MyEducationLab. Click on Videos and watch the video entitled "**Using Manipulatives**" to see a third-grade teacher work with students to solve a problem using manipulatives.

Contextual Problems

Many of the issues surrounding addition and subtraction also apply to multiplication and need not be discussed in depth again. It remains important to use contextual problems whenever reasonable instead of more sterile story problems. Just as with additive structures, it is a good idea to build multiplicative lessons around only two or three problems. Students should solve problems using whatever techniques they wish. What is important is that they explain—preferably in words, pictures, and numbers—what they did and why it makes sense.

Symbolism for Multiplication and Division. When students solve simple multiplication story problems before learning about multiplication symbolism, they will most likely write repeated-addition equations to represent what they did. This is your opportunity to introduce the multiplication sign and explain what the two factors mean.

The usual convention is that 4×8 refers to four sets of eight, not eight sets of four. There is no reason to be rigid about this convention. The important thing is that the students can tell you what each factor in *their* equations represents. In vertical form, it is usually the bottom factor that indicates the number of sets. Again, this distinction is not terribly important.

The quotient 24 divided by 6 is represented in three different ways: $24 \div 6$, $6\overline{)24}$, and $\frac{24}{6}$. Students should understand that these representations are equivalent. The fraction notation becomes important at the middle school level. Children often mistakenly read $6\overline{)24}$ as "6 divided by 24" due to the left-right order of the numerals. Generally this error does not match what they are thinking.

Compounding the difficulty of division notation is the unfortunate phrase, "six goes into twenty-four." This phrase carries little meaning about the division concept, especially in connection with a fair-sharing or partitioning context. The "goes into" (or "guzinta") terminology is simply engrained in adult parlance; it has not been in textbooks for years. If you tend to use that phrase, it is probably a good time to consciously abandon it.

Choosing Numbers for Problems. When selecting numbers for multiplicative story problems or activities, there is a tendency to think that large numbers pose a burden to students or that 3×4 is somehow easier to understand than 4×17. An understanding of products or quotients is not affected by the size of numbers as long as the numbers are within the grasp of the students. Little is gained by restricting early explorations of multiplication to small numbers. Even in early third grade, students can work with larger numbers using whatever counting strategies they have at their disposal. A contextual problem involving 14×8 is not too large for third graders even before they have learned a computation technique. When given these challenges, children are likely to invent computational strategies.

Remainders

More often than not in real-world situations, division does not result in a simple whole number. For example, problems with 6 as a divisor will result in a whole number only one time out of six. In the absence of a context, a remainder can be dealt with in only two ways: It can either remain a quantity left over or be partitioned into fractions. In Figure 9.10, the problem $11 \div 4$ is modeled to show fractions.

In real contexts, remainders sometimes have three additional effects on answers:

- The remainder is discarded, leaving a smaller whole-number answer.
- The remainder can "force" the answer to the next highest whole number.
- The answer is rounded to the nearest whole number for an approximate result.

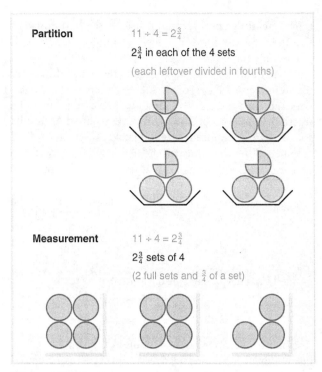

Figure 9.10 Remainders expressed as fractions.

The following problems illustrate all five possibilities.

1. **You have 30 pieces of candy to share fairly with 7 children. How many pieces of candy will each child receive?**
   Answer: **4 pieces of candy and 2 left over. (*left over*)**

2. **Each jar holds 8 ounces of liquid. If there are 46 ounces in the pitcher, how many jars will that be?**
   Answer: **5 and $\frac{6}{8}$ jars. (*partitioned as a fraction*)**

3. **The rope is 25 feet long. How many 7-foot jump ropes can be made?**
   Answer: **3 jump ropes. (*discarded*)**

4. **The ferry can hold 8 cars. How many trips will it have to make to carry 25 cars across the river?**
   Answer: **4 trips. (*forced to next whole number*)**

5. **Six children are planning to share a bag of 50 pieces of bubble gum. About how many pieces will each child get?**
   Answer: **About 8 pieces for each child. (*rounded, approximate result*)**

Students should not just think of remainders as "R 3" or "left over." Remainders should be put in context and dealt with accordingly.

—————————— *Pause and Reflect*

It is useful for you to make up problems in different contexts. Include continuous quantities such as length, time, and volume. See if you can come up with division problems for equal-group and comparison structures that would have remainders dealt with as fractions or as rounded-up or rounded-down results.

It is important to provide story problems for both multiplication and division in the same lesson so that you can be certain children are interpreting the meaning of the problems and not simply taking the two numbers and using "today's" operation.

When modeling multiplicative problems or using their own strategies for solving them, children will not always use an approach that matches the problem. For example, if solving a problem involving 12 sets of 4, many children will add 4 twelves rather than 12 fours. Rather than be concerned about this, view it as an indication that students likely accept or understand that 12×4 and 4×12 give the same result. However, when students solve a problem such as this in different ways, it is a great opportunity for meaningful discussion. ◆

Model-Based Problems

In the beginning, children will be able to use the same models—sets and number lines—for all four operations. A model not generally used for addition but extremely important and widely used for multiplication and division is the array. An *array* is any arrangement of things in rows and columns, such as a rectangle of square tiles or blocks (see Blackline Master 12).

To make clear the connection to addition, early multiplication activities should also include writing an addition sentence for the same model. A variety of models are shown in Figure 9.11. Notice that the products are not included—only addition and multiplication "names" are written. This is another way to avoid the tedious counting of large sets. A similar approach is to write one sentence that expresses both concepts at once, for example, $9 + 9 + 9 + 9 = 4 \times 9$.

As with additive problems, children benefit from a few activities with models and no context. The purpose of such activities is to focus on the meaning of the operation and the associated symbolism. Activity 9.4 has a good problem-solving spirit. The language you use depends on what you have previously used with your children.

Activity **9.4**

Finding Factors

Start by assigning a number that has several factors—for example, 12, 18, 24, 30, or 36. Have students find

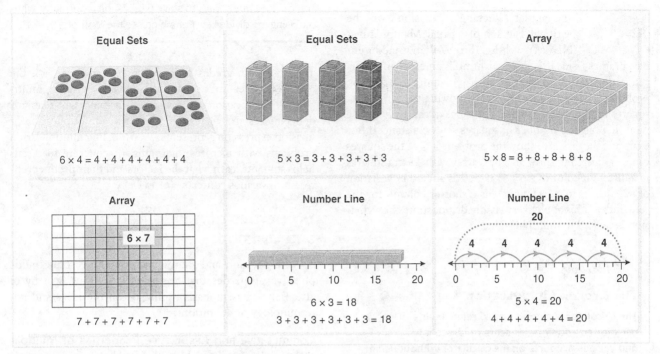

Figure 9.11 Models for equal-group multiplication.

as many multiplication expressions for their assigned number as possible. With counters, students attempt to find a way to separate the counters into equal subsets. With arrays (perhaps made from square tiles or cubes or drawn on grid paper), students try to build rectangles that have the given number of squares. For each such arrangement of sets or appropriate rectangles, both an addition and a multiplication equation should be written. This activity is available as an applet at http://illuminations.nctm.org/ActivityDetail .aspx?id=64.

Activity 9.4 can also include division concepts. When children have learned that 3 and 6 are factors of 18, they can write the equations $18 \div 3 = 6$ and $18 \div 6 = 3$ along with $3 \times 6 = 18$ and $6 + 6 + 6 = 18$ (assuming that three sets of six were modeled). The following variation of the same activity focuses on division. Having children create word problems is another excellent elaboration of this activity. Require children to explain how their story problems fit with what they did with the counters.

Activity 9.5

Learning about Division

Provide children with an ample supply of counters and some way to place them into small groups. Small paper cups work well. Have children count out a number of counters to be the whole or total set. They record this number: "Start with 31." Next specify either the number of equal sets to be made or the size of the sets to be made: "Separate your counters into four equal-sized sets," or "Make as many sets of four as is possible." Next have the children write the corresponding multiplication equation for what their materials show; under that, have them write the division equation.

Be sure to include both types of exercises: number of equal sets and size of sets. Discuss with the class how these two are different, yet each is related to multiplication and each is written as a division equation. You can show the different ways to write division equations at this time. Do Activity 9.5 several times. Start with whole quantities that are multiples of the divisor (no remainders) but soon include situations with remainders. (Note that it is technically incorrect to write $31 \div 4 = 7$ R 3. However, in the beginning, that form may be the most appropriate to use.)

The activity can be varied by changing the model. Have children build arrays using square tiles or blocks or by having them draw arrays on centimeter grid paper. Present the exercises by specifying how many squares are to be in the array. You can then specify the number of rows that should be made (partition) or the length of each row (measurement). How could children model fractional answers using drawings of arrays on grid paper?

The applet "Rectangle Division" on the National Library of Virtual Manipulatives (NLVM) website (http://nlvm.usu.edu/en/nav/Frames_asid_193_g_2_+_1.html) is an excellent interactive illustration of division with remainders. A division problem is presented with an array showing the number of squares in the product. The dimensions of the array can be modified but the number of squares stays constant. If, for example, the task is to show the problem 52 ÷ 8, the squares can be adjusted to show an 8 by 6 array with 4 extra squares in a different color (8 × 6 + 4) as well as any other variation of 52 squares in a rectangle plus a shorter column for the remainder. This applet very vividly demonstrates how division is related to multiplication. ◆

Activity 9.6

The Broken Multiplication Key

The calculator is a good way to relate multiplication to addition. Students can be told to find various products on the calculator without using the ⊗ key. For example, 6 × 4 can be found by pressing ⊞ 4 ⊜ ⊜ ⊜ ⊜ ⊜ ⊜. (Successive presses of ⊜ add 4 to the display each time. You began with zero and added 4 six times.) Students can be challenged to demonstrate their result with sets of counters. But note that this same technique can be used to determine products such as 23 × 459 (⊞ 459 and then 23 presses of ⊜). Students will want to compare to the same product using the ⊗ key.

"The Broken Multiplication Key" can profitably be followed by "The Broken Division Key."

Activity 9.7

The Broken Division Key

Have children work in groups to find methods of using the calculator to solve division exercises without using the divide key. The problems can be posed without a story context. "Find at least two ways to figure out 61 ÷ 14 without pressing the divide key." If the problem is put in a story context, one method may actually match the problem better than another. Good discussions may follow different solutions with the same answers. Are they both correct? Why or why not?

◗◗ ———————— *Pause and Reflect*

There is no reason ever to show children how to do Activity 9.7. However, it would be a good idea for *you* to see if you can find *three* ways to solve 61 ÷ 14 on a calculator without using the divide key. For a hint, see the footnote.*

"In grades 3–5, students should focus on the meanings of, and relationship between, multiplication and division. It is important that students understand what each number in a multiplication or division expression represents. . . . Modeling multiplication problems with pictures, diagrams, or concrete materials helps students learn what the factors and their product represent in various contexts" (p. 151). ◆

Properties of Multiplication and Division

As with addition and subtraction, there are some multiplicative properties that are useful and, thus, worthy of attention. The emphasis should be on the ideas and not terminology or definitions.

Commutative and Associative Properties of Multiplication. It is not intuitively obvious that 3 × 8 is the same as 8 × 3 or that, in general, the order of the numbers makes no difference (the *commutative* property). A picture of 3 sets of 8 objects cannot immediately be seen as 8 piles of 3 objects. Eight hops of 3 land at 24, but it is not clear that 3 hops of 8 will land at the same point.

The array, by contrast, is quite powerful in illustrating the commutative property, as shown in Figure 9.12. Children should draw or build arrays and use them to demonstrate why each array represents two different multiplications with the same product. As in addition, there is an associative property of multiplication that allows numbers in an expression to be paired in any order.

Zero and Identity Properties. Zero and, to a lesser extent, 1 as factors often cause conceptual challenges for children. In one third-grade textbook, a lesson on factors of 0 and 1 has children use a calculator to examine a wide range of products involving 0 or 1 (423 × 0, 0 × 28, 1536 × 1, etc.) and look for patterns. The pattern suggests the rules for factors of 0 and 1 but not a reason. In the same lesson, a word problem asks how many grams of fat there are in 7 servings of celery with 0 grams of fat in each serving. This approach is far preferable to an arbitrary rule, since it asks students to reason. Make up interesting word problems involving 0 or 1, and discuss the results. Problems with 0 as a first factor are really strange. Note that on a number line, 5 hops of 0 land at 0 (5 × 0). What would 0 hops of 5 be? Another fun activity is to try to model 6 × 0 or 0 × 8 with an array. (Try it!) Arrays for factors of 1 are also worth investigating.

---

*There are two measurement approaches to find out how many 14s are in 61. A third way is essentially related to partitioning or finding 14 times what number is close to 61.

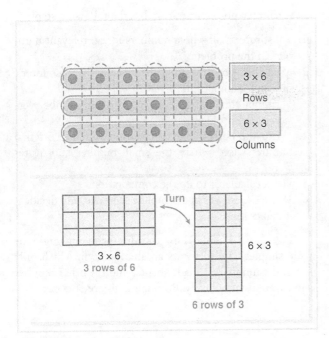

Figure 9.12 Two ways an array can be used to illustrate the commutative property for multiplication.

Distributive Property.   The *distributive property of multiplication over addition* refers to the idea that one of two factors in a product can be split into two or more parts and each part multiplied separately and then added. The result is the same as when the original factors are multiplied. For example, 6×9 is the same as $(6 \times 5) + (6 \times 4)$. The 9 has been split into 5 and 4. The concept involved is very useful in relating one basic fact to another, and it is also involved in the development of two-digit computation. Figure 9.13 illustrates how the array model can be used to illustrate that a product can be broken up into two parts.

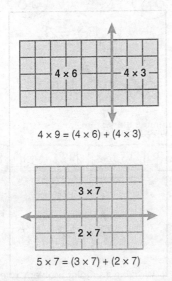

Figure 9.13 Models for the distributive property of multiplication over addition.

The next activity is designed to help children discover how to partition factors or, in other words, learn about the distributive property of multiplication over addition.

Activity 9.8

Slice It Up

Supply students with several sheets of centimeter grid paper or color tiles. Assign each pair of students a product such as 6×8. (Products can vary across the class or all be the same.) The task is to find all of the different ways to make a single slice through the rectangle. For each slice students write an equation. For a slice of one row of 8, students would write $6 \times 8 = (5 \times 8) + (1 \times 8)$. This might be a good time to discuss order of operations. The individual equations can be written in the arrays as shown in Figure 9.13.

Why Not Division by Zero?   Some children are simply told "Division by zero is not allowed," often when teachers do not fully understand this concept (Quinn, Lamberg, & Perrin, 2008). To avoid an arbitrary rule, pose problems to be modeled that involve zero: "Take thirty counters. How many sets of zero can be made?" or "Put twelve blocks in zero equal groups. How many in each group?"

 Figure This! is a wonderful collection of explorations that is available at www.figurethis.org. The 80 challenges are designed for middle grade students. Although not simple story problems, many involve an understanding of the operations. Each problem has interesting follow-up questions and all are designed to engage students and families in real-world applications of mathematics. A version in Spanish is available. ◆

Strategies for Solving Contextual Problems

Often students see context or story problems and are at a loss for what to do. Also struggling readers or ELL students may need support in understanding the problem. In this section you will learn some techniques for helping them.

Analyzing Context Problems

Consider the following problem:

In building a road through a subdivision, workers filled in a large hole in the land with dirt hauled in by trucks. The complete fill required 638 truckloads of dirt. The average truck carried $6\frac{1}{4}$ cubic yards of dirt, which weighed 17.3 tons. How many tons of dirt were used in the fill?

Typically, in fifth- to eighth-grade textbooks, problems of this type are found as part of a series of problems revolving around a single context or theme. Data may be found in a graph or chart or perhaps a short news item or story. Most likely the problems will include all four of the operations. Students have difficulty deciding on the correct operation and even finding the appropriate data for the problem. Many students will find two numbers in the problem and guess at the correct operation. These children simply do not have any tools for analyzing problems. At least two strategies can be taught that are very helpful: Think about the answer before solving the problem, or solve a simpler problem that is just like this one.

Think about the Answer Before Solving the Problem.

Poor problem solvers fail to spend adequate time thinking about the problem and what it is about. They rush in and begin doing calculations, believing that "number crunching" is what solves problems. That is simply not the case. Rather, students should spend time talking about (later, thinking about) what the answer might look like. For our sample problem, it might go as follows:

> *What is happening in this problem?* Some trucks were bringing dirt in to fill up a big hole.
> *What will the answer tell us?* How many tons of dirt were needed to fill the hole.
> *Will that be a small number of tons or a large number of tons?* Well, there were 17.3 tons on a truck, but there were a lot of trucks, not just one. It's probably going to be a lot of tons.
> *About how many tons do you think it will be?* It's going to be a lot. If there were just 100 trucks, it would be 1730 tons. It might be close to 10,000 tons.

In this type of discussion, three things are happening. First, the students are asked to focus on the problem and the meaning of the answer instead of on numbers. The numbers are not important in thinking about the structure of the problem. Second, with a focus on the structure of the problem, students can identify the numbers that are important as well as numbers that are not important to the problem. Third, the thinking leads to a rough estimate of the answer. In any event, thinking about what the answer tells and about how large it might be is a useful first step.

Work a Simpler Problem.

The reason that models are rarely used with problems such as the dirt problem is that the large numbers are impossible to model easily. Dollars and cents, distances in thousands of miles, and time in minutes and seconds are all examples of data likely to be found in the upper grades, and all are difficult to model. The general problem-solving strategy of "try a simpler problem" can almost always be applied to problems with unwieldy numbers.

A simpler-problem strategy has the following steps:

1. Substitute small whole numbers for all relevant numbers in the problem.
2. Model the problem using the new numbers (counters, drawing, number line, array).
3. Write an equation that solves the small-number version of the problem.
4. Write the corresponding equation with the original numbers used where the small-number substitutes were.
5. Use a calculator to do the computation.
6. Write the answer in a complete sentence, and decide if it makes sense.

Figure 9.14 shows how the dirt problem might be made simpler. It also shows an alternative in which only one of the numbers is made smaller and the other number is illustrated symbolically. Both methods are effective.

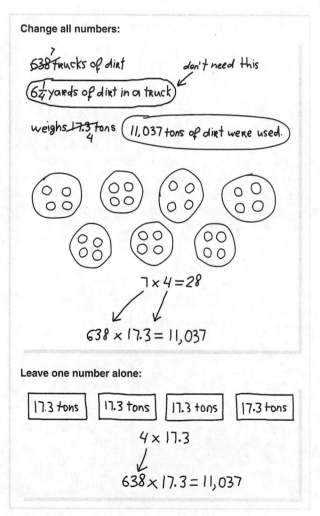

Figure 9.14 Working a simpler problem: two possibilities.

The idea is to provide a tool students can use to analyze a problem and not just guess at what computation to do. It is much more useful to have students do a few problems where they must use a model of a drawing to justify their solution than to give them a lot of problems where they guess at a solution but don't know if their guess is correct.

Caution: Avoid Relying on the Key Word Strategy!   It is often suggested that students should be taught to find "key words" in story problems. Some teachers even post lists of key words with their corresponding meanings. For example, "altogether" and "in all" mean you should add and "left" and "fewer" indicate you should subtract. The word "each" suggests multiplication. To some extent, teachers have been reinforced by the overly simple and formulaic story problems sometimes found in textbooks and other times by their own reading skills (Svlentic-Dowell, Beal, & Capraro, 2006). When problems are written in this way, it may appear that the key word strategy is effective.

In contrast with this belief, researchers and mathematics educators have long cautioned against the strategy of key words (e.g., Burns, 2000; Carpenter, 1985; Clement & Bernhard, 2005; Goldin, 1985; Sowder, 1988). Here are three arguments against relying on the key word approach.

1. Key words are often misleading. Many times the key word or phrase in a problem suggests an operation that is incorrect. The following problem shared by Drake and Barlow (2007) demonstrates this possibility.

There are three boxes of chicken nuggets on the table. Each box contains six chicken nuggets. How many chicken nuggets are there in all? (p. 272)

Drake and Barlow found that one student generated the answer of 9, using the words "how many in all" as a suggestion to add 3 + 6, generating 9 as the answer. Instead of making sense of the situation, the student used the key word approach as a shortcut in making an operational decision.

2. Many problems have no key words. Except for the overly simple problems found in primary textbooks, a large percentage of problems have no key words. A child who has been taught to rely on key words is left with no strategy. For example, both the additive and the multiplicative problems in this chapter include numerous examples with no key words. And this is from a collection of overly simple problems designed to help you with structure.

3. The key word strategy sends a terribly wrong message about doing mathematics. The most important approach to solving any contextual problem is to analyze it and make sense of it. The key word approach encourages students to ignore the meaning and structure of the problem and look for an easy way out. Mathematics is about reasoning and making sense of situations. A sense-making strategy will *always* work.

Two-Step Problems

Students often have difficulty with multistep problems. First, be sure they can analyze one-step problems in the way that we have discussed. The following ideas, adapted from suggestions by Huinker (1994), are designed to help children see how two problems can be chained together.

1. Give students a one-step problem and have them solve it. Before discussing the answer, have each student or group use the answer to the first problem to create a second problem. The rest of the class can then be asked to solve the second problem, as in the following example:

Given problem: It took $3\frac{1}{3}$ hours for the Jones family to drive the 195 miles to Washington, D.C. What was their average speed?

Second problem: The Jones children remember crossing the river at about 10:30, or 2 hours after they left home. About how far from home is the river?

2. Make a "hidden question." Repeat the first exercise by beginning with a one-step problem. Give different problems to different groups. This time have students write a second problem as before. Then write a single combined problem that leaves out the question from the first problem. That question from the first problem is the "hidden question," as in the following simple example:

Given problem: Tony bought three dozen eggs for 89 cents a dozen. How much was the bill?

Second problem: How much change did Tony get back from $5?

Hidden-question problem: Tony bought three dozen eggs for 89 cents a dozen. How much change did Tony get back from $5?

Have other students identify the hidden question. Since all students are working on a similar task but with different problems (be sure to mix the operations), they will be more likely to understand what is meant by a hidden question.

3. Pose standard two-step problems, and have the students identify and answer the hidden question. Consider the following problem:

Willard Sales Company bought 275 widgets wholesale for $3.69 each. In the first month, the company sold 205 widgets at $4.99 each. How much did Willard make or lose on the widgets? Do you think Willard Sales should continue to sell widgets?

Begin by considering the questions that were suggested earlier: "What's happening in this problem?" (Something is being bought and sold at two different prices.) "What will the answer tell us?" (How much profit or loss there was.) These questions will get you started. If students are stuck, you can ask, "Is there a hidden question in this problem?"

 The value of student discussions to help develop meaning throughout mathematics including understanding the operations is quite evident in the *Standards*. At the K–2 level: "When students struggle to communicate ideas clearly, they develop a better understanding of their own thinking" (p. 129). At the 3–5 level: "The use of models and pictures provides a further opportunity for understanding and conversation. Having a concrete referent helps students develop understandings that are clearer and more easily shared" (p. 197). ◆

 One of the best ways to assess students' knowledge of the meaning of the operations is to have them generate story problems for a given equation or result (Drake & Barlow, 2007; Whitin & Whitin, 2008). For example, give students the result "24 cents" and ask them to write a subtraction problem that will generate that answer or a division problem or any other appropriate type of problem. Another option is to give them an expression such as 5 × 7 and ask them to write a story problem representing the expression. Students who can ably match scenarios to the computation will demonstrate their understanding, whereas struggling students will reveal areas of weakness. Students can also use the context from a piece of children's literature to write word problems that emphasize the meaning of the four operations. ◆

Reflections on Chapter 9

Writing to Learn

1. Make up a comparison story problem. Next change the problem to provide an example of all six different possibilities for comparison problems.
2. Why might a contextual problem be more effective than a simple story problem?
3. Explain how missing-part activities prepare students for mastering subtraction facts.
4. Make up multiplication story problems to illustrate the difference between equal groups and multiplicative comparison. Can you create problems involving rates or continuous quantities such as area?
5. Make up two different story problems for 36 ÷ 9. Create one problem as a measurement problem and one as a partition problem?
6. Make up realistic measurement and partition division problems where the remainder is dealt with in each of these three ways: (a) it is discarded (but not left over); (b) it is made into a fraction; (c) it forces the answer to the next whole number.
7. Why is the use of key words not a good strategy to teach children?

For Discussion and Exploration

1. *Cognitively Guided Instruction* is not a curriculum program but a professional development program in which teachers learn to use students' thinking to guide instruction. The predominant thrust of CGI is the use of story problems, not only for learning the operations but also for number and fact development and even for computation development with larger numbers. Select either basic fact mastery or computation development and describe how you think these goals might be achieved primarily through story problems. If possible, view some of the video clips on the CD that comes with *Children's Mathematics: Cognitively Guided Instruction* (Carpenter et al., 1999) to compare your thoughts with theirs.
2. See how many different types of story problems you can find in a textbook. In the primary grades, look for join, separate, part-part-whole, and compare problems. For grades 4 and up, look for the four multiplicative types. (Examine the multiplication and division chapters and also any special problem-solving lessons.) Are the various types of problems well represented?

Resources for Chapter 9

Literature Connections

There are many books with stories or pictures concerning sets, buying items, measures, and so on, that can be used to pose problems or, better, to stimulate children to invent their own problems. Perhaps the most widely mentioned book in this context is *The Doorbell Rang* by Pat Hutchins (1986). You can check that one out yourself, as well as the following four additional suggestions.

How Many Snails? *Giganti, 1988*

Appropriate for the pre-K–2 set, this book includes a variety of pictures in which the objects belonging to one collection have various subcollections (parts and wholes). For example, a sky full of clouds has various types of clouds. The text asks, "How many clouds are there? How many clouds are big and fluffy? How many clouds are big and fluffy and gray?" These pages lead directly to addition and subtraction situations matching the part-part-whole concepts. Of special note is the opportunity to have missing-part thinking for subtraction. Children can then pose their own questions about the drawing and add appropriate number sentences or draw pictures with subcollections on their own equation and how it fits the picture.

One Hundred Hungry Ants *Pinczes, 1999*

This book, written by a grandmother for her grandchild, helps students explore the operation of multiplication (and division). It tells the tale of 100 ants on a trip to a picnic. In an attempt to speed their travel, the ants move from their single-file line of 100 to two rows of 50, four rows of 25, and so forth. This story uses the visual representation of arrays to explore several options for a group of 100 ants. Students can be given different sizes of ant groups to explore other groupings.

Remainder of One *Pinczes, 1995*

Similar to her other book, Elinor Pinczes describes the trials and tribulations of a parade formation of 25 bugs. As the queen is viewing the outline of the parading bugs she notices that one bug is not with the group, trailing behind. The group tries to create different numbers of rows and columns (arrays) but again the one bug is always a "leftover" (remainder). Here too students can be given different parade groups and they can generate formations that will leave one, two, or none out of the group.

Each Orange Had 8 Slices *Giganti, 1992*

Each two-page spread shows objects grouped in three ways. For example, one illustration has four trees, three bird's nests in each tree, and two eggs in each nest. The author asks three questions: "How many trees? How many nests? How many eggs?" The three questions with each picture extend multiplication to a three-factor product. In the case of the trees, nests, and eggs, the number of eggs is the product of $4 \times 3 \times 2$. After children get a handle on the predictable arrangement of the book's pictures, they can write different multiplication stories that go with the pictures or make up illustrations of their own. For example, what similar situations can be found in the classroom? Perhaps desks, books, and pages or bookshelves, shelves, and books.

Recommended Readings

Articles

Clement, L., & Bernhard, J. (2005). A problem-solving alternative to using key words. *Mathematics Teaching in the Middle School, 10*(7), 360–365.

This article explores the use of key words as a replacement for sense making in reading word problems. The authors emphasize the meanings of the operations as they sort out common student misconceptions. They describe ways to emphasize having students understand the quantities and relationships between quantities rather than just focusing on the values.

Jung, M., Kloosterman, P., & McMullen, M. (2007). Research in review: Young children's intuition for solving problems in mathematics. *Young Children, 62*(5), 50–57.

This article explores how students in pre-K through the second grade solve problems using the Cognitively Guided Instruction (CGI) approach as a foundation. The authors share classroom vignettes and then they debrief what they learned about children's thinking.

Books

Carpenter, T. P., Fennema, E., Franke, M. L., Levi, L., & Empson, S. (1999). *Children's mathematics: Cognitively guided instruction.* Portsmouth, NH: Heinemann. (Also published by NCTM)

For teachers, this is the best book available for understanding the CGI approach to operations and the use of story problems to develop number, basic facts, and computational procedures. The classifications of word problems for all operations, as discussed in this chapter, are explained in detail along with methods for using these problems with students. With the book come two CDs, one with classroom clips of CGI classrooms and the other showing children using the various strategies described in the book.

Schifter, D., Bastable, V., & Russell, S. J. (1999b). *Developing mathematical understanding: Numbers and operations, Part 2, Making meaning for operations (Casebook).* Parsippany, NJ: Dale Seymour Publications.

In this casebook, teachers in grades K–7 share their stories of working with children as they develop meanings for the four operations. The teachers discuss the kinds of actions and situations that students use as they come to understand the operations.

Online Resources

Broken Calculators
http://my.nctm.org/eresources/view_article.asp?article_id=7457&page=11&add=Y
www.fi.uu.nl/toepassingen/00014/toepassing_wisweb.en.html

These two applets demonstrate the broken calculator activity as mentioned in Activities 9.6 and 9.7. The first allows for problems at any level, whereas the second is more appropriate for intermediate or middle grade students, as it includes a problem-solving feature.

Number Line Arithmetic
http://nlvm.usu.edu/en/nav/frames_asid_156_g_1_t_1.html

This number-line applet can be used to model whole-number operations in addition, subtraction, multiplication, and division.

Thinking Blocks: Addition and Subtraction
www.thinkingblocks.com/ThinkingBlocks_AS/TB_AS_Main.html

Thinking Blocks: Multiplication and Division
www.thinkingblocks.com/ThinkingBlocks_MD/TB_MD_Main.html

These teacher-developed tools links to the various types of problems discussed earlier in the chapter. The difference is the use of two-digit numbers and problems with multiple steps, including compare, part-part-whole, and change examples. There is an emphasis on identifying and solving for an unknown quantity. Because the ideas are presented in game formats, you should view the introduction to be able to play.

All About Multiplication (Grades 3–5)
http://illuminations.nctm.org/LessonDetail.aspx?id=U109

Four lessons with links to other activities and student recording sheets highlight the models of the number line, equal groups, arrays, and balanced equations. Lesson 3 explores the order property, the zero property, and the identity property. Lesson 4 has an engaging applet called the *Product Game*.

The Factor Game
http://illuminations.nctm.org/ActivityDetail.aspx?ID=12

This game puts two players into competition to collect the factors for given numbers.

Field Experience Guide Connections

This is a good time to use FEG Field Experiences 3.1, 3.4, and 3.6, all of which target conceptual and procedural understanding. FEG Activity 10.2 ("Odd or Even?") is a problem-based activity that includes addition and looking for patterns. FEG Expanded Lesson 9.1 focuses on subtraction, and FEG Expanded Lesson 9.4 focuses on connecting subtraction to division. Skip counting, a precursor to multiplication, is the focus of FEG Activity 10.1 ("The Find!"). Factors, which are important in division, are the focus of FEG Activity 10.3 ("Factor Quest"). FEG Activity 10.5 ("Target Number") helps students develop number sense for all the operations.

Chapter 10

Helping Children Master the Basic Facts

Basic facts for addition and multiplication refer to combinations where both addends or both factors are less than 10. Subtraction and division facts correspond to addition and multiplication facts. Thus, $15 - 8 = 7$ is a subtraction fact because the corresponding addition parts are less than 10.

Mastery of a basic fact means that a child can give a quick response (in about 3 seconds) without resorting to non-efficient means, such as counting. According to NCTM's *Curriculum Focal Points*, addition and subtraction concepts should be learned in first grade, with quick recall of basic addition and subtraction facts mastered in grade 2. Relatedly, concepts of multiplication and division should be learned in third grade, with quick recall of the facts mastered in grade 4.

Developing quick and accurate recall with the basic facts is a developmental process—just like every topic in this book! It is critical that students know their facts well—and teaching them well requires much more than flash cards and timed tests. This chapter explains strategies for helping students learn their facts, including instructional approaches to use—and others to avoid.

Big Ideas

1. Number relationships provide the foundation for strategies that help students remember basic facts. For example, knowing how numbers are related to 5 and 10 helps students master facts such as 3 + 5 (think of a ten-frame) and 8 + 6 (since 8 is 2 away from 10, take 2 from 6 to make 10 + 4 = 14).

2. "Think-addition" is the most powerful way to think of subtraction facts. Rather than 13 "take away 6," which requires counting backward while also keeping track of how many counts, students can think 6 and what makes 13. They might add up to 10 or they may think double 6 is 12 so it must be 7.

3. Because mastery of the basic facts is a developmental process, students move through stages, starting with counting, then to more efficient reasoning strategies, and eventually to quick recall. Instruction must help students move through these phases, without rushing them to memorization.

Mathematics Content Connections

As described in the Big Ideas, basic fact mastery is not really new mathematics; rather, it is the development of fluency with ideas that have already been learned.

- **Number and Operations** (Chapters 8 and 9): Fact mastery relies significantly on how well students have constructed relationships about numbers and how well they understand the operations.

  Fluency with basic facts allows for ease of computation, especially mental computation, and therefore aids in the ability to reason numerically in every number-related area. Although calculators and tedious counting are available for students who do not have command of the facts, reliance on these methods for simple number combinations is a serious handicap to mathematical growth.

Developmental Nature of Basic Fact Mastery

Teaching basic facts well requires the essential understanding that students progress through stages that eventually result in "just knowing" that 2 + 7 is 9 or that 5 × 4 is 20. Arthur Baroody, a mathematics educator who does research on basic facts, describes three phases in this process (2006, p. 22):

Phase 1: Counting Strategies—using object counting (e.g., blocks or fingers) or verbal counting to determine the answer.

Example: 4 + 7. Student starts with 7 and counts on verbally 8, 9, 10, 11.

Phase 2: Reasoning Strategies—using known information to logically determine an unknown combination.

Example: 4 + 7. Student knows that 7 + 3 is 10, so 7 + 4 is one more, 11.

Phase 3: Mastery—efficient (fast and accurate) production of answers.

Example: 4 + 7. Student quickly responds, "It's 11; I just know it."

Figure 10.1 outlines the methods for solving basic addition and subtraction problems that students move through developmentally.

Much research over many years supports the notion that basic facts mastery is dependent on the development of reasoning strategies (Baroody, 2003, 2006; Brownell & Chazal, 1935; Carpenter & Moser, 1984; Fuson, 1992; Henry & Brown, 2008). This chapter focuses on reasoning strategies and effective ways to teach students to use reasoning to master the basic facts.

Approaches to Fact Mastery

In attempting to help children master their basic facts, three somewhat different approaches can be identified. First is to work on memorization of each fact in isolation. A second approach that can be traced at least as far back as the 1970s (Rathmell, 1978) suggests that for various classes of basic facts we teach students a collection of strategies or thought patterns that have been found to be efficient and teachable. The third approach, "guided invention," also focuses on the use of strategies to learn facts; however, the strategies are generated, or reinvented, by students. Each of these approaches is briefly discussed in the following sections.

Memorizing Facts.   Some textbooks and teachers move from presenting concepts of addition and multiplication straight to memorization of facts, skipping the process of developing strategies. This means that students have 100 separate addition facts (0–9) and 100 separate multiplication facts. They may even have to memorize subtraction and division separately. However, the reality that many students in the fourth and fifth grades have not mastered addition and subtraction facts, and that students in middle school and beyond do not know their multiplication facts strongly, suggests that this method simply does not work well. You may be tempted to respond that you learned your facts in this manner, as did many other students. However, studies by Brownell and Chazal as long

> **myeducationlab**
>
> Go to the Activities and Application section of Chapter 10 of MyEducationLab. Click on Videos and watch the video entitled "**John Van de Walle on Approaches to Fact Mastery**" to see him talk with teachers about approaches to help all children master basic facts.

	Addition	Subtraction
Counting	Direct modeling (counting objects and fingers) • Counting all • Counting on from first • Counting on from larger	Counting objects • Separating from • Separating to • Adding on
	Counting abstractly • Counting all • Counting on from first • Counting on from larger	Counting fingers • Counting down • Counting up
		Counting abstractly • Counting down • Counting up
Reasoning	Properties • $a + 0 = a$ • $a + 1$ = next whole number • Commutative property	Properties • $a - 0 = a$ • $a - 1$ = previous whole number
	Known-fact derivations (e.g., $5 + 6 = 5 + 5 + 1$; $7 + 6 = 7 + 7 - 1$)	Inverses/complement of known additions facts (e.g., $12 - 5$ is known because $5 + 7 = 12$)
	Redistributed derived facts (e.g., $7 + 5 = 7 + (3 + 2) = (7 + 3) + 2 = 10 + 2 = 12$)	Redistributed derived facts (e.g., $12 - 5 = (7 + 5) - 5 = 7 + (5 - 5) = 7$)
Retrieval	Retrieval from long-term memory	Retrieval from long-term memory

Figure 10.1 The developmental process for basic fact mastery for addition and subtraction.

Source: Henry, V. J., & Brown, R. S. (2008). "First-Grade Basic Facts: An Investigation into Teaching and Learning of an Accelerated, High-Demand Memorization Standard." *Journal for Research in Mathematics Education, 39*(2), p. 156. Reprinted with permission.

ago as 1935 concluded that children develop a variety of different thought processes or strategies for basic facts in spite of the amount of isolated drill that they experience. Unfortunately, drill does not encourage or support the refinement of these strategies. Moreover, Baroody (2006) notes that this approach to basic facts instruction works against the development of the five strands of mathematics proficiency (see pp. 24–25), pointing out the following limitations:

- *Inefficiency.* Too many facts to memorize.
- *Inappropriate applications.* Students misapply the facts and don't check their work.
- *Inflexibility.* Students don't learn flexible strategies for finding the sums (or products) and therefore continue to use counting.

Drill is also an equity issue. Struggling learners and students with learning disabilities often have difficulty memorizing so many isolated facts but can be *very* successful at using strategies. In addition, drill can cause unnecessary anxiety and undermine student interest and confidence in mathematics.

Explicit Strategy Instruction. For approximately 3 decades, it has been popular to show students an efficient strategy that is applicable to a collection of facts. Students then practice the strategy as it was shown to them. There is strong evidence to indicate that such a method can be effective (e.g., Baroody, 1985; Bley & Thornton, 1995; Fuson, 1984, 1992; Rathmell, 1978; Thornton & Toohey, 1984). Many of the ideas developed and tested by these researchers are discussed in this chapter.

Teaching explicit strategies is intended to support student thinking rather than force students to use a strategy they have memorized. Sometimes textbooks or teachers focus on memorizing the strategy and which facts work with that strategy. However, this doesn't work. When students memorize strategies that don't make sense to them they are likely to misapply them. In reality, a recent study found that teachers who relied heavily on textbooks (which focused on memorizing basic fact strategies) had students with lower number sense proficiency (Henry & Brown, 2008). Moreover, students don't memorize well, so they resort to counting. The key is to help students see the possibilities and then let them choose strategies that help them get to the solution without counting.

Guided Invention. The third option might be called "guided invention" (Gravemeijer & van Galen, 2003). In this effective approach, fact mastery is intricately connected to students' collection of number relationships. Some students may think of 6 + 7 as "double 6 is 12 and one more is 13." In the same class, others may note that 7 is 3 away from 10 and so take 3 from the 6 to put with the 7 to make 10. They then add on the remaining 3. Still other students may take 5 from each addend to make 10 and then add

the remaining 1 and 2. What is significant is that students are using number combinations and relationships that they own and that make sense to them.

Gravemeijer and van Galen call this approach *guided invention* because many of the strategies that are efficient will not be developed by all students without some guidance. That is, we cannot simply place all of our efforts on number relationships and the meanings of the operations and assume that fact mastery will happen by magic. Class discussions based on student solutions to story problems and other number tasks and games will bring a variety of strategies into the classroom. Children select and adapt the ideas that are meaningful to them. The teacher's job is to design tasks and problems that will promote the invention of effective strategies by students and to be sure that these strategies are clearly articulated and shared in the classroom. It is vitally important that teachers attend to the development of a rich collection of number relationships, as described in Chapter 8.

Guiding Strategy Development

In order for you to guide your students to use effective strategies, you yourself need to have a command of as many good strategies as possible. With this knowledge, you will be able to recognize effective strategies as your students develop them and help others capitalize on their ideas.

You need to plan experiences which help students move from counting to strategies to recall. One critical approach uses simple story problems designed in such a manner that students are most likely to develop a strategy as they solve it. In discussing student strategies, you can focus attention on the methods that are most useful.

Second, teach the reasoning strategies. This can help students expand their own collection of mental strategies and move away from counting. We caution, however, that this instruction should be about highlighting strategies, not about having students memorize or be required to use them.

Story Problems. Story problems provide context that can help students understand the situation and apply flexible strategies for doing the computation. Consider, for example, that the class is working on the × 3 facts. The teacher poses the following question:

In 3 weeks we will be going to the zoo. How many days until we go to the zoo?

Suppose that Aidan explains how she figured out 3 × 7 by starting with double 7 (14) and then adding 7 more. She knew that 6 added onto 14 is 20 and one more is 21. You can ask another student to explain what Aidan just shared. This requires students to attend to ideas that come from their

Grade 1, Unit 6, Number Games and Crayon Puzzles
Lesson: Making Arrays

1. Max's soccer team has 15 balls.
   His team let Rosa's team borrow 6 balls.
   How many balls does Max's team have left?

Grade 4, Unit 1, Factors, Multiples, and Arrays
Lesson: Addition and Subtraction Story Problems

2. A package of juice boxes has 8 juice boxes.
   How many juice boxes are in 3 packages?
   How many juice boxes are in 6 packages?
   How many juice boxes are in 9 packages?

Figure 10.2 Story problems from the *Investigations in Number, Data, and Space* curriculum to develop basic fact reasoning strategies.

classmates. Now explore with the class to learn what other facts would work with Aidan's strategy. This discussion may include a variety of strategies. Some may notice that all of the facts with a 3 in them will work for the double-and-add-one-more strategy. Others may say that you can always add one more set on if you know the smaller fact. For example, for 6×8 you can start with 5×8 and add 8.

The *Thinking with Numbers* program (Rathmell, Leutzinger, & Gabriele, 2000) consists of a large collection of simple story problems developed in sets designed to promote particular strategies or ways of thinking about a particular collection of facts. Teachers pose one problem each day for students to solve mentally. This is followed by a brief discussion of the ideas that students use. A similar approach is shown in Figure 10.2, which includes story examples intended to support reasoning strategies from grade 1 and grade 4 of *Investigations in Number, Data, and Space*. Research has found that when a strong emphasis is placed on students' solving problems, they not only become better problem solvers but also they master more basic facts than students in a fact drill program (NRC, 2001).

Reasoning Strategies.   A second approach is to directly model a reasoning strategy. A lesson may be designed to have students examine a specific collection of facts for which a particular type of strategy is appropriate. You can discuss how these facts are all alike in some way, or you might suggest an approach and see if students are able to use it on similar facts.

Avoid the temptation to tell students to use a strategy and then have them practice it. Continue to discuss strategies invented in your class and plan lessons that encourage strategies. Don't expect to have a strategy introduced and understood with just one word problem or one exposure. Children need lots of opportunities to make a strategy their own. Many children will simply not be ready to use an idea the first few days, and then all of a sudden something will click and a useful idea will be theirs.

It is a good idea to write new strategies on the board or make a poster of strategies students develop. Give the strategies names that make sense. (*Double and add one more set. Aidan's idea. Use with 3s.* Include an example.)

No student should be forced to adopt someone else's strategy, but every student should be encouraged to understand strategies that are brought to the discussion.

Different students will likely invent or adopt different strategies for the same collection of facts. For example, there are several methods or strategies that use 10 when adding 8 or 9. Therefore, a drill that includes all of the addition facts with an 8 or a 9 can accommodate any child who has a strategy for that collection. Two children can be playing a spinner drill game, each using different strategies.

 Critics of the reform movement in mathematics education often try to suggest that the *Standards* are "soft on the basics," especially mastery of facts. Nothing could be further from the truth. Among several similar statements that could be selected from the *Standards* document is this quotation: "Knowing the basic number combinations—single-digit addition and multiplication pairs and their counterparts for subtraction and division—is essential" (p. 32). ◆

Reasoning Strategies for Addition Facts

The strategies that students can and will invent for addition facts are directly related to one or more number relationships. In Chapter 8, numerous activities were suggested to develop these relationships. Now the teaching task is to help children connect these number relationships to the basic facts.

The "big idea" behind using reasoning strategies is for students to make use of known facts and relationships to solve basic facts. Of the two ways students might do this, one is to use a *known fact* (like $7 + 3 = 10$) to solve an unknown fact, such as $7 + 5$, which is two more than the known fact. The second is to use *derived facts*. In this case, the student might solve $7 + 5$ by taking 7 apart into $5 + 2$, then adding the $5 + 5$ and then 2 more (Henry & Brown, 2008). Keep this "big idea" in mind as you review each of the reasoning strategies described in this section.

myeducationlab

Go to the Activities and Application section of Chapter 10 of MyEducationLab. Click on Videos and watch the video entitled "**John Van de Walle on Reasoning Strategies for Addition Facts**" to see him talk with teachers about strategies for addition.

One More Than and Two More Than

Each of the 36 facts highlighted in the following chart has at least one addend of 1 or 2. These facts are a direct application of the one-more-than and two-more-than relationships described in Chapter 8.

Story problems in which one of the addends is a 1 or a 2 are easy to make up. For example, *When Tommy was at the circus, he saw 7 clowns come out in a little car. Then 2 more clowns came out on bicycles. How many clowns did Tommy see in all?* Ask different students to explain how they got the answer of 9. Some will count on from 7. Some may still need to count 7 and 2 and then count all. Others will say they knew that 2 more than 7 is 9. The last response gives you an opportunity to talk about facts where you can use the two-more-than idea.

+	0	1	2	3	4	5	6	7	8	9
0		1	2							
1	1	2	3	4	5	6	7	8	9	10
2	2	3	4	5	6	7	8	9	10	11
3				4	5					
4				5	6					
5				6	7					
6				7	8					
7				8	9					
8				9	10					
9				10	11					

Activity 10.1

How Many Feet in the Bed?

Read *How Many Feet in the Bed?* On the second time through the book ask students how many more feet are in the bed when a new person gets in. Ask students to record the equation (e.g., 6 + 2) and tell how many. Two less can be considered as family members getting out of the bed.

The different responses will provide you with a lot of information about students' number sense. As students are ready to use the two-more-than idea without "counting all," they can begin to practice with activities such as the following.

Activity 10.2

One More Than and Two More Than with Dice and Spinners

Make a die labeled +1, +2, +1, +2, "one more," and "two more." Use with another die labeled 3, 4, 5, 6, 7, and 8 (or whatever values students need to practice). After each roll of the dice, children should say the complete fact: "Four and two more is six." Alternatively, roll one die and use a spinner with +1 on one half and +2 on the other half.

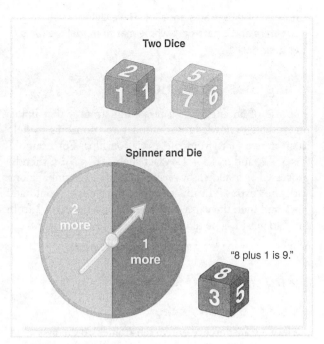

Figure 10.3 One-more and two-more activities.

Figure 10.3 illustrates the ideas in Activity 10.2. Notice that activities such as these can be modified for almost all of the strategies in the chapter.

Adding Zero

Nineteen facts have zero as one of the addends. Though such problems are generally easy, some children overgeneralize the idea that answers to addition problems are bigger than the addends. Word problems involving zero will be especially helpful. In the discussion, use drawings that show two parts with one part empty.

+	0	1	2	3	4	5	6	7	8	9
0	0	1	2	3	4	5	6	7	8	9
1	1									
2	2									
3	3									
4	4									
5	5									
6	6									
7	7									
8	8									
9	9									

Activity 10.3

What's Alike? Zero Facts

Write about ten zero facts on the board, some with the zero first and some with the zero second. Discuss

how all of these facts are alike. Have children use counters and a part-part-whole mat to model the facts at their desks.

Using 5 as an Anchor

The use of an anchor is a reasoning strategy that builds on students' knowledge of number relationships to help them derive facts from these relationships. For example, 7 is 5 + 2, and 6 is 5 + 1. A fact such as 6 + 7 can then be processed by a student by seeing the 5 in each number along with the "extras." In this example, the student would add 5 + 5 and then the extra 1 from the 6 and the extra 2 from the 7 to get 13. The ten-frames discussed in Chapter 8 can help students see numbers as 5 and some more.

Activity 10.4

Using 10 as an Anchor

Place a transparency of two ten-frames on the overhead projector. Place counters on each—for example, 6 on one and 7 on the other. Flash on the overhead for about 5 seconds; then turn it off. First ask students how many counters there were and then have students explain how they saw them. See Blackline Masters 11 and 16.

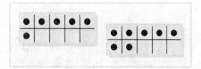

Activity 10.5

Say the 10 Fact

Hold up a ten-frame card, and have children say the "10 fact." For a card with seven dots, the response is "seven and three is ten." Later, with a blank ten-frame drawn on the board, say a number less than 10. Children start with that number and complete the "10 fact." If you say, "four," they say, "four plus six is ten." Use the same activities in independent or small-group modes. See Blackline Master 16.

10 Facts

Perhaps the most important strategy for students to know is the Make 10 strategy, or the combinations that make 10. Story problems using two numbers that make 10 or that ask how many are needed to make 10 can assist this process. The ten-frame is also a very useful tool. Place counters on one ten-frame and ask, "How many more to make 10?" This activity can be done over and over until students have

mastered all the combinations to make 10. Knowing combinations that make 10 not only helps with basic facts mastery, it builds foundations for working on addition with higher numbers, as well as understanding place-value concepts.

Up Over 10

Some facts have sums greater than 10. Students use their known facts that equal 10 to solve these basic fact problems. For example, students solving 6 + 8 might start with the larger number and see that it is 2 away from 10; therefore, they take 2 from the 6 to get 10 and then add on the remaining 4 to get 14.

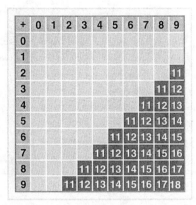

This reasoning strategy is extremely important and often not emphasized enough in U.S. textbooks or classrooms (Henry & Brown, 2008). In fact, this strategy is heavily emphasized in high-performing countries (Korea, China, Taiwan, and Japan) where students memorize facts sooner and more accurately than U.S. students. A recent study of California first graders found that the Make 10 strategy contributed more to memorizing over-10 facts (e.g., 7 + 8) than using doubles (even though using doubles had been emphasized by teachers and textbooks in the study). Also, notice how many of the basic addition facts can be solved using the Make 10 strategy. Moreover, this strategy can be later applied to adding up over 20 or 50 or other benchmark numbers. Thus, this reasoning strategy deserves significant attention in teaching addition (and subtraction) facts.

Activity 10.6

Move to Make 10

Adapt Activity 10.4 by asking students to visualize moving counters to fill one of the ten-frames to figure out how many. After students have found a total, have students share and record the equations. Alternatively, start with the equation and have students visualize "making 10" and then tell the answer. See Blackline Master 11.

Activity 10.7

Make 10 on the Ten-Frame

Give students a mat with two ten-frames. Flash cards are placed next to the ten-frames, or a fact can be given orally. The students model each number in the two ten-frames and then decide on the easiest way to find the total without counting. Get students to explain what they did. Focus especially on the idea that counters can be taken from one of the frames and moved to the other frame to make 10. Then you have 10 and whatever is left. See Blackline Master 11.

Activity 10.8

Frames and Facts

Use the little ten-frame cards (Blackline Masters 15 and 16). Make a transparency set for the overhead. Show an 8 (or 9) card on the overhead. Place other cards beneath it one at a time as students respond with the total. Have students say orally what they are doing. For 8 + 4, they might say, "Take 2 from the 4 and put it with 8 to make 10. Then 10 and 2 left over is 12." Move to harder cards, like 7 + 6. The activity can be done independently with the little ten-frame cards. Ask students to record each equation, as shown in Figure 10.4.

Frames and Facts

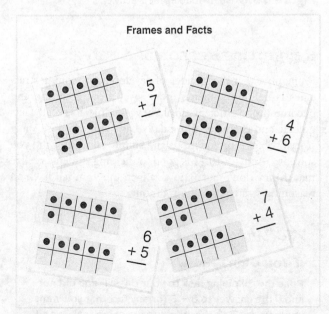

Figure 10.4 Frames and facts activity.

Doubles

There are ten doubles facts from 0 + 0 to 9 + 9, as shown here. Students often know doubles, perhaps because of their rhythmic nature. These factors can be anchors for other facts.

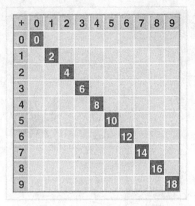

Activity 10.9

Double Images

Have students make picture cards for each of the doubles and include the basic fact on the card as shown in Figure 10.5.

Word problems can focus on pairs of like addends. *Alex and Zack each found 7 seashells at the beach. How many did they find together?*

A simple "doubling machine" can be drawn on the board or created from a shoe box. Cards are made with an "input number" on the front side and the double of the number on the reverse. The card is flipped front to back as it goes "through" the double machine. A pair of students or a small group can use input/output machines, with one student flipping the card and the other(s) stating the fact.

Activity 10.10

Calculator Doubles

Use the calculator and enter the "double maker" (2 ×). Let one child say, for example, "Seven plus seven." The child with the calculator should press 7, try to give the double (14), and then press = to see the correct double on the display. (Note that the calculator is also a good way to practice +1 and +2 facts.)

Near-Doubles

Near-doubles are also called the "doubles-plus-one" or "doubles-minus-one" facts and include all combinations

Figure 10.5 Doubles facts.

where one addend is one more or less than the other. This is a strategy that uses a known fact to generate an unknown fact. The strategy is to double the smaller number and add 1. Be sure students know the doubles before you focus on this strategy.

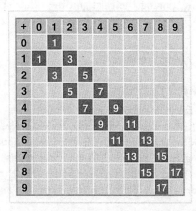

In addition to story problems involving near-doubles, you can introduce the strategy to the class by writing about ten near-doubles facts on the board. Use vertical and horizontal formats and vary which addend is the smaller.

Have students work independently to write the answers. Then discuss their ideas for "good" (that is, efficient) strategies of answering these facts. Some may double the smaller number and add one and others may double the larger and subtract. If no one uses a near-double strategy, write the corresponding doubles for some of the facts and ask how these facts could help.

Activity 10.11

On the Double

Create an activity board (on the board or on paper) that illustrates the doubles (see Figure 10.6). Prepare cards with near-doubles (e.g., 4 + 5). Ask students to find the fact that could help them solve the fact they have on the card and place it on that spot. Ask students if there are other doubles that could help.

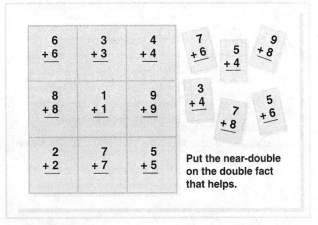

Figure 10.6 Near-doubles facts activity.

Reinforcing Reasoning Strategies

Remember that the big idea of developing reasoning strategies is helping students move away from counting and become more efficient until they are able to recall facts quickly and correctly. On a daily basis you can pose short story problems or equations and simply ask, "How did you solve it?" Activity 10.12 is good for helping students realize that if they don't "just know" a fact, they can fall back on reasoning strategies to figure it out.

Activity 10.12

If You Didn't Know

Pose the following task to your class: If you did not know the answer to 8 + 5 (or any fact that you want students to think about), what are some really good ways to get the answer? Explain that "really good" means that you don't have to count and you can do it in your head. Encourage students to come up with more than one way. Use a think-pair-share approach in which students discuss their ideas with a partner before they share them with the class.

 Many students will have latched on to counting strategies for addition facts. Often these children become so adept at counting that you may not be aware that they are doing so. Speed in counting is not a substitute for fact mastery. It is useful to find out just how your students are thinking when they respond to facts. This may require a short diagnostic interview that includes fact groups you think the student may not have mastered. Once the student records or states the answer, say "Tell me how you were thinking to get this answer." ◆

Pause and Reflect

Many of the addition facts lend themselves to a variety of different reasoning strategies. What strategies might students use to get the answer to 8 + 6? Name at least three.

Reasoning Strategies for Subtraction Facts

Subtraction facts prove to be more difficult than addition. This is especially true when children have been taught subtraction through a "count-count-count" approach; for 13 − 5, *count* 13, *count* off 5, *count* what's left. As discussed earlier in the chapter, counting is a very early step in reaching basic fact mastery. Figure 10.1 at the beginning of the chapter lists the ways students might subtract, from counting to mastery. Without opportunities to learn and use reasoning strategies, students may continue to rely on counting strategies to come up with subtraction facts, a slow and often inaccurate approach.

myeducationlab

Go to the Activities and Application section of Chapter 10 of MyEducationLab. Click on Videos and watch the video entitled "**John Van de Walle on Reasoning Strategies for Subtraction Facts**" to see him talk with teachers about strategies for subtraction.

Subtraction as Think-Addition

In Figure 10.7, subtraction is modeled in such a way that students are encouraged to think, "What goes with this part to make the total?" When done in this *think-addition* manner, the child uses known addition facts to produce the unknown quantity or part. (You might want to revisit the discussion of missing-part activities in Chapter 8 and part-part-whole subtraction concepts in Chapter 9.) If this important relationship between parts and wholes—between addition and subtraction—can be made, subtraction facts will be much easier. Like with addition facts, it is helpful to begin with the facts that have totals of 10 or less (e.g., 8 − 3, 9 − 7) before working on facts that have a total (minuend) higher than 10 (e.g., 13 − 4).

When children see 9 − 4, you want them to think spontaneously, "Four and *what* makes nine?" By contrast, consider a third-grade child who struggles with this fact. The idea of thinking addition never occurs. Instead, the child will begin to count either back from 9 or up from 4. The value of think-addition cannot be overstated.

However, if think-addition is to be used effectively, it is essential that addition facts be mastered first. Evidence suggests that children learn very few, if any, subtraction facts without first mastering the corresponding addition facts. In other words, mastery of 3 + 5 can be thought of as prerequisite knowledge for learning the facts 8 − 3 and 8 − 5.

Story problems that promote think-addition are those that sound like addition but have a missing addend: *join, initial part unknown; join, change unknown;* and *part-part-whole, part unknown* (see Chapter 9). Consider this problem: *Janice had 5 fish in her aquarium. Grandma gave her some more fish. Then she had 12 fish. How many fish did Grandma give Janice?* Notice that the action is join and, thus, suggests addition. There is a high probability that students will think *5 and how many more makes 12.* In the discussion in which you use problems such as this, your task is to connect this thought process with the subtraction fact, 12 − 5.

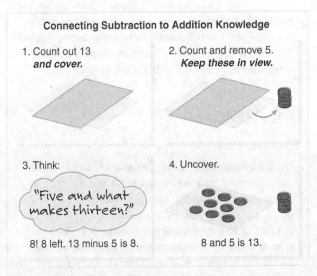

Figure 10.7 Using a think-addition model for subtraction.

Down Over 10

⏸ ——————— *Pause and Reflect*

Before reading further, look at the three subtraction facts shown here, and try to reflect on what thought process you use to get the answers. Even if you "just know them," think about what a likely process might be.

$$14 \qquad 12 \qquad 15$$
$$-9 \qquad -6 \qquad -6$$

You may have applied a think-addition strategy to any of these. For example, on the first problem counting from 9 up 1 to 10 and then 4 more to 14 for a difference of 5. If you instead started with the 14 and counted down, perhaps reasoning that it is 4 down to 10 and then down 1 more to get to 9, so a total difference of 5, then you used a reasoning strategy called Down-Over-10. If you didn't already use this strategy, try it with the other two examples.

This reasoning strategy is a derived fact strategy, as students use what they know (that 14 minus 4 is 10) to figure out a related fact (14 – 5). Like the Make 10 strategy discussed in addition facts, this strategy is one emphasized in high-performing countries (Fuson & Kwon, 1992). This strategy shows great promise for helping students move to mastery while supporting their number sense, yet it does not receive the attention in U.S. textbooks and classrooms that it should.

Activity 10.13

Apples in the Trees

Place a double ten-frame transparency on the overhead (or an interactive whiteboard) with chips covering the first ten-frame and some of the second (e.g., for 16, cover 10 in the first frame and 6 on the second frame). Tell students some apples have fallen to the ground—you will tell them how many and they will tell you how many are still in the trees. Repeat activity often and as needed. See Blackline Master 11.

Activity 10.14

Subtract to 10

On the board write five or six pairs of facts in which the difference for the first fact is 10 and the second fact is either 8 or 9: for example, 16 – 6 and 16 – 7 or 14 – 4 and 14 – 6. Have students complete all of the facts and then discuss their strategies. The idea is to connect the two facts in each pair. The second fact is either one or two less than 10. On a subsequent day repeat the activity without using the facts

that equal 10—for example, the following story problem:

> **Becky had 16 cents. She spent 7 cents to buy a small toy. How much money does she have left?**

Take from the 10

This strategy is not well known or used in the United States but is consistently used in high-performing countries. It also takes advantage of students' knowledge of the combinations that make 10. It works for all subtraction problems where the starting value (minuend) is over 10. For example, take the problem 16 – 8. Students take the minuend apart into 10 + 6. Subtracting from the 10 (because they know this fact), 10 – 8 is 2. Then they add the 6 back on to get 8. Try it on these examples:

$$15 - 8 = \qquad 17 - 9 = \qquad 14 - 8 =$$

You can see that while this may seem unusual at first, it is a great reasoning strategy. It can be used for all the subtraction facts having minuends greater than 10 (the "toughies") by just knowing how to subtract from 10 and knowing addition facts with sums less than 10.

Activity 10.15

Apples in Two Trees

Adapting Activity 10.13, explain that each ten-frame is a different tree. Tell students you will tell them how many apples fall out of the "full" tree and they will tell you how many apples are left (on both trees). Each time ask students to explain their thinking.

Activity 10.16

Missing-Number Cards

Show students families of numbers with the sum circled as in Figure 10.8(a). Ask why they think the numbers go together and why one number is circled. When this number family idea is understood, draw a different card and cover one of the numbers with your thumb, saying, "What's missing?" Ask students how they figured it out. After modeling, students can do this with partners. Alternatively, you can create cards with one number replaced by a question mark, as in Figure 10.8(b).

When students understand this activity, explain that you have made some missing-number cards based on this idea, as in Figure 10.8(c). Ask students to name the missing number and explain their thinking.

As a follow-up to Activity 10.16 students can complete "cards" on a missing-number handout. Make copies of the

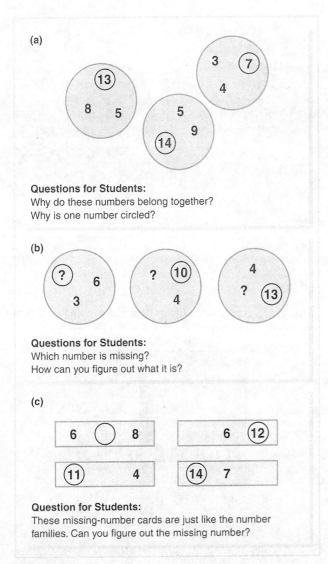

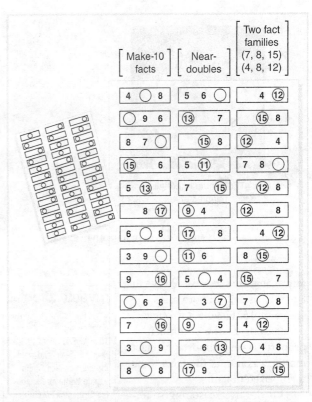

Figure 10.9 Missing-number handouts. The blank version can be used to fill in any sets of facts you wish to emphasize (see Blackline Master 13). Labels (in brackets) are not included on student pages.

able to give the missing part in a family but do not connect this knowledge with subtraction.

Teachers often ask when students should have mastered the addition and subtraction facts. According to the *Curriculum Focal Points*, in grade 2 students will develop, "quick recall of addition facts and related subtraction facts" (p. 14). ◆

Figure 10.8 Introducing missing-number cards.

Missing Part worksheet found in Blackline Master 13 to make a wide variety of drill exercises. In a column of 13 "cards," put all of the combinations from two families with different numbers missing, some parts and some wholes. Put blanks in different positions. An example is shown in Figure 10.9. After filling in numbers, make copies and have students fill in the missing numbers. Another idea is to group facts from one strategy or number relation or perhaps mix facts from two strategies on one page. Remember to let students select the strategy they want to use. Have students write an addition fact and a subtraction fact to go with each missing-number card. This is an important step because many children are

myeducationlab

Go to the Building Teaching Skills and Dispositions section of Chapter 10 of MyEducationLab. Click on Expanded Lessons to download the Expanded Lesson for "**Missing Number Cards**" and complete the related activities.

Reasoning Strategies for Multiplication Facts

Multiplication facts can also be mastered by relating new facts to existing knowledge. Using a problem-based approach and focusing on reasoning strategies is just as important, if not more so, for developing mastery of the multiplication and related division facts (Baroody, 2006; Wallace & Gurganus, 2005). As with addition and subtraction facts, you should use story problems throughout your work on different reasoning strategies.

It is imperative that students completely understand the commutative property (see page 160 and Figure 9.12). This can be visualized by using arrays. For example a 2-by-8

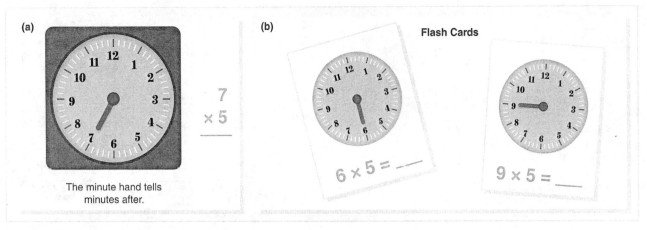

Figure 10.10 Using clocks to help learn fives facts.

array can be described as 2 rows of 8 or 8 rows of 2. In both cases, the answer is 16. Having a strong understanding of the commutative property is very important in fact mastery, as it cuts the facts to be memorized in half.

Of the five reasoning strategies discussed next, the first four are generally easier and cover 75 of the 100 multiplication facts. These strategies are suggestions, not rules, and the instructional approach is to have students discuss ways that *they* use reasoning strategies to determine the basic facts.

myeducationlab

Go to the Activities and Application section of Chapter 10 of MyEducationLab. Click on Videos and watch the video entitled **"John Van de Walle on Reasoning Strategies for Multiplication"** to see him talk with teachers about strategies for multiplication.

Doubles

Facts that have 2 as a factor are equivalent to the addition doubles and should already be known by students who know their addition facts. Help students realize that not only is 2 × 7 double 7, but so is 7 × 2. Try word problems where 2 is the number of sets. Later use problems where 2 is the size of the sets. *George was making sock puppets. Each puppet needed 2 buttons for eyes. If George makes 7 puppets, how many buttons will he need for the eyes?*

×	0	1	2	3	4	5	6	7	8	9
0			0							
1			2							
2	0	2	4	6	8	10	12	14	16	18
3			6							
4			8							
5			10							
6			12							
7			14							
8			16							
9			18							

Fives

This group consists of all facts with 5 as the first or second factor, as shown here.

×	0	1	2	3	4	5	6	7	8	9
0						0				
1						5				
2						10				
3						15				
4						20				
5	0	5	10	15	20	25	30	35	40	45
6						30				
7						35				
8						40				
9						45				

Practice skip counting by fives to at least 45. Connect counting by fives with arrays that have rows of five dots. Point out that such an array with six rows is a model for 6 × 5, eight rows is 8 × 5, and so on.

Activity 10.17

Clock Facts

Focus on the minute hand of the clock. When it points to a number, how many minutes after the hour is it? See Figure 10.10(a). Connect this idea to the multiplication facts with 5. Hold up a flash card as in Figure 10.10(b) and then point to the number on the clock corresponding to the other factor. In this way, the fives facts become the "clock facts."

Zeros and Ones

Thirty-six facts have at least one factor that is either 0 or 1. These facts, though apparently easy, tend to get confused with "rules" that some children learned for addition. The fact 6 + 0 stays the same, but 6 × 0 is always zero. The 1 + 4 fact is a one-more idea, but 1 × 4 stays the same. The concepts behind these facts can be developed best through story problems. Alternatively, ask students to put words to the equations. For example, say that 6 × 0 is six groups with zero in them (or six rows of chairs with no people in each). For 0 × 6, there are six in the group, but you have zero groups. For example, you worked 0 hours babysitting at $6 an hour. Avoid rules that sound arbitrary and without reason such as "Any number multiplied by zero is zero."

×	0	1	2	3	4	5	6	7	8	9
0	0	0	0	0	0	0	0	0	0	0
1	0	1	2	3	4	5	6	7	8	9
2	0	2								
3	0	3								
4	0	4								
5	0	5								
6	0	6								
7	0	7								
8	0	8								
9	0	9								

Nifty Nines

Facts with a factor of 9 include the largest products but can be among the easiest to learn. The table of nines facts includes some nice patterns that are fun to discover. Two of these patterns are useful for mastering the nines: (1) The tens digit of the product is always one less than the "other" factor (the one other than 9), and (2) the sum of the two digits in the product is always 9. These two ideas can be used together to get any nine fact quickly. For 7 × 9, *1 less than 7 is 6, 6 and 3 make 9, so the answer is 63.*

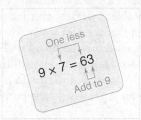

×	0	1	2	3	4	5	6	7	8	9
0										0
1										9
2										18
3										27
4										36
5										45
6										54
7										63
8										72
9	0	9	18	27	36	45	54	63	72	81

Children are not likely to invent this strategy simply by solving word problems involving a factor of 9. Therefore, consider building a lesson around the following task.

Activity 10.18

Patterns in the Nines Facts

In column form, write the nines table on the board (9 × 1 = 9, 9 × 2 = 18, . . . , 9 × 9 = 81). The task is to find as many patterns as possible in the table. (Do not ask students to think of a strategy.) As you listen to the students work on this task, be sure that somewhere in the class the two patterns necessary for the strategy have been found. After discussing all the patterns, a follow-up task is to use the patterns to think of a clever way to figure out a nines fact if you didn't know it. (Note that even for students who know their nines facts, this remains a valid task.)

Once children have invented a strategy for the nines, a tactile way to help students remember the nifty nines is to use fingers—but not for counting. Here's how: Hold up both hands. Starting with the pinky on your left hand, count over for which fact you are doing. For example, for 4 × 9, you move to the fourth finger (your pointer). Bend it down. Look at your fingers: You have three to the left of the folded finger representing 3 tens and six to the right—36! (Barney, 1970). See Figure 10.11.

Warning: Although the nines strategy can be quite successful, it also can cause confusion. Because two steps are involved and a conceptual connection is not apparent, children may confuse the two steps or attempt to apply the idea to other facts. It is not, however, a "rule without reason." It is an idea based on a very interesting pattern that exists in the base-ten numeration system. In fact, you can challenge students to think about why this pattern exists.

An alternative strategy for the nines is almost as easy to use. Notice that 7 × 9 is the same as 7 × 10 less one set of 7,

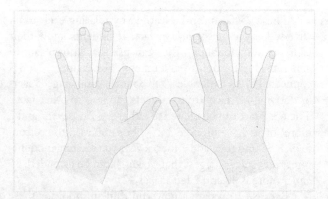

Figure 10.11 Nifty nines using fingers to show 4 × 9.

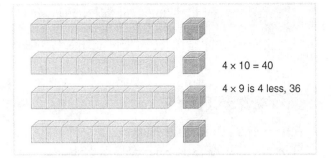

Figure 10.12 Using tens to think of the nines.

or 70 – 7. For students who can easily subtract 6 from 60, 7 from 70, and so on, this strategy may be preferable.

You might introduce this idea by showing a set of bars such as those in Figure 10.12 with only the end cube a different color. After explaining that every bar has ten cubes, ask students if they can think of a good way to figure out how many are yellow.

Using Known Facts to Derive Other Facts

The following chart shows the remaining 25 multiplication facts. It is worth pointing out to children that there are actually only 15 facts remaining to master because 20 of them consist of 10 pairs of turnarounds.

×	0	1	2	3	4	5	6	7	8	9
0										
1										
2										
3				9	12			18	21	24
4				12	16			24	28	32
5										
6				18	24			36	42	48
7				21	28			42	49	56
8				24	32			48	56	64
9										

These 25 facts can be learned by relating each to an already known fact or *helping* fact. If students know their facts for × 2 (doubling), they can use that known fact to generate facts for times 3 and times 4. For example, 3 × 8 is connected to 2 × 8 (double 8 and 8 more). Knowing × 5 facts or deriving × 3 facts from × 2 facts can lead to other facts. The 6 × 7 fact can be related to either 5 × 7 (5 sevens and 7 more) or to 3 × 7 (double 3 × 7). For example, to go from 5 × 7 is 35 and then add 7 for 6 × 7. If you see finger counting at that stage, suggest that Make 10 can be extended: 35 and 5 more is 40 and 2 left makes 42.

Because arrays are a powerful thinking tool for these strategies, provide students with copies of the ten-by-ten dot

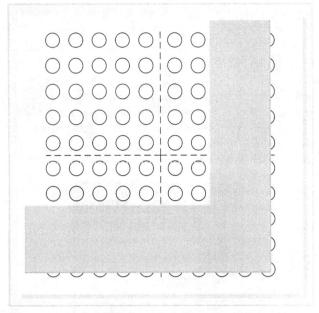

Figure 10.13 An array is a useful model for developing strategies for the hard multiplication facts (see Blackline Master 12).

array (Figure 10.13; also Blackline Master 12). A tagboard *L* (shaded area) is used to outline arrays for specific products. The lines in the array make counting the dots easier and often suggest the use of the easier fives facts as helpers. For example, 7 × 7 is 5 × 7 plus double 7, or 35 + 14.

How to find a helping fact that is useful varies with different facts and sometimes depends on which factor you focus on. Figure 10.14 illustrates models for four overlapping groups of facts and the thought process associated with each.

The *double and double again* strategy shown in Figure 10.14(a) is applicable to all facts with 4 as one of the factors. Remind children that the idea works when 4 is the second factor as well as when it is the first. For 4 × 8, double 16 is also a difficult fact. Help children with this by noting, for example, that 15 + 15 is 30, and 16 + 16 is two more, or 32. Adding 16 + 16 on paper defeats the purpose.

The *double and one more set* strategy shown in Figure 10.14(b) is a way to think of facts with one factor of 3. With an array or a set picture, the double part can be circled, and it is clear that there is one more set. Two facts in this group involve more difficult mental additions (8 × 3 and 9 × 3).

If either factor is even, a *half then double* strategy as shown in Figure 10.14(c) can be used. Select the even factor, and cut it in half. If the smaller fact is known, that product is doubled to get the new fact.

Many children prefer to go to a fact that is "close" and then *add one more set* to this known fact as shown in Figure 10.14(d). For example, think of 6 × 7 as 6 sevens. Five sevens is close: That's 35. Six sevens is one more seven, or 42. When using 5 × 8 to help with 6 × 8, the set language "6

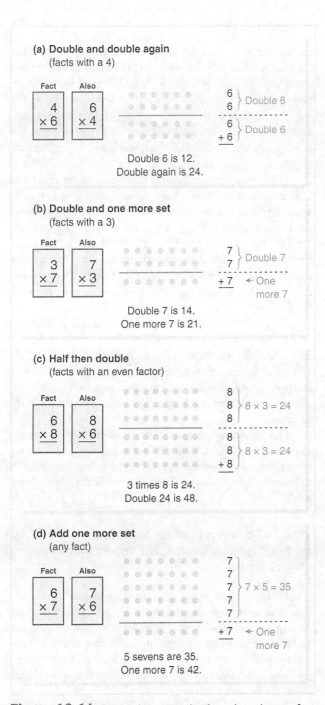

Figure 10.14 Reasoning strategies for using a known fact to derive an unknown fact.

eights" is very helpful in remembering to add 8 more and not 6 more. This "close" fact reasoning strategy is critically important. First, it has no limits—it can be used for any fact. Second, it reinforces students' sense of number and of relationships among numbers. Asking students if they know a nearby fact to derive the new fact over time will become an automatic mental process for students. In fact, many adults use this strategy for the particularly difficult facts. The mental process goes something like this: "What

is seven times eight? Oh, that's 49 and 7 more—56." Similarly, students may use 5 facts to generate 4 and 6 facts.

The relationships between easy and hard facts are fertile ground for good problem-based tasks. Say to students, "If you didn't know what 6 × 8 is, how could you figure it out by using something that you do know?" Students should be challenged to find as many ways as possible to answer a hard multiplication fact.

Pause and Reflect

Select what you consider a "hard fact" and see how many of the reasoning strategies in Figure 10.14 you can use to derive the fact.

Word problems can also be structured to prompt a strategy. *Carlos and Jose kept their baseball cards in albums with 6 cards on each page. Carlos had 4 pages filled, and Jose had 8 pages filled. How many cards did each boy have?* (Do you see the half-then-double strategy?)

It should be clear that the array plays a large part in helping students establish multiplication facts and relationships. In both third and fourth grades, the *Investigations in Number, Data, and Space* curriculum places a significant emphasis on arrays. They are used to help with multiplication facts, the relationship between multiplication and division, and in the development of computational procedures for multiplication.

Division Facts and "Near Facts"

An interesting question to ask is, "When children are working on a page of division facts, are they practicing division or multiplication?" There is undoubtedly some value in limited practice of division facts. However, mastery of multiplication facts and connections between multiplication and division are the key elements of division fact mastery. Word problems continue to be a key vehicle to create this connection.

Pause and Reflect

What thought process do you use to recall facts such as 48 ÷ 6 or 36 ÷ 9?

If we are trying to think of 36 ÷ 9, we tend to think, "Nine times what is thirty-six?" For most, 42 ÷ 6 is not a separate fact but is closely tied to 6 × 7. (Would it not be wonderful if subtraction were so closely related to addition? It can be!)

Exercises such as 50 ÷ 6 might be called "near facts." Divisions that do not result in a whole number are much more prevalent in computations and in real situations than those that do. To determine the answer to $50 \div 6$, most people run through a short sequence of the multiplication facts, comparing each product to 50: "6 times 7 (low), 6 times 8 (close), 6 times 9 (high). Must be 8. That's 48 and 2 left over." Children should be able to do problems with one-digit divisors and one-digit answers with remainders mentally and with reasonable speed.

Activity 10.19

How Close Can You Get?

As illustrated below, the idea is to find the one-digit factor that makes the product as close as possible to the target without going over. Help children develop the process of going through the multiplication facts that were just described. This can be a whole class activity by preparing a list for the overhead or Power-Point, or it can be a partner or individual written task.

> Find the largest factor without going over the target number.

$4 \times \boxed{} \longrightarrow 23, \boxed{}$ left over

$7 \times \boxed{} \longrightarrow 52, \boxed{}$ left over

$6 \times \boxed{} \longrightarrow 27, \boxed{}$ left over

$9 \times \boxed{} \longrightarrow 60, \boxed{}$ left over

NCTM Standards What does the *Standards* document tell us about multiplication and division facts? "Through skip-counting, using area models, and relating unknown combinations to known ones, students will learn and become fluent with unfamiliar combinations [multiplication facts]. . . . If by the end of the fourth grade, students are not able to use multiplication and division strategies efficiently, then they must either develop strategies so that they are fluent with these combinations or memorize the 'harder' combinations" (p. 153). ◆

Mastering the Basic Facts

There is little doubt that strategy development and general number sense (number relationships and operation meanings) are the best contributors to fact mastery. Drill in the absence of these factors has repeatedly been demonstrated as ineffective. However, drill strengthens memory and retrieval capabilities (Ashcraft & Christy, 1995).

Effective Drill

Drill—repetitive non-problem-based activity—is appropriate for children who have a strategy that they understand and know how to use, but with which they have not yet become facile. Drill with an in-place strategy focuses students' attention on that strategy and helps to make it more automatic. Drill plays a significant role in fact mastery, and the use of methods such as flash cards and fact games can be effective if used wisely.

When you are comfortable that children are able to use a strategy and are beginning to use it mentally, it may be appropriate to create drill activities for special groupings of facts. You might have as many as ten different activities for each strategy or group of facts. File folders or boxed activities can be used by children individually, in pairs, or even in small groups. With a large number of activities, children can work on strategies they understand and on the facts that they need the most.

Flash cards are among the most useful approaches to fact strategy practice. For each strategy or related group of facts, make several sets of flash cards using all of the facts that fit that strategy. On the cards, you can label the strategy or use drawings or cues to remind the children of the strategy. Several such examples have been shown in this chapter.

Drill is appropriate only after students have developed reasoning strategies. Drill can help students move to mastery, but it can also interfere. Therefore, it is important to be aware of methods you should use and others you should avoid.

What to Do When Teaching Basic Facts. The following list of recommendations can support the development of quick recall.

1. *Ask students to self-monitor.* The importance of this recommendation cannot be overstated. Across all learning, having a sense of what you don't know and what you need to learn is important. It certainly holds true with memorizing facts. Students should be able to identify their "toughies" and continue to work on reasoning strategies to help them derive those facts.

2. *Focus on self-improvement.* This point follows from self-monitoring. If you are working on improving students' quickness at recalling facts, then the only persons the students should be competing with are themselves. Students can keep track of how long it took them to go through their "four stack" for example, and then, two days later, pull the same stack and see if they are quicker (or more accurate) than the last time.

3. *Drill in short time segments.* You can flash numerous examples on a transparency of double ten-frames in relatively little time. Or you can do a story problem a day—taking five minutes to share strategies. You can also have

each student pull a set of flash cards from storage, pair with another student, and go through each other's set in two minutes. Long periods (ten minutes or more) are not effective. Using the first five to ten minutes of the day, or extra time just before lunch, can provide continued support on fact development without taking up mathematics instructional time better devoted to other topics.

4. *Work on facts over time.* Rather than do a unit on fact memorization, work on facts over months and months, working on reasoning strategies and then on memorization, and then continued review and monitoring.

5. *Involve families.* Share the big plan of how you will work on learning facts over the year. One idea is to let parents or guardians know that during the second semester of second grade (or fourth grade), for example, you will have one or two "Take Home Facts of the Week." Ask family members to help students by using reasoning strategies when they don't know a fact.

6. *Make drill enjoyable.* There are many games designed to reinforce facts that are not competitive or anxiety inducing, as shown in the following activity.

Activity 10.20

Salute!

Place students in groups of three and give each group a deck of cards (without face cards and using aces as 1s). Two of the students draw a card without looking at it and place it on their forehead facing out (so the other two can see it). The student with no card tells the sum (or product). The first of the other two to correctly say what number is on their forehead "wins" the card set. Competition can be removed by having each student write down the card they think they have (within five seconds) and getting a point if they are correct.

7. *Use technology.* When students work on the computer or with the calculator they get immediate feedback and reinforcement, helping them to self-monitor. See the Tech Note below and the websites listed at the end of this chapter for ideas.

8. *Emphasize the importance of quick recall of facts.* Without trying to create pressure or anxiety, emphasize to students that in real life and in the rest of mathematics they will be recalling these facts all the time—they really must learn them and learn them well. Celebrate student successes.

 There are literally hundreds of software programs that offer drill of basic facts. Nearly all fact programs offer games or exercises at various difficulty levels. Unfortunately, there do not seem to be any programs that emphasize strategy development. It should be clear that computerized fact practice should be used only after students have developed reasoning strategies.

One good example of available software is *FASTT Math* (Tom Snyder Productions software, *not* free). This is a diagnostic tool with ongoing assessment. The program is student paced, provides "self-progress tracking," and includes practice games. See www.tomsnyder.com/products/product.asp?SKU=FASFAS.

In *Math Munchers Deluxe* (Riverdeep Interactive Learning, 2005), students move their muncher in a three-dimensional grid format. By answering questions, they can avoid six Troggles that chase the muncher and try to eat it. *Math Munchers* encourages speed and is highly motivating. It is aimed at grades 3 to 6.

Another popular program is *Math Blaster* (Knowledge Adventure), which promotes speed through an arcade format. Like most programs, *Math Blaster* includes drills for more than just facts, including multidigit computation, decimals, fractions, percents, estimation, and other topics, all in the same format. ◆

What Not to Do When Teaching Basic Facts. The following list shows some strategies that may have been designed with good intentions but work against student memorization of the basic facts.

1. *Don't use lengthy timed tests.* Students get distracted by the pressure and abandon their reasoning strategies. If they miss some, they don't get the chance to see which ones they are having trouble with, so the assessment doesn't help them move forward. Students develop anxiety, which works against learning mathematics. Having students self-monitor the time it takes them to go through a small set of facts can help with their speed.

2. *Don't use public comparisons of mastery.* You may have experienced the bulletin board that shows which students are on which step of a staircase to mastering their multiplication facts. Imagine how the student who is on the third step feels when others are on step 6. It is great to celebrate student successes, but avoid comparisons among students.

3. *Don't proceed through facts in order from 0 to 9.* It is better to work on collections based on the strategies and to "knock out" those that students know rather than proceed in a rigid fashion by going in order. In reality, the more that facts are mixed up, the more likely it is that students will rely on their reasoning strategies and number sense and not forget the facts mastered last week.

4. *Don't move to memorization too soon.* This has been addressed throughout the chapter, but is worth repeating. Quick recall or mastery can be obtained only after students are ready—meaning they have a robust collection of reasoning strategies to apply as needed.

5. *Don't use facts as a barrier to good mathematics.* Students who have total command of basic facts do not necessarily *reason better* than those who, for whatever reason, have not yet mastered facts. Today, mathematics is not solely about computation, especially pencil-and-paper computation. Mathematics is about reasoning and patterns and making sense of things. Mathematics is problem solving. There is no reason that a child who has not yet mastered all basic facts should be excluded from real mathematical experiences.

If there is any purpose for a timed test of basic facts it may be for diagnosis—to determine which combinations are mastered and which remain to be learned. Even for diagnostic purposes timed tests should only occur once every couple of weeks. ◆

Fact Remediation

Students who have not mastered their basic facts by the fifth or sixth grade are in need of something other than more drill. They have certainly seen and practiced facts countless times in previous grades and yet not remembered them. There is no reason to believe that the drills *you* provide will somehow be more effective than last year's. These students need something better. The following key ideas can guide your efforts to help these older students.

1. *Recognize that more drill will not work.* Students' fact difficulties are due to a failure to develop or to connect concepts and relationships such as those that have been discussed in this chapter, not a lack of drill. At best, more drill will provide temporary results. At worst, it will cause negative attitudes about mathematics.

2. *Provide hope.* Students who have experienced difficulty with fact mastery often believe that they cannot learn facts or that they are doomed to finger counting forever. Let these children know that you will help them and that you will provide some new strategies that will help them as well.

3. *Inventory the known and unknown facts for each student in need.* Find out from each student which facts are known quickly and comfortably and which are not. Fifth-grade or older students can do this diagnosis for you. Provide sheets of all facts for one operation in random order, and have the students circle the facts they are hesitant about and answer all others. To achieve an honest assessment, emphasize that you need this information so that you can help the student.

4. *Diagnose strengths and weaknesses.* Observe what students do when they encounter one of their unknown facts. Do they count on their fingers? Add up numbers in the margins? Guess? Try to use a related fact? Write down times tables? Are they able to use any of the helpful relationships suggested in this chapter?

You can conduct a ten-minute diagnostic interview with each student in need. Simply pose unknown facts and ask the student how he or she approaches them. Don't try to teach; just find out. Again, students can provide some of this information by writing about what they do when they don't know a fact.

5. *Focus on reasoning strategies.* Using a problem-solving strategy to focus on fact mastery is very effective (Baroody, 2006; Crespoki, Kyriakides, & McGee, 2005). Because students will likely be working alone or with a small group in this remediation program, they will not have the benefit of class discussion nor the time required over weeks and months to develop their own strategies. Therefore, with these students it is reasonable to share with them strategies that you "have seen other students use." Be certain that they have a conceptual understanding of the strategy and are able to use it.

6. *Build in success.* As you begin a well-designed fact program for a child who has experienced failure, be sure that successes come quickly and easily. Begin with easier and more useful reasoning strategies like "Up Over 10" for addition. Success builds success! With strategies as an added assist, success comes even more quickly. Point out to students how one idea, one strategy, is all that is required to learn many facts. Use fact charts to show the set of facts you are working on. It is surprising how the chart quickly fills up with mastered facts. Keep reviewing newly learned facts and those that were already known.

7. *Provide engaging activities for drill.* See Activity 10.20 as one idea of drill that has an element of fun. The following activity integrates all four operations.

Activity 10.21

Bowl a Fact

In this activity, you draw circles placed in triangular fashion to look like bowling pins, with the front circle labeled 1 and the next labeled consecutively through 10.

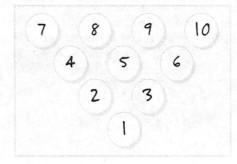

Take three dice and roll them. Students use the three dice to come up with equations that result in answers that are on the pins. For example, if you roll 4, 2, and 3, they can get 5 by 4 × 2 − 3, thereby "knocking down" that "pin." If they can produce equations to knock down all ten pins, they get a strike. If not, roll again and see if they can knock the rest down for a spare. After doing this with the whole class, students can work in small groups. (Shoecraft, 1982)

Your extra effort beyond class time can be a motivation to a student to make some personal effort on his or her own time. During class, these students should continue to work with all students on the regular curriculum. You must believe and communicate to these students that the reason they have not mastered basic facts is not a reflection of their ability. With efficient strategies and individual effort, success will come. Believe!

Reflections on Chapter 10

Writing to Learn

1. Describe advantages of a developmental approach to helping students master basic facts.
2. For the fact 8 + 6 list at least three reasoning strategies that a student might use.
3. What is meant by subtraction as "think-addition"? How can you help children develop a think-addition thought pattern for subtraction?
4. Give an example of a story problem that would promote a think-addition strategy for subtraction facts.
5. For the multiplication fact 6 × 7 describe three reasoning strategies a student might use.
6. Describe how to use drill effectively.
7. Describe positive and negative ways to use timed tests for basic fact mastery.
8. Describe three key ideas you will use in working with students to remediate basic fact mastery.

For Discussion and Exploration

1. Explore a Web-based or software program for drilling basic facts. What features does your program have that are good? Not so good? How would you use such software in a classroom with only one or two available computers?
2. One view of thinking strategies is that they are little more than a collection of tricks for kids to memorize. Discuss the question, "Is teaching children thinking strategies for basic fact mastery in keeping with a constructivist view of teaching mathematics?"
3. Assume you are teaching a grade that expects mastery of facts (grade 2 for addition and subtraction or grade 4 for multiplication and division). How will you design fact mastery across the semester or year? Include timing, strategy development, involvement of families, and so forth.

Resources for Chapter 10

Literature Connections

The children's books described in Chapters 8 and 9 are also good choices when working on the basic facts. In addition to those, consider these opportunities to develop and practice basic facts.

One Less Fish *Toft, 1998*

This beautiful book with an important environmental message starts with 12 fish and counts back to zero fish. On a page with eight fish, ask, "How many fish are gone?" and "How did you figure it out?" Encourage students to use the

Down Over 10 strategy. Any counting-up or counting-back book can be used in this way!

The Twelve Days of Summer *Andrews, 2005*

You will quickly recognize the style of this book with five bumble bees, four garter snakes, three ruffed grouse, and so on. The beautiful illustrations and motions make this a wonderful book. Students can figure out how many of each item appear by the end of the book, applying multiplication facts. (For example, three ruffed grouse appear on days 3, 4, 5, and so on.)

Recommended Readings

Articles

Baroody, A. J. (2006). Why children have difficulties mastering the basic fact combinations and how to help them. *Teaching Children Mathematics, 13*(1), 22–31.
Baroody suggests that basic facts are developmental in nature and contrasts "conventional wisdom" with a number sense view. Great activities are included as exemplars.

Buchholz, L. (2004). Learning strategies for addition and subtraction facts: The road to fluency and the license to think. *Teaching Children Mathematics, 10*(7), 362–367.
A second-grade teacher explains how her students developed and named their strategies and even extended them to work with two-digit numbers. She found her "lower ability" students were very successful using reasoning strategies.

Crespo, S., Kyriakides, A. O., & McGee, S. (2005). Nothing "basic" about basic facts: Exploring addition facts with fourth graders. *Teaching Children Mathematics, 12*(2), 60–67.
This article provides evidence of the critical importance of addressing remediation through a focus on reasoning strategies and number sense.

Kamii, C., & Anderson, C. (2003). Multiplication games: How we made and used them. *Teaching Children Mathematics, 10*(3), 135–141.
Constance Kamii, a well-known constructivist, teams up with a third-grade teacher and describes a collection of games that were used to help Title I school students master multiplication facts.

Books

Fennema, E., & Carpenter, T. P. (with Levi, L., Franke, M. L., & Empson, S.) (1997). *Cognitively guided instruction: Professional development in primary mathematics.* Madison, WI: Wisconsin Center for Education Research.
The CGI program is based on the belief that students develop their own strategies for mastering the basic facts. They are helped in this process by solving well-selected story problems. Teachers listen carefully to students' emerging processes and encourage increasingly efficient methods.

Rathmell, E. C., Leutzinger, L. P., & Gabriele, A. J. (2000). *Thinking with numbers.* Cedar Falls, IA: Thinking with Numbers.
This resource is a set of small cards, each with several simple story problems. The cards are organized by strategies for each of the operations. As children solve these problems (5 minutes per day), they invent their own strategies and share them with the class.

Online Resources

Arithmetic Four
www.shodor.org/interactivate/activities/ArithmeticFour/index.html
> The game is like "Connect Four." Players must answer an arithmetic fact to be able to enter a piece of their color on the board. Operations can be selected and timer set for answering each fact.

Cross the Swamp (BBC)
www.bbc.co.uk/schools/starship/maths/crosstheswamp.shtml
> This British applet asks students to supply a missing operation (+/– or ×/÷) and a number to complete an equation (e.g., 4 __ __ = 12). There are five questions in a set, each with three levels of difficulty.

Diffy (NLVM—Applet/Game)
http://nlvm.usu.edu/en/nav/frames_asid_326_g_1_t_1.html
> Diffy is a classic mathematics puzzle that involves finding the differences of given numbers.

Let's Learn Those Facts (NCTM's Illuminations—Lessons, Grades 1–2)
http://illuminations.nctm.org/LessonDetail.aspx?id=U58
> These six lessons, including links to resources and student recording sheets, target addition facts.

Multiplication: It's in the Cards (NCTM's Illuminations—Lessons, Grades 3–5)
http://illuminations.nctm.org/LessonDetail.aspx?id=U110
> These four lessons, including links to resources and student recording sheets, use the properties of multiplication to help students master the multiplication facts. See also "Six and Seven as Factors" (NCTM's Illuminations—Lessons, Grades 3–5), two lessons on products where 6 or 7 is a factor (http://illuminations.nctm.org/LessonDetail.aspx?ID=U150).

Number Invaders
www.mathplayground.com/balloon_invaders.html
> This game is like "Space Invaders." Players choose an operation (×, ÷) and a factor, and use the space bar and arrow keys to launch the "number (product) popper."

Number Puzzles (NLVM—Applet)
http://nlvm.usu.edu/en/nav/frames_asid_157_g_3_t_1.html
> In this applet, students are required to arrange numbers on a diagram so that all numbers in a line add up to a given value.

The Product Game (NCTM's Illuminations—Lessons, Grades 3–8)
http://illuminations.nctm.org/LessonDetail.aspx?id=U100
> These four lessons use the engaging and effective games "Factor Game" and "Product Game" to help students see the relationship between products and factors.

SpeedMath Deluxe (Jefferson Lab)
http://education.jlab.org/smdeluxe/index.html
> Players are given four numbers between which they must enter one of the four operation signs so that the resulting expression equals a given number. Requires an understanding of order of operations and occasionally integers.

Field Experience Guide Connections

> FEG Expanded Lesson 9.3 provides an exploration to help students develop and build fluency in a basic facts strategy of two more or two less. Similarly, FEG Expanded Lesson 9.12 helps students notice that 7 + 7 is the same as 8 + 6—relationships that help in memorizing the basic facts.

Chapter 11

Developing Whole-Number Place-Value Concepts

A complete understanding of place value, including the extension to decimal numeration, develops across the elementary and middle grades. For whole numbers, the most critical period in this development occurs in grades pre-K to 3. As described in the 2006 *Curriculum Focal Points*, in grades K and 1 children count and are exposed to patterns in the numbers to 100. Most importantly, they begin to think about groups of ten objects as a unit. By second grade, these initial ideas of patterns and groups of ten are formally connected to our place-value system of numeration. In grades 3 and 4 children extend their understanding to numbers up to 10,000 in a variety of contexts. In fourth and fifth grades, the ideas of whole numbers are extended to decimals.

As a significant part of this development, students should begin to work at putting numbers together and taking them apart in a wide variety of ways as they solve addition and subtraction problems with two- and three-digit numbers. Children's struggles with the invention of their own methods of computation will both enhance their understanding of place value and provide a firm foundation for flexible methods of computation.

Big Ideas

1. Sets of ten (and tens of tens) can be perceived as single entities. For example, three sets of ten and two singles is a base-ten method of describing 32 single objects. This is the major principle of *base-ten* numeration.

2. The positions of digits in numbers determine what they represent and which size group they count. This is the major principle of *place-value* numeration.

3. There are patterns to the way that numbers are formed. For example, each decade has a symbolic pattern reflective of the 1-to-9 sequence.

4. The groupings of ones, tens, and hundreds can be taken apart in different ways. For example, 256 can be 1 hundred, 14 tens, and 16 ones but also 250 and 6. Decomposing and composing multidigit numbers in flexible ways is a significant skill for computation.

5. "Really big" numbers are best understood in terms of familiar real-world referents. It is difficult to conceptualize quantities as large as 1000 or more. However, the number of people that will fill the local sports arena is, for example, a meaningful concept for those who have experienced that crowd.

Mathematics Content Connections

The base-ten place-value system is the way that we communicate and represent anything that we do with whole numbers and later with decimals.

- **Whole-Number Computation and Number Sense** (Chapters 12 and 13): Flexible methods of computation including various mental methods, pencil-and-paper methods, estimation skills, and even effective use of technology depend completely on an understanding of place value. Computational strategies for addition and subtraction can and should be developed along with an understanding of place value.

- **Decimal and Percents** (Chapter 17): Whole-number place-value ideas are extended to allow for representation of the full range of rational numbers and approximations of irrational numbers.

- **Measurement** (Chapter 19): Problem-based tasks involving real measures can be used to help students structure ideas about grouping by tens. Through measures, people develop benchmarks and meaningful referents for numbers.

Pre-Base-Ten Concepts

Children know a lot about numbers with two digits (10 to 99) even as early as kindergarten. After all, most kindergartners can and should learn to count to 100 and count out sets with as many as 20 or 30 objects. They do daily calendar activities, count children in the room, turn to specified page numbers in their books, and so on. However, their understanding is quite different from yours. It is based on a one-more-than or count-by-ones approach to quantity.

Children's Pre-Base-Ten View of Numbers

Ask first- or second-grade children to count out 53 tiles, and most will be able to do so or will make only careless errors. If you watch closely, you will note that the children count out the tiles one at a time and put them into the pile with no use of any type of grouping. Have the children write the number that tells how many tiles they just counted. Most children will be able to write it. Some may write "35" instead of "53," a simple reversal.

So far, so good. Now ask the children to write the number that is 10 more than the number they just wrote. Most will begin to count, probably starting from 53. When counting on from 53, they find it necessary to keep track of the counts, probably on their fingers. Many, if not most, children in the first and early second grades will not be successful at this task, and very few will know immediately that 10 more is 63. Asking for the number that is 10 less is even more problematic.

Finally, show a large collection of cards, each with a ten-frame drawn on it. Explain that the cards each have ten spaces and that each will hold ten tiles. Demonstrate putting tiles on the cards by filling up one of the ten-frames with tiles. Now ask, "How many cards like this do you think it will take if we want to put all of these tiles [the 53 counted out] on the cards?" A response of "53" is not unusual. Other children will say they do not know, and a few will need to put the tiles on the cards to figure it out.

Count by Ones

The children just described know that there are 53 tiles "because I counted them." Writing the number and saying the number are usually done correctly, but their understanding of 53 derives from and is connected to the count by ones. Children do not easily or quickly develop a meaningful use of groups of ten to represent quantities.

> **myeducationlab**
>
> Go to the Activities and Application section of Chapter 11 of MyEducationLab. Click on Videos and watch the video entitled "**John Van de Walle on Pre-Base-Ten Concepts**" to see him talk with teachers about children's pre-base-ten view of numbers.

With minimal instruction, children can tell you that in the numeral 53, the 5 is in the tens place or that there are "3 ones." However, it is likely that this is simply a naming of the positions with little understanding. If children have been exposed to base-ten materials, they may name a rod of ten as a "ten" and a small cube as a "one." These same children, however, may not be readily able to tell how many ones are required to make a ten. It is easy to attach words to both materials and groups without realizing what the materials or symbols represent.

Children do know that 53 is "a lot" and that it's more than 47 (because you count past 47 to get to 53). They think of the "53" that they write as a single numeral. They do not know that the 5 represents five groups of ten things and the 3 three single things (Fuson, 2006). Fuson and her colleagues refer to children's pre-base-ten understanding of number as "unitary." That is, there are no groupings of ten, even though a two-digit number is associated with the quantity. They rely on unitary counts to understand quantities.

Basic Ideas of Place Value

Place-value understanding requires an integration of new and difficult-to-construct concepts of grouping by tens (the base-ten concept) with procedural knowledge of how groups are recorded in our place-value scheme, how numbers are written, and how they are spoken.

Integration of Base-Ten Groupings with Count by Ones

Recognizing that children can count out a set of 53, we want to help them see that making groupings of tens and leftovers is a way of counting that same quantity. Each of the groups in Figure 11.1 has 53 tiles. We want children to construct the idea that all of these are the same and that the sameness is clearly evident by virtue of the groupings of tens.

There is a subtle yet profound difference between two groups of children: those who know that group B is 53 because they understand the idea that five groups of 10 and 3 more is the same amount as 53 counted by ones and those who simply say, "It's 53," because they have been told that when things are grouped this way, it's called 53. The latter children may not be sure how many they will get if they count the tiles in set B by ones or if the groups were "ungrouped" how many there would then be. The children who understand will see no need to count set B by ones. They understand the "fifty-threeness" of sets A and B to be the same.

‖ ——————— *Pause and Reflect*

The ideas in the preceding paragraph are important for you to understand so that the activities discussed later will make sense. Be sure you can talk about children who do and children who do not understand place value.

Recognition of the equivalence of groups B and C is another step in children's conceptual development. Groupings with fewer than the maximum number of tens can be referred to as *equivalent groupings* or *equivalent representations*. Understanding the equivalence of B and C indicates that grouping by tens is not just a rule that is followed but that any grouping by tens, including all or some of the singles, can help tell how many. Many computational techniques are based on equivalent representations of numbers.

Role of Counting

Counting plays a key role in constructing base-ten ideas about quantity and connecting these concepts to symbols and oral names for numbers.

Children can count sets such as those in Figure 11.1 in three different ways. Each way helps children think about the quantities in a different way (Thompson, 1990).

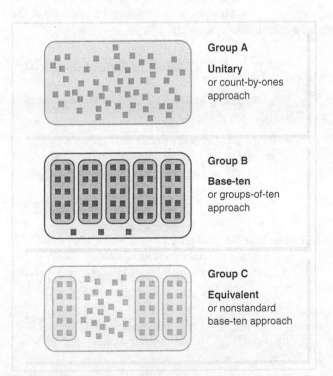

Group A

Unitary
or count-by-ones approach

Group B

Base-ten
or groups-of-ten approach

Group C

Equivalent
or nonstandard base-ten approach

Figure 11.1 Three equivalent groupings of 53 objects. Group A is 53 because "I counted them (by ones)." Group B has 5 tens and 3 more. Group C is the same as B, but now some groups of ten are broken into singles.

1. *Counting by ones.* This is the method children have to begin with. Initially, a count by ones is the only way they are able to name a quantity or "tell how many." All three of the sets in Figure 11.1 can be counted by ones. Before base-ten ideas develop, a count by ones is the only way children can be convinced that all three sets are the same.

2. *Counting by groups and singles.* In group B in Figure 11.1, counting by groups and singles would go like this: "One, two, three, four, five bunches of ten, and one, two, three singles." Consider how novel this method would be for a child who had never thought about counting a group of objects as a single item. Also notice how this counting does not tell directly how many items there are. This counting must be coordinated with a count by ones before it can be a means of telling "how many."

3. *Counting by tens and ones.* This is the way adults would probably count group B and perhaps group C: "Ten, twenty, thirty, forty, fifty, fifty-one, fifty-two, fifty-three." Although this count ends by saying the number that is there, it is not as explicit as the second method in counting the number of groups. Nor will it convey an understanding of "how many" unless it is coordinated with the more meaningful count by ones.

Regardless of the specific activity that you may be doing with children, helping them integrate the grouping-by-tens concept with what they know about number from counting by ones should be your foremost objective. If first counted by ones, the question might be, "What will happen if we count these by groups and singles (or by tens and ones)?" If a set has been grouped into tens and singles and counted accordingly, "How can we be really certain that there are 53 things here?" or "How many do you think we will get if we count by ones?" It is inadequate to *tell* children that these counts will all be the same. That is a relationship they must construct themselves through reflective thought, not because the teacher says it works that way.

Integration of Groupings with Words

The way we say a number such as "fifty-three" must also be connected with the grouping-by-tens concept. The counting methods provide a connecting mechanism. The count by tens and ones results in saying the number of groups and singles separately: "five tens and three." This is an acceptable, albeit nonstandard, way of naming this quantity. Saying the number of tens and singles separately in this fashion can be called *base-ten language* for a number. Children can associate the base-ten language with the usual language: "five tens and three—fifty-three."

There are several variations of the base-ten language for 53—5 tens and 3; 5 tens and 3 ones; 5 tens and 3 singles; and so on. Each may be used interchangeably with the standard name, "fifty-three."

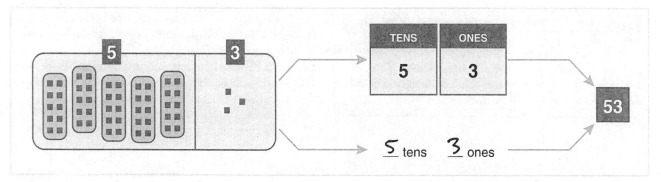

Figure 11.2 Groupings by 10 are matched with numerals, placed in labeled places, and eventually written in standard form.

It can easily be argued that base-ten language should be used throughout the second grade, even in preference to standard oral names.

Integration of Groupings with Place-Value Notation

In like manner, the symbolic scheme that we use for writing numbers (ones on the right, tens to the left of ones, and so on) must be coordinated with the grouping scheme. Activities can be designed so that children physically associate a tens and ones grouping with the correct recording of the individual digits, as Figure 11.2 indicates.

Language again plays a key role in making these connections. The explicit count by groups and singles matches the individual digits as the number is written in the usual left-to-right manner. A similar coordination is necessary for hundreds and other place values.

> *NCTM Standards* "Making a transition from viewing 'ten' as simply the accumulation of 10 ones to seeing it both as 10 ones *and* as 1 ten is an important first step for students toward understanding the structure of the base-ten number system" (p. 33). ◆

Figure 11.3 summarizes the ideas that have been discussed so far.

- The conceptual knowledge of place value consists of the base-ten grouping ideas.

  - When a collection of objects is grouped in sets of ten and some leftover singles, counting the groups of ten and adding the singles tells how many are in the collection.
  - There can be equivalent representations with fewer than the maximum groupings.

- The base-ten grouping ideas must be integrated with oral and written names for numbers.
- In addition to counting by ones, children use two other ways of counting: by groups and singles separately and by tens and ones. All three methods of counting are coordinated as the principal method of integrating the concepts, the written names, and the oral names.

Base-Ten Concepts

Standard and equivalent groupings meaningfully used to represent quantities

Counting
- By ones
- By groups and singles
- By tens and ones

Oral Names ⟷ **Written Names**

Standard:
Thirty-two
Base-Ten:
Three tens and two

Figure 11.3 Relational understanding of place value integrates three components, shown as the corners of the triangle: base-ten concepts, oral names for numbers, and written names for numbers.

⏸ ———————— *Pause and Reflect*

Think of Figure 11.3 as a triangle with the conceptual ideas of place value at the top. The procedural ideas of how we say and write numbers are the other two corners. Counting is the main tool children use to help connect these ideas. Before moving further, be sure that you have a good feel for how these ideas are related. Remember that the conceptual ideas must first be built on the count-by-ones concept of quantity that children bring to this array of ideas.

Models for Place Value

Physical models for base-ten concepts can play a key role in helping children develop the idea of "a ten" as both a single entity and as a set of ten units. Remember, though, that the models do not "show" the concept to the children. The children must mentally construct the concept and impose it on the model.

Base-Ten Models and the Ten-Makes-One Relationship

A good base-ten model for ones, tens, and hundreds is one that is *proportional*. That is, a ten model is physically ten times larger than the model for a one, and a hundred model is ten times larger than the ten model. Base-ten models can be categorized as *groupable* and *pregrouped*.

Groupable Models

Models that most clearly reflect the relationships of ones, tens, and hundreds are those for which the ten can actually be made or grouped from the singles. When children put ten beans in a portion cup, the cup of ten literally *is the same as* the ten single beans. This is a particularly important process for students with special needs. Examples of these groupable models are shown in Figure 11.4(a). These could also be called "put-together-take-apart" models.

Of the groupable models, beans or counters in portion cups are the cheapest and easiest for children to use. Plastic connecting cubes are attractive and provide a good transition to pregrouped tens sticks. Bundles of wooden craft sticks or coffee stirrers are a well-known model, but small hands have trouble with rubber bands and actually making the bundles. With most groupable materials, hundreds are possible but are generally not practical.

As children become more and more familiar with these models, collections of tens can be made up in advance by the children and kept as ready-made tens. Lids can be purchased for the plastic portion cups, and the connecting

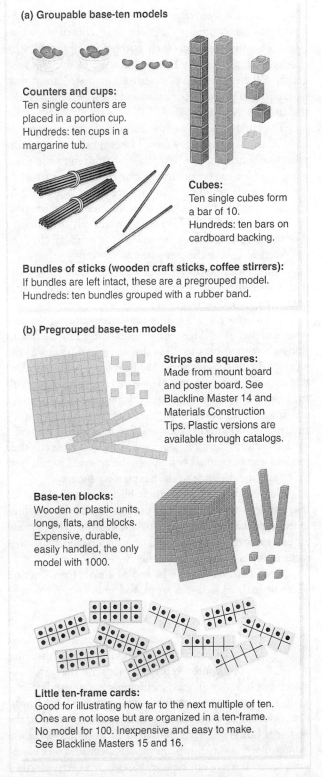

(a) Groupable base-ten models

Counters and cups:
Ten single counters are placed in a portion cup. Hundreds: ten cups in a margarine tub.

Cubes:
Ten single cubes form a bar of 10. Hundreds: ten bars on cardboard backing.

Bundles of sticks (wooden craft sticks, coffee stirrers):
If bundles are left intact, these are a pregrouped model. Hundreds: ten bundles grouped with a rubber band.

(b) Pregrouped base-ten models

Strips and squares:
Made from mount board and poster board. See Blackline Master 14 and Materials Construction Tips. Plastic versions are available through catalogs.

Base-ten blocks:
Wooden or plastic units, longs, flats, and blocks. Expensive, durable, easily handled, the only model with 1000.

Little ten-frame cards:
Good for illustrating how far to the next multiple of ten. Ones are not loose but are organized in a ten-frame. No model for 100. Inexpensive and easy to make. See Blackline Masters 15 and 16.

Figure 11.4 Groupable and pregrouped base-ten models.

cubes can be left prebundled. This is a good transition to the pregrouped models described next.

Pregrouped or Trading Models

Models that are pregrouped are commonly shown in textbooks and are commonly used in instructional activities. With pregrouped models such as those in Figure 11.4(b), children cannot actually take pieces apart or put them together. When ten single pieces are accumulated, they must be exchanged or *traded* for a ten, and likewise, tens must be traded for hundreds.

The chief advantage of these models is their ease of use and the efficient way they model large numbers. A significant disadvantage is the potential for children to use them without reflecting on the ten-to-one relationships or without really understanding what they are doing. For example, if children are told to trade 10 ones for a ten, it is quite possible for them to make this exchange without attending to the "tenness" of the piece they call a ten. Similarly, children can learn to "make the number 42" by simply selecting 4 tens and 2 ones pieces without understanding that if the pieces all came apart there would be 42 ones pieces that could be counted by ones.

In this category, the little ten-frame cards are somewhat unique. If children have been using ten-frames to think about numbers to 20 as discussed in Chapter 8, the value of the filled ten-frame may be more meaningful than it is with strips and squares of base-ten materials. Although the ones are fixed on the cards, this model has the distinct advantage of always showing the distance to the next multiple of ten. When 47 is shown with 4 ten cards and a seven card, it is clear that three more will make 50. With all other models, the ones must continually be counted to tell how many and the distance to the next ten is obscure.

No model, including a groupable model, will guarantee that children are reflecting on the ten-to-one relationships in the materials. With pregrouped models we need to make an extra effort to see that children understand that a ten piece really is the same as 10 ones.

(See Blackline Master 14 and Materials Construction Tips for making base-ten strips and squares and the ten-frame cards.)

 Tech NOTES Electronic versions of base-ten manipulatives are becoming more popular. Usually these are computer representations of the three-dimensional base-ten blocks, including the thousands piece. With simple mouse clicks children can place units, rods, flats, or cubes on the screen. In the Base Block applets at the National Library of Virtual Manipulatives (http://nlvm.usu.edu/en/nav/vlibrary.html), the models are placed on a place-value chart. If ten of one type are lassoed by a rectangle, they snap together. If a piece is dragged one column to the right, the pieces break apart. Pearson Education's *eTools* has a similar place-value tool with a bit more flexibility. This applet is available free at www.kyrene.org/mathtools. Choose "Place Value Blocks" and if you wish under "workspaces" on

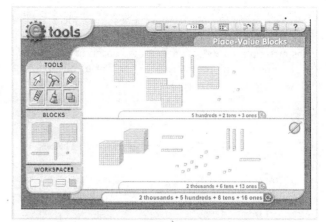

Figure 11.5 Pearson Scott Foresman's *eTools* includes a computer model of base-ten blocks.
Source: Scott Foresman Addison-Wesley Math Electronic-Tools CD-ROM Grade K Through 6. Copyright © 2004 Pearson Education, Inc., or its affiliate(s). Used by permission. All rights reserved.

the bottom left, select the two-part mat as in Figure 11.5. Then select the base-ten pieces of your choice and add ones, tens, or hundreds. With the *eTools* "Number Blocks," place-value columns can be turned off, and up to three different numbers can be modeled separately. The "odometer" option can show the number 523 as *5 hundreds + 2 tens + 3 ones*, as *500 + 20 + 3*, or as *five hundred twenty-three*. A hammer icon will break a piece into smaller pieces and a glue bottle icon is used to group ten pieces together.

Compared to real base-ten models, virtual blocks are free, are easily grouped and ungrouped, can be shown to the full class on a monitor, and are available in "endless" supply, even the thousands blocks. Computer models allow students to print their work and, thus, create a written record of what they've done. On the other hand, the computer model is no more conceptual than a physical model and, like the physical model, is only a representation for students who understand the relationships involved. ◆

Nonproportional Models

Nonproportional models can be used by students who no longer need to understand how ten units makes "a ten" or by some students who need to return to place-value concepts as they struggle with more advanced computations. These are models, such as money, that do not show the model for a ten as physically ten times larger than the one. Many students can grasp place-value relationships using pennies, dimes, and dollars to represent the ones, tens, and hundreds on their place-value mat. Using coin representations they can display amounts and exchange ten dimes for a dollar and represent and carry out a variety of calculations. Like a bead-frame with same-sized beads on different columns (wires) or colored chips that are given different place values by color, these nonproportional representations are *not* for introducing place-value concepts. They are used when students already have a conceptual understanding of the numeration system and need additional reinforcement. Oftentimes money is a useful tool for middle grade students with special needs who understand the relationships between the place values yet need support in developing other mathematical concepts. These older children sometimes do not want to use beans, blocks, and connecting cubes, because they perceive them as tools for much younger children.

Developing Base-Ten Concepts

Now that you have a sense of the task of helping children develop place-value concepts, we can begin to focus on activities that can help with this task. This section focuses on the top of the triangle of ideas in Figure 11.3: base-ten concepts or grouping by tens. The central idea of counting groups of ten to describe quantities is clearly the most important component to be developed. The connections of these critical ideas with the place-value system of writing numbers and with the way we say numbers—the bottom two corners of the triangle in Figure 11.3—are discussed separately to help you focus on the conceptual objective. However, in the classroom, the oral and written names for numbers can and should be developed in concert and nearly always with connections to conceptual ideas using models.

Grouping Activities

Because children come to their development of base-ten concepts with a count-by-ones idea of number, you must begin there. You cannot arbitrarily impose grouping by ten on children. We want children to experiment with showing amounts in groups of like size and perhaps to come to an agreement that ten is a very useful size to use. The following activity could be done in late first grade or second grade and is designed as an example of a first effort at developing grouping concepts.

Activity 11.1

Counting in Groups

Find a collection of items that children might be interested in counting—perhaps the number of eyes in the classroom or the number of shoes, a mystery jar of buttons or cubes, a long chain of plastic links, or the number of crayons in the crayon box. The quantity should be countable, somewhere between 25 and 100. Pose the question, "How could we count our shoes in some way that would be easier than counting by ones?" Whatever suggestions you get, try to implement them. After trying several methods, you can have a discussion of what worked well and what did not. If no one suggests counting by tens, you might casually suggest that as possibly another idea.

One teacher had her second-grade students find a good way to count all the connecting cubes being held by the children after each had been given a cube for each of their pockets. The first suggestion was to count by sevens. That was tried but did not work very well because none of the second graders could count by sevens. In search of a faster way, the next suggestion was to count by twos. This did not seem to be much better than counting by ones. Finally, they settled on counting by tens and realized that this was a pretty good method, although counting by fives also worked well.

This and similar activities provide you with the opportunity to suggest that materials actually be arranged into groups of tens before the "fast" way of counting is begun. Remember that children may count "ten, twenty, thirty, thirty-one, thirty-two" but not fully realize the "thirty-two-ness" of the quantity. To connect the count-by-tens method with their understood method of counting by ones, the children need to count both ways and discuss why they get the same result.

The idea in the next activity is for children to make groupings of ten and record or say the amounts. Number words are used so that children will not mechanically match tens and ones with individual digits. It is important that children confront the actual quantity in a manner meaningful to them.

Activity 11.2

Groups of 10

Prepare bags of counters of different types such as toothpicks, buttons, beans, plastic chips, connecting cubes, craft sticks, or other items. Children have a record sheet similar to the top example in Figure 11.6. The bags can be placed at stations around the room, or given to pairs of children. Children dump out and count the contents. The amount is recorded as a number word. Then the counters are grouped in as many tens as possible. The groupings are recorded on the form. Bags are traded, or children move to another station after returning all counters to the bag.

Variations of the "Groups of 10" activity are suggested by the other recording sheets in Figure 11.6. In "Get This Many," the children count the dots and then count out the corresponding number of counters. Small portion cups to put the groups of ten in should be provided. Notice that the

Name ....

Bag of	Number word		
Toothpicks		Tens	
		Singles	
Beans		Tens	
		Singles	
Washers		Tens	
		Singles	

Get this many.

○○○○○ ○○○○○ ○
○ ○ ○ ○ ○
○ ○ ○ ○ ○
○ ○ ○ ○ ○
○ ○○○○○ ○○○○○

Write the number word.	
_____	
Tens	
Singles	

Fill the tens.

Get forty-seven beans.

Fill up ten-frames. Draw dots.

Tens _____   Singles _____

Loop this many.

Loop [sixty-two] in groups of ten.

○○
○○
○○
○○

Tens _____   Singles _____

Figure 11.6 Activities involving number words and making groups of 10.

activity requires students to first count the set in a way they understand, record the amount in words, and then make the groupings. The activity starts with meaningful student counts and develops the idea of groups. "Fill the Tens" and "Loop This Many" begin with a verbal name (number word), and students must count the indicated amount and then make groups.

As you watch children doing these activities, you will be able to learn a lot about their base-ten concept development. For example, how do children count out the objects? Do they make groupings of ten? Do they count to 10 and then start again at 1? Children who do that are already using the base-ten structure. But what you will more likely see early on is children counting a full set without any stopping at tens and without any effort to group the materials in piles. A second-grade teacher had her students count a jar of small beans. After they had recorded the number, they were to ask for portion cups in which to make groups of ten. Several children, when asked how many cups they thought they might need, had no idea or made random guesses. What would you know about these students' knowledge of place value? ◆

It is quite easy to integrate grouping concepts along with measurement activities. This will save time in your curriculum as well as add interest to both areas. As you will read in Chapter 19, including an estimation component to early measurement activities is important to help students understand measurement concepts. In the following mea-

surement activity, the estimation also serves to help students think about quantities as groupings of ten.

Activity 11.3

Estimating Groups of Tens and Ones

Show students a length that they are going to measure—for example, the length of a student lying down or the distance around a sheet of newspaper. At one end of the length, line up ten units (e.g., ten connecting cubes, toothpicks, rods, or blocks). On a recording sheet (see Figure 11.7), students write down an estimate of how many groups of ten and ones they think will fit into the length. Next they find the actual measure, placing units along the full length. These are counted by ones and also grouped in tens. Both results are recorded.

Notice that all place-value components are included in Activity 11.3. Children can work in pairs to measure several lengths around the room. A similar estimation approach could be added to "Groups of 10" (Activity 11.2), where students first estimate the quantity in the bags. Estimation requires reflective thought concerning quantities expressed in groups.

Listening to students' estimates is also a useful assessment opportunity that tells you a lot about children's concepts of numbers in the range of your current activities. ◆

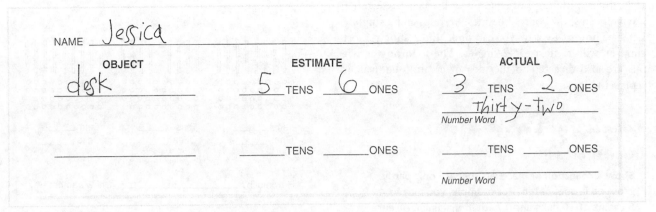

Figure 11.7 Recording sheet for estimating groups of tens and ones.

The Strangeness of *Ones, Tens,* and *Hundreds*

Reflect for a moment on how strange it must sound to say "seven ones." Certainly children have never said they were "seven ones" years old. The use of the word *ten* as a singular group name is even more mysterious. Consider the phrase "Ten ones makes one ten." The first *ten* carries the usual meaning of 10 things, the amount that is 1 more than 9 things. But the other *ten* is a singular noun, a thing. How can something the child has known for years as the name for a lot of things suddenly become one thing? Bunches, bundles, cups, and groups of 10 make more sense in the beginning than "a ten."

As students begin to make groupings of 10, the language of these groupings must also be introduced. At the start, language such as "groups of tens and ones" or "bunches of tens and singles" is most meaningful. For tens, use whatever terminology fits: bars of 10, cups of 10, bundles of 10. Eventually you can abbreviate this simply to "ten." There is no hurry to use the word "ones" for the leftovers. Language such as "four tens and seven" works very well.

The word *hundred* is equally strange and yet usually gets less attention. It must be understood in three ways: as 100 single objects, as 10 tens, and as a singular thing. These word names are not as simple as they seem!

Grouping Tens to Make 100

So far we have focused mainly on helping students move from counting by ones to understanding how groups of ten can be used more effectively. In second grade, numbers from 100 to 999 become important. Here the issue is not one of connecting a count-by-ones concept to a group of 100, but rather, seeing how a group of 100 can be understood as a group of 10 tens as well as 100 single ones. In textbooks, this connection is often illustrated on one page showing how 10 sticks of ten can be put together to make

1 hundred. This quick demonstration may be lost on many students.

As a means of introducing hundreds as groups of 10 tens and also 100 singles, consider the following estimation activity.

Activity 11.4

Too Many Tens

Show students any quantity with 150 to 1000 items. For example, you might use a jar of lima beans. Alternatives include a long chain of connecting links or paper clips or a box of Styrofoam packing peanuts. First, have students make and record estimates of how many beans are in the jar. Discuss with students how they came to select their estimates. Give portions of the beans to pairs or triads of students to put into cups of ten beans. Collect leftover beans and put these into groups of ten as well. Now ask, "How can we use these groups of ten to tell how many beans we have? Can we make new groups from the groups of ten? What is ten groups of ten called?" If using cups of beans, be prepared with some larger containers into which ten cups can be placed. When all groups are made, count the hundreds, the tens, and the ones separately. Record on the board as "4 hundreds + 7 tens + 8 ones."

In the last activity it is important to use a groupable model so that students can see how the ten groups make the 100 items. This is often lost in the rather simple display of a 100 flat or square in the pregrouped base-ten models.

Equivalent Representations

An important variation of the grouping activities is aimed at the equivalent representations of numbers. For example, with children who have just completed the "Groups of

10" activity with a bag of counters, ask, "What is another way you can show your 42 besides 4 groups and 2 singles? Let's see how many ways you can find." Interestingly, most children will go next to 42 singles. The following activities are also directed to the idea of creating equivalent representations.

Activity 11.5

Odd Groupings

Show a collection of materials that are only partly grouped in sets of ten. For example, you may have 5 chains of 10 links and 17 additional links. Be sure the children understand that the groups each have ten items. Count the number of groups, and also count the singles. Ask, "How many in all?" Record all responses, and discuss before you count. Let the children use whatever way they wish to count. Next change the groupings (make a ten from the singles, or break apart one of the tens) and repeat the questions and discussion. Do not change the total number from one time to the next. Once students begin to understand that the total does not change, ask in what other ways the items could be grouped if you use tens and ones.

If you are teaching in grade 3, equivalent representations for hundreds as groups of tens can help with the concept of a hundred as 10 tens. The next activity is similar to "Odd Groupings" but is done using pregrouped materials and includes hundreds.

Activity 11.6

Three Other Ways

Students work in groups or pairs. First they show "four hundred sixty-three" on their desks with strips and squares in the standard representation. Next they find and record at least three other ways of representing this number.

A variation of "Three Other Ways" is to challenge students to find a way to show an amount with a specific number of pieces. "Can you show 463 with 31 pieces?" (There is more than one way to do this.) Students in grades 3 or 4 can get quite involved with finding all the ways to show a three-digit number.

After children have had sufficient experiences with pregrouped materials, a semiabstract "dot, stick, and square" notation can be used for recording ones, tens, and hundreds. By third grade, children can use small squares for hundreds, as shown in Figure 11.8. Use the drawings as a

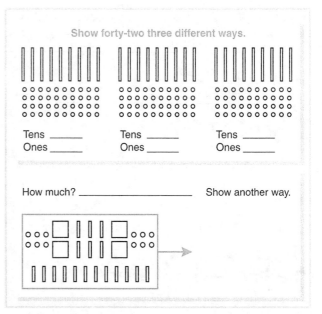

Figure 11.8 Equivalent representation exercises using square-stick-dot pictures.

means of telling the children what materials to get out to solve the problems and also as a way for children to record results.

The next activity begins to incorporate oral language with equivalent representation ideas.

Activity 11.7

Base-Ten Riddles

Base-ten riddles can be presented orally or in written form. In either case, children should use base-ten materials to help solve them. The examples here illustrate a variety of different levels of difficulty. Have children write new riddles when they complete these.

I have 23 ones and 4 tens. Who am I?

I have 4 hundreds, 12 tens, and 6 ones. Who am I?

I have 30 ones and 3 hundreds. Who am I?

I am 45. I have 25 ones. How many tens do I have?

I am 341. I have 22 tens. How many hundreds do I have?

I have 13 tens, 2 hundreds, and 21 ones. Who am I?

If you put 3 more tens with me, I would be 115. Who am I?

I have 17 ones. I am between 40 and 50. Who am I? How many tens do I have?

Oral and Written Names for Numbers

In this section we focus on helping children connect the bottom two corners of the triangle in Figure 11.3—oral and written names for numbers—with their emerging base-ten concepts of using groups of ten as efficient methods of counting. Note that the ways we say and write numbers are conventions rather than concepts. Students must learn these by being told rather than through problem-based activities. It is also worth remembering that for ELL students, the convention or pattern in our English number words is probably not the same as it is in their native language. This is especially true of the numbers 11 to 19.

Two-Digit Number Names

In first and second grades, children need to connect the base-ten concepts with the oral number names they have used many times. They know the words but have not thought of them in terms of tens and ones.

Almost always use base-ten models while teaching oral names. Initially, rather than using standard number words, a more explicit *base-ten language* can be used. In base-ten language, rather than saying "forty-seven" you would say "four tens and seven ones." Base-ten language is rarely misunderstood. As it seems appropriate, begin to pair base-ten language with standard language. Emphasize the teens as exceptions. Acknowledge that they are formed "backward" and do not fit the patterns. The next activity is useful for introducing oral names for numbers.

Activity 11.8

Counting Rows of 10

Use a 10 × 10 array of dots on the overhead projector. Cover up all but two rows, as shown in Figure 11.9. "How many tens? [2.] Two tens is called *twenty*." Have the class repeat. Show another row. "Three tens is called *thirty*. Four tens is *forty*. Five tens could have been *fivety* but is just *fifty*." The names *sixty*, *seventy*, *eighty*, and *ninety* all fit the pattern. Slide the cover up and down the array, asking how many tens and the name for that many.

Use the same 10 × 10 array to work on names for tens and ones. Show, for example, four full lines, "forty." Next expose one dot in the fifth row. "Four tens and one. Forty-one." Add more dots one at a time. "Four tens and two. Forty-two." "Four tens and three. Forty-three." This is shown in Figure 11.9. When that pattern is established, repeat with other decades from twenty through ninety.

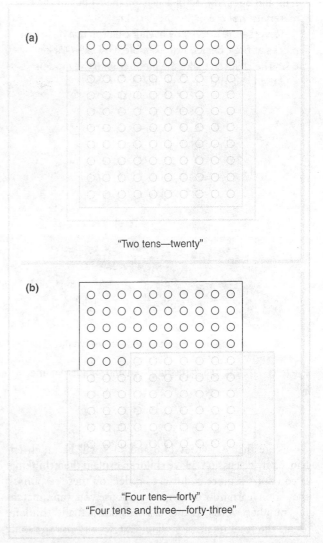

(a)

"Two tens—twenty"

(b)

"Four tens—forty"
"Four tens and three—forty-three"

Figure 11.9 10 × 10 dot arrays are used to model sets of tens and ones (Blackline Master 12).

Repeat this basic approach with other base-ten models. The next activity shows how this might be done.

Activity 11.9

Counting with Base-Ten Models

Show some tens pieces on the overhead or electronic whiteboard or just placed on the carpet in a mixed arrangement as shown in Figure 11.10. Ask how many tens. Add a ten or remove a ten and repeat the questions. Next add some ones. Always have children give the base-ten name and the standard name. Continue to make changes in the materials displayed by adding or removing 1 or 2 tens and by adding and removing ones. By avoiding the standard left-to-right order for tens and ones, the emphasis is on the names of the materials, not the order they are in.

Reverse the activity by having children use base-ten pieces at their desks. For example, you say, "Make 63." The children make the number with the models and then give the base-ten name.

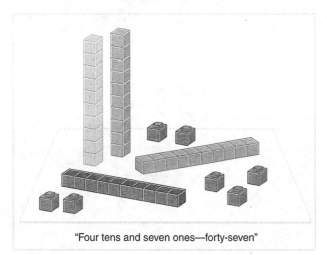

"Four tens and seven ones—forty-seven"

Figure 11.10 Using the base-ten and standard name for 47.

Note that Activities 11.8 and 11.9 will be much enhanced by discussion. Have children explain their thinking. If you don't require children to reflect on these responses, they soon learn how to give the response you want, matching number words to models, without actually thinking about the total quantities. The next activity has the same objective.

Activity 11.10

Tens, Ones, and Fingers

Ask your class, "How can you show 6 [or another amount less than 10] fingers?" Then ask, "How can you show 37 fingers?" Some children will figure out that at least four children are required. Line up four children, and have three hold up 10 fingers and the last child 7 fingers. Have the class count the fingers by tens and ones. Ask for other children to show different numbers. Emphasize the number of sets of 10 fingers and the single fingers (base-ten language) and pair this with standard language.

Three-Digit Number Names

The approach to three-digit number names is essentially the same as for two-digit names. Show mixed arrangements of base-ten materials. Have children give the base-ten name and the standard name. Vary the arrangement from one example to the next by changing only one type of piece. That is, add or remove only ones or only tens or only hundreds.

Similarly, have children at their desks model numbers that you give to them orally using the standard names. By the time that children are ready for three-digit numbers, the two-digit number names, including the difficulties with the teens, have usually been mastered. The major difficulty is with numbers involving no tens, such as 702. As noted earlier, the use of base-ten language is quite helpful here. The zero-tens difficulty is more pronounced when writing numerals. Children frequently write 7002 for "seven hundred two." The emphasis on the meaning in the oral base-ten language form will be a significant help.

Written Symbols

Place-value mats are simple mats divided into two or three sections to hold ones and tens or ones, tens, and hundreds pieces as shown in Figure 11.11. You can suggest to your students that the mats are a good way to organize their materials when working with base-ten pieces. Explain that the standard way to use a place-value mat is with the space for the ones on the right and tens and hundreds places to the left.

Although not commonly seen in traditional textbooks, it is strongly recommended that two ten-frames be drawn in the ones place as shown. (See Blackline Master 17.) That

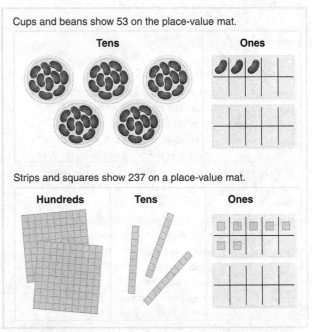

Figure 11.11 Place-value mats with two ten-frames in the ones place organize the counters and promote the concept of groups of ten.

way, the amount of ones on the ten-frames is always clearly evident, eliminating the need for frequent and tedious counting. The ten-frame also makes it very clear how many additional counters would be needed to make the next set of ten. If children are modeling two numbers at the same time, one ten-frame can be used for each number.

As children use their place-value mats, they can be shown how the left-to-right order of the pieces is also the way that numbers are written. The place-value mat becomes a link between the base-ten models and the written form of the numbers. Once again, be aware of how easy it would be for a child to show a number on a mat using tens and ones pieces and learn to write the number without any conceptual understanding of what the number represents. First- and second-grade textbooks often show a model and have children record numbers in this manner:

$$\underline{7} \text{ tens and } \underline{3} \text{ ones is } \underline{73} \text{ in all.}$$

It is all too easy to copy down the number of strips and single squares and rewrite these digits in a single number 73 and not confront what these symbols stand for.

The next three activities are designed to help children make connections among all three representations: models, oral language, and written forms. They can be done with two- or three-digit numbers in grades 1 to 4.

Activity 11.11

Say It/Press It

Display some models of ones and tens (and hundreds) in a mixed arrangement. (Use the overhead projector or interactive whiteboard or simply draw on the board using the square-stick-dot method.) Students say the amount shown in base-ten language ("four hundreds, one ten, and five") and then in standard language ("four hundred fifteen"), and finally they enter it on their calculators. Have someone share his or her display and defend it. Make a change in the materials and repeat.

"Say It/Press It" is especially good for helping with teens (note the example in the activity description) and for three-digit numbers with zero tens. If you show 7 hundreds and 4 ones, the class says "seven hundreds, zero tens, and four—seven hundred (*slight pause*) four." The pause and the base-ten language suggest the correct three-digit number to press or write. As mentioned previously, many students have trouble with this example and write "7004," writing exactly what they hear in the standard name. This activity will help. The next activity simply changes the first representation that is presented to the students.

Activity 11.12

Show It/Press It

Say the standard name for a number (with either two or three digits). At their desks, students use their own base-ten models to show that number and press it on their calculators (or write it). Again, pay special attention to the teens and the case of zero tens.

The following activity has been popular for decades and remains a useful challenge for students in the early stages of place-value development.

Activity 11.13

Digit Change

Have students enter a specific two- or three-digit number on the calculator. The task is to then change one of the digits in the number without simply entering the new number. For example, change 48 to 78. Change 315 to 305 or to 295. Changes can be made by adding or subtracting an appropriate amount. Students should write or discuss explanations for their solutions.

Children are often able to disguise their lack of understanding of place value by following directions, using the tens and ones pieces in prescribed ways, and using the language of place value.

The diagnostic tasks presented here are designed to help you look more closely at children's understanding of place value. Designed for diagnostic interviews rather than full-class activities, these tasks have been used by several researchers and are adapted primarily from Labinowicz (1985), Kamii (1985), and Ross (1986).

Write the number 342. Have the child read the number. Then have the child write the number that is 1 more. Next ask for the number that is 10 more than the number. You may wish to explore further with models. One less and 10 less can be checked the same way.

The next task, referred to as the *Digit Correspondence Task*, has been used widely in the study of place-value development. Take out 36 blocks. Ask the child to count the blocks, and then have the child write the number that tells how many there are. Circle the 6 in 36 and ask, "Does this part of your 36 have anything to do with how many blocks there are?" Then circle the 3 and repeat the question exactly. Do not give clues. Based on responses to the task, Ross (1989, 2002) has identified five distinct levels of understanding of place value:

1. *Single numeral.* The child writes 36 but views it as a single numeral. The individual digits 3 and 6 have no meaning by themselves.

2. *Position names.* The child identifies correctly the tens and ones positions but still makes no connections between the individual digits and the blocks.
3. *Face value.* The child matches 6 blocks with the 6 and 3 blocks with the 3.
4. *Transition to place value.* The 6 is matched with 6 blocks and the 3 with the remaining 30 blocks but not as 3 groups of 10.
5. *Full understanding.* The 3 is correlated with 3 groups of 10 blocks and the 6 with 6 single blocks. ◆

Patterns and Relationships with Multidigit Numbers

In this section we want to move beyond this snapshot view of individual numbers toward an orientation that looks at the full number rather than just the digits. Here the focus will be on the patterns in our number system and how numbers are related to one another. We are interested in the relationships of numbers to important special numbers—relationships that begin to overlap with or provide a basis for computation. In the standards-based curricula, ideas similar to those found in this section comprise nearly all of the place-value development with lesser attention given to the ideas discussed earlier.

The Hundreds Chart

The hundreds chart (Figure 11.12) is such an important tool in the development of place-value concepts that it deserves special attention. K–2 classrooms should have a hundreds chart displayed prominently.

An extremely useful version of the chart is made of transparent pockets into which each of the 100 numeral cards can be inserted. You can hide a number by inserting a blank card in front of a number in the pocket. You can also insert colored pieces of paper in the slots to highlight various number patterns. And you can remove the number cards and have students replace them in their correct positions.

An overhead transparency or representation on the interactive whiteboard of a hundreds chart is almost as flexible as the pocket chart version. Numbers can be hidden by placing opaque counters on them. Patterns can be marked with a pen or with transparent counters. A transparency of a blank 10 × 10 grid serves as an empty hundreds chart on which you can write numbers. These transparencies can be made from Blackline Master 21.

At the kindergarten and first-grade levels, students can be helped to count and recognize two-digit numbers with the hundreds chart long before they develop a base-ten understanding of these numbers.

1	2	3	4	5	6	7	8	9	10
11	12	13	14	15	16	17	18	19	20
21	22	23	24	25	26	27	28	29	30
31	32	33	34	35	36	37	38	39	40
41	42	43	44	45	46	47	48	49	50
51	52	53	54	55	56	57	58	59	60
61	62	63	64	65	66	67	68	69	70
71	72	73	74	75	76	77	78	79	80
81	82	83	84	85	86	87	88	89	90
91	92	93	94	95	96	97	98	99	100

Figure 11.12 A hundreds chart (Blackline Master 22).

Activity 11.14

Patterns on the Hundreds Chart

Have children work in pairs to find patterns on the hundreds chart. Solicit ideas orally from the class. Have children explain patterns found by others to be sure that all understand the ideas that are being suggested.

There are lots of patterns on the hundreds chart. In a discussion, different children will describe the same pattern in several ways. Accept all ideas. Here are some of the patterns they may point out:

- The numbers in a column all end with the same number, which is the same as the number at the top.
- In a row, one number "counts" (the ones digit goes 1, 2, 3, . . . , 9, 0); or the "second" number goes up by ones, but the first number (tens digit) stays the same.
- In a column, the first number (tens digit) "counts" or goes up by ones.
- You can count by tens going down the right-hand column.
- The numbers under the 2 are all even numbers. (Every alternating number in the rows is even.)
- If you count by fives, you get two columns, the 5 column and the last column.

For children, these patterns are not at all obvious or trivial. For example, one child may notice the pattern in the column under the 4—every number ends in a 4. Two minutes later another child will "discover" the parallel pattern in the column headed by 7. That there is a pattern like this in every column may not be completely obvious.

Other patterns you might have students explore include numbers that have a 7 in them, numbers where the digits add up to four, numbers where both digits are the same (11, 22, etc.), and various skip-count patterns.

Activity 11.15

Skip-Count Patterns

As a full class activity, have students skip-count by twos, threes, fours, and so on. After skip-counting as a class, have students record a specific skip-count pattern on their own copy of the hundreds chart by coloring in each number they count. Every skip count produces an interesting pattern on the chart. You should also discuss the patterns in the numbers. For example, when you skip-count by fours, you only land on numbers that you get when you count by twos. Which counts make column patterns and which counts make diagonal patterns?

In the beginning, skip counting may be quite difficult for children. As they become more comfortable with skip counts, you can challenge students to skip-count without the aid of the hundreds chart. Skip-counting skills show a readiness for multiplication combinations and also help children begin to look for interesting and useful patterns in numbers.

Activity 11.16

Missing Numbers

Provide students with a hundreds chart on which some of the number cards have been removed. Use the classroom pocket chart or, for a full-class activity, you can use the overhead transparency. The students' task is to replace the missing numbers or tell what they are. Beginning versions of this activity have only a random selection of individual numbers removed. Later, remove sequences of several numbers from three or four different rows. Finally, remove all but one or two rows or columns. Eventually, challenge children to replace all of the numbers in a blank chart. (See Blackline Master 21.)

Replacing the number cards or tiles from a blank chart is a good station activity for two students to work on together. By listening to how students go about finding the correct places for numbers you can assess how well they have constructed an understanding of the 1-to-100 sequence.

Activity 11.17

More and Less on the Hundreds Chart

Begin with a blank or nearly blank chart (Blackline Master 21). Circle a particular missing number. Students are to fill in the designated number and its "neighbors," the numbers to the left, right, above, and below. This can be done with the full class on the overhead projector or whiteboard, or worksheets can be prepared using a blank hundreds chart or 10 × 10 grid. After students become comfortable naming the neighbors of a number, ask what they notice about the neighbor numbers. The numbers to the left and right are one more and one less than the given number. Those above and below are ten less and ten more, respectively. What about those on the diagonal? By discussing these relationships on the chart, students begin to see how the sequence of numbers is related to the numeric relationships in the numbers.

Notice that children will first use the hundreds chart to learn about the patterns in the sequence of numbers. Many students, especially at the K or grade 1 level, will not understand the corresponding numeric relationships such as those discussed in the last activity. In the following activity, number relationships on the chart are made more explicit by including the use of base-ten models.

Activity 11.18

Models with the Hundreds Chart

Use any physical model for two-digit numbers with which the students are familiar. The little ten-frame cards are recommended.

- Give children one or more numbers to first make with the models and then find on the chart. Use groups of two or three numbers either in the same row or the same column.
- Indicate a number on the chart. What would you have to change to make each of its neighbors (the numbers to the left, right, above, and below)?

The hundreds chart can extend even very young students' concepts of number. Children can use a hundreds chart to find combinations for any number they are familiar with. Students use patterns on the chart to see how big numbers are related in a similar manner as little numbers.

It is becoming more and more popular to have a chart that extends to 200, even in the first grade. Perhaps a more powerful idea is to extend the hundreds chart to 1000.

Activity 11.19

The Thousands Chart

Provide students with several sheets of the blank hundreds charts from Blackline Master 21. Assign groups of three or four students the task of creating a 1-to-1000 chart. The chart is made by taping ten charts together in a long strip. Students should decide how they are going to divide up the task with different students taking different parts of the chart.

The thousands chart should be discussed as a class to examine how numbers change as you count from 1 hundred to the next, what the patterns are, and so on. In fact, the earlier hundreds chart activities can all be extended to a thousands chart.

Several Web-based resources include hundreds charts that allow students to explore patterns. *Learning about Number Relationships* is an e-Example from NCTM's *e-Standards* that has a calculator and hundreds chart and allows for a fairly open exploration. Patterns are colored on the chart as students skip-count with the calculator. Students can skip-count by any number and also begin their counts at any number. Any two patterns can be overlapped using two colors. The chart also extends to 1000. The *Number Patterns* applet from NLVM (http://nlvm.usu.edu/en/nav/vlibrary.html) presents students with number patterns to complete. ◆

Relationships with Landmark Numbers

One of the most valuable features of both the hundreds chart and the little ten-frame cards is how clearly they illustrate the distance to the next multiple of ten—the end of the row on the chart or the blank spaces on the ten-frame card. Multiples of 10, 100, and occasionally other special numbers such as multiples of 25, are referred to in the *Investigations in Number, Data, and Space* program as *landmark numbers*. Students learn to use this term as they work with informal methods of computation. When finding the difference between 74 and 112, a child might say, "First I added 6 onto 74 to get to a landmark number. Then I added 2 more tens onto 80 to get to 100 because that's another landmark number. . . ." Whatever terminology is used, understanding how numbers are related to these special numbers is an important step in students' development of number sense.

In addition to the hundreds chart, the number line is an excellent way to explore these relationships. The next two activities are suggestions for using number lines.

Activity 11.20

Who Am I?

Sketch a line labeled 0 and 100 at opposite ends. Mark a point with a ? that corresponds to your secret number. (Estimate the position the best you can.) Students try to guess your secret number. For each guess, place and label a mark on the line. Continue marking each guess until your secret number is discovered. As a variation, the endpoints can be other than 0 and 100. For example, try 0 and 1000, 200 and 300, or 500 and 800.

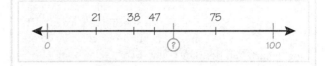

Activity 11.21

Who Could They Be?

Label two points on a number line (not necessarily the ends) with landmark numbers.

Show students different points labeled with letters and ask what numbers they might be and why they think that. In the example shown here, B and C are less than 100 but probably more than 60. E could be about 180. You can also ask where 75 might be or where 400 is. About how far apart are A and D? Why do you think D is more than 100?

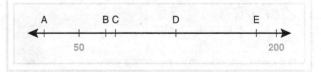

The next two activities are extensions of part-part-whole ideas that were explored in Chapter 9. In the first of these, one of the parts is a landmark number. In the second, the landmark number is the whole.

Activity 11.22

50 and Some More

Say or write a number between 50 and 100. Students respond with "50 and ____." For 63, the response is "50 and 13." Any landmark number can be used instead of 50. For example, you could use any number that ends in 50. You can also do this with numbers such as 70 or 230.

Landmark numbers are often broken apart in computations. The next activity is aimed at what may be the most important landmark number, 100.

Activity 11.23

The Other Part of 100

Two students work together with a set of little ten-frame cards. One student makes a two-digit number. Then both students work mentally to determine what goes with the ten-frame amount to make 100. They write their solutions on paper and then check by making the other part with the cards to see if the total is 100. Students take turns making the original number. Figure 11.13 shows three different thought processes that students might use.

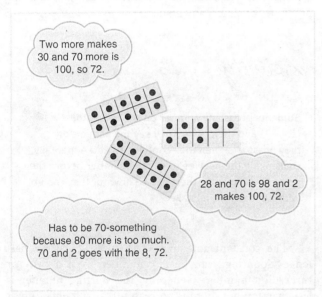

Two more makes 30 and 70 more is 100, so 72.

28 and 70 is 98 and 2 makes 100, 72.

Has to be 70-something because 80 more is too much. 70 and 2 goes with the 8, 72.

Figure 11.13 Using little ten-frames to help think about the "other part of 100."

Being able to give the other part of 100 should become a skill focus at grades 2 to 4 because it is so useful for flexible methods of computation.

If your students are adept at parts of 100, you can change the whole from 100 to another number. At first try other multiples of 10 such as 70 or 80. Then extend the whole to any number less than 100.

myeducationlab

Go to the Building Teaching Skills and Dispositions section of Chapter 11 of MyEducationLab. Click on Expanded Lessons to download the Expanded Lesson for "**The Other Part of 100**" and complete the related activities.

—— Pause and Reflect

Suppose that the whole is 83. Sketch four little ten-frame cards showing 36. Looking at your "cards," what goes with 36 to make 83? How did you think about it?

What you just did in finding the other part of 83 was subtract 36 from 83. You did not borrow or regroup. Most likely you did it in your head. With more practice you (and students as early as the third grade) can do this without the aid of the cards.

Compatible numbers for addition and subtraction are numbers that go together easily to make nice numbers. Numbers that make tens or hundreds are the most common examples. Compatible sums also include numbers that end in 5, 25, 50, or 75, since these numbers are easy to work with as well. The teaching task is to get students accustomed to looking for combinations that work together and then looking for these combinations in computational situations.

Activity 11.24

Compatible Pairs

Searching for compatible pairs can be done as an activity with the full class. Prepare a transparency or use the whiteboard to duplicate a page with a search task. Four possibilities of different difficulty levels are shown in Figure 11.14. Students name or connect the compatible pairs as they see them.

Make 50
41 28
37
13 19 9
12 38
22
31

Make 500
240 415
165 125
150 350 335
375 85
260

Using fives to make 100
45 65
35
75
95
15 55

Make 1000
365 720
760 450
635
280 185
435 550

Figure 11.14 Compatible-pair searches.

The next activity has children apply some of the same ideas about landmark numbers that we have been exploring.

Activity 11.25

Close, Far, and In Between

Put any three numbers on the board. If appropriate, use two-digit numbers.

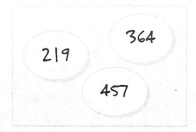

With these three numbers as referents, ask questions such as the following, encouraging discussion of all responses:

Which two are closest? Why?

Which is closest to 300? To 250?

Name a number between 457 and 364.

Name a multiple of 25 between 219 and 364.

Name a number that is more than all of these.

About how far apart are 219 and 500? 219 and 5000?

If these are "big numbers," what are some small numbers? Numbers that are about the same? Numbers that make these seem small?

Number Relationships for Addition and Subtraction

If you examine any textbook for grades 1 to 5 you will find chapters on place value and other chapters on computational strategies. The same, of course, is true of this book. However, evidence suggests that there is an interaction between learning about numeration and learning about computational techniques (NRC, 2001). That is, it is not necessary to complete the development of numeration concepts before exploring computation.

Jerrika, in January of the first grade, solves a story problem for 10 + 13 + 22 using connecting cubes. Her written work is shown in Figure 11.15. She is beginning to use one 10 but most likely counted on the remaining cubes by ones. Her classmate, Monica, solved the same problem but has clearly utilized more base-ten ideas (Figure 11.15). Ideas such as these continue to grow with additional problem solving and sharing of ideas during class discussion.

 The *Standards* authors also suggest a blending of numeration and computation. "It is not necessary to wait for students to fully develop place-value understandings before giving them opportunities to solve problems with two- and three-digit numbers. When such problems arise in interesting contexts, students can often invent ways to solve them that incorporate and deepen their understanding of place value, especially when students have the opportunities to discuss and explain their invented strategies and approaches" (p. 82). ◆

The activities in this section are designed to both further students' understanding of base-ten concepts and also to prepare them for computation—especially addition and subtraction. (Don't forget that simple story problems such as those shown in Figure 11.15 are also effective.) The first of these bridging activities involves skip counting using the calculator. By adjusting the numbers, it can be made appropriate for almost any grade.

Activity 11.26

Calculator Challenge Counting

Students press any number on the calculator (e.g., 7) and then ⊞ 4. They say the sum before they press ⊟. Then they continue to add 4 mentally, challenging themselves to say the number before they press ⊟. Challenge them to see how far they can go without making a mistake.

The constant addend (⊞ 4) in "Calculator Challenge Counting" can be any number, even a two- or three-digit number. Generally, the starting number is less than ten but there is no reason that students cannot begin, for example, with 327 or any other number. Young students will even find jumps of five fairly challenging if the starting number is not also a multiple of five. Skip counting by 20 or 25 will be easier than counting by 7 or 12 and will help to develop important patterns and relationships.

"Calculator Challenge Counting" can also go in reverse. That is, enter a number such as 123 in the calculator and press ⊟ 6. As before, students say the result before pressing ⊟. Each successive press will subtract six or whatever constant was entered.

Two children can work together quite profitably on this activity. The flexibility of the activity allows for it to be used over and over at various skill levels, always challenging students and improving their mental skills with numbers.

The next activity combines symbolism with base-ten representations.

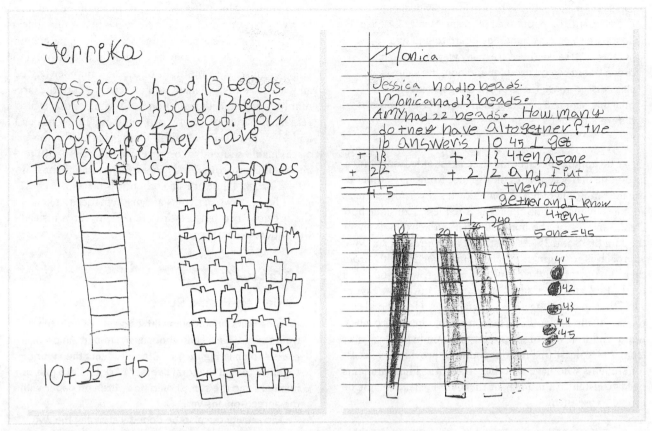

Figure 11.15 The work of two first-grade children in January. They both solved the problem 10 + 13 + 22. Jerrika's work shows she does not yet use tens in her computation whereas Monica is clearly adding groups of ten.

Activity 11.27

Numbers, Squares, Sticks, and Dots

As illustrated in Figure 11.16, prepare a worksheet or a transparency on which a numeral and some base-ten pieces are shown. Use small squares, sticks, and dots to keep the drawings simple. The task is to mentally compute the totals.

If this activity is done as a full class, discuss each exercise before going to the next. If you use a worksheet format, include only a few examples and have students write how they went about solving them. It is still important to have a discussion with the class.

The next activity extends the use of the hundreds board.

Activity 11.28

Hundreds Board Addition

For this activity it is best to have a classroom hundreds board (or a thousands board) that all students

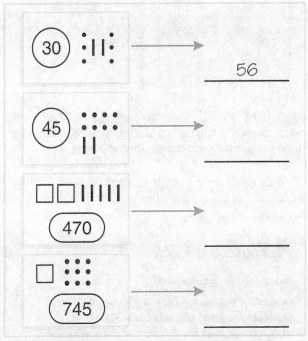

Figure 11.16 Flexible counting on or addition using both models and numerals.

can see. An alternative is to provide individual hundreds boards on paper (see Blackline Master 22). Students are to use the hundreds board to add two numbers. Because there are many ways that the hundreds board can be used for addition, the value is in class discussions. Therefore, it is a good idea to do only one sum at a time and then have a discussion of different methods.

The hundreds chart can be seen as a folded-up number line—one that accentuates the distance from any number to the next multiple of ten. A jump down a row is the same as adding ten and a jump up a row is ten less. Consider how a child might use the hundreds chart to help think about the sum of 38 and 25. As illustrated in Figure 11.17(a), one approach is to begin at 38 and count over 2 to 40. From there a student might count down two rows to 60 for a total of 22 and then add 3 more in the next row. Figure 11.17(b) shows adding 38 beginning at 25. Here the idea is to add 40 and back off 2. There are also other approaches. Many children will simply count on 25 individual squares from 38. At least this tedious counting provides an access for students who have no other strategies. These students need to listen to the ideas of their classmates but not be forced to use them.

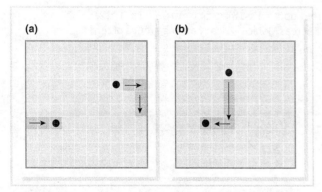

Figure 11.17 Two methods of adding 38 + 25 on the hundreds chart. It is important to stress the idea that moving down a row in the column is the same as adding 10.

The following activity is similar to "Hundreds Board Addition" but looks forward to the idea of adding up as a method of subtraction.

Activity 11.29

How Much Between?

Students must have access to a hundreds board. Students are given two numbers. Their task is to determine how much from one number to the next.

In "How Much Between?" the choice of the two numbers will have an impact on the strategies that some students will use. The easiest pairs are those in the same column, such as 24 and 64. This may be a good place to begin. If the larger number is to the right of the first number (e.g., 24 and 56), students will likely add on tens to get to the target number's row and then add ones. Of course, this is also a reasonable strategy for any two numbers. But consider 17 and 45, with 45 being left of 17 on the chart. With this pair, a reasonable strategy is to move down 3 rows (+30) to 47 and then count back 2 (–2) to 45. The total count is now 30 – 2 or 28. There are also other possible approaches.

The next two activities are mathematically parallel to the previous two but use little ten-frame cards instead of the hundreds chart.

Activity 11.30

Little Ten-Frame Sums

Provide pairs of students with two sets of little ten-frame cards. Each child chooses a number. An example is shown in Figure 11.18(a). Students then work together to find the total number of dots. Each pair of numbers and the sum should be written on paper with the agreed-on answer.

The activity can also be done by showing the two numbers on the overhead projector and having students work in pairs at their desks.

Activity 11.31

How Far to My Number?

Students work in pairs with a single set of little ten-frame cards. One student uses the cards to make a number less than 50. In the meantime, the other student writes a number larger than 50 on a piece of paper, as shown in Figure 11.18(b). You may choose to limit the size of this number but it is not necessary. The task is for the students to work together to find out how much more must be added to the ten-frame number to get to the written number. Students should try to do this without using any more cards. Once an answer is determined, they should make their answer with cards and see if the total is the same as the written numbers.

ll —————————— *Pause and Reflect*

Try your hand at the two examples in Figure 11.18. How many ways can you imagine that two students might do these? Share your ideas with a colleague.

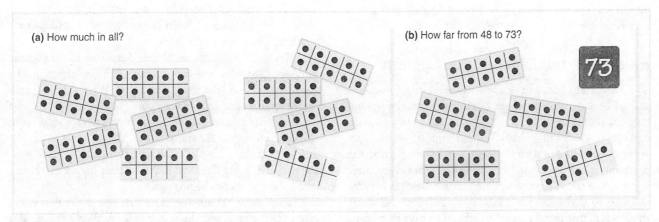

(a) How much in all?

(b) How far from 48 to 73?

73

Figure 11.18 Two tasks that can be done with little ten-frame cards.

Chapter 12 will discuss a variety of solution strategies that students use to add and subtract numbers. Students should have ample opportunities to develop their ideas in activities like those in this section. Notice, however, that students may still be developing their ideas about numbers and the distances between them. These ideas are as much about place-value understanding as about addition and subtraction. The little ten-frames and the hundreds chart are good models to support the development of these relationships.

Students who exhibit difficulty with any of these activities may also have difficulty with almost any type of invented computation. For example, how do students go about the exercises in Activity 11.27, "Numbers, Squares, Sticks, and Dots"? That activity requires that children have sufficient understanding of base-ten concepts to use them in meaningful counts. If students are counting by ones, perhaps on their fingers, then more practice with these activities may be misplaced. Rather, consider additional counting and grouping activities in which students have the opportunity to see the value of groups of ten. Using the little ten-frame cards may also help.

"How Far to My Number?" (Activity 11.31) is also a useful task for a diagnostic interview. As you listen to how children solve these problems, you will realize that there is a lot more information to be found out about their thinking beyond simply getting the correct answer. ◆

Connections to Real-World Ideas

We should not permit children to study place-value concepts without encouraging them to see number in the world about them. You do not need a prescribed activity to bring real numbers into the classroom.

Children in the second grade should be thinking about numbers under 100 first and, soon after, numbers up to 1000. Quantities larger than that are difficult to think about. Where are numbers like this? Around your school: the number of children in each class, the numbers on the school buses, the number of minutes devoted to mathematics each day and then each week, the number of cartons of chocolate and plain milk served in the cafeteria each day, the numbers on the calendar (days in a week, month, year), the number of days since school has started. And then there are measurements, numbers at home, numbers on a field trip, numbers in the news, and so on.

What do you do with these numbers? Turn them into interesting graphs, write stories using them, make up problems, devise contests.

As children get a bit older, the interest in numbers can expand beyond the school and classroom. All sorts of things can and should be measured to create graphs, draw inferences, and make comparisons. For example, what numbers are associated with the "average" fifth grader? Height, weight, arm span, age in months, number of siblings, distance from home to school, length of standing broad jump, number of pets, hours spent watching TV in a week. How can you find the average for these or other numbers that may be of interest to the students in your room? Is anyone really average?

The particular way you bring number and the real world together in your class is up to you. But do not underestimate the value of connecting the real world to the classroom.

Numbers Beyond 1000

For children to have good concepts of numbers beyond 1000, the conceptual ideas that have been carefully developed must be extended. This is sometimes difficult to do because physical models for thousands are not commonly available, or you may just have one large cube to show. At the same time, number sense ideas must also be developed. In many ways, it is these informal ideas about very large numbers that are the most important.

Extending the Place-Value System

Two important ideas developed for three-digit numbers should be extended to larger numbers. First, the grouping idea should be generalized. That is, ten in any position makes a single thing (group) in the next position, and vice versa. Second, the oral and written patterns for numbers in three digits are duplicated in a clever way for every three digits to the left. These two related ideas are not as easy for children to understand as adults seem to believe. Because models for large numbers are so difficult to have or picture, textbooks must deal with these ideas in a predominantly symbolic manner. That is not sufficient!

Activity 11.32

What Comes Next?

Have a "What Comes Next?" discussion with the use of base-ten strips and squares. The unit or ones piece is a 1-centimeter (cm) square. The tens piece is a 10 × 1 strip. The hundreds piece is a square, 10 cm × 10 cm. What is next? Ten hundreds is called a thousand. What shape? It could be a strip made of 10 hundreds squares. Tape 10 hundreds together. What is next? (Reinforce the idea of "ten makes one" that has progressed to this point.) Ten one-thousand strips would make a square measuring 1 meter (m) on a side. Once the class has figured out the shape of the thousand piece, the problem-based task is "What comes next?" Let small groups work on the dimensions of a ten-thousand piece.

If your students become interested in seeing the big pieces from "What Comes Next?" engage them in measuring them out on paper. Ten ten-thousand squares (100,000) go together to make a huge strip. Draw this strip on a long sheet of butcher paper, and mark off the ten squares that make it up. You will have to go out in the hall.

How far you want to extend this square, strip, square, strip sequence depends on your class. The idea that 10 in one place makes 1 in the next can be brought home dramatically. It is quite possible with older children to make the next 10 m × 10 m square using chalk lines on the playground. The next strip is 100 m × 10 m. This can be measured out on a large playground with kids marking the corners. By this point, the payoff includes an appreciation of the increase in size of each successive amount as well as the ten-makes-one progression. The 100 m × 10 m strip is the model for 10 million, and the 10 m × 10 m square

models 1 million. The difference between 1 million and 10 million is dramatic. Even the concept of 1 million tiny centimeter squares is dramatic.

Try the "What Comes Next?" discussion in the context of these three-dimensional models. The first three shapes are distinct: a *cube*, a *long*, and a *flat*. What comes next? Stack ten flats and they make a cube, same shape as the first one, only 1000 times larger. What comes next? (See Figure 11.19.) Ten *cubes* make another *long*. What comes next? Ten big *longs* make a big *flat*. The first three shapes have now repeated! Ten big flats will make an even bigger cube, and the triplet of shapes begins again.

Each cube has a name. The first one is the *unit* cube, the next is a *thousand*, the next a *million*, then a *billion*, and so on. Each long is 10 cubes: 10 units, 10 thousands, 10 millions. Similarly, each flat shape is 100 cubes.

To read a number, first mark it off in triples from the right. The triples are then read, stopping at the end of each to name the unit (or cube shape) for that triple (see Figure 11.20). Leading zeros in each triple are ignored. If students can learn to read numbers like 059 (fifty-nine) or 009 (nine), they should be able to read any number. To write a number, use the same scheme. If first mastered orally, the system is quite easy. Remind students not to use the word "and" when reading a whole number. For example, 106 should be read as "one hundred six," not "one hundred *and* six." The word "and" will be needed to signify a decimal point. Please make sure you read numbers accurately.

It is important for children to realize that the system does have a logical structure, is not totally arbitrary, and can be understood.

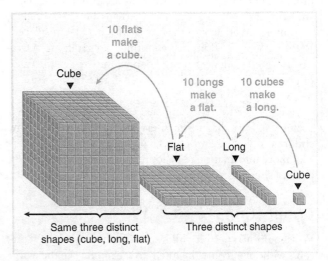

Figure 11.19 With every three places, the shapes repeat. Each cube represents a 1, each long represents a 10, and each flat represents a 100.

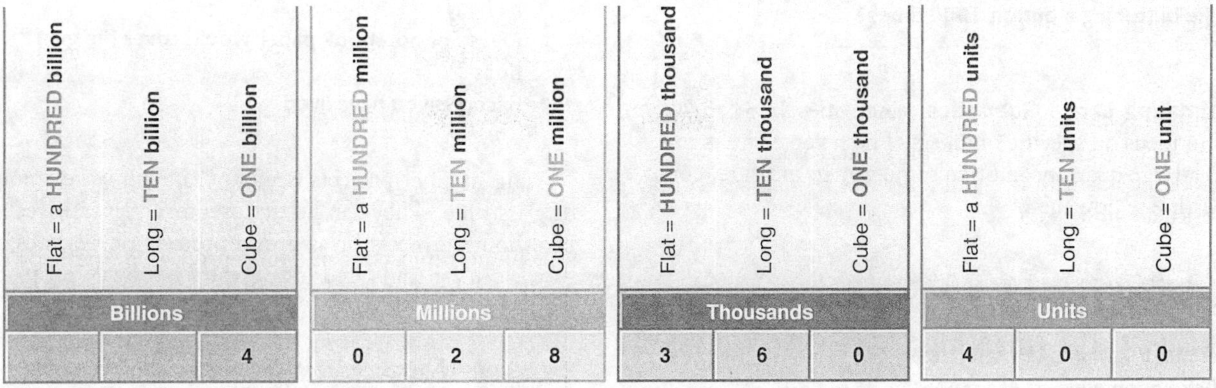

Flat = a HUNDRED billion	Long = TEN billion	Cube = ONE billion	Flat = a HUNDRED million	Long = TEN million	Cube = ONE million	Flat = HUNDRED thousand	Long = TEN thousand	Cube = ONE thousand	Flat = a HUNDRED units	Long = TEN units	Cube = ONE unit
Billions			**Millions**			**Thousands**			**Units**		
		4	0	2	8	3	6	0	4	0	0

"Four billion, twenty-eight million, three hundred sixty thousand, four hundred."

Figure 11.20 The triples system for naming large numbers.

Conceptualizing Large Numbers

The ideas just discussed are only partially helpful in thinking about the actual quantities involved in very large numbers. For example, in extending the square, strip, square, strip sequence, some appreciation for the quantities of 1000 or of 100,000 is acquired. But it is hard for anyone to translate quantities of small squares into quantities of other items, distances, or time.

⏸ ──────────── *Pause and Reflect*

How do you think about 1000 or 100,000? Do you have any real concept of a million?

Creating References for Special Big Numbers.   In these activities, numbers like 1000, 10,000 (see Blackline Master 29), or even 1 million are translated literally or imaginatively into something that is easy or fun to think about. Interesting quantities become lasting reference points or benchmarks for large numbers and thereby add meaning to numbers encountered in real life.

Activity 11.33

Collecting 10,000

Collections. As a class or grade-level project, collect some type of object with the objective of reaching some specific quantity—for example, 1000 or 10,000 buttons, walnuts, old pencils, soda can poptops, or pieces of junk mail. If you begin aiming for 100,000 or 1 million, be sure to think it through. One teacher spent nearly 10 years with her classes before amassing a million bottle caps. It takes a small dump truck to hold that many!

Activity 11.34

Showing 10,000

Illustrations. Sometimes it is easier to create large amounts. For example, start a project where students draw 100 or 200 or even 500 dots on a sheet of paper. Each week different students contribute a specified number. Another idea is to cut up newspaper into pieces the same size as dollar bills to see what a large quantity would look like. Paper chain links can be constructed over time and hung down the hallways with special numbers marked. Let the school be aware of the ultimate goal.

Activity 11.35

How Long?/How Far?

Real and imagined distances. How long is a million baby steps? Other ideas that address length: toothpicks, dollar bills, or candy bars end to end; children holding hands in a line; blocks or bricks stacked up; children lying down head to toe. Real measures can also be used: feet, centimeters, meters.

Activity 11.36

A Long Time

Time. How long is 1000 seconds? How long is a million seconds? A billion? How long would it take to count to 10,000 or 1 million? (To make the counts all the same, use your calculator to do the counting. Just press the [=].) How long would it take to do some task like buttoning a button 1000 times?

Estimating Large Quantities. Activities 11.33 through 11.36 focus on specific numbers. The reverse idea is to select a large quantity and find some way to measure, count, or estimate how many.

Activity 11.37

Really Large Quantities

Ask how many

- Candy bars would cover the floor of your room
- Steps an ant would take to walk around the school building
- Grains of rice would fill a cup or a gallon jug
- Quarters could be stacked in one stack floor to ceiling

- Pennies can be laid side by side down the entire hallway
- Pieces of notebook paper would cover the gym floor
- Seconds you have lived

Big-number projects need not take up large amounts of class time. They can be explored over several weeks as take-home projects or as group projects or, perhaps best of all, can be translated into great schoolwide estimation contests.

 The *Standards* document also recognizes the need for relating large numbers to the real world. "A third-grade class might explore the size of 1000 by skip-counting to 1000, building a model of 1000 using ten hundred charts, gathering 1000 items such as paper clips and developing efficient ways to count them, or using strips that are 10 or 100 centimeters long to show the length of 1000 centimeters" (p. 149). ◆

Reflections on Chapter 11

Writing to Learn

1. Explain how a child who has not yet developed base-ten concepts understands quantities as large as, say, 85. Contrast this with a child who understands these same quantities in terms of base-ten groupings.
2. What is meant by *equivalent representations*?
3. Explain the three ways one can count a set of objects and how these methods of counting can be used to coordinate concepts and oral and written names for numbers.
4. Describe the three types of physical models for base-ten concepts. What is the significance of the differences among these models?
5. How do children learn to write two- and three-digit numbers in a way that is connected to the base-ten meanings of ones and tens or ones, tens, and hundreds?
6. Describe some patterns that can be found on the hundreds chart. In addition to looking for patterns, describe another activity with the hundreds chart.

7. What are landmark numbers? Describe the relationships you want children to develop concerning landmark numbers. Describe an activity that addresses these relationships.
8. How can place-value concepts and computation skills be developed at the same time? Describe two activities that can be used to address these dual agendas.

For Discussion and Exploration

1. Based on the suggestions in this chapter, design a diagnostic interview for a child at a particular grade level and conduct the interview. It is a good idea to take a friend to act as an observer or to use a tape recorder or video recorder to keep track of how the interview went. Analyze the child's understanding of the comments and suggest your next instructional steps.

Resources for Chapter 11

Literature Connections

Books that emphasize groups of things, even simple counting books, are a good beginning to the notion of ten things in a single group. Many books have wonderful explorations of large quantities and how they can be combined and separated.

Moira's Birthday *Munsch, 1987*

As Moira plans her birthday party, she invites more and more children until she has invited all the children in the kindergarten, first, second, third, fourth, fifth,* and sixth grades. Then she needs to order food. She orders 200 cakes and 200 pizzas. Wonderful bedlam ensues. A second-grade teacher, Diane Oppedal (1995), used this story as a background for the question "How can you show 200 things in different ways?" As children work on this or similar projects, they can be encouraged to use some form of groups to keep track of their collections.

100th Day Worries *Cuyler, 2000*
100 Days of School *Harris, 1999*

Both of these books focus on the 100th day of school, which is one way to recognize the landmark number of 100. Through a variety of ways to think about 100 either through collections of 100 items or 10 salty peanuts every minute for 10 minutes, students will be able to use these stories to think about the relative size of 100 or ways to make 100 using a variety of combinations.

How Much Is a Million? *Schwartz, 1985*
If You Made a Million *Schwartz, 1989*
On Beyond a Million: An Amazing Math Journey
Schwartz, 1999
Magic of a Million Activity Book—Grades 2–5
Schwartz & Whitin, 1998

David Schwartz has generated a series of entertaining and conceptually sound children's books about the powers of ten or what makes a million—from visual images of students standing on one another's shoulders in a formation that reaches the moon to various monetary collections. In addition, the activity book by Schwartz and Whitin provides a series of powerful activities to help students interpret large numbers.

The King's Commissioners *Friedman, 1994*

The king has so many commissioners, he can't keep track of how many there are. In a hilarious tale, the commissioners are marched into the throne room to be counted. One person tries to count them by twos and another by fives. The princess convinces the king that there are many other excellent ways to count. The story is a natural background for place-value concepts, including grouping and different counting methods, large numbers, and informal early computation challenges.

A Million Fish . . . More or Less *McKissack, 1992*

This story, which takes place in lower Louisiana, is a tall tale of a boy who catches three fish . . . and then a million more. The story is full of exaggerations such as a turkey that weighs 500 pounds and a jump-rope contest (using a snake) where the story's hero wins with 5553 jumps. "Could these things be true? How long would it take to jump 5553 times? Could Hugh put a million fish in his wagon? How do you write half of a million?"

Recommended Readings

Articles

Ellett, K. (2005). Making a million meaningful. *Mathematics Teaching in the Middle School, 10*(8), 416–423.
This amazing collection of ideas for helping students think about large numbers, especially 1 million, is found in the MTMS focus issue on Mathematics and Literature. Ellett gives examples of student projects and ways for students to conceptualize a million, shows student work, and connects many of these ideas to literature.

Kari, A. R., & Anderson, C. B. (2003). Opportunities to develop place value through student dialogue. *Teaching Children Mathematics, 10*(2), 78–82.
These two teachers describe a mixed first/second-grade classroom illustrating in vivid detail how children's understanding of two-digit numbers can at first be quite mistaken and then developed conceptually with the aid of discussion. Much of the discussion revolves around one child's belief that any 1 in a number stands for ten. This student is convinced that 11 + 11 + 11 is 60. Reading this article emphasizes the wide range of student ideas and the value of classroom discourse.

Books

Burns, M. (1994). *Math by all means: Place value, grades 1–2.* Sausalito, CA: Math Solutions Publications.
Burns provides 25 very detailed lessons in place value. There are ample examples of children's written work and descriptions of interactions that took place in actual classrooms.

Richardson, K. (2003). *Assessing math concepts: Grouping tens.* Bellingham, WA: Mathematical Perspectives.
This is one of a nine-part series on using diagnostics interviews and other assessment tools to understand children's grasp of a concept—in this case, grouping by tens. Tips are shared about conducting careful observations and suggestions for instruction. Blackline Masters are included to support the assessments.

Online Resources

Base-Ten Blocks
http://nlvm.usu.edu/en/nav/topic_t_1.html

There are several variations of the basic base-ten blocks applet here. Blocks appear on a place-value chart and can be grouped or broken apart. The addition and subtraction versions pose problems and allow blocks in two colors to model two separate numbers.

Comparison Estimator
www.shodor.org/interactivate/activities/estim2/index.html

Two sets of small objects are shown and the task is to decide which set has more. The actual counts are then given. The same applet also allows for comparisons of length and areas.

Hundreds Board and Calculator
http://standards.nctm.org/document/eexamples/chap4/4.5/index.htm

A calculator is used to create skip-counting patterns on a hundreds chart. You can start the pattern on any number and skip by any number. The chart extends to 1000. A second pattern will show with red dots on top of the first pattern.

Lots of Dots and a Million Dots on One Page
www.vendian.org/envelope

These explorations of big numbers are only a hint at the array of ideas found on this website. A lot is beyond the elementary school, but anyone interested in big numbers and measures will certainly be intrigued. See a dot for every second of the day!

The MegaPenny Project
www.kokogiak.com/megapenny/default.asp

A fascinating look at large numbers in terms of stacks of pennies. Stacks from 1 penny to a trillion pennies are shown with visual referents, value, weight, height if stacked, and more. Great for large-number concepts.

The Place Value Game (Jefferson Lab)
http://education.jlab.org/placevalue/index.html

The goal is to make the largest possible number from the digits the computer gives you. Digits are presented one at a time. The player must place the digit in the number without knowing what the next digits will be. It's fun and also good for understanding ordering of numbers.

Field Experience Guide Connections

FEG Expanded Lesson 9.5 focuses on estimating tens and ones, building important concepts in place value. In FEG Expanded Lesson 9.2 ("Close, Far, and In Between"), students estimate the relative size of a number between 0 and 100, strengthening their conceptual understanding of number size and place value.

Chapter 12

Developing Strategies for Whole-Number Computation

Much of the public sees computational skill as the hallmark of what it means to know mathematics at the elementary school level. Although this is far from the truth, the issue of computational skills with whole numbers is, in fact, a very important part of the elementary curriculum, especially in grades 1 to 6.

Rather than a single method of subtracting (or any operation), the most appropriate method can and should change flexibly as the numbers and the context change. In the spirit of the *Standards*, the issue is no longer a matter of "knows how to subtract three-digit numbers"; rather, it is the development over time of an assortment of flexible skills, including the ability to compute mentally, that will best serve students in the real world.

It is quite possible that you do not have these skills, but you can acquire them. Work at them as you learn about them. Equip yourself with a flexible array of computational strategies.

Big Ideas

1. Flexible methods of computation involve taking apart and combining numbers in a wide variety of ways. Most of the partitions of numbers are based on place value or "compatible" numbers—number pairs that work easily together, such as 25 and 75.

2. "Invented" strategies are flexible methods of computing that vary with the numbers and the situation. Successful use of the strategies requires that they be understood by the one who is using them—hence, the term *invented*.

3. Flexible methods for computation require a good understanding of the operations and properties of the operations, especially the commutative property and the distributive property for multiplication. How the operations are related—addition

to subtraction, addition to multiplication, and multiplication to division—is also an important ingredient.

4. The traditional algorithms are clever strategies for computing that have been developed over time. Each is based on performing the operation on one place value at a time with transitions to an adjacent position (trades or regrouping). Traditional algorithms tend to make us think in terms of digits rather than the composite number that the digits make up. These algorithms work for all numbers but are often not the most efficient or useful methods of computing.

Mathematics Content Connections

Flexible computation is built on the ideas found in the preceding three chapters. Flexible methods for computing, especially mental methods, allow one to reason much more effectively in every area of mathematics involving numbers.

- **Operation Meanings and Fact Mastery** (Chapters 9 and 10): Children can and should explore contextual problems involving multidigit numbers as they develop their understanding of the operations. Without basic facts, students will be severely disadvantaged in any computational endeavor. Furthermore, many strategies and number concepts used to master basic facts can be extended to computation.

- **Place Value** (Chapter 11): Place value is not only a basis for computation; students can also develop place-value understanding as a *result* of finding their own methods of computing.

- **Computational Estimation** (Chapter 13): Computational estimation involves substituting "nice" numbers in a computation so that the new computation can be done mentally or at least with minimal effort.

Toward Computational Fluency

With today's technology the need for doing tedious computations by hand has essentially disappeared. A study done in 1957, well before the commonplace use of calculators, found that adults used pencil-and-paper computation methods for only 25 percent of the calculations they did (Wandt & Brown in Northcote & McIntosh, 1999). We now know that there are numerous methods of computing that can be handled either mentally or with pencil-and-paper support. In most everyday instances, these alternative strategies for computing are easier and faster, can often be done mentally, and contribute to our overall number sense. The traditional algorithms (procedures for computing) do not have these benefits.

Consider the following problem.

Mary had 114 spaces in her photo album. So far she has 89 photos in the album. How many more photos can she put in before the album is full?

 ———————— *Pause and Reflect*

Try solving the photo album problem using some method other than the one you were taught in school. If you want to begin with the 9 and the 4, try a different approach. Can you do it mentally? Can you do it in more than one way? Work on this before reading further.

Here are just four of many methods that have been used by students in the primary grades to solve the computation in the photo album problem:

89 + 11 is 100. 11 + 14 is 25.

90 + 10 is 100 and 14 more is 24 plus 1 (for 89, not 90) is 25.

Take away 14 and then take away 11 more or 25 in all.

89, 99, 109 (that's 20). 110, 111, 112, 113, 114 (keeping track on fingers) is 25.

Strategies such as these can be done mentally, are generally faster than the traditional algorithms, and make sense to the person using them. Every day, students and adults resort to traditional, often error-prone strategies when other, more meaningful methods would be faster and less susceptible to error. Flexibility with a variety of computational strategies is an important tool for successful daily living. It is time to broaden our perspective of what it means to compute.

Figure 12.1 lists three general types of computing. The initial, inefficient direct modeling methods can, with guid-

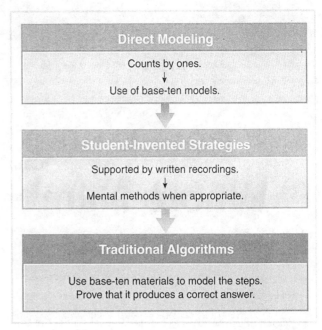

Figure 12.1 Three types of computational strategies.

ance, develop into an assortment of student-invented strategies that are flexible and useful. As noted in the diagram, many of these methods can be handled mentally, although no special methods are designed specifically for mental computation. The traditional pencil-and-paper algorithms remain in the mainstream curricula. However, the emphasis given to them should, at the very least, be considered.

NCTM Standards "Equally essential [with basic facts] is computational fluency—having and using efficient and accurate methods for computing. Fluency might be manifested in using a combination of mental strategies and jottings on paper or using an algorithm with paper and pencil, particularly when the numbers are large, to produce accurate results quickly. Regardless of the particular methods used, students should be able to explain their method, understand that many methods exist, and see the usefulness of methods that are efficient, accurate, and general" (p. 32). ◆

Direct Modeling

The developmental step that usually precedes invented strategies is called *direct modeling*: the use of manipulatives or drawings along with counting to represent directly the meaning of an operation or story problem. Figure 12.2 provides an example using base-ten materials, but often students use simple counters and count by ones.

Students who consistently count by ones most likely have not developed base-ten grouping concepts. That does not mean that they should not continue to solve prob-

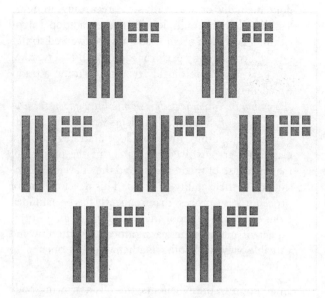

Figure 12.2 A possible direct modeling of 36 × 7 using base-ten models.

lems involving two-digit numbers. As you work with these children, suggest (don't force) that they group counters by tens as they count. Some students will use the ten-stick as a counting device to keep track of counts of ten, even though they are counting each segment of the stick by ones.

Students using direct modeling will soon transfer their ideas to methods that do not rely on materials or counting. The direct-modeling phase provides a necessary background of ideas. These developmental strategies are also important because they provide students who are not ready for more efficient methods a way to explore the same problems as classmates who have progressed beyond this stage. It is important not to push students prematurely to abandon manipulative approaches.

Student-Invented Strategies

Carpenter, Franke, Jacobs, Fennema, and Empson (1998) refer to any strategy other than the traditional algorithm or that does not involve the use of physical materials or counting by ones as an *invented strategy*. We will use this term also, although *personal and flexible strategies* might be equally appropriate. At times, invented strategies become mental methods after the ideas have been explored, used, and understood. For example, 75 + 19 is not difficult to do mentally (75 + 20 is 95, less 1 is 94). For 847 + 256, some students may write down intermediate steps to aid remembering as they work through the problem. (Try that one yourself.) In the classroom, some written support is often encouraged as strategies develop. Written records of thinking are more easily shared and help students focus on the ideas. The distinction between written, partially written,

and mental is not important, especially in the development period.

Over the past two decades, a number of research projects have focused attention on how children handle computational situations when they have not been taught a specific algorithm or strategy.* "There is mounting evidence that children both in and out of school can construct methods for adding and subtracting multi-digit numbers without explicit instruction" (Carpenter et al., 1998, p. 4). Data supporting students' construction of useful methods for multiplication and division have also been gathered (Baek, 2006; Fosnot & Dolk, 2001; Kamii & Dominick, 1997; Schifter, Bastable, & Russell, 1999b).

Not all students invent their own strategies. Strategies invented by class members are shared, explored, and tried out by others. However, students should not be permitted to use any strategy without understanding it (Campbell, Rowan, & Suarez, 1998).

Contrasts with Traditional Algorithms.   There are significant differences between student-invented strategies and traditional algorithms.

1. *Invented strategies are number oriented rather than digit oriented.* For example, an invented strategy for 68 × 7 begins 7 × 60 is 420 and 56 more is 476. The first product is 7 times *sixty*, not the digit 6, as would be the case in the traditional algorithm. Using the traditional algorithm for 45 + 32, children never think of 40 and 30 but rather 4 + 3. Kamii, long a crusader against traditional algorithms, claims that they "unteach" place value (Kamii & Dominick, 1998).
2. *Invented strategies are left-handed rather than right-handed.* Invented strategies begin with the largest parts of numbers, those represented by the leftmost digits. For 26 × 47, invented strategies will begin with 20 × 40 is 800, providing some sense of the size of the eventual answer in just one step. The traditional algorithm begins with 7 × 6 is 42. By beginning on the right with a digit orientation, traditional methods may hide the result until the end. Long division is an exception.
3. *Invented strategies are flexible rather than "one right way."* Invented strategies tend to change with the numbers involved in order to make the computation easier. Try each of these mentally: 465 + 230 and 526 + 98. Did

---

*The Cognitively Guided Instruction (CGI) project, directed by Carpenter, Fennema, and Franke at the University of Wisconsin; the Conceptually Based Instruction (CBI) project, directed by Hiebert and Wearne at the University of Delaware; the Problem Centered Mathematics Project (PCMP), directed by Human, Murray, and Olivier at the University of Stellenbosch, South Africa; the Supporting Ten-Structured Thinking (STST) project, directed by Fuson at Northwestern University; and ongoing research by Kamii at the University of Alabama are all examples of efforts that have informed thinking about invented strategies for computation.

you use the same method? The traditional algorithm suggests using the same tool on all problems. The traditional algorithm for 7000 – 25 typically leads to student errors, yet a mental strategy is relatively simple.

Benefits of Student-Invented Strategies. The development of invented strategies delivers more than computational facility. Both the development of these strategies and their regular use have positive benefits that are difficult to ignore.

- *Students make fewer errors.* Research indicates that students using methods they understand make many fewer errors than when strategies are learned without understanding (Gravemeijer & van Galen, 2003; Kamii & Dominick, 1997). After decades of good intentions with the traditional algorithms, many students do not understand the concepts that support them. Not only do these students make errors, but also the errors are often systematic and difficult to remediate. Errors with invented strategies are less frequent and almost never systematic.
- *Less reteaching is required.* Teachers often complain that students' early efforts with alternative strategies are slow and time consuming. The time-consuming struggle in these early stages, however, results in ideas that are meaningful and well integrated in a web of ideas that are robust and long lasting. An increase in development time is made up for with a significant decrease in the need for reteaching and remediation.
- *Students develop number sense.* "More than just a means to produce answers, computation is increasingly seen as a window on the deep structure of the number system" (NRC, 2001, p. 182). Students' development and use of number-oriented, flexible algorithms offer them a rich understanding of the number system. In contrast, students frequently use traditional algorithms without being able to explain why they work (Carroll & Porter, 1997). Such rules without reasons have few benefits.
- *Invented strategies are the basis for mental computation and estimation.* When invented strategies are the norm for computation, there is no need to teach other methods or even to talk about mental computation as if it were a separate skill. Often students who have been taught to record their thinking with invented strategies or to write down intermediate steps will ask if this writing is really required since they find they can do the procedures more efficiently mentally. Computational estimation does involve a separate set of skills; the development of flexible, number-oriented strategies plays a significant role in most of these skills (NRC, 2001).
- *Flexible methods are often faster than the traditional algorithms.* Consider the product 64 × 8. A simple invented strategy might involve 60 × 8 = 480 and 8 × 4 = 32. The sum of 480 and 32 is 500 + 12 more—512. This is easily done mentally, or even with some recording, in much less time than the multiple steps of the traditional algorithm. Those who become adept with invented strategies will consistently perform addition and subtraction computations more quickly than those using a traditional algorithm.
- *Algorithm invention is itself a significantly important process of "doing mathematics."* Students who invent a strategy for computing, or who adopt a strategy from a classmate, are involved intimately in the process of making sense of mathematics and they develop a confidence in their ability to do so. This development of procedures is a process that frequently has been hidden from elementary school students. By engaging in this aspect of mathematics, a significantly different and valuable view of "doing mathematics" is opened to young children.

In addition to these benefits, there is a growing body of evidence that students' computational skills do not suffer in contrast to those taught the traditional strategies. Data collected from school systems using standards-based programs reveal that those students consistently outperform their traditional program counterparts on measures of understanding and problem solving. In the area of multidigit computation, most studies find that the standards-based students are either on a par with students in traditional programs or outperform them (Fuson, 2003). Students in the Netherlands are not taught to use traditional algorithms and they perform at least as well as U.S. students (Gravemeijer & van Galen, 2003; Torrence, 2003).

Mental Computation. A mental computation strategy is simply any invented strategy that is done mentally. What may be a mental strategy for one student may require written support by another. Initially, students should not be asked to do computations mentally, as this may threaten students who have not yet developed a reasonable invented strategy or who are still at the direct-modeling stage. At the same time, you may be quite amazed at the ability of students (and at your own ability) to do computations mentally.

Try your own hand with this example:

$$342 + 153 + 481$$

Pause and Reflect

For the addition task just shown, try this method: Begin by adding the hundreds, saying the totals as you go—*3 hundred, 4 hundred, 8 hundred.* Then add on to this the tens in successive manner and finally the ones. Give it a try.

When the computations are a bit more complicated, the challenge is more interesting and generally there are more alternatives. For 7 × 28, the *Standards* lists three paths to a solution but there are at least two more (NCTM, 2000, p. 152). How many ways can you find?

As your students become more adept, they can and should be challenged from time to time to do computations mentally. Do not expect the same skills of all students.

Traditional Algorithms

With the exception of *Investigations*, every commercial curriculum teaches the traditional algorithms. More than a century of tradition plus pressures from families are at least partly responsible for our unwillingness to abandon these approaches. Other arguments generally revolve around efficiency and the need for methods that will work with all numbers. For addition and subtraction, one can easily counter that well-understood and practiced invented strategies are more than adequate. However, it is certainly true that a computation such as 486 × 372 is difficult with invented strategies. But should those computations be done with technology?

No matter the growing interest in invented strategies, and no matter how compelling the arguments against the traditional algorithms may be, few classroom teachers will be able to abandon the traditional approaches.

Delay! Delay! Delay! Students are not likely to invent the traditional algorithms. You will need to introduce and explain each algorithm to them and help them understand how and why they work. No matter how carefully you introduce these algorithms into your classroom as simply another alternative, students are likely to sense that "this is the real way" or the "right way" to compute. Once having begun with traditional algorithms, it is extremely difficult to suggest to students that they learn other methods. Notice how difficult it is for you to begin computations by working from the left rather than the right and to think in terms of whole numbers rather than digits. These habits, once established, are difficult to change.

Can the traditional algorithms be taught meaningfully? Absolutely! Meaningful approaches for teaching each algorithm are discussed later in this chapter. If you plan to teach the traditional algorithms, you are well advised to first spend a significant time with invented strategies—months, not weeks. Do not feel that you must rush to the traditional algorithms. Delay! Spend your effort on invented methods. The understanding children gain from working with invented strategies will make it much easier for you to teach the traditional algorithms.

Traditional Algorithms Will Happen. Children often pick up the traditional algorithms from older siblings, last year's teacher, and family members ("My dad showed me an easy way"). Such students who already know a traditional method often resist the invention of more flexible strategies. What do you do then?

First and foremost, apply the same rule to traditional algorithms as to all strategies: *If you use it, you must understand why it works and be able to explain it.* In an atmosphere that says, "Let's figure out why this works," students can profit from making sense of these algorithms just like any other. But the responsibility should be theirs, not yours.

Accept a traditional algorithm (once it is understood) as one more strategy to put in the class "tool box" of methods. But reinforce the idea that like the other strategies, it may be more useful in some instances than in others. Pose problems where a mental strategy is much more useful, such as 504 − 498 or 75 × 4. Discuss which method seems best. Point out that for a problem such as 4568 + 12,813, the traditional algorithm has some advantages. But in the real world, most people do those computations on a calculator.

Cultural Differences in Algorithms. Although we may assume that mathematics is easier than other subjects for students who are English learners, through the belief that the language of numbers is universal, the reality is that there are many differences in notation, conventions, and algorithms. Knowing more about the diverse algorithms students bring to the classroom and their ways of recording symbols for "doing mathematics" will assist you in supporting students and responding to families (see also "Culturally Relevant Mathematics Instruction" in Chapter 6), particularly knowing that what we may call a "traditional algorithm" is not the tradition in other countries. Awareness of alternative algorithms will help you explore the procedures and ways to record answers that your students know from prior experiences in schools outside of the United States or from approaches taught to them by their families.

For example, one popular subtraction algorithm used in most Latin and European countries is known as "equal addition" or "add tens to both" and is based on the knowledge that adding the same amount to both the minuend and the subtrahend will not change the difference (answer). Therefore, if the expression to be solved is 15 − 5, there is no change to the answer (or the difference) if you add 10 to the minuend and subtrahend and solve 25 − 15. There is still a difference of 10. Let's look at 62 − 27 to think about this. Using the algorithm that you may think of as "traditional" and familiar, you would likely regroup by crossing out the 6, adding the 10 with a small "1" to the 2 in the ones column (making 12) and then subtracting the 7 from the 12 and so forth. In the "equal addition" approach you add ten to 62 by just mentally adding a small "1" (to represent ten) to the 2 in the ones column and thereby having 12. You would then counteract that addition of 10 to the minuend by mentally adding 10 to the 27 (subtrahend), but doing that by increasing the tens column by one and then subtracting 37. This may sound confusing to you—but try it. Especially when there are zeros in the minuend (e.g., 302 − 178) you may find this an interesting approach. More importantly, your possible confusion can give you the sense of how your students (and their families) may react to a completely different procedure than the one they know and find successful.

Another key component to understanding differences in cultures regarding algorithms is the heavy emphasis on mental mathematics in other countries. This often surprises teachers, especially when a student writes down just an answer with no apparent partial products, intermediate calculations, or notations. Awkwardly, this is sometimes interpreted by teachers not aware of this emphasis as the student's possibly copying another's work (Perkins & Flores, 2002). In fact, students are taught to pride themselves on their ability to do this work mentally.

Learning more about what your students, particularly those from other cultural backgrounds, are doing and thinking as they explore operations with numbers is often an opportunity to expand your own repertoire.

Development of Student-Invented Strategies

Students do not spontaneously invent wonderful computational methods while the teacher sits back and watches. Among different experimental programs, students tended to develop or gravitate toward different strategies, suggesting that teachers and the programs do have an effect on the methods students develop (Fuson et al., 1997). The following section discusses general pedagogical methods for helping children develop invented strategies that are appropriate at all grades and for all four operations.

myeducationlab

Go to the Building Teaching Skills and Dispositions section of Chapter 12 of MyEducationLab. Click on Videos and watch the video entitled **"Equations"** to see students solving equations and discussing the strategies they used.

Creating an Environment for Inventing Strategies

Invented strategies are developed out of a strong understanding of numbers. The standard development of place value often leaves students ill prepared for the challenges of inventing computational strategies. For example, some third- and fourth-grade students have difficulty naming a number that is ten more or ten less than a given two-digit number without resorting to counting. Therefore, students need a classroom environment where they can act like mathematicians and explore ideas without trepidation.

Students who are attempting to investigate these new ideas in mathematics need to find their classroom a safe place for expressing those naïve or rudimentary thoughts. Some of the very characteristics described earlier in this

book regarding the development of a problem-solving environment need to be reiterated here to establish the climate for testing conjectures and trying new approaches. Here are some factors to keep in mind:

- Expect and encourage student-to-student interactions, discussions, and conjectures
- Celebrate when students clarify previous knowledge and attempt to construct new ideas
- Encourage curiosity and an open mind to trying new things
- Talk about both right and wrong ideas in a nonevaluative or threatening way
- Move unsophisticated ideas to more sophisticated thinking through coaxing, coaching, and guided questioning
- Use contexts and story problems to capture student interest
- Consider carefully whether you should step in or step back when students are formulating new ideas (when in doubt—step back)

The three-part lesson format described in Chapter 3 is a good structure for an invented-strategy lesson. Whether the task is one or two story problems or even a bare computation, the method of solution should always be discussed. Sometimes you can provide variations with different numbers to different groups to adjust for difficulty.

Models to Support Invented Strategies

Activities that focus on the patterns in our number system and that explore addition and subtraction through place-value models such as the hundreds chart, the little ten-frame cards, or base-ten blocks can both prepare students for invented strategies and improve their number sense. A collection of appropriate activities focusing on number relationships and informal addition and subtraction strategies can be found in Chapter 11 (see pp. 199 to 206).

Note also that many of the strategies for addition and subtraction are extensions of basic fact and place-value strategies, especially those that use 10 as a bridge (see Chapter 10). For example, as students are exploring methods for mastering facts with an 8 or 9, extend these ideas to 38 or 69. As another example, double 4 can be extended to double 40.

The notion of "splitting" a number into parts is a useful strategy for all operations. Both the word *split* and the use of a visual diagram, as shown, have been found to help students develop strategies (Sáenz-Ludlow, 2004). Try using arrows or lines to indicate how two computations are joined together as shown in Figure 12.3(a).

The *empty number line* shown in Figure 12.3(b) is a technique developed in the Netherlands that is increasingly being suggested in the United States (Fosnot & Dolk, 2001; Gravemeijer & van Galen, 2003; Ineson, 2007; Varol & Farran,

(a) How much is 86 and 47?

S: I know that 80 and 20 more is 100.

T: Where do the 80 and the 20 come from?

S: I split the 47 into 20 and 20 and 7 and the 86 into 80 and 6.

T: (illustrates the splitting with lines)
    So then you added one of the 20s to 80?

S: Yes, 80 and 20 is 100. Then I added the other 20 and got 120.

T: (writes the equations on the board)

S: Then I added the 6 and the 7 and got 13.

T: (writes this equation)

S: Then I added the 120 to the 13 and got 133.

T: Indicates with joining lines.

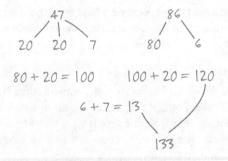

(b) How much is 4 times 68?

S: I used 70s because they were easier than 68s. First I did 70 and 70 is 140.

Then I doubled 140 to get 280.

T: Why did you double 140?

S: Because that would make four 70s, and I already had two 70s. Then I had to take off four sets of 2 because I used 70 instead of only 68. That got me to 272.

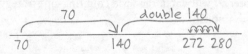

Figure 12.3 Two methods of recording students' thought processes on the board so that the class can see the strategy.

2007.) Initially, the empty number line is a good way to help you model a student's thinking for the class. Soon it will become a tool for students to use in creating their own thinking (Klein, Beishuizen, & Treffers, 1998). These researchers found that the empty number line is much more flexible than the usual number line because it can be used with any numbers and students are not confused with hash marks and the spaces between them. The hops on the line can be recorded as the students share or explain each step of their solution.

Student-Invented Strategies for Addition and Subtraction

Research has demonstrated that children will invent a lot of different strategies for addition and subtraction. Your goal might be that each of your children has at least one or two methods that are reasonably efficient, mathematically correct, and useful with lots of different numbers. Expect different children to settle on different strategies.

There is no clear-cut progression to follow that will dictate what problems you should pose to your students. You must learn to listen to the kind of reasoning they are using and the strategies that are being suggested. The numbers involved in a computation and also the type of story problems used will tend to influence how students approach a problem. Even so, you will discover many variations of thought processes. The following sections suggest a variety of invented strategies that children often use. These are presented not as a curriculum but rather to give you some idea of the range of possibilities.

Adding and Subtracting Single-Digit Numbers

When adding or subtracting a small amount, or finding the difference between two numbers that are reasonably close, many students will use counting to solve the problems. One goal should be to extend students' knowledge of basic facts and the ten-structure of the number system so that counting is not required. When the difference crosses a ten (e.g., 58 + 6), using the distance up to or down to the multiple of ten is extremely helpful.

Tommy was on page 47 of his book. Then he read 8 more pages. What page did he end up on?

How far is it from 68 to 75?

Ruth had 52 cents. She bought a small toy for 8 cents. How much does she have left?

Each of these problems crosses a ten and involves a change or a difference of less than ten. Listen for children who are counting on or counting back without paying attention to the ten. For these children, you might suggest using either the hundreds chart or the little ten-frames as shown in Figure 12.4. Also, find out how they solve fact combinations such as 8 + 6 or 13 − 5. The use of ten for these facts is essentially the same as for the higher-decade problems. Related activities are "Calculator Challenge Counting" (11.26), "How Much Between?" (11.29), or "Little Ten-Frame Sums" (11.30), all found in Chapter 11. ◆

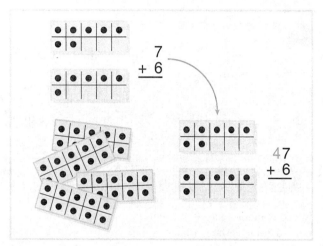

Figure 12.4 Little ten-frame cards can help children extend the Make 10 idea to larger numbers (see Blackline Masters 15–16).

As you move students from single-digit to two-digit numbers, adding and subtracting tens and hundreds is an important transition. Sums and differences involving multiples of 10 or 100 are easily computed mentally. Write a problem such as the following on the board:

$$300 + 500 + 20$$

Challenge children to solve it mentally. Ask students to share how they did it. Look for use of place-value words: "3 *hundred* and 5 *hundred* is 8 *hundred*, and 20 is 820."

Use base-ten models to help children begin to think in terms of tens and hundreds. Early examples should not include any trades. The exercise 420 + 300 involves no trades, whereas 70 + 80 may be more difficult.

Adding Two-Digit Numbers

Problems involving the sum of 2 two-digit numbers will provoke a wide variety of strategies. Some of these will involve starting with one or the other number and working from that point, either by adding on to get to the next ten or by adding tens from one number to the other. That is, for 46 + 35 a student may add on 4 to the 46 to get to 50 and then add 31 more, or, first add 30 to 46 and then add 4 to get to 80 and 1 more. In either case there is a clear ad-

vantage to the utilization of ten. Many children will count past these multiples without stopping at ten.

Other approaches involve splitting the numbers into parts and adding the easier parts separately. Usually the split will involve tens and ones, or students may use other parts of numbers such as 50 or 25 as a "nice" part of a number to work with.

Students will often use a counting-by-tens-and-ones technique. That is, instead of "46 + 30 is 76," they may count "46 → 56, 66, 76." These counts can be written down as they are said to help students keep track.

Figure 12.5 illustrates four different strategies for addition of 2 two-digit numbers. The ways that the solutions are recorded are suggestions. Note the use of the empty number line. The following story problem is a suggestion.

> **The two Scout troops went on a field trip. There were 46 Girl Scouts and 38 Boy Scouts. How many Scouts went on the trip?**

The Move to Make 10 and compensation strategies are useful when one of the numbers ends in 8 or 9. To promote that strategy, present problems with addends like 39 or 58. Note that it is only necessary to adjust one of the two numbers.

⏸ ———————— *Pause and Reflect*

Try adding 367 + 155 in as many different ways as you can. How many of your ways are like those in Figure 12.5?

Subtracting by Counting Up

This is an amazingly powerful way to subtract. Students working on the *think-addition* strategy for their basic facts can also be solving problems with larger numbers. The concept is the same. For 38 − 19, the idea is to think, "How much do I add to 19 to get to 38?" Notice that this strategy is probably not efficient for 42 − 6. Using *join with change unknown* problems or *missing-part* problems (discussed in Chapter 9) will encourage the counting-up strategy. Here is an example of each.

> **Sam had 46 baseball cards. He went to a card show and got some more cards for his collection. Now he has 73 cards. How many cards did Sam buy at the card show?**

> **Juanita counted all of her crayons. Some were broken and some not. She had 73 crayons in all. 46 crayons were not broken. How many were broken?**

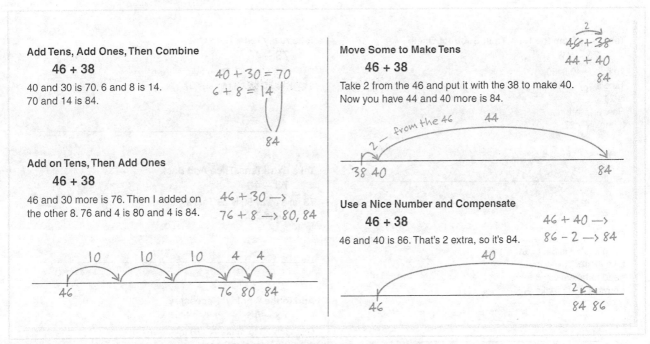

Figure 12.5 Four different invented strategies for addition with two-digit numbers.

The numbers in these problems are used in the strategies illustrated in Figure 12.6. Simply asking for the difference between two numbers may also prompt this strategy.

Take-Away Subtraction

Using a take-away action is considerably more difficult to do mentally. However, take-away strategies are common,

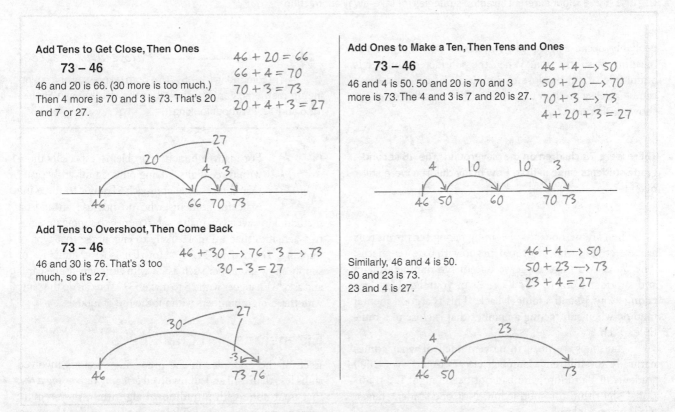

Figure 12.6 Three different invented strategies for subtraction by counting up.

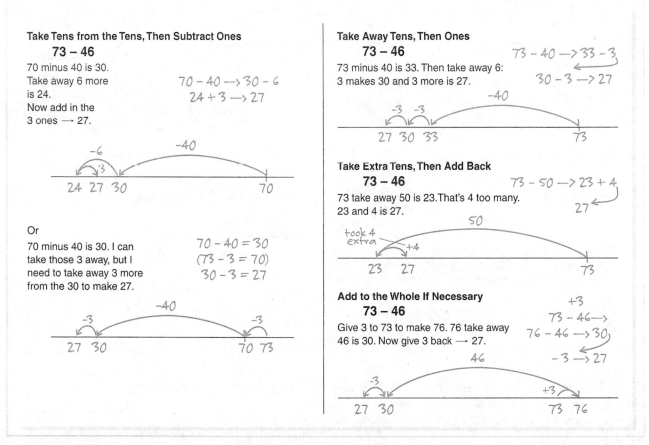

Figure 12.7 Four different invented strategies for take-away subtraction.

probably because textbooks emphasize take-away as the meaning of subtraction. When the subtracted number is a multiple of ten or close to a multiple of ten, take-away can be an easy method to use. Four different strategies are shown in Figure 12.7.

There were 73 children on the playground. The 46 second-grade students came in first. How many children were still outside?

The two methods that begin by taking tens from tens are reflective of what most students do with base-ten pieces. The other two methods leave one of the numbers intact and subtract from it. Try 83 – 29 in your head by first taking away 30 and adding 1 back. This is a good mental method when subtracting a number that is close to a multiple of ten.

Sometimes we need to be reminded of what comes naturally to children. Campbell (1997) tested over 2000 students in Baltimore who had not been taught the traditional algorithm for subtraction. Not one student began with the ones place!

Pause and Reflect

Try computing 82 – 57. Use both take-away and counting up methods. Can you use all of the strategies in Figures 12.6 and 12.7 without looking?

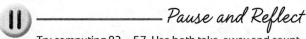

For many subtraction problems, especially those with three digits, adding on is significantly easier than a take-away approach. Try not to force the issue for students who do not use an add-on method. However, you may want to return to simple missing-part activities that are more likely to encourage that type of thinking. Try Activity 11.31, "How Far Is My Number?" or simply show a number such as 28 with little ten-frame cards and ask, "What goes with 28 to make 53?" You can do the same with three-digit numbers without the use of models. ◆

Extensions and Challenges

Each of the examples in the preceding sections involved sums less than 100 and all involved *bridging* or *crossing a ten;* that is, if done with a traditional algorithm, they require regrouping or trading. Bridging, the size of the numbers, and the potential for doing problems mentally are all issues to consider.

Bridging.   For most of the strategies, it is easier to add or subtract when bridging is not required. Try each strategy with 34 + 52 or 68 − 24 to see how it works. Easier problems instill confidence. They also permit you to challenge your students with a "harder one." There is also the issue of bridging 100 or 1000. Try 58 + 67 with different strategies. Bridging across 100 is also an issue for subtraction. Problems such as 128 − 50 or 128 − 45 are more difficult than ones that do not cross 100.

Larger Numbers.   Most curricula will expect third graders to add and subtract three-digit numbers. Your state standards may even require work with four-digit numbers. Try seeing how *you* would do these without using the traditional algorithms: 487 + 235 and 623 − 247. For subtraction, a counting-up strategy is usually the easiest. Occasionally, other strategies appear with larger numbers. For example, "chunking off" multiples of 50 or 25 is often a useful method. For 462 + 257, pull out 450 and 250 to make 700. That leaves 12 and 7 more → 719.

 The Number and Operation standards at both the pre-K–2 and 3–5 grade bands will clearly demonstrate that the *Standards* are supportive of the approaches described in this chapter. For example, "When students compute with strategies they invent or choose because they are meaningful, their learning tends to be robust—they are able to remember and apply their knowledge. Children with specific learning disabilities can actively invent and transfer strategies if given well-designed tasks that are developmentally appropriate" (p. 86). ◆

Traditional Algorithms for Addition and Subtraction

If you teach the traditional computation strategies for addition and subtraction, remember that a serious effort of several months with invented strategies is still well worth it. Because your students will not likely invent the traditional algorithms, your instruction will necessarily be more directed. Students may infer from this that this "new" way that you are explaining must be preferred and many will abandon their invented strategies. Try to avoid this complete switch to the traditional algorithms by presenting them as another alternative and then maintain practice with invented methods.

The traditional algorithms require an understanding of *regrouping*, exchanging 10 in one place-value position for 1 in the position to the left—or the reverse, exchanging 1 for 10 in the position to the right. The corresponding terms *carrying* and *borrowing* are obsolete and conceptually misleading. The word *regroup* may have little meaning for young children. A preferable term to use initially is *trade*. Ten ones

are *traded* for a ten. A hundred is *traded* for 10 tens. Notice that none of the invented strategies involves regrouping.

It is a serious error to work for mastery of problems that do not involve regrouping before tackling regrouping. Keeping these problems separate has been the documented source of many error patterns. Teaching problems that do not require regrouping first causes bad habits that children must later unlearn.

Addition Algorithm

Explain to the students that they are going to learn a method of adding that most adults learned when they were in school. It is not the only way or even the best way; it is just another method you want them to learn.

Begin with Models Only.   In the beginning, avoid any written work except for the possible recording of an answer. Provide children with place-value mats and base-ten models. The mat with two ten-frames in the ones place (Blackline Master 17) is suggested.

Have students make one number at the top of the mat and a second beneath it as shown in the top portion of Figure 12.8. If children are still developing base-ten

Figure 12.8 Working from right to left in addition (see Blackline Master 17).

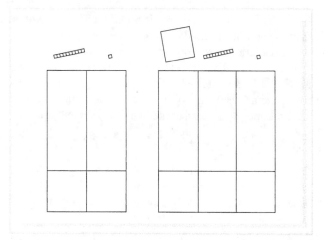

Figure 12.9 Blank recording charts are helpful (see Blackline Master 19).

concepts, a groupable model such as counters in cups is helpful.

Explain this one rule: *You begin in the ones column.* "This is a way people came up with a time ago, and it worked for them." Let students solve the problem on their own. Provide plenty of time, and then have students explain what they did and why. Let students use overhead or interactive whiteboard models or magnetic pieces to help with their explanations.

One or two problems in a lesson with lots of discussion is much more productive than a lot of problems based on rules children don't understand.

Develop the Written Record. Reproduce pages with simple place-value charts similar to those shown in Figure 12.9. The charts will help young children record numerals in columns. The general idea is to have children record on these pages each step of the procedure they do with the base-ten models *as it is done.* The first few times you do this,

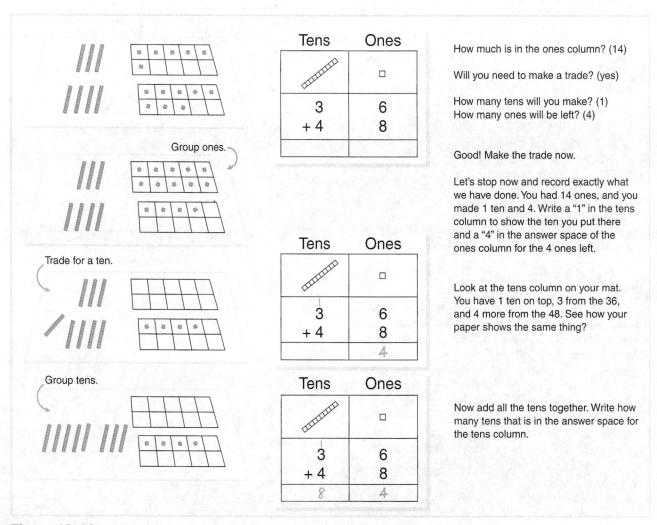

Figure 12.10 Help students record on paper each step they do on their place-value mats (see Blackline Masters 17 and 19).

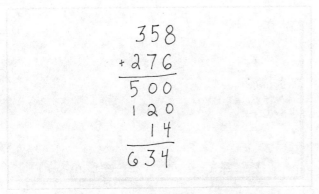

$$\begin{array}{r} 358 \\ + 276 \\ \hline 500 \\ 120 \\ 14 \\ \hline 634 \end{array}$$

Figure 12.11 An alternative recording scheme for addition. Notice that this can be used from left to right as well as from right to left.

guide each step carefully, as illustrated in Figure 12.10. A similar approach would be used for three-digit problems.

A suggestion is to have children work in pairs. One child is responsible for the models and the other records the steps. They can reverse roles with each problem.

Figure 12.11 shows a variation of the traditional recording scheme that is quite reasonable, at least for up to three digits. It avoids the little "carried ones" and focuses attention on the value of the digits. If students were permitted to start adding on the left as they are inclined to do, this would just be a vertical recording scheme for the invented strategy "Add tens, add ones, then combine" (Figure 12.5).

Subtraction Algorithm

The general approach to developing the subtraction algorithm is the same as for addition. When the procedure is completely understood with models, a do-and-write approach connects it with a written form.

Begin with Models Only. Start by having children model the top number in a subtraction problem on the top half of their place-value mats. For the amount to be subtracted, have children write each digit on a small piece of paper and place these pieces near the bottom of their mats in the respective columns, as in Figure 12.12. To avoid errors, suggest making all trades first. That way, the full amount on the paper slip can be taken off at once. Also explain to children that they are to begin working with the ones column first, as they did with addition.

Anticipate Difficulties with Zeros. Exercises in which zeros are involved anywhere in the problem tend to cause special difficulties. Give extra attention to these cases while still using models.

The very common error of "regrouping across zero" is best addressed at the modeling stage. For example, in

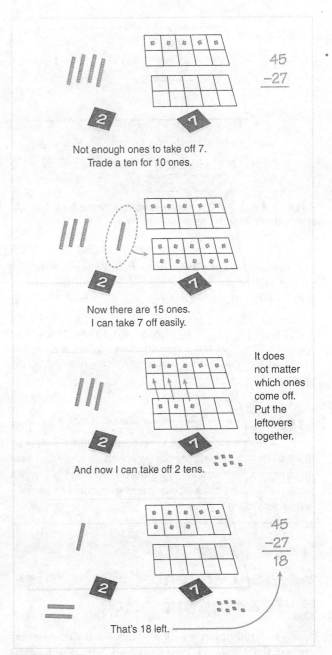

Not enough ones to take off 7.
Trade a ten for 10 ones.

Now there are 15 ones.
I can take 7 off easily.

It does not matter which ones come off. Put the leftovers together.

And now I can take off 2 tens.

That's 18 left.

Figure 12.12 Two-place subtraction with models.

403 – 138, a double trade must be made: trading a hundreds piece for 10 tens and then a tens piece for 10 ones.

Develop the Written Record. The process of recording each step as it is done is the same as was suggested for addition. The same recording sheets (Figure 12.9) are also recommended.

When children can explain the use of symbols involved in the recording process, that is a signal for moving them away from the use of physical materials on to a completely symbolic level. Again, be attentive to problems with zeros.

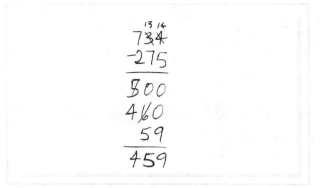

Figure 12.13 A left-hand recording scheme for subtraction. Other methods can also be devised.

If students are permitted to follow their natural instincts and begin with the big pieces (from the left instead of the right), recording schemes similar to that shown in Figure 12.13 are possible. The trades are made from the pieces remaining *after* the subtraction in the column to the left has been done. A "regroup across zero" difficulty will still occur in problems like 462 – 168. Try it.

⏸ —————————— *Pause and Reflect*

Contrast the difficulties of teaching children to regroup in subtraction, especially regrouping across zero, with the ease of adding on. For example, try solving this: 428 and how much makes 703? Now think about teaching students to regroup across zero to solve 703 – 428.

Student-Invented Strategies for Multiplication

For multiplication, the ability to break numbers apart in flexible ways is even more important than in addition or subtraction. The distributive property of multiplication over addition is another concept that is important in multiplication computation. For example, to multiply 43 × 5, one might think about breaking 43 into 40 and 3, multiplying each by 5, and then adding the results. Children require ample opportunities to develop these concepts by making sense of their own ideas and those of their classmates.

Useful Representations

The problem 6 × 34 may be represented in a number of ways, as illustrated in Figure 12.14. Often the choice of a model is influenced by a story problem. To determine

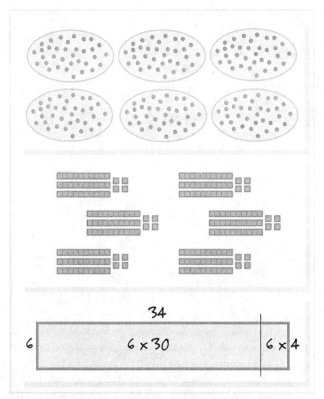

Figure 12.14 Different ways to model 6 × 34 may support different computational strategies.

how many oranges 6 classes need if there are 34 children in each class, children may model 6 sets of 34. If the problem is about the area of a rectangle that is 34 cm by 6 cm, then some form of an array is likely. But each representation is appropriate for thinking about 34 × 6 regardless of the context, and students should get to a point where they select ways to think about multiplication that are meaningful to them.

How children represent a product interacts with their methods for determining answers. The groups of 34 might suggest repeated additions—perhaps taking the sets two at a time. Double 34 is 68 and there are three of those, so 68 + 68 + 68. From there, various methods are possible.

The six sets of base-ten pieces might suggest breaking the numbers into tens and ones: 6 times 3 tens or 6 × 30 and 6 × 4. Some children use the tens individually: 6 tens make 60. So that's 60 and 60 and 60 (180). Then add on the 24 to make 204.

All of these ideas should be part of students' repertoire of models for multidigit multiplication. Introduce different representations (one at a time) as ways to explore multiplication until you are comfortable that the class has a collection of useful ideas. At the same time, do not force students who reason very well without drawings to use models when they are not needed.

Multiplication by a Single-Digit Multiplier

As with addition and subtraction, it is helpful to place multiplication tasks in contextual story problems. Let students model the problems in ways that make sense to them. Do not be concerned about reversing factors (6 sets of 34 or 34 sets of 6). Nor should you be timid about the numbers you use. The problem 3 × 24 may be easier than 7 × 65, but the latter provides challenge. The types of strategies that students use for multiplication are much more varied than for addition and subtraction. However, the following three categories can be identified from the research to date.

Complete-Number Strategies. Children who are not yet comfortable breaking numbers into parts will approach the numbers in the sets as single groups. Most likely these early strategies will be based on repeated addition. Often students will list long columns of numbers and add them up. In an attempt to shorten this tedious process, students soon realize that if they add two numbers, the next two will have the same sum and so on down the line. This doubling process can become the principle approach for many students, although it is certainly not very efficient (Ambrose, Baek, & Carpenter, 2003; Fosnot & Dolk, 2001b). Figure 12.15 illustrates two methods they may use. These children will benefit from listening to children who use base-ten models. They may also need more work with base-ten grouping activities where they take numbers apart in different ways.

Partitioning Strategies. Children break numbers up in a variety of ways that reflect an understanding of base-ten concepts, at least four of which are illustrated in Figure

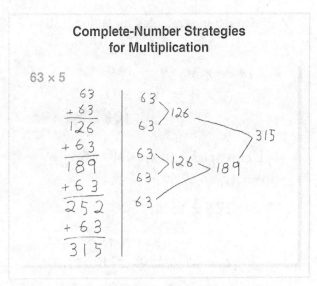

Complete-Number Strategies for Multiplication

Figure 12.15 Children who use a complete-number strategy do not break numbers apart into decades or tens and ones.

12.16. The "By Decades" (or "By Hundreds" etc.) approach is the same as the traditional algorithm except that students always begin with the large values. It extends easily to three digits and is very powerful as a mental math strategy. Another valuable strategy for mental methods is found in the "Other Partitions" example. It is easy to compute mentally with multiples of 25 and 50 and then add or subtract a small adjustment. All partition strategies rely on the distributive property.

Compensation Strategies. Children and adults look for ways to manipulate numbers so that the calculations are easy. In Figure 12.17, the problem 27 × 4 is changed to an easier

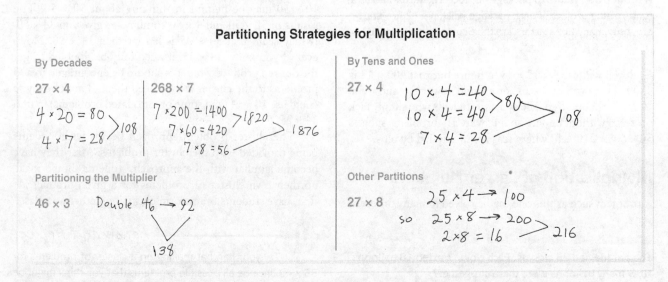

Partitioning Strategies for Multiplication

Figure 12.16 Four different ways to make easier partial products.

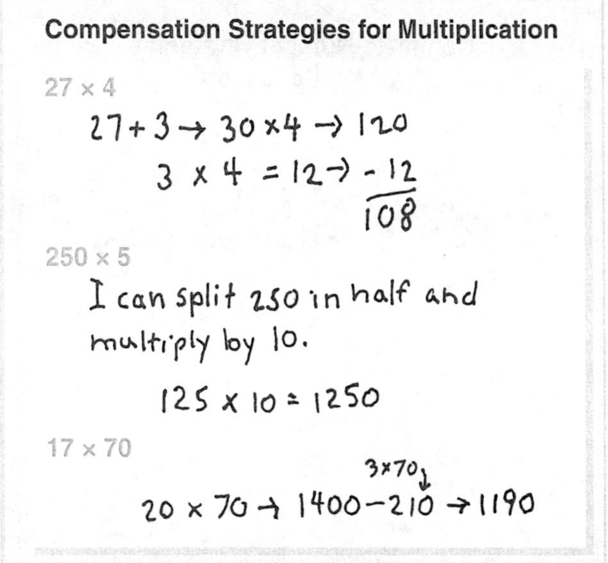

Compensation Strategies for Multiplication

27 × 4

$$27 + 3 \rightarrow 30 \times 4 \rightarrow 120$$
$$3 \times 4 = 12 \rightarrow -12$$
$$\overline{108}$$

250 × 5

I can split 250 in half and
multiply by 10.

$$125 \times 10 = 1250$$

17 × 70

$$3 \times 70$$
$$20 \times 70 \rightarrow 1400 - 210 \rightarrow 1190$$

Figure 12.17 Compensation methods use a product related to the original. A compensation is made in the answer, or one factor is changed to compensate for a change in the other factor.

one, and then an adjustment or compensation is made. In the second example, one factor is cut in half and the other doubled. This is often used when a 5 or a 50 is involved. Because these strategies are so dependent on the numbers involved, they can't be used for all computations. However, they are powerful strategies, especially for mental math and estimation.

Transitioning from Single-Digit to Two-Digit Factors. As you move students from single-digit to two-digit factors, there is a value in exposing students early to products involving multiples of 10 and 100.

A Scout troop wants to package up 400 fire starter kits as a fund-raising project. If each package will have 12 fire starters, how many fire starters are the Scouts going to need?

Children will use 4 × 12 = 48 to figure out that 400 × 12 is 4800. There will be discussion around how to say and write "forty-eight hundred." Be aware of students who simply tack on zeros without understanding why. Try problems such as 30 × 60 or 210 × 40 where tens are multiplied by tens.

Multiplication of Larger Numbers

A problem such as this one can be solved in many different ways:

The parade had 23 clowns. Each clown carried 18 balloons. How many balloons were there altogether?

Some children look for smaller products such as 6 × 23 and then add that result three times. Another method is to do 20 × 23 and then subtract 2 × 23. Others will calculate four separate partial products: 10 × 20 = 200, 8 × 20 = 160, 10 × 3 = 30, and 8 × 3 = 24. And still others may add up a string of 23s. Two-digit multiplication is both complex and challenging. But students can solve these problems in a variety of interesting ways, many of which will contribute to the development of the traditional algorithm or one that is just as efficient. Figure 12.18 shows the work of three fourth-grade students who had not been taught the traditional algorithm for multiplication. Kenneth's "parting" refers to *partitioning*, a strategy label provided earlier by the teacher. Briannon is content with adding. She needs to see other strategies developed by her classmates. Nick's method is conceptually very similar to the traditional algorithm. As students begin partitioning numbers along place-value lines, the strategies are often like the traditional algorithm but without the traditional recording schemes.

Cluster Problems. In the fourth and fifth grades of *Investigations in Number, Data, and Space*, one approach to multidigit multiplication is called "cluster problems." This approach encourages students to use facts and combinations they know in order to figure out more complex computations. For example, the following cluster could be used in a lesson: 7 × 6, 5 × 6, 10 × 6, 50 × 6, and **57 × 6.** The goal is to figure out the final product (shown in bold) using the other problems as support.

It is useful to have students make an estimate of the final product before doing any of the problems in the cluster. For example, in a cluster for 34 × 50, 3 × 50 and 10 × 50 may be helpful in thinking about 30 × 50. The results of 30 × 50 and 4 × 50 combine to give you 34 × 50. It may seem that 34 × 25 is harder than 34 × 50. However, if you know 34 × 25, it need only be doubled to get the desired product. Students should be encouraged to add problems to the cluster if they need them. Think how you could use 10 × 34 (and some other related problems) to find 34 × 25.

The cluster problem approach begins with students being provided with the cluster problems. After they have become familiar with the approach, students should make up their own cluster of problems for a given product. At first, have students brainstorm clusters together as a class.

myeducationlab

Go to the Activities and Application section of Chapter 12 of MyEducationLab. Click on Videos and watch the video entitled "**John Van de Walle on Multiplication of Larger Numbers**" to see him explain examples of student work with two-digit multipliers.

⏸ ———————— *Pause and Reflect*

Try your hand at making up a cluster of problems for 86 × 42. Include all possible problems that you think might be helpful, even if they are not all related to one approach to find-

There were 35 dogsleds. Each sled was pulled by 12 dogs. How many dogs were there in all?

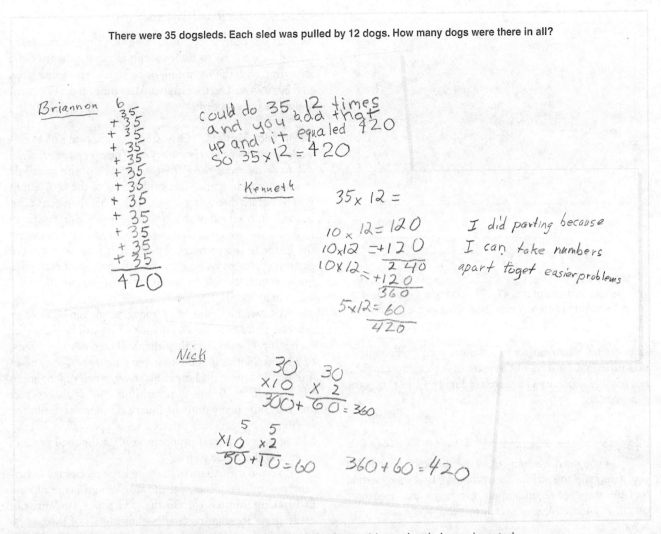

Figure 12.18 Three fourth-grade students solve a multiplication problem using their own invented strategies. Each is at a different place in developing a reasonably efficient method.

ing the product. Then use your cluster to find the product. Is there more than one way?

Here are some of the problems that might be in your cluster.

$$2 \times 80 \quad 4 \times 80 \quad 2 \times 86 \quad 40 \times 80$$
$$6 \times 40 \quad 10 \times 86 \quad 40 \times 86$$

Of course, your cluster may have included products not shown here. All that is required to begin the cluster problem approach is that your cluster eventually leads to a solution. Besides your own cluster, see if you can use the problems in this cluster to find 86×42.

Cluster problems help students think about ways that they can break factors apart—or split numbers—into easier parts. The strategy of splitting numbers and multiplying the parts—the distributive property—is an extremely valuable technique for flexible computation. It is also fun to find

different clever paths to the solution. For many problems, finding a workable cluster is actually faster than using an algorithm.

Area Models. A valuable exploration is to prepare large rectangles for each group of two or three students. The rectangles should be measured carefully, with dimensions between 25 cm and 60 cm, and drawn accurately with square corners. The students' task is to determine how many small ones pieces (base-ten materials) will fit inside. Wooden or plastic base-ten pieces are best, but cardboard strips and squares are adequate. Alternatively, students can simply be given the task verbally: *What is the area of a rectangle that is 47 cm by 36 cm?*

Most children will fill the rectangle first with as many hundreds pieces as possible. One obvious approach is to put the 12 hundreds in one corner. This will leave narrow regions on two sides that can be filled with tens pieces and a final small rectangle that will hold ones. Especially if

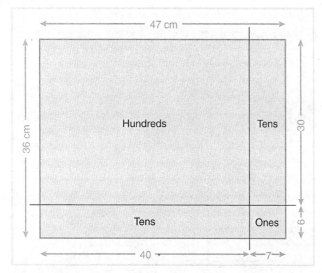

Figure 12.19 Ones, tens, and hundreds pieces fit exactly into the four sections of this 47 × 36 rectangle. Figure the size of each section to determine the size of the whole rectangle.

students have had earlier experiences with finding products in arrays, figuring out the size of each subrectangle is not terribly difficult. The sketch in Figure 12.19 shows the four regions.

❚❚ ——————— *Pause and Reflect*

If you did not already know the algorithm, how would you determine the size of the rectangle? Use your method (not the standard algorithm) on a rectangle that measures 68 cm × 24 cm. Make a sketch to show and explain your work.

As you will see in the discussion of the traditional algorithm, the area model leads to a reasonable approach to multiplying numbers.

Traditional Algorithm for Multiplication

The traditional multiplication algorithm is probably the most difficult of the four algorithms if students have not had plenty of opportunities to explore their own strategies. The multiplication algorithm can be meaningfully developed using either a repeated addition model or an area model. For single-digit multipliers, the difference is minimal. When you move to two-digit multipliers, the area model has some advantages. For that reason, the discussion here will use the area model. Again, you are reminded of the need for a more directed approach than when developing invented strategies.

One-Digit Multipliers

As with the other algorithms, as much time as necessary should be devoted to the conceptual development of the algorithm with the recording or written part coming later. In contrast, most textbooks spend less time on development and more time on drill.

Begin with Models. Give students a drawing of a rectangle 47 cm by 6 cm. *How many small square centimeter pieces will fit in the rectangle?* (What is the area of the rectangle in square centimeters?) Let students solve the problem in groups before discussing it as a class. This simple task can be made into a good problem for students. Challenge them to find a way to determine the number of unit squares on the inside of the rectangle by slicing it into two or more parts in such a way that they can tell the size of each part. For example, it could be sliced into two sections of 20 × 6 and one of 7 × 6.

As shown in Figure 12.20, the rectangle can be sliced or separated into two parts so that one part will be 6 ones by 7 ones, or 42 ones, and the other will be 6 ones by 4 tens, or 24 tens. Notice that the base-ten language "6 ones times 4 tens is 24 tens" tells how many *pieces* (strips of ten) are in the big section. To say "6 times 40 is 240" is also correct and tells how many units or square centimeters are in the section. Each section is referred to as a *partial product*. By adding the two partial products, you get the total product or area of the rectangle.

To avoid the tedium of drawing large rectangles and arranging base-ten pieces, use the base-ten grid paper found in Blackline Master 18. On the grid paper, students can easily draw accurate rectangles showing all of the pieces. Do not force any recording technique on students until they understand how to use the two dimensions of a rectangle to get a product.

Develop the Written Record. To help with a recording scheme, provide sheets with base-ten columns on which students can record problems. When the two partial

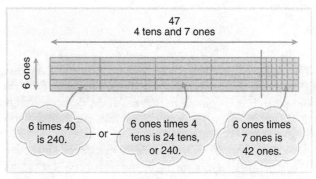

Figure 12.20 A rectangle filled with base-ten pieces is a useful model for two-digit-by-one-digit multiplication.

products are written separately as in Figure 12.21(a), there is little new to learn. Students simply record the products and add them together. As illustrated, it is possible to teach students how to write the first product with a carried digit so that the combined product is written on one line. This recording scheme is known to be a source of errors. The little carried digit is often the difficulty—it gets added in before the second multiplication or is forgotten.

There is no practical reason why students can't be allowed to record both partial products and avoid the errors related to the carried digit. When you accept that, it makes no difference in which order the products are written. Why not simply permit students to do written multiplication as shown in Figure 12.21(b)? When the factors are in a word problem, chart, or other format, all that is really necessary is to write down all the partial products and add. Furthermore, that is precisely how this is done mentally.

Most standard curricula progress from two digits to three digits with a single-digit multiplier. Students can make this progression easily. They still should be permitted to write all three partial products separately and not have to bother with carrying.

Two-Digit Multipliers

With the area model, the progression to a two-digit multiplier is relatively straightforward. Rectangles can be drawn on base-ten grid paper, or full-sized rectangles can be filled

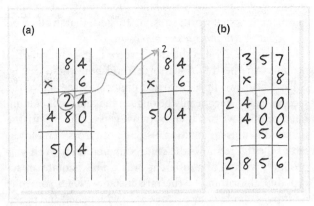

Figure 12.21 (a) In the standard form, the product of ones is recorded first. The tens digit of this first product can be written as a "carried" digit above the tens column. (b) It is quite reasonable to abandon the carried digit and permit the partial products to be recorded in any order. (See Blackline Master 20.)

in with base-ten pieces. There will be four partial products, corresponding to four different sections of the rectangle.

Several variations in language might be used. Consider the product 47 × 36 as illustrated in Figure 12.22. In the partial product 40 × 30, if base-ten language is used—*4 tens times 3 tens is 12 hundreds*—the result tells how many hundreds pieces are in that section. Verbally, the product "forty times thirty" is formidable. Try to avoid "four times

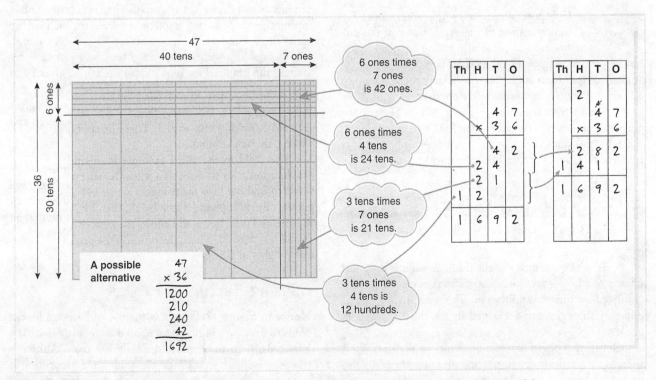

Figure 12.22 47 × 36 rectangle filled with base-ten pieces. Base-ten language connects the four partial products to the traditional written format. Note the possibility of recording the products in some other order.

three," which promotes thinking about digits rather than numbers. It is well worth stressing the idea that in all cases, a product of *tens times tens is hundreds.*

Figure 12.22 also shows the recording of four partial products in the traditional order and how these can be collapsed to two lines if carried digits are used. Here the second "carry" technically belongs in the hundreds column but it rarely is written there. Often it gets confused with the first and is thus an additional source of errors. The lower left of the figure shows the same computation with all four products written in a different order. This is quite an acceptable algorithm. In the rare instance when someone multiplies numbers such as 538×29 with pencil and paper, there would be six partial products. But far fewer errors would occur, requiring less instructional time and much less remediation.

 "As students move from third to fifth grade, they should consolidate and practice a small number of computational algorithms for addition, subtraction, multiplication and division that they understand well and can use routinely. . . . Having access to more than one method for each operation allows students to choose an approach that best fits the numbers in a particular problem. For example, 298×42 can be thought of as $(300 \times 42) - (2 \times 42)$, whereas 41×16 can be computed by multiplying 41×8 to get 328 and then doubling 328 to get 656" (p. 155). ◆

 Computer versions of the area model for multiplication can alleviate some of the difficulties of physically filling in place-value blocks into rectangles. On the NLVM website, the Rectangle Multiplication applet will model any rectangle up to 30×30 (http://nlvm.usu.edu/en/nav/frames_asid_192_g_2_t_1.html?from=category_g_2_t_1_html). The rectangle is split into two parts rather than four, corresponding to the tens and ones digits in the multiplier. The result is nicely correlated to the traditional algorithm. ◆

Student-Invented Strategies for Division

Even though many adults think division is the most onerous of the computational operations, it can be considerably easier than multiplication. Typically, division computation strategies are developed in the third and fourth grades.

Recall that there are two concepts of division. First there is the partition or fair-sharing idea, illustrated by this story problem:

The bag has 783 jelly beans, and Aidan and her four friends want to share them equally. How many jelly beans will Aidan and each of her friends get?

Then there is the measurement or repeated subtraction concept:

Jumbo the elephant loves peanuts. His trainer has 625 peanuts. If he gives Jumbo 20 peanuts each day, how many days will the peanuts last?

Students should be challenged to solve both types of problems. However, the fair-share problems are often easier to solve with base-ten pieces. Furthermore, the traditional algorithm is built on this idea. Eventually, students will develop strategies that they will apply to both types of problem, even when the process does not match the action of the story.

Figure 12.23 shows some strategies that fourth-grade children have used to solve division problems. The first example illustrates $92 \div 4$ using base-ten pieces and a sharing process. A ten is traded when no more tens can be passed out. Then the 12 ones are distributed, resulting in 23 in each set. This direct modeling approach with base-ten pieces is quite easy even for third-grade students to understand and use.

In the second example, the student sets out the base-ten pieces and draws a "bar graph" with six columns. After noting that there are not enough hundreds for each kid, he splits the 3 hundreds in half, putting 50 in each column. That leaves him with 1 hundred, 5 tens, and 3 ones. After trading the hundred for tens (now 15 tens), he gives 20 to each, recording 2 tens in each bar. Now he is left with 3 tens and 3 ones, or 33. He knows that 5×6 is 30, so he gives each kid 5, leaving him with 3. These he splits in half and writes $\frac{1}{2}$ in each column.

The child in the third example is solving a sharing problem but tries to do it as a measurement process. She wants to find out how many eights are in 143. Initially she guesses. By multiplying 8 first by 10, then by 20 (work not shown), and then by 14, she knows the answer is more than 14 and less than 20. Then, she rethinks the problem as how many eights in 100 and how many in 40.

Missing-Factor Strategies

Notice in Figure 12.23(a) how the use of base-ten blocks tends to develop a digit-oriented approach—first share the hundreds, then the tens, and finally the ones. Although this is good background for the traditional algorithm, it does not help develop complete-number strategies that

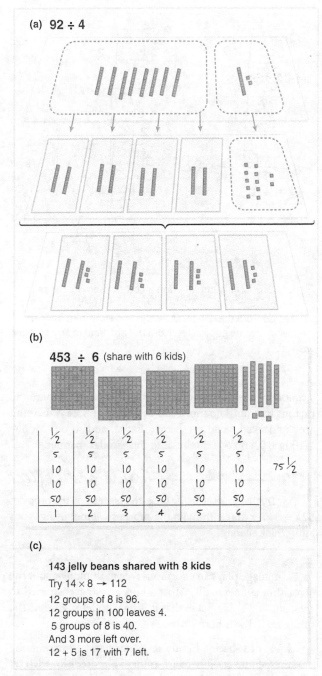

(a) 92 ÷ 4

(b)

453 ÷ 6 (share with 6 kids)

½	½	½	½	½	½	
5	5	5	5	5	5	
10	10	10	10	10	10	
10	10	10	10	10	10	75 ½
50	50	50	50	50	50	
1	2	3	4	5	6	

(c)

143 jelly beans shared with 8 kids

Try 14 × 8 → 112

12 groups of 8 is 96.
12 groups in 100 leaves 4.
5 groups of 8 is 40.
And 3 more left over.
12 + 5 is 17 with 7 left.

Figure 12.23 Students use both models and symbols to solve division tasks.
Source: Adapted from *Developing Mathematical Ideas: Numbers and Operations, Part I, Casebook* by Deborah Schifter, Virginia Bastable, and Susan Jo Russell. Copyright © 2000 by the Education Development Center, Inc. Used by permission of Pearson Education, Inc. All rights reserved.

are also quite useful. In Figure 12.23(c), the student is using a multiplicative approach. She is trying to find out, "What number times 8 will be close to 143 with less than 8 remaining?"

❙❙ ———————— *Pause and Reflect*

Try to determine the quotient of 318 ÷ 7 by figuring out *what number times 7* (or *7 times what number*) is close to 318 without going over. Do not use the standard algorithm.

There are several places to begin solving this problem. For instance, since 10 × 7 is only 70 and 100 × 7 is 700, the answer has to be between 10 and 100. You might start with multiples of 10. Thirty 7s are 210. Forty 7s are 280. Fifty 7s are 350. So 40 is not enough and 50 is too much. It has to be forty-something. At this point you could guess at numbers between 40 and 50. Or you might add on 7s. Or you could notice that forty 7s (280) leaves you with 20 plus 18 or 38. Five 7s will be 35 of the 38 with 3 left over. In all, that's 40 + 5 or 45 with a remainder of 3.

This missing-factor approach is likely to be invented by some students if they are solving measurement problems such as the following:

Grace can put 6 pictures on one page of her photo album. If she has 82 pictures, how many pages will she need?

Alternatively, you can simply pose a task such as 82 ÷ 6 and ask students, "What number times 6 would be close to 82?" and continue from there.

Cluster Problems

Another approach to developing missing-factor strategies is to use cluster problems as discussed for multiplication. Here are two examples:

100 × 4	10 × 72
500 ÷ 4	5 × 70
4 × 25	2 × 72
6 × 4	4 × 72
527 ÷ 4	5 × 72
	381 ÷ 72

Notice that the missing-factor strategy works equally well for one-digit divisors as for two-digit divisors. Also notice that it is okay to include division problems in the cluster. In the first example, 400 ÷ 4 could easily have replaced 100 × 4, and 125 × 4 could replace 500 ÷ 4. The idea is to keep multiplication and division as closely connected as possible.

Cluster problems provide students with a sense that problems can be solved in different ways and with different starting points. Therefore, rather than cluster problems, you can provide students with a variety of first steps for solving a problem. Their task is to select one of the starting points and solve the problem from there.

For example, here are four possible starting points for 514 ÷ 8:

$$10 \times 8 \quad 400 \div 8 \quad 60 \times 8 \quad 80 \div 8$$

When students are first asked to solve problems using two methods, they often use a primitive or completely inefficient method for their second approach (or revert to a standard algorithm). For example, to solve 514 ÷ 8, a student might perform a very long string of repeated subtractions (514 – 8 = 506, 506 – 8 = 498, 498 – 8 = 490, and so on) and count how many times he or she subtracted 8. Others will actually draw 514 tally marks and loop groups of 8. These students have not developed sufficient flexibility to think of other efficient methods. The idea just suggested of posing a variety of starting points can nudge students into other more profitable alternatives. Class discussions will also help students begin to see more flexible approaches. ◆

Traditional Algorithm for Division

Long division is the one traditional algorithm that starts with the left-hand or big pieces. The conceptual basis for the algorithm most often taught in textbooks is the partition or fair-share method, the method we will explore in detail. Another well-known algorithm is based on repeated subtraction and may be viewed as a good way to record the missing-factor approach with partial products recorded in a column to the right of the division computation. As shown by the two examples in Figure 12.24, one advantage is that there is total flexibility in the factors selected at each step of the way.

One-Digit Divisors

Typically, the division algorithm with one-digit divisors is introduced in the third grade. If done well, it should not have to be retaught, and it should provide the basis for two-digit divisors. Students in the upper grades who are having difficulty with the division algorithm can also benefit from a conceptual development.

Begin with Models. Traditionally, if we were to do a problem such as 4)583, we might say "4 goes into 5 one time." This is quite mysterious to children. How can you just ignore the "83" and keep changing the problem? Preferably, you want students to think of the 583 as 5 hundreds, 8 tens, and 3 ones, not as the independent digits 5, 8, and 3. One idea is to use a context such as candy bundled in boxes of ten with 10 boxes to a carton. Then the problem becomes *We have 5 cartons, 8 boxes, and 3 pieces of candy to share between*

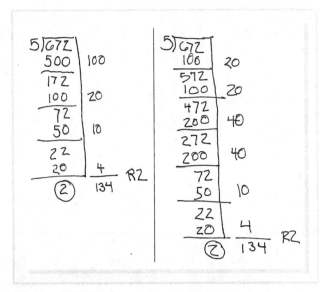

Figure 12.24 In the division algorithm shown, the numbers on the side indicate the quantity of the divisor being subtracted from the dividend. As the two examples indicate, the divisor can be subtracted from the dividend in any amount desired.

4 schools evenly. In this context, it is reasonable to share the cartons first until no more can be shared. Those remaining are "unpacked," and the boxes shared, and so on. Money ($100, $10, and $1) can be used in a similar manner.

▌▌ ——————— *Pause and Reflect*

Try this yourself using base-ten pieces and the problem 524 ÷ 3. Try to talk through the process without using "goes into." Think sharing.

Language plays an enormous role in thinking about the algorithm conceptually. Most adults are so accustomed to the "goes into" language that it is hard to let it go. For the problem 583 ÷ 4, here is some suggested language:

- I want to share 5 hundreds, 8 tens, and 3 ones among these four sets. There are enough hundreds for each set to get 1 hundred. That leaves 1 hundred that I can't share.
- I'll trade the hundred for 10 tens. That gives me a total of 18 tens. I can give each set 4 tens and have 2 tens left over. Two tens is not enough to go around the four sets.
- I can trade the 2 tens for 20 ones and put those with the 3 ones I already had. That makes a total of 23 ones. I can give 5 ones in each of the four sets. That leaves me with 3 ones as a remainder. In all I gave out to each group 1 hundred, 4 tens, and 5 ones with 3 left over.

Develop the Written Record.   The recording scheme for the long-division algorithm is not completely intuitive. You will need to be quite directive in helping children learn to record the fair sharing with models. There are essentially four steps:

1. *Share* and record the number of pieces put in each group.
2. *Record* the number of pieces shared in all. Multiply to find this number.
3. *Record* the number of pieces remaining. Subtract to find this number.
4. *Trade* (if necessary) for smaller pieces, and combine with any that are there already. Record the new total number in the next column.

When students model problems with a one-digit divisor, steps 2 and 3 seem unnecessary. Explain that these steps really help when you don't have the pieces there to count.

Record Explicit Trades.   Figure 12.25 details each step of the recording process just described. On the left, you see the traditional algorithm. To the right is a suggestion that matches the actual action with the models by explicitly recording the trades. Instead of the somewhat mysterious "bring-down" procedure, the traded pieces are crossed out, as is the number of existing pieces in the next column. The combined number of pieces is written in this column using a two-digit number. In the example, 2 hundreds are traded for 20 tens, combined with the 6 that were there for a total of 26 tens. The 26 is, therefore, written in the tens column.

Students who are required to make sense of the long-division procedure find the explicit-trade method easier to follow. Blank division charts with wide place-value columns are highly recommended. These can be found in Blackline Master 20. Without the charts, it is important to spread out the digits in the dividend when writing down the problem. (*Author note:* The explicit-trade method is an invention of John Van de Walle. It has been used successfully in grades 3 to 8. You will not find it in other textbooks.)

Both the explicit-trade method and the use of place-value columns will help with the problem of leaving out a middle zero in a problem (see Figure 12.26).

Two-Digit Divisors

Explore your state and local standards for guidance on when children master division with two-digit divisors. A large chunk of the fourth, fifth, and sometimes sixth grade is frequently spent on this skill. The cost in terms of time and students' attitudes toward mathematics is enormous. Only a few times in any adult's life will an exact result to such a computation be required and a calculator not be available.

With a two-digit divisor, it is hard to come up with the right amount to share at each step. A guess too high or too low means you have to erase and start all over. Start by using the same division in several problems. That will help students estimate more successfully while allowing them to focus on the process.

An Intuitive Idea.   Suppose that you were sharing a large pile of candies with 36 friends. Instead of passing them out one at a time, you conservatively estimate that each person could get at least 6 pieces. So you give 6 to each of your friends. Now you find there are more than 36 pieces left. Do you have everyone give back the 6 pieces so you can then give them 7 or 8? That would be silly! You simply pass out more.

The candy example gives us two good ideas for sharing in long division. First, always underestimate how much can be shared. You can always pass out some more. To avoid ever overestimating, always pretend there are more sets among which to share than there really are. For example, if you are dividing 312 by 43 (sharing among 43 sets or "friends"), pretend you have 50 sets instead. Round *up* to the next multiple of 10. You can easily determine that 6 pieces can be shared among 50 sets because 6 × 50 is an easy product. Therefore, since there are really only 43 sets, clearly you can give *at least* 6 to each. Always consider a larger divisor; *always round up*.

Using the Idea Symbolically.   These ideas are used in Figure 12.27. Both the traditional method and the explicit-trade method of recording are illustrated. The rounded-up divisor, 70, is written in a little "think bubble" above the real divisor. Rounding up has another advantage: It is easy to run through the multiples of 70 and compare them to 374. Think about sharing base-ten pieces (thousands, hundreds, tens, and ones). Work through the problem one step at a time, saying exactly what each recorded step stands for.

This approach has proved successful with children in the fourth grade learning division for the first time and with children in the sixth to eighth grades in need of remediation. It reduces the mental strain of making choices and essentially eliminates the need to erase. If an estimate is too low, that's okay. And if you always round up, the estimate will never be too high. The same is true of the explicit-trade notation.

 The following comes from the 3–5 chapter of the *Standards:* "Although the expectation is that students develop fluency in computing with whole numbers, frequently they should use calculators to solve complex computations involving large numbers or as part of an extended problem" (p. 155). ◆

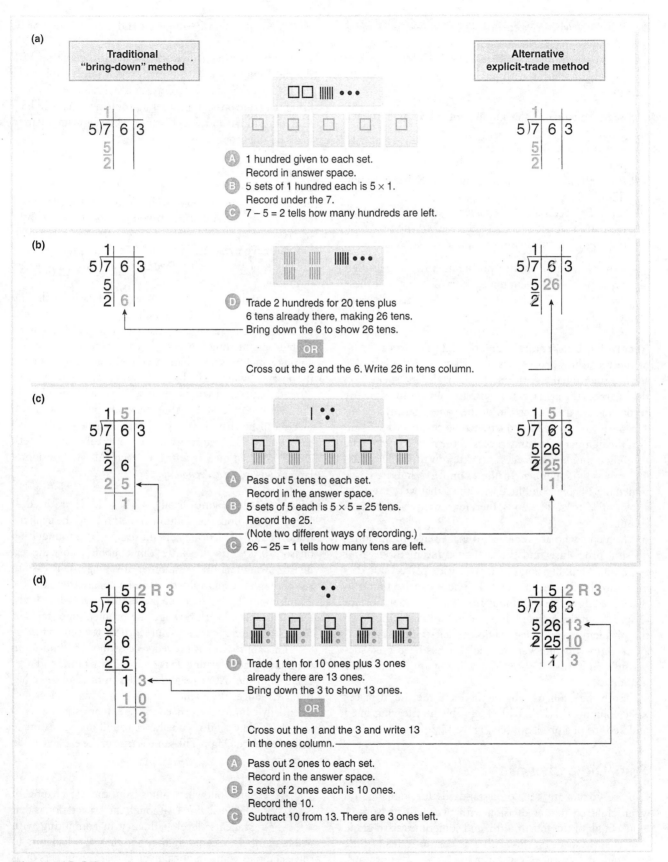

Figure 12.25 The traditional and explicit-trade methods are connected to each step of the division process. Every step can and should make sense (see Blackline Master 20).

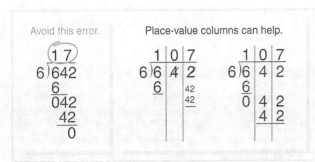

Figure 12.26 Using lines to mark place-value columns can help avoid forgetting to record zeros.

 When teaching a traditional algorithm for any operation, you may give quizzes or use chapter-end tests found in your textbook. Whether students do well or not so well, it is important to ask yourself if you really can assess what students understand or do not understand from a strictly computational test. When students make a systematic error in an algorithm, it will likely show up in the same way in repeated problems. What you do not know is what conceptual knowledge children are using—or not using. Don't mistake correct use of a standard algorithm for conceptual understanding.

To assess this very important background understanding for algorithms, during class discussions, call on different students to explain individual steps. Keep track of students' responses in a simple chart or other recording technique, indicating how well they seem to understand the algorithm you are working on. For struggling students, you may want to conduct a short diagnostic interview to explore in more detail their level of understanding.

A diagnostic interview might begin by having the student complete a computation. When finished, ask for explanations for specific steps in the process. If there is difficulty explaining the symbolic process, have the student use base-ten blocks to perform the same computation. Then ask for

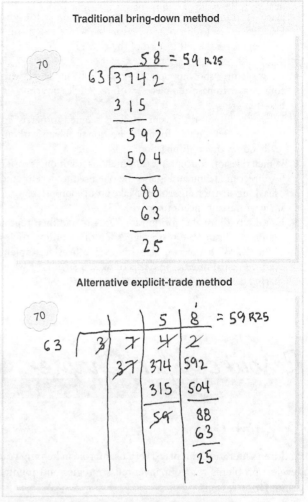

Figure 12.27 Round the divisor up to 70 to think with, but multiply what you share by 63. In the ones column, share 8 with each set. Oops! 88 left over. Just give 1 more to each set.

connections between what was done with the models and what was done symbolically. ◆

Reflections on Chapter **12**

Writing to Learn

1. What is the difference between solving a problem with direct modeling and solving a problem with an invented strategy? What is a traditional algorithm?
2. How are traditional algorithms different from student-invented strategies? Explain the benefits of invented strategies over traditional algorithms.
3. Illustrate three different strategies for adding 46 + 39. Which ones are easy to do mentally? Is there a strategy that is easier because 39 is close to 40? What strategies work well for sums such as 538 + 243? For each strategy you work with, think about how you could record it on the board so that other students will be able to follow what is being done.
4. Use two different adding-up strategies for 93 − 27 and for 545 − 267. Make up a story problem that would encourage an adding-up strategy.
5. Describe how you would go about developing the traditional algorithms for addition and subtraction. How would you

deal with the issue of beginning on the right with the ones place when students' natural tendency is to begin on the left? Use 385 + 128 to illustrate a reasonable written algorithm that begins on the left instead of the right. Do the same for 453 − 278.

6. Draw pictures showing how 57 × 4 could be modeled: with counters, with base-ten pieces, with rectangles or arrays on base-ten grids.

7. What would you do if your students seemed to persist in using repeated addition for multiplication problems without really doing any multiplication?

8. Which division concept, measurement or partition, is easier for direct modeling and is also the one used to develop the usual long-division algorithm? Make up an appropriate word story with that concept to go with 735 ÷ 6.

9. Use the traditional algorithm for 735 ÷ 6, and then repeat the process using the text's suggestion of recording trades explicitly. With the two algorithms side by side, explain every recorded number in terms of what it stands for when sharing base-ten pieces.

10. Why is some form of assessment that gets at student understanding so important when teaching traditional algorithms?

For Discussion and Exploration

1. Conduct a four-person panel discussion debating whether or not the traditional computational algorithms for whole numbers should continue to be taught. Have two persons represent each view. Arguments should show the benefits of each approach, efficiency of various methods, students' understanding of "doing mathematics," the issue of available technology in the real world, the need for computation of various types outside of the classroom, high-stakes testing, and the desires of families. Two intermediate views are also possible: including traditional algorithms only for multiplication and division, and withholding teaching of the traditional algorithms until seventh or eighth grade after flexible strategies and better number sense have been developed.

Resources for Chapter 12

Literature Connections

Children's literature can play a very useful role in helping you develop problems for your invented strategies and mental computation lessons.

The Breakfast Cereal Gourmet *Hoffman, 2005*
The History of Everyday Life *Landau, 2006*
The Pop Corn Book *de Paola, 1978*
Math and Non-Fiction: Grades 6–8 (a resource book for teachers) *Bay-Williams & Martinie, 2008*

These nonfiction books include interesting facts and figures that can be used for a variety of calculations and investigations. Hoffman's book provides fun information about breakfast eating habits; for example, the average person eats 160 bowls of cereal a year. Such facts can be used to find how many bowls are eaten in 5 years, or how many consumed in a month. In the *History of Everyday Life*, inventions are discussed, including facts and figures about the toilet. If the toilet uses about 3 or 4 gallons of water for every flush, how much water are you using at home? Can the school keep track of its usage for one day? *The Pop Corn Book* is representative of books that combine stories with numerical data. If 500,000,000 pounds of popcorn are popped in a year, how many 100-pound children would it take to weigh as much? Look for other titles on your bookshelf, or explore facts in your own local newspaper to bring children into the mathematical calculations that naturally emerge from real situations. The teacher resource book by Bay-Williams and Martinie shares other titles and activities in all mathematics content areas including whole-number computations.

Alice Ramsey's Grand Adventure *Brown, 1997*
Wilma Unlimited *Krull, 1996*

Brown and Krull both write about strong females who made their mark in history and sports. Alice Ramsey was the first woman to drive across the continental United States, and Wilma Rudolph was an Olympic track athlete who had polio as a young child. Again, these are representative of many pieces of children's literature that link actual information to possible calculations and comparisons. The first book can lead to considering trips across the United States by car in which students can use road maps to explore distances between locations, tallying up mileage across states or regions. Alice's first trip (of 31) took 59 days and there are interesting problems that can be generated to compare that to cross-country car trips today or to figure how many days she was in the car on the total of 31 trips. In *Wilma Unlimited*, there are obvious connections to the length of her races or how any race can be divided into a relay of a given number of people leading to calculations of the length of each segment. Of course additional problems can emerge from calculating how long ago these women lived. Biographies of pioneers and leaders are a good source of data for addition, subtraction, multiplication, and division problems.

Is a Blue Whale the Biggest Thing There Is?
Wells, 2005

This is one of the most intriguing books you will find about large objects and large distances. Blue whales look small next to Mount Everest, which in turn looks small next to the earth. The data in the book allow children to make other comparisons, such as the number of fourth graders that would have the same weight or volume as a blue whale or would fill the gymnasium. These comparisons are the perfect place for estimations and discussions about how much precision is necessary to make a meaningful comparison.

Recommended Readings

Articles

National Council of Teachers of Mathematics. (2003). Computational fluency [Focus Issue]. *Teaching Children Mathematics, 9*(6).

How to help children achieve skills and understanding in the area of computation is the focus of this entire journal, which can be purchased separately from NCTM. Each of the nine articles is well worth reading, including a discussion of teaching computation to English language learners, an article on computational fluency written by an internationally prominent mathematician, a reprint of a classic article on meaning and skill by William Brownell, plus other worthwhile articles by both classroom teachers and researchers in the area of computation.

O'Loughlin, T. A. (2007). Using research to develop computational fluency in young mathematicians. *Teaching Children Mathematics, 14*(3), 132–138.

Written by a second-grade teacher, this article describes her journey to improve her students' computational fluency through research-based practice. Using the Fosnot and Dolk (2001) books referred to in the "Books" section below, she encourages student-invented strategies to explore her students' thinking and understanding. The interesting collection of student work and thought-provoking associated debriefing will demonstrate various methods, such as place-value strategies and empty number line representations.

Russell, S. J. (2000). Developing computational fluency with whole numbers. *Teaching Children Mathematics, 7,* 155–158.

In just four pages, Russell provides an articulate view of what Principles and Standards *means by computational fluency. Russell accompanies each of her points with examples from children. She explains that teaching for fluency is a complex task requiring the teacher's understanding of the mathematics, selecting appropriate tasks, and recognizing when to capitalize on students' ideas.*

Books

Duncan, N., Geer, C., Huinker, D., Leutzinger, L., Rathmell, E., & Thompson, C. (2007). *Navigating through number and operations in grades 3–5.* Reston, VA: NCTM.

This book (particularly Chapters 3 and 4) is a perfect companion to this chapter, reflecting on how to introduce and develop the four operations with the ultimate goal of developing computational fluency and mathematical proficiency. There is also follow-up on how to assess and interpret student work. Part of the publication is a CD that includes blackline masters that correspond to a variety of activities in the book and a collection of related articles and chapters from NCTM publications.

Fosnot, C. T., & Dolk, M. (2001). *Young mathematicians at work: Constructing multiplication and division.* Portsmouth, NH: Heinemann.

Fosnot, C. T., & Dolk, M. (2001). *Young mathematicians at work: Constructing number sense, addition, and subtraction.* Portsmouth, NH: Heinemann.

These are two in a series of three books by Fosnot (a U.S. mathematics educator) and Dolk (a mathematics educator in the Netherlands). The books are products of a collaborative research effort of working with teachers to examine how children learn and how to support that learning. They show children's work constructing ideas about number, operations, and computation in ways not found elsewhere. (Their third book is on fractions and decimals.)

Online Resources

Base Blocks Addition
http://nlvm.usu.edu/en/nav/frames_asid_154_g_2_t_1.html

Base Blocks Subtraction
http://nlvm.usu.edu/en/nav/frames_asid_155_g_2_t_1.html

These two similar applets use base-ten blocks on a place-value chart. You can form any problem you wish up to four digits. The subtraction model shows the bottom number in red instead of blue. When the top blocks are dragged onto the red blocks, they disappear. Although you can begin in any column, the model forces a regrouping strategy as well as a take-away model for subtraction. Good for reinforcing the traditional algorithms.

Rectangle Division
http://nlvm.usu.edu/en/nav/frames_asid_193_g_1_t_1.html

This applet uses an array model to represent any two-digit number as a product of two numbers. Remainders are included.

Rectangle Multiplication
http://nlvm.usu.edu/en/nav/frames_asid_192_g_1_t_1.html

This applet nicely models two-digit by two-digit products up to 30 × 30.

Whole Number Algorithms and a Bit of Algebra!
http://mason.gmu.edu/%7Emmankus/whole/base10/asmdb10.htm

The purpose of this website is to assist the user in looking at addition, subtraction, multiplication, and division of whole numbers connecting the conceptual and procedural understandings. The site uses explanations with manipulatives to demonstrate the different algorithms.

Field Experience Guide Connections

There a number of Expanded Lessons and Activities that support student understanding of computation for whole numbers. FEG Activity 10.2 ("Odd or Even?") is a problem-based activity that includes addition and looking for patterns. FEG Expanded Lesson 9.1 on subtraction and Expanded Lesson 9.4 on division focus on building meaning for computation. FEG Activity 10.4 ("Interference") focuses on multiples and FEG Activity 10.3 ("Factor Quest") focuses on factors. FEG Activity 10.5 ("Target Number") helps students develop number sense for all the operations. Finally, the FEG Balanced Assessment Item 11.1 ("Magic Age Rings") is an excellent assessment for order of operations.

Chapter 13

Using Computational Estimation with Whole Numbers

Recall that *Principles and Standards* defined computational fluency as "having and using efficient and accurate methods for computing" (NCTM, 2000, p. 32). Computational estimation skills round out a full development of flexible and fluent thinking with whole numbers. *Curriculum Focal Points* (NCTM, 2006) includes computational estimation with whole numbers alongside expectations with related computation across grades 1 through 4, stating that the goal is for students to be able to "select and apply appropriate methods."

Mental computation and computational estimation are highly related yet quite different skills. Estimates are made using mental computations with numbers that are easier to work with than the actual numbers involved. Thus, estimation depends on students' mental computational skills. However, because of the importance of estimation—both in the real world and in much of mathematics—and because the strategies for computational estimation are quite different from those discussed in the preceding chapter, it makes sense to address computational estimation separately.

Big Ideas

1. Multidigit numbers can be built up or taken apart in a wide variety of ways. When the parts of numbers are easier to work with, these parts can be used to create estimates in calculations rather than using the exact numbers involved. For example, 36 is 30 and 6 or 25 and 10 and 1. 483 can be thought of as $500 - 20 + 3$.

2. Nearly all computational estimations involve using easier-to-handle parts of numbers or substituting difficult-to-handle numbers with close "nice" numbers so that the resulting computations can be done mentally.

Mathematics Content Connections

Estimation skills once developed are a tool for everyday living as well as a tool for sense making in other areas of mathematics.

- **Operations, Place Value, and Whole-Number Computation** (Chapters 9, 11, and 12): Many of the skills of estimation grow directly out of invented strategies for computation. For example, to estimate $708 \div 27$ you might compute 20×27 (540) and then 5×27 (135, for a total of 675). Thus, the quotient is a little more than 25. To compute these two products requires an understanding of place value. To understand how multiplication can help with the division estimate requires an understanding of how multiplication and division are related.

- **Estimation with Fractions, Decimals, and Percents** (Chapters 16 and 17): Once students have an understanding of what an estimate is and have developed strategies for whole-number estimation, few new strategies are required for estimation with other types of numbers. To estimate $3.45 + 24.06 - 0.0057$ requires no new estimation skills, only a good conceptual understanding of the decimals involved. Similar statements are true of fractions and percents.

Introducing Computational Estimation

Whenever we are faced with a computation in real life or in school, we have a variety of choices to make concerning how we will handle the computation. As pointed out in the 1989 *Standards* document, the first decision is: "Do we need an exact answer or will an approximate answer be okay?" If an exact answer is called for, we can use an invented or mental strategy, a pencil-and-paper algorithm, a calculator, or even a computer. A computer is called for when there are many repetitive computations that lend themselves to spreadsheet formats. Often, however, we do not need an exact answer and so we can use an estimate. How good an estimate—how close it must be to the actual computation—is a matter of context, as was the original decision to use an estimate.

The goal of computational estimation is to be able to flexibly and quickly produce an approximate result for a computation that will be adequate for the situation. In everyday life, estimation skills are valuable time savers. Many situations do not require an exact answer, so reaching for a calculator or a pencil is not necessary if one has good estimation skills. However, computational estimation is a higher-level thinking skill as it requires many decisions by the estimator (Sowder, 1989). Students are not as good at computational estimation as they are at producing exact answers and find computational estimation uncomfortable (Hanson & Hogan, 2000; Reys, Reys, & Penafiel, 1991; Reys, Reys, Nohda, Ishida, Yoshikawa, & Shimizu, 1991).

Good estimators tend to employ a variety of computational strategies they have developed over time. Teaching these strategies to children has become a regular part of the curriculum. As early as grade 2, we can help children develop an understanding of what it means to estimate a computation and start to develop some early strategies that may be useful. From then on through middle school, children should continue to develop and add to their estimation strategies and skills.

Understanding Computational Estimation

By itself, the term *estimate* refers to a number that is a suitable approximation for an exact number given the particular context. This concept of an estimate applies to measures and quantities as well as computation.

Three Types of Estimation. In the K–8 mathematics curriculum, *estimation* refers to three quite different ideas:

- *Measurement estimation*—determining an approximate measure without making an exact measurement. For example, we can estimate the length of a room or the weight of a watermelon in the grocery store.
- *Quantity estimation*—approximating the number of items in a collection. For example, we might estimate the number of students in the auditorium or jelly beans in the "estimation jar."
- *Computational estimation*—determining a number that is an approximation of a computation that we cannot or do not wish to determine exactly. For example, we might want to know the approximate gas mileage

in our car if we travel 326 miles on 16 gallons of gas (326 ÷ 16). In some instances, it is sufficient to know that a computation is either more or less than a given number. Do I have enough money to buy six boxes at $3.29 each? We have 28 dozen donuts. Are there enough for the 117 students to have two each?

Estimate or Guess. Many children confuse the idea of estimation with guessing. None of the three types of estimation involves outright guessing. Each involves some form of reasoning. Computational estimation, for example, involves some computation; it is not a guess at all. It is therefore important to (1) not use the word *guessing* when working on estimation and (2) explicitly help students see the difference between a guess and an estimate.

Computational Estimation in the Curriculum. Computational estimation may be underemphasized in your textbook and even in your state standards, but it is an important part of being able to do mathematics. In *Curriculum Focal Points* statements are made about computational estimation of whole numbers across four years—evidence of how important it is. Here is a synopsis of those statements. Key terms are highlighted in bold.

Grade 2 [within Focal Point on fluency with multidigit addition and subtraction]

[Students] select and apply appropriate methods to **estimate** sums and differences or calculate them mentally, depending on the context and numbers involved. (p. 14)

Grade 3 [within Connections to Number and Operations]

[Students] develop their understanding of numbers by building their facility with mental computation (addition and subtraction in special cases, such as 2500 + 6000 + 5000), by using **computational estimation,** and by performing paper-and-pencil computation. (p. 15)

Grade 4 [within Focal Point on fluency with multiplication]

[Students] select and apply appropriate methods to **estimate** products or calculate them mentally, depending on the context and numbers involved. (p. 16)

Grade 5 [within Focal Point on fluency with division of whole numbers]

[Students] select and apply appropriate methods to **estimate** quotients or calculate them mentally, depending on the context and numbers involved. (p. 17)

Notice that all work with estimation includes a decision (based on the context) of whether one should compute or estimate and the selection of a strategy.

NCTM *Standards* "Teachers should help students learn how to decide when an exact answer or an estimate would be more appropriate, how to choose the computational methods that would be best to use, and how to evaluate the reasonableness of answers to computations. Most calculations should arise as students solve problems in context" (p. 220). ◆

Suggestions for Teaching Computational Estimation

Here are some general principles that are worth keeping in mind as you help your students develop computational estimation skills.

Use Real Examples of Estimation. Discuss situations in which computational estimations are used in real life. Some simple examples include dealing with grocery store situations (doing comparative shopping, determining if there is enough to pay the bill), adding up distances in planning a trip, determining approximate yearly or monthly totals of all sorts of things (school supplies, haircuts, lawn-mowing income, time watching TV), and figuring the cost of going to a sporting event or show including transportation, tickets, and snacks. Discuss why exact answers are not necessary in some instances but are necessary in others. Look in a newspaper or magazine to find where numbers are the result of estimation and where they are the result of exact computations. Real examples are also a way to motivate students—for example, asking middle school students, "Are you a million seconds old? How can you find out?" Students enjoy exchanging information about birthdays and estimating how many seconds old they are (Martinie & Coates, 2007).

Use the Language of Estimation. Words and phrases such as *about, close, just about, a little more* (or *less) than,* and *between* are part of the language of estimation. Students should understand that they are trying to get as close as possible using quick and easy methods, but there is no correct estimate. Language can help convey that idea.

Use Context to Help with Estimates. Situations play a role in estimation. For example, for thirty 69-cent soft drinks, it is much easier to focus on 7×3 and use a result that makes sense than to compute 0.69×30 and try to place the decimal correctly. Is $2.10, $21, or $210 most reasonable? Similar assists come from knowing if the cost of a car would likely be $950 or $9500. Could attendance at the school play be 30 or 300 or 3000? A simple computation can provide the important digits, with knowledge of the context providing the rest.

Accept a Range of Estimates. Since they are based on computation, how can there be different answers to estimates? The answer, of course, is that any particular estimate depends on the strategy used and the kinds of adjustments in the numbers that might be made. Estimates also tend to vary with the need for the estimate. Estimating your gas mileage is quite different from trying to decide if your last $5 will cover the three items you need at the Fast Mart. These are new and difficult ideas for young students.

What estimate would you give for 27×325? If you use 20×300, you might say 6000. Or you might use 25 for the 27, noting that four 25s make 100. Since $325 \div 4$ is about 81, that would make 8100. If you use 30×300, your estimate is 9000, and 30×320 gives an estimate of 9600. Is one of these "right"?

By listing the estimates of many students and letting students discuss how and why different estimates resulted, they can begin to see that estimates generally fall in a range around the exact answer. Different approaches provide different results. And don't forget the context. Some situations call for more careful estimates than others and all results should be judged on their reasonableness.

Important teacher note: Do not reward or emphasize the answer that is the closest. It is already very difficult for students to handle "approximate" answers; worrying about accuracy and pushing for the closest answer only exacerbates this problem. Instead, focus on whether the answers given are *reasonable* for the situation or problem at hand.

Focus on Flexible Methods, Not Answers. Remember that your primary concern is to help students develop strategies for making computational estimates quickly. Reflection on the strategies therefore will lead to strategy development. Class discussion of strategies for estimation is just as important as it was for the development of invented methods of computation. For any given estimation, there are often several very good but different methods of estimation. Students will learn strategies from each other. The discussion of different strategies will also help students understand that there is no "right" estimate.

⏸ ———————————— *Pause and Reflect*

Estimate this product: 438×62. Use the first idea that comes to your head and write down the result. Then return to the task and try a different approach, perhaps using different numbers in your approach to the estimate.

Sometimes different strategies produce the same estimates. For 438×62, you might have thought about using 450×60 as a first step. Then suppose you think 10×450 is 4500. Double 4500 is 9000 and 3×9000 is 27,000. You might also have thought 6×45 is $240 + 30$ or 270. But this is not 6×45 but 60 times 450 so you add two more zeros—27,000.

Alternatively, you could have used 400 × 60 and gotten 24,000 and then recognized that you rounded both numbers down. You lost at least 38 sets of 62 or about 40 × 60. So add 2400 to the 24,000 to get 26,400.

If just a "ballpark" estimate were OK, you might have thought 500 × 60 is 30,000 and realized that it was a bit high. But the exact answer is also at least 400 × 60 or 24,000. So it's between 24 and 30 thousand.

You've just seen four of many possible estimation strategies for one computation. The more strategies you experience, the more you will learn. The more strategies you have, the better you can select one that best suits the situation at hand. Students will learn like this as well. In contrast, if you tell students to use a given strategy (e.g., round each number to one significant digit and multiply), they won't develop the skills to pick different strategies for different situations. Sometimes rounding is cumbersome and other strategies are quicker or more accurate.

Ask for Information, But No Answer. Consider the threat a third-grade student perceives when you ask for an estimate of the sum $349.29 + $85.99 + $175.25. The requirement to come up with *a number* can result in students' trying to quickly calculate an exact answer and then round it—a common strategy, especially among poor estimators (Hanson & Hogan, 2000). To counter this, ask questions that provide a possible result, using prompts like "Is it over or under 1000?" or "Will $500 be enough to pay for the tickets?" For the three prices, the question "About how much?" is quite different from "Is it more than $600?" How would you answer each of those questions?

Each activity that follows suggests a format for estimation in which a specific numeric response is not required.

Activity 13.1

Over or Under?

Prepare several estimation exercises on a transparency. With each, provide an "over or under number." In Figure 13.1, each is either over or under $1.50, but the number need not be the same for each task.

The last activity need not be very elaborate. Here are some more "over/under" examples:

37 + 75	over/under 100
712 − 458	over/under 300
17 × 38	over/under 400
349 ÷ 45	over/under 10

A meaningful context can be added to the examples to make the task accessible to more learners. Simple, noncontextual

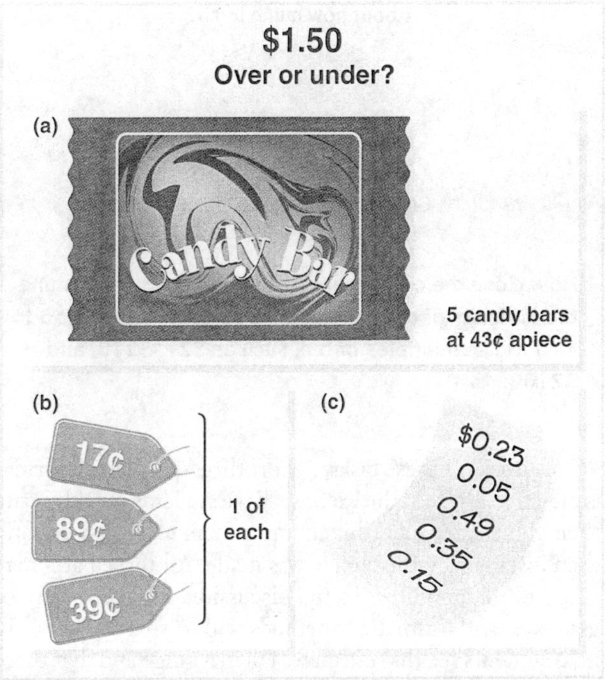

Figure 13.1 "Over or Under?" is a good beginning estimation activity.

tasks such as these can be prepared quickly. After presenting each, have students select their choice and then discuss their reasoning. The next activity is similar. It is adapted from an activity in the *Investigations in Number, Data, and Space* fifth-grade materials.

myeducationlab
Go to the Building Teaching Skills and Dispositions section of Chapter 13 of MyEducationLab. Click on Expanded Lessons to download the Expanded Lesson for **"High or Low?"** and complete the related activities.

Activity 13.2

High or Low?

Display a computation and three or more possible computations that might be used to create an estimate. The students' task is to decide if the estimation will be higher or lower than the actual computation. For example, present the computation 736 × 18. For each of the following, decide if the result will be higher or lower than the exact result and explain why you think so.

750 × 10	730 × 15
700 × 20	750 × 20

Activity 13.3

Best Choice

For any single estimation task, offer three or four possible estimates.

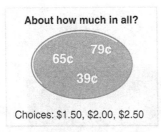

About how much in all?

65¢ 79¢ 39¢

Choices: $1.50, $2.00, $2.50

How close the choices are to each other will determine the difficulty of the estimation. Sometimes it is a good idea to use multiples of ten, such as $21, $210, and $2100.

With all of these tasks, a short three-part lesson format is effective. Present the exercise, have students quickly write their choice on paper (this commits them to an answer), and then discuss why the choice was made. All three parts may take only 10 minutes. In the discussion, a wide variety of estimates and estimation methods will be shared. This will help students see that estimates fall in a range and that there is no single correct (or best) estimate or method.

Computational Estimation from Invented Strategies

Estimation, like invented strategies, depends on using number relationships (Menon, 2003). Suppose that you were asked to compute the sum of 64 and 28. You might begin by adding 60 and 20 or 64 and 30. For each of these beginnings, you would need to make one or two additional computations before arriving at the answer. However, either of these beginnings is actually a reasonable estimate.

Stop Before the Details

Often it is the first step or two in an invented computation that is good enough for the estimate. In the 64 × 28 example, even a third grader would probably continue to the exact answer. But estimations are generally called for because an exact answer is too tedious or not necessary. When students have a good repertoire of invented strategies, one approach to an estimate is to simply begin to compute until you've gotten close to the exact answer.

Activity 13.4

That's Good Enough

Present students with a computation that is reasonably difficult for their skills. For example: *T-shirts with the school logo cost $6 wholesale. The Pep Club has saved $257. How many shirts can they buy for their*
fund-raiser? **The task is to describe the steps they would take to get an exact answer but not do them.**

Share students' ideas. Next, have students actually do one or two steps. Stop and see whether that is a good estimate.

The example in "That's Good Enough" may have seemed difficult to you. Try the same idea with a sum of four to six numbers: 47 + 29 + 74 + 55. Try it with a difficult difference: 7021 − 4583. Try it with a product: 86 × 29. The methods that students will come up with will be based on the ideas that they have learned for computing. In most instances, the beginnings of these computations are good estimates. By using the first steps of an invented strategy students are also improving their understanding of invented strategies and enhancing their number sense.

Use Related Problem Sets

In Chapter 12, the use of related cluster problem sets, or cluster problems, was explained as a technique to help students develop invented strategies for multiplication and division. (See p. 228.) The cluster problem approach, adapted from the *Investigations* curriculum, has students solve a collection of problems related to but easier than the target problem. These problems are then used to solve the harder problem. An important aspect of the cluster problem approach is that students first make (and write down) an estimate of the target computation.

Pause and Reflect

What follows are some cluster problems for each of the operations. The last problem is the target problem. Give these a try. Don't forget to first make an estimate of the target. Then solve all of the problems in the set. Use problems in the set to estimate the target. Which choices lead to good estimates?

4 + 5 + 6	600 − 300
400 + 500 + 600	600 − 400
400 + 600	85 + 15
60 + 30 + 100	15 + 13
60 + 20 + 90	85 − 13
467 + 528 + 693	**613 − 385**

10 ÷ 7	6 × 7
70 ÷ 7	6 × 8
7 × 11	70 × 7
7 × 12	60 × 7
87 ÷ 7	**68 × 7**

40 × 20	5 × 20
50 × 4	5 × 22
48 × 2	5 × 10
48 × 4	22 × 10
50 × 20	2 × 22
48 × 24	**147 ÷ 22**

There are many possible paths to the results. Notice, however, that some of the related problems (not the target) are actually good problems to use in making estimates. Once students are comfortable with sets of problems, try the following task.

Activity 13.5

Make a Little Cluster

Give students a target problem for a related problem set. It can be any operation that you are working on. The task is to create a set of two to three problems that will help produce a reasonable estimate. Once students have made the little set cluster, they should use their problems to estimate the target.

Computational Estimation Strategies

Estimation strategies are specific algorithms that produce approximate results. As you work through the strategies in this section, you should recognize many of the same approaches that students are likely to have developed from their invented methods. It is also likely that some of the strategies in this section will not have been developed and you will need to introduce these to your students. Be very clear whenever you suggest a strategy that the intention is to create a good full "basket" of strategies. Those that you introduce are no more correct or important than ideas that they have devised.

 NCTM *Standards* "Instructional attention and frequent modeling by the teacher can help students develop a range of computational estimation strategies including flexible rounding, the use of benchmarks, and front-end strategies. Students should be encouraged to frequently explain their thinking as they estimate" (p. 156). ◆

Front-End Methods

Front-end methods focus on the leading or leftmost digits in numbers, ignoring the rest. After an estimate is made on the basis of only these front-end digits, an adjustment can be made by noticing how much has been ignored.

For students who have had a lot of experience with invented strategies, the front-end strategy will make a lot of sense since invented strategies often begin with the large part of the numbers involved. The front-end approach is an especially good place to begin the topic of estimation for students who use only the traditional algorithms. They will have to work hard at the idea of looking first at the left portion of numbers in a computation.

Front-End Addition and Subtraction.   A front-end approach is reasonable for addition or subtraction when all or most of the numbers have the same number of digits. Figure 13.2 illustrates the idea. Notice that when a number has fewer digits than the rest, that number is initially ignored.

After adding or subtracting the front digits, an adjustment is made to correct for the digits or numbers that were ignored. Making an adjustment is actually a separate skill. For young children, practice first just using the front digits.

The leading-digit strategy can be easy to use because it does not require rounding or changing numbers. The numbers used are there and visible, so children can estimate without changing the numbers. You do need to be sure that students pay close attention to place value and only consider digits in the largest place, especially when the numbers vary in the number of digits in each.

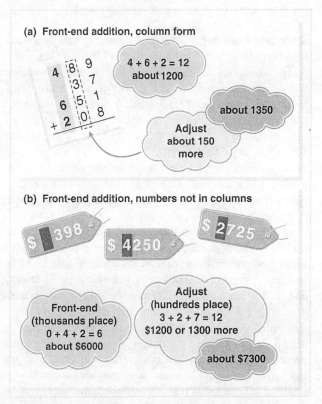

Figure 13.2 Front-end estimation in addition.

Front-End Multiplication and Division. For multiplication and division, the front-end method uses the first digit in each factor. The computation is then done using zeros in the other positions. For example, a front-end estimation of 48 × 7 is 40 times 7, or 280. When both numbers have more than one digit, the front ends of both are used. For 452 × 23, consider 400 × 20, or 8000. Because of the greater error that occurs in estimating with multiplication it is important to adjust these estimates.

For division, one approach is to think multiplication. Avoid presenting problems using the computational form (7)3482) because this tends to suggest a computation rather than an estimate and encourages a "goes into" approach. Present problems in context or using the algebraic form: 3482 ÷ 7. For this problem the front-end digit is determined by first getting the correct position. (100 × 7 is too low. 1000 × 7 is too high. It's in the hundreds.) There are 34 hundreds in the dividend, so since 34 ÷ 7 is between 4 and 5, the front-end estimate is 400 or 500. In this example, because 34 ÷ 7 is almost 5, the closer estimate is 500.

Rounding Methods

The most familiar form of estimation is rounding, which is a way of changing the numbers in the problem to others that are easier to compute mentally. To be useful in estimation, rounding should be flexible and well understood conceptually. Like front-end methods answers can be adjusted as a final step in order to get a closer estimate.

Rounding Concept. To round a number simply means to substitute a "nice" number that is close so that some computation can be done more easily. The close number can be any nice number and need not be a multiple of 10 or 100, as has been traditional. It should be whatever makes the computation or estimation easier or simplifies numbers sufficiently in a story, chart, or conversation. You might say, "Last night it took me 57 minutes to do my homework" or "Last night it took me about one hour to do my homework." The first expression is more precise; the second substitutes a rounded number for better communication.

A number line with nice numbers highlighted can be useful in helping children select near-nice numbers. An unlabeled number line like the one shown in Figure 13.3 can be made using three strips of poster board taped end to end. Labels are written above the line on the chalkboard. The ends can be labeled 0 and 100, 100 and 200, . . . , 900 and 1000. The other markings then show multiples of 25, 10, and 5. Indicate a number above the line that you want to round. Discuss the marks (nice numbers) that are close. (*Author note:* The term "nice number" is not always found in textbooks. It refers to numbers that would make the problem easier to compute mentally.)

Figure 13.3 A blank number line can be labeled in different ways to help students with near and nice numbers.

Rounding in Addition and Subtraction. When several numbers are to be added, it is usually a good idea to round them to the same place value. Keep a running sum as you round each number. Figure 13.4 shows an example of rounding.

For addition and subtraction problems involving only two terms, one strategy is to round only one of the two numbers. For example, you can round only the subtracted number (e.g., 6724 – 1863 becomes 6724 – 2000, resulting in 4724). You can stop here, or you can adjust. Adjusting might go like this: You took away a bigger number, so the result must be too small. Adjust to about 4800.

Rounding to "nice" numbers depends on what you, the estimator, consider "nice." For example, in 625 + 385, you may want to round 385 to 375 or 400. The point is that there are no rigid rules. Choices depend on the relationships held by the estimator, on how quickly the estimate is needed, and on how accurate an estimate needs to be.

Rounding in Multiplication and Division. The rounding strategy for multiplication is no different from that for other operations. However, the error involved can be

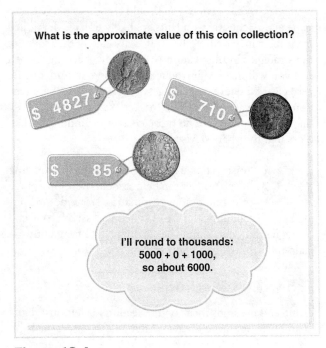

Figure 13.4 Rounding in addition.

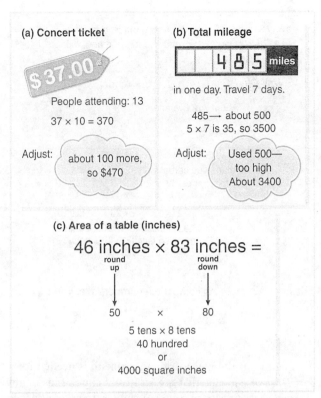

Figure 13.5 Rounding in multiplication.

significant, especially when both factors are rounded. In Figure 13.5, several multiplication situations are illustrated, and rounding is used to estimate each.

If one number can be rounded to 10, 100, or 1000, the resulting product is easy to determine without adjusting the other factor. Figure 13.5(a) shows a similar process.

When one factor is a single digit, examine the other factor. Consider the product 7 × 485. If 485 is rounded to 500, the estimate is relatively easy but is too high by 7 × 15. If a more accurate result is required, subtract about 100 (an estimate of 7 × 15). See Figure 13.5(b).

Another good rounding strategy for multiplication is to round one factor up and the other down (even if that is not the closest round number). When estimating 86 × 28, 86 is between 80 and 90, but 28 is very close to 30. Try rounding 86 down to 80 and 28 up to 30. The actual product is 2408, only 8 off from the 80 × 30 estimate. If both numbers were rounded to the nearest 10, the estimate would be based on 90 × 30, with an error of nearly 300 (see Figure 13.5(c) for another example).

When rounding in division, the key is to find two nice numbers, rather than round to the nearest benchmark. For example, 4325 ÷ 7 can be estimated by rounding to the close nice number, 4200, to yield an estimate of 600. Rounding to the nearest hundred results in a dividend of 4300, which does not make the division easier to do mentally.

Compatible Numbers

It is sometimes useful to look for two or three numbers that can be grouped to make benchmark values (e.g., 10, 100, 500). If numbers in the list can be adjusted slightly to produce these groups, that will make finding an estimate easier. This approach is illustrated in Figure 13.6.

In subtraction, it is often possible to adjust only one number to produce an easily observed difference, as illustrated in Figure 13.7.

One of the best uses of the compatible numbers strategy is in division. The two exercises shown in Figure 13.8 illustrate adjusting the divisor or dividend (or both) to create a division that results in a whole number and is, therefore, easy to do mentally. Many percent, fraction, and rate situations involve division, and the compatible numbers strategy is quite useful, as shown in Figure 13.9.

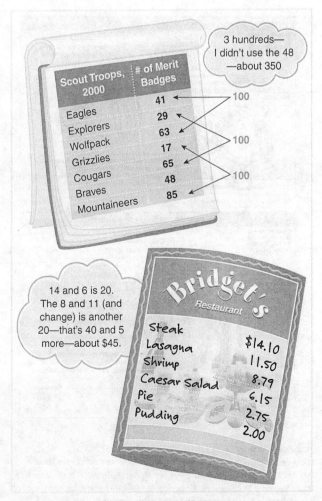

Figure 13.6 Compatibles used in addition.

Figure 13.7 Compatibles can mean an adjustment that produces an easy difference.

Figure 13.8 Adjusting to simplify division.

Source: GUESS (Guide to Using Estimation Skills and Strategies) Box 2 (cards 2 and 3), by Barbara J. Reys and Robert E. Reys, White Plains, NY: Dale Seymour Publications. Copyright © 1984 Pearson Education, Inc., or its affiliate(s). Used by permission. All rights reserved.

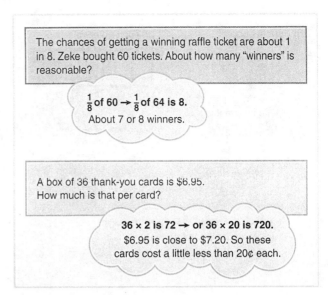

Figure 13.9 Using compatible numbers in division.

Clustering

Frequently in the real world, an estimate is needed for a large list of addends that are relatively close. This might happen with a series of prices of similar items, attendance at a series of events in the same arena, cars passing a point on successive days, or other similar data. In these cases, as illustrated in Figure 13.10, a nice number can be selected as representative of each, and multiplication can be used to determine the total.

Use Tens and Hundreds

Sometimes one of the numbers in the problem can be changed to take advantage of how easy it is to multiply or

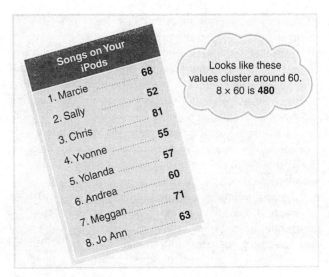

Figure 13.10 Estimating sums using clustering.

divide by tens, hundreds, and thousands (Menon, 2003). For example, take 456 × 5. Five is really 10/2 (so substitute 10 ÷ 2 to solve mentally). Multiply 456 by 10 to get 4560 and then estimate what half of that is—about 2300. See if you can apply this strategy to a larger problem: 786 × 48. You may have first thought that 48 is almost 50, which is the same as 100 ÷ 2. Since 786 times 100 equals 78,600, that is about 80,000 and half of that equals 40,000. Alternatively, you can divide by the two first and then multiply by 10 or 100. In the last example, that would mean taking half of 786, which is about 400, and multiplying by 100 to get 40,000.

This works with division, too. Consider 429 ÷ 5. Think: 429 ÷ 10 × 2 (or 429 × 2 ÷ 10). 429 ÷ 10 is about 42 and double that is 84. This can be a particularly useful strategy as the numbers get larger, like the following:

2309 ÷ 53
45,908 ÷ 517

This strategy can also be extended to numbers close to 25 (which is 100/4). For example: 786 ÷ 23 can be thought of this way: 786 × 4 ÷ 100. So 786 is close to 800, times 4 is 3200, then divided by 100 is 32.

 Since computational estimation involves a certain element of speed, teachers often wonder how they can test it so that students are not computing on paper and then rounding the answer to look like an estimate. One method is to prepare a short list of about three estimation exercises on a transparency. The cards in the GUESS boxes (Reys & Reys, 1983) are a ready source for these, or you can simply write computations. Students have their paper ready as you very briefly show one exercise at a time on the overhead, perhaps for 20 seconds, depending on the task. Students write their estimate immediately and indicate if they think their estimate is "low" or "high"—that is, lower or higher than the exact computation. They are not to do any written computation. Continue until you are finished. Then show all the exercises and have students write down how they did each estimate. They should also indicate if they think the estimate was a good estimate or not so good and why. By only doing a few estimates but having the students reflect on them in this way, you actually receive more information than you would with just the answers to a longer list. ◆

Estimation Experiences

The examples presented here are not designed to teach estimation strategies but offer useful formats to provide your students with practice using estimation skills as they are being developed. These will be a good addition to any estimation program.

Because students are less comfortable (and have less ability) with estimation as opposed to calculation, it is im-

portant to include regular experiences and activities that help students improve their estimation skills. The following activity works well on the overhead projector as do many whole-class estimation activities. This activity is also good for engaging students in discussions of estimation strategies.

Activity 13.6

What Was Your Method?

Select a problem with an estimation given. For example, 139 × 43 might be estimated as 6000. Ask questions concerning this estimate: "How do you think that estimate was arrived at? Was that a good approach? How should it be adjusted? Why might someone select 150 instead of 140 as a substitute for 139?" Almost every estimate can involve different choices and methods. Alternatives make good discussions, helping students see different methods and learn that there is no single correct estimate.

Activity 13.7

Jump to It

This activity focuses on division concepts. Students begin with a start number and estimate how many times they will add that start number to reach the goal. Here are a few to get you started (the numbers can vary to meet the needs and experiences of your students):

Jump Number	Goal	Estimate of Jumps	Was Estimate Reasonable?
5	72		
11	97		
7	150		
14	135		
47	1200		

To check estimates on the calculator, students can enter 0 + [jump number] and key ⊟ once for every estimated jump, or multiply [jump number] ⊠ [estimate of jumps].

Calculator Activities

The calculator is not only a good source of estimation activities but also one of the reasons estimation is so important. In the real world, we frequently hit a wrong key, leave off a zero or a decimal, or simply enter numbers incorrectly. An estimate of the expected result alerts us to these errors. The calculator as an estimation teaching tool lets students work independently or in pairs in a challenging, fun way without fear of embarrassment.

Activity 13.8

The Range Game

This is an estimation game for any of the four operations. First pick a start number and an operation. Students then take turns entering the start number, ☒, a number of choice, and ☐ to try to make the result land in the target range. The following example for multiplication illustrates the activity:

> Start Number: 17
>
> Range: 800–830

If the first number tried is 25, pressing 17 ☒ 25 gives 425. This is not in the range, so the calculator is passed to the partner, who clears the screen and picks a different number—for example, a number close to 50 because the first product was about half of the target range. A second guess might be 17 ☒ 45, or 765. This is closer, but still not in the range. The calculator goes back to the first person. Continue to clear each guess and start again until someone gets a product that lands in the range. Figure 13.11 gives examples for all four operations. Prepare a list of start numbers and target ranges. Let students play in pairs to see who can hit the most targets on the list (Wheatley & Hersberger, 1986).

"The Range Game" can also be played on an overhead calculator with the whole class. The span of the range and the type of numbers used can all be adjusted to suit the level of the class.

Activity 13.9

The Range Game: Continuous Input

Select a target range as before. Next enter the starting number in the calculator, and hand it to the first player. For addition and subtraction, the first player then presses either ☐ or ☐, followed by a number, and then ☐. If the result is not in the range, the calculator (with answer still on the screen) is handed to the next player, who begins his or her turn by entering ☐ or ☐ and an appropriate number. If the target is 423 to 425, a sequence of turns might go like this:

Start with 119.

Player 1 ☐ 350 ☐ ⟶ 469 (too high)
Player 2 ☐ 42 ☐ ⟶ 427 (a little over)
Player 1 ☐ 3 ☐ ⟶ 424 (success)

For multiplication or division, only one operation is used through the whole game. After the first or second turn, decimal factors are usually required. This variation provides excellent understanding of multiplication or division by decimals. A sequence for a target of 262 to 265 might be like this:

Start with 63.

Player 1 ☒ 5 ☐ ⟶ 315 (too high)
Player 2 ☒ 0.7 ☐ ⟶ 220.5 (too low)
Player 1 ☒ 1.3 ☐ ⟶ 286.65 (too high)
Player 2 ☒ 0.9 ☐ ⟶ 257.985 (too low)
Player 1 ☒ 1.03 ☐ ⟶ 265.72455 (very close!)

(What would you press next?)

Try a target of 76 to 80, begin with 495, and use only division.

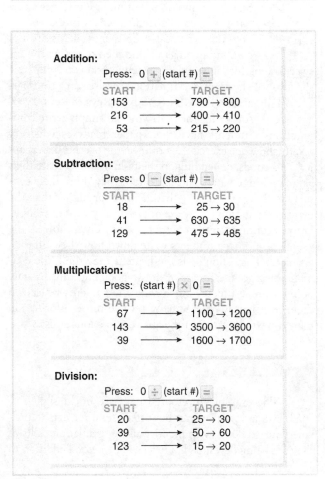

Addition:

Press: 0 ☐ (start #) ☐

START		TARGET
153	⟶	790 → 800
216	⟶	400 → 410
53	⟶	215 → 220

Subtraction:

Press: 0 ☐ (start #) ☐

START		TARGET
18	⟶	25 → 30
41	⟶	630 → 635
129	⟶	475 → 485

Multiplication:

Press: (start #) ☒ 0 ☐

START		TARGET
67	⟶	1100 → 1200
143	⟶	3500 → 3600
39	⟶	1600 → 1700

Division:

Press: 0 ÷ (start #) ☐

START		TARGET
20	⟶	25 → 30
39	⟶	50 → 60
123	⟶	15 → 20

Figure 13.11 "The Range Game."

The following activity is a blend of mental computation and estimation. Figuring out where the numbers go to create the exact solution involves estimation.

Activity 13.10

Box Math

Give students three digits to use (e.g., 3, 5, 7) and two operations (+ and −), preferably on cut-out cardstock so they can manipulate the numbers easily. Give students a set of equations with answers only and ask them to use only their digits (in the squares) and operations (in the circle) to get to the answer, as shown in the following display.

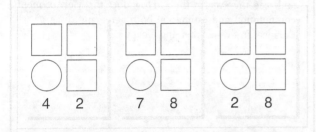

There are at least nine different possible answers. The same can be done with multiplication and division, though it must be written horizontally to account for both operations (adapted from Coates & Thompson, 2003).

Using Whole Numbers to Estimate Rational Numbers

It might be argued that much of the estimation in the real world involves fractions, decimals, and percents. A few examples are suggested here:

Sale! Original price of a jacket is 58.00. It is marked one-fourth off. What is the sale price?

About 62 percent of the 834 students bought their lunch last Wednesday. How many bought lunch?

Tickets sold for $1.25. If attendance was 3124, about how much was the total income?

I drove 337 miles on 12.35 gallons of gas. How many miles per gallon did my car get?

⏸ ——————— Pause and Reflect

Suppose you were to make estimates in each of the previous situations. Without actually getting an estimate, decide what numbers you would use in each case. For instance, in the first example you would not use 51.99 but perhaps 50 or 52. What about the fractions, decimals, and percents in the other problems? Think about that now before reading on.

The first example is basically asking for an estimate of $\frac{1}{4}$ off or $\frac{3}{4}$ of $58.00. To get $\frac{3}{4}$ of a quantity requires dividing by 4 and multiplying by 3. Those are whole-number computations, but they require an understanding of fraction multiplication.

In the next example, the problem is finding a way to deal with 62 percent. Well, that's close to 60 percent, which is $\frac{3}{5}$ or equivalently, 6 times 10 percent. In either case, the required computations involve whole numbers. The translation of 62 percent requires an understanding of percents.

In the third example, an understanding of decimals and fractions converts the problem to $1\frac{1}{4}$ of 3125. The computations involve dividing 3125 (perhaps 3200) by 4 and adding that to 3125—all whole-number computations. Similarly, the final example requires an understanding of decimals followed by whole-number computations.

The point is that when fractions, decimals, and percents are involved, an understanding of numeration is often the first thing required to make an estimate. That understanding often translates the situation into one involving only whole-number computations.

Of course, this is not always the case for fractions and decimals. Consider what is required to make estimates for the following:

$$2\frac{3}{8} + 4\frac{1}{9} - 1\frac{1}{12}$$

$$42.5 \times 0.46$$

A reasonable estimate in each case requires an understanding of rational numbers. There are very few new estimation skills required. These types of problems are discussed in Chapter 16.

Reflections on Chapter 13

Writing to Learn

1. How is computational estimation different from other types of estimation?
2. Why might computational estimation be uncomfortable for students?
3. What are some important considerations for teaching computational estimation?
4. What is the purpose of activities like "Over or Under" where students do not actually produce an answer?
5. Describe in general terms how estimation can grow out of the development of invented strategies.
6. Describe each of these estimation strategies. Be able to make up a good example and use it in your explanation.
   a. Front-end
   b. Rounding
   c. Compatibles
   d. Clustering
   e. Adapting to use 10s, 100s, and so forth.

For Discussion and Exploration

1. You notice a student is estimating by doing the computation and rounding the answer. Why might the student be using this strategy? What experiences might you plan to improve the student's ability to estimate?
2. *Adding It Up* (NRC, 2001) devotes less than five pages to the topics of mental arithmetic and estimation (pp. 214–218). Read these few pages with special attention to the discussion of estimation and the related skills that are needed for estimation. You can access the full text of *Adding It Up* on the Web at www.nap.edu/books/0309069955/html/index.html and read the excerpt there. How does this view of mental computation and estimation both agree and disagree with the ideas in this chapter and Chapter 12?

Resources for Chapter 13

Literature Connections

Literature often provides excellent contexts for which estimates, not exact answers, are the goal, as in the following two engaging examples.

Counting on Frank *Clement, 1991*

This popular book has a narrator who uses his dog, Frank, as a counting reference. For example, he explains that 24 Franks would fit in his room. Since the book offers approximations, there are limitless opportunities to do computational estimation. For example, how many Franks would fit in five rooms? If there were 24 Franks, how many cans of dog food (discussed on a later page) might be needed? The back of the book offers a series of estimation questions to get you started.

"How Many, How Much" from *A Light in the Attic* *Silverstein, 1981*

This very short poem is a nice lead-in to lessons on estimation, especially as it asks some unanswerable estimates, like how many slices in a loaf of bread (depends on how you slice it!). No answers are given, but students can estimate how many

eggs in 15 dozen, how many crayons in 70 boxes (boxes with 8, 16, or any amount), or how many weeks in their lifetime.

Recommended Readings

Books

Bresser, R., & Holtzman, C. (1999). *Developing number sense: Grades 3–6*. Sausalito, CA: Math Solutions Publications.
   This book includes 13 worthwhile number sense activities covering a range of topics including estimation. Activities include extensions, practical suggestions, and examples of students' work.

Reys, B. (1991). *Developing number sense*. Addenda Series, Grades 5–8. Reston, VA: NCTM.
   This is (still) a fabulous resource—providing a discussion about number sense and including a great collection of activities, some of which focus on computational estimation.

Online Resources

Count on Math (NCTM's Illuminations—Lessons, Grades 6–8)
http://illuminations.nctm.org/LessonDetail.aspx?id=U96
   The two lessons here provide activities for older students to estimate and develop number sense through data collection activities.

Estimate!

www.fi.uu.nl/toepassingen/00062/schatten/welcome_en.html

This is a fun fast-paced estimation applet for all four operations (go to "options" to select the ones you want to do). You click on start and a timer records how long until you get your answer entered. After ten problems you get a score, based on speed and accuracy.

Estimate Sums

www.ixl.com/math/practice/grade-2-estimate-sums

This site has various applets to practice skills for pre-K–3 students. There is a range of rounding and estimating activities for grades 2 and 3.

Estimation—Hundreds

www.quia.com/mc/65924.html

Players select squares on a board that round to the same hundred. A concentration version is also available.

Estimator Quiz (Shodor's Project Interactivate)

www.shodor.org/interactivate/activities/EstimatorQuiz

Similar to Estimate!, this applet allows a student to practice estimation for addition, multiplication, and percentage problems, getting instant feedback, but this site gives one problem at a time. A timer and instant feedback allow for independent practice and reinforcement.

Field Experience Guide Connections

Computational estimation is the focus of FEG Activity 10.5 ("Target Number"), as students use numbers on dice to try to reach a desired target number. Computational estimation is an excellent topic for a student interview. See FEG 7.2 for a template to design an interview with a student about their abilities to estimate with each operation.

Chapter 14

Algebraic Thinking: Generalizations, Patterns, and Functions

Algebra is an established content strand in most, if not all, state standards for grades K to 12 and is one of the five content standards in NCTM's *Principles and Standards*. Although there is much variability in the algebra requirements at the elementary and middle school levels, one thing is clear: The algebra envisioned for these grades—and for high school as well—is not the algebra that you most likely experienced in high school. That typical algebra course of the eighth or ninth grade previously consisted primarily of symbol manipulation procedures and artificial applications with little connection to the real world. The focus now is on the type of thinking and reasoning that prepares students to think mathematically across all areas of mathematics.

Algebraic thinking or algebraic reasoning involves forming generalizations from experiences with number and computation, formalizing these ideas with the use of a meaningful symbol system, and exploring the concepts of pattern and functions. Far from a topic with little real-world use, algebraic thinking pervades all of mathematics and is essential for making mathematics useful in daily life.

Big Ideas

1. Algebra is a useful tool for generalizing arithmetic and representing patterns in our world.

2. Symbolism, especially involving equality and variables, must be well understood conceptually for students to be successful in mathematics, particularly algebra.

3. Methods we use to compute and the structures in our number system can and should be generalized. For example, the generalization that $a + b = b + a$ tells us that $83 + 27 = 27 + 83$ without computing the sums on each side of the equal sign.

4. Patterns, both repeating and growing, can be recognized, extended, and generalized.

5. Functions in K–8 mathematics describe in concrete ways the notion that for every input there is a unique output.

6. Understanding is strengthened with functions that are explored across representations, as each one provides a different view of the same relationship.

Mathematics Content Connections

As Kaput (1998) notes, it is difficult to find an area of mathematics that does not involve generalizing and formalizing in some central way. In fact, this type of reasoning is at the heart of mathematics as a science of pattern and order.

- **Number, Place Value, Basic Facts, and Computation** (Chapters 8, 10, 11, and 12): The most important generalizations at the core of algebraic thinking are those made about number and computation—arithmetic. Not only does algebraic thinking generalize from number and computation, but also the generalizations themselves add to understanding and facility with computation. We can use our understanding of 10 to add $5 + 8$ ($5 + 8 = 3 + 2 + 8 = 3 + 10$) or $5 + 38$ ($5 + 38 = 3 + 2 + 38 = 3 + 40$). The generalized idea is that 2 can be taken from one addend and moved to the other: $a + b = (a - 2) + (b + 2)$. Although students may not symbolize this general idea, seeing that this works is algebraic thinking.

- **Operation Concepts** (Chapter 9): As children learn about the operations, they also learn that there are regularities in the way that the operations work. Examples include the commutative properties ($a + b = b + a$ and $a \times b = b \times a$) as well as the way that operations are related to one another.

- **Proportional Reasoning** (Chapter 18): Every proportional situation gives rise to a linear (straight-line) function with a graph that goes through the origin. The constant ratio in the proportion is the slope of the graph.

- **Measurement** (Chapter 19): Measures are a principal means of describing relationships in the physical world, and these relationships are often algebraic. Measurement formulas, such as circumference of a circle, are functions. You can say that the height of a building is a function of how many stories it has.

- **Geometry** (Chapter 20): Geometric patterns are some of the first that children experience. Growing patterns give rise to functional relationships. Coordinates are used to generalize distance concepts and to control transformations. And, of course, functions are graphed on the coordinate plane to visually show algebraic relationships.

- **Data Analysis** (Chapter 21): When data are gathered, the algebraic thinker is able to examine them for regularities and patterns. Functions are used to approximate trends or describe the relationships in mathematically useful ways.

Algebraic Thinking

Algebraic thinking begins in prekindergarten and continues through high school. According to *Curriculum Focal Points* (NCTM, 2006), in prekindergarten, "Children recognize and duplicate simple sequential patterns (e.g., square, circle, square, circle, square, circle, . . .)" (p. 11). Algebraic thinking continues to be included in every grade level, with the primary topics being (1) the use of patterns leading to generalizations (especially with the operations), the study of change, and the concept of function. Seeley & Schielack (2008) in their look at algebraic thinking in *Curriculum Focal Points* note:

> Underlying all these particular topics is the fundamental idea that, for students to be prepared to succeed in algebra, one of the best tools they can have is a deep understanding of the number system, its operations, and the properties related to those operations. (p. 266)

In fact, this chapter follows the chapters on these concepts so that you can see how closely related number concepts, operations, and algebraic thinking are.

Kaput (1999), a leader in crafting appropriate algebra curriculum across the grades, talks about algebra that "involves generalizing and expressing that generality using increasingly formal languages, where the generalizing begins in arithmetic, in modeling situations, in geometry, and in virtually all the mathematics that can or should appear in the elementary grades" (pp. 134–135). Although many authors and researchers have written about algebraic thinking, Kaput's description is the most complete, encompassing the ideas of many other contributors. He describes five different forms of algebraic reasoning:

1. Generalization from arithmetic and from patterns in all of mathematics
2. Meaningful use of symbols
3. Study of structure in the number system
4. Study of patterns and functions
5. Process of mathematical modeling, integrating the first four list items

Thus, algebraic thinking is not a singular idea but is composed of different forms of thought and an understanding of symbols. It is a separate strand of the curriculum but should also be embedded in all areas of mathematics. There is general agreement that we must begin the development of these forms of thinking from the very beginning of school so that students will learn to think productively with the powerful ideas of mathematics—basically so that they can think mathematically.

In this chapter, these five themes are used to discuss algebraic thinking. The categories themselves are not developmental, but within each category there are important developmental considerations. Therefore, in reading this chapter, you will find that each category offers considerations and effective instructional activities across the pre-K–8 curriculum.

Generalization from Arithmetic and from Patterns

The process of creating generalizations from number and arithmetic begins as early as kindergarten and continues as students learn about all aspects of number and computation, including basic facts and meanings of the operations. Therefore, algebraic thinking is very much connected to the ideas in Chapters 9 through 13.

Generalization with Addition

Young children explore addition families and in the process learn how to decompose and recompose numbers. The monkeys and trees problem illustrated in Figure 14.1 provides students a chance to not only consider ways to decompose 7, but also to see generalizable characteristics, such as that increasing the number in the small tree by one means reducing the number in the large tree by one.

Students may be asked to find all the ways the monkeys can be in the two trees. The significant question is how to decide when all of the solutions have been found. At one level, students will just not be able to think of any more and many will forget about using 0. Other children may try to use each number from 0 to 7 for one tree. The student who explains that for each number 0 to 7 there is one

myeducationlab

Go to the Activities and Application section of Chapter 14 of MyEducationLab. Click on Videos and watch the video entitled **"Pre-Algebra Strategies"** to see students engaged in prealgebra activities such as looking for patterns and generalizing to solve word problems.

Figure 14.1 Seven monkeys want to play in two trees, one big and one small. Show all the different ways that the seven monkeys could play in the two trees.
Source: Adapted from Yackel, E. (1997). "A Foundation for Algebraic Reasoning in the Early Grades." *Teaching Children Mathematics, 3*(6), 276–280. A similar task was explored in Carpenter, T. P., Franke, M. L., and Levi, L. (2003). *Thinking Mathematically: Integrating Arithmetic and Algebra in Elementary School.* Portsmouth, NH: Heinemann.

solution is no longer partitioning 7 into parts but is making a generalization that yields the number of solutions without even listing them (Yackel, 1997). That reasoning can be generalized to the number of ways 376 monkeys occupy the two trees. Second graders have articulated that there is always one more solution than the number of monkeys (Carpenter et al., 2003). Notice how this is a generalization that no longer depends on the numbers involved.

Generalizing does not need to involve symbols, but it is an important inclusion for older students (see the next major section). Seventh graders, for example, doing a problem like the monkeys but with 8 mice in a green or a blue cage, discovered three equations to describe the situation: $b + g = 8$, $8 - g = b$, and $8 - b = g$ (Stephens, 2005).

This is just one example of how algebraic thinking can and should be infused into work with number. To do so requires planning in advance—thinking of what questions you can ask to help students think about generalized characteristics within the problem they are working (when the number of monkeys in one tree goes down, the number in the other goes up by one) and to other problems that have the same pattern (376 monkeys).

Generalization in the Hundreds Chart

The hundreds chart is a rich field for exploring number relationships and should not be thought of solely as a device for teaching numeration. In Chapter 11, children colored skip counts on the hundreds chart and looked for pat-

terns (see Activities 11.14–11.19 and Activity 11.28). Here are some additional tasks you might explore in a similar manner.

- Which numbers make diagonal patterns? Which make column patterns? Can you make up a rule for explaining when a number will have a diagonal or column pattern? (See Figure 14.2, noting that the patterns depend on how many columns the charts contain.)
- If you move down two and over one on the hundreds chart what is the relationship between the original number and the new number?
- Can you find two skip-count patterns with one "on top of" the other? That is, all of the shaded values for one pattern are part of the shaded values for the other. How are these two skip-count numbers related? Is this true for any pair of numbers that have this relationship. Will this be true on hundreds charts with different widths? Why or why not?
- Find any value on the hundreds chart. Add it with the number to the left and the one to the right, then divide by 3. What did you get? Why?

These examples are just some of the many questions that extend number concepts to algebraic thinking concepts. "Can you find a rule?," "Why does this work?," and "When will this be true?" are questions that require justification and reasoning, which in turn strengthen students' understanding of number and of algebra.

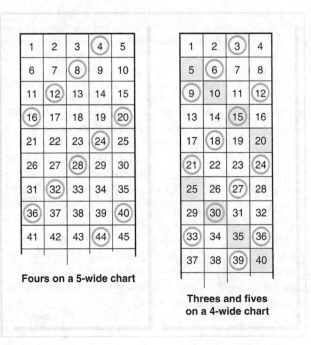

Fours on a 5-wide chart

Threes and fives on a 4-wide chart

Figure 14.2 Patterns on hundreds charts of different widths.

Generalization Through Exploring a Pattern

One of the most interesting and perhaps most valuable methods of searching for generalization is to find it in the growing physical pattern. One method of doing this is to examine only one growth step of a physical pattern and ask students to find a method of counting the elements without simply counting each by one. The following problem is a classic example of such a task, described in many resources including Burns and McLaughlin (1990) and Boaler and Humphreys (2005).

Activity 14.1

The Border Problem

On centimeter grid paper, have students draw an 8×8 square representing a swimming pool. Next, have them shade in the surrounding squares, the tiles around the pool (see Figure 14.3). The task is to find a way to count the border tiles without counting them one by one. Students should use their drawings, words, and number sentences to show how they counted the squares.

There are at least five different methods of counting the border tiles around a square other than counting them one at a time.

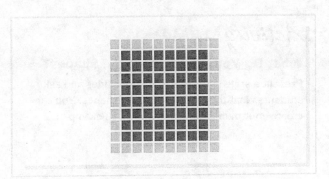

Figure 14.3 How many different ways can you find to count the border tiles of an 8×8 pool without counting them one at a time?

⏸ ——————— *Pause and Reflect*

Before reading further, see if you can find four or five different counting schemes for the border tiles problem. Apply your method to a square border of other dimensions.

A very common solution is to notice that there are ten squares across the top and also across the bottom, leaving eight squares on either side. This might be written as:

$$10 + 10 + 8 + 8 = 36 \text{ or } 2 \times 10 + 2 \times 8 = 36$$

Each of the following expressions can likewise be traced to looking at the squares in various groupings:

$$4 \times 9$$

$$4 \times 8 + 4$$

$$4 \times 10 - 4$$

$$100 - 64$$

More expressions are possible, since students may use addition instead of multiplication in the expressions. In any case, once the generalizations are created, students need to justify how the elements in the expression map to the physical representation.

Another approach to the Border Problem is to have students build a series of pools in steps, each with one more tile on the side (3×3, 4×4, 5×5, etc.) and then find a way to count the elements of each step using an algorithm that handles the step numbers in the same manner at each step. Students can find, for example, number sentences parallel to what they wrote for the 8×8 to find a 6×6 pool and a 7×7 pool. Eventually, this can result in a generalized statement, for example, taking $2 \times 10 + 2 \times 8$ and generalizing it to $2 \times (n + 2) + 2(n)$.

One important idea in generalization is recognizing a new situation where it can apply and adapting it appropriately. For example, students may explore other perimeter-related growing patterns, such as a triangle with 3, 4, and 5 dots on each side. Students should reason that this is the same type of pattern, except that it has three sides, and be able to use their previous generalization for this specific problem (Steele, 2005).

Meaningful Use of Symbols

Perhaps one reason that students are unsuccessful in algebra is that they do not have a strong understanding of the symbols they are using. For many adults, the word algebra elicits memories of simplifying long equations with the goal of finding x. These experiences of manipulating symbols were often devoid of meaning and resulted in such a strong dislike for mathematics that algebra has become a favorite target of cartoonists and Hollywood writers. In reality, symbols represent real events and should be seen as useful tools for solving important problems that aid in decision making (e.g., calculating how many we need to sell to make x dollars or at what rate do a given number of employees need to work to finish the project on time). Students cannot make sense of such questions without meaningful instruction on two very important (and poorly understood) topics: the equal sign and variables.

The Meaning of the Equal Sign

The equal sign is one of the most important symbols in elementary arithmetic, in algebra, and in all mathematics using numbers and operations. At the same time, research dating from 1975 to the present indicates clearly that "=" is a very poorly understood symbol (RAND Mathematics Study Panel, 2003).

❚❚ ——————— *Pause and Reflect*

In the following expression, what number do you think belongs in the box?

$$8 + 4 = \boxed{} + 5$$

How do you think students in the early grades or in middle school typically answer this question?

In one study, no more than 10 percent of students at any grade from 1 to 6 put the correct number (7) in the box. The common responses were 12 and 17. (How did students get these answers?) In grade 6, not one student out of 145 put a 7 in the box (Falkner, Levi, & Carpenter, 1999). Earlier studies found similar results (Behr, Erlwanger, & Nichols, 1975; Erlwanger & Berlanger, 1983).

Where do such misconceptions come from? Most, if not all, equations that students encounter in elementary school looks like this: 5 + 7 = ___ or 8 × 45 = ___ or 9(3 + 8) = ___. Naturally, students come to know = to signify "and the answer is" rather than a symbol to indicate equivalence (Carpenter, Franke, & Levi, 2003; McNeil & Alibali, 2005; Molina & Ambrose, 2006).

Why is it so important that students correctly understand the equal sign? First, it is important for students to see, understand, and symbolize the relationships in our number system. The equal sign is a principal method of representing these relationships. For example, 6 × 7 = 5 × 7 + 7. This is not only a fact strategy but also an application of the distributive property. The distributive property allows us to multiply each of the parts separately: (1 + 5) × 7 = (1 × 7) + (5 × 7). Other number properties are used to convert this last expression to 5 × 7 + 7. When these ideas, initially and informally developed through arithmetic, are generalized and expressed symbolically, powerful relationships are available for working with other numbers in a generalized manner.

A second reason is that when students fail to understand the equal sign, they typically have difficulty when it is encountered in algebraic expressions (Knuth et al., 2006). Even solving a simple equation such as $5x - 24 = 81$ requires students to see both sides of the equal sign as equivalent expressions. It is not possible to "do" the left-hand side. However, if both sides are the same, then they will remain the same when 24 is added to each side.

Conceptualizing the Equal Sign as a Balance.   Helping students understand the idea of equivalence can be developed concretely, beginning in the elementary grades. The next two activities illustrate how tactile objects and visualizations can reinforce the "balancing" notion of the equal sign (ideas adapted from Mann, 2004).

Activity 14.2

Seesaw Students

Ask students to raise their arms to look like a seesaw. Explain that you have big juicy oranges, all weighing the same, and tiny little apples, all weighing the same. Ask students to imagine that you have placed an orange in each of their left hands (students should bend to lower left side). Ask students to imagine that you place another orange on the right side (students level off). Next, with oranges still there, ask students to imagine an apple added to the left. Finally, say you are adding another apple, but tell students it is going on the left (again). Then ask them to imagine it moving over to the right.

After acting out the seesaw several times, ask students to write Seesaw Findings (e.g., "If you have a balanced seesaw and add something to one side, it will tilt to that side," and "If you take away the same object from both sides of the seesaw, it will still be balanced").

Activity 14.3

What Do You Know about the Shapes?

Present a scale with objects on both sides and ask students what they know about the shapes. You can create your own, but here is one as an example:

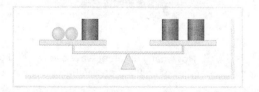

The red cylinders weigh the same. The yellow balls weigh the same. What do you know about the weights of the balls and the cylinders? Figure 14.4 illustrates how one third grader explained what she knew. (Notice that these tasks, appropriate for early grades, are good beginnings for the more advanced balancing tasks later in this chapter.)

After students have experiences with shapes, they can then explore numbers, eventually going on to variables.

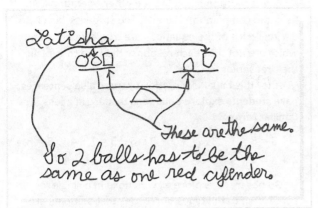

Figure 14.4 Latisha's work on the problem.
Source: Figure 4 from Mann, R. L. (2004). "Balancing Act: The Truth Behind the Equals Sign." *Teaching Children Mathematics, 11*(2), p. 68. Reprinted with permission. Copyright © 2004 by the National Council of Teachers of Mathematics, Inc. www.nctm.org. All rights reserved.

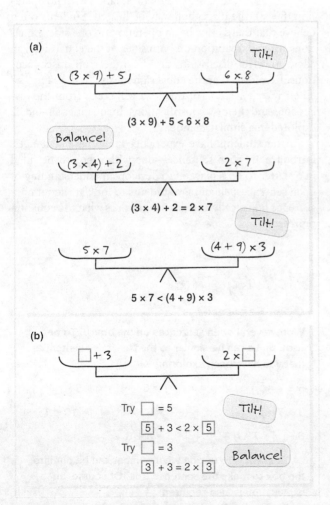

Figure 14.5 Using expressions and variables in equations and inequalities. The two-pan balance helps develop the meaning of =.

Figure 14.5 offers examples that connect the balance to the related equation. This two-pan-balance model also illustrates that the expressions on each side represent a number.

The balance is a concrete tool that can help students understand that if you add or subtract a value from one side, you must add or subtract a like value from the other side to keep the equation balanced.

Figure 14.6 shows solutions for two equations, one in a balance and the other without. Even after you have stopped using the balance, it is a good idea to refer to the scale or balance-pan concept of equality and the idea of keeping the scales balanced.

As students begin to develop equations they wish to graph, the equations will often be in a form in which neither variable is isolated. For example, in the equation $3A - B = 2A$, they may want A in terms of B or B in terms of A. The same technique of solving for one variable can be used to solve for one variable in terms of the other by adjusting the expressions on both sides while keeping the equation in balance.

 An NCTM Illuminations applet titled *Pan Balance—Expressions* provides a virtual balance where students can enter what they believe to be equivalent expressions (with numbers or symbols) each in a separate pan to see if, in fact, the expressions balance. ◆

True/False and Open Sentences. Carpenter, Franke, and Levi (2003) suggest that a good starting point for helping students with the equal sign is to explore equations as either true or false. Clarifying the meaning of the equal sign is just one of the outcomes of this type of exploration, as seen in the following activity.

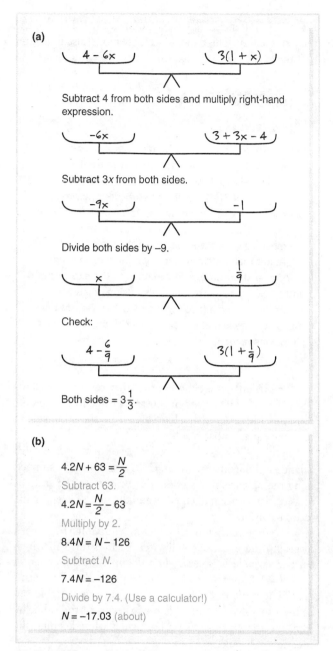

(a)

Subtract 4 from both sides and multiply right-hand expression.

Subtract 3x from both sides.

Divide both sides by –9.

Check:

Both sides = $3\frac{1}{3}$.

(b)

$4.2N + 63 = \dfrac{N}{2}$

Subtract 63.

$4.2N = \dfrac{N}{2} - 63$

Multiply by 2.

$8.4N = N - 126$

Subtract N.

$7.4N = -126$

Divide by 7.4. (Use a calculator!)

$N = -17.03$ (about)

Figure 14.6 Using a balance scale to think about solving equations.

Activity 14.5

True or False

Introduce true/false sentences or equations with simple examples to explain what is meant by a true equation and a false equation. Then put several simple equations on the board, some true and some false. The following are appropriate for primary grades:

$5 + 2 = 7 \qquad 4 + 1 = 6$

$4 + 4 = 8 \qquad 8 = 10 - 1$

Your collection might include other operations but keep the computations simple. The students' task is to decide which of the equations are true equations and which are not. For each response they are to explain their reasoning.

After this initial exploration of true/false sentences, have students explore equations that are in a less familiar form:

$4 + 5 = 8 + 1 \quad 3 + 7 = 7 + 3 \quad 6 - 3 = 7 - 4 \quad 8 = 8$

$4 + 5 = 4 + 5 \quad 9 + 5 = 14 \qquad 9 + 5 = 14 + 0$

Do not try to explore all variations in a single lesson. Listen to the types of reasons that students are using to justify their answers and plan additional equations accordingly for subsequent days.

Students will generally agree on equations where there is an expression on one side and a single number on the other, although initially the less familiar form of $7 = 2 + 5$ may cause some discussion. For an equation with no operation $(8 = 8)$, the discussion may be heated. Students often believe that there must be an operation on one side. Equations with an operation on both sides of the equal sign can elicit powerful discussions and help clear up misconceptions. Reinforce that the equal sign means "is the same as." Their internalization of this idea will come from the discussions and their own justifications. Inequalities should be explored in a similar manner.

After students have experienced true/false sentences, introduce an open sentence—one with a box to be filled in or letter to be replaced. To develop an understanding of open sentences, encourage students to look at the number sentence holistically and discuss in words what the equation represents.

Activity 14.6

Open Sentences

Write several open sentences on the board. To begin with, these can be similar to the true/false sentences that you have been exploring.

$5 + 2 = \square \qquad 4 + \square = 6 \qquad 4 + 5 = \square - 1$

$3 + 7 = 7 + \square \qquad \square + 4 = 8 \qquad \square = 10 - 1$

$6 - \square = 7 - 4 \qquad \square + 5 = 5 + 8$

The task is to decide what number can be put into the box to make the sentence true. Of course, an explanation is also required.

For grades 3 and above, include multiplication as well as addition and subtraction.

Initially, some students will revert to doing computations and putting the answer in the box. This is a result of too many exercises where an answer is to be written as a single number following an equal sign. In fact, the box is a forerunner of a variable, not an answer holder.

Relational Thinking. Once students understand that the equal sign means that the quantities on both sides are the same, they can use relational thinking in solving problems. Relational thinking takes place when a student observes and uses numeric relationships between the two sides of the equal sign rather than actually computing the amounts. Relational thinking of this sort is a first step toward generalizing relationships found in arithmetic so that these same relationships can be used when variables are involved rather than numbers.

Consider two distinctly different explanations for placing a 5 in the box for the open sentence $7 - \square = 6 - 4$.

a. Since $6 - 4$ is 2, you need to take away from 7 to get 2. $7 - 5$ is 2, so 5 goes in the box.
b. Seven is one more than the 6 on the other side. That means that you need to take one more away on the left side to get the same number. One more than 4 is 5 so 5 goes in the box.

⏸ ———————————— *Pause and Reflect*

How are these two correct responses actually quite different? How would each of these students solve this open sentence? $534 + 175 = 174 + \square$

The first student computes the result on one side and adjusts the result on the other to make the sentence true. The second student is using a relationship between the expressions on either side of the equal sign. This student does not need to compute the values on each side. When the numbers are large, the relationship approach is much more useful. Since 174 is one less than 175, the number in the box must be one more than 534 to make up the difference. The first student will need to do the computation and will perhaps have difficulty finding the correct addend.

In order to nurture relational thinking and the meaning of the equal sign, continue to explore an increasingly complex series of true/false and open sentences with your class. Select equations designed to elicit good thinking and challenges rather than computation. Use large numbers that make computation difficult (not impossible) to push them toward relational thinking.

True/False

$674 - 389 = 664 - 379$ $5 \times 84 = 10 \times 42$
$37 + 54 = 38 + 53$ $64 \div 14 = 32 \div 28$

Open Sentences

$73 + 56 = 71 + \square$ $126 - 37 = \square - 40$
$20 \times 48 = \square \times 24$ $68 + 58 = 57 + 69 + \square$

⏸ ———————————— *Pause and Reflect*

One of the true/false statements is false. Can you explain why using relational thinking?

Marta Molina and Rebecca Ambrose (2006), researchers in mathematics education, used the true/false and open-ended prompts with third graders, none of whom understood the equal sign in a relational way at the start of their study. For example, all 13 students answered $8 + 4 = \_\_\_ + 5$ with 12. They found that asking students to write their own open sentences was particularly effective in helping students solidify their understanding of the equal sign. The following forms were provided as guidance (though students could use multiplication and division if they wanted):

$$\_\_\_ + \_\_\_ = \_\_\_ + \_\_\_$$

$$\_\_\_ - \_\_\_ = \_\_\_ - \_\_\_$$

$$\_\_\_ + \_\_\_ = \_\_\_ - \_\_\_.$$

Activity 14.7

Writing True/False Sentences

After students have had ample time to discuss true/false and open sentences, ask them to make up their own true/false sentences that they can use to challenge their classmates. Each student should write a collection of three or four sentences with at least one true and at least one false sentence. Encourage them to include one "tricky" one. Their equations can either be traded with a partner or used in full-class discussions.

Repeat for open sentence problems.

When students write their own true/false sentences, they often are intrigued with the idea of using large numbers and lots of numbers in their sentences. This encourages them to create sentences involving relational thinking.

 As students explore true/false and open sentence activities, look for two developments. First, are students acquiring an appropriate understanding of the equal sign? Look to see if they are comfortable using operations on both sides of the equal sign and can use the meaning of *equal* as "is the same as" to solve open sentences.

Second, look for an emergence of relational thinking. Students who rely on relationships found in the operations on each side of the equal sign rather than on direct computation have moved up a step in their algebraic thinking. ◆

The Meaning of Variables

Expressions or equations with variables allow for the expression of generalizations. When students can work with expressions involving variables without even thinking about the specific number or numbers that the letters may stand for, they have achieved what Kaput (1999) refers to as manipulation of opaque formalisms—they can look at and work with the symbols themselves. Variables can be used as unique unknown values or as quantities that vary. Unfortunately, students often think of the former and not the latter. Experiences in elementary and middle school should focus on building meaning for both, as delineated in the next two sections.

Variables Used as Unknown Values. Students' first experiences with variables tend to focus exclusively on variables as unknown values. In the open sentence explorations, the □ is a precursor of a variable used in this way. Early on, you can begin using various letters instead of a box in your open sentences. Rather than ask students what number goes in the box, ask what number the letter could stand for to make the sentence true. Initial work with finding the value of the variable that makes the sentence true—solving the equation—should initially rely on relational thinking. Later, students will develop specific techniques for solving equations when these relationships are insufficient.

The balancing ideas described in the previous section can also serve this purpose. NCTM Illuminations, for example, uses an applet titled "Pan Balance—Shapes," along with two excellent pre-K–2 lesson plans, for having students (virtually) weigh different shapes to figure out what number each shape represents.

Consider the following open sentence: □ + □ + 7 = □ + 17 (or, equivalently, $n + n + 7 = n + 17$). A convention for the use of multiple variables is that the same symbol or letter in an equation stands for the same number every place it occurs. Carpenter et al. (2003) refer to it as "the mathematician's rule." In the preceding example, the □ must stand for 10.

Many story problems involve a situation in which the variable is a specific unknown, as in the following basic example:

> **Gary ate five strawberries and Jeremy ate some, too. The container of 12 was gone! How many did Jeremy eat?**

Although students can solve this problem without using algebra, they can begin to learn about variables by expressing it in symbols: $5 + s = 12$. These problems can grow in difficulty over time.

With a context, students can even explore three variables, each one standing for an unknown value, as in the activity below.

Activity **14.8**

Balls, Balls, Balls

How much does each ball weigh given the following three facts:

1.	baseball + football	= 1.25 pounds
2.	baseball + soccer ball	= 1.35 pounds
3.	soccer ball + football	= 1.9 pounds

Ask students to look at each fact and make observations that help them generate other facts. For example, they might notice that the soccer ball weighs 0.1 pounds more than the football. Write this in the same fashion as the other statements. Continue until these discoveries lead to finding the weight of each ball. Encourage students to use models to represent and explore the problem (activity adapted from Maida, 2004).

One possible approach: Add equations 1 and 2:

baseball + baseball + football + soccer ball = 2.6 pounds

Then take away the football and soccer ball, reducing the weight by 1.9 pounds (based on the information in equation 3), and you have two baseballs that weigh 0.7 pounds. Divide by 2, so one baseball is 0.35 pounds.

You may have recognized this last example as a system of equations presented in a concrete manner. This type of work is accessible to upper elementary and middle school students when presented in this manner and helps build the foundation for working with systems of equations later.

Another concrete way to work on systems of equations is through balancing. Notice the work done in building the concept of the equal sign is now applied to understanding and solving for variables.

In Figure 14.7, a series of examples shows scale problems in which each shape on the scales represents a different value. Two or more scales for a single problem provide different information about the shapes or variables. Problems of this type can be adjusted in difficulty for children across the grades. Greenes and Findell (1999a,b) have developed a whole collection of these and similar activities in books for grades 1 to 7.

When no numbers are involved, as in the top two examples of Figure 14.7, students can find combinations of numbers for the shapes that make all of the balances balance. If an arbitrary value is given to one of the shapes, then values for the other shapes can be found accordingly.

In the second example, if the sphere equals 2, then the cylinder must be 4 and the cube equals 8. If a different value is given to the sphere, the other shapes will change accordingly.

Pause and Reflect

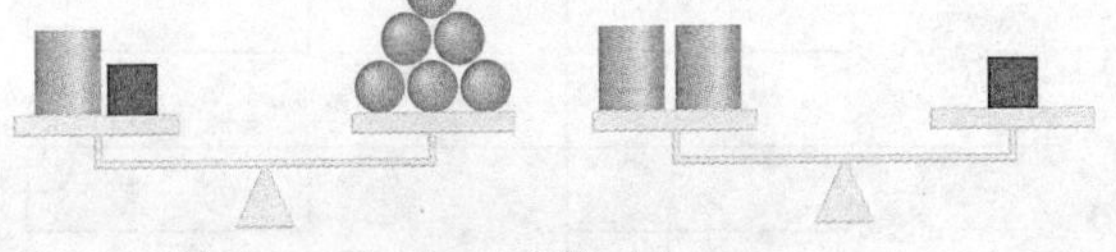

How would you solve the last problem in Figure 14.7? Can you solve it in two ways?

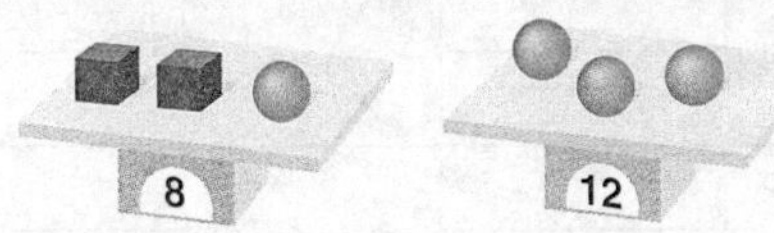

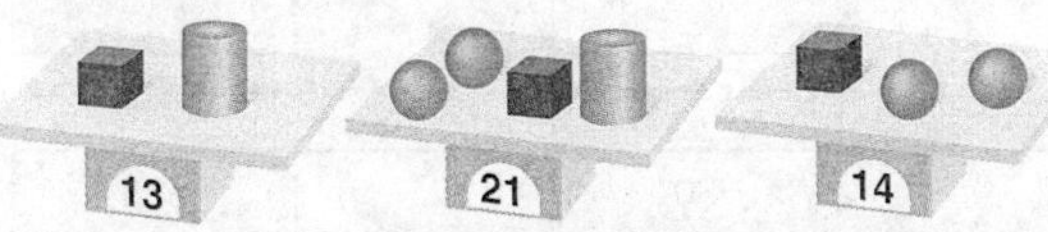

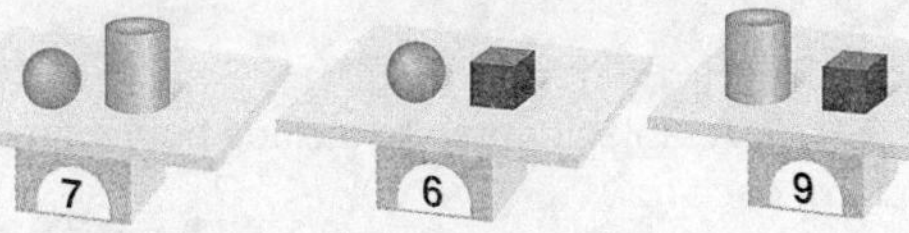

You (and your students) can tell if you are correct by checking your solutions with the original scale positions.

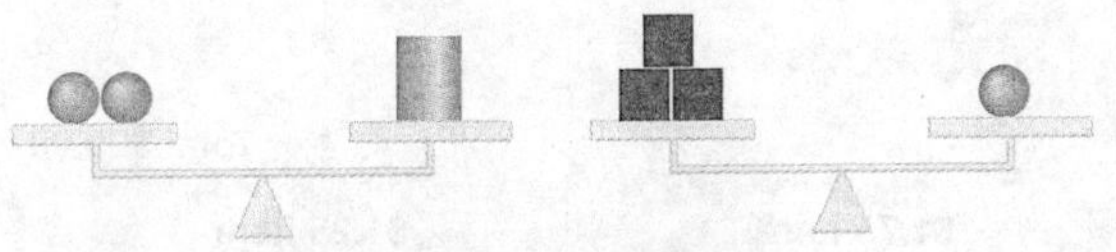

Believe it or not, you have just solved a series of simultaneous equations, a skill generally left to a formal algebra class.

Simplifying Expressions and Equations. As noted earlier, simplifying equations and solving for *x* have often been meaningless tasks, and students are unsure of what steps to do when. Still, knowing how to simplify and recognizing equivalent expressions are essential skills to working algebraically. In *Curriculum Focal Points* (NCTM, 2006), one of the three focal points is about algebra: "Writing, interpreting, and using mathematical expressions and equations."

Students need an understanding of how to apply mathematical properties and how to preserve equivalence as they simplify. One way to do this is to have students look at simplifications that have errors and explain how to fix the errors (Hawes, 2007). Figure 14.8 shows how three students have justified the correct simplification of $(2x + 1) - (x + 6)$.

Figure 14.7 Examples of problems with multiple variables and multiple scales.

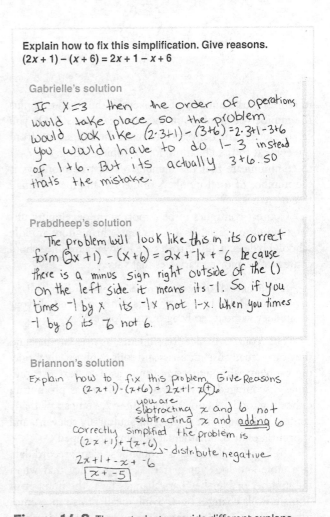

Figure 14.8 Three students provide different explanations for fixing the flawed simplification given.
Source: Figure 3 from Hawes, K. (2007). "Using Error Analysis to Teach Equation Solving." *Mathematics Teaching in the Middle School, 12*(5), p. 241. Reprinted with permission. Copyright © 2007 by the National Council of Teachers of Mathematics, Inc. www.nctm.org. All rights reserved.

Variables Used as Quantities That Vary. As noted earlier, the important concept that variables can represent more than one missing value is not well understood by students and is not as present in the elementary and middle school curriculum as it should be. When there are different variables in a single equation, each variable can represent many, even infinite, numbers. In the middle school grades, variables that are used to describe functions (e.g., $y = 3x - 5$) are variables that have many possible numeric solutions. This shift from the variable as an unknown to a variable representing a relationship can be difficult for students. This difficulty can be alleviated if students have experiences with variables that vary in the elementary curriculum.

Recall the monkeys in two trees problem in Figure 14.1 of this chapter. Even very young students can represent the possible solutions using symbols. For example, they might draw

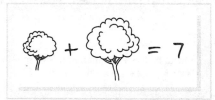

to represent the number of monkeys in the small tree plus the number of monkeys in the big tree equals 7. Or you can use letters and help students make the connection from the context to the equation, for example writing: $b = 7 - s$ to communicate that the number of big tree monkeys is the number of total monkeys minus the number of small tree monkeys.

Context continues to be important in developing understanding of variables for students throughout middle school. Hyde et al. (2006) offer the following middle school context for exploring variables that vary:

> If you have $10 to spend on $2 Hershey bars and $1 Tootsie Rolls, how many ways can you spend all your money without receiving change? (p. 262)

This context is nice for students, as it is familiar and they can actually use minibars and rolls to physically model the problem, although using candy as a context is sometimes discouraged, as it can be interpreted as promoting unhealthy foods. As noted in Chapter 2, you can pick any context that you think is engaging, culturally relevant, and appropriate for the mathematics being developed.

To begin exploring this problem, students record data in a table and look for patterns. They notice that when the number of Hershey bars changes by 1, the number of Tootsie Rolls changes by 2. Symbolically, this representation is $2H + T = \$10$, where H is the number of Hersheys and T is the number of Tootsie Rolls. It is also important to include decimal and fraction values in the exploration of variables. As any algebra teacher will confirm, students struggle most with these numbers—again resulting from the lack of earlier, more concrete, and visual experiences mixing fractions and decimals with variables. For example, if you were buying $1.75 pencils and $1.25 erasers from the school store, and spending all of $35.00, how many combinations are possible? What equation represents this situation?

For students with special needs or students who might be unfamiliar with using a table, it is helpful to adapt the table to include both how many and how much, as shown in Figure 14.9 (Hyde et al., 2006). Reinforce the two elements with each entry (how many and how much). In addition, calculators can facilitate exploration of possible solutions. To increase the challenge for advanced or gifted students, ask students to graph the values or to consider more complex situations.

Once students have the expression in symbols (in this case, $1.75x + 1.25y = 35.00$), ask students to tie each number and variable back to the context. In this way, students can make sense of what is normally poorly understood and really develop a strong foundation for the algebra they will study in high school.

	$1.75 item		$1.25 item	Total $35.00
	$35.00		$0	
20		0		
	$0		$35	
0		28		

Figure 14.9 A table adapted to include how many and how much for each row.
Source: Hyde, A., George, K., Mynard, S., Hull, C., Watson, S., & Watson, P. (2006). "Creating Multiple Representations in Algebra: All Chocolate, No Change," *Mathematics Teaching in the Middle School, 11*(6), 262–268. Reprinted with permission. Copyright © 2006 by the National Council of Teachers of Mathematics, Inc. www.nctm.org. All rights reserved.

Making Structure in the Number System Explicit

Chapter 9 discusses a few properties for each operation (see p. 153 and pp. 160–161) that are important for students as they learn basic facts and strategies for computation. For example, the commutative or order property for both addition and multiplication reduces substantially the number of facts necessary to learn. These and other properties are likely to be used informally as students develop relational thinking while working with true/false and open sentences as described in previous sections.

A next step is to have students examine these structures or properties explicitly and express them in general terms without reference to specific numbers. For example, a student solving $394 + 176 = N + 394$ may say that N must be 176 because $394 + 176$ is the same as $176 + 394$. This is a specific instance of the commutative property. To articulate this (and other structural properties of our number system) in a form such as $a + b = b + a$, noting that it is true for all numbers, is the goal of looking at structure. When made explicit and understood, these structures not only add to students' tools for computation but also enrich their understanding of the number system and provide a base for even higher levels of abstraction (Carpenter et al., 2003).

Making Conjectures about Properties

Properties of the number system can be built into students' explorations with true/false and open number sentences. For example, third-grade students will generally agree that the true/false sentence $41 \times 3 = 3 \times 41$ is true. The pivotal question, however, asks "Is this true for any numbers?" Some students will argue that although it seems to be true all of the time, there may be two numbers that haven't been tried yet for which it does not work.

The following classroom problem and discussion was focused on investigating the distributive and associative properties, not on whether the equation was true or false (from Baek, 2008):

Ms. J: [*Pointing at* $(2 \times 8) + (2 \times 8) = 16 + 16$ *on the board*] Is it true or false?

LeJuan: True, because two 8 is 16 and two 8 is 16.

Lizett: $(2 \times 8) + (2 \times 8)$ is 32 and $16 + 16$ is 32.

Carlos: 8 plus 8 is 16, so 2 times 8 is 16, and 8 plus 8 is 16, and 2 times 8 is 16.

Ms. J: [*Writing* $4 \times 8 = (2 \times 8) + (2 \times 8)$ *on the board*] True or false?

Students: True.

Ms. J: What does the 2 stand for?

Reggie: Two boxes of eight.

Ms. J: So how many boxes are there?

Students: Four.

Ms. J: [*Writing* $32 + 16 = (4 \times 8) + (a \times 8)$ *on the board*] What is a?

Michael: Two, because 4 times 8 is 32, and 2 times 8 is 16.

Ms. J: [*Writing* $(4 \times 8) + (2 \times 8) = (b \times 8)$ *on the board*] What is b?

Students: 6. (pp. 151–152)

Notice how the teacher is developing the aspects of these properties in a conceptual manner—focusing on exemplars to guide students to generalize, rather than presenting the properties as they appear in Table 14.1 as their first experience, which can be a meaningless, rote activity.

You can follow specific examples, such as those used in the dialogue, by asking students to try to state the idea in words without using a specific number. For example, when multiplying a number by a second number, you can split the first number and multiply each part by the second number, and you will get the same answer. If a generalization is not clear or entirely correct, have students discuss the wording until all agree that they understand what it means. Write this verbal statement of the property on the board. Call it a conjecture and explain that it is not necessarily a true statement just because we think that it is true. Until someone either proves it or finds a counterexample—an instance for which the conjecture is not true—it remains a conjecture.

Students can make conjectures about properties as early as first or second grade. By third or fourth grade, students should be challenged to translate verbal conjectures into open sentences. The preceding conjecture can be written using any two letters as follows: $a \times b = (c \times b) + (d \times b)$, where $c + d = a$. Ask students to state conjectures verbally before moving to the symbolic statement of the same idea. Then have them explain what each variable in the symbolic form means.

Activity 14.9

Conjecture Creation

Once students have seen a couple of conjectures developed out of your explorations of true/false sentences, challenge students to make up conjectures on their own—creating statements about numbers and computation that they believe are always true. It is best to have them state the conjectures in words. The full class should discuss the various conjectures, asking for clarity or challenging conjectures with counterexamples. Conjectures can be added to a class list written in words and in symbols.

Table 14.1 lists basic properties of the number system for which students may make conjectures.

Students are almost certainly not going to know or understand why division by zero is not possible. You will need to provide contexts for them to make sense of this property.

Table 14.1

Properties of the Number System	
Number Sentence	Student Statement of Conjecture
Addition and Subtraction	
$a + 0 = a$	When you add zero to a number, you get the same number you started with.
$a - 0 = a$	When you subtract zero from a number, you get the number you started with.
$a - a = 0$	When you subtract a number from itself, you get zero.
$a + b = b + a$	You can add numbers in one order and then change the order and you will get the same number.
Multiplication and Division	
$a \times 1 = a$	When you multiply a number by 1, you get the number you started with.
$a \div 1 = a$	When you divide a number by 1, you get the number you started with.
$a \div a = 1, a \neq 0$	When you divide a number that is not zero by itself, you get 1.
$a \times 0 = 0$	When you multiply a number times zero, you get zero.
$0 \div a = 0, a \neq 0$	When you divide zero by any number except zero, you get zero.
$a \times b = b \times a$	When you multiply two numbers, you can do it in any order and you will get the same number.
Conjectures Derived from Basic Properties	
$a + b - b = a$	When you add a number to another number and then subtract the number that you added, you will get the number that you started with.
$a \times b \div b = a, b \neq 0$	When you multiply a number by another number that is not zero and then divide by the same number, you get the number you started with.

Source: Adapted from Carpenter, T. P., Franke, M. L., and Levi, L. (2003). *Thinking Mathematically: Integrating Arithmetic & Algebra in Elementary School.* Portsmouth, NH: Heinemann.

Justifying Conjectures

Attempting to justify that a conjecture is true is a significant form of algebraic reasoning and is at the heart of what it means to do mathematics. How young students attempt to prove that something is always true is a relatively new and interesting area of research (Ball & Bass, 2003; Carpenter, Franke, & Levi, 2003; Schifter, 1999; Schifter, Monk, Russell, & Bastable, 2007). These researchers all believe that there is a real value in challenging students even as early as second grade to justify that the conjectures they make are always true. Therefore, when conjectures are made in class, rather than respond with an answer, ask, "Do you think that is always true? How can we find out?" Students need to reason through ideas based on their own thinking rather than simply relying on the word of others.

The most common form of justification, especially in elementary school, is the use of examples. Students will try lots of specific numbers in a conjecture. "See, it works for any number you try." They may try very large numbers as substitutes for "any" number and they may try rational fractions or decimal values. Proof by example will hopefully lead to someone asking, "How do we know there aren't some numbers that it doesn't work for?"

Less commonly, students will attempt to use some form of logic. Often these efforts include the use of physical materials to show the reasoning behind the conjecture. For example, a student attempting to prove that $a + b = b + a$ might show two bars of snap cubes, one with 8 cubes and the other with 6. The bars are used to show that the number of blocks does not change when the order of the two bars is reversed. What moves this beyond just an example is the student's statement or explanation that the number of cubes in the bars is not part of the argument: "It would work this way no matter how many blocks are in each bar."

At the elementary level, not all students will be able to create arguments and some may not even follow those constructed by others (Carpenter et al., 2003). However, at all levels it is important to push students to reason using logic and not be content with appeals to authority or the use of examples. Remember that your goal is for students' thinking to be involved in these justifications; there is little value in making a good argument *for* your students.

Odd and Even Relationships

An interesting category of number structures is that of odd and even numbers. Students will often observe that the sum of two even numbers is even, that the sum of two odd numbers is even, or that the sum of an even and an odd number is always odd. Similar statements can be made about multiplication.

Pause and Reflect

Before reading on, think for a moment about how you might prove that the sum of two odd numbers is always even.

Students will provide a variety of interesting proofs of odd/even conjectures. As with other conjectures, they typically begin by trying lots of numbers. But here it is a bit easier to imagine that there just might be two numbers "out there" that don't work. Then students turn to the definition or a model that illustrates the definition. For example, if a number is odd and you split it in two, there will be a leftover. If you do this with the second odd number, it will have a leftover also. So if you put these two numbers together, the two leftovers will go together so there won't be a leftover in the sum. Students frequently use models such as bars of snap cubes to strengthen their arguments.

The following calculator activity helps students explore properties of odd and even numbers.

Activity 14.10

Broken Calculator: Can You Fix It?

Explore these two challenges, and afterward ask students for conjectures they might make about odds and evens.

1. If you cannot use any of the even keys (0, 2, 4, 6, 8), can you create an even number in the calculator display? If so, how?

2. If you cannot use any of the odd keys (1, 3, 5, 7, 9), can you create an odd number in the calculator display? If so, how?

It is not important that all students initiate conjectures. It is important that all students actively consider the validity of all conjectures made by classmates. When deciding if a conjecture is always true, have students write their ideas before sharing with the class. If you begin with a class discussion, only a few students are likely to participate, with others content to listen whether or not they are following the arguments. You can then use both what the students write as well as their input in discussions to assess what level of reasoning they are at: authority, use of examples, or an appeal to logic. ◆

Study of Patterns and Functions

Patterns are found in all areas of mathematics. Learning to search for patterns and how to describe, translate, and extend them is part of doing mathematics and thinking algebraically.

Repeating Patterns

The concept of a repeating pattern and how a pattern is extended or continued can be introduced to the full class in several ways. One possibility is to draw simple shape patterns on the board and extend them in a class discussion. Oral patterns can be recited. For example, "do, mi, mi, do, mi, mi" is a simple singing pattern. Body movements such as arm up, down, and sideways provides three movements with which to make patterns: up, side, side, down, up, side, side, down. Boy-girl patterns or stand-sit patterns are also good movement patterns.

Children's books often have repeating patterns. For example, a very long repeating pattern can be found in *If You Give a Mouse a Cookie* (Numeroff, 1985) in which each event eventually leads back to giving a mouse a cookie, with the implication that the sequence would be repeated.

Identifying and Extending Repeating Patterns. An important concept in working with repeating patterns is for students to identify the core of the pattern (Warren & Cooper, 2008). The *core* of a repeating pattern is the string of elements that repeats. In addition, it is important to use knowledge of the core to extend the pattern.

Activity 14.11

Making Pattern Strips

Students can work independently or in groups of two or three to extend patterns made from simple materials: buttons, colored blocks, connecting cubes, toothpicks, geometric shapes—items you can gather easily. For each set of materials, draw two or three complete repetitions of a pattern on strips of tagboard about 5 cm by 30 cm. The students' task is to use actual materials, copy the pattern shown, and extend it as far as they wish. Figure 14.10 illustrates one possible pattern for each of various manipulatives. You can also select one manipulative and make ten different pattern strips so that students can work with partners and then trade and work on identifying the core and extending patterns.

Young children make a significant generalization when they see that two patterns constructed with different materials are actually the same pattern. For example, in creating a repeating pattern with cubes, as in Figure 14.10, you can ask students to find a pattern block pattern with the same pattern (from one of the strips), or ask them to build such a pattern.

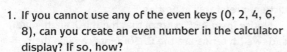

"[S]tudents should recognize that the color pattern 'blue, blue, red, blue, blue, red' is the same in form as 'clap, clap, step, clap, clap, step.' This

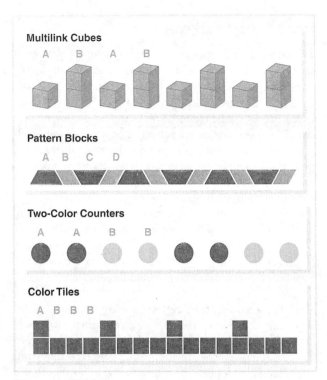

Multilink Cubes

A   B   A   B

Pattern Blocks

A   B   C   D

Two-Color Counters

A   A   B   B

Color Tiles

A   B   B   B

Figure 14.10 Examples of repeating patterns using manipulatives.

recognition lays the foundation for the idea that two very different situations can have the same mathematical features and thus are the same in some important ways. Knowing that each pattern above could be described as having the form AABAAB is for students an early introduction to the power of algebra" (pp. 91–92). ◆

The following activities reflect the powerful algebraic concept of repeating patterns just described in the quotation from *Principles and Standards*.

Activity 14.12

Pattern Match

Using the chalkboard or overhead projector, show six or seven different patterns (e.g., ABAB, ABCABC, etc.) with different materials or pictures (e.g., smileys, arrows pointing in different directions, etc.). Place students in pairs. One in each pair closes his or her eyes while the partner uses the A, B, C scheme to identify the core of a pattern that they have selected.

After hearing the pattern, the students who had their eyes closed examine the patterns and try to decide which pattern was selected. If two of the patterns in the list have the same structure, the discussion can be very interesting.

Conversely, give students the A, B, C label of the core of a pattern (e.g., ABCD or ABB) and ask them to create a pattern of this kind using two or three different models. Translation of a pattern from one medium to another is an alternative way of helping students separate the relationship in a pattern from the materials used to build it.

Predicting with Repeating Patterns: Linking to Divisibility. Prediction is an important part of algebraic thinking. The next activity focuses on prediction as a forerunner to looking at the functions.

Activity 14.13

Predict down the Line

For most repeating patterns, the elements of the pattern can be numbered 1, 2, 3, and so on. Provide students with a pattern to extend. Before students begin to extend the pattern, have them predict exactly what element will be in, say, the fifteenth position. Students should be required to provide a reason for their prediction, preferably in writing.

Notice in an ABC pattern that the third, sixth, ninth, and twelfth terms are the C. Students can use their developing concepts of multiplication and division to predict what the eighteenth and twenty-fifth items would be. Ask them to predict the hundredth item. Since $100 \div 3 = 33$ remainder 1, it would be the A item in the pattern. If predicting the hundredth element, students will not be able to check the prediction by extending the pattern. Justification focuses on students' knowledge of multiplication and division (Warren & Cooper, 2008).

Using Real Contexts. Though geometric patterns and motions, like clapping, are good ways to introduce patterns, it is important that students see patterns in the world around them. The seasons, days of the week, and months of the year are just a beginning. Students might be able to think of AB patterns in their daily activities, for example "to school, home from school" or "set table before eating, clear table after eating."

Predicting what happens down the line has some interesting real-world contexts appropriate for upper elementary and middle school students. One context is the Olympics (Bay-Williams & Martinie, 2004). The Summer Olympics are held in 2008, 2012, and every four years after that. The Winter Olympics are held in 2010, 2014, and so on. This makes the ABCD or ABAC pattern: No Olympics, Summer Olympics, No Olympics, Winter Olympics.

A second context is the names of hurricanes, which are in an ABCDEF repeating pattern by letter in the alphabet, meaning that for each letter of the alphabet, there are six names that are used and then repeated (except that a name is retired when a major hurricane is given that name, like Katrina) (Fernandez & Schoen, 2008). The A names, for example, are: 2006—Alberto, 2007—Andrea, 2008—Arthur, 2009—Ana, 2010—Alex, and 2011—Arlene. (Good for you if you noticed the ABAB pattern regarding gender!). Assuming the names don't get retired, ask students questions such as:

- In what year will the first hurricane of that year be named Alex?
- What will be the first hurricane's name in the year 2020? 2050?
- Can you describe in words how to figure out the name of a hurricane, given the year?

Number Patterns. In the same way that contexts can be used to predict a number down the line, number patterns can be engaging for students, varying in complexity from simple repeating patterns such as 1, 2, 1, 2 to much more advanced. In this way, they can provide an interesting challenge for gifted students or be part of a learning station and explored by those who finish other work early. Here are a few:

2, 4, 6, 8, 10, . . .   (even numbers; add 2 each time)
1, 4, 7, 10, 13, . . .   (start with 1; add 3 each time)
1, 4, 9, 16, . . .   (squares)
0, 1, 5, 14, 30, . . .   (add the next square number)
2, 5, 11, 23, . . .   (double the number and add 1)
2, 6, 12, 20, 30, . . .   (multiply pairs of counting numbers)
3, 3, 6, 9, 15, 24, . . . (add the two preceding numbers—an example of a Fibonacci sequence)

For each of these patterns, students predict the thirteenth number or one hundredth number, to eventually find a general rule to produce any number in the sequence.

The calculator provides a powerful approach to patterns. For a good example, see the discussion of "Start and Jump Numbers" in Chapter 2 (p. 15).

Growing Patterns

Beginning at about the fourth grade and extending through the middle school years, students can explore patterns that involve a progression from step to step. In technical terms, these are called sequences; we will simply call them growing patterns. With these patterns, students not only extend patterns but also look for a generalization or an algebraic relationship that will tell them what the pattern will be at any point along the way. Growing patterns can be functions, and growing patterns used in school textbooks tend to be

functions. Figure 14.11(a) is a growing pattern in which design 1 requires three triangles, design 2 requires six triangles, and so on—so we can say that the number of triangles needed is a function of which design it is (which happens to be the function triangles = 3 × design number). The Border Problem discussed earlier in this chapter can be adapted to be a growing pattern by simply having a swimming pool that is 5 by 5, then 6 by 6, then 7 by 7, and so on.

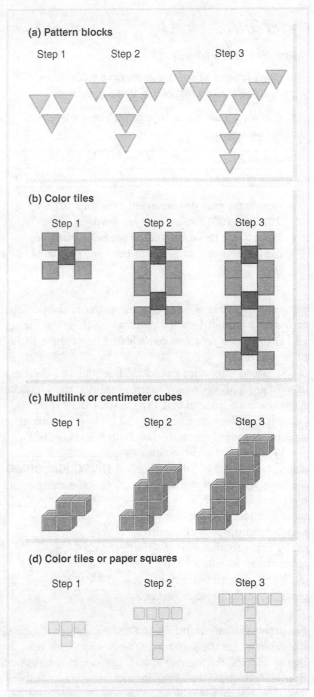

Figure 14.11 Geometric growing patterns using manipulatives.

Geometric patterns make good exemplars because the pattern is easy to see and because students can manipulate the objects. Figure 14.11 shows one growing pattern for four different manipulatives, though the possibilities are endless.

The questions in Activity 14.14, mapped to the pattern in Figure 14.11(a), are commonly used (and good ones to use!) to help students begin to think about the functional relationship.

Activity 14.14

Predict How Many

Working in pairs or small groups, have students explore a pattern and respond to these questions:

- Complete a table that shows number of triangles for each step.

Step Number	1	2	3	4	5 ...	10	20
Number of Triangles							

- How many triangles are needed for step 10? Step 20? Step 100? Explain your reasoning.
- Write a rule (in words and/or symbols) that gives the total number of pieces to build any step number (*n*).

Students' experiences with growing patterns should start with fairly straightforward patterns (such as in Figure 14.11) to somewhat more complicated (see Figure 14.12) to very difficult.

It is also important to include fractions and decimals in working with growing patterns. In 2003, the National Assessment of Educational Progress (NAEP) tested 13-year-olds on the item in Figure 14.13. Only 27 percent of students answered correctly (Lambdin & Lynch, 2005).

When looking for relationships, some students will focus on the table and others will focus on the physical pattern. It is important for students to see that whatever relationships they discover, they exist in both forms. So if a relationship is found in a table, challenge students to see how that plays out in the physical version.

myeducationlab

Go to the Building Teaching Skills and Dispositions section of Chapter 14 of MyEducationLab. Click on Videos and watch the video entitled **"Use Symbols"** to see a first-grade class creating patterns.

Recursive Patterns and Formulas.
For most students, it is easier to see the patterns from one step to the next. In Figure 14.12(a) the number in each step can be determined from the previous step by adding successive even numbers. The description that tells how a pattern changes from step to step is known as a *recursive* pattern (Bezuszka & Kenney, 2008).

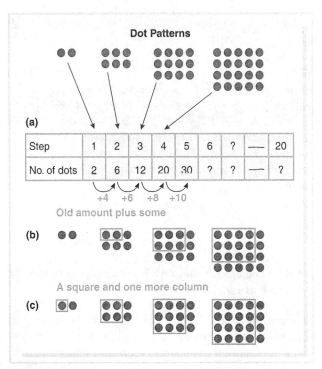

Figure 14.12 Two different ways to analyze relationships in the "dot pattern."

The recursive pattern can also be observed in the physical pattern. In Figure 14.12(b), notice that in each step, the previous step has been outlined. That lets you examine the amount added and see how it creates the pattern of adding on even numbers.

Recursive formulas are equations that show you how to get the next quantity, given the one you have. For example, in Figure 14.11, the first design grows by 3 trian-

Term	1	2	3	4
Fraction	$\frac{1}{2}$	$\frac{2}{3}$	$\frac{3}{4}$	$\frac{4}{5}$

If the list of fractions above continues in the same pattern, which term will be equal to 0.95?

Ⓐ The 100th
Ⓑ The 95th
Ⓒ The 20th
Ⓓ The 19th
Ⓔ The 15th

Figure 14.13 NAEP item for 13-year-olds.
Source: Lambdin, D. V., & Lynch, K. (2005). "Examining Mathematics Tasks from the National Assessment of Educational Progress." *Mathematics Teaching in the Middle School, 10*(6), 314–318. Reprinted with permission. Copyright © 2005 by the National Council of Teachers of Mathematics, Inc. www.nctm.org. All rights reserved.

gles each time, so the recursive formula can be written as NEXT = NOW + 3. If NOW is the step 5 quantity, then NEXT is the step 6 quantity. Try to write a recursive formula for the other three patterns in Figure 14.11.

Explicit Formulas. To find the table entry for the hundredth step, the only way a recursive formula can help is to find all of the prior 99 entries in the table. If a formula can be discovered that connects the number of the step to the number of objects in a step, any table entry can be determined without building or calculating all of the previous entries. A rule that determines the number of elements in a step from the step number is called the *explicit formula*. Activities and textbooks in elementary and middle school often call the explicit formula the "rule" for the growing pattern.

> ⏸ ———————— *Pause and Reflect*
>
> Can you determine an explicit formula for the pattern in Figure 14.12? How did you find the formula?

There is no single best method for finding this relationship between step number and step, and students are likely to see it different ways. Some will analyze the table and notice that if they multiply the step number by the next step number, they will get the number of circles for that step. This leads the explicit formula: $d = n(n + 1)$, where d is number of dots and n is the step number.

Some will examine the physical pattern to see what is changing. In Figure 14.12(c), a square array is outlined for each step. Each successive square is one larger on a side. In this example, the side of each square is the same as the step number. The column to the right of each square is also the step number. At this point, writing a numeric expression for each step number can help students write the explicit formula. For example, the first four steps in Figure 14.12 are $1^2 + 1$, $2^2 + 2$, $3^2 + 3$, and $4^2 + 4$. The explicit formula is therefore $d = n^2 + n$.

Regardless of whether students use the table or the model, they will likely be able to describe the explicit formula in words before they can write it in symbols. If the goal of your lesson is to be able to find the rule, then stopping with the verbal formula is appropriate. In this case, you may have some students that are ready to represent the formula in symbols and they can be challenged to do so as a form of differentiating your instruction. If your instructional goal is to write formulas using symbols, then ask students to first write the formula, or rule, in words and then think about how they can translate that statement to numbers and symbols.

NCTM Standards "In grades 3–5, students should investigate numerical and geometric patterns and express them mathematically in words or symbols. They should analyze the structure of the pattern and how it grows or changes, organize this information systematically, and use their analysis to develop generalizations about the mathematical relationships in the pattern" (p. 159). ◆

Graphs of Functions. So far, growing patterns have been represented by (1) the physical materials or drawings, (2) a table, (3) words, and (4) symbols. A graph adds a fifth representation. Figure 14.14 shows the graph for the Border Problem and the Dot Pattern. Notice that the first is a straight-line (linear) relationship and the other is a curved line that would make half of a parabola if the points were joined. The horizontal axis is always used for the step numbers, the independent variable.

Graphs provide visuals that allow students to readily see relationships among growing patterns. Consider strings of a single color of pattern blocks (Figure 14.15) and the corresponding perimeters. This is a good pattern to explore in the same manner as the Border Problem, beginning with

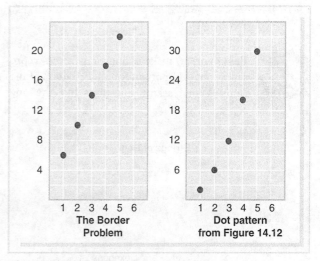

Figure 14.14 Graphs of two growing patterns.

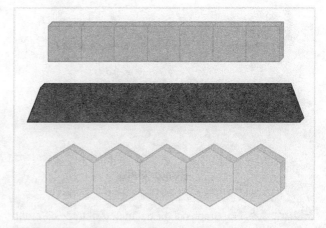

Figure 14.15 For each string of pattern blocks, can you determine the perimeter for *N* pattern blocks?

a string of seven or eight blocks and finding ways to determine the perimeter without counting. Again, there are at least five different ways to find the perimeter, each resulting in a general formula that appears on the surface to be different from the others.

Having graphs of three related growing patterns offers the opportunity to compare and connect the graphs to the patterns and to the tables (see Figure 14.16). For example, ask students to discuss how to get from one coordinate to the next (up six, over one) and then ask how that information can be found in the table. Second, you can point at a particular point on the graph and ask what it tells about the pattern.

See if you can answer the following questions, which you can also pose to students to help them understand the graphical representation of the function:

- How does each graph represent each of the string patterns?
- Why is there not a line connecting the dots?
- Why is one line steeper than the others?
- Why is there no dot on the *y*-axis?
- If the dots were plotted on the *y*-axis, what would they be for each string? Why?

Being able to make connections across representations is important for understanding functions. When asking questions like the ones

listed above, look to see if students are able to link the graph to the context, to the table, and to the formula. ◆

Not all functions have straight-line graphs. For example, in building a rectangular pen with 24 yards of fence, if you increase the width, you will decrease the length. The area will vary accordingly (see Figure 14.17). An explicit formula for the width is $w = 12 - l$ (*l* is the length), which decreases at a constant rate, therefore looking like a line. By contrast, the explicit formula for area of the pen is $a = l(12 - l)$—it rises in a curve, reaches a maximum value, and then goes back down.

Graphs and Contexts. It is important for students to be able to interpret and construct graphs related to real situations, including sketching the shape of a graph without using any specific data, equations, or numbers. The advantage of activities such as these is the focus on how a graph can express the relationships involved.

Activity 14.15

Sketch a Graph

Sketch a graph for each of these situations. No numbers or formulas are to be used.

a. **The temperature of a frozen dinner from 30 minutes before it is removed from the freezer until it is removed from the microwave and placed on the table. (Consider time 0 to be the moment the dinner is removed from the freezer.)**
b. **The value of a 1970 Volkswagen Beetle from the time it was purchased to the present. (It was kept by a loving owner and is in top condition.)**
c. **The level of water in the bathtub from the time you begin to fill it to the time it is completely empty after your bath.**
d. **Profit in terms of number of items sold.**
e. **The height of a baseball from when it is thrown to the time it hits the ground.**
f. **The speed of the baseball in the situation in item e.**

⏸ ——————— *Pause and Reflect*

Stop for a moment and sketch graphs for each situation in the last activity.

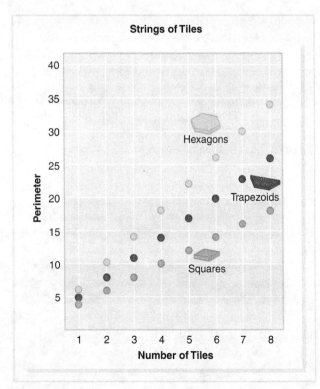

Figure 14.16 Graphs of the perimeters of three different pattern-block strings. The lines are not drawn because for this context, there are no solutions between the points.

In a classroom, it is fun to have students sketch their graphs on transparencies without identifying which situation they selected (no labels on the graphs). Let students examine the graph to see if they can determine which situation goes with each graph that is presented. Figure 14.18 contains six graphs that match the six situations described in

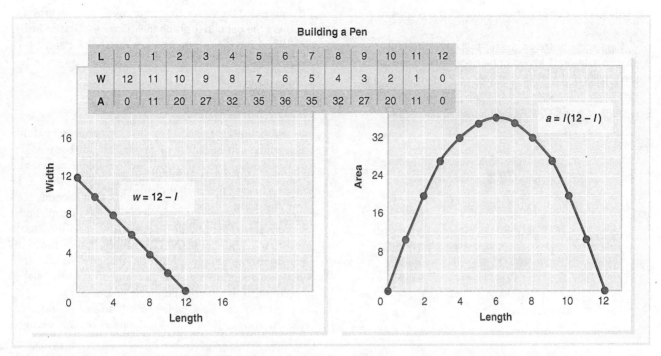

Building a Pen

L	0	1	2	3	4	5	6	7	8	9	10	11	12
W	12	11	10	9	8	7	6	5	4	3	2	1	0
A	0	11	20	27	32	35	36	35	32	27	20	11	0

$w = 12 - l$

$a = l(12 - l)$

Figure 14.17 The width and area graphs as functions of the length of a rectangle with a fixed perimeter of 24 units.

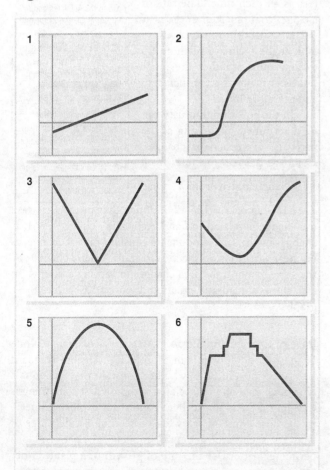

Figure 14.18 Match each graph with the situations described in Activity 14.15. Talk about what change is happening in each case.

the "Sketch a Graph" activity. Can you match these graphs with the six situations?

Graphs and Rate of Change.   Notice that the analysis of the graphs focuses on how the graphs increase or decrease and how steeply or gradually. A graph is a picture of the rate of change of one variable in terms of the other. Essentially, graphs can only have one of the seven characteristics shown in Figure 14.19 or some combination of these. These types of change will be seen in the following activity.

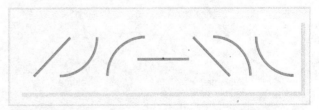

Figure 14.19 Seven ways that graphs can change. A graph often has combinations of these characteristics.

Activity 14.16

Bottles and Volume Graphs

Figure 14.20 shows six vases and six graphs. Assume that the bottles are filled at a constant rate. Because of their shapes, the height of the liquid in the bottles will increase either more slowly or more quickly as the bottle gets wider or narrower. Match the graphs with the bottles.

Find some vases or glasses that have different shapes. Give each group or pair one vase to use for the activity. Fill a small container (e.g., medicine cup or test tube) with water and empty it into the vase, recording in a table the number of containers used and the height of the water after pouring. After each group gathers the data, they graph their findings. Graphs are collected and then students try to match the graph with the vase.

Linear Functions

Linear functions are a subset of growing patterns and functions, which can be linear or nonlinear. But because linearity is a major focus of middle school mathematics, and because growing patterns in elementary school tend to be linear situations, it appears here in its own section. *Curriculum Focal Points* emphasizes the importance of linear functions across the middle grades, with a specific focus on linearity in eighth grade (NCTM, 2006). Linear functions are defined quite simply as functions that grow in a linear or constant manner. In a graph, this can be easily established by seeing that the plotted points lie on one line.

Linearity can be established by looking at the other representations. If you make a table for the hexagon perimeter task in Figure 14.15 you will notice that the recursive pattern is +4 each time. The rate of change from one step to the next is constant (+4). You can always look at the recursive relationship to determine whether the function is growing at a constant rate and therefore linear.

In the equation, linearity can be determined by looking at the part of the expression that changes. Compare the two formulas from the rectangular pen problem. One was $w = 12 - l$ and the other was $a = l(12 - l)$ or $a = 12l - l^2$. Notice that in the first case the change is related to l and each time l changes by 1, w changes by the same amount—a constant rate of change, as in linear situations. In the area formula, when l changes by the same amount, the area changes in varying amounts. In fact, this is a quadratic situation. Figure 14.17 shows these graphs.

Rate of Change and Slope. An analysis of change is one of the four components in the NCTM Algebra standard (see Appendix A). Rate, whether constant or varying, is a type of change often associated with how fast something is traveling. Rate is an excellent context for exploring linearity, because constant rates can be seen in a wide range of contexts, such as the geometric model of the pattern block perimeter pattern or the rate of growth of a plant. Other rate contexts in numerical situations include hourly wages, gas mileage, profit, and even the cost of an item, such as a bus ticket.

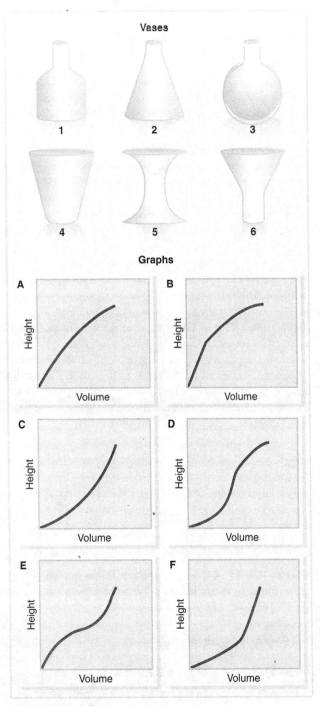

Figure 14.20 Assuming bottles are filled at a constant rate, match the graphs with the vases.

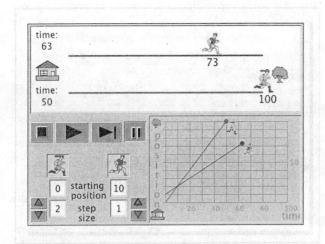

Figure 14.21 Applet 5.2, "Understanding Distance, Speed, and Time Relationships Using Simulation Software." Used with permission from NCTM *e-Standards.* Copyright © 2003 by the National Council of Teachers of Mathematics, Inc. All rights reserved. The presence of the screenshot from NCTM *e-Standards*, http://standards .nctm.org/document/eexamples/chap5/5.2/index.htm, does not constitute or imply an endorsement by NCTM.

 The NCTM e-Examples has two applets that target rate, making the connection between a real-world context and graphs. In Applet 5.2 students can adjust the speed, direction, and starting position of two runners. As the runners are set in motion, a time–distance graph is generated dynamically for each runner (see Figure 14.21). ◆

The NCTM applet compares two rates through two representations (visual model and the graph). Many real-world situations can be similarly described. Another NCTM applet (6.2), for example, explores phone call rates in this manner. Another example is shown by Figure 14.16. The three graphs are increasing at different rates. Notice each slant or slope is different. *Slope* is the numeric value that describes the rate of change for a linear function.

One of the explicit formulas for the hexagon growing pattern is $y = 4x + 2$. Note that the rate of change is 4 because the perimeter increases by 4 with each new piece. All linear functions can be written in this form: $y = mx + b$ (including $y = mx$ when $b = 0$). The value m in this formula is the rate of change or the slope of the line.

Conceptually, then, slope signifies how much y increases when x increases by 1. If a line contains the points $(2, 4)$ and $(3, -5)$, then you can see that as x increases by 1, y decreases by 9. So the rate of change, or slope, is -9. For the points $(4, 3)$ and $(7, 9)$, you can see that when x increases by 3, y increases by 6. Therefore, an increase of 1 in x results in a change of 2 in y (dividing 6 by 3). After further exploration and experiences, your students will begin to notice that you can find the rate of change or slope by finding the difference in the y values and dividing by the difference in the x values.

Sometimes an equation may not look like the familiar form $y = mx + b$. For example, in the rectangular pen problem, if the l and w represent the length and width and the perimeter is 24, then $2l + 2w = 24$ is an equation that relates the length to the width, but can be simplified to $w = -1l + 12$, a linear equation with a slope of -1 and an initial value of 12.

Zero Slope and No Slope. Understanding these two easily confused slopes requires contexts, such as walking rates. Consider this story:

You walk for 10 minutes at a rate of 1 mile per hour, stop for 3 minutes to watch a nest of baby birds, then walk for 5 more minutes at 2 miles per hour.

What will the graph look like for the 3 minutes when you stop? What is your rate when you stop? In fact, your rate is 0 and since you are at the same distance for 3 minutes, the graph will be a horizontal line.

Let's say that you see a graph of a walking story that includes a vertical line. What would this mean? That you traveled a distance with no time passing! Now, even if you were a world record sprinter, this would be impossible, and therefore a vertical line has no slope. Remember rate is based a change of 1 in the x value, and a vertical line will never have a change in the x variable.

Proportional and Nonproportional Situations. Linear functions can be proportional or nonproportional. The rate example just described is *proportional*. The distance you walk is proportional to how much time you have walked. As another example, your paycheck is proportional to the hours you work. But it is not the case that the perimeter of the pattern block growing problem is proportional to the number of blocks used. Although you have a constant increase factor of 4, there is an extra 2 units of perimeter. Said another way, you cannot get from the input (number of blocks) to the perimeter by multiplying by a factor, as you can in proportional situations.

All proportional situations, then, are equations in the form $y = mx$. Notice that the graphs of all proportional situations are straight lines that pass through the origin. Students will find that the slope of these lines is also the rate of change between the two variables.

This distinction is important from a teaching perspective because proportional situations are easier to generalize; you should be careful to select growing patterns that are proportional before moving to ones that are not. Figure 14.11(a)–(c) show proportional representations. However, if you slightly altered the patterns, they would become nonproportional. For example, in the first pattern, if the triangles were added on to only two of the prongs, like an upside-down V, then you could no longer find the nth term simply by multiplying the step number by a factor. Pattern (d) demonstrates such a situation—it grows by three with an initial value of 4 squares.

⏸ —————————— *Pause and Reflect*

Can you determine the explicit formula for the upside-down V pattern? Its first steps require 3, 5, 7, and 9 triangles, respectively.

———————————————————

Typical proportion problems can be adapted for an algebraic approach. Consider the following example:

Two out of every three students who eat in the cafeteria drink a pint of white milk. If 450 students eat in the cafeteria, how many pints of milk are consumed?

As the problem is stated, there are a fixed number of students (450) and a single answer to the problem. Students would be expected to set up a proportion and solve for the unknown. But if only the first sentence of the problem is provided, students can be asked to find a rule (explicit formula) that shows the amount of milk in terms of the number of students, $m = \frac{2}{3}s$, where s is number of students and m is the number of pints of milk.

In nonproportional situations, one value is constant. In the perimeter pattern problem, for example, no matter which step number you are on, there are 2 units (one on each end that must be included). Similarly, the Border Problem always has the 4 corners. If you were walking, but had a head start of 50 meters, or if you were selling something and had an initial expense, those values are constants in the linear function that make it not proportional. The constant value, or initial value, of a linear function ends up being where the graph crosses the y-axis. We can find out the initial value in the table by using 0 as a step number, in the equation by using $x = 0$ and simplifying, or on the graph by seeing where the line would cross the y-axis.

Nonproportional situations are more challenging for students to generalize. Students want to use the recursive value (e.g., +4) as the factor (×4), without considering what constant or initial values are part of the situation. Students often make the common error of using the table to find the tenth step and doubling it to find the twentieth step, which works in proportional situations but not in nonproportional situations. Mathematics education researchers have found that having students analyze their errors is essential in helping support their learning of mathematics concepts (Lannin, Arbaugh, Barker, & Townsend, 2006).

Parallel and Perpendicular Lines. Consider the situation of Larry and Mary, each earning $30 a week for the summer months. Mary starts the summer $50 dollars in the hole and Larry already has $20. When will Mary and Larry have the same amount of money? In week 3, how much more money does Larry have? How much more does he have in week 7? In any week, what is the difference in their wealth? The rate for Larry and Mary's earnings are the same—and the graphs would therefore go up at the same rate; that is, the slopes would be the same. We can tell that the graphs of $y = 30x + 20$ (Larry's money) and $y = 30x - 50$ (Mary's money) are parallel without even making the graphs because the rates (or slopes) are the same.

Slopes can also tell us when two lines are perpendicular, but it is less obvious. A little bit of analysis using similar triangles will show that for perpendicular lines, the slope of one is the negative reciprocal of the other.

Mathematical Modeling

Kaput (1999) defines modeling as the process of beginning with real phenomena and attempting to mathematize them. Mathematical models, or equations, are used to predict other phenomena. Mathematical models are not to be confused with the models that use manipulatives or visuals for building a pattern (such as a pattern block).

We have already seen many examples of mathematical models. How is modeling used to predict? Take the example of selling widgets marked up at some percentage over wholesale. Once a formula is derived for a given price and markup, it can be used to determine the profit at different sales levels. Furthermore, it is relatively easy to make adjustments in the price and markup percentage, allowing for further predictions. That is, the equation, or mathematical model, allows us to find values that cannot be observed in the real phenomenon.

Consider creating a mathematical model to describe the depreciation of a car at 20 percent each year. Determining the model might progress in the following steps: If the car loses 20 percent of its value in 1 year, then it must be worth 80 percent of its value after a year. So after 1 year, the $15,000 car is worth $15,000 × 0.8. In the second year, it loses 20 percent of that value, so it will be worth only 80 percent of its value at the end of year one, which was $15,000 × 0.8. The value at the end of year 2 would be ($15,000 × 0.8) × 0.8, and so on. At the end of y years, the value of the car can be expressed in this equation: value = $15,000 × 0.8^y$. Figure 14.22 shows the graph and the table of values on a graphing calculator.

The next activity provides another context appropriate for developing a mathematical model.

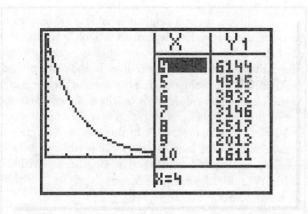

Figure 14.22 The graph and table for $V = 15,000 \times 0.8^y$. Years, the independent variable, are shown under X and value, the dependent variable, is shown under Y1.

Activity 14.17

How Many Gallons Left?

A car gets 23 miles per gallon of gas. It has a gas tank that holds 20 gallons. Suppose that you were on a trip and had filled the tank at the outset. Determine a mathematical model that describes the gallons left given number of miles traveled?

Notice that the word *rule* could replace "mathematical model." In this case, one possible equation is $g = 20 - \frac{m}{23}$. Use the model, or equation, to make predictions. For example, "How can you tell from the model how much gas will be left after driving 300 miles?" "How many miles can you drive before the gas tank has only 3 gallons left?" Two more engaging contexts are provided in Figure 14.23.

Sometimes a model is provided and the important task is for students to understand and use the formula. Consider the following pumping water problem and related equation from the Michigan Algebra Project (Herbel-Eisenmann & Phillips, 2005):

Suppose you turn a pump on and let it run to empty the water out of a pool. The amount of water in the pool (*W*, measured in gallons) at any time (*T*, measured in hours) is given by the following equation: $W = -350 (T - 4)$.

❚❚ ————————— *Pause and Reflect*

What questions might you pose to middle school students to help them make sense of this equation? Try to think of three.

1. Pleasant's Hardware buys widgets for $4.17 each, marks them up 35 percent over wholesale, and sells them at that price. Create a mathematical model to relate widgets sold (*w*) to profit (*p*). The manager asks you to determine the formula if she were to put the widgets on sale for 25 percent off. What is your formula or mathematical model for the sale, comparing widgets sold (*s*) to profit (*p*)?

2. In Arches National Park in Moab, Utah, there are sandstone cliffs. A green coating of color, called cyanobacteria, covers some of the sandstone. Bacteria grow by splitting into two (or doubling) in a certain time period. If the sandstone started with 50 bacteria, create a mathematical model for describing the growth of cyanobacteria on the sandstone.

Figure 14.23 Mathematical modeling problems for further exploration.
Source: Adapted from Buerman, M. (2007). "The Algebra of the Arches." *Mathematics Teaching in the Middle School, 12*(7), 360–365.

In the Michigan Algebra Project, students were asked to solve several problems and explain how the equation was used to find the answer. Those questions and one student's responses are provided in Figure 14.24.

🐚 Teaching Considerations

It is important to emphasize some key considerations that will lead students to feel empowered to do algebra. Some of these ideas have already been implied in the previous discussions of algebraic concepts.

Emphasize Appropriate Algebra Vocabulary

A large part of understanding mathematics is the ability to communicate mathematically, so it is important to use appropriate terminology in teaching algebra. This is far more than a vocabulary list; it is the practice of consistently using, and having students use, appropriate words for situations. Creating word walls and keeping a journal of terms are ways to help all students but especially English language learners (ELLs). Having graphs, models, or tables to illustrate the words is essential. Here we briefly share some important vocabulary terms.

Independent and Dependent Variables. Although the meanings of "independent" and "dependent" variables are implied by the words themselves, they can still be challenging for students. The independent variable is the step number, or the input, or whatever value is being used to

A. How many gallons of water are being pumped out each hour?

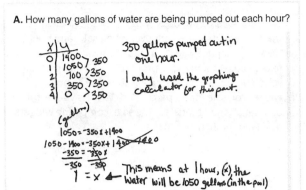

350 gallons pumped out in one hour.

I only used the graphing calculator for this part.

$1050 = -350x + 1400$

$1050 - 1400 = -350x + 1400 - 1400$

$-350 = -350x$

$\frac{-350}{-350} = \frac{-350x}{-350}$

$1 = x$ ← This means at 1 hour, (x) the water will be 1050 gallons (in the pool)

B. How much water was in the pool when the pumping started?

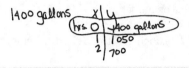

1400 gallons

hrs	0	1400 gallons
	1	1050
	2	700

C. How long will take for the pump to empty the pool completely?

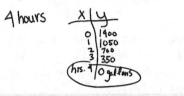

4 hours

x	y
0	1400
1	1050
2	700
3	350
hrs. 4	0 gallons

D. Write an equation that is equivalent to $W = -350(T - 4)$. What does this second equation mean about the situation?

$-350x - {}^-1400$ OR $-350x + 1400$

This second equation tells me how much water was in the pool in the beginning (the 1400), and the $-350x$ is how much water is pumped out of the pool each hour. (350 gallons are pumped OUT of the pool each hour) (x is the # hours)

E. Describe what the graph of the relationship between W and T looks like.

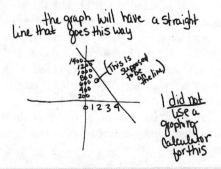

the graph will have a straight line that goes this way

(This is supposed to be a line)

I did not use a graphing calculator for this.

Figure 14.24 One student's explanations of questions regarding what a mathematical model means.
Source: Figure 3 from Herbel-Eisenmann, B. A., & Philips, E. D. (2005). "Using Student Work to Develop Teachers' Knowledge of Algebra." *Mathematics Teaching in the Middle School*, 11(2), p. 65. Reprinted with permission.

find another value. For example, in the case of the strings of pattern blocks the independent variable is the number of blocks in the string. The dependent variable is the number of objects needed, the output, or whatever value you get from using the independent variable. In the pattern block problem, it is the perimeter. You can say that the perimeter of the block structure depends on the number of blocks. Recall the two equations and graphs representing a pen of 24 meters in Figure 14.17. In this case, the length has been selected as the independent variable (though it could have as easily been the width) and the dependent variable is width. What are the independent and dependent variables for the problem in Figure 14.24?

Discrete and Continuous. In elementary school, the discussion of functions, especially graphical representations, should include a discussion of whether the points plotted on the graph should be connected or not and why. In the pattern block perimeter problem, the answer is no because you will only have whole number values. When isolated or selected values are the only ones appropriate for a context, the function is *discrete*. If all values along a line or curve are solutions to the function, then it is *continuous*. The pen example is continuous—the length can be any value up to a certain maximum and the width (or area) would change accordingly.

Domain and Range. The *domain* of a function comprises the possible values for the independent variable. If it is discrete, like the pattern block perimeter problem, it may include all positive whole numbers. For the 24-meter rectangular pen, the domain is all real numbers between 0 and 12. The *range* is the corresponding possible values for the dependent variable. In the pattern block perimeter problem, the range is the positive whole numbers; in the rectangular pen, the range for the length is the same as the domain—real numbers between 0 and 12.

Multiple Representations

Functions can be represented in any of five ways: (1) the pattern itself, which we can refer to as the context; (2) the table; (3) the verbal description; (4) the symbolic equation; and (5) the graph. In both the repeating and the growing pattern sections, each example has included at least two representations (e.g., context and the table) and as many as all five (e.g., the dot pattern in Figure 14.12). It is important to see that each representation is a way of looking at the function, each providing a different way of looking at or thinking about the function. The value of each representation is in the way that it helps us see and understand the function in a different manner than the others do. To illustrate this point, we will use the context of a hot dog vendor.

Brian is trying to make money to help pay for college by selling hot dogs from a hot dog cart at the coliseum during major performances and ball games. He pays the cart owner $35 per night for the use of the cart. He sells hot dogs for $1.25 each. His costs for the hot dogs, condiments, napkins, and other paper products are about 60 cents per hot dog on average. The profit from a single hot dog is, therefore, 65 cents.

Context. This function begins with a context: selling hot dogs and the resulting profit. We are interested in Brian's profit in terms of the number of hot dogs sold. The more hot dogs Brian sells, the more profit he will make. Brian does not begin to make a profit immediately because he must pay the $35 rent on the vending cart. Nonetheless, Brian's profit is dependent on—is a function of—the number of hot dogs he sells.

The context helps students make sense of what changes (number of hot dogs sold) and what stays the same ($35 rental), which can help them figure out the explicit formula. The context supports students' conceptual understanding of the other more abstract representations and illustrates that algebra is a tool for describing real-world phenomena. The context alone, though, is not sufficient—carefully selected prompts to connect the context to other representations are needed to support students' algebraic thinking (Earnest & Balti, 2008).

Table. Brian might well sit down and calculate some possible income figures based on anticipated sales. This will give him some idea of how many hot dogs he must sell to break even and what his profit might be for an evening. A table of values might resemble Table 14.2.

The number of hot dogs shown in the table is purely a matter of choice. One could calculate the profit for 10,000 hot dogs (10,000 × 0.65 – 35), even though it is not reasonable in this context. The table provides a concise way to look at the recursive pattern and the explicit pattern. The recursive pattern can lead to seeing what changes, if it changes at a constant rate, and how that can help find the explicit formula.

Table 14.2

Number of Hot Dogs Sold (Independent Variable) and the Profit (Dependent Variable)	
Hot Dogs Sold	**Profit**
0	−35.00
50	−2.50
100	30.00
150	62.50

Verbal Description. In the hot dog vendor situation, Brian's profit depends on the number of hot dogs that are sold. In functional language, we can say, "Profit is a function of the number of hot dogs sold." The phrase "is a function of" expresses the dependent relationship. The profit depends on—is a function of—the hot dog sales. The verbal description of the explicit formula for the hot dog stand might be stated by students as, "You multiply each hot dog sold by $0.65; then you subtract the $35 for the cart."

The verbal explanation of the explicit formula provides a connection from the context to the symbolic representation. Students may struggle with using variables, and being able to first describe the formula in words is an important stepping-stone for being able to use symbols (Lannin, Townsend, Armer, Green, & Schneider, 2008).

Symbols. Suppose that we pick a letter—say, h—to represent the number of hot dogs Brian sells. Brian's profit is represented by the equation $p = (0.65 \times h) - 35$, where p is the letter selected to stand for profit. This equation defines a mathematical relationship between two values or two variables, profit and hot dogs.

By expressing a function as an equation, it is possible to find the profit for any number of hot dogs. Conversely, if Brian wants to make $100, he can figure out how many hot dogs he needs to sell. Because it is abstract, it is particularly important that students explain what each number and each variable represents.

The equation can be entered into a graphing calculator, and the calculator can do the calculations to produce a table or draw a graph. This enables students to make connections across representations without having to do the tedious work of creating each one by hand.

Graphs. In Figure 14.25, four different values of hot dog sales are plotted on a graph. The horizontal axis represents the number of hot dogs sold, and the vertical axis, the profit. As we have already established, the profit goes up as the sales go up. There is, in this situation, a linear pattern to the six values. In this context it means that the profit is going up at a constant rate, namely at 0.65 per hot dog.

The graphical representation allows one to see "at a glance" that the relationship between sales and profits is linear—a straight line—and is increasing. It also can be used to get quick approximate answers to questions about Brian's profits, such as, "How many hot dogs must be sold to break even?" "How many will need to be sold to earn $100?" (It looks to be near 210 or 215.) The context gives meaning to the graph, and the graph adds understanding to the context.

The graph indicates the pattern in the data, but in terms of the context, all values may not make sense for the context. In this case, it would not make sense to extend the

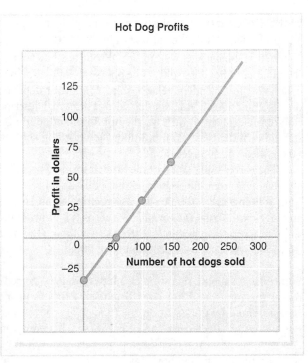

Figure 14.25 A graph showing profit as a function of hot dogs sold.

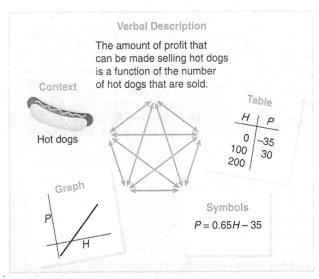

Figure 14.26 Five different representations of a function. For any given function, students should see that all these representations are connected and illustrate the same relationship.

line to the left of the vertical axis, as this would mean selling a negative quantity of hot dogs. Nor is it reasonable to talk about sales of millions of hot dogs (unless he develops a national chain!).

 In the past, when students had to plot points and do by hand all the computations that were involved, functions were limited to examples using whole numbers to avoid the tedium of computing and plotting fractional values. Thanks to technology, we can now explore realistic contexts involving more precise and "messy" numbers. ◆

Connect Representations

Figure 14.26 illustrates the five representations of functions for the hot dog context. The most important idea is to see that, for a given function, each of these representations illustrates the same relationship and that students should be able to explain connections across representations in a conceptual manner. This is a different experience than you might have experienced in an Algebra I textbook that gave instructions such as, "Graph the function, given the equation," along with a set of steps to follow. The difference lies in whether the movement among representations is about following a rote procedure or about making sense of the function. The latter is your goal as a teacher.

The seventh-grade *Connected Mathematics Project* (CMP II) has an entire unit titled "Variables and Patterns,"

in which students explore and use different representations of functions in real contexts. The excerpt on the next page is a lesson focused on tables and graphs.

 "By the middle grades, students should be able to understand the relationships among tables, graphs, and symbols and to judge the advantages and disadvantages of each way of representing relationships for practical purposes. As they work with multiple representations of functions—including numeric, graphic, and symbolic—they will develop a more comprehensive understanding of functions" (p. 38). ◆

 A good formative or summative assessment prompt for the hot dog problem (which can be adapted to any task) is: "Can you show me how to use each representation to find the profit for selling 225 hot dogs?" ◆

Algebraic Thinking Across the Curriculum

One reason the phrase "algebraic thinking" is used instead of "algebra" is that the practice of looking for patterns and generalizations goes beyond curriculum topics that are usually categorized as algebra topics. You have already experienced some of this integration—looking at geometric growing patterns and working with perimeter and area. In fact, in *Curriculum Focal Points* (NCTM, 2006), many of the focal points that include algebra connect it to other content areas. In the sections that follow, the emphasis of the content moves to be on the other content areas, with algebraic

Connected Mathematics

Grade 7, *Variables and Patterns*
Investigation 3: Analyzing Graphs and Tables

Context

Much of this unit is built on the context of a group of students who take a multiday bike trip from Philadelphia to Williamsburg, Virginia, and who then decide to set up a bike tour business of their own. Students explore a variety of functional relationships between time, distance, speed, expenses, profits, and so on. When data are plotted as discrete points, students consider what the graph might look like between points. For example, what interpretations could be given to each of these five graphs showing speed change from 0 to 15 mph in the first 10 minutes of a trip?

Task Description

In this investigation, the fictional students in the unit began gathering data in preparation for setting up their tour business. As their first task, they sought data from two different bike rental companies as shown here, given by one company in the form of a table and by the other in the form of a graph. The task is interesting because of the firsthand way in which students experience the value of one representation over another, depending on the need of the situation. In this unit students are frequently asked whether a graph or a table is the better source of information.

In the tasks that follow, students are given a table of data showing results of a phone poll that asked at which price former tour riders would take a bike tour. Students must find the best way to graph this data. After a price for a bike tour is established, graphs for estimated profits are created with corresponding questions about profits depending on different numbers of customers.

The investigations use no formulas at this point. The subsequent investigation is called "Patterns and Rules"

2.1 Renting Bicycles

The tour operators decide to rent bicycles for their customers. They get information from two bike shops.

Rocky's Cycle Center sends a table of weekly rental fees for bikes.

Rocky's Weekly Rental Rates for Bikes

Number of Bikes	5	10	15	20	25	30	35	40	45	50
Rental Fee	$400	$535	$655	$770	$875	$975	$1,070	$1,140	$1,180	$1,200

Adrian's Bike Shop sends a graph of their weekly rental fees. Because the rental fee depends on the number of bikes, they put the number of bikes on the *x*-axis.

Adrian's Weekly Rental Rates for Bikes

Problem 2.1   Analyzing a Table and a Graph

A. Which bike shop should Ocean Bike Tours use? Explain.

B. Suppose you make a graph from the table for Rocky's Cycle Center. Would it make sense to connect the points? Explain.

C. How much do you think each company charges to rent 32 bikes?

D. 1. What patterns do you find in the table and in the graph?

  2. Based on the patterns you found in part (1), how can you predict values that are not included in the table or graph?

E. 1. Describe a way to find the costs for renting any number of bikes from Adrian's Bike Shop.

  2. Describe a way to find the costs for renting any number of bikes from Rocky's Cycle Center.

ACE Homework starts on page 35.

Investigation 2 Analyzing Graphs and Tables   **31**

---

and begins the exploration of connecting equations or rules to the representations of graphs and tables. In the final investigation, students use graphing calculators to explore how graphs change in appearance when the rules that produce the graphs change.

thinking used as a tool for discovery. This brief discussion will be developed more fully in later chapters.

Measurement and Algebra. Soares, Blanton, and Kaput (2006) describe how to "algebrafy" the elementary curriculum. One measurement example they give uses *Spaghetti and Meatballs for All*, looking at the increasing number of chairs needed given the number of tables put together.

Geometric formulas relate various dimensions, areas, and volumes of shapes. Each of these formulas involves at least one functional relationship. Consider any familiar formula for measuring a geometric shape. For example, the circumference of a circle is $c = 2\pi r$. The radius is the independent variable and circumference is the dependent variable. We can say that the circumference is dependent on the radius. Even nonlinear formulas like volume of a cone ($V = 1/3\pi r^2 h$) are functions. Here the volume is a function of both the height of the cone and the radius. If the radius is held constant, the volume is a function of the height. Similarly, for a fixed height, the volume is a function of the radius.

The following activity explores how the volume of a box varies as a result of changing the dimensions.

Activity 14.18

Designing the Largest Box

Begin with a rectangular sheet of cardstock, and from each corner, cut out a square. Fold up the four resulting flaps, and tape them together to form an open box. The volume of the box will vary depending on the size of the squares (see Figure 14.27). Write a formula that gives the volume of the box as a function of the size of the cutout squares. Use the function to determine what size the squares should be to create the box with the largest volume.

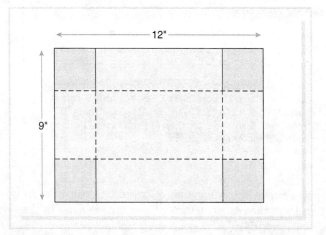

Figure 14.27 If squares are cut from a 9-by-12-inch piece of cardboard so that the four flaps can be folded up, what size squares should be cut so that the volume of the box is the largest possible?

Data and Algebra. Data can be obtained from sports records, census reports, the business section of the newspaper, and many other sources. Students can gather data such as measurement examples or survey data. As noted toward the end of Chapter 7, the Internet has many sites where data can be found.

 "When doing experiments or dealing with real data, students may encounter 'messy data,' for which a line or a curve may not be an exact fit. They will need experience with such situations and assistance from the teacher to develop their ability to find a function that fits the data well enough to be useful as a prediction tool" (p. 228). ◆

Experiments. There are many experiments that students can explore to see the functional relationships, if any, that exist between two variables. Gathering real data is an excellent way to engage a range of learners and to see how mathematics can be used to describe real phenomena.

Data should be collected and then represented in a table or on a graph. The goal is to determine if there is a relationship between the independent and dependent variables, and if so, whether it is linear or nonlinear, as in the following engaging experiments:

- How long would it take for 100 students standing in a row to complete a wave similar to those seen at football games? Experiment with different numbers of students from 5 to 25. Can the relationship predict how many students it would take for a given wave time?
- How far will a Matchbox car roll off of a ramp, based on the height the ramp is raised?
- How is the flight time of a paper airplane affected by the number of paper clips attached to the nose of the plane?
- What is the relationship between the number of dominoes in a row and the time required for them to fall over? (Use multiples of 100 dominoes.)
- Make wadded newspaper balls using different numbers of sheets of newspaper, using rubber bands to help hold the paper in a ball. What is the relationship between the number of sheets and the distance the ball can be thrown?
- What is the relationship between the number of drops of colored water dropped on a paper towel and the diameter of the spot? Is the relationship different for different brands of towels?
- How much weight can a toothpick bridge hold? Lay toothpicks in a bunch to span a 2-inch gap between two boards. From the toothpicks, hang a bag or other container into which weights can be added until the toothpicks break. Begin with only one toothpick (McCoy, 1997).

Experiments like these are fun and accessible to a wide range of learners. They also provide an opportunity for students to engage in experimental design. Students need practice in identifying independent and dependent variables, controlling experiments for other variables, measuring and recording results, and analyzing data. This is a perfect blend of mathematics and science.

Scatter Plots. Often in the real world, phenomena are observed that seem to suggest a functional relationship but not necessarily as clean or as well defined as some of the situations we have described so far. Certainly this would be true of the experiments described above. However, even in the case of measuring the increasing height of a stack of identical books as each new one is added—a linear situation—measuring error will lead to values that are not exactly on a line. In such cases, the data are generally plotted on a graph to produce a scatter plot of points.

A visual inspection of the graphed data may suggest what kind of relationship, if any, exists. If a linear relationship seems to exist, for example, students can approximate a line of best fit or use graphing technology to do a linear regression to find the line of best fit (along with the equation). They do not need to understand what linear regression is to use this function on the graphing calculator—just that it is a statistical method for finding the line of best fit.

Not all scatter plots will show a straight-line relationship. Suppose students were figuring out the time it takes for balloons of various diameters to deflate (another engaging experiment!). A parabolic or cubic function might better approximate the shape of the data. Graphing calculators can also find best-fitting curves. These brief examples of algebraic thinking in other content areas illustrate the importance of algebra in the K–8 curriculum

Reflections on Chapter 14

Writing to Learn

1. Kaput lists five types of algebraic thinking. Rather than list each of these, describe algebraic thinking in no more than three sentences in a manner that encompasses Kaput's main ideas and the spirit of this chapter.
2. What misconceptions do students have regarding the equal sign? What causes these misconceptions and how can instruction clear these up?
3. What misconceptions do students have regarding variables? What causes these misconceptions and how can instruction clear these up?
4. Explain how to solve the equation $4x + 3 = x + 12$ on the pan balance.
5. What is a recursive relationship? Where in a table for a growing pattern would you look for the recursive relationship? What would it mean in terms of the pattern itself?
6. How can you tell from the recursive relationship whether the graph of the growing pattern will be straight or curved?

7. How can you determine if a function is linear in each of the five representations?

For Discussion and Exploration

1. The idea of having students make connections from arithmetic to algebra is a relatively new idea for the elementary curriculum. What examples can you find in the number strand for taking an algorithm and presenting it in a way that it becomes a process for generalizing a rule? (See the "Generalization with Addition" section for an example.)
2. Explore some of the online applets that focus on functions (see "Online Resources" at the end of the chapter). For each consider what the technology provides in terms of learning opportunities. How might the technology be used to support the diversity in a classroom?

Resources for Chapter 14

Literature Connections

Many teachers find pattern explorations sufficiently interesting that they may not think of using literature to provide a springboard for student explorations. However, the following three examples of books are excellent beginnings for patterns and chart building.

Anno's Magic Seeds *Anno, 1994*

Anno's Magic Seeds has several patterns. A wise man gives Jack two magic seeds, one to eat and one to plant. The planted seed will produce two new seeds by the following year. Several years later, Jack decides to plant both seeds. Then he has a family and starts to sell seeds.

At each stage of the story, there is an opportunity to develop a chart and extend the current pattern into the future. Austin and Thompson (1997) describe how they used the story to develop patterns and charts with sixth- and seventh-grade students.

Bats on Parade *Appelt, 1999*

This story includes the pattern of bats walking 1 by 1, then 2 by 2, and so on. One activity from this enjoyable book is determining the growing pattern of the number of bats given the array length (e.g., 3 for the 3-by-3 array). There is also one mouse, so this can be included in a second investigation. Activity sheets for these two ideas and two others can be found in Roy and Beckmann, 2007.

Pattern *Pluckrose, 1988*

This book brings pattern from the real world to the classroom in the form of brilliantly colored photographs. Pattern is seen in the soles of tennis shoes, dishes, butterflies, leaves, and flowers. The book provides a jumping-off point for an exploration of repeating patterns in the world around us.

Two of Everything: *A Chinese Folktale*
Hong, 1993

The magic pot discovered by Mr. Haktak doubles whatever goes in it, including his wife! This idea of input–output is great for exploring functions from grades 2 through 8; just vary the rule of the magic pot from doubling to something more complex. For more details and handouts, see Suh (2007) and Wickett, Kharas, and Burns (2002).

Recommended Readings

Articles

Joram, E., Hartman, C., & Trafton, P. R. (2004). "As people get older, they get taller": An integrated unit on measurement, linear relationships, and data analysis. *Teaching Children Mathematics, 10*(7), 344–351.
This is a wonderful unit for second grade showing students using real data to answer the question of how much taller students in the fourth grade were compared to students in the second grade. They used a best-fit line to create a function from the scatter plot data.

Kalman, R. (2008). Teaching algebra without algebra. *Mathematics Teaching in the Middle School, 13*(6), 334–339.
This article includes three contexts that involve simplifying equations and effectively explains how to make sense of the simplification by relating it to the context. An excellent resource for helping middle school students make sense of symbols and properties.

Molina, M., & Ambrose, R. C. (2006). Fostering relational thinking while negotiating the meaning of the equals sign. *Teaching Children Mathematics, 13*(2), 111–117.
This article helps us understand the conceptual considerations related to the equal sign while simultaneously illustrating the value of errors and misconceptions in creating opportunities for learning.

Books

Carpenter, T. P., Franke, M. L., & Levi, L. (2003). *Thinking mathematically: Integrating arithmetic and algebra in elementary school*. Portsmouth, NH: Heinemann.
This book is a detailed look at helping children in the primary grades develop the thinking and create the generalizations of algebra. The included CD shows classroom-based examples of the ideas discussed. Many of the ideas about equality, true/false sentences, and generalizations discussed in this chapter were influenced by this book.

Driscol, M. (1999). *Fostering algebraic thinking: A guide for teachers, grades 6–10*. Portsmouth, NH: Heinemann.
Driscol's book is one of the most popular algebra resources—full of rich problems to use and helpful for expanding the reader's understanding of algebra.

Greenes, C. E., & Rubenstein, R. (Eds.). (2008). *Algebra and algebraic thinking in school mathematics*. NCTM 70th Yearbook. Reston, VA: NCTM.
NCTM Yearbooks are always excellent collections of articles for grades pre-K–12. This one is no exception, offering a wealth of thought-provoking and helpful articles about algebraic thinking.

NCTM's Navigations Series

Cuevas, G. J., & Yeatts, K. (2001). *Navigating through algebra in grades 3–5*. Reston, VA: NCTM.

Friel, S., Rachlin, S., & Doyle, D. (2001). *Navigating through algebra in grades 6–8*. Reston, VA: NCTM.

Greenes, C., Cavanagh, M., Dacey, L., Findell, C., & Small, M. (2001). *Navigating through algebra in prekindergarten–grade 2*. Reston, VA: NCTM.
These books offer high-quality algebra activities that reflect the Principles and Standards. Each book includes a CD-ROM with blackline masters for the activities, applets, and selected articles.

Online Resources

Algebra Balance Scales and Algebra Balance Scales—Negative
http://nlvm.usu.edu/en/nav/frames_asid_324_g_3_t_2.html
Linear equations are presented on a two-pan balance with variables on each side. The user can solve equations in the same way as described in the text. The negative version uses balloons for negative values and negative variables.

Graph Sketcher
www.shodor.org/interactivate/activities/GraphSketcher
Works very much like a graphing calculator for graphing functions of any type. A good demonstration tool for making graphs of equations.

Learning about Rate of Change (e-Example)
http://standards.nctm.org/document/eexamples/chap6/6.2/index.htm
A nice interactive lesson in which the cost per minute to make a phone call (the slope) can be adjusted and then the graph of the cost can be displayed. A slider helps connect points on the two graphs.

Pan Balance—Shapes
http://illuminations.nctm.org/ActivityDetail.aspx?id=33

With each problem, four shapes are assigned unknown values. By stacking shapes on the two balance pans, the user attempts to balance the scale and then create additional balances. A numbers version and an expressions version are extensions of this applet.

Patterns, Relations and Functions (eNLVM module)
http://enlvm.usu.edu/ma/nav/toc.jsp?sid=__shared&cid=emready@patterns_relations_functions&bb=course

This site encourages students to generate rules and functions for geometric sequences, describing relationships between the pattern number and characteristics of the pattern.

Slope Slider
www.shodor.org/interactivate/activities/slopeslider

A good interactive tool for illustrating the meaning of slope and the y-intercept for a linear equation of the form $y = mx + b$. The user can use a slider to change the value of m or b and see the graph change dynamically.

Function Machine Applets

Function Machine (NLVM)
http://nlvm.usu.edu/en/nav/frames_asid_191_g_3_t_1.html

Function Machine (Math Playground)
www.mathplayground.com/functionmachine.html

This is a nice, Flash-based tool.

Stop That Creature! (PBS Kids' CyberChase)
http://pbskids.org/cyberchase/games/functions/functions.html

In this fun game, figure out the rule that runs the game to shut down the creature cloning machine.

Function Machine (Shodor Project Interactivate)
www.shodor.org/interactivate/activities/FunctionMachine

The functions on this site have one of the following forms: $y = x \times \_\_$, $y = x + \_\_$, $y = x - \_\_$, where the underline can be any integer between -10 and 10.

Linear Function Machine (Shodor Project Interactivate)
www.shodor.org/interactivate/activities/LinearFunctMachine

Field Experience Guide Connections

The focus on multiple representations and meaning in this chapter are a good match for FEG Field Experiences 1.2 and 4.1. Number patterns and geometric growing patterns are the focus of FEG Expanded Lessons 9.12 and 9.13 and FEG Activity 10.8. Expanded Lesson 9.14 for grades 6–8 connects graphs to stories—an excellent integration of writing. In addition, Activities 10.9 ("Compensation Decision") and 10.10 ("Solving the Mystery") are excellent applications of algebra. Balanced Assessment Item 11.2 ("Grocery Store") is an excellent assessment for finding a rule to describe a growing pattern.

Chapter 15

Developing Fraction Concepts

Fractions have always represented a considerable challenge for students, even into the middle grades. Results of NAEP testing have consistently shown that students have a weak understanding of fraction concepts (Sowder & Wearne, 2006; Wearne & Kouba, 2000). This lack of understanding is then translated into difficulties with fraction computation, decimal and percent concepts, and the use of fractions in other content areas, particularly algebra (NMP, 2008).

Curriculum Focal Points (NCTM, 2006) places initial development of foundational fraction concepts in grade 3 as one of three focal points: *Developing an understanding of fractions and fraction equivalence.* Fraction concepts are also emphasized at each grade following grade 3, focusing on topics such as computation and proportional reasoning. Elementary and middle school programs must provide students with adequate time and experiences to develop a deep conceptual understanding of this important area of the curriculum. This chapter explores conceptual development of fraction concepts in order to help students construct a firm foundation.

Big Ideas

1. For students to really understand fractions, they must experience fractions across many constructs, including part of a whole, ratios, and division.

2. Three categories of models exist for working with fractions—area (e.g., $\frac{1}{3}$ of a garden), length (e.g., $\frac{3}{4}$ of an inch), and set or quantity (e.g., $\frac{1}{2}$ of the class).

3. Partitioning and iterating are ways for students to understand the meaning of fractions, especially numerator and denominator.

4. Students need many experiences estimating with fractions.

5. Understanding equivalent fractions is critical. Two equivalent fractions are two ways of describing the same amount by using different-sized fractional parts. For example, in the fraction $\frac{6}{8}$, if the eighths are taken in twos, then each pair of eighths is a fourth. Six-eighths then can be seen to be equivalent to three-fourths.

Mathematics Content Connections

What students bring to the topic of fractions is an understanding of fair sharing. Other whole-number ideas actually interfere in early fraction development, as discussed later in this chapter. However, fraction concepts are intimately connected to other areas of the curriculum. In addition to the clear content connections just listed, fractions are used frequently in measurement (Chapter 19) and in probability (Chapter 22).

* **Algebraic Thinking** (Chapter 14): As described in Chapter 14, fractions are a part of algebra. Equations with variables often involve fractions or can be solved using fractions. For example, $\frac{x}{4} = \frac{5}{16}$ is an equation involving equivalent fractions.

* **Fraction Computation** (Chapter 16): Without a firm conceptual understanding of fractions, computation with fractions is relegated to rules without reasons.

* **Decimals and Percents** (Chapter 17): A key idea for students is that decimal notation and percent notation are simply two other representations of fractions. By making the connections among these three representations, the load of new ideas to be learned is significantly reduced.

* **Ratio and Proportion** (Chapter 18): A part-to-whole concept of a fraction is just one form of ratio. The same fraction notation can be used for part-to-part ratios (e.g., the ratio of boys to girls in the room is 3 to 5 or $\frac{3}{5}$).

Meanings of Fractions

Fractions are a critical foundation for students, as they are used in measurement across various professions, and they are essential to the study of algebra and more advanced mathematics. This understanding must go well beyond recognizing that $\frac{3}{5}$ of a region is shaded. This chapter begins with a look at the multiple concepts related to fractions and how these relate to students' knowledge of whole numbers.

Fraction Constructs

Understanding fractions means understanding all the possible concepts that fractions can represent. One of the commonly used meanings of fraction is part-whole, including examples when part of a whole is shaded. In fact, part-whole is so ingrained in elementary textbooks as the way to represent fractions, it may be difficult for you to think about what else fractions might represent. Although the part-whole model is the most used in textbooks, many who research fraction understanding believe students would understand fractions better with more emphasis across other meanings of fractions (Clarke, Roche, & Mitchell, 2008; Siebert & Gaskin, 2006).

⏸ ——————————— *Pause and Reflect*

Beyond shading a region of a shape, how else are fractions modeled? Try to name three ideas.

Part-Whole. Part-whole is one meaning of fractions and in fact goes beyond shading a region. For example, it could be part of a group of people ($\frac{3}{5}$ of the class went on the field trip) or it could be part of a length (we walked $3\frac{1}{2}$ miles). Cramer, Wyberg, and Leavitt (2008), researchers on rational numbers, note that the circle model is particularly effective in illustrating the part-whole relationship. Perhaps these were among the ideas you listed in responding to the Pause and Reflect. The following paragraphs present some other meanings that are important for students to experience to achieve a deep understanding with many connections among ideas, as discussed in Chapter 2.

Measure. Measurement involves identifying a length and then using that length as a measurement piece to determine the length of an object. For example, in the fraction $\frac{5}{8}$, you can use the unit fraction $\frac{1}{8}$ as the selected length and then count or measure to show that it takes five of those to reach $\frac{5}{8}$. This concept focuses on how much rather than how many parts, which is the case in part-whole situations (Behr, Lesh, Post, & Silver, 1983; Martinie, 2007).

Division. Consider the idea of sharing $10 with 4 people. This is not a part-whole scenario, but it still means that each person will receive one-fourth ($\frac{1}{4}$) of the money, or $2\frac{1}{2}$ dollars. Division is often not connected to fractions, which is unfortunate. Students should understand and feel comfortable with the example here written as $\frac{10}{4}$, $4)\overline{10}$, $10 \div 4$, $2\frac{2}{4}$, and $2\frac{1}{2}$ (Flores, Samson, & Yanik, 2006). Division of fractions is addressed in detail in the next chapter.

Operator. Fractions can be used to indicate an operation, as in $\frac{4}{5}$ of 20 square feet or $\frac{2}{3}$ of the audience was holding banners. These situations indicate a fraction of a whole number, and students may be able to use mental math to determine the answer. Researchers note that this construct is not emphasized enough in school curricula (Usiskin, 2007) and that just knowing how to represent fractions doesn't mean students will know how to operate with fractions, such as when working in other areas of the curriculum where fractions occur (Johanning, 2008).

Ratio. Discussed at length in Chapter 18, the concept of ratio is yet another context in which fractions are used. For example, the fraction $\frac{1}{4}$ can mean that the probability of an event is one in four.

Ratios can be part-part or part-whole. For example, the ratio $\frac{3}{4}$ could be the ratio of those wearing jackets (part) to those not wearing jackets (part); or it could be part-whole, meaning those wearing jackets (part) to those in the class (whole). When working with ratios, students have to attend to part-part and part-whole relationships, which requires attention to the context.

Building on Whole-Number Concepts

As described in Chapter 2, students build on their prior knowledge, meaning that when they encounter situations with fractions, they naturally use what they know about whole numbers to solve the problems. Their prior knowledge of whole numbers both supports and inhibits their work with fractions. It is important for a teacher to help students see how fractions are like and different from whole numbers. The following list shows some common misapplications of whole numbers to fractions:

1. Students think that the numerator and denominator are separate values. It is hard for them to see that $\frac{3}{4}$ is one number. Finding fraction values on a number line or ruler can help students develop this notion. Also, avoid the phrase "three *out of* four" (unless talking about ratios or probability) or "three over four" and instead say "three *fourths*" (Siebert & Gaskin, 2006).

2. In thinking of the numbers separately, students may think that $\frac{2}{3}$ means any two parts, not equal-sized parts. For example, students may think that the shape below shows $\frac{3}{4}$ green, rather than $\frac{1}{2}$ green.

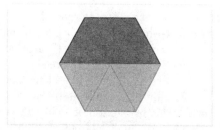

3. Students think that a fraction such as $\frac{1}{5}$ is smaller than a fraction such as $\frac{1}{10}$ because 5 is less than 10. Many visuals and contexts that show parts of the whole are essential in helping students understand. For example, ask students if they would rather go outside for $\frac{1}{2}$ of an hour, $\frac{1}{4}$ of an hour, or $\frac{1}{10}$ of an hour.

4. Students mistakenly use the operation "rules" for whole numbers to compute with fractions, for example, $\frac{1}{2} + \frac{1}{2} = \frac{2}{4}$. The explorations in the estimation section of this chapter can help students understand that this answer is not reasonable. See Chapter 16 for more on helping students understand the operations of fractions.

Only One Size for the Whole. A key idea about fractions that students must come to understand is that a fraction does not say anything about the size of the whole or the size of the parts. A fraction tells us only about the *relationship between* the part and the whole. Consider the following situation.

Mark is offered the choice of a third of a pizza or a half of a pizza. Because he is hungry and likes pizza, he chooses the half. His friend Jane gets a third of a pizza but ends up with more than Mark. How can that be?

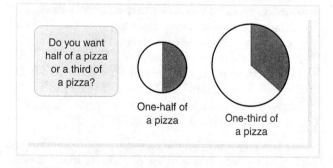

The visual illustrates how Mark got misdirected in his choice. The point of the "pizza fallacy" is that whenever two or more fractions are discussed in the same context, one cannot assume (as Mark did in choosing a half of a pizza) that the fractions are all parts of the same size whole.

Comparisons with any model can be made only if both fractions are parts of the same size whole. For example,

when using Cuisenaire rods, $\frac{2}{3}$ of a light green strip cannot be compared to $\frac{2}{5}$ of an orange strip.

 The *Standards* supports a strong conceptual development of fractions in grades 3 to 5, with computation primarily a middle school topic. "During grades 3–5, students should build their understanding of fractions as parts of a whole and as division. They will need to see and explore a variety of models of fractions, focusing primarily on fractions such as halves, thirds, fourths, fifths, sixths, eighths, and tenths" (p. 150). ◆

Models for Fractions

There is substantial evidence to suggest that the use of models in fraction tasks is important (Cramer & Henry, 2002; Siebert & Gaskin, 2006). Unfortunately, even teachers who use models do not always employ manipulatives or spend adequate time for students to make sense of fractions in light of the model. Properly used, however, models can help students clarify ideas that are often confused in a purely symbolic mode. Sometimes it is useful to do the same activity with two quite different models; from the viewpoint of the students, the activities will be quite different.

Different models offer different opportunities to learn. For example, an area model helps students visualize parts of the whole. A linear model shows that there is always another fraction to be found between any two fractions—an important concept that is underemphasized in the teaching of fractions. Also, some students are able to make sense of one model, but not another. Using appropriate models and using models of each type broaden and deepen students (and teachers) understanding of fractions. This section focuses on three categories of models: region/area, length, and set.

Region or Area Models

In the discussion of sharing, all of the tasks involved sharing something that could be cut into smaller parts. The fractions are based on parts of an area or region. This is a good place to begin and is almost essential when doing sharing tasks. There are many good region models, as shown in Figure 15.1.

Circular fraction piece models are the most commonly used area model. (See Blackline Masters 24–26.) One advantage of the circular region is that it emphasizes the part-whole concept of fractions and the meaning of the relative size of a part to the whole (Cramer, Wyberg, & Leavitt, 2008). The other models in Figure 15.1 demonstrate how different shapes can be the whole. Paper grids, several of which can be found in the Blackline Masters, are

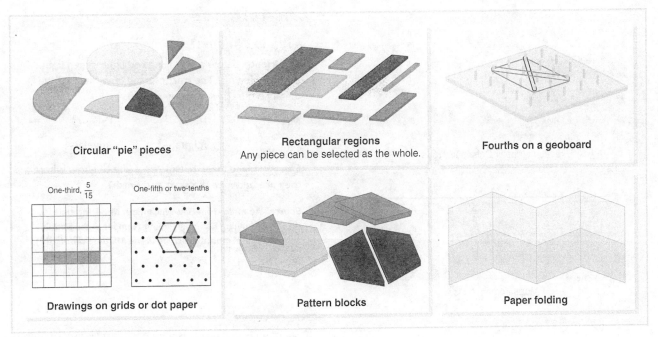

Circular "pie" pieces

Rectangular regions
Any piece can be selected as the whole.

Fourths on a geoboard

One-third, $\frac{5}{15}$

One-fifth or two-tenths

Drawings on grids or dot paper

Pattern blocks

Paper folding

Figure 15.1 Area or region models for fractions.

especially flexible and do not require management of materials. Commercial versions of area models are available in a wide variety, including circular and rectangular regions. The following activity is an example of how area models can be used to help students develop concepts of equal shares.

Activity 15.1

Playground Fractions

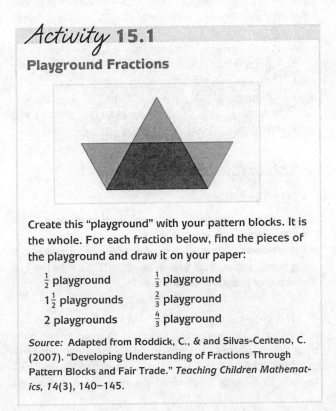

Create this "playground" with your pattern blocks. It is the whole. For each fraction below, find the pieces of the playground and draw it on your paper:

$\frac{1}{2}$ playground $\frac{1}{3}$ playground

$1\frac{1}{2}$ playgrounds $\frac{2}{3}$ playground

2 playgrounds $\frac{4}{3}$ playground

Source: Adapted from Roddick, C., & and Silvas-Centeno, C. (2007). "Developing Understanding of Fractions Through Pattern Blocks and Fair Trade." *Teaching Children Mathematics, 14*(3), 140–145.

Length Models

With length models, lengths or measurements are compared instead of areas. Either lines are drawn and subdivided, or physical materials are compared on the basis of length, as shown in Figure 15.2.

Cuisenaire rods have pieces in lengths of 1 to 10 measured in terms of the smallest strip or rod. Each length is a different color for ease of identification. Strips of paper or adding-machine tape can be folded to produce student-made fraction strips.

Rods or strips provide flexibility because any length can represent the whole. For example, if you wanted students to work with $\frac{1}{4}$s and $\frac{1}{8}$s, select the brown Cuiseniare rod, which is 8 units long. Therefore, the four rod (purple) becomes $\frac{1}{2}$, the two rod (red) becomes $\frac{1}{4}$ and the one rod (white) becomes $\frac{1}{8}$. For exploring twelfths, put the orange rod and red rod together to make a whole that is 12 units long.

Cuisenaire rods consist of the following colors and lengths:

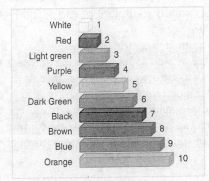

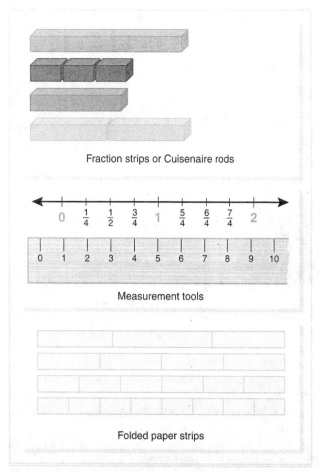

Figure 15.2 Length or measurement models for fractions.

Source: Adapted from Bay-Williams, J. M., & Martinie, S. L. (2003). "Thinking Rationally about Number in the Middle School." *Mathematics Teaching in the Middle School, 8*(6), 282–287.

The number line is a significantly more sophisticated measurement model (Bright, Behr, Post, & Wachsmuth, 1988). In fact, many researchers in mathematics education have found it to be an essential model that should be emphasized more in the teaching of fractions (Clarke, Roche, & Mitchell, 2008; Flores, Samson, & Yanik, 2006; Middleton, van den Heuvel-Panhuizen, & Shew, 1998; Usiskin, 2007; Watanabe, 2006). Linear models are closely connected to the real-world contexts in which fractions are commonly used—measuring. Music, for example, is an excellent opportunity to explore $\frac{1}{2}$s, $\frac{1}{4}$s, $\frac{1}{8}$s, and $\frac{1}{16}$s (Goral & Wiest, 2007).

The number line also emphasizes that a fraction is one number as well as its relative size to other numbers, which is not as clear when using area models. Importantly, the number line reinforces that there is always one more fraction to be found between two fractions. The following activity is a fun way to use a real-world context to engage students in thinking about fractions through a linear model.

Activity 15.2

Who Is Winning?

The friends below are playing red light–green light. Who is winning? The fractions tell how much of the distance they have already moved.

Mary—$\frac{3}{4}$ Harry—$\frac{1}{2}$ Larry—$\frac{5}{6}$

Han—$\frac{5}{8}$ Miguel—$\frac{5}{9}$ Angela—$\frac{2}{3}$

Can you place these friends on a line to show where they are between the start and finish?

Set Models

In set models, the whole is understood to be a set of objects, and subsets of the whole make up fractional parts. For example, 3 objects are one-fourth of a set of 12 objects. The set of 12, in this example, represents the whole or 1. The idea of referring to a collection of counters as a single entity makes set models difficult for some children. Students will frequently focus on the size of the set rather than the number of equal sets in the whole. For example, if 12 counters make a whole, then a set of 4 counters is one-*third*, not one-fourth, since 3 equal sets make the whole. However, the set model helps establish important connections with many real-world uses of fractions and with ratio concepts. Figure 15.3 illustrates several set models for fractions.

Counters in two colors on opposite sides are frequently used. They can easily be flipped to change their color to model various fractional parts of a whole set.

The activity below can be done as an energizer or as a quick activity when you find you have five minutes.

Activity 15.3

Class Fractions

Use a group of students as the whole—for example, six students if you want to work on $\frac{1}{3}$s, $\frac{1}{2}$s, and $\frac{1}{6}$s. Ask students, "What fraction of our friends [are wearing tennis shoes, have brown hair, etc.]?" Change the number of people over time.

It is important to remember that students must be able to explore fractions across models. If they never see fractions represented as a length, they will struggle to solve any problem or context that is linear. As a teacher, you will not know if they really understand the meaning of a fraction

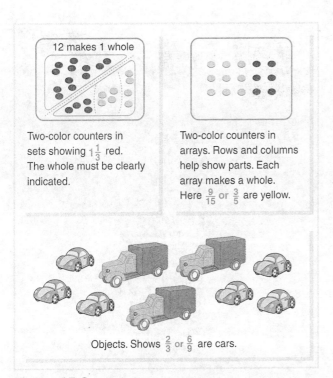

Two-color counters in sets showing $1\frac{1}{3}$ red. The whole must be clearly indicated.

Two-color counters in arrays. Rows and columns help show parts. Each array makes a whole. Here $\frac{9}{15}$ or $\frac{3}{5}$ are yellow.

Objects. Shows $\frac{2}{3}$ or $\frac{6}{9}$ are cars.

Figure 15.3 Set models for fractions.

such as $\frac{1}{4}$ unless you have seen a student model one-fourth using different contexts and models.

A straightforward way to assess students' knowledge of a fractional amount is to give them a piece of paper, fold it into thirds, and at the top of each section write *area, length,* and *set* and have them show you a picture and write a sentence for the fraction (e.g., $\frac{3}{4}$) in all three ways (NCTM, 2007, p. 32). This can be done exactly for commonly used fractions or can be an estimation activity with fractions like $\frac{31}{58}$.

Concept of Fractional Parts

The first goal in the development of fractions should be to help children construct the idea of *fractional parts of the whole*—the parts that result when the whole or unit has been partitioned into *equal-sized portions* or *fair shares*.

Children seem to understand the idea of separating a quantity into two or more parts to be shared fairly among friends. They eventually make connections between the idea of fair shares and fractional parts. Sharing tasks are, therefore, good places to begin the development of fractions.

Sharing Tasks

Considerable research has been done with children from first through eighth grades to determine how they go about the process of forming fair shares and how the tasks posed to students influence their responses (e.g., Empson, 2002; Lamon, 1996; Mack, 2001; Pothier & Sawada, 1983).

Sharing tasks are generally posed in the form of a simple story problem. *Suppose there are four square brownies to be shared among three children so that each child gets the same amount. How much (or show how much) will each child get?* Task difficulty changes with the numbers involved, the types of things to be shared (regions such as brownies, discrete objects such as pieces of chewing gum), and the presence or use of a model.

Students initially perform sharing tasks (division) by distributing items one at a time. When this process leaves leftover pieces students must think of how to subdivide so that every group (or person) gets a fair share. Contexts that lend to subdividing an area include brownies (rectangles), sandwiches, pizzas, crackers, cake, candy bars, and so on. The problems and variations that follow are adapted from Empson (2002).

Four children are sharing ten brownies so that each one will get the same amount. How much can each child have?

Problem difficulty is determined by the relationship between the number of things to be shared and the number of sharers. Because children's initial strategies for sharing involve halving, a good place to begin is with two, four, or even eight sharers. For ten brownies and four sharers, many children will deal out two to each child and then halve each of the remaining brownies (see Figure 15.4).

Consider these variations in numbers:

5 brownies shared with 2 children
2 brownies shared with 4 children
5 brownies shared with 4 children
7 brownies shared with 4 children
4 brownies shared with 8 children
3 brownies shared with 4 children

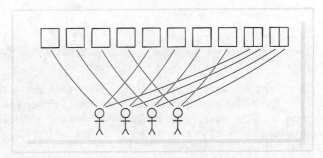

Figure 15.4 Ten brownies shared with four children.

⏸ ———————————— *Pause and Reflect*

Try drawing pictures for each of the preceding sharing tasks. Which do you think is most difficult? Which of these represent essentially the same degree of difficulty?

The last example, three brownies shared with four children, was significantly more challenging. Figure 15.5 shows how one third-grader, who easily solved the first three, worked hard to solve this problem. Her guess and check strategy involved first subdividing each brownie in two parts, five parts, six parts, seven parts, and then dropping back to four parts.

When the numbers allow for some items to be distributed whole (five shared with two), some students will first share whole items and then cut up the leftovers. Others will slice every piece in half and then distribute the halves. When there are more sharers than items, some partitioning must happen at the beginning of the solution process.

When students who are still using a halving strategy try to share five things among four children, they will eventually get down to two halves to give to four children. For some, the solution is to cut each half in half; that is, "each child gets a whole (or two halves) and a half of a half."

As always, it is important to meet the needs of the range of learners in your classroom. The level of difficulty of these tasks varies, so a tiered lesson can be implemented to provide appropriate tasks for different students, while still enabling all students to learn the important mathematics of the lesson (fair sharing as a meaning of fractions). Figure 15.6 shows how one teacher offers these three tiers for her lesson on sharing brownies (Williams, 2008, p. 326).

As students report their answers, it is important to emphasize the equivalence of different representations (Flores & Klein, 2005). For example, in the case of three people sharing four brownies the answer might be noted on the board this way:

$$\tfrac{4}{3} = 1\tfrac{1}{3} = 1 + \tfrac{1}{3}$$

It is a progression to move to three or six sharers because this will force children to confront their halving strategies.

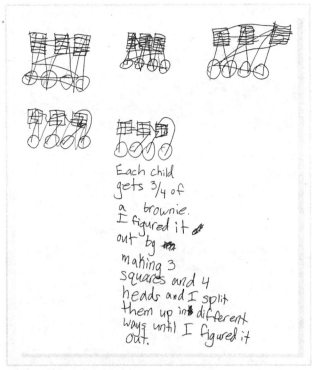

Each child gets 3/4 of a brownie. I figured it out by making 3 squares and 4 heads and I split them up in different ways until I figured it out.

Figure 15.5 Elizabeth partitions to find the fair shares for 3 brownies shared with 4 people.

⏸ ———————————— *Pause and Reflect*

Try solving the following variations using drawings. Can you do them in different ways?

4 pizzas shared with 6 children
7 pizzas shared with 6 children
5 pizzas shared with 3 children
5 pizzas shared with 4 children

Subdividing a region into a number of parts other than a power of two (four, eight, etc.) is more challenging for students. Figure 15.7 shows how a student partitioned to solve the third pizza problem. This took much guess and check, at which point the teacher asked, "Can you see a pattern in how you have divided the pizza and how many

Tier 1 task: for students who still need experience with halving	Tier 2 task: for students comfortable with halving and ready to try other strategies.	Tier 3 task: for students ready to solve tasks where students combine halving with new strategies
How can 2 people share 3 brownies?	How can 4 people share 3 brownies?	How can 3 people share 5 brownies?
How can 2 people share 5 brownies?	How can 3 people share 4 brownies?	How can 3 people share 2 brownies?
How can 4 people share 3 brownies?	How can 3 people share 5 brownies?	How can 6 people share 4 brownies?
How can 3 people share 4 brownies?	How can 6 people share 4 brownies?	How can 5 people share 4 brownies?

Figure 15.6 Example of a tiered lesson for the sharing brownies problem.

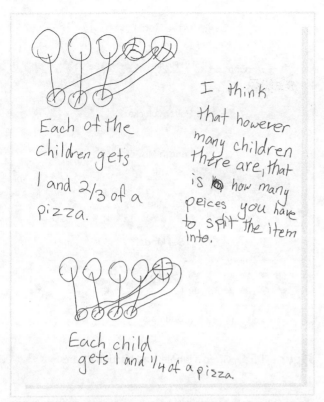

Each of the children gets 1 and 2/3 of a pizza.

I think that however many children there are, that is how many peices you have to split the item into.

Each child gets 1 and 1/4 of a pizza.

Figure 15.7 Student explains a pattern for finding equal shares of a pizza.

people are eating?" At this point the student noticed a pattern: if there are three people, the remaining pizzas need to be partitioned into thirds. She used this fact to quickly solve the fourth problem. This points out the importance of a teacher not telling students what to think, but rather asking questions that lead students to pause and analyze their work. Notice that the context and the model match—both are circles. It is important to use a range of contexts and to encourage a range of representations across the different types of models (area, length, and set).

Fraction bars, Cuisenaire rods, and fraction circles can be subdivided. Another possibility is to cut out construction paper circles or squares. Some students may need to cut and physically distribute the pieces. Students can use connecting cubes to make bars that they can separate into pieces. Or they can use more traditional fraction models such as circular "pie" pieces.

Fraction Language

During the discussions of students' solutions (and discussions are essential!) is a good time to introduce the vocabulary of fractional parts. When a brownie or other region has been broken into equal shares, simply say, "We call these *fourths*. The whole is cut into four parts. All of the parts are the same size—fourths."

When partitioning a whole, children need to be aware of two aspects or components of fractional parts: (1) the

number of parts determines the fractional amount (e.g., partitioning into 4 parts, means each part is $\frac{1}{4}$ of the unit) and (2) the parts must be the same size, though not necessarily the same shape. Emphasize that the number of parts that make up a whole determines the name of the fractional parts or shares. They will be familiar with halves but should quickly learn to describe thirds, fourths, fifths, and so on.

In addition to helping children use the words *halves*, *thirds*, *fourths*, *fifths*, and so on, be sure to make regular comparison of fractional parts to the whole. Make it a point to use the terms *whole*, or *one whole*, or simply *one* so that students have a language that they can use regardless of the model involved.

A physical model, like color tiles, can mislead students to believe that fractional parts must be the same *shape* as well as the same size. For example:

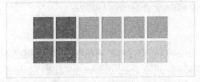

Class discussions that challenge students' thinking and expose their ideas are the best ways to both help students develop accurate concepts and to find out what they understand.

Equivalent Size of Fraction Pieces

Too often students see shapes that are already all the same shape and size when they are asked questions about what fraction is shaded. The result is that students think that equal shares might need to be the same shape, which is not the case. Young children, in particular, tend to focus on shape, when the focus should be on equal-*sized* parts.

The following activity focuses on this, having examples that are (1) same shape, same size; (2) different shape, same size; (3) different shape, different size; and (4) same shape, different size. The first two categories are then examples of fair shares, or equivalent shares. The activity is a simple extension of the sharing tasks. It is important that students can tell when a region has been separated into a particular type of fractional part.

Activity **15.4**

Correct Shares

Draw regions like the ones in Figure 15.8, showing examples and nonexamples of fractional parts. Have students identify the wholes that are correctly divided into requested fractional parts and those that are not. For each response, have students explain their reasoning. The activity should be done with a variety of models, including length and set models.

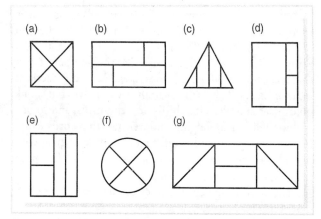

Figure 15.8 Students learning about fractional parts should be able to tell which of these figures are correctly partitioned in fourths. They should also be able to explain why the other figures are not showing fourths.

In the "Correct Shares" activity, it is important to have students explain why they do or do not think the shape is partitioned correctly. The diagrams in the task fall in each of the following categories:

1. Same shape, same size: (a) and (f) [equivalent]
2. Different shape, same size: (e) and (g) [equivalent]
3. Different shape, different size: (b) and (c) [not equivalent]
4. Same shape, different size: (d) [not equivalent]

The "Correct Shares" task is a good formative assessment to see whether students understand that it is the *size* that matters, not the shape. If students only miss (e) and (g), they do not have this concept and you need to plan future tasks that focus on equivalence—for example, asking students to take a square and subdivide a picture themselves, as in Activity 15.5. ◆

Activity 15.5

Finding Fair Shares

Give students dot paper and have them find halves, fourths, or other fractional parts of an enclosed region. The activity is especially interesting when different shapes represent equivalent areas.

Partitioning

Sectioning a shape into equal-sized pieces is called *partitioning*, a major part of developing fraction concepts with young children. In the previous section you were partitioning regions or shapes, which fall under area models. It is also important to partition lengths and quantities. The number line with only 0 and 1 can be used, as well as paper

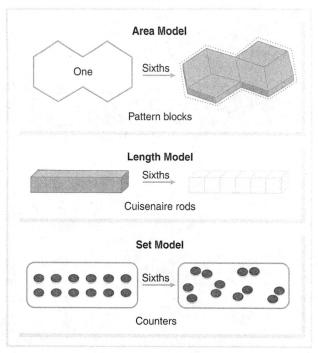

Figure 15.9 Given a whole, find fractional parts.

strips. Students can partition sets of objects such as coins, counters, or baseball cards.

Notice when partitioning sets that children may confuse the number of counters in a share with the name of the share. In the example in Figure 15.9, the 12 counters are partitioned into 6 sets—*sixths*. Each share or part has two counters, but it is the number of shares that makes the partition show *sixths*.

Using Fraction Language and Symbols

Fraction symbols represent a fairly complex convention that is often misleading to children. It is well worth your time to help students develop a strong understanding of what the numerator and denominator of a fraction tell us.

Counting Fraction Parts: Iteration

Counting fractional parts to see how multiple parts compare to the whole creates a foundation for the two parts of a fraction. Students should come to think of counting fractional parts in much the same way as they might count apples or any other objects. If you know the kind of part you are counting, you can tell when you get to one, when you get to two, and so on.

This counting or repeating a piece is called *iterating*. Like partitioning, iterating is an important part of being able to understand and use fractions. There is evidence that an iterative notion of fractions, one that views a fraction such as $\frac{3}{4}$ as a count of three parts called *fourths*, is an important idea for children to develop (Post, Wachsmuth, Lesh, & Behr, 1985; Siebert & Gaskin, 2006; Tzur, 1999). The iterative concept is most clear when focusing on these two ideas about fraction symbols:

- The top number *counts*. (numerator)
- The bottom number tells *what is being counted*. (denominator)

The *what* of fractions are the fractional parts. They can be counted. Fraction symbols are just a shorthand for saying *how many* and *what*.

Iterating makes sense with length models because iteration is much like measuring. Consider that you have a $2\frac{1}{2}$ feet of ribbon and are trying to figure out how many fourths you have. You can draw a strip and start counting (iterating) the fourths:

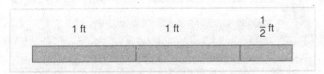

Using a ribbon that is $\frac{1}{4}$ of a foot long as a measuring tool, a student marks off ten-fourths:

Students can participate in many tasks that involve iterating lengths, progressing in increasing difficulty. For example, give the students a strip of paper and tell them that it is $\frac{3}{4}$ of the whole. Ask them to find: $\frac{1}{2}$, $1\frac{1}{2}$, $2\frac{1}{4}$, 3, and so on. To find these, students should partition the piece into three sections to find $\frac{1}{4}$ and then iterate the $\frac{1}{4}$ to find the fractions listed.

Iterating can be done with area models as well. Display some circular fractional pieces in groups as shown in Figure 15.10. For each collection, tell students what type of piece is being shown and simply count them together: "*one*-fourth, *two*-fourths, *three*-fourths, *four*-fourths, *five*-fourths." Ask, "If we have five-fourths, is that more than one whole, less than one whole, or the same as one whole?" To reinforce the piece size even more, you can slightly alter your language to say, "one $\frac{1}{4}$, two $\frac{1}{4}$s, three $\frac{1}{4}$s," and so on.

As students count each collection of parts, discuss the relationship to one whole. Make informal comparisons between different collections. "Why did we get almost two wholes with seven-fourths, and yet we don't even have one whole with ten-twelfths?"

Also take this opportunity to lay verbal groundwork for mixed fractions. "What is another way that we could say seven-thirds?" (Two wholes and one more third or one whole and four-thirds.)

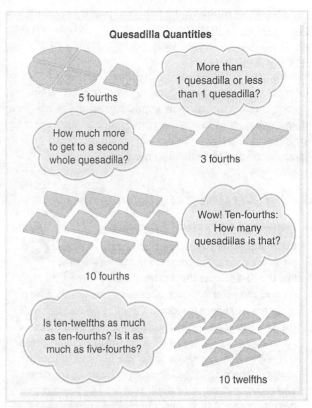

Figure 15.10 Iterating fractional parts in an area model. (See Blackline Masters 24–26.)

With this introduction, students are ready for the following task.

Activity 15.6

More, Less, or Equal to One Whole

Give students a collection of fractional parts (all the same size pieces) and indicate the kind of fractional part they have. Parts can be drawn on a worksheet or physical models can be placed in plastic baggies with an identifying card. For example, if done with Cuisenaire rods or fraction strips, the collection might have seven light green rods/strips with a caption or note indicating "each piece is $\frac{1}{8}$." The task is to decide if the collection is less than one whole, equal to one whole, or more than one whole. Ask students to draw pictures or use symbols to explain their answer.

Try Activity 15.6 with several different fraction models and then with no model, using mental imagery only. Iteration can also be done with set models, although this can be confusing for students. For example, show a collection of two-color counters and ask questions such as, "If 5 counters is one-fourth, how much is 15 counters?"

Other questions can be engaging puzzles for students. For example: "Three counters represent $\frac{1}{8}$ of my set; how big is my set?" "Twenty counters represents $\frac{2}{3}$ of my set; how big is my set?"

Similar activities can be adapted to meet a range of learners. For example, adding a context such as people, candy, crayons, or an item familiar to students will help them understand the problem. Students who are very strong at doing these puzzles can create their own "puzzle statements" and pose them to the class.

Activity 15.7

Calculator Fraction Counting

Calculators that permit fraction entries and displays are now quite common in schools. Many, like the TI-15, now display fractions in correct fraction format and offer a choice of showing results as mixed numbers or simple fractions. Counting by fourths with the TI-15 is done by first storing $\frac{1}{4}$ in one of the two operation keys: Op1 + 1 n 4 d Op1. To count, press 0 Op1 Op1 Op1, repeating to get the number of fourths wanted. The display will show the counts by fourths and also the number of times that the Op1 key has been pressed. Ask students questions such as the following: "How many $\frac{1}{4}$s to get to 3?" "How many $\frac{1}{5}$s to get to 5?" These can get increasingly more challenging: "How many $\frac{1}{4}$s to get to $4\frac{1}{2}$?" "How many $\frac{2}{3}$s to get to 6? Estimate and then count by $\frac{2}{3}$s on the calculator." Students should coordinate their counts with fraction models, adding a new fourths piece to the pile with each count. At any time, the display can be shifted from mixed form to simple fractions with a press of a key. The TI-15 can be set so that it will not simplify fractions automatically, the appropriate setting prior to the introduction of equivalent fractions.

Fraction calculators provide a powerful way to help children develop fractional symbolism. A variation on Activity 15.7 is to show children a mixed number such as $3\frac{1}{8}$ and ask how many counts of $\frac{1}{8}$ on the calculator it will take to count that high. The students should try to stop at the correct number ($\frac{25}{8}$) before pressing the mixed-number key.

Fraction Notation

After experiences with partitioning and iterating, students are ready to learn the symbolic notations for fractions. The way that we write fractions with a top and a bottom number and a bar between is a convention—an arbitrary agreement for how to represent fractions, so it is one of the concepts that you simply tell students. However, understanding of the convention can be clarified by giving a demonstra-

tion that will encourage students to tell *you* what the top and bottom numbers stand for. The following procedure is recommended even if your students have been "using" symbolic fractions for several years.

Display several collections of fractional parts in a manner similar to those in Figure 15.10. Have students count the parts together. After each count, write the correct fraction, indicating that this is how it is written as a symbol. Include sets that are more than one, but write them as simple or "improper" fractions and not as mixed numbers. Include at least two pairs of sets with the same numerators such as $\frac{4}{8}$ and $\frac{4}{3}$. Likewise, include sets with the same denominators. After the class has counted and you have written the fraction for at least six sets of fractional parts, pose the following questions:

> What does the bottom number in a fraction tell us?
> What does the top number in a fraction tell us?

❚❚ ——————— *Pause and Reflect*

Imagine counting a set of 5 eighths and a set of 5 fourths and writing the fractions for these sets. Use children's language in your formulations and try to come up with a way to explain what the numbers on top and on the bottom mean.

Here are some likely explanations for the top and bottom numbers from second or third graders.

- *Top number:* This is the counting number. It tells how many shares or parts we have. It tells how many have been counted. It tells how many parts we are talking about. It counts the parts or shares.
- *Bottom number:* This tells what is being counted. It tells how big the part is. If it is a 4, it means we are counting *fourths;* if it is a 6, we are counting *sixths;* and so on.

This formulation of the meanings of the numerator and denominator may seem unusual to you. It is often said that the top number tells "how many." (This phrase seems unfinished. How many *what*?) The bottom number is said to tell "how many parts it takes to make a whole." This may be correct but can be misleading. For example, a $\frac{1}{6}$ piece is often cut from a cake without making any slices in the remaining $\frac{5}{6}$ of the cake. That the cake is only in two pieces does not change the fact that the piece taken is $\frac{1}{6}$. Or if a pizza is cut in 12 pieces, two pieces still make $\frac{1}{6}$ of the pizza. In neither of these instances does the bottom number tell how many pieces make a whole.

Fractions Greater Than 1

In the previous section, fractions less than and greater than 1 were mixed together. This was done intentionally and should similarly be done with students as they are learning fractions. Too often students aren't exposed to numbers greater than one (e.g., $\frac{5}{2}$ or $4\frac{1}{4}$) and then when they are added into the mix (no pun intended!), students find them confusing.

The term *improper fraction* is used to describe fractions such as $\frac{5}{2}$ that are greater than one. This term can be a source of confusion as the word *improper* implies that this representation is not acceptable, which is not the case at all—in fact, in algebra it is often the preferred representation. Instead, try not to use this phrase and instead use "fractions" or "fractions greater than 1." If you do use the term (because it is in the state standards, for example), then be sure to share with students that it is really not improper to write fractions greater than one as a single fraction.

In the fourth National Assessment of Educational Progress, about 80 percent of seventh graders could change a mixed number to an improper fraction, but fewer than half knew that $5\frac{1}{4}$ was the same as $5 + \frac{1}{4}$ (Kouba et al., 1988a). The result indicates that many children are using procedures without understanding them.

If you have counted fractional parts beyond a whole, as in the previous section, your students already know how to write $\frac{13}{6}$ or $\frac{13}{5}$. Ask students to use a model to illustrate these values and find equivalent representations. Neumer (2007), a fifth-grade teacher, found that using Unifix cubes (Multilink cubes could also be used) was the most effective way to help students see both forms for recording fractions greater than 1. Figure 15.11 illustrates how to use Unifix cubes. Students identify one cube as the unit fraction ($\frac{1}{5}$) for the problem ($\frac{12}{5}$). They count out 12 fifths and build wholes. Conversely, they could start with the mixed number, build it, and find out how many total cubes (or fifths) were used. This procedure is an example of a length model. Repeated experiences in building and solving these tasks will lead students to see a pattern of multiplication and division that closely resembles the algorithm for moving between these two forms.

Context can help students understand the equivalency of these two ways to record fractions, which is the focus of Activity 15.8.

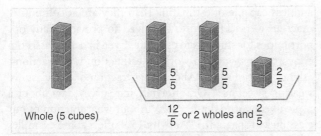

Figure 15.11 Unifix cubes are used to represent the equivalence of $\frac{12}{5}$ and $2\frac{2}{5}$.

Whole (5 cubes)

$\frac{12}{5}$ or 2 wholes and $\frac{2}{5}$

$\frac{5}{5}$ $\frac{5}{5}$ $\frac{2}{5}$

Activity 15.8

Pitchers and Cups

Show students a pitcher that can hold enough to fill six cups with juice. You can even use an actual pitcher and actual cups for sharing with the class. Ask questions such as the following: "If I have $3\frac{1}{2}$ pitchers, how many cups will I be able to fill?" "If we have 16 students in our class, how many pitchers will I need?" Alter the amount the pitcher can hold to involve other fractions.

After a while, challenge students to figure out the two equivalent forms without using models. A good explanation for $3\frac{1}{4}$ might be that there are 4 fourths in one whole, so there are 8 fourths in two wholes and 12 fourths in three wholes. The extra fourth makes 13 fourths in all, or $\frac{13}{4}$. (Note the iteration concept playing a role.)

Do not push the traditional algorithm (multiply the bottom by the whole number and add the top) as it can interfere with students making sense of the relationship between the two and their equivalency. This procedure can readily be developed by the students in their own words and with complete understanding by looking at patterns in their work.

Assessing Understanding

Present exercises that ask students to demonstrate their understanding of fractional parts as well as the meanings of the top and bottom numbers in a fraction. Models are used to represent wholes and parts of wholes. Examples of each type of exercise are provided in Figures 15.12 and 15.13. Each figure includes examples with a region model (freely drawn rectangles), a length model (Cuisenaire rods or fraction strips), and set model (counters).

— Pause and Reflect

Work through the exercises in Figure 15.2 and 15.3. If you do not have access to rods or counters, just draw lines or circles. What can you learn about student understanding if they are able to solve problems in 15.12 but not 15.13? What if students are able to use paper but not the Cuisenaire rods? If students are stuck, what contexts for each model can be used to support their thinking?

Two or three challenging parts-and-whole questions can make an excellent performance assessment. The tasks should be presented to the class in just the same form as in the figures. Physical models are often the best way to present the tasks so that students can use a trial-and-error approach to determine their results. As with all tasks, it should be clear that an explanation is required to justify each answer. As students build their solutions, you can walk

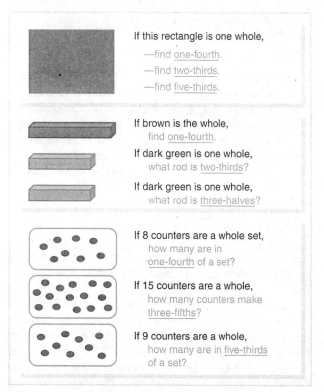

Figure 15.12 Given the whole and the fraction, find the part.

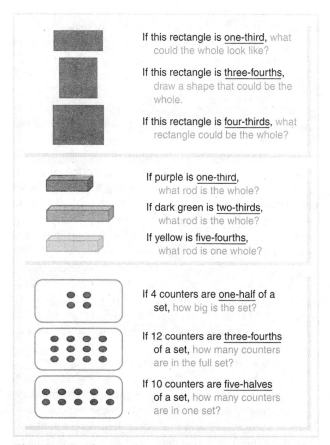

Figure 15.13 Given the part and the fraction, find the whole.

around observing and asking questions to assess students' understanding.

As noted throughout this book, it is a good idea to create simple story problems or contexts that ask the same questions.

Mr. Samuels has finished $\frac{3}{4}$ of his patio. It looks like this:

Draw a picture that might be the shape of the finished patio.

Questions involving unit fractions are generally the easiest. The hardest questions usually involve fractions greater than 1. For example, *If 15 chips are five-thirds of one whole set, how many chips are in a whole set?* However, in every question, the unit fraction plays a significant role. If you have $\frac{5}{3}$ and want the whole, you first need to find $\frac{1}{3}$.

The parts-and-whole questions are challenging yet very effective at helping students reflect on the meanings of the numerator and denominator. They also are a good diagnostic assessment to see if students really understand the meanings of the numerator and denominator since the

tasks require students to *use* those meanings, not simply recite a definition.

Estimating with Fractions

The focus on fractional parts is an important beginning, but number sense with fractions demands more—it requires that students have some intuitive feel for fractions. They should know "about" how big a particular fraction is and be able to tell easily which of two fractions is larger.

Like with whole numbers, students are less confident and less capable of estimating than they are at computing exact answers. Therefore, you need to provide many opportunities for students to estimate. Even in daily classroom conversations, you can work on estimation with fractions, asking questions like "About what fraction of our class are wearing sweaters?" Or, after tallying survey data about a topic like favorite dinner, ask, "About what fraction of our class picked spaghetti?" Activity 15.9 offers some examples of visual estimating activities.

Activity 15.9

About How Much?

Draw a picture like one of those in Figure 15.14 (or prepare some ahead of time for the overhead). Have each student write down a fraction that he or she thinks is a good estimate of the amount shown (or the indicated mark on the number line). Listen to the ideas of several students, and ask them whether a particular estimate is a good one. There is no single correct answer, but estimates should be "in the ballpark." If children have difficulty coming up with an estimate, ask whether they think the amount is closer to 0, $\frac{1}{2}$, or 1.

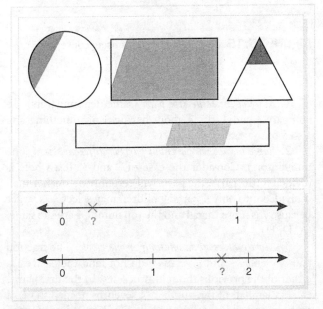

Figure 15.14 About how much? Name a fraction for each drawing and explain why you chose that fraction.

Benchmarks of Zero, One-Half, and One

As suggested in Activity 15.9, the most important reference points or benchmarks for fractions are 0, $\frac{1}{2}$, and 1. For fractions less than 1, simply comparing them to these three numbers gives quite a lot of information. For example, $\frac{3}{20}$ is small, close to 0, whereas $\frac{3}{4}$ is between $\frac{1}{2}$ and 1. The fraction $\frac{9}{10}$ is quite close to 1. Since any fraction greater than 1 is a whole number plus an amount less than 1, the same reference points are just as helpful: $3\frac{3}{7}$ is almost $3\frac{1}{2}$.

Activity 15.10

Zero, One-Half, or One

On a set of cards, write a collection of 10 to 15 fractions, one per card. A few should be greater than 1

($\frac{9}{8}$ or $\frac{11}{10}$), with the others ranging from 0 to 1. Let students sort the fractions into three groups: those close to 0, close to $\frac{1}{2}$, and close to 1. For those close to $\frac{1}{2}$, have them decide if the fraction is more or less than $\frac{1}{2}$. The difficulty of this task largely depends on the fractions. The first time you try this, use fractions such as $\frac{1}{20}$, $\frac{53}{100}$, or $\frac{9}{10}$ that are very close to the three benchmarks. On subsequent days, mostly use fractions with denominators less than 20. You might include one or two fractions such as $\frac{2}{8}$ or $\frac{3}{4}$ that are exactly in between the benchmarks. Ask students to explain how they are using the numerator and denominator to decide.

The next activity is also aimed at developing the same three reference points for fractions. In "Close Fractions," however, the students must come up with the fractions rather than sort fractions already provided.

Activity 15.11

Close Fractions

Have your students name a fraction that is close to 1 but not more than 1. Next have them name another fraction that is even closer to 1 than the first. For the second response, they have to explain why they believe the fraction is closer to 1 than the previous fraction. Continue for several fractions in the same manner, each one being closer to 1 than the previous fraction. Similarly, try close to 0 or close to $\frac{1}{2}$ (either under or over). The first several times you try this activity, let the students use models to help with their thinking. Later, see how well their explanations work when they cannot use models or drawings.

Focus discussions on the important idea that there are infinitely many fractions, so they can always find one in between.

Using Number Sense to Compare

The ability to tell which of two fractions is greater is another aspect of number sense with fractions. That ability is built around concepts of fractions, not on an algorithmic skill or symbolic tricks. In the 2000 NAEP test, only 21 percent of fourth-grade students could explain why one unit fraction was larger or smaller than another—for example, $\frac{1}{5}$ and $\frac{1}{4}$ (Kloosterman et al., 2004). For eighth graders, only 41 percent were able to correctly order three fractions given in simplified form (Sowder, Wearne, Martin, & Strutchens, 2004). As these researchers note, "How students can work meaningfully with fractions if they do not have a sense of the relative size of the fractions is difficult to imagine" (p. 116).

Comparing Unit Fractions. Children have a tremendously strong mind-set about numbers, which can cause difficulties with the relative size of fractions. In their experience, larger numbers mean "more," which can translate to: "Seven is more than four, so sevenths should be bigger than fourths" (Mack, 1995). The inverse relationship between number of parts and size of parts cannot be told but must be a creation of each student's own thought process through many experiences.

Activity 15.12

Ordering Unit Fractions

List a set of unit fractions such as $\frac{1}{3}$, $\frac{1}{8}$, $\frac{1}{5}$, and $\frac{1}{10}$. Ask children to put the fractions in order from least to most. Challenge children to defend the way they ordered the fractions. The first few times you do this activity, have them illustrate their ideas by using models.

Students may notice that larger bottom numbers mean smaller fractions, but this is not a rule to be memorized. Revisit this basic idea periodically. Children will seem to understand one day and revert to their more comfortable ideas about big numbers a day or two later. Repeat Activity 15.12 with all numerators equal to some number other than 1. You may be surprised to see that this is much harder for students.

Comparing Any Fractions. You have probably learned rules or algorithms for comparing two fractions. The usual approaches are finding common denominators and using cross-multiplication. These rules can be effective in getting correct answers but require no thought about the size of the fractions. If children are taught these rules before they have had the opportunity to think about the relative sizes of various fractions, there is little chance that they will develop any familiarity with or number sense about fraction size. Comparison activities (which fraction is more?) can play a significant role in helping children develop concepts of relative fraction sizes. Reflective thought is the goal, not an algorithmic method of choosing the correct answer.

Pause and Reflect

Assume for a moment that you do not know the common denominators or cross-multiplication techniques. Now examine the pairs of fractions in Figure 15.15 and select the larger of each pair using a reasoning approach that a fourth grader might use.

The following numbered list shows ways that the fractions in Figure 15.15 might have been compared:

Which fraction in each pair is greater?
Give one or more reasons. Try not to use drawings or models.
Do not use common denominators or cross-multiplication.

A.	$\frac{4}{5}$ or $\frac{4}{9}$	G.	$\frac{7}{12}$ or $\frac{5}{12}$
B.	$\frac{4}{7}$ or $\frac{5}{7}$	H.	$\frac{3}{5}$ or $\frac{3}{7}$
C.	$\frac{3}{8}$ or $\frac{4}{10}$	I.	$\frac{5}{8}$ or $\frac{6}{10}$
D.	$\frac{5}{3}$ or $\frac{5}{8}$	J.	$\frac{9}{8}$ or $\frac{4}{3}$
E.	$\frac{3}{4}$ or $\frac{9}{10}$	K.	$\frac{4}{6}$ or $\frac{7}{12}$
F.	$\frac{3}{8}$ or $\frac{4}{7}$	L.	$\frac{8}{9}$ or $\frac{7}{8}$

Figure 15.15 Comparing fractions using concepts.

1. *More of the same-size parts* (same denominators). To compare $\frac{3}{8}$ and $\frac{5}{8}$, think about having 3 of something and also 5 of the same thing. (B, G)

2. *Same number of parts but parts of different sizes* (same numerators). Consider the case of $\frac{3}{4}$ and $\frac{3}{7}$. If a whole is divided into 7 parts, the parts will certainly be smaller than if divided into only 4 parts. Children may select $\frac{3}{7}$ as larger because 7 is more than 4 and the top numbers are the same. (A, D, H)

3. *More and less than one-half or one whole.* The fraction pairs $\frac{3}{7}$ versus $\frac{5}{8}$ and $\frac{5}{4}$ versus $\frac{7}{8}$ do not lend themselves to either of the previous thought processes. In the first pair, $\frac{3}{7}$ is less than half of the number of sevenths needed to make a whole, and so $\frac{3}{7}$ is less than a half. Similarly, $\frac{5}{8}$ is more than a half. Therefore, $\frac{5}{8}$ is the larger fraction. The second pair is determined by noting that one fraction is less than 1 and the other is greater than 1. (A, D, F, G, H)

4. *Closeness to one-half or one whole.* Why is $\frac{9}{10}$ greater than $\frac{3}{4}$? Each is one fractional part away from one whole, and tenths are smaller than fourths. Similarly, notice that $\frac{5}{8}$ is smaller than $\frac{4}{6}$ because it is only one-eighth more than a half, while $\frac{4}{6}$ is a sixth more than a half. Can you use this basic idea to compare $\frac{3}{5}$ and $\frac{5}{9}$? (*Hint:* Each is half of a fractional part more than $\frac{1}{2}$.) Also try $\frac{5}{7}$ and $\frac{7}{9}$. (C, E, I, J, K, L)

How did your reasons for choosing fractions in Figure 15.15 compare to these ideas? It is important that you are comfortable with these informal comparison strategies as a major component of your own number sense as well as for helping children develop theirs. Notice that some of the comparisons, such as D and H, could have been solved using more than one of the strategies listed.

Tasks you design for your students should assist them in developing these and possibly other methods of comparing two fractions. It is important that the ideas come from your students and their discussions. To teach "the four ways to compare fractions" would be adding four more mysterious rules and defeats the purpose of encouraging students to apply their number sense.

To develop these methods for comparing fractions, select pairs of fractions that will likely elicit desired comparison strategies. On one day, for example, you might have two pairs with the same denominators and one with the same numerators. On another day, you might pick fraction pairs in which each fraction is exactly one part away from a whole. Try to build strategies over several days by the strategic choice of fraction pairs.

The use of a region or number-line model may help students who are struggling to reason mentally. Place greater emphasis on students' reasoning and connect it to the visual models.

The next activity extends the comparison task a bit more.

Activity 15.13

Line 'Em Up

Select four or five fractions for students to put in order from least to greatest. Have them indicate approximately where each fraction belongs on a number line labeled only with the points 0 and 1. Adding-machine paper can be used as the number line. Students can compare their lines with others and explain how they decided where to place the fractions.

To place fractions on the number line, students must also make estimates of fraction size in addition to simply ordering the fractions.

Including Equivalent Fractions. The discussion to this point has somewhat artificially ignored the idea that students might use equivalent-fraction concepts in making comparisons. Equivalent-fraction concepts are such an important idea that the entire following section is devoted to the development of that idea. However, equivalent-fraction concepts need not be put off until last and certainly should be embedded in the discussions of which fraction is more.

Smith (2002) suggests that the comparison question to ask is "Which of the following two (or more) fractions is greater, *or are they equal*?" (p. 9, emphasis added). He points out that this question leaves open the possibility that two fractions that may look different can, in fact, be equal.

In addition to this point, with equivalent fraction concepts, students can adjust how a fraction looks so that they can use ideas that make sense to them. Burns (1999) describes how fifth graders compared $\frac{6}{8}$ to $\frac{4}{5}$. (You might want to stop for a moment and think how you would compare these fractions.) One child changed the $\frac{4}{5}$ to $\frac{8}{10}$ so that

both fractions would be two parts away from the whole and he reasoned from there. Another changed both fractions to a common *numerator* of 12.

Be absolutely certain to revisit the comparison activities and include pairs such as $\frac{8}{12}$ and $\frac{2}{3}$ in which the fractions are equal but do not appear to be.

Equivalent-Fraction Concepts

As discussed in Chapter 14, equivalence is a critical but often poorly misunderstood concept. This is particularly true with fraction equivalence.

Conceptual Focus on Equivalence

 ——————— *Pause and Reflect*

How do you know that $\frac{4}{6} = \frac{2}{3}$? Before reading further, think of at least two different explanations.

Here are some possible answers to the above question.

1. They are the same because you can simplify $\frac{4}{6}$ and get $\frac{2}{3}$.
2. If you have a set of 6 items and you take 4 of them, that would be $\frac{4}{6}$. But you can make the 6 into 3 groups and the 4 would be 2 groups out of the 3 groups. That means it's $\frac{2}{3}$.

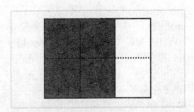

3. If you start with $\frac{2}{3}$, you can multiply the top and the bottom numbers by 2, and that will give you $\frac{4}{6}$, so they are equal.
4. If you had a square cut into 3 parts and you shaded 2, that would be $\frac{2}{3}$ shaded. If you cut all 3 of these parts in half, that would be 4 parts shaded and 6 parts in all. That's $\frac{4}{6}$, and it would be the same amount.

All of these answers are correct. But let's think about what they tell us. Responses 2 and 4 are conceptual, although not as efficient. The procedural responses, 1 and 3, are efficient but do not indicate conceptual understanding. All students should eventually be able to write an equivalent fraction for a given fraction. At the same time, the procedures should never be taught or used until the students understand what the result means. Consider how different the procedure and the concept appear to be.

Concept: Two fractions are equivalent if they are representations for the same amount or quantity—if they are the same number.

Algorithm: To get an equivalent fraction, multiply (or divide) the top and bottom numbers by the same nonzero number.

In a problem-based classroom, students can develop an understanding of equivalent fractions and also develop from that understanding a conceptually based algorithm. As with most algorithms, it is a serious instructional error to rush too quickly to the rule. Be patient! Intuitive methods are always best at first.

Equivalent-Fraction Models

The general approach to helping students create an understanding of equivalent fractions is to have them use contexts and models to find different names for a fraction. Consider that this is the first time in their experience that a fixed quantity can have multiple names (actually an infinite number). The following activities are possible starting places.

Activity 15.14

Different Fillers

Using a region model for fractions that is familiar to your students, prepare a worksheet with two or at most three outlines of different fractions, as in Figure 15.16. Do not limit yourself to unit fractions. For example, if the model is circular fraction pieces, you might draw an outline for $\frac{2}{3}$, $\frac{1}{2}$, and $\frac{3}{4}$. The students' task is to use their own fraction pieces to find as many equivalent fractions for the region as possible. After completing the three examples, have students write about the ideas or patterns they may have noticed in finding the names. Follow the activity with a class discussion.

In the class discussion following the "Different Fillers" activity, a good question to ask involves what names could be found if students had other sized pieces. For example, ask students "What equivalent fractions could you find if we had sixteenths in our fraction kit? What names could you find if you could have a piece of any size at all?"

The following activity is a variation of "Different Fillers." Instead of using a manipulative, the task is constructed on dot paper.

Activity 15.15

Dot Paper Equivalencies

Create a worksheet using a portion of either isometric or square dot grid paper (see Blackline Masters 37–40).

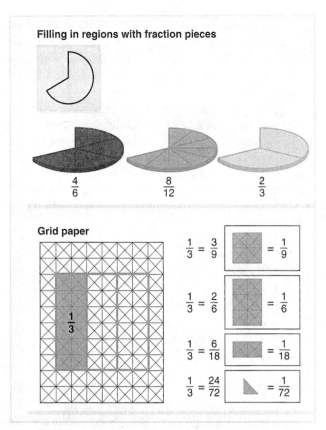

Figure 15.16 Area models for equivalent fractions.

On the grid, draw the outline of a region and designate it as one whole. Draw a part of the region within the whole. The task is to use different parts of the whole determined by the grid to find names for the part. See Figure 15.16, which includes an example drawn on an isometric grid. Students should draw a picture of the unit fractional part that they use for each fraction name. The larger the size of the whole, the more names the activity will generate.

The "Dot Paper Equivalencies" activity is a form of what Lamon (2002) calls "unitizing," that is, given a quantity, finding different ways to chunk the quantity into parts in order to name it. She points out that this is a key ability related not only to equivalent fractions but also to proportional reasoning, especially in the comparison of ratios. (See also Lamon, 1999a,b.)

Length models can be used to create activities similar to the "Different Fillers" task. For example, as shown in Figure 15.17, rods or paper strips can be used to designate both a whole and a part. Students use smaller rods to find fraction names for the given part. To have larger wholes and,

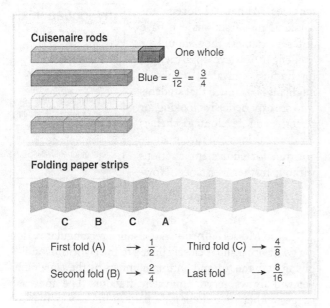

Figure 15.17 Length models for equivalent fractions.

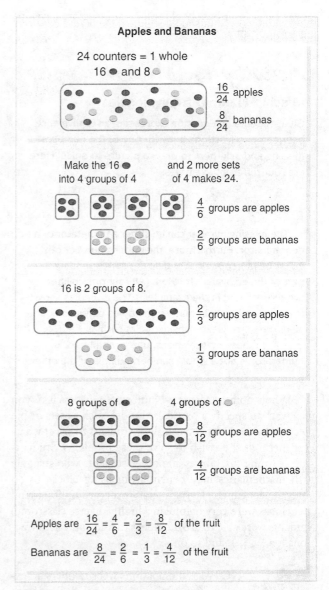

Figure 15.18 Set models for illustrating equivalent fractions.

thus, more possible parts, use a train of two or three rods for the whole and the part. Folding paper strips is another method of creating fraction names. In the example shown in Figure 15.17, one-half is subdivided by successive folding in half. Other folds would produce other names and these possibilities should be discussed if no one tries to fold the strip in an odd number of parts.

The following activity is also a unitizing activity in which students look for different units or chunks of the whole in order to name a part of the whole in different ways. This activity utilizes a set model.

Activity 15.16

Apples and Bananas

Have students set out a specific number of counters in two colors—for example, 24 counters, 16 of them red (apples) and 8 yellow (bananas). The 24 make up the whole. The task is to group the counters into different fractional parts of the whole and use the parts to create fraction names for the fractions that are apples and fractions that are bananas. In Figure 15.18, 24 counters are arranged in different groups. You might also suggest arrays (see Figure 15.19).

In Lamon's version of the latter activity, she prompts students with questions such as "If we make groups of four, what part of the set is red?" With these prompts you can suggest fraction names that students are unlikely to think of.

In the activities so far, there has only been a hint of a rule for finding equivalent fractions. The following activity

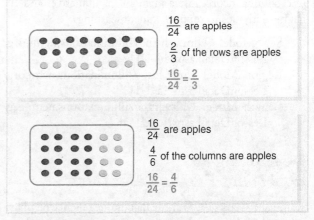

Figure 15.19 Arrays for illustrating equivalent fractions.

moves a bit closer but should still be done before developing an algorithm.

Activity 15.17

Missing-Number Equivalencies

Give students an equation expressing an equivalence between two fractions but with one of the numbers missing and ask them to draw a picture to solve. Here are four different examples:

$$\frac{5}{3} = \frac{\square}{6} \qquad \frac{2}{3} = \frac{6}{\square} \qquad \frac{8}{12} = \frac{\square}{3} \qquad \frac{9}{12} = \frac{3}{\square}$$

The missing number can be either a numerator or a denominator. Furthermore, the missing number can either be larger or smaller than the corresponding part of the equivalent fraction. (All four possibilities are represented in the examples.) The examples shown involve simple whole-number multiples between equivalent fractions. Next, consider pairs such as $\frac{6}{8} = \frac{\square}{12}$ or $\frac{9}{12} = \frac{6}{\square}$. In these equivalencies, one denominator or numerator is not a whole number multiple of the other.

When doing "Missing-Number Equivalencies" you may want to specify a particular model, such as sets or pie pieces. Alternatively, you can allow students to select whatever methods they wish to solve these problems. Students with learning disabilities and other students who struggle with mathematics may benefit from using clocks to do equivalence. Chick, Tierney, and Storeygard (2007) found that clocks were very helpful in a highly diverse classroom. Students were able to use the clocks to find equivalent fractions for $\frac{10}{12}$, $\frac{3}{4}$, $\frac{4}{6}$, and so on.

 NCTM's Illuminations website offers an excellent set of three units called "Fun with Fractions." Each unit uses one of the model types (set, region, or length) and focuses on comparing and ordering fractions and equivalency. The five to six lessons in each unit incorporate a range of manipulatives and engaging activities to support student learning.

Set Model Unit: http://illuminations.nctm.org/ LessonDetail.aspx?id=U112

Region Model Unit: http://illuminations.nctm.org/ LessonDetail.aspx?id=U113

Length Model Unit: http://illuminations.nctm.org/ LessonDetail.aspx?id=U152 ◆

Developing an Equivalent-Fraction Algorithm

Kamii and Clark (1995) argue that undue reliance on physical models does not help children construct equivalence

schemes. When children understand that fractions can have different names, they should be challenged to develop a method for finding equivalent names. It might also be argued that students who are experienced at looking for patterns and developing schemes for doing things can invent an algorithm for equivalent fractions without further assistance. However, the following approach will certainly improve the chances of that happening.

A Region Model Approach. Using a rectangular region is a good visual and is closely linked to the algorithm: multiplying both the top and bottom numbers by the same number will always get an equivalent fraction. The approach suggested here is to look for a pattern in the way that the fractional parts in both the part as well as the whole are counted. Activity 15.18 is a beginning, but a good class discussion following the activity will also be required.

myeducationlab

Go to the Activities and Application section of Chapter 15 of MyEducationLab. Click on Videos and watch the video entitled "**John Van de Walle on Developing an Equivalent-Fraction Algorithm**" to see him work with teachers to develop an algorithm for equivalent-fraction problems.

Activity 15.18

Slicing Squares

Give students a worksheet with four squares in a row, each approximately 3 cm on a side. Have them shade in the same fraction in each square using vertical dividing lines. You can use the context of a garden or farm. For example, slice each square in fourths and shade three-fourths as in Figure 15.20. Next, tell students to slice each square into equal-sized horizontal slices. Each square must be partitioned differently, using from one to eight slices. For each sliced square, they record an equation showing the equivalent fractions. Have them examine their equations and drawings to look for any patterns. You can repeat this with four more squares and a different fraction.

Following this activity, write on the board the equations for four or five different fraction names found by the students. Discuss any patterns they discovered. To focus the discussion, show on the overhead a square illustrating $\frac{4}{5}$ made with vertical slices as in Figure 15.21. Turn off the overhead and slice the square into six parts in the opposite direction. Cover all but two edges of the square as shown in the figure. Ask, "What is the new name for my $\frac{4}{5}$?"

The reason for this exercise is that many students simply count the small regions and never think to use multiplication. With the covered square, students can see that there are four columns and six rows to the shaded part, so there must be 4×6 parts shaded. Similarly, there must be

Start with each square showing $\frac{3}{4}$.

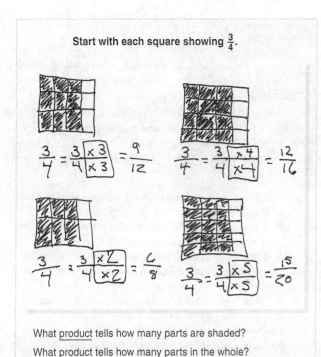

$$\frac{3}{4} = \frac{3}{4}\boxed{\begin{array}{c}\times 3\\ \times 3\end{array}} = \frac{9}{12}$$

$$\frac{3}{4} = \frac{3}{4}\boxed{\begin{array}{c}\times 4\\ \times 4\end{array}} = \frac{12}{16}$$

$$\frac{3}{4} = \frac{3}{4}\boxed{\begin{array}{c}\times 2\\ \times 2\end{array}} = \frac{6}{8}$$

$$\frac{3}{4} = \frac{3}{4}\boxed{\begin{array}{c}\times 5\\ \times 5\end{array}} = \frac{15}{20}$$

What <u>product</u> tells how many parts are shaded?

What <u>product</u> tells how many parts in the whole?

Notice that the same factor is used for both part and whole.

Figure 15.20 A model for developing the equivalent-fraction algorithm.

5×6 parts in the whole. Therefore, the new name for $\frac{4}{5}$ is $\frac{4 \times 6}{5 \times 6}$, or $\frac{24}{30}$.

Using this idea, have students return to the fractions on their worksheet to see if the pattern works for other fractions.

Examine examples of equivalent fractions that have been generated with other models, and see if the rule of multiplying top and bottom numbers by the same number holds there also. If the rule is correct, how can $\frac{6}{8}$ and $\frac{9}{12}$ be equivalent?

Writing Fractions in Simplest Terms. The multiplication scheme for equivalent fractions produces fractions with larger denominators. To write a fraction in *simplest*

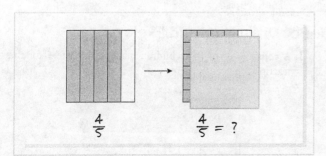

$$\frac{4}{5} \qquad \frac{4}{5} = ?$$

Figure 15.21 How can you count the fractional parts if you cannot see them all?

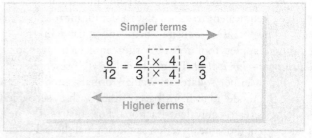

Figure 15.22 Using the equivalent-fraction algorithm to write fractions in simplest terms.

terms means to write it so that numerator and denominator have no common whole-number factors. (Some texts use the name *lowest terms* instead of *simplest terms*.) One meaningful approach to this task of finding simplest terms is to reverse the earlier process, as illustrated in Figure 15.22. The search for a common factor or a simplified fraction should be connected to grouping.

Two additional notes:

1. Notice that the phrase *reducing fractions* was not used. This terminology implies making a fraction smaller and is rarely used anymore in textbooks. Fractions are simplified, not reduced.

2. Teachers may tell students that fraction answers are incorrect if not in simplest or lowest terms. This also misinforms students about the equivalency of fractions. When students add $\frac{1}{6} + \frac{1}{2}$ both $\frac{2}{3}$ and $\frac{4}{6}$ are correct. It is best to reinforce that they are both correct and are equivalent.

Multiplying by One. Many middle school textbooks use a strictly symbolic approach to equivalent fractions. It is based on the multiplicative property that says that any number multiplied by 1 remains unchanged. Any fraction of the form $\frac{n}{n}$ can be used as the identity element. Therefore, $\frac{3}{4} = \frac{3}{4} \times 1 = \frac{3}{4} \times \frac{2}{2} = \frac{6}{8}$. Furthermore, the numerator and denominator of the identity element can also be fractions. In this way, $\frac{6}{12} = \frac{6}{12} \times \left(\frac{1/6}{1/6}\right) = \frac{1}{2}$.

This explanation relies on an understanding of the multiplicative identity property, which most students in grades 4 to 6 do not fully appreciate. It also relies on the procedure for multiplying two fractions. Finally, the argument uses solely deductive reasoning based on an axiom of the rational number system. It does not lend itself to intuitive modeling. A reasonable conclusion is to delay this important explanation until at least seventh or eighth grade in an appropriate prealgebra context and not as a method or a rationale for producing equivalent fractions.

 In the NCTM e-Examples (http://standards .ctm.org/document/eexamples/index.htm), there is a motivating fraction game for two players (Applet 5.1, *Communicating about Mathematics Using*

Games). The game uses a number-line model, and knowledge of equivalent fractions plays a significant role.

The NLVM website (http://nlvm.usu.edu) has a limited applet tool for exploring equivalent fractions, *Fractions—Equivalent*. Proper fractions are presented randomly in either square or circular formats. Students can slice the model in as many parts as they wish to see which slicings create equivalent fractions. For squares, the new slices go in the same direction as the original slices. For circles, it is a bit hard to distinguish new slices from old. Students enter an equivalent fraction and then click a button to check their response. ◆

Teaching Considerations for Fraction Concepts

Because the teaching of fractions is so important, and because fractions are often not well understood even by adults, a recap of the big ideas is needed. Hopefully you have recognized that one reason fractions are not well understood is that there is a lot to know about them—from part-whole relationships to division. In addition, building understanding means representing across area, length, and set models—and including contexts that fit these models. Using estimation activities can

> **myeducationlab**
>
> Go to the Building Teaching Skills and Dispositions section of Chapter 15 of MyEducationLab. Click on Videos and watch the video entitled **"A Lesson on Fractions"** to see a class use fraction pieces to learn about equivalent fractions.

support student understanding of fractions and is an important skill in and of itself.

Equivalence is a central idea for which students must have sound understanding and skill. Connecting visuals with the procedure and not rushing the algorithm too soon are important aspects of the process.

Clarke, Roche, and Mitchell (2008), well-known researchers of fraction teaching and learning, offer "10 Practical Tips for Making Fractions Come Alive and Make Sense." These tips are listed here as an effective summary of this chapter:

1. Give a greater emphasis to the meaning of fractions than on the procedures for manipulating them.
2. Develop a generalizable rule for explaining the numerator and denominator of a fraction.
3. Emphasize that fractions are numbers, making extensive use of number lines in representing fractions and decimals.
4. Take opportunities early to focus on improper fractions and equivalencies.
5. Provide a variety of models to represent fractions.
6. Link fractions to key benchmarks and encourage estimation.
7. Give emphasis to fractions as division.
8. Link fractions, decimals, and percents wherever possible.
9. Take the opportunity to interview several students one on one . . . to gain awareness of their thinking strategies.
10. Look for examples and activities that can engage students in thinking about fractions in particular and rational number ideas in general. (pp. 374–378)

Reflections on Chapter 15

Writing to Learn

1. Describe what is meant by sharing activities. What is the goal of these activities? When would you implement them?
2. Give examples of manipulatives within each of the three categories of fraction models.
3. What does partitioning mean? Explain and illustrate.
4. What does iteration mean? Explain and illustrate.
5. Describe how a student might explain what the numerator and denominator mean.
6. What are two ways you can support students' development of estimating with fractions?
7. Describe two ways to compare $\frac{5}{12}$ and $\frac{5}{8}$ (not common denominator or cross-product methods).
8. What are two ways to build the conceptual relationship between $\frac{11}{4}$ and $2\frac{3}{4}$?

9. What contexts might you use to develop the concept of equivalence within each of the models—area, length, and set?
10. How can you help children develop the algorithm for equivalent fractions?

For Discussion and Exploration

1. A common error that children make is to write $\frac{3}{5}$ for the fraction represented here:

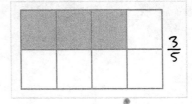

Why do you think that they do this? What activity or strategy would you use to try to address this misconception?

2. Fractions are often named by adults and in cartoons as a dreaded math topic. Why do you think this is true? How might your fraction instruction alter this perception for your students?

Resources for Chapter 15

Literature Connections

Context takes children away from rules and encourages them to explore ideas in a more open and meaningful manner. The way that children approach fraction concepts in these contexts may surprise you.

How Many Snails? A Counting Book *Giganti, 1988*

Each page of this book has a similar pattern of questions. For example, "I went walking and I wondered: How many clouds were there? How many clouds were big and fluffy? How many were big and fluffy and gray?" Students can look at the pictures and find the fraction of the objects (e.g., clouds) that have the particular characteristic (big and fluffy). Whitin and Whitin (2006) describe how a class used this book to write their own stories in this pattern and record the fractions for each subset of the objects.

The Doorbell Rang *Hutchins, 1986*

Often used to investigate whole-number operations of multiplication and division, this book is also an excellent early introduction to fractions. The story is a simple tale of two children preparing to share a plate of 12 cookies. Just as they have figured out how to share the cookies, the doorbell rings and more children arrive. You can change the number of children to create a sharing situation that requires fractions (e.g., 5 children).

The Man Who Counted: A Collection of Mathematical Adventures *Tahan, 1993*

This book contains a story, "Beasts of Burden," about a wise mathematician, Beremiz, and the narrator, who are traveling together on one camel. They are asked by three brothers to solve an argument. Their father has left them 35 camels to divide among them: half to one brother, one-third to another, and one-ninth to the third. The story provides an excellent context for discussing fractional parts of sets and how fractional parts change as the whole changes. However, if the whole is changed from 35 to, say, 36 or 34, the problem of the indicated shares remains unresolved. The sum of $\frac{1}{2}$, $\frac{1}{3}$, and $\frac{1}{9}$ will never be one whole, no matter how many camels are involved. Bresser (1995) describes three days of activities with his fifth graders.

Recommended Readings

Articles

Clarke, D. M., Roche, A., & Mitchell, A. (2008). Ten practical tips for making fractions come alive and make sense. *Mathematics Teaching in the Middle School, 13*(7), 373–380.

This article has the ten suggestions listed in the summary of this chapter. Each is discussed and favorite activities are shared. An excellent overview of teaching fractions.

Flores, A., & Klein, E. (2005). From students' problem-solving strategies to connections in fractions. *Teaching Children Mathematics, 11*(9), 452–457.

This article offers a very realistic view (complete with photos of student work) of how children develop initial fraction concepts and an understanding of notation as they engage in sharing tasks like those described in this chapter.

Reys, B. J., Kim, O., & Bay, J. M. (1999). Establishing fraction benchmarks. *Mathematics Teaching in the Middle School, 4*(8), 530–532.

This short article describes a simple three-question interview administered to 20 fifth-grade students. The results are both sad and surprising. A significant conclusion is that the teaching of benchmarks for fractions, specifically 0, $\frac{1}{2}$, and 1, is generally neglected in the standard curriculum.

Stump, S. (2003). Designing fraction counting books. *Teaching Children Mathematics, 9*(9), 546–549.

This article describes the work of several preservice teachers whose students created counting books in which they count by unit fractions.

Books

Burns, M. (2001). *Teaching arithmetic: Lessons for introducing fractions, grades 4–5.* Sausalito, CA: Math Solutions Publications.

Typical of Marilyn Burns, this book offers well-designed lessons with lots of details, sample student dialogue, and Blackline Masters. These are introductory ideas for fraction concepts. Five lessons cover one-half as a benchmark. Assessments are also included.

Online Resources

Cyberchase (PBS)
www.pbs.org/teachers/search/results.html?q=fractions&x=0&y=0&num=100&loggedin=0&loggedin=0&active=audio video

Cyberchase is a very popular television series targeting important mathematics. The site offers videos that model fractions with real-world connections. Also offered are activities such as "Make a Match" (http://pbskids.org/cyberchase/games/equivalentfractions/index.html), in which students examine the concept of equivalent fractions and match a fraction with a graphic representation of that fraction. Another activity is "Thirteen Ways of Looking at a Half" (http://pbskids.org/cyberchase/games/fractions/index.html), in which students explore fractions of geometric shapes—in particular, the thirteen ways half of an eight-piece square can be arranged.

Fraction Bars (Math Playground)
http://mathplayground.com/Fraction_bars.html

The user sets the total parts and then the shaded parts for each bar. Explore fractional parts, the concept of numerator and denominator, and equivalency. The user can turn the numbers on or off.

Fraction Concepts (eNLVM Module)
http://enlvm.usu.edu/ma/nav/toc.jsp?sid=_shared&cid= emready@fraction_concepts&bb=published

These part-whole activities provide practice in writing and comparing fractions. A full lesson plan with NCTM standards correlations and worksheets is provided, and the teacher can log in to see how students performed.

Fraction Track
http://standards.nctm.org/document/eexamples/chap5/ 5.1/index.htm

Players position fractions on number lines with different denominators. Fractions can be split into parts. A challenging game involving equivalent-fraction concepts.

Fraction Pointer
www.shodor.org/interactivate/activities/FractionPointer

A good applet for connecting an area model with the number line. After creating area models for two fractions, the user must then create a new fraction between the first two. Similar to the *Illuminations* applet, "Equivalent Fractions."

National Library of Virtual Manipulatives
http://nlvm.usu.edu

This site offers numerous models for exploring fractions, including fraction bars and fraction pieces. Also there is an applet for comparing and visualizing fractions.

Field Experience Guide Connections

Because fractions are not as well understood as whole numbers, they are a good content area for the Chapter 3 field experiences, especially 3.1, 3.4, 3.5, and 3.6, which target conceptual and procedural understanding. FEG Expanded Lesson 9.6 is a dot paper activity focused on fraction equivalencies. FEG Expanded Lesson 9.10 and FEG Activity 10.6 ("Fraction Find") target an important concept of fractions—the idea that you can always find one more fraction between any two fractions.

Chapter 16

Developing Strategies for Fraction Computation

A fifth-grade student asks, "Why is it when we times 29 times two-ninths that the answer goes down?" (Taber, 2002, p. 67). Although generalizations from whole numbers can confuse students, you should realize that their ideas about the operations were developed with whole numbers. Students need to build on their ideas of whole-number operations. We can use their prior understanding of the whole-number operations to give meaning to fraction computation. This, combined with a firm understanding of fractions, provides the foundation for understanding fraction computation. Without this foundation, your students will almost certainly be learning rules without reasons, an unacceptable goal.

Big Ideas

1. The meanings of each operation on fractions are the same as the meanings for the operations on whole numbers. Operations with fractions should begin by applying these same meanings to fractional parts.

   - For addition and subtraction, the numerator tells the number of parts and the denominator the type of part. It is the parts that are added or subtracted.

   - For multiplication by a fraction, repeated addition and area models support development of the algorithm for multiplication of fractions.

   - For division by a fraction, the two ways of thinking about the operation—partition and measurement—will lead to two different thought processes for division. Both are important.

2. Estimation in fraction computation is tied almost entirely to concepts of the operations and relative sizes of fractions. A computation algorithm is not required for making estimates. Estimation should be an integral part of computation development to keep students' attention on the meanings of the operations and the expected sizes of the results.

Mathematics Content Connections

As just noted, computation with fractions is built on an understanding of the operations for whole numbers and on fraction sense (Chapters 12 and 15). Understanding fraction computation has connections in these areas as well.

- **Algebraic Thinking** (Chapter 14): Equations with variables often involve fractions or can be solved using fractions. For example, $\frac{3}{4}x = 15$ could be solved mentally, if fraction multiplication is understood *and* the procedure for solving it requires multiplication (or division) of fractions.

- **Decimals and Percents** (Chapter 17): Because decimals and percents are alternative representations for fractions, they can often help with computational fluency, especially in the area of estimation. For example, 2.452×0.513 is about $2\frac{1}{2} \times \frac{1}{2}$ or $1\frac{1}{4} = 1.25$. Twenty-five percent off of the $132 list price is easily computed as $\frac{1}{4}$ of 132.

- **Proportional Reasoning** (Chapter 18): Fraction multiplication helps us to think about fractions as operators. This in turn is connected to the concepts of ratio and proportion, especially the ideas of scaling and scale factors.

- **Measurement** (Chapter 19): Not only does measuring often involve adding, subtracting, multiplying, and dividing with fractions, but the models for understanding the operations include a measurement interpretation (How many $\frac{1}{2}$" segments can you get from 5" of string?).

Number Sense and Fraction Algorithms

Today it is important to be able to compute with fractions, primarily for the purpose of making estimates and for understanding computations in algebra, measurement, and other mathematics strands.

Conceptual Development Takes Time

It is important to give students ample opportunity to develop fraction number sense prior to and during instruction about common denominators and other procedures for computation. Even in grade 7 or 8 it makes sense to delay computation and work on concepts if students are not conceptually ready.

Premature attention to rules for fraction computation has a number of serious drawbacks. None of the algorithms helps students think about the operations and what they mean. When students follow a procedure they do not understand, they have no means of assessing their results to see if they make sense. Second, mastery of the poorly understood algorithm in the short term is quickly lost. When mixed together, the differing procedures for each operation soon become a meaningless jumble. Students ask, "Do I need a common denominator, or do I just add or multiply the bottom numbers?" "Which one do you invert, the first or the second number?" When the numbers in a problem are altered slightly, for example, a mixed number appears, students think the algorithm does not apply.

 Principles and Standards suggests that the main focus on fractions and decimals in grades 3–5 should be on the development of number sense and informal approaches to addition and subtraction. In grades 6–8, students should expand their skills to include all operations with fractions, decimals, and percents. ◆

A Problem-Based Number Sense Approach

Even if your curriculum guidelines call for teaching all four of the operations with fractions, you must still delay a rush to algorithmic procedures until it becomes clear that students are ready. Students can become adequately proficient using informal student-invented methods that they understand.

The following guidelines should be kept in mind when developing computational strategies for fractions:

1. *Begin with simple contextual tasks.* This should seem like déjà vu, as this recommendation applies to nearly every topic. Huinker (1998) makes an excellent case for using contextual problems and letting students develop their own methods of computation with fractions. Problems or contexts need not be elaborate. What you want is a context for both the meaning of the operation and the fractions involved.

2. *Connect the meaning of fraction computation with whole-number computation.* To consider what $2\frac{1}{2} \times \frac{3}{4}$ might mean, we should ask, "What does 2×3 mean?" Follow this with "What might $2 \times 3\frac{1}{2}$ mean?," slowly moving to a fraction times a fraction. The concepts of each operation are the same, and benefits can be had by connecting to whole number operations, explicitly discussing what is similar and what is different.

3. *Let estimation and informal methods play a big role in the development of strategies.* "Should $2\frac{1}{2} \times \frac{1}{4}$ be more or less than 1? More or less than 2?" Estimation keeps the focus on the meanings of the numbers and the operations, encourages reflective thinking, and helps build informal number sense with fractions. Can you reason to get an exact answer without using the standard algorithm? One way is to apply the distributive property, splitting the mixed number and multiplying both parts by $\frac{1}{4}$: $(2 \times \frac{1}{4}) + (\frac{1}{2} \times \frac{1}{4})$. Two $\frac{1}{4}$s is $\frac{2}{4}$ or $\frac{1}{2}$ and a half of a fourth is $\frac{1}{8}$. So, add an eighth to a half and you have $\frac{5}{8}$.

4. *Explore each of the operations using models.* Use a variety of models. Have students defend their solutions using the models, including simple student drawings. You will find that sometimes it is possible to get answers with models that do not seem to help with pencil-and-paper approaches. That's fine! The ideas will help children learn to think about the fractions and the operations, contribute to mental methods, and provide a useful background when you eventually do get to the standard algorithms.

These four steps are embedded in each of the sections in this chapter.

Computational Estimation

A frequently quoted result from the Second National Assessment of Educational Progress (Post, 1981) concerns the following item:

> Estimate the answer to $\frac{12}{13} + \frac{7}{8}$. You will not have time to solve the problem using paper and pencil.

Here is how 13-year-olds answered:

Response	Percent of 13-Year-Olds
1	7
2	24
19	28
21	27
Don't know	14

A more recent study of sixth- and eighth-grade Taiwanese students included this same item. The results were nearly identical to those in the NAEP study (Reys, 1998).

In the Taiwanese study, a significantly higher percentage of students (61 percent and 63 percent) were able to correctly compute the sum, a process that requires finding the common denominator of thirteenths and eighths! Notice that to estimate this sum requires no skill whatsoever with computation—only a feeling for the size of the two fractions.

Addition and Subtraction.   The development of fraction number sense should most certainly include estimation of fraction sums and differences—even before computational strategies are introduced. The following activity can be done regularly as a short full-class warm-up for any fraction lesson.

Activity 16.1

First Estimates

Tell students that they are going to estimate a sum or difference of two fractions. They are to decide only if the exact answer is more or less than 1. On the overhead projector, for no more than about 10 seconds, show a fraction addition or subtraction problem involving two fractions. Students write down on paper or a mini whiteboard their choice of more or less than one. Do several problems in a row. Then return to each problem and discuss how students decided on their estimate.

Activity 16.1, estimating to over or under 1, is the beginning of related tasks that are more complicated. When students are ready for a tougher challenge, choose from the following variations:

- Use a target answer that is different than 1. For example, estimate more or less than $\frac{1}{2}$, $1\frac{1}{2}$, 2, or 3.
- Choose fractions both less than and greater than 1. Estimate to the nearest half.

In the discussions following these estimation exercises, ask students if they think that the exact answer is more or less than the estimate that they gave.

Figure 16.1 shows six sample sums and differences that might be used in a "First Estimates" activity.

— *Pause and Reflect*

Test your own estimation skills with the sample problems in Figure 16.1. Look at each computation for only about 10 seconds and write down an estimate. After writing down all six of your estimates, look at the problems and decide whether your estimate is higher or lower than the actual computation. Don't guess! Have a good reason.

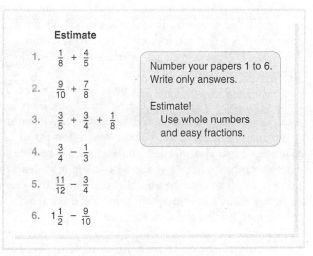

Figure 16.1 Example of fraction estimation expressions.

In most cases students' estimates should not be much more than $\frac{1}{2}$ away from the exact sum or difference.

 "The development of rational-number concepts is a major goal for grades 3–5, which should lead to informal methods for calculating with fractions. For example, a problem such as $\frac{1}{4} + \frac{1}{2}$ should be solved mentally with ease because students can picture $\frac{1}{2}$ and $\frac{1}{4}$ or can use decomposition strategies, such as $\frac{1}{4} + \frac{1}{2} = \frac{1}{4} + (\frac{1}{4} + \frac{1}{4})$" (p. 35). ◆

Multiplication and Division.   How would you estimate the answer to $3\frac{2}{3} \times 2\frac{1}{4}$? Using the estimation technique of rounding one factor up and the other down, this product might be estimated as 4×2. That simple estimation may be all that is required in a real setting. It is also good enough to help students know if their calculated answer is in the right ballpark.

In the real world, there are many instances when whole numbers times fractions must be multiplied and mental estimates or even exact answers are quite useful. For example, sale items are frequently listed as "$\frac{1}{4}$ off" or we read of a "$\frac{1}{3}$ increase" in the number of registered voters. Also, fractions are excellent substitutes for percents, as you will see in the next chapter. To get an estimate of 60 percent of $36.69, it is useful to think of 60 percent as $\frac{3}{5}$ or as a little less than $\frac{2}{3}$.

These products of fractions and large whole numbers can be calculated mentally by thinking of the meanings of the top and bottom numbers. For example, $\frac{3}{5}$ is 3 *one*-fifths. So if you want $\frac{3}{5}$ of 350, for example, first think about *one*-fifth of 350, or 70. If *one*-fifth is 70, then *three*-fifths is 3×70, or 210. Although this example has very compatible numbers, it illustrates a process for mentally multiplying a large number by a fraction: First determine the unit fractional part, and then multiply by the number of parts you want.

When numbers are not so nice, encourage students to use compatible numbers. To estimate $\frac{3}{5}$ of $36.69, a useful compatible is $35. One-fifth of 35 is 7, so three-fifths is 3×7, or 21. Now adjust a bit—perhaps add an additional 50 cents, for an estimate of $21.50.

Understanding division can be greatly supported by using estimation. Consider the problem $12 \div 4$. This can mean "How many fours in 12?" Similarly, $12 \div \frac{1}{4}$ means "How many fourths in 12?" There are 48 fourths in 12. With this basic idea in mind, students should be able to estimate problems like $4\frac{1}{3} \div \frac{1}{2}$ and $3\frac{4}{5} \div \frac{2}{3}$. Asking students to first use words to describe what these equations are asking (e.g., how many halves in $4\frac{1}{3}$) can help them think about the meaning of division and then estimate.

As with the other operations, using context is important in estimating with division. An example is: "We have 5 submarine sandwiches. A serving for one person is $\frac{2}{5}$ of a sandwich. About how many people will get a full serving?"

Addition and Subtraction

Addition and subtraction of fractions are usually taught together in fifth or sixth grade. *Curriculum Focal Points* (NCTM, 2006) includes addition and subtraction of fractions and decimals as a fifth-grade focal point and stresses ability to model and represent, ability to estimate, and fluency.

As with whole-number computation, provide computational tasks without giving rules or procedures for completing them. Expect that students will use a variety of methods and that the methods will vary widely with the fractions encountered in the problems.

Students should find a variety of ways to solve problems with fractions, and their invented approaches will contribute to the development of the standard algorithms (Huinker, 1998; Lappan & Mouck, 1998; Schifter, Bastable, & Russell, 1999c).

Invented Strategies

Invented strategies are critical for developing an understanding of fractions, as they tend to use a student's number sense. Besides, most of the fractions people add in their adult lives involve halves, fourths, eighths—fractions that can be added mentally in whatever ways people find most comfortable. Apply the same strategies discussed in Chapter 12, encouraging students to model the problem or solve it in a way that makes sense to them.

Consider the following problem.

Mark bought $4\frac{1}{4}$ pounds of candy for his mom. The candy looked so good that he ate $\frac{7}{8}$ of a pound of it. How much did he give to his mom?

A fifth-grade class was asked to solve this problem in two ways. Many students attempted or correctly used a standard subtraction algorithm for mixed numbers as one method. However, not a single drawing or other explanation could be found in the class for the algorithm. As shown in Figure 16.2, Christian makes an error with the algorithm but draws a correct picture showing $4\frac{1}{4} = \frac{34}{8}$ and gets a correct answer of $\frac{27}{8}$. However, he is not confident in his drawing and crosses it out. Although many students do not understand their procedural methods, if not asked to justify their methods, they will believe in the algorithm more than their own reasoning.

A drawing method used by many in the class involved taking the $\frac{1}{8}$ left from the $\frac{7}{8}$ and adding it onto the $\frac{1}{4}$ as shown in Brandon's drawing. Only DaQuawn does this first in a symbolic manner. His "second method" is a drawing supporting his work. When DaQuawn shares with the class he says, "I took this from eighths so I could minus it from $\frac{7}{8}$. That leaves $\frac{1}{8}$. Then change [points to quarter circle] to $\frac{1}{8}$. Minus $\frac{1}{8}$ from . . . no, add it to $\frac{1}{8}$ equals $\frac{2}{8}$ plus $\frac{1}{8}$ equals $\frac{3}{8}$."

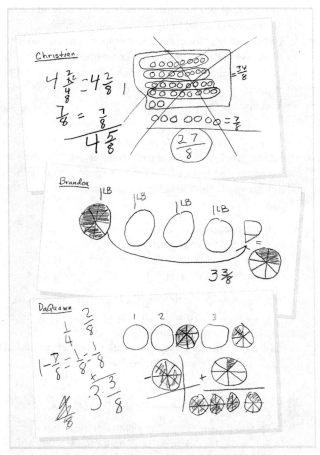

Figure 16.2 Fifth-grade students show how they solved the problem $4\frac{1}{4} - \frac{7}{8}$. For most students, their methods based on drawings have little to do with their symbolic algorithms. The work of DaQuawn, a student who struggles, is an exception.

DaQuawn's teacher notes that he "struggles with reading and writing although he has good number sense." This teacher values students' thinking and carefully distinguishes mathematics learning from students' abilities to express their ideas.

These examples illustrate how written work can provide insights into students' thinking—in this case showing that students have difficulty connecting symbols and pictures.

Fraction Circles. Students seem to have a preference for drawing circles to represent fractions. Perhaps that says something about an overuse of that model. The drawings in Figure 16.2 are not carefully drawn—the partitioning does not show equal parts. However, the students are not making conclusions based on the size of the pieces, but rather they are drawing to count sections. As long as students know that sections should be equivalent, do not be concerned with poorly drawn fraction models.

Cramer, Wyberg, and Leavitt (2008), well-known researchers in the area of rational numbers, have found circles to be the best model for adding and subtracting fractions because circles allow students to develop mental images of the sizes of different pieces (fractions) of the circle. Figure 16.3 shows how students estimate first (including marking a number line), and then explain how they added the fraction using fraction circles.

How you ask students to solve a problem can make a difference in what occurs in the classroom. For example, consider this problem:

Jack and Jill ordered two medium pizzas, one cheese and one pepperoni. Jack ate $\frac{5}{6}$ of a pizza and Jill ate $\frac{1}{2}$ of a pizza. How much pizza did they eat together?

⏸ ——————————— *Pause and Reflect*

Try to think of two ways that students might solve this problem without using a common-denominator symbolic approach.

If students draw circles as in the earlier example, some will try to fill in the $\frac{1}{6}$ gap in the pizza. Then they will need to figure out how to get $\frac{1}{6}$ from $\frac{1}{2}$. If they can think of $\frac{1}{2}$ as $\frac{3}{6}$, they can use one of the sixths to fill in the gap. Another approach, after drawing the two pizzas, is to notice that there is a half plus 2 more sixths in the $\frac{5}{6}$ pizza. Put the two halves together to make one whole and there are $\frac{2}{6}$ more—1 $\frac{2}{6}$. These are certainly good solutions that represent the type of thinking you want to encourage.

Number Lines. Another helpful model for using invented strategies to add or subtract fractions is the number line. One advantage of the number line is that it can be connected to the ruler, which is a familiar context for exploring

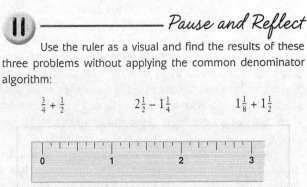

$$\frac{1}{5} + \frac{1}{10} =$$

Estimate first by putting an X on the number line.

Solve with Fraction Circles. Draw pictures of what you did with the circles below.

Record what you did with the circles with symbols.

Figure 16.3 A student estimates and then adds fractions using a fraction circle.

fraction addition and subtraction. The number line is also a more challenging model than the circle model, because it requires that the student not only understand $\frac{3}{4}$ as 3 out of 4, but as a value between 0 and 1 (Izsak, Tillema, & Tunc-Pekkam, 2008). Using the number line in addition to area representations like the circle can strengthen student understanding (Clarke, Roche, & Mitchell, 2008; Cramer, Wyberg, & Leavitt, 2008; Usiskin, 2007)

⏸ ——————————— *Pause and Reflect*

Use the ruler as a visual and find the results of these three problems without applying the common denominator algorithm:

$$\frac{3}{4} + \frac{1}{2} \qquad 2\frac{1}{2} - 1\frac{1}{4} \qquad 1\frac{1}{8} + 1\frac{1}{2}$$

Think about how you solved the problems in Pause and Reflect. Do you think there are other ways? In the first problem, students might use 1 as a benchmark (in the way that 10 or 100 is used as a benchmark with whole numbers). They use $\frac{1}{4}$ from the $\frac{1}{2}$ to get to one whole, and then have $\frac{1}{4}$ more to add on—so $1\frac{1}{4}$. Similarly, they could take the $\frac{1}{2}$ from the $\frac{3}{4}$ to make a whole with the $\frac{1}{2}$ and then add on the $\frac{1}{4}$ or, they might just know that $\frac{1}{2}$ is $\frac{2}{4}$ and then count to get $\frac{5}{4}$ (or $1\frac{1}{4}$).

Adding a context (that fits a linear situation) can also support students' use of invented strategies. In the second problem posed in the Pause and Reflect, for example, one context might be: Desmond runs $2\frac{1}{2}$ miles a day. If he has just passed the $1\frac{1}{4}$ mile marker, how far does he still need to go? Students may first subtract the whole numbers to get $1\frac{1}{2} - \frac{1}{4}$, and then know that $\frac{1}{2} - \frac{1}{4}$ is $\frac{1}{4}$, or they might prefer to change $\frac{1}{2}$ to $\frac{2}{4}$.

Given a different context, stories could be different. For example, Desmond is at mile marker $2\frac{1}{2}$ and James is at mile marker $1\frac{1}{4}$. How far does James need to go to catch up to where Desmond is? In this case, students may use a counting up strategy, noting that it takes $\frac{3}{4}$ to get to 2, then another $\frac{1}{2}$ added to $\frac{3}{4}$ would be $1\frac{1}{4}$. The more students can share strategies and illustrate them on the number line, the more flexible they will become in choosing how to add or subtract a fraction. As with whole numbers, sometimes invented strategies are the best and most efficient, but sometimes the numbers don't lend themselves to a mental strategy, in which case an algorithm can be very useful.

Suppose that you had asked the students to solve the Jack and Jill problem but changed the context to submarine sandwiches, asking students to use Cuisenaire rods or fraction strips to model the problem. The first decision that must be made is what strip to use as the whole. That decision is not required with a circular model. The whole must be the same for both fractions although there is a tendency to use the easiest whole for each fraction. Again, this issue does not arise with circles. In this case, the smallest strip that will work is the 6 rod or the dark green strip. Figure 16.4(a) illustrates a solution.

What if instead, you asked students to compare the quantity that Jack and Jill ate? Figure 16.4(b) illustrates lining up the "sandwiches" to compare their lengths. Recall that subtraction can be thought of as "separate" where the total is known and a part is removed, "comparison" as two amounts being compared to find the difference, and "how many more are needed" as starting with a smaller value and asking how much more to get to the higher value. This sandwich example is a comparison—be sure to include more than "take away" examples in the stories and examples you create.

As we saw in the very first example (Figure 16.2), students can and do use invented methods for subtraction as well as addition. This reasoning is extremely important. Students should become comfortable with different methods

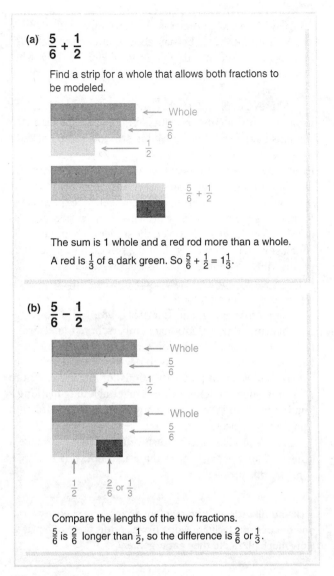

(a) $\frac{5}{6} + \frac{1}{2}$

Find a strip for a whole that allows both fractions to be modeled.

← Whole

$\frac{5}{6}$

$\frac{1}{2}$

$\frac{5}{6} + \frac{1}{2}$

The sum is 1 whole and a red rod more than a whole.
A red is $\frac{1}{3}$ of a dark green. So $\frac{5}{6} + \frac{1}{2} = 1\frac{1}{3}$.

(b) $\frac{5}{6} - \frac{1}{2}$

← Whole

$\frac{5}{6}$

$\frac{1}{2}$

← Whole

$\frac{5}{6}$

$\frac{1}{2}$ $\frac{2}{6}$ or $\frac{1}{3}$

Compare the lengths of the two fractions.
$\frac{5}{6}$ is $\frac{2}{6}$ longer than $\frac{1}{2}$, so the difference is $\frac{2}{6}$ or $\frac{1}{3}$.

Figure 16.4 Using rods to add and subtract fractions.

of taking simple fractions apart and recombining them in ways that make sense. Keep the fractions in your problems "friendly" with denominators no greater than 12. There is rarely a need to add fifths and sevenths or even fifths and twelfths. With numbers like that, drawings are difficult, as the common denominators are quite large. Although forcing the use of a model such as fraction strips or sets can cause students to prepare for common denominators, it is best to delay that emphasis in the beginning.

Why Are Common Denominators "Required"? Teachers commonly tell students, "In order to add or subtract fractions, you must first get common denominators." The explanation usually goes something like, "After all, you can't add apples and oranges." This well-intentioned statement is essentially false. A correct statement might be, "In order *to use the standard algorithm* to add or subtract fractions, you must first get common denominators." And the explanation is then, "The algorithm is designed to work only with common denominators because it is based on the idea of adding parts that are the same size."

Using their own invented strategies, students will see that many correct solutions are found without ever getting a common denominator. Consider these sums and differences:

$$\frac{3}{4} + \frac{1}{8} \qquad \frac{1}{2} - \frac{1}{8} \qquad \frac{2}{3} + \frac{1}{2} \qquad 1\frac{1}{2} - \frac{3}{4} \qquad 1\frac{2}{3} + \frac{3}{4}$$

Working with the ways different fractional parts are related one to another often provides solutions without common denominators. For example, halves, fourths, and eighths are easily related because $\frac{1}{8}$ is half of $\frac{1}{4}$ and $\frac{1}{4}$ is half of $\frac{1}{2}$. Also, picture three-thirds making up a whole in a circle as in Figure 16.5. Have you ever noticed that one-half of the whole is a third plus a half of a third or a sixth? Similarly, the difference between a third and a fourth is a twelfth.

As noted, the number line is also a tool that can be used mentally to solve addition and subtraction without finding a common denominator. Students instead may start with finding one fraction on the number line or ruler and then "jump" the value of the other fraction. For example, in $3\frac{1}{4} - 1\frac{1}{2}$, students can find $3\frac{1}{4}$, jump down one to $2\frac{1}{4}$, and then jump $\frac{1}{2}$, which takes them to $1\frac{3}{4}$.

Developing an Algorithm

Students can build on their invented strategies and knowledge of equivalence to develop the common-denominator approach for adding and subtracting fractions. As discussed in Chapter 15, in the section on equivalent fractions, having a strong conceptual foundation of equivalence is important in many other mathematics topics, one of which is computation of fractions. Students that have a level of fluency in

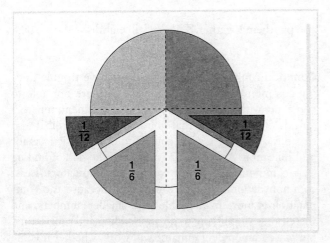

Figure 16.5 There are lots of fractional relationships that can be observed simply by looking at how halves, thirds, fourths, sixths, and twelfths fit into a partitioned circle.

moving between $\frac{1}{2}$, $\frac{2}{4}$, $\frac{4}{8}$, and $\frac{8}{16}$, or $\frac{3}{4}$, $\frac{6}{8}$, and $\frac{12}{16}$ can adjust the fractions as needed to combine or subtract fractions. Whether using an area, length, or set model, establishing equivalence is foundational and needs continued reinforcement during instruction on addition and subtraction of fractions. For example, have students complete a sum such as $\frac{3}{8} + \frac{4}{8}$ and write the finished equation on the board. Then, beneath this equation, write a second sum made of easily seen equivalents for each fraction as shown here:

$$\frac{3}{8} + \frac{4}{8} = \frac{7}{8}$$

$$\frac{6}{16} + \frac{1}{2} = ?$$

Discuss briefly the fact that $\frac{3}{8}$ is equivalent to $\frac{6}{16}$ as is $\frac{4}{8}$ to $\frac{1}{2}$. Now have students write the answer to the second equation and give a reason for their answer. Students should see that the answer is $\frac{7}{8}$. The second sum is the same as the first because although the fractions *look* different, they are actually the same numbers.

Like Denominators. Most lists of objectives first specify addition and subtraction with like denominators. If students have a good foundation with fraction concepts, they should be able to add or subtract fractions with like denominators. Students who are not confident solving problems such as $\frac{3}{4} + \frac{2}{4}$ or $3\frac{7}{8} - 1\frac{3}{8}$ may lack fraction concepts and need more experience manipulating models. The idea that the top number counts and the bottom number tells what is counted makes addition and subtraction of like fractions the same as adding and subtracting whole numbers. When working on adding with like denominators, however, it is important to be sure that students are focusing on the key idea—the units are the same, so they can be combined (Mack, 2004).

 The ease with which students can or cannot add like-denominator fractions should be viewed as an important concept assessment before pushing students forward to an algorithm. As just noted, students who do not see these sums or differences as trivial likely do not understand the meanings of the numerator and denominator. Any further symbolic development will almost certainly be without understanding. ◆

Unlike Denominators. To begin adding and subtracting fractions with unlike denominators, consider a task such as $\frac{5}{8} + \frac{1}{4}$ where only one fraction needs to be changed. Let students use any method. As students explain how they solved it, someone is likely to explain that $\frac{1}{4}$ is the same as $\frac{2}{8}$. Write equations on the board that show the initial equation and the equation rewritten with $\frac{2}{8}$ in place of $\frac{1}{4}$. Ask "Is this still the same equation? Why would we want to change the $\frac{1}{4}$?" Have students use models or drawings to explain why the original problem and also the converted problem should have the same answer.

Next try some examples where both fractions need to be changed—for example, $\frac{2}{3} + \frac{1}{4}$. Encourage students to solve these problems without using models or drawings if possible. Suggest (don't require) that the use of equivalent fractions might be an easier tool than a drawing. In the discussion of student solutions, focus attention on the idea of *rewriting the problem* to make it easier to add or subtract. Be certain that students understand that the rewritten problem is the same as the original and, therefore, must have the same answer. If your students express any doubt about the equivalence of the two problems ("Is $\frac{8}{12} + \frac{3}{12}$ really the answer to $\frac{2}{3} + \frac{1}{4}$?"), that should be a clue that the concept of equivalent fractions is not well understood, and more experience using visual or concrete models is needed.

As students continue to explore solutions to sums and differences of fractions, models should remain available for use. The three examples in Figure 16.6 show how models might be used. Note that each model requires students to think about the size of a whole that can be partitioned into the units of both fractions (e.g., fifths and halves require tenths).

The most common error in adding fractions is to add both numerators and denominators. Rather than jump in and attempt to correct this error directly, capitalize on the opportunity for a wonderful class discussion. One idea is to show students the following solution for adding $\frac{1}{2} + \frac{1}{3}$ that you "saw" offered by a fictional student in another class:

$$\frac{1}{2} \, \bullet \bullet \qquad \frac{1}{3} \, \bullet \bullet \bullet$$

$$\text{add} \quad \bullet \bullet \bullet \bullet \bullet$$

$$\text{Therefore, } \frac{1}{2} + \frac{1}{3} = \frac{2}{5}.$$

Add tops and bottoms.

Ask students to decide whether the student could be right. If not, what is wrong with the solution?

‖ ———————— *Pause and Reflect*

Why can't the answer be $\frac{2}{5}$ and what is wrong with the student's reasoning?

Focus first on the answer. The sum of $\frac{2}{5}$ is smaller than $\frac{1}{2}$ when, in fact, $\frac{1}{2} + \frac{1}{3}$ must be more than $\frac{1}{2}$. When students are convinced that the sum cannot be $\frac{2}{5}$, there is real value in letting them decide what is wrong with the reasoning. You must first see where students are in their understanding. For example, Nancy Mack, a researcher and teacher, asked her fifth graders if the following were correct: $\frac{3}{8} + \frac{2}{8} = \frac{5}{16}$. A student correctly replied, "No, because they are eighths (*holds up one-eighth of a fraction circle*). If you put them together you still have eighths (*shows this with the fraction circles*). See, you didn't make them into sixteenths when

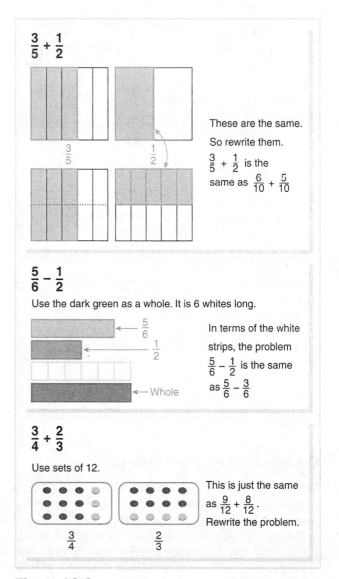

Figure 16.6 Rewriting addition and subtraction problems involving fractions so they have a common denominator.

you put them together. They're still eighths" (Mack, 2004, p. 229).

Common Multiples. Many students have trouble finding common denominators because they are not able to come up with common multiples of the denominators quickly. That is a skill that you may wish to drill. It also depends on having a good command of the basic facts for multiplication. Activity 16.2 is aimed at the skill of finding least common multiples or common denominators. Least common denominators are preferred because the computation is more manageable with smaller numbers, and there is less simplifying to do after adding and subtracting, but *any* common denominator will work, whether it is the smallest or not. Do not require least common multiples—support all common denominators and in discussion students will see that finding the smallest multiple is more efficient.

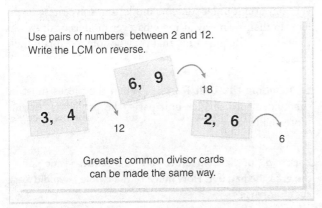

Use pairs of numbers between 2 and 12.
Write the LCM on reverse.

6, 9   18

3, 4   12   2, 6   6

Greatest common divisor cards
can be made the same way.

Figure 16.7 Least common multiple (LCM) flash cards.

Mixed Numbers and Improper Fractions

A separate algorithm for mixed numbers in addition and subtraction is not necessary even though mixed numbers are often treated as separate topics in traditional textbooks and in some lists of objectives. Include mixed numbers in all of your activities with addition and subtraction, and let students solve these problems in ways that make sense to them. Students will tend to naturally add or subtract the whole numbers and then the fractions. Sometimes this is all that needs to be done, but in other cases regrouping across the whole number and fraction is needed. In subtraction, this happens when the second fraction is larger than the first, and it occurs in addition when the answer of the fraction sum is more than 1.

Dealing with the whole numbers first still makes sense. Consider this problem: $5\frac{1}{8} - 3\frac{5}{8}$. After subtracting 3 from 5, students will need to deal with the $\frac{5}{8}$. Some will take $\frac{5}{8}$ from the whole part, 2, leaving $1\frac{3}{8}$, and then $\frac{1}{8}$ more is $1\frac{4}{8}$. Others may take away the $\frac{1}{8}$ that is there and then take $\frac{4}{8}$ from the remaining 2. A third but unlikely method is to trade one of the wholes for $\frac{8}{8}$, add it to the $\frac{1}{8}$, and then take

$\frac{5}{8}$ from the resulting $\frac{9}{8}$. This last method is the same as the traditional algorithm.

One underemphasized technique that is nevertheless a great strategy is to change the mixed numbers to single, or improper, fractions. You may have been taught that this was the process used for multiplication, but that is part of the "rules without reason" approach of having one way to do one procedure. Let's revisit $5\frac{1}{8} - 3\frac{5}{8}$. This can be rewritten as $\frac{41}{8} - \frac{29}{8}$. (See Chapter 15 for conceptual ways for helping students do this.) Because 41 – 29 is 12, the solution is $\frac{12}{8}$ or $1\frac{1}{2}$. This is certainly efficient and will always work. The message here is to provide options to students and you will find that more students understand and are able to solve these problems successfully.

Multiplication

Multiplication of fractions is often taught in middle school, though informal fraction activities that reflect multiplication, such as "What is $\frac{2}{3}$ of 30?" are introduced earlier. *Curriculum Focal Points* (NCTM, 2006) has fluency with multiplication and division of fractions placed at sixth grade. Fluency means that a student can not only do the algorithm, but also understands it and can model problems, solve situations that involve multiplication and division of fractions, and estimate.

It is important to emphasize the application component of fluency, as very few people have learned multiplication and division of fractions such that they are able to do much more than the basic procedure. If you fall in this category, then read the examples in this section carefully and try to solve the problems—many figures are provided to help illustrate the meaning of multiplication of fractions.

When working with whole numbers, we would say that 3 × 5 means "3 sets of 5" (repeated addition) or "3 rows of 5" (area or array). The first factor tells how much of the second factor you have or want. This is a good place to begin using contexts and simple story problems are a significant help in this development.

Developing the Concept

The story problems that you use to pose multiplication tasks to children need not be elaborate, but it is important to think about the numbers that you use in the problems. A possible progression of problem difficulty is developed in the sections that follow.

Fractions of Whole Numbers. Students' first experiences with multiplication should involve finding fractions of whole numbers. In Chapter 15, several examples of finding fractions of the whole are provided, such as, "If the whole is 45, how much is $\frac{1}{5}$ of the whole?" A more challenging example is, "If the whole is 24, what is $\frac{3}{8}$ of the whole?" These reasoning tasks can lead into discussions of what multiplication of fractions means. Consider the following three problems as good starting tasks:

There are 15 cars in Michael's matchbox car collection. Two-thirds of the cars are red. How many red cars does Michael have?

How might students think through this problem? They might partition 15 into three groups, five in each group, and then see how many are in two groups. Recording this in symbols ($\frac{2}{3}$ of 15) gives the following result: $15 \div 3 \times 2$.

This can be adapted to involve a length context:

The walk from school to the public library takes 15 minutes. When I asked my mom how far we had gone, she said that we had gone $\frac{2}{3}$ of the way. Can you tell me how many minutes we have walked? (Assume constant walking rate.)

Tasks can have lower whole numbers—for example, $\frac{1}{4} \times 2$. What does this mean? How might you solve it? What about $\frac{1}{4} \times 5$? $\frac{3}{4}$ of 5?

Problems in which the first factor or multiplier is a whole number are also important.

Wayne filled 5 glasses with $\frac{2}{3}$ liter of soda in each glass. How much soda did Wayne use?

Notice that this situation is "5 groups of $\frac{2}{3}$" and not "$\frac{2}{3}$ of a group of 5." Although the commutative property means that these numbers can be switched, it is important that students understand each type as representations whose meanings are different. The problem might be solved in a counting-up strategy. It may be solved by repeated addition: $\frac{2}{3} + \frac{2}{3} + \frac{2}{3} + \frac{2}{3} + \frac{2}{3} = \frac{10}{3}$. Students may notice that what they did was multiply the numerator by 5, so $5 \times \frac{2}{3} = (5 \times 2)/3 = \frac{10}{3}$.

This problem may be solved in different ways. Some children will put the thirds together, making wholes as they go. Others will count all of the thirds and then find out how many whole liters are in 10 thirds.

Unit Parts Without Subdivisions. To expand on the ideas just presented, consider these three problems:

You have $\frac{3}{4}$ of a pizza left. If you give $\frac{1}{3}$ of the leftover pizza to your brother, how much of a whole pizza will your brother get?

Someone ate $\frac{1}{10}$ of the loaf of bread, leaving $\frac{9}{10}$. If you use $\frac{2}{3}$ of what is left to make French toast how much of a whole loaf will you have used?

Gloria used $2\frac{1}{2}$ tubes of blue paint to paint the sky in her picture. Each tube holds $\frac{4}{5}$ ounce of paint. How many ounces of blue paint did Gloria use?

Intentionally the units or fractional parts in these problems do not need to be subdivided further. The first problem is $\frac{1}{3}$ of three things, the second is $\frac{2}{3}$ of nine things, and the last is $2\frac{1}{2}$ of four things. The focus remains on the number of unit parts in all, and then the size of the parts determines the number of wholes. Figure 16.8 shows how problems of this type might be modeled. However, it is very important to let students model and solve these problems in their own way, using whatever models or drawings they choose. Require only that they be able to explain their reasoning.

Subdividing the Unit Parts. When the pieces must be subdivided into smaller unit parts, the problems become more challenging.

Zack had $\frac{2}{3}$ of the lawn left to cut. After lunch, he cut $\frac{3}{4}$ of the grass he had left. How much of the whole lawn did Zack cut after lunch?

The zookeeper had a huge bottle of the animals' favorite liquid treat, Zoo Cola. The monkey drank $\frac{1}{5}$ of the bottle. The zebra drank $\frac{2}{3}$ of what was left. How much of the bottle of Zoo Cola did the zebra drink?

❚❚ —————— *Pause and Reflect*

Pause for a moment and figure out how you would solve each of these problems. Draw pictures to help you, but do not use a computational algorithm.

In Zack's lawn problem, it is necessary to find fourths of two things, the 2 *thirds* of the grass left to cut. In the Zoo Cola problem, you need thirds of four things, the 4 *fifths* of the cola that remain. Again, the concepts of the top number counting and the bottom number naming what is counted play an important role. Figure 16.9 shows a possible solution for Zack's lawn problem. A similar approach can be used

myeducationlab

Go to the Building Teaching Skills and Dispositions section of Chapter 16 of MyEducationLab. Click on Expanded Lessons to download the Expanded Lesson for "**Using Visuals to Multiply Fractions**" and complete the related activities.

Task	Finding the starting amount	Showing the fraction of the starting amount	Solution
Pizza Find $\frac{1}{3}$ of $\frac{3}{4}$ (of a pizza) or $\frac{1}{3} \times \frac{3}{4}$	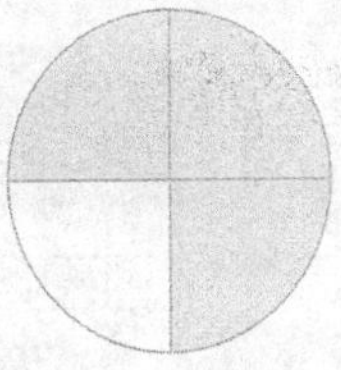	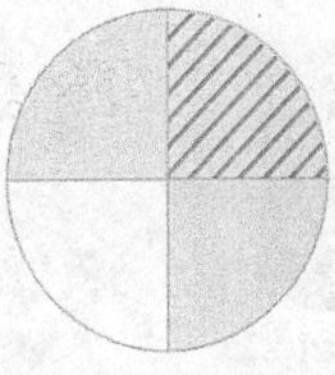	$\frac{1}{3}$ of the $\frac{3}{4}$ is $\frac{1}{4}$ of the original pizza. $\frac{1}{3} \times \frac{3}{4} = \frac{1}{4}$
Bread Find $\frac{2}{3}$ of $\frac{9}{10}$ (of a loaf of bread) or $\frac{2}{3} \times \frac{9}{10}$	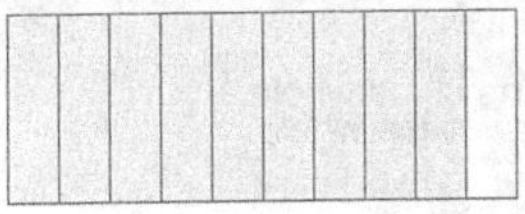	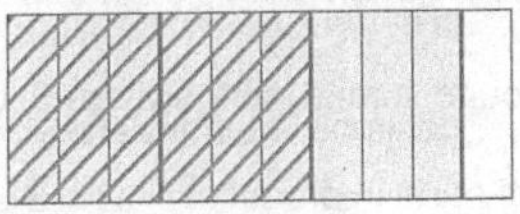	$\frac{2}{3}$ of the $\frac{9}{10}$ is 6 slices of the loaf or $\frac{6}{10}$ of the whole. $\frac{2}{3} \times \frac{9}{10} = \frac{6}{10}$
Paint Find $2\frac{1}{2}$ of $\frac{4}{5}$ (ounces of paint) or $2\frac{1}{2} \times \frac{4}{5}$	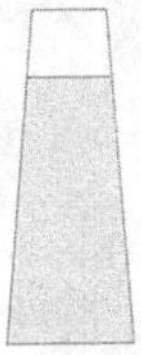	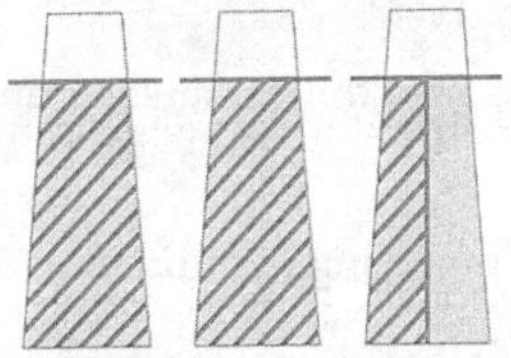	$2\frac{1}{2}$ of the $\frac{4}{5}$ is $\frac{4}{5} + \frac{4}{5} + \frac{2}{5} = \frac{10}{5}$

Figure 16.8 Models that illustrate three problems involving multiplication.

for the Zoo Cola problem. You may have used different drawings, but the ideas should be the same.

Using a paper strip and partitioning it is an effective way to solve multiplication problems, especially when they require additional partitioning (Siebert & Gaskin, 2006). Figure 16.9 illustrates how to use paper strips for the prob-

lem $\frac{3}{5} \times \frac{2}{3}$. (*Three-fifths of $\frac{2}{3}$ of a whole is how much of a whole?*) Solving this problem requires that the thirds be subdivided.

Multiplication of fractions can be modeled with counters (see Figure 16.10). Do not discourage students from using counters, but be prepared to help them find ways to determine the whole.

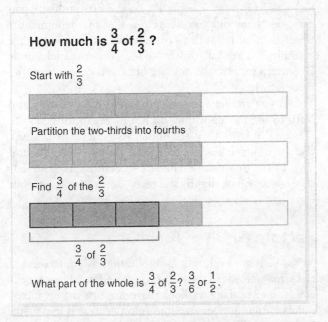

Figure 16.9 Solutions to a multiplication problem when the parts must be subdivided.

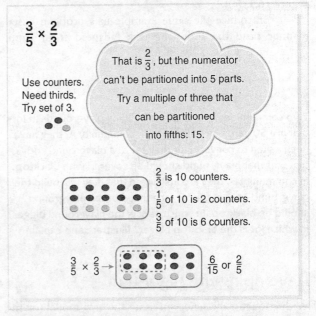

Figure 16.10 Modeling multiplication of fractions with counters.

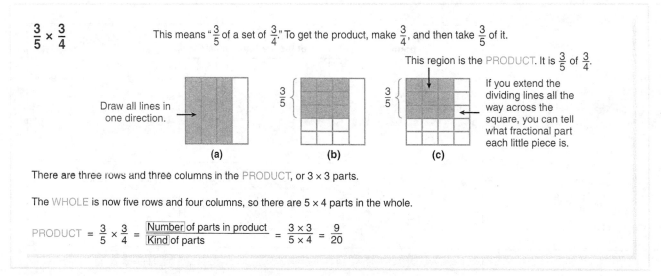

Figure 16.11 Development of the algorithm for multiplication of fractions.

Area Model. The area model for modeling fraction multiplication has several advantages. First, it works for problems where partitioning a length can get tedious. Second, it provides a nice visual to show that a result can be quite a bit smaller than either of the fractions used or that if the fractions are both close to 1, then the result is also close to one. Third, it is a good model for connecting to the standard algorithm for multiplying fractions.

Provide students with a square as in Figure 16.11 and ask them to illustrate the first fraction. For example in $\frac{3}{5} \times \frac{3}{4}$, you are finding $\frac{3}{5}$ of $\frac{3}{4}$, so you first must show $\frac{3}{4}$ (see Figure 16.11(a)). To find fifths of the $\frac{3}{4}$, draw five horizontal lines through the $\frac{3}{4}$ (see Figure 16.11(b)) or all the way across the square so that the whole is in the same-sized partitions (see Figure 16.11(c)).

To introduce the same example in a problem-based manner pose the following task (adapted from Imm, Stylianou, & Chae, 2008, p. 459):

Playground Problem

Two communities, A and B, are building playgrounds in lots that are 50 yards by 100 yards. In community A, they have been asked to convert $\frac{3}{4}$ of their lot to a playground and that $\frac{2}{5}$ of that playground should be covered with blacktop. In community B, they are instructed that they will build their playground on $\frac{2}{5}$ of the lot, and that $\frac{3}{4}$ of the playground should be blacktop. In which park is the playground bigger? In which lot is the blacktop bigger? Illustrate and explain.

Developing the Algorithm

With enough experiences in using the area model (or the linear model), students will start to notice a pattern. Re-member that "enough" is probably a lot more than is usually provided—in other words, this does not mean two or three examples, but several days, even weeks, working with different examples and problems. These exercises will lead students to focus on how the denominators relate to how the grid (or line) is partitioned and how the numerator affects the solution to the problem.

When students are ready to start using the algorithm, ask them to solve three examples such as the following:

$$\frac{5}{6} \times \frac{1}{2} \qquad \frac{3}{4} \times \frac{1}{5} \qquad \frac{1}{3} \times \frac{9}{10}$$

For each one, use a square and partition it vertically and horizontally to model the problems. Ask, "How did you figure out how what the unit of the fraction [the denominator] was?" Or more specifically, on the first problem, you can ask, "How did you figure out that the denominator would be twelfths? Is this a pattern that is true on the other examples?" Then ask students to see if they can find a similar pattern for how the number of parts is determined (the numerator).

As you are helping students focus on the pattern and learn to use the algorithm, do not forget to focus on the meaning of what they are doing. Ask questions that ask them to estimate how big they think the answer will be and why. In the first example here, a student might note that the answer will be slightly less than $\frac{1}{2}$ since $\frac{5}{6}$ is close to, but less than, 1.

Factors Greater Than One

As students are exploring multiplication, begin to include tasks in which one of the factors is a mixed number—for example, $\frac{3}{4} \times 2\frac{1}{2}$. Many textbooks have students change mixed numbers to improper fractions in order to multiply them. In fact, students can make improper fractions or use mixed numbers. Either way, area representations can be used to model the problem, as illustrated in Figure 16.12. This is an efficient way to solve these types of problems, but it is not the only way. Students who understand that $2\frac{1}{2}$ means $2 + \frac{1}{2}$ might multiply $\frac{3}{4} \times 2$ and $\frac{3}{4} \times \frac{1}{2}$ and add the results—the distributive property.

When both factors are mixed numbers, there are four partial products, just as there are when multiplying 2 two-digit numbers.

⏸ ———————— *Pause and Reflect*

Find the four partial products in this multiplication: $3\frac{2}{3} \times 2\frac{1}{4}$.

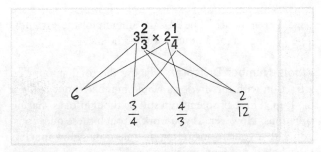

Figure 16.13 When multiplying two mixed numbers, there will be four partial products. These can then be added up to get the total product or an estimate may be enough. Here the answer is about 8.

Figure 16.13 shows how this product might be worked out by multiplying the individual parts. In most cases, the resulting fractions are not likely to be difficult to work with. More importantly, the process is more conceptual and also lends itself to estimation—either before the partial products are determined or after. Notice that the same four partial products of Figure 16.13 can be found in the rectangle in Figure 16.12.

🐚 Division

Invert the divisor and multiply is probably one of the most mysterious rules in elementary mathematics. We want to avoid this mystery at all costs. It makes sense to examine division with fractions from a more familiar perspective.

As with the other operations, go back to the meaning of division with whole numbers. Recall that there are two meanings of division: partitive and measurement (Gregg & Gregg, 2007; Krib-Zalita, 2008; Tirosh, 2000). We will review each briefly and look at some story problems that involve fractions. (Can you make up a word problem right now that would go with the computation $2\frac{1}{2} \div \frac{1}{4}$?)

You should have students explore both measurement and partitive problems. Here we will discuss each type of problem separately for the purpose of clarity. In the classroom, the types of problems should eventually be mixed. As with multiplication, how the numbers relate to each other in the problems tends to affect the difficulty.

Partitive Interpretation of Division

Too often we think of the partition problems strictly as sharing problems: 24 apples to be shared with 4 friends. How many will each friend get? Recall from Chapter 9, however, that this same sharing structure applies to rate problems: If you walk 12 miles in 3 hours, how many miles do you walk per hour? Both of these problems, in fact, are partition problems, asking the questions, "How much is one?" "How

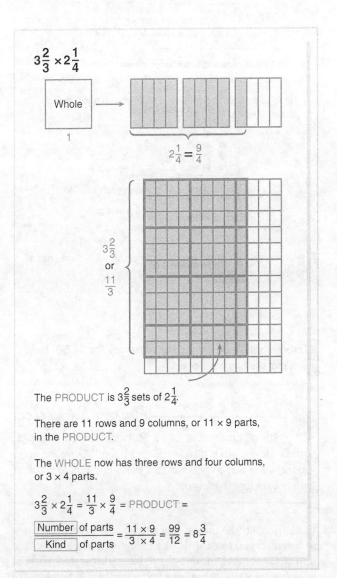

The PRODUCT is $3\frac{2}{3}$ sets of $2\frac{1}{4}$.

There are 11 rows and 9 columns, or 11 × 9 parts, in the PRODUCT.

The WHOLE now has three rows and four columns, or 3 × 4 parts.

$3\frac{2}{3} \times 2\frac{1}{4} = \frac{11}{3} \times \frac{9}{4} = \text{PRODUCT} =$

$\dfrac{\boxed{\text{Number}} \text{ of parts}}{\boxed{\text{Kind}} \text{ of parts}} = \dfrac{11 \times 9}{3 \times 4} = \dfrac{99}{12} = 8\frac{3}{4}$

Figure 16.12 The same approach used to develop the algorithm for fractions less than 1 can be expanded to mixed numbers.

much is the amount for *one* friend?" "How many miles are walked in *one* hour?" The 24 is the amount for the 4 friends. The 12 miles is the amount for the 3 hours.

Whole-Number Divisors.   Having the total amount be a fraction with the divisor a whole number is not really a big leap. These problems can still be thought of as sharing situations. However, as you work through these questions, notice that you are answering the question, "How much is the whole?" or "How much for one?"

> **Cassie has $5\frac{1}{3}$ yards of ribbon to make four bows for birthday packages. How much ribbon should she use for each bow if she wants to use the same length of ribbon for each?**

When the $5\frac{1}{3}$ is thought of as fractional parts, there are 16 thirds to share, or 4 thirds for each ribbon. Alternatively, one might think of first allotting 1 yard per bow, leaving $1\frac{1}{3}$ yards. These 4 thirds are then shared, one per bow, for a total of $1\frac{1}{3}$ yards for each bow. The unit parts (thirds) required no further partitioning in order to do the division. In the following problem, the parts must be split into smaller parts.

> **Mark has $1\frac{1}{4}$ hours to finish his three household chores. If he divides his time evenly, how many hours can he give to each?**

Note that the question is "How many hours for one chore?" The 5 fourths of an hour that Mark has do not split neatly into three parts. So some or all of the parts must be partitioned. Figure 16.14 shows three different models for figuring this out. In each case, all of the fourths are subdivided into three equal parts, producing twelfths. There are a total of 15 twelfths, or $\frac{5}{12}$ hour for each chore. (Test this answer against the solution in minutes: $1\frac{1}{4}$ hours is 75 minutes, which divided among 3 chores is 25 minutes per chore.)

Fractional Divisors.   The sharing concept appears to break down when the divisor is a fraction. However, it is enormously helpful to keep in mind that for partition and rate problems the fundamental question is "How much is one?" Interestingly, this is exactly the second type of question in the parts-and-whole tasks from Chapter 15: Given the part, find the whole—how much is one? For example, if 18 counters represents $2\frac{1}{4}$ sets, how much is one whole set? (See Figure 15.13 for more examples.) In solving these problems, the first task is to find the number in one-fourth and then multiply by 4 to get four-fourths or *one*. Let's see if we can see the same process in the following problem:

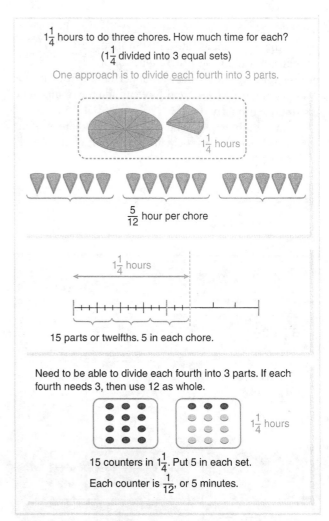

Figure 16.14 Three models of partition division with a whole-number divisor.

> **Elizabeth bought $3\frac{1}{3}$ pounds of tomatoes for $2.50. How much did she pay per pound?**

⏸ ——————————— *Pause and Reflect*

The given amount of $2.50 is distributed across $3\frac{1}{3}$ pounds. How much is distributed to 1 pound? Solve the problem the same way as you would a parts-and-whole problem. Try it now before reading on.

In $3\frac{1}{3}$ there are 10 thirds. Since the $2.50 covers (or is distributed across) ten-thirds, the first step is to partition and find out how much for one-third. If ten-thirds is $2.50, then one-third is $0.25. There are 3 thirds in one. Therefore, 75 cents must cover 1 pound, or 75 cents per pound.

Try the following problems using a similar strategy.

Dan paid $2.40 for a $\frac{3}{4}$-pound box of cereal. How much is that per pound?

Aidan found out that if she walks really fast during her morning exercise, she can cover $2\frac{1}{2}$ miles in $\frac{3}{4}$ of an hour. She wonders how fast she is walking in miles per hour.

With both problems, first find the amount of one-fourth (partitioning) and then the value of one whole (iterating). Aidan's walking problem is a bit harder because the $2\frac{1}{2}$ miles, or 5 half miles, do not neatly divide into three parts. If this was difficult for you, try dividing each half into three parts. Draw pictures or use models if that will help.

Measurement Interpretation of Division

The measurement interpretation is also called repeated subtraction or equal groups (NCTM, 2006a). In these situations an equal group is taken away from the total repeatedly. For example, *If you have 13 quarts of lemonade, how many canteens holding 3 quarts each can you fill?* Notice that this is not a sharing situation but rather an equal subtraction situation.

Since this is the concept of division that is almost always seen in textbooks and will be used to develop an algorithm for dividing fractions, it is important for students to explore this idea in contextual situations.

Students readily understand problems such as this:

You are going to a birthday party. From Ben and Jerry's ice cream factory, you order 6 pints of ice cream. If you serve $\frac{3}{4}$ of a pint of ice cream to each guest, how many guests can be served? (Schifter, Bastable, & Russell, 1999b, p. 120)

Students typically draw pictures of six items divided into fourths and count out how many servings of $\frac{3}{4}$ can be found. The difficulty is in seeing this as $6 \div \frac{3}{4}$, and that part will require some direct guidance on your part. One idea is to compare the problem to one involving whole numbers (6 pints, 2 per guest) and make a comparison.

Gregg and Gregg (2007) produced a method for developing the concept of division of fractions through servings, a measurement context. In tasks that progress in difficulty, they pose problems and include visuals of the size of the pieces. Figure 16.15 includes a subset of these tasks.

As the figure shows, moving very slowly to more complex examples will enable students to use their whole-number concepts to build an understanding of division with fractions. Over time students will be able to take on prob-

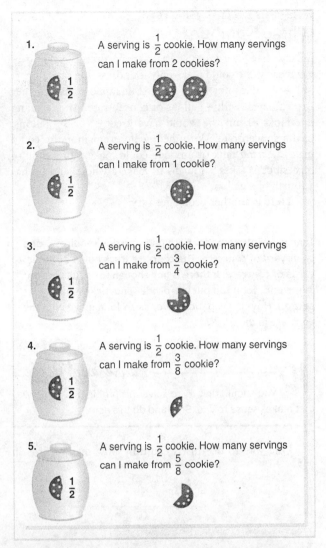

Figure 16.15 Tasks that use the measurement interpretation of "How many servings?" to develop the concept of division. *Source:* Gregg, J., & Gregg, D. W. (2007). "Measurement and Fair-Sharing Models for Dividing Fractions." *Mathematics Teaching in the Middle School, 12*(9), p. 491. Reprinted with permission. Copyright © 2008 by the National Council of Teachers of Mathematics, Inc. www.nctm.org. All rights reserved.

lems that are more complex in context and in the numbers involved, as in the following example.

Farmer Brown found that he had $2\frac{1}{4}$ gallons of liquid fertilizer concentrate. It takes $\frac{3}{4}$ gallon to make a tank of mixed fertilizer. How many tankfuls can he mix?

Try solving this problem yourself. Use any model or drawing you wish to help explain what you are doing. Notice that you are trying to find out *How many sets of 3 fourths are in a set of 9 fourths?* Your answer should be 3 tankfuls (not 3 fourths).

Answers That Are Not Whole Numbers

If Linda had 5 yards of material to make dresses needing $1\frac{1}{6}$ yards each, she could make only four dresses because a part of a dress does not make sense. But suppose that Farmer Brown began with 4 gallons of concentrate. After making five tanks of mix, he would have used $\frac{15}{4}$, or $3\frac{3}{4}$ gallons, of the concentrate. With the $\frac{1}{4}$ gallon remaining he could make a *partial* tank of mix. He could make $\frac{1}{3}$ of a tank of mix, since it takes *3 fourths* to make a whole, and he has *1 fourth* of a gallon.

Here is another problem to try:

John is building a patio. Each patio section requires $\frac{1}{3}$ of a cubic yard of concrete. The concrete truck holds $2\frac{1}{2}$ cubic yards of concrete. If there is not enough for a full section at the end, John can put in a divider and make a partial section. How many patio sections can John make with the concrete in the truck?

⏸ ─────────── *Pause and Reflect*

You should first try to solve this problem in some way that makes sense to *you*. Stop and do this now.

One way to do this is counting how many thirds in $2\frac{1}{2}$?

Here you can see that you get 3 patio sections from the yellow whole, 3 more from the orange whole, and then you get 1 more full section and $\frac{1}{2}$ of what you need for another patio section. So, the answer is $7\frac{1}{2}$. Students will want to write the "remainder" as $\frac{1}{3}$ since they were measuring in thirds, but the question is how many sections can be made—$7\frac{1}{2}$.

Will common denominators work for multiplication? Let's see. In the problem you just solved, $2\frac{1}{2} \div \frac{1}{3}$, the problem would become $2\frac{3}{6} \div \frac{2}{6}$, or it could be $\frac{15}{6} \div \frac{2}{6}$. The question becomes, *How many sets of 2 sixths are in a set of 15 sixths?* Or, *How many 2s in 15?* $7\frac{1}{2}$. This is as efficient as the traditional algorithm, and it may make more sense to students to do it this way.

Figure 16.16 shows two division problems solved in this same way, each with a different model. That is, both the dividend or given quantity and the divisor are expressed in the same type of fractional parts. This results in a whole-number division problem. (In the concrete problem, after

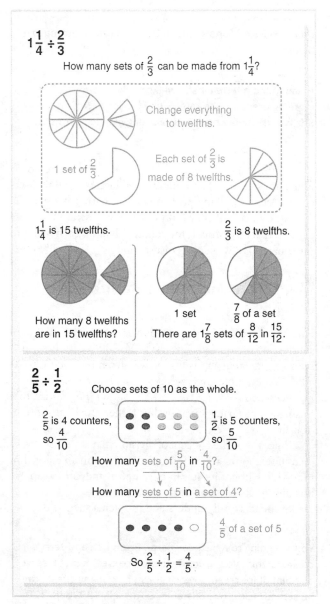

Figure 16.16 Common denominators can be used to solve division of fraction problems.

changing the numbers to twelfths, the answer is the same as $15 \div 8$.) In the classroom, after students have solved problems such as this using their own methods, suggest this common-unit approach.

Developing the Algorithms

There are two different algorithms for division of fractions. Methods of teaching both algorithms are discussed here.

Common-Denominator Algorithm. The common-denominator algorithm relies on the measurement or repeated subtraction concept of division. Consider the problem $\frac{5}{3} \div \frac{1}{2}$. As shown in Figure 16.17, once each num-

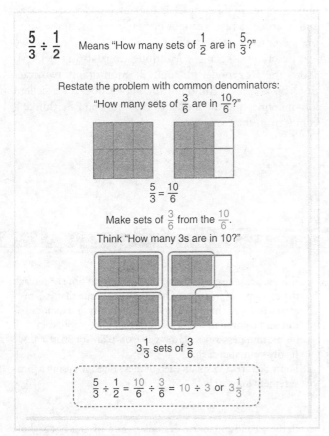

Figure 16.17 Models for the common-denominator method for fraction division.

ber is expressed in terms of the same fractional part, the answer is exactly the same as the whole-number problem $10 \div 3$. The name of the fractional part (the denominator) is no longer important, and the problem is one of dividing the numerators. The resulting algorithm, therefore, is as follows: *To divide fractions, first get common denominators, and then divide numerators.* For example, $\frac{5}{3} \div \frac{1}{4} = \frac{20}{12} \div \frac{3}{12} = 20 \div 3 = \frac{20}{3} = 6\frac{2}{3}$.

Try using circular fraction pieces, fraction strips, and then sets of counters to model $1\frac{2}{3} \div \frac{3}{4}$ using a common-denominator approach.

Invert-and-Multiply Algorithm. To invert the divisor and multiply may be one of the most poorly understood procedures in the K–8 curriculum. (Do you know why invert-and-multiply works?) Interestingly, in a much discussed study of Chinese and U.S. teachers, Liping Ma (1999) found that most Chinese teachers not only use and teach this algorithm, but they also understand why it works. U.S. teachers were found to be sadly lacking in their understanding of fraction division.

Providing a series of tasks and having students look for patterns in how they are finding the answers can help students discover the algorithm. For example, consider this

first set, in which the divisor is a unit fraction. Remember to pose the related question that goes with each equation. Servings of food can be the context.

$3 \div \frac{1}{2} =$ (How many servings of $\frac{1}{2}$ in 3 containers?)
$5 \div \frac{1}{4} =$ (How many servings of $\frac{1}{4}$ in 5 containers?)
$3\frac{3}{4} \div \frac{1}{2} =$ (How many servings of $\frac{1}{2}$ in $3\frac{3}{4}$ containers?)
$6 \div \frac{1}{3} =$ (How many servings of $\frac{1}{3}$ in 6 containers?)
$8 \div \frac{1}{5} =$ (How many servings of $\frac{1}{5}$ in $8\frac{1}{2}$ containers?)

In looking across these problems (and more if you are working with students) and looking for a pattern, students will notice they are multiplying by the denominator of the second fraction. For example, in the last example, a student might say, "You get five for every whole container, so 5×8 is 40."

Then take similar problems, but with a second fraction that is not a unit fraction:

$5 \div \frac{3}{4} =$
$6 \div \frac{2}{3} =$
$8 \div \frac{2}{5} =$

Have students compare these responses to the corresponding problems in the first set. Notice that if there are 40 one-fifths in 8, then when you group the fifths in pairs (two-fifths), you will have half as many—20. Stated in servings, if the serving is twice as big, you will have half the number of servings. Similarly, if the fraction is $\frac{3}{4}$, after finding how many fourths, you will group in threes, which means you will get $\frac{1}{3}$ the number of servings. You can see that this means you must divide by 3.

The examples given were measurements because the size of the group (serving) was known, but not the number of groups. Using partitioning, or sharing, examples nicely illustrates the standard algorithm. Consider this example:

You have $1\frac{1}{2}$ oranges, which is $\frac{3}{5}$ of an adult serving. How many oranges (and parts of oranges) make up 1 adult serving? (Kribs-Zaleta, 2008)

You may be thinking that you first need to find what one fifth would be—which would be one-third of the oranges you have—or $\frac{1}{2}$ an orange (notice you are dividing by the numerator). Then, to get the whole serving you multiply $\frac{1}{2}$ by 5 (the denominator) to get $2\frac{1}{2}$ oranges in 1 adult serving.

In either the measurement or the partitive interpretations, the denominator leads you to find out how many fifths, eighths, or sixths you have, and the numerator tells you the size of the serving, so you group according to how many are in the serving. So the process means to multiply by the denominator and divide by the numerator. At some point someone thought, well, if they just flip the fraction, then it would be more straightforward—multiplying by the top and dividing by the bottom—and that is why we have learned to "invert and multiply."

 The NLVM website (http://nlvm.usu.edu/en/nav/NAV/vlibrary.html) has a nice collection of fraction applets. Number Line Bars-Fractions allows the user to place bars of any fractional length along a number line. The number line can be adjusted to have increments from $\frac{1}{2}$ to $\frac{1}{15}$, but the user must decide. For example, if bars of $\frac{1}{4}$ and $\frac{1}{3}$ are placed end to end, the result cannot be read from the applet until the increments are in twelfths.

Fractions Rectangle Multiplication (also at NLVM) shows the area model for multiplication of any two fractions up to 2×2. Although the applet does an excellent job of connecting the model to the equation, the thinking comes from the user. ◆

Reflections on Chapter 16

Writing to Learn

1. When should estimation of fraction computation be taught to students? Why is it important to teach computational estimation with fractions?
2. A student adds $\frac{4}{5} + \frac{2}{3}$ and gets $\frac{6}{8}$. How will you help the student understand that this is incorrect and how would you redirect him or her to do it correctly?
3. For the problem $3\frac{1}{4} - 1\frac{1}{2}$ think of a story problem that would be a "take away" situation and one that would be a "comparison" situation.
4. Explain at least one mental method (estimation or mental computation) for each of these:

$$\frac{3}{4} \times 5\frac{1}{2} \qquad 1\frac{1}{8} \text{ of } 40$$

5. Make up a word problem with a fraction as a divisor. Is your problem a measurement problem or a partition problem? Make up a second word problem with fractions of the other type (measurement or partition).

For Discussion and Exploration

1. Imagine teaching fraction computation in the sixth or seventh grade, a subject required by your curriculum. You quickly find that your students have a very weak understanding of fractions. Your textbook primarily targets the algorithms. Some teachers argue that there is no time to reteach the concepts of fractions. Others would argue that it is necessary to teach the meanings of numerators and denominators and equivalent fractions or else all the computation will be meaningless rules. How will you plan for instruction? Justify your approach.

2. Draw pictures to explain each of these divisions using a measurement approach:

$$\frac{2}{4} \div \frac{1}{4} \qquad 2\frac{1}{3} \div \frac{2}{3} \qquad \frac{3}{4} \div \frac{1}{8} \qquad 2\frac{3}{4} \div \frac{2}{3}$$

In the second and fourth examples, the answer is not a whole number. To help you explain the fractional part of the answer, use a set of counters to explain why $13 \div 5 = 2\frac{3}{5}$, also using a measurement approach. (That is, how many sets of 5 are in a set of 13?) Use the same problems and explain a common-denominator algorithm for division. Use the same rationale to explain why $\frac{13}{79} \div \frac{5}{79} = 13 \div 5 = \frac{13}{5}$.

3. Several calculators are now available that do computations in fractional form as well as in decimal form. Some of these automatically give results in simplest terms. If you have access to such a calculator, discuss how it might be used in teaching fractions and especially fraction computation. If such calculators become commonplace, should we continue to teach fraction computation?

Resources for Chapter 16

Literature Connections

Alice's Adventures in Wonderland
Carroll, 1865/1982

This well-known children's story needs no introduction. Because Alice shrinks in the story, there is an opportunity to explore multiplication by fractions. S. B. Taber (2007) describes in detail how she used this story to engage students in understanding the meaning of multiplication of fractions. She begins by asking if Alice was originally 54″ tall, but was shrunk to $\frac{1}{9}$ of her height, how tall would she be? Later, what if she was restored, but to only $\frac{5}{6}$ her original height? The students were then asked to write their own Alice explanations to multiplication equations.

The Man Who Made Parks *Wishinsky, 1999*

This nonfiction novel explains the remarkable story of Frederick Olmsted, who decided he was going to design a park for New York City—what became Central Park. Creating a park design, students can be given fractional amounts for what needs to be included in the park—for example, $\frac{2}{5}$ gardens, $\frac{1}{10}$ playgrounds, $\frac{1}{2}$ natural habitat (streams and forest), and the rest special features (like a baseball arena). Students can build the plan for their park on a rectangular grid. To include multiplication of fractions include guidelines such as that $\frac{3}{4}$ of the park is natural habitat, with $\frac{1}{3}$ of that to be wooded and $\frac{1}{6}$ to be water features, and so on.

Recommended Readings

Articles

Cramer, K., Wyberg, T., & Leavitt, S. (2008). The role of representations in fraction addition and subtraction. *Mathematics Teaching in the Middle School, 13*(8), 490–496.

This article provides illustrations and student work to show how to teach addition using the fraction circle. Essential considerations of effective instruction are emphasized.

Gregg, J., & Gregg, D. U. (2007). Measurement and fair-sharing models for dividing fractions. *Mathematics Teaching in the Middle School, 12*(9), 490–496.

These authors provide specific series of tasks to develop the concept of division of fractions—a must read for a teacher needing more experiences exploring division or trying to plan a good sequence for her students.

Huinker, D. (1998). Letting fraction algorithms emerge through problem solving. In L. J. Morrow (Ed.), *The teaching and learning of algorithms in school mathematics* (pp. 170–182). Reston, VA: NCTM.

Huinker takes the idea of students inventing algorithms as described for whole numbers in Chapter 12 and applies it to problems involving fractions. With examples of children's work, this article makes a good case for avoiding rules and letting students work with ideas that make sense.

Imm, K. L., Stylianou, D. A., & Chae, N. (2008). Student representations at the center: Promoting classroom equity. *Mathematics Teaching in the Middle School, 13*(8), 458–463.

These authors explain how to use a park context to teach multiplication of fractions. Equity and a culture for learning are at the center of their discussion of the lessons.

Perlwitz, M. D. (2005). Dividing fractions: Reconciling self-generated solutions with algorithmic answers. *Mathematics Teaching in the Middle School, 10*(6), 278–282.

On the surface, this article is about dealing with the remainder in fraction division. The discussion gets at the importance of under-standing algorithms, wrestling with the minimal knowledge that many teachers bring to this subject, and the value of classroom discourse.

Online Resources

Diffy
http://nlvm.usu.edu/en/nav/frames_asid_326_g_3_t_1.html

The goal in a Diffy puzzle is to find differences between the numbers on the corners of the square, working to a desired difference in the center. When working with fractions, the difference of two fractions is a fraction that can be written in many different ways and students must recognize equivalent forms.

Fraction Bars
http://nlvm.usu.edu/en/nav/frames_asid_203_g_2_t_1.html

Much like Cuisenaire rods, this applet places bars over a number line on which the step size can be adjusted, providing a flexible model that can be used for all four operations.

Fractions—Adding
http://nlvm.usu.edu/en/nav/frames_asid_106_g_2_t_1.html

Two fractions and an area model for each are given. The user must find a common denominator to rename and add the fractions.

Field Experience Guide Connections

The link sheet in FEG 3.4 is an excellent planning tool and an assessment tool, as it focuses on four representations for a topic such as multiplication of fractions. Both FEG 3.4 and FEG 7.2 could be used to interview students to find out what they know about fraction computation. FEG Expanded Lessons 9.7 and 9.9 are designed to help students understand fraction multiplication and division, respectively. In addition, FEG 10.3 ("Factor Quest"), which targets factors, and FEG 10.4 ("Interference"), which targets multiples, are good activities to use when teaching computation of fractions.

Chapter 17

Developing Concepts of Decimals and Percents

The U.S. curriculum typically follows the recommendations of the *Curriculum Focal Points* (NCTM, 2006) and introduces decimals in the fourth grade, with most of the computation work on decimals occurring in the fifth grade and repeated later in grades 6 and 7. This fractions-first, decimals-later sequence is arguably the best approach. However, the unfortunate fact is that the topics of fractions and decimals are too often developed separately. Linking the ideas of fractions to decimals can be extremely useful, both from a pedagogical view as well as a practical view. Most of this chapter focuses on that connection.

Big Ideas

1. Decimal numbers are simply another way of writing fractions. Both notations have value. Maximum flexibility is gained by understanding how the two symbol systems are related.

2. The base-ten place-value system extends infinitely in two directions: to tiny values as well as to large values. Between any two place values, the ten-to-one ratio remains the same.

3. The decimal point is a convention that has been developed to indicate the units position. The position to the left of the decimal point is the unit that is being counted as singles or ones.

4. Percents are simply hundredths and as such are a third way of writing both fractions and decimals.

5. Addition and subtraction with decimals are based on the fundamental concept of adding and subtracting the numbers in like position values—a simple extension from whole numbers.

6. Multiplication and division of two numbers will produce the same digits, regardless of the positions of the decimal point. As a result, for most practical purposes, there is no reason to develop new rules for decimal multiplication and division. Rather, the computations can be performed as whole numbers with the decimal placed by way of estimation.

Mathematics Content Connections

The most important connections for decimals are built within this chapter—between decimal numbers and the concepts of fractions.

- **Fraction Concepts** (Chapter 15): Both decimal and fraction symbolism represents the same ideas—the rational numbers.

- **Proportional Thinking** (Chapter 18): Percents are a part-to-whole ratio and can be extended to proportion concepts.

- **Measurement** (Chapter 19): The metric system is modeled after the base-ten system, and all metric measures are expressed in decimals rather than fractions. Conversion from one metric measure to another is quite simple, given an understanding of the decimal system.

- **Real Number System** (Chapter 23): Decimal numeration is helpful in characterizing and understanding the density of the rational numbers and also for approximating irrational numbers.

Connecting Fractions and Decimals

In a world where almost everything can be measured, people need to be able to interpret decimals for such varied needs as reading metric measures, calculating distances, or understanding sports statistics such as those at the Olympics where winners and losers are separated by hundredths of a second and in baseball where hitters (and fans) evaluate performances to thousandths of points. Decimals are important in many occupations, ranging from nurses and pharmacists to workers building airplanes where the level of precision impacts safety for the general public. Because children have been shown to have greater difficulty understanding decimals than fractions (Martinie, 2007), conceptual understanding of decimals and their connections to fractions must be carefully developed.

The symbols 3.75 and $3\frac{3}{4}$ represent the same quantity, yet on the surface the two appear quite different. For children especially, the world of fractions and the world of decimals are very distinct. Even adults tend to think of fractions as sets or regions (three-fourths *of* something), whereas we think of decimals as being more like numbers. When we tell children that 0.75 is the same as $\frac{3}{4}$, this can be especially confusing because in decimal fractions, the denominators are hidden. Even though different ways of writing the numbers have been invented, the numbers themselves are not different. A significant goal of instruction in decimal and fraction numeration should be to help students see that both systems represent the same concepts.

There are at least three ways to help students see the connection between fractions and decimals. First, we can use familiar fraction concepts and models to explore rational numbers that are easily represented by decimals: tenths, hundredths, and thousandths. Second, we can help them see how the base-ten system can be extended to include numbers less than 1 as well as large numbers. Third, we can help children use models to make meaningful translations between fractions and decimals. These three components are discussed in turn.

Base-Ten Fractions

Fractions with denominators of 10, 100, 1000, and so on will be referred to in this chapter as *base-ten fractions*. This is simply a convenient label and is not one commonly found in the literature. Fractions such as $\frac{7}{10}$ or $\frac{63}{100}$ are examples of base-ten fractions.

Base-Ten Fraction Models. Most of the common manipulative models for fractions are somewhat limited for the purpose of depicting base-ten fractions. Generally, the familiar fraction models cannot show hundredths or thousandths. It is important to provide models for these fractions using the same conceptual approaches that were used for fractions such as thirds and fourths.

Two very useful region models can be used to model base-ten fractions. First, to model tenths and hundredths, circular disks such as the one shown in Figure 17.1 can be printed on cardstock (see Blackline Master 28). Each disk is marked with 100 equal intervals around the edge and is cut along one radius. Two disks of different colors, slipped together as shown, can be used to model any fraction less than 1. Fractions modeled on this rational number wheel can be read as base-ten fractions by noting the spaces around the edge but are still reminiscent of the traditional circle model.

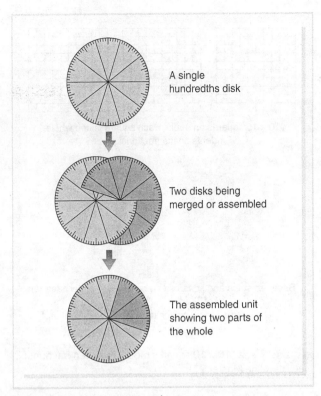

A single hundredths disk

Two disks being merged or assembled

The assembled unit showing two parts of the whole

Figure 17.1 Rational number wheel. For example, turn the wheel to show $\frac{25}{100}$ on the blue plate (also $\frac{1}{4}$ of the circle) (see Blackline Master 28).

However, the most common regional model for base-ten fractions is a 10 × 10 square (see Figure 17.2 and Blackline Master 27). An important variation is to use base-ten place-value strips and squares. As a fraction model, the 10-cm square that was used as the hundreds model for whole numbers is taken as the whole or 1. Each strip is then 1 tenth, and each small square is 1 hundredth. Blackline Master 29 provides a large square that is subdivided into 10,000 tiny squares. When shown on an overhead projector, individual squares or ten-thousandths can easily be identified and shaded in with a pen.

One of the best length models is a meter stick. Each decimeter is one-tenth of the whole stick, each centimeter is one-hundredth, and each millimeter is one-thousandth. Any number-line model broken into 100 subparts is likewise a useful model for hundredths.

Blank number lines are also very useful in helping students compare decimals and think about scale and place value (Martinie & Bay Williams, 2003). Given two or more decimals, students can use the blank number line to position the values, revealing what they know about the size of these decimals using zero, one, other whole numbers, or other decimal values as benchmarks. Again, the use of multiple representations will broaden not only students' understanding but your understanding of their level of performance.

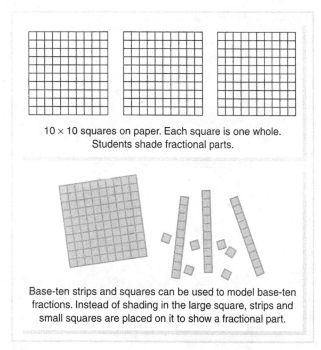

10 × 10 squares on paper. Each square is one whole. Students shade fractional parts.

Base-ten strips and squares can be used to model base-ten fractions. Instead of shading in the large square, strips and small squares are placed on it to show a fractional part.

Figure 17.2 10 × 10 squares model base-ten fractions (see Blackline Master 27).

Many teachers use money as a model for decimals, and to some extent this is helpful. However, for children, money is almost exclusively a two-place system: Numbers like 3.2 or 12.1389 do not relate to money and can cause confusion (Martinie, 2007). Children's initial contact with decimals should be more flexible, and so money is not recommended as a decimal model, at least not at the introductory level. Money is certainly an important *application* of decimal numeration.

Multiple Names and Formats. Early work with base-ten fractions is designed primarily to acquaint students with the models, to help them begin to think of quantities in terms of tenths and hundredths, and to learn to read and write base-ten fractions in different ways.

Have students show a base-ten fraction using any base-ten fraction model. Once a fraction, say, $\frac{65}{100}$, is modeled, the following ideas can be explored:

- Is this fraction more or less than $\frac{1}{2}$? Than $\frac{2}{3}$? Than $\frac{3}{4}$? Some familiarity with base-ten fractions can be developed by comparison with fractions that are easy to think about.
- What are some different ways to say this fraction using tenths and hundredths? ("6 tenths and 5 hundredths," "65 hundredths") Include thousandths when appropriate.

- Show two ways to write this fraction ($\frac{65}{100}$ or $\frac{6}{10} + \frac{5}{100}$).

The last two questions are very important. When base-ten fractions are later written as decimals, they are usually read as a single fraction. That is, 0.65 is read "sixty-five hundredths." But to understand them in terms of place value, the same number must be thought of as 6 tenths and 5 hundredths. A mixed number such as $\frac{513}{100}$ is usually read the same way as a decimal: 5.13 is "five and thirteen-hundredths." Please note that it is accurate to use the word "and," which represents your decimal point. For purposes of place value, it should also be understood as $5 + \frac{1}{10} + \frac{3}{100}$.

The expanded forms will be helpful in translating these fractions to decimals. Given a model or a written or oral fraction, students should be able to give the other two forms of the fraction, including equivalent forms where appropriate.

Extending the Place-Value System

Before considering decimal numerals with students, it is advisable to review some ideas of whole-number place value. One of the most basic of these ideas is the 10-to-1 relationship between the value of any two adjacent positions. In terms of a base-ten model such as strips and squares, 10 of any one piece will make 1 of the next larger, and vice versa.

A Two-Way Relationship. The 10-makes-1 rule continues indefinitely to larger and larger pieces or positional values. As you learned in Chapter 11, if you are using the strip-and-square model, for example, the strip and square shapes alternate in an infinite progression as they get larger and larger. Having established the progression to larger pieces, focus on the idea that each piece to the right in this string gets smaller by one-tenth. The critical question becomes "Is there ever a smallest piece?" In the students' experience, the smallest piece is the centimeter square or unit piece. But couldn't even that piece be divided into 10 small strips? And couldn't these small strips be divided into 10 very small squares, and so on? In the mind's eye, there is no smallest strip or smallest square.

The goal of this discussion is to help students see that a 10-to-1 relationship can extend *infinitely in two directions*. There is no smallest piece and no largest piece. The relationship between adjacent pieces is the same regardless of which two adjacent pieces are being considered. Figure 17.3 illustrates this idea.

The Role of the Decimal Point. An important idea to be realized in this discussion is that there is no built-in reason

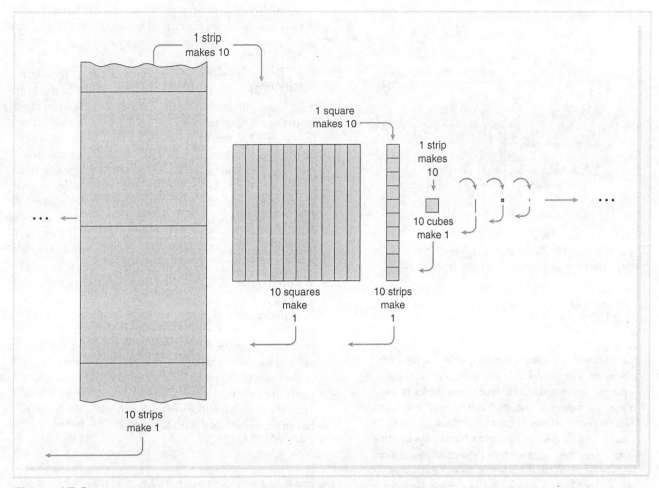

Figure 17.3 Theoretically, the strips and squares extend infinitely in both directions.

why any one position (or base-ten piece) should naturally be chosen to be the unit or ones position. In terms of strips and squares, for example, which piece is the ones piece? The small centimeter square? Why? Why not a larger or a smaller square? Why not a strip? *Any piece could effectively be chosen as the ones piece.*

As shown in Figure 17.4, a given quantity can be written in different ways, depending on the choice of the unit or what piece is used to count the entire collection. The decimal point is placed between two positions with the convention that the position to the left of the decimal is the units or ones position. Thus, the role of the decimal point is *to designate the units position*, and it does so by sitting just to the right of that position.

A fitting caricature for the decimal is shown in Figure 17.5. The "eyes" of the decimal always focus up toward the name of the units or ones. If the "smiling" decimal point were placed between the squares and strips in Figure 17.4, the squares would then be designated as the units, and 16.24 would be the correct written form for the model.

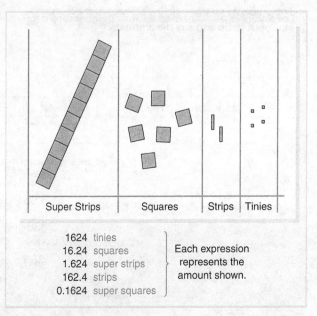

1624	tinies	
16.24	squares	Each expression represents the amount shown.
1.624	super strips	
162.4	strips	
0.1624	super squares	

Figure 17.4 The placement of the decimal point indicates which position is the units.

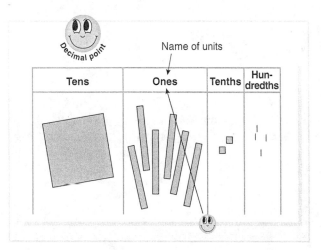

Figure 17.5 The decimal point always "looks up at" the name of the units position. In this case, we have 16.24.

Activity 17.1

The Decimal Names the Unit

Have students display a certain number of base-ten pieces on their desks. For example, put out three squares, seven strips, and four tinies. Refer to the pieces as "squares," "strips," and "tinies," and reach an agreement on names for the theoretical pieces both smaller and larger. To the right of tinies can be "tiny strips" and "tiny squares." To the left of squares can be "super strips" and "super squares." Each student should also have a smiling decimal point. Now ask students to write and say how many squares they have, how many super strips, and so on, as in Figure 17.4. The students position their decimal point accordingly and both write and say the amounts.

Activity 17.1 illustrates vividly the convention that the decimal indicates the named unit and that the unit can change without changing the quantity.

The Decimal with Measurement and Monetary Units. The notion that the decimal "looks at the units place" is useful in a variety of contexts. For example, in the metric system, seven place values have names. As shown in Figure 17.6, the decimal can be used to designate any of these places as the unit without changing the actual measure. Our monetary system is also a decimal system. In the amount $172.95, the decimal point designates the dollars position as the unit. There are 1 hundred (of dollars), 7 tens, 2 singles, 9 dimes, and 5 pennies or cents in this amount of money regardless of how it is written. If pennies were the designated unit, the same amount would be written as 17,295 cents or 17,295.0 cents. It could just as correctly be 0.17295 thousands of dollars or 1729.5 dimes.

In the case of measures such as metric lengths or weights or the U.S. monetary system, the name of the unit is written after the number rather than above the digit as on a place-value chart. You may be 1.62 meters tall, but it does not make sense to say you are "1.62 tall." In the paper, we may read about Congress spending $7.3 billion. Here the units are billions of dollars, not dollars. A city may have a population of 2.4 million people. That is the same as 2,400,000 individuals.

Fraction-Decimal Connection

To connect fractions and decimals, students should make concept-oriented translations—that is, translations based on understanding rather than a rule or algorithm. The purpose of such activities has less to do with the skill of

kilometer	hectometer	dekameter	meter	decimeter	centimeter	millimeter
			3	8	5	

3 meters, 8 decimeters,
and 5 centimeters =

3.85   meters
3850   millimeters
0.00385   kilometers   Unit names
385   centimeters

Figure 17.6 In the metric measurement system, each place-value position has a name. The decimal point can be placed to designate which length is the unit length. Again, the decimal point will "look up" at the unit length. The arrows point to the corresponding location of the decimal point.

converting a fraction to a decimal than with construction of the concept that both systems are used to express the same ideas. The place to begin is with base-ten fractions.

Activity 17.2

Base-Ten Fractions to Decimals

For this activity, have students use their place-value strips and squares (Blackline Master 14). Agree that the large square represents one. Have students cover a base-ten fractional amount of the square using their strips and tinies. For example, have them cover $2\frac{35}{100}$ of the square. Whole numbers require additional squares. The task is to decide how to write this fraction as a decimal and demonstrate the connection using their physical models.

For the last activity, a typical (and correct) reason why $2\frac{35}{100}$ is the same as 2.35 is that there are 2 wholes, 3 tenths, and 5 hundredths. It is important to see this physically. The exact same materials that are used to represent $2\frac{35}{100}$ of the square can be rearranged or placed on an imaginary place-value chart with a paper decimal point used to designate the units position as shown in Figure 17.7.

The reverse of this activity is also worthwhile. Give students a decimal number such as 1.68 and have them show it with base-ten pieces. Their task is to write it as a fraction and show it as a fractional part of a square.

Although these translations between decimals and base-ten fractions are rather simple, the main agenda is

for students to learn from the beginning that decimals are simply fractions.

The calculator can also play a significant role in decimal concept development.

Activity 17.3

Calculator Decimal Counting

Recall how to make the calculator "count" by pressing ⊞ 1 ⊟ ⊟ . . . Now have students press ⊞ 0.1 ⊟ ⊟ . . . When the display shows 0.9, stop and discuss what this means and what the display will look like with the next press. Many students will predict 0.10 (thinking that 10 comes after 9). This prediction is even more interesting if, with each press, the students have been accumulating base-ten strips as models for tenths. One more press would mean one more strip, or 10 strips. Why should the calculator not show 0.10? When the tenth press produces a display of 1 (calculators are not usually set to display trailing zeros to the right of the decimal), the discussion should revolve around trading 10 strips for a square. Continue to count to 4 or 5 by tenths. How many presses to get from one whole number to the next? Try counting by 0.01 or by 0.001. These counts illustrate dramatically how small one-hundredth and one-thousandth really are. It requires 10 counts by 0.001 to get to 0.01 and 1000 counts to reach 1.

The fact that the calculator counts 0.8, 0.9, 1, 1.1 instead of 0.8, 0.9, 0.10, 0.11 should give rise to the question "Does this make sense? If so, why?"

Calculators that permit entry of fractions also have a fraction-decimal conversion key. On some calculators a decimal such as 0.25 will convert to the base-ten fraction $\frac{25}{100}$ and allow for either manual or automatic simplification. Graphing calculators can be set so that the conversion is either with or without simplification. The ability of fraction calculators to go back and forth between fractions and decimals makes them a valuable tool as students begin to connect fraction and decimal symbolism.

Developing Decimal Number Sense

So far, the discussion has revolved around the connection of decimals with base-ten fractions. Number sense implies more. It means having intuition about or a friendly understanding of numbers. To this end, it is useful to connect decimals to the fractions with which children are familiar, to be able to compare and order decimals readily, and to approximate decimals with useful familiar numbers.

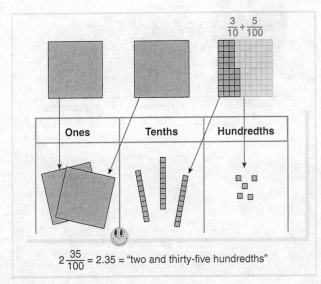

$2\frac{35}{100} = 2.35 =$ "two and thirty-five hundredths"

Figure 17.7 Translation of a base-ten fraction to a decimal.

Familiar Fractions Connected to Decimals

Chapter 15 showed how to help students develop a conceptual familiarity with simple fractions, especially halves, thirds, fourths, fifths, and eighths. We should extend this familiarity to the same concepts expressed as decimals. One way to do this is to have students translate familiar fractions to decimals by means of a base-ten model.

The following two activities have the same purpose—to help students think of decimals in terms of familiar fraction equivalents and to make this connection in a conceptual manner.

Activity 17.4

Friendly Fractions to Decimals

Students are given a "friendly" fraction to convert to a decimal. They first model the fraction using either a 10 × 10 grid or the base-ten strips and squares. With the model as a guide, they then write and draw an explanation for the decimal equivalent. If strips and squares are used, be sure that students draw pictures as part of their explanations.

A good sequence is to start with halves and fifths, then fourths, and possibly eighths. Thirds are best done as a special activity.

Figure 17.8 shows how translations in the last activity might go with a 10 × 10 grid. For fourths, students will often shade a 5 × 5 section (half of a half). The question

then becomes how to translate this to decimals. Ask these students how they would cover $\frac{1}{4}$ with strips and squares if they were only permitted to use nine or fewer tinies. The fraction $\frac{3}{8}$ represents a wonderful challenge. A hint might be to find $\frac{1}{4}$ first and then notice that $\frac{1}{8}$ is half of a fourth. Remember that the next smaller pieces are tenths of the little squares. Therefore, a half of a little square is $\frac{5}{1000}$.

Because the circular model carries such a strong mental link to fractions, it is well worth the time to do some fraction-to-decimal conversions with the rational number wheel shown in Figure 17.1 (see Blackline Master 28).

Activity 17.5

Estimate, Then Verify

With the blank side of the wheel facing them, have students adjust the wheel to show a particular friendly fraction, for example, $\frac{3}{4}$. Next they turn the wheel over and record how many hundredths they estimate were in the section (note that the color reverses when the wheel is turned over). Finally, they should make an argument for the correct number of hundredths and the corresponding decimal equivalent.

The estimation component of the last activity adds the visual "feeling" for fractions. In one fifth-grade class that was having difficulty finding a decimal equivalent for their rational number wheel fraction, the teacher cut up some extra disks into tenths and hundredths so that these parts of the fraction could be placed on a chart (see Figure 17.9).

The exploration of modeling $\frac{1}{3}$ as a decimal is a good introduction to the concept of an infinitely repeating decimal.

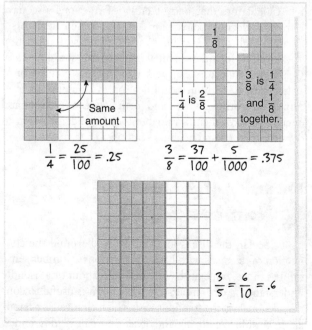

Figure 17.8 Familiar fractions converted to decimals using a 10 × 10 square.

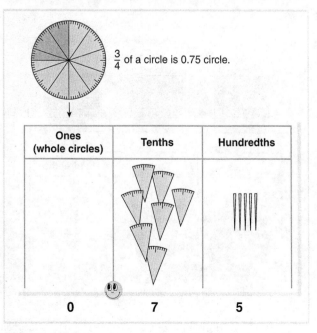

Figure 17.9 Fraction models could be decimal models.

Try to partition the whole 10×10 square into 3 parts using strips and little squares. Each part receives 3 strips with 1 strip left over. To divide the leftover strip, each part gets 3 little squares with 1 left over. To divide the little square, each part gets 3 small strips with 1 left over. (Recall that with base-ten pieces, each smaller piece must be $\frac{1}{10}$ of the preceding size piece.) It becomes obvious that this process is never-ending. As a result, $\frac{1}{3}$ is the same as $0.333333\ldots$ or $0.\overline{3}$. For practical purposes, $\frac{1}{3}$ is about 0.333. Similarly, $\frac{2}{3}$ is a repeating string of sixes, or about 0.667. Later, students will discover that many fractions cannot be represented by a finite decimal.

The number line is another good connecting model. Students are more apt to think of decimals as numbers that appear on the number line than they are to think of fractions in that way. The following activity continues the development of fraction-decimal equivalences.

Activity 17.6

Decimals on a Friendly Fraction Line

Give students five decimal numbers that have friendly fraction equivalents. Keep the numbers between two consecutive whole numbers. For example, use 3.5, 3.125, 3.4, 3.75, and 3.66. Show a number line encompassing the same whole numbers. The subdivisions on the number line should be only fourths, only thirds, or only fifths but without labels. The students' task is to locate each of the decimal numbers on the number line and to provide the fraction equivalent for each.

Results of National Assessment of Educational Progress (NAEP) examinations consistently reveal that students have difficulties with the fraction-decimal relationship. Kouba et al. (1988a) note that students could express proper fractions as decimals but only 40 percent of seventh graders could give a decimal equivalent for a mixed number. In the sixth NAEP, students had difficulty placing decimals on a number line where the subdivisions were fractions (Kouba, Zawojewski, & Strutchens, 1997). In the 2005 NAEP, only 56 percent of eighth graders correctly placed decimal numbers on a number line when the increments were multiples of 0.2—not even in fraction increments. Division of the numerator by the denominator may be a means of converting fractions to decimals, but it contributes nothing to understanding the resulting equivalence. Note that this method has not been and will not be suggested in this chapter.

A simple yet powerful assessment of decimal understanding has students represent two related decimal numbers, such as 0.6 and 0.06, using each of three or four different representations: a number line (not provided but student drawn), a

10×10 grid, money, and base-ten materials (Martinie & Bay-Williams, 2003). For additional information, have students give reasons for their representations. If students have significantly more difficulty with one model than others, this may mean that they have learned how to use certain models but have not necessarily developed true conceptual understanding of decimal fractions. Placement of decimals on a blank number line is perhaps the most interesting—and the most telling—task (see Figure 17.10). ◆

Approximation with a Nice Fraction

In the real world, decimal numbers are rarely those with exact equivalents to nice fractions. What fraction would you say approximates the decimal 0.52? In the sixth NAEP exam, only 51 percent of eighth graders selected $\frac{1}{2}$. The other choices were $\frac{1}{50}$ (29 percent), $\frac{1}{5}$ (11 percent), $\frac{1}{4}$ (6 percent), and $\frac{1}{3}$ (4 percent) (Kouba et al., 1997). Again, a possible explanation for this performance is a reliance on rules. Students need to wrestle with the size of decimal numbers and begin to develop a sense of familiarity with them.

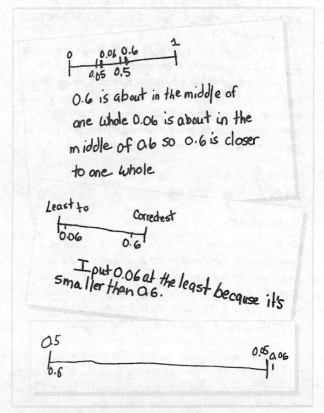

Figure 17.10 Three different sixth-grade students attempt to draw a number line and show the numbers 0.6 and 0.06.

Source: Reprinted with permission from Martinie, S. L., & Bay-Williams, J. (2003). "Investigating Students' Conceptual Understanding of Decimal Fractions Using Multiple Representations." *Mathematics Teaching in the Middle School, 8,* p. 246. Copyright © 2003 by the National Council of Teachers of Mathematics, Inc. www.nctm.org. All rights reserved.

As with fractions, the first benchmarks that should be developed are 0, $\frac{1}{2}$, and 1. For example, is 7.3962 closer to 7 or 8? Why? (Would you accept this response: "Closer to 7 because 3 is less than 5"?) Is it closer to 7 or $7\frac{1}{2}$? Often the 0, $\frac{1}{2}$, or 1 benchmarks are good enough to make sense of a situation. If a closer approximation is required, students should be encouraged to consider the other nice fractions (thirds, fourths, fifths, and eighths). In this example, 7.3962 is close to 7.4, which is $7\frac{2}{5}$. A good number sense with decimals would imply the ability to think quickly of a meaningful fraction that is a close substitute for almost any number.

To develop this type of familiarity with decimals, children do not need new concepts or skills. They do need the opportunity to apply and discuss the related concepts of fractions, place value, and decimals in activities such as the following.

Activity 17.7

Close to a Friendly Fraction

Make a list of about five decimals that are close to but not exactly equal to a nice or friendly fraction equivalent. For example, use 24.8025, 6.59, 0.9003, 124.356, and 7.7.

The students' task is to decide on a decimal number that is close to each of these decimals and that also has a friendly fraction equivalent that they know. For example, 6.59 is close to 6.6, which is $6\frac{3}{5}$. They should write an explanation for their choices. Different students may select different equivalent fractions, providing for a discussion of which is closer.

Activity 17.8

Best Match

On the chalkboard or whiteboard, list a scattered arrangement of five familiar fractions and at least five decimals that are close to the fractions but not exact. Students are to pair each fraction with the decimal that best matches it. The difficulty is determined by how close the various fractions are to one another.

In Activities 17.7 and 17.8, students will have a variety of reasons for their answers. Sharing their thinking with the class provides a valuable opportunity for all to learn. Do not focus on the answers but on the rationales.

 The connections between models and the two symbol systems for rational numbers—fractions and decimals—provide good tasks for a diagnostic interview. Provide students with a number represented in any one of these three ways and have

them provide the other two along with an explanation. Here are a few examples:

- Write the fraction $\frac{5}{8}$ as a decimal. Use a drawing or a physical model (meter stick or 10×10 grid) and explain why your decimal equivalent is correct.
- What fraction is also represented by the decimal 2.6? Use words, pictures, and numbers to explain your answer.
- Use both a fraction and a decimal to tell what point might be indicated on this number line. Explain your reasoning.

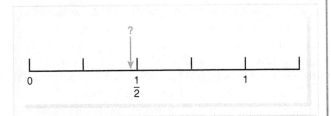

In the last example, it is especially interesting to see which representation students select first—fraction or decimal. Furthermore, do they then translate this number to the other representation or make a second independent estimate?

Ordering Decimal Numbers

Putting a list of decimal numbers in order from least to greatest is a skill closely related to the one just discussed. Consider the following list: 0.36, 0.058, 0.375, and 0.4. The most common error is to select the number with more digits as largest, an incorrect application of whole-number ideas. Another common error is the idea that because digits far to the right represent very small numbers, longer numbers are smaller (Steinle & Stacey, 2004). Both errors reflect a lack of conceptual understanding of how decimal numbers are constructed. The following activities can help promote discussion about the relative sizes of decimal numbers.

Activity 17.9

Line 'Em Up

Prepare a list of four or five decimal numbers that students might have difficulty putting in order. They should all be between the same two consecutive whole numbers. Have students first predict the order of the numbers, from least to greatest. Require students to use a model of their choice to defend their ordering. As students wrestle with representing the numbers with a model (perhaps a number line with 100 subdivisions or the 10,000 grid), they will necessarily confront the idea of which digits contribute the most to the size of a decimal.

In the world outside of classrooms, we almost never have to even think about the order of "ragged" decimals—decimals with different numbers of digits after the decimal point. The real purpose of exercises such as "Line 'Em Up" is not to develop a skill—but rather to create a better understanding of decimal numeration. Tasks such as this will, however, continue to be on standardized tests because they are good assessments of decimal understanding.

Activity **17.10**

Close "Nice" Numbers

Write a four-digit decimal on the board—3.0917, for example. Start with the whole numbers: "Is it closer to 3 or 4?" Then go to the tenths: "Is it closer to 3.0 or 3.1?" Repeat with hundredths and thousandths. At each answer, challenge students to defend their choices with the use of a model or other conceptual explanation. A large number line without numerals, shown in Figure 17.11, is useful.

Other Fraction-Decimal Equivalents

Recall that the denominator is a divisor and the numerator is a multiplier. For example, $\frac{3}{4}$, therefore, means the same as $3 \times (1 \div 4)$ or $3 \div 4$. So how would you express $\frac{3}{4}$ on a simple four-function calculator? Simply enter $3 \div 4$. The display will read 0.75.

Too often students think that dividing the denominator into the numerator is simply an algorithm for converting fractions to decimals, and they have no understanding of why this might work. Use the opportunity to help students develop the idea that in general $a/b = a \div b$. (See Chapter 15, p. 287.)

The calculator is an important tool when developing familiarity with decimal concepts. Finding the decimal equivalents with a calculator can produce some interesting patterns and observations. For example, here are some questions to explore:

- Which fractions have decimal equivalents that terminate? Is the answer based on the numerator, the denominator, or both?
- For a given fraction, how can you tell the maximum length of the repeating part of the decimal? Try dividing by 7 and 11 and 13 to reach an answer.
- Explore all of the ninths—$\frac{1}{9}, \frac{2}{9}, \frac{3}{9}, \ldots \frac{8}{9}$. Remember that $\frac{1}{3}$ is $\frac{3}{9}$ and $\frac{2}{3}$ is $\frac{6}{9}$. Use only the pattern you discover to predict what $\frac{9}{9}$ should be. But doesn't $\frac{9}{9} = 1$?
- How can you find what fraction produces this repeating decimal: 3.454545 . . . ?

The last question in the list can be generalized for any repeating decimal, illustrating that every repeating decimal is a rational number. It is not at all useful for students to become skillful at this.

 Much of what was discussed in this section is recommended by the *Standards*. "Students in [grades 3 to 5] should use models and other strategies to represent and study decimal numbers. For example, they should count by tenths (one-tenth, two-tenths, three-tenths, . . .) verbally or use a calculator to link and relate whole numbers with decimal numbers. . . . They should also investigate the relationship between fractions and decimals, focusing on equivalence" (p. 150). ◆

Introducing Percents

The term *percent* is simply another name for *hundredths* and as such is a standardized ratio with a denominator of 100. If students can express common fractions and simple decimals as hundredths, the term *percent* can be substituted for the term *hundredth*. Consider the fraction $\frac{3}{4}$. As a fraction expressed in hundredths, it is $\frac{75}{100}$. When $\frac{3}{4}$ is written in decimal form, it is 0.75. Both 0.75 and $\frac{75}{100}$ are read in exactly the same way, "seventy-five hundredths." When used as operators, $\frac{3}{4}$ of something is the same as 0.75

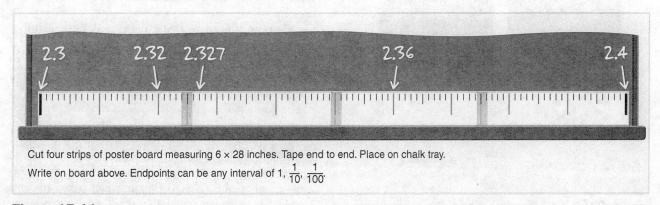

Cut four strips of poster board measuring 6 × 28 inches. Tape end to end. Place on chalk tray.

Write on board above. Endpoints can be any interval of 1, $\frac{1}{10}$, $\frac{1}{100}$.

Figure 17.11 A decimal number line.

or 75 percent of that same thing. Thus, percent is merely a new notation and terminology, not a new concept.

The results of the NAEP tests and numerous other studies have consistently shown that students have difficulty with problems involving percents (Wearne & Kouba, 2000). For example, on the 2005 NAEP, only 37 percent of eighth graders could determine an amount following a given percent of increase. Most are likely to select the answer obtained by adding the percent itself to the original amount. That is, for a 10 percent increase, they would select the answer that was 10 more than the original amount. Only 30 percent of the students could accurately calculate the tip percentage when given the cost of the meal and the amount of the tip left by the diners. A reason for this continual dismal performance is a failure to develop percent concepts meaningfully. In this book we explore percentages twice. Here we will connect them to fractions and decimals. In Chapter 18 we will revisit percent as a ratio as part of the study of proportional reasoning.

Models and Terminology

Models provide the main link among fractions, decimals, and percents, as shown in Figure 17.12 (see Blackline Masters 27 and 28). Base-ten fraction models are suitable for fractions, decimals, and percents, since they all represent the same idea. Students should use base-ten models for percents in much the same way as for decimals. The wheel (Figure 17.1) with 100 markings around the edge is now a model for percents as well as a fraction model for hundredths. The same is true of a 10 × 10 square. Each little square inside is 1 percent of the square. Each row or

strip of 10 squares is not only a tenth but also 10 percent of the square.

Zambo (2008) suggests linking fractions to percent using the 10 × 10 blank hundreds chart. By marking one out of every four squares on the chart students can discover the link between $\frac{1}{4}$ and $\frac{25}{100}$ or 25 percent. He goes on to suggest that even more complex representations such as $\frac{1}{8}$ can lead to interesting discussions about the remaining squares left at the end resulting in $12\frac{1}{2}$ out of 100 squares or $12\frac{1}{2}$ percent.

Similarly, the familiar fractions (halves, thirds, fourths, fifths, and eighths) should become familiar in terms of percents as well as decimals. Three-fifths, for example, is 60 percent as well as 0.6. One-third of an amount is frequently expressed as $33\frac{1}{3}$ percent instead of 33.3333 . . . percent. Likewise, $\frac{1}{8}$ of a quantity is $12\frac{1}{2}$ percent or 12.5 percent of the quantity. These ideas should be explored with base-ten models and not as rules about moving decimal points.

One representation that can be used to link percentages with data collection is a percent necklace. Using fishing cord or other sturdy string, link 100 beads and knot them in a tight, circular necklace. Anytime a circle graph is created or observed in class the percent necklace can provide an estimation tool to help think about the percent that falls in any given category. Given any circle graph, even one of humans as shown in Figure 21.8 on page 445, place the necklace in a circle so that its center coincides with the center of the circle, rather than trying to align with the outside edge of the circle graph. If the necklace makes a wider concentric circle, the students can use a ruler to extend the lines distinguishing the different categories straight out to meet the necklace. If the circle is larger than the necklace, as it would be in Figure 21.8 you will use the actual radial lines marking off the categories. Have students explore the number of beads between any two given lines that represent a wedge of the circle. For example, they might find that 24 beads are in the section of the circle graph that shows how many students like blue as their favorite color. That is an estimate that approximately 24 percent of the students favor blue. Such counting of beads gives students an informal approach to estimating percent, while investigating a meaningful model for thinking about the per one hundred concept.

Percent concepts can be developed through other powerful visual representations that link to proportional thinking. One option is the use of a three-part model to represent the original amount, the decrease/increase, and the final amount (Parker, 2004). Using three rectangles that can be positioned and divided, students can analyze components and consider each piece of the model. The rectangles can be a particularly useful representation for the often confusing problems that include a percentage increase to find an amount greater than the original, as in the previously mentioned 2005 NAEP item, which asked students to calculate how many employees there were at a company

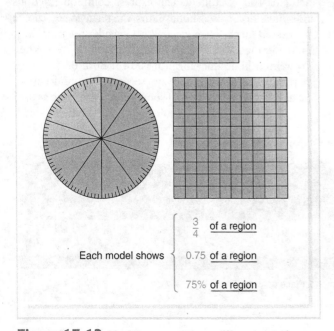

Each model shows
$\frac{3}{4}$ of a region
0.75 of a region
75% of a region

Figure 17.12 Models connect three different notations.

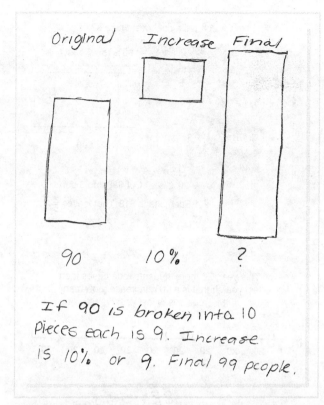

Figure 17.13 A proportional model for reasoning about percent.

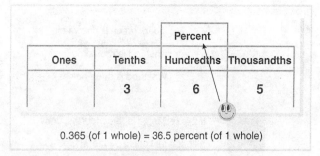

Figure 17.14 Hundredths are also known as percents.

whose workforce increased by 10 percent over the previous level of 90. Using Parker's suggested model, you can see in Figure 17.13 how a student used this proportional model to come up with a correct solution. The use of the proportional model to think about percents will be revisited in the next chapter on proportional reasoning.

Another helpful approach to the terminology of percent is through the role of the decimal point. Recall that the decimal identifies the units. When the unit is ones, a number such as 0.659 means a little more than 6 tenths of 1. The word *ones* is understood (6 tenths of 1 *one* or one *whole*). But 0.659 is also 6.59 tenths and 65.9 hundredths and 659 thousandths. The name of the unit must be explicitly identified, or else the unit would change with each position of the decimal. Since *percent* is another name for *hundredths*, when the decimal identifies the hundredths position as the units, the word *percent* can be specified as a synonym for *hundredths*. Thus, 0.659 (of some whole or 1) is 65.9 hundredths or 65.9 percent of that same whole. As illustrated in Figure 17.14, the notion of placing the decimal point *to identify the percent position* is conceptually more meaningful than the apparently arbitrary rule: "To change a decimal to a percent, move the decimal two places to the right." A more conceptually focused idea is to equate hundredths with percent both orally and in notation.

Realistic Percent Problems

Some middle school teachers may talk about "the three percent problems." The sentence "_____ is _____ percent of _____" has three spaces for numbers; for example, "20 is 25 percent of 80." The classic three percent problems come from this sterile expression; two of the numbers are given, and the students are asked to produce the third. Students learn very quickly that you either multiply or divide the two given numbers, and sometimes you have to move a decimal point. But they have no way of determining when to do what, which numbers to divide, or which way to shift the decimal point. As a result, performance on percentage problems is very poor. Furthermore, commonly encountered expressions using percent terminology, such as sales figures, taxes, census data, political information, and trends in economics, are almost never in the "_____ is _____ percent of _____" format. So when asked to solve a realistic percent problem, students are frequently at a loss.

Chapter 15 explored exercises with fractions in which one element—part, whole, or fraction—was unknown. Students used models and simple fraction relationships in those exercises, which are actually the same as the three percent problems. Developmentally, then, it makes sense to help students make the connection between the exercises done with fractions and those done with percents. How? Use the same types of models and the same terminology of parts, wholes, and fractions. The only thing that is different is that the word *percent* is used instead of *fraction*. In Figure 17.15, the three-part whole-fraction exercises demonstrate the link between fractions and percents.

Teaching Percents. Though students must have some experience with the noncontextual situations in Figure 17.15, it is important to have them explore percent relationships in real contexts. Find or make up percent problems, and present them in the same way that they appear in newspapers, on television, and in other real contexts. In addition to realistic problems and formats, follow these maxims for your instruction on percents:

- Limit the percents to familiar fractions (halves, thirds, fourths, fifths, and eighths) or easy percents ($\frac{1}{10}$, $\frac{1}{100}$),

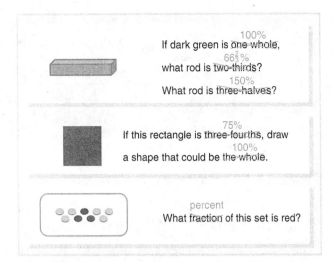

Figure 17.15 Part-whole fraction exercises can be translated into percent exercises.

and use numbers compatible with these fractions. The focus of these exercises is the relationships involved, not complex computational skills.

- Do not suggest any rules or procedures for different types of problems. Do not categorize or label problem types.
- Use the terms *part*, *whole*, and *percent* (or *fraction*). *Fraction* and *percent* are interchangeable. Help students see these percent exercises as the same types of exercises they did with simple fractions.
- Require students to use models or drawings to explain their solutions. It is wiser to assign three problems requiring a drawing and an explanation than to give 15 problems requiring only computation and answers. Remember that the purpose is the exploration of relationships, not computational skill.
- Encourage mental computation.

The following sample problems meet these criteria for familiar fractions and compatible numbers. Try working each problem, identifying each number as a part, a whole, or a fraction. Draw length or area models to explain or work through your thought process. Examples of this informal reasoning are illustrated with additional problems in Figure 17.16.

1. **The PTA reported that 75 percent of the total number of families were represented at the meeting last night. If children from 320 families go to the school, how many were represented at the meeting?**

2. **The baseball team won 80 percent of the 25 games it played this year. How many games were lost?**

3. **In Mrs. Carter's class, 20 students, or $66\frac{2}{3}$ percent, were on the honor roll. How many students are in her class?**

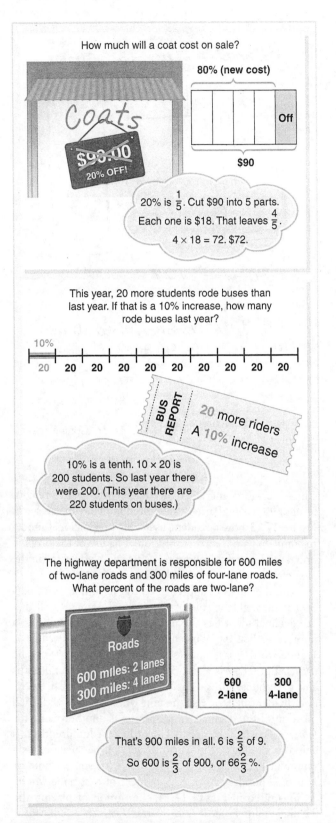

Figure 17.16 Real percent problems with compatible numbers. Simple drawings help with reasoning.

4. Zane bought his new computer at a $12\frac{1}{2}$ percent discount. He paid $700. How many dollars did he save by buying it at a discount?

5. If Nicolas has read 60 of the 180 pages in his library book, what percent of the book has he read so far?

6. The hardware store bought widgets at 80 cents each and sold them for $1 each. What percent did the store mark up the price of each widget?

Pause and Reflect

Examine the examples in Figure 17.16. Notice how each problem is solved with simple fractions and mental math. Then try each of the six problems just listed. Each can be done easily and mentally using familiar fraction equivalents. Use a model or drawing that you think your students might use.

Realistic percent problems are still the best way to assess a student's understanding of percent. Assign one or two, and have students explain why they think their answer makes sense. You might take a realistic percent problem and substitute fractions for percents (e.g., use $\frac{1}{8}$ instead of 12.5 percent) to see how students handle these problems with fractions compared to percents.

If your focus is on reasons and justifications rather than number of problems correct, you will be able to collect all the assessment information you need. ◆

Estimation

Of course, not all real percent problems have nice numbers. Frequently in real life an approximation or estimate in percent situations is all that is required or is enough to help one think through the situation. Even if a calculator will be used to get an exact answer, an estimate based on an understanding of the relationship can confirm that a correct operation was performed or that the decimal point was positioned correctly.

To help students with estimation in percent situations, two ideas that have already been discussed can be applied. First, when the percent is not a "nice" one, substitute a close percent that is easy to work with. Second, select numbers that are compatible with the percent involved, to make the calculation easy to do mentally. In essence, convert the not-nice percent problem into one that is nice. Here are some examples.

1. The 83,000-seat stadium was 73 percent full. How many people were at the game?

2. The treasurer reported that 68.3 percent of the dues had been collected, for a total of $385. How much

more money could the club expect to collect if all dues are paid?

3. Max McStrike had 217 hits in 842 at-bats. What was his batting average?

Pause and Reflect

Use nice fractions and compatible numbers to estimate solutions to each of these last three problems. Do this before reading on.

Possible Estimates

1. (Use $\frac{3}{4}$ and 80,000) ⟶ about 60,000

2. (Use $\frac{2}{3}$ and $380; will collect $\frac{1}{3}$ more) ⟶ about $190

3. ($4 \times 217 > 842$; $\frac{1}{4}$ is 25 percent, or 0.250) ⟶ a bit more than 0.250

Here are three more percent problems with two sets of numbers. The first number in the set is a nice number that allows the problem to be worked mentally using fraction equivalents. The second number requires a substitution with an approximation allowing for an estimate as in the last activity.

1. The school enrolls {480, 547} students. Yesterday {$12\frac{1}{2}$ percent, 13 percent} of the students were absent. How many came to school?

2. Mr. Carver sold his lawn mower for {$45, $89}. This was {60 percent, 62 percent} of the price he paid for it new. What did the mower cost when it was new?

3. When the box fell off the shelf {90, 63} of the {720, 500} widgets broke. What percentage was lost in the breakage?

The first problem asks for a part (whole and fraction given), the second asks for a whole (part and fraction given), and the third asks for a fraction (part and whole given).

It is also convenient at times to use simple base-ten equivalents: 1 percent and 10 percent and multiples of these (including halves). For example, we often use 10 percent plus half of that much to compute a 15 percent tip at a restaurant. To find 0.5 percent we can think of half of 1 percent.

There are several rules of thumb for estimating percentages in real-world situations. As students gain full conceptual understanding and flexibility, there are ways to think about percents that are useful as you are shopping or in situations that bring thinking about percents to the forefront. As mentioned previously to figure a tip you can find 10 percent of the amount and then half of that again to make 15 percent. The same approach is used for adding on sales tax. Depending on your amount, you can find 10 percent, take half of that, and then find 1 percent and add or subtract that amount as needed. But you can encourage other approaches as well. First, students should realize that finding percents is a process of multiplication; therefore, finding 50 percent of 16 will generate the same result as finding 16 percent of 50. This is an important estimation tool when you are "on the go." Also, a 30 percent decrease is the same as 70 percent of the original amount, and sometimes, depending on the original amount, using one of those percents is easier to use in mental calculations than the other. Again, these are nothing more than using the full understanding of percent concepts to your advantage.

Computation with Decimals

Certainly, students should develop computational fluency with decimal numbers. In the past, decimal computation was dominated by the following rules: Line up the decimal points (addition and subtraction), count the decimal places (multiplication), and shift the decimal point in the divisor and dividend so that the divisor is a whole number (division). Some textbooks continue to emphasize these rules. The position taken in this book and in some of the

> **myeducationlab**
>
> Go to the Activities and Application section of Chapter 17 of MyEducationLab. Click on Videos and watch the video entitled **"John Van de Walle on Computation with Decimals"** to see him lead activities with teachers that focus on computation with decimals.

standards-based curricula is that specific rules for decimal computation are not really necessary, especially if computation is built on a firm understanding of place value and a connection between decimals and fractions.

 At the 3–5 level, the *Standards* says that students should "develop and use strategies to estimate computations involving fractions and decimals in situations relevant to students' experience" (p. 148). At the 6–8 level, students are to "select appropriate methods and tools for computing with fractions and decimals from among mental computation, estimation, calculators or computers, and paper and pencil, depending on the situation" (p. 214). ◆

The Role of Estimation

Students should become adept at estimating decimal computations well before they learn to compute with pencil and paper. For many decimal computations, rough estimates can be made easily by rounding the numbers to nice whole numbers or simple base-ten fractions. A minimum goal for your students should be to have the estimate contain the correct number of digits to the left of the decimal—the whole-number part. Start your instruction by selecting problems for which estimates are not terribly difficult.

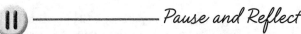
Pause and Reflect

Before going on, try making whole-number estimates of the following computations. Do not spend time with fine adjustments in your estimates.

1. 4.907 + 123.01 + 56.1234
2. 459.8 − 12.345
3. 24.67 × 1.84
4. 514.67 ÷ 3.59

Your estimates might be in the following ranges:

1. Between 175 and 200
2. More than 400, or about 425 to 450
3. More than 25, closer to 50 (1.84 is more than 1 and close to 2)
4. More than 125, less than 200 (500 ÷ 4 = 125 and 600 ÷ 3 = 200)

In these examples, an understanding of decimal numeration and some simple whole-number estimation skills can produce rough estimates. When estimating, focus on the meanings of the numbers and the operations and not on counting decimal places. However, students who are taught to focus on the pencil-and-paper rules for decimal computation do not even consider the actual values of the numbers, much less estimate.

Therefore, a good *place* to begin decimal computation is with estimation. Not only is it a highly practical skill, but it also helps children look at answers in terms of a reasonable range and can form a check on calculator computation.

A good *time* to begin computation with decimals is as soon as a conceptual background in decimal numeration has been developed. An emphasis on estimation is very important, even for students in the seventh and eighth grades who have been exposed to and have used rules for decimal computation, especially for multiplication and division. Many students who are totally reliant on rules for decimals make mistakes without being aware, as they are not using number sense.

Addition and Subtraction

Consider this problem:

Jessica and MacKenna each timed her own quarter-mile run with a stopwatch. Jessica says that she ran the quarter in 74.5 seconds. MacKenna was more accurate. She reported her run as 81.34 seconds. How many seconds faster did Jessica run than MacKenna?

Students who understand decimal numeration should first of all be able to tell approximately what the difference is—close to 7 seconds. With an estimate as a beginning, students should then be challenged to figure out the exact difference. The estimate will help them avoid the common error of lining up the 5 under the 4. A variety of student strategies are possible. For example, students might note that 74.5 and 7 is 81.5 and then figure out how much extra that is. Others may count on from 74.5 by adding 0.5 and then 6 more seconds to get to 81 seconds and then add on the remaining 0.34 second. These and other strategies will eventually confront the difference between the 0.5 and 0.34. Students can resolve this issue by returning to their understanding of place value. Similar story problems for addition and subtraction, some involving different numbers of decimal places, will help develop students' understanding of these two operations. Always require an estimate prior to computation.

After students have had several opportunities to solve addition and subtraction story problems, the following activity is reasonable.

Activity 17.11

Exact Sums and Differences

Give students a sum involving different numbers of decimal places. For example: 73.46 + 6.2 + 0.582. The first task is to make an estimate and explain how the estimate was made. The second task is to compute the exact answer and explain how that was done (no calculators). In the third and final task students devise a method for adding and subtracting decimal numbers that they can use with any two numbers.

When students have completed these three tasks, have students share their strategies for computation and test them on a new computation that you provide. The same task can be repeated for subtraction.

The earlier estimation practice will focus students' attention on the meanings of the numbers. Remember, students can also think about rewriting decimals as fractions with the same denominator to make connections. It is reasonable to expect that students will develop an algorithm that is essentially the same as aligning the decimal points.

If students have difficulty with Activity 17.11, it is an indication that they have a weak understanding of decimal concepts and the role of the decimal point. This is true even for students who get a correct sum by using a rule they learned in an earlier grade but who have difficulty with their explanations. Rather than focus on how to add or subtract decimals, return or shift your focus to decimal concepts as discussed earlier in the chapter. ◆

Multiplication

Estimation should play a significant role in developing an algorithm for multiplication. As a beginning point, consider this problem:

The farmer fills each jug with 3.7 liters of cider. If you buy 4 jugs, how many liters of cider is that?

Begin with an estimate. Is it more than 12 liters? What is the most it could be? Could it be 16 liters? Once an estimate of the result is decided on, let students use their own methods for determining an exact answer. Many will use repeated addition: 3.7 + 3.7 + 3.7 + 3.7. Others may begin by multiplying 3 × 4 and then adding up 0.7 four times. Eventually, students will agree on the exact result of 14.8 liters. Explore other problems involving whole-number multipliers. Multipliers such as 3.5 or 8.25 that involve nice fractional parts—here, one-half and one-fourth—are also reasonable.

As a next step, have students compare a decimal product with one involving the same digits but no decimal. For example, how are 23.4 × 6.5 and 234 × 65 alike? Interestingly, both products have exactly the same digits: 15210. (The zero may be missing from the decimal product.) Using a calculator, have students explore other products that are alike except for the location of the decimals involved. The digits in the answer are always alike. After seeing how the digits remain the same for these related products, do the following activity.

Activity 17.12

Where Does the Decimal Go?: Multiplication

Have students compute the following product: 24 × 63. Using only the result of this computation and estimation, have them give the exact answer to each of the following:

   0.24 × 6.3   24 × 0.63   2.4 × 63   0.24 × 0.63

For each computation they should write a rationale for how they made the placement of the decimal point in each answer. They can check their results with a calculator. Any errors must be acknowledged and the rationale that produced the error adjusted.

❚❚ ——————— *Pause and Reflect*

The product of 24 × 63 is 1512. Use this information to give the answer to each of the products in the previous activity. Do *not* count decimal places. Remember your fractional equivalents.

The method of placing the decimal point in a product by way of estimation is more difficult as the product gets smaller. For example, knowing that 54×83 is 4482 does not make it easy to place the decimal in the product 0.0054×0.00083. Even the product 0.054×0.83 is hard. A reasonable algorithm for multiplication is: *Ignore the decimal points, and do the computation as if all numbers were whole numbers. When finished, place the decimal by estimation.* Even if students have already learned the traditional algorithm, they need to know the conceptual rationale centered on place value and the powers of ten for "counting" and shifting the decimal places. By focusing on rote applications of rules, students lose out on approaches that emphasize opportunities to understand the meaning and effects of operations and are more prone to misapply procedures (Martinie & Bay-Williams, 2003).

Questions such as the following keep the focus on number sense and provide useful information about your students' understanding.

1. Consider these two computations: $3\frac{1}{2} \times 2\frac{1}{4}$ and 2.276×3.18. Without doing the calculations, which product do you think is larger? Provide a reason for your answer that can be understood by someone else in this class.

2. How much larger is 0.76×5 than 0.75×5? How can you tell without doing the computation (Kulm, 1994)?

Student discussions and explanations as they work on these or similar questions can provide insights into their decimal and fraction number sense and the connections between the two representations. ◆

Division

Division can be approached in a manner exactly parallel to multiplication. In fact, the best approach to a division estimate generally comes from thinking about multiplication rather than division. Consider the following problem:

The trip to Washington was 282.5 miles. It took exactly $4\frac{1}{2}$ hours or 4.5 hours to drive. What was the average miles per hour?

To make an estimate of this quotient, think about what times 4 or 5 is close to 280. You might think $60 \times 4.5 = 240 + 30 = 270$. So maybe about 61 or 62 miles per hour.

Here is a second example without context. Make an estimate of $45.7 \div 1.83$. Think only of what times $1\frac{8}{10}$ is close to 45.

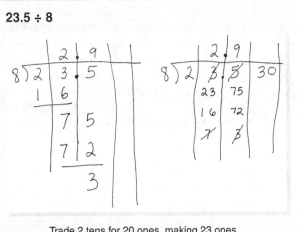

23.5 ÷ 8

Trade 2 tens for 20 ones, making 23 ones.
Put 2 ones in each group, or 16 in all.
That leaves 7 ones.

Trade 7 ones for 70 tenths, making 75 tenths.
Put 9 tenths in each group, or 72 tenths in all.
That leaves 3 tenths.

Trade the 3 tenths for 30 hundredths.

(Continue trading for smaller pieces as long as you wish.)

Figure 17.17 Extension of the division algorithm.

▌▌ ———————————— *Pause and Reflect*

Will the answer be more or less than 45? Why? Will it be more or less than 20? Now think about 1.8 being close to 2. What times 2 is close to 46? Use this to produce an estimate.

Since 1.83 is close to 2, the estimate is near 22. And since 1.83 is less than 2 the answer must be greater than 22—say 25 or 26. (The actual answer is 24.972677.)

Okay, so estimation can produce a reasonable result, but you may still require a pencil-and-paper algorithm to produce the digits the way it was done for multiplication. Figure 17.17 shows division by a whole number and how that can be carried out to as many places as you wish. (The explicit-trade method described in Chapter 12 is shown on the right.) It is not necessary to move the decimal point up into the quotient. Leave that to estimation.

Activity **17.13**

Where Does the Decimal Go?: Division

Provide a quotient such as 146 ÷ 7 = 20857 correct to five digits but without the decimal point. The task is to use only this information and estimation to give a fairly precise answer to each of the following:

$$146 \div 0.7 \quad 1.46 \div 7 \quad 14.6 \div 0.7 \quad 1460 \div 70$$

For each computation students should write a rationale for their answers and then check their results with a calculator. Any errors should be acknowledged, and the rationale that produced the error adjusted.

A reasonable algorithm for division is parallel to that for multiplication: *Ignore the decimal points, and do the computation as if all numbers were whole numbers. When finished, place the decimal by estimation.* This is reasonable for divisors greater than 1 or close to a familiar value (e.g., .1, .5, .01). If students have a method for dividing by 45, they can divide by 0.45 and 4.5.

Reflections on Chapter **17**

Writing to Learn

1. Describe three different base-ten models for fractions and decimals, and use each to illustrate how base-ten fractions can easily be represented.
2. How can we help students think about very small place values such as thousandths and millionths in the same way we get students to think about very large place values such as millions and billions?
3. Use an example involving base-ten pieces to explain the role of the decimal point in identifying the units position. Relate this idea to changing units of measurement as in money or metric measures.
4. For addition and subtraction of decimals, the line-up-the-decimals rule can be reasonably developed through practice with estimation. Explain.
5. Give an example explaining how, in most problems, multiplication and division with decimals can be replaced with estimation and whole-number methods.

For Discussion and Exploration

1. One way to order a series of decimal numbers is to annex zeros to each number so that all numbers have the same number of decimal places. For example, rewrite

0.34		0.3400
0.3004	as	0.3004
0.059		0.0590

Now ignore the decimal points and any leading zeros, and order the resulting whole numbers. Discuss the merits of teaching this approach to children. If taught this procedure, what would students learn about decimal numeration? How will you ensure that this process is not just a "rule without reason"?

Resources for Chapter **17**

Literature Connections

In the daily paper and weekly magazines, you will find decimal and percent situations with endless real-world connections. One issue with percents in news stories is the frequent omission of the base amount or the whole on which the percent is determined. "March sales of video games were reported to be up 3.6 percent." Does that mean an increase over February or over March of the previous year? Increase and decrease by percents are interesting to project over several years. If the consumer price index rises 3 percent a year, how much will a $100 basket of groceries cost by the time your students are 21 years old?

The Phantom Tollbooth *Juster, 1961*

References to mathematical ideas abound throughout this book about Milo's adventures in Digitopolis, where everything is number-oriented. There, Milo meets a boy who is only half of a boy, appearing in the illustration to be the left half of a boy cut top to bottom. As it turns out, the boy is actually 0.58 since he is a member of the average family: a mother, father, and 2.58 children. The boy is the 0.58. One advantage, he explains, is that he is the only one who can drive the 0.3 of a car—the average family owning 1.3 cars. This section of the tale involves a great discussion of averages that come out in decimal numbers.

An obvious extension of the story is to explore averages of things that are interesting to the students (average number of siblings, average arm span, etc.) and see where these odd decimal fractions come from. In the case of measures of length, for example, an average length can be a real length even if no one has it. But an average number of something like pets can be very humorous.

This same book can be used to develop mathematical concepts such as time (when Milo visits the Doldrums), data collection and analysis through percents (How do students in the class spend their day?), measurement with distances to Digitopolis given in various measures on a chart, and humorous discussions and in some cases misunderstandings of such concepts as infinity and proportional thinking. This book is a gem for use with intermediate and middle grade students.

Piece = Part = Portion: Fraction = Decimal = Percent *Gifford & Thaler, 2008*

Illustrated with vivid photos, this is a beginning look at how fractions relate to corresponding decimals and percents. Written by an elementary classroom teacher, the links between the concepts are drawn through common representations, such as one sneaker representing $\frac{1}{2}$ a pair of shoes, 0.50 in decimal form or 50 percent. Real-world links such as one-seventh of a week and one-eleventh of a soccer team will connect with students. Note that some decimals and percents are rounded. The book is available in English and Spanish.

Recommended Readings

Articles

Irwin, K. C. (2001). Using everyday knowledge of decimals to enhance understanding. *Journal for Research in Mathematics Education, 32*(4), 399–420.
Irwin's article describes her work with 16 children, ages 11 and 12. The students worked in eight pairs, half of whom solved problems given in contexts. The other four pairs solved the same problems but without contexts. The article is enlightening on a number of fronts, particularly the transcriptions that clearly indicate the students' misconceptions of decimal numeration.

Martinie, S. L., & Bay-Williams, J. (2003). Investigating students' conceptual understanding of decimal fractions using multiple representations. *Mathematics Teaching in the Middle School, 8*(5), 244–247.
This article describes the results of 43 sixth-grade students who were asked to represent 0.6 and 0.06 with four different representations: a number line, a 10 × 10 grid, money, and base-ten materials. The results indicate that students may appear to understand decimals with one model but not with another. The authors make an argument for using multiple models in teaching decimals.

Books

Albert, L., & McAdam, J. (2007). Making sense of decimal fraction algorithms using base-ten blocks. In W. Gary Martin, Marilyn Strutchens, and Portia Elliott (Eds.), *The learning of mathematics: Sixty-ninth yearbook of the National Council of Teachers of Mathematics* (pp. 303–315). Reston, VA: NCTM.
This chapter emphasizes the critical need for precise mathematical language in the development of algorithms for multiplying decimal fractions. A classroom example details how teachers can use place-value knowledge and arrays of base-ten blocks to build students' conceptual understanding of decimals. Since the article is about prospective teachers' learning of this material, it is easy to relate to the challenges and connections readers may be experiencing.

Online Resources

Base Blocks—Decimals
http://nlvm.usu.edu/en/nav/frames_asid_264_g_3_t_1 .html
Base-ten blocks can be placed on a place-value chart. The number of decimal places can be selected, thus designating any of the four blocks as the unit. Addition and subtraction problems can be created or can be generated randomly.

Circle 3
http://nlvm.usu.edu/en/nav/frames_asid_187_g_3_t_1 .html
This game challenges students to use logic as they combine decimals to add to 3. Not as easy as it sounds.

Concentration
http://illuminations.nctm.org/ActivityDetail.aspx?ID=73
This is an engaging matching game using representations of percents, fractions, and a regional model.

Fractions Bar Applet
www.arcytech.org/java/fractions/fractions.html
This applet develops the relationships among fractions, decimals, and percents. Bars for one whole are displayed and can be partitioned according to selected fraction, decimal, or percent values and then labeled in any of these representations. This makes equivalencies easy to explore.

Fraction Model—Version 3
http://illuminations.nctm.org/tools/tool_detail.aspx?id=45
The equivalence of fraction, decimal, and percent representations in a circle, set, or rectangle model is demonstrated.

Percentages
http://nlvm.usu.edu/en/nav/frames_asid_160_g_3_t_1 .html?open=activities
The user enters any two of the values—whole, part, and percent—and clicks on Compute. Although the computer does the work, the applet nicely models percent problems.

Railroad Repair
http://pbskids.org/cyberchase/games/decimals/decimals
.html

This fun activity has students repairing a railroad by choosing and combining different sized decimal pieces of railroad tracks to help get Cybertrain back to the station.

Sock
www.interactivestuff.org/sums4fun/sock.html

Click on directional arrows to guide the sphere into pushing the green cubes into holes that contain the decimals that will make the target number.

Field Experience Guide Connections

Expanded Lesson 9.8 is an engaging lesson with the goal of helping students be able to fluently convert common fractions to their decimal equivalencies. In Expanded Lesson 9.10 ("How Close Is Close?") students shade 10 × 10 grids to explore density of fractions and decimals, thus learning that for any two decimals, another decimal can be found between them.

Chapter 18

Proportional Reasoning

Proportional reasoning has been referred to as the capstone of the elementary curriculum and the cornerstone of algebra and beyond (Lesh, Post, & Behr, 1987). It begins with the ability to understand multiplicative relationships, distinguishing them from relationships that are additive. The development of proportional reasoning is one of the most important goals of the 5–8 curriculum.

Proportional reasoning goes well beyond the notion of setting up a proportion to solve a problem—it is a way of reasoning about multiplicative situations. In fact, proportional reasoning, like equivalence, is considered a unifying theme in mathematics. You will see this evidence in the many content connections listed on this page.

Big Ideas

1. A ratio is a multiplicative comparison of two quantities or measures. A key developmental milestone is the ability of a student to begin to think of a ratio as a distinct entity, different from the two measures that made it up.

2. Ratios and proportions involve multiplicative rather than additive comparisons. Equal ratios result from multiplication or division, not from addition or subtraction.

3. Proportional thinking is developed through activities involving comparing and determining the equivalence of ratios and solving proportions in a wide variety of problem-based contexts and situations without recourse to rules or formulas.

Mathematics Content Connections

Proportional reasoning is indeed the cornerstone of a wide variety of essential topics in the middle and high school curriculum.

- **Algebra** (Chapter 14): Much of algebra concerns a study of change and, hence, rates of change (ratios) are particularly im-

portant. In this chapter you will see that the graphs of equivalent ratios are straight lines passing through the origin. The slope of the line is the unit ratio.

- **Fractions** (Chapter 15): Equivalent fractions are found through a multiplicative process; numerators and denominators are multiplied or divided by the same number. Equivalent ratios can be found in the same manner. In fact, part-whole relationships (fractions) are an example of ratio. Fractions are also one of the principal methods of representing ratios.

- **Percents** (Chapter 17): Percents are a way of describing an amount as if it were out of 100. This is a part-whole ratio. For example a 65 percent approval rating means the ratio of those approving to those asked is 65 to 100.

- **Geometry** (Chapter 20): When two figures are the same shape but different sizes (i.e., similar), they constitute a visual example of a proportion. The ratios of linear measures in one figure will be equal to the corresponding ratios in the other.

- **Data Graphs** (Chapter 21): A relative frequency histogram shows the frequencies of different related events compared to all outcomes (visual part-to-whole ratios). A box-and-whisker plot shows the relative distribution of data along a number line and can be used to compare distributions of populations of very different sizes.

- **Probability** (Chapter 22): A probability is a ratio that compares the number of outcomes in an event to the total possible outcomes. Proportional reasoning helps students understand these ratios, especially in comparing large and small sample sizes.

Ratios

Regardless of how the objectives are stated in your curriculum concerning the ability to solve proportions or percent problems, the ultimate goal for your students should be focused on the development of proportional reasoning, not a collection of skills. To this end it is useful to have a good idea of what constitutes a ratio and a proportion and in what contexts these mathematical ideas appear. With this information we can then examine what it means to reason proportionally and begin to work toward helping students achieve that goal.

According to *Curriculum Focal Points* (NCTM, 2006), ratios and rates are a focus in sixth grade, developed by looking at pairs of rows (or columns) on the multiplication table and in drawings. In seventh grade ratios are extended to understanding and applying proportional reasoning—for example, investigating contexts such as interest, taxes, and tips as well as connecting to work with similar figures, graphing, and slope. That is not to say that proportional reasoning doesn't begin until middle school. Understanding one-to-one correspondence, place value, fraction concepts, and multiplicative reasoning are among topics that involve early proportional reasoning (Seeley & Schieleck, 2007).

Types of Ratios

A *ratio* is a number that relates two quantities or measures within a given situation in a multiplicative relationship (in contrast to a difference or additive relationship). A ratio can be applied to another situation where the relative amounts of the quantities or measures are the same as in the first situation (Smith, 2002). Ratios appear in a variety of different contexts. Part of proportional reasoning is the ability to recognize ratios in these various settings. To the student just beginning to develop an understanding of ratio, different settings or contexts may well seem like different ideas even though they are essentially the same from a mathematical viewpoint.

Research on Chinese and U.S. teachers shows that Chinese teachers spend more time making sense of the subtle differences among fractions, ratios, and division, whereas U.S. teachers connect ratios quickly to percents without discussion of these interrelated concepts (Cai and Wang, 2006). Table 18.1 offers comparisons among fractions, ratios, and division similar to those used in Chinese lessons as prompts for students to discuss the relationships among these ideas.

Part-to-Whole Ratios. Ratios can express comparisons of a part to a whole, for example, the ratio of the number of girls in a class to the number of students in the class. Because fractions are also part-whole ratios, it follows that every fraction is also a ratio. In the same way, percentages are ratios, and in fact, percentages are sometimes used to express ratios. Probabilities are ratios of a part of the sample space to the whole sample space.

Part-to-Part Ratios. A ratio can also relate one part of a whole to another part of the same whole. For example, the number of girls in the class can be compared to the number of boys. The ratio of the length to the width of a rectangle is a part-to-part relationship. Although the probability of an event is a part-to-whole ratio, the *odds* of an event happening is a ratio of the number of ways an event can happen to the number of ways it cannot happen—a part-to-part ratio.

Rates as Ratios. Both part-to-whole and part-to-part ratios compare two measures of the same type of thing. A ratio can also be a *rate*. A rate is a comparison of the measures of two different things or quantities; the measuring unit is different for each value.

For example, if 4 similar boats carry 36 passengers, then the comparison of 4 boats to 36 passengers is a ratio. Boats and passengers are different types of things. The rate would be the passengers per boat: $\frac{p}{b} = \frac{36}{4} = \frac{9}{1}$. The ratio of passengers to boats is 36:4, which can also be written as $\frac{36}{4}$ or 36 to 4. The rate is 9 passengers per boat. Similarly, all rates of speed are ratios that compare distance to time, such as driving at 55 miles per hour or jogging at 9 minutes per mile.

Miles per gallon, square yards of wall coverage per gallon of paint, passengers per busload, and roses per bouquet are all rates. Relationships between two units of measure are also rates or ratios, for example, inches per foot, milliliters per liter, and centimeters per inch.

Examples of Ratio. In geometry, the ratios of corresponding parts of similar geometric figures are always the same. The diagonal of a square is always $\sqrt{2}$ times a side; that is, the ratio of the diagonal of a square to its side

Table 18.1

Comparison of Fractions, Ratios, and Division				
Concept	First Value	Symbol	Second Value	Result
Ratio	First term	: Colon	Second term	Value of ratio
Fraction	Numerator	— Fraction line	Denominator	Value of fraction
Division	Dividend	÷ Division sign	Divisor	Quotient

Source: Adapted from Cai and Wang, 2006.

is $\sqrt{2}$. The value π (pi) is the ratio of the circumference of a circle to the diameter. The trigonometric functions can be developed from ratios of sides of right triangles.

The slope of a line or of a roof is a ratio of rise for each unit of horizontal distance or run. Slope is an extremely important ratio in algebra. Not only does it describe the steepness of a line, but also it tells us the rate of change of one variable in terms of another.

In nature, the ratio known as the *golden ratio* is found in many spirals, from nautilus shells to the swirls of a pine-cone or a pineapple. Artists and architects have used the same ratio in creating shapes that are naturally pleasing to the eye.

Recall that a ratio is a number that expresses a multiplicative relationship that can be applied to a second situation where the relative quantities or measures are the same as in the first situation.

Proportional Reasoning

Proportional reasoning is difficult to define in a simple sentence or two. It is not something that you either can or cannot do. It is both a qualitative and quantitative process. According to Lamon (1999), the following are a few of the characteristics of proportional thinkers:

- Proportional thinkers have a sense of covariation. That is, they understand relationships in which two quantities vary together and are able to see how the variation in one coincides with the variation in another.
- Proportional thinkers recognize proportional relationships as distinct from nonproportional relationships in real-world contexts.
- Proportional thinkers develop a wide variety of strategies for solving proportions or comparing ratios, most of which are based on informal strategies rather than prescribed algorithms.
- Proportional thinkers understand ratios as distinct entities representing a relationship different from the quantities they compare.

It is estimated that more than half of the adult population cannot be viewed as proportional thinkers (Lamon, 1999). That means that we do not acquire the habits and skills of proportional reasoning simply by getting older. On the other hand, Lamon's research and that of others indicate that instruction that focuses on reasoning (rather than a formula) can have an effect on a student's ability to reason proportionally, which begins early with multiplicative reasoning. Chinese students begin their formal exploration of ratio and proportion in the elementary grades (Cai & Sun, 2002, 2006). In the United States, these concepts are typically taught in grades 6 to 9. However, merely focusing on the procedure of finding the missing value in a proportion encourages students to apply rules without thinking and, thus, the ability to reason proportionally often does not develop.

Such rote work is particularly troubling in the area of proportional reasoning, which is at the core of so many important concepts students will encounter during and after middle school, including "similarity, relative growth and size, dilations, scaling, pi, constant rate of change, slope, speed, rates, percent, trigonometric ratios, probability, relative frequency, density, and direct and inverse variations" (Heinz & Sterba-Boatwright, 2008, p. 528). Wow!

Considerable research has been conducted to determine how children reason in various proportionality tasks and to determine if developmental or instructional factors are related to proportional reasoning (for example, see Bright, Joyner, & Wallis, 2003; Karplus, Pulos, & Stage, 1983; Lamon, 1993, 2002; Lo & Watanabe, 1997; Noelting, 1980; and Post, Behr, & Lesh, 1988).

The research provides direction for how to help children develop proportional thought processes. These ideas are summarized in the following list:

1. Provide ratio and proportion tasks in a wide range of contexts, including situations involving measurements, prices, geometric and other visual contexts, and rates of all sorts.
2. Encourage discussion and experimentation in predicting and comparing ratios. Help children distinguish between proportional and nonproportional comparisons by providing examples of each and discussing the differences.
3. Help children relate proportional reasoning to existing processes. The concept of unit fractions is very similar to unit rates. Research indicates that the use of a unit rate for comparing ratios and solving proportions is the most common approach among middle school students even when cross-product methods have been taught. (This approach is explained later.)
4. Recognize that symbolic or mechanical methods, such as the cross-product algorithm, for solving proportions do not develop proportional reasoning and should not be introduced until students have had many experiences with intuitive and conceptual methods.

 In 1989, the *Curriculum Standards* noted that proportional reasoning "was of such great importance that it merits whatever time and effort must be expended to assure its careful development" (NCTM, 1989, p. 82). The emphasis on proportional reasoning is similarly reflected in *Principles and Standards*, where emphasis is on the need for an integrative approach, one that involves "percent, similarity, scaling,

myeducationlab
Go to the Activities and Application section of Chapter 18 of MyEducationLab. Click on Videos and watch the video entitled "**John Van de Walle on Proportional Reasoning**" to see him talk with teachers about proportional reasoning.

linear equations, slope, relative frequency histograms, and probability" (NCTM, 2000, p. 212). ◆

Additive Versus Multiplicative Situations

Consider the following problem adapted from the book *Adding It Up* (National Research Council, 2001).

Two weeks ago, two flowers were measured at 8 inches and 12 inches, respectively. Today they are 11 inches and 15 inches tall. Did the 8-inch or 12-inch flower grow more?

■■ ──────── *Pause and Reflect*

Before reading further, find and defend two different answers to this problem.

One answer is that they both grew the same amount—3 inches. This correct response is based on additive reasoning. That is, a single quantity was added to each measure to result in the two new measures. A second way to look at the problem is to compare the amount of growth to the original height of the flower. The first flower grew $\frac{3}{8}$ of its height while the second grew $\frac{3}{12}$. Based on this multiplicative view ($\frac{3}{8}$ *times as much* more), the first flower grew more. This is a proportional view of this change situation. Here, both the additive reasoning and multiplicative reasoning produce valid, albeit different, answers. Discussions should focus on the comparison and, thus, highlight the distinction between additive and multiplicative comparisons. An ability to understand the difference between these situations is an indication of proportional reasoning.

 To further help you understand the complexities of proportional reasoning, consider the five-item assessment shown in Figure 18.1, devised to examine students' appropriate use of additive or multiplicative reasoning (Bright, Joyner, & Wallis, 2003). Notice the way each item addresses the possibility of using additive versus multiplicative reasoning. This instrument could easily be used in the classroom as a preassessment, as a series of good classroom tasks to then be discussed, or as a summative assessment to see how well students have acquired an understanding of multiplicative comparisons. In item 1, you might want to explain that the 200 percent setting doubles each dimension of the photo. ◆

■■ ──────── *Pause and Reflect*

Answer the questions in Figure 18.1. Discuss your answers with your colleagues. Which item is not a proportional situation? What is the difference between items 2 and 4?

For each problem, circle the correct answer.

1. Mrs. Allen took a 3-inch by 5-inch photo of the Cape Hatteras Lighthouse and made an enlargement on a photocopier using the 200% option. Which is "more square," the original photo or the enlargement?

   a. The original photo is "more square."
   b. The enlargement is "more square."
   c. The photo and the enlargement are equally square.
   d. There is not enough information to determine which is "more square."

2. The Science Club has four separate rectangular plots for experiments with plants:

1 foot by 4 feet	7 feet by 10 feet
17 feet by 20 feet	27 feet by 30 feet

   Which rectangular plot is most square?

   a. 1 foot by 4 feet
   b. 7 feet by 10 feet
   c. 17 feet by 20 feet
   d. 27 feet by 30 feet

3. Sue and Julie were running equally fast around a track. Sue started first. When Sue had run 9 laps, Julie had run 3 laps. When Julie completed 15 laps, how many laps had Sue run?

   a. 45 laps
   b. 24 laps
   c. 21 laps
   d. 6 laps

4. At the midway point of the basketball season, you must recommend the best free-throw shooter for the all-star game. Here are the statistics for four players:

Novak: 8 of 11 shots	Peterson: 22 of 29 shots
Williams: 15 of 19 shots	Reynolds: 33 of 41 shots

   Which player is the best free-throw shooter?

   a. Novak   b. Peterson   c. Williams   d. Reynolds

5. Write your answer to this problem.

   A farmer has three fields. One is 185 feet by 245 feet, one is 75 feet by 114 feet, and one is 455 feet by 508 feet. If you were flying over these fields, which one would seem most square? Which one would seem least square? Explain your answers.

Figure 18.1 Five items to assess proportional reasoning.
Source: Reprinted with permission from Bright, G. W., Joyner, J. J., & Wallis, C. (2003). "Assessing Proportional Thinking." *Mathematics Teaching in the Middle School, 9*(3), p. 167. Copyright © 2003 by the National Council of Teachers of Mathematics, Inc. www.nctm.org. All rights reserved.

Notice that the items involving rectangles (1, 2, and 5) cannot be answered correctly using additive reasoning, as could the flower-growth problem discussed previously. For a group of 132 eighth- and ninth-grade students, item

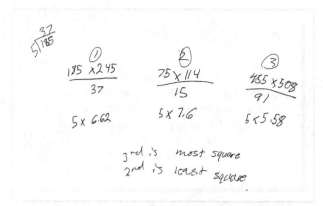

Figure 18.2 Jacob noticed that each length was divisible by 5; therefore, he simplified each ratio to have a side of 5 and then compared the widths.

2 was the easiest (67 percent correct). The percentage correct on the other three multiple-choice items ranged only from 45 percent to 59 percent correct. The open-response item, number 5, proved quite difficult (37 percent correct for most square, 28 percent correct for least square). Over 52 percent of the students selected the 75 × 114 rectangle as the most square, and 45 percent selected the 185 × 245 rectangle as the least square.

Item 5 was given to an eighth grader, who first solved it incorrectly, using an additive strategy (subtracting the sides). When asked if a very large rectangle, 1,000,000 by 1,000,050 would look less square, he replied, "No—oh, this is a proportional situation." He then solved it using a novel strategy (see Figure 18.2).

Identifying Multiplicative Relationships

As noted earlier, students may confuse additive situations for multiplicative situations. Making explicit the type of relationships that exist between two values can greatly support students' understanding of ratios and proportions. Using the multiplication chart, as recommended in *Curriculum Focal Points* (NCTM, 2006), is one way to nurture this understanding. Consider the following sample problem suggested by Cai and Sun in their discussion of how teachers in Chinese classrooms introduce the concept of ratio (2002, p. 196):

> Miller Middle School has 16 sixth-grade students, and 12 of them say that they are basketball fans. The remaining students are not basketball fans.

Students are asked to describe whatever relationships they can between students who are basketball fans and those who are not. Once it is determined that there are four nonfans, there are now several different possibilities including the following:

- There are eight more fans than nonfans.
- There are three times as many fans as nonfans.
- For every three students who like basketball, there is one who does not.

Of these, the first is an additive relationship—focusing on the difference between the two numbers. The other two are variations of the multiplicative relationship, each expressing the 3-to-1 ratio of fans to nonfans in a slightly different way. A discussion helps to contrast the multiplicative relationship with the additive one.

In the following activities, two ratios are compared. As with the earlier flower-growing problem, the choices can be made using either additive or multiplicative reasoning, providing your class with a helpful distinction between the two types of relationships without your attempt to define ratio for them.

Activity 18.1

Which Has More?

Provide students with two or three situations similar to those in Figure 18.3. Whether students work individually or in groups, a follow-up class discussion is imperative. This discussion can provide you with insights into how students are thinking and can also provide opportunities for students to help others see the situations from different perspectives.

Do not prompt students by telling them to look for a multiplicative relationship, but wait to see what sort of answers the students provide.

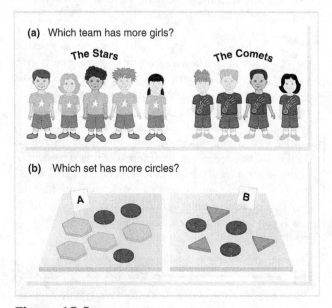

Figure 18.3 Two pictorial situations that can be interpreted with either additive or multiplicative comparisons.

The situations in Figure 18.3 can be interpreted either additively or multiplicatively. The ambiguity is the key: If students recognize and understand the difference between the additive and multiplicative approaches, this is a beginning to being able to reason proportionally. As with the flower problem, both interpretations are correct. You are looking for an awareness that there is a different way of looking at the situation. If at first they do not voluntarily suggest another way, ask a different question: for example, "Amy says it is the second group. Can you explain why she made that choice?" or "Which class team has a larger proportion of girls?"

Return for a moment to item 3 in Figure 18.1. This item has been used in other studies showing that students try to solve this as a proportion problem when it is strictly an additive situation. The two runners will end up six laps apart, which is how they began. Watson and Shaughnessy (2004) note that often the way that we word problems is a dead giveaway that a proportion is involved. Students also recognize the current unit of study is proportional reasoning and then set up proportions even when it is not appropriate, as in item 3. Students have learned how to arrange four quantities in a proportion, but they aren't paying attention to whether there is a multiplicative relationship between the numbers. They are focused on the structure of the proportion, not the concept of the proportion (Heinz & Boatwright, 2008).

The next problem is similar to the flower problem discussed earlier, allowing an additive or multiplicative interpretation.

Activity 18.2

Weight Loss

Show students the data in the following chart:

Week	Max	Moe	Minnie
0	210	158	113
2	202	154	108
4	196	150	105

Max, Moe, and Minnie are each on a diet and have recorded their weight at the start of their diet and at two-week intervals. After four weeks, which person is the most successful dieter?

The task is to make three different arguments—each favoring a different dieter.

The way that the task in "Weight Loss" is presented, the students are forewarned that there are differing arguments and the results will assure a good discussion. (The argument for Moe is that he is the most steady in his loss.)

Equivalent Ratios

In selection activities, a ratio is presented, and students select an equivalent ratio from others presented. The focus should be on an intuitive rationale for why the pairs selected are in the same ratio. Sometimes numeric values will play a part to help students develop numeric methods to explain their reasoning. In later activities, students will be asked to construct an equivalent ratio without choices being provided.

It is extremely useful in these activities to include pairs of ratios that are not proportional but have a common difference. For example, $\frac{5}{8}$ and $\frac{9}{12}$ are not equivalent ratios, but the corresponding differences are the same: $8 - 5 = 12 - 9$. Students who focus on this additive relationship are not seeing the multiplicative relationship of proportionality. Using contexts in comparing ratios helps students articulate their multiplicative or proportional thinking. Activity 18.3 uses sides of a rectangle as the context (linking to the important concepts of similarity and scale drawings).

Activity 18.3

Look-Alike Rectangles

Provide groups of students with a copy of Blackline Masters 30 and 31 shown in Figure 18.4 and have them cut out the ten rectangles. Three of the rectangles (A, I, and D) have sides in the ratio of 3 to 4. Rectangles C, F, and H have sides in the ratio of 5 to 8. J, E, and G have sides in the ratio of 1 to 3. Rectangle B is a square, so its sides are in the ratio of 1 to 1.

The task is to group the rectangles into three sets of three that "look alike" with one "oddball." If your students know the word *similar* from geometry, you can use that instead of "look alike." To explain what "look alike" means, draw three rectangles on the

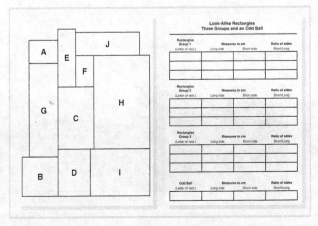

Figure 18.4 Blackline Masters 30 and 31 for use with Activity 18.3.

board with two that are similar and one that is clearly dissimilar to the other two, as in the following example. Have students use their language to explain why rectangles 1 and 3 are alike.

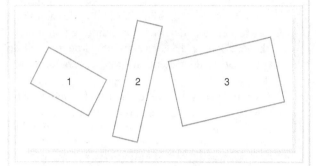

When students have decided on their groupings, stop and discuss the reasons they classified the rectangles as they did. Be prepared for some students to try to match sides or look for rectangles that have the same amount of difference between them. Next have the students measure and record the sides of each rectangle to the nearest half-centimeter. They should then calculate the ratios of the short to long sides for each. Blackline Master 31 can be used to record the data. Discuss these results and ask students to offer explanations of how the ratios and groupings are related. If the groups are formed of proportional (similar) rectangles, the ratios within each group will all be the same.

From a geometric standpoint, "Look-Alike Rectangles" is an activity concerning similarity. The two concepts—proportionality and similarity—are closely connected.

Another characteristic of proportional rectangles can be observed by stacking like rectangles aligned at one corner, as in Figure 18.5. Place a straightedge across the diagonals, and you will see that opposite corners also

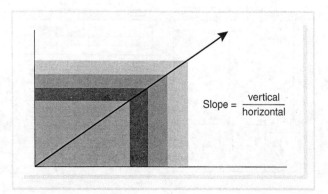

$$\text{Slope} = \frac{\text{vertical}}{\text{horizontal}}$$

Figure 18.5 The slope of a line through a stack of proportional rectangles is equal to the ratio of the two sides.

line up. If the rectangles are placed on a coordinate axis with the common corner at the origin, the slope of the line joining the corners is the ratio of the sides. Here is a connection between proportional reasoning and algebra.

Activity 18.4

Different Objects, Same Ratios

Prepare cards with distinctly different objects, as shown in Figure 18.6. Given one card, students are to select a card on which the ratio of the two types of objects is the same. This task moves students toward a numeric approach rather than a visual one and introduces the notion of ratios as rates. In this context, it makes the most sense to find the boxes per truck as the rate (rather than trucks per box). Finding the rate (amount for 1 unit) for pairs of quantities facilitates comparisons (like the unit prices provided in grocery stores to allow you to compare different products).

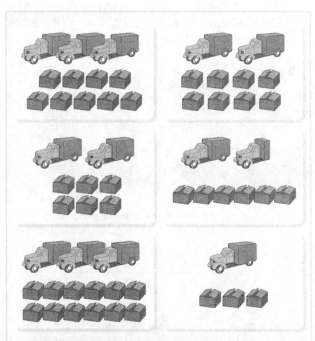

1. On which cards is the ratio of trucks to boxes the same?
2. What is the rate of boxes per truck for each card?

Figure 18.6 Ratio cards for exploring ratios and rates.

Differerent Ratios

An understanding of proportional situations includes being able to compare two ratios as well as to identify equivalent ratios. The following activity has been used in various studies of proportional reasoning.

Activity 18.5

Lemonade Recipes

Show students a picture of two lemonade pitchers as in Figure 18.7. The pitchers each have the same amount of lemonade. The little squares indicate the recipes used in each pitcher. A yellow square is a cup of lemonade concentrate and the blue square is a cup of water. Ask which pitcher will have the stronger lemonade flavor or whether they will both taste the same. Ask them to justify their answers.

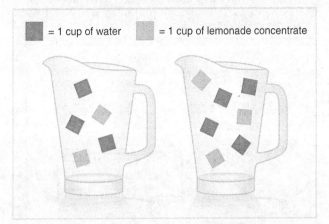

= 1 cup of water   = 1 cup of lemonade concentrate

Figure 18.7 A comparing ratios problem: Which pitcher will have the stronger lemon flavor, or will they be the same?

⏸ ————————— *Pause and Reflect*

Solve the lemonade problem and write down your reasoning. Is there more than one way to justify the answer?

The task in "Lemonade Recipes" is challenging for many students. It is interesting because of how many ways there are to make the comparison. A common method is to figure out how much water goes with each cup of lemonade mix. As we will see later, this is using a unit rate: cups of water per cup of lemonade mix ($1\frac{1}{2}$ vs. $1\frac{1}{3}$). Other approaches use fractions instead of unit rates and attempt to compare the fractions: lemonade mix compared to water ($\frac{2}{3}$ vs. $\frac{3}{4}$) or the reverse, and also lemonade mix as a fraction of the total ($\frac{2}{5}$ vs. $\frac{3}{7}$). This can also be done with water as a fraction of the total. Some students may also use percentages instead of fractions, creating the same arguments. Another way to justify is to use multiples of one or both of the pitchers until either the water or the lemonade mix is equal in both.

One interesting argument is that the pitchers will taste the same: If the lemonade mix and water are matched up in

myeducationlab

Go to the Building Teaching Skills and Dispositions section of Chapter 18 of MyEducationLab. Click on Expanded Lessons to download the Expanded Lesson for "**Lemonade Recipes**" and complete the related activities.

each pitcher, then there will be one cup of water left in each recipe. Although incorrect (can you tell why?), your class will likely have a spirited discussion of these ideas.

The lemonade task can be adjusted for difficulty. As given, the two mixtures are reasonably close and there are no simple relationships between the two pitchers. If the solutions are 3 to 6 and 4 to 8 (equal flavors), the task is much simpler. For a 2-to-5 recipe versus a 4-to-9 recipe, it is easy to double the first and compare it to the second. When a 3-to-6 recipe is compared to a 2-to-5 recipe, the unit rates are perhaps more obvious (1 to 2 vs. 1 to $2\frac{1}{2}$).

The following problem also is adapted from the research literature.

Two camps of Scouts are having pizza parties. The Bear Camp ordered enough so that every 3 campers will have 2 pizzas. The leader of the Raccoons ordered enough so that there would be 3 pizzas for every 5 campers. Did the Bear campers or the Raccoon campers have more pizza to eat?

Figure 18.8 shows two different reasoning strategies. When the pizzas are sliced up into fractional parts as in Figure 18.8(a), the approach is to look for a unit rate—pizzas per camper. A sharing approach has been used for each ratio just as described for fractions in Chapter 15. But notice that this problem does not say that the camps have only 3 and 5 campers, respectively. Any multiples of 2 to 3 and 3 to 5 can be used to make the appropriate comparison, the same as making multiple pitchers of lemonade. This is the approach used in Figure 18.8(b). Three "clones" of the 2-to-3 ratio and two clones of the 3-to-5 ratio are made so that the number of campers getting a like number of pizzas can be compared. From a vantage of fractions, this is

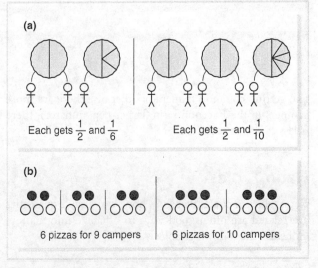

(a)

Each gets $\frac{1}{2}$ and $\frac{1}{6}$ Each gets $\frac{1}{2}$ and $\frac{1}{10}$

(b)

6 pizzas for 9 campers   6 pizzas for 10 campers

Figure 18.8 Two reasoning methods for comparing two ratios.

Connected Mathematics

Grade 7, *Comparing and Scaling*
Investigation 3: Comparing and Using Ratios

Context

This investigation occurs in the second week of the unit on ratio and proportions. In earlier activities, students explored ratios and percents to compare survey data from large populations with similar data gathered from their own class. Students used fractions, decimals, and percents to express ratios, and they compared ratios using their own strategies.

Task Description

In the juice problem shown (2.1: Mixing Juice), students apply proportional reasoning to figure out which recipe is the most orangey and which is the least orangey. Students are to apply their knowledge of ratios to reason to a solution. Students have solved this task in a variety of ways, including:

1. Make equal amounts of each recipe to compare (e.g., make 120 cups of each).

2. Make the cups of concentrate the same and look at how much water goes with each (e.g., for 30 cups of concentrate, how much water is needed for each recipe?).

3. Find part-to-whole fractions, find common denominators, and compare.

4. Find part-to-whole fractions, convert to percents, and compare.

5. Draw pictures to show how much water per cup of concentrate. For example, for Mix D:

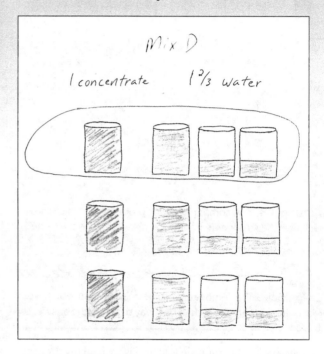

like getting common numerators. Because there are more campers in the Raccoon ratio (larger denominator), there is less pizza for each camper.

Ratio Tables

Ratio tables or charts that show how two variable quantities are related are often good ways to organize information. Consider the following table:

Acres	5	10	15	20	25			
Pine trees	75	150	225					

If the task is to find the number of trees for 65 acres of land or the number of acres needed for 750 trees, students can proceed by using addition. That is, they can add 5s along the top row until they reach 65. As discussed in Chapter 14, this is a recursive pattern, or repeated addition strategy. The pattern that connects acres to pine trees ($\times 15$) is the generative pattern and the multiplicative relationship between the values. The equation for this situation is $y = 15x$, a proportional situation, as discussed in Chapter 14 as a subset of linear equations.

Ratio tables may not always be in organized lists where a pattern can be found. In fact, ratio tables can be used when only one ratio is known and you are trying to find a

Mixing Juice

Julia and Mariah attend summer camp. Everyone at the camp helps with the cooking and cleanup at meal times.

One morning, Julia and Mariah make orange juice for all the campers. They plan to make the juice by mixing water and frozen orange-juice concentrate. To find the mix that tastes best, they decide to test some mixes.

Mix A		Mix B	
2 cups concentrate	3 cups cold water	5 cups concentrate	9 cups cold water

Mix C		Mix D	
1 cup concentrate	2 cups cold water	3 cups concentrate	5 cups cold water

Problem 2.1 Developing Comparison Strategies

A. Which mix will make juice that is the most "orangey"? Explain.

B. Which mix will make juice that is the least "orangey"? Explain.

C. Which comparison statement is correct? Explain.

$\frac{5}{9}$ of Mix B is concentrate. $\frac{5}{14}$ of Mix B is concentrate.

D. Assume that each camper will get $\frac{1}{2}$ cup of juice.

    1. For each mix, how many batches are needed to make juice for 240 campers?

    2. For each mix, how much concentrate and how much water are needed to make juice for 240 campers?

E. For each mix, how much concentrate and how much water are needed to make 1 cup of juice?

ACE Homework starts on page 24.

Investigation 2 Comparing Ratios, Percents, and Fractions   **19**

The context of this problem, a familiar one, allows students to apply their own creative and clever strategies to solve a proportional situation without instructions on *how* to solve the problem.

The full unit contains six investigations, each with numerous real contexts. Scaling, the use of unit rates, and percentages are suggested techniques for solving the proportional situations.

specific equivalent ratio. Then the ratio table can be used as a strategy for solving a proportion. The following activity provides examples and Figure 18.9 gives illustrations of this use of a ratio table.

Activity 18.6

Using Ratio Tables

Build a ratio table and use it to answer the question. Tasks are adapted from Lamon (1999, p. 183).

• A person who weighs 160 pounds on Earth will weigh 416 pounds on the planet Jupiter. How much will a person weigh on Jupiter who weighs 120 pounds on earth?

• At the local college, five out of every eight seniors live in apartments. How many of the 30 senior math majors are likely to live in an apartment?

• The tax on a purchase of $20 is $1.12. How much tax will there be on a purchase of $45.50?

• When in Australia you can exchange $4.50 in U.S. dollars for $6 Australian. How much is $17.50 Australian in U.S. dollars?

The tasks in this activity are typical "solve the proportion" tasks. One ratio and part of a second are given

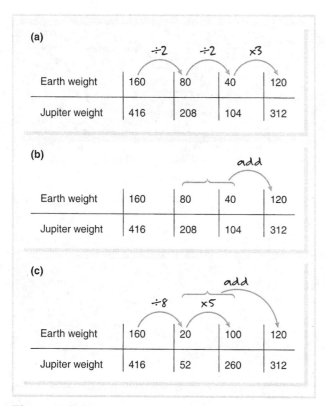

	Pounds	Cost	Notes
A	1	4.25	Given
B	10	42.50	A × 10
C	2	8.50	A × 2
D	0.1	0.425	A ÷ 10
E	12.1	51.425	B + C + D
F	0.01	0.0425	D ÷ 10
G	0.03	0.1275	F × 3
H	12.13	51.5525	E + G

Figure 18.10 A more structured ratio table. The Notes column shows what was done in each step. The task is to find the cost of 12.13 pounds.

Cheese is $4.25 per pound. How much will 12.13 pounds cost?

The format in Figure 18.10 allows for easier tracing of what was done at each step. The format is just that—a format. It is not the same as an algorithm. For any problem there are likely to be several different reasonable ratio tables. In applying this technique, students are using multiplicative relationships to transform a given ratio into an equivalent ratio. As Lamon points out, the process is not at all random. Students should mentally devise a plan for getting from one number to another.

The tasks suggested in Activity 18.6 have quite reasonable numbers. However, as you can see from the cheese example, it is quite possible to use this technique with almost any numbers. By using easy multiples and divisors, often the arithmetic can be done mentally.

It should be clear to students why the same factor must be used on both entries in a ratio table. For example, in row B of Figure 18.10, both the 1 and 4.25 are multiplied by 10. In row G, both parts are multiplied by 3. Each pair of entries comprises a ratio. An equivalent ratio is found by multiplying both parts by the same number. ◆

Figure 18.9 160 pounds on Earth is 416 pounds on Jupiter. If something weighs 120 pounds on Earth, how many pounds would it weigh on Jupiter? Three solutions using ratio tables.

with the task being to find the fourth number. However, tasks such as these should come long before any formal approach is suggested. Further note that in no case is it easy to simply add or subtract to get to the desired entry. Rather, the student should use a ratio table to find equivalent ratios that lead to a desired result. Figure 18.9 shows three different ways to solve the Jupiter weight task using ratio tables.

The format of these ratio tables is not at all important. Some students may not use a table format at all and simply draw arrows and explain in words how they got from one ratio to another. You may find value in a more structured format.

Ⅱ ———————— *Pause and Reflect*

Use a ratio table strategy to solve the last three problems from Activity 18.6. Describe any advantages this approach has over a cross-product algorithm?

The following problem and the table in Figure 18.10 are taken from Lamon (1999, p. 233). Notice that the numbers are not "nice" at all.

Proportional Reasoning Across the Curriculum

As noted at the start of this chapter, proportional reasoning is essential to many concepts in the curriculum. Here are some brief examples in algebra, measurement and geometry, statistics, and number.

Algebra

Graphing ratios provides a powerful connection to algebra. As discussed earlier in this chapter and in Chapter 14, proportional situations are linear situations. In fact, ratios are a special case of linear situations that will always go through the origin, since they are multiplicative relationships. The ratio or rate is the slope of the graph.

Any ratio table provides data that can be graphed. Make each axis correspond to one of the quantities in the table. This idea is developed in the next activity.

Activity 18.7

Rectangle Ratios—Revisited

Have students make a graph of the data from a collection of equal ratios that they have scaled or discussed. The graph in Figure 18.11 is based on the ratios of two sides of similar rectangles. If only a few ratios have actually been plotted, the graph can be drawn carefully and then used to determine other equivalent ratios. In the rectangle example, students can draw rectangles with sides determined by the graphs and compare them to the original rectangles. A unit ratio can be found by locating the point on the line at x = 1 or at y = 1. Ask students to find the rate each way. Ask students to see if they can find a rectangle that has a noninteger side (e.g., 4½ units). Ask students how, if they know the short side, they could find the long side (and vice versa).

Graphs provide another way of thinking about proportions, and they connect proportional thought to algebraic interpretations. All graphs of equivalent ratios fall along straight lines that pass through the origin. If the equation of one of these lines is written in the form $y = mx$, the slope m is always one of the equivalent ratios. Note that the slope of any line through the origin is the ratio of the y-coordinate at any point with the x-coordinate of the same point.

Measurement and Geometry

In these activities, students make measurements or construct physical or visual models of equivalent ratios in order to provide a tangible example of a proportion as well as look at numeric relationships.

Activity 18.8

Different Units, Equal Ratios

Cut strips of adding machine tape all the same length, and give one strip to each group in your class. Each group is to measure the strip using a different nonstandard unit. Possible units include different Cuisenaire rods, a piece of chalk, a pencil, or the edge of a book or index card. When every group has measured the strip, ask for the measure of one of the groups, and display the unit of measure. Next, hold up the unit of measure used by another group, and have the class compare it with the first unit. See if the class can estimate the measurement that the second group found. The ratio of the measuring units should be the inverse of the measurements made with those units. For example, if two units are in a ratio of 2 to 3, the respective measures will be in a ratio of 3 to 2. Examine measurements made with other units. Finally, present a unit that no group has used, and see if the class can predict the measurement when made with that unit.

Activity 18.8 can be extended by providing each group with an identical set of four strips of quite different lengths. Good lengths might be 20, 50, 80, and 120 cm. As before, each group is given a different unit to measure the strips.

This time, have each group enter data into a common spreadsheet. (Alternatively, share group data so that all groups can enter data on their own spreadsheets.) Figure 18.12 shows what a spreadsheet might look like for three

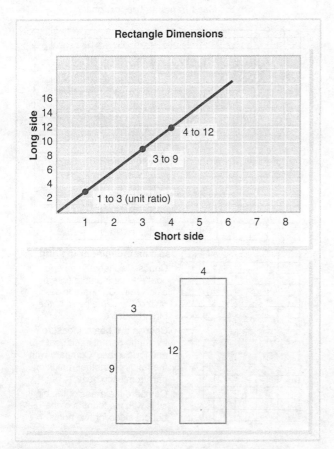

Figure 18.11 Graphs show ratios of sides in similar rectangles.

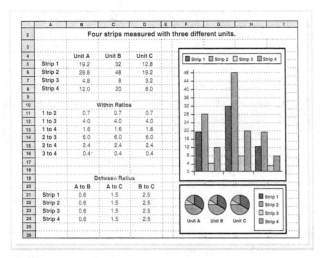

Figure 18.12 A spreadsheet can be used to record data, create tables of interesting ratios, and produce bar and circle graphs.

Source: Screen reprinted with permission from Apple Computer, Inc.

groups. A template can be prepared ahead of time, or students can create their own spreadsheets. Almost all spreadsheets will offer a variety of graphing options. In this activity, bar graphs show the actual measurements for each group and circle graphs show each measure in ratio to the sum of the measures (i.e., a percentage of total measures.)

Once the graphs are completed, there are numerous opportunities to observe and explore multiplicative relationships within and between ratios. The bar graphs, though different in size, all look "alike." Since the circle graphs illustrate the ratios rather than the actual measurements, they will be identical or nearly so. Within ratios (for a set of strips) and between ratios (one unit to another) are easily calculated with the spreadsheet. (Within and between ratios are discussed later in the chapter.)

Continue the exploration by introducing a new strip. If you know its measure with any one of the units, what will its measure be with the other units? Similarly, if a new unit of measure is introduced, how can the measures of the strips be determined? Can this be done by comparing the new unit with an old one? If a known strip is measured with the new unit, can all other measures and ratios be determined?

The task just described may take several days to complete with students, but the time is well spent, as students are able to solidify the different multiplicative relationships through numeric and graphic representations.

Scale Drawings

The connection between proportional reasoning and the geometric concept of similarity is very important. Similar figures provide a visual representation of proportions, and proportional thinking enhances the understanding of simi-

larity. Discussion of the similar figures should focus on the ratios between and within the figures. The next activity is aimed at this connection.

Activity 18.9

Scale Drawings

On grid or dot paper (see Blackline Masters 34–37), have students draw a simple shape using straight lines with vertices on the dots. After one shape is complete, have them draw a larger or smaller shape that looks similar to the first. This can be done on a grid of the same size or a different size, as shown in Figure 18.13. First compare ratios within (see the first problem in Figure 18.13). Then compare ratios between the figures (see the second problem in Figure 18.13).

Corresponding sides from one figure to the next should all be in the same ratio. The ratio of two sides within one figure should be the same as the ratio of the corresponding two sides in another figure.

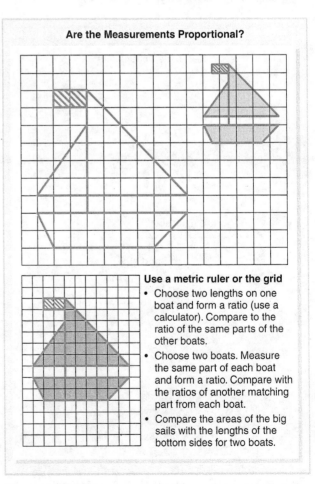

Figure 18.13 Comparing similar figures drawn on grids.

Part three of Activity 18.9 involves area as well as length. Comparisons of corresponding lengths, areas, and volumes in proportional figures lead to some interesting patterns. If two figures are proportional (similar), any two linear dimensions you measure will be in the same ratio on each, say, 1 to k (the variable k is often used with proportions, whereas m is used with equations to describe slope—both refer to the rate or ratio between two values). That means if a similar figure is twice the length of the original figure, then each corresponding side is in a ratio of original to new figure of 1:2. To find the length of a new side, you multiply by 2, which is the value of k in this case.

Imagine you have a square that is 3 by 3 and you create a new square that is 6 by 6. The ratio between the lengths is 1:2. What is the ratio between the two areas? Why is it 1:4? Try the same concept for volume of a cube—what is the relationship of the original to the new volume? Why? Returning to the sailboat in Figure 18.13, what would you conjecture is the ratio between the areas of the two sailboats? Measure and test your hypothesis.

As a means of contrasting proportional situations with additive ones, try starting with a figure on a grid or a building made with blocks and adding two units to every dimension in the figure. The result will be larger but will be a similar shape. Try this with a simple rectangle that is 1 cm by 15 cm. The new rectangle is twice as "thick" (2 cm) but only a bit longer. It will not appear to be the same shape as the original.

Dynamic geometry software such as *GeoGebra* (a free download from www.geogebra.org/cms) or *The Geometer's Sketchpad* (Key Curriculum Press) offers a very effective method of exploring the idea of ratio. In Figure 18.14, two lengths are drawn on a grid using the "snap-to-grid" option. The lengths are measured, and two ratios are computed. As the length of either line is changed, the measures and ratios are updated instantly. A screen similar to this could be used to discuss ratios of lengths as well as inverse ratios with your full class. In this example, notice that the second pair of lines has the same difference but that the ratios are not the same. A similar drawing could be prepared for the overhead on a transparency of a centimeter dot grid if software is not available.

You can also explore similar figures and corresponding measures. Using the Dilate feature, a figure can be drawn and then dilated (reduced or enlarged proportionally) according to any scale factor of your choosing. The ratios of beginning and ending measures (lengths and areas) can then be compared to the scale factor. All of the computations can be done within the software program. ◆

More interesting situations to consider for scale drawings are shown in the following list:

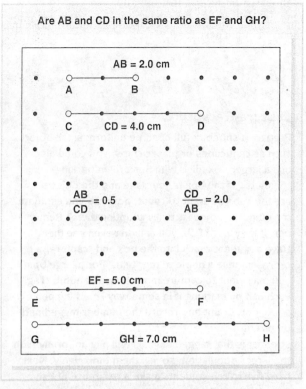

Figure 18.14 Dynamic geometry software or just a centimeter grid can be used to discuss ratios of two lengths.
Source: From *The Geometer's Sketchpad*, Key Curriculum Press, 1150 65th Street, Emeryville, CA 94608, 1-800-995-MATH, www.keypress.com. Reprinted by permission.

- If you wanted to make a scale model of the solar system and use a Ping-Pong ball for the earth, how far away should the sun be? How large a ball would you need?
- What scale should be used to draw a scale map of your city (or some interesting region) so that it will nicely fit onto a standard piece of poster board?
- Use the scale on a map to estimate the distance and travel time between two points of interest.
- Roll a toy car down a ramp, timing the trip with a stopwatch. How fast was the car traveling in miles per hour? If the speed is proportional to the size of the car, how fast would this have been for a real car?
- Your little sister wants a table and chair for her doll. Her doll is 14 inches tall. How big should you make the table?
- Determine the various distances that a ten-speed bike travels in one turn of the pedals. You will need to count the sprocket teeth on the front and back gears.

Statistics

Have you ever wondered how scientists estimate wildlife counts such as the number of bass in a lake or the number of monarch butterflies that migrate each year to Mexico? One method often used is a capture-recapture technique modeled in the next activity.

Activity 18.10

Capture-Recapture

Prepare a shoebox full of some uniform small object such as centicubes or plastic chips. You could also use a larger box filled with Styrofoam packing "peanuts." If the box is your lake and the objects are the fish you want to count, how can you estimate the number without actually counting them? Remember, if they were fish, you couldn't even see them! Have a student reach into the box and "capture" a representative sample of the "fish." For a large box, you may want to capture more than a handful. "Tag" each fish by marking it in some way—marking pen or sticky dot. Count and record the number tagged and then return them to the box. The assumption of the scientist is that tagged animals will mix uniformly with the larger population, so mix them thoroughly. Next, have five to ten students make a recapture of fish from the box. Each counts the total captured and the number in the capture that are tagged. Accumulate these data.

   Now the task is to use all of the information to estimate the number of fish in the lake. The recapture data provide an estimated ratio of tagged to untagged fish. The number tagged to the total population should be in the same ratio. After solving the proportion, have students count the actual items in the box to see how close their estimate is.

For a more detailed description of the "Capture-Recapture" activity, see the NCTM Addenda Series book *Understanding Rational Numbers and Proportions* (Curcio & Bezuk, 1994).

Number: Fractions and Percent

Percent has traditionally been included as a topic with ratio and proportion because percent is one form of ratio, a part-to-whole ratio. In Chapter 17, it was shown that percent problems can be connected to fraction concepts. Here the same part-to-whole fraction concept of percent will be extended to ratio and proportion concepts. Ideally, all of these ideas (fractions, decimals, ratio, proportion, and percent) should be conceptually integrated. The better that students connect these ideas, the more flexible and useful their reasoning and problem-solving skills will be.

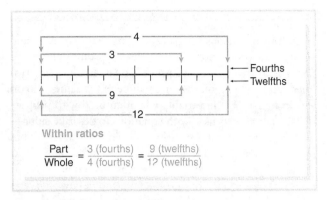

Within ratios

$$\frac{\text{Part}}{\text{Whole}} = \frac{3 \text{ (fourths)}}{4 \text{ (fourths)}} = \frac{9 \text{ (twelfths)}}{12 \text{ (twelfths)}}$$

Figure 18.15 Equivalent fractions as proportions.

Equivalent Fractions. First consider how equivalent fractions can be interpreted as a proportion using the same simple models already used. In Figure 18.15, a line segment is partitioned in two different ways: in fourths on one side and in twelfths on the other. In the previous examples, proportions were established based on two amounts of apples, two different distances or runs, and two different sizes of drawings. Here only one thing is measured—the part of a whole—but it is measured or partitioned two ways: in fourths and in twelfths.

A simple line segment drawing similar to the one in Figure 18.15 could be drawn to set up a proportion to solve any equivalent-fraction problem, even ones that do not result in whole-number numerators or denominators. An example is shown in Figure 18.16.

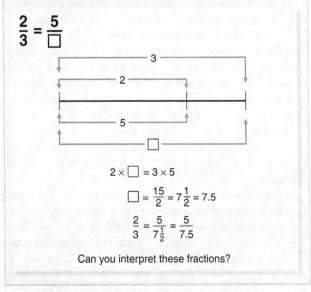

$$2 \times \square = 3 \times 5$$

$$\square = \frac{15}{2} = 7\frac{1}{2} = 7.5$$

$$\frac{2}{3} = \frac{5}{7\frac{1}{2}} = \frac{5}{7.5}$$

Can you interpret these fractions?

Figure 18.16 Solving equivalent-fraction problems as equivalent ratios using cross-products.

Percents. All percent problems are exactly the same as the equivalent-fraction examples. They involve a part and a whole measured in some unit and the same part and whole measured in hundredths—that is, in percents. A simple line segment drawing can be used for each of the three types of percent problems. Let the measures on one side of the line correspond to the numbers or measures in the problem. On the opposite side of the line, indicate the corresponding values in terms of percents. Label the segments of the line rather than endpoints. Examples of each type of problem are shown in Figure 18.17.

Notice how flexible this simple line model is for every type of percent problem. It allows modeling of not only part-whole scenarios but also increase-decrease situations and those in which there is a comparison between two distinct quantities. One of each of these is included in Figure 18.17. Another advantage of the line model is that it does not restrict students from thinking about percents greater than 100 as does a circle graph or a 10 × 10 grid (Parker, 2004).

Proportions

The activities to this point have been designed to lead students to an intuitive concept of ratio and proportion to help in the development of proportional reasoning.

One practical value of proportional reasoning is to use observed proportions to find unknown values. Knowledge of one ratio can often be used to find a value in the other. Comparison pricing, using scales on maps, and solving percentage problems are just a few everyday instances where solving proportions is required. Students need to learn to set up proportions symbolically and to solve them.

 "Attention to developing flexibility in working with rational numbers contributes to students' understanding of, and facility with, proportionality. Facility with proportionality involves much more than setting two ratios equal and solving for a missing term. It involves recognizing quantities that are related proportionally and using numbers, tables, graphs, and equations to think about the quantities and their relationship" (p. 217). ◆

A *proportion* is a statement of equality between two ratios. If 4 boats carry 36 passengers, then 2 boats of the same size will carry 18 passengers, 3 boats will carry 27 passengers, and 20 boats will carry 180 passengers. Here the ratio of 4 to 36 can be applied to each of these situations even though the measures are different in each case.

In 1960, U.S. railroads carried 327 million passengers. Over the next 20 years, there was a 14 percent decrease in passengers. How many passengers rode the railroads in 1980?

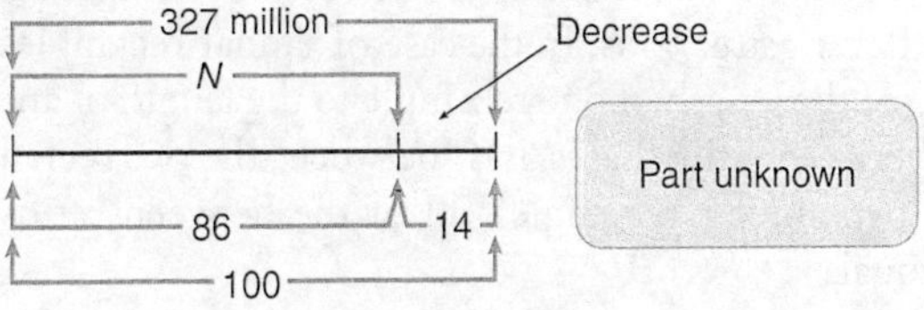

Part unknown

$$\frac{N}{327 \text{ million}} = \frac{86}{100} = 0.86$$

$N = 0.86 \times 327$ million → about 281 million

Sylvia's new boat cost $8950. She made a down payment of $2000. What percent of the sales price was Sylvia's down payment?

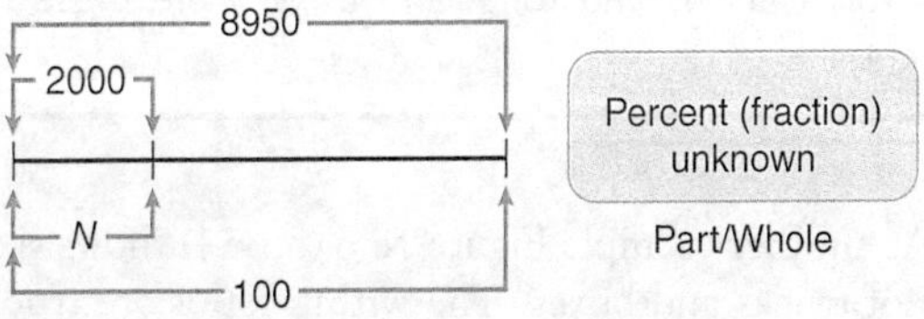

Percent (fraction) unknown

Part/Whole

$$\frac{\$2000}{\$8950} = \frac{N}{100}$$

$8950N = 200,000$ → $N = 22.35$, or about 22%

The seventh- and eighth-grade classes at Robious Middle School had a contest to see which class would sell more raffle tickets at the school festival. The eighth grade sold 592 tickets. However, this turned out to be only 62.5 percent of the number of tickets sold by the seventh grade. How many tickets did the seventh grade sell?

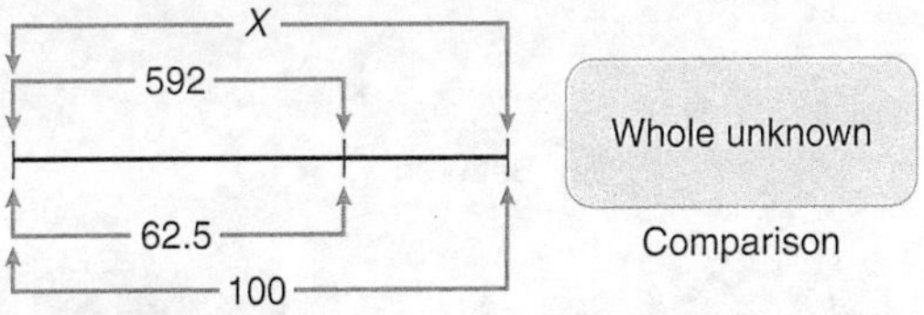

Whole unknown

Comparison

$$\frac{592 \text{ tickets}}{X \text{ tickets}} = \frac{62.5}{100}$$

$62.5X = 59,200$ → $X = 947.2$, or 947 tickets.

Figure 18.17 Percentage problems solved by setting up a proportion using a simple line-segment model.

Within and Between Ratios

When examining two ratios, it is useful to think of them as being either *within* ratios or *between* ratios. A ratio of two measures in the same setting is a *within* ratio. For example, in the case of similar rectangles, the ratio of length to width for any one rectangle is a within ratio, that is, it is "within" the context of that rectangle. For all similar rectangles, corresponding within ratios will be equal.

A *between* ratio is a ratio of two corresponding measures in different situations. In the case of similar rectangles, the ratio of the length of one rectangle to the length of another is a between ratio; that is, it is "between" the two rectangles. For two similar rectangles, all of the between ratios will be equal.

Pause and Reflect

Consider three rectangles A, B, and C. A measures 2 × 6, B measures 3 × 9, and C measures 8 × 24. Find the within ratio for each rectangle. This should convince you that the rectangles are similar. Now examine the between ratios for A and B and for A and C. Why are these ratios different?

As another example Figure 18.6 (p. 354) shows six pictures of trucks and boxes. The within ratios are trucks to boxes (within one picture). The between ratios are from trucks to trucks and boxes to boxes.

The drawing in Figure 18.18 is an effective way of looking at two ratios and determining if a ratio is between or within. A drawing similar to this will be very helpful to students in setting up proportions, especially students who struggle with abstract representatives. Pick any two equivalent truck and box pictures and place the numbers in this figure.

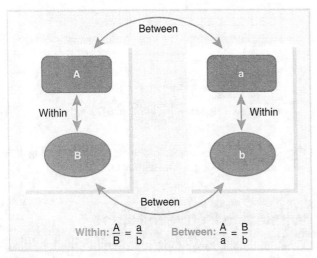

Figure 18.18 Given a proportional situation, the two between ratios and the two within ratios will be equivalent.

Reasoning Approaches

Traditional textbooks show students how to set up an equation of two ratios involving an unknown, "cross-multiply," and solve for the unknown. This can be a very mechanical approach and can lead to confusion and error. Although you may wish eventually to cover the cross-product algorithm, it is well worth the time for students to find ways to solve proportions using their own ideas. If you have been exploring proportions and discussing between and within relationships, students will have a good foundation on which to build their own approaches.

To illustrate some intuitive approaches for solving typical proportion tasks, consider the following:

Tammy bought 3 widgets for $2.40. At the same price, how much would 10 widgets cost?

Tammy bought 4 widgets for $3.75. How much would a dozen widgets cost?

Pause and Reflect

Before reading further, solve these two problems using an approach other than the cross-product algorithm.

In the first situation, it is perhaps easiest to determine the cost of one widget—the unit rate or unit price. This can be found by dividing the price of three widgets by 3. Multiplying this unit rate of $0.80 per widget by 10 will produce the answer. This approach is referred to as a *unit-rate* method of solving proportions. Notice that the unit rate is a within ratio.

In the second problem, a unit-rate approach could be used, but the division does not appear to be easy. Since 12 is a multiple of 4, it is easier to notice that the cost of a dozen is 3 times the cost of 4. This is called a *scale factor* method. It could have been used on the first problem but would have been awkward. The scale factor between 3 and 10 is $3\frac{1}{3}$. Multiplying $2.40 by $3\frac{1}{3}$ will produce the correct answer. (When you multiply entries in a ratio table, you are using a scale factor.) Although the scale factor method is a useful way to think about proportions, it is most frequently used when the numbers are compatible. Students should be given problems in which the numbers lend themselves to both approaches so that they will explore both methods. The scale factor is a between ratio.

Try using the unit-rate method or scale factors to solve the next two problems. You can set up the proportions using the format in Figure 18.18.

At the Office Super Store, you can buy plain #2 pencils, 4 for 59 cents. The store also sells the same pencils in a large box of 5 dozen pencils for $7.79. How much do you save by buying the large box?

The price of a box of 2 dozen candy bars is $4.80. Bridget wants to buy 5 candy bars. What will she have to pay?

To solve the pencil problem, you might notice that the between ratio of pencils to pencils is 4 to 60, or 1 to 15. If you multiply the 59 cents by 15, the factor of change, you will get the price of the box of 60 if the pencils were sold at the same price. In the candy problem, the within ratio of 24 to $4.80 is easy to use to get the unit rate of 20 cents per candy bar.

It is important to follow these tasks with problems that have more difficult numbers, asking students to still apply the same strategies to reason to an answer. For example, try to apply both strategies to the next problem.

Brian can run 5 km in 18.4 minutes. If he keeps on running at the same speed, how far can he run in 23 minutes?

Cross-Product Approach

"The central challenge of developing students' capacity to think with ratios (to reason proportionally) is to teach ideas and restrain the quick path to computation" (Smith, 2002, p. 15).

The methods just described come close to being well-defined algorithms, though they are a bit more flexible than cross-product methods. The reality is that the computations involved are exactly the same as in cross-multiplication. Sixth- and seventh-grade students rarely use cross-multiplication to solve proportion problems, even when that method has been taught (Smith, 2002). A possible reason is that, although the method is relatively efficient, it does not appear on the surface to look like the earlier conceptual approaches. If teaching cross-products, connect the unit-rate and/or scale factor approaches to this procedure.

Draw a Simple Model.   Given a ratio word problem, the greatest difficulty students have is setting up a correct proportion or equation of two ratios, one of which includes the missing value. "Which fractions do I make? Where does the x go?"

Rather than drill and drill in the hope that they will somehow eventually get it, show students how to sketch a simple picture that will help them determine what parts are related. In Figure 18.19, a simple model is drawn

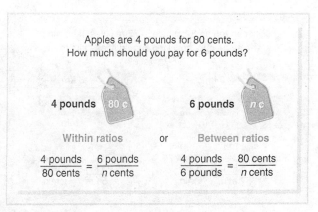

Figure 18.19 A simple drawing helps to establish correct proportion equations.

for a typical rate or price problem. The two equations in the figure come from setting up within and between ratios.

Solve the Proportion.   Examine the left (within) ratios. Find out what to multiply the left fraction by to get the right. You may see that this is a scale factor of 1.5, or you can divide to find the scale ($6 \div 4$). Then multiply 80 cents by the same scale factor to get $1.20.

$$\tfrac{6}{4} \times 80$$

Looking at the same left equation in Figure 18.19, we could also determine the unit price or the price for 1 pound by dividing the 80 cents by 4 and then multiplying this result by 6 to determine the price of 6 pounds:

$$\tfrac{80}{4} \times 6$$

Now look what happens if we cross-multiply in the original equation:

$$4n = 6 \times 80$$

$$n = \tfrac{6 \times 80}{4}$$

This equation can be solved by dividing the 6 by 4 and multiplying by 80 or dividing 80 by 4 and multiplying by 6. These are exactly the two devices we employed in the other two approaches (scale factor and unit rate). If you cross-multiply the between ratios, you get exactly the same result. Furthermore, you get the same result if you had written the two ratios inverted, that is, with the reciprocals of each fraction. Try it!

So if you want to develop a cross-product algorithm, it is not unreasonable to do problems like these while encouraging students to use their own methods. If the cross-product approach is understood and presented as one strategy, and not necessarily the only approach or the best approach, students will be more likely to continue to reason and chose the strategy that makes sense given the context and the numbers involved in the problem.

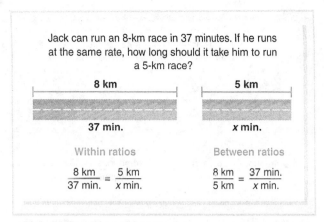

Figure 18.20 Line segments can be used to model both time and distance.

Providing visual cues to set up proportions is a very effective way to support a wide range of learners. In Figure 18.20 the visual of the road is used to help students consider the quantities involved and set up ratios appropriately. Notice how the visual is much like the ratio table and much like the picture in Figure 18.19. Different students will find different strategies more logical—encourage students to select a strategy that makes sense to them.

Reflections on Chapter 18

Writing to Learn

1. Describe the idea of a ratio in your own words. Explain how your idea fits with each of the following statements:
   a. A fraction is a ratio.
   b. Ratios can compare things that are not at all alike.
   c. Ratios can compare two parts of the same whole.
   d. Rates such as prices or speeds are ratios.
2. Describe a situation in which the comparison involved could be interpreted both in an additive sense as well as multiplicatively. Why might you want to explore a situation such as this early on in your discussion of ratio and proportion?
3. What can you say about the graph of a collection of equivalent ratios?
4. Make up a realistic proportional situation that can be solved mentally by a scale factor approach and another that can be solved mentally by a unit-rate approach.
5. Consider this problem: If 50 gallons of fuel oil cost $56.95, how much can be purchased for $100? Draw a sketch to illustrate the proportion, and set up the equation in two different ways. One equation should equate within ratios and the other between ratios.

6. Make up a realistic percentage problem and set up a line-segment model to represent it. Then write a proportion.

For Discussion and Exploration

1. Proportional reasoning is a unifying theme in mathematics. For each of the content strands (number, algebra, measurement, geometry, and data analysis and probability) think about content that involves proportional reasoning and explain the connections among all of these ideas.
2. In Chapter 17, the three percent problems were developed around the theme of which element was missing—the part, the whole, or the fraction that related the two. In this chapter, percent is related to proportions, an equality of two ratios with one of these ratios a comparison to 100. How are these two approaches alike? How are they different? Explain how 100 percent could, in some problems, be a part rather than a whole.

Resources for Chapter 18

Literature Connections

Literature brings an exciting dimension to the exploration of proportional reasoning. Many books and stories discuss comparative sizes, concepts of scale as in maps, giants and miniature people who are proportional to regular people, comparative rates, especially rates of speed, and so on. For example, Beckman, Thompson, and Austin (2004) explore the popular *Harry Potter* stories, *The Lord of the Rings*, and *The*

Perfect Storm for exciting contexts for proportional reasoning activities.

If You Hopped Like a Frog *Schwartz, 1999*

David Schwartz, the author of *How Much Is a Million?* and *If You Made a Million*, uses proportional reasoning to determine what it would be like if we had the skills or dimensions of familiar animals. "If you hopped like a frog, you could jump from home plate to first base in one mighty leap." This short picture book contains 12 more fascinating comparisons. At the end of the book, Schwartz provides some factual data on which the proportions are based. Students can figure out how strong or tall they would be if they were one of the featured animals.

Holes *Sachar, 2000*

A popular book and movie, this novel tells the story of boys in a "camp" digging holes every day, which provides an opportunity to look at daily rates of dirt removal. Pugalee et al. (2008) describe an excellent activity with this book that not only involves proportional reasoning, but also measurement and algebra.

Literature with Large and/or Small People

There is a plethora of literature involving very little or very big people (or animals). With any of these books, body parts can be compared as a way to explore within and between ratios. The following list of some great literature can lead to wonderful lessons on proportional reasoning:

Alice's Adventures in Wonderland
Carroll, 1865/1982

In this classic, Alice becomes very small and very tall, opening doors to many ratio and proportion investigations.

The Borrowers *Norton, 1953*

A classic tale of little folk living in the walls of a house. Furnishings are created from odds and ends of the full-sized human world.

Gulliver's Travels *Swift, 1726, amended 1735/1999*

Yet another classic story. In this case Gulliver first visits the Lilliputians, where he is 12 times their size, and then goes to Brobdingnag, where he is $\frac{1}{10}$ the size of the inhabitants.

Jim and the Beanstalk *Briggs, 1970*

What happened to the giant after Jack? Jim comes along. Jim wants to help the poor, pessimistic giant. This heartwarming story is great for multiplicative or proportional reasoning across grades K–8.

Kate and the Beanstalk *Osborne, 2000*

This version of *Jack and the Beanstalk* includes a giantess. The giantess falls to earth and Kate finds out the castle belongs to her family.

"One Inch Tall" in *Where the Sidewalk Ends*
Silverstein, 1973

Shel Silverstein is a hit with all ages. This poems asks what it would be like if you were one inch tall.

Swamp Angel *Isaacs, 1999*

A swamp angel named Angelica is born very tiny but grows into a giant. Students can explore birth height to current height or compare Angelica's measurements to their own.

Recommended Readings

Articles

Langrall, C. W., & Swafford, J. (2000). Three balloons for two dollars. *Mathematics Teaching in the Middle School, 6*(4), 254–261.
The authors describe and give examples of four levels of proportional reasoning using examples from the classroom. A good article on a difficult topic.

Lo, J., Watanabe, T., & Cai, J. (2004). Developing ratio concepts: An Asian perspective. *Mathematics Teaching in the Middle School, 9*(7), 362–367.
These well-known researchers discuss the way that the concepts of ratio and proportion are developed in Asian countries. They share a sequence of activities adapted from textbooks used in China, Taiwan, and Japan. The series of examples will certainly be useful in your classroom.

Books

Lamon, S. J. (1999). *Teaching fractions and ratios for understanding: Essential content knowledge and instructional strategies for teachers.* Mahwah, NJ: Lawrence Erlbaum.
Lamon is one of the most prolific researchers and writers on the subject of fractions, ratios, and proportional reasoning. This book is full of specific practical examples of activities and is freely illustrated with children's work. Many of the ideas found in this chapter are adapted from this book and other works by Lamon.

Litwiller, B. (Ed.). (2002). *Making sense of fractions, ratios, and proportions: 2002 yearbook.* Reston, VA: NCTM.
Eleven of the 26 short chapters in this NCTM yearbook discuss explicitly the issue of multiplicative relationships and/or proportional reasoning. The remaining chapters are on various aspects of fraction concepts and fraction computation, many illustrating the connection with proportional thinking. Accompanying the yearbook is a book of Classroom Activities *complete with Blackline Masters.*

Online Resources

Fibonacci Sequence
http://nlvm.usu.edu/en/nav/frames_asid_315_g_3_t_1
.html

The applet simply computes successive terms of the Fibonacci sequence and shows in both fraction and decimal forms the ratio of successive terms of the sequence. This ratio converges to the *golden ratio*. For what may be the most information assembled anywhere on the Fibonacci sequence, go to www.mcs.surrey.ac.uk/Personal/R.Knott/Fibonacci.

Fish Simulation Applet I
http://mathforum.org/escotpow/puzzles/fish/applet
.html

A collection of two colors of fish is to be placed into three ponds to create specified ratios within each pond. Students should find out if there is more than one solution and then make up similar problems for their classmates.

Learning about Length, Area, Volume, Surface Area of Similar Objects (e-Example 6.3)
http://standards.nctm.org/document/eexamples

A two-part exploration complete with extensive teacher notes. The applets compare two rectangles or two prisms showing ratios of measures in both numeric and graphical form.

Understanding Ratios of Inscribed Figures (e-Example 7.3)
http://standards.nctm.org/document/eexamples

A nice geometry/measurement link to ratio. The user explores the ratio of figures inscribed in polygons formed by joining midpoints of sides. These points can also be adjusted. The supporting lesson and activity suggestions are quite good.

Ameba (The Math Forum's Teacher Exchange)
http://mathforum.org/te/exchange/hosted/ameba

In this game, students select a total number of pellets to eat that is equal to the target ratio given at the top of the board, then return to the start/finish location.

The Futures Channel
www.thefutureschannel.com

This site provides lessons and includes video clips. Two related to proportional reasoning are "How Tall?," which engages students in finding the heights of people and objects using proportional thinking, and "Snow," which explores the ratio of inches of snowfall to liquid water.

Field Experience Guide Connections

Because ratios and proportions are important to many topics in the curriculum, they are the topic for many of the field experiences in Part I of the *Field Experience Guide*. For example, any of the proportional reasoning tasks in this chapter (including the assessment in Figure 18.1) can be used for FEG 7.2. FEG 3.5 ("Create a Web of Ideas") can be done by you to prepare for a lesson, or by students to see if they connect ideas of ratio, fraction, division, and rate. This chapter includes many literature links; see Field Experience 2.6 for designing (and teaching) a lesson using children's literature. In Part II, FEG Expanded Lesson 9.11 provides interesting problem-solving contexts to explore proportional situations. FEG Activity 10.7 helps students connect representations for ratios.

Chapter 19

Developing Measurement Concepts

Measurement is one of the most useful mathematics content strands as it is an important component in everything from occupational tasks to life skills for the mathematically literate citizen. From gigabytes that measure amounts of information to font size on computers, from miles per gallon to recipes for a meal, people are surrounded daily with measurement concepts that apply to a variety of real-world situations. However, measurement is not an easy topic for students to understand. Data from both international studies (TIMSS) and from NAEP consistently indicate that students are weaker in the area of measurement than any other topic in the curriculum (Thompson & Preston, 2004). Although learning both the metric and the customary measurement systems may be a contributing factor, the poor performance is more likely a function of how the subject is taught—too much reliance on pictures and worksheets rather than hands-on experiences and a focus on skills with less attention to the concepts of measurement.

In this chapter you will learn how to help students develop a conceptual understanding of the measurement process and the tools of measurement. You will also learn about nonstandard and standard units of measurement, estimation in measurement including the use of benchmarks, and the development of measurement formulas.

Big Ideas

1. Measurement involves a comparison of an attribute of an item or situation with a unit that has the same attribute. Lengths are compared to units of length, areas to units of area, time to units of time, and so on.

2. Meaningful measurement and estimation of measurements depend on a personal familiarity with the unit of measure being used.

3. Estimation of measures and the development of benchmarks for frequently used units of measure help students increase their familiarity with units, preventing errors and aiding in the meaningful use of measurement.

4. Measurement instruments are devices that replace the need for actual measurement units. It is important to understand how measurement instruments work.

5. Area and volume formulas provide a method of measuring these attributes by using only measures of length.

6. Area, perimeter, and volume are related. For example, as the shapes of regions or three-dimensional objects change while maintaining the same areas or volumes, there is a predictable effect on the perimeters and surface areas.

Mathematics Content Connections

In order to provide more time for students to engage in meaningful measurement activities, measurement should be integrated across the mathematics curriculum as well as the science curriculum.

- **Number** (Chapter 8): Early measurement activities are a very meaningful context for counting. Measurement of important objects in the familiar environment connects ideas of number to the real world, enhancing number sense.

- **Place Value** (Chapter 11): Multiples of ten are profitably used by young children in counting nonstandard measures. The metric system of measurement is built on the base-ten system of numeration.

- **Algebra** (Chapter 14): Measurement formulas are themselves functions. Measurement provides data from which generalizations and functional relationships can be derived.

- **Fractions** (Chapter 15): The need for increased precision leads to fractional parts of units.

- **Proportional Reasoning** (Chapter 18): The use of benchmarks in estimating measures promotes multiplicative thinking. Measures are used in scale drawings. Proportions are used to find unknown measures of similar figures.

- **Geometry** (Chapter 20): The development and understanding of perimeter, area, and volume formulas require an understanding of the shapes and relationships involved. Measures help to describe shapes, and angular measures play a significant role in the properties of shapes.

- **Data** (Chapter 21): Statistics and graphs are used to describe our world and help us answer questions about it. Often this description is in terms of measures.

The Meaning and Process of Measuring

Suppose that you asked your students to measure an empty bucket. The first thing they would need to know is *what* about the bucket is to be measured. They might measure the height, depth, diameter (distance across), or circumference (distance around). All of these are length measures. The surface area of the side could be determined. A bucket also has volume (or capacity) and weight. Each of these aspects that can be measured is an *attribute* of the bucket.

Once students determine the attribute to be measured, they need to choose a unit that has the attribute being measured. Length is measured with units that have length, volume with units that have volume, and so on.

Technically, a *measurement* is a number that indicates a comparison between the attribute of the object (or situation, or event)

being measured and the same attribute of a given unit of measure. We commonly use small units of measure to determine a numeric relationship (the measurement) between what is measured and the unit. For example, to measure a length, the comparison can be done by lining up copies of the unit directly against the length being measured. To measure weight, which is a pull of gravity or a force, the weight of the object might first be applied to a spring. Then the comparison is made by finding out how many units of weight produce the same effect on the spring. In either case, the number of units is the measure of the object.

For most of the attributes that are measured in schools, we can say that *to measure* means that the attribute being measured is "filled" or "covered" or "matched" with a unit of measure with the same attribute (as illustrated in Figure 19.1).

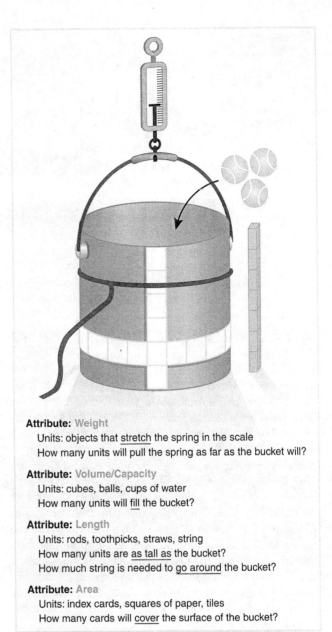

Attribute: Weight
Units: objects that <u>stretch</u> the spring in the scale
How many units will pull the spring as far as the bucket will?

Attribute: Volume/Capacity
Units: cubes, balls, cups of water
How many units will <u>fill</u> the bucket?

Attribute: Length
Units: rods, toothpicks, straws, string
How many units are <u>as tall as</u> the bucket?
How much string is needed to <u>go around</u> the bucket?

Attribute: Area
Units: index cards, squares of paper, tiles
How many cards will <u>cover</u> the surface of the bucket?

Figure 19.1 Measuring different attributes of a bucket.

In summary, to measure something, one must perform three steps:

1. Decide on the attribute to be measured.
2. Select a unit that has that attribute.
3. Compare the units, by filling, covering, matching, or using some other method, with the attribute of the object being measured. The number of units required to match the object is the measure.

Standard measuring instruments such as rulers, scales, protractors, and clocks are devices that make the filling, covering, or matching process easier.

Concepts and Skills

If a typical group of first graders attempt to measure the length of their classroom by laying strips 1 meter long end to end the strips sometimes overlap, and the line can weave in a snakelike fashion. Do they understand the concept of length as an attribute of the classroom? Do they understand that each 1-meter strip has this attribute of length? Do they understand that their task is to fill or match smaller units of length into the length of the classroom? What they most likely understand is that they are supposed to be making a line of strips stretching from wall to wall (and from their vantage point, they are doing quite well). They are performing this task procedurally without conceptual understanding. The skill of measuring with a unit must be explicitly linked to the concept of measuring as a process of comparing attributes, using measuring units and using measuring instruments. A sequence of experiences for measurement instruction is summarized in Table 19.1 and the following discus-

myeducationlab

Go to the Building Teaching Skills and Dispositions section of Chapter 19 of MyEducationLab. Click on Videos and watch the video entitled "**Measurement Lesson**" to see students learn how to measure perimeter.

Table 19.1

Measurement Instruction—A Sequence of Experiences

Step One—Making Comparisons
Goal: Students will understand the attribute to be measured.
Type of Activity: Make comparisons based on the attribute. For example, longer/shorter, heavier/lighter. Use direct comparisons whenever possible.
Notes: When it is clear that the attribute is understood, there is no further need for comparison activities.

Step Two—Using Models of Measuring Units
Goal: Students will understand how filling, covering, matching, or making other comparisons of an attribute with measuring units produces a number called a *measure*.
Type of Activity: Use physical models of measuring units to fill, cover, match, or make the desired comparison of the attribute with the unit.
Notes: Begin with nonstandard units. Progress to the direct use of standard units when appropriate and certainly before using formulas or measuring tools.

Step Three—Using Measuring Instruments
Goal: Students will use common measuring tools with understanding and flexibility.
Type of Activity: Make measuring instruments and use them in comparison with the actual unit models to see how the measurement tool is performing the same function as the individual units. Be certain to make direct comparisons between the student-made tools and the standard tools.
Notes: Student-made tools are usually best made with nonstandard units. Without a careful comparison with the standard tools, much of the value in making the tools can be lost.

sion suggests the types of activities that will develop these skills.

Making Comparisons. The first and most critical goal is for students to understand the attribute they are going to measure. When students compare objects on the basis of some measurable attribute, that attribute becomes the focus of the activity. For example, is the capacity of one box more than, less than, or about the same as the capacity of another? No measurement is required, but some manner of comparing one volume to the other must be devised. The attribute of "capacity" (how much a container can hold) is inescapable.

Many attributes can be compared directly, such as placing one length directly in line with another. In the case of volume or capacity, some indirect method is probably required, such as filling one box with beans and then pouring the beans into the other box. Using a string to compare the height of a wastebasket to the distance around is another example of an indirect comparison. The string is the intermediary, as it is impossible to compare these two lengths directly.

Constructing or making something that is the same in terms of a measurable attribute is another type of comparison activity—for example, "Cut the straw to be about as long as this piece of chalk" or "Draw a rectangle that is about the same size (has the same area) as this triangle."

Using Physical Models of Measuring Units. The second goal is for students to understand what units of measure are appropriate for the particular attribute in question and how these units are used to produce a measurement. Regardless of grade level, you cannot make assumptions that students have an understanding of measuring units. For most attributes that are measured in elementary schools, it is possible to have physical models of the units of measure. Time and temperature are exceptions. (Many other attributes not commonly measured in school also do not have physical units of measure. Light intensity, speed, loudness, viscosity, and radioactivity are just a few examples.) Unit models can be found for both nonstandard (sometimes referred to as informal) units and standard units. For length, for example, drinking straws (nonstandard) or tagboard strips 1 foot long (standard) might be used as units.

The most easily understood use of unit models is actually to use as many copies of the unit as are needed to fill or match the attribute measured. To measure the area of the desktop with an index card as your unit, you can literally cover the entire desk with index cards. Somewhat more difficult, especially for younger children, is to use a single copy of the unit with an iteration process. That would mean the same desktop area can be measured with a single index card by repeatedly moving it from position to position and keeping track of which areas the card has covered.

It is useful to measure the same object with different-sized units. Results should be estimated in advance and discussed afterward. This will help students understand that the unit used is important. The fact that smaller units produce larger numeric measures, and vice versa, is hard for young children to understand. This inverse relationship can only be mentally constructed by predicting, then experimenting, and finally reflecting on measurements with varying-sized units.

Using Measuring Instruments. Understanding the devices we use for measuring is the third goal. In the 2003 National Assessment of Educational Progress (Blume, Galindo, & Walcott, 2007), only 20 percent of fourth-grade students could give the correct measure of an object not aligned with the end of a ruler, as in Figure 19.2. These results point to the difference between using a measuring device and understanding how it works. Students also experienced difficulty when the increments on a measuring device were not one unit.

If students actually make simple measuring instruments using unit models with which they are familiar, it is more likely that they will understand how an instrument measures. A ruler is a good example. If students line up individual physical units along a strip of tagboard and mark them off, they can see that it is the *spaces* on rulers and not the hash marks or numbers that are important. It is essential that students discuss how measurement with individual units compares with measurement using an instrument. Without this comparison and discussion, students may not understand that these two methods are essentially the same.

A discussion of student-made measuring instruments for various attributes is provided in the text and on the Web. Of course, children should also use standard, ready-made instruments such as rulers and scales and should compare the use of these devices with the use of the models they constructed.

Nonstandard Units and Standard Units: Reasons for Using Each

It is common in primary grades to use nonstandard units to measure length and sometimes area. Unfortunately, measurement activities in the upper grades, where other attri-butes are measured, often do not begin with nonstandard units. The use of nonstandard units for beginning measurement activities is beneficial at all grade levels for the following reasons:

- Nonstandard units make it easier to focus directly on the attribute being measured. For example, in a discussion of how to measure the area of an irregular shape, units such as lima beans, square tiles, or circular counters may be suggested. Each unit covers area and each will give a different result. The discussion should then focus on what it means to measure area.
- The use of nonstandard units can avoid conflicting objectives in the same beginning lesson. Is your lesson about what it means to measure area or about understanding square centimeters?
- Nonstandard units provide a good rationale for using standard units. A discussion of the need for a standard unit can have more meaning after groups in your class have measured the same objects with their own units and arrived at different and sometimes confusing answers.
- Using nonstandard units can be motivating.

The use of standard units is also important in your measurement program at any grade level for these reasons:

- Knowledge of standard units is an essential objective of a measurement program. Students must not only develop a familiarity with standard units but must also learn appropriate relationships between them.
- Once a measuring concept is fairly well developed, standard units can be effectively introduced. If there is no good instructional reason for nonstandard units, use standard units to increase students' experience and familiarity with the unit.

The amount of time that should be spent using nonstandard unit models varies with the age of the children and the attributes being measured. Pre-K–grade 1 children need a lot of experience with a variety of nonstandard units of length, weight, and capacity. Conversely, the benefits of nonstandard measuring units may last only a day or two for measurements of angles at the middle school level. When nonstandard units have served their purpose, move on.

The Role of Estimation and Approximation

Always have students estimate a measurement before they make it. This is true with both nonstandard and standard units. There are at least four good reasons for including estimation in measurement activities:

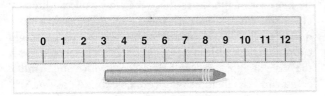

Figure 19.2 "How long is this crayon?"

- Estimation helps students focus on the attribute being measured and the measuring process. Think how you would estimate the area of the front of this book using standard playing cards as the unit. To do so, you have to think about what area is and how the units might be placed on the book cover.
- Estimation provides intrinsic motivation to measurement activities. It is interesting to see how close you can come in your estimate.
- When standard units are used, estimation helps develop familiarity with the unit. If you estimate the height of the door in meters before measuring, you have to think about the size of a meter.
- The use of a benchmark to make an estimate promotes multiplicative reasoning. The width of the building is about one-fourth of the length of a football field—perhaps 25 yards.

In all measuring activities, emphasize the use of approximate language. The desk is *about* 15 orange rods long. The chair is *a little less than* 4 straws high. The use of approximate language is very useful for younger children because many measurements do not result in whole numbers. Older children will begin to search for smaller units or will use fractional units to try to measure exactly. Here is an opportunity to develop the idea that all measurements include some error. First acknowledge that each smaller unit or subdivision produces a greater degree of *precision*. For example, a length measure can never be more than one-half unit in error. And yet, since there is mathematically no "smallest unit," there is always some error involved.

NCTM Standards   The Measurement Standard in *Principles and Standards* for grades 3–5 states that "students should understand that measurements are approximations and understand how differences in units affect precision" (NCTM, 2000, p. 398). In grades 6–8, NCTM states that "middle school students should select and apply techniques and tools to accurately find length, area, volume, and angle measure to appropriate levels of precision" (p. 300). ◆

Length

Length is usually the first attribute students learn to measure. Be aware, however, that length measurement is not immediately understood by young children. Likewise, upper elementary and middle school students may have challenges with the concept of length as they attempt to investigate problems that include perimeter and circumference.

Comparison Activities

At the pre-K–kindergarten level, children should begin with direct comparisons of two or more lengths.

Activity 19.1

Longer, Shorter, Same

Make several sorting-by-length learning stations at which students sort objects as longer, shorter, or about the same as a specified object. The reference object can be changed to produce different sorts. A similar task involves putting objects in order from shortest to longest.

Activity 19.2

Length (or Unit) Hunt

Give pairs of students a strip of tagboard, a stick, a length of rope, or some other object with an obvious length dimension. The task on one day might be to find five things in the room that are shorter than, longer than, or about the same length as their target unit. They can draw pictures or write the names of the things they find.

By making the target length a standard unit (e.g., a meter stick or a 1-meter length of rope), the activity can be repeated to provide familiarity with important standard units.

It is important to compare lengths that are not in straight lines. One way to do this is by using string or rope. Students can wrap string around objects in a search for things that are, for example, as long around as the distance from the floor to their belly button or as long as the distance around one's head or waist. Body measures are always fun.

Indirect comparisons are used in the "Crooked Paths" activity that follows.

Activity 19.3

Crooked Paths

Make some crooked or curvy paths on the floor (or outside) with masking tape or chalk. The task is to determine which path is longest, next longest, and so on. The students should suggest ways to measure the crooked paths so that they can be compared easily. If you wish to offer a hint, provide pairs of students with a long piece of rope. The task is easier if the rope is longer than the crooked paths. Have students explain how they solved the problem.

Units of Length

Students can use a variety of nonstandard units to begin measuring length—for example:

- *Giant footprints:* Make about 20 copies of a large footprint about $1\frac{1}{2}$ to 2 feet long on poster board and cut them out.
- *Measuring ropes:* Cut cotton clothesline into lengths of 1 m. These can measure the perimeter and the circumference of objects such as the teacher's desk, a tree trunk, or the class pumpkin.
- *Plastic straws:* Drinking straws provide large quantities of a useful unit. Straws are easily cut into smaller units or linked together with a long string. The string of straws is an excellent bridge to a ruler or measuring tape.
- *Short units:* Toothpicks, connecting cubes, wooden cubes, and paper clips are all useful nonstandard units for measuring shorter lengths. Cuisenaire rods are a good choice for a set of units because they come in ten different lengths, are readily placed end to end, and can easily be related to each other. They are also metric (cms) and thus make an excellent bridge to a ruler.

The temptation is to carefully explain to students how to use these units to measure and then send them off to practice measuring. This approach will shift students' attention to the procedure (following your instruction) and away from developing an understanding of measurement using units. In the following activity students are provided with a measuring task but are required to develop their own approach.

Activity 19.4

How Long Is the Teacher?

Explain that you have just received an important request from the principal. She needs to know exactly how tall each teacher in the building is. The students are to decide how to measure the teachers and write a note to the principal explaining how tall their teacher is and detailing the process that they used. If you wish to give a hint, have students make marks at your feet and head and draw a straight line between these marks.

Explain that the principal says they can use any ONE of several nonstandard units to measure with (provide choices). For each choice of unit, supply enough units to more than cover your length. Put students in pairs and allow them to select one unit with which to measure.

The value of the last activity will come from the discussion. Good questions include "How did you get your measurement?" "Did students who measured with the same unit get the same answers? Why not?" "How could the principal make a line that was just as long as the teacher?" In your discussion, focus on the value of lining units up carefully, end to end. Discuss what happens if you overlap units, have a gap in the units, or don't stay in a straight line.

The following activity adds an estimation component.

Activity 19.5

Estimate and Measure

Make lists of items in the room to measure (see Figure 19.3). For younger children, run a piece of masking tape along the dimension of objects to be measured. On the list, designate the units to be used. Do not forget to include curves or other distances that are not straight lines. Include estimates before the measures. Remember that young children have probably had limited experiences with estimating distances.

For students beginning to learn about estimation, add the following component to the "Estimate and Measure" activity: Have students make a row or chain of exactly ten units to use in helping them with their estimates. They

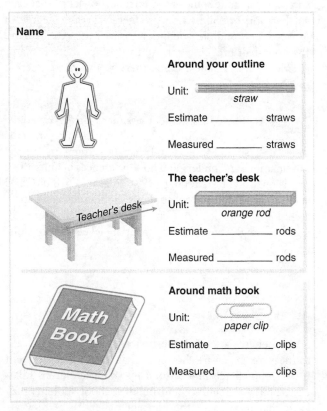

Figure 19.3 Example recording sheet for measuring with nonstandard length units.

first lay ten units against the object and then make their estimate.

It is a challenge to explain to students that larger units will produce a smaller measure and vice versa. Instead, engage students in an activity like the following where this issue is a focus.

Activity 19.6

Changing Units

Have students measure a length with a specified unit. Then provide them with a different unit that is either twice as long or half as long as the original unit. Their task is to predict the measure of the same length using the new unit. Students should write down their estimations and explanations of how they were made. Stop and have a discussion about their estimations and then have them make the actual measurement. Cuisenaire rods are excellent for this activity. Older students can be challenged with units that are more difficult multiples of the original unit.

In "Changing Units," you are looking first for the basic idea that when the unit is longer the measure is smaller and vice versa. This is a good activity to do just before you discuss unit conversion with standard units. For example, if the doorway is 80 inches high, how many feet is that? Changing measurement units is an excellent proportional reasoning task for middle school students.

 Observation and discussion during activities such as those just described provide evidence of how well your students understand length measurement. Additional tasks that can be used as assessments in a diagnostic interview format are:

- Provide a box with assorted units of different sizes (i.e., Cuisenaire rods). Have the students use the materials in the box to measure a given length. Observe whether students understand that all units must be of equal lengths. If different units are used, ask how the students would describe their measurement.
- Ask students to draw a line or mark off a distance of a prescribed number of units. Observe whether the students know to align the units in a straight line without overlaps or gaps.
- Have students measure two different objects. Then ask how much longer is the longer object. Observe whether students can use the measurements to answer or whether a third measurement must be made of the difference.
- Provide a length of string and tell students that the string is 6 units long. Ask how could they use the

string to make a length of 3 units. Ask how could they make a length of 9 units? In this task, you are looking to see if students can mentally subdivide the given length (string) based on an understanding of its measure. That is, can students visualize that 6 units are matched to the string length and half of these are 3 units? ◆

Fractional Parts of Units.   Children are sometimes perplexed when their measurements do not result in a whole number. One suggestion you might make to younger students is to use a smaller unit to fill in the remaining gap, as in Figure 19.4. Another idea is to suggest that fractions be used. In the metric system, units are rarely mixed, and fractional units are expressed in decimal form (e.g., 3.2 m). In the customary system a measurement of 4 feet 3 inches is sometimes reported as 51 inches or as $4\frac{1}{4}$ feet. The use of fractional units can help students understand subdivision marks on a ruler. The children's book *Inchworm and a Half* provides a nice way to introduce the idea of fractional units (see the literature section at the end of the chapter).

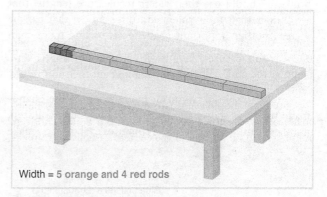

Width = 5 orange and 4 red rods

Figure 19.4 Using two units to measure length.

Making and Using Rulers

The jump from measuring with nonstandard units to using standard rulers is challenging. One of the best methods of helping students understand rulers is to have them make their own rulers out of actual units.

Activity 19.7

Make Your Own Ruler

Precut narrow strips of construction paper 5 cm long and about 2 cm wide. Use two different colors. Discuss how the strips could be used to measure by laying them end to end. Provide long strips of tagboard about 3 cm wide. Without explicit guided direction, have students make their own ruler by gluing the units onto the tagboard. Have a list of a few things to measure. Students use their new rulers to measure the items on the list. Discuss the results. It is possible that there will be discrepancies due to rulers that were not made properly or to a failure to understand how a ruler works.

The same activity can be done using larger nonstandard units such as tracings of students' footprints glued onto strips of adding machine tape. Older children can use a standard unit (centimeter, inch, foot) to make marks on the strips and color in the spaces with alternating colors.

This activity makes the construction of a ruler a problem-based experience. By not overguiding students in how to make their rulers, you will get formative assessment information concerning students' understanding of the measurement process. At the conclusion of this process, all students should have correctly made a ruler. The multiple copies of units on the student-made rulers (rather than markings and numbers) maximize the connection between the spaces on the ruler and the actual units. Students should use their rulers to measure lengths that are longer than their rulers and discuss how that can be done. Another important challenge is to find more than one way to measure a length with a ruler. Do you have to begin at the end? What if you begin at another unit in the center?

Students should eventually put numbers on their handmade rulers, as shown in Figure 19.5. For young children, numbers can be written in the center of each unit to make it clear that the numbers are a way of precounting the units. When numbers are written in the standard way, at the ends of the units, the ruler becomes a number line. This format is more sophisticated and should be carefully discussed with children.

Much of the value of student-made rulers can be lost if you do not transfer this knowledge to standard rulers. Give children a standard ruler, and discuss how it is like and how it differs from the ones they have made. What are the units? Could you make a ruler with paper units the same as this? What do the numbers mean? What are the other marks for? Where do the units begin?

 Research indicates that when students see standard rulers with the numbers on the hash marks, they often believe that the numbers are counting the marks rather than indicating the units or spaces between the marks. This is an incorrect understanding of rulers that can lead to wrong answers when using them. As an assessment, provide students a ruler with hash marks but no numbers. Have students use the ruler to measure an item that is shorter than the ruler. A correct understanding of rulers is indicated if students count spaces between the hash marks.

Another good assessment of ruler understanding is to have students measure with a "broken" ruler, one with the first two units broken off. Some students will say that it is impossible to measure with such a ruler because there is no starting point. Those who understand rulers will be able to match and count the units meaningfully in their measures. (See Barrett, Jones, Thornton, & Dickson, 2003, for a complete discussion of student development of length measurement, including the use of rulers.)

Observing how children use a ruler to measure an object that is longer than the ruler is also informative. Children who simply read the last mark on the ruler may struggle because they do not understand how a ruler is a representation of a continuous row of units. ◆

Area

Area is the two-dimensional space inside a region. As with other attributes, students must first understand the attribute of area before measuring. Data from the 2003 NAEP suggest that fourth- and eighth-grade students have an incomplete understanding of area (Blume, Galindo, & Walcott, 2007).

Comparison Activities

One of the purposes of comparison activities with areas is to help students distinguish between size (or area) and shape, length, and other dimensions. A long, skinny rectangle may have less area than a triangle with shorter sides.

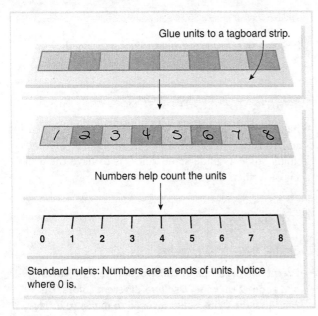

Glue units to a tagboard strip.

1 2 3 4 5 6 7 8
Numbers help count the units

0 1 2 3 4 5 6 7 8
Standard rulers: Numbers are at ends of units. Notice where 0 is.

Figure 19.5 Give meaning to numbers on rulers.

Investigations
in Number, Data, and Space

Grade 3, *Perimeter, Angles, and Area*

Context

The perimeter activity continues the development of ideas about linear measurement. At the point of this lesson, it is assumed that students understand the need for standard units and can use tools that measure length in both the metric and customary systems. Students are able to recognize that perimeter is the measure around the outside edges of a two-dimensional shape.

Task

In this investigation, students select real-world objects and measure the perimeter or rim (Hint for students: the word rim is in pe**rim**eter). Key in this process will be the choices the students make, such as whether the object they choose has a perimeter that is regular, like the top of a desk, or more challenging, like the top of a waste paper basket. They also need to choose the tool that will be best for measuring, given yardsticks or metersticks, or adding machine tape or string. At first, students are asked as a group to suggest an object. Then one student traces with a finger the perimeter that will be measured. All students are asked to include this object in the exploration that follows. In this way, students will be able to compare the results of at least one common item, providing a basis for discussing any measurement errors. Students can be asked to include an estimate of the perimeter on their chart prior to actually measuring. During the "after" period of the lesson, students should discuss how they measured objects that were larger than the tool they were using and how they

Name		Date

Perimeter, Angles, and Area

Finding and Measuring Perimeters (page 1 of 2)

Choose 5 objects in the classroom that have perimeters you can measure, such as a bulletin board, the top of a table, or the side of the teacher's desk. Measure their perimeters and record your work below.

Object	Drawing of What I Am Measuring	Perimeter
Example: Top of my desk	30 in. / 18 in. / 18 in. / 30 in.	96 inches
1.		
2.		

Sessions 1.2, 1.3   Unit 4   **5**

knew when to use a "flexible" measuring tool such as the string or adding machine tape.

This is an especially difficult concept for young children to understand. In addition, many 8- or 9-year-olds do not understand that rearranging areas into different shapes does not affect the amount of area.

Direct comparison of two areas is nearly always impossible except when the shapes involved have some common dimension or property. For example, two rectangles with the same width can be compared directly, as can any two circles. Comparison of these special shapes, however, fails to deal with the attribute of area. Instead, activities in which one area is rearranged are suggested. Cutting a shape into

two parts and reassembling it in a different shape can show that the before and after shapes have the same area, even though they are different shapes. This idea is not at all obvious to children in the K–2 grade range.

Activity 19.8

Two-Piece Shapes

Cut a large number of rectangles of the same area, about 3 inches by 5 inches. Each pair of students will need six rectangles. Have students fold and cut the rectangles on the diagonal, making two identical triangles. Next, have them rearrange the triangles into different shapes, including the original rectangle. The rule is that only sides of the same length can be matched up and must be matched exactly. Have each group find all the shapes that can be made this way, gluing the triangles on paper as a record of each shape (see Figure 19.6). Discuss the area and shape of the different results. Is one shape bigger than the rest? How is it bigger? Did one take more paper to make? Help children conclude that although each figure is a different shape, all the figures have the same *area*.

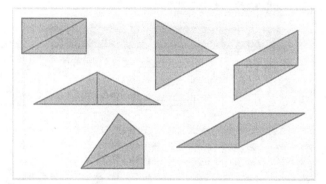

Figure 19.6 Different shapes, same area.

Tangrams, a very old and popular set of puzzle shapes, can be used for the same purpose. The standard set of seven tangram pieces is cut from a square, as shown in Figure 19.7. The two small triangles can be used to

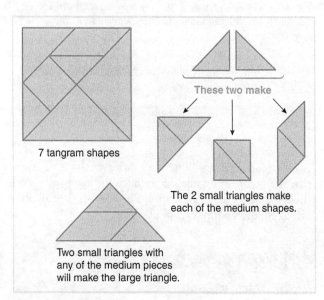

7 tangram shapes

These two make

The 2 small triangles make each of the medium shapes.

Two small triangles with any of the medium pieces will make the large triangle.

Figure 19.7 Tangrams provide an opportunity to investigate area concepts (see Blackline Master 51).

make the parallelogram, the square, and the medium triangle. This permits a similar discussion about the pieces having the same size (area) but different shapes (Seymour, 1971). (Tangram pieces can be found in Blackline Master 51.)

Activity **19.9**

Tangram Areas

Draw the outline of several shapes made with tangram pieces, as in Figure 19.8. Let students use tangrams to decide which shapes are the same size, which are larger, and which are smaller. Shapes can be duplicated on paper, and children can work in groups. Let students explain how they came to their conclusions. Use the animal shapes from *Grandfather Tang's Story* (Tompert, 1997) for additional investigations.

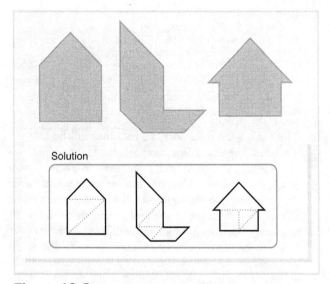

Solution

Figure 19.8 Compare shapes made of tangram pieces.

II ———— *Pause and Reflect*

You might pause here, get a set of tangrams, and make the area comparisons suggested in Figure 19.8.

Units of Area

Although squares are the most common units of area, any tile that conveniently fills up a plane region can be used. Even filling a region with uniform circles or lima beans provides a useful idea of what it means to measure area. Here are some suggestions for area units that are easy to gather or make in large quantities.

- Round plastic chips, pennies, or lima beans can be used. It is not necessary at a beginning stage that the area units fit with no gaps.
- Color tiles (1-inch plastic squares).
- Squares cut from cardboard. Large squares (about 20 cm on a side) work well for large areas. Smaller units should be about 5 to 10 cm on a side.
- Sheets of newspaper make excellent units for very large areas.

Children can use units to measure surfaces in the room such as desktops, bulletin boards, or books. Large regions can be outlined with masking tape on the floor. Small regions can be duplicated on paper so that students can work at their desks. Odd shapes and curved surfaces provide more challenge and interest. The surface of a watermelon or of the side of the wastebasket provide useful challenges.

In area measurements, there may be lots of units that only partially fit. You may wish to begin with shapes in which the units fit by building a shape with units, and drawing the outline. According to *Curriculum Focal Points* (NCTM, 2006), in fourth grade, students should begin to wrestle with partial units and mentally put together two or more partial units to count as one. Figure 19.9 shows one possible measurement exercise.

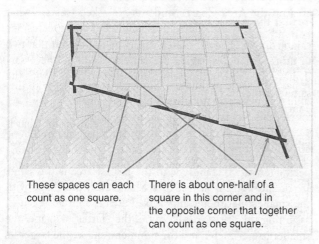

These spaces can each count as one square.

There is about one-half of a square in this corner and in the opposite corner that together can count as one square.

Figure 19.9 Measuring the area of a large shape drawn with tape on the floor. Units are pieces of tagboard all cut to squares of the same size.

The following activity is a good starting point to see what ideas your students bring to their understanding of units of area.

Activity 19.10

Fill and Compare

Draw two rectangles and a blob shape on a sheet of paper. Make it so that the three areas are not the same but with no area that is clearly largest or small-est. The students' task is to first make an estimate about which is the smallest and the largest of the three shapes. After recording their estimate, they should use a filler of their choice to decide. Students should explain in writing what they found out.

Your objective in the beginning is to develop the idea that area is measured by covering. Do not introduce formulas. Groups are very likely to come up with different measures for the same region. Discuss these differences with the children and point to the difficulties involved in making estimates around the edges. Avoid the idea that there is a "right" answer.

By fourth grade, students should begin to relate the concept of multiplication using arrays to the area of rectangles. The following comparison activity is a good step in that direction.

Activity 19.11

Rectangle Comparison—Square Units

Students are given a pair of rectangles that are either the same or very close in area. They are also given a model or drawing of a single square unit and a ruler that measures the appropriate unit. The students are not permitted to cut out the rectangles. They may draw on them if they wish. The task is to use their rulers to determine, in any way that they can, which rectangle is larger or whether they are the same. They should use words, pictures, and numbers to explain their conclusions. Some suggested pairs are as follows:

4×10 and 5×8

5×10 and 7×7

4×6 and 5×5

The goal of this activity is not necessarily to develop an area formula but to apply students' developing concepts of multiplication to the area of rectangles. Not all students will use a multiplicative approach. In order to count a single row of squares along one edge, and then multiply by the length of the other edge, the first row must be thought of as a unit that is then replicated to fill in the rectangle (Outhred & Mitchelmore, 2004). Many students will attempt to draw in all the squares. However, some may use their rulers to determine the number of squares that will fit along each side and, from that, use multiplication to determine the total area (see Figure 19.10). By having students share their strategies, more students can be exposed to the use of multiplication in this context.

Grids. Grids of various types can be thought of as "area rulers." A grid of squares for area does exactly what a ruler

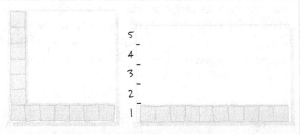

This rectangle is covered | Five rows of 10 squares is 5 × 10 or
by 49 squares: 7 × 7 is 49. | 50 squares. This rectangle is larger.

Figure 19.10 Some students use multiplication to tell the total number of square units.

does for length. It lays out the units for you. Square grids to make transparencies are available in Blackline Masters 34–36. Have students place the grid over a region to be measured and count the units inside. An alternative method is to trace around a region on a paper grid.

The Relationship Between Area and Perimeter

Area and perimeter (the distance around a region) are continually a source of confusion for students. Perhaps it is because both involve regions to be measured or because students are taught formulas for both concepts at about the same time and tend to get formulas confused. Whatever the reason, expect that students even in the fifth and sixth grades will confuse these two ideas. An interesting approach to alleviating this confusion is to contrast the two ideas as in the next activities.

Activity 19.12

Fixed Perimeters

Give students a loop of nonstretching string that is exactly 24 centimeters in circumference. The task is to decide what different-sized rectangles can be made with a perimeter of 24 cm. Students may want to use a 1-cm grid to place their strings on. Each different rectangle can be recorded on grid paper with the area noted inside the figure.

An alternative to the string loop is to simply use grid paper and ask students to find rectangles with perimeters of 24 cm.

Activity 19.13

Fixed Areas

Provide students with centimeter grid paper. The task is to see how many rectangles can be made

with an area of 36—that is, to make filled-in rectangles, not just borders. Each new rectangle should be recorded by sketching the outline and the dimensions on grid paper. For each rectangle, students should determine and record the perimeter inside the figure. (See the "Fixed Areas" lesson on pp. 74–75.)

II *Pause and Reflect*

Before reading further, think about the two previous activities. For "Fixed Areas," will all of the perimeters be the same? If not, what can you say about the shapes with longer or shorter perimeters? For "Fixed Perimeters," will the areas remain the same? Why or why not?

As students complete Activities 19.12 and 19.13 in small groups, have them keep track of the areas and perimeters by writing them on the rectangles (area = 12 cm²). Then they should cut out all the figures, keeping the fixed perimeters in one pile and the fixed areas in another. Labeling either two charts or locations on the board with "Perimeter" and "Area," the teams should come up and place their figures (left to right) from smallest perimeter to largest perimeter on the Perimeter Chart and from smallest area to largest area on the Area Chart. Students are asked to state what they observe, make conjectures, and see if any conclusions can be drawn. They are often surprised to find out that two or more rectangles having the same areas do not necessarily have the same perimeters. Similarly two shapes with the same perimeters do not always have the same areas. And, of course, this fact is not restricted to rectangles.

Students will notice that there is a relationship that is fairly interesting. When the area is fixed, the shape with the smallest perimeter is a square or "square-like." For a fixed perimeter, the rectangle with the largest area is the same. If you allowed for any shapes whatsoever, the shape with the smallest perimeter and a fixed area is a circle. That is, assuming the areas are the same, the "fatter" a shape, the smaller its perimeter and the skinnier a shape, the larger its perimeter. (A corresponding result is true in three dimensions. Replace perimeter with surface area and area with volume.)

Volume and Capacity

Volume and *capacity* are both terms for measures of the "size" of three-dimensional regions. The term *capacity* is generally used to refer to the amount that a container will hold. Standard units of capacity include quarts and gallons or liters and milliliters. The term *volume* can be used to refer to the capacity of a container but is also used for the size of solid objects. Standard units of volume are expressed in terms of length units, such as cubic inches or cubic centimeters.

Comparison Activities

Comparing the volumes of solid objects is very difficult. For children at the primary level, it is appropriate to focus on capacity. A simple method of comparing capacity is to fill one container with something and then pour this amount into the comparison container. By third grade most students will understand the concept of "holds more" with reference to containers. The concept of volume for solid objects may not be as readily understood.

In pre-K settings, young children should have lots of experiences directly comparing the capacities of different containers. Collect a large assortment of cans, small boxes, and plastic containers. Gather as many different shapes as possible. Also gather some plastic scoops. Cut a plastic 2-liter bottle in half, and use the top portion as a funnel. Rice or dried beans are good fillers to use. Sand and water are both possible, particularly if there is a water table available.

Activity 19.14

Capacity Sort

Provide a collection of labeled containers, with one marked as the "target." The students' task is to sort the collection into those that hold more than, less than, or about the same amount as the target container. Provide a recording sheet on which each container is listed and a place to circle "holds more," "holds less," and "holds about the same." List the choices twice for each container. The first choice is to record an estimation made by observation. The second is to record "what was found." Provide a filler (such as beans or rice), scoops, and funnels. Avoid explicit directions, but later discuss students' ideas for solving the task.

Do not expect students to be able to accurately predict which of two containers holds more. Even adults have difficulty making this judgment. Try the following task yourself as well as with students. Take two sheets of construction paper. Make a tube shape (cylinder) by taping the two long edges together. Make a shorter, fatter cylinder from the other sheet by taping the short edges together. When placed upright, which cylinder holds more, or do they have the same capacity?

Before doing this with your class, survey them to see how many select which option. Most groups split roughly in thirds: short and fat, tall and skinny, or same capacity. Use a filler such as Styrofoam packing peanuts or lima beans. Place the skinny cylinder inside the fat one. Fill the inside tube and then lift it up, allowing the filler to empty into the fat cylinder.

The apparent volumes of solid objects are sometimes misleading, and a method of comparison is also difficult. To compare volumes of solids such as a ball and an apple, some method of displacement must be used. Provide students with two or three containers that will each hold the objects to be compared and a filler such as rice or beans. With this equipment some students may be able to devise their own comparison method. One approach is to first fill a container completely and then pour it into an empty holding container. Next, place an object in the first container and fill it again to the top, using filler from the holding container. The volume of filler remaining is equal to the volume of the object. Mark the level of the leftover filler in the holding container before repeating the experiment with other objects. By comparing the level of the leftover filler for two or more objects, the volumes of the objects can be compared.

The following activity is a three-dimensional version of Activity 19.13, "Fixed Areas." Here the volume is fixed and students look for changes in surface area.

Activity 19.15

Fixed Volume: Comparing Prisms

Give each pair of students a supply of centimeter cubes or wooden cubes. Their task is, for a fixed number of cubes, to build different rectangular prisms and record the surface area for each prism formed. A good number of cubes to suggest is 64, since a minimal surface area will occur with a 4 × 4 × 4 cube. With 64 cubes a lot of prisms can be made. However, if you are short of cubes, other good choices are 24 or 36 cubes. Using the tables students construct, they should observe any patterns that occur. In particular, what happens to the surface area as the prism becomes less like a tall, skinny box and more like a cube?

The goal here is for students to realize that volume does not dictate surface area and to recognize the pattern between surface area and volume is similar to the one found between area and perimeter. Namely, prisms that are more cubelike have less surface area than prisms with the same volume that are long and narrow.

Once students have developed formulas for computing area and volume, they can continue to explore the relationships between surface area and volume without actually building the prisms.

Units of Volume and Capacity

Two types of units can be used to measure volume and capacity: solid units and containers. Solid units are objects like wooden cubes or old tennis balls that can be used to fill the container being measured. The other type of unit model is a small container that is filled and poured repeatedly into the container being measured. The following are a few examples of units that you might want to collect:

- Plastic caps and liquid medicine cups.
- Plastic jars and containers of almost any size.
- Wooden cubic blocks or blocks of any shape (as long as you have a lot of the same size).
- Styrofoam packing peanuts (which still produce conceptual measures of volume despite not packing perfectly).

The following activity is similar to Activity 19.11, "Rectangle Comparison—Square Units."

Activity 19.16

Box Comparison—Cubic Units

Provide students with a pair of small boxes that you have folded up from poster board (see Figure 19.11). Use unit dimensions that match the blocks that you have for units. Students are given two boxes, exactly one block, and an appropriate ruler. (If you use 2-cm cubes, make a ruler with the unit equal to 2 centimeters.) The students' task is to decide which box has the greater volume or if they have the same volume.

Here are some suggested box dimensions ($L \times W \times H$):

6 × 3 × 4   5 × 4 × 4   3 × 9 × 3   6 × 6 × 2   5 × 5 × 3

Students should use words, drawings, and numbers to explain their conclusions.

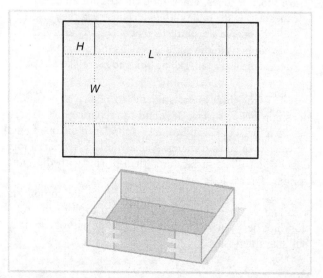

Figure 19.11 Make small boxes by starting with a rectangle and drawing a square on each corner as shown. Cut on the solid lines and fold the box up, wrapping the corner squares to the outside and tape them to the sides as shown.

A useful hint in the last activity is to first figure out how many cubes will fit on the bottom of the box. Some students, although certainly not all, will discover a multiplicative rule for the volume. The boxes can be filled with cubes to confirm conclusions. No formulas should be used unless students can explain them. The development of a formula is not necessarily the goal of this activity.

Using Measuring Cups. Instruments for measuring capacity are generally used for small amounts of liquids or pourable materials such as rice or water. These tools are commonly found in kitchens and laboratories. Students should use measuring cups to explore recipes for food products as well as to create papier-mâché for art or Oobleck for science experiments (Google "making Oobleck" for recipes). The *Better Homes and Gardens New Junior Cookbook* (2004) is a great place to start for student-friendly recipes and multiple measuring experiences with units of capacity.

Weight and Mass

Weight is a measure of the pull or force of gravity on an object. *Mass* is the amount of matter in an object and a measure of the force needed to accelerate it. On the moon, where gravity is much less than on earth, an object has a smaller weight but the identical mass as on earth. For practical purposes, on the earth, the measures of mass and weight will be about the same. In this discussion, the terms *weight* and *mass* will be used interchangeably.

Comparison Activities

The most conceptual way to compare the weights of two objects is to hold one in each hand, extend your arms, and experience the relative downward pull on each—effectively communicating to a pre-K–1 child what "heavier" or "weighs more" means. This personal experience can then be transferred to one of two basic types of scales—balances and spring scales.

When children place the objects in the two pans of a balance, the pan that goes down can be understood to hold the heavier object. Even a relatively simple balance will detect small differences. If two objects are placed one at a time in a spring scale, the heavier object pulls the pan down farther. Both balances and spring scales have real value in the classroom. (Technically, spring scales measure weight and balance scales measure mass. Why?)

With either scale, estimating, sorting, and ordering tasks are possible with very young children. For older children, comparison activities for weight are not necessary. (Why?)

Units of Weight or Mass

Any collection of uniform objects with the same mass can serve as weight units. For very light objects, large paper clips, wooden blocks, or plastic cubes work well. Large metal washers found in hardware stores are effective for weighing slightly heavier objects. You will need to rely on standard weights to weigh things as heavy as a kilogram or more.

Weight cannot be measured directly. Either a two-pan balance or a spring scale must be used. In a balance scale, place an object in one pan and weights in the other until the two pans balance. In a spring scale, first place the object in and mark the position of the pan on a piece of paper taped behind the pan. Remove the object and place just enough weights in the pan to pull it down to the same level. Discuss how equal weights will pull the spring or rubber band with the same force.

While the concept of heavier and lighter is learned rather early, the notion of units of weight or mass is a bit more challenging. At any grade level, even a brief experience with informal unit weights is good preparation for standard units and scales.

Time

Time is a bit different from the other attributes that are commonly measured in school because it cannot be seen or felt and because it is more difficult for students to comprehend units of time or how they are matched against a given time period or duration.

Duration

Time can be thought of as the duration of an event from its beginning to its end. As with other attributes, for students to adequately understand the attribute of time, they should make comparisons of events that have different durations. If two events begin at the same time, the shorter duration will end first and the other last longer. For example, which top spins longer? However, this form of comparison focuses on the ending of the duration rather than the duration itself. In order to think of time as something that can be measured, it is helpful to compare two events that do not start at the same time. This requires that some form of measurement of time be used from the beginning.

An informal unit of time might be the duration of a pendulum swing made with a tennis ball suspended on a long string from the ceiling. The long string produces a slow swing and, thus, keeps the counting manageable. The steady drip of a water faucet into an empty container is another option. The level of the water is marked at the end of the period. When the marked container is emptied and used to time a second duration, the two markings can

be compared. One advantage of the water drip method is that there are no units to count. Simple tasks that address duration include the following:

- Stacking ten blocks one at a time and then removing them one at a time
- Printing the alphabet
- Walking slowly around a designated path
- Making a bar of 15 connecting cubes

Only one student does each task, so that there is no competition or racing.

Students also need to learn about seconds, minutes, and hours and to develop some concept of how long these units are. You can help by making a conscious effort to note the duration of short and long events during the day. Timing small events of $\frac{1}{2}$ minute to 2 minutes is fun and useful. TV shows and commercials are a good standard. Have students time familiar events in their daily lives: brushing teeth, eating dinner, riding to school, spending time doing homework.

Activity 19.17

Be Ready for the Bell

Give students a recording sheet with a set of clock faces (see Blackline Master 33). Secretly set a timer to go off at the hour, half hour, or minute. When the bell rings, students should look up and record the time on the clock face and in numerals. This highly engaging activity motivates students to not only think about telling time, but to consider the relationship between the analog clock reading and digital recording. Elapsed time can also be explored by discussing the time between timer rings.

Clock Reading

The common instrument for measuring time is the clock. However, learning to tell time has little to do with time measurement and more to do with the skills of learning to read a dial-type instrument. Clock reading can be a difficult skill to teach.

Some Challenges. Starting in first grade, children are usually taught first to read clocks to the hour, then the half and quarter hours, and finally to 5- and 1-minute intervals in the grades that follow. In the early stages of this sequence, children are shown clocks set exactly to the hour or half hour. Thus, many children who can read a clock at 7:00 or 2:30 are initially challenged by 6:58 or 2:33.

Digital clocks permit students to read times easily but do not relate times very well. To know that a digital reading of 7:58 is nearly 8 o'clock, the child must know that there are 60 minutes in an hour, that 58 is close to 60, and that 2 minutes is not a very long time. These concepts have not been developed by most first-grade and many second-grade children. The analog clock (with hands) shows "close to" times visually without the need for understanding big numbers or even how many minutes in an hour.

Suggested Approach. The following suggestions can help students understand and read analog clocks.

1. Begin with a one-handed clock. A clock with only an hour hand can be read with reasonable accuracy. Use lots of approximate language: "It's about 7 o'clock." "It's a little past 9 o'clock." "It's halfway between 2 o'clock and 3 o'clock" (see Figure 19.12).

2. Discuss what happens to the big hand as the little hand goes from one hour to the next. When the big hand is at 12, the hour hand is pointing exactly to a number. If the hour hand is about halfway between numbers, about where would the minute hand be? If the hour hand is a little past or before an hour (10 to 15 minutes), about where would the minute hand be?

3. Use two real clocks, one with only an hour hand and one with two hands. (Break off the minute hand from an old clock.) Cover the two-handed clock. Periodically during the day, direct attention to the one-handed clock. Discuss the time in approximate language. Have students predict where the minute hand should be. Uncover the other clock and check.

4. Teach time after the hour in 5-minute intervals. After step 3 has begun, count by fives going around the clock. Instead of predicting that the minute hand is pointing at the 4, encourage students to say it is about 20 minutes after the hour. As skills develop, suggest that students always look first at the little or hour hand to learn approximately what time it is and then focus on the minute hand for precision.

5. Predict the reading on a digital clock when shown an analog clock, and vice versa; set an analog clock when shown a digital clock. This can be done with both one-handed and two-handed clocks.

As students learn more about two-digit numbers, the time after the hours can also be related to the time left before the hour. This is helpful not only for telling time but for number sense as well. Note that in the sequence

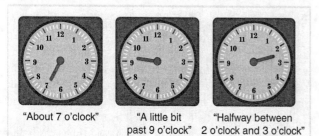

"About 7 o'clock"   "A little bit past 9 o'clock"   "Halfway between 2 o'clock and 3 o'clock"

Figure 19.12 Approximate time with one-handed clocks.

suggested, time after the hour is stressed almost exclusively. Time before or till the hour can come later.

The following activity can be used to help students in the second grade and beyond, even if the earlier sequence of one-handed clocks has not been followed.

Activity 19.18

One-Handed Clocks

Prepare a page of clock faces (see Blackline Master 33). On each clock draw an hour hand. Include placements that are approximately a quarter past the hour, a quarter until the hour, half past the hour, and some that are close to but not on the hour. For each clock face, the students' task is to write the digital time and draw a minute hand on the clock where they think it would be.

"One-Handed Clocks" is a good assessment of students' clock reading. If students in the third grade or above are having difficulty reading clocks, working with a one-handed clock as suggested earlier will offer a different approach. ◆

Elapsed Time

Determining elapsed time is a skill required by most state curricula starting in about grade 3. It is also a skill that can be challenging for students, especially when the period of time includes noon or midnight. Students must know how many minutes are in an hour. On the 2003 NAEP assessment, only 26 percent of fourth graders and 55 percent of eighth-grade students could solve a problem involving the conversion of one measure of time to another (Blume, Galindo, & Walcott, 2007). If given the digital time or the time after the hour, students must be able to tell how many minutes to the next hour. This should certainly be a mental process of counting on for multiples of 5 minutes. Avoid having students use pencil and paper to subtract 25 from 60.

Figuring the time from, say, 8:15 A.M. to 11:45 A.M. is a multistep task regardless of how it is done. Keeping track of the intermediate steps is difficult, as is deciding what to do first. In this case you could count hours from 8:15 to 11:15 and add on 30 minutes. But then what do you do if the endpoints are 8:45 and 11:15? To propose a singular method or algorithm is not helpful.

Next is the issue of A.M. and P.M. The problem is due less to the fact that students don't understand what happens on the clock at noon and midnight as it is that they now have trouble counting the intervals.

In the discussion so far, we have only addressed one form of the problem. There is also the task of finding the

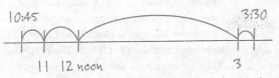

(a) School began late today at 10:45 A.M. If you get out at 3:30, how much time will you be in school today?

Four hours from 11 to 3. Then 15 minutes in front and 30 minutes at the end—45 minutes. Three hours 45 minutes in all.

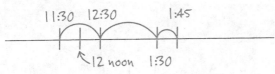

(b) The game begins at 11:30 A.M. If it lasts 2 hours and 15 minutes, when will it be over?

One hour after 11:30 is 12:30 and a second hour gets you to 1:30 and then 15 minutes more is 1:45. It's P.M. because it is after noon.

Figure 19.13 A sketch of an empty time line can be useful in solving elapsed time problems.

end time given the start time and elapsed time, or finding the start time given the end time and the elapsed time. In keeping with the spirit of problem solving and the use of models, consider the following.

As a general model for all of these elapsed time problems, suggest that students sketch an empty time line (similar to the empty number line discussed in Chapter 12 for computation). Examples are shown in Figure 19.13. It is important not to be overly prescriptive in telling students how to use the time line since there are various alternatives (Dixon, 2008). For example, in Figure 19.13, a student might count by full hours from 10:45 (11:45, 12:45, 1:45, 2:45, 3:45) and then subtract 15 minutes.

Money

Here is a list of the money ideas and skills typically required in the primary grades:

- Coin recognition
- Values of coins
- Using the values of coins
- Counting sets of coins (including comparing two sets)
- Equivalent collections of coins (same amounts, different coins)
- Selecting coins for a given amount
- Making change

These ideas and skills will be discussed in the following sections.

Coin Recognition and Values

The names of our coins are conventions of our social system. Students learn these names the same way that they learn the names of physical objects in their daily environment—through exposure and repetition.

The value of each coin is also a convention that students must simply be told. For these values to make sense, students must have an understanding of 5, 10, and 25. More than that, they need to be able to think of these quantities without seeing countable objects. Nowhere else do we say, "this is 5," while pointing to a single item. A child whose number concepts remain tied to counts of objects will be challenged to understand the values of coins. Coin value lessons should focus on purchase power—a dime can *buy the same thing* that 10 pennies can buy.

Counting Sets of Coins

To name the total value of a group of coins is the same as mentally adding their values except that there are no numerals visible. Ironically, most state standards require coin counting before they require students to mentally do the symbolic sum. Yet, second-grade students can be asked to do the mental math required in counting a collection of coins. Even though it is actually mental computation, the numbers are fortunately restricted to multiples of 5 and 10 with some 1s added at the end. The next activity is a preparation for counting money.

Activity **19.19**

Money Skip Counts

Explain to students that they will start skip-counting by one number and at your signal they will shift to a count by a different number. Begin with only two different amounts, say, 25 and 10. Write these numbers on the board. Point to the larger number (25), and have students begin to skip-count. After three or more counts, raise your hand to indicate a pause in the counting. Then lower your hand and point to the smaller number (10). Children continue the skip count from where they left off but now count by 10s. Use any two of these numbers: 100, 50, 25, 10, 5, 1. Always start with the larger. Later, try three numbers, still in descending order.

Remember that working with coins requires not only adding up the values but also first mentally giving each coin a value and then ordering the coins.

When discussing solutions to situations involving counting of coins, be sure to value any approach that works. However, pay special attention to those students who begin with the larger values and those who put nice combinations together utilizing thinking with 10s.

Making Change

Because adding on to find a difference is such a valuable skill—much easier than using the usual subtraction algorithm—it makes sense to give students a lot of experience with adding on to find differences before asking them to make change. As students become more skillful at adding on, they can see the process of making change as an extension of a skill already acquired.

This sequence of suggested activities is not a surefire solution to the difficulties students experience with money. It is designed to build on prerequisite number and place-value skills and concepts without or before using coins.

Angles

Angle measurement can be a challenge for two reasons: The attribute of angle size is often misunderstood, and protractors are introduced and used without understanding how they work.

Comparison Activities

The attribute of angle size might be called the "spread of the angle's rays." Angles are composed of two rays that are infinite in length with a common vertex. The only difference in their size is how widely or narrowly the two rays are spread apart.

To help children conceptualize the attribute of the spread of the rays, two angles can be directly compared by tracing one and placing it over the other. Be sure to have students compare angles with sides of different lengths. A wide angle with short sides may seem smaller than a narrow angle with long sides. This is a common misconception among students (Munier, Devichi, & Merle, 2008). As soon as students can tell the difference between a large angle and a small one, regardless of the length of the sides, you can move on to measuring angles.

Units of Angular Measure

A unit for measuring an angle must be an angle (see Blackline Master 32). Nothing else has the same attribute of spread that we want to measure. (Contrary to what many people think, you do not need to use degrees to measure angles.)

Activity 19.20

A Unit Angle

Give each student an index card or a small piece of tagboard. Have students draw a narrow angle on the tagboard (or use the wedges in Blackline Master 32) using a straightedge and then cut it out. The resulting wedge can then be used as a unit of angular measure by counting the number that will fit in a given angle as shown in Figure 19.14. Pass out a worksheet with assorted angles on it, and have students use their unit to measure them. Because students made their own unit angles, the results will differ and can be discussed in terms of unit size.

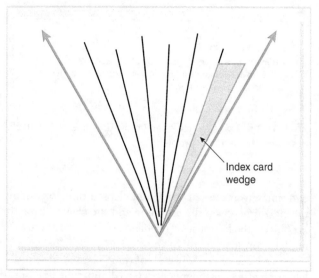

Index card wedge

Figure 19.14 Using a small wedge cut from an index card as a unit angle, this angle measures about $7\frac{1}{2}$ wedges. Accuracy of measurement with these nonstandard angles is less important than the idea of how an angle is used to measure the size of another angle.

Activity 19.20 illustrates that measuring an angle is the same as measuring length or area; unit angles are used to fill or cover the spread of an angle just as unit lengths fill or cover a length. Once this concept is well understood, you can move on to the use of measuring instruments.

Using Protractors and Angle Rulers

The protractor is one of the most poorly understood measuring instruments. Part of the difficulty arises because the units (degrees) are so small. It would be physically impossible for students to cut out and use a single degree to measure an angle accurately. In addition, the numbers that appear on most protractors run clockwise and counterclockwise along the edge, making the scale hard to interpret without a strong conceptual foundation.

Students can make nonstandard waxed-paper protractors (see Figure 19.15), but it is likely that they will move rapidly to standard instruments. To best understand the measures on a protractor or angle ruler, they need an approximate mental image of angle size. Then false readings of the protractor scale will be eliminated. One approach is to use a wheel like the rational number wheel in Figure 17.1 on page 329. Rather than measuring hundredths, the wheel in this case would be used as an "angle fixer." Two paper dessert plates, one white and the other a vivid color, would be cut and merged as in Figure 17.1. You can then rotate the plates to create an "angle fixer" that can match angles of interest and eventually be used to estimate important benchmark angles such as 30, 45, 60, 90, 135, 180, and 270 degrees. If students have a strong grasp of the approximate sizes of angles, that will give them the background they need to move to standard measuring tools such as the protractor and angle ruler (see Figure 19.16).

Introducing Standard Units

As pointed out earlier, there are a number of reasons for teaching measurement using nonstandard units. However, measurement sense demands that children be familiar with standard measurement units and that they be able to make estimates in terms of these units and meaningfully interpret measures depicted with standard units.

Perhaps the biggest error in measurement instruction is the failure to recognize and separate two types of ob-

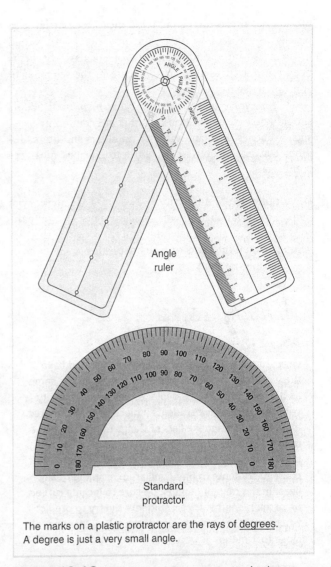

Angle ruler

Standard protractor

The marks on a plastic protractor are the rays of <u>degrees</u>. A degree is just a very small angle.

Figure 19.16 Different tools to measure angles (see Blackline Master 32).

jectives: (1) understanding the meaning and technique of measuring a particular attribute and (2) learning about the standard units commonly used to measure that attribute.

Instructional Goals

Teaching standard units of measure can be organized around three broad goals:

1. *Familiarity with the unit.* Students should have a basic idea of the size of commonly used units and what they measure. It is more important to know approximately how much 1 liter of water is or to be able to estimate a shelf as 5 feet long than to have the ability to measure either of these accurately.

2. *Ability to select an appropriate unit.* Students should know what is a reasonable unit of measure in a given situation. The choice of an appropriate unit is also a matter

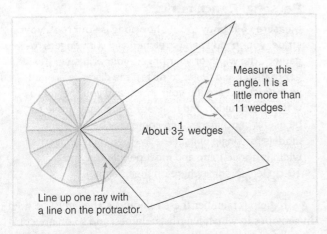

Measure this angle. It is a little more than 11 wedges.

About $3\frac{1}{2}$ wedges

Line up one ray with a line on the protractor.

Figure 19.15 Measuring angles in a polygon using a waxed-paper protractor.

of required precision. (Would you measure your lawn to purchase grass seed with the same precision as you would use in measuring a window to buy a pane of glass?) Students need practice in using common sense in the selection of appropriate standard units.

3. *Knowledge of relationships between units.* Students should know those relationships that are commonly used, such as inches, feet, and yards or milliliters and liters. Tedious conversion exercises do little to enhance measurement sense.

Developing Unit Familiarity. Two types of activities can help develop familiarity with standard units: (1) comparisons that focus on a single unit and (2) activities that develop personal referents or benchmarks for single units or easy multiples of units.

Activity 19.21
About One Unit

Give students a model of a standard unit, and have them search for objects that measure about the same as that one unit. For example, to develop familiarity with the meter, give students a piece of rope 1 meter long. Have them make lists of things that are about 1 meter. Keep separate lists for things that are a little less (or more) or twice as long (or half as long). Encourage students to find familiar items in their daily lives. In the case of lengths, be sure to include curved or circular lengths. Later, students can try to predict whether a given object is more than, less than, or close to 1 meter.

The same activity can be done with other unit lengths. Families can be enlisted to help students find familiar distances that are about 1 mile or about 1 kilometer. Suggest in a letter that they check the distances around the neighborhood, to the school or shopping center, or along other frequently traveled paths. If possible, send home (or use in class) a 1-meter or 1-yard trundle wheel to measure distances.

For capacity units such as cup, quart, and liter, students need a container that holds or has a marking for a single unit. They should then find other containers at home and at school that hold about as much, more, and less. Remember that the shapes of containers can be very deceptive when estimating their capacity.

For the standard weights of gram, kilogram, ounce, and pound, students can compare objects on a two-pan balance with single copies of these units. It may be more effective to work with 10 grams or 5 ounces. Students can be encouraged to bring in familiar objects from home to compare on the classroom scale.

Standard area units are in terms of lengths such as square inches or square feet, so familiarity with lengths is important. Familiarity with a single degree is not as important as some idea of 30, 45, 60, and 90 degrees.

The second approach to unit familiarity is to begin with very familiar items and use their measures as references or benchmarks. A doorway is a bit more than 2 meters high and a doorknob is about 1 meter from the floor. A bag of flour is a good reference for 5 pounds. A paper clip weighs about a gram and is about 1 centimeter wide. A gallon of milk weighs a little less than 4 kilograms.

Activity 19.22
Familiar References

Use the book *Measuring Penny* (Leedy, 2000) to get students interested in the variety of ways familiar items can be measured. In this book, the author bridges between nonstandard (e.g., dog biscuits) and standard units to measure Penny the pet dog. Have your students use the idea of measuring Penny to find something at home (or in class) to measure in as many ways as they can think using standard units. The measures should be rounded to whole numbers (unless children suggest adding a fractional unit to be more precise). Discuss in class the familiar items chosen and their measures so that different ideas and benchmarks are shared.

Of special interest for length are benchmarks found on our bodies. These become quite familiar over time and can be used as approximate rulers in many situations. Even though young children grow quite rapidly, it is useful for them to know the approximate lengths that they carry around with them.

Activity 19.23
Personal Benchmarks

Measure your body. About how long is your foot, your stride, your hand span (stretched and with fingers together), the width of your finger, your arm span (finger to finger and finger to nose), the distance around your wrist and around your waist, and your height to waist, to shoulder, and to head? Some may prove to be useful benchmarks, and some may be excellent models for single units. (The average child's fingernail width is about 1 cm, and most people can find a 10-cm length somewhere on their hands.)

To help remember these references, they must be used in activities in which lengths, volumes, and so on are compared to the benchmarks to estimate measurements.

Choosing Appropriate Units. Should the room be measured in feet or inches? Should the concrete blocks be weighed in grams or kilograms? The answers to questions such as these involve more than simply knowing how big the units are, although that is certainly required. Another consideration involves the need for precision. If you were measuring your wall in order to cut a piece of molding or woodwork to fit, you would need to measure it very precisely. The smallest unit would be an inch or a centimeter, and you would also use small fractional parts. But if you were determining how many 8-foot molding strips to buy, the nearest foot would probably be sufficient.

Activity **19.24**

Guess the Unit

Find examples of measurements of all types in newspapers, on signs, or in other everyday situations. Present the context and measures but without units. The task is to predict what units of measure were used. Have students discuss their choices.

Important Standard Units and Relationships

Both the customary and metric systems include many units that are rarely if ever used in everyday life. Your state or local curriculum is the best guide to help you decide which units your students should learn. NCTM's position statement on the metric system (2006) states: "To equip students to deal with diverse situations in science and other subject areas, and to prepare them for life in a global society, schools should provide students with rich experiences in working with both the metric and the customary systems of measurement while developing their ability to solve problems in either system." The statement goes on to explain that several countries have passed laws stating that international commerce must use metric units, as almost all nations in the world use the metric system. If U.S. students are going to be prepared for the global workplace, they must be knowledgeable and comfortable with commonly used metric units. Results of the 2004 NAEP reveal that only 40 percent of fourth graders were able to identify how many kilograms a bicycle weighed given the choices of 1.5, 15, 150, and 1500 kg. Among eighth graders, only 37 percent knew how many milliliters were in a liter (Perie, Moran, & Lutkus, 2005). Interestingly, although performance on national assessments reveals measurement as a weak area, U.S. students do better on metric units than customary units (Preston & Thompson, 2004).

The relationships between units within either the metric or customary systems are conventions. As such, students must simply be told what the relationships are, and in-

structional experiences must be devised to reinforce them. It can be argued that knowing about how much liquid makes a liter, or being able to pace off 3 meters—unit familiarity—is more important than knowing how many cubic centimeters are in a liter. However, in the intermediate grades, knowing basic relationships becomes more important for testing purposes. Your curriculum should be your guide.

The customary system has very few patterns or rules to guide students in converting units. On the other hand, the metric system was designed systematically around powers of ten. An understanding of the role of the decimal point as indicating the units position is a powerful concept for making metric conversions (see Chapter 17, Figure 17.6). As students begin to appreciate the structure of decimal notation, the metric system can and should be developed with all seven places: three prefixes for smaller units (*deci-*, *centi-*, *milli-*) and three for larger units (*deka-*, *hecto-*, *kilo-*). Avoid mechanical rules such as "To change centimeters to meters, move the decimal point two places to the left." When the students themselves do not create conceptual, meaningful methods for conversions, arbitrary-sounding rules are bound to be misused and forgotten.

Exact conversions between the metric and the customary system should be avoided. As long as we live in a country that uses two systems of measurement, "friendly" conversions are useful. For example, a liter is a "gulp more" than a quart, and a meter is a bit longer than a yard. The same is true of familiar references. One hundred meters is about one football field plus one end zone, or about 110 yards.

 In assessing students' understanding and familiarity with standard units, there is a danger of focusing on the traditional conversion problems. Consider the following two tasks:

1. 4 feet = _____ inches.
2. Estimate the length of this rope in feet and then in inches. How did you decide on your estimate?

Both tasks relate feet and inches. However, the second task requires students to have a familiarity with the units as well. With the estimation task we can observe whether the student uses the first estimate to make the second (understanding and *using* the feet-inches relationship) or rather makes two separate estimates. This task also allows us to see how an estimate is made—information that is unavailable in the first task. ◆

Estimating Measures

Measurement estimation is the process of using mental and visual information to measure or make comparisons without the use of measuring instruments. It is a practical skill used almost every day. Do I have enough sugar to make cookies? Can you throw the ball 15 meters? Is this suitcase over the weight limit? About how long is the fence?

Besides its value outside the classroom, estimation in measurement activities helps students focus on the attribute being measured, adds intrinsic motivation, and helps develop familiarity with standard units. Therefore, measurement estimation both improves measurement understanding and develops a valuable life skill.

Strategies for Estimating Measurements

Just as for computational estimation, specific strategies exist for estimating measures. There are four strategies that can be taught specifically:

1. *Develop and use benchmarks or referents for important units.* Research has shown that students who have both acquired mental benchmarks or reference points for measurements *and* have practiced using them in class activities are much better estimators than students who have not learned to use benchmarks (Joram, 2003). Referents should be things that are easily envisioned by the student. One example is the height of a child, as shown in Figure 19.17. Students should have a good referent for single units and also useful multiples of standard units.

2. *Use "chunking" when appropriate.* Figure 19.17 shows an example. It may be easier to estimate the shorter chunks along the wall than to estimate the whole length. The weight of a stack of books is easier if some estimate is given to an "average" book.

3. *Use subdivisions.* This is a similar strategy to chunking, with the chunks imposed on the object by the estima-

tor. For example, if the wall length to be estimated has no useful chunks, it can be mentally divided in half and then in fourths or even eighths by repeated halving until a more manageable length is arrived at. Length, volume, and area measurements all lend themselves to this technique.

4. *Iterate a unit mentally or physically.* For length, area, and volume, it is sometimes easy to mark off single units visually. You might use your hands or make marks or folds to keep track as you go. If you know, for example, that your stride is about $\frac{3}{4}$ meter, you can walk off a length and then multiply to get an estimate. Hand and finger widths are useful for shorter measures.

Tips for Teaching Estimation

Each of the four strategies just listed should be taught directly and discussed with students. Suggested benchmarks for useful measures can be developed and recorded on a class chart. Include items found at home. But the best approach to improving estimation skills is to have students do a lot of estimating. Keep the following tips in mind:

1. Help students learn strategies by having them use a specified approach. Later activities should permit students to choose whatever techniques they wish.

2. Discuss how different students made their estimates. This will help students understand that there is no single right way to estimate and also remind them of different approaches that are useful.

3. Accept a range of estimates. Think in relative terms about what is a good estimate. Within 10 percent for length is quite good. Even 30 percent off may be reasonable for weights or volumes. Do not promote a "winning" estimate.

Estimate the room length.

Use: windows, bulletin board, and spaces between as "chunks."

Use: mental benchmark—"My height is about 5 feet long. I could get 5 kids lying down in here plus maybe 3 more feet. Say, 28 feet."

Figure 19.17 Estimating measures by using benchmarks and chunking.

4. Encourage students to give a range of measures that they believe includes the actual measure. This not only is a practical approach in real life but also helps focus on the approximate nature of estimation.

5. Make measurement estimation an ongoing activity. A daily measurement to estimate can be posted. Students can turn in their estimates on paper and discuss them in a 5-minute period. Older students can even be given the task of determining the measurements to estimate, with a student or team of students assigned this task each week.

Measurement Estimation Activities

Estimation activities need not be elaborate. Any measurement activity can have an "estimate first" component. For more emphasis on the process of estimation itself, simply think of measures that can be estimated, and have students estimate. Here are two suggestions.

Activity 19.25

Estimation Quickie

Select a single object such as a box, a pumpkin, a jar, or even the principal. Each day, select a different attribute or dimension to estimate. For a pumpkin, for example, students can estimate its height, circumference, weight, volume, and surface area.

Activity 19.26

Estimation Scavenger Hunt

Conduct estimation scavenger hunts. Give teams a list of measurements, and have them find things that are close to having those measurements. Do not permit the use of measuring instruments. A list might include the following items:

   A length of 3.5 m

   Something that weighs more than 1 kg but less than 2 kg

   A container that holds about 200 ml

   An angle of 45 degrees or 135 degrees

Let students suggest how to judge results in terms of accuracy.

Estimation tasks are a good way to assess students' understanding of both measurement and standard units. Use real objects and distances within the room as well as outside. Time and long distances should be estimated with comparisons to events and distances that are meaningful to the students.

Have students explain how they arrived at their estimates to get a more complete picture of their measurement knowledge. Asking only for a numeric estimate can mask a lack of understanding and will not give you the information you need to provide appropriate remediation. ◆

Developing Formulas for Area and Volume

Do not make the mistake of bypassing formula development with your students even if your state and local testing programs allow students access to formulas during the test. When students develop formulas, they gain conceptual understanding of the ideas and relationships involved and they engage in one of the real processes of doing mathematics. There is less likelihood that students will confuse area and perimeter or that they will select the incorrect formula on the test. General relationships are developed. For example, students can see how all area formulas are related to one idea: length of the base times the height. And students who understand where formulas come from do not see them as mysterious, tend to remember them, and reinforce the idea that mathematics makes sense. Rote use of formulas from a book offers none of these advantages.

Students' Misconceptions

The results of National Assessment of Educational Progress (NAEP) testing indicate clearly that students do not have a very good understanding of formulas. For example, in the 2007 NAEP, only 39 percent of fourth-grade students were able to give the area of a carpet 15 feet long and 12 feet wide. A common error is to confuse formulas for area and perimeter. Such results are largely due to an overemphasis on formulas with little or no conceptual background.

The tasks in Figure 19.18 cannot be solved with simple formulas; they require an understanding of concepts and

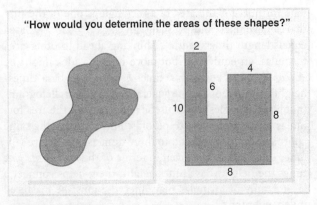

Figure 19.18 Understanding the attribute of area.

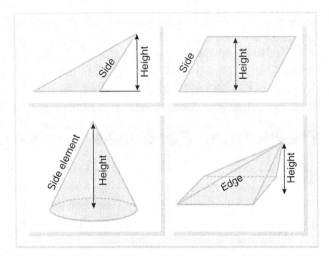

Figure 19.19 Heights of figures are not always measured along an edge or a surface.

how formulas work. "Length times width" is not a definition of area.

Another common error when students use formulas comes from failure to conceptualize the meaning of height and base in both two- and three-dimensional geometric figures. The shapes in Figure 19.19 each have a slanted side and a height given. Students tend to confuse these two. Any side or flat surface of a figure can be called a *base* of the figure. For each base that a figure has, there is a corresponding height. If the figure were to slide into a room on a selected base, the *height* would be the height of the shortest door it could pass through without tipping—that is, the perpendicular distance to the base. Students have a lot of early experiences with the length-times-width formula for rectangles, in which the height is exactly the same as the length of a side. Perhaps this is the source of the confusion. Before formulas involving heights are discussed, students should be able to identify where a height could be measured for any base that a figure has.

Areas of Rectangles, Parallelograms, Triangles, and Trapezoids

The formula for the area of a rectangle is one of the first that is developed and is usually given as $A = L \times W$, "area equals length times width." Thinking ahead to other area formulas, an equivalent but more unifying idea might be $A = b \times h$, "area equals *base* times *height*." The base-times-height formulation can be generalized to all parallelograms (not just rectangles) and is useful in developing the area formulas for triangles and trapezoids. Furthermore, the same approach can be extended to three dimensions, where volumes of cylinders are given in terms of the *area of the base* times the height. Base times height, then, helps connect a large family of formulas that otherwise must be mastered independently.

Rectangles. Research suggests that it is a significant leap for students to move from counting squares inside of a rectangle to a conceptual development of a formula. Battista (2003) found that students often try to fill in empty rectangles with drawings of squares and then count the result one square at a time.

An important concept to review is the meaning of multiplication as seen in arrays. Show students rows and columns of objects or of squares and discuss why multiplication tells the total amount. We count either a single row or column and then find out how many columns or rows there are in all. This is the same concept that they will need to apply to the area of a rectangle. When we multiply a length times a width, we are not multiplying "squares times squares." Rather, the *length* of one side indicates how many squares will fit on that side. If this set of squares is taken as a unit, then the *length* of the other side (not a number of squares) will tell how many of these *rows of squares* can fit in the rectangle.

A good activity to begin your exploration of area formulas is to revisit Activity 19.11, "Rectangle Comparison—Square Units" (p. 379). Students who are drawing in all of the squares and counting them have not thought about a row of squares as a single row that can be replicated. Related tasks, based on the work of Battista (2003), are shown in Figure 19.20.

When your students have formulated an approach to area based on the idea of a row of squares (determined by the length of a side) multiplied by the number of these rows

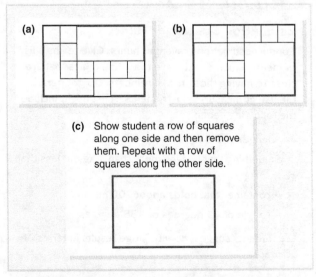

Figure 19.20 Three different activities in sequential order for determining area. Students in each case are to tell how many squares will fill the rectangles.

Source: Based on suggestions by Battista, M. T. (2003). "Understanding Students; Thinking about Area and Volume Measurement." In D. H. Clements (Ed.), *Learning and Teaching Measurement* (pp. 122–142). Reston, VA: NCTM.

that will fit the rectangle (determined by the length of the other side), it is time to consolidate these ideas. Explain to students that you like the idea of measuring one side to tell how many squares will fit in a row along that side. You would like them to call or think of this side as the *base* of the rectangle even though some people call it the length or the width. Then the other side you can call the *height*. But which side is the base? Be sure that students conclude that either side could be the base. If you use the formula $A = b \times h$, then the same area will result using either side as the base.

From Rectangles to Other Parallelograms.   Once students understand the base-times-height formula for rectangles, the next challenge is to determine the areas of parallelograms. Do not provide a formula or other explanation. Rather, try the following activity, which again asks students to devise their own formula.

Activity 19.27

Area of a Parallelogram

Give students two or three parallelograms either drawn on grid paper or, for a slightly harder challenge, drawn on plain paper with all dimensions—the lengths of all four sides and the height. Their task is to use what they have learned about the area of rectangles to determine the areas of these parallelograms. Students should find a method that will work for any parallelogram, even if not drawn on a grid.

If students are stuck, ask them to examine ways that the parallelogram is like a rectangle or how it can be changed into a rectangle. As shown in Figure 19.21, a parallelogram can always be transformed into a rectangle with the same

base, the same height, and the same area. Thus, the formula for the area of a parallelogram is exactly the same as for a rectangle: base times height.

From Parallelograms to Triangles.   With that background, the area of a triangle is relatively simple. Again, use a problem-based approach as in the next activity.

Activity 19.28

Area of a Triangle

Provide students with at least two triangles drawn on grid paper. Avoid right triangles because they are an easier special case. The challenge for students is to use what they have learned about the area of parallelograms to find the area of each of the triangles and to develop a method that will work for any triangle. They should be sure that their method works for all the triangles given to them as well as at least one more that they draw.

There are several hints that you might offer if students are stuck. *Can you find a parallelogram that is related to your triangle?* If this is not sufficient, suggest that they fold a piece of paper in half, draw a triangle on the folded paper, and cut it out, making two identical copies. They should use the copies to find out how a triangle is related to a parallelogram.

As shown in Figure 19.22 below, two congruent triangles can always be arranged to form a parallelogram with the same base and the same height as the triangle. The area of the triangle will, therefore, be one-half as much as that of the parallelogram. Have students further explore all three possible parallelograms, one for each triangle side that serves as a base. Will the computed areas always be the same?

From Parallelograms to Trapezoids.   After developing formulas for parallelograms and triangles, your students may be interested in tackling trapezoids. (See Figure 3.1, p. 36, for an example of a completely open challenge.) There are at least ten different methods of arriving at a

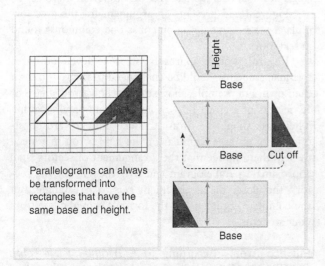

Parallelograms can always be transformed into rectangles that have the same base and height.

Figure 19.21 Transforming a parallelogram into a rectangle.

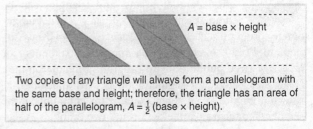

$A = \text{base} \times \text{height}$

Two copies of any triangle will always form a parallelogram with the same base and height; therefore, the triangle has an area of half of the parallelogram, $A = \frac{1}{2}(\text{base} \times \text{height})$.

Figure 19.22 Two congruent triangles always make a parallelogram.

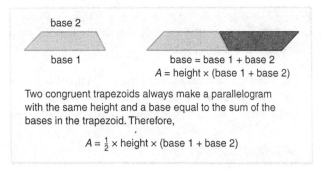

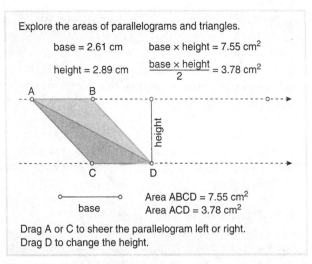

Explore the areas of parallelograms and triangles.

base = 2.61 cm   base × height = 7.55 cm^2

height = 2.89 cm $\frac{\text{base} \times \text{height}}{2} = 3.78$ cm^2

Area ABCD = 7.55 cm^2
Area ACD = 3.78 cm^2

Drag A or C to sheer the parallelogram left or right.
Drag D to change the height.

Figure 19.24 Dynamic geometry software shows that figures with the same base and height maintain the same area.

Figure 19.23 Two congruent trapezoids always form a parallelogram.

formula for trapezoids, each related to the area of parallelograms or triangles. One method uses the same general approach that was used for triangles. Suggest that students try working with two trapezoids that are identical, just as they did with triangles. Figure 19.23 shows how this method results in the formula. Not only are all of these formulas connected, but similar methods were used to develop them as well.

Here are a few hints, each leading to a different approach to finding the area of a trapezoid.

- Make a parallelogram inside the given trapezoid using three of the sides.
- Make a parallelogram using three sides that surround the trapezoid.
- Draw a diagonal forming two triangles.
- Draw a line through the midpoints of the nonparallel sides. The length of that line is the average of the lengths of the two parallel sides.
- Draw a rectangle inside the trapezoid leaving two triangles and then put those two triangles together.

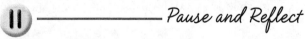

—— *Pause and Reflect*

Do you think that students should learn special formulas for the area of a square? Why or why not? Do you think students need formulas for the perimeters of squares and rectangles?

The relationship among the areas of rectangles, parallelograms, and triangles can be dramatically illustrated using a dynamic geometry program such as *The Geometer's Sketchpad* (Key Curriculum Press), *Cabri Geometry* (Texas Instruments), or *Wingeom* (free public domain program available online). Draw two congruent segments on two parallel lines, as shown in Figure 19.24. Then connect the endpoints of the segments to form a parallelogram and two triangles. A segment between the parallel lines and perpendicular to each indicates the height. Either of the two line segments can be dragged left or right to "sheer" the parallelogram and triangle but without changing the base or height. All area measures remain fixed! ◆

Circumference and Area of Circles

The relationship between the *circumference* of a circle (the distance around or the perimeter) and the length of the *diameter* (a line through the center joining two points on the circle) is one of the most interesting that children can discover. The circumference of every circle is about 3.14 times as long as the diameter. The exact ratio is an irrational number close to 3.14 and is represented by the Greek letter π. So π = C/D, the circumference divided by the diameter. In a slightly different form, C = πD. Half the diameter is the radius (r), so the same equation can be written C = 2πr. (Activity 20.10 in Chapter 20 will discuss in detail the concept of π and how students can discover this important ratio.)

Figure 19.25 presents an argument for the area formula $A = \pi r^2$. This development is one commonly found in textbooks.

Regardless of the approach you use to develop the area formula, students should be challenged to figure it out on their own. For example, show students how to arrange 8 or 12 sectors of a circle into an approximate parallelogram. Their task should be to use this as a hint toward development of an area formula for the circle. You may need to help them notice that the arrangement of sectors is an approximate parallelogram and that the smaller the sectors, the closer the arrangement gets to a rectangle. But the complete argument for the formula should come from your students.

Surface Area. According to *Curriculum Focal Points* (NCTM, 2006), in the fifth grade students will explore

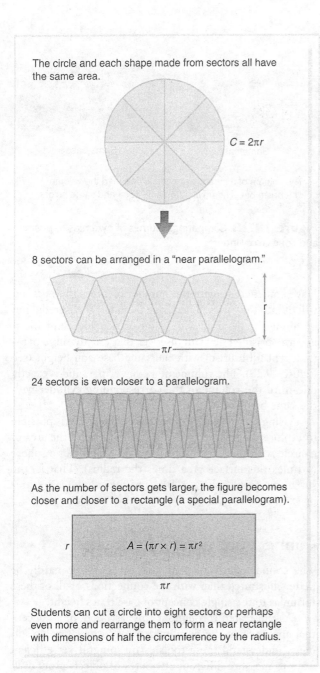

The circle and each shape made from sectors all have the same area.

$C = 2\pi r$

8 sectors can be arranged in a "near parallelogram."

r

πr

24 sectors is even closer to a parallelogram.

As the number of sectors gets larger, the figure becomes closer and closer to a rectangle (a special parallelogram).

r

$A = (\pi r \times r) = \pi r^2$

πr

Students can cut a circle into eight sectors or perhaps even more and rearrange them to form a near rectangle with dimensions of half the circumference by the radius.

Figure 19.25 Development of the circle area formula.

surface area of prisms and by seventh grade cylinders will be investigated. Build on the knowledge students have of the areas of two-dimensional figures. If they think of each face of a solid as its two-dimensional counterpart, they can find the area of each face and sum the amount. One of the best approaches to teaching the surface area of three-dimensional figures is to create several cardstock rectangular prisms, cubes, or cylinders that have sides held together by small pieces of Velcro. In this way students can think about the components or the "net" of the figure as they break the solid into faces and calculate the surface area.

Volumes of Common Solid Shapes

The relationships between the formulas for volume are completely analogous to those for area. As you read, notice the similarities between rectangles and prisms, between parallelograms and "sheered" (oblique) prisms, and between triangles and pyramids. Not only are the formulas related, but the process for developing the formulas is similar.

Volumes of Cylinders. A *cylinder* is a solid with two congruent parallel bases and sides with parallel elements that join corresponding points on the bases. There are several special classes of cylinders, including *prisms* (with polygons for bases), *right prisms*, *rectangular prisms*, and *cubes* (see Chapter 20). Interestingly, all of these solids have the same volume formula, and that one formula is analogous to the area formula for parallelograms.

Activity 19.29

Volume of a Box

Provide students with some cardboard shoe boxes or similar cardboard boxes, a few cubes of the same size, and a ruler. As was done with rectangles, the task is to determine how many cubes will fit inside the box. Most likely your boxes will not have whole-number dimensions, so tell students to ignore any fractional parts of cubes. Although they may have seen or used a volume formula before, for this task they may not rely on a formula. Rather, they must come up with a method using the cubes that they can explain or justify. If a hint is required, suggest that they begin by finding out how many cubes will fit on the bottom of the box.

The development of the volume formula from this box exploration is parallel to the development of the formula for the area of a rectangle, as shown in Figure 19.26. The *area* of the base (instead of *length* of the base for rectangles)

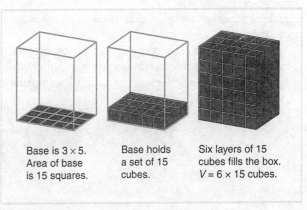

Base is 3 × 5. Area of base is 15 squares.

Base holds a set of 15 cubes.

Six layers of 15 cubes fills the box. $V = 6 \times 15$ cubes.

Figure 19.26 Volume of a right prism: *Area* of the base × height.

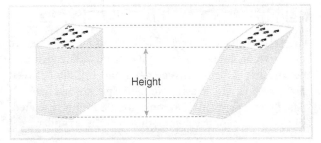

Figure 19.27 Two prisms with the same base and height have the same volume.

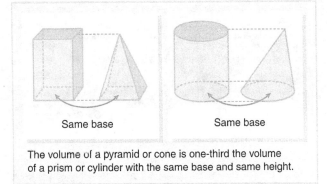

The volume of a pyramid or cone is one-third the volume of a prism or cylinder with the same base and same height.

Figure 19.28 Comparing volumes of pyramids to prisms and cones to cylinders.

determines how many *cubes* can be placed on the base forming a single unit—a layer of cubes. The *height* of the box then determines how many of these *layers* will fit in the box just as the height of the rectangle determined how many *rows* of squares would fill the rectangle.

Recall that a parallelogram can be thought of as a "sheered" rectangle, as was illustrated with the dynamic geometry software (see Figure 19.24). Show students a stack of three or four decks of playing cards (or a stack of books or paper). When stacked straight, they form a rectangular solid. The volume, as just discussed, is $V = A \times h$, with A equal to the area of one playing card. Now if the stack is sheered or slanted to one side as shown in Figure 19.27, what will the volume of this new figure be? Students should be able to argue that this figure has the same volume (and same volume formula) as the original stack.

What if the cards in this activity were some other shape? If they were circular, the volume would still be the area of the base times the height; if they were triangular, still the same. The conclusion is that the volume of *any* cylinder is equal to the *area of the base* times the *height*.

Volumes of Cones and Pyramids. Recall that when parallelograms and triangles have the same base and height, the areas are in a 2-to-1 relationship. Interestingly, the relationship between the volumes of cylinders and cones with the same base and height is 3 to 1. That is, *area* is to *two*-dimensional figures what *volume* is to *three*-dimensional figures. Furthermore, triangles are to parallelograms as cones are to cylinders.

To investigate this relationship use plastic models of these related shapes such as translucent Power Solids (available through Learning Resources or other companies).

Have students estimate the number of times the pyramid will fit into the prism. Then have them test their prediction by filling the pyramid with water or rice and emptying it into the prism. They will discover that exactly three pyramids will fill a prism with the same base and height (see Figure 19.28). The volume of a cone or pyramid is exactly one-third the volume of the corresponding cylinder with the same base and height.

Using the same idea of base times height, it is possible to explore the surface area of a sphere (4 times the area of a circle with the same radius) and the volume of a sphere ($\frac{1}{3}$ times the surface area times the radius). That is, the surface area of a sphere is $4\pi r^2$ and the volume is $\frac{1}{3}(4\pi r^2)r$ or $\frac{4}{3}\pi r^3$.

Connections among Formulas

The connectedness of mathematical ideas can hardly be better illustrated than with the connections of all of these formulas to the single concept of base times height.

As illustrated throughout this last section, a conceptual approach to the development of formulas helps students understand these tools as meaningful yet efficient ways to measure different attributes of objects around us. After having developed formulas in meaningful ways, students are no longer required to memorize them as isolated pieces of mathematical facts but can instead derive formulas from what they already know. Mathematics does make sense!

Reflections on Chapter 19

Writing to Learn

1. Explain what it means to measure something. Does your explanation work equally well for length, area, weight, volume, and time?

2. A general instructional plan for measurement has three steps. Explain how the type of activity to use at each step accomplishes the instructional goal.

3. Four reasons were offered for using nonstandard units instead of standard units in instructional activities. Which of these seem most important to you, and why?

4. Develop in a connected way the area formulas for rectangles, parallelograms, triangles, and trapezoids. Draw pictures and provide explanations.

5. Explain how the area of a circle can be determined using the basic formula for the area of a parallelogram. (If you have a set of fraction circular pieces, these can be used as sectors of a circle.)

For Discussion and Exploration

1. Frequently, a textbook chapter on measurement will cover length, area, volume, and capacity with both metric and customary units. Get a teacher's edition of a textbook for any grade level, and look at the chapters on measurement. How well does the book cover metric measurement ideas? How would you modify or expand on the lessons found there?

Resources for Chapter 19

Literature Connections

How Big Is a Foot? *Myller, 1990*

The story in this concept book is very attractive to young children. The king measures his queen using his feet and orders a bed made that is 6 feet long and 3 feet wide. The chief carpenter's apprentice, who is very small, makes the bed according to his own feet, demonstrating the need for standard units.

Every Minute on Earth: Fun Facts That Happen Every 60 Seconds *Murrie & Murrie, 2007*

This is an amazing book that is not just about the concept of time. The authors provide fun facts about what can happen in 60 seconds: a snow avalanche travels 4.2 miles (6.8 kilometers); the adult heart pumps 3.3 liters (3.5 quarts) of blood; movie film travels 90 feet (27.4 meters) through a projector; a garden snail moves 0.31 inches (7.8 millimeters); people in the United States throw away 18,315 pounds (8325 kilograms) of food; and consumers spend $954.00 on chewing gum. Students can use the facts provided or identify others as they think and discuss these relationships.

Inchworm and a Half *Pinczes, 2001*

In this wonderfully illustrated book, an inchworm happily goes about measuring various garden vegetables. One day a measurement does not result in a whole number, and the worm gets very upset. Fortunately, a smaller worm drops onto the vegetable and measures a half unit. Eventually, other fraction-measuring worms appear. (Be wary of the $\frac{1}{3}$ worm as $\frac{1}{3}$ is not a common measurement unit.) The story provides a great connection between fractions and measurement concepts, especially for the introduction of fractional units in measurement. Moyer and Mailley (2004) describe a nice series of activities inspired by the book.

Recommended Readings

Articles

Austin, R., Thompson, D., & Beckmann, C. (2005). Exploring measurement concepts through literature: Natural links across disciplines. *Mathematics Teaching in the Middle School, 10*(5), 218–224.

This article includes a rich collection of almost 30 children's books that emphasize overall systems of measurement, length, weight, capacity, speed, area, perimeter, and volume. Three books are described in detail as the authors share how to link measurement to science, history, geography, and economics.

National Council of Teachers of Mathematics. (2004). Measurement [Focus Issue]. *Mathematics Teaching in the Middle School, 9.*

This focus issue of NCTM's middle school journal is full of great information for teachers at that level. Of particular note are several articles that involve scale drawings or other aspects of proportional reasoning, which is a great way to integrate measurement into the curriculum.

Pumala, V. A., & Klabunde, D. A. (2005). Learning measurement through practice. *Mathematics Teaching in the Middle School, 10*(9), 452–460.

A mathematics teacher and a science teacher collaborated on a series of six activities to help their students learn about measurement.

Included in the article are descriptions of the activities and detailed rubrics, along with samples of student work.

Whitin, D. (2008). Learning our way to one million. *Teaching Children Mathematics, 14*(8), 448–453.

Through an exploration of the topic of one million, Whitin suggests ways for children in grades 2–5 to explore several mathematics topics, including length, area, and money. All investigations emphasize the need for active problem solving in real-world contexts that reflect students' interests.

Books

Clements, D. H. (Ed.). (2003). *Learning and teaching measurement: 2003 Yearbook.* Reston, VA: NCTM.

This book brings both a practical and a research perspective on measurement that expands and provides additional details concerning the ideas in this chapter. Discussions include beginning measurement in the pre-K–2 classroom, assessment strategies, and the importance of benchmarks in estimation.

Online Resources

Area Tool
http://illuminations.nctm.org/ActivityDetail.aspx?ID=108

There are three separate applets that explore how changes in the base and height of these shapes affect the area.

Clock Wise
www.shodor.org/interactivate/activities/clockwise

A clock face is shown and the user enters the digital time. Four difficulty levels.

Cubes
http://illuminations.nctm.org/ActivityDetail.aspx?ID=6

An excellent interactive applet that illustrates the volume of a rectangular prism (box). Units of single cubes, rows of cubes, or layers of cubes can be used to fill a prism.

Geoboard
http://nlvm.usu.edu/en/nav/frames_asid_279_g_4_t_3 .html

This electronic geoboard measures the area and perimeter of any shape made. What is nice is that the measures are not shown until the user clicks the Measure button. Students can be challenged to make shapes with specified areas and/or perimeters.

How High
http://nlvm.usu.edu/en/nav/frames_asid_275_g_3_t_4 .html

Two cylinders are shown along with the area of the base shown as a grid of squares. One cylinder is filled to a specified height. The task is to determine the height of this same liquid when it is poured into the second container.

Image Tool
www.shodor.org/interactivate/activities/imagetool/index .html

The user can measure angles, distances, and areas in several different images (choices include maps, aerial photos, and others). A scale feature allows the user to set the scale used for measuring distances and areas. Unique!

Money
http://nlvm.usu.edu/en/nav/frames_asid_325_g_2_t_4 .html

This site gives students an opportunity to make a dollar, find an exact amount, or fill in how much money is shown.

Perimeter Explorer
www.shodor.org/interactivate/activities/Perimeter Explorer

The user sets a fixed number of square units and the applet randomly creates shapes on a grid with this area. The object is to determine the perimeter. There is also an *Area Explorer* (fixes the perimeter) and a *Shape Explorer*, which asks the user for both the area and perimeter of the randomly produced shapes.

What Time Will It Be?
http://nlvm.usu.edu/en/nav/frames_asid_318_g_2_t_4 .html

Elapsed-time problems are presented in word format. Two clocks are shown, one with the start time and the other to be set. Some problems are digital, others analog.

Field Experience Guide Connections

Because measurement is so much a part of real-life experiences, lessons in measurement should be too. Use FEG 2.3 and 2.4 to analyze tasks or lessons to see whether they provide students with authentic opportunities to measure and understand measurement concepts. FEG Expanded Lessons 9.15 ("Crooked Paths") and 9.16 ("Fixed Areas") are engaging lessons about length and area and perimeter, respectively. The Fixed Areas Expanded Lesson can also be found on pages 74–75 in this book. FEG Activity 10.11 ("Cover All") uses manipulatives to explore area, and Balanced Assessment Task 11.3 ("Bolts and Nuts!") is a task to analyze student thinking about measuring length and analyzing patterns.

Chapter 20

Geometric Thinking and Geometric Concepts

Geometry is a strand of the curriculum in nearly every state and district. This is due in large part to the influence of the NCTM standards movement beginning in 1989 and the growing use of geometry in everything from global positioning systems to computer animation. Increased attention to a theoretical perspective that has helped us understand how students reason about spatial concepts is another significant influence.

Big Ideas

1. What makes shapes alike and different can be determined by geometric properties. For example, shapes have sides that are parallel, perpendicular, or neither; they have line symmetry, rotational symmetry, or neither; they are similar, congruent, or neither.

2. Shapes can be moved in a plane or in space. These changes can be described in terms of translations (slides), reflections (flips), and rotations (turns).

3. Shapes can be described in terms of their location in a plane or in space. Coordinate systems can be used to describe these locations precisely. In turn, the coordinate view of shape offers ways to understand certain properties of shapes, changes in position (transformations), and how they appear or change size (visualization).

4. Shapes can be seen from various perspectives. The ability to perceive shapes from different viewpoints helps us understand relationships between two- and three-dimensional figures and mentally change the position and size of shapes.

Mathematics Content Connections

A rich understanding of geometry has clear and important implications for other areas of the curriculum. Take advantage of these connections whenever possible.

- **Algebra** (Chapter 14): Coordinate graphing provides an analytic view of the concept of slope and, in turn, of perpendicular and parallel relationships. Transformations of shapes (slides, flips, and turns) can be described in terms of coordinates, allowing for the digital manipulation of shapes.

- **Proportional Reasoning** (Chapter 18): Similar geometric objects have proportional dimensions and provide visual representations of proportionality.

- **Measurement** (Chapter 19): Measurement is aligned in the development of area and volume formulas and in an understanding of area/perimeter and surface area/volume relationships. Coordinate geometry provides new ways to determine lengths, areas, and volumes. The Pythagorean relationship is at once an algebraic, geometric, and metric relationship.

- **Integers** (Chapter 23): Both positive and negative numbers are used in the description of position in the plane and in space.

Geometry Goals for Students

It is useful to think about your geometry objectives in terms of two related frameworks: (1) spatial sense and geometric reasoning, and (2) the specific geometric content found in your state or district objectives. The first framework has to do with the way students think and reason about shape and space. There is a well-researched theoretical basis for organizing the development of geometric thought that guides this framework. The second framework is content in the more traditional sense—knowing about symmetry, triangles, parallel lines, and so forth. The NCTM *Principles and Standards for School Mathematics* and *Curriculum Focal Points* help describe content goals across the grades. We need to understand both aspects of geometry—reasoning and content—so that we can best help students grow.

Spatial Sense and Geometric Reasoning

Spatial sense can be defined as an intuition about shapes and the relationships among shapes. Spatial sense includes the ability to mentally visualize objects and spatial relationships—to turn things around in your mind. It includes a comfort with geometric descriptions of objects and position. People with well-developed spatial sense appreciate geometric form in art, nature, and architecture. They are able to use geometric ideas to describe and analyze their world.

Some people say they aren't very good with shape or that they have poor spatial sense. The typical belief is that you either are or are not born with spatial sense. This simply is not true! We now know that rich experiences with shape and spatial relationships, when provided consistently over time, can and do develop spatial sense. Between 1990 and 2000, NAEP data indicated a steady, continuing improvement in students' geometric reasoning at grade 8 (Sowder & Wearne, 2006). Students did not just get smarter. Instead, there has been an increasing emphasis on geometry at all grades. Still, much more needs to be done if U.S. children are to rise to the same level as their European and Asian counterparts.

 ──────── *Pause and Reflect*

Reflect for a moment about your own beliefs concerning an individual's abilities in the area of spatial sense. What do you think causes some people to have better spatial sense than others?

───────────────────────────────

NCTM Standards The *Standards* supports the notion that all students can grow in their geometric skills and understandings. "The notion of building understanding in geometry across the grades, from informal to more formal thinking, is consistent with the thinking of theorists and researchers" (p. 41). ◆

Geometric Content

For too long, the geometry curriculum in the United States has emphasized the learning of terminology. At the same time, however, the growing focus on geometry has spawned a huge assortment of wonderful tasks for students. As with each of the NCTM content standards, the geometry standard has a number of goals that apply to all grade levels. The four content goals for geometry can be summarized in the following four categories:

- *Shapes and Properties* includes a study of the properties of shapes in both two and three dimensions, as well as a study of the relationships built on properties.

- *Transformation* includes a study of translations, reflections, rotations (slides, flips, and turns), the study of symmetries, and the concept of similarity.
- *Location* refers primarily to coordinate geometry or other ways of specifying how objects are located in the plane or in space.
- *Visualization* includes the recognition of shapes in the environment, developing relationships between two- and three-dimensional objects, and the ability to draw and recognize objects from different perspectives.

Because of these content goals, a content framework finally exists that bridges grades so that both teachers and curriculum planners can examine growth from year to year. To get a more detailed look at these areas of the curriculum, turn to Appendix A in this book and examine the NCTM goals and expectations for each of these areas across the grades. To assist you, the activities in this chapter are grouped according to these four categories.

The Development of Geometric Thinking

Although not all people think about geometric ideas in the same manner, we are all capable of growing and developing in our ability to think and reason in geometric contexts. The research of two Dutch educators, Pierre van Hiele and Dina van Hiele-Geldof (husband and wife), has provided insight into the differences in geometric thinking and how the differences come to be.

The van Hieles' work began in 1959 and immediately attracted a lot of attention in the former Soviet Union but for nearly two decades got little notice in the United States (Hoffer & Hoffer, 1992). But today, the van Hiele theory has become the greatest influence in the American geometry curriculum.

The van Hiele Levels of Geometric Thought

The most prominent feature of the model is a five-level hierarchy of ways of understanding spatial ideas. Each of the five levels describes the thinking processes used in geometric contexts (see Figure 20.1). The levels describe how we think and what types of geometric ideas we think about, rather than how much knowledge we have. A significant difference from one level to the next is the objects of thought—what we are able to think about geometrically.

Level 0: Visualization

The objects of thought at level 0 are shapes and what they "look like."

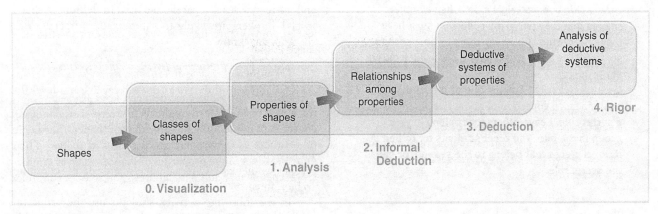

Figure 20.1 The van Hiele theory of geometric thought.

Students at level 0 recognize and name figures based on the global visual characteristics of the figure. For example, a square is defined by a level 0 student as a square "because it looks like a square." Because appearance is dominant at this level, appearances can overpower properties of a shape. For example, a square that has been rotated so that all sides are at a 45-degree angle to the vertical may now be a diamond and no longer a square. Students at this level will sort and classify shapes based on their appearances—"I put these together because they are all pointy" (or "fat," or "look like a house," and so on). With a focus on the appearances of shapes, students are able to see how shapes are alike and different. As a result, students at this level can create and begin to understand classifications of shapes.

The products of thought at level 0 are classes or groupings of shapes that seem to be "alike."

The emphasis at level 0 is on the shapes that students can observe, feel, build, take apart, or work with in some manner. The general goal is to explore how shapes are alike and different and to use these ideas to create classes of shapes (both physically and mentally). Some of these classes of shapes have names—rectangles, triangles, prisms, cylinders, and so on. Properties of shapes, such as parallel sides, symmetry, right angles, and so on, are included at this level but only in an informal, observational manner.

Although the van Hiele theory applies to students of all ages learning any geometric content, it may be easier to apply the theory to the shapes-and-property category. The following is a good representation of an activity appropriate for level 0.

Activity 20.1

Shape Sorts

Have students work in groups of four with a set of 2-D shapes similar to those in Figure 20.2, doing the following related activities in order:

- Each child selects a shape. In turn, the students tell one or two things they find interesting about their shape. There are no right or wrong responses.
- Children each randomly select two shapes and try to find something that is alike about their two shapes and something that is different.
- The group selects one shape at random and places it in the center of the workspace. Their task is to find all other shapes that are like the target shape according to the same rule. For example, if they say "This shape is like the target shape because it has a

Figure 20.2 An assortment of shapes for sorting. See Blackline Masters 41–47 for a larger collection of shapes.

curved side and a straight side," then all other shapes that they put in the collection must have these properties. Challenge them to do a second sort with the same target shape but using a different property.

- Do a "secret sort." You (or one of the students) create a small collection of about five shapes that fit a secret rule. Leave others that belong in your group in the pile. The other students try to find additional pieces that belong to the set and/or guess the secret rule.

Depending on the grade level, these activities will elicit a wide variety of ideas as students examine the shapes. For the most part these will be ideas such as "curvy" or "looks like a rocket" rather than typical geometric concepts. But students may begin to notice more sophisticated properties and the teacher can take the opportunity to attach appropriate names to them as the students describe them. For example, students may notice that some shapes have corners "like a square" (right angles) or that "these shapes are the same on both sides" (line symmetry).

What clearly makes this a level-0 activity, however, is not the presence or the absence of traditional geometric properties or terms. Rather, students are operating on the shapes that they see in front of them. Furthermore, for level-0 students, the shapes may even "change" or have different properties as they are rearranged or rotated. The objective of the activity is for students to begin to see that there are likenesses and differences in shapes. By forming groups of shapes, they may begin to imagine shapes belonging to these classes that are not there.

Level 1: Analysis

The objects of thought at level 1 are classes of shapes rather than individual shapes.

Students at the analysis level are able to consider all shapes within a class rather than a single shape on their desk. Instead of talking about *this* rectangle, it is possible to talk about *all* rectangles. By focusing on a class of shapes, students are able to think about what makes a rectangle a rectangle (four sides, opposite sides parallel, opposite sides same length, four right angles, congruent diagonals, etc.). The irrelevant features (e.g., size or orientation) fade into the background and students begin to appreciate that a collection of shapes goes together because of properties. If a shape belongs to a particular class such as cubes, it has the corresponding properties of that class. "All cubes have six congruent faces, and each of those faces is a square." These properties were only implicit at level 0. Students operating at level 1 may be able to list all the properties of squares, rectangles, and parallelograms but may not see that these are subclasses of one another, that all squares are rectangles

and all rectangles are parallelograms. In defining a shape, level-1 thinkers are likely to list as many properties of a shape as they know.

The products of thought at level 1 are the properties of shapes.

A significant difference between level 1 and level 0 is the object of students' thought. While level-1 students will continue to use models and drawings of shapes, they begin to see these as representatives of classes of shapes. Their understanding of the properties of shapes—such as symmetry, perpendicular and parallel lines, and so on—continues to be refined.

In the following activity, students use the properties of shapes they learned in earlier activities, possibly while operating at level 0. These include ideas such as symmetry, angle classification (right, obtuse, acute), parallel and perpendicular, and the concept of congruent line segments and angles.

Activity 20.2

Property Lists for Quadrilaterals

Prepare worksheets for parallelograms, rhombi, rectangles, and squares. (See Blackline Masters 54–57 and Figure 20.3.) Assign students working in groups of three or four to one type of quadrilateral. Their task is to list as many properties as they can that are applicable to all of the shapes on their sheet. They will need an index card to check right angles, to compare

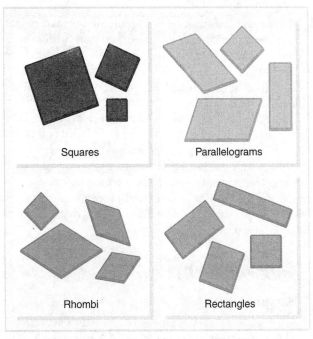

Figure 20.3 Shapes for the "Property Lists for Quadrilaterals" activity (see Blackline Masters 54–57).

side lengths, and to draw straight lines. Mirrors (to check line symmetry) and tracing paper (for angle congruence and rotational symmetry) are also useful tools. Encourage students to use the words "at least" when describing how many of something: for example, "rectangles have at least two lines of symmetry," because squares—included in the rectangles—have four.

Have students prepare their property lists under these headings: Sides, Angles, Diagonals, and Symmetries. Groups then share their lists with the class and eventually a class list for each category of shape will be developed.

Both this activity and the earlier classification activity involve an examination of shapes focusing on geometric properties. What distinguishes this activity from the level-0 classification activity is the object of students' thinking. Students must assess whether the properties apply to all shapes in the category. If they are working on the squares, for example, their observations must apply to a square mile as well as a square centimeter.

Level 2: Informal Deduction

The objects of thought at level 2 are the properties of shapes.

As students begin to be able to think about properties of geometric objects without the constraints of a particular object, they are able to develop relationships between and among these properties. "If all four angles are right angles, the shape must be a rectangle. If it is a square, all angles are right angles. If it is a square, it must be a rectangle." With greater ability to engage in "if-then" reasoning, shapes can be classified using only minimum defining characteristics. For example, four congruent sides and at least one right angle can be sufficient to define a square. Rectangles are parallelograms with a right angle. Observations go beyond properties themselves and begin to focus on logical arguments *about* the properties. Students at level 2 will be able to follow and appreciate an informal deductive argument about shapes and their properties. "Proofs" may be more intuitive than rigorously deductive; however, there is an appreciation that a logical argument is compelling. An appreciation of the axiomatic structure (an agreed-on set of rules) of a formal deductive system, however, remains under the surface.

The products of thought at level 2 are relationships among properties of geometric objects.

The hallmark of level-2 activities is the inclusion of informal logical reasoning. Since students have developed an understanding of various properties of shapes, it is now time to encourage conjecture and to ask "Why?" or "What if?" Contrast the required thinking in the following activity.

Activity 20.3

Minimal Defining Lists

(This activity must be done as a follow-up to Activity 20.2, "Property Lists.") Once property lists for the parallelogram, rhombus, rectangle, and square (and possibly the kite and trapezoid) have been agreed on by the class, have these lists posted. Have students work in groups to find "minimal defining lists," or MDLs, for each shape. An MDL is a subset of the properties for a shape that is defining and "minimal." "Defining" here means that any shape that has all the properties on the MDL must be that shape. "Minimal" means that if any single property is removed from the list it is no longer defining. For example, one MDL for a square is a quadrilateral with four congruent sides and four right angles. Students should try to find at least two or three MDLs for their shape. A proposed list can be challenged as either not minimal or not defining. A list is not defining if a counterexample—a shape other than one being described—can be produced using only the properties on the list.

The hallmark of this and other level-2 activities is the logic component. "*If* a quadrilateral has these properties, *then* it must be a square." Logic is also involved in proving that a list is faulty—either not minimal or not defining. Here students begin to learn the nature of a definition and the value of counterexamples. In fact, any minimal defining list (MDL) is a potential definition. The other aspect of this activity that clearly sets it into the level-2 category is that students focus on the lists of properties of the shapes—the very factors that were products of the earlier level-1 activity. As a result of the MDL activity, students are creating a collection of new relationships that exist between and among properties.

Level 3: Deduction

The objects of thought at level 3 are relationships among properties of geometric objects.

At level 3, students are able to examine more than just the properties of shapes. Their earlier thinking has produced conjectures concerning relationships among properties. Are these conjectures "true"? As this analysis of the informal arguments takes place, the structure of a system complete with axioms, definitions, theorems, corollaries, and postulates begins to develop and can be appreciated as the necessary means of establishing geometric truth. The student at this level is able to work with abstract statements about geometric properties and make conclusions based more on logic than intuition. A student operating at level 3 is aware that the diagonals of a rectangle bisect each other. However, at level 3, there is an appreciation of the need to prove this from a series of deductive arguments. The level-2 thinker, by contrast, follows the argument but fails to appreciate the need for more.

The products of thought at level 3 are deductive axiomatic systems for geometry.

The type of reasoning that characterizes a level-3 thinker is the same that is required in a typical high school geometry course. There students build on a list of axioms and definitions to create theorems. They also prove theorems using clearly articulated logical reasoning, whereas the reasoning at level 2 may be quite informal. In the best geometry courses, students would engage in activities in which they would discover the relationships they later prove.

In a very global sense, high school geometry students are working on the creation of a complete geometric deductive system. Usually this is the Euclidean system that describes best the world in which we live. They may also explore other geometric systems, such as the geometry where all lines are drawn on the surface of a sphere or "taxicab geometry" where lines may only follow a rectangular grid of "streets."

Level 4: Rigor

The objects of thought at level 4 are deductive axiomatic systems for geometry.

At the highest level of the van Hiele hierarchy, the objects of attention are axiomatic systems themselves, not just the deductions within a system. There is an appreciation of the distinctions and relationships between different axiomatic systems. For example, spherical geometry is based on lines drawn on a sphere rather than in a plane or ordinary space. This geometry has its own set of axioms and theorems. This is generally the level of a college mathematics major who is studying geometry as a branch of mathematical science.

The products of thought at level 4 are comparisons and contrasts among different axiomatic systems of geometry.

Characteristics of the van Hiele Levels. You no doubt noticed that the products of thought at each level are the same as the objects of thought at the next. This object-product relationship between levels of the van Hiele theory is illustrated in Figure 20.1. The objects (ideas) must be created at one level so that relationships among these objects can become the focus of the next level. In addition, the van Hiele levels have several common characteristics:

- The levels are sequential. To arrive at one level, students must move through prior levels.
- The products of thought at each level are the same as the objects of thought at the next.
- The levels are not age dependent. A third grader or a high school student could be at level 0.

- Geometric experiences are the greatest single factor influencing advancement through the levels. Students should explore, talk about, and interact with content at the next level while increasing experiences at their current level.
- When instruction or language is at a level higher than that of the student, there will be a lack of communication. A student can memorize a fact (e.g., all squares are rectangles) without having constructed that relationship.

The first three of the five van Hiele levels will continue as the focus of this chapter. Most students in pre-K through grade 8 will fall within these three categories. The emphasis of your work in geometry will be reflected by these ideas.

Implications for Instruction

If the van Hiele theory is correct—and there is much evidence to support it—then a major goal of the pre-K–8 curriculum must be to advance students' level of geometric thought. If students are to be adequately prepared for the deductive geometry curriculum of high school and beyond, then it is important for their thinking to have grown to at least level 2 by the end of the eighth grade.

All teachers should be aware that the experiences they provide are the single most important factor in moving children up this developmental ladder. Every teacher should be able to see some growth in students' geometric thinking over the course of the year.

The van Hiele theory and the developmental perspective of this book highlight the necessity of teaching at the child's level of thought. However, almost any activity can be modified to span two levels of thinking, even within the same classroom. For many activities, how we interact with individual children will adapt the activity to their levels while challenging them to operate at the next higher level.

The following sections contain descriptions of the types of activity and questioning that are appropriate for each of the first three levels. Apply these descriptors to the tasks that you pose to students, and use them to guide your interaction with students. The use of physical materials, drawings, and computer models is a must at every level.

Instruction at Level 0. Instructional activities in geometry appropriate for level 0 should:

- Involve lots of sorting and classifying. Seeing how shapes are alike and different is the primary focus of level 0. As students learn more content, the relationships that they notice will become more sophisticated.

- Students need ample opportunities to draw, build, make, put together (compose), and take apart (decompose) shapes in both two and three dimensions. These activities should be built around specific characteristics or properties so that students develop an understanding of geometric properties and begin to use them naturally.

To help students move from level 0 to level 1, students should be challenged to test ideas about shapes for a variety of examples from a particular category. Say to them, "Let's see if that is true for other rectangles," or "Can you draw a triangle that does *not* have a right angle?" In general, students should be challenged to see if observations made about a particular shape apply to other shapes of a similar kind.

Instruction at Level 1. Instructional activities in geometry appropriate for level 1 should:

- Focus more on the properties of figures rather than on simple identification. As new geometric concepts are learned, the number of properties that figures have can be expanded.
- Apply ideas to entire classes of figures (e.g., *all* rectangles, *all* prisms) rather than on individual models. For example, find ways to sort all possible triangles into groups. From these groups, define types of triangles.

To assist students in moving from level 1 to level 2, challenge them with questions such as "Why?" and those that involve reasoning. For example, "If the sides of a four-sided shape are all congruent, will you always have a square?" and "Can you find a counterexample?"

Instruction at Level 2. Instructional activities in geometry appropriate for level 2 should:

- Encourage the making and testing of hypotheses or conjectures. "Do you think that will work all the time?" "Is that true for all triangles or just equilateral ones?"
- Examine properties of shapes to determine necessary and sufficient conditions for different shapes or concepts. "What properties of diagonals do you think will guarantee that you will have a square?"
- Use the language of informal deduction: *all, some, none, if . . . then, what if,* and so on.
- Encourage students to attempt informal proofs. As an alternative, require them to make sense of informal proofs that other students or you have suggested.

Task Selection and Levels of Thought. If you teach at the pre-K–3 level, nearly all of your students will be at level 0. In the upper grades you may have children at two or even three levels within the same classroom. How do you discover the level of each student? Once you know, how will you select the right activities to match your students' levels?

No simple assessment exists to identify the exact level at which a student is functioning. However, examine the descriptors for the first two levels. As you conduct an activity, listen to students' observations. Can they talk about shapes as classes? Do they refer, for example, to "rectangles" rather than basing discussion around a particular rectangle? Do they understand that shapes do not change when the orientation or size changes? With careful observations such as these, you will soon be able to distinguish between levels 0 and 1.

At the upper grades, attempt to move students from level 1 to level 2. If students are not able to follow or appreciate logical arguments and are not comfortable with conjectures and if-then reasoning, these students are likely still at level 1 or below.

The remainder of this chapter offers a sampling of activities organized broadly around the four content goals of the NCTM standards: Shapes and Properties, Location, Transformations, and Visualization. Within each of these content groupings, activities are further sorted according to the first three van Hiele levels. Understand that all of these subdivisions are quite fluid. An activity found at one level can easily be adapted to an adjacent level simply by the way it is presented to the students.

Learning about Shapes and Properties

This is the content area that most people think about when they think about geometry in the pre-K–8 classroom; children are working with both two- and three-dimensional shapes. They are finding out what makes these shapes alike and different and in the process they begin to discover properties of the shapes, including the conventional names for these properties. With sufficient experiences, students develop classifications of special shapes—triangles, parallelograms, cylinders, pyramids, and so on—and learn that some properties apply to full classes. Eventually, they will investigate how properties of shapes impose logical consequences on geometric relationships and the ability to reason about shapes and properties will be developed.

Shapes and Properties for Level-0 Thinkers

Young children need experience with a rich variety of both two- and three-dimensional shapes. Triangles should be more than just equilateral and not always shown with the vertex at the top. Shapes should have curved sides, straight sides, and combinations of these. Along the way, the names of shapes and their properties can be introduced.

Sorting and Classifying.   As young students work at classification of shapes, be prepared for them to notice features that you do not consider to be "real" geometric attributes, such as "dented" or "looks like a tree." Children at this level will also attribute to shapes ideas that are not part of the shape, such as "points up" or "has a side that is the same as the edge of the board."

For variety in two-dimensional shapes, create your own materials. A good set of assorted shapes is found in Blackline Masters 41–47. Make multiple copies so that groups of children can all work with the same shapes. Once you have your sets constructed, a good beginning is Activity 20.1, "Shape Sorts," on pages 401–402.

In any sorting activity, the students should decide how to sort, not the teacher. This allows the students to do the activity using ideas *they* own and understand. By listening to the kinds of attributes that they use in their sorting, you will be able to tell what properties they know and use and how they think about shapes. Figure 20.4 illustrates a few of the many possible ways a set might be sorted.

The secret sorting portion of Activity 20.1 is one option for introducing a new property. For example, sort the shapes so that all have at least one right angle or "square corner." When students discover your rule, you have an opportunity to talk more about that property.

The following activity is also done with the 2-D shapes.

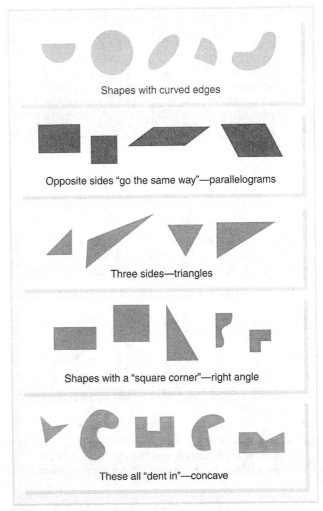

Shapes with curved edges

Opposite sides "go the same way"—parallelograms

Three sides—triangles

Shapes with a "square corner"—right angle

These all "dent in"—concave

Figure 20.4 By sorting shapes, students begin to recognize properties.

Activity 20.4

What's My Shape?

From Blackline Masters 41–47, make a double set of 2-D assorted shapes on cardstock. Cut out one set of shapes and glue each inside a folded half-sheet of construction paper to make "secret shape" folders.

In a group, one student is designated the leader and given a secret-shape folder. The other students are to find the shape that matches the shape in the folder by asking questions to which the leader can answer only "yes" or "no." The group can eliminate shapes as they ask questions to help narrow down the possibilities. They are not allowed to point to a piece and ask, "Is it this one?" Rather, they must continue to ask questions about properties or characteristics that reduce the choices to one shape. The final piece is checked against the one in the leader's folder.

The difficulty of Activity 20.4 is largely dependent on the shape in the folder. The more shapes in the collection that resemble the secret shape, the more difficult the task.

Most of the activities in "Shape Sorts" can and should be done with three-dimensional shapes. The difficulty is finding or making a collection that has sufficient variability. Geoblocks are a large set of wooden blocks available through various distributors. The variety is good, but no blocks have curved surfaces. Check catalogs for other collections. Consider combining several different sets to get variation. Another option is to collect real objects such as cans, boxes, balls, and Styrofoam shapes. Figure 20.5 illustrates some classifications of solids.

The ways in which children describe shapes in "Shape Sorts" and similar activities with three-dimensional shapes are good evidence of their level of thinking. The classifications made by level-0 thinkers will generally be restricted to the shapes that they have in front of them. As they begin to think in terms of the properties of shapes, they will create categories based on properties and their language will indicate that there are many more shapes in the group than those that

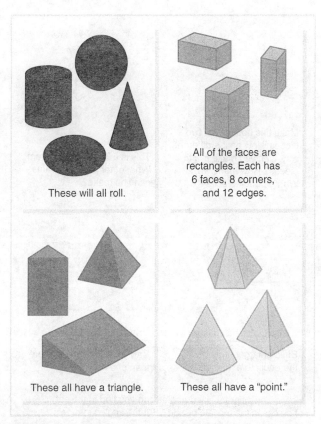

Figure 20.5 Early classifications of three-dimensional shapes.

These will all roll.

All of the faces are rectangles. Each has 6 faces, 8 corners, and 12 edges.

These all have a triangle.

These all have a "point."

are physically present (Mack, 2007). Students may say things like, "These shapes have square corners sort of like rectangles," or "These look like boxes. All the boxes have square [rectangular] sides." ◆

Composing and Decomposing Shapes. Children need to freely explore how shapes fit together to form larger shapes and how larger shapes can be made of smaller shapes. Among two-dimensional shapes for these activities, pattern blocks and tangrams are the best known. In a 1999 article, Pierre van Hiele describes an interesting set of tiles he calls the mosaic puzzle (see Figure 20.6). Patterns for the mosaic puzzle and tangrams can be found in Blackline Master 51.

Figure 20.7 shows four different types of tangram puzzles in increasing order of difficulty. NCTM's e-Examples includes a tangram applet (Example 4.4) with a set of challenges. One form of the applet includes eight puzzle figures that can be made using all seven of the pieces. The e-version of tangrams has the advantage of motivation and the fact that you must be much more deliberate in arranging the shapes.

The value of van Hiele's mosaic puzzle is partly due to the fact that the set contains five different angles (see Figure 20.8). You can use the pieces to talk about square corners (*right* angles) and angles that are more and less than a right angle (*obtuse* and *acute* angles).

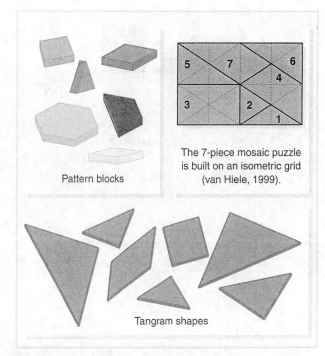

Pattern blocks

The 7-piece mosaic puzzle is built on an isometric grid (van Hiele, 1999).

Tangram shapes

Figure 20.6 Assorted tiles for activities.

The geoboard is one of the best devices for "drawing" two-dimensional shapes. The following activities are just three of many possible activities appropriate for level 0.

Activity 20.5

Geoboard Copy

Copy shapes, designs, and patterns from an overhead or projected geoboard. Begin with designs using one band; then create more complex designs (see Figure 20.9 on p. 409).

Activity 20.6

Congruent Parts

Copy a shape from a card, and have students subdivide or decompose it into smaller shapes on their geoboards. Specify the number of smaller shapes. Also specify whether they are all to be congruent or simply of the same type as shown in Figure 20.10 (p. 409).

Have lots of geoboards available in the classroom. It is better for two or three children to have 10 or 12 boards at a station than for each to have only one. That way, a variety of shapes can be made and compared before they are changed.

Teach students from the very beginning to record their geoboard designs. Paper copies (see Blackline Masters 49–50) permit students to create complete sets of

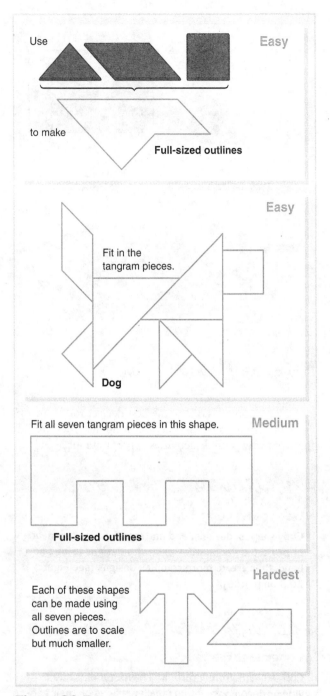

Figure 20.7 Four types of tangram puzzles (see Blackline Master 51).

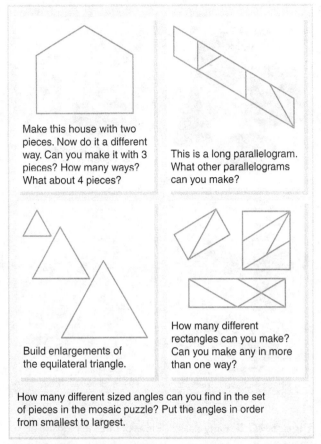

Make this house with two pieces. Now do it a different way. Can you make it with 3 pieces? How many ways? What about 4 pieces?

This is a long parallelogram. What other parallelograms can you make?

Build enlargements of the equilateral triangle.

How many different rectangles can you make? Can you make any in more than one way?

How many different sized angles can you find in the set of pieces in the mosaic puzzle? Put the angles in order from smallest to largest.

Figure 20.8 A sample of activities with the mosaic puzzle (see Blackline Master 51).

Source: Based on van Hiele, P. M. (1999). "Developing Geometric Thinking Through Activities That Begin with Play." *Teaching Children Mathematics,* 5(6), 310–316. Reprinted with permission. Copyright © 1999 by the National Council of Teachers of Mathematics, Inc. www.nctm.org. All rights reserved.

Tech NOTES The e-Examples found at the NCTM website under "Standards Focal Points" provide a good electronic geoboard (Applet 4.2). Although found in the K–2 section and entitled "Investigating the Concept of a Triangle," this is a great geoboard applet for any grade. It allows you to select and delete bands and vertices. The *Geoboard* applet from the National Library of Virtual Manipulatives (http://nlvm.usu.edu/en/nav/vlibrary .html) is essentially the same but with instant calculation of perimeter and area by clicking the "measures" button. ◆

Pause and Reflect

If you have never used a geoboard, explore one of these electronic geoboards. If you know about geoboards but have never used an e-geoboard, now would be a good time to try one.

drawings that fulfill a particular task. To help children in the very early grades copy geoboard designs, suggest that they first mark the dots for the corners of their shape ("second row, end peg"). With the corners identified, it is much easier for them to draw lines to make the shape.

Drawings can be placed in groups for classification and discussion, made into booklets illustrating a new idea that is being discussed, and sent home to families.

Building three-dimensional shapes is a little more difficult compared with two-dimensional shapes. A variety of

Have children copy shapes from pattern cards onto a geoboard.

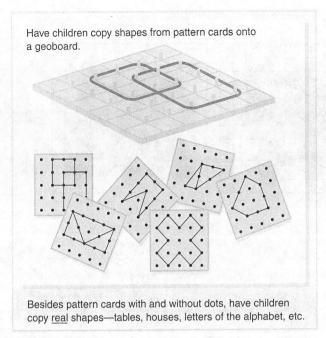

Besides pattern cards with and without dots, have children copy <u>real</u> shapes—tables, houses, letters of the alphabet, etc.

Figure 20.9 Shapes on geoboards (see Blackline Masters 49 and 50).

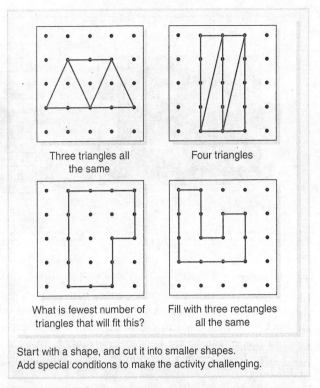

Three triangles all the same

Four triangles

What is fewest number of triangles that will fit this?

Fill with three rectangles all the same

Start with a shape, and cut it into smaller shapes. Add special conditions to make the activity challenging.

Figure 20.10 Subdividing shapes (see Blackline Masters 49 and 50).

commercial materials permit fairly creative construction of geometric solids (for example, 3D Geoshapes, Polydron, and the Zome System). The following are three highly recommended handmade approaches to skeletal models.

- *Plastic coffee stirrers with twist ties or modeling clay.* Plastic stirrers can be easily cut to different lengths. Use twist ties inserted into the ends or small chunks of clay (about 2 cm in diameter) to connect the corners.
- *Plastic drinking straws.* Cut the straws lengthwise with scissors from the top down to the flexible joint. These slit ends can then be inserted into the uncut bottom ends of other straws, making a strong but flexible joint. Three or more straws are joined in this fashion to form two-dimensional polygons. Use tape or twist ties to join polygons.
- *Rolled newspaper rods.* Fantastic super large skeletons can be built using newspaper and masking or duct tape (see Figure 20.11).

With these handmade models, students should compare the rigidity of a triangle with the lack of rigidity of polygons with more than three sides. Point out that triangles are used in many bridges, in the long booms of construction cranes, and in the structural parts of buildings. Discuss why this may be so. As children build large skeleton structures, they will find that they need to add diagonal pieces to form triangles for strength. The more triangles, the less likely their structure will collapse. Primary-grade students can benefit from creating free-form structures. Older students can be challenged to make more well-defined shapes.

Roll three full sheets of newspaper very tightly on the diagonal. Secure with tape. Tight rolls make stronger sticks.

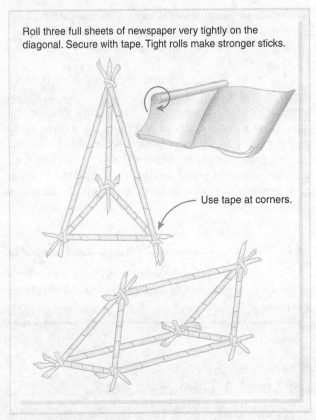

Use tape at corners.

Figure 20.11 Large skeletal structures and special shapes can be built with tightly rolled newspaper.

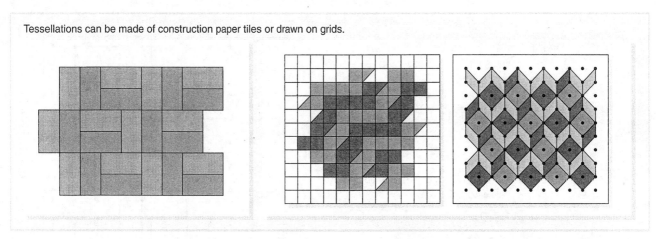

Tessellations can be made of construction paper tiles or drawn on grids.

Figure 20.12 Tessellations (see Blackline Masters 34–40).

Tessellations. A *tessellation* is a tiling of the plane using one or more shapes in a repeated pattern with no gaps or overlaps. Making tessellations is an artistic way for level-0 students from first grade to eighth grade to explore patterns in shapes and to see how shapes combine to form other shapes. Tessellation activities can vary considerably in difficulty.

Single-shape tessellations are more easily made with some shapes than others. For example, squares or equilateral triangles self-tessellate quite easily, although these provide only a minimal geometric challenge. When the shapes can be put together in more than one pattern, both the problem-solving level and the creativity increase. Literally hundreds of shapes can be used as tiles for tessellations (see Figure 20.12).

For their first experiences with tessellations, most children will benefit from using actual tiles to create patterns. Simple construction paper tiles can be cut quickly on a paper cutter or several of the pattern block pieces work well. Older children may be able to use dot or line grids (Blackline Masters 34–40) and plan their tessellations with pencil and paper. To plan a tessellation, use only one color so that the focus is on the spatial relationships.

⏸ ——————— *Pause and Reflect*

Look at the center tessellation in Figure 20.12. What single tile (a combination of squares and half squares) made this pattern?

Shapes and Properties for Level-1 Thinkers

As students move to level-1 thinking, the attention turns more to properties possessed by the traditional classifi-

Table 20.1

Categories of Two-Dimensional Shapes	
Shape	Description
Simple Closed Curves	
Concave, convex	An intuitive definition of *concave* might be "having a dent in it." If a simple closed curve is not concave, it is *convex*. A more precise definition of *concave* may be interesting to explore with older students.
Symmetrical, nonsymmetrical	Shapes may have one or more lines of symmetry and may or may not have rotational symmetry. These concepts will require more detailed investigation.
Polygons	Simple closed curves with all straight sides.
Concave, convex	
Symmetrical, non-symmetrical	
Regular	All sides and all angles are congruent.
Triangles	
Triangles	Polygons with exactly three sides.
Classified by sides	
Equilateral	All sides are congruent.
Isosceles	At least two sides are congruent.
Scalene	No two sides are congruent.
Classified by angles	
Right	Has a right angle.
Acute	All angles are smaller than a right angle.
Obtuse	One angle is larger than a right angle.
Convex Quadrilaterals	
Convex quadrilaterals	Convex polygons with exactly four sides.
Kite	Two opposing pairs of congruent adjacent sides.
Trapezoid	At least one pair of parallel sides.
Isosceles trapezoid	A pair of opposite sides is congruent.
Parallelogram	Two pairs of parallel sides.
Rectangle	Parallelogram with a right angle.
Rhombus	Parallelogram with all sides congruent.
Square	Parallelogram with a right angle and all sides congruent.

cations of shapes. During this period it makes sense for students to learn the proper names for shapes and their properties.

For the sake of clarity, the important definitions of two- and three-dimensional shapes are provided here. You will notice that shape definitions include relationships between and among shapes.

Special Categories of Two-Dimensional Shapes.
Table 20.1 (p. 410) lists some important categories of two-dimensional shapes. Examples of these shapes can be found in Figure 20.13.

In the classification of quadrilaterals and parallelograms, some subsets overlap. For example, a square is a rectangle and a rhombus. All parallelograms are trapezoids,

but not all trapezoids are parallelograms.* Children at level 1 continue to have difficulty seeing this type of subrelationship. They may quite correctly list all the properties of a square, a rhombus, and a rectangle and still might classify a square as a "nonrhombus" or a "nonrectangle." By fourth or fifth grade, encourage students to be more precise in their classifications. Burger (1985) points out that upper elementary students correctly use such classification

---

*Some definitions of trapezoid specify *only one* pair of parallel sides, in which case parallelograms would not be trapezoids. The University of Chicago School Mathematics Project (UCSMP) uses the "at least one pair" definition, meaning that parallelograms and rectangles are trapezoids.

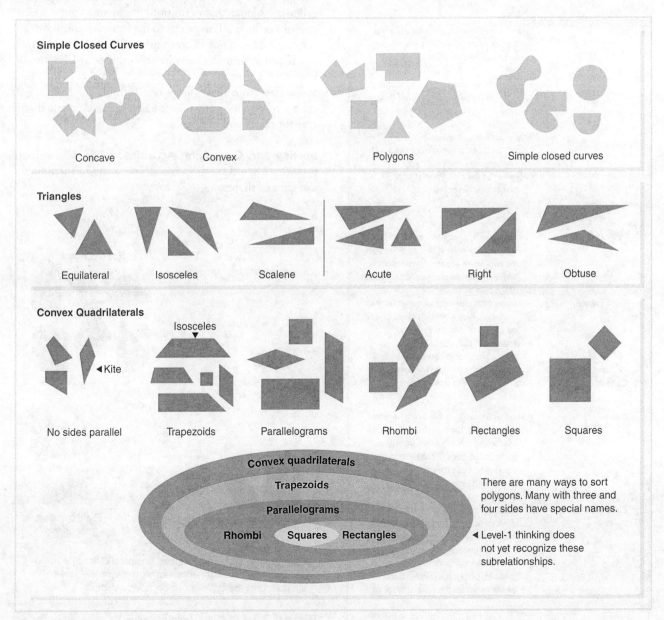

Figure 20.13 Classification of two-dimensional shapes.

schemes in other contexts. For example, individual students in a class can belong to more than one club. A square is an example of a quadrilateral that belongs to two other clubs.

Table 20.2

Categories of Three-Dimensional Shapes	
Shape	**Description**
Sorted by Edges and Vertices	
Spheres and "egglike" shapes	Shapes with no edges and no *vertices* (corners).
	Shapes with *edges* but no *vertices* (e.g., a flying saucer).
	Shapes with *vertices* but no *edges* (e.g., a football).
Sorted by Faces and Surfaces	
Polyhedron	Shapes made of all faces (a *face* is a flat surface of a solid). If all surfaces are faces, all the edges will be straight lines.
	Some combination of faces and rounded surfaces (circular cylinders are examples, but this is not a definition of a cylinder).
	Shapes with all curved surfaces.
	Shapes with and without edges and with and without vertices.
	Faces can be parallel. Parallel faces lie in planes that never intersect.
Cylinders	
Cylinder	Two congruent, parallel faces called *bases*. Lines joining corresponding points on the two bases are always parallel. These parallel lines are called *elements* of the cylinder.
Right cylinder	A cylinder with elements perpendicular to the bases. A cylinder that is not a right cylinder is an *oblique cylinder*.
Prism	A cylinder with polygons for bases. All prisms are special cases of cylinders.
Rectangular prism	A cylinder with rectangles for bases.
Cube	A square prism with square sides.
Cones	
Cone	A solid with exactly one face and a vertex that is not on the face. Straight lines (elements) can be drawn from any point on the edge of the base to the vertex. The base may be any shape at all. The vertex need not be directly over the base.
Circular cone	Cone with a circular base.
Pyramid	Cone with a polygon for a base. All faces joining the vertex are triangles. Pyramids are named by the shape of the base: *triangular* pyramid, *square* pyramid, *octagonal* pyramid, and so on. All pyramids are special cases of cones.

Special Categories of Three-Dimensional Shapes. Important and interesting shapes and relationships also exist in three dimensions. Table 20.2 describes classifications of solids. Figure 20.14 shows examples of cylinders and prisms. Note that prisms are defined here as a special category of cylinder—a cylinder with a polygon for a base. Figure 20.15 shows a similar grouping of cones and pyramids.

▌▌ ———————— *Pause and Reflect*

Explain the following: Prisms are to cylinders as pyramids are to cones. How is this relationship helpful in learning volume formulas?

Many textbooks define cylinders strictly as circular cylinders. These books do not have special names for other cylinders. Under that definition, the prism is not a special case of a cylinder. This points to the fact that definitions are conventions, and not all conventions are universally agreed on. If you return to the volume formulas in Chapter 19, you will see that the more inclusive definition of cylinders and cones given here allows one formula for any type of cylinder—hence, prisms—with a similar statement that is true for cones and pyramids.

Sorting and Classifying Activities. The next activity provides a good method when you want to introduce a category of shapes.

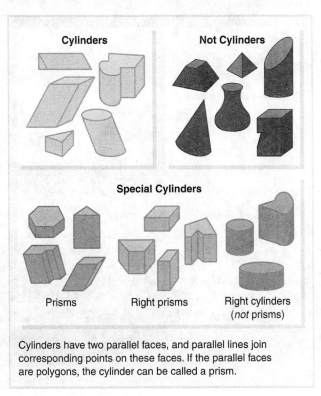

Cylinders have two parallel faces, and parallel lines join corresponding points on these faces. If the parallel faces are polygons, the cylinder can be called a prism.

Figure 20.14 Cylinders and prisms.

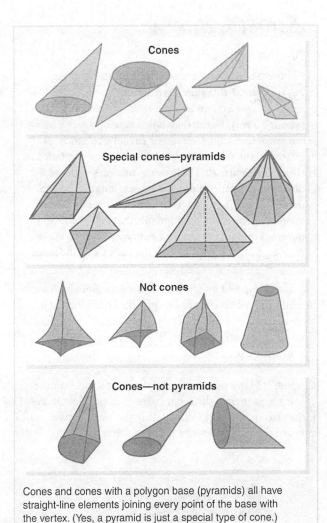

Cones and cones with a polygon base (pyramids) all have straight-line elements joining every point of the base with the vertex. (Yes, a pyramid is just a special type of cone.)

Figure 20.15 Cones and pyramids.

Activity **20.7**

Mystery Definition

Use the overhead or whiteboard to conduct logic activities such as the example in Figure 20.16. For your first collection be certain that you have allowed for all possible variables. In Figure 20.16, for example, a square is included in the set of rhombi. Similarly, choose nonexamples to be as close to the positive examples as is necessary to help with an accurate definition. The third or mixed set should also include those nonexamples with which students are most likely to be confused. Students should justify their choices.

The value of the "Mystery Definition" approach is that students develop ideas and definitions based on their own concept development. After their definitions have been

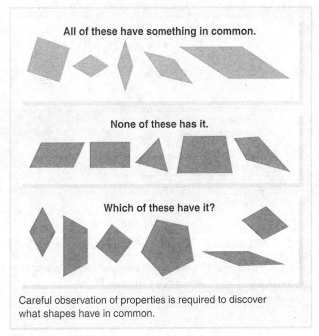

Careful observation of properties is required to discover what shapes have in common.

Figure 20.16 A mystery definition.

discussed and compared, you can offer the usual "book" definition for the sake of clarity.

For defining types or categories of triangles, the next activity is especially good and uses a different approach.

Activity **20.8**

Triangle Sort

Make copies of the Assorted Triangles sheet (see Blackline Master 58). Note the examples of right, acute, and obtuse triangles; examples of equilateral, isosceles, and scalene triangles; and triangles that represent every possible combination of these categories. Have students cut them out. The task is to sort the entire collection into three discrete groups so that no triangle belongs to two groups. When this is done and descriptions of the groupings have been written, students should then find a second criterion for creating three different groupings. Students may need a hint to look only at angle sizes or only at the issue of congruent sides, but hold these hints if you can.

"Triangle Sort" results in definitions of the six different types of triangles without having to list these definitions on the board and have students memorize them. As a follow-up activity, make a chart such as the following.

Challenge students to sketch a triangle in each of the nine cells.

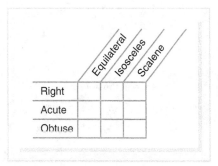

——————————— *Pause and Reflect*

Of the nine cells in the chart, two of them are impossible to fill. Can you tell which ones and why?

Quadrilaterals (polygons with four sides) are an especially rich source of investigations. Once students are familiar with the concepts of right, obtuse, and acute angles, congruence of line segments and angles, and symmetry (both line and rotational), Activity 20.2 "Property Lists for Quadrilaterals" on pages 402–403, is a good way to bring these ideas together and begin to see how different collections of properties apply to special classes of shapes. In this activity, students work to create lists of all the properties that they can find for a particular class of shapes. Students should share lists beginning with parallelograms, then rhombi, then rectangles, and finally squares.

The class must agree with everything that is put on the list. As new relationships come up in this presentation-and-discussion period, you can introduce proper terminology. For example, if two diagonals intersect in a square corner, then they are *perpendicular*. Other terms such as *parallel*, *congruent*, *bisect*, *midpoint*, and so on can be clarified as you help students write their descriptions. This is also a good time to introduce symbols such as ≅ for "congruent" or ‖ for "parallel." As an extension, repeat Activity 20.2 using kites and trapezoids. Furthermore, similar activities can be used to introduce three-dimensional shape definitions.

Construction Activities. Students' building or drawing shapes continue to be important at level 1. Dynamic geometry software (*The Geometer's Sketchpad, Cabri,* and *Wingeom*) dramatically enhances the exploration of shapes at this level.

In the next activity, students examine the diagonals of various classes of quadrilaterals.

Activity 20.9

Diagonal Strips

For this activity, students need three strips of tagboard about 2 cm wide. Two should be the same length (about 30 cm) and the third somewhat shorter (about 20 cm). Punch nine holes equally spaced along the strip. Use a brass fastener to join two strips. A quadrilateral is formed by joining the four end holes as shown in Figure 20.17. Provide students with the list of possible relationships for angles, lengths, and ratios of parts. Their task is to use the strips to determine the properties of diagonals that will produce different quadrilaterals. Students may want to make drawings on dot grids to test the various hypotheses.

Every type of quadrilateral can be uniquely described in terms of its diagonals using only the conditions of length, ratio of parts, and whether or not they are perpendicular. A dynamic geometry program is also an excellent vehicle for this investigation.

Circles. Many interesting relationships can be observed among measures of different parts of the circle. One of the most astounding and important is the ratio between measures of the circumference and the diameter.

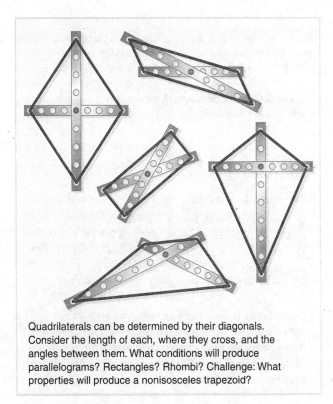

Quadrilaterals can be determined by their diagonals. Consider the length of each, where they cross, and the angles between them. What conditions will produce parallelograms? Rectangles? Rhombi? Challenge: What properties will produce a nonisosceles trapezoid?

Figure 20.17 Diagonals of quadrilaterals.

Activity 20.10

Discovering Pi

Have groups of students carefully measure both the circumference and diameter of circular items such as jar lids, tubes, cans, and wastebaskets. To measure circumference, wrap string once around the object and then measure that length of string. Also measure large circles marked on gym floors and playgrounds. Use a trundle wheel or rope to measure the circumference.

Collect measures of circumference and diameter from all groups and enter them in a table. Ratios of the circumference to the diameter should also be computed for each circle. A scatter plot of the data should be made with the horizontal axis representing diameters and the vertical axis circumferences.

Most ratios should be in the neighborhood of 3.1 or 3.2. The scatter plot should approximate a straight line through the origin. The slope of the line should also be close to 3.1. (Recall from Chapter 18 that graphs of equivalent ratios are always straight lines through the origin.) The exact ratio is an irrational number, about 3.14159, represented by the Greek letter π (pi).

What is most important in Activity 20.10 is that students develop a clear understanding of π as the ratio of circumference to diameter in any circle. The quantity π is not some strange number that appears in math formulas; it is a naturally occurring and universal ratio.

Dynamic Geometry Software.   In a dynamic geometry program, points, lines, and geometric figures are easily constructed on the computer using only a mouse or a stylus. Once drawn, the geometric objects can be moved about and manipulated in endless variety. Distances, lengths, areas, angles, slopes, and perimeters can be measured. As the figures are changed, the measurements update instantly.

Lines can be drawn perpendicular or parallel to other lines or segments. Angles and segments can be drawn congruent to other angles and segments. A point can be placed at the midpoint of a segment. A figure can be produced that is a reflection, rotation, or dilation of another figure. The most significant idea is that when a geometric object is created with a particular relationship to another, that relationship is maintained no matter how either object is moved or changed.

myeducationlab
Go to the Building Teaching Skills and Dispositions section of Chapter 20 of MyEducationLab. Click on Videos and watch the video entitled "**Geometer's Sketchpad**" to see a teacher work with dynamic geometry software.

The best known dynamic geometry programs are *The Geometer's Sketchpad* (Key Curriculum Press), *Wingeom* (open source from Peanut Software), *Geogebra* (open source), and *Cabri Geometry II* (Texas Instruments). Originally designed for high school students, all can be used starting about grade 4.

Dynamic Geometry Examples.   To appreciate the potential (and the fun) of dynamic geometry software, you really need to experience it. In the meantime, an example is offered here in an attempt to illustrate how these programs work.

In Figure 20.18, the midpoints of a freely drawn quadrilateral ABCD have been joined. The diagonals of the resulting quadrilateral (EFGH) are also drawn and measured. No matter how the points A, B, C, and D are dragged around the screen, even inverting the quadrilateral, the other lines will maintain the same relationships (joining midpoints and diagonals), and the measurements will be instantly updated.

Remember that at level 1, the objects of thought are *classes* of shapes. In a dynamic geometry program, if a quadrilateral is drawn, only one shape is observed, as would be the case on paper or on a geoboard. But now that quadrilateral can be stretched and altered in endless ways, so students actually explore not one shape but an enormous number of examples from that class of shapes. If a property or constructed relationship does not change when the figure changes, the property is attributable to the *class* of shapes rather than any particular shape.

Another example in Figure 20.19 shows how dynamic geometry software can be used to investigate quadrilaterals starting with the diagonals. By creating the drawing in this manner, the diagonals of ACBD will always bisect each

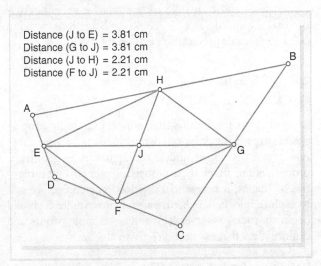

Figure 20.18 A *Sketchpad* construction illustrating an interesting property of quadrilaterals.

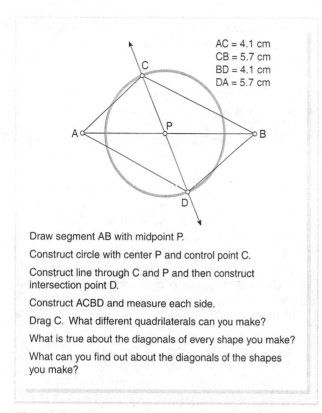

AC = 4.1 cm
CB = 5.7 cm
BD = 4.1 cm
DA = 5.7 cm

Draw segment AB with midpoint P.

Construct circle with center P and control point C.

Construct line through C and P and then construct intersection point D.

Construct ACBD and measure each side.

Drag C. What different quadrilaterals can you make?

What is true about the diagonals of every shape you make?

What can you find out about the diagonals of the shapes you make?

Figure 20.19 Quadrilaterals with diagnonals that bisect each other.

other no matter how the drawing is altered. By dragging point C around, ACBD can be made into a parallelogram, rectangle, rhombus, and square. For each of these figures, additional information about the diagonals can be determined by looking at the drawing.

Dynamic geometry programs are also powerful for investigating concepts of symmetry and transformations (slides, flips, and turns). There are many excellent activities that are appropriate for level-1 investigations found in NCTM journals publications and on the Web.

Shapes and Properties for Level-2 Thinkers

At level 2, the focus shifts from simply examining properties of shapes to explorations that include logical reasoning. As students develop an understanding of various geometric properties and attach these properties to important categories of shapes, it is essential to encourage conjecture and to explore informal deductive arguments. Students should begin to attempt—or at least follow—simple proofs and explore ideas that connect directly to algebra.

Definitions and Proofs. The previously described activities of "Property Lists for Quadrilaterals" (Activity

20.2), which is a level-1 activity, and "Minimal Defining Lists" (Activity 20.3), a level-2 activity, really clarify the distinction between these two levels. (See Groth, 2006, for more information.) The parallelogram, rhombus, rectangle, and square each has at least four MDLs. One of the most interesting MDLs for each shape consists only of the properties of its diagonals. For example, a quadrilateral with diagonals that bisect each other and are perpendicular (intersect at right angles) is a rhombus.

Notice that the MDL activity is actually more involved with logical thinking than in examining shapes. Students are engaged in the general process of deciding, "*If* we specify only this list of properties, will that guarantee this particular shape?" A second feature is the opportunity to discuss what constitutes a definition. In fact, any MDL could be the definition of the shape. The definitions we usually use are MDLs that have been chosen probably due to the ease with which we can understand them. A quadrilateral with diagonals that bisect each other does not immediately call to mind a parallelogram although that is a defining list of properties.

The next activity is also a good follow-up to the "Property Lists" activity, although it is not restricted to quadrilaterals and can include three-dimensional shapes as well. Notice again the logic involved.

Activity 20.11

True or False?

Prepare a set of true and false statements of the following forms: "If it is a _____, then it is also a _____." "All _____ are _____." "Some _____ are _____."

A few examples are suggested here but numerous possibilities exist.

- If it is a square, then it is a rhombus.
- All squares are rectangles.
- Some parallelograms are rectangles.
- All parallelograms have congruent diagonals.
- If it has exactly two lines of symmetry, it must be a quadrilateral.
- If it is a cylinder, then it is a prism.
- All prisms have a plane of symmetry.
- All pyramids have square bases.
- If a prism has a plane of symmetry, then it is a right prism.

The task is to decide if the statements are true or false and to present an argument to support the decision. Four or five true-or-false statements will make a good lesson. Once this format is understood, let students challenge their classmates by making their own lists of five statements. Each list should have a mix of true and false statements. See the suggested article by Renne (2004) for additional ideas. Students' lists can then be used in subsequent lessons.

Pause and Reflect

Use the property list for squares and rectangles to prove "All squares are rectangles." Notice that you must use logical reasoning to understand this statement. It does little good to simply force it on students who are not ready to develop the relationship.

The following activity was designed by Sconyers (1995) to demonstrate that students can create proofs in geometry well before high school.

Activity 20.12

Two Polygons from One

Pose the following problem:

> **Begin with a convex polygon with a given number of sides. Connect two points on the polygon with a line segment forming two new polygons. How many sides do the two resulting polygons have together?**

Demonstrate with a few examples (see Figure 20.20). Have students explore by drawing polygons and slicing them. Encourage students to make a table showing sides in the original and resulting sides. Students should first make conjectures about a general rule. When groups are comfortable with their conjecture, they should try to reason why their statement is correct—that is, prove their conjecture.

Obviously, the number of resulting sides depends on where the slice is made. With the exception of triangles, there are three possibilities. For each case, a clear argument can be made. The appropriate conjecture and proof are left to you, but trust that students working together can do this task.

Notice that in this task, as in others we have explored, the statements to be proved come from students. If you write a theorem on the board and ask students to prove it, you have already told them that it is true. If, by contrast, a student makes a statement about a geometric situation the class is exploring, it can be written on the board with a question mark as a *conjecture*, a statement whose truth has not yet been determined. You can ask, "Is it true? Always? Can we prove it? Can we find a counterexample?" Reasonable deductive arguments can be forged out of discussions (Boats, Dwyer, Laing, & Fratella, 2003).

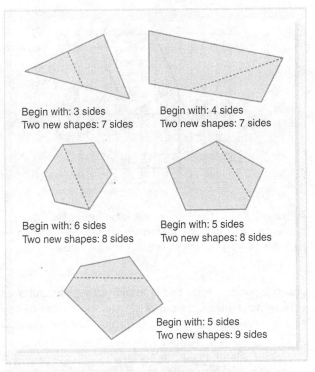

Begin with: 3 sides
Two new shapes: 7 sides

Begin with: 4 sides
Two new shapes: 7 sides

Begin with: 6 sides
Two new shapes: 8 sides

Begin with: 5 sides
Two new shapes: 8 sides

Begin with: 5 sides
Two new shapes: 9 sides

Figure 20.20 Start with a polygon, and draw a segment to divide it into two polygons. How many sides will the two new polygons have?

The Pythagorean Relationship. The *Pythagorean relationship* is so important that it deserves special attention. In geometric terms, this relationship states that if a square is constructed on each side of a right triangle, the areas of the two smaller squares will together equal the area of the square on the longest side, the hypotenuse. To discover this relationship, consider the following activity.

Activity 20.13

The Pythagorean Relationship

Have students draw a right triangle on half-centimeter grid paper (see Blackline Master 36). Assign each student a different triangle by specifying the lengths of the two legs. Students are to draw a square on each leg and the hypotenuse and find the area of all three squares. (For the square on the hypotenuse, the exact area can be found by making each of the sides the diagonal of a rectangle. See Figure 20.21.) Make a table of the area data (Sq. on leg 1, Sq. on leg 2, Sq. on hyp.), and ask students to look for a relationship between the squares.

As an extension to the last activity, students can explore drawing other figures on the legs of right triangles

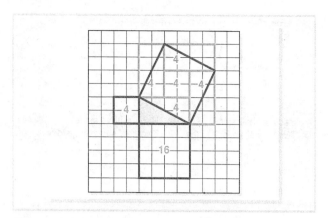

Figure 20.21 The Pythagorean relationship. Note that if drawn on a grid, the area of all squares is easily determined. Here 4 + 16 = area of the square on the hypotenuse.

and computing areas. For example, draw semicircles or equilateral triangles instead of squares. The areas of any regular polygons drawn on the three sides of right triangles will have the same relationship.

What about proof? Both large congruent squares in Figure 20.22 together show a nonverbal proof of the Pythagorean theorem (Nelson, 2001). Note that both squares contain four triangles that are the same but arranged differently. By adding up the areas of the squares and the triangles and setting them equal, the Pythagorean relationship can be found by subtracting out the common areas in both squares. An algebraic recording of the thinking process is shown below the drawings.

❚❚ ——————————— *Pause and Reflect*

Use the two drawings in Figure 20.22 to create a proof of the Pythagorean relationship.

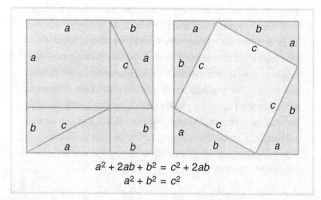

$$a^2 + 2ab + b^2 = c^2 + 2ab$$
$$a^2 + b^2 = c^2$$

Figure 20.22 The two squares together are a "proof without words." Can you supply the words?

The e-Examples found at the NCTM website under "Standards & Focal Points" includes a dynamic proof without words that is worth sharing with your students (Applet 6.5). Because it requires knowing that parallelograms and rectangles with the same base and height have the same area (see Chapter 19), it is also a good review. ◆

Finding Versus Explaining Relationships. At level 2, the focus is on reasoning or deductive thinking. Can dynamic geometry software programs help students develop deductive arguments to support the relationships they come to believe through inductive reasoning? Consider the following situation.

Suppose that you have students use a dynamic geometry program to draw a triangle, measure all of the angles, and add them up. As the triangle vertices are dragged around, the sum of the angles would remain steadfast at 180 degrees. Students can conjecture that the sum of the interior angles of a triangle is always 180 degrees, and they would be completely convinced of the truth of this conjecture based on this inductive experience. (Several noncomputer activities lead to the same conclusion.) However, the experience just described fails to explain *why it is so*. Consider the following activity, which can be done easily with paper and scissors or quite dramatically with a dynamic geometry program.

Activity 20.14

Angle Sum in a Triangle

Have all students cut out three congruent triangles. (Stack three sheets of paper, and cut three shapes at one time.) Place one triangle on a line and the second directly next to it in the same orientation. Place the third triangle in the space between the triangles as shown in Figure 20.23(a). Based on this experience, what conjecture can you make about the sum of the angles in a triangle?

In a dynamic geometry program, the three triangles in Figure 20.23(a) can be drawn by starting with one triangle, translating it to the right the length of AC, and then rotating the same triangle about the midpoint of side BC. When vertices of the original triangle are dragged, the other triangles will change accordingly and remain congruent. We still do not know why the angle sum is always a straight angle, but this exploration allows students to see why it might be so. In the figure, there are lines parallel to each side of the original triangle. By using properties of angles formed by cutting parallel lines with a transverse

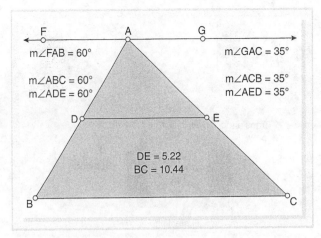

Figure 20.24 The midsegment of a triangle is always parallel to the base and half as long.

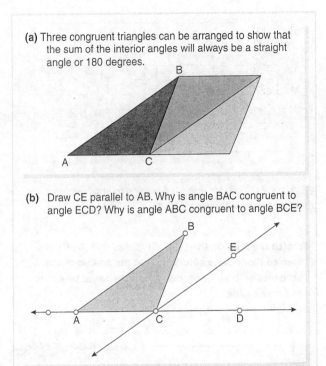

(a) Three congruent triangles can be arranged to show that the sum of the interior angles will always be a straight angle or 180 degrees.

(b) Draw CE parallel to AB. Why is angle BAC congruent to angle ECD? Why is angle ABC congruent to angle BCE?

Figure 20.23 Deductive, logical reasoning is necessary to prove relationships that appear true from observations.

line, it is easy to argue that the sum of the angles will always be a straight line. See Figure 20.23(b); the proof is left to you.

Dynamic geometry software can be enormously powerful for helping students observe geometric relationships and make conjectures. The truth of the conjectures will often be obvious. At level 2, however, we must begin to ask why. The following activity further illustrates the point.

Activity 20.15

Triangle Midsegments

Using a dynamic geometry program, draw a triangle, and label the vertices A, B, and C. Draw the segment joining the midpoints of AB and AC, and label this segment DE, as in Figure 20.24. Measure the lengths of DE and BC. Also measure angles ADE and ABC. Drag points A, B, and C. What conjectures can you make about the relationships between segment DE, the *midsegment* of ABC, and BC, the base of ABC?

It is very clear that the midsegment is half the length of the base and parallel to it, but why is this so? Students will

need a bit more guidance, but you should not necessarily have to provide the argument for them. Suggest that they draw a line through A parallel to BC. List all pairs of angles that they know are congruent. Why are they congruent? Note that triangle ABC is similar to triangle ADE. Why is it similar? With hints such as these, many middle grade students can begin to make logical arguments for why the things they observe to be true are in fact true.

Learning about Transformations

Transformations are changes in position or size of a shape. Movements that do not change the size or shape of the object moved are called "rigid motions." Usually, three rigid-motion transformations are discussed: *translations* or slides, *reflections* or flips, and *rotations* or turns. Interestingly, the study of symmetry is also included under the study of transformations. Do you know why?

Transformations for Level-0 Thinkers

Transformations at this level involve an introduction to the basic concepts of slides, flips, and turns and the initial development of line symmetry and rotational symmetry.

Slides, Flips, and Turns. At the primary level, the terms *slide*, *flip*, and *turn* are adequate. The early goal is to help students recognize these transformations and to begin to explore their effects on simple shapes. You can use a nonsymmetric shape to introduce these terms (see Figure 20.25). Most likely your textbook will use only the center of a shape as the point of rotation and restrict reflections to vertical

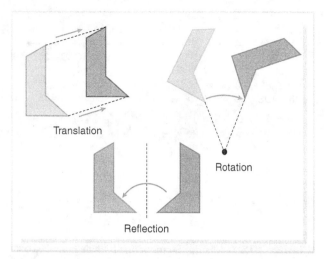

Figure 20.25 Translation (slide), reflection (flip), rotation (turn).

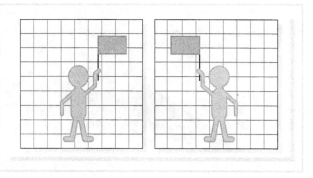

Figure 20.26 Motion Man is used to show slides, flips, and turns (see Blackline Masters 52 and 53).

and horizontal lines through the center. These restrictions are not necessary and may even be misleading.

The Motion Man activity described next can also be used to introduce students to the terms *slide*, *flip*, and *turn*. In the activity, rotations are restricted to $\frac{1}{4}$, $\frac{1}{2}$, and $\frac{3}{4}$ turns in a clockwise direction. The center of the turn will be the center of the figure. Reflections will be flips over vertical or horizontal lines. These restrictions are for simplicity. In the general case, the center of rotation can be anywhere on or off the figure. Lines of reflection can also be anywhere.

Activity 20.16

Motion Man

Using Blackline Masters 52–53, make copies of the first Motion Man and then copy the mirror image on the backs of these copies. (See Figure 20.26.) Experiment first. You want the back image to match the front image when held to the light. Cut off the excess paper to leave a square. Give all students a two-sided Motion Man.

Demonstrate each of the possible motions. A slide is simply that. The figure does not rotate or turn over. Demonstrate turns. Emphasize that only clockwise turns will be used for this activity. Similarly, demonstrate a horizontal flip (top goes to bottom) and a vertical flip (left goes to right). Practice by having everyone start with his or her Motion Man in the same orientation. As you announce one of the moves, students slide, flip, or turn Motion Man accordingly.

Then display two Motion Men side by side in any orientation. The task is to decide what motion or combination of motions will get the man on the left to

match the man on the right. Students use their own man to work out a solution. Test the solutions that students offer. If both men are in the same position, call that a slide.

⏸ ———————— *Pause and Reflect*

Begin with the Motion Man in the left position shown in Figure 20.26. Now place a second Motion Man next to the first. Will it take one move or more than one move (transformation) to get from the first to the second Motion Man? Can you describe all of the positions that require more than one move? Are there any positions that require more than two moves?

At first, students will be confused when they can't get their Motion Man into the new position with one move. This causes an excellent problem. Don't be too quick to suggest that it may take two moves. If flips across each of the two diagonals are added to the motions along with vertical and horizontal flips, Motion Man can assume any new position in exactly one move. This provides a challenge for students. Two students begin with their Motion Man figures in the same position. One student then changes his or her Motion Man and challenges the other student to say what motion is required to make the two Motion Men match. The solution is then tested and the roles reversed.

Line and Rotational Symmetry. If a shape can be folded on a line so that the two halves match, then it is said to have *line symmetry* (or mirror symmetry). Notice that the fold line is actually a line of reflection—the portion of the shape on one side of the line is reflected onto the other side, demonstrating a connection between line symmetry and transformations.

One way to introduce line symmetry to children is to show examples and nonexamples using an all-of-these/none-of-these approach as in Figure 20.16, p. 413. Another possibility is to have students fold a sheet of paper in half and cut out a shape of their choosing. When they open the paper, the fold line will be a line of symmetry. A third way is to use mirrors or Miras. (The Mira is a red, plastic image reflector that can be used to explore concepts of symmetry and congruence.) When you place a mirror on a picture or design so that the mirror is perpendicular to the table, you see a shape with symmetry when you look in the mirror.

The following activity explores line symmetry.

Activity 20.17

Pattern Block Mirror Symmetry

Students need a plain sheet of paper with a straight line through the middle. Using about six to eight pattern blocks, students make a design completely on one side of the line that touches the line in some way. The task is to make the mirror image of their design on the other side of the line. When finished, they use a mirror (or Mira) to check their work. They place the mirror on the line and look into it from the side of the original design. With the mirror in place they should see exactly the same image as they see when they lift the mirror. You can also challenge them to make designs with more than one line of symmetry.

Building symmetrical designs with pattern blocks tends to be easier if the line is vertical. With the line oriented horizontally or diagonally, the task is harder.

The same task can be done with a geoboard. First, stretch a band down the center or from corner to corner. Make a design on one side of the line and its mirror image on the other. Check with a mirror. This can also be done on either isometric or square dot grids (Blackline Masters 34 and 38) as shown in Figure 20.27 or with dynamic geometry software.

A plane of symmetry in three dimensions is analogous to a line of symmetry in two dimensions. Figure 20.28 illustrates a shape built with cubes that has a plane of symmetry.

Activity 20.18

Plane Symmetry Buildings

With cubes, build a building that has a plane of symmetry. If the plane of symmetry goes between cubes, slice the shape by separating the building into two symmetrical parts. Try making buildings with two or three planes of symmetry. Build various prisms. Do not forget that a plane can slice diagonally through the blocks.

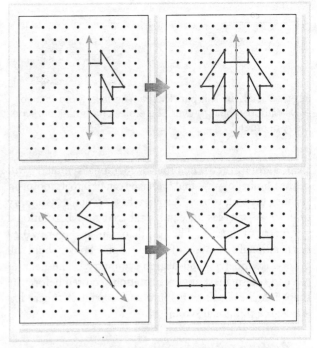

Figure 20.27 Exploring symmetry on dot grids (Blackline Masters 37 and 39).

A shape has *rotational symmetry* (also referred to as *point symmetry*) if it can be rotated about a point and land in a position exactly matching the one in which it began. A square has rotational symmetry as does an equilateral triangle.

A good way to understand rotational symmetry is to take a shape with rotational symmetry, such as a square, and trace around it on a piece of paper. Call this tracing the

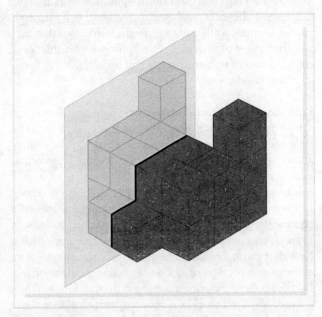

Figure 20.28 A block building with one plane of symmetry.

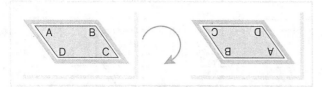

Figure 20.29 This parallelogram fits in its footprint two ways without flipping it over. Therefore, it has rotational symmetry of order 2.

shape's "footprint." The order of rotational symmetry will be the number of ways that the shape can fit into its footprint without flipping it over. A square has rotational symmetry of *order* 4, whereas an equilateral triangle has rotational symmetry of *order* 3. The parallelogram in Figure 20.29 has rotational symmetry of order 2. Some books would call order-2 symmetry "180-degree symmetry." The degrees refer to the smallest angle of rotation required before the shape matches itself or fits into its footprint. A square has 90-degree rotational symmetry.

Activity 20.19

Pattern Block Rotational Symmetry

Have students construct designs with pattern blocks having different rotational symmetries. They should be able to make designs with order 2, 3, 4, 6, or 12 rotational symmetry. Which of the designs have mirror symmetry as well?

Transformations for Level-1 Thinkers

Within the context of transformations, students moving into level-1 thinking can begin to analyze transformations a bit more analytically and to apply them to shapes that they see. Two types of activities seem appropriate at this level: compositions of transformations and using transformations to create tessellations.

Composition of Transformations. One transformation can be followed by another. For example, a figure can be reflected over a line, and then that figure can be rotated about a point. A combination of two or more transformations is called a *composition.*

Have students experiment with compositions of two or even three transformations using a simple shape on a rectangular dot grid. For example, have students draw an L-shape on a dot grid and label it L_1 (refer to Figure 20.30). Reflect it through a line, and then rotate the image $\frac{1}{4}$ turn clockwise about a point not on the shape. Call this image L_2, the image of a composition of a reflection followed by a rotation. Notice that if L_1 is rotated $\frac{1}{4}$ turn clockwise about the same point used before to L_3 there is a relationship

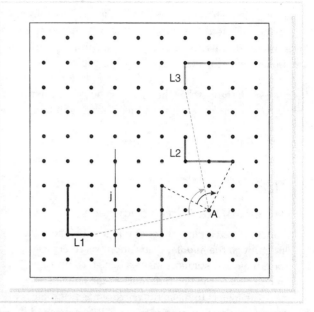

Figure 20.30 Shape L_1 was reflected across line j and rotated $\frac{1}{4}$ turn about point A resulting in L_2. L_1 was also rotated $\frac{1}{4}$ turn about point A. How are L_2 and L_3 related? Will this always work?

between L_2 and L_3. Continue to explore different combinations of transformations. Don't forget to include translations (slides) in the compositions. Compositions do not have to involve different types of transformations. For example, a reflection can be followed by another reflection.

 In NCTM's e-Examples found at the NCTM website under "Standards & Focal Points," "Understanding Congruence, Similarity, and Symmetry" (Applet 6.4) is one of the best examples of a simple yet valuable interactive applet. In the first part of the applet, students develop an understanding of all three rigid motions. In the second part, a transformation is complete and the student uses a guess-and-check procedure to determine what exact transformation was done. In the last two parts, students can explore compositions of reflections and then other compositions of up to three transformations. This applet is strongly recommended. ◆

Similar Figures and Proportional Reasoning. In Chapter 18 on proportional reasoning, we saw a good first definition of similar figures as shapes that "look alike but are different sizes" (see Activity 18.3, p. 353). More precisely, two figures are *similar* if all of their corresponding angles are congruent and the corresponding sides are proportional. Other proportional reasoning activities are also good connections to geometry, such as Activity 18.9, which involves scale drawings and proportional relationships in figures that are similar.

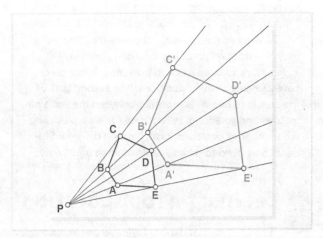

Figure 20.31 Begin with figure ABCDE and place point P anywhere at all. Draw lines from P through each vertex. Place point A′ twice as far from P as A is from P (scale factor of 2). Do similarly for the other points. ABCDE is congruent with A′B′C′D′E′.

A *dilation* is a nonrigid transformation that produces similar figures. Figure 20.31 shows how a given figure can be *dilated* to make larger or smaller figures. If different groups of students dilate the same figure using the same scale factor, they will find that the resulting figures are all congruent, even with each group using different dilation points. Dynamic geometry software makes the results of this exercise quite dramatic. The software allows for the scale factors to be set at any value. Once a dilation is made, the dilation point can be dragged around the screen and the size and shape of the image clearly stay unchanged. Scale factors less than 1 produce smaller figures.

Tessellations Revisited.   Either by using transformations or by combining compatible polygons, students at level 1 can create tessellations that are artistic and quite complex.

The Dutch artist M. C. Escher is well known for his tessellations, where the tiles are very intricate and often take the shape of things like birds, horses, angels, or lizards. Escher took a simple shape such as a triangle, parallelogram, or hexagon and performed transformations on the sides. For example, a curve drawn along one side might be translated (slid) to the opposite side. Another idea was to draw a curve from the midpoint of a side to the adjoining vertex. This curve was then rotated about the midpoint to form a totally new side of the tile. These two ideas are illustrated in Figure 20.32. Dot paper is used to help draw the lines. *Escher-type tessellations*, as these have come to be called, are important applications of transformations for students in grades 5 and up. Once a tile has been designed, it can be cut from two different colors of construction paper instead of drawing the tessellation on a dot grid.

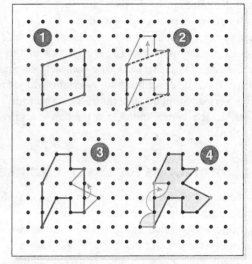

① Start with a simple shape.

② Draw the same curve on two opposite sides. This tile will stack up in columns.

③ Rotate a curve on the midpoint of one side.

④ Rotate a curve on the midpoint of the other side. Use this tile for tessellation (below).

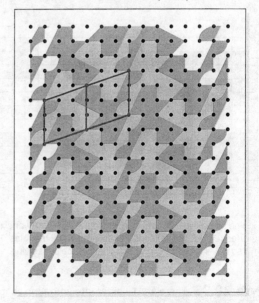

A column of the resulting tile will now match a like column that is rotated one complete turn. Find these rotated columns in the tessellation shown here.

Figure 20.32 Creating an Escher-type tessellation (see Blackline Master 37).

A *regular tessellation* is made of a single tile that is a regular polygon (all sides and angles congruent). Each vertex of a regular tessellation has the same number of tiles meeting at that point. A checkerboard is a simple example of a regular tessellation. A *semiregular tessellation* is made of two or more tiles, each of which is a regular polygon. At each vertex of a semiregular tessellation, the same collection of regular polygons come together in the same order. A vertex (and, therefore, the complete semiregular tessellation) can be described by the series of shapes meeting at a vertex. Students can figure out which polygons are possible at a vertex and design their own semiregular tessellations.

Transformations for Level-2 Thinkers

The following activity is a challenge for students to use their understanding of symmetries and transformations to establish an interesting relationship between these two ideas. The shapes used for this activity are called *pentominoes*—shapes made from 5 squares, each square touching at least one other square by sharing a full side. The search to see how many different pentominoes there are is a well-known geometry activity (see Activity 20.27). For our purposes in discussing transformations and symmetries, the collection of 12 pentominoes simply serves as a convenient collection of shapes, as shown in Figure 20.33.

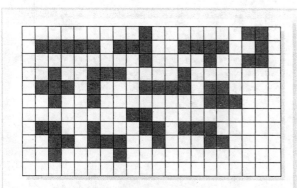

There are 12 pentominoes.

Finding all possible shapes made with five squares—or six squares (called "hexominoes") or six equilateral triangles and so on—is a good exercise in spatial problem solving.

Figure 20.33 There are 12 different pentomino shapes. An exploration to find these shapes is Activity 20.27 on page 429.

Activity 20.20

Pentomino Positions

Have students cut out a set of 12 pentominoes from 2-cm grid paper (see Figure 20.33). Mark one side of each piece to help remember if it has been flipped over. The first part of the task is to determine how many different positions on the grid each piece has (Walter, 1970). Call positions "different" if a reflection or a turn is required to make them match. Therefore, the cross-shaped piece has only one position. The strip of five squares has two positions. Some pieces have as many as eight positions. The second part of the task is to find a relationship between the line symmetries and rotational symmetries for each piece and the number of positions it can have on the grid. Students may need to make a table of what they know.

Learning about Location

The location standard in *Principles and Standards* says that students should "specify locations and describe spatial relationships using coordinate geometry and other representational systems" (NCTM, 2000, p. 42). After early development of terms for how objects are located with respect to other objects (e.g., the ball is *under* the table), location activities involve analysis of paths from point to point as on a map and the use of coordinate systems.

Location for Level-0 Thinkers

In pre-K and kindergarten, children learn about everyday positional descriptions—*over, under, near, far, between, left,* and *right*. These are the beginnings of the *Standards* goal of specifying locations. However, helping students refine the way they answer questions of direction, distance, and location enhances spatial understandings. Geometry, measurement, and algebra are all supported by the use of a grid system with numbers or coordinates attached that can specify location on a grid. As students become more sophisticated, their use of coordinates progresses along with them. Importantly, students at the primary level can begin to think in terms of a grid system to identify location.

The next activity can serve as a readiness task for coordinates and help students see the value of having a way to specify location without pointing.

Activity 20.21

Hidden Positions

For the game boards, draw an 8-inch square on tagboard. Subdivide the squares into a 3 × 3 grid. Two students sit with a "screen" separating their desktop space so that neither student can see the other's grid (see Figure 20.34). Each student has four different pattern blocks. The first player places a block on four different sections of the grid. He then tells the other player where to put blocks on her grid to match his own. When all four pieces are positioned, the two grids are checked to see if they are alike. Then the players switch roles. Model the game once by taking the part of the first student. Use words such as *top row, middle, left,* and *right.* Students can play in pairs as a station activity.

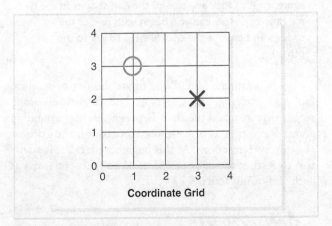

Figure 20.34 The "Hidden Positions" game.

The "Hidden Positions" game can easily be extended to grids up to 6 × 6. As the grid size increases, the need for a system of labeling positions increases. Students can begin to use a simple coordinate system as early as the first grade. Use a coordinate grid like the one shown in Figure 20.35 (see Blackline Master 48). Explain how to use two numbers to designate an intersection point on the grid. The first number tells how far to move to the right. The second number tells how far to move up. For younger children use the words along with the numbers: 3 right and 0 up. Be sure to include 0 in your introduction. Select a point on the grid and have students decide what two numbers name that point. If your point is at (2,4) and students incorrectly

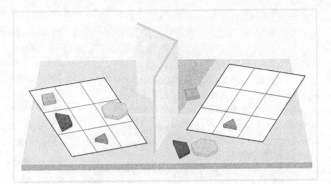

Figure 20.35 A simple coordinate grid. The X is at (3, 2) and the O is at (1, 3). Use the grid to play Three in a Row (like Tic-Tac-Toe). Put marks on intersections, not spaces (see Blackline Master 48).

say "four, two," then simply indicate where the point is that they named. Another way for students to visualize the difference is to compare students in the second row fourth seat to the fourth row second seat.

The next activity explores the notion of different paths on a grid.

Activity 20.22

Paths

On a sheet of 2-cm grid paper (see Blackline Master 34), mark two different points A and B as shown in Figure 20.36. Using the overhead, whiteboard, or floor tiles, demonstrate how to describe a path from A to B. For the points in the figure, one path is "up 5 and right 6." Another path might be "right 2, up 2, right 2, up 3, right 2." Count the length of each path. As long as you always move toward the target point (in this case either right or up), the path lengths will always be the same. Here they are 11 units long. Students draw three paths on their papers from A to B using different-colored crayons. For each path they write directions that describe their paths. Ask, "What is the greatest number of turns that you can make in your path?" "What is the smallest number?" "Where would A and B have to be in order to get there with no turns?"

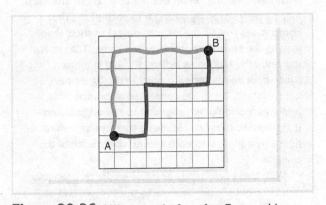

Figure 20.36 Different paths from A to B on a grid.

If you add a coordinate system on the grid in "Paths," students can describe their paths with coordinates: For example: (1, 2) ⟶ (3, 2) ⟶ (3, 5) ⟶ (7, 5) ⟶ (7, 7).

The e-Examples found at the NCTM website under "Standards & Focal Points" contains a nice applet (Applet 4.3) that is similar to the previous activity but offers some additional challenges. Students move a ladybug by issuing directions.

The task is to make a list of directions to hide the ladybug beneath a leaf. When the directions are complete, the ladybug is set in motion to follow them. The ladybug is also used to draw shapes such as a rectangle in a tilted position or to travel through mazes. This applet is a very basic version of the powerful computer programming language Logo. ◆

Location for Level-1 Thinkers

At level 1, one use of the coordinate grid is to examine transformations in a more analytic manner. There is not a lot of new knowledge about coordinates to learn except for the extension to four quadrants with the use of negative numbers. Even fourth- and fifth-grade students can use negative integers so that the full plane can be represented. The activities here suggest how coordinates can be used to examine transformations.

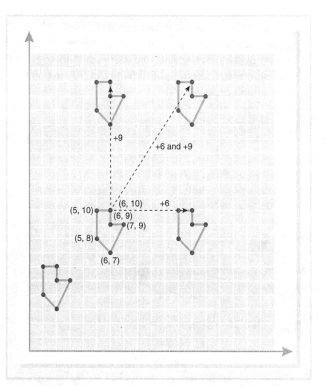

Figure 20.37 Begin with a simple shape and record the coordinates. By adding or subtracting from the coordinates, new shapes are found that are translations (slides) of the original.

Activity 20.23

Coordinate Slides

Students will need a sheet of centimeter grid paper on which to draw two coordinate axes near the left and bottom edges. Have them plot and connect about five or six points on the grid to form a small shape (see Figure 20.37.) If you direct them to use only coordinates between 5 and 12, the figure will be reasonably small and near the center of the paper. Next, students make a new shape by adding 6 to each of the first coordinates (called the *x*-coordinates) of their shape, leaving the second coordinates the same. That is, for the point (5, 10) a new point, (11, 10) is plotted. When new points for each point in the figure have been plotted, these are connected as before. This new figure should be congruent to the original and translated to the right. Students then create a third figure by adding 9 to each second coordinate of the original.

With these two slides as initial guidance, stop and discuss what should be done to the coordinates to move the figure along a diagonal line up and to the right. Have students make and test their conjectures. Figure 20.37 shows a slide that was created by adding 6 to all of the first coordinates and adding 9 to all of the second coordinates. As long as all first coordinates are changed by the same amount and all second coordinates by the same amount, the figure will be translated without distortion. Challenge students to figure out how to change the coordinates to make the figure slide down and to the left. (Subtract from the coordinates instead of add.) Students' papers should show their original shape and four copies, each in a different location on the grid.

Help students summarize what they've learned: What does adding (or subtracting) a number from the first coordinates cause? What if the number is added or subtracted from the second coordinates? From both coordinates? Have students draw lines connecting corresponding points in the original figure with one of those where both coordinates were changed. What do they notice? (The lines are parallel and the same length.) Pick any two of the five shapes in the final drawing. How can you begin with one of the shapes and change the coordinates to get to the other?

In "Coordinate Slides" the figure did not twist, turn, flip over, or change size or shape. The shape "slid" along a path that matched the lines between the corresponding points. Reflections can be explored on a coordinate grid just as easily as translations. At this beginning level, it is advisable to restrict the lines of reflection to the *x*- or *y*-axis as in the following activity.

Activity 20.24

Coordinate Reflections

Have students draw a five-sided shape in the first quadrant on coordinate grid paper using grid points for vertices. Label the Figure ABCDE and call it Figure 1. Use the *y*-axis as a line of symmetry and draw the reflection of the shape in the second quadrant. Call it Figure 2 (for second quadrant) and label the reflected points A′B′C′D′E′. Now use the *x*-axis as the line of symmetry. Reflect both Figure 2 and Figure 1 into the third and fourth quadrants, respectively, and call these Figures 3 and 4. Label the points of these figures with double and triple primes (A″ and A‴, and so on). Write in the coordinates for each vertex of all four figures.

- How is Figure 3 related to Figure 4? How else could you have gotten Figure 3? How else could you have found Figure 4?
- How are the coordinates of Figure 1 related to its image in the *y*-axis, Figure 2? What can you say about the coordinates of Figure 4?
- Make a conjecture about the coordinates of a shape reflected in the *y*-axis and a different conjecture about the coordinates of a shape reflected in the *x*-axis.
- Draw lines from the vertices of Figure 1 to the corresponding vertices of Figure 2. What can you say about these lines? How is the *y*-axis related to each of these lines?

Refer to Figure 20.38 to answer these questions.

Students who have done the preceding activities should have a general way to describe translations and reflections across an axis, all in terms of coordinates. Rotations can also be explored with the use of coordinates. In the following activity, multiplying a constant times

the coordinates is a transformation that is not a rigid motion.

Activity 20.25
Coordinate Dilations

Students begin with a four-sided shape in the first quadrant. They then make a list of the coordinates and make a new set of coordinates by multiplying each of the original coordinates by 2. They plot the resulting shape. What is the result? Now have students multiply each of the original coordinates by $\frac{1}{2}$ and plot that shape. What is the result? Next, students draw a line from the origin to a vertex of the largest shape on their paper. Repeat for one or two additional vertices and ask for observations. (An example is shown in Figure 20.39.)

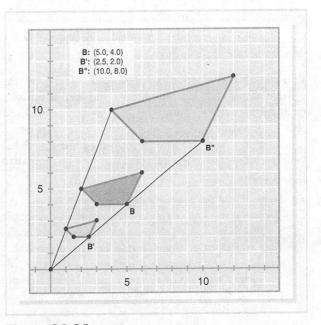

Figure 20.39 Dilations with coordinates.

Pause and Reflect

How do the lengths of sides and the areas of the shapes compare when the coordinates are multiplied by 2? What if they are multiplied by 3 or by $\frac{1}{2}$?

When the coordinates of a shape are multiplied as in the last activity, each by the same factor, the shape either gets larger or smaller. The size is changed but not the shape. The new shape is similar to the old shape. This is called a *dilation*, a transformation that is *not* rigid because the shape changes.

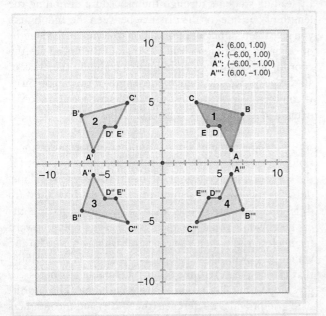

Figure 20.38 Exploring reflections on a coordinate grid.

Your students may enjoy exploring this phenomenon a bit further. If they start with a line drawing of a simple face, boat, or some other shape drawn with straight lines connecting vertices, they will create an interesting effect by multiplying just the first coordinates, just the second coordinates, or using a different factor for each. When only the second coordinate is multiplied, the vertical dimensions alone are dilated, so the figure is proportionately stretched (or shrunk) in a vertical manner. Students can explore this process to distort shapes in various ways.

It is impressive to see how an arithmetic operation can control a figure. Imagine being able to control slides, flips, turns, and dilations, not just in the plane but also for three-dimensional figures. The process is identical to computer animation techniques.

Location for Level-2 Thinkers

On the surface, there may not be a clear distinction between coordinate activities for level 1 and those for level 2. However, the move to level-2 thinking is highlighted by the infusion of logical reasoning.

Coordinate Transformations Revisited. It is quite reasonable that a class has both level-1 and level-2 thinkers or at least students who are ready to move on to logical reasoning. While exploring the transformation activities in the last section, students who are ready might be challenged with questions such as the following that are a bit more than simple explorations:

- How should the coordinates be changed to cause a reflection if the line of reflection is not the *y*-axis but is parallel to it?
- Can you discover a single rule for coordinates that would cause a reflection across one of the axes followed by a rotation of a quarter turn? Is that rule the same for the reverse order—a quarter turn followed by a reflection?
- If two successive slides are made with coordinates and you know what numbers were added or subtracted, what number should be added or subtracted to get the figure there in only one move?
- What do you think will happen if, in a dilation, different factors are used for different coordinates?

Tech NOTES Once students begin to explore questions of this type, they may well come up with their own questions and explorations. Dynamic geometry software includes an optional coordinate grid. If drawings are made with the points "snapped" to the grid, coordinate transformations can be explored much more easily. ◆

Applying the Pythagorean Relationship. The geometric version of the Pythagorean relationship is about areas. The following activity has students use the coordinate grid and the Pythagorean relationship to develop a formula for the distance between points.

Activity **20.26**

The Distance Formula

Have students draw a line between two points in the first quadrant that are not on the same horizontal or vertical line. The task is to use only the coordinates of the endpoints to find the distance between them in terms of the units on the grid. To this end, suggest that they draw a right triangle using the line as the hypotenuse. The vertex at the right angle will share one coordinate from each endpoint. Students compute the areas of the squares on the legs and add to find the area of the square on the hypotenuse. Now the length of the original line segment (the distance between the points) is the number whose square is the area of the square on the hypotenuse. (This last sentence is a geometric interpretation of square root.) Have students follow these directions to compute the length of the line.

Next, have them look through all of their calculations and see how the coordinates of the two endpoints were used. Challenge students to use the same type of calculations to get the distance between two new points without drawing any pictures.

Level-2 students do not necessarily construct proofs but should be able to follow the rationale if shown proofs. By leading students through the procedure of finding the length of one line (or the distance between the endpoints), you give them sufficient information to compute the lengths of other lines. Students will see that all they need are the coordinates of the two endpoints to compute the areas of all three squares and, hence, the length of the hypotenuse. If you then help them substitute letters for specific coordinates, a general distance formula results.

Slope. The topic of slope is another important connection between geometry and algebra and need not wait for the study of linear equations. To begin a discussion of slope, draw several different slanted lines. Discuss how they are different. Some are steeper than others. Some go up, others go down. If you agree that "up" means sloping upward from left to right, then you can agree which ones go up and which go down. This "steepness" of a line is an attribute that can be measured like other measurable attributes. To give slope a number requires a reference line. The coordinate grid provides a reference (the *x*-axis) and the numbers

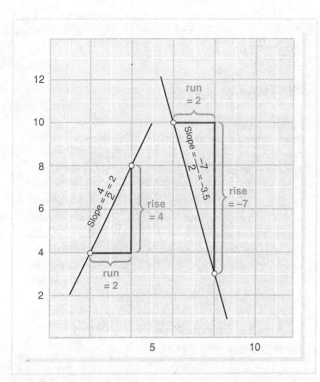

Figure 20.40 The slope of a line is equal to rise ÷ run.

to use in the measurement. Spend some time having students invent their own methods for attaching a number to the concept of steepness.

The convention for measuring the steepness of a line or the *slope* is based on the ideas of the *rise* and *run* between any two points on the line. The *rise* is the vertical change from the left point to the right point—positive if up, negative if down. The *run* is the horizontal distance from the left point to the right point. Slope is then defined as *rise ÷ run* or the ratio of the vertical change to the horizontal change (see Figure 20.40). By agreement, vertical lines have no slope or the slope is said to be "undefined." Horizontal lines have a slope of 0 as a result of the definition.

Once students are given the definition, they should be able to compute the slopes of any nonvertical line drawn on a coordinate grid without further assistance and *without formulas*. A good problem-based task is to figure out what can be said about the slopes of parallel lines and perpendicular lines.

Learning about Visualization

Visualization might be called "geometry done with the mind's eye." It involves being able to create mental images of shapes and then turn them around mentally,

thinking about how they look from different perspectives—predicting the results of various transformations. It includes the mental coordination of two and three dimensions—predicting the unfolding of a box (or net) or understanding a two-dimensional drawing of a three-dimensional shape. Any activity that requires students to think about a shape mentally, to manipulate or transform a shape mentally, or to represent a shape as it is seen visually will contribute to the development of students' visualization skills.

Visualization for Level-0 Thinkers

At level 0, students are quite bound to thinking about shapes in terms of the way they look. Visualization activities at this level will have students using a variety of physical shapes and drawings and will challenge them to think about these shapes in different orientations.

Finding out how many different shapes can be made with a given number of simple tiles demands that students mentally flip and turn shapes in their minds and find ways to decide if they have found them all. That is the focus of the next activity.

Activity 20.27

Pentominoes

A pentomino is a shape formed by joining five squares as if cut from a square grid. Each square must have at least one side in common with another. Provide students with five square tiles and a sheet of square grid paper for recording. Challenge them to see how many different pentomino shapes they can find. Shapes that are flips or turns of other shapes are not considered different. Do not tell students how many pentomino shapes there are. Good discussions will come from deciding if some shapes are really different and if all shapes have been found.

Once students have decided that there are just 12 pentominoes (revisit Figure 20.33), the 12 pieces can then be used in a variety of activities. Glue the grids with the children's pentominoes onto tagboard, and let them cut out the 12 shapes.

It is also fun to explore the number of shapes that can be made from six equilateral triangles or from four 45-degree right triangles (halves of squares), as shown in Figure 20.41. With the right triangles, sides that touch must be the same length. How many of each of these "ominoes" do you think there are?

Lots of activities can be done with pentominoes. For example, try to fit all 12 pieces into a 6 × 10 or 5 × 12 rectangle. Also, each of the 12 shapes can be used as a tessellation tile. Another task is to examine each of the 12 pentominoes

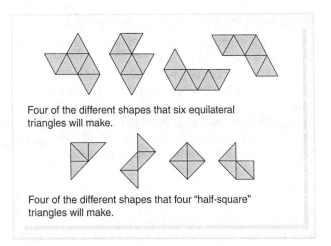

Four of the different shapes that six equilateral triangles will make.

Four of the different shapes that four "half-square" triangles will make.

Figure 20.41 Finding possible shapes with triangles.

and decide which will fold up to make an open box, also called a *net*. For those that are "box makers," which square is the bottom?

Another aspect of visualization for young children is to be able to think about solid shapes in terms of their faces or sides. For these activities you will need to make "face cards" by tracing around the different faces of a shape, making either all faces on one card or a set of separate cards with one face per card (see Figure 20.42).

Activity 20.28

Face Matching

There are two versions of the task: Given a face card, find the corresponding solid, or given a solid, find the face card. With a collection of single-face cards, students can select the cards that go with a particular block. For another variation, stack all of the single-face cards for one block face down. Turn them up one at a time as clues to finding the block.

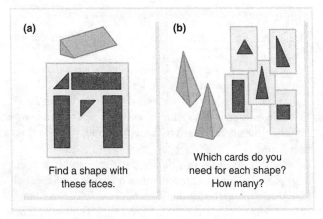

(a)

Find a shape with these faces.

(b)

Which cards do you need for each shape? How many?

Figure 20.42 Matching face cards with solid shapes.

The following activity has been adapted from NCTM's *Principles and Standards* and is found in the pre-K–2 section on geometry (NCTM, 2000, p. 101).

Activity 20.29

Quick Images

Draw some simple sketches on transparencies so that they can be shown to students one figure at a time. They should be drawings that students can easily reproduce. Some examples are shown in Figure 20.43. On the overhead projector or whiteboard display one of the figures for about 5 seconds. Then have students attempt to reproduce it on their own. Show the same figure again for a few seconds and allow students to modify their drawings. Repeat with additional figures.

In your discussions with students, ask them to tell how they thought about the figure or to describe it in words that helped them remember what they saw. As students learn to verbally describe what they see, their visual memory will improve.

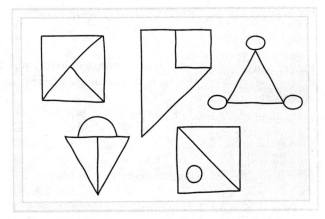

Figure 20.43 Examples of designs to use in the "Quick Images" activity.

In the last activity, visual memory as well as the ability to think about positions of lines and features of the figure are important.

Visualization for Level-1 Thinkers

In identifying a visualization task as either level 0 or level 1, one consideration is the degree of attention that must be given to the particular properties of shapes. The activities in this section are almost certainly too difficult for students at level 0.

One of the main goals of the visualization strand of the Geometry Standard is to be able to identify and draw two-dimensional images of three-dimensional figures and to build three-dimensional figures from two-dimensional images. Activities aimed at this goal often involve drawings of small "buildings" made of one-inch cubes.

Activity 20.30

Viewpoints

- In the first version, students begin with a building and draw the left, right, front, and back direct views. In Figure 20.44, the building plan shows a top view of the building and the number of blocks in each position. After students build a building from a plan like this, their task is to draw the front, right, left, and back direct views as shown in the figure.
- In the reverse version of the task, students are given a right and front view. The task is to build the building that has those views. To record their solution, they draw a building plan (top view with numbers).

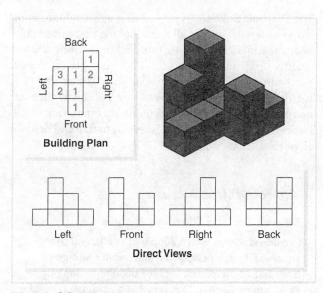

Building Plan

Direct Views

Figure 20.44 "Viewpoints" task.

Notice that front and back direct views are symmetric, as are the left and right views. That is why only one of each is given in the second part of the activity.

In "Viewpoints," students made "buildings" out of 1-inch cubes and coordinated these with direct views of the sides and top. A significantly more challenging activity is to draw perspective views of these block buildings or to match perspective drawings with a building. Isometric dot grids (Blackline Masters 38 and 39) are used for the drawings. The next activity provides a glimpse at this form of visualization activity.

Activity 20.31

Perspective Drawings

- In the first version, students begin with a perspective drawing of a building. The assumption is that there are no hidden blocks. From the drawing the students build the actual building with their blocks. To record the result, they draw a building plan indicating the number of blocks in each position.
- In the second version, students are given either a block plan or the five direct views (see Figure 20.45). They build the building accordingly and draw two or more of the perspective views. There are four possible perspectives from above the table: the front left and right, and the back left and right. It is useful to build the building on a sheet of paper with the words "front," "back," "left," and "right" written on the edges to keep from getting different viewpoints confused.

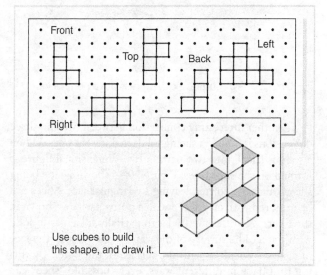

Use cubes to build this shape, and draw it.

Figure 20.45 Block "buildings" on isometric grids.

 An amazing computer tool for drawing two- and three-dimensional views of block buildings is the Isometric Drawing Tool, available on the Illuminations website (http://illuminations.nctm .org/ActivityDetail.aspx?ID=125). This applet requires only mouse clicks to draw either whole cubes, any single face of a cube, or just lines. The drawings, however, are actually "buildings" and can be viewed as three-dimensional objects. They can be rotated in space so that they can be seen from any vantage. Prepared investigations are informative and also lead students through the features of the tool. ◆

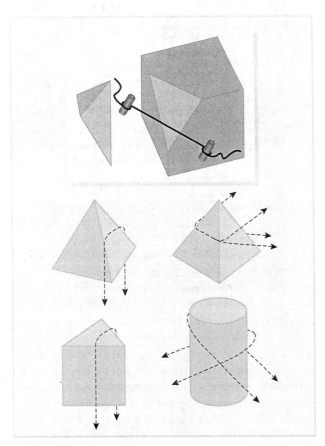

Figure 20.46 Cutting a clay model with a potter's wire.

Another interesting connection between two and three dimensions is found in slicing solids in different ways. When a solid is sliced into two parts, a two-dimensional figure is formed on the slice faces. Figure 20.46 shows a cube being sliced off at the corner, leaving a triangular face. Slices can be explored with clay sliced with a potter's wire as shown in the figure. A niftier method is to partially fill a plastic solid with water. The surface of the water is the same as the face of a slice coinciding with the surface of the water. By tilting the shape in different ways, every possible "slice" can be observed. Small plastic solids such as Power Solids are excellent for this.

Visualization for Level-2 Thinkers

Once again, we see that logical reasoning is what distinguishes activities for level-2 thinkers from those for level 1. It is important to note, however, that visualization is an area of geometry where the distinction is not particularly sharp. The activities described for level 1 can easily be modified to challenge level-2 thinkers. Likewise, the activities in this section will help to push level-1 students forward in their thinking.

Connecting Earlier Activities to Level-2 Visualization. Students who are ready can be challenged to make predictions about the types of slices that are possible. For example, given a particular solid, prior to testing with water as described previously they might go through a list of types of triangles and quadrilaterals and decide which can be made and which are impossible. For those they think are impossible, they should offer a reason for that hypothesis.

The following are extensions of pentomino activities that are appropriate visualization tasks for level 2:

- How many *hexominoes* are there? A hexomino is made of six squares following the same rule as for pentominoes. Since there are quite a few hexominoes (35), devising a good logical scheme for categorizing the shapes is one of the few ways there are of knowing they have all been found.
- Instead of putting together five squares, students can find all of the arrangements of five cubes. These shapes are called *pentominoids*. In general, shapes made of cubes in which adjoining cubes share a complete face are called *polyominoids*.

The Platonic Solids. A *polyhedron* is a three-dimensional shape with polygons for all faces. Among the various polyhedra, the Platonic solids are especially interesting. *Platonic solids* is the name given to the set of completely regular polyhedrons. "Completely regular" means that each face is a regular polygon and every vertex has exactly the same number of faces joining at that point. An interesting visualization task appropriate for this level is to find and describe all of the Platonic solids.

Activity **20.32**

Search for the Platonic Solids

Provide students with a supply of equilateral triangles, squares, regular pentagons, and regular hexagons from one of the plastic sets for building solids (e.g., *Polydron* or *Geofix*). Explain what a completely regular solid is. The task is to find as many different completely regular solids as possible.

Some students, particularly those with special needs, may need additional structure. Therefore, you might suggest a systematic approach as follows. Since the smallest number of sides a face can have is three, begin with triangles, then squares, then pentagons, and so on. Furthermore, since every vertex must have the same number of faces, try three faces at a point, then four, and so on. (It is clearly impossible to have only two faces at a point.)

With this plan, students will find that for triangles they can have three, four, or five triangles coming to a point. For each of these, they can begin with a "tent" of triangles and then add more triangles so that each vertex has the same number. With three at a point you get a four-sided solid called a *tetrahedron* (in Greek *tetra* = four). With four at each point you get an eight-sided solid called an *octahedron* (*octa* = eight). It is really exciting to build the solid with five triangles at each point. It will have 20 sides and is called an *icosahedron* (*icosa* = twenty).

In a similar manner, students will find that there is only one solid made of squares—three at each point and six in all—a *hexahedron* (*hex* = six), also called a cube. And there is only one solid with pentagons, three at each point, 12 in all. This is called a *dodecahedron* (*dodeca* = twelve).

⏸ ——————————— *Pause and Reflect*

Why are there no regular polyhedra with six or more triangles or four or more squares? Why are there no regular polyhedra made with hexagons or with polygons with more than six sides? The best way to answer these questions is to experiment with the polygons and explain the answers in your own words. Students should do the same.

A fantastic skeletal icosahedron can be built out of the newspaper rods described earlier (see Figure 20.11, p. 409.) Since five triangles converge at each point, there are also five edges at each point. Simply work at bringing five rods to each vertex and remember that each face is a triangle. This icosahedron will be about 4 feet across and will be amazingly sturdy.

Reflections on Chapter 20

Writing to Learn

1. Describe in your own words the first three van Hiele levels of geometric thought (levels 0, 1, and 2). Note in your description the object of thought and the product of thought. How would activities aimed at levels 0, 1, and 2 differ?
2. Briefly describe the nature of the content in each of the four geometric strands featured in this chapter and in the *Standards:* Shapes and Properties, Location, Transformations, and Visualization.
3. What can you do when the students in your classroom are at different van Hiele levels of thought?
4. Find one of the suggested applets for geometry or explore *Wingeom* and explain how it can be used. What are the advantages of using the computer in geometry instead of the corresponding hands-on materials or drawings?
5. How can a teacher assess students in terms of general geometric growth or spatial sense? Assuming that the van Hiele theory is correct, why is it important to understand where your students are in terms of that theory?

For Discussion and Exploration

1. Examine the teacher's edition of a textbook at any grade level. Select any lesson on geometry. What evidence do you find that the lesson responds to the van Hiele levels? How might the lesson be adapted for your students who may be at several different levels?
2. At the elementary and middle school levels, technology should be an important component of your instructional tools. If you are not familiar with the types of technology discussed in this chapter, play around to learn what each suggested digital tool or program can do. (Learning about a dynamic geometry program is highly recommended.)

Resources for Chapter 20

Literature Connections

The Greedy Triangle *Burns, 1995*

This delightful book starts off with the story of a triangle that is very busy being a sail or musical instrument, or fitting into the crook of someone's arm when standing with hand on hip. It isn't long before he becomes bored and travels to the local shapeshifter for a change. Adding a new side and angle and becoming a quadrilateral gives the triangle new things to try as he fits into different four-sided figures in the environment. The greedy triangle goes through several other shape-shifts. This book links well with activities at level 0 and level 1. Using a meter-long loop of yarn for every pair of students (or three ace bandages in a loop for a class demonstration), have students follow and discuss events in the book by creating appropriate shapes with the loop (holding it in the air between their hands). First they can explore the different triangles that were made and eventually they can investigate properties as they shift from one shape to the next.

Snowflake Bentley *Martin, 1998*

This amazing true story describes the life of a persistent young scientist in Vermont who wanted to learn more about snowflakes. Living in an area averaging 120 inches of snow a year, Wilson Bentley established a lifelong dedication to this work. Using a photographic innovation he created, Bentley was able to produce beautiful and detailed images of these short-lived wonders. This book is a natural to use with symmetry and hexagonal shapes.

Color Farm, 1990
Color Zoo, 1989 *Ehlert*

These visually motivating books can engage young children in thinking about shapes. Using cut-out overlays of circles, rectangles, ovals, triangles, and other familiar shapes, images of either farm or zoo animals are created. The reader turns the page to remove a shape, transforming the image into a new animal. Because this book reinforces shapes, animals, and colors, it is a good vocabulary development book to engage English language learners and their families.

Cubes, Cones, Cylinders and Spheres, 2000
Shapes, Shapes, Shapes, 1996
So Many Circles, So Many Squares, 1998 *Hoban*

These books without words are a collection of vivid photographs on a geometric theme. Each one can engage students of all ages in thinking about and locating shapes in the environment. It is easy to see how students can use digital cameras to create their own Hoban-like books that invite readers to seek and identify two- and three-dimensional shapes in the world around them. Student-made books are great for children to take home to their families, for students in upper grades to make for younger children, or to add to the collection in the school or classroom library.

Recommended Readings

Articles

Glass, B. (2004). Transformations and technology: What path to follow? *Mathematics Teaching in the Middle School, 9*(7), 393–397.

Glass explores compositions of transformations with his middle school students. Part of their discourse revolve around this question: Is a composition of two or more transformations the same as the single transformation that will accomplish the same thing? For those exploring transformations at the upper grades, this is a useful article.

Koester, B. A. (2003). Prisms and pyramids: Constructing three-dimensional models to build understanding. *Teaching Children Mathematics, 9*(8), 436–442.
Koester's activities and explorations with third to fifth graders involves building models using straws and pipe cleaners. The activities involve classification and definitions of shapes and also Euler's formula relating faces, vertices, and edges.

Renne, C. G. (2004). Is a rectangle a square? Developing mathematical vocabulary and conceptual understanding. *Teaching Children Mathematics, 10*(5), 258–263.
The voices of children in this article are clear examples of the difficulty that students at level-1 reasoning have in attempting to make logical conclusions about geometric properties and relationships.

Books

Findell, C. R., Small, M., Cavanagh, M., Dacey, L., Greenes, C. E., & Sheffield, L. J. (2001). *Navigating through geometry in prekindergarten–grade 2*. Reston, VA: NCTM.

Gavin, M. K., Sinelli, A. M., & St. Marie, J. (2001). *Navigating through geometry in grades 3–5*. Reston, VA: NCTM.

Pugalee, D. K., Frykholm, J., Johnson, A., Slovin, H., Malloy, C., & Preston, R. (2002). *Navigating through geometry in grades 6–8*. Reston, VA: NCTM.
Each of these three excellent books from the Navigations Series provides both a perspective on the geometry standard and also a collection of excellent activities appropriate for the grade band of the book.

Online Resources

Cutting Corners
http://illuminations.nctm.org/tools/CutTool/CutTool.asp
A cutting tool allows any one of three simple shapes to be sliced into parts along any straight line. Shapes can be rearranged, rotated, and flipped.

Geoboards
http://nlvm.usu.edu/en/nav/category_g_2_t_3.html
The NLVM library has four geoboards. The first measures areas and perimeters. The circular board has pins in a circular arrangement. The isometric board has pins in a triangular arrangement (like isometric dot paper). The coordinate board shows coordinates for each peg when the cursor is on it. It measures the slope and distance between two points joined by a band and then the perimeter and area of banded shapes.

GeoGebra
www.geogebra.org/cms
This is a free downloadable dynamic geometry software that emphasizes geometry and algebra. Like *Geometer's Sketchpad*, you can construct with points, segments, and lines.

Maze Game

www.shodor.org/interactivate/activities/coords/index.html

The maze game provides practice with coordinates. The user plots points to guide a robot through a mine field.

Mirror Tool

http://illuminations.nctm.org/ActivityDetail.aspx?ID=24

A nice tool for early investigations of mirror or line symmetry.

Space Blocks

http://nlvm.usu.edu/en/nav/frames_asid_195_g_3_t_3
.html?open=activities

This applet allows the user to create "buildings" made of cubic blocks rather easily. Use it to explore surface area.

Tangrams

http://nlvm.usu.edu/en/nav/frames_asid_268_g_1_t_3
.html

These virtual tangrams can be manipulated freely. Plus, there are 14 puzzle shapes to fill in with all 7 tangrams.

Visualizing Transformations

http://standards.nctm.org/document/eexamples/chap6/
6.4/index.htm

This four-part applet provides an excellent exploration of the three rigid-motion transformations including composition of two transformations.

Field Experience Guide Connections

This chapter includes many literature links; see Field Experience 2.6 for designing and teaching a lesson using children's literature. What van Hiele developmental level have students achieved within an area such as shapes and properties? Use Field Experience 7.2 to prepare an interview to find out! The FEG Expanded Lessons 9.17, 9.18, and 9.19 target geometric concepts for grades K–3, 5–7, and 7–8, respectively. These explorations are engaging opportunities to explore concepts of shapes and their properties.

Chapter 21

Developing Concepts of Data Analysis

Graphs and statistics bombard the public in areas such as advertising, opinion polls, reliability estimates, population trends, health risks, and progress of students in schools. We hear that the average amount of rainfall this summer is more than it was last summer or that the average American household consists of 1.86 people. We read on the U.S. Census website (www.census.gov) that the median home price in 2000 was $119,600, and in May 2008 it was $281,000. The mean home price in May 2008 was $311,300. Knowing these statistics should raise a range of questions: How were these data gathered? What was the purpose? What does it mean to have an average of 1.86 people? Why are the median and the mean for home sales so different? Which statistic makes more sense for communicating about home sales?

Statistical literacy is critical to understanding the world around us. Misuse of statistics occurs even in trustworthy sources like newspapers, where graphs are often designed to exaggerate a finding. Students in pre-K through grade 8 should have meaningful experiences with basic concepts of statistics throughout their school years. At the pre-K–grade 2 level, students can begin this understanding by learning how data can be categorized and displayed in various graphical forms. In grades 3–5, students should have many experiences collecting and organizing sets of data as well as representing data in frequency tables, bar graphs, line plots, and picture graphs. As they mature in understanding, they should be introduced to new data representations such as box-and-whisker plots, scatter plots, and stem-and-leaf plots. Students should also study measures of center—for example, median and mean (NCTM, 2006; Schrelack & Seeley, 2007).

Big Ideas

1. Statistics is its own field different from mathematics; one key difference is focus on variability of data in statistical reasoning.

2. Doing statistics involves a four-step process: formulating questions, collecting data, analyzing data, and interpreting results.

3. Data are gathered and organized in order to answer questions about the populations from which the data come. With data from only a sample of the population, inferences are made about the population.

4. Different types of graphs and other data frameworks provide different information about the data and, hence, the population from which the data were taken. The choice of graphical representation can impact how well the data are understood.

5. Measures that describe data with numbers are called *statistics*. Data can be organized in various graphical forms to visually convey information. The use of a particular graph or statistic can mediate what the data tell about the population.

6. Both graphs and statistics can provide a sense of the shape of the data, including how spread out or how clustered they are. Having a sense of the shape of data is having a big picture of the data rather than a collection of numbers.

Mathematics Content Connections

Statistics involves using data in the form of numbers and graphs to describe our world. Certainly, there are connections to the numeric areas of the curriculum. However, the connection to algebra is perhaps one of the most important mathematical connections.

- **Number Sense** (Chapter 8): Young children create graphs of class data (such as "What color socks?" or "How many buttons?") and use the graphs to talk about quantity.

- **Algebra** (Chapter 14): Algebra is used to analyze and describe relationships. Whenever data are gathered on two related variables (e.g., height and arm span, age and growth), algebra can be used to describe the relationship between the variables. The resulting relationship can then be used to predict outcomes for which no data have yet been gathered. The better that the data are approximated by the algebraic relationship or function, the more predictive value the function has.

Fractions, Decimals, and Percents (Chapters 15 and 17): Fractions, decimals, and percents are used to describe data.

Proportional Reasoning (Chapter 18): Statistical reasoning *is* proportional reasoning. When a population is sampled (a subset selected), that sample is assumed to be proportional to the larger population.

Measurement (Chapter 19): Much of the real-world data that are gathered consist of measurements. Pedagogically, measurement can be interwoven with data analysis as students make measurements to answer questions and create data to be analyzed.

What Does It Mean to Do Statistics?

A look back at Chapter 2 will find the same header about doing mathematics. Doing statistics is in fact, a different process from doing mathematics, a notion that has recently received much attention by standards documents and research (Burrill & Elliott, 2006; Franklin et al., 2005; Shaugnessy, 2003). As Richard Scheaffer, past president of the American Statistics Association notes,

> Mathematics is about numbers and their operations, generalizations and abstractions; it is about spatial configurations and their measurement, transformations, and abstractions. . . . Statistics is also about numbers—but numbers in context: these are called data. Statistics is about variables and cases, distribution and variation, purposeful design or studies, and the role of randomness in the design of studies, and the interpretation of results. (Scheaffer, 2006, pp. 310–311)

This section describes some of the big ideas regarding statistics and explains a general process for doing statistics. Each of the four steps in the process is used as a major section in the organization of this chapter.

Is It Statistics or Is It Mathematics?

Statistics and mathematics are two different fields; however, statistical questions are often asked in assessments with questions that are mathematical in nature rather than statistical. The harm in this is that students are not focusing on statistical reasoning, as shown by the following excellent exemplars from Scheaffer (2006).

Ⅱ ─────── *Pause and Reflect*

Read the questions below and code each as "doing mathematics" or "doing statistics."

1. The average weight of 50 prize-winning tomatoes is 2.36 pounds. What is the combined weight, in pounds, of these 50 tomatoes? (NAEP sample question)
   a. 0.0472　　b. 11.8　　c. 52.36　　d. 59　　e. 118

2. Joe had three test scores of 78, 76, and 74, whereas Mary had scores of 72, 82, and 74. How did Joe's average (mean) compare to Mary's average (mean) score? (TIMSS eighth-grade released item)
   a. Joe's was one point higher.
   b. Joe's was one point lower.
   c. Both averages were the same.
   d. Joe's was 2 points higher.
   e. Joe's was 2 points lower.

3. Table 21.1 gives the times each girl has recorded for seven runnings of the 100-meter dash this year. Only one girl may compete in the upcoming tournament. Which girl would you select for the tournament and why?

Table 21.1

Race Times for Three Runners							
	Race						
Runner	1	2	3	4	5	6	7
Suzie	15.2	14.8	15.0	14.7	14.3	14.5	14.5
Tanisha	15.8	15.7	15.4	15.0	14.8	14.6	14.5
Dara	15.6	15.5	14.8	15.1	14.5	14.7	14.5

Which of these involves statistical reasoning? All of them? None of them? As explained by Schaeffer, only the last is statistical in nature. The first requires knowing the formula for averages, but the task required is to work backwards through a formula—mathematical thinking, not statistical thinking. Similarly in the second problem, one must know the formula for the mean, but the question is about the computational process of using the formula. In both of these, you might notice that the context is irrelevant to the problem. The final question is statistical in nature because the situation requires analysis—graphs or averages might be used to determine a solution. The mathematics here is basic; the focus is on statistics. Notice the context is central to the question.

In statistics the context is essential to analyzing and interpreting the data (Franklin & Garfield, 2006; Franklin et al., 2005; Rossman, Chance, & Medina, 2006; Schaeffer, 2006). Looking at the spread, or shape, of data and considering the meaning of unusual data points (outliers) are determined based on the context.

Variability

The second concept that is critical and unique in statistics is variability. Statisticians must deal with variability in the data (Franklin & Garfield, 2006; Franklin et al., 2005; Rossman, Chance, & Medina, 2006; Schaeffer, 2006). Students do not have a clear understanding of variability, perhaps because the mathematical process of analyzing data dominates the data analysis phase. Shaughnessy (2006), a noted researcher on statistics education, summarized the findings on what students know about variability in the following list, starting with basic notions and progressing to more sophisticated ideas:

1. Focusing only on outliers or extremes (but not on the full distribution of the data).
2. Considering change over time (can lead into discussions of other types of variation).
3. Examining variability as the full range of data. Range is everything that occurs but doesn't reveal the frequency of different events within the range.
4. Considering variability as the likely range or expected value.
5. Looking at how far data points are from the center (e.g., the mean).
6. Looking at how far off a set of data is from some fixed value.

All of these are accessible to students in elementary and middle school, when students are engaged in doing experiments to answer questions (Shaughnessy, 2006). In order to be prepared to teach students variability beyond outliers and extremes, it is important to know about the way that variability occurs in statistics.

Variability can occur in numerous ways. The *Guidelines for Assessment and Instruction in Statistics Education* (GAISE) report (Franklin et al., 2005) discusses three levels of statistical thinking, which although developmental in nature can be roughly mapped to elementary, middle, and secondary level curriculum. The report states that the variability that should be the focus at the elementary level includes variability within a group—for example, the varying lengths of students' names, varying family sizes, and so on. When students create a bar graph of class data and compare the data collected, they are discussing the variability within a group.

At the next level, variability within a group continues, but groups of data are also considered. Students might compare the variability of fifth-graders' favorite music choices with eighth-graders' music choices, an example of variability between groups. In addition, middle school students study how the change in one variable relates to change in another variable—yes, algebra! Students analyze two variables to see whether there is a relationship (discussed in more depth in the section on scatter plots).

Another type of relevant variability in pre-K–8 is sampling variability (Franklin et al., 2005). When students flip a coin 10 times, as a sample, they may get 5 heads and 5 tails, but they also may get many other results (even 0 heads and 10 tails). This is sampling variability. The larger the sample, the more the data reflect the expected values (50 percent heads, 50 percent tails). Sampling is discussed in Chapter 22 (probability).

Finally, at the third level, students can examine natural and induced variability. For example, plants grow at different rates. When one flower naturally grows taller than the one right next to it in the garden, that is natural variability. If the two plants were in two different gardens, then other variables come into play: fertilization, amount of sunlight, amount of water, and so on, which can "induce" different growth rates. Knowing these variability terms is less important than knowing that in designing an experiment to look at one factor (e.g., sunlight), all other factors should be kept the same. This is at the heart of doing statistics (Franklin & Garfield, 2006).

Students need to understand variability. One way to help students do this is including questions on variability in the discussion of data. Friel, O'Conner, and Mamer (2006), using the context of heart rates, suggest the following questions as an example of how to get students to focus on data and variability:

- If the average heart rate for 9- to 11-year-olds is 88 beats per minute, does this mean every student this age has a heart rate of 88 beats per minute? (Note the range is actually quite large—from 60 to 110 beats per minute.)
- If we found the heart rate for everyone in the class (of 30), what might the distribution of data look like?
- If another class (of 30) was measured, would their distribution look like our class?
- Would the distribution of data from 200 students look like the data from the two classes?

The Shape of Data

A big conceptual idea in data analysis can be referred to as the *shape of data*: a sense of how data are spread out or grouped, what characteristics about the data set as a whole can be described, and what the data tell us in a global way about the population from which they are taken.

There is no single technique that can tell us what the shape of the data is. Across the pre-K–8 curriculum, students begin looking at the shape of data by examining various graphs. Different graphing techniques or types of graphs can provide a different snapshot of the data as a whole. For example, bar graphs and circle graphs (percentage graphs) each show how the data cluster in different categories. The circle graph focuses more on the relative values of this clustering whereas the bar graph adds a dimension of quantity. The choice of which and how many categories to use in these graphs will cause different pictures of the shape of the data.

Part of understanding the shape of data is being aware of how spread out or clustered the data are. In the early grades this can be discussed informally by looking at almost any graph.

For numeric data, there are statistics that tell us how data are spread. The simplest of these is the *range*. Averages (the *mean* and the *median*) tell us where the "center" of the data is. In high school students will learn about the standard deviation statistic, which is also a measure of spread. At the middle school level, a simple graphical technique called the *box-and-whisker plot* is designed to give us visual information about the spread of data.

Process of Doing Statistics

Just as learning addition involves much more than the procedure for combining, doing statistics is much more than the computational procedures for finding the mean or the process of creating a circle graph. To engage students *meaningfully* in learning and doing statistics, they should be involved in the full process, from asking and defining questions to interpreting results. This broad approach provides a framework and purpose under which students learn how to create graphs, compute the mean, and analyze data in other ways. This chapter is organized around this process, which is presented in Figure 21.1.

I. Formulate Questions
- Clarify the problem at hand
- Formulate one (or more) questions that can be answered with data

II. Collect Data
- Design a plan to collect appropriate data
- Employ the plan to collect the data

III. Analyze Data
- Select appropriate graphical and numerical methods
- Use these methods to analyze the data

IV. Interpret Results
- Interpret the analysis
- Relate the interpretation to the original question

Figure 21.1 Process of doing statistics.
Source: Franklin, C., Kader, G., Mewborn, D., Moreno, J., Peck, R., Perry, M., & Scheaffer, R. (2005, August). *Guidelines for Assessment and Instruction in Statistics Education (GAISE) Report: A Pre-K–12 Curriculum Framework*, p. 11. Reprinted with permission. Copyright 2005 by the American Statistical Association. All rights reserved.

Formulating Questions

Statistics is about more than making graphs and analyzing data. It includes both asking and answering questions about our world. The first goal in the Data Analysis and Probability standard of *Principles and Standards* says that students should "formulate questions that can be addressed with data and collect, organize, and display relevant data to answer them" (NCTM, 2000, p. 48). Notice that data collection should be for a purpose, to answer a question, just as in the real world. Then the analysis of data actually adds information about some aspect of our world, just as political pollsters, advertising agencies, market researchers, census takers, wildlife managers, medical researchers, and hosts of others gather data to answer questions.

Students should be given opportunities to generate their own questions, decide on appropriate data to help answer these questions, and determine methods of collecting the data. For example, in a second-grade class studied by Susan Jo Russell (lead author of *Investigations*), a student wanted to know how many houses were on her street (Russell, 2006). Or a teacher may ask, "How many sisters and brothers do you have?" Whether the question is teacher initiated or student initiated, students should engage in conversations about how well defined the question is. In the house example, students wondered whether they should include houses that weren't finished yet or whether apartments counted. In the second case, there is a need to discuss half-siblings, for example.

When students formulate the questions they want to ask, the data they gather become more meaningful. How they organize the data and the techniques for analyzing them have a purpose.

Ideas for Questions

Often the need to gather data will come from the class naturally in the course of discussion or from questions arising in other content areas. Science, of course, is full of measurements and, thus, abounds in data requiring analysis. Social studies is also full of opportunities to pose questions requiring data collection. The next few sections suggest some additional ideas.

Classroom Questions. Students want to learn about themselves, their families and pets, measures such as arm span or time to get to school, their likes and dislikes, and so on. The easiest questions to deal with are those that can be answered by each class member contributing one piece of data. Here are a few ideas:

- *Favorites:* TV shows, games, movies, ice cream, video games, sports teams, music CDs. (When there are lots of possibilities, suggest that students restrict the number of choices.)
- *Numbers:* Number of pets, sisters, or brothers; hours watching TV or hours of sleep; bedtime; time spent on the computer.
- *Measures:* Height, arm span, area of foot, long-jump distance, shadow length, seconds to run around the track, minutes spent on the bus.

Beyond One Classroom. The questions in the previous section are designed for students to contribute data about themselves. These questions can be expanded by asking,

"How would this compare to another class?" Comparison questions are a good way to help students focus on the data they have collected and the variability within that data (Russell, 2006). As children get older, they can begin to think about various populations and differences between them. For example, how are fifth graders similar or different from middle school students? Students might examine questions concerning boys versus girls, adults or teachers versus students, or categories of workers or college graduates. These situations involve issues of sampling and making generalizations and comparisons. In addition, students can ask questions about things beyond the classroom. Discussions about communities provide a good way to integrate social studies and mathematics.

The newspaper suggests all sorts of data-related questions. For example, how many full-page ads occur on different days of the week? What types of stories are on the front page? Which comics are really for kids and which are not?

Science is another area where questions can be asked and data gathered. For example, what is the width of oak leaves that fall to the ground. How many times do different types of balls bounce when each is dropped from the same height? How many days does it take for different types of bean, squash, and pea seeds to germinate when kept in moist paper towels?

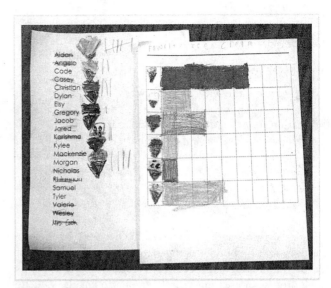

Figure 21.2 Kindergartners collect data on ice cream flavor choices, keeping track of who they have surveyed, tallying the data, and then creating a horizontal bar graph.

Source: Cook, C. D. (2008). "I Scream, You Scream: Data Analysis with Kindergartners." *Teaching Children Mathematics, 14*(9), p. 539. Reprinted with permission. Copyright © 2008 by the National Council of Teachers of Mathematics, Inc. www.nctm.org. All rights reserved.

Data Collection

Gathering data is not easy for students, especially young students. In a first-grade class, a teacher asked students to gather data on "Are you 6?" Upon receiving the prompt, 18 eager students began asking others in the class if they were 6 and tallying the yes and no responses. The problem? They had no idea whom they had asked more than once or whom they had not asked at all. This provided an excellent entry into a discussion about how statisticians must gather data. Carolyn Cook, a kindergarten teacher, asked her students to help think of an organized manner to gather the data from their classmates on favorite ice cream flavors. These students decided a class list (see Figure 21.2) would allow them to keep track (Cook, 2008).

Gathering data also must take into consideration variability. Young children can understand that asking a group of first graders their favorite TV show will produce different answers than asking a group of fifth graders. Answers also may vary based on the day the question is asked or whether a particular show has been recently discussed.

For older students (GAISE recommends this at the second level of statistical thinking), planning data collection includes gathering data from more than one

classroom to seek a more representative sample, or even using random sampling. In fact, for middle school students, it is important that they engage in the whole process of doing statistics, including designing an experiment in which most variables (induced) are kept the same so that one variable can be analyzed.

Using Existing Data Sources

Data do not have to be collected by survey; data abound in various places, such as the following sources of print and Web data.

Print Resources. Newspapers, almanacs, sports record books, maps, and various government publications are possible sources of data that may be used to answer student questions.

Children's literature is an excellent and engaging resource. Young students can tally words in a repeating verse like "Hickory, Dickory, Dock" (Niezgoda & Moyer-Packenham, 2005). Similarly, books like *Good Night Moon* (Brown, 1947) or *Green Eggs and Ham* (Dr. Seuss, 1960) have many repeated words or phrases. Nonfiction literature can be a source of data, especially for older students. For example, the *Book of Lists: Fun Facts, Weird Trivia, and Amazing Lists on Nearly Everything You Need to Know!* (Buckley & Stremme, 2006) reports on various statistics and includes surveys at the end of every section. Books on sports, such as *A Negro League Scrapbook* (Weatherform, 2005), can have very interesting statistics about historic periods that students can explore and compare.

myeducationlab

Go to the Building Teaching Skills and Dispositions section of Chapter 21 of MyEducationLab. Click on Videos and watch the video entitled "**Food Survey Lesson**" to see a class collect, display, and analyze data.

Websites.   Students may be interested in facts about another country as a result of a social studies unit or a country in the news. Olympic records in various events over the years or data related to space flight are other examples of topics around which student questions may be formulated. For these and hundreds of other questions, data can be found on the World Wide Web. Here are four websites with a lot of interesting data.

- U.S. Census Bureau (www.census.gov): This website contains copious statistical information by state, county, or voting district.
- Economic Research Service, USDA (www.ers.usda.gov/data/foodconsumption): Here you can find wonderful data sets on the availability and consumption of hundreds of foods. Per capita estimates on a yearly basis often go back as far as 1909.
- The World Fact Book (https://www.cia.gov/library/publications/the-world-factbook/index.html): This website provides demographic information for every nation in the world, including population; age distributions; death and birth rates; and information on the economy, government, transportation, and geography. Maps are included as well.
- Internet Movie Database (www.imdb.com): This website offers information about movies of all genres.

Data Analysis: Classification

Classification involves *making decisions about how to categorize things*, a basic activity that is fundamental to data analysis. In order to formulate questions and decide how to represent data that have been gathered, decisions must be made about how things might be categorized. Young children might group farm animals, for example, by number of legs; by type of product they provide; by those that work, provide food, or are pets; by size or color; by the type of food they eat; and so on. Each of these groupings is based on a different attribute of the animals.

Young children need experiences with categorizing things in different ways in order to learn to make sense of real-world data. Attribute activities are explicitly designed to develop this flexible reasoning about the characteristics of data.

Attribute Materials

Attribute materials can be any set of objects that lend themselves to being sorted and classified in different ways—for example, seashells, leaves, the children themselves, or the set of the children's shoes. The *attributes* are the ways that the materials can be sorted. For example, hair color, height, and gender are attributes of children. Each attribute has

a number of different *values*: for example, blond, brown, black, or red (for the attribute of hair color); tall or short (for height); male or female (for gender). An example of a teacher-made attribute set is displayed in Figure 21.3. These cards are available in Blackline Master 59.

Commercially available attribute blocks are sets of 60 plastic attribute materials, with each piece having four attributes: color (red, yellow, blue), shape (circle, triangle, rectangle, square, hexagon), size (big, little), and thickness (thick, thin). The specific values, number of values, or number of attributes that a set may have is not important.

 "Organizing data into categories should begin with informal sorting experiences, such as helping to put away groceries. . . . Young children should continue activities that focus on attributes of objects and data so that by the second grade, they can sort and classify simultaneously, using more than one attribute" (pp. 109–110). ◆

Activities with Attribute Materials.   Most attribute activities are best done with young children sitting on the floor in a large circle where all can see and have access to the materials. Kindergarten classes can have fun with simple Venn diagram activities. With the use of words such as *and*,

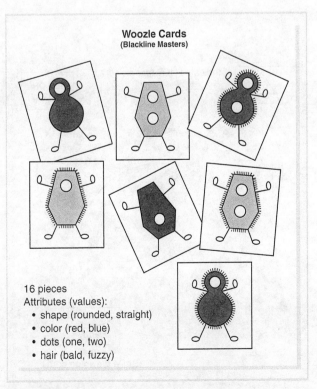

Woozle Cards
(Blackline Masters)

16 pieces
Attributes (values):
- shape (rounded, straight)
- color (red, blue)
- dots (one, two)
- hair (bald, fuzzy)

Figure 21.3 Woozle Cards can be duplicated on card stock colored with red and blue bodies, and then laminated and cut into individual cards (see Blackline Master 59).

or, and *not,* the loop activities become quite challenging, even for fifth graders.

Activity 21.1

What about "Both"

Give children two large loops of yarn or string and attribute blocks. Direct them to put all the red pieces inside one string and all triangles inside the other. Let the children try to resolve the difficulty of what to do with the red triangles. When the notion of overlapping the strings to create an area common to both loops is clear, more challenging activities can be explored.

Affix or draw labels on each loop and have students take turns placing pieces in the appropriate regions. As shown in Figure 21.4, the labels need not be restricted to single attributes. If a piece does not fit in any region, it is placed outside all of the loops.

It is important to introduce labels for negative attributes such as "not red" or "not small." Also important is the eventual use of *and* and *or* connectives, as in "red and square" or "big or happy." This use of *and, or,* and *not* significantly widens children's classification schemes.

An engaging and challenging activity is to infer how things have been classified when the loops are not labeled.

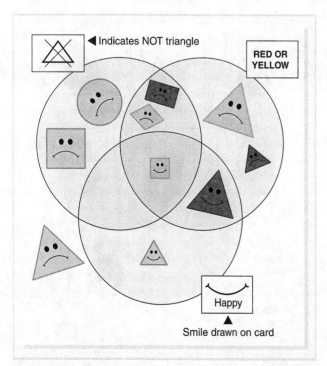

Figure 21.4 A Venn Diagram activity with attribute pieces. A rule is written on each card.

The following activities require students to make and test conjectures about how things are being classified.

Activity 21.2

Guess My Rule

For this activity, try using students instead of shapes as attribute "pieces." Decide on an attribute of your students such as "blue jeans" or "stripes on clothing," but do not tell your rule to the class. Silently look at one child at a time and move the child to the left or right according to this attribute rule. After a number of students have been sorted, have the next child come up and ask students to predict which group he or she belongs in. Before the rule is articulated, continue the activity for a while so that others in the class will have an opportunity to determine the rule. This same activity can be done with virtually any materials that can be sorted, such as students' shoes, shells, or buttons.

Activity 21.3

Hidden Labels

Select label cards for the loops of string, and place the cards face down. Ask students to select a piece for you to place. Begin to sort pieces according to the turned-down labels. As you sort, have students try to determine what the labels are for each of the loops. Let students who think they have guessed the labels try to place a piece in the proper loop, but avoid having them guess the labels aloud. Students who think they know the labels can be asked to "play teacher" and respond to the guesses of the others. Point out that one way to test an idea about the labels is to select pieces that you think might go in a particular section. Do not turn the cards up until most students have figured out the rule. With simple one-value labels and only two loops, this activity can easily be played in kindergarten.

"Guess My Rule" can and should be repeated with real-world materials connected to students' current explorations. For example, if you were doing a unit on animals in the backyard, you can use pictures of animals (see Figure 21.5). The loops used with the attribute materials provide a first form of data presentation. The class can "graph" data about themselves by placing information in loops with labels. A graph of "Our Pets" might consist of a picture of each student's pet or favorite stuffed animal (in lieu of a pet) and be affixed to a wall display showing how the pets were classified.

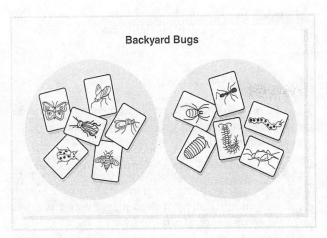

Backyard Bugs

Figure 21.5 Can you guess the rule that was used to sort these bugs?

Data Analysis: Graphical Representations

How data are organized should be directly related to the question that caused you to collect the data in the first place. For example, suppose that students want to know how many pockets they have on their clothing (Burns, 1996; Russell et al., 2007). Each student in the room counts his or her pockets and the data are collected.

Pause and Reflect

If your second-grade class had collected these data, what methods might you suggest they use for organizing and graphing them? Is one of your ideas better than others for answering the question about how many pockets?

If a large bar graph is made with a bar for every student, that will certainly tell how many pockets each student has. However, is it the best way to answer the question? If the data were categorized by number of pockets, then a graph showing the number of students with two pockets, three pockets, and so on will easily show which number of pockets is most common and how the number of pockets varies across the class.

Students should be involved in deciding how they want to represent their data. However, for children lacking experience with the various methods of picturing data, you can suggest alternatives.

Once students have made the display, they can discuss its value. Analyzing data that are numerical (number of pockets) versus categorical (color of socks) is an added challenge for students as they struggle to make sense of the graphs (Russell, 2006). If for example, the graph has seven stickers above the five, students may think that five people have seven pockets or seven people have five pockets.

The emphasis or goal of this instruction should be to help children see that graphs and charts tell about information and that different types of representations tell different things about the same data. The value of having students actually construct their own graphs is not so much that they learn the techniques but that they are personally invested in the data and that they learn how a graph conveys information. Once a graph is constructed, the most important activity is discussing what it tells the people who see it, especially those who were not involved in making the graph. Discussions about graphs of real data that the children have themselves been involved in gathering will help them analyze and interpret other graphs and charts that they see in newspapers and on TV.

What we should *not* do is get overly anxious about the tedious details of graph construction. The issues of analysis and communication are your agendas and are much more important than the technique! In the real world, technology will take care of details.

Students should construct graphs or charts by hand and with technology. First, you can encourage students to make charts and graphs that make sense to them and that they feel communicate the information they wish to convey. Young students may feel more personally invested in their work when creating by hand and not distracted by the techniques of technology. The intent is to get the students involved in accurately communicating a message about their data.

Technology use is very common in graphical representations. Computer programs and graphing calculators can provide various graphical displays with very little effort. Discussion can then focus on the information that each display provides. Students can make their own selections among different graphs and justify their choice based on their own intended purposes. ◆

Bar Graphs and Tally Charts

Bar graphs and tally charts are some of the first ways to group and present data and are especially useful in grades pre-K–3. At this early level, bar graphs should be made so that each bar consists of countable parts such as squares, objects, tallies, or pictures of objects. Figure 21.6 illustrates a few techniques that can be used to make a graph quickly with the whole class.

A "real graph" uses the actual objects being graphed. Examples include types of shoes, seashells, and books. Each item can be placed in a square or on a floor tile so that comparisons and counts are easily made.

Picture graphs use a drawing of some sort that represents what is being graphed. Students can make their own drawings, or you can duplicate drawings to be colored or cut out to suit particular needs.

Symbolic graphs use something like squares, blocks, tallies, or Xs to represent the items being counted in the graph. An easy idea is to use sticky notes as elements of a graph. These can be stuck directly to the chalkboard or other chart and rearranged if needed.

Recall that analyzing data in this way is step 3 of the process of doing statistics. A question is posed and data are collected based on the categories that will be graphed. Figure 21.6 illustrates two quick ways to gather information so that it is already displayed in a bar, combining steps 2 and 3 of doing statistics. A class of 25 to 30 students can make a graph in less than 10 minutes, leaving ample time to use it for questions and observations.

Once a graph has been constructed, engage the class in a discussion of what information the graph tells or conveys. "What can you tell about our class by looking at this shoe graph?" Graphs convey factual information (more people wear sneakers than any other kind of shoe) and also provide opportunities to make inferences that are not directly observable in the graph (kids in this class do not like to wear leather shoes). The difference between actual facts and inferences is an important idea in graph construction and is also an important idea in science. Older students can examine graphs found in newspapers or magazines and discuss the *facts* in the graphs and the *message* that may have been intended by the person who made the graph.

Circle Graphs

Typically, we think of circle graphs as showing percentages and, as such, these would probably not be appropriate for primary students. However, notice in Figure 21.7 that the circle graph could be set up to only indicate the number of data points (in that case, students) in each of five categories. Many computer graphing programs will create a similar graph. An understanding of percentages is not required when the computer creates the graph.

Notice also that the circle graph shows information that is not as easily available from the other graphs. For example, when comparisons are made between two populations of very different size, the circle graph offers visual ratios that allow for these comparisons. In Figure 21.7, the two graphs shows the percentages of students with different numbers of siblings. One graph is based on classroom data and the other on schoolwide data. Because circle graphs display ratios rather than quantities, the small set of class data can be compared to the large set of school data, which could not be done with bar graphs.

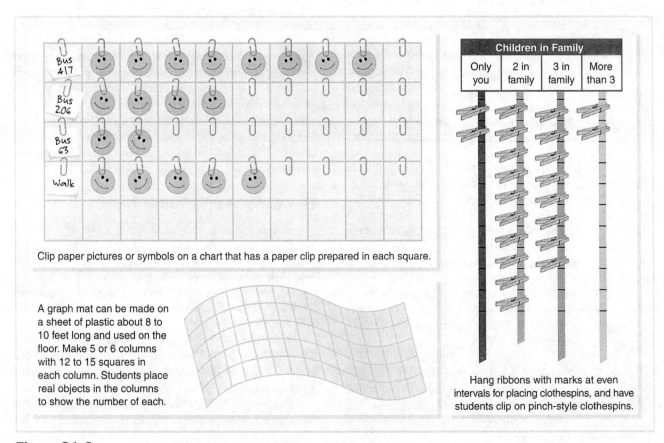

Clip paper pictures or symbols on a chart that has a paper clip prepared in each square.

A graph mat can be made on a sheet of plastic about 8 to 10 feet long and used on the floor. Make 5 or 6 columns with 12 to 15 squares in each column. Students place real objects in the columns to show the number of each.

Hang ribbons with marks at even intervals for placing clothespins, and have students clip on pinch-style clothespins.

Figure 21.6 Some ideas for quick graphs that can be used again and again.

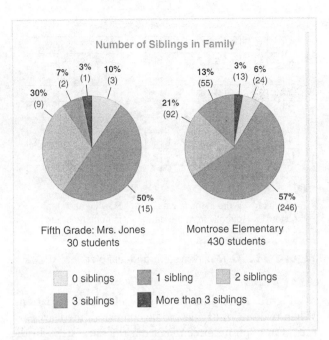

Number of Siblings in Family

Fifth Grade: Mrs. Jones
30 students

7% (2)   3% (1)   10% (3)
30% (9)
50% (15)

Montrose Elementary
430 students

13% (55)   3% (13)   6% (24)
21% (92)
57% (246)

☐ 0 siblings   ☐ 1 sibling   ☐ 2 siblings
☐ 3 siblings   ☐ More than 3 siblings

Figure 21.7 Circle graphs show ratios of part to whole and can be used to compare ratios.

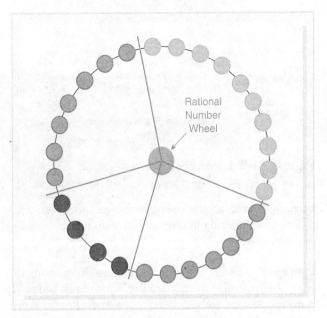

Rational Number Wheel

Figure 21.8 A human circle graph: Students are arranged in a circle, with string stretched between them to show the divisions.

Easily Made Circle Graphs. Circle graphs of the students in your room can be made quickly and quite dramatically. Suppose, for example, that each student picked his or her favorite basketball team in the NCAA tournament's "Final Four." Line up all of the students in the room so that students favoring the same team are together. Now form the entire group into a circle of students. Tape the ends of four long strings to the floor in the center of the circle, and extend them to the circle at each point where the teams change. Voilà! A very nice circle graph with no measuring and no percentages. If you copy and cut out a rational number wheel (see Blackline Master 28) and place it on the center of the circle, the strings will show approximate percentages for each part of your graph (see Figure 21.8). Percent necklaces as described in Chapter 17 or a loop with 100 pieces of colored cereal, like Froot Loops, can be used in a similar fashion.

Another easy approach to circle graphs is similar to the human circle graph. Begin by having students make a bar graph of the data. Once complete, cut out the bars themselves, and tape them together end to end. Next, tape the two ends together to form a circle. Estimate where the center of the circle is, draw lines to the points where different bars meet, and trace around the full loop. You can estimate percentages using the rational number wheel or percent necklace as before.

Determining Percentages. If students have experienced either of the two methods just described, using their own calculations to make circle graphs will make more sense. The numbers in each category are added to form the total

or whole. (That's the same as taping all of the strips together or lining up the students.) By dividing each of the parts by the whole with a calculator, students will find the decimals and convert to percents. It is an interesting proportional problem for students to convert between percents and degrees, since one is out of 100 and the other out of 360. It is helpful to start students with obvious values, like 50 percent, 25 percent, and 10 percent before moving to more difficult values.

As you evaluate students in the area of graphing, it is important not to focus undue attention on the skills of constructing a graph. It is more important to think about the choice of graphs that the students make to help answer their questions or complete their projects. Your goal is for students to understand that a graph helps answer a question and provides a picture of the data. Different graphs tell us different things about the data.

Students should write about their graphs, explaining what the graph tells and why they selected that type of graph to illustrate the data. Use this information for your assessment. ◆

Continuous Data Graphs

Bar graphs or picture graphs are useful for illustrating categories of data that have no numeric ordering—for example, colors or TV shows. When data are grouped along a continuous scale, they should be ordered along a number line. Examples of such information include temperatures that

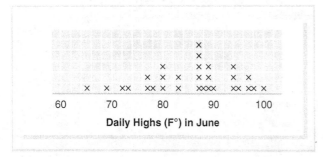

Figure 21.9 Line plot of temperatures.

occur over time, height or weight over age, and percentages of test takers scoring in different intervals along the scale of possible scores.

Line Plots. *Line plots* are counts of things along a numeric scale. To make a line plot, a number line is drawn and an X is made above the corresponding value on the line for every corresponding data element. One advantage of a line plot is that every piece of data is shown on the graph. It is also a very easy type of graph for students to make. It is essentially a bar graph with a potential bar for every possible value. A simple example is shown in Figure 21.9.

Stem-and-Leaf Plots. *Stem-and-leaf plots* are a form of bar graph in which numeric data are graphed and displayed as a list. By way of example, suppose that the American League baseball teams had posted the following record of wins over the past season:

Baltimore	45	Tampa Bay	91
Boston	94	Minnesota	98
Los Angeles	85	New York	100
Chicago	72	Oakland	101
Cleveland	91	Seattle	48
Detroit	102	Toronto	64
Kansas City	96	Texas	65

If the data are to be grouped by tens, list the tens digits in order and draw a line to the right, as shown in Figure 21.10(a). These form the "stem" of the graph. Next, go through the list of scores, and write the ones digits next to the appropriate tens digit, as shown in Figure 21.10(b). These are the "leaves." The process of making the graph groups the data for you. Furthermore, every piece of data can be retrieved from the graph. (Notice that stem-and-leaf plots are best made on graph paper so that each digit takes up the same amount of space.) The graph can be quickly rewritten, ordering each leaf from least to most, as shown in Figure 21.10(c).

Stem-and-leaf graphs are not limited to two-digit data. For example, if the data ranged from 600 to 1300, the stem could be the numerals from 6 to 13 and the leaves made of two-digit numbers separated by commas.

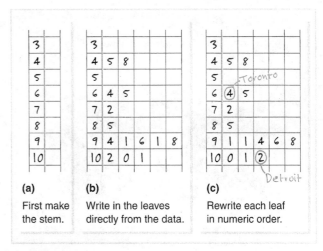

Figure 21.10 Making a stem-and-leaf plot.

Figure 21.11 illustrates two additional variations. When two sets of data are to be compared, the leaves can extend in opposite directions from the same stem. In the same example, notice that the data are grouped by fives instead of tens. When plotting 62, the 2 is written next to the 6; for 67, the 7 is written next to the dot below the 6.

Notice that the stem-and-leaf plot in Figure 21.11 clearly shows the shape of the data. You can observe how the data spread and how they cluster. From observation, students can find the range, median, mode, and any outliers. In Figure 21.11, again using rows grouped by fives instead of by tens illustrates the spread of the

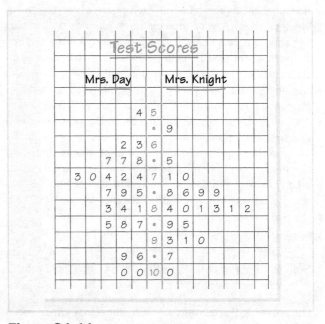

Figure 21.11 Stem-and-leaf plots can be used to compare two sets of data.

data, perhaps to illustrate particular grades (e.g., B from B+). Determining how to set up the stem-and-leaf plot depends on the context and on the question being asked.

Histograms. A *histogram* is a form of bar graph in which the categories are consecutive equal intervals along a numeric scale. The height or length of each bar is determined by the number of data elements falling into that particular interval. Histograms are not difficult in concept but can cause problems for the students constructing them. What is the appropriate interval to use for the bar width? What is a good scale to use for the length of the bars? That all of the data must be grouped and counted within each interval causes further difficulty. Figure 21.12 shows a histogram for the same temperature data used in Figure 21.9. Notice how similar the two displays are in illustrating the spread and clustering of data. Histograms can be created with graphing calculators or by computer software, making the process of creation immediate.

Line Graphs. A *line graph* is used when there is a numeric value associated with equally spaced points along a continuous number scale. Points are plotted to represent two related pieces of data, and a line is drawn to connect the points. For example, a line graph might be used to show how the length of a flagpole shadow changed from one hour to the next during the day. The horizontal scale would be time, and the vertical scale would be the length of the shadow. Discrete points can be plotted and straight lines drawn connecting them. In the previous example, a shadow was present at all times, but its length did not jump or drop from one plotted value to the other. It changed continuously as suggested by the graph. See the example in Figure 21.13 for a line graph on temperature change. Line graphs were discussed thoroughly in Chapter 14.

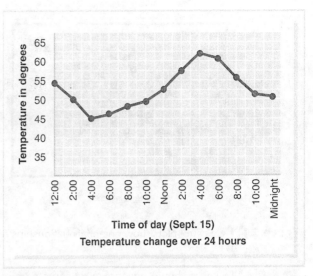

Figure 21.13 Line graph of one day's temperatures.

Scatter Plots

Data are often analyzed to search for or demonstrate relationships between two sets of data or phenomena. For example, what are the relationships, if any, between time spent watching television and overall grades?

All sorts of real situations exist in which we are interested in relationships between two variables or two numeric phenomena. How far does a toy car roll beyond an inclined plane as the angle of the plane varies? Is there a relationship between the air in a balloon and the time it takes to deflate? Such data are generally gathered from some sort of experiment that is set up and observed, with measurements taken.

Data that may be related are gathered in pairs. For example, if you were going to examine the possible relationship between hours of TV watched and grades, each person in the survey or sample would produce a pair of numbers, one for TV time and one for grade point average.

Data involving two variables can be plotted on a *scatter plot*, a graph of points on a coordinate grid with each axis representing one of the two variables. Each pair of numbers from the two sets of data, when plotted, produces a visual image of the data as well as a hint concerning any possible relationships. Suppose that the following information was gathered from 25 eighth-grade boys: height in inches, weight in pounds, and number of letters in their last name. The two graphs in Figure 21.14 show two possibilities. Graph (a) is a scatter plot of height to weight, and graph (b) is a plot of name length to weight.

As you would expect, the boys' weights seem to increase as their heights increase. However, the relationship is far from perfect. There is no reason to expect any relationship between name length and weight, and indeed the dots appear to be almost randomly distributed.

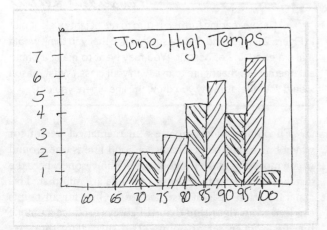

Figure 21.12 Histogram of June high temperatures.

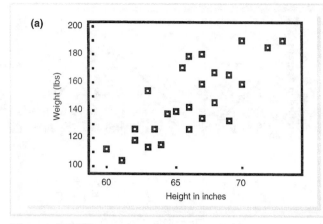
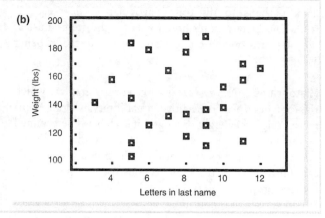

Figure 21.14 Scatter plots show potential relationships or lack of relationships.

 NCTM Standards "Teachers should encourage students to plot many data sets and look for relationships in the [scatter] plots; computer graphing software and graphing calculators can be very helpful in this work. Students should see a range of examples in which plotting data sets suggests linear relationships, and no apparent relationships at all" (p. 253). ◆

Best-Fit Lines. If your scatter plot indicates a relationship, it can be simply described in words. "As boys get taller, they tend to get heavier." This is correct but not particularly useful. What exactly is the relationship? If I knew the height of a boy, could I predict what his weight might be based on this information? Like much of statistical analysis, the value of a statistic is to predict what has not yet been observed. We poll a small sample of voters before an election to predict how the full population will vote. Here, can a sample of 30 students predict the weights of other students? The line of best fit helps students develop conjectures.

The relationship in these cases is not a number like a mean or a standard deviation but rather a line or curve. Is there a line that can be drawn through the scatter plot that represents the "best" approximation of all of the dots and reflects the observed trend? If the scatter plot seems to indicate a steadily increasing or steadily decreasing relationship (as in the height–weight graph), you would probably try to find a straight line that approximates the dots. Sometimes the plot will indicate a curved relationship, in which case you might try to draw a smooth curve like a parabola to approximate the dots.

What Determines Best Fit? From a strictly visual standpoint, the line you select defines the observed relationship and could be used to predict other values not in the data set. The more closely the dots in the scatter plot hug the line you select, the greater the confidence you would have in the predictive value of the line. Certainly you could try to

draw a straight line somewhere in the name length–weight graph, but you would not have much faith in its predictive capability because the dots would be quite dispersed from any line you might draw.

Activity **21.4**

Best-Fit Line

Once students have collected related data and prepared a scatter plot, duplicate an accurate version of the plot for each group of students. Provide the groups with an uncooked piece of spaghetti to use as a line. The task is to tape the line on the plot so that it is the "best" line to represent the relationship in the dots. Furthermore, the students are to develop a rationale for why they positioned the line as they did.

Using an overhead transparency of the plot, compare the lines chosen by various groups and their rationales.

⏸ ————————— *Pause and Reflect*

Before reading further, return to the height–weight plot in Figure 21.14(a) and draw a straight line that you think would make a good line of best fit. (You may want to make a photo enlargement of that figure to use with your class.) What reason would you offer for why you drew the line where you did?

Encourage students to use a "mathematical" reason for why a line might be best. Since a good line is one around which most dots cluster, a good-fitting line is one where the distances from all of the dots to the line are minimal. This general notion of least distance to the line for all points can lead to an algorithm that will always produce a unique line for a given set of points. Two such algorithms are well known and used in statistics. The more complicated approach is called the *least squares regression* line. It is an algebraic procedure that is not accessible to middle grade students and is also rather tedious to compute. The second algorithm produces what is called the *median-median* line, which is easier to determine. It basically involves dividing the data into three sets and finding the medians of each. The medians are plotted and further manipulated to find a best-fit line. More specific information can be found by online searching.

Scatter plots and best-fit lines are also discussed in the section on functions in Chapter 14. The connection among the real world, statistics, and algebraic ideas is a valuable one to make.

 Data analysis is an area of the curriculum in which technology really changes the way we teach. In the past, the emphasis was on *how* to create the graph and *how* to compute the statistic. Students had to labor over graph paper, drawing scales, labeling axes, coloring the graphs, and so on. Today, every graphical technique and every statistic mentioned in this chapter is readily available in a variety of technologies, with the possible exception of stem-and-leaf plots. With the help of technology, the focus of instruction in data analysis can and should shift to the big ideas of using graphs and statistics: to describe data, to get a sense of the shape of data, to answer questions with data, and to communicate this information to others.

Spreadsheets will compute any statistic for columns or rows of data. If the data are changed, the statistics change instantly. Spreadsheets also make very nice bar graphs, line graphs, and circle graphs. Teachers should also check to see if the publisher of their textbook offers graphing software.

The graphing calculator puts data analysis technology in the hands of every student. The TI-73 calculator is designed for middle grade students. It will produce eight different kinds of plots or graphs, including circle graphs, bar graphs, and picture graphs and will compute and graph best-fit lines.

An argument can be made for having students do some graphing and computing of statistics without technology. Appropriate methods have been suggested in this chapter. However, the intent of by-hand methods should always be to analyze the question posed and interpret results. ◆

Data Analysis: Measures of Center

Although graphs provide visual images of data, measures of the data are a different and important way to describe data. The most common numerical descriptions of a set of data relate to the spread (the *range*) and the center (a *mean*, *median*, or *mode*), and dispersion within the range (the *variance* or *dispersion*). Students can get an idea of the importance of these statistics by exploring the ideas informally.

Averages

The term *average* is heard quite frequently in everyday usage. Sometimes it refers to an exact arithmetic average, as in "the average daily rainfall." Sometimes it is used quite loosely, as in "She is about average height." In either situation, an average is a single number or measure that is descriptive of a larger collection of numbers. If your test average is 92, it is assumed that somehow all of your test scores are reflected by this number.

The *mean*, *median*, and *mode* are specific types of averages, also called *measures of center* or *measures of central tendency*. The *mode* is the value that occurs most frequently in the data set.

The *mean* is computed by adding all of the numbers in the set and dividing the sum by the number of elements added.

The *median* is the middle value in an ordered set of data. Half of all values lie at or above the median and half at or below. The median is easier to understand and to compute and is not affected, as the mean is, by one or two extremely large or extremely small values outside the range of the rest of the data. Median is also more accessible to elementary age students. Many researchers and curriculum developers find median is appropriate for upper elementary, but that mean should be delayed until middle school (Russell, 2006). *Curriculum Focal Points* places descriptive statistics as a focus in eighth grade, integrated with number and algebra (NCTM, 2006).

As mentioned earlier, the context in statistics is important. The context of a situation will determine whether the mode, mean, or median is the measure you want to use. For example, in reporting home prices (see p. 436), the median is quite different from the mean, with the mean being higher. Which better portrays the cost of housing? Very expensive homes can drive the mean up, so typically the median is a more common measure for describing the center of housing costs. If a travel agent gathered data on the number of days that families usually travel as part of planning a promotional vacation package, the agent would be more interested in the mode, because the other measures would not be as helpful in answering the question.

Understanding the Mean: Two Interpretations

There are actually two different ways to think about the mean. First, it is a number that represents what all of the data items would be if they were leveled out. In this sense, the mean represents all of the data items. Statisticians prefer to think of the mean as a central balance point. This concept of the mean is more in keeping with the notion of a measure of the "center" of the data or a measure of central tendency. Both concepts are discussed in the following sections.

Leveling Interpretation.   Suppose that the average number of family members for the students in your class is 5. One way to interpret this is to think about distributing the entire collection of moms, dads, sisters, and brothers to each of the students so that each would have a "family" of the same size. To say that you have an average score of 93 for the four tests in your class is like spreading the total of all of your points evenly across the four tests. It is as if each student had the same family size and each test score were the same, but the totals matched the actual distributions. This concept of the mean has the added benefit that it connects to the algorithm for computing the mean.

Activity 21.5

Leveling the Bars

Have students make a bar graph of some data using plastic connecting cubes. Choose a situation with 5 or 6 values. For example, the graph in Figure 21.15 shows prices for six toys. The task for students is to use the graph itself to determine what the price would be if all of the toys were the same price, assuming that the total for all the toys remained the same. Students will use various techniques to rearrange the cubes in the graph but will eventually create six equal bars, possibly with some leftovers that could mentally be distributed in fractional amounts.

Explain to students that the size of the leveled bars is the *mean* of the data—the amount that each item would cost if all items cost the same amount but the total of the prices remained fixed.

Follow "Leveling the Bars" with the next activity to help students develop an algorithm for finding the mean.

Activity 21.6

The Mean Foot

Pose the following question: What is the mean length of our feet in inches? Have each student cut a strip of adding machine tape that matches the length of his or her foot. Students record their names and the length of their feet in inches on the strips. Suggest that before finding a mean for the class, you will first get means for smaller groups. Put students into groups of four, six, or eight students. (Groups of five or seven

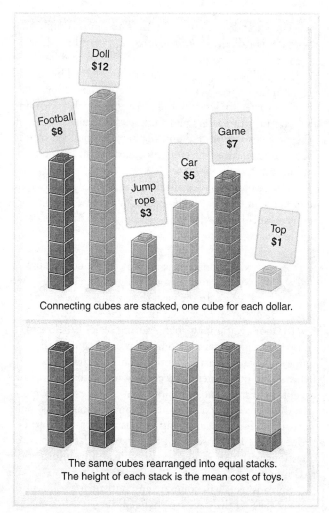

Connecting cubes are stacked, one cube for each dollar.

The same cubes rearranged into equal stacks. The height of each stack is the mean cost of toys.

Figure 21.15 Understanding the mean as a leveling of the data.

will prove to be problematic.) In each group, have the students tape their foot strips end to end. The task for each group is to come up with a method of finding the mean without using any of the lengths written on the strips. They can only use the combined strip. Each group will share their method with the class. From this work, they will devise a method for determining the mean for the whole class.

⏸ ─────────── *Pause and Reflect*

Before reading on, what is a method that the students could use in "The Mean Foot"?

─────────────────────────────

To evenly distribute the inches for each student's foot among the members of the group, they can fold the strip into equal parts so that there are as many sections as students in the group. Then they can measure the length of any one part.

How can you find the mean for the whole class? Suppose there are 23 students in the class. Using the strips already taped together, make one very long strip for the whole class. It is not reasonable to fold this long strip into 23 equal sections. But if you wanted to know how long the resulting strip would be, how could that be done? The total length of the strip is the sum of the lengths of the 23 individual foot strips. To find the length of one section if the strip were actually folded in 23 parts, simply divide by 23. In fact, students can mark off "mean feet" along the strip. There should be very close to 23 equal-length "feet." This dramatically illustrates the algorithm for finding the mean.

Balance Point Interpretation.   Statisticians think about the mean as a point on a number line where the data on either side of the point are balanced. To help think about the mean in this way, it is useful to think about the data placed on a line plot. What is important is not how many pieces of data are on either side of the mean or balance point but the distances of data from the mean.

To illustrate, draw a number line on the board, and arrange eight sticky notes above the number 3 as shown in Figure 21.16(a). Each sticky note represents one family. The notes are positioned on the line to indicate how many pets are owned by the family. Stacked up like this would indicate that all families have the same number of pets. The mean is three pets. But different families are likely to have different numbers of pets. So we could think of eight families with a range of numbers of pets. Some may have zero pets, and some may have as many as ten or even more. How could you change the number of pets for these eight families so that the mean remains at 3? Students will suggest moving the sticky notes in opposite directions, probably in pairs. This will result in a symmetrical arrangement. But what if one of the families has eight pets, a move of five spaces from the 3? This might be balanced by moving two families to the left, one three spaces to the 0 and one two spaces to the 1. Figure 21.16(b) shows one way the families could be rearranged to maintain a mean of 3. You should stop here and find at least two other distributions of the families, each having a mean of 3.

Use the next activity to find the mean or balance point given the data.

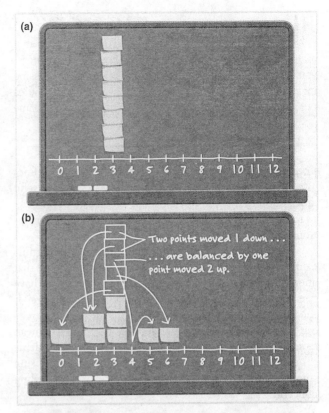

Figure 21.16 (a) If all data points are the same, the mean is that value. (b) By moving data points away from the mean in a balanced manner, different distributions can be found that have the same mean.

tation. The task is to determine the actual mean by moving the sticky notes in toward the "center." That is, the students are finding out what price or point on the number line balances out the six prices on the line. For each move of a sticky one space to the left (a toy with a lower price), a different sticky must be moved one space to the right (a toy with a higher price). Eventually, all stickies should be stacked above the same number, the balance point or mean.

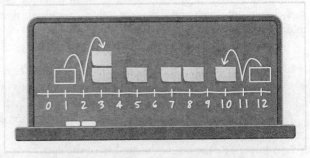

Figure 21.17 Move data points in toward the center or balance point without changing the balance around that point. When you have all points at the same value, that is the balance or the mean.

Activity **21.7**

Finding the Balance Point

Have students draw a number line from 0 to 12 with about an inch between the numbers. Use six small sticky notes to represent the prices of six toys as shown in Figure 21.17. Have them place a light pencil mark on the line where they think the mean might be. For the moment, avoid the add-up-and-divide compu-

Pause and Reflect

Stop now and try this exercise yourself. Notice that after any pair of moves that keep the distribution balanced, you actually have a new distribution of prices with the same mean. The same was true when you moved the sticky notes out from the mean when they were all stacked on the same point.

Changes in the Mean.   Notice that the mean only defines a "center" of a set of data and so by itself is not a very useful description of the shape of the data. The balance approach to the mean clearly illustrates that many different distributions can have the same mean.

Especially for small sets of data, the mean is significantly affected by extreme values. For example, suppose that another toy with a price of $20 is added to the six we have been using in the examples. How will the mean change? If the $1 toy were removed, how would the mean be affected? Suppose that one new toy is added that increases the mean from $6 to $7. How much does the new toy cost? Students should be challenged with questions such as these using small sets of data and either the balance or the leveling concept.

NCTM Standards   In the e-Examples found at the NCTM website under Standards & Focal Points, Applet 6.6, "Comparing Properties of the Mean and the Median," shows seven data points that can be dragged back and forth along a number line with the mean and median updated instantly. The applet allows students to see how stable the median is and how changing one point can affect the mean. ◆

Box-and-Whisker Plots

Box-and-whisker plots (or just *box plots*) are a method for visually displaying not only the center (median) but also information about the range and distribution or variance of data. In Figure 21.18, the ages in months for 27 sixth-grade students are given, along with stem-and-leaf plots for the full class and the boys and girls separately. Box-and-whisker plots are shown in Figure 21.19.

Each box-and-whisker plot has these three features:

1. A box that contains the "middle half" of the data, one-fourth to the left and right of the median. The ends of the box are at the *lower quartile*, the median of the lower half of the data, and the *upper quartile*, the median of the upper half of the data.
2. A line inside the box at the median of the data.
3. A line extending from the end of each box to the *lower extreme* and *upper extreme* of the data. Each line, therefore, covers the upper and lower fourths of the data.

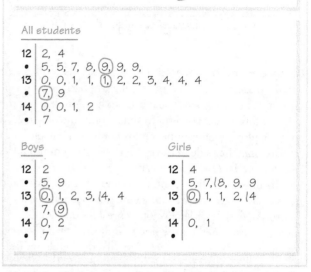

Figure 21.18 Ordered stem-and-leaf plots grouped by fives. Medians and quartiles are circled or are represented by a bar (I) if they fall between two elements.

Look at the information these box plots provide at a glance! The box and the lengths of the lines provide a quick indication of how the data are spread out or bunched

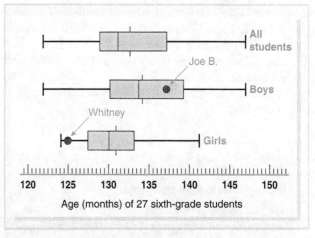

Figure 21.19 Box-and-whisker plots show a lot of information. In addition to showing how data are distributed, data points of particular interest can be shown.

together. Since the median is shown, this spreading or bunching can be determined for each quarter of the data. The entire class in this example is much more spread out in the upper half than the lower half. The girls are much more closely grouped in age than either the boys or the class as a whole. It is immediately obvious that at least three-fourths of the girls are younger than the median age of the boys. The *range* of the data (difference between upper and lower extremes) is represented by the length of the plot, and the extreme values can be read directly. The mean is indicated by the small marks above and below each box. A box plot provides useful visual information to help understand the shape of a data set.

To make a box-and-whisker plot, put the data in order. Next, find the median. Simply count the number of values and determine the middle one. This can be done on stem-and-leaf plots as in Figure 21.18. To find the two quartiles, ignore the median itself, and find the medians of the upper and lower halves of the data. Mark the two extremes, the two quartiles, and the median above an appropriate number line. Draw the box and the lines. Box plots can also be drawn vertically.

Note that the means for the data in our example are each just slightly higher than the medians (class = 132.4; boys = 133.9; girls = 130.8). For this example, the means themselves do not provide nearly as much information as the box plots.

Tech NOTES Graphing calculators and several computer programs draw box-and-whisker plots, making this process even more accessible. The TI-73, TI-84, and TI Nspire calculators can draw box plots for up to three sets of data on the same axis. Remember that a box-and-whisker plot, like any graph, is a tool for learning about the question posed, not an end in itself (McClain, Leckman, Schmitt, & Regis, 2006). Because a box-and-whisker plot offers so much information on the spread and center of the data, much can be learned from careful examination, and particularly from comparing two box-and-whisker plots with related data. ◆

❚❚ *Pause and Reflect*

Notice that in Figure 21.19 the box for the boys is actually a bit longer than the box for the whole class. How can that be when there are clearly more students in the full class than there are boys? How would you explain this apparent discrepancy to a class of seventh graders?

Interpreting Results

Interpretation is the fourth step in the process of doing statistics. As seen in the sample test items shown earlier, sometimes questions focus on mathematical ideas rather than statistical ideas. Although it is helpful to ask mathematical questions, it is essential to ask questions that are statistical in nature. That means the questions focus on the context of the situation and seeing what can be learned or inferred from the data. In addition, they should focus on the key ideas of statistics, such as variability, center of the data, and the shape of the data. During interpretation, students might want to loop back and create a different data display to get a different look at the data, or might want to gather data from a different population to see if their results are representative.

Different researchers have recommended questions that focus on statistical thinking (Franklin et al., 2005; Friel, O'Conner, & Mamer, 2006; Russell, 2006; Shaughnessy, 2006). Here are some ideas from their lists to get you started on having meaningful discussions interpreting data:

- What do the numbers (symbols) tell us about our class (or other population)?
- If we asked another class (population), how would our data look? What if we asked a larger group, how would the data look?
- How do the numbers in this graph (population) *compare* to this graph (population)?
- Where are the data "clustering"? How much of the data are in the cluster? How much are *not* in the cluster? About what percent is or is not in the cluster?
- What kinds of variability might need to be considered in interpreting these data?
- Would the results be different if . . . [change of sample/population or setting]? (Example: Would gathered data on word length in a third-grade book be different for a fifth-grade book? Would a science book give different results than a reading book?)
- How strong is the association between two variables (scatter plot)? How do you know? What does that mean if you know x? If you know y?
- What does the graph *not* tell us? What might we infer?
- What new questions arise from these data?

This section is shorter than the sections on data analysis, but only because these prompts apply across many data displays. It certainly should be a major focus of your instruction. Consider it the *after* phase of your lesson, though some of these questions will be integrated in the *during* phase as well.

Our world is inundated with data, from descriptive statistics to different graphs. It is essential that we prepare students to be literate about what can be interpreted from data and what cannot be interpreted from data, what is important to pay attention to and what can be discarded as misleading or poorly designed statistics. This is important for success in school, as well as for being a mathematically literate citizen.

Reflections on Chapter 21

Writing to Learn

1. How is statistics different from mathematics? In a lesson on the mean, what mathematical questions and what statistical questions might you ask?
2. What is meant by the "shape of data"?
3. Explain why attribute activities are important in the development of data analysis skills.
4. Data should be collected to answer questions. What are some examples of questions that students might explore with data at the K–2 level and what are some for the upper grades?
5. What kinds of graphs can be used for data that can be put into categories?
6. What is the difference between a bar graph and a histogram? What kinds of data are required for a histogram?
7. What are three ways to make a circle graph? What does a circle graph tell you that a bar graph does not? What does it not tell?
8. Give an example of a context in which you would you choose to use median over mean and when would you choose mean over median (not the ones given in the text).
9. Describe two different concepts of the mean. How can each be developed? Which idea leads to the method of computing the mean?
10. Pick one of the contexts from this chapter and give three questions that you would ask students that focus on statistical thinking.

For Discussion and Exploration

1. Select a popular news weekly such as *Time* or *Newsweek*. Look through at least one issue carefully to see graphs and statistical information a typical reader would be expected to understand. Note that you will not be able to do this by simply looking for graphs. Statistics are frequently used without any corresponding graphs.
2. The process of doing statistics must be clear to students, even when they are working on a piece (e.g., circle graphs) within the process. Pick a grade band (pre-K–2, 3–5, 6–8), and consider possibilities for authentic and engaging (and researchable) questions. Then discuss how you would plan instruction in order to include the four-step process and engage students in statistical thinking.

Resources for Chapter 21

Literature Connections

Literature is full of situations in which things must be sorted, compared, or measured. Each of these can be the springboard for a data-collection and representation activity. As noted earlier in this chapter, books of lists also are fruitful beginnings for data explorations. Students can use the data in the books and/or compare similar data collected themselves.

The Best Vacation Ever *Murphy, 1997*

This is in the MathStart series, designed as a collection of single-concept books to generate simple activities in mathematics. In this book, appropriate for first or second grade, a little girl gathers data from her family on what is important to them to decide where the family would have the best vacation.

This book nicely introduces the concept of gathering data to answer a question. Use the book as an introduction to this important topic.

Frog and Toad Are Friends *Lobel, 1970*

When Frog and Toad go walking, Frog loses a button. As they search to find the button, they find many buttons. Whenever one of Frog's friends asks, "Is this your button?" Frog responds (with a touch of frustration), "No, that is not my button! That button is _____, but my button was _____."

This classic story is a perfect lead-in to sorting activities as described in this chapter. Young students can model the story directly with sets of buttons, shells, attribute blocks, Woozle Cards (Blackline Master 59), or other objects with a variety of attributes.

200% of Nothing: An Eye-Opening Tour Through the Twists and Turns of Math Abuse and Innumeracy *Dewdney, 1993*

This middle school–friendly chapter book has explanations of the many ways that "statistics are turned" to mislead the common person. Because the examples are *real*, provided by readers of *Scientific American*, this book is an excellent tool for showing the power of statistics and how important it is to be statistically literate in today's society. Reading the examples can launch a mathematics project into looking for error in advertisements and at how overlapping groups (as in a Venn Diagram) can be reported separately to mislead readers. (See Bay-Williams and Martinie, 2009, for more ideas connected with this book.)

If the World Were a Village: A Book about the World's People *Smith, 2002*

This is a favorite as well as important book about how wealth, culture, language, and other influences play out in the world. Each beautiful two-page spread shares the statistics for the topic (e.g., language). This book can give rise to other questions about the world, which can be researched and interpreted into the village metaphor. The data can also be compared to other populations (e.g., within the school).

The Inch Boy *Morimoto, 1991*
Swamp Angel *Isaacs and Zelinsky, 2000*

Both of these are examples of books with a character who is *not* average. The Inch Boy is very small and the Swamp Angel is very large. These books create interest in gathering descriptive statistics and seeing the impact of outliers on the mean and median. Beyond height, many things can be measured—weight of backpacks, shoulder width, shoe length, and so on. For an engaging investigation with *The Inch Boy*, see Foss (2008).

Recommended Readings

Articles

Harper, S. R. (2004). Students' interpretations of misleading graphs. *Mathematics Teaching in the Middle Grades, 9*(6), 340–343.
Harper explores some of the types of misleading graphing techniques that are often seen in the popular press and discusses how she explored these graphs with students. This is a very short version of a few of the ideas found in the classic book How to Lie with Statistics *(Huff, 1954/1993).*

Manchester, P. (2002). The lunchroom project: A long-term investigative study. *Teaching Children Mathematics, 9*(1), 43–47.
A third-grade teacher describes how her class decided to do something about their dislike of the cafeteria food. She explains the difficulty of designing appropriate questions and gathering the data. Student work shows how the students dealt with the data collected.

Books

Burrill, G. F., & Elliott, P. C. (Eds.). (2006). *Thinking and reasoning about data and chance: Sixty-eighth yearbook.* Reston, VA: NCTM.
This NCTM Yearbook is full of excellent articles that can inform and improve your understanding and teaching of statistics. Many of the articles are cited in this chapter.

Franklin, C., Kader, G., Mewborn, D., Moreno, J., Peck, R., Perry, M., & Scheaffer, R. (2005). *Guidelines for assessment and instruction in statistics education* (GAISE Report). Alexandria, VA: American Statistical Association.
The examples provided in this excellent framework for teaching statistics, prepared by statistics educators, are great tasks to use with students in pre-K–8.

Sheffield, L. J., Cavanagh, M., Dacey, L., Findell, C. R., Greenes, C. E., & Small, M. (2002). *Navigating through data analysis and probability in prekindergarten–grade 2.* Reston, VA: NCTM.

Chapin, S., Koziol, A., MacPherson, J., & Rezba, C. (2002). *Navigating through data analysis and probability in grades 3–5.* Reston, VA: NCTM.

Bright, G. W., Brewer, W., McClain, K., & Mooney, E. S. (2003). *Navigating through data analysis in grades 6–8.* Reston, VA: NCTM.
Each of these books is strongly suggested as a reference for excellent activities and explorations with students.

Online Resources

Bar Graph
www.shodor.org/interactivate/activities/BarGraph
The user of this applet can enter data as well as manipulate the *y*-axis values to create a bar graph. The ability to manipulate the *y*-axis values allows the creation of potentially misleading graphs, a good source of discussion.

Box Plotter
http://illuminations.nctm.org/ActivityDetail.aspx?ID=77
The user can enter data and create box-and-whisker plots.

Circle Grapher
http://illuminations.nctm.org/ActivityDetail.aspx?ID=60
Make your own circle graph with your own data, or display a circle graph from a given set of data.

Collecting, Representing, and Interpreting Data Using Spreadsheets and Graphing Software
http://standards.nctm.org/document/eexamples/chap5/5.5/index.htm
Data are provided in a spreadsheet. The data can be changed and/or ordered in different ways with simple buttons. Scatter plots and bar graphs are also easily made with various combinations of data. Lesson suggestions are provided.

Histograms
http://illuminations.nctm.org/ActivityDetail.aspx?ID=78
Each of these sites offers an interactive applet allowing the user to create and manipulate histograms. User data can be entered or data are supplied.

Stem-and-Leaf Plot
www.shodor.org/interactivate/activities/StemAndLeafPlotter
Enter data and calculate mean, median, and mode.

Field Experience Guide Connections

Field Experiences 1.2, 1.3, and 1.5 focus on an environment for learning and can be used to explore the extent to which lessons incorporate the process of *doing* statistics. FEG Expanded Lesson 9.20 is a lesson on using the four-step process of doing statistics; it can be used by itself, or with Field Experiences 1.5 ("Establishing Your Environment") or 2.5 ("Planning a Problem-Based Lesson"). FEG Expanded Lesson 9.22 engages students in comparing different ways to graph data, analyzing the differences in the two. FEG Expanded Lesson 9.24 explores the impact of outliers in data sets.

Chapter 22

Exploring
Concepts of Probability

References to probability are all around us: The weather forecaster predicts a 60 percent chance of snow; medical researchers predict people with certain diets have a high chance of heart disease; investors calculate risks of specific stocks; and so on. Simulations of complex situations are frequently based on probabilities and are then used in the design process of such undertakings as spacecraft, highways and storm sewers, or plans for responding to disasters. Because the ideas and methods of probability are so prevalent in today's world, this strand of mathematics has risen in visibility in the school curriculum.

Realistic concepts of chance require considerable development before children are ready to construct formal ideas about the probability of a future event. This development occurs most optimally as children consider and discuss with their peers the outcomes of a wide variety of probabilistic situations. The emphasis should be on exploration rather than rules and formal definitions. If done well, these informal experiences will provide a useful background from which more formal ideas can be developed in middle and high school. In *Curriculum Focal Points* (NCTM, 2006) probability is a connection to content in seventh grade.

Big Ideas

1. Chance has no memory. For repeated trials of a simple experiment, the outcomes of prior trials have no impact on the next. The chance occurrence of six heads in a row has no effect on getting a head on the next toss of the coin. That chance remains 50–50.

2. The probability that a future event will occur can be characterized along a continuum from impossible to certain.

3. The *probability* of an event is a number between 0 and 1 that is a measure of the chance that a given event will occur. A probability of 0 indicates impossibility and that of 1 indicates

certainty. A probability of $\frac{1}{2}$ indicates an even chance of the event occurring.

4. The relative frequency of outcomes (from *experiments*) can be used as an estimate of the probability of an event. The larger the number of trials, the better the estimate will be. The results for a small number of trials may be quite different from those experienced in the long run.

5. For some events, the exact probability can be determined by an analysis of the event itself. A probability determined in this manner is called a *theoretical probability*.

6. *Simulation* is a technique used for answering real-world questions or making decisions in complex situations in which an element of chance is involved. To see what is likely to happen in the real event, a model must be designed that has the same probabilities as the real situation.

Mathematics
Content Connections

Probability and data analysis have long been joined when talking about the mathematics curriculum and there is a real mathematical connection as students reach the upper grades.

- **Fractions and Percents** (Chapters 15 and 17): Students can see fractional parts of spinners or sets of counters in a bag and use these fractions to determine probabilities. Percents provide useful common denominators for comparing ratios (e.g., rolling a 7 three times in the first 20 rolls, or 15%, and 16 times in 80 rolls, or 20%).

- **Ratio and Proportion** (Chapter 19): Comparing probabilities means relating part-to-whole ratios. To understand these comparisons requires proportional reasoning.

- **Data Analysis** (Chapter 21): The purpose of probability is to answer statistics-related questions. When performing a probability experiment, the results are data—a sample of the theoretically infinite experiments that could be done.

Introducing Probability

Young children's concept of the likelihood of a future event is often surprising. Children can be absolutely convinced that the next roll of the die will be a 3 "because I just know it's going to happen" or "because 3 is my lucky number."

Likely or Not Likely

To change these early misconceptions, a good place to begin is with a focus on possible and not possible (Activity 22.1) and later impossible, possible, and certain (Activity 22.2). In preparation for these activities, discuss the words *impossible* and *certain*. *Certain* is the more difficult of these words for children.

Activity 22.1

Nursery Rhyme Possibilities

Create a table, labeling one column "Impossible" and the other "Possible." Take a nursery rhyme verse, such as "Hey, Diddle, Diddle" (or a picture book) and for each line, ask students if it goes in the impossible or possible column. Record each statement in the appropriate column.

Activity 22.2

Is It Likely?

Ask students to judge various events as *certain, impossible,* or *possible* ("might happen"). Consider these examples:

- It will rain tomorrow.
- Drop a rock in water and it will sink.
- Trees will talk to us in the afternoon.
- The sun will rise tomorrow morning.
- Three students will be absent tomorrow.
- George will go to bed before 8:30 tonight.
- You will have two birthdays this year.

Have children describe or make up events that are certain, impossible, or possible. For each event, they should justify their choice of likelihood.

The key idea to developing chance or probability on a continuum is to help children see that some of these possible events are more likely or less likely than others. For instance, if a group of students has a running race, the chance that Gregg, a really fast runner, will be first is not certain but is very likely. It is more likely that Gregg will be near the front of the group than near the back of the pack.

The use of random devices that can be analyzed (e.g., spinners, number cubes, coins to toss, colored cubes drawn from a bag) can help students make predictions about the likelihood of an event. The process of exploring the likeliness of an event maps to the *before, during, after* lesson plan model. In the *before* phase, students make predictions of what they think will be likely; in the *during* phase, students experiment to explore the likeliness of the event; and in the *after* phase, students analyze the experimental results to determine the likeliness of the event.

The following activity or variations of it should be repeated often either using the same random devices or with a variety of devices.

Activity 22.3

Race to the Top

Show students the spinner in Figure 22.1 and ask: "If we count spins that land on red and ones that land on blue, which one will reach the top first." Two players take turns spinning the spinner. Each game requires a simple recording sheet with ten rows or spaces. Figure 22.1 shows a sheet for the two-color spinner. In the simplest version of the game, use only one spinner: one-fourth red and three-fourths blue. Before playing, each student predicts which color will win, red or blue. (Note that it is *color* that wins, not a player!) After each spin, an X is drawn in the appropriate column. Play continues until one color reaches the top of the chart.

Students should play "Race to the Top" several times. After all students have played, ask "Which color is likely to win? Why do you think so?"

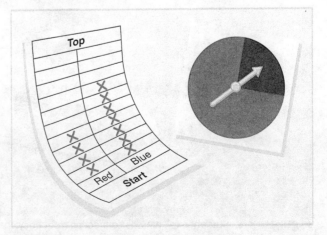

Figure 22.1 Students take turns spinning a spinner and recording the result. The first color to reach the top is the winner.

In activities such as "Race to the Top," use a variety of spinners. Use spinners that have two colors with the same area—and colors covering different areas, as shown here.

As a random device, spinners have the advantage that students can see the relative portion of the whole given to each color or outcome. Students do not always see that the first two spinners, or a spinner divided into just two sections, have the same likelihood of getting blue (Cohen, 2006; Jones, Langrall, Thornton, & Magill, 1997; Nicolson, 2005). Therefore, it is important to use spinners that are partitioned in different ways. Spinner faces can easily be made to adjust the chances of different outcomes. An effective way to connect the idea that the larger region on the spinner is more likely to have a spin land there is to have

students use frequency charts to record data. In Figure 22.2 a student explains how she knows which frequency table goes with which circle graph.

Devices other than spinners should also be used for "Race to the Top" and similar activities. Colored dots can be stuck on the sides of a wooden cube to create different color probabilities. Similarly, opaque bags with eight red and two blue tiles, or some other ratio of red to blue, can be used. Students draw a tile from the bag and then return it after each draw. In the *after* phase of each experience, focus on what is likely/unlikely and certain/impossible.

The following activity is a game of chance with unequal outcomes. However, students will not readily be able to predict which result is most likely, so it provides a good opportunity for discussion.

Activity 22.4

Add, Then Tally

Make number cubes with sides as follows: 1, 1, 2, 3, 3, 3. Each game requires two cubes. Students take turns rolling the two cubes and recording the sum of

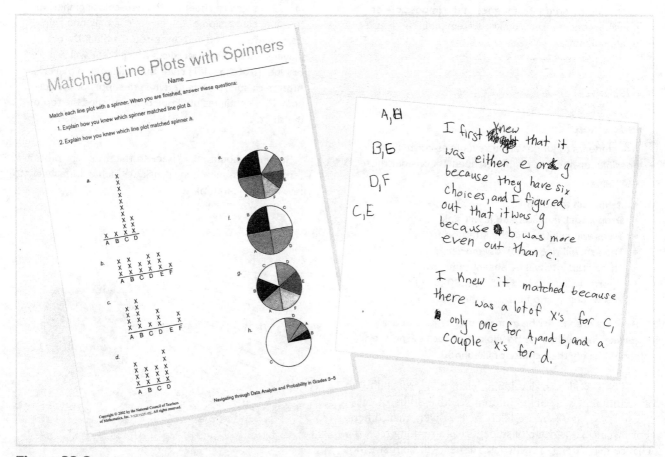

Figure 22.2 Student explanations connecting frequency charts to spinners.

Source: Adapted from Chapin, S., Kozial, A., MacPherson, J., & Rezba, C. (2002). *Navigating Through Data Analysis and Probability in Grades 3–5*. Reston, VA: NCTM, p. 116. Reprinted with permission. Copyright © 2002 by the National Council of Teachers of Mathematics, Inc. www.nctm.org. All rights reserved.

the two numbers. To record the results, run off tally sheets with six rows of ten squares, labeled 1 through 6 (see Figure 22.3). Students continue to roll the cubes until one of the rows is full. They can repeat the game on a new tally sheet as long as time permits. Before play begins ask students to predict which row will fill the fastest.

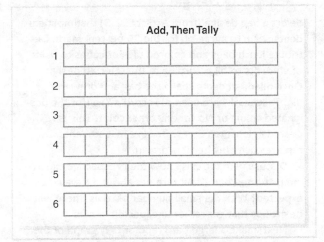

Add, Then Tally

1

2

3

4

5

6

Figure 22.3 A recording sheet for "Add, Then Tally."

It is important to talk with students after they have played "Add, Then Tally." Which numbers "won" the most and the least often? If they were to play again, which number would they pick to win and why? Furthermore, although an outcome of 1 is impossible, all of the other outcomes, 2 through 6, are possible. A sum of 4 is the most likely. Sums of 2 or 3 are the least likely.

Students' ideas about chance must develop from experience. Students' experiences with likely events can lead to misconceptions about chance.

For example, some students think a 1 is not as likely as rolling a 5 on a dice, perhaps because they play a game where 1 is desirable. The 1 is not likely compared to the other 5 choices, but it is as likely as any other number (Nicolson, 2005; Watson & Moritz, 2003). During discussions, your task is to elicit their ideas. The main idea is that the sum rolled is not necessarily just pure luck, but that some results are clearly more or less likely because of the design of the spinner or dice. ◆

The Probability Continuum

To begin refining the concept that some events are more or less likely to occur than others, introduce the idea of a continuum of likelihood between impossible and certain. Draw a long line on the board, as in Figure 22.4. Label the left end "Impossible" and the right end "Certain." Write "Chances of Spinning Blue" above the line. Discuss various positions on the line and what the corresponding spinner would look like. To review these ideas, show the spinners one at a time and ask which marks represent the chance of getting blue for that spinner. Also name events (e.g., having a snow day) and ask where they would go (or have students think of events for selected points on the line).

In the next activity students design random devices that they think will create chances for various designated positions on the probability line.

Activity **22.5**

Design a Bag

(Note that students must be introduced to the idea of a probability continuum as just described.)
    Use the worksheet shown in Figure 22.5 (see Blackline Master 60) and provide students with a copy. On the board mark a place on a probability line

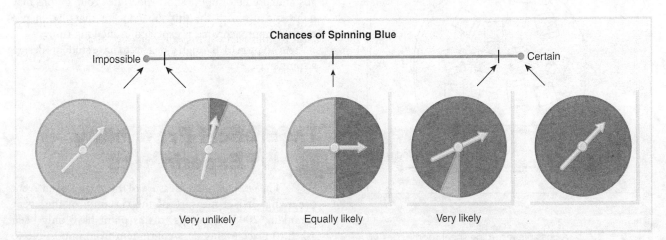

Chances of Spinning Blue

Impossible   Certain

Very unlikely   Equally likely   Very likely

Figure 22.4 The probability continuum. Use these spinner faces to help students see how chance can be at different places on a continuum between impossible and certain.

at roughly the 20 percent position. At this time do not use percent or fraction language with the children. Students are to mark this position on their worksheet probability lines. Students should color the square indicated by "Color" at the top of the page. Explain that they are going to decide what color tiles should be put in bags of 12 total tiles so that the chance of drawing this designated color is about the same as the chance indicated on the probability line. Before students begin to design their bags, ask for ideas about which colors of tiles might be put in the bag if the mark were very close to the middle of the line. Show how the real bags will be filled based on the design on the page. Emphasize that the tiles will be shaken up so that which particular squares on the bag design are colored will not reflect the actual position in the bag.

At the bottom of each sheet (and on the reverse if needed), students explain why they chose their tiles. Give them an example: *We put in 8 red and 4 of other colors because _____.*

Collect and display the designs made by the students in "Design a Bag." Discuss the ideas that students had for the number of designated colors to put in the bag. (Expect some variation.)

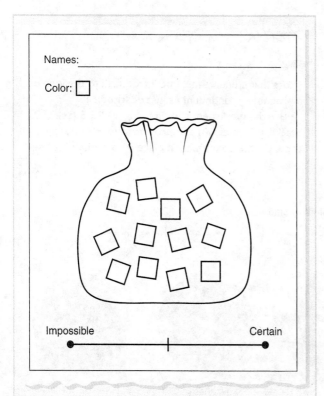

Figure 22.5 A possible recording sheet for the "Design a Bag" activity (see Blackline Master 60).

The "Design a Bag" activity provides useful information about how your students conceive of chance as appearing on a continuum. The next follow-up activity focuses on doing an experiment to see if the design predicted was reasonable.

Activity 22.6

Testing Bag Designs

Select a bag design (from Activity 22.5) that most students seem to agree on for the 20 percent mark. Distribute lunch bags and colored tiles or cubes to pairs of students to fill according to the selected design. Once filled, students shake the bag and draw out one tile. Tally marks are used to record a Yes (for the designated color) or No for any other color. This is repeated at least ten times. Be sure that students replace each tile after it is drawn.

Discuss with the class how their respective experiments turned out. Did it turn out about the way they expected? With the small number of trials, there will be groups that get rather unexpected results.

Next, make a large bar graph or tally graph of the data from all of the groups together. This should show many more No's than Yes's. Here the discussion can help students see that if the experiment is repeated a lot of times, the results are closer to what was predicted.

The dual activities of "Design a Bag" and "Testing Bag Designs" can and should be repeated for two or three other marks on the probability line. Try marks at about $\frac{1}{3}$, $\frac{1}{2}$, and $\frac{3}{4}$.

"Design a Bag" and "Testing Bag Designs" are important activities. Because no numbers are used for the probabilities, there are no "right" answers. The small-group testing of a design shows students that chance is not an absolute predictor in the short run. The group graphs may help students with the difficult concept that the chance tends to approach what is expected in the long run.

A variation of "Design a Bag" is to have students design a spinner.

Theoretical Probability and Experiments

The *probability* is a measure of the chance of an event occurring. It is a measure of the certainty of the event (Franklin, 2005). Students to this point have only been asked to place events on a continuum from impossible to certain or to compare the likelihood of one event with another. So how do you measure a chance? In many situations, there are actually two ways to determine this measure.

Probability has two distinct types. The first type involves any specific event whose likelihood of occurrence is known (e.g., that a fair die has a $\frac{1}{6}$ chance of producing each number). When the likeliness of an event is known, probability can be established theoretically by examining all the possibilities.

The second case involves any event whose likeliness of occurrence isn't observable—but can be established through *empirical data*, or evidence from past experiments or data collection (Colgan, 2006; Nicolson, 2005). Examples include a basketball player's likelihood of making free throws in a game (based on the player's previous record), the chance that a telecommunicator will be successful (based on prior rates of success), or the chance of rain (based on how often it rained under equivalent conditions). Although this latter type of probability is less common in the school curriculum, it is the most applicable to most fields that use probability and therefore important to include in your teaching (Franklin et al., 2005).

In both cases, *experiments* or *simulations* can be designed to explore the phenomena being examined (sometimes in the K–12 curriculum this is referred to as *experimental probability* although this terminology is not employed by statisticians).

Coin flips have a known likelihood of occurrence. Logically, we can argue that if it is a fair coin, obtaining a head is just as likely as obtaining a tail. Since there are two possible outcomes that are equally likely, each has a probability of $\frac{1}{2}$. Hence, the theoretical probability of obtaining a head is $\frac{1}{2}$. When all possible outcomes of a simple experiment are equally likely, the *theoretical probability* of an event is

$$\frac{\text{Number of outcomes in the event}}{\text{Number of possible outcomes}}$$

Instead, consider the question, "Is this coin fair?" This is a statistics problem that can only be answered by doing an experiment and establishing the frequency of heads and tails over the long run (Franklin et al., 2005). The answer requires empirical data and the probability will be:

$$\frac{\text{Number of observed occurrences of the event}}{\text{Total number of trials}}$$

Because it is impossible to conduct an infinite number of trials, we can only consider the relative frequency for a very large number of trials as an approximation of the theoretical probability. This emphasizes the notion that probability is more about predictions over the long term than predictions of individual events.

Theoretical Probability

A problem-based way to introduce theoretical probability is to engage students in an activity with an unfair game and have students later examine the possibilities within the game to determine theoretically if it is fair. In the following activity, the results of the game will likely be contrary to students' intuitive ideas. This in turn will provide a real reason to analyze the game in a logical manner and find out why things happened as they did—theoretical probability.

Activity 22.7

Fair or Unfair?

Three students toss 2 like coins (e.g., 2 pennies or 2 nickels) and are assigned points according to the following rules: Player A gets 1 point if the coin toss results in "two heads"; player B gets 1 point if the toss results in "two tails"; and player C gets 1 point if the toss results are "mixed" (one head, one tail). The game is over after 20 tosses. The player who has the most points wins. Have students play the game at least two or three times. After each game, the players are to stop and discuss if they think the game is fair and make predictions about who will win the next game.

When the full class has played the game several times, conduct a discussion on the fairness of the game. Challenge students to make an argument *not* based on the data as to whether the game is fair or not and why.

A common analysis of the game in Activity 22.7 goes something like this: There are three outcomes: two tails, one head and one tail, or two heads. Each has an equal chance. The game should be fair. However, after playing "Fair or Unfair?" students will find that player C (gets points for a mixed result) appears to have an unfair advantage (especially if they have played several games or the class has pooled its data). This observation seems to contradict the notion that the outcomes are equally likely.

Rubel (2006, 2007) used a similar two-coin task with students from fifth to eleventh grades, asking for the probability of getting a head and a tail with two coins. She found that about half (54 percent) answered this problem correctly (across grades), but that many of the fifth and seventh graders used faulty reasoning, having picked that answer believing there is a 50–50 chance in any experiment. About 25 percent of the students said the probability was $\frac{1}{3}$—because three things could happen (two heads, one of each, two tails).

Encourage students to analyze the situation and generate all the possible outcomes. A student explanation may be as follows:

There is only one way for two heads to occur and one way for two tails to occur, but there are two ways for a head and a tail to occur: Either the first coin is heads and the second tails, or vice versa. That makes a total of four possible outcomes, not three. [See Figure 22.6.] Getting a head and a tail happens in two out of the four possible outcomes. Since each outcome is equally likely, getting a head and a tail has a probability of $\frac{2}{4}$ or $\frac{1}{2}$.

First Coin	Second Coin
Head	Head
Head	Tail
Tail	Head
Tail	Tail

Figure 22.6 Four possible outcomes of flipping two coins.

This theoretical probability is based on a logical analysis of the experiment, not on experimental results.

Another great context is the game of "rock, paper, scissors," which can be played in the normal way, or adapted so "same" scores 1 point and "different" scores 1 point for the other player. Decide whether this is a fair game (Ellis, Yeh, & Stump, 2007).

Experiments

As noted earlier, some probabilities cannot be analyzed by the theoretical likeliness of an event or the theoretical probability. The probability of these events can be determined only through empirical data, which may be preexisting or may be established through experimentation, conducting a sufficiently large number of trials to become confident that the resulting relative frequency is an approximation of the theoretical probability. The following activity provides students with such a situation.

Activity 22.8

Cup Toss

Provide a small plastic cup to pairs of students. Ask them to list the possible ways that the cup could land if they tossed it in the air and let it land on the floor. Which of the possibilities (upside down, right side up, or on its side) do they think is most and least likely? Why? Have students toss the cup 20 times, each time recording how it lands. Students should agree on a uniform method of tossing the cups to ensure unbiased data (e.g., dropping the cups from the same height). Record each pair's data in a class chart. Discuss the differences and generate reasons for them. Have students predict what will happen if they pool their data. Pool the data and compute the three ratios (upside down, right side up, and on the side) to the total number of tosses. The relative frequency of the combined data should approximate the actual probability.

In the cup-tossing experiment there is no practical way to determine the results before you start. However, once you have results for 200 tosses (empirical data), you would undoubtedly feel more confident in predicting the results of the next 100 tosses. After gathering data for 1000 trials, you would feel even more confident. The more tosses that are made, the more confident you become. You have determined a probability of $\frac{4}{5}$ or 80 percent for the cup to land on its side. It is empirical data because it is based on the results of an experiment rather than a theoretical analysis of the cup.

myeducationlab

Go to the Building Teaching Skills and Dispositions section of Chapter 22 of MyEducationLab. Click on Videos and watch the video entitled **"Probability Lesson: Rolling a Die"** to see students use a dice-rolling activity to determine the probability of a certain number coming up.

The Law of Large Numbers. The phenomenon that the relative frequency becomes a closer approximation of the actual probability or the theoretical probability as the size of the data set (sample) increases is referred to as *the law of large numbers*. The larger the size of the data set, the more representative the sample is of the population. Thinking about statistics, a survey of 1000 people provides more reliable and convincing data about the larger population than a survey of 5 people. The larger the number of trials (people surveyed), the more confident you can be that the data reflect the larger population. The same is true when you are attempting to determine the probability of an event through data collection.

Although critical to understanding probability, this concept is difficult for students to grasp. Students commonly think that a probability should play out in the short term, a misconception sometimes referred to as "the law of small numbers" (Flores, 2006; Tarr, Lee, & Rider, 2006). Therefore, students think that if a coin, for example, has had a series of heads, it is more likely to have several tails. But a coin has no memory, and the likelihood of heads and tails is still 50–50. The next activity emphasizes the large variability of data in the short run (only a small number of trials).

Activity 22.9

Get All 6!

Ask students to list the numbers 1 through 6 at the bottom of a frequency table. Ask students to roll a die and to mark an X over each number until they have rolled each number at least once. Repeat five or six times. Discuss how the frequency charts compare in each case. Students will see that in some cases there are many 4s, for example, and it took 25 rolls before getting all numbers, while in other cases, they got all the numbers in only 10 rolls. Focus discussion on the fact that in the short run, data varies a lot—it is over the long run that the data "evens out." This activity can also be done on a graphing calculator (Flores, 2006).

Truly random events often occur in unexpected groups; a fair coin may turn up heads five times in a row. A 100-year flood may hit a town twice in ten years. Hands-on random devices such as spinners, dice, or cubes drawn from a bag give students an intuitive feel for the imperfect distribution of randomness. Students believe in the unbiased outcomes of these devices. The downside is that hands-on devices require a lot of time to produce a large number of trials. This is where technology can help enormously.

The next activity is designed to help students with this difficult idea without resorting to comparing ratios expressed as fractions.

Activity 22.10

What Are the Chances?

Make a transparency of Blackline Master 61 shown in Figure 22.7. Provide pairs of students with a spinner face that is half red and half blue. Discuss the chances of spinning blue. Mark the $\frac{1}{2}$ point on the Impossible–Certain continuum and draw a vertical line down through all of the lines below this point. Then have each pair of students spin their spinner 20 times, tallying the number of red and blue spins. Mark the number of blue spins on the second line. For example, if there are 13 blue and 7 red, place a mark at about 13 on the 0-to-20 number line. If the result of these 20 spins was not exactly 10 and 10, discuss possible reasons why this may be so.

Now have student pairs each spin their spinners 20 more times. Collect these results and add them to the tallies for the first 20 spins. Mark the total in the right-hand box of the third line and indicate the number of blue spins on the line as before. Repeat this at least

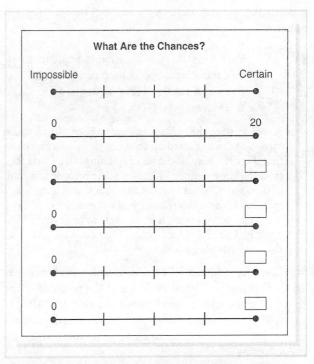

Figure 22.7 This activity is used to explore probability in the short run and the long run (see Blackline Master 61).

two more times, continuing to add the results of new spins to the previous results. Each time, enter the total in the right-hand box to create a new number line but with the same length as before. If possible, try to get the total number of spins to be at least 200. Using a graphing calculator, even 1000 trials is possible in a short amount of time.

The successive number lines used in "What Are the Chances" each have the same length and each represent the total number of trials. When the results are plotted on any one number line, the position shows the fraction of the total spins as a visual portion of the whole line. With more trials, the marks will get closer and closer to the $\frac{1}{2}$ mark you drew at the top of the page. Note that 240 blue spins out of 500 is 48 percent, or very close to one-half. This is so even though there are 20 more red spins (260) than blue. To be that close with only 100 spins, the results would need to be 48 and 52.

The same Blackline Master and the same process of accumulating data in stages can and should be used for other experiments as well. For example, try using this approach with the "Cup Toss" experiment. Rather than draw a vertical line before collecting data, decide on the best guess at the actual probability after the numbers have gotten large. Then draw the vertical line at that time to observe how more and more trials brought the results closer to the line. For students who have an understanding of percentages, the probabilities at each stage can be expressed as percents.

Pose the following situation to students to assess their ideas about long-run results versus short-run results. Have students write about their ideas.

Margaret spun the spinner ten times. Blue turned up on three spins. Red turned up on seven spins. Margaret says that there is a 3-in-10 chance of spinning blue. Carla then spun the same spinner 100 times. Carla recorded 53 spins of blue and 47 spins of red. Carla says that the chance of spinning blue on this spinner is about even.

> Who do you think is more likely to be correct: Margaret or Carla? Explain. Draw a spinner that you think they may have been using.

Look for evidence that students understand that even 10 spins is not very good evidence of the probability and that 100 spins tells us more about the chances. Also, to assess whether students understand the big idea that chance has no memory, have students either write about or discuss the following:

> Duane has a lucky coin that he has tossed many, many times. He is sure that it is a fair coin—that there is an even chance of heads or tails. Duane tosses his coin six times and heads come up six times in a row. Duane is sure that the next toss will be tails because he has never been able to toss heads seven times in a row. What do you think the chances are of Duane tossing heads on the next toss? Explain your answer.

In this case you are looking for the idea that each toss of the coin is independent of prior tosses. ◆

Implications for Instruction

There are many reasons why an experimental approach to probability, actually conducting experiments and examining outcomes, is important in the middle grades classroom.

- It develops an appreciation for a simulation approach to solving problems. Many real-world problems are actually solved by conducting experiments or doing simulations.
- It is significantly more intuitive. Results begin to make sense and do not come from some abstract rule.
- It eliminates guessing at probabilities and wondering, "Did I get it right?" Counting or trying to determine the number of elements in a sample space can be very difficult without some intuitive background information.
- It provides an experiential background for examining the theoretical model. When you begin to sense that the probability of two heads is $\frac{1}{4}$ instead of $\frac{1}{3}$, the analysis in Figure 22.6 seems more reasonable.

- It helps students see how the ratio of a particular outcome to the total number of trials begins to converge to a fixed number. For an infinite number of trials, the relative frequency and theoretical probability would be the same.
- It is a lot more fun and interesting! Even searching for a correct explanation in the theoretical model is more interesting.

Try to use an experimental approach in the classroom whenever possible, posing interesting problems to investigate. If a theoretical analysis (such as with the two-coin experiment in "Fair or Unfair?") is possible, it should also be examined, and the results compared to the expected outcome.

The experimental approach is much like the inquiry approach that is the basis of the *before, during,* and *after* lesson format. In an experiment, you start with a problem (*before*), design and implement a way to explore it (*during*), and analyze the results of the experiment (*after*).

Use of Technology in Experiments

Electronic devices, including some relatively simple calculators and graphing calculators, are designed to produce random outcomes at the press of a button. Computer software is available that flips coins, spins spinners, or draws numbers from a hat. Calculators produce random numbers that can then be interpreted in terms of the desired device. As long as students accept the results generated by the technology as truly random or equivalent to the hands-on device, they offer significant advantages for performing experiments.

Technology makes some content more accessible, and this is certainly the case with probability experiments. Using software or a graphing calculator has the advantage of enabling many more trials in much less time. These devices can also explore across a variety of tools (virtual dice, coins, cards, etc.) and show graphical displays of the trials. For teachers, technology means that dice can be "loaded" and that spinners can easily be created with different partitions (Beck & Huse, 2007; Phillips-Bey, 2004). One particular website to explore is the National Library of Virtual Manipulatives. This site has been recommended in many chapters, but it is worth emphasizing here, as it is an outstanding site for doing virtual experiments.

Software for exploring probability concepts can generally be described as computer-animated random devices. Graphics show students the coins being flipped or the spinner being spun. Most allow different speeds. In a slow version, students may watch each spin of a spinner or coin flip. Faster speeds show the recording of each trial but omit the graphics. An even quicker mode simply shows the cumulative results. The number of trials can be set by the user.

Sample Spaces and Probability of Two Events

Understanding the concepts of outcome and sample space is central to understanding probability. The *sample space* for an experiment or chance situation is the set of all possible outcomes for that experiment. For example, if a bag contains two red, three yellow, and five blue tiles, the sample space consists of all ten tiles. An *event* is a subset of the sample space. The event of drawing a yellow tile has three elements or outcomes in the sample space and the event of drawing a blue tile has five elements in the sample space. For rolling a single number cube, the sample space always consists of the numbers 1 to 6.

Rolling a single die, drawing one colored chip from a bag, or the occurrence of rain tomorrow are all examples of one-event experiments. A two-event experiment is an experiment that requires two (or more) activities to determine an outcome. Examples include rolling two dice, drawing two cubes from a bag, or the occurrence of rain and forgetting your umbrella.

When exploring two-event experiments, there is another factor to consider: Does the occurrence of the event in one stage have an effect on the occurrence of the event in the other? In the following sections we will consider two-event experiments of both types—those with *independent* events and those with *dependent* events.

Independent Events

Recall that in Activity 22.7, "Fair or Unfair?," students explored the results of tossing two coins. The toss of one coin had no effect on the other. These were examples of *independent events*; the occurrence or nonoccurrence of one event has no effect on the other. The same is true of rolling two dice—the result on one die does not affect the other. The common error for both tossing two coins or rolling two dice is a failure to distinguish between the two events, especially when the outcomes are combined, as in "a head and a tail" or adding the numbers on two dice.

We've already solved the problem of tossing two coins. Let's explore rolling two dice and adding the results. Suppose that your students tally the sums that they get for two dice. The results might look like Figure 22.8. Clearly, these events are not equally likely and in fact the sum of 7 appears to have the best chance of occurring. To explain this, students might look for the combinations that make 7: 1 and 6, 2 and 5, and 3 and 4. But there are also three combinations for 6 and for 8. It seems as though 6 and 8 should be just as likely as 7, and yet they are not.

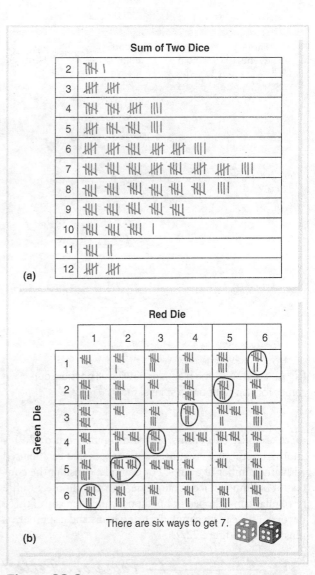

Figure 22.8 Tallies can account only for the total (a) or keep track of each die (b).

Now suppose that the experiment is repeated. This time, for the sake of clarity, suggest that students roll two different-colored dice and that they keep the tallies in a chart like the one in part (b) of Figure 22.8.

The results of a large number of dice rolls indicate what one would expect, namely, that all 36 cells of this chart are equally likely. But there are more cells with a sum of 7 than any other number. Therefore, students were really looking for the event consisting of any of the six ways, not three ways, that two dice can add to 7. There are six outcomes in the desired event out of a total of 36, for a probability of $\frac{6}{36}$, or $\frac{1}{6}$.

To create the sample space for two independent events, it is helpful to use a chart or diagram that keeps the two events separate and illustrates all possible combinations. The matrix in Figure 22.8(b) is one good suggestion when

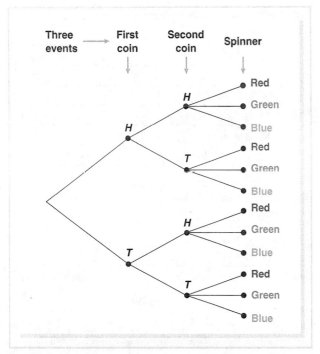

Figure 22.9 A tree diagram showing all possible outcomes for two coins and a spinner that is $\frac{2}{3}$ red.

there are only two events. A tree diagram (Figure 22.9) is another method of creating sample spaces that can be used with any number of events. For example, consider the context of building an ice cream cone. You can choose a waffle or regular cone, dipped or not dipped, and then any of three flavors. This can be simulated using coins and a spinner, as illustrated in Figure 22.9.

⏸ ── *Pause and Reflect*

Use a chart and/or tree diagram to analyze the sum of two number cubes each with sides 1, 1, 2, 3, 3, and 3. (These were the cubes used in "Add, Then Tally," Activity 22.4.) What is the probability of each sum, 1 through 6?

───────────────────

Activity 22.11

Exploring Multistage Events

The following are examples of multistage events composed of independent events.

- Rolling an even sum with two dice
- Spinning blue twice on a spinner
- Having a tack or a cup land up if each is tossed once
- Getting at *least* two heads from tossing four coins

Have students first make and defend a prediction of the probability of the event. Then they should conduct an experiment with a large number of trials, comparing their results to their predicted probabilities. Finally, they should reconcile differences. Where appropriate, students can try to determine the theoretical probability as part of their final analysis of the experiment.

Words and phrases such as *and, or, at least*, and *no more than* can also cause students some trouble. Of special note is the word *or*, since its everyday usage is generally not the same as its strict logical use in mathematics. In mathematics, *or* includes the case of *both*. So in the tack-and-cup example, the event includes tack up, cup up, and *both* tack *and* cup up.

Two-Event Probabilities with an Area Model

One way to determine the theoretical probability of a multistage event is to list all possible outcomes and count the number of outcomes that make up the event. This is effective, but has some limitations. First, what if the events are not all equally likely? For example, the spinner may be only $\frac{1}{4}$ blue. Second, it can get tedious when there are many possibilities. An area model approach has been used successfully with students as young as fifth grade and is quite helpful for some reasonably difficult problems.

Students like to explore data about themselves. Consider the context of birthdays of the entire seventh-grade class. Asking students which animal represents their Chinese birth year and which season they were born represents two independent events. Figure 22.10 illustrates how to model this using an area model, with 64 percent of the class born in the year of the tiger and 36 percent born in the year of the rabbit. Seasons are assumed to be equally likely.

In Figure 22.10(b) you can visually see that students in the tiger and spring groups make up $\frac{1}{4}$ of 64 percent or 16 percent of the population. This should look very familiar, as the same process is used for multiplying fractions. In Figure 22.10(c), the situation is more complex because it is an OR situation. Half of the students are born in summer or fall and 36 percent are born in the year of the rabbit. But some students are both, and they have been double counted. The diagram shows this case as the overlap of the shaded columns with the shaded rows. In the situation under consideration that amount is $\frac{1}{2}$ of 36, or 18 percent. Therefore, the population that is summer or fall or born in the year of the rabbit is 50 + 36 − 18 = 68 percent of the population.

The area approach is accessible to a range of learners, as it is less abstract than equations or tree diagrams. For more than two independent events, further subdivision of each region is required but is still quite reasonable. The use

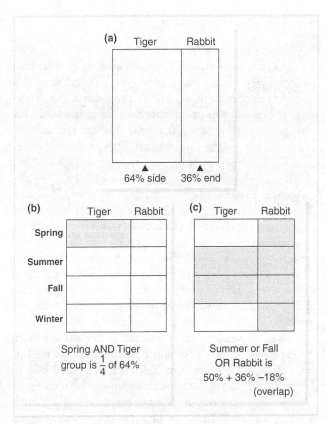

Figure 22.10 An area model for determining probabilities.

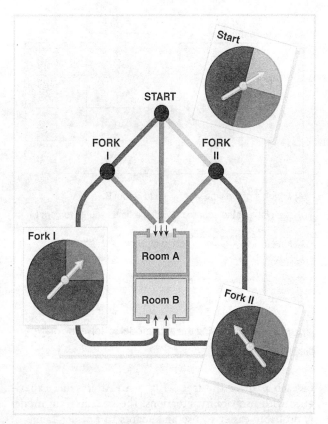

Figure 22.11 Should you place your key to freedom in Room A or Room B? At each fork, the spinner determines your path.

of *and* and *or* connectives can be modeled effectively. It is clear to students, without memorization of formulas, how to find probabilities of independent events.

Dependent Events

Dependent events occur when the second event depends on the result of the first. For example, suppose that there are two identical boxes. In one box is a dollar bill and two counterfeit bills. In the other box is one of each. You may choose one box and from that box select one bill without looking. What are your chances of getting a genuine dollar? Here there are two events: selecting a box and selecting a bill. The probability of getting a dollar in the second event depends on which box is chosen in the first event. These events are *dependent*, not independent.

As a whimsical but engaging context, suppose that you are a prisoner in a faraway land. The king has pity on you and gives you a chance to leave. He shows you the maze in Figure 22.11. At the start and at each fork in the path, you must spin the spinner and follow the path that it points to. You may request that the key to freedom be placed in one of the two rooms. In which room should you place the key to have the best chance of freedom? Notice that the prob-

ability of ending the maze in any one room is dependent on the result of the first spin.

Either of these two problems could be explored with an experimental approach, a simulation. Remember that experiments are a good lead-in to theoretical probability. You can use the area model to determine the theoretical probabilities. An area model solution to the prisoner problem is shown in Figure 22.12. How would the area model for the prisoner problem be different if the spinner at Forks I and II were $\frac{1}{3}$ A and $\frac{2}{3}$ B spinners?

Pause and Reflect

Try the area approach for the problem of the counterfeit bills. The chance of getting a dollar is $\frac{5}{12}$. Can you get this result?

The area model will not solve all probability problems. However, it fits very well into a developmental approach to the subject because it is conceptual, it is based on existing knowledge of fractions, and more symbolic approaches can be derived from it. Figure 22.13 shows a tree diagram for the same problem, with the probability

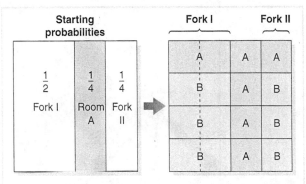

At Fork I, $\frac{3}{4}$ of the time you will go to Room B.

(Note: Not $\frac{3}{4}$ of the square but $\frac{3}{4}$ of the times you go to Fork I.)

At Fork II, $\frac{3}{4}$ of these times (or $\frac{3}{16}$ of total time) you will go to Room B.

Therefore, you will end up in Room A $\frac{7}{16}$ of the time and Room B $\frac{9}{16}$ of the time.

Figure 22.12 Using the area model to solve the maze problem.

of each path of the tree written in. After some experience with probability situations, the tree diagram model is probably easier to use and adapts to a wider range of situations. You should be able to match up each branch of the tree diagram in Figure 22.13 with a section of the square in Figure 22.12. Use the area model to explain why the probability for each complete branch of the tree is determined by multiplying the probabilities along the branch.

Simulations

Simulation is a technique used for answering real-world questions or making decisions in complex situations where an element of chance is involved. Many times simulations are conducted because it is too dangerous, complex, or expensive to manipulate the real situation. To see what is likely to happen in the real event, a model must be designed that has the same probabilities as the real situation. For example, in designing a rocket, a large number of related systems all have some chance of failure. Various combinations of failures might cause serious problems with the rocket. Knowing the probability of serious failures will help determine if redesign or backup systems are required. It is not reasonable to make repeated tests of the actual rocket. Instead, a model that simulates all of the chance situations is designed and run repeatedly with the help of a computer. The computer model can simulate thousands of flights, and an estimate of the chance of failure can be made.

The following problem and model are adapted from the excellent materials developed by the Quantitative Literacy Project (Gnanadesikan, Schaeffer, & Swift, 1987). In Figure 22.14, a diagram shows water pipes for a pumping system connecting A to B. The five pumps are aging, and it is estimated that at any given time, the probability of pump failure is $\frac{1}{2}$. If a pump fails, water cannot pass that station. For example, if pumps 1, 2, and 5 fail, water can flow only through 4 and 3. Consider the following questions that might well be asked about such a system:

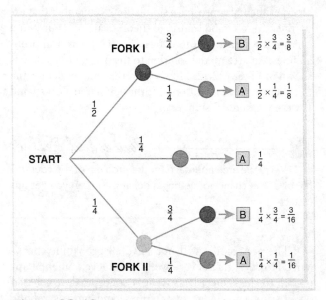

Figure 22.13 A tree diagram is another way to model the outcomes of two or more dependent events.

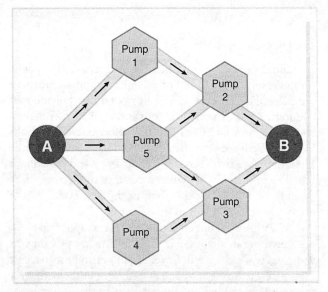

Figure 22.14 Each of these five pumps has a 50 percent chance of failure. What is the probability that some path from A to B is working?

- What is the probability that water will flow at any time?
- On the average, about how many stations need repair at any time?
- What is the probability that the 1–2 path is working at any time?

For any simulation, the following steps can serve as a useful guide.

1. *Identify key components and assumptions of the problem.* The key component in the water problem is the condition of a pump. Each pump is either working or not. The assumption is that the probability that a pump is working is $\frac{1}{2}$.

2. *Select a random device for the key components.* Any random device can be selected that has outcomes with the same probability as the key component—in this case, the pumps. Here a simple choice might be tossing a coin, with heads representing a working pump.

3. *Define a trial.* A *trial* consists of simulating a series of key components until the situation has been completely modeled one time. In this problem, a trial could consist of tossing a coin five times, each toss representing a different pump.

4. *Conduct a large number of trials and record the information.* For this problem, it would be good to keep the record of heads and tails in groups of five because each set of five is one trial and represents all of the pumps.

5. *Use the data to draw conclusions.* There are four possible paths for the water, each flowing through two of the five pumps. As they are numbered in the drawing, if any one of the pairs 1–2, 5–2, 5–3, and 4–3 is open, it makes no difference whether the other pumps are working. By counting the trials in which at least one of these four pairs of coins both came up heads, we can estimate the probability of water flowing. To answer the second question, the number of tails per trial can be averaged.

❙❙ ——————— *Pause and Reflect*

How would you answer the third question concerning the 1–2 path's being open?

The interesting problem-solving aspects of simulation activities are in the first three steps, where the real-world situation is translated into a model. Steps 4 and 5 are the same as solving a probability problem by experimental means. Translation of real-world information into models is the essence of applied mathematics.

Here are a few more examples of problems for which a simulation can be used to gather empirical data.

In a true-or-false test, what is the probability of getting 7 out of 10 questions correct by guessing alone? (**Key component:** answering a question. **Assumption:** Chance of getting it correct is $\frac{1}{2}$.)
   Simulation option: Flip a coin 10 times for one trial.

In a group of five people, what is the chance that two were born in the same month? (**Key component:** month of birth. **Assumption:** All 12 months are equally likely.)
   Simulation option: 12-sided dice or 12 cards. Draw/roll one, replace, and draw/roll again.

Casey's batting average is .350. What is the chance he will go hitless in a complete nine-inning game? (**Key component:** getting a hit. **Assumptions:** Probability of a hit for each at-bat is .35. Casey will get to bat four times in the average game.)
   Simulation option: Spinner with 35 percent shaded. Spin 4 times for one trial.

Students often have trouble selecting an appropriate random device for their simulations. Spinners are an obvious choice since faces can be adjusted to match probabilities. Coins or two-colored chips are useful for probabilities of $\frac{1}{2}$. A standard die can be used for probabilities that are multiples of $\frac{1}{6}$. There are also dice available from educational distributors with 4, 8, 12, and 20 sides.

 Many relatively simple calculators include a key that will produce random numbers that can be used to simulate experiments (e.g., 1 means true, 2 means false). Usually, the random numbers generated are between 0 and 1. Students who are going to use these random number generators will need some direction in using them to their advantage. Each number generated will likely have eight or more decimal places. A list of five numbers might look like this:

0.8904433368
0.0232028877
0.1669322714
0.1841957303
0.5523714952

How could a list of decimals like this replace flipping a coin or spinning a spinner? Suppose each was multiplied by 2. The results would be between 0 and 2. If you ignore the decimal part, you would have a series of zeros and ones that could stand for heads and tails, boys and girls, true and false, or any other pair of equally likely outcomes. For three outcomes, the same as a $\frac{1}{4}$-$\frac{1}{4}$-$\frac{1}{2}$ spinner, you might decide to look at the first two digits of the number and assign values from 0 to 24 and 25 to 49 to the two quarter portions and values 50 to 99 for the one-half portion. Alternatively, each number could be multiplied by 4, the decimal part ignored, resulting in random numbers 0, 1, 2, and 3. These could then be assigned to the desired outcomes. In effect, random numbers can simulate any simple random device.

With graphing calculators, the random number generator can be used inside of a simple program that produces the numbers and stores them in a list. The list can then be displayed graphically. The program in Figure 22.15 is for a TI-83 calculator. It will "roll" as many dice as you request. At the end of the program, a histogram displays the totals for each sum. With the TRACE feature, the value for each bar in the graph is displayed. The figure shows the result of rolling two dice 1000 times. It took about $2\frac{1}{2}$ minutes to run the program and produce the graph. (Computer programs produce the result almost instantly.) The TI-73 calculator designed for middle school has a built-in coin and dice function. ◆

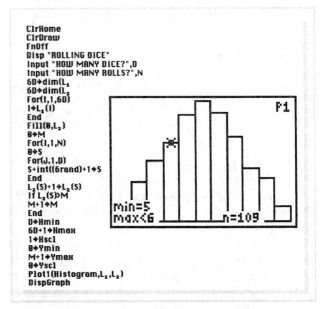

```
ClrHome
ClrDraw
FnOff
Disp "ROLLING DICE"
Input "HOW MANY DICE?",D
Input "HOW MANY ROLLS?",N
6D→dim(L₁
6D→dim(L₂
For(I,1,6D)
I→L₁(I)
End
Fill(0,L₂)
0→M
For(I,1,N)
0→S
For(J,1,D)
S+int((6rand)+1→S
End
L₂(S)+1→L₂(S)
If L₂(S)>M
M+1→M
End
D→Hmin
6D+1→Hmax
1→Hscl
0→Ymin
M+1→Ymax
0→Yscl
Plot1(Histogram,L₁,L₂)
DispGraph
```

Figure 22.15 This TI-83 program can be used to simulate thousands of dice rolls and accumulate the results.

Reflections on Chapter 22

Writing to Learn

1. What are the first ideas about probability that students should develop? How can you help students with these ideas?
2. Activities 22.3 and 22.4 ("Race to the Top" and "Add, Then Tally") are each designed to help students see that some outcomes are more likely than others. What is the difference between these two activities? Why might this difference be useful in helping students?
3. Explain what is meant by the statement "Chance has no memory."
4. Describe the difference between experimental probability and theoretical probability. Will these ever be the same? Which is the "correct" probability?
5. What are the advantages of having students conduct experiments even before they attempt to figure out a theoretical probability?
6. Explain the law of large numbers. Describe an activity that might help students to appreciate this idea.
7. Describe the difference between a single-stage and a multistage experiment. In multistage experiments, what are independent events and dependent events? Give an example of each.
8. Use an area model and a tree diagram to determine the probability for the following situation:

   Dad puts a $5 bill and three $1 bills in the first box. In a second box, he puts another $5 bill with just one $1 bill. For washing the car, Junior gets to take one bill from the first box without looking and put it in the second box. After these are well mixed, he then gets to take one bill from the second box. What is the probability that he will get $5?

   Design a simulation for the problem and try it out. Does your simulation agree with your theoretical probability?
9. The three outcomes of a sample space have probabilities of $\frac{1}{3}$, $\frac{1}{6}$, and $\frac{1}{2}$. Describe how you could use a random number generator on a calculator or computer to simulate these probabilities.

For Discussion and Exploration

1. The "Monty Hall Problem" has become a classic. In the game show, the contestant chooses from one of three doors. Behind one of the three doors is a big prize. Monty shows the contestant a goat behind one of the doors not selected and then offers the contestant the opportunity to switch doors. Does the contestant have a better chance of winning the big prize by switching, staying with the original choice, or is there no difference? There are numerous methods of answering this question. Make a convincing argument for your own answer based on the ideas and techniques in this chapter.
2. Go to the Illuminations website and find the activities related to probability. Explore the tasks for various trials. Discuss (a) the advantages and disadvantages of virtual experiments and (b) content within this chapter that could be discussed following student exploration on these applets.

Resources for Chapter **22**

Literature Connections

The books described here offer both fanciful and real-life data for investigating probability. Also, listed in Recommended Readings is an article with two more great literature links.

Go Figure! A Totally Cool Book about Numbers *Ball, 2005*

This wonderful book could be placed in every chapter of this book. About 40 different topics are covered, one of which is called "Take a Chance." This two-page spread is full of interesting contexts for probability, including a match-dropping experiment and genetics.

Harry Potter Books *Rowling, 1998, 1999a, 1999b, 2000, 2003, 2005, 2007*

The game of Qidditch can lend itself to creating a simulation to explore the likelihood of winning. Wagner and Lachance (2004) suggest that sums of two dice be linked to Qidditch actions. For example, a roll of 7 means a player scores a Quaffle, which is worth 10 points. Rolls of 2 or 12 mean the player catches the snitch and the game ends, 150 points; 3, 5, 9, 11 means hit by bludger—lose a turn; 4, 6, 8, 10 means dodge a bludger, no points.

Do You Wanna Bet? Your Chance to Find Out about Probability *Cushman, 1991*

The two characters in this book, Danny and Brian, become involved in everyday situations both in and out of school. Each situation has an element of probability involved. For example, two invitations to birthday parties are for the same day. What is the chance that two friends would have the same birthday? In another situation, Danny flips heads several times and readers are asked about Brian's chances on the next flip. An excellent opportunity to explore this possible misconception. These and other situations lead to a probability experiment or discussion. Students might create simulations to examine some of the ideas.

My Little Sister Ate One Hare *Grossman, 1996*

This counting book will appeal to the middle school set as well as to young children due to the somewhat gross thought of a little girl eating one rabbit, two snakes, three ants, and so on, including bats, mice, worms, and lizards. Upon eating ten peas, she throws up everything she ate.

Bay-Williams and Martinie (2004) used this tale with middle school students to create a wonderful introductory lesson in probability. If one of the things the little sister "spilled" on the floor is picked up at random in the process of cleaning up, what is the probability of getting a polliwog (or other animal or category of animal)? Students can use cards for the correct number of each thing eaten and approach the task experimentally and also compare the results to the theoretical probability.

Recommended Readings

Articles

Coffey, D. C., & Richardson, M. G. (2005). Rethinking fair games. *Mathematics Teaching in the Middle School, 10*(6), 298–303.

Students explore the fairness of a matching game both experimentally and using a theoretical model. They then set out to create a variation of the game that would be fair by assigning points to a match and to a mismatch. A TI-73 program is included that simulates the revised game.

Edwards, T. G., & Hensien, S. M. (2000). Using probability experiments to foster discourse. *Teaching Children Mathematics, 6*(8), 524–529.

Fifth-grade students experiment with outcomes of flipping a coin, spinning a spinner, and rolling a die. The discourse is directed to the disparity between the observed outcomes and the theoretical probabilities. For example, is it reasonable that there are 77 heads out of 150 tosses?

Lawrence, A. (1999). From *The Giver* to *The Twenty-One Balloons:* Explorations with probability. *Mathematics Teaching in the Middle School, 4*(8), 504–509.

Lawrence uses two award-winning books to motivate some nontrivial explorations for her middle school students. One task was to decide how often in a series of 50 births there will be 25 boys and 25 girls. In a related task, students tried to find out if it was more likely to have the same number of girls and boys in a small family or a large family. The ideas here are quite challenging and the results are interesting.

McMillen, S. (2008). Predictions and probability. *Teaching Children Mathematics, 14*(8), 454–463.

This article provides a series of high-quality probability lessons—various contexts and models are used, as well as calculators. The lessons include a number of key concepts discussed in this chapter and two handouts are provided.

Books

Shaughnessy, J. M. (2003). Research on students' understanding of probability. In J. Kilpatrick, W. G. Martin, & D. Schifter (Eds.), *A research companion to Principles and Standards for School Mathematics* (pp. 216–226). Reston, VA: NCTM.

Shaughnessy's chapter offers interesting insights from research and makes useful recommendations. Teachers serious about the teaching of probability will benefit from checking this out.

Online Resources

Adjustable Spinner (Shodor)
www.shodor.org/interactivate/activities/AdjustableSpinner

A virtual spinner can be adjusted to have any number of sections of any size. It can then be spun any number of times in increments of 100,000.

A Better Fire! (Shodor's Project Interactivate)
www.shodor.org/interactivate/activities/ABetterFire

This site offers a realistic simulation of actual forest fires, with controls for wind speed and direction to add more realism. The simulation uses a virtual "die" to see if a tree should be planted for each square. Then the fire is set and allowed to burn. An excellent authentic use of simulations.

Box Model (NLVM)
http://nlvm.usu.edu/en/nav/frames_asid_146_g_3_t_5
.html

The applet permits creating a box of up to 16 colored cubes, including the possibility of duplicates. Cubes can then be drawn at random (with replacement). A bar graph shows the results that can be compared to the theoretical results.

Coin Tossing (NLVM)
http://nlvm.usu.edu/en/nav/frames_asid_305_g_3_t_5
.html

A single coin can be "tossed" any number of times. The results are shown in order, which can help with the concept of randomness. A bar graph shows results.

Marble Mania
www.sciencenetlinks.com/interactives/marble/marble
mania.html

This applet explores randomness and probability. You'll be able to control how many and what color marbles to place in a virtual marble bag. An advantage of this applet is that you can run a large number of different trials in a short amount of time.

Probability (Shodor)
www.shodor.org/interactivate/activities/ExpProbability/
index.html

A spinner can be created with up to four regions or two like dice can be made with each side adjustable from 1 to 6. The devices can then be used in experiments.

Spinners (NLVM)
http://nlvm.usu.edu/en/nav/frames_asid_186_g_1_t_1
.html

This site provides a spinner that can be customized and used for experiments.

Field Experience Guide Connections

Children have very interesting notions about probability. Use Diagnostic Interview 7.2 with activities from this chapter to find out what students think is likely or not likely and why they think so. Or adapt Student Interview 4.5 to focus on attitudes about probability. FEG Expanded Lesson 9.21 ("Create a Game") engages students in designing a fair game, and FEG Expanded Lesson 9.23 ("Testing Bag Designs") provides more details on using this activity (see page 460 in this chapter).

Chapter 23

Developing Concepts of Exponents, Integers, and Real Numbers

Students in the middle grades need to develop a more complete understanding of the number system, which includes extending whole numbers to integers and starting to think of fractions as rational numbers (both positive and negative). In these ways and others they can begin to appreciate the completeness of the real number system.

The ideas presented in this chapter build on ideas that have been developed throughout this book. Exponents are used in algebraic expressions and add to the operations. Scientific notation expands how large and small numbers are represented, building on place-value concepts. Integers open up the counting numbers less than 0 and therefore extend the number line (as well as operations) to include negative values. The *Curriculum Focal Points* (NCTM, 2006) states that seventh graders should be "developing an understanding of operations on all rational numbers and solving linear equations" (p. 19) and that in eighth grade, "Students use exponents and scientific notation to describe very large and very small numbers. They use square roots when they apply the Pythagorean theorem." (p. 20).

Big Ideas

1. Exponential notation is a way to express repeated products of the same number. Specifically, powers of 10 express very large and very small numbers in an economical manner.

2. Integers add to the number system the negative (and positive) counting numbers, so that every number has both size and a positive or negative relationship to other numbers. A negative number is the opposite of the positive number of the same size.

3. Whole numbers, fractions, and integers are rational numbers. Every rational number can be expressed as a fraction.

4. Many numbers are not rational; the irrationals can be expressed only symbolically or approximately using a close rational number. Examples include $\sqrt{2} \approx 1.41421\ldots$ and $\pi \approx 3.14159\ldots$

Mathematics Content Connections

The ideas in this chapter represent an expansion of the ways in which we represent numbers. These representations expand or enhance earlier ideas of whole numbers, fractions, and decimals.

- **Whole-Number Place Value, Fractions, and Decimals** (Chapters 11, 15, and 17): When exponential notation is combined with decimal notation, very small and very large numbers can be written efficiently. Decimals and fractions help to describe the difference between rational and irrational numbers. Negative numbers extend the number line in both directions.

- **Algebra** (Chapter 14): The symbolic manipulation of numbers, including the rules for order of operations, is exactly the same as is used with variables. The study of integers helps with the notion of "opposite," represented by a negative sign: $^-6$ is the opposite of $^+6$ and ^-x is the opposite of ^+x, regardless of whether x is negative or positive. Exponents can also be variables, giving rise to exponential functions.

Exponents

As numbers in our technological world get very small or very large, expressing them in standard form is cumbersome. Exponential notation is much more efficient for conveying numeric or quantitative information.

Exponents in Expressions and Equations

In algebra classes, students get confused trying to remember the rules of exponents. For example, when you raise numbers to powers, do you add or multiply the exponents? This is an example of procedural knowledge that is often learned without supporting conceptual knowledge. Before algebra, students should have ample opportunity to explore exponents with whole numbers rather than with letters or variables. By doing so, they are able to deal directly with the concept and actually generate the rules themselves.

A *whole-number exponent* is simply shorthand for repeated multiplication of a number times itself; for example, $3^4 = 3 \times 3 \times 3 \times 3$.

Conventions of symbolism must also be learned. These are arbitrary rules with no conceptual basis. The first is that *an exponent applies to its immediate base.* For example, in the expression $2 + 5^3$, the exponent 3 applies only to the 5, so the expression is equal to $2 + (5 \times 5 \times 5)$. However, in the expression $(2 + 5)^3$, the 3 is an exponent of the quantity $2 + 5$ and is evaluated as $(2 + 5) \times (2 + 5) \times (2 + 5)$, or $7 \times 7 \times 7$.

Students' first encounter with exponents should be squares and cubes, numbers that can be represented geometrically. For example, consider the following problem:

Minia knows that square animal pens are the most economical for the amount of space they provide. Can you provide a table for Minia that shows the areas of square pens that have between 4 meters and 10 meters of fence on each side?

Students may set up a table similar to Figure 23.1, showing possible areas for the pen.

Students can also explore algebraic growing patterns involving squares and/or cubes. The Painted Cube Problem, which involves both squares and cubes, is a popular investigation that appears in many places, including the *Connected Mathematics* curriculum (see Figure 23.2). In this problem the faces of the cube are squares. Therefore, the

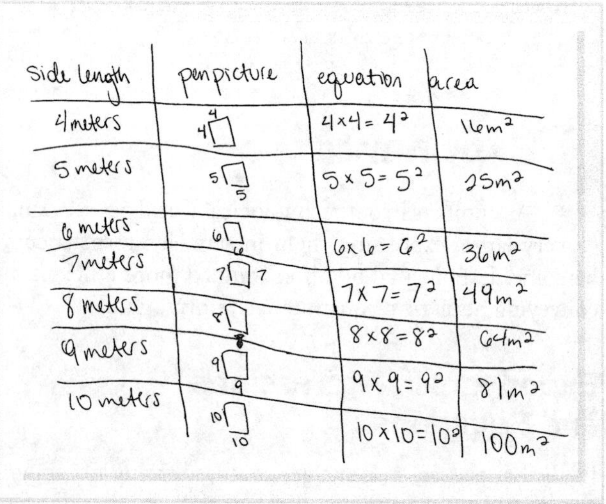

Figure 23.1 A student records possibilities for making a square pen.

sides getting painted are also squares, and the growth pattern is a square. The cubes getting no sides painted are those hidden inside the painted cube. In a $2 \times 2 \times 2$, there are 0 inside cubes, but in a $3 \times 3 \times 3$ there is one hidden cube inside that will not get painted. This "hidden cube" grows at a cubic rate. In exploring the pattern, students get experience with squares and cubes.

Order of Operations. The other convention involves the *order of operations:* Multiplication and division are always done before addition and subtraction. Since exponentiation is repeated multiplication, it also is done before addition and subtraction. In the expression $5 + 4^2 - 6 \div 3$, 4^2 and $6 \div 3$ are done first. Therefore, the expression is evaluated as $5 + 16 - 2 = 21 - 2 = 19$.

❚❚ ———————— *Pause and Reflect*

Try evaluating the same expression in left-to-right order. Do you get 4?

Parentheses are used to group operations that are to be done first. Therefore, in $(5 + 4) \times 2 - 6 \div 3$, the addition can be done inside the parentheses first, or the distributive property can be used, and the final result is 16. The phrase "*P*lease *e*xcuse *m*y *d*ear *A*unt *S*ally" is sometimes used to help students recall that operations inside *p*arentheses are done first, then *e*xponentiation, and then *m*ultiplication and *d*ivision before *a*ddition and *s*ubtraction.

Although this phrase is a good mnemonic, it can lead students to think that addition is done before subtraction and multiplication comes before division. An improvement might involve writing it as a verse in rows that show the last four words as pairs. Another option is to just use the acronym "PEMDAS," with the letters listed in rows to indicate order:

P = parenthesis
E = exponents
MD = multiplication and division (whichever is first from left to right)
AS = addition and subtraction (whichever is first from left to right)

Sometimes, students' only experience is to simplify expressions applying the order. You can both assess and strengthen their understanding of this process by having them write equations that indicate the proper order of operations, as in the activity below.

Activity **23.1**

Guess My Number

This algebraic activity involves the teacher giving hints about a number and students thinking backwards to

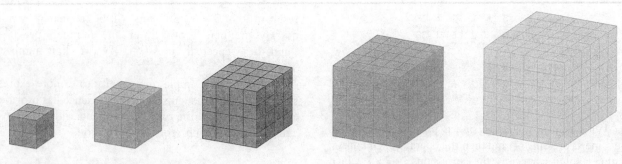

Organize your data in a table like the one below.

Edge Length of Large Cube	Number of Centimeter Cubes	Number of Centimeter Cubes Painted On			
		3 faces	2 faces	1 face	0 faces
2					
3					
4					
5					
6					

Study the patterns in the table.

1. Describe the relationship between the edge length of the large cube and the total number of centimeter cubes.

2. Describe the relationship between the edge length of the large cube and the number of centimeter cubes painted on.

   a. three faces   **b.** two faces   **c.** one face   **d.** zero faces

Figure 23.2 The Painted Cube Problem provides a context for exploring squares and cubes.

Source: Adapted from *Connected Mathematics: Frogs, Fleas and Painted Cubes: Quadratic Relationships* by Glenda Lappan, James T. Fey, William M. Fitzgerald, Susan N. Friel, & Elizabeth Difanis Phillips. Copyright © 2006 by Michigan State University. Used by permission of Pearson Education, Inc. All rights reserved.

find it (using logical reasoning). Students create equations, using parentheses appropriately to reflect the clues the teacher gives, as in the following three examples:

- **I am thinking of a number; I add 5, double it, and get 22. $[(n + 5) \times 2 = 22]$**
- **I am thinking of a number; I subtract 2, square it, and get 36. $[(n - 2)^2 = 36]$**
- **I am thinking of a number; I double it, add 2, cube it, and get 1000. $[(2n + 2)^3 = 1000]$**

The writing stories activity is another excellent tool for learning and applying the order of operations. Students can be asked to write an expression using all the operations and parentheses—for example, $(4 + 2)^2 \times 2 \div 4$—and then write a story, using a context of their choice, to fit the expression they have created (Golembo, 2000).

Writing stories is an excellent assessment of students' understanding of the order of operations. Golembo (2006) includes a student page and assessment pages. As students write expressions or stories, determine whether they realize that multiplication and division (and addition and subtraction) are equal in order and should be solved left to right. Also, ask students questions to see whether they understand when parentheses are optional and when they are necessary. ◆

Exponent Notation on the Calculator. Most scientific calculators employ "algebraic logic" that evaluates expressions using the order of operations and also allows grouping with parentheses. However, with the exception of the TI-MathMate and other newer calculators designed specifically for school use, most simple four-function calculators do not use algebraic logic. Operations are processed as they are entered. On calculators without algebraic logic, the following two keying sequences produce the same results:

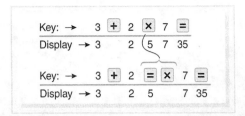

Whenever an operation sign is pressed, the effect is the same as pressing $=$ and then the operation. Of course, neither result is correct for the expressions $3 + 2 \times 7$, which should be evaluated as $3 + 14$, or 17. Calculators designed for middle grades do use algebraic logic and include parenthesis keys so that both $3 + 2 \times 7$ and $(3 + 2) \times 7$ can be keyed in the order that the symbols appear. See the difference in the following displays:

Key: →   3 + 2 × 7 =
Display → 3   2   7 17

Notice that the following display does not change when $\times$ is pressed and a right parenthesis is never displayed. Instead, the expression that the right parenthesis encloses is calculated and that result displayed.

Key: →   (3 + 2) × 7 =
Display → [3   2 5   7 35

Some basic calculators and graphing calculators show the expression $3 + 2 \times (6^2 - 4)$. Nothing is evaluated until you press Enter or EXE. Then the result appears on the next line to the right of the screen:

$$3 + 2 * (6^2 - 4) \qquad 67$$

Moreover, the last expression entered can be recalled and edited so that students can see how different expressions are evaluated. Only minimum key presses are required.

$3 + 2 * (6^2 - 4)$	67
$(3 + 2) * (6^2 - 4)$	160
$(3 + 2) * 6^2 - 4$	176
$3 + 2 * 6^2 - 4$	71

The simple four-function calculator remains a powerful tool for exploration. For example, to evaluate 3^8, press

3 × = = = = = = =. (The first press of $=$ will result in 9, or 3×3.) Students will be fascinated by how quickly numbers grow. Enter any number, press $\times$, and then repeatedly press $=$. Try two-digit numbers. Try 0.1.

Give students ample opportunity to explore expressions involving exponents. When experience has provided a firm background, the rules of exponents will make sense and should not require rote memorization.

Activity 23.2

Entering Expressions

Provide students with numeric expressions to evaluate with simple four-function calculators. Ask: "How will you have to enter these to correctly apply the order of operations?" Rewrite the expression the way it will be entered. Here are some examples of expressions:

$3 + 4 \times 8$ $4 \times 8 + 3$	$3^6 + 2^6$ $(3 + 2)^6$	$3^4 \times 7 - 5^2$ $(3 \times 7)^4 - 5 \times 2$	$3^4 \times 5^2$ $(3 \times 5)^6$

$\dfrac{5^3 \times 5^2}{5^6}$	$4 \times 3 - 2^3 \times 5 + 23 \times 9$	$\dfrac{4 \times 3^5}{2} \qquad 4 + \dfrac{3^5}{2}$

When experiencing difficulty with exponents, students should write equivalent expressions without exponents or include parentheses to indicate explicit groupings. For example:

$$
\begin{aligned}
(7 \times 2^3 - 5)^3 &= (7 \times (2 \times 2 \times 2) - 5) \times \\
&\quad (7 \times (2 \times 2 \times 2) - 5) \times \\
&\quad (7 \times (2 \times 2 \times 2) - 5) \\
&= ((7 \times 8) - 5) \times \\
&\quad ((7 \times 8) - 5) \times \\
&\quad ((7 \times 8) - 5) \\
&= (56 - 5) \times (56 - 5) \times (56 - 5) \\
&= 51 \times 51 \times 51
\end{aligned}
$$

For many expressions, there is more than one way to proceed, and sharing different ways is important.

Of course, calculators with algebraic logic will automatically produce correct results. Yet it remains important for students to know these rules, and the calculator should not replace an understanding of the order of operations. These rules apply to symbolic manipulation in algebra and must be understood for mental calculations or for using a basic calculator.

Negative Exponents

When students begin to explore exponents and have also experienced negative integers, it is interesting to consider what it might mean to raise a number to a negative power. For example, what does 2^{-4} mean? The following two related options can help students explore the possibilities of negative exponents. First, based on the importance of patterns in mathematics, examine a pattern of numbers, and see how it might best be expanded. The powers of 10 are good to explore because they are directly related to place value. Have students consider 10^N as follows:

$$10^4 = 10,000$$
$$10^3 = 1000$$
$$10^2 = 100$$
$$10^1 = 10$$
$$10^0 = ?$$
$$10^{-1} = ?$$

In this sequence, the most obvious entry for 10^0 is 1, which is the *definition* of 10^0. That is, it is a convention that 10 or any other nonzero number raised to the power 0 is 1. So what is 10^{-1}? If the pattern is to continue, the 1 should move to the right of the decimal:

$$10^0 = 1$$
$$10^{-1} = 0.1$$
$$10^{-2} = 0.01$$
$$10^{-3} = 0.001$$

and so on. Notice how each of these numbers is written as a fraction:

$$10^{-1} = 0.1 = \frac{1}{10}$$
$$10^{-2} = 0.01 = \frac{1}{100} = \frac{1}{10^2}$$
$$10^{-3} = 0.001 = \frac{1}{1000} = \frac{1}{10^3}$$

Second, students can explore negative exponents on a calculator. For example, tell students, "Use a calculator to see if you can figure out what 4^{-3} or 2^{-5} equal." The calculator should, of course, never be seen as the *reason* for anything in mathematics, but here you are exploring notation convention. If the calculator has decimal-to-fraction conversion, suggest that students use that feature to help develop the meaning of negative exponents. Figure 23.3 gives an example of how this might look on a graphing calculator.

Scientific Notation

The more common it becomes to find very large or very small numbers in our daily lives, the more important it is to have convenient ways to represent them. One option is to say and write numbers in their common form. However, this practice can at times be cumbersome. Another option is to use exponential notation and our base-ten place-value system—scientific notation. In scientific notation, a number is changed to be the product of a number greater than or equal to 1 and less than ten (meaning only one digit in front of the decimal) multiplied by a multiple of 10. For example,

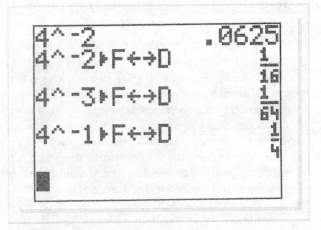

Figure 23.3 Graphing calculators evaluate expressions as decimals. However, they also convert decimals to fractions. This figure shows the screen of a TI-73 calculator. The F–D key converts fractions to decimals (and decimals to fractions) as shown here.

3,414,000,000 can be written as 3.414×10^9. Since you have moved the decimal back nine places (divided by 1 billion) to place the decimal, to keep the number equivalent, you must multiply by 1 billion (10^9).

Different notations have different purposes and values. Consider this fact: In 1990, the population of the world was more than 5,050,700,000 persons, about 1 billion fewer than in the year 2000. This can be expressed in various ways:

5 billion 50 million 700 thousand
5,050,700,000
5.0507×10^9
Less than 5.1 billion
A little more than 5 billion

Each way of stating the number has value and purpose in different contexts. Rather than spend time with exercises converting numbers from standard form to scientific notation, consider large numbers found in newspapers, magazines, and atlases. How are they written? How are they said aloud? When are they rounded? When not and why? What forms of the numbers seem best for the purposes?

The *Standards* reminds us that large numbers and scientific notation are used in various contexts. "A newspaper headline may proclaim, 'Clean-Up Costs from Oil Spill Exceed $2 Billion!' or a science textbook may indicate that the number of red blood cells in the human body is about 1.9×10^{13}" (p. 217). ◆

Contexts for Very Large Numbers. The real world is full of very large quantities and measures. We see references to huge numbers in the media all the time. Unfortunately, most of us have not developed an appreciation for extremely large numbers, such as the following examples:

- A state lottery with 44 numbers from which to pick 6 has over 7 million possible combinations of 6 numbers. There are $44 \times 43 \times 42 \times 41 \times 40 \times 39$ possible ways that the balls could come out of the hopper (5,082,517,440). But generally the order in which they are picked is not important. Since there are $6 \times 5 \times 4 \times 3 \times 2 \times 1 = 720$ different arrangements of 6 numbers, each collection appears 720 times. Therefore, there are *only* $5,082,517,440 \div 720$ possible lottery numbers, or in other words, 1 out of 7,059,052 chances to win.
- The estimated size of the universe is 40 billion light-years. One light-year is the number of miles light travels in *one year*. The speed of light is 186,281.7 miles per *second*, or 16,094,738,880 miles in a single day.
- The human body has about 100 billion cells.
- The distance to the sun is about 150 million kilometers.
- The population of the world in 2008 was about 6.71 billion.

Connecting these large numbers to meaningful points of reference can help students get a handle on their true magnitude. For example, suppose students determine the population in their city or town is about 500,000 people. They can then figure that it would take about 12,500 cities of the same population size to generate the population of the world. Or suppose students determine that it is about 4600 km between San Francisco, California, and Washington, DC. This would mean that it would take over 32,000 trips back and forth between these two cities to equal the distance between the earth and the sun. Building from such familiar or meaningful reference points can help students develop benchmarks to work with and make sense of large numbers.

The following activity uses real data and asks students to use scientific notation and create a scale drawing.

Activity 23.3

How Far Away from the Sun?

A problem-based way to explore scientific notation is to have students research planetary distances from the sun (in km), record the data in scientific notation, and create a scaled illustration of the distances. Alternatively, the following figures can be provided:

Mercury	57,909,000	Jupiter	778,400,000
Venus	108,200,000	Saturn	1,423,600,000
Earth	149,600,000	Uranus	2,867,000,000
Mars	227,940,000	Neptune	4,488,400,000

Contexts for Very Small Numbers. It is extremely important to use real examples of very small numbers. Without real contexts, you may be tempted to resort to drill exercises that have little meaning for students. As with large numbers, connecting these small numbers to points of reference can help students conceptualize how very tiny these numbers really are, as shown by the following real-world examples:

- The length of a DNA strand in a cell is about 10^{-7} m. This is also measured as 1000 *angstroms*. (Based on this information, how long is an angstrom?) For perspective, the diameter of a human hair is about 2.54×10^{-5} m.
- Human hair grows at the rate of 10^{-8} miles per hour. Garden snails have been clocked at about 3×10^{-2} mph.
- The chances of winning the Virginia lottery, based on selecting six numbers from 1 to 44, is 1 in 7.059 million. That is a probability of less than 1.4×10^{-10}.
- The mass of one atom of hydrogen is 0.000 000 000 000 000 000 000 001 675 g compared to the mass of one paper clip at about 1 g.
- It takes sound 0.28 second (2.8×10^{-1}) to travel the length of a football field. In contrast, a TV signal travels a full mile in about 0.000005368 second, or 5.3×10^{-6} second. A TV viewer at home hears the football being kicked before the receiver on the field does.

Scientific Notation on the Calculator. Students in elementary school learn how to multiply by 10, by 100, and by 1000 by simply adding the appropriate number of zeros. Help students expand this idea by examining powers of 10 on a calculator that handles exponents.

Activity 23.4

Exploring Powers of 10

Have students use any calculator that permits entering exponents to explore some of the following:

- Explore 10^N for various values of *N*. What patterns do you notice. What does 1E15 mean? (1E15 is the typical calculator form of 1×10^{15}.)
- Find different expressions for one thousand, one million, one billion, one trillion. What patterns are there in expressions you found?
- Enter 45 followed by a string of zeros. How many will your calculator permit? What happens when you press Enter ? What does 4.5E10 mean?
- What does 5.689E6 mean? Can you enter this another way?
- Try sums like $(4.5 \times 10^N) + (27 \times 10^K)$ for different values of *N* and *K*. What can you find out?
- What happens with products of numbers like those in the previous item?

It is useful to become comfortable with the power-of-10 expressions in Activity 23.4. Students should eventually discover that when scientific or graphing calculators display numbers with more digits than the display will hold, they use scientific notation. For example, on a TI-73, the product of 45,000,000 × 8,000,000 is displayed as 3.6E14, meaning 3.6×10^{14}, or 360,000,000,000,000 (360 trillion).

Ask students why there are only 13 zeros. What happens when the numbers in the computation do not involve a lot of zeros?

Pause and Reflect

With each factor in the product expressed in scientific notation: $(4.5 \times 10^7) \times (8 \times 10^6)$, or 4.5E7 × 8.0E6, can you compute the result mentally?

Notice the advantages of scientific notation, especially for multiplication and division. Here the significant digits can be multiplied mentally (4.5 × 8 = 36) and the exponents added to produce almost instantly 36×10^{13} or 3.6×10^{14}.

Integers

Almost every day students have some interaction with negative numbers or experience phenomena that negative numbers can model, as shown in the following list:

Temperature
Altitude (above and below sea level)
Golf
Money
Time lines (including BC)
Football yardage (gains/losses)

In fact, almost any concept that is quantified and has direction probably has both positive and negative values.

Generally, negative values are introduced with *integers*—the whole numbers and their negatives or opposites—instead of with fractions or decimals.

However, it is a mistake to stop with integer values, because students must understand where numbers like ⁻4.5 and ⁻1¾ belong in relation to the integers. In fact, research has shown that students often place ⁻1¾ between ⁻1 and 0 instead of between ⁻2 and ⁻1.

Contexts for Exploring Integers

As with any new topic or type of number, it is important to start with familiar contexts so that students can use this prior knowledge to build meaning. With integers, students often get confused as to which number is bigger or which direction they are moving when they do operations, so having a context is particularly important. As students learn to compare and compute, they can use the contexts

to ground their thinking and justify their answers. For example, some contexts for integers involve quantities and some contexts are linear.

Pause and Reflect

Review the list of contexts in the introduction to this section. Which do you think are quantity contexts and which are linear contexts? In the following sections, both quantity and linear contexts are discussed, followed by models for illustrating integers for both types.

Quantity Contexts

Golf Scores. In golf, scores are often written in relationship to a number considered par for the course. So, if par is 70 for the course, a golfer who ends the day at 67 has a score of ⁻3. Consider a player in a tournament with day-end scores of ⁺5, ⁻2, ⁻3, ⁺1. What would be his or her final result for the tournament? How did you think about it? You could match up the positive and the negatives (in this case, ⁺5 with ⁻2 and ⁻3 to get a net result of 0), and then see what is left (in this case, ⁺1). The notion that opposites (5 and ⁻5) equal zero is a big idea in the teaching of integers. You can post a mixed-up leader board of golf scores and ask students to order them from first through tenth place. Emphasize that first place is the *lowest* score—and therefore the *smallest* number. As you can see, golf scores provide a great context for comparing and computing with integers.

Money: Debits and Credits. Suppose that you are the bookkeeper for a small business. At any time, your records show how many dollars the company has in its account. There are always so many dollars in cash (credits or receipts) and so many dollars in accounts payable (debits). The difference between the debit and credit totals tells the value of the account. If there are more credits than debits, the account is positive, or "in the black." If there are more debits than credits, the account is in debt, showing a negative cash value, or "in the red." With the bookkeeping context, it is possible to explore addition and subtraction of integers, as in the example illustrated in Figure 23.4. An advantage of money is that it can be used for negative values that are not integers, specifically decimals. As noted earlier, it is important to engage students in thinking about negative numbers that are decimals and fractions once they have explored integer values.

Linear Contexts. Many of the real contexts for negative numbers are linear. In addition, the number line provides a good tool for learning the operations that relates well to what the students have done with whole number and fraction operations.

| Credits | | Debits | | Balance |
In	Out	In	Out	**Begin** 0
50				+50
		30		+20
	10			+10
		50		−40
25				−15
			20	+5

Debit
$20

Figure 23.4 A ledger sheet context for integers.

Temperature. The "number line" measuring temperature is vertical. This context demonstrating negative integers may be the most familiar to students, as they have either experienced temperatures below zero or know about temperatures on the North or South Pole. A good starting activity for students is finding where various temperatures belong on a thermometer. For example, Figure 23.5 displays a thermometer marked in increments of five degrees, and students are asked to place on the number line the following temperatures from a week in North Dakota: 8, ⁻2,

⁻12, 4, ⁻8. Ask students to order them from the coldest to the warmest (least to greatest). Temperatures as a context have the advantage that you can also use fractional and decimal values.

Altitude. Another vertical number-line model, altitude, is also a good context for integers. The altitudes of sites below sea level are negative, such as the town of Dead Sea, Israel, with an altitude of ⁻1371 feet and in the United States, Badwater, California, in Death Valley has an altitude of ⁻282 feet. Positive values for altitude include Mount McKinley (tallest mountain in North America) at 20,322 feet. Students can order the altitudes of various places around the United States or around the world (data easily found through a Google search on the Web) or find the difference between the altitudes of two different places—a good context for subtraction of integers. Beyond exploring real altitudes, using a model of a hill and a valley over which a toy car moves up and down can be a graphic way to explore integer operations.

Time Lines. Asking students to place historical events on a time line is an excellent interdisciplinary opportunity. The time line is useful for examples with larger values (e.g., 1950) as well as negative values (e.g., ⁻3000). Or students can explore their own personal time line (Weidemann, Mikovch, & Hunt, 2001), in which students find out key events that happened before they were born (e.g., birth of an older sibling) and since they have been alive (e.g., move to a new house). They then place these events on a number line. By partitioning a year into months, students can gain experience with rational numbers (twelfths) on the number line. Continue to reinforce the connection to the size of numbers, asking students, "Which number (year) is the smallest (earliest)?

Football. A statistic reported on every play in a football game is yards gained and yards lost, which provides a good context for exploring integers, especially when it comes to comparing and adding integers. Students can be asked questions like "If the Steelers started their drive on the 20 yard line and the first three plays were recorded as ⁻4, ⁺9, ⁺3, did they get a first down?" or "On the Broncos first play, the yardage is ⁻4. Where are they in relation to the line of scrimmage (using negatives, if behind the line of scrimmage, in this case ⁻4) and where are they in relation to the first down marker (⁻14)?"

Activity **23.5**

Football Statistics

Look up the average yards gained for some of the best running backs in the NFL or from college teams popular with your students. Ask students to use average yards gained per down to create a possible list of

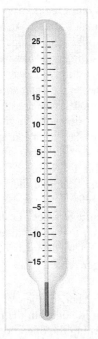

Figure 23.5 Thermometers provide an excellent tool for exploring positive and negative numbers.

yardage gains and losses for that player. For example, if a player had an average of 4 yards per carry in a game, the following could have been his data:

10, ‾3, ‾2, 21, ‾5, 3, ‾1, 5, ‾1, 13

You may want to do one like this together and then have students create their own. The football context provides an excellent way to *use* integers meaningfully, integrated with the important concept of averages.

The calculator is a tool that might be explored early in the discussion of integers. It gives correct and immediate results that students can justify on a number line or with one of the contexts described.

Have students explore subtraction problems such as 5 – 8 = ?, and discuss the results. (Be aware that the negative sign appears in different places on different calculators.)

Students can benefit by using the calculator along with the intuitive models and questions mentioned earlier. For example, how can you get from ‾5 to ‾17 by addition? 13 minus *what* is 15?

Meaning of Negative Numbers

Negative numbers are defined in terms of whole numbers. Therefore, the definition of negative 3 is the solution to the equation 3 + ? = 0. In general, the *opposite of n* is the solution to n + ? = 0. If n is a positive number, the *opposite of n* is a negative number. The set of integers, therefore, consists of the positive whole numbers, the opposites of the whole numbers, or negative numbers, and 0, which is neither positive nor negative. This is the definition found in student textbooks. Like many aspects of mathematics, abstract or symbolic definitions are best understood when conceptual connections link to the formal mathematics.

Absolute Value. The distance between two points, either on the number line or in the plane, is often an important concern, especially in applications of mathematics. We need to be able, for example, to tell a computer how far a train is from a station regardless of whether it is to the north or the south on the track. "Distance" can also refer to a mathematical distance as in the amount of possible error between a measurement and the true value, and the measures could be weight, time, voltage, and so on.

The *absolute value of a number* is defined as the distance between that number and zero. The notation for absolute value consists of two vertical bars on either side of the number. Thus, the absolute value of a number n is |n|. Opposites, such as ‾12 and 12, are the same distance from zero, and therefore have the same absolute value.

In most middle school books, students are asked only to evaluate numeric expressions such as |‾8| or |6 – 10|. The unfortunate consequence of these exercises is that stu-

dents quickly learn to simply do the computation and then ignore or "remove" the negative sign if there is one.

Notations. Because students have only seen the negative sign when doing subtraction, the symbolic notation for integers may be confusing. It is important to help students understand and use the appropriate symbols. Students may find it confusing that sometimes the negative sign appears at different heights (e.g., –7 and ‾7). Also, sometimes parentheses are placed around the number so that it is separate from the operation—for example, 8 – (–5). Students have not seen parentheses used in this way and may think there is multiplication involved. It is important to connect to their prior knowledge and add to it. In this case, therefore, you might ask students, "When do we use parentheses in mathematics?" Students might say they are used for grouping a series of computations to show what to do first and that it can also mean multiplication. Point out that parentheses are also used to make a number sentence more readable—separating the negative number from the operation.

On graphing calculators, these expressions are entered using the "negative" key and the "subtraction" key. The difference between those two symbols is evident in the display. The redundant superscript plus signs are not shown. Students can see that 3 + ‾5 and 3 – 5 each results in ‾2 and that 3 – ‾5 and 3 + 5 are equal. ◆

Two Models for Teaching Integers

Two models, one denoted by quantity and the other by linear operations, are popular for helping students understand comparisons and the four operations (+, –, ×, and ÷) with integers.

Counters. One model consists of counters in two different colors, one for positive counts and one for negative counts. Two counters of each type result in zero (⁺1 + ‾1 = 0). Consider money: If yellows are credits and reds are debits, 5 yellows and 7 reds is the same as 2 reds or 2 debits and is represented as ‾2 (see Figure 23.6). It is important in using this model for students to understand that it is always possible to add to or remove from a pile any number of pairs consisting of one positive and one negative counter

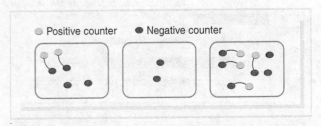

Figure 23.6 Each collection is a model of negative 2.

without changing the value of the pile. (Intuitively, this is like adding equal quantities of debits and credits.)

Number Lines. The number line is the second model. For instance, a thermometer would be considered a number line. A number line has several advantages. First, it shows the distance from 0 (or the absolute value of the number). In addition, it is an excellent tool for modeling the operations. Jumps can be shown in the same way as with whole numbers and fractions (see Chapters 12 and 16). Students can see that integer moves to the left go to smaller numbers and moves to the right go to larger numbers. Also, the number line allows students to explore noninteger negative and positives values (e.g., $-4\frac{1}{2} + 3\frac{1}{4}$) that cannot be modeled very well with counters.

In modeling operations, arrows can be used to show distance and direction. For example, 4 can be modeled with an arrow four units long pointing to the right, and -3 can be modeled with an arrow three units long pointing to the left (see Figure 23.7). The arrows help students think of integer quantities as directed distances. A positive arrow never points left, and a negative arrow never points right. Furthermore, each arrow is a quantity with both length (magnitude or absolute value) and direction (sign). These properties are constant for each arrow regardless of its position on the number line.

Which Model to Use. Although the two models appear quite different, they are alike mathematically. Integers involve two concepts—*quantity* and *opposite*. Quantity is modeled by the number of counters or the length of the arrows. Opposite is represented as different colors or different directions.

Many teachers decide to use only the model that students like or understand better. This is a mistake! Remember that the concepts are not in the models but rather must be constructed by the students and imposed on the models. Seeing integers across two models can help students extract the intended concepts. Students should experience both models and, perhaps even more important, discuss how the two are alike.

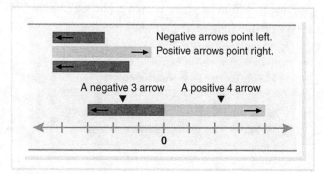

Figure 23.7 Number-line model for integers.

Operations with Integers

Once your students understand how integers are represented by each of the models, you can present the operations for the integers in the form of problems. In other words, rather than explaining how addition of integers works and showing students how to solve exercises with the models, you pose an integer computation and let students use their models to find a solution. When solutions have been reached, the groups can compare and justify their results using one of the contexts or models described earlier in this chapter.

Addition and Subtraction

Since middle school students may not have used counters or number lines for some time, it would be good to begin work with either of these models using positive whole numbers. After a few examples to help students become familiar with the model for addition or subtraction with whole numbers, have them work through an example with integers using exactly the same reasoning. Remember, the emphasis should be on the rationale and not on how quickly students can get correct answers.

Introduce negative values using one of the contexts discussed earlier in this chapter. For example, golf scores can be used as a context. Personalize the story by telling students that each weekend you golf a round on Saturday and on Sunday. The first weekend your results were $+3$ and $+5$, the next weekend you scored $+3$ and -5, and on the last weekend you scored -6 and $+2$. How did you do overall each weekend? Because this is a quantity model, counters are a good choice for modeling (though number lines can also be used). A linear context could be football yards gained and lost on two plays. See Figure 23.8 for illustrations of how to use both models for addition.

Several examples of addition are modeled in Figure 23.8, each in two ways: with positive and negative counters and with the number-line-and-arrow model. First examine the counter model. After the two quantities are joined, any pairs of positive and negative counters combine to equal zero, and students can remove these, making it easier to see the result.

To add using the arrow model, note that each added arrow begins at the arrowhead end of the previous arrow. Recall that subtraction can be used for take-away situations (e.g., start with 7 and take away 10) or in comparisons (What is the difference between 7 and -3?). The quantity model is appropriate for take away and the number line can be used for either take away or comparisons.

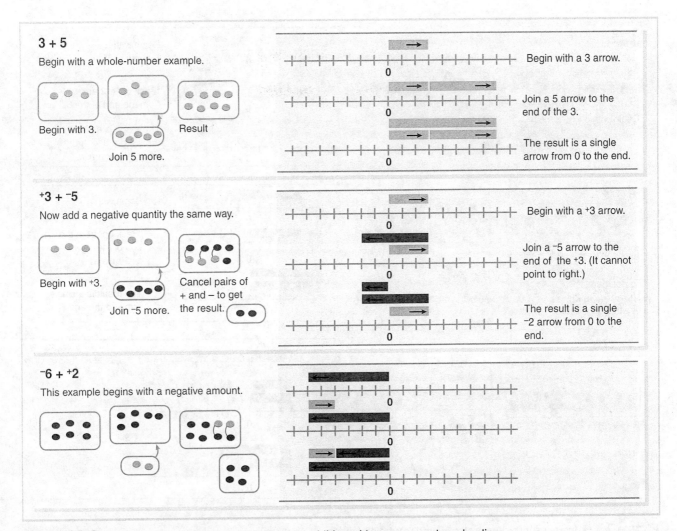

Figure 23.8 Relate integer addition to whole-number addition with counters and number lines.

Consider the problem ⁻5 – ⁺2, the second example modeled in Figure 23.9 (the first being a whole number example for the sake of making the connection). If using a quantity model, the context could be money, such as, "I start with a debt of $5 and then charge (take out) $2 more to my account. What balance will my bank account show (if no fees have been charged yet for my overdrawn account)? To model it, you start with the five red counters. To remove two positive counters from a set that has none, a different representation of ⁻5 must first be made. Since any number of neutral pairs (one positive, one negative) can be added without changing the value of the set, two pairs are added so that two positive counters can be removed. The net effect is to have more negative counters.

In a number model, subtraction can be modeled using arrows. When subtracting positive values, as in the second example in Figure 23.9, this works just as with whole numbers, moving to the left. Using temperature as a context, the explanation could be: "The day begins at 5 below zero. Then the temperature drops +2°, which means it just got colder and is now ⁻7°. The difficulty comes when trying to

provide an authentic explanation of subtracting a negative value. For example, ⁻4 – ⁻7 (see Figure 23.9, third example). In this case you start with thinking about taking away, but because it is negative temperature (or coldness) that is being taken away, you are in fact doing the opposite—warming up by 7 degrees. Modeling on the number line, you start at ⁻4, then reverse the arrow going left to one going right 7 moves. Number lines can also be used for comparison or distance. What is the difference between ⁻7 and ⁻4? In other words, how do you get from ⁻7 to ⁻4? You count up 3.

⏸ ──────── *Pause and Reflect*

Before reading further, go through each example in Figures 23.8 and 23.9. Explain each problem using both a quantity and a linear context. You should become comfortable with both models.

Have your students draw pictures to accompany integer computations. Set pictures are easy enough; they may consist of Xs and Os, for example. For the number line,

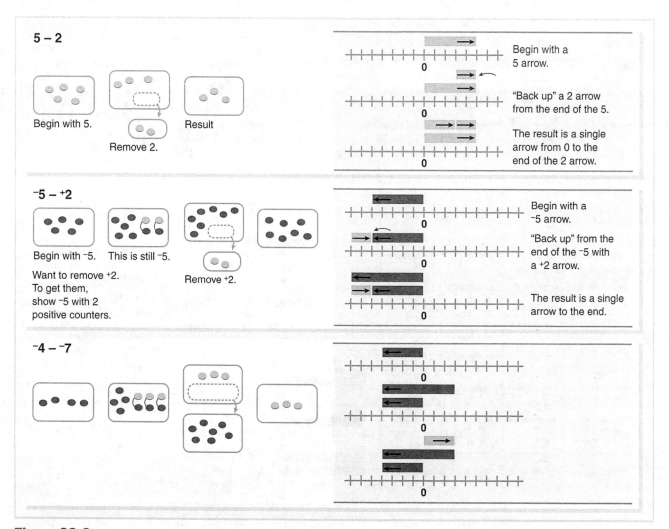

Figure 23.9 Integer subtraction is also related to whole numbers.

arrows can be used. Figure 23.10 illustrates how a student might draw arrows for simple addition and subtraction exercises without even sketching the number line.

It is important for students to see that $^+3 + {}^-5$ is the same as $^+3 - {}^+5$ and that $^+2 - {}^-6$ is the same as $^+2 + {}^+6$. With modeling addition and subtraction problems in both ways, students will see the connection and recognize that while these expressions are quite distinguishable, they have the same result.

Multiplication and Division

Multiplication of integers should be a direct extension of multiplication for whole numbers, just as addition and subtraction were connected to whole-number concepts. We frequently refer to whole-number multiplication as repeated addition. The first factor tells how many sets there are or how many are added in all, beginning with 0. This translates to integer multiplication quite readily when the

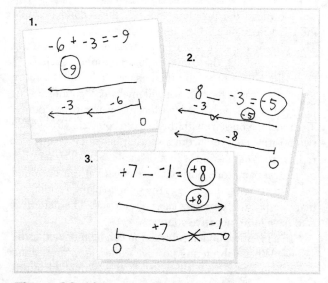

Figure 23.10 Students can use simple arrow sketches to represent addition and subtraction with integers.

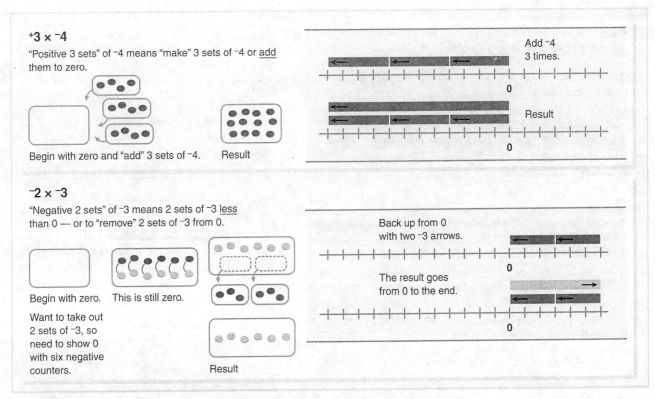

Figure 23.11 Multiplication by a positive first factor is repeated addition. Multiplication by a negative first factor is repeated subtraction.

first factor is positive, regardless of the sign of the second factor. The first example in Figure 23.11 illustrates a positive first factor and a negative second factor.

What could the meaning be when the first factor is negative, as in ⁻2 × ⁻3? If a positive first factor means repeated addition (how many times added to 0), a negative first factor should mean repeated subtraction (how many times subtracted from 0). The second example in Figure 23.11 illustrates how multiplication with the first factor negative can be modeled.

The deceptively simple rules of "like signs yield positive products" and "unlike signs yield negative products" are quickly established. These models allow students to understand why those rules work.

With division of integers, again explore the whole-number case first. Recall that 8 ÷ 4 with whole numbers has two possible meanings corresponding to two missing-factor expressions: 4 × ? = 8 asks, "Four sets of *what* make eight?" whereas ? × 4 = 8 asks, "How many fours make eight?" Generally, the measurement approach (? × 4) is the one used with integers, although both concepts can be exhibited with either model. It is helpful to think of building the dividend with the divisor from 0, or repeated addition—to find the missing factor.

The first example in Figure 23.12 illustrates how the two models work for whole numbers. Following that is an example where the divisor is positive but the dividend is negative.

Pause and Reflect

Try using both models to compute ⁻8 ÷ ⁺2. Draw pictures using Xs and Os and also arrows. Check your understanding with the examples in Figure 23.12. Once you understand that example, try ⁺9 ÷ ⁻3 and also ⁻12 ÷ ⁻4.

Understanding of integer division rests on a good concept of a negative first factor for multiplication and a knowledge of the relationship between multiplication and division.

Do not rush your students into difficult problems. It is much better that they first think about how to model the whole-number situation and then figure out, with some guidance from you, how to deal with integers.

NCTM *Standards* "Positive and negative integers should be seen as useful for noting relative changes or values. Students can also appreciate the utility of negative integers when they work with equations whose solution requires them, such as $2x + 7 = 1$" (p. 218). ◆

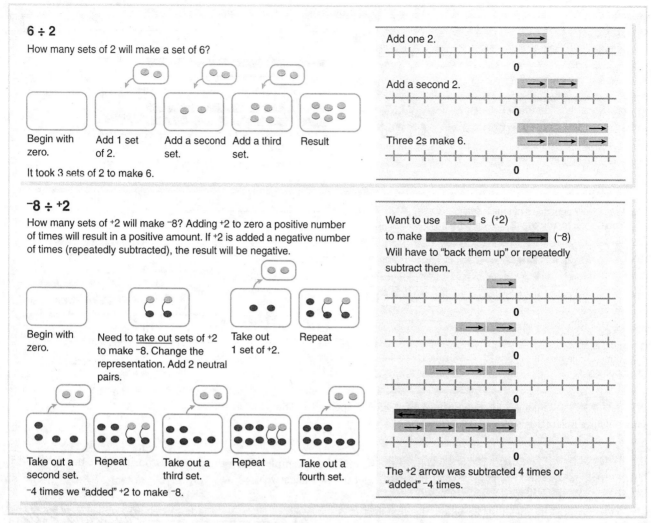

Figure 23.12 Division of integers following a measurement approach.

Real Numbers

Section II of this book began with whole numbers, then moved to rational numbers, and now, in this chapter, has explored integers. All of these are rational numbers. Irrational numbers are numbers such as $\sqrt{2}$—numbers whose value cannot be written as a fraction and whose value can only be estimated. All these numbers are part of the *real numbers*, which are the only types of numbers students explore until high school where they consider the square roots of negative numbers, called *imaginary numbers*. Each of these sets of numbers are interrelated, and some are subsets of other sets. Figure 23.13 provides an illustration of the types of numbers and how they are interrelated.

Rational Numbers

Rational numbers comprise the set of all numbers that can be represented as a fraction—or a ratio of an integer to an inte-

ger. Even when numbers are written as whole numbers or as terminating decimals, they can also be written as fractions and thus are rational numbers. In fact, in most textbooks and state curriculum guides the term *rational numbers* is often used to refer to fractions, decimals (terminating and

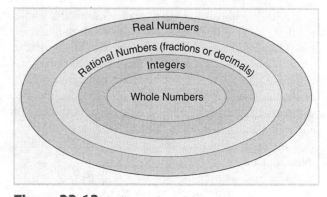

Figure 23.13 An illustration of the real numbers.

repeating), and percents. These are rational numbers, but so are integers, including whole numbers. To help build this notion of rational numbers, it is important to be able to move between fractions and decimals and between fractions and whole numbers.

Moving among Representations. Because children tend to think of fractions as parts of sets or objects, they remain, in the minds of children, more physical object than number. This is one reason that students can have such a difficult time placing fractions on a number line. A significant leap toward thinking about fractions as numbers is made when students begin to understand that a decimal is a representation of a fraction. In Chapter 17, we explored the idea of the "friendly" fractions (halves, thirds, fourths, fifths, eighths) in terms of their decimal equivalents.

In the middle grades, it is time to combine all of these ideas:

- $4\frac{3}{5}$ is 4.6 because $\frac{3}{5}$ is six-tenths of a whole, so 4 wholes and six-tenths is 4.6.
- $4\frac{3}{5}$ is $\frac{23}{5}$, and that is the same as $23 \div 5$, or 4.6 if I use decimals.
- 4.6 is read "four and six-tenths," so I can write that as $4\frac{6}{10} = 4\frac{3}{5}$.

Similarly, compare these three expressions:

$$\tfrac{1}{4} \text{ of } 24 \qquad \tfrac{24}{4} \qquad 24 \div 4$$

This discussion can lead to a general development of the idea that a fraction can be thought of as division of the numerator by the denominator or that $\frac{a}{b}$ is the same as $a \div b$.

What becomes clear in a discussion building on students' existing ideas is that any number, positive or negative, that can be written as a fraction can also be written as a decimal number. You can also reverse this idea and convert decimal numbers to fractions. Keep in mind that the purpose is to see that there are different symbolic notations for the same quantities—not to become skilled at conversions.

When a fraction is converted to a decimal, it is interesting to note that the decimal either terminates (e.g., 3.415) or repeats (e.g., 2.5141414 . . .).

Is there a way to tell if a given fraction is a terminating decimal or a repeating decimal? The answer lies in the denominator. The following activity can be used to discover why.

Activity *23.6*

Repeater or Terminator

Have students generate a table listing in one column the first 20 unit fractions ($\frac{1}{2}, \frac{1}{3}, \frac{1}{4}, \dots \frac{1}{21}$). In the second column they list the prime factorization of the denominators and in the third column the decimal equivalent for the fraction. Have students use calculators to get the decimal form.

After completing the table, the task is to see if they can discover a rule that will tell in advance if the decimal will repeat or terminate. They can test the rule with fractions with denominators beyond 21. They may also wish to confirm that it makes no difference what the numerator is.

If you try the last activity yourself, you will quickly discover that the only fractions with terminating decimals have denominators that factor with all 2s and/or 5s. The explanation for why this is so is also within the reach of students. As students work on this task, they will notice various patterns, as can be seen in the student work provided in Figure 23.14.

Irrational Numbers

Students have encountered *irrational numbers* as early as fifth grade when they learn about π. However, the discussion of what an irrational number is occurs later in middle school, probably seventh or eighth grade. As noted, *irrational* numbers are not rational, meaning they cannot

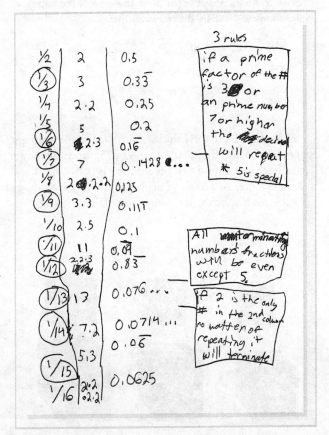

Figure 23.14 A student notes patterns as he explores the "Repeater or Terminator" activity.

be put in fraction form. The irrationals together with the rational numbers make up the *real* numbers. The real numbers fill in all the holes on the number line even when the holes are infinitesimally small. Students' first experience with irrational numbers typically occurs when exploring roots of whole numbers.

Introducing the Concept of Roots. The following activity provides a good introduction to square roots and cube roots. From this beginning, the notion of roots of any degree is easily developed.

Activity 23.7

Edges of Squares and Cubes

Show students pictures of three squares (or three cubes) as in Figure 23.15. The edges of the first and last figure are consecutive whole numbers. The areas (volumes) of all three figures are provided. The students' task is to use a calculator to find the edge of the figure in the center. Explain to students that they are not to use the square root key, but to estimate what they think the side would be and test it by squaring it. Ask students to continue to estimate until they have found a value to the hundredths place that gets as close to 45 as possible (or 30 in the case of the cube). Solutions will satisfy these equations:

$\square \times \square = 45,$ or $\square^2 = 45$

and

$\square \times \square \times \square = 30,$ or $\square^3 = 30$

For example, to solve the cube problem, students might start with 3.5 and find that 3.5^3 is 42.875, much too large. Quickly, they will find that the solution is between 3.1 and 3.2. But where? Although a calculator can find these square or cube roots quickly, the estimation activity strengthens

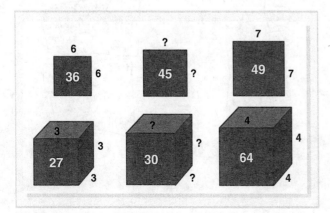

Figure 23.15 A geometric interpretation of square roots and cube roots.

students' understanding of squares and square roots and the relative sizes of numbers.

 ——————— *Pause and Reflect*

Use a calculator to continue getting a better approximation of the cube root of 30 to the hundredths place.

From this simple introduction, students can be challenged to find solutions to equations such as $\square^2 = 8$. These students are now prepared to understand the general definition of the *nth root* of a number N as the number that when raised to the nth power equals N. The *square* and *cube roots* are simply other names for the second and third roots. The notational convention of the radical sign comes last. It should then be clear that $\sqrt{6}$ is a number rather than a computation. The cube root of eight is the same as $\sqrt[3]{8}$, which is just another way of writing 2.

In middle school, students encounter irrational numbers primarily when working with the Pythagorean theorem ($a^2 + b^2 = c^2$), which is used to find the distance between two points (the distance being the diagonal or c). If $a = 3$ and $b = 4$, then $c = 5$. All sides are rational numbers. But this case is the exception to the rule. More often sides will be something like 4 and 7 units, in which case $c = \sqrt{16 + 49} = \sqrt{65}$. Although sometimes there is a perfect square that can be simplified, in this case there is not one and the distance is $\sqrt{65}$, an irrational number.

An engaging middle school project applies the Pythagorean theorem and irrational numbers to create a Wheel of Theodorus, as described in Activity 23.8. Theodorus was one of the early believers that irrational numbers existed (quite a contentious issue for the Pythagoreans, who were against the idea of irrationals!).

Activity 23.8

Wheel of Theodorus

Ask students to construct a right triangle that measures 1 centimeter on each side adjacent to the right angle and then draw the hypotenuse and record its measure. They then use the hypotenuse as a side and draw a new right triangle with this as side *a* along with a side *b* that is 1 cm. Draw and record the new hypotenuse ($\sqrt{3}$). Create the next triangle, which will have sides of $\sqrt{3}$ and 1 and a hypotenuse of $\sqrt{4}$ or 2, and so on. Doing this about 30 times will form a wheel. (See Bay-Williams & Martinie, 2009, for a complete lesson or search online for instructions and diagrams.)

NCTM *Standards*

"In grades 6–8, students frequently encounter squares and square roots when they use the Pythagorean relationship. They can use the inverse relationship to determine the approximate location of square roots between whole numbers on a number line"

(p. 220). As examples, the authors note that $\sqrt{27}$ is a little more than 5 because $5^2 = 25$ and $\sqrt{99}$ is a little less than 10 since $10^2 = 100$. ◆

Density of the Real Numbers

One important aspect of real numbers that is not well understood by students is that they are infinite. This means that for two values, such as $\frac{7}{9}$ and $\frac{8}{9}$, you can find infinitely many rational numbers between them. This is a concept that warrants exploration and discussion, which is the intent of Activity 23.9.

If the density of the rationals is impressive, even more astounding is that the irrationals are also dense. And the irrationals and the rationals are all mixed up together. The density of the irrationals is not as easy to demonstrate and is not within the scope of the middle school.

The following activity can help students develop a better understanding of the structure of the rational number system.

Activity 23.9

How Close Is Close?

Have students select any two fractions or any two decimals that they think are "really close." It makes no difference what numbers students pick or even how close together they really are. Now challenge them to find at least ten more numbers (fractions or decimals) that are between these two numbers.

"How Close Is Close?" is an opportunity to find out how your students understand fractions and decimals. (The activity should be done in both forms eventually.) The activity offers a great opportunity for discussion, assessment of individual students' fraction and decimal concepts, and the introduction of perhaps the most interesting feature of the rational number system: density. The rational numbers are said to be *dense* because between any two rational numbers there exists an *infinite* number of other rational numbers.

 Ask students "How many numbers are between these two numbers?" for each of the following:

$$\frac{3}{5} \text{ and } \frac{4}{5}$$

$$0.6 \text{ and } 0.7$$

$$^-2 \text{ and } ^-3$$

As part of this "interview" assessment, ask students to provide examples and to explain how they are finding the numbers in between. Students should be able to manipulate the numbers to find values in between and should know there are infinitely many.

If they are stuck and say there are none, ask if they can write an equivalent form of the numbers to help them find a number in between. ◆

Reflections on Chapter 23

Writing to Learn

1. What strategies can you use to help students understand and appropriately use the order of operations?
2. How can a calculator be used to explore the order of operations?
3. Explain how powers of 10 are used to write very small and very large numbers. What is the particular form of the power-of-10 symbolism used in scientific notation and on calculators?
4. Use a context and a model to solve the following:
   $^-10 + {}^+13 = {}^+3$ $^-4 - {}^-9 = {}^+5$ $^+6 - {}^-7 = {}^+13$
   $^-4 \times {}^-3 = {}^+12$ $^+15 \div {}^-5 = {}^-3$ $^-12 \div {}^-3 = {}^+4$
5. For each of the following numbers, tell all the kinds of numbers it is (real, rational, integer, whole). For example, $^-8\frac{1}{2}$ is real and rational.
   $^-3$ 120 $\frac{4}{5}$ $\sqrt{5}$ $.323232\ldots$ $^-1.4$
6. How would you explain the difference between a rational and an irrational number to a middle school student?

7. What does $\sqrt{6}$ mean? How is $\sqrt{6}$ different from $\sqrt{4}$? How are they the same?
8. What does it mean to say that the rational numbers are dense?

For Discussion and Exploration

1. How might teachers help students become fluent in moving between equivalent representations of numbers, for example, changing fractions to decimals flexibly to fit the situation?
2. Some exponent values are easily confused by students. Two of the most common cases are listed below. For each example,
   - Explain how the values are different in meaning.
   - Draw a representation to show how they are different.
   - Describe what investigation you would plan to help students see the differences in these values.
   Case 1: 2^3 and 2×3 and 3^2
   Case 2: $2n$ and n^2 and 2^n

Resources for Chapter 23

Literature Connections

Some topics in this chapter present opportunities for "playing around" with ideas and numbers. In the middle grades using literature is a great springboard for doing mathematics. The following ideas offer a change of pace in the upper grades.

The Number Devil *Enzensberger, 1997*

Full of humor and wit, *The Number Devil* lays out a collection of interesting ideas about numbers in 12 easily read chapters. Robert, a boy who hates mathematics, meets up with a crafty number devil in each of 12 dreams. On the fourth night's dream, Robert learns about infinitely repeating decimals and the "Rutabaga of two" (the square root of two), providing a connection to rational and irrational numbers.

Oh, Yikes! History's Grossest, Wackiest Moments *Masoff, 2006*

In this picture-rich reference book, the author describes important historical events and people with facts that are interesting to middle schoolers. Her topics include, "Aztec Antics," "Cruel Constructions," "Humongous Hoaxes," "Pirates," and so on. In several cases, she takes a topic, such as brushing teeth and briefly describes how this was handled across all of history, which provides the opportunity to do time lines that include dates such as 2500 BC. Students can create a time line that is proportionally accurate to tell the events related to the topic they have selected. In addition to integers, this lesson includes measuring, proportional reasoning, and fractions.

Recommended Readings

Articles

Graeber, A. O., & Baker, K. M. (1992). Little into big is the way it always is. *Arithmetic Teacher, 39*(8), 18–21.

This is one of the few articles that discusses the issue of a fraction as an indicated division. The authors look at practices in the elementary school that suggest why the difficulty exists and make practical suggestions for working with middle school students.

Reeves, C. A., & Webb, D. (2004). Balloons on the rise: A problem-solving approach to integers. *Mathematics Teaching in the Middle School, 9*(9), 476–482.

Expanding on a discussion of the possibility of helium party balloons making you weigh less if held while on a scale, the fifth-grade students in this article generalize the concepts of integers and use their ideas for addition and subtraction. The authors point clearly to the value of a context to help students develop a new concept.

Online Resources

The Evolution of the Real Numbers
www.themathpage.com/areal/real-numbers.htm
This is an interesting description of many topics related to the real number system. Although mostly text, the pages are filled with interactive questions.

National Library of Virtual Manipulatives (NLVM)
http://nlvm.usu.edu
Among the many applets on this site are "Color Chips—Addition," "Color Chips—Subtraction," "Rectangle Multiplication of Integers," and "Integer Arithmetic." These applets focus on using models for integer computation.

Tic-Tac-Go Negative Numbers (Freudenthal Institute)
www.fi.uu.nl/toepassingen/03088/toepassing_wisweb
.en.html
In this game, students pick addition, subtraction, or multiplication and find the equation to match an answer, trying to get three in a row.

Volt Meter (Illuminations)
http://illuminations.nctm.org/ActivityDetail.aspx?ID=152
Click and drag batteries with negative and positive voltage to explore integer addition and subtraction.

Exponential Growth (Otherwise)
www.otherwise.com/population/exponent.html
This site offers an applet to experiment with population (exponential) growth.

The Next Billion (Illuminations)
http://illuminations.nctm.org/LessonDetail.aspx?id=L715
In 1999 the world population passed 6 billion. In this lesson, students predict when it will reach 7 billion. Students discuss their predictions, past trends in population growth, and social factors—a good interdisciplinary opportunity.

Field Experience Guide Connections

This chapter covers a range of topics, so there are a number of excellent lessons and resources in the *Field Experience Guide*. FEG 3.5 ("Web of Ideas") can be an excellent task for teachers and students to explore the relationships among rational numbers (integers, fractions, whole numbers, etc.). FEG Expanded Lesson 9.2 ("Close, Far, and In Between") focuses on the relative magnitude of numbers and FEG Expanded Lesson 9.10 ("How Close Is Close?") focuses on the density of rational numbers. The order of operations is the focus of FEG Activity 10.5 ("Target Number") and Balanced Assessment Task 11.1 ("Magic Age Rings").

Appendix **A**

Principles and Standards for School Mathematics

Content Standards and
Grade Level Expectations

Number and Operations

STANDARD

Instructional programs from prekindergarten through grade 12 should enable all students to—

Expectations

In prekindergarten through grade 2 all students should—

Understand numbers, ways of representing numbers, relationships among numbers, and number systems	• count with understanding and recognize "how many" in sets of objects; • use multiple models to develop initial understandings of place value and the base-ten number system; • develop understanding of the relative position and magnitude of whole numbers and of ordinal and cardinal numbers and their connections; • develop a sense of whole numbers and represent and use them in flexible ways, including relating, composing, and decomposing numbers; • connect number words and numerals to the quantities they represent, using various physical models and representations; • understand and represent commonly used fractions, such as $\frac{1}{4}$, $\frac{1}{3}$, and $\frac{1}{2}$.
Understand meanings of operations and how they relate to one another	• understand various meanings of addition and subtraction of whole numbers and the relationship between the two operations; • understand the effects of adding and subtracting whole numbers; • understand situations that entail multiplication and division, such as equal groupings of objects and sharing equally.
Compute fluently and make reasonable estimates	• develop and use strategies for whole-number computations, with a focus on addition and subtraction; • develop fluency with basic number combinations for addition and subtraction; • use a variety of methods and tools to compute, including objects, mental computation, estimation, paper and pencil, and calculators.

Grades 3–5

Expectations

In grades 3–5 all students should—

- understand the place-value structure of the base-ten number system and be able to represent and compare whole numbers and decimals;
- recognize equivalent representations for the same number and generate them by decomposing and composing numbers;
- develop understanding of fractions as parts of unit wholes, as parts of a collection, as locations on number lines, and as divisions of whole numbers;
- use models, benchmarks, and equivalent forms to judge the size of fractions;
- recognize and generate equivalent forms of commonly used fractions, decimals, and percents;
- explore numbers less than 0 by extending the number line and through familiar applications;
- describe classes of numbers according to characteristics such as the nature of their factors.

- understand various meanings of multiplication and division;
- understand the effects of multiplying and dividing whole numbers;
- identify and use relationships between operations, such as division as the inverse of multiplication, to solve problems;
- understand and use properties of operations, such as the distributivity of multiplication over addition.

- develop fluency with basic number combinations for multiplication and division and use these combinations to mentally compute related problems, such as 30×50;
- develop fluency in adding, subtracting, multiplying, and dividing whole numbers;
- develop and use strategies to estimate the results of whole-number computations and to judge the reasonableness of such results;
- develop and use strategies to estimate computations involving fractions and decimals in situations relevant to students' experience;
- use visual models, benchmarks, and equivalent forms to add and subtract commonly used fractions and decimals;
- select appropriate methods and tools for computing with whole numbers from among mental computation, estimation, calculators, and paper and pencil according to the context and nature of the computation and use the selected method or tool.

Grades 6–8

Expectations

In grades 6–8 all students should—

- work flexibly with fractions, decimals, and percents to solve problems;
- compare and order fractions, decimals, and percents efficiently and find their approximate locations on a number line;
- develop meaning for percents greater than 100 and less than 1;
- understand and use ratios and proportions to represent quantitative relationships;
- develop an understanding of large numbers and recognize and appropriately use exponential, scientific, and calculator notation;
- use factors, multiples, prime factorization, and relatively prime numbers to solve problems;
- develop meaning for integers and represent and compare quantities with them.

- understand the meaning and effects of arithmetic operations with fractions, decimals, and integers;
- use the associative and commutative properties of addition and multiplication and the distributive property of multiplication over addition to simplify computations with integers, fractions, and decimals;
- understand and use the inverse relationships of addition and subtraction, multiplication and division, and squaring and finding square roots to simplify computations and solve problems.

- select appropriate methods and tools for computing with fractions and decimals from among mental computation, estimation, calculators or computers, and paper and pencil, depending on the situation, and apply the selected methods;
- develop and analyze algorithms for computing with fractions, decimals, and integers and develop fluency in their use;
- develop and use strategies to estimate the results of rational-number computations and judge the reasonableness of the results;
- develop, analyze, and explain methods for solving problems involving proportions, such as scaling and finding equivalent ratios.

Algebra

STANDARD

Instructional programs from prekindergarten through grade 12 should enable all students to—

In prekindergarten through grade 2 all students should—

Understand patterns, relations, and functions	<ul><li>sort, classify, and order objects by size, number, and other properties;</li><li>recognize, describe, and extend patterns such as sequences of sounds and shapes or simple numeric patterns and translate from one representation to another;</li><li>analyze how both repeating and growing patterns are generated.</li></ul>
Represent and analyze mathematical situations and structures using algebraic symbols	<ul><li>illustrate general principles and properties of operations, such as commutativity, using specific numbers;</li><li>use concrete, pictorial, and verbal representations to develop an understanding of invented and conventional symbolic notations.</li></ul>
Use mathematical models to represent and understand quantitative relationships	<ul><li>model situations that involve the addition and subtraction of whole numbers, using objects, pictures, and symbols.</li></ul>
Analyze change in various contexts	<ul><li>describe qualitative change, such as a student's growing taller;</li><li>describe quantitative change, such as a student's growing two inches in one year.</li></ul>

Grades 3–5

Expectations

In grades 3–5 all students should—

- describe, extend, and make generalizations about geometric and numeric patterns;
- represent and analyze patterns and functions, using words, tables, and graphs.

- identify such properties as commutativity, associativity, and distributivity and use them to compute with whole numbers;
- represent the idea of a variable as an unknown quantity using a letter or a symbol;
- express mathematical relationships using equations.

- model problem situations with objects and use representations such as graphs, tables, and equations to draw conclusions.

- investigate how a change in one variable relates to a change in a second variable;
- identify and describe situations with constant or varying rates of change and compare them.

Grades 6–8

Expectations

In grades 6–8 all students should—

- represent, analyze, and generalize a variety of patterns with tables, graphs, words, and, when possible, symbolic rules;
- relate and compare different forms of representation for a relationship;
- identify functions as linear or nonlinear and contrast their properties from tables, graphs, or equations.

- develop an initial conceptual understanding of different uses of variables;
- explore relationships between symbolic expressions and graphs of lines, paying particular attention to the meaning of intercept and slope;
- use symbolic algebra to represent situations and to solve problems, especially those that involve linear relationships;
- recognize and generate equivalent forms for simple algebraic expressions and solve linear equations.

- model and solve contextualized problems using various representations, such as graphs, tables, and equations.

- use graphs to analyze the nature of changes in quantities in linear relationships.

Geometry

STANDARD

Instructional programs from prekindergarten through grade 12 should enable all students to—

In prekindergarten through grade 2 all students should—

STANDARD	Expectations
Analyze characteristics and properties of two- and three-dimensional geometric shapes and develop mathematical arguments about geometric relationships	• recognize, name, build, draw, compare, and sort two- and three-dimensional shapes; • describe attributes and parts of two- and three-dimensional shapes; • investigate and predict the results of putting together and taking apart two- and three-dimensional shapes.
Specify locations and describe spatial relationships using coordinate geometry and other representational systems	• describe, name, and interpret relative positions in space and apply ideas about relative position; • describe, name, and interpret direction and distance in navigating space and apply ideas about direction and distance; • find and name locations with simple relationships such as "near to" and in coordinate systems such as maps.
Apply transformations and use symmetry to analyze mathematical situations	• recognize and apply slides, flips, and turns; • recognize and create shapes that have symmetry.
Use visualization, spatial reasoning, and geometric modeling to solve problems	• create mental images of geometric shapes using spatial memory and spatial visualization; • recognize and represent shapes from different perspectives; • relate ideas in geometry to ideas in number and measurement; • recognize geometric shapes and structures in the environment and specify their location.

Grades 3–5

Expectations

In grades 3–5 all students should—

- identify, compare, and analyze attributes of two- and three-dimensional shapes and develop vocabulary to describe the attributes;
- classify two- and three-dimensional shapes according to their properties and develop definitions of classes of shapes such as triangles and pyramids;
- investigate, describe, and reason about the results of subdividing, combining, and transforming shapes;
- explore congruence and similarity;
- make and test conjectures about geometric properties and relationships and develop logical arguments to justify conclusions.

- describe location and movement using common language and geometric vocabulary;
- make and use coordinate systems to specify locations and to describe paths;
- find the distance between points along horizontal and vertical lines of a coordinate system.

- predict and describe the results of sliding, flipping, and turning two-dimensional shapes;
- describe a motion or a series of motions that will show that two shapes are congruent;
- identify and describe line and rotational symmetry in two- and three-dimensional shapes and designs.

- build and draw geometric objects;
- create and describe mental images of objects, patterns, and paths;
- identify and build a three-dimensional object from two-dimensional representations of that object;
- identify and build a two-dimensional representation of a three-dimensional object;
- use geometric models to solve problems in other areas of mathematics, such as number and measurement;
- recognize geometric ideas and relationships and apply them to other disciplines and to problems that arise in the classroom or in everyday life.

Grades 6–8

Expectations

In grades 6–8 all students should—

- precisely describe, classify, and understand relationships among types of two- and three-dimensional objects using their defining properties;
- understand relationships among the angles, side lengths, perimeters, areas, and volumes of similar objects;
- create and critique inductive and deductive arguments concerning geometric ideas and relationships, such as congruence, similarity, and the Pythagorean relationship.

- use coordinate geometry to represent and examine the properties of geometric shapes;
- use coordinate geometry to examine special geometric shapes, such as regular polygons or those with pairs of parallel or perpendicular sides.

- describe sizes, positions, and orientations of shapes under informal transformations such as flips, turns, slides, and scaling;
- examine the congruence, similarity, and line or rotational symmetry of objects using transformations.

- draw geometric objects with specified properties, such as side lengths or angle measures;
- use two-dimensional representations of three-dimensional objects to visualize and solve problems such as those involving surface area and volume;
- use visual tools such as networks to represent and solve problems;
- use geometric models to represent and explain numerical and algebraic relationships;
- recognize and apply geometric ideas and relationships in areas outside the mathematics classroom, such as art, science, and everyday life.

Measurement

STANDARD

Instructional programs from prekindergarten through grade 12 should enable all students to—

Pre-K–2

Expectations

In prekindergarten through grade 2 all students should—

Understand measurable attributes of objects and the units, systems, and processes of measurement

- recognize the attributes of length, volume, weight, area, and time;
- compare and order objects according to these attributes;
- understand how to measure using nonstandard and standard units;
- select an appropriate unit and tool for the attribute being measured.

Apply appropriate techniques, tools, and formulas to determine measurements

- measure with multiple copies of units of the same size, such as paper clips laid end to end;
- use repetition of a single unit to measure something larger than the unit, for instance, measuring the length of a room with a single meterstick;
- use tools to measure;
- develop common referents for measures to make comparisons and estimates.

Grades 3–5

Expectations

In grades 3–5 all students should—

- understand such attributes as length, area, weight, volume, and size of angle and select the appropriate type of unit for measuring each attribute;
- understand the need for measuring with standard units and become familiar with standard units in the customary and metric systems;
- carry out simple unit conversions, such as from centimeters to meters, within a system of measurement;
- understand that measurements are approximations and understand how differences in units affect precision;
- explore what happens to measurements of a two-dimensional shape such as its perimeter and area when the shape is changed in some way.

- develop strategies for estimating the perimeters, areas, and volumes of irregular shapes;
- select and apply appropriate standard units and tools to measure length, area, volume, weight, time, temperature, and the size of angles;
- select and use benchmarks to estimate measurements;
- develop, understand, and use formulas to find the area of rectangles and related triangles and parallelograms;
- develop strategies to determine the surface areas and volumes of rectangular solids.

Grades 6–8

Expectations

In grades 6–8 all students should—

- understand both metric and customary systems of measurement;
- understand relationships among units and convert from one unit to another within the same system;
- understand, select, and use units of appropriate size and type to measure angles, perimeter, area, surface area, and volume.

- use common benchmarks to select appropriate methods for estimating measurements;
- select and apply techniques and tools to accurately find length, area, volume, and angle measures to appropriate levels of precision;
- develop and use formulas to determine the circumference of circles and the area of triangles, parallelograms, trapezoids, and circles and develop strategies to find the area of more-complex shapes;
- develop strategies to determine the surface area and volume of selected prisms, pyramids, and cylinders;
- solve problems involving scale factors, using ratio and proportion;
- solve simple problems involving rates and derived measurements for such attributes as velocity and density.

Data Analysis and Probability

STANDARD

Instructional programs from prekindergarten through grade 12 should enable all students to—

STANDARD	Pre-K–2
	Expectations In prekindergarten through grade 2 all students should—
Formulate questions that can be addressed with data and collect, organize, and display relevant data to answer them	• pose questions and gather data about themselves and their surroundings; • sort and classify objects according to their attributes and organize data about the objects; • represent data using concrete objects, pictures, and graphs.
Select and use appropriate statistical methods to analyze data	• describe parts of the data and the set of data as a whole to determine what the data show.
Develop and evaluate inferences and predictions that are based on data	• discuss events related to students' experiences as likely or unlikely.
Understand and apply basic concepts of probability	

Grades 3–5

Expectations

In grades 3–5 all students should—

- design investigations to address a question and consider how data-collection methods affect the nature of the data set;
- collect data using observations, surveys, and experiments;
- represent data using tables and graphs such as line plots, bar graphs, and line graphs;
- recognize the differences in representing categorical and numerical data.

- describe the shape and important features of a set of data and compare related data sets, with an emphasis on how the data are distributed;
- use measures of center, focusing on the median, and understand what each does and does not indicate about the data set;
- compare different representations of the same data and evaluate how well each representation shows important aspects of the data.

- propose and justify conclusions and predictions that are based on data and design studies to further investigate the conclusions or predictions.

- describe events as likely or unlikely and discuss the degree of likelihood using such words as certain, equally likely, and impossible;
- predict the probability of outcomes of simple experiments and test the predictions;
- understand that the measure of the likelihood of an event can be represented by a number from 0 to 1.

Grades 6–8

Expectations

In grades 6–8 all students should—

- formulate questions, design studies, and collect data about a characteristic shared by two populations or different characteristics within one population;
- select, create, and use appropriate graphical representations of data, including histograms, box plots, and scatter plots.

- find, use, and interpret measures of center and spread, including mean and interquartile range;
- discuss and understand the correspondence between data sets and their graphical representations, especially histograms, stem-and-leaf plots, box plots, and scatter plots.

- use observations about differences between two or more samples to make conjectures about the populations from which the samples were taken;
- make conjectures about possible relationships between two characteristics of a sample on the basis of scatter plots of the data and approximate lines of fit;
- use conjectures to formulate new questions and plan new studies to answer them.

- understand and use appropriate terminology to describe complementary and mutually exclusive events;
- use proportionality and a basic understanding of probability to make and test conjectures about the results of experiments and simulations;
- compute probabilities for simple compound events, using such methods as organized lists, tree diagrams, and area models.

Standards for Teaching Mathematics

NCTM has developed standards for pre-K–12 students, teaching, and assessment. The first pre-K–12 standards document came out in 1989 and was titled *Curriculum and Evaluation Standards for School Mathematics*. In 1991, a companion document that focused on teaching was released. It was titled *Professional Standards for Teaching Mathematics*. In 2000, NCTM again published a pre-K–12 standards document, *Principles and Standards for School Mathematics*, offering more precision and direction for educators and increased attention to teaching with the inclusion of the Teaching Principle. This standards document is featured throughout the textbook (noted by the NCTM Standards icon) and in Appendix A. In 2007, *Mathematics Teaching Today* was released. This resource elaborates on the Teaching Principle and offers a revision of the teaching standards from the *Professional Standards for Teaching Mathematics*. These teaching standards continue to be a guide to mathematics educators on the knowledge, skills, and dispositions required for effective mathematics teaching.

Source: National Council of Teachers of Mathematics. (2007). *Mathematics Teaching Today*. Reston, VA: NCTM.

STANDARD 1 Knowledge of Mathematics and General Pedagogy

Teachers of mathematics should have a deep knowledge of—

* sound and significant mathematics;
* theories of student intellectual development across the spectrum of diverse learners;
* modes of instruction and assessment; and
* effective communication and motivational strategies.

STANDARD 2 Knowledge of Student Mathematical Learning

Teachers of mathematics must know and recognize the importance of—

* what is known about the ways students learn mathematics;
* methods of supporting students as they struggle to make sense of mathematical concepts and procedures;
* ways to help students build on informal mathematical understandings;
* a variety of tools for use in mathematical investigation and the benefits and limitations of those tools; and
* ways to stimulate engagement and guide the exploration of the mathematical processes of problem solving, reasoning and proof, communication, connections, and representations.

STANDARD 3 Worthwhile Mathematical Tasks

The teacher of mathematics should design learning experiences and pose tasks that are based on sound and significant mathematics and that—

* engage students' intellect;
* develop mathematical understandings and skills;
* stimulate students to make connections and develop a coherent framework for mathematical ideas;
* call for problem formulation, problem solving, and mathematical reasoning;
* promote communication about mathematics;
* represent mathematics as an ongoing human activity; and
* display sensitivity to, and draw on, students' diverse background experiences and dispositions.

STANDARD 4 Learning Environment

The teacher of mathematics should create a learning environment that provides—

* the time necessary to explore sound mathematics and deal with significant ideas and problems;
* a physical space and appropriate materials that facilitate students' learning of mathematics;
* access and encouragement to use appropriate technology;
* a context that encourages the development of mathematical skill and proficiency;
* an atmosphere of respect and value for students' ideas and ways of thinking;

* an opportunity to work independently or collaboratively to make sense of mathematics;
* a climate for students to take intellectual risks in raising questions and formulating conjectures; and
* encouragement for the student to display a sense of mathematical competence by validating and supporting ideas with a mathematical argument.

STANDARD 5 Discourse

The teacher of mathematics should orchestrate discourse by—

* posing questions and tasks that elicit, engage, and challenge each student's thinking;
* listening carefully to students' ideas and deciding what to pursue in depth from among the ideas that students generate during a discussion;
* asking students to clarify and justify their ideas orally and in writing and by accepting a variety of presentation modes;
* deciding when and how to attach mathematical notation and language to students' ideas;
* encouraging and accepting the use of multiple representations;
* making available tools for exploration and analysis;
* deciding when to provide information, when to clarify an issue, when to model, when to lead, and when to let students wrestle with a difficulty; and
* monitoring students' participation in discussions and deciding when and how to encourage each student to participate.

STANDARD 6 Reflection on Student Learning

The teacher of mathematics should engage in ongoing analysis of students' learning by—

* observing, listening to, and gathering information about students to assess what they are learning so as to ensure that every student is learning sound and significant mathematics and is developing a positive disposition toward mathematics;
* challenge and extend students' ideas;
* adapt or change activities while teaching;
* describe and comment on each student's learning to parents and administrators; and
* provide regular feedback to the students themselves.

STANDARD 7 Reflection on Teaching Practice

The teacher of mathematics should engage in ongoing analysis of teaching by—

* reflecting regularly on what and how they teach;
* examining effects of the task, discourse, and learning environment on students' mathematical knowledge, skills, and dispositions;
* seeking to improve their teaching and practice by participating in learning communities beyond their classroom;
* analyzing and using assessment data to make reasoned decisions about necessary changes in curriculum; and
* collaborating with colleagues to develop plans to improve instructional programs.

Guide to Blackline Masters

This Appendix contains images of all of the Blackline Masters (BLM) that are listed below. The actual masters can be found in either of two places:

- In hard copy at the end of the *Field Experience Guide* (Blackline Masters 62–77 are connected to Expanded Lessons provided in the *Field Experience Guide*.)
- On the MyEducationLab website (www.myeducationlab.com)

0.5-cm square grid   36
1-cm isometric dot grid   39
1-cm square/diagonal grid   40
1-cm square dot grid   37
1-cm square grid   35
2-cm isometric grid   38
2-cm square grid   34
2 more than   63
2 less than   64
10 × 10 grids   27
10 × 10 multiplication array   12
10,000 grid   29
Addition and subtraction recording charts   19
Assorted shapes   41–47
Assorted triangles   58
Base-ten grid paper   18
Base-ten materials   14
Blank hundreds chart (10 × 10 square)   21
Circular fraction pieces   24–26

Clock faces   33
Coordinate grid   48
Create a journey story   71
Crooked paths   72
Degrees and wedges   32
Design a bag   60
Dot cards   3–8
Double ten-frame   11
Five-frame   9
Fixed area recording sheet   74
Four small hundreds charts   23
Fraction names   66
Geoboard pattern   49
Geoboard recording sheets   50
How long?   65
Hundreds chart   22
It's a matter of rates   68
Little ten-frames   15–16
Look-alike rectangles   30
Look-alike rectangles recording sheet   31
Looking at collections   62

Missing-part worksheet   13
More-or-less cards   1
Motion man   52–53
Multiplication and division recording charts   20
Number cards   2
Place-value mat (with ten-frames)   17
Predict how many   69–70
Properties of quadrilateral diagonals   75
Property lists for quadrilaterals   54–57
Rational number wheel   28
Rectangles made with 36 tiles   73
Solving problems involving fractions   67
Tangrams and mosaic puzzle   51
Ten-frame   10
Toying with measures   77
Toy purchases   76
What are the chances?   61
Woozle cards   59

Suggestions for Use and Construction of Materials

Card Stock Materials

A good way to have many materials made quickly and easily for students is to have them duplicated on card stock. Card stock is a heavy paper that comes in a variety of colors and can be laminated and then cut into smaller pieces, if desired. Laminate first, and then cut into pieces afterward. Otherwise you will need to cut each piece twice.

Materials are best kept in clear freezer bags with zip-type closures. Punch a hole near the top of the bag so that you do not store air. Lots of small bags can be stuffed into the largest bags.

The following list is a suggestion for materials that can be made from card stock using the masters in this section. Quantity suggestions are also given.

Dot Cards—3–8

One complete set of cards will serve four to six children. Duplicate each set in a different color so that mixed sets can be separated easily. Laminate and then cut with a paper cutter.

Five-Frames and Ten-Frames—9–10

Five-frames and ten-frames are best duplicated on light-colored card stock. Do not laminate; if you do, the mats will curl and counters will slide around.

10 × 10 Multiplication Array—12

Make one per student in any color. Lamination is suggested. Provide each student with an L-shaped piece of tagboard.

Base-Ten Materials—14

Run copies on white card stock. One sheet will make 4 hundreds and 10 tens or 4 hundreds and 100 ones. Cut into pieces with a paper cutter. It is recommended that you *not* laminate the base-ten pieces. A kit consisting of 10 hundreds, 30 tens, and 30 ones is adequate for each student or pair of students.

Little Ten-Frames—15–16

There are two masters for these materials. One has full ten-frames and the other has 1 to 9 dots, including two with 5 dots. Copy the 1-to-9 master on one color of card stock and the full ten-frames on another. Cut off most of the excess stock (do not trim) and then laminate. Cut into little ten-frames. Each set consists of 20 pieces: 10 full ten-frames and 10 of the 1-to-9 pieces, including 2 fives. Make a set for each child.

Place-Value Mat (with Ten-Frames)—17

Mats can be duplicated on any pastel card stock. It is recommended that you not laminate these because they tend to curl and counters slide around. Make one for every child.

Circular Fraction Pieces—24–26

First make three copies of each page of the master. Cut the disks apart and tape onto blank pages with three of the same type on a page. You will then have a separate master for each size with three full circles per master. Duplicate each master on a different color card stock. Laminate and then cut the circles out. A kit for one or two students should have two circles of each size piece.

Rational Number Wheel—28

These disks can be made on paper but are much more satisfying on card stock. Duplicate the master on two contrasting colors. Laminate and cut the circles and also the slot on the dotted line. Make a set for each student.

Tangrams and Mosaic Puzzle—51

Both tangrams and the mosaic puzzle should be copied on card stock. For younger children, the card stock should first be mounted on poster board to make the pieces a bit thicker and easier to put together in puzzles. Prepare one set of each per student.

Woozle Cards—59

Copy the Woozle Card master on white or off-white card stock. You need two copies per set. Before laminating, color one set one color and the other a different color. An easy way to color the cards is to make one pass around the inside of each Woozle, leaving the rest of the creature white. If you color the entire Woozle, the dots may not show up. Make one set for every four students.

Transparencies and Overhead Models

A copy of any page can be made into a transparency with a photocopier. Alternatively, the PDF files can be printed directly onto transparency masters (use the appropriate transparency film for your printer). If you have an opaque projector, just use the hard copies.

Some masters lend themselves to demonstration purposes on the overhead. The 10 × 10 array, the blank hundreds board, and the large geoboard are examples. The five-frame and ten-frame work well with counters. The place-value mat can be used with strips and squares or with counters and cups directly on the overhead. The missing-part blank and the record blanks for the four algorithms are pages that you may wish to use as write-on transparencies.

A transparency of the 10,000 grid is the easiest way there is to show 10,000 or to model four-place decimal numbers.

A transparency of the degrees and wedges page is the very best way to illustrate what a degree is and also to help explain protractors.

All of the line and dot grids are useful to have available as transparencies. You may find it a good idea to make several copies of each and keep them in a folder where you can get to them easily.

For the Woozle Cards, dot cards, little ten-frames, and assorted shapes, make a reduction of the master on a photocopy machine. Then make transparencies of the small cards, cut them apart, and use them on the overhead.

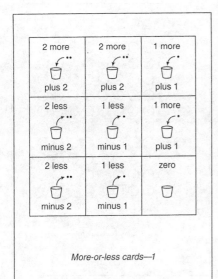

More-or-less cards—1

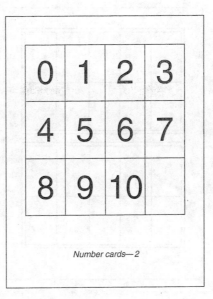

Number cards—2

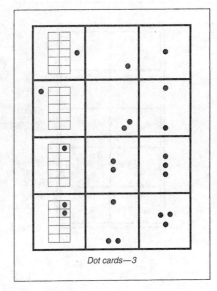

Dot cards—3

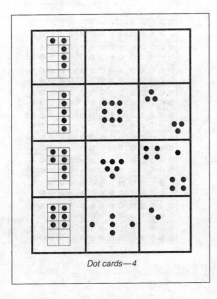

Dot cards—4

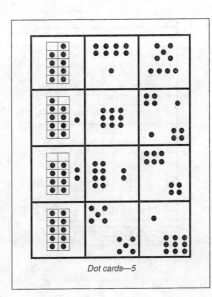

Dot cards—5

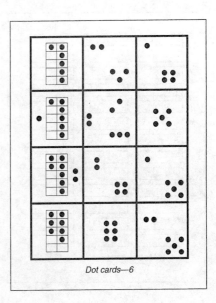

Dot cards—6

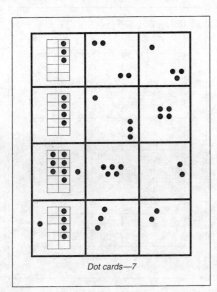

Dot cards—7

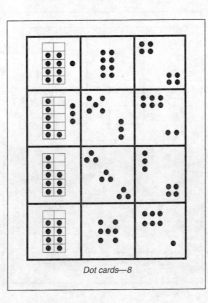

Dot cards—8

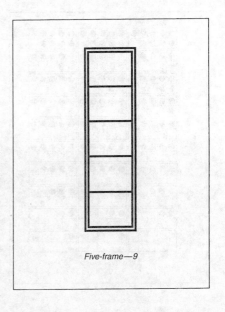

Five-frame—9

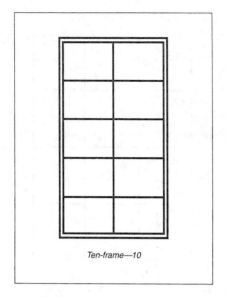

Ten-frame—10

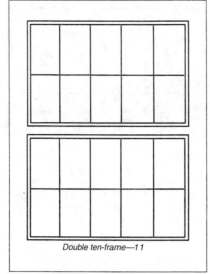

Double ten-frame—11

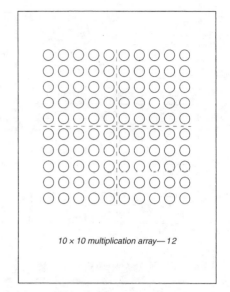

10 × 10 multiplication array—12

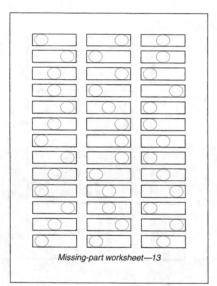

Missing-part worksheet—13

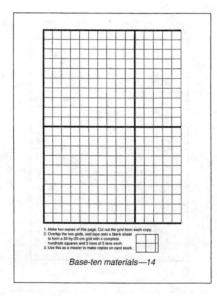

1. Make two copies of this page. Cut out the grid from each copy.
2. Overlap the two grids, and tape onto a blank sheet to form a 20-by-25-cm grid with 4 complete hundreds squares and 2 rows of 5 tens each.
3. Use this as a master to make copies on card stock.

Base-ten materials—14

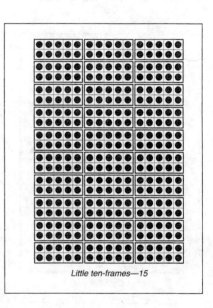

Little ten-frames—15

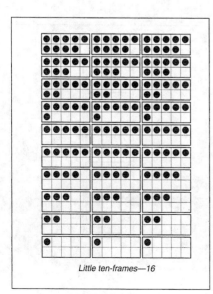

Little ten-frames—16

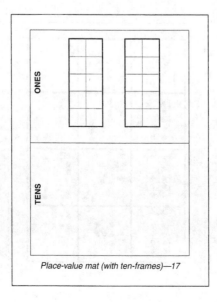

ONES

TENS

Place-value mat (with ten-frames)—17

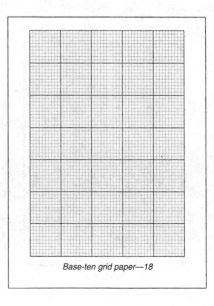

Base-ten grid paper—18

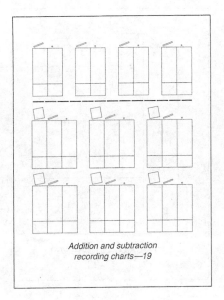

Addition and subtraction recording charts—19

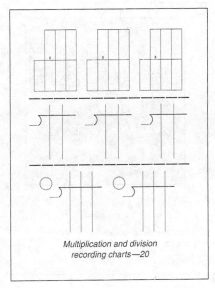

Multiplication and division recording charts—20

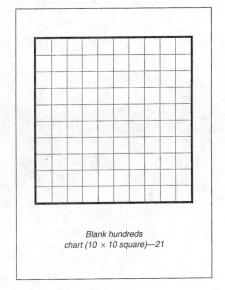

Blank hundreds chart (10 × 10 square)—21

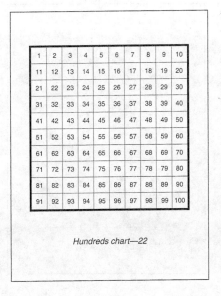

Hundreds chart—22

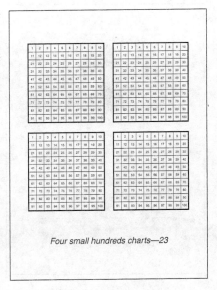

Four small hundreds charts—23

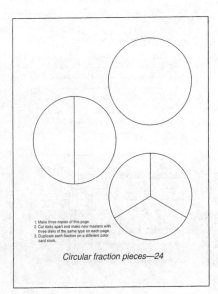

Circular fraction pieces—24

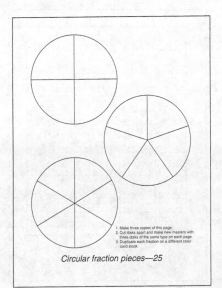

Circular fraction pieces—25

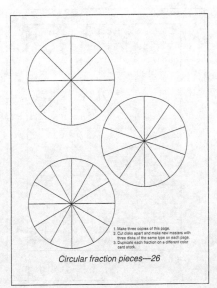

Circular fraction pieces—26

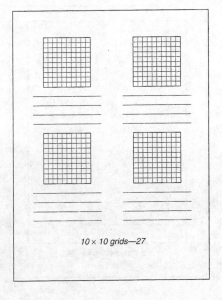

10 × 10 grids—27

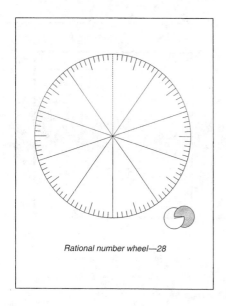

Rational number wheel—28

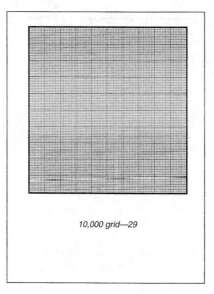

10,000 grid—29

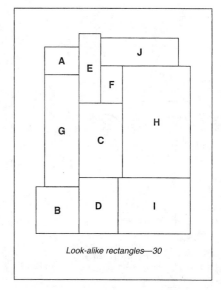

Look-alike rectangles—30

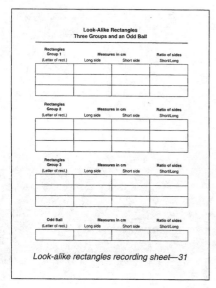

Look-alike rectangles recording sheet—31

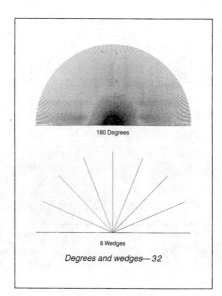

Degrees and wedges—32

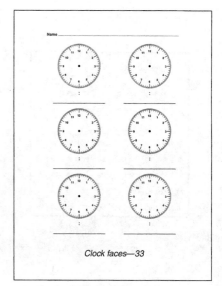

Clock faces—33

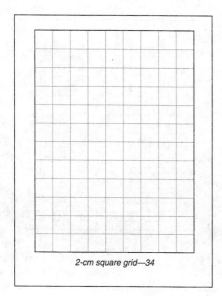

2-cm square grid—34

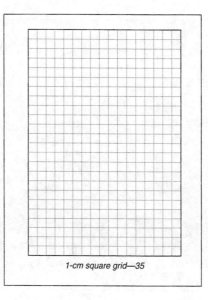

1-cm square grid—35

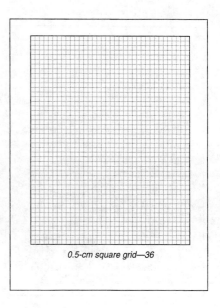

0.5-cm square grid—36

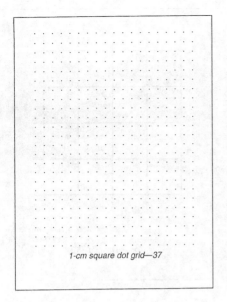

1-cm square dot grid—37

2-cm isometric grid—38

1-cm isometric dot grid—39

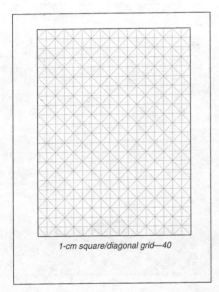

1-cm square/diagonal grid—40

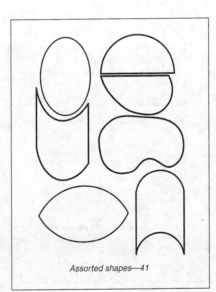

Assorted shapes—41

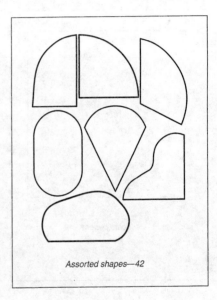

Assorted shapes—42

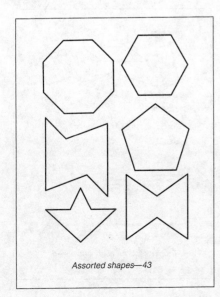

Assorted shapes—43

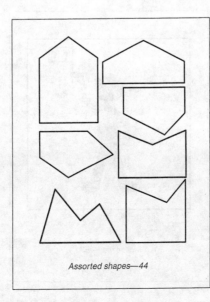

Assorted shapes—44

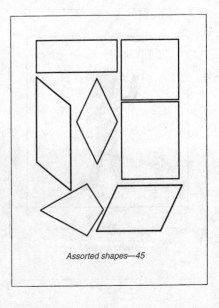

Assorted shapes—45

Assorted shapes—46

Assorted shapes—47

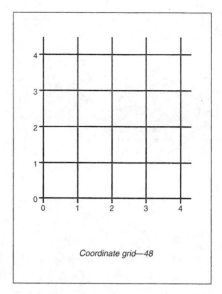

Coordinate grid—48

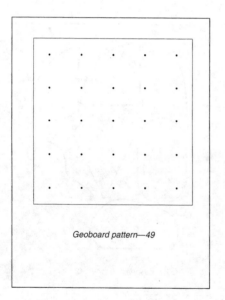

Geoboard pattern—49

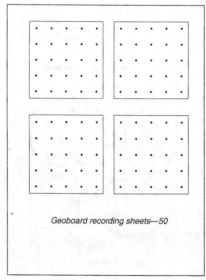

Geoboard recording sheets—50

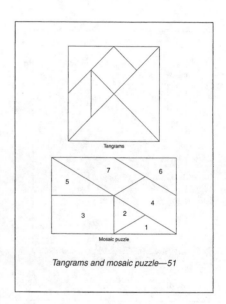

Tangrams and mosaic puzzle—51

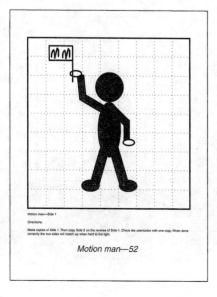

Motion man—52

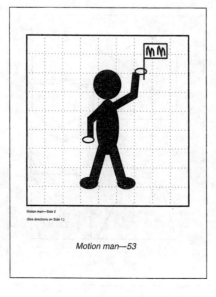

Motion man—53

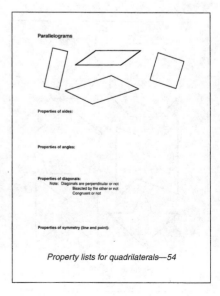

Property lists for quadrilaterals—54

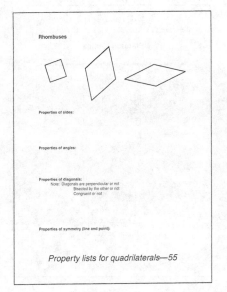

Rhombuses

Properties of sides:

Properties of angles:

Properties of diagonals:
Note: Diagonals are perpendicular or not
Bisected by the other or not
Congruent or not

Properties of symmetry (line and point):

Property lists for quadrilaterals—55

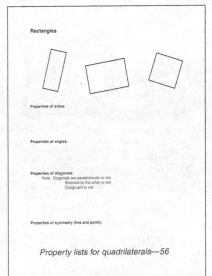

Rectangles

Properties of sides:

Properties of angles:

Properties of diagonals:
Note: Diagonals are perpendicular or not
Bisected by the other or not
Congruent or not

Properties of symmetry (line and point):

Property lists for quadrilaterals—56

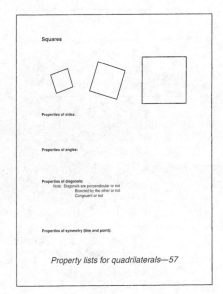

Squares

Properties of sides:

Properties of angles:

Properties of diagonals:
Note: Diagonals are perpendicular or not
Bisected by the other or not
Congruent or not

Properties of symmetry (line and point):

Property lists for quadrilaterals—57

Assorted triangles—58

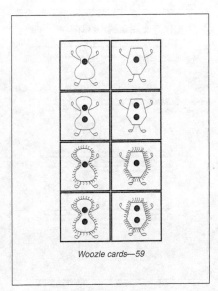

Woozle cards—59

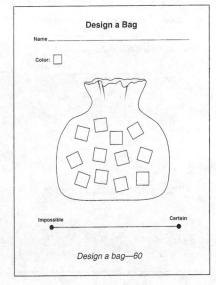

Design a Bag

Name _____

Color: ☐

Impossible ———————————— Certain

Design a bag—60

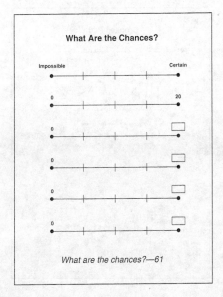

What Are the Chances?

Impossible | Certain

0 | 20

0 ☐

0 ☐

0 ☐

0 ☐

What are the chances?—61

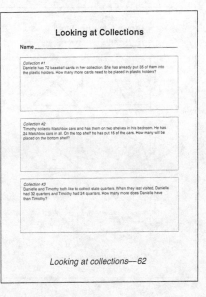

Looking at Collections

Name _____

Collection #1
Danielle has 72 baseball cards in her collection. She has already put 35 of them into the plastic holders. How many more cards need to be placed in plastic holders?

Collection #2
Timothy collects Matchbox cars and has them on two shelves in his bedroom. He has 24 Matchbox cars in all. On the top shelf he has put 16 of the cars. How many will be placed on the bottom shelf?

Collection #3
Danielle and Timothy both like to collect state quarters. When they last visited, Danielle had 32 quarters and Timothy had 24 quarters. How many more does Danielle have than Timothy?

Looking at collections—62

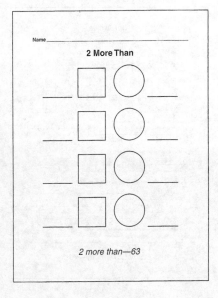

Name _____

2 More Than

2 more than—63

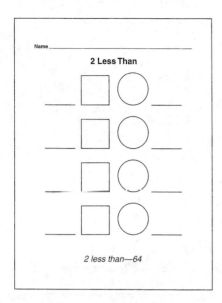

2 less than—64

How long?—65

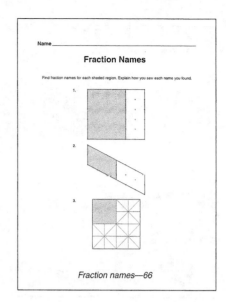

Fraction names—66

Solving Problems Involving Fractions

Name _____

Solve these problems. Use words and drawings to explain how you got your answer.

1. You have 3/4 of a pizza left. If you give 1/3 of the leftover pizza to your brother, how much of a whole pizza will your brother get?

2. Someone ate 1/10 of the cake, leaving only 9/10. If you eat 2/3 of the cake that is left, how much of a whole cake will you have eaten?

3. Gloria used 2 1/2 tubes of blue paint to paint the sky in her picture. Each tube holds 4/5 ounce of paint. How many ounces of blue paint did Gloria use?

Solving problems involving fractions—67

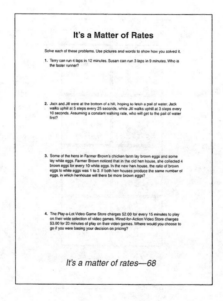

It's a matter of rates—68

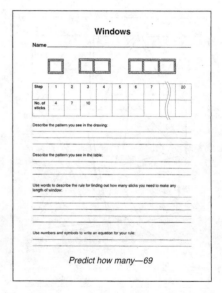

Predict how many—69

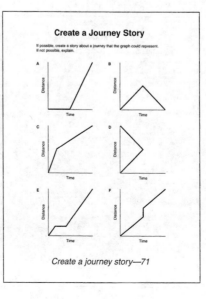

Predict how many—70

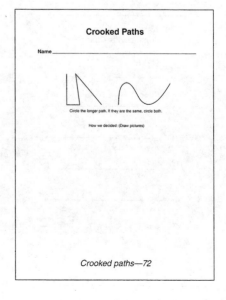

Create a journey story—71

Crooked Paths

Name _____

Circle the longer path. If they are the same, circle both.

How we decided: (Draw pictures)

Crooked paths—72

Rectangles Made with 36 Tiles

Name _____

Rectangle Dimensions	Area	Perimeter

Rectangles made with 36 tiles—73

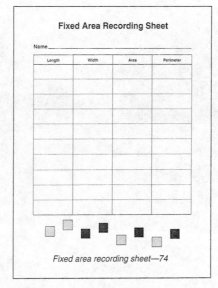

Fixed Area Recording Sheet

Name _____

Length	Width	Area	Perimeter

Fixed area recording sheet—74

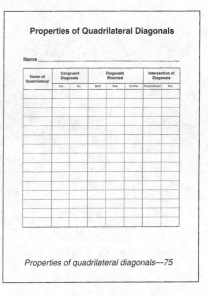

Properties of Quadrilateral Diagonals

Name _____

Name of Quadrilateral	Congruent Diagonals		Diagonals Bisected			Intersection of Diagonals	
	Yes	No	Both	One	Neither	Perpendicular	Not

Properties of quadrilateral diagonals—75

Toy Purchases

Toy purchases—76

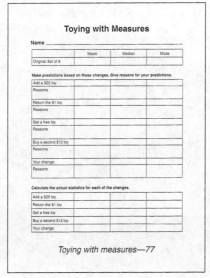

Toying with Measures

Name _____

	Mean	Median	Mode
Original Set of 6			

Make predictions based on these changes. Give reasons for your predictions.

Add a $20 toy			
Reasons			
Return the $1 toy			
Reasons			
Get a free toy			
Reasons			
Buy a second $12 toy			
Reasons			
Your change:			
Reasons			

Calculate the actual statistics for each of the changes.

Add a $20 toy			
Return the $1 toy			
Get a free toy			
Buy a second $12 toy			
Your change:			

Toying with measures—77

References

AIMS. (2001). *Looking at lines: Interesting objects and linear functions.* Fresno, CA: AIMS Education Foundation.

Ambrose, R., Baek, J., & Carpenter, T. P. (2003). Children's invention of multidigit multiplication and division algorithms. In A. J. Baroody & A. Dowker (Eds.), *The development of arithmetic concepts and skills: Constructing adaptive expertise* (pp. 305–336). Mahwah, NJ: Erlbaum.

Ashcraft, M. H., & Christy, K. S. (1995). The frequency of arithmetic facts in elementary texts: Addition and multiplication in grades 1–6. *Journal for Research in Mathematics Education, 26*(5), 396–421.

Austin, R., & Thompson, D. (1997). Exploring algebraic patterns through literature. *Mathematics Teaching in the Middle School, 2*(4), 274–281.

Backhouse, J., Haggarty, L., Pirie, S., & Stratton, J. (1992). *Improving the learning of mathematics.* Portsmouth, NH: Heinemann.

Baek, J. M. (1998). Children's invented algorithms for multidigit multiplication problems. In L. J. Morrow (Ed.), *The teaching and learning of algorithms in school mathematics* (pp. 151–160). Reston, VA: NCTM.

Baek, J. M. (2006). Children's mathematical understanding and invented strategies for multidigit multiplication. *Teaching Children Mathematics, 12*(5), 242–247.

Baek, J. M. (2008). Developing algebraic thinking through exploration in multiplication. In Greenes, C. E., & Rubenstein, R. (Eds.), *Algebra and algebraic thinking in school mathematics: 70th NCTM yearbook* (pp. 141–154). Reston, VA: NCTM.

Baker, A., & Baker, J. (1991). *Math's in the mind: A process approach to mental strategies.* Portsmouth, NH: Heinemann.

Baker, J., & Baker, A. (1990). *Mathematics in process.* Portsmouth, NH: Heinemann.

Baker, S., Gersten, R., & Lee, D. S. (2002). A synthesis of empirical research on teaching mathematics to low-achieving students. *Elementary School Journal, 10*, 51–73.

Ball, D. L. (1992). Magical hopes: Manipulatives and the reform of math education. *American Educator, 16*(2), 14–18, 46–47.

Ball, D. L. (2008). *The work of teaching and the challenges for teacher education.* Presentation at the American Association of Colleges of Teacher Education annual meeting, New Orleans, LA, February 2008.

Ball, L., & Bass, H. (2003). Making mathematics reasonable in school. In J. Kilpatrick, W. G. Martin, & D. Schifter (Eds.), *A research companion to Principles and Standards for School Mathematics* (pp. 27–44). Reston, VA: NCTM.

Ball, L., & Stacey, K. (2005). Teaching strategies for developing judicious technology use. In W. J. Masalski & P. C. Elliott (Eds.), *Technology-supported mathematics learning environments* (pp. 3–15). Reston, VA: NCTM.

Baratta-Lorton, M. (1976). *Mathematics their way.* Menlo Park, CA: AWL Supplemental.

Barnett, R. C. (2007). As the twig is bent: Early and powerful influences on whether girls choose careers in math and science. Presentation at Boston University, October 5, 2007.

Barney, L. (1970, April). Your fingers can multiply! *Instructor,* pp. 129–130.

Baroody, A. J. (1985). Mastery of the basic number combinations: Internalization of relationships or facts? *Journal for Research in Mathematics Education, 16*(2), 83–98.

Baroody, A. J. (1987). *Children's mathematical thinking: A developmental framework for preschool, primary, and special education teachers.* New York: Teachers College Press.

Baroody, A. J. (2003). The development of adaptive expertise and flexibility: The integration of conceptual and procedural knowledge. In A. J. Baroody & A. Dowker (Eds.), *The development of arithmetic concepts and skills: Constructing adaptive expertise* (pp. 1–34). Mahwah, NJ: Erlbaum.

Baroody, A. J. (2006). Why children have difficulties mastering the basic number combinations and how to help them. *Teaching Children Mathematics, 13*(1), 22–31.

Baroody, A. J., & Wilkins, J. L. M. (1999). The development of informal counting, number, and arithmetic skills and concepts. In J. V. Copley (Ed.), *Mathematics in the early years* (pp. 48–65). Reston, VA: NCTM.

Barrett, J. E., Jones, G., Thornton, C., & Dickson, S. (2003). Understanding children's developing strategies and concepts of length. In D. H. Clements (Ed.), *Learning and teaching measurement* (pp. 17–30). Reston, VA: NCTM.

Battista, M. C. (1999). The mathematical miseducation of America's youth: Ignoring research and scientific study in education. *Phi Delta Kappan, 80*(6), 424–433.

Battista, M. T. (2003). Understanding students' thinking about area and volume measurement. In D. H. Clements (Ed.), *Learning and teaching measurement* (pp. 122–142). Reston, VA: NCTM.

Bay-Williams, J., & Herrera, S. (2007). Is "just good teaching" enough to support English language learners: Insights from sociocultural learning theory. In W. G. Martin & M. E. Struchens (Eds.), *The learning of mathematics: 69th NCTM yearbook.* Reston, VA: NCTM.

Bay-Williams, J. M., & Martinie, S. L. (2003). Thinking rationally about number in the middle school. *Mathematics Teaching in the Middle School, 8*(6), 282–287.

Bay-Williams, J. M., & Martinie, S. (2004a). What does algebraic thinking look like? *Mathematics Teaching in the Middle School, 10*(4), 198–199.

Bay-Williams, J. M., & Martinie, S. L. (2004b). *Math and literature: Grades 6–8.* Sausalito, CA: Math Solutions Publications.

Bay-Williams, J. M., & Martinie, S. L. (2009). *Math and nonfiction: Grades 6–8.* Sausalito, CA: Marilyn Burns Books.

Beck, S. A., & Huse, V. E. (2007). A virtual spin on probability. *Teaching Children Mathematics, 13*(9), 482–486.

Becker, J. R., & Jacobs, J. E. (2001). Introduction. In J. E. Jacobs, J. R. Becker, & G. F. Gilmer (Eds.), *Changing the faces of mathematics: Perspectives on gender* (pp. 1–8). Reston, VA: NCTM.

Becker, J. P., & Shimada, S. (Eds.). (1997). *The open-ended approach: A new proposal for teaching mathematics.* Reston, VA: NCTM.

Beckman, C. E., Thompson, D., & Austin, R. A. (2004). Exploring proportional reasoning through movies and literature. *Mathematics Teaching in the Middle School, 9*(5), 256–262.

Behr, M. J., Lesh, R., Post, T. R., & Silver, E. A. (1983). Rational number concepts. In R. Lesh & M. Landau (Eds.), *Acquisition of mathematics concepts and processes* (pp. 91–126). New York: Academic Press.

Bell, E. S., & Bell, R. N. (1985). Writing and mathematical problem solving: Arguments in favor of synthesis. *School Science and Mathematics, 85*(3), 210–21.

Bell, M. (1998–1999, Winter). Problems with implementing new curricula: The example of the K–6 *Everyday Mathematics* curriculum. *UCSMP Newsletter, 24*, 1–2.

Benard, B. (1991). *Fostering resiliency in kids: Protective factors in the family, school and community.* Portland, OR: Northwest Regional Educational Laboratory.

Bezuszka, S. J., & Kenney, M. J. (2008). The three R's: Recursive thinking, recursion, and recursive formulas. In Greenes, C. E., & Rubenstein, R. (Eds.), *Algebra and algebraic thinking in school mathematics: 70th NCTM yearbook* (pp. 81–97). Reston, VA: NCTM

Bishop, A. (1991). *Mathematical enculturation: A cultural perspective on mathematics education.* Dordrecht, Holland: Kluwer.

Bley, N. S., & Thornton, C. A. (1995). *Teaching mathematics to students with learning disabilities* (3rd ed.). Austin, TX: Pro-Ed.

Blote, A., Lieffering, L., & Ouwehand, K. (2006). The development of many-to-one counting in 4-year old children. *Cognitive Development, 21*(3), 332–348.

Blume, G., Galindo, E., & Walcott, C. (2007). Performance in measurement and geometry from the viewpoint of *Principles and Standards for School Mathematics.* In P. Kloosterman & F. Lester, Jr. (Eds.), *Results and interpretations of the 2003 mathematics assessment of the National Assessment of Educational Progress* (pp. 95–138). Reston, VA: NCTM.

Boaler, J. (1998). Open and closed mathematics: Student experiences and understandings. *Journal for Research in Mathematics Education, 29*(1), 41–62.

Boaler, J. (2002). *Experiencing school mathematics: Traditional and reform approaches to teaching and their impact on student learning.* Mahwah, NJ: Erlbaum.

Boaler, J., & Humphreys, C. (2005). *Connecting mathematical ideas: Middle school video cases to support teaching and learning.* Portsmouth, NH: Heinemann.

Boat, J., Dwyer, N., Laing, S., & Fratella, M. (2003). Geometric conjectures: The importance of counterexamples. *Mathematics Teaching in the Middle School, 9*(4), 210–215.

Bransford, J., Brown, A., & Cocking, R., Eds. (2000). *How people learn: Brain, mind, experience, and school: Expanded edition.* Washington, DC: National Academy Press.

Bresser, R. (1995). *Math and literature (grades 4–6).* Sausalito, CA: Math Solutions.

Bright, G. W., Behr, M. J., Post, T. R., & Wachsmuth, I. (1988). Identifying fractions on number lines. *Journal for Research in Mathematics Education, 19*(3), 215–232.

Bright, G. W., Joyner, J. M., & Wallis, C. (2003). Assessing proportional thinking. *Mathematics Teaching in the Middle School, 9*(3), 166–172.

Brooks, J. G., & Brooks, M. G. (1993). *In search of understanding: The case for the constructivist classroom.* Alexandria, VA: Association for Supervision and Curriculum Development.

Brownell, W., & Chazal, C. (1935). The effects of premature drill in third grade arithmetic. *Journal of Educational Research, 29*(1), 17–28.

Burger, W. F. (1985). Geometry. *Arithmetic Teacher, 32*(6), 52–56.

Burns, M. (1992). *Math and literature (K–3).* Sausalito, CA: Math Solutions Publications.

Burns, M. (1995a). Timed tests. *Teaching Children Mathematics, 1*(7), 408–409.

Burns, M. (1995b). *Writing in math class.* White Plains, NY: Cuisenaire (distributor).

Burns, M. (1996). *50 problem-solving lessons: Grades 1–6.* Sausalito, CA: Math Solutions.

Burns, M. (1999). *Making sense of mathematics: A look toward the twenty-first century.* Presentation at the annual meeting of the National Council of Teachers of Mathematics, San Francisco.

Burns, M. (2000). *About teaching mathematics: A K–8 resource* (2nd ed.). Sausalito, CA: Math Solutions Publications.

Burns, M., & McLaughlin, C. (1990). *A collection of math lessons from grades 6 through 8.* Sausalito, CA: Math Solutions Publications.

Burrill, G. F., & Elliot, P. (2006). *Thinking and reasoning with data and chance: 68th NCTM yearbook.* Reston, VA: NCTM.

Burris, C. C., & Welner, K. (2005). Closing the achievement gap by detracking. *Phi Delta Kappan, 86*(8), 594–598.

Buschman, L. (2003a). Children who enjoy problem solving. *Teaching Children Mathematics, 9*(9), 539–544.

Buschman, L. (2003b). *Share and compare: A teacher's story about helping children become problem solvers in mathematics.* Reston, VA: NCTM.

Cai, J., & Sun, W. (2002). Developing students' proportional reasoning: A Chinese perspective. In B. Litwiller (Ed.), *Making sense of fractions, ratios, and proportions* (pp. 195–205). Reston, VA: NCTM.

Cai, J., & Wang, T. (2006). U.S. and Chinese teachers' conceptions and constructions of representations: A case of teaching ratio concept. *International Journal of Science and Mathematics Education, 4*(1), 145–186.

Campbell, P. B. (1995). Redefining the "girl problem in mathematics." In W. G. Secada, E. Fennema, & L. B. Adajian (Eds.), *New directions for equity in mathematics education* (pp. 225–241). New York: Cambridge University Press.

Campbell, P. F. (1996). Empowering children and teachers in the elementary mathematics classrooms of urban schools. *Urban Education, 30*(4), 449–475.

Campbell, P. F. (1997, April). *Children's invented algorithms: Their meaning and place in instruction.* Presented at the annual meeting of the National Council of Teachers of Mathematics, Minneapolis, MN.

Campbell, P. F., & Johnson, M. L. (1995). How primary students think and learn. In I. M. Carl (Ed.), *Prospects for school mathematics* (pp. 21–42). Reston, VA: NCTM.

Campbell, P. F., Rowan, T. E., & Suarez, A. R. (1998). What criteria for student-invented algorithms? In L. J. Morrow (Ed.), *The teaching and learning of algorithms in school mathematics* (pp. 49–55). Reston, VA: NCTM.

Campione, J. C., Brown, A. L., & Connell, M. L. (1989). Metacognition: On the importance of understanding what you are doing. In R. I. Charles & E. A. Silver (Eds.), *The teaching and assessing of mathematical problem solving* (pp. 93–114). Reston, VA: NCTM.

Carpenter, T. P. (1985). Learning to add and subtract: An exercise in problem solving. In E. A. Silver (Ed.), *Teaching and learning mathematical problem solving: Multiple research perspectives* (pp. 17–40). Hillsdale, NJ: Lawrence Erlbaum.

Carpenter, T. P., Ansell, E., Franke, M. L., Fennema, E., & Weisbeck, L. (1993). A study of kindergarten children's problem-solving processes. *Journal for Research in Mathematics Education, 24*(5), 428–441.

Carpenter, T. P., Carey, D. A., & Kouba, V. L. (1990). A problem-solving approach to the operations. In J. N. Payne (Ed.), *Mathematics for the young child* (pp. 111–131). Reston, VA: NCTM.

Carpenter, T. P., Fennema, E., Franke, M. L., Levi, L., & Empson, S. B. (1999). *Children's mathematics: Cognitively guided instruction.* Portsmouth, NH: Heinemann.

Carpenter, T. P., Franke, M. L., Jacobs, V. R., Fennema, E., & Empson, S. B. (1998). A longitudinal study of invention and understanding in children's multidigit addition and subtraction. *Journal for Research in Mathematics Education, 29*(1), 3–20.

Carpenter, T. P., Franke, M. L., & Levi, L. (2003). *Thinking mathematically: Integrating arithmetic and algebra in elementary school.* Portsmouth, NH: Heinemann.

Carpenter, T. P., & Moser, J. M. (1984). The acquisition of addition and subtraction concepts in grades one through three. *Journal for Research in Mathematics Education, 15*(3), 179–202.

Carroll, W. M., & Porter, D. (1997). Invented strategies can develop meaningful mathematical procedures. *Teaching Children Mathematics, 3*(7), 370–374.

Chapin, S. H., O'Conner, C., & Anderson, N. C. (2003). *Classroom discussions: Using math talk to help students learn.* Sausalito, CA: Math Solutions Publications.

Charles, R. I., Chancellor, D., Harcourt, L., Moore, D., Schielack, J. F., Van de Walle, J., & Wortzman, R. (1998). *Scott Foresman—Addison Wesley MATH (Grades K to 5).* Glenview, IL: Addison Wesley Longman.

Chick, C., Tierney, C., & Storeygard, J. (2007). Seeing students' knowledge of fractions: Candace's inclusive classroom. *Teaching Children Mathematics, 14*(1), 52–57.

Clark, F. B., & Kamii, C. (1996). Identification of multiplicative thinking in children in grades 1–5. *Journal for Research in Mathematics Education, 27*(1), 41–51.

Clarke, D., Cheeseman, J., Clarke, B., Gervasoni, A., Gronn, D., Horne, M., McDonough, A., Montgomery, P., Rowley, G., & Sullivan, P. (2001). *Understanding, assessing and developing young children's mathematical thinking: Research as a powerful tool for professional growth.* Keynote paper at the annual conference of the Mathematics Education Research Group of Australia, Sydney, July.

Clarke, D. M., Roche, A., & Mitchell, A. (2008). 10 practical tips for making fractions come alive and make sense. *Mathematics Teaching in the Middle School, 13*(7), 373–380.

Clement, L., & Bernhard, J. (2005). A problem-solving alternative to using key words. *Mathematics Teaching in the Middle School, 10*(7), 360–365.

Clements, D. H., & Battista, M. T. (1990). Constructivist learning and teaching. *Arithmetic Teacher, 38*(1), 34–35.

Clements, D. H., & Battista, M. T. (2001). *Logo and geometry.* Reston, VA: NCTM.

Clements, D. H., & Sarama, J. (2005). Young children and technology: What's appropriate? In W. Masalski & P. C. Elliott (Eds.), *Technology-supported mathematics learning environments: 67th NCTM yearbook* (pp. 51–73). Reston, VA: NCTM.

Coates, G. D., & Thompson, V. (2003). *Family Math II: Achieving Success in Mathematics.* Berkeley, CA: EQUALS Lawrence Hall of Science.

Cobb, P. (1988). The tension between theories of learning and instruction in mathematics education. *Educational Psychologist, 23*(2), 87–103.

Cobb, P. (1994) Where is the mind? Constructivist and sociocultural perspectives on mathematical development. *Educational Researcher, 23*(7), 13–20

Cohen, R. (2006). How do students think? *Mathematics Teaching in the Middle School, 11*(9), 434–436.

Colgan, M. D. (2006). March math madness: The mathematics of the NCAA basketball tournament. *Mathematics Teaching in the Middle School, 11*(7), 334–342.

Cook, C. D. (2008). I scream, you scream: Data analysis with kindergartners. *Teaching Children Mathematics, 14*(9), 538–540.

Cramer, K., & Henry, A. (2002). Using manipulative models to build number sense for addition of fractions. In B. Litwiller (Ed.), *Making sense of fractions, ratios, and proportions* (pp. 41–48). Reston, VA: NCTM.

Cramer, K., Wyberg, T., & Leavitt, S. (2008). The role of representations in fraction addition and subtraction. *Mathematics Teaching in the Middle School, 13*(8), 490–496.

Crespo, S., Kyriakides, A. O., & McGee, S. (2005). Nothing "basic" about basic facts: Exploring addition facts with fourth graders. *Teaching Children Mathematics, 12*(2), 60–67.

Cummins, J. (1994). Primary language instruction and the education of language minority students. In C. F. Leyba (Ed.), *Schooling and language minority students: A theoretical framework* (pp. 3–46). Los Angeles, CA: California State University, National Evaluation, Dissemination and Assessment Center.

Curcio, F. R., & Bezuk, N. S. (1994). *Understanding rational numbers and proportions: Addenda Series, grades 5–8.* Reston, VA: NCTM.

Davis, R. B. (1986). *Learning mathematics: The cognitive science approach to mathematics education.* Norwood, NJ: Ablex.

Dennis v. U.S. (1950). 339 US 162, p. 184.

Dewdney, A.K. (1993). *200% of nothing: An eye-opening tour through the twists and turns of math abuse and innumeracy.* New York: John Wiley and Sons.

Dixon, J. (2008) Tracking time: Representing elapsed time on an open timeline. *Teaching Children Mathematics, 15*(1), 18–24.

Drake, J., & Barlow, A. (2007). Assessing students' level of understanding multiplication through problem writing. *Teaching Children Mathematics, 14*(5), 272–277.

Earnest, D., & Balti, A. A. (2008). Instructional strategies for teaching algebra in elementary school: Findings from a research-practice partnership. *Teaching Children Mathematics, 14*(9), 518–522.

Echevarria, J., Vogt, M. E., & Short, D. (2008). *Making content comprehensible for English learners: The SIOP model* (3rd ed.). Boston: Allyn & Bacon.

Ellington, A. (2003). A meta-analysis of the effects of calculators on students' achievement and attitude levels in precollege mathematics classes. *Journal for Research in Mathematics Education, 34*(5), 433–463.

Elliott, P., & Garnett, C. (1994). Mathematics power for all. In C. A. Thornton & N. S. Bley (Eds.), *Windows of opportunity: Mathematics for students with special needs* (pp. 3–17). Reston, VA: NCTM.

Ellis, M., Yeh, C., & Stump, S. (2007/2008). Rock-paper-scissors and solutions to the broken calculator problem. *Teaching Children Mathematics, 14*(5), 309–314.

Empson, S. B. (2002). Organizing diversity in early fraction thinking. In B. Litwiller (Ed.), *Making sense of fractions, ratios, and proportions* (pp. 29–40). Reston, VA: NCTM.

English, L. (2003). Engaging children in problem posing in an inquiry oriented mathematics classroom. In F. Lester, Jr. *Teaching mathematics through problem solving: Prekindergarten–grade 6* (pp. 187–198). Reston, VA: NCTM.

Falkner, K. P., Levi, L., & Carpenter, T. P. (1999). Children's understanding of equality: A foundation for algebra. *Teaching Children Mathematics, 6*(4), 232–236.

Feather, N. (1982) Human values and the prediction of action: An expectancy-valence analysis. In N. T. Feather, (Ed.), *Expectations and actions: Expectancy-value models in psychology* (pp. 263–289). Hillsdale, NJ: Erlbaum.

Fennema, E., Carpenter, T. P., Franke, M. L., & Carey, D. A. (1993). Learning to use children's mathematics thinking: A case study. In R. B. Davis & C. A. Maher (Eds.), *School, mathematics, and the world of reality* (pp. 93–117). Boston: Allyn & Bacon.

Fennema, E., Carpenter, T., Levi, L., Franke, M. L., & Empson, S. (1997). *Cognitively guided instruction: Professional development in primary mathematics.* Madison, WI: Wisconsin Center for Education Research.

Fernandez, M. L., & Schoen, R. C. (2008). Teaching and learning mathematics through hurricane tracking. *Mathematics Teaching in the Middle School, 13*(9), 500–512.

Fischer, F. E. (1990). A part-part-whole curriculum for teaching number in the kindergarten. *Journal for Research in Mathematics Education, 21*(3), 207–215.

Flores, A. (2006). Using graphing calculators to redress beliefs in the "law of small numbers." *Thinking and reasoning about data and chance: 68th NCTM yearbook* (pp. 139–149). Reston, VA: NCTM.

Flores, A., & Klein, E. (2005). From students' problem solving strategies to connections with fractions. *Teaching Children Mathematics, 11*(9), 452–457.

Flores, A., Samson, J., Yanik, H. B. (2006). Quotient and measurement interpretations of rational numbers. *Teaching Children Mathematics, 13*(1), 34–39.

Forman, E. A. (2003). A sociocultural approach to mathematics reform: Speaking, inscribing, and doing mathematics within communities of practice. In J. Kilpatrick, G. Martin, & D. Schifter (Eds.), *A research companion to the NCTM Standards* (pp. 333–352). Reston, VA: NCTM.

Forman, E. A., & McPhail, J. (1993). A Vygotskian perspective on children's collaborative problem-solving activities. In E. A. Forman, N. Minick, & C. A. Stone (Eds.), *Contexts for learning: Sociocultural dynamics in children's development* (pp. 213–229). New York: Oxford University Press.

Fosnot, C. T. (1996). Constructivism: A psychological theory of learning. In C. T. Fosnot (Ed.), *Constructivism: Theory, perspectives, and practice* (pp. 8–33). New York: Teachers College Press.

Fosnot, C. T., & Dolk, M. (2001). *Young mathematicians at work: Constructing number sense, addition, and subtraction.* Portsmouth, NH: Heinemann.

Foss, S. M. (2008). Literature in the mathematics classroom: Introducing *The Inch Boy* to middle school students. *Mathematics Teaching in the Middle School, 13*(9), 538–542.

Franklin, C., Kader, G., Mewborn, D., Moreno, J., Peck, R., Perry, M., & Scheaffer, R. (2005). *Guidelines for assessment and instruction in statistics education (GAISE) report.* Alexandria, VA: American Statistical Association.

Franklin, C. A., & Garfield, J. B. (2006). The *GAISE* Project: Developing statistics education guidelines for grades PreK–12 and college courses. In G. F. Burrill & P. C. Elliott (Eds.), *Thinking and reasoning about data and chance: 68th NCTM yearbook* (pp. 345–376). Reston, VA: NCTM.

Friedman, Thomas (2007). *The world is flat 3.0: A brief history of the twenty-first century.* New York: Picador.

Friel, S. N., Mokros, J. R., & Russell, S. J. (1992). Statistics: Middles, means, and in-betweens. A unit of study for grades 5–6 from *Used numbers: Real data in the classroom.* White Plains, NY: Cuisenaire—Dale Seymour.

Friel, S. N., O'Conner, W., & Mamer, J. D. (2006). More than "meanmedianmode" and a bar graph: What's needed to have a statistical conversation? In G. F. Burrill & P. C. Elliott (Eds.), *Thinking and reasoning about data and chance: 68th NCTM yearbook* (pp. 117–138). Reston, VA: NCTM.

Fuchs, L. S., & Fuchs, D. (2001). Principles for the prevention and intervention of mathematics difficulties. *Learning Disabilities Research and Practice, 16*(2), 85–95.

Fuchs, L. S., & Fuchs, D. (2005). Enhancing mathematical problem solving for students with disabilities. *Journal of Special Education, 39*(1), 45–57.

Fuchs, L. S., & Fuchs, D. (2007). A framework for implementing responsiveness to intervention. *Teaching Exceptional Children, 39*(5), 14–20.

Fuchs, L. S., Fuchs, D., Yazdian, L., & Powell, S. R. (2002). Enhancing first-grade children's mathematics development with peer-assisted learning strategies. *School Psychology Review, 31*(4), 569–583.

Fuson, K. (2003). Developing mathematical power in whole number operations. In J. Kilpatrick, W. G. Martin, and D. Schifter (Eds.), *A research companion to Principles and Standards in School Mathematics* (pp. 68–94). Reston, VA: NCTM.

Fuson, K. (2006). Research on whole number addition and subtraction. In D. Grouws (Ed.), *Handbook of research on mathematics teaching and learning* (pp. 243–275). Charlotte, NC: Information Age Publishing.

Fuson, K. C. (1984). More complexities in subtraction. *Journal for Research in Mathematics Education, 15*(3), 214–225.

Fuson, K. C. (1988). *Children's counting and concepts of number.* New York: Springer-Verlag.

Fuson, K. C. (1992). Research on whole number addition and subtraction. In D. A. Grouws (Ed.), *Handbook of research on teaching and learning* (pp. 243–275). Old Tappan, NJ: Macmillan.

Fuson, K. C., Carroll, W. M., & Drueck, J. V. (2000). Achievement results for second and third graders using the *Standards*-based curriculum *Everyday Mathematics. Journal for Research in Mathematics Education, 31*(3), 277–295.

Fuson, K. C., & Hall, J. W. (1983). The acquisition of early number word meanings: A conceptual analysis and review. In H. P. Ginsburg (Ed.), *The development of mathematical thinking* (pp. 49–107). Orlando, FL: Academic Press.

Fuson, K. C., & Kwon, Y. (1992). Korean children's single-digit addition and subtraction: Numbers structured by ten. *Journal for Research in Mathematics Education, 23*(2), 148–165.

Fuson, K. C., Wearne, D. Hiebert, J. C., Murray, H. G., Human, P. G., Olivier, A. I., Carpenter, T. P., & Fennema, E. (1997). Children's conceptual structures for multidigit numbers and methods of multidigit addition and subtraction. *Journal for Research in Mathematics Education, 28*(2), 130–162.

Futrell, M. H., & Gomez, J. (2008). How tracking creates a poverty of learning. *Educational Leadership, 65*(8), 74–78.

Fuys, D., Geddes, D., & Tischler, R. (1988). The van Hiele model of thinking in geometry among adolescents. *Journal for Research in Mathematics Education Monograph, 3.*

Gagnon, J., & Maccini, P. (2001). Preparing students with disabilities for algebra. *Teaching Exceptional Children, 34*(1), 8–15.

Gallagher, J., & Gallagher, S. (1994). *Teaching the gifted child.* Boston: Allyn and Bacon.

Garofalo, J. (1987). Metacognition and school mathematics. *Arithmetic Teacher, 34*(9), 22–23.

Garrison, L. (1997). Making the NCTM's Standards work for emergent English speakers. *Teaching Children Mathematics, 4*(3), 132–138.

Garrison, L., & Mora, J. K. (1999). Adapting mathematics instruction for English-language learners: The language-concept connection. In L. Ortiz-Franco, N. G. Hernandez, & Y. De La Cruz (Eds.), *Changing the faces of mathematics perspectives on Latinos* (pp. 45–47). Reston, VA: NCTM.

Geddes, D., & Fortunato, I. (1993). Geometry: Research and classroom activities. In D. T. Owens (Ed.), *Research ideas for the classroom: Middle grades mathematics* (pp. 199–222). New York: Macmillan.

Gelman, R., & Gallistel, C. R. (1978). *The child's understanding of number.* Cambridge, MA: Harvard University Press.

Gelman, R., & Meck, E. (1986). The notion of principle: The case of counting. In J. Hiebert (Ed.), *Conceptual and procedural knowledge: The case of mathematics* (pp. 29–57). Hillsdale, NJ: Erlbaum.

Gersten, R., Chard, D., Jayanthi, M., & Baker, S. (2006). *Experimental and quasi-experimental research on instructional approaches for teaching mathematics to students with learning disabilities: A research synthesis.* Signal Hill, CA: Center of Instruction Research Group.

Ginsburg, H. P. (1977). *Children's arithmetic: The learning process.* New York: Van Nostrand.

Glenn, J. (2000). *Before it's too late: Report to the nation from the National Commission on mathematics and science teaching for the 21st century.* Washington, DC: U.S. Department of Education.

Gnanadesikan, M., Schaeffer, R. L., & Swift, J. (1987). *The art and techniques of simulation: Quantitative literacy series.* Palo Alto, CA: Dale Seymour.

Goldin, G. A. (1985). Thinking scientifically and thinking mathematically: A discussion of the paper by Heller and Hungate. In E. A. Silver (Ed.), *Teaching and learning mathematical problem solving: Multiple research perspectives* (pp. 113–122). Hillsdale, NJ: Lawrence Erlbaum.

Golembo, V. (2000). Writing a PEMDAS story. *Mathematics Teaching in the Middle School, 5*(9), 574–579.

Goos, M. (2004). Learning mathematics in a classroom community of inquiry. *Journal for Research in Mathematics Education, 35*(4), 258–291.

Goral, M. B., & Wiest, L. R. (2007). An arts-based approach to teaching fractions. *Teaching Children Mathematics, 14*(2), 74–80.

Gravemeijer, K., & van Galen, F., (2003). Facts and algorithms as products of students' own mathematical activity. In J. Kilpatrick, W. G. Martin, & D. Schifter (Eds.), *A research companion to Principles and Standards for School Mathematics* (pp. 114–122). Reston, VA: NCTM.

Greenes, C., & Findell, C. (1999a). *Groundworks: Algebra puzzles and problems* (separate books for grades 4 to 7). Chicago: Creative Publications.

Greenes, C., & Findell, C. (1999b). *Groundworks: Algebraic thinking* (separate books for grades 1 to 3). Chicago: Creative Publications.

Greer, B. (1992). Multiplication and division as models of situations. In D. A. Grouws (Ed.), *Handbook of research on mathematics teaching and learning* (pp. 276–295). Old Tappan, NJ: Macmillan.

Gregg, J., & Gregg, D. U. (2007). Measurement and fair-sharing models for dividing fractions. *Mathematics Teaching in the Middle School, 12*(9), 490–496.

Groff, P. (1996). It is time to question fraction teaching. *Mathematics Teaching in the Middle School, 1*(8), 604–607.

Groth, R. E. (2006). Expanding teachers' understanding of geometric definition: The case of the trapezoid. *Teaching Children Mathematics, 12*(7), 376–380.

Gutstein, E., Lipman, P., Hernandez, P., & Reyes, R. (1997). Culturally relevant mathematics teaching in a Mexican American context. *Journal for Research in Mathematics Education, 28*(6), 709–737.

Gutstein, E., & Romberg, T. A. (1995). Teaching children to add and subtract. *Journal of Mathematical Behavior, 14*(3), 283–324.

Hanson, S. A., & Hogan, T. P. (2000). Computational estimation skill of college students. *Journal for Research in Mathematics Education, 31*(4), 483–499.

Hawkins, D. (1965). Messing about in science. *Science and Children, 2*(5), 5–9.

Heck, T. *Team building games on a shoestring.* Retrieved August 22, 2008, from www.teachmeteamwork.com.

Heinz, K., & Sterba-Boatwright, B. (2008). The when and why of using proportions. *Mathematics Teacher, 101*(7), 528–533.

Hembree, R., & Dessert, D. (1986). Effects of hand-held calculators in precollege mathematics education: A meta analysis. *Journal of Research in Mathematics Education, 17*(2), 83–99.

Hembree, R., & Dessert, D. (1992). Research on calculators in mathematics education. In J. Fey & C. R. Hirsch (Eds.), *Calculators in mathematics education* (pp. 23–32). Reston, VA: NCTM.

Henry, V. J., & Brown, R. S. (2008). First-grade basic facts: An investigation into teaching and learning of an accelerated, high-demand memorization standard. *Journal for Research in Mathematics Education, 39*(2), 153–183.

Herbel-Eisenmann, B. A., & Phillips, E. D. (2005). Using student work to develop teachers' knowledge of algebra. *Mathematics Teaching in the Middle School, 11*(2), 62–66.

Hiebert, J. (2003). What research says about the NCTM standards. In J. Kilpatrick, W. G. Martin, & D. Schifter (Eds.), *A research companion to Principles and Standards for School Mathematics* (pp. 5–23). Reston, VA: NCTM.

Hiebert, J., & Carpenter, T. P. (1992). Learning and teaching with understanding. In D. A. Grouws (Ed.), *Handbook of research on mathematics teaching and learning* (pp. 65–97). Old Tappan, NJ: Macmillan.

Hiebert, J., Carpenter, T. P., Fennema, E., Fuson, K., Human, P., Murray, H., Olivier, A., & Wearne, D. (1996). Problem solving as a basis for reform in curriculum and instruction: The case of mathematics. *Educational Researcher, 25*(4), 12–21.

Hiebert, J., Carpenter, T. P., Fennema, E., Fuson, K., Wearne, D., Murray, H., Olivier, A., & Human, P. (1997). *Making sense: Teaching and learning mathematics with understanding.* Portsmouth, NH: Heinemann.

Hiebert, J., Gallimore, R., Garnier, H., Givvin, K. B., Hollingsworth, H., Jacobs, J., Chui, A. M-Y., Wearne, D., Smith, M., Kersting, N., Manaster, A., Tseng, E., Etterbeek, W., Manaster, C., Gonzales, P., & Stigler, J. (2003). *Teaching mathematics in seven countries: Results from the TIMSS 1999 video study.* Washington, DC: National Center for Education Statistics, U.S. Department of Education.

Hiebert, J., & Lindquist, M. M. (1990). Developing mathematical knowledge in the young child. In J. N. Payne (Ed.), *Mathematics for the young child* (pp. 17–36). Reston, VA: NCTM.

Hiebert, J., & Wearne, D. (1996). Instruction, understanding, and skill in multidigit addition and subtraction. *Cognition and Instruction, 14*(3), 251–283.

Hiebert, J., & Wearne, D. (2003). Developing understanding through problem solving. In H. L. Schoen & R. I. Charles (Eds.), *Teaching mathematics through problem solving* (pp. 3–14). Reston, VA: NCTM.

Hilliard, A. (1991). Do we have the will to educate all children? *Educational Leadership, 49*(1), 31–36.

Hoffer, A. R., & Hoffer, S. A. K. (1992). Ratios and proportional thinking. In T. R. Post (Ed.), *Teaching mathematics in grades K–8: Research-based methods* (2nd ed., pp. 303–330). Boston: Allyn & Bacon.

Howden, H. (1989). Teaching number sense. *Arithmetic Teacher, 36*(6), 6–11.

Hughes, C., & Rusch, F. R. (1989). Teaching supported employees with severe mental retardation to solve problems. *Journal of Applied Behavior Analysis, 22*(4), 365–372.

Huinker, D. (1994, April). *Multi-step word problems: A strategy for empowering students.* Presented at the annual meeting of the National Council of Teachers of Mathematics, Indianapolis, IN.

Huinker, D. (1998). Letting fraction algorithms emerge through problem solving. In L. J. Morrow (Ed.), *The teaching and learning of algorithms in school mathematics* (pp. 170–182). Reston, VA: NCTM.

Hyde, J., Lindberg, S., Linn, M., Ellis, A., & Williams, C. (2008). Gender similarities characterize mathematics performance, *Science 25, 321*(5888), 494–495.

Imm, K. L., Stylianou, D. A., & Chae, N. (2008). Student representations at the center: Promoting classroom equity. *Mathematics Teaching in the Middle School, 13*(8), 458–463.

Individuals With Disabilities Education Act, Pub. L. No. 101–476, 104 Stat. 1142 (1990).

Individuals with Disabilities Education Act of 1997, Pub. L. No. 105–17 (1997) (codified as amended at 20 U.S.C.A. sec. 1400 (West 2000 & Supp. 2006)).

Individuals with Disabilities Education Improvement Act of 2004, Pub. L. No. 108–446, 118 Stat. 37 (2004) (codified at 20 U.S.C.A. sec. 1400 et. seq. (West 2003 & Supp. 2006)) (amending IDEA).

Ineson, G. (2007). Year 6 children: Has the new British mathematics curriculum helped their mental calculation? *Early Child Development and Care, 177*(5), 541–555.

Izsak, A., Tillema, E., Tunc-Pekkam, Z. (2008). Teaching and learning fraction addition on number lines. *Journal for Research in Mathematics Education, 39*(1), 1, 33–62.

Janvier, C. (Ed.). (1987). *Problems of representation in the teaching and learning of mathematics.* Hillsdale, NJ: Erlbaum.

Johanning, D. J. (2008). Learning to use fractions: Examining middle school students' emerging fraction literacy. *Journal for Research in Mathematics Education, 39*(3), 281–310.

Jones, A. (1999). *Team building activities for every group.* Richland, WA: Rec Room Publishing.

Jones, G., Langrall, C., Thornton, C., & Mogill, A. (1997). A framework for assessing and nurturing young children's thinking in probability. *Educational Studies in Mathematics, 32*(3), 101–125.

Jones, G. A., Thornton, C. A., Langrall, C. W., & Tarr, J. E. (1999). Understanding students' probabilistic reasoning. In L. V. Stiff (Ed.), *Developing mathematical thinking in grades K–12* (pp. 146–155). Reston, VA: NCTM.

Joram, E. (2003). Benchmarks as tools for developing measurement sense. In D. H. Clements (Ed.), *Learning and teaching measurement* (pp. 57–67). Reston, VA: NCTM.

Kamii, C. K. (1985). *Young children reinvent arithmetic.* New York: Teachers College Press.

Kamii, C. K. (1989). *Young children continue to reinvent arithmetic: 2nd grade.* New York: Teachers College Press.

Kamii, C. K., & Clark, F. B. (1995). Equivalent fractions: Their difficulty and educational implications. *The Journal of Mathematical Behavior, 14*(4), 365–378.

Kamii, C. K., & Dominick, A. (1997). To teach or not to teach the algorithms. *Journal of Mathematical Behavior, 16*(1), 51–62.

Kamii, C. K., & Dominick, A. (1998). The harmful effects of algorithms in grades 1–4. In L. J. Morrow (Ed.), *The teaching and learning of algorithms in school mathematics* (pp. 130–140). Reston, VA: NCTM.

Kaput, J. J. (1998). Transforming algebra from an engine of inequity to an engine of mathematical power by "algebrafying" the K–12 curriculum. In *The nature and role of algebra in the K–12 curriculum: Proceedings of national symposium* (pp. 25–26). Washington, DC: National Academy Press.

Kaput, J. J. (1999). Teaching and learning a new algebra. In E. Fennema & T. A. Romberg (Eds.), *Mathematics classrooms that promote understanding* (pp. 133–155). Mahwah, NJ: Erlbaum.

Karp, K. (1991). Elementary school teachers' attitudes towards mathematics: Impact on students' autonomous learning skills. *School Science and Mathematics, 91*(6), 265–270.

Karp, K., Brown, E. T., Allen, L., & Allen, C. (1998). *Feisty females: Inspiring girls to think mathematically.* Portsmouth, NH: Heinemann.

Karp, K., & Howell, P. (2004). Building responsibility for learning in students with special needs. *Teaching Children Mathematics, 11*(3), 118–126.

Karplus, R., Pulos, S., & Stage, E. K. (1983). Proportional reasoning of early adolescents. In R. A. Lesh & M. Landau (Eds.), *Acquisition of mathematics concepts and processes* (pp. 45–90). Orlando, FL: Academic Press.

Khisty, L. L. (1997). Making mathematics accessible to Latino students: Rethinking instructional practice. In M. Kenney & J. Trentacosta (Eds.), *Multicultural and gender equity in the mathematics classroom: The gift of diversity* (pp. 92–101). Reston, VA: NCTM.

Kingore, B. (2006, Winter). Tiered instruction: Beginning the process. *Teaching for High Potential,* 5–6.

Klein, A. S., Beishuizen, M., & Treffers, A. (1998). The empty number line in Dutch second grade: *Realistic* versus *gradual* program design. *Journal for Research in Mathematics Education, 29*(4), 443–464.

Kliman, M., & Russell, S. J. (1998). *The number system: Building number sense (Grade 1).* Glenview, IL: Scott Foresman.

Kloosterman, P., Warfield, J., Wearne, D., Koc, Y., Martin, W. G., & Strutchens, M. (2004). Fourth-grade students' knowledge of mathematics and perceptions of learning mathematics. In P. Kloosterman & F. K. Lester, Jr., *Results and interpretations of the 1990–2000 mathematics assessments of the National Assessment of Educational Progress* (pp. 71–103). Reston, VA: NCTM.

Knowledge Adventure. (n.d.). *Math for the real world.* Pleasantville, NY: Author.

Knuth, E. J., Stephens, A. C., McNeil, N. M., & Alabali, M. W. (2006). Does understanding the equal sign matter? Evidence from solving equations. *Journal for Research in Mathematics Education, 37*(4), 297–312.

Kohler, A., & Lazarin, M. (2007). Hispanic education in the United States. *National Council of La Raza (NCLR) Statistical Brief, 8,* 1–16.

Kohn, A. (1993). *Punished by rewards: The trouble with gold stars, incentive plans, A's, praise, and other bribes.* Boston: Houghton Mifflin.

Kouba, V. L. (1989). Children's solution strategies for equivalent set multiplication and division word problems. *Journal for Research in Mathematics Education, 20*(2), 147–158.

Kouba, V. L., Brown, C. A., Carpenter, T. P., Lindquist, M. M., Silver, E. A., & Swafford, J. O. (1988a). Results of the fourth NAEP assessment of mathematics: Number, operations, and word problems. *Arithmetic Teacher, 35*(8), 14–19.

Kouba, V. L., Zawojewski, J. S., & Strutchens, M. E. (1997). What do students know about numbers and operations? In P. A. Kenney & E. Silver (Eds.), *Results from the sixth mathematics assessment of the National Assessment of Educational Progress* (pp. 87–140). Reston, VA: NCTM.

Kribs-Zalet, C. (2008). Oranges, poster, ribbons, and lemonade: Concrete computational strategies for dividing fractions. *Mathematics Teaching in the Middle School, 13*(8), 453–457.

Kulm, G. (1994). *Mathematics and assessment: What works in the classroom.* San Francisco: Jossey-Bass.

Labinowicz, E. (1985). *Learning from children: New beginnings for teaching numerical thinking.* Menlo Park, CA: AWL Supplemental.

Lambdin, D. V., & Lynch, K. (2005). Examining mathematics tasks from the National Assessment of Educational Progress. *Mathematics Teaching in the Middle School, 10*(6), 314–318.

Lamon, S. J. (1993). Ratio and proportion: Connecting content and children's thinking. *Journal for Research in Mathematics Education, 24*(1), 41–61.

Lamon, S. J. (1996). The development of unitizing: Its role in children's partitioning strategies. *Journal for Research in Mathematics Education, 27*(2), 170–193.

Lamon, S. J. (1999a). *More: In-depth discussion of the reasoning activities in "Teaching fractions and ratios for understanding."* Mahwah, NJ: Lawrence Erlbaum.

Lamon, S. J. (1999b). *Teaching fractions and ratios for understanding: Essential content knowledge and instructional strategies for teachers.* Mahwah, NJ: Lawrence Erlbaum.

Lamon, S. J. (2002). Part-whole comparisons with unitizing. In B. Litwiller (Ed.), *Making sense of fractions, ratios, and proportions* (pp. 79–86). Reston, VA: NCTM.

Lannin, J. K., Arbaugh, F., Barker, D. D., & Townsend, B. E. (2006). Making the most of student errors. *Teaching Children Mathematics, 13*(3), 182–186.

Lannin, J. K., Townsend, B. E., Armer, N., Green, S., & Schneider, J. (2008). Developing meaning for algebraic symbols: Possibilities and pitfalls. *Mathematics Teaching in the Middle School, 13*(8), 478–483.

Lapp, D. (2001). *How do students learn with data collection devices?* Presentation given at the annual International Teachers Teaching with Technology Conference, Columbus, Ohio.

Lappan, G., & Briars, D. (1995). How should mathematics be taught? In I. M. Carl (Ed.), *Prospects for school mathematics* (pp. 115–156). Reston, VA: NCTM.

Lappan, G., & Even, R. (1989). *Learning to teach: Constructing meaningful understanding of mathematical content* (Craft Paper 89–3). East Lansing: Michigan State University.

Lappan, G., & Mouck, M. K. (1998). Developing algorithms for adding and subtracting fractions. In L. J. Morrow (Ed.), *The teaching and learning of algorithms in school mathematics* (pp. 183–197). Reston, VA: NCTM.

Leder, G. C. (1995). Equity inside the mathematics classroom: Fact or artifact? In W. G. Secada, E. Fennema, & L. B. Adajian (Eds.), *New directions for equity in mathematics education* (pp. 209–224). New York: Cambridge University Press.

Lee, H., & Jung, W. S. (2004). Limited-English-Proficient (LEP) students' mathematical understanding. *Mathematics Teaching in the Middle School, 9*(5), 269–272.

Leeming, C. (2007, November 3). "Cool Cash" card confusion. *Manchester Evening News,* Manchester, England. Retrieved September 4, 2008, from www.manchester eveningnews.co.uk/news/s/1022757_cool_cash_card_ confusion

Leinwand, S. (2007). Four teacher-friendly postulates for thriving in a sea of change. *Mathematics Teacher, 100*(9), 582–584.

Lesh, R. A., Post, T. R., & Behr, M. J. (1987). Representations and translations among representations in mathematics learning and problem solving. In C. Janvier (Ed.), *Problems of representation in the teaching and learning of mathematics* (pp. 33–40). Hillsdale, NJ: Erlbaum.

Lester, F. K., Jr. (1989). Reflections about mathematical problem-solving research. In R. I. Charles & E. A. Silver (Eds.), *The teaching and assessing of mathematical problem solving* (pp. 115–124). Reston, VA: NCTM.

Lo, J., & Watanabe, T. (1997). Developing ratio and proportion schemes: A story of a fifth grader. *Journal for Research in Mathematics Education, 28*(2), 216–236.

Lynch, S. (1992). Fast paced high school science for the academically talented: A six-year perspective. *Gifted Child Quarterly, 36*(3), 147–154.

Ma, L. (1999). *Knowing and teaching elementary mathematics: Teachers' understanding of fundamental mathematics in China and the United States.* Mahwah, NJ: Lawrence Erlbaum.

Mack, N. K. (1995). Confounding whole-number and fraction concepts when building on informal knowledge. *Journal for Research in Mathematics Education, 26*(5), 422–441.

Mack, N. K. (2001). Building on informal knowledge through instruction in a complex content domain: Partitioning, units, and understanding multiplication of fractions. *Journal for Research in Mathematics Education, 32*(3), 267–295.

Mack, N. K. (2004). Connecting to develop computational fluency with fractions. *Teaching Children Mathematics, 11*(4), 226–232.

Mack, N. K. (2007). Gaining insights into children's geometric knowledge. *Teaching Children Mathematics, 14*(4), 238–245.

Madell, R. (1985). Children's natural processes. *Arithmetic Teacher, 32*(7), 20–22.

Maida, P. (2004). Using algebra without realizing it. *Mathematics Teaching in the Middle School, 9*(9), 484–488.

Martin, R., Sexton, C., Wagner, K., & Gerlovich, J. (1997). *Teaching science for all children.* Boston: Allyn & Bacon.

Martinie, S. L. (2007). *Middle school rational number knowledge.* Unpublished doctoral dissertation, Kansas State University.

Martinie, S. L., & Bay-Williams, J. M. (2003). Investigating students' conceptual understanding of decimal fractions using multiple representations. *Mathematics Teaching in the Middle School, 8*(5), 244–247.

Martinie, S., & Coates, G. D. (2007). A push for number sense makes good sense. *Mathematics Teaching in the Middle Schools, 13*(2), 88–90.

Mathematical Sciences Education Board, National Research Council. (1989). *Everybody counts: A report to the nation on the future of mathematics education.* Washington, DC: National Academy of Sciences Press.

Mau, T. S., & Leitze, A. R. (2001). Powerless gender or genderless power? The promise of constructivism for females in the mathematics classroom. In J. E. Jacobs, J. R. Becker, & G. F. Gilmer (Eds.), *Changing the faces of mathematics: Perspectives on gender* (pp. 37–41). Reston, VA: NCTM.

McClain, K., Leckman, J., Schmitt, P., & Regis, T. (2006). Changing the face of statistical data analysis in the middle grades: Learning by doing. In G. F. Burrill & P. C. Elliott (Eds.), *Thinking and reasoning about data and chance: 68th NCTM yearbook* (pp. 229–240). Reston, VA: NCTM.

McCoy, L. (1997). Algebra: Real-life investigations in a lab setting. *Mathematics Teaching in the Middle School, 2*(4), 220–224.

McGraw, R., Lubienski, S., & Strutchens, M. (2006). A closer look at gender in NAEP mathematics achievement and affect data: Intersections with achievement, race/ethnicity, and socioeconomic status. *Journal for Research in Mathematics Education, 37*(2), 129–150.

Middleton, J. A., van den Heuvel-Panhuizen, M., & Shew, J. A. (1998). Using bar representations as a model for connecting concepts of rational number. *Mathematics Teaching in the Middle School, 3*(4), 302–312.

Mishra, P., & Koehler, M. J. (2006). Technological pedagogical content knowledge: A new framework for teacher knowledge. *Teachers College Record, 108*(6), 1017–1054.

Mokros, J., Russell, S. J., & Economopoulos, K. (1995). *Beyond arithmetic: Changing mathematics in the elementary classroom.* Palo Alto, CA: Dale Seymour Publications.

Moyer, P. S., & Mailley, E. (2004). *Inchworm and a Half:* Developing fraction and measurement concepts using mathematical representations. *Teaching Children Mathematics,* *10*(5), 244–252.

Mulligan, J. T., & Mitchelmore, M. C. (1997). Young children's intuitive models of multiplication and division. *Journal for Research in Mathematics Education,* *28*(3), 309–330.

Mullis, I., Martin, M., Gonzalez, E., & Chrostowski, S. (2004). *Findings from IEA's Trends in International Mathematics and Science Study at the Fourth and Eighth Grades.* Chestnut Hill, MA: TIMSS & PIRLS International Study Center, Boston College.

Munier, V., Devichi, C., & Merle, H. (2008). A physical situation as a way to teach angle. *Teaching Children Mathematics,* *14*(7), 402–407.

Myren, C. (1995). *Posing open-ended questions in the primary classroom.* San Leandro, CA: Teaching Resource Center.

National Association for Gifted Children (NAGC). (2007). Retrieved May 10, 2008, from www.nagc.org

National Center for Educational Statistics. (2007). *The nation's report card mathematics 2007 (National Assessment of Educational Progress at grades 4 and 8).* Washington, DC: Institute for Education Sciences.

National Center for Technology Innovation. (2008). www.techmatrix.org

National Council of Teachers of Mathematics. (1989). *Curriculum and evaluation standards for school mathematics.* Reston, VA: NCTM.

National Council of Teachers of Mathematics. (1991). *Professional standards for teaching mathematics.* Reston, VA: NCTM.

National Council of Teachers of Mathematics. (1995). *Assessment standards for school mathematics.* Reston, VA: NCTM.

National Council of Teachers of Mathematics. (2000). *Principles and standards for school mathematics.* Reston, VA: NCTM.

National Council of Teachers of Mathematics. (2004). *News Bulletin 40*(6). Reston, VA: NCTM.

National Council of Teachers of Mathematics. (2005). *Position Statement on Computation, Calculators and Common Sense.* Retrieved from www.nctm.org/about/content.aspx?id=6358

National Council of Teachers of Mathematics. (2006a). *Curriculum focal points for prekindergarten through grade 8 mathematics: A quest for coherence.* Reston, VA: NCTM.

National Council of Teachers of Mathematics (2006b). *Navigating through number and operations in Grades 6–8.* Reston, VA: NCTM.

National Council of Teachers of Mathematics. (2006c). *Teaching the metric system for America's future.* Reston, VA: NCTM.

National Council of Teachers of Mathematics. (2007a). *Mathematics teaching today.* Reston, VA: NCTM.

National Council of Teachers of Mathematics. (2007b). *Research Brief: Effective Strategies for Teaching Students with Difficulties in Mathematics.* Retrieved May 10, 2008, from www.nctm.org/news/content.aspx?id=8452

National Council of Teachers of Mathematics. (2008, January). Position Statement on Equity in Mathematics Education. Retrieved May 10, 2008, from www.nctm.org/about/content.aspx?id=13490

National Mathematics Advisory Panel. (2008). *Foundations for success.* Jessup, MD: U.S. Department of Education. (Also available online at www.ed.gov/MathPanel.)

National Research Council. (2001). Adding it up: Helping children learn mathematics. In J. Kilpatrick, J. Swafford, & B. Findell (Eds.), *Mathematics learning study committee, center for education division of behavioral and social sciences and education.* Washington, DC: National Academy Press.

Nelson, R. (2001). *Proofs without words II: More exercises in visual thinking.* Washington, DC: Mathematical Association of America.

Neumer, C. (2007). Mixed numbers made easy: Building and converting mixed numbers and improper fractions. *Teaching Children Mathematics,* *13*(9), 488–492.

Nicolson, C. P. (2005). Is chance fair? One student's thoughts on probability. *Teaching Children Mathematics,* *12*(2), 83–89.

Niess, M. (2008). Guiding preservice teachers in developing TPCK. In AACTE Committee on Innovation and Technology (Eds.), *Handbook of technological pedagogical content knowledge (TCPK) for educators* (pp. 223–250). Routledge/Taylor and Francis Group.

Niezgoda, D. A., & Moyer-Packenham, P. S. (2005). Hickory, dickory, dock: Navigating through data analysis. *Teaching Children Mathematics,* *11*(6), 292–300.

Noddings, N. (1988, December 7). Schools face crisis in caring. *Education Week,* p. 32.

Noddings, N. (1993). Constuctivism and caring. In R. B. Davis & C. A. Maher (Eds.), *Schools, mathematics, and the world of reality* (pp. 35–50). Boston: Allyn & Bacon.

Noelting, G. (1980). The development of proportional reasoning and the ratio concept: Part 1–Differentiation of stages. *Educational Studies in Mathematics,* *11*(2), 217–253.

Northcote, N., & McIntosh, A. (1999). What mathematics do adults really do in everyday life? *Australian Primary Mathematics Classroom,* *4*(1), 19–21.

Nosek, B., Banaji, M., & Greenwald, A. (2002). Math = male, me = female, therefore me ≠ math. *Journal of personality and social psychology,* *83*(1), 44–59.

Nyquist, J. B. (2003). *The benefits of reconstruing feedback as a larger system of formative assessment: A meta-analysis.* Unpublished master's thesis. Vanderbilt University, Nashville, TN.

O'Brien, T. C. (1999). Parrot math. *Phi Delta Kappan,* *80*(6), 434–438.

Oppedal, D. C. (1995). Mathematics is something good. *Teaching Children Mathematics,* *2*(1), 36–40.

Outhred, L., & Mitchelmore, M. (2004). Students' structuring of rectangular arrays. In M. J. Hoines & A. B. Fuglestad (Eds.), *Proceedings of the 28th PME International Conference,* *3*, 465–472.

Papert, S. (1980). *Mindstorms: Children, computers, and powerful ideas.* New York: Basic Books.

Parker, M. (2004). Reasoning and working proportionally with percent. *Mathematics Teaching in the Middle School, 9*(6), 326–330.

Perie, M., Moran, R., & Lutkus, A. (2005). *NAEP 2004 trends in academic progress: Three decades of student performance in reading and mathematics.* Washington, DC: National Center for Education Statistics.

Perkins, I., & Flores, A. (2002). Mathematical notations and procedures of recent immigrant students. *Mathematics Teaching in the Middle School, 7*(6), 346–351.

Petersen, J. (2004). *Math and nonfiction: Grades K–2.* Sausalito, CA: Math Solutions Publications.

Philipp, R. A., Schappelle, B., Siegfried, J., Jacobs, V., & Lamb, L. (2008). *The effects of professional development on the mathematical content knowledge of K–3 teachers.* Paper presented at the American Educational Research Association annual meeting, New York City, NY, April 2008.

Phillips-Bey, C. K. (2004). TI-73 calculator activities. *Mathematics Teaching in the Middle School, 9*(9), 500–508.

Popham, W. J. (2008). *Transformative assessment.* Alexandria, VA: Association for Supervision and Curriculum Development.

Poplin, M. S. (1988a). Holistic/constructivist principles of the teaching/learning process: Implications for the field of learning disabilities. *Journal of Learning Disabilities, 21*(7), 401–416.

Poplin, M. S. (1988b). The reductionistic fallacy in learning disabilities: Replicating the past by reducing the present. *Journal of Learning Disabilities, 21*(7), 389–400.

Post, T. R. (1981). Fractions: Results and implications from the national assessment. *Arithmetic Teacher, 28*(9), 26–31.

Post, T. R., Behr, M. J., & Lesh, R. A. (1988). Proportionality and the development of prealgebra understandings. In A. F. Coxford (Ed.), *The ideas of algebra, K–12* (pp. 78–90). Reston, VA: NCTM.

Post, T. R., Wachsmuth, I., Lesh, R. A., & Behr, M. J. (1985). Order and equivalence of rational numbers: A cognitive analysis. *Journal for Research in Mathematics Education, 16*(1), 18–36.

Pothier, Y., & Sawada, D. (1983). Partitioning: The emergence of rational number ideas in young children. *Journal for Research in Mathematics Education, 14*(4), 307–317.

Powell, C. A., & Hunting, R. P. (2003). Fractions in the early-years curriculum: More needed, not less. *Teaching Children Mathematics, 10*(1), 6–7.

Preston, R., & Thompson, T. (2004). Integrating measurement across the curriculum. *Mathematics Teaching in the Middle School, 9*(8), 436–441.

Pugalee, D. K. (2005). *Writing for mathematical understanding.* Norwood, MA: Christopher Gordon Publishers.

Pugalee, D., Arbaugh, F., Bay-Williams, J. M., Farrell, A., Mathews, S., &. Royster, D. (2008). *Navigating through mathematical connections in grades 6–8.* Reston, VA: NCTM.

Quinn, R., Lamberg, T., & Perrin, J. (2008). Teacher perceptions of division by zero. *Clearing House, 81*(3), 101–104.

Ramakrishnan, M. (2003). Using number relationships for estimation and mental computation. *Mathematics Teaching in the Middle Schools, 8*(9), 476–479.

Rasmussen, C., Yackel, E., & King, K. (2003). Social and sociomathematical norms in the mathematics classroom. In H. L. Schoen & R. I. Charles (Eds.), *Teaching mathematics through problem solving: Grades 6–12* (pp. 143–154). Reston, VA: NCTM.

Rathmell, E. C. (1978). Using thinking strategies to teach the basic skills. In M. N. Suydam (Ed.), *Developing computational skills* (pp. 13–38). Reston, VA: NCTM.

Rathmell, E. C., Leutzinger, L. P., & Gabriele, A. (2000). *Thinking with numbers.* (Separate packets for each operation.) Cedar Falls, IA: Thinking with Numbers.

Renne, C. G. (2004). Is a rectangle a square? Developing mathematical vocabulary and conceptual understanding. *Teaching Children Mathematics, 10*(5), 258–263.

Renzulli, J. S. (1986). The three-ring conception of giftedness: A developmental model for creative productivity. In R. J. Sternberg & J. E. Davidson (Eds.), *Conceptions of giftedness* (pp. 53–92). New York: Cambridge University Press.

Renzulli, J., Smith, L. H., & Reis, S. (1982). Curriculum compacting: An essential strategy for working with gifted students. *Elementary School Journal, 82*(3), 185–194.

Resnick, L. B. (1983). A developmental theory of number understanding. In H. P. Ginsburg (Ed.), *The development of mathematical thinking* (pp. 109–151). New York: Academic Press.

Resnick, L. B., Nesher, P., Leonard, F., Magone, M., Omanson, S., & Peled, I. (1989). Conceptual bases of arithmetic errors: The case of decimal fractions. *Journal for Research in Mathematics Education, 20*(1), 8–27.

Reys, B. (1991). *Developing number sense.* Addenda Series, Grades 5–8. Reston, VA: NCTM.

Reys, B., Chval, K., Dingman, S., McNaught, M., Regis, T., & Togashi, J. (2007). Grade-level learning expectation: A new challenge for elementary mathematics teachers. *Teaching Children Mathematics, 14*(1), 6–11.

Reys, B., & Lappan, G. (2007). Consensus or confusion? The intended math curriculum in state-level standards. *Phi Delta Kappan, 88*(9), 676–680.

Reys, B. J., & Reys, R. E. (1995). Japanese mathematics education: What makes it work. *Teaching Children Mathematics, 1*(8), 474–475.

Reys, B. J., Reys, R. E., & Penafiel, A. F. (1991). Estimation performance and strategy use of Mexican 5th and 8th grade student sample. *Educational Studies in Mathematics, 22*(4), 353–375.

Reys, B. J., Robinson, E., Sconiers, S., & Mark, J. (1999). Mathematics curricula based on rigorous national standards: What, why, and how? *Phi Delta Kappan, 80*(6), 454–456.

Reys, R. E. (1998). Computation versus number sense. *Mathematics Teaching in the Middle School, 4*(2), 110–113.

Reys, R. E., & Reys, B. J. (1983). *Guide to using estimation skills and strategies (GUESS)* (Boxes I and II). Palo Alto, CA: Dale Seymour.

Reys, R. E., Reys, B. J., Nohda, N., Ishida, J., Yoshikawa, S., & Shimizu, K. (1991). Computational estimation performance and strategies used by fifth and eighth-grade Japanese students. *Journal for Research in Mathematics Education, 22*(1), 39–58.

Riordin, J. E., & Noyce, P. E. (2001). The impact of two *Standards*-based mathematics curricula on student achievement in Massachusetts. *Journal for Research in Mathematics Education, 32*(4), 368–398.

Riverdeep. (1995). *Math munchers deluxe*. Mahwah, NJ: Author.

Roberts, S., & Tayeh, C. (2007). It's the thought that counts: Reflecting on problem solving. *Mathematics Teaching in the Middle School, 12*(5), 232–237.

Roddick, C., & Silvas-Centeno, C. (2007). Developing understanding of fractions through pattern blocks and fair trade. *Teaching Children Mathematics, 14*(3), 140–145.

Ross, S. H. (1986). *The development of children's place-value numeration concepts in grades two through five*. Presented at the annual meeting of the American Educational Research Association, San Francisco. (ERIC Document Reproduction Service No. ED 2773 482)

Ross, S. H. (1989). Parts, wholes, and place value: A developmental perspective. *Arithmetic Teacher, 36*(6), 47–51.

Rossman, A., Chance, B., & Median, E. (2006). Some important comparisons between statistics and mathematics, and why teachers should care. In G. F. Burrill, & P. C. Elliott (Eds.), *Thinking and reasoning about data and chance: 68th NCTM yearbook* (pp. 323–334). Reston, VA: NCTM.

Rotigel, J., & Fellow, S. (2005). Mathematically gifted students: How can we meet their needs? *Gifted Child Today, 27*(4), 46–65.

Rowan, T. E. (1995, March). Helping children construct mathematical understanding with IMPACT. Presented at the regional meeting of the National Council of Teachers of Mathematics, Chicago, IL.

Rowan, T. E., & Bourne, B. (1994). *Thinking like mathematicians: Putting the K–4 standards into practice*. Portsmouth, NH: Heinemann.

Roy, J. A., & Beckmann, C. E. (2007). Batty functions: Exploring quadratic functions through children's literature. *Mathematics Teaching in the Middle School, 13*(1), 52–64.

Rubel, L. (2006). Students' probabilistic thinking revealed: The case of coin tosses. In G. Burrill & P. C. Elliott (Eds.), *Thinking and reasoning about data and chance: Sixty-eighth yearbook* (pp. 49–60). Reston, VA: NCTM.

Rubel, L. (2007). Middle school and high school students' probabilistic reasoning on coin tasks. *Journal for Research in Mathematics Education, 38*(5), 531–557.

Rubenstein, R. N. (2000). Word origins: Building communication connections. *Mathematics Teaching in the Middle School, 5*(8), 493–498.

Russell, S. J. (1997, April). *Using video to study students' strategies for whole-number operations*. Paper presented at the annual meeting of the National Council of Teachers of Mathematics, Minneapolis, MN.

Russell, S. J. (2006). What does it mean that "5 has a lot"? From the world to data and back. In G. F. Burrill & P. C. Elliott (Eds.), *Thinking and reasoning about data and chance: 68th NCTM yearbook* (pp. 17–30). Reston VA: NCTM.

Russell, S. J., & Economopoulos, K. (2008). *Investigations in number, data, and space*. New York: Pearson.

Sadler, P., & Tai, R. (2007). The two pillars supporting college science. *Science, 317*(5837), 457–458.

Sáenz-Ludlow, A. (2004). Metaphor and numerical diagrams in the arithmetical activity of a fourth-grade class. *Journal for Research in Mathematics Education, 35*(1), 34–56.

Samara, T. R. (2007). *Obstacles to opportunity: Alexandria, Virginia students speak out*. Alexandria, VA: Alexandria United Teens, George Mason University.

Scheaffer, R. L. (2006). Statistics and mathematics: On making a happy marriage. In G. F. Burrill, & P. C. Elliott (Eds.), *Thinking and reasoning about data and chance: Sixty-eighth yearbook* (pp. 309–322). Reston, VA: NCTM.

Schielack, J., & Seeley, C. (2007). A look at the development of data representation and analysis in *Curriculum Focal Points: A Quest of Coherence. Mathematics Teaching in the Middle School, 13*(4), 208–210.

Schifter, D. (1999). Reasoning about operations: Early algebraic thinking, grades K through 6. In L. Stiff & F. Curcio (Eds.), *Developing mathematical reasoning in grades K–12* (pp. 62–81). Reston, VA: NCTM.

Schifter, D. (2001). Perspectives from a mathematics educator. In Center for Education, *Knowing and Learning Mathematics for Teaching* (pp. 69–71). Washington, DC: National Academies Press.

Schifter, D., Bastable, V., & Russell, S. J. (1999a). *Developing mathematical understanding: Numbers and operations, Part 1, Building a system of tens (Casebook)*. Parsippany, NJ: Dale Seymour Publications.

Schifter, D., Bastable, V., & Russell, S. J. (1999b). *Developing mathematical understanding: Numbers and operations, Part 2, Making meaning for operations (Casebook)*. Parsippany, NJ: Dale Seymour Publications.

Schifter, D., Bastable, V., & Russell, S. J. (1999c). *Developing mathematical understanding: Numbers and operations, Part 2, Making meaning for operations (Facilitator's Guide)*. Parsippany, NJ: Dale Seymour Publications.

Schifter, D., Bastable, V., Russell, S. J., & Monk, S. (in press). *Developing mathematical ideas: Number and operations, Part 3, Reasoning algebraically about operations (Facilitator's Guide)*. Parsippany, NJ: Dale Seymour Publications.

Schifter, D., & Fosnot, C. T. (1993). *Reconstructing mathematics education: Stories of teachers meeting the challenge of reform*. New York: Teachers College Press.

Schmidt, W. H., McKnight, C. C., & Raizen, S. A. (1996). *Executive summary of a splintered vision: An investigation of U.S. science and mathematics education*. Boston: Kluwer.

Schoenfeld, A. H. (1992). Learning to think mathematically: Problem solving, metacognition, and sense making in mathematics. In D. A. Grouws (Ed.), *Handbook of research on teaching and learning* (pp. 334–370). Old Tappan, NJ: Macmillan.

Schroeder, T. L., & Lester, F. K., Jr. (1989). Developing understanding in mathematics via problem solving. In P. R. Trafton (Ed.), *New directions for elementary school mathematics* (pp. 31–42). Reston, VA: NCTM.

Schwartz, S. L. (1996). Hidden messages in teacher talk: Praise and empowerment. *Teaching Children Mathematics, 2*(7), 396–401.

Sconyers, J. M. (1995). Proof and the middle school mathematics student. *Mathematics Teaching in the Middle School, 1*(7), 516–518.

Seattle Times News Services. (2008, July 25). In math, girls and boys are equal. *The Seattle Times.*

Seeley, C., & Schielack, J. F. (2007). A look at the development of ratios, rates, and proportionality. *Mathematics Teaching in the Middle School, 13*(3), 140–142.

Seeley, C., & Schielack, J. F. (2008). A look at the development of algebraic thinking in Curriculum Focal Points. *Mathematics Teaching in the Middle School, 13*(5), 266–269.

Seymour, D. (1971). *Tangramath.* Palo Alto, CA: Creative Publications.

Shaughnessy, J. M. (2003). Research on students' understanding of probability. In J. Kilpatrick, W. G. Martin, & D. Schifter (Eds.), *A research companion to Principles and Standards for School Mathematics* (pp. 216–226). Reston, VA: NCTM.

Shaughnessy, J. M. (2006). Research on students' understanding of some big concepts in statistics. In G. F. Burrill, & P. C. Elliott (Eds.), *Thinking and reasoning about data and chance: 68th NCTM yearbook* (pp. 77–98). Reston, VA: NCTM.

Sheffield, L. J. (1997). From Doogie Howser to dweebs—or how we went in search of Bobby Fischer and found that we are dumb and dumber. *Mathematics Teaching in the Middle School, 2*(6), 376–379.

Sheffield, S. (1995). *Math and literature (K–3)* (Vol. 2). Sausalito, CA: Math Solutions Publications.

Sheffield, S., & Gallagher, K. (2004). *Math and nonfiction: Grades 3–5.* Sausalito, CA: Math Solutions Publications.

Shoecraft, P. (1982). "Bowl-A-Fact: A game for reviewing the number facts," *Arithmetic Teacher, 29*(8), 24–25.

Shulman, L. (1986). Those who understand: Knowledge growth in teaching. *Educational Researcher, 15*(2), 4–14.

Siebert, D., & Gaskin, N. (2006). Creating, naming, and justifying fractions. *Teaching Children Mathematics, 12*(8), 394–400.

Sikes, S. (1995). *Feeding the zircon gorilla and other team building activities.* Tulsa, OK: Learning Unlimited Corporation.

Silver, E. A., & Kenney, P. A. (Eds.) (2000). *Results from the seventh mathematics assessment of the National Assessment of Educational Progress.* Reston, VA: NCTM.

Silver, E. A., Smith, M. S., & Nelson, B. S. (1995). The QUASAR project: Equity concerns meet mathematics education reform in the middle school. In W. G. Secada, E. Fennema, & L. B. Adajian (Eds.), *New directions for equity in mathematics education* (pp. 9–56). New York: Cambridge University Press.

Silver, E. A., & Stein, M. K. (1996). The QUASAR project: The "revolution of the possible" in mathematics instructional reform in urban middle schools. *Urban Education, 30*(4), 476–521.

Simon, M. A. (1995). Reconstructing mathematics pedagogy from a constructivist perspective. *Journal for Research in Mathematics Education, 26*(2), 114–145.

Skemp, R. (1978). Relational understanding and instrumental understanding. *Arithmetic Teacher, 26*(3), 9–15.

Smith, A. (1997a). Testing the surf: Criteria for evaluating Internet information resources, *The Public-Access Computer Systems Review, 8*(3), 5–23.

Smith, B. A. (1997b). A meta-analysis of outcomes from the use of calculators in mathematics education. (Doctoral dissertation, Texas A&M University, 1996.) *Dissertation Abstracts International, 58,* 787A.

Smith, J. P., III. (2002). The development of students' knowledge of fractions and ratios. In B. Litwiller (Ed.), *Making sense of fractions, ratios, and proportions* (pp. 3–17). Reston, VA: NCTM.

Soares, J., Blanton, M. L., & Kaput, J. J. (2006). Thinking algebraically across the elementary school curriculum. *Teaching Children Mathematics, 12*(5), 228–234.

Sowder, J. (1989). Developing understanding of computational estimation. *Arithmetic Teacher, 36*(5), 25 27.

Sowder, J. T., Wearne, D., Martin, W. G., & Strutchens, M. (2004). What do 8th-grade students know about mathematics? Changes over a decade. In P. Kloosterman & F. K. Lester, Jr., *Results and interpretations of the 1990–2000 mathematics assessments of the National Assessment of Educational Progress* (pp. 105–143). Reston, VA: NCTM.

Sowder, J., & Wearne, D. (2006). What do we know about eighth-grade student achievement? *Mathematics Teaching in the Middle School, 11*(6), 285–293.

Sowder, L. (1988). Children's solutions of story problems. *Journal of Mathematical Behavior, 7*(3), 227–238.

Steele, D. F. (2005). Using schemas to develop algebraic thinking. *Mathematics Teaching in the Middle School, 11*(1), 40–46.

Steele, D. F. (2007). Understanding students' problem-solving knowledge through their writing. *Mathematics Teaching in the Middle School, 13*(2), 102–109.

Steen, L. A. (1997). Preface: The new literacy. In L. A. Steen (Ed.), *Why numbers count.* New York: College Entrance Examination Board.

Stein, M. K., & Bovalino, J. W. (2001). Manipulatives: One piece of the puzzle. *Teaching Children Mathematics, 6*(6), 356–359.

Stein, M. K., Grover, B. W., & Henningsen, M. (1996). Building student capacity for mathematical thinking and reasoning: An analysis of mathematical tasks used in reform classrooms. *American Educational Research Journal, 33*(2), 455–488.

Stein, M. K., & Lane, S. (1996). Instructional tasks and the development of student capacity to think and reason: An analysis of the relationship between teaching and learning in a reform mathematics project. *Educational Research and Evaluation, 2*(1), 50–58.

Steinberg, L., Brown, B., & Dornbusch, S. (1996). *Beyond the classroom.* New York: Simon & Schuster.

Steinle, V., & Stacey, K. (2004). Persistence of decimal misconceptions and readiness to move to expertise. *Proceedings of the 28th conference of the International Groups for the Psychology of Mathematics Education, 4,* 225–232.

Stenmark, J. K. (1989). *Assessment alternatives in mathematics: An overview of assessment techniques that promote learning.* Berkeley: EQUALS, University of California.

Stenmark, J. K., & Bush, W. S. (Eds.). (2001). *Mathematics assessment: A practical handbook for grades 3–5.* Reston, VA: NCTM.

Stenmark, J. K., Thompson, V., & Cossey, R. (1986). *Family math.* Berkeley: University of California, Lawrence Hall of Science.

Stephan, M., & Whitenack, J. (2003). Establishing classroom social and sociomathematical norms for problem solving. In F. K. Lester, Jr., & R. I. Charles (Eds.), *Teaching mathematics through problem solving: Grades pre-K–6* (pp. 149–162). Reston, VA: NCTM.

Stephens, A. C. (2005). Developing students' understanding of variable. *Mathematics Teaching in the Middle School, 11*(2), 96–100.

Stoessiger, R., & Edmunds, J. (1992). *Natural learning and mathematics.* Portsmouth, NH: Heinemann.

Style, E. (1988). *Listening for all voices.* Summit, NJ: Oak Knoll School Monograph.

Suh, J. M. (2007). Developing "algebra-'rithmetic" in the elementary grades. *Teaching Children Mathematics, 14*(4), 246–253.

Suh, J. M. (2007). Tying it all together: Building mathematics proficiency for all students. *Teaching Children Mathematics, 14*(3), 163–169.

Sulentic-Dowell, M. M., Beal, G., & Capraro, R. (2006). How do literacy experiences affect the teaching propensities of elementary pre-service teachers? *Journal of Reading Psychology, 27*(2–3), 235–255.

Taber, S. B. (2002). Go ask Alice about multiplication of fractions. In B. Litwiller (Ed.), *Making sense of fractions, ratios, and proportions* (pp. 61–71). Reston, VA: NCTM.

Taber, S. B. (2007). Using Alice in Wonderland to teach multiplication of fractions. *Mathematics Teaching in the Middle School, 12*(5), 244–250.

Tarr, J. E., Lee, H. S., & Rider, R. L. (2006). When data and chance collide: Drawing inferences from empirical data. In G. Burrill & P. C. Elliott (Eds.), *Thinking and reasoning about data and chance: 68th NCTM yearbook* (pp. 139–149). Reston, VA: NCTM.

Teachers of English to Speakers of Other Languages (TESOL). (1997). *TESOL ESL standards for pre-K–12 students.* Alexandria, VA: Author.

Theissen, D., Matthias, M., & Smith, J. (1998). *The wonderful world of mathematics: A critically annotated list of children's books in mathematics* (2nd ed.). Reston, VA: NCTM.

Thomas, K. R. (2006). Students THINK: A framework for improving problem solving. *Teaching Children Mathematics, 13*(2), 86–95.

Thompson, C. S. (1990). Place value and larger numbers. In J. N. Payne (Ed.), *Mathematics for the young child* (pp. 89–108). Reston, VA: NCTM.

Thompson, P. W. (1994). Concrete materials and teaching for mathematical understanding. *Arithmetic Teacher, 41*(9), 556–558.

Thompson, T. D., & Preston, R. V. (2004). Measurement in the middle grades: Insights from NAEP and TIMSS. *Mathematics Teaching in the Middle School, 9*(9), 514–519.

Thornton, C. A. (1982). Doubles up—easy! *Arithmetic Teacher, 29*(8), 20.

Thornton, C. A. (1990). Strategies for the basic facts. In J. N. Payne (Ed.), *Mathematics for the young child* (pp. 133–151). Reston, VA: NCTM.

Thornton, C. A., & Toohey, M. A. (1984). *A matter of facts: (Addition, subtraction, multiplication, division).* Palo Alto, CA: Creative Publications.

Tirosh, D. (2000). Enhancing prospective teachers' knowledge of children's conceptions: The case of division of fractions. *Journal for Research in Mathematics Education, 31*(1), 1, 5–25.

Tobias, S. (1995). *Overcoming math anxiety.* New York: W. W. Norton & Company.

Tomlinson, C. A. (1999). *The differentiated classroom: Responding to the needs of all learners.* Alexandria, VA: Association for Supervision and Curriculum Development.

Torgesen, J. K. (2002). The prevention of reading difficulties. *Journal of School Psychology, 40*(1), 7–26.

Torrence, E. (2003). Learning to think: An American third grader discovers mathematics in Holland. *Teaching Children Mathematics, 10*(2), 90–93.

Tortolani, M. (2007, February). Presentation at the 2007 National Association of Multicultural Engineering Program Advocates National Conference, Baltimore, MD.

Trafton, P. R., & Claus, A. S. (1994). A changing curriculum for a changing age. In C. A. Thornton & N. S. Bley (Eds.), *Windows of opportunity: Mathematics for students with special needs* (pp. 19–39). Reston, VA: NCTM.

Tsuruda, G. (1994). *Putting it together: Middle school math in transition.* Portsmouth, NH: Heinemann.

Tzur, R. (1999). An integrated study of children's construction of improper fractions and the teacher's role in promoting learning. *Journal for Research in Mathematics Education, 30*(4), 390–416.

U.S. Department of Education. (2000). *Before it's too late: A report to the nation from the national commission on mathematics and science teaching for the 21st century.* Retrieved April 16, 2008, from www.ed.gov/americacounts/glenn

U.S. Department of Education. (2008). *The condition of education.* Retrieved March 24, 2008, from nces.ed.gov/programs/coe

U.S. Department of Education, Office of Educational Research and Improvement. (1996). *Pursuing excellence: A study of U.S. eighth-grade mathematics and science teaching, learning, curriculum, and achievement in international context.* NCES 97-198, by L. Peak. Washington, DC: U.S. Government Printing Office.

U.S. Department of Education, Office of Educational Research and Improvement. (1997a). *Introduction to TIMSS.* Washington, DC: U.S. Government Printing Office.

U.S. Department of Education, Office of Educational Research and Improvement. (1997b). *Moderator's guide to eighth-grade mathematics lessons: United States, Japan, and Germany.* Washington, DC: U.S. Government Printing Office.

U.S. Department of Education, Office of Educational Research and Improvement. (1997c). *Pursuing excellence: A study of U.S. fourth-grade mathematics and science achievement in international context.* NCES 97-255. Washington, DC: U.S. Government Printing Office.

Usiskin, Z. (2007). Some thoughts about fractions. *Mathematics Teaching in the Middle School, 12*(7), 370–373.

Van de Walle, J. A., & Lovin, L. H. (2006). *Teaching student-centered mathematics: Grades 5–8.* Boston: Allyn and Bacon.

van Hiele, P. M. (1999). Developing geometric thinking through activities that begin with play. *Teaching Children Mathematics, 5*(6), 310–316.

Van Tassel-Baska, Joyce (1998). *Excellence in educating gifted and talented learners.* Denver, CO: Love.

Varol, F., & Farran, D. (2007). Elementary school students' mental computation proficiencies. *Early Childhood Education Journal, 35*(1), 89–94.

von Glasersfeld, E. (1990). An exposition of constructivism: Why some like it radical. In R. B. Davis, C. A. Maher, & N. Noddings (Eds.), *Constructivist views on the teaching and learning of mathematics* (pp. 19–29). Reston, VA: NCTM.

von Glasersfeld, E. (1996). Introduction: Aspects of constructivism. In C. T. Fosnot (Ed.), *Constructivism: Theory, perspectives, and practice* (pp. 3–7). New York: Teachers College Press.

Vygotsky, L. S. (1978). *Mind and society.* Cambridge, MA: Harvard University Press.

Wagner, M. M., & Lachance, A. (2004). Mathematical adventures with Harry Potter. *Teaching Children Mathematics, 10*(5), 274–277.

Wakefield, D. V. (2000). Math as a second language. *The Educational Forum, 64*(3), 272–279.

Wallace, A. H. (2007). Anticipating student responses to improve problem solving. *Mathematics Teaching in the Middle School, 12*(9), 504–511.

Wallace, A. H., & Gurganus, S. P. (2005). Teaching for mastery of multiplication. *Teaching Children Mathematics, 12*(1), 26–33.

Walter, M. I. (1970). *Boxes, squares and other things: A teacher's guide for a unit in informal geometry.* Reston, VA: NCTM.

Wandt, E. & Brown, G. W. (1957). Non-occupational uses of mathematics: Mental and written—Approximate and exact. *Arithmetic Teacher, 4*(4), 151–154

Ward, R. A. (2006). *Numeracy and literacy: Teaching K–8 mathematics using children's literature.* Colorado Springs, CO: PEAK Parent Center.

Wareham, K. (2005). *Hand-held calculators and mathematics achievement: What the 1996 national assessment of educational progress eighth-grade mathematics exam scores tell us.* Unpublished doctoral dissertation, Utah State University.

Warren, E., & Cooper, T. J. (2008). Patterns that support early algebraic thinking in elementary school. In C. E. Greenes & R. Rubenstein (Eds.), *Algebra and algebraic thinking in school mathematics: 70th NCTM yearbook,* (pp. 113–126). Reston, VA: NCTM.

Watanabe, T. (2001). Let's eliminate fractions from the primary curricula! *Teaching Children Mathematics, 8*(2), 70–72.

Watanabe, T. (2006). The teaching and learning of fractions: A Japanese perspective. *Teaching Children Mathematics, 12*(7), 368–374.

Watson, J. M., & Moritz, J. B. (2003). Fairness of dice: A longitudinal study of students' beliefs and strategies for making judgments. *Journal for Research in Mathematics Education, 34* (4), 270–304.

Watson, J. M., & Shaughnessy, J. M. (2004). Proportional reasoning: Lessons learned from research in data and chance. *Mathematics Teaching in the Middle School, 10*(2), 104–109.

Wearne, D., & Kouba, V. L. (2000). Rational numbers. In E. A. Silver & P. A. Kenney (Eds.), *Results from the seventh mathematics assessment of the National Assessment of Educational Progress* (pp. 163–191). Reston, VA: NCTM.

Weidemann, W., Mikovch, A. K., & Hunt, J. B. (2001). Using a lifeline to give rational numbers a personal touch. *Mathematics Teaching in the Middle School, 7*(4), 210–215.

Welchman-Tischler, R. (1992). *How to use children's literature to teach mathematics.* Reston, VA: NCTM.

Wheatley, G. H., & Hersberger, J. (1986). A calculator estimation activity. In H. Schoen (Ed.), *Estimation and mental computation* (pp. 182–185). Reston, VA: NCTM.

Whitin, D. J., & Whitin, P. (2004). *New visions for linking literature and mathematics.* Urbana, IL: National Council of Teachers of English; Reston, VA: NCTM.

Whitin, D. J., & Wilde, S. (1992). *Read any good math lately? Children's books for mathematical learning, K–6.* Portsmouth, NH: Heinemann.

Whitin, D. J., & Wilde, S. (1995). *It's the story that counts: More children's books for mathematical learning, K–6.* Portsmouth, NH: Heinemann.

Whitin, P., & Whitin, D. J. (2006). Making connections through math-related book pairs. *Teaching Children Mathematics, 13*(4), 196–202.

Whitin, P., & Whitin, D. (2008). Learning to solve problems in the primary grades. *Teaching Children Mathematics, 14*(7), 426–432.

Wickett, M., Kharas, K., & Burns, M. (2002). *Lessons for algebraic thinking.* Sausalito, CA: Math Solutions Publications.

Wiliam, D. (2007). Content *then* process: Teacher learning communities in the service of formative assessment. In D. B. Reeves (Ed.), *Ahead of the curve: The power of assessment to transform teaching and learning* (pp. 183–204). Bloomington, IN: Solution Tree.

Wiliam, D. (2008). Changing classroom practice. *Educational Leadership, 65*(4), 36–41.

Williams, L. (2008). Tiering and scaffolding: Two strategies for providing access to important mathematics. *Teaching Children Mathematics, 14*(6), 324–330.

Winter, M. J., Lappan, G., Phillips, E., & Fitzgerald, W. (1986). *Middle grades mathematics project: Spatial visualization.* Menlo Park, CA: AWL Supplemental.

Wood, T., Cobb, P., Yackel, E., & Dillon, D. (Eds.). (1993). *Rethinking elementary school mathematics: Insights and issues* (*Journal for Research in Mathematics Education* Monograph No. 6). Reston, VA: NCTM.

Wood, T., & Sellers, P. (1996). Assessment of a problem-centered mathematics program: Third grade. *Journal for Research in Mathematics Education, 27*(2), 337–353.

Wood, T., & Sellers, P. (1997). Deepening the analysis: Longitudinal assessment of a problem-centered mathematics program. *Journal for Research in Mathematics Education, 28*(2), 163–168.

Wood, T., & Turner-Vorbeck, T. (2001). Extending the conception of mathematics teaching. In T. Wood, B. S. Nelson, & J. Warfield (Eds.), *Beyond classical pedagogy: Teaching elementary school mathematics* (pp. 185–208). Mahwah, NJ: Erlbaum.

Wood, T., Williams, G., & McNeal, B. (2006). Children's mathematical thinking in different classroom cultures.

Journal for Research in Mathematics Education, 37(3), 222–255

Wyner, J. S., Bridgeland, J. M., & Dilulio, J. Jr. (2007). *Achievement trap: How America is failing millions of high-achieving students from lower-income families.* Lansdowne, VA: Jack Kent Cooke Foundation.

Yackel, E., & Cobb, P. (1996). Sociomathematical norms, argumentation, and autonomy in mathematics. *Journal for Research in Mathematics Education, 27*(4), 458–477.

Yackel, E., Cobb, P., Wood, T., Wheatley, G. H., & Merkel, G. (1990). The importance of social interaction in children's construction of mathematical knowledge. In T. J. Cooney (Ed.), *Teaching and learning mathematics in the 1990s* (pp. 12–21). Reston, VA: NCTM.

Ysseldyke, J. (2002). Response to "Learning Disabilities: Historical Perspectives." In R. Bradley, L. Danielson, & D. Hallahan (Eds.), *Identification of learning disabilities: Research to practice* (pp. 89–98). Mahwah, NJ: Erlbaum.

Zambo, R. (2008). Percents can make sense. *Mathematics Teaching in the Middle School, 13*(7), 418–422.

Children's Literature References

Anno, M. (1982). *Anno's counting house.* New York: Philomel Books.

Anno, M. (1994). *Anno's magic seeds.* New York: Philomel Books.

Anno, M., & Anno, M. (1983). *Anno's mysterious multiplying jar.* New York: Philomel Books.

Ash, R. (1996). *Incredible comparisons.* New York: Dorling Kindersley.

Better Homes and Gardens. (2004). *New junior cookbook.* Des Moines, IA: Author.

Briggs, R. (1970). *Jim and the beanstalk.* New York: Coward-McCann.

Brown, D. (1997). *Alice Ramsey's grand adventure.* Boston: Houghton Mifflin Company.

Brown, M. W. (1947). *Goodnight moon.* New York: Harper and Row.

Buckley, J., Jr., & Stremme, R. (2006). *Book of lists: Fun facts, weird trivia, and amazing lists on nearly everything you need to know!* Santa Barbara, CA: Scholastic.

Burns, M. (1982). *Math for smarty pants.* New York: Little, Brown.

Burns, M. (1995). *The greedy triangle.* New York: Houghton Mifflin.

Carle, E. (1969). *The very hungry caterpillar.* New York: Putnam.

Chalmers, M. (1986). *Six dogs, twenty-three cats, forty-five mice, and one hundred sixteen spiders.* New York: HarperCollins.

Chwast, S. (1993). *The twelve circus rings.* San Diego, CA: Gulliver Books, Harcourt Brace Jovanovich.

Clement, R. (1991). *Counting on Frank.* Milwaukee: Gareth Stevens Children's Books.

Cushman, R. (1991). *Do you wanna bet? Your chance to find out about probability.* New York: Clarion Books.

de Paola, T. (1978). *The pop corn book.* New York: Holiday House.

Dee, R. (1988). *Two ways to count to ten.* New York: Holt.

DiSalvo-Ryan, D. (1994). *City green.* New York: William Morrow and Company.

Ehlert, L. (1989). *Color zoo.* New York: Harper Collins.

Ehlert, L. (1990). *Color farm.* New York: Harper Collins.

Enzensberger, H. M. (1997). *The number devil.* New York: Metropolitan Books.

Friedman, A. (1994). *The king's commissioners.* New York: Scholastic.

Gag, W. (1928). *Millions of cats.* New York: Coward-McCann.

Giganti, P. (1988). *How many snails? A counting book.* New York: Greenwillow.

Giganti, P. (1992). *Each orange had 8 slices.* New York: Greenwillow.

Grossman, B. (1996). *My little sister ate one hare.* New York: Crown.

Hoban, T. (1981). *More than one.* New York: Greenwillow.

Hoban, T. (1996). *Shapes, shapes, shapes.* New York: Harper Trophy.

Hoban, T. (1998). *So many circles, so many squares.* New York: Greenwillow

Hoban, T. (2000). *Cubes, cones, cylinders and shapes.* New York: Greenwillow.

Hoffman, D. (2005). *The breakfast cereal gourmet: Fortified with essential facts and figures!* Kansas City, MO: Andrews McMeel Publishing.

Hong, L. T. (1993). *Two of everything: A Chinese folktale.* New York: Albert Whitman & Company.

Hutchins, P. (1986). *The doorbell rang.* New York: Greenwillow.

Jaspersohn, W. (1993). *Cookies.* Old Tappan, NJ: Macmillan.

Juster, N. (1961). *The phantom tollbooth.* New York: Random House.

Krull, K. (1996). *Wilma unlimited: How Wilma Rudolph became the world's fastest woman.* New York: Harcourt Brace.

Landau, E. (2006). *The history of everyday life.* Brookfield, CT: Twenty-First Century Books.

Leedy, L. (2000). *Measuring Penny.* New York: Holt.

Lobal, A. (1970). *Frog and Toad are friends.* New York: HarperCollins.

Martin, J. B. (1998). *Snowflake Bentley.* New York: Houghton Mifflin.

Mathews, L. (1979). *Gator pie.* New York: Dodd, Mead.

Mathis, S. B. (1986). *The hundred penny box.* New York: Viking Juvenile Books.

McKissack, P. C. (1992). *A million fish . . . more or less.* New York: Knopf.

Munsch, R. (1987). *Moira's birthday.* Toronto: Annick Press.

Murrie, S., & Murrie, M. (2007). *Every minute on earth.* New York: Scholastic.

Myller, R. (1990). *How big is a foot?* New York: Dell.

Norton, M. (1953). *The borrowers.* New York: Harcourt Brace.

Numeroff, L. J. (1985). *If you give a mouse a cookie.* New York: HarperCollins.

Parker, T. (1984). *In one day.* Boston: Houghton Mifflin.

Pluckrose, H. (1988). *Pattern.* New York: Franklin Watts.

Rowling, J. K. (1998). *Harry Potter and the sorcerer's stone.* New York: A. A. Lewine.

Schwartz, D. (1985). *How much is a million?* New York: Lothrop, Lee & Shepard.

Schwartz, D. (1989). *If you made a million.* New York: Lothrop, Lee & Shepard.

Schwartz, D. M. (1999). *If you hopped like a frog.* New York: Scholastic Press.

Scieszka, J., & Smith, L. (1995). *Math curse.* New York: Viking Penguin.

Seuss, Dr. (1960). *Green eggs and ham.* New York: Random House.

Sharmat, M. W. (1979). *The 329th friend.* New York: Four Winds Press.

Silverstein, S. (1974). One inch tall. In *Where the sidewalk ends* (p. 55). New York: Harper & Row.

Silverstein, S. (1981). *A light in the attic.* New York: Harper-Collins Publishers.

Smith, D. (2002). *If the world were a village: A book about the world's people.* Tonawanda, NY: Kids Can Press Ltd.

St. John, G. (1975). *How to count like a Martian.* New York: Walck.

Tahan, M. (1993). *The man who counted: A collection of mathematical adventures* (Trans. L. Clark & A. Reid). New York: Norton.

Tompert, A. (1997). *Grandfather Tang's story.* New York: Dragonfly Books.

Weatherform, C. B. (2005). *A Negro League Scrapbook.* Honesdale, PA: Boyds Mills Press.

Weiss, A. E. (1991). *Lotteries: Who wins, who loses.* Hillsdale, NJ: Enslow.

Wells, R. E. (1993). *Is a blue whale the biggest thing there is?* Morton Grove, IL: Whitman.

Wolkstein, D. (1972). *8,000 stones.* New York: Doubleday.

Index